COLLINS GEM

SPANISH DICTIONARY

SPANISH · ENGLISH
ENGLISH · SPANISH

Collins Gem

An imprint of HarperCollinsPublishers

grijalbo

first published in this edition 1982
fourth edition 1998

© William Collins Sons & Co. Ltd. 1982, 1989
© HarperCollins Publishers 1993, 1998

latest reprint 2000

ISBN 0-00-470750-8

Collins Gem® and Bank of English® are registered trademarks
of HarperCollins Publishers Limited

The Collins Gem website address is
www.collins-gem.com

---

*based on previous editions by/basada en las
ediciones anteriores de*
Mike Gonzalez, Alicia de Benito de Harland
Soledad Pérez-López, José Ramón Parrondo
Bob Grossmith, Teresa Álvarez García

contributors/colaboradores
Joyce Littlejohn, Claire Evans, Sharon Hunter,
Val McNulty, Jeremy Butterfield

Grijalbo Mondadori, S.A.
Aragó, 385, 08013 Barcelona

www.grijalbo.com

ISBN 84-253-3211-7

Typeset by Morton Word Processing Ltd, Scarborough

*Printed and bound in Great Britain by
Caledonian International Book Manufacturing Ltd, Glasgow*

ÍNDICE

CONTENTS

INTRODUCCIÓN

Estamos muy satisfechos de que hayas decidido comprar el Diccionario de Inglés Collins y esperamos que lo disfrutes y que te sirva de gran ayuda ya sea en el colegio, en el trabajo, en tus vacaciones o en casa.

Esta introducción pretende darte algunas indicaciones para ayudarte a sacar el mayor provecho de este diccionario; no sólo de su extenso vocabulario, sino de toda la información que te proporciona cada entrada. Esta te ayudará a leer y comprender — y también a comunicarte y a expresarte — en inglés moderno.

El Diccionario de Inglés Collins Gem comienza con una lista de abreviaturas utilizadas en el texto y con una ilustración de los sonidos representados por los símbolos fonéticos. Al final del diccionario encontrarás una tabla de los verbos irregulares del inglés, y para terminar, una sección sobre el uso de los números y de las expresiones de tiempo.

EL MANEJO DE TU DICCIONARIO COLLINS GEM

La amplia información que te ofrece este diccionario aparece presentada en distintas tipografías, con caracteres de diversos tamaños y con distintos símbolos, abreviaturas y paréntesis. Los apartados siguientes explican las reglas y símbolos utilizados.

Entradas

Las palabras que consultas en el diccionario — las "entradas" — aparecen ordenadas alfabéticamente y en **caracteres gruesos** para una identificación más rápida. Las dos palabras que ocupan el margen superior de cada página indican la primera y la última entrada de la página en cuestión.

La información sobre el uso o la forma de determinadas entradas aparece entre paréntesis, detrás de la transcripción fonética, y generalmente en forma abreviada y en cursiva (p.ej.: *(fam)*, *(COM)*).

En algunos casos se ha considerado oportuno agrupar palabras de una misma familia (**nación, nacionalismo; accept, acceptance**) bajo una misma entrada, en caracteres gruesos de tamaño algo más pequeño que los de la entrada principal.

Las expresiones de uso corriente en las que aparece una entrada se dan en negrita (p.ej.: **to be in a hurry**).

Símbolos fonéticos

La transcripción fonética de cada entrada (que indica su pronunciación) aparece entre corchetes, inmediatamente después de la entrada (p.ej.: **knead** [ni:d]). En la página x encontrarás una lista de los símbolos fonéticos utilizados en este diccionario.

Traducciones

Las traducciones de las entradas aparecen en caracteres normales, y en los casos en los que existen significados o usos diferentes, éstos aparecen separados mediante un punto y coma. A menudo encontrarás también otras palabras en cursiva y entre paréntesis antes de las traducciones. Estas sugieren contextos en los que la entrada podría aparecer (p.ej.: **rough** (*voice*) o (*weather*)) o proporcionan sinónimos (p.ej.: **rough** (*violent*)).

Palabras clave

Particular relevancia reciben ciertas palabras inglesas y españolas que han sido consideradas palabras "clave" en cada lengua. Estas pueden, por ejemplo, ser de utilización muy corriente o tener distintos usos (**de, haber; get, that**). La combinación de rombos ♦ y números te permitirá distinguir las diferentes categorías gramaticales y los diferentes significados. Las indicaciones en cursiva y entre paréntesis proporcionan además importante información adicional.

Información gramatical

Las categorías gramaticales aparecen en forma abreviada y en cursiva después de la transcripción fonética de cada entrada (*vt, adv, conj*).

También se indican la forma femenina y los plurales irregulares de los sustantivos del inglés (**child, ~ren**).

INTRODUCTION

We are delighted you have decided to buy the Collins Gem Spanish Dictionary and hope you will enjoy and benefit from using it at school, at home, on holiday or at work.

This introduction gives you a few tips on how to get the most out of your dictionary — not simply from its comprehensive wordlist but also from the information provided in each entry. This will help you to read and understand modern Spanish, as well as communicate and express yourself in the language.

The Collins Gem Spanish Dictionary begins by listing the abbreviations used in the text and illustrating the sounds shown by the phonetic symbols. You will find Spanish verb tables at the back, followed by a final section on numbers and time expressions.

USING YOUR COLLINS GEM DICTIONARY

A wealth of information is presented in the dictionary, using various typefaces, sizes of type, symbols, abbreviations and brackets. The conventions and symbols used are explained in the following sections.

Headwords

The words you look up in a dictionary — "headwords" — are listed alphabetically. They are printed in **bold type** for rapid identification. The two headwords appearing at the top of each page indicate the first and last word dealt with on the page in question.

Information about the usage or form of certain headwords is given in brackets after the phonetic spelling. This usually appears in abbreviated form and in italics (e.g. *(fam)*, *(COMM)*).

Where appropriate, words related to headwords are grouped in the same entry (**nación, nacionalismo; accept, acceptance**) in a slightly smaller bold type than the headword.

Common expressions in which the headword appears are shown in a different bold roman type (e.g. **hacer calor**).

Phonetic spellings

The phonetic spelling of each headword (indicating its pronunciation) is given in square brackets immediately after the headword (e.g. **dónde** ['donde]). A list of these symbols is given on page x.

Translations

Headword translations are given in ordinary type and, where more than one meaning or usage exists, these are separated by a semi-colon. You will often find other words in italics in brackets before the translations. These offer suggested contexts in which the headword might appear (e.g. **grande** (*de tamaño*) or provide synonyms (e.g. **grande** (*alto*) *o* (*distinguido*)).

"Key" words

Special status is given to certain Spanish and English words which are considered as "key" words in each language. They may, for example, occur very frequently or have several types of usage (e.g. **de, haber**). A combination of lozenges ♦ and numbers helps you to distinguish different parts of speech and different meanings. Further helpful information is provided in brackets and in italics.

Grammatical information

Parts of speech are given in abbreviated form in italics after the phonetic spellings of headwords (e.g. *vt, adv, conj*).

Genders of Spanish nouns are indicated as follows: *nm* for a masculine and *nf* for a feminine noun. Feminine and irregular plural forms of nouns are also shown (**irlandés, esa; luz,** (*pl* **luces**)).

ABREVIATURAS

ABBREVIATIONS

abreviatura	ab(b)r	abbreviation
adjetivo, locución adjetiva	adj	adjective, adjectival phrase
administración	ADMIN	administration
adverbio, locución adverbial	adv	adverb, adverbial phrase
agricultura	AGR	agriculture
América Latina	AM	Latin America
anatomía	ANAT	anatomy
arquitectura	ARQ, ARCH	architecture
el automóvil	AUT(O)	the motor car and motoring
aviación, viajes aéreos	AVIAT	flying, air travel
biología	BIO(L)	biology
botánica, flores	BOT	botany
inglés británico	BRIT	British English
química	CHEM	chemistry
comercio, finanzas, banca	COM(M)	commerce, finance, banking
informática	COMPUT	computers
conjunción	conj	conjunction
construcción	CONSTR	building
compuesto	cpd	compound element
cocina	CULIN	cookery
economía	ECON	economics
electricidad, electrónica	ELEC	electricity, electronics
enseñanza, sistema escolar y universitario	ESCOL	schooling, schools and universities
España	Esp	Spain
especialmente	esp	especially
exclamación, interjección	excl	exclamation, interjection
femenino	f	feminine
lengua familiar (! vulgar)	fam (!)	colloquial usage (! particularly offensive)
ferrocarril	FERRO	railways
uso figurado	fig	figurative use
fotografía	FOTO	photography
(verbo inglés) del cual la partícula es inseparable	fus	(phrasal verb) where the particle is inseparable
generalmente	gen	generally
geografía, geología	GEO	geography, geology
geometría	GEOM	geometry
uso familiar (! vulgar)	inf (!)	colloquial usage (! particularly offensive)
infinitivo	infin	infinitive
informática	INFORM	computers
invariable	inv	invariable
irregular	irreg	irregular
lo jurídico	JUR	law
América Latina	LAM	Latin America
gramática, lingüística	LING	grammar, linguistics

ABREVIATURAS

ABBREVIATIONS

masculino	m	masculine
matemáticas	MATH	mathematics
masculino/femenino	m/f	masculine/feminine
medicina	MED	medicine
lo militar, ejército	MIL	military matters
música	MUS	music
sustantivo, nombre	n	noun
navegación, náutica	NAUT	sailing, navigation
sustantivo numérico	num	numeral noun
complemento	obj	(grammatical) object
	o.s.	oneself
peyorativo	pey, pej	derogatory, pejorative
fotografía	PHOT	photography
fisiología	PHYSIOL	physiology
plural	pl	plural
política	POL	politics
participio de pasado	pp	past participle
preposición	prep	preposition
pronombre	pron	pronoun
psicología, psiquiatría	PSICO, PSYCH	psychology, psychiatry
tiempo pasado	pt	past tense
química	QUÍM	chemistry
ferrocarril	RAIL	railways
religión	REL	religion
	sb	somebody
enseñanza, sistema escolar y universitario	SCH	schooling, schools and universities
singular	sg	singular
España	SP	Spain
	sth	something
sujeto	su(b)j	(grammatical) subject
subjuntivo	subjun	subjunctive
tauromaquia	TAUR	bullfighting
también	tb	also
técnica, tecnología	TEC(H)	technical term, technology
telecomunicaciones	TELEC, TEL	telecommunications
imprenta, tipografía	TIP, TYP	typography, printing
televisión	TV	television
universidad	UNIV	university
inglés norteamericano	US	American English
verbo	vb	verb
verbo intransitivo	vi	intransitive verb
verbo pronominal	vr	reflexive verb
verbo transitivo	vt	transitive verb
zoología	ZOOL	zoology
marca registrada	®	registered trademark
indica un equivalente cultural	≈	introduces a cultural equivalent

SPANISH PRONUNCIATION

Consonants

c	[k]	caja	c before a, o or u is pronounced as in cat
ce, ci	[θe, θi]	cero cielo	c before e or i is pronounced as in thin
ch	[tʃ]	chiste	ch is pronounced as ch in chair
d	[d, ð]	danés ciudad	at the beginning of a phrase or after l or n, d is pronounced as in English. In any other position it is pronounced like th in the
g	[g, ɣ]	gafas paga	g before a, o or u is pronounced as in gap, if at the beginning of a phrase or after n. In other positions the sound is softened
ge, gi	[xe, xi]	gente girar	g before e or i is pronounced similar to ch in Scottish loch
h		haber	h is always silent in Spanish
j	[x]	jugar	j is pronounced similar to ch in Scottish loch
ll	[ʎ]	talle	ll is pronounced like the lli in million
ñ	[ɲ]	niño	ñ is pronounced like the ni in onion
q	[k]	que	q is pronounced as k in king
r, rr	[r, rr]	quitar garra	r is always pronounced in Spanish, unlike the silent r in dancer. rr is trilled, like a Scottish r
s	[s]	quizás isla	s is usually pronounced as in pass, but before b, d, g, l, m or n it is pronounced as in rose
v	[b, ß]	vía dividir	v is pronounced something like b. At the beginning of a phrase or after m or n it is pronounced as b in boy. In any other position the sound is softened
z	[θ]	tenaz	z is pronounced as th in thin

b, f, k, l, m, n, p, t and x are pronounced as in English.

Vowels

a	[a]	p*a*ta	not as long as *a* in f*a*r. When followed by a consonant in the same syllable (i.e. in a closed syllable), as in am*a*nte, the *a* is short, as in b*a*t
e	[e]	m*e*	like *e* in th*ey*. In a closed syllable, as in g*e*nte, the *e* is short as in p*e*t
i	[i]	p*i*no	as in m*ea*n or mach*i*ne
o	[o]	l*o*	as in l*o*cal. In a closed syllable, as in c*o*ntrol, the *o* is short as in c*o*t
u	[u]	l*u*nes	as in r*u*le. It is silent after *q*, and in g*ue*, g*ui*, unless marked g*üe*, g*üi* e.g. antig*üe*dad

Diphthongs

ai, ay	[ai]	b*ai*le	as *i* in r*i*de
au	[au]	*au*to	as *ou* in sh*ou*t
ei, ey	[ei]	bu*ey*	as *ey* in gr*ey*
eu	[eu]	d*eu*da	both elements pronounced independently [e]+[u]
oi, oy	[oi]	h*oy*	as *oy* in t*oy*

Stress

The rules of stress in Spanish are as follows:
(a) when a word ends in a vowel or in *n* or *s*, the second last syllable is stressed: pat*a*ta, pat*a*tas, c*o*me, c*o*men
(b) when a word ends in a consonant other than *n* or *s*, the stress falls on the last syllable: par*e*d, habl*a*r
(c) when the rules set out in a and b are not applied, an acute accent appears over the stressed vowel: com*ú*n, geograf*í*a, ingl*é*s

In the phonetic transcription, the symbol ['] precedes the syllable on which the stress falls.

PRONUNCIACIÓN INGLESA

Vocales y diptongos

	Ejemplo inglés	*Ejemplo español/explicación*
ɑː	f**a**ther	Entre *a* de p**a**dre y *o* de n**o**che
ʌ	b**u**t, c**o**me	*a* muy breve
æ	m**a**n, c**a**t	Se mantienen los labios en la posición de *e* en p**e**na y luego se pronuncia el sonido *a*
ə	f**a**ther, **a**go	Sonido indistinto parecido a una *e* u *o* casi mudas
əː	b**i**rd, h**ea**rd	Entre *e* abierta, y *o* cerrada, sonido alargado
ɛ	g**e**t, b**e**d	como en p**e**rro
ɪ	**i**t, b**i**g	Más breve que en s**i**
iː	t**ea**, s**ee**	Como en f**i**no
ɔ	h**o**t, w**a**sh	Como en t**o**rre
ɔː	s**a**w, **a**ll	Como en p**o**r
u	p**u**t, b**oo**k	Sonido breve, más cerrado que b**u**rro
uː	t**oo**, y**ou**	Sonido largo, como en **u**no
aɪ	fl**y**, h**i**gh	Como en fr**ai**le
au	h**ow**, h**ou**se	Como en p**au**sa
ɛə	th**ere**, b**ear**	Casi como en v**ea**, pero el sonido *a* se mezcla con el indistinto [ə]
eɪ	d**ay**, ob**ey**	*e* cerrada seguida por una *i* débil
ɪə	h**ere**, h**ear**	Como en man**ía**, mezclándose el sonido *a* con el indistinto [ə]
əu	g**o**, n**o**te	[ə] seguido por una breve *u*
ɔɪ	b**oy**, **oi**l	Como en v**oy**
uə	p**oo**r, s**ure**	*u* bastante larga más el sonido indistinto [ə]

Consonantes

	Ejemplo inglés	Ejemplo español/explicación
d	men*d*ed	Como en con*d*e, an*d*ar
g	*g*o, *g*et, bi*g*	Como en *g*rande, *g*ol
dʒ	*g*in, *j*udge	Como en la *ll* andaluza y en *G*eneralitat (catalán)
ŋ	si*ng*	Como en ví*n*culo
h	*h*ouse, *h*e	Como la jota hispanoamericana
j	*y*oung, *y*es	Como en *y*a
k	*c*ome, mo*ck*	Como en *c*aña, Es*c*ocia
r	*r*ed, t*r*ead	Se pronuncia con la punta de la lengua hacia atrás y sin hacerla vibrar
s	*s*and, ye*s*	Como en *c*asa, *s*esión
z	ro*s*e, *z*ebra	Como en de*s*de, mi*s*mo
ʃ	*sh*e, ma*ch*ine	Como en *ch*ambre (francés), ro*x*o (portugués)
tʃ	*ch*in, ri*ch*	Como en *ch*ocolate
v	*v*alley	Como en f, pero se retiran los dientes superiores vibrándolos contra el labio inferior
w	*w*ater, *wh*ich	Como en la *u* de h*u*evo, p*u*ede
ʒ	vi*s*ion	Como en *j*ournal (francés)
θ	*th*ink, my*th*	Como en re*c*eta, *z*apato
ð	*th*is, *th*e	Como en la *d* de habla*d*o, verda*d*

b, p, f, m, n, l, t iguales que en español

El signo * indica que la r final escrita apenas se pronuncia en inglés británico cuando la palabra siguiente empieza con vocal.

El signo ['] indica la sílaba acentuada.

ESPAÑOL • INGLÉS
SPANISH • ENGLISH

ESPAÑOL - INGLÉS
SPANISH - ENGLISH

A, a

PALABRA CLAVE

a [a] (a+ el = al) prep **1** (dirección) to; **fueron ~ Madrid/Grecia** they went to Madrid/Greece; **me voy ~ casa** I'm going home

2 (distancia): **está ~ 15 km de aquí** it's 15 km from here

3 (posición): **estar ~ la mesa** to be at table; **al lado de** next to, beside; ver tb **puerta**

4 (tiempo): **~ las 10/~ medianoche** at 10/midnight; **~ la mañana siguiente** the following morning; **~ los pocos días** after a few days; **estamos ~ 9 de julio** it's the ninth of July; **~ los 24 años** at the age of 24; **al año/~ la semana** (AM) a year/week later

5 (manera): **~ la francesa** the French way; **~ caballo** on horseback; **~ oscuras** in the dark

6 (medio, instrumento): **~ lápiz** in pencil; **~ mano** by hand; **cocina ~ gas** gas stove

7 (razón): **~ 30 ptas el kilo** at 30 pesetas a kilo; **~ más de 50 km/h** at more than 50 kms per hour

8 (dativo): **se lo di ~ él** I gave it to him; **vi al policía** I saw the policeman; **se lo compré ~ él** I bought it from him

9 (tras ciertos verbos): **voy ~ verle** I'm going to see him; **empezó ~ trabajar** he started working o to work

10 (+ infin): **al verle, le reconocí inmediatamente** when I saw him I recognized him at once; **el camino**

~ recorrer the distance we (etc) have to travel; **¡~ callar!** keep quiet!; **¡~ comer!** let's eat!

---

abad, esa [a'βað, 'ðesa] nm/f abbot/abbess; **~ía** nf abbey

abajo [a'βaxo] adv (situación) (down) below, underneath; (en edificio) downstairs; (dirección) down, downwards; (hacia lo bajo): **ver tb puerta** the parts flat; **la parte de ~** the lower part; **¡~ el gobierno!** down with the government!; **cuesta/río ~** downhill/downstream; **de arriba ~** from top to bottom; **el ~ firmante** the undersigned; **más ~** lower o further down

abalanzarse [aβalan'θarse] vr: **~ sobre** o **contra** to throw o.s. at

abandonado, a [aβando'naðo, a] adj derelict; (desatendido) abandoned; (desierto) deserted; (descuidado) neglected

abandonar [aβando'nar] vt to leave; (persona) to abandon, desert; (cosa) to abandon, leave behind; (descuidar) to neglect; (renunciar a) to give up; (INFORM) to quit; **~se** vr: **~se a** to abandon o.s. to; **abandono** nm (acto) desertion, abandonment; (estado) abandon, neglect; (renuncia) withdrawal, retirement; **ganar por abandono** to win by default

abanicar [aβani'kar] vt to fan; **abanico** nm fan; (NAUT) derrick

abaratar [aβara'tar] vt to lower the price of; **~se** vr to go o come down in price

abarcar [aβar'kar] vt to include, embrace; (AM) to monopolize

abarrotado, a [aβarro'taðo, a] adj packed

abarrotar [aβarro'tar] vt (local, estadio, teatro) to fill, pack

abarrotero, a [aβarro'tero, a] (AM) nm/f grocer; **abarrotes** nmpl (AM) groceries, provisions

abastecer [aβaste'θer] vt: ~ **(de)** to supply (with); **abastecimiento** nm supply

abasto [a'βasto] nm supply; **no dar ~ a** to be unable to cope with

abatido, a [aβa'tiðo, a] adj dejected, downcast

abatimiento [aβati'mjento] nm (depresión) dejection, depression

abatir [aβa'tir] vt (muro) to demolish; (pájaro) to shoot o bring down; (fig) to depress; **~se** vr to get depressed; **~se sobre** to swoop o pounce on

abdicación [aβðika'θjon] nf abdication

abdicar [aβði'kar] vi to abdicate

abdomen [aβ'ðomen] nm abdomen; **abdominales** nmpl (tb: ejercicios abdominales) sit-ups

abecedario [aβeθe'ðarjo] nm alphabet

abedul [aβe'ðul] nm birch

abeja [a'βexa] nf bee

abejorro [aβe'xorro] nm bumblebee

abertura [aβer'tura] nf = apertura

abeto [a'βeto] nm fir

abierto, a [a'βjerto, a] pp de **abrir** ♦ adj open; (AM) generous

abigarrado, a [aβiɣa'rraðo, a] adj multi-coloured

abismal [aβis'mal] adj (fig) vast, enormous

abismar [aβis'mar] vt to humble, cast down; **~se** vr to sink; **~se en** (fig) to be plunged into

abismo [a'βismo] nm abyss

abjurar [aβxu'rar] vi: ~ **de** to abjure, forswear

ablandar [aβlan'dar] vt to soften; **~se**

vr to get softer

abnegación [aβneɣa'θjon] nf self-denial

abnegado, a [aβne'ɣaðo, a] adj self-sacrificing

abocado, a [aβo'kaðo, a] adj: **verse ~ al desastre** to be heading for disaster

abochornar [aβotʃor'nar] vt to embarrass

abofetear [aβofete'ar] vt to slap (in the face)

abogado, a [aβo'ɣaðo, a] nm/f lawyer; (notario) solicitor; (en tribunal) barrister (BRIT), attorney (US); **~ defensor** defence lawyer o attorney (US)

abogar [aβo'ɣar] vi: ~ **por** to plead for; (fig) to advocate

abolengo [aβo'lengo] nm ancestry, lineage

abolición [aβoli'θjon] nf abolition

abolir [aβo'lir] vt to abolish; (cancelar) to cancel

abolladura [aβoʎa'ðura] nf dent

abollar [aβo'ʎar] vt to dent

abominable [aβomi'naβle] adj abominable

abonado, a [aβo'naðo, a] adj (deuda) paid(-up) ♦ nm/f subscriber

abonar [aβo'nar] vt (deuda) to settle; (terreno) to fertilize; (idea) to endorse; **~se** vr to subscribe; **abono** nm payment; fertilizer; subscription

abordar [aβor'ðar] vt (barco) to board; (asunto) to broach

aborigen [aβo'rixen] nm/f aborigine

aborrecer [aβorre'θer] vt to hate, loathe

abortar [aβor'tar] vi (malparir) to have a miscarriage; (deliberadamente) to have an abortion; **aborto** nm miscarriage; abortion

abotonar [aβoto'nar] vt to button (up), do up

abovedado, a [aβoβe'ðaðo, a] adj vaulted, domed

abrasar [aβra'sar] vt to burn (up);

(AGR) to dry up, parch

abrazar [aβra'θar] vt to embrace, hug

abrazo [a'βraθo] nm embrace, hug; **un ~ (en carta)** with best wishes

abrebotellas [aβreβo'teʎas] nm inv bottle opener

abrecartas [aβre'kartas] nm inv letter opener

abrelatas [aβre'latas] nm inv tin (BRIT) o can opener

abreviar [aβre'βjar] vt to abbreviate; (texto) to abridge; (plazo) to reduce; **abreviatura** nf abbreviation

abridor [aβri'ðor] nm bottle opener; (de latas) tin (BRIT) o can opener

abrigar [aβri'var] vt (proteger) to shelter; (suj: ropa) to keep warm; (fig) to cherish

abrigo [a'βrivo] nm (prenda) coat, overcoat; (lugar protegido) shelter

abril [a'βril] nm April

abrillantar [aβriʎan'tar] vt to polish

abrir [a'βrir] vt to open (up) ♦ vi to open; **~se** vr to open (up); (extenderse) to open out; (cielo) to clear; **~se paso** to find o force a way through

abrochar [aβro'tʃar] vt (con botones) to button (up); (zapato, con broche) to do up

abrumar [aβru'mar] vt to overwhelm; (sobrecargar) to weigh down

abrupto, a [a'βrupto, a] adj abrupt; (empinado) steep

absceso [aβs'θeso] nm abscess

absentismo [aβsen'tismo] nm absenteeism

absolución [aβsolu'θjon] nf (REL) absolution; (JUR) acquittal

absoluto, a [aβso'luto, a] adj absolute; **en ~** adv not at all

absolver [aβsol'βer] vt to absolve; (JUR) to pardon; (: acusado) to acquit

absorbente [aβsor'βente] adj absorbent; (interesante) absorbing

absorber [aβsor'βer] vt to absorb; (embeber) to soak up

absorción [aβsor'θjon] nf absorption;

(COM) takeover

absorto, a [aβ'sorto, a] pp de **absorber** ♦ adj absorbed, engrossed

abstemio, a [aβs'temjo, a] adj teetotal

abstención [aβsten'θjon] nf abstention

abstenerse [aβste'nerse] vr: **~ (de)** to abstain o refrain (from)

abstinencia [aβsti'nenθja] nf abstinence; (ayuno) fasting

abstracción [aβstrak'θjon] nf abstraction

abstracto, a [aβs'trakto, a] adj abstract

abstraer [aβstra'er] vt to abstract; **~se** vr to be o become absorbed

abstraído, a [aβstra'iðo, a] adj absent-minded

absuelto [aβ'swelto] pp de **absolver**

absurdo, a [aβ'surðo, a] adj absurd

abuchear [aβutʃe'ar] vt to boo

abuelo, a [a'βwelo, a] nm/f grandfather/mother; **~s** nmpl grandparents

abulia [a'βulja] nf apathy

abultado, a [aβul'taðo, a] adj bulky

abultar [aβul'tar] vi to be bulky

abundancia [aβun'danθja] nf: **una ~** de plenty of; **abundante** adj abundant, plentiful

abundar [aβun'dar] vi to abound, be plentiful

aburguesarse [aβurve'sarse] vr to become middle-class

aburrido, a [aβu'rriðo, a] adj (hastiado) bored; (que aburre) boring; **aburrimiento** nm boredom, tedium

aburrir [aβu'rrir] vt to bore; **~se** vr to be bored, get bored

abusar [aβu'sar] vi to go too far; **~ de** to abuse

abusivo, a [aβu'siβo, a] adj (precio) exorbitant

abuso [a'βuso] nm abuse

abyecto, a [aβ'jekto, a] adj wretched, abject

acá [a'ka] *adv* (*lugar*) here; ¿de
cuándo ~? since when?

acabado, a [aka'βaðo, a] *adj* finished,
complete; (*perfecto*) perfect; (*agotado*)
worn out; (*fig*) masterly ♦ *nm* finish

acabar [aka'βar] *vt* (*llevar a su fin*) to
finish, complete; (*consumir*) to use up;
(*rematar*) to finish off ♦ *vi* to finish,
end; ~**se** *vr* to finish, stop; (*terminarse*)
to be over; (*agotarse*) to run out;
~ **con** to put an end to; ~ **de llegar**
to have just arrived; ~ **por hacer** to
end (up) by doing; **¡se acabó!** it's all
over!; (*¡basta!*) that's enough!

acabóse [aka'βose] *nm*: **esto es el ~**
this is the last straw

academia [aka'ðemja] *nf* academy;
académico, a *adj* academic

acaecer [akae'θer] *vi* to happen, occur

acallar [aka'ʎar] *vt* (*persona*) to silence;
(*protestas, rumores*) to suppress

acalorado, a [akalo'raðo, a] *adj*
(*discusión*) heated

acalorarse [akalo'rarse] *vr* (*fig*) to get
heated

acampar [akam'par] *vi* to camp

acantilado [akanti'laðo] *nm* cliff

acaparar [akapa'rar] *vt* to monopolize;
(*acumular*) to hoard

acariciar [akari'θjar] *vt* to caress;
(*esperanza*) to cherish

acarrear [akarre'ar] *vt* to transport;
(*fig*) to cause, result in

acaso [a'kaso] *adv* perhaps, maybe;
(por) si ~ (just) in case

acatamiento [akata'mjento] *nm*
respect; (*ley*) observance

acatar [aka'tar] *vt* to respect; (*ley*) obey

acatarrarse [akata'rrarse] *vr* to catch a
cold

acaudalado, a [akauða'laðo, a] *adj*
well-off

acaudillar [akauði'ʎar] *vt* to lead,
command

acceder [akθe'ðer] *vi*: ~ **a** (*petición etc*)
to agree to; (*tener acceso a*) to have
access to; (*INFORM*) to access

accesible [akθe'siβle] *adj* accessible

acceso [ak'θeso] *nm* access, entry;
(*camino*) access, approach; (*MED*)
attack, fit

accesorio, a [akθe'sorjo, a] *adj, nm*
accessory

accidentado, a [akθiðen'taðo, a] *adj*
uneven; (*montañoso*) hilly; (*azaroso*)
eventful ♦ *nm/f* accident victim

accidental [akθiðen'tal] *adj*
accidental; **accidentarse** *vr* to have
an accident

accidente [akθi'ðente] *nm* accident;
~**s** *nmpl* (*de terreno*) unevenness *sg*

acción [ak'θjon] *nf* action; (*acto*)
action, act; (*COM*) share; (*JUR*) action,
lawsuit; **accionar** *vt* to work, operate;
(*INFORM*) to drive

accionista [akθjo'nista] *nm/f*
shareholder, stockholder

acebo [a'θeβo] *nm* holly; (*árbol*) holly
tree

acechar [aθe'tʃar] *vt* to spy on;
(*aguardar*) to lie in wait for; **acecho**
nm: **estar al acecho (de)** to lie in
wait (for)

aceitar [aθei'tar] *vt* to oil, lubricate

aceite [a'θeite] *nm* oil; (*de oliva*) olive
oil; ~**ra** *nf* oilcan; **aceitoso, a** *adj* oily

aceituna [aθei'tuna] *nf* olive

acelerador [aθelera'ðor] *nm*
accelerator

acelerar [aθele'rar] *vt* to accelerate

acelga [a'θelγa] *nf* chard, beet

acento [a'θento] *nm* accent;
(*acentuación*) stress

acentuar [aθen'twar] *vt* to accent; to
stress; (*fig*) to accentuate

acepción [aθep'θjon] *nf* meaning

aceptable [aθep'taβle] *adj* acceptable

aceptación [aθepta'θjon] *nf*
acceptance; (*aprobación*) approval

aceptar [aθep'tar] *vt* to accept;
(*aprobar*) to approve

acequia [a'θekja] *nf* irrigation ditch

acera [a'θera] *nf* pavement (*BRIT*),
sidewalk (*US*)

acerca [a'θerka]: ~ **de** prep about, concerning

acercar [aθer'kar] vt to bring o move nearer; ~**se** vr to approach, come near

acerico [aθe'riko] nm pincushion

acero [a'θero] nm steel

acérrimo, a [a'θerrimo, a] adj (partidario) staunch; (enemigo) bitter

acertado, a [aθer'taðo, a] adj correct; (apropiado) apt; (sensato) sensible

acertar [aθer'tar] vt (blanco) to hit; (solución) to get right; (adivinar) to guess ♦ vi to get it right, be right; ~ **a** to manage to; ~ **con** to happen o hit on

acertijo [aθer'tixo] nm riddle, puzzle

achacar [atʃa'kar] vt to attribute

achacoso, a [atʃa'koso, a] adj sickly

achantar [atʃan'tar] (fam) vt to scare, frighten; ~**se** vr to back down

achaque etc [a'tʃake] vb ver **achacar** ♦ nm ailment

achicar [atʃi'kar] vt to reduce; (NAUT) to bale out

achicharrar [atʃitʃa'rrar] vt to scorch, burn

achicoria [atʃi'korja] nf chicory

aciago, a [a'θjaɣo, a] adj ill-fated, fateful

acicalar [aθika'lar] vt to polish; (persona) to dress up; ~**se** vr to get dressed up

acicate [aθi'kate] nm spur

acidez [aθi'ðeθ] nf acidity

ácido, a ['aθiðo, a] adj sour, acid ♦ nm acid

acierto etc [a'θjerto] vb ver **acertar** ♦ nm success; (buen paso) wise move; (solución) solution; (habilidad) skill, ability

aclamación [aklama'θjon] nf acclamation; (aplausos) applause

aclamar [akla'mar] vt to acclaim; (aplaudir) to applaud

aclaración [aklara'θjon] nf clarification, explanation

aclarar [akla'rar] vt to clarify, explain;

(ropa) to rinse ♦ vi to clear up; ~**se** vr (explicarse) to understand; ~**se la garganta** to clear one's throat

aclaratorio, a [aklara'torjo, a] adj explanatory

aclimatación [aklimata'θjon] nf acclimatization

aclimatar [aklima'tar] vt to acclimatize; ~**se** vr to become acclimatized

acné [ak'ne] nm acne

acobardar [akoβar'ðar] vt to intimidate

acodarse [ako'ðarse] vr: ~ **en** to lean on

acogedor, a [akoxe'ðor, a] adj welcoming; (hospitalario) hospitable

acoger [ako'xer] vt to welcome; (abrigar) to shelter; ~**se** vr to take refuge

acogida [ako'xiða] nf reception; refuge

acometer [akome'ter] vt to attack; (emprender) to undertake; **acometida** nf attack, assault

acomodado, a [akomo'ðaðo, a] adj (persona) well-to-do

acomodador, a [akomoða'ðor, a] nm/f usher(ette)

acomodar [akomo'ðar] vt to adjust; (alojar) to accommodate; ~**se** vr to conform; (instalarse) to install o.s.; (adaptarse) ~**se (a)** to adapt (to)

acompañar [akompa'ɲar] vt to accompany; (documentos) to enclose

acondicionar [akondiθjo'nar] vt to arrange, prepare; (pelo) to condition

acongojar [akoŋgo'xar] vt to distress, grieve

aconsejar [akonse'xar] vt to advise, counsel; ~**se** vr: ~**se con** to consult

acontecer [akonte'θer] vi to happen, occur; **acontecimiento** nm event

acopio [a'kopjo] nm store, stock

acoplamiento [akopla'mjento] nm coupling, joint; **acoplar** vt to fit; (ELEC) to connect; (vagones) to couple

acorazado, a [akora'θaðo, a] adj

armour-plated, armoured ♦ *nm* battleship

acordar |akor'ðar| *vt* (*resolver*) to agree, resolve; (*recordar*) to remind; ~**se** *vr* to agree; ~**se (de algo)** to remember (sth); **acorde** *adj* (*MUS*) harmonious; **acorde con** (*medidas etc*) in keeping with ♦ *nm* chord

acordeón |akorðe'on| *nm* accordion

acordonado, a |akorðo'naðo, a| *adj* (*calle*) cordoned-off

acorralar |akorra'lar| *vt* to round up, corral

acortar |akor'tar| *vt* to shorten; (*duración*) to cut short; (*cantidad*) to reduce; ~**se** *vr* to become shorter

acosar |ako'sar| *vt* to pursue relentlessly; (*fig*) to hound, pester; **acoso** *nm* harassment; **acoso sexual** sexual harassment

acostar |akos'tar| *vt* (*en cama*) to put to bed; (*en suelo*) to lay down; ~**se** *vr* to go to bed; to lie down; ~**se con uno** to sleep with sb

acostumbrado, a |akostum'braðo, a| *adj* usual; ~ **a** used to

acostumbrar |akostum'brar| *vt*: ~ **a uno a algo** to get sb used to sth ♦ *vi*: ~ **(a) hacer** to be in the habit of doing; ~**se** *vr*: ~**se a** to get used to

acotación |akota'θjon| *nf* marginal note; (*GEO*) elevation mark; (*de límite*) boundary mark; (*TEATRO*) stage direction

ácrata |'akrata| *adj, nm/f* anarchist

acre |'akre| *adj* (*olor*) acrid; (*fig*) biting ♦ *nm* acre

acrecentar |akreθen'tar| *vt* to increase, augment

acreditar |akreði'tar| *vt* (*garantizar*) to vouch for, guarantee; (*autorizar*) to authorize; (*dar prueba de*) to prove; (*COM: abonar*) to credit; (*embajador*) to accredit; ~**se** *vr* to become famous

acreedor, a |akree'ðor, a| *adj*: ~ **de** worthy of ♦ *nm/f* creditor

acribillar |akriβi'ʎar| *vt*: ~ **a balazos** to riddle with bullets

acróbata |a'kroβata| *nm/f* acrobat

acta |'akta| *nf* certificate; (*de comisión*) minutes *pl*, record; ~ **de nacimiento/de matrimonio** birth/marriage certificate; ~ **notarial** affidavit

actitud |akti'tuð| *nf* attitude; (*postura*) posture

activar |akti'ßar| *vt* to activate; (*acelerar*) to speed up

actividad |aktißi'ðað| *nf* activity

activo, a |ak'tißo, a| *adj* active; (*vivo*) lively ♦ *nm* (*COM*) assets *pl*

acto |'akto| *nm* act, action; (*ceremonia*) ceremony; (*TEATRO*) act; **en el** ~ immediately

actor |ak'tor| *nm* actor; (*JUR*) plaintiff ♦ *adj*: **parte** ~ a prosecution

actriz |ak'triθ| *nf* actress

actuación |aktwa'θjon| *nf* action; (*comportamiento*) conduct, behaviour; (*JUR*) proceedings *pl*; (*desempeño*) performance

actual |ak'twal| *adj* present(-day), current; ~**idad** *nf* present; ~**idades** *nfpl* (*noticias*) news *sg*; **en la** ~**idad** at present; (*hoy día*) nowadays

actualizar |aktwali'θar| *vt* to update, modernize

actualmente |aktwal'mente| *adv* at present; (*hoy día*) nowadays

actuar |ak'twar| *vi* (*obrar*) to work, operate; (*actor*) to act, perform ♦ *vt* to work, operate; ~ **de** to act as

acuarela |akwa'rela| *nf* watercolour

acuario |a'kwarjo| *nm* aquarium; (*ASTROLOGÍA*): **A~** Aquarius

acuartelar |akwarte'lar| *vt* (*MIL*) to confine to barracks

acuático, a |a'kwatiko, a| *adj* aquatic

acuchillar |akutʃi'ʎar| *vt* (*TEC*) to plane (down), smooth

acuciante |aku'θjante| *adj* urgent

acuciar |aku'θjar| *vt* to urge on

acudir |aku'ðir| *vi* (*asistir*) to attend; (*ir*) to go; ~ **a** (*fig*) to turn to; ~ **en**

ayuda de to go to the aid of
acuerdo etc [a'kwerðo] vb ver **acordar**
♦ nm agreement; **¡de ~!** agreed!; **de ~ con** (persona) in agreement with; (acción, documento) in accordance with; **estar de ~** to be agreed, agree
acumular [akumu'lar] vt to accumulate, collect
acuñar [aku'nar] vt (moneda) to mint; (frase) to coin
acupuntura [akupun'tura] nf acupuncture
acurrucarse [akurru'karse] vr to crouch; (ovillarse) to curl up
acusación [akusa'θjon] nf accusation
acusar [aku'sar] vt to accuse; (revelar) to reveal; (denunciar) to denounce
acuse [a'kuse] nm: **~ de recibo** acknowledgement of receipt
acústica [a'kustika] nf acoustics pl
acústico, a [a'kustiko, a] adj acoustic
adaptación [aðapta'θjon] nf adaptation
adaptador [aðapta'ðor] nm (ELEC) adapter
adaptar [aðap'tar] vt to adapt; (acomodar) to fit
adecuado, a [aðe'kwaðo, a] adj (apto) suitable; (oportuno) appropriate
adecuar [aðe'kwar] vt to adapt; to make suitable
a. de J.C. abr (= antes de Jesucristo) B.C.
adelantado, a [aðelan'taðo, a] adj advanced; (reloj) fast; **pagar por ~** to pay in advance
adelantamiento [aðelanta'mjento] nm (AUTO) overtaking
adelantar [aðelan'tar] vt to move forward; (avanzar) to advance; (acelerar) to speed up; (AUTO) to overtake ♦ vi to go forward, advance; **~se** vr to go forward, advance
adelante [aðe'lante] adv forward(s), ahead ♦ excl come in!; **de hoy en ~** from now on; **más ~** later on; (más allá) further on

adelanto [aðe'lanto] nm advance; (mejora) improvement; (progreso) progress
adelgazar [aðelɣa'θar] vt to thin (down) ♦ vi to get thin; (con régimen) to slim down, lose weight
ademán [aðe'man] nm gesture; **ademanes** nmpl manners; **en ~ de** as if to
además [aðe'mas] adv besides; (por otra parte) moreover; (también) also; **~ de** besides, in addition to
adentrarse [aðen'trarse] vr: **~ en** to go into, get inside; (penetrar) to penetrate (into)
adentro [a'ðentro] adv inside, in; **mar ~** out at sea; **tierra ~** inland
adepto, a [a'ðepto, a] nm/f supporter
aderezar [aðere'θar] vt (ensalada) to dress; (comida) to season; **aderezo** nm dressing; seasoning
adeudar [aðeu'ðar] vt to owe; **~se** vr to run into debt
adherirse [aðe'rirse] vr: **~ a** to adhere to; (partido) to join
adhesión [aðe'sjon] nf adhesion; (fig) adherence
adicción [aðik'θjon] nf addiction
adición [aði'θjon] nf addition
adicto, a [a'ðikto, a] adj: **~ a** addicted to; (dedicado) devoted to ♦ nm/f supporter, follower; (toxicómano etc) addict
adiestrar [aðjes'trar] vt to train, teach; (conducir) to guide, lead; **~se** vr to practise; (enseñarse) to train o.s.
adinerado, a [aðine'raðo, a] adj wealthy
adiós [a'ðjos] excl (para despedirse) goodbye!, cheerio!; (al pasar) hello!
aditivo [aði'tiβo] nm additive
adivinanza [aðiβi'nanθa] nf riddle
adivinar [aðiβi'nar] vt to prophesy; (conjeturar) to guess; **adivino, a** nm/f fortune-teller
adj abr (= adjunto) encl.
adjetivo [aðxe'tiβo] nm adjective

adjudicación [aðxuðika'θjon] nf award; adjudication

adjudicar [aðxuði'kar] vt to award; **~se** vr: **~se algo** to appropriate sth

adjuntar [aðxun'tar] vt to attach, enclose; **adjunto, a** adj attached, enclosed ♦ nm/f assistant

administración [aðministra'θjon] nf administration; (dirección) management; **administrador, a** nm/f administrator; manager(ess)

administrar [aðminis'trar] vt to administer; **administrativo, a** adj administrative

admirable [aðmi'raßle] adj admirable

admiración [aðmira'θjon] nf admiration; (asombro) wonder; (LING) exclamation mark

admirar [aðmi'rar] vt to admire; (extrañar) to surprise; **~se** vr to be surprised

admisible [aðmi'sißle] adj admissible

admisión [aðmi'sjon] nf admission; (reconocimiento) acceptance

admitir [aðmi'tir] vt to admit; (aceptar) to accept

admonición [aðmoni'θjon] nf warning

adobar [aðo'ßar] vt (CULIN) to season

adobe [a'ðoße] nm adobe, sun-dried brick

adoctrinar [aðoktri'nar] vt: **~ en** to indoctrinate with

adolecer [aðole'θer] vi: **~ de** to suffer from

adolescente [aðoles'θente] nm/f adolescent, teenager

adonde [a'ðonde] conj (to) where

adónde [a'ðonde] adv = **dónde**

adopción [aðop'θjon] nf adoption

adoptar [aðop'tar] vt to adopt

adoptivo, a [aðop'tißo, a] adj (padres) adoptive; (hijo) adopted

adoquín [aðo'kin] nm paving stone

adorar [aðo'rar] vt to adore

adormecer [aðorme'θer] vt to put to sleep; **~se** vr to become sleepy;

(dormirse) to fall asleep

adornar [aðor'nar] vt to adorn

adorno [a'ðorno] nm ornament; (decoración) decoration

adosado, a [aðo'saðo, a] adj: **casa adosada** semi-detached house

adquiero etc vb ver **adquirir**

adquirir [aðki'rir] vt to acquire, obtain

adquisición [aðkisi'θjon] nf acquisition

adrede [a'ðreðe] adv on purpose

adscribir [aðskri'ßir] vt to appoint

adscrito pp de **adscribir**

aduana [a'ðwana] nf customs pl

aduanero, a [aðwa'nero, a] adj customs cpd ♦ nm/f customs officer

aducir [aðu'θir] vt to adduce; (dar como prueba) to offer as proof

adueñarse [aðwe'narse] vr: **~ de** to take possession of

adulación [aðula'θjon] nf flattery

adular [aðu'lar] vt to flatter

adulterar [aðulte'rar] vt to adulterate

adulterio [aðul'terjo] nm adultery

adúltero, a [a'ðultero, a] adj adulterous ♦ nm/f adulterer/adulteress

adulto, a [a'ðulto, a] adj, nm/f adult

adusto, a [a'ðusto, a] adj stern; (austero) austere

advenedizo, a [aðßene'ðiðo, a] nm/f upstart

advenimiento [aðßeni'mjento] nm arrival; (al trono) accession

adverbio [að'ßerßjo] nm adverb

adversario, a [aðßer'sarjo, a] nm/f adversary

adversidad [aðßersi'ðað] nf adversity; (contratiempo) setback

adverso, a [að'ßerso, a] adj adverse

advertencia [aðßer'tenθja] nf warning; (prefacio) preface, foreword

advertir [aðßer'tir] vt to notice; (avisar): **~ a uno de** to warn sb about o of

Adviento [að'ßjento] nm Advent

advierto etc vb ver **advertir**

adyacente [aðja'θente] adj adjacent

aéreo, a [a'ereo, a] *adj* aerial

aerobic [ae'roβik] *nm* aerobics *sg*

aerodeslizador [aeroðesliθa'ðor] *nm* hovercraft

aeromozo, a [aero'moθo, a] (*AM*) *nm/f* air steward(ess)

aeronáutica [aero'nautika] *nf* aeronautics *sg*

aeronave [aero'naβe] *nm* spaceship

aeroplano [aero'plano] *nm* aeroplane

aeropuerto [aero'pwerto] *nm* airport

aerosol [aero'sol] *nm* aerosol

afabilidad [afaβili'ðað] *nf* friendliness; **afable** *adj* friendly

afamado, a [afa'maðo, a] *adj* famous

afán [a'fan] *nm* hard work; (*deseo*) desire

afanar [afa'nar] *vt* to harass; (*fam*) to pinch; **~se** *vr*: **~se por hacer** to strive to do

afear [afe'ar] *vt* to disfigure

afección [afek'θjon] *nf* (*MED*) disease

afectación [afekta'θjon] *nf* affectation; **afectado, a** *adj* affected

afectar [afek'tar] *vt* to affect

afectísimo, a [afek'tisimo, a] *adj* affectionate; **suyo ~** yours truly

afectivo, a [afek'tiβo, a] *adj* (*problema etc*) emotional

afecto [a'fekto] *nm* affection; **tenerle ~ a uno** to be fond of sb

afectuoso, a [afek'twoso, a] *adj* affectionate

afeitar [afei'tar] *vt* to shave; **~se** *vr* to shave

afeminado, a [afemi'naðo, a] *adj* effeminate

Afganistán [afɣanis'tan] *nm* Afghanistan

afianzamiento [afjanθa'mjento] *nm* strengthening; security

afianzar [afjan'θar] *vt* to strengthen; to secure; **~se** *vr* to become established

afiche [a'fitʃe] (*AM*) *nm* poster

afición [afi'θjon] *nf* fondness, liking; **la ~** the fans *pl*; **pinto por ~** I paint as a

hobby; **aficionado, a** *adj* keen, enthusiastic; (*no profesional*) amateur ♦ *nm/f* enthusiast; fan; amateur; **ser aficionado a algo** to be very keen on o fond of sth

aficionar [afiθjo'nar] *vt*: **~ a uno a algo** to make sb like sth; **~se** *vr*: **~se a algo** to grow fond of sth

afilado, a [afi'laðo, a] *adj* sharp

afilar [afi'lar] *vt* to sharpen

afiliarse [afi'ljarse] *vr* to affiliate

afín [a'fin] *adj* (*parecido*) similar; (*conexo*) related

afinar [afi'nar] *vt* (*TEC*) to refine; (*MUS*) to tune ♦ *vi* (*tocar*) to play in tune; (*cantar*) to sing in tune

afincarse [afin'karse] *vr* to settle

afinidad [afini'ðað] *nf* affinity; (*parentesco*) relationship; **por ~** by marriage

afirmación [afirma'θjon] *nf* affirmation

afirmar [afir'mar] *vt* to affirm, state; **afirmativo, a** *adj* affirmative

aflicción [aflik'θjon] *nf* affliction; (*dolor*) grief

afligir [afli'xir] *vt* (*apenar*) to distress; **~se** *vr* to grieve

aflojar [aflo'xar] *vt* to slacken; (*desatar*) to loosen, undo; (*relajar*) to relax ♦ *vi* to drop; (*bajar*) to go down; **~se** *vr* to relax

aflorar [aflo'rar] *vi* to come to the surface, emerge

afluente [aflu'ente] *adj* flowing ♦ *nm* tributary

afluir [aflu'ir] *vi* to flow

afmo, a *abr* (= *afectísimo(a) suyo(a)*) Yours

afónico, a [a'foniko, a] *adj*: **estar ~** to have a sore throat; to have lost one's voice

aforo [a'foro] *nm* (*de teatro etc*) capacity

afortunado, a [afortu'naðo, a] *adj* fortunate, lucky

afrancesado, a [afranθe'saðo, a] *adj*

francophile; (*pey*) Frenchified

afrenta [aˈfrenta] *nf* affront, insult; (*deshonra*) dishonour, shame

África [ˈafrika] *nf* Africa; **africano, a** *adj*, *nm/f* African

afrontar [afronˈtar] *vt* to confront; (*poner cara a cara*) to bring face to face

afuera [aˈfwera] *adv* out, outside; **~s** *nfpl* outskirts

agachar [ayaˈtʃar] *vt* to bend, bow; **~se** *vr* to stoop, bend

agalla [aˈɣaʎa] *nf* (*ZOOL*) gill; **tener ~s** (*fam*) to have guts

agarradera [ayarraˈðera] (*esp AM*) *nf* handle

agarrado, a [ayaˈrraðo, a] *adj* mean, stingy

agarrar [ayaˈrrar] *vt* to grasp, grab; (*AM*) to take, catch; (*recoger*) to pick up ♦ *vi* (*planta*) to take root; **~se** *vr* to hold on (tightly)

agarrotar [ayarroˈtar] *vt* (*persona*) to squeeze tightly; (*reo*) to garrotte; **~se** *vr* (*motor*) to seize up; (*MED*) to stiffen

agasajar [ayasaˈxar] *vt* to treat well, fête

agazaparse [ayaθaˈparse] *vr* to crouch down

agencia [aˈxenθja] *nf* agency; **~ inmobiliaria** estate (*BRIT*) o real estate (*US*) agent's (office); **~ de viajes** travel agency

agenciarse [axenˈθjarse] *vr* to obtain, procure

agenda [aˈxenda] *nf* diary

agente [aˈxente] *nm/f* agent; (*de policía*) policeman/policewoman; **~ inmobiliario** estate agent (*BRIT*), realtor (*US*); **~ de seguros** insurance agent

ágil [ˈaxil] *adj* agile, nimble; **agilidad** *nf* agility, nimbleness

agilizar [axiliˈθar] *vt* (*trámites*) to speed up

agitación [axitaˈθjon] *nf* (*de mano etc*) shaking, waving; (*de líquido etc*)

stirring; (*fig*) agitation

agitado, a [axiˈtaðo, a] *adj* hectic; (*viaje*) bumpy

agitar [axiˈtar] *vt* to wave, shake; (*líquido*) to stir; (*fig*) to stir up, excite; **~se** *vr* to get excited; (*inquietarse*) to get worried o upset

aglomeración [aylomeraˈθjon] *nf*: **~ de tráfico/gente** traffic jam/mass of people

aglomerar [aylomeˈrar] *vt* to crowd together; **~se** *vr* to crowd together

agnóstico, a [ayˈnostiko, a] *adj*, *nm/f* agnostic

agobiar [ayoˈβjar] *vt* to weigh down; (*oprimir*) to oppress; (*cargar*) to burden

agolparse [ayolˈparse] *vr* to crowd together

agonía [ayoˈnia] *nf* death throes *pl*; (*fig*) agony, anguish

agonizante [ayoniˈθante] *adj* dying

agonizar [ayoniˈθar] *vi* to be dying

agosto [aˈɣosto] *nm* August

agotado, a [ayoˈtaðo, a] *adj* (*persona*) exhausted; (*libros*) out of print; (*acabado*) finished; (*COM*) sold out

agotador, a [ayotaˈðor, a] *adj* exhausting

agotamiento [ayotaˈmjento] *nm* exhaustion

agotar [ayoˈtar] *vt* to exhaust; (*consumir*) to drain; (*recursos*) to use up, deplete; **~se** *vr* to be exhausted; (*acabarse*) to run out; (*libro*) to go out of print

agraciado, a [ayraˈθjaðo, a] *adj* (*atractivo*) attractive; (*en sorteo etc*) lucky

agradable [ayraˈðaβle] *adj* pleasant, nice

agradar [ayraˈðar] *vt*: **él me agrada** I like him

agradecer [ayraðeˈθer] *vt* to thank; (*favor etc*) to be grateful for; **agradecido, a** *adj* grateful; **¡muy agradecido!** thanks a lot!; **agradecimiento** *nm* thanks *pl*;

gratitude

agradezco etc vb ver **agradecer**

agrado [a'γraðo] nm: **ser de tu** etc ~ to be to your etc liking

agrandar [aγran'dar] vt to enlarge; (fig) to exaggerate; **~se** vr to get bigger

agrario, a [a'γrarjo, a] adj agrarian, land cpd; (política) agricultural, farming

agravante [aγra'ßante] adj aggravating ♦ nm: **con el ~ de que ...** with the further difficulty that ....

agravar [aγra'ßar] vt (pesar sobre) to make heavier; (irritar) to aggravate; **~se** vr to worsen, get worse

agraviar [aγra'ßjar] vt to offend; (ser injusto con) to wrong; **~se** vr to take offence; **agravio** nm offence; wrong; (JUR) grievance

agredir [aγre'ðir] vt to attack

agregado, a [aγre'γaðo, a] nm/f: **A-** ≈ teacher (who is not head of department) ♦ nm aggregate; (persona) attaché

agregar [aγre'γar] vt to gather; (añadir) to add; (persona) to appoint

agresión [aγre'sjon] nf aggression

agresivo, a [aγre'sißo, a] adj aggressive

agriar [a'γrjar] vt to (turn) sour; **~se** vr to turn sour

agrícola [a'γrikola] adj farming cpd, agricultural

agricultor, a [aγrikul'tor, a] nm/f farmer

agricultura [aγrikul'tura] nf agriculture, farming

agridulce [aγri'ðulθe] adj bittersweet; (CULIN) sweet and sour

agrietarse [aγrje'tarse] vr to crack; (piel) to chap

agrimensor, a [aγrimen'sor, a] nm/f surveyor

agrio, a [a'γrjo, a] adj bitter

agrupación [aγrupa'θjon] nf group; (acto) grouping

agrupar [aγru'par] vt to group

agua ['aγwa] nf water; (NAUT) wake; (ARQ) slope of a roof; **~s** nfpl (de piedra) water sg, sparkle sg; (MED) water sg, urine sg; (NAUT) waters; **~s abajo/arriba** downstream/upstream; **~ bendita/destilada/potable** holy/distilled/drinking water; **~ caliente** hot water; **~ corriente** running water; **~ de colonia** eau de cologne; **~ mineral (con/sin gas)** mineral water; **~ oxigenada** hydrogen peroxide; **~s jurisdiccionales** territorial waters

aguacate [aγwa'kate] nm avocado (pear)

aguacero [aγwa'θero] nm (heavy) shower, downpour

aguado, a [a'γwaðo, a] adj watery, watered down

aguafiestas [aγwa'fjestas] nm/f inv spoilsport, killjoy

aguanieve [aγwa'njeße] nf sleet

aguantar [aγwan'tar] vt to bear, put up with; (sostener) to hold up ♦ vi to last; **~se** vr to restrain o.s.; **aguante** nm (paciencia) patience; (resistencia) endurance

aguar [a'γwar] vt to water down

aguardar [aγwar'ðar] vt to wait for

aguardiente [aγwar'ðjente] nm brandy, liquor

aguarrás [aγwa'rras] nm turpentine

agudeza [aγu'ðeθa] nf sharpness; (ingenio) wit

agudizar [aγuði'θar] vt (crisis) to make worse; **~se** vr to get worse

agudo, a [a'γuðo, a] adj sharp; (voz) high-pitched, piercing; (dolor, enfermedad) acute

agüero [a'γwero] nm: **buen/mal ~** good/bad omen

aguijón [aγi'xon] nm sting; (fig) spur

águila ['aγila] nf eagle; (fig) genius

aguileño, a [aγi'leɲo, a] adj (nariz) aquiline; (rostro) sharp-featured

aguinaldo [aγi'naldo] nm Christmas

box

aguja [a'γuxa] nf needle; (de reloj) hand; (ARQ) spire; (TEC) firing-pin; ~s nfpl (ZOOL) ribs; (FERRO) points

agujerear [aγuxere'ar] vt to make holes in

agujero [aγu'xero] nm hole

agujetas [aγu'xetas] nfpl stitch sg; (rigidez) stiffness sg

aguzar [aγu'θar] vt to sharpen; (fig) to incite

ahí [a'i] adv there; **de ~ que** so that, with the result that; **~ llega** here he comes; **por ~** that way; (allá) over there; **200 o por ~** 200 or so

ahijado, a [ai'xaðo, a] nm/f godson/daughter

ahínco [a'inko] nm earnestness

ahogar [ao'γar] vt to drown; (asfixiar) to suffocate, smother; (fuego) to put out; **~se** vr (en el agua) to drown; (por asfixia) to suffocate

ahogo [a'oγo] nm breathlessness; (fig) financial difficulty

ahondar [aon'dar] vt to deepen, make deeper; (fig) to study thoroughly ♦ vi: **~ en** to study thoroughly

ahora [a'ora] adv now; (hace poco) a moment ago, just now; (dentro de poco) in a moment; **~ voy** I'm coming; **~ mismo** right now; **~ bien** now then; **por ~** for the present

ahorcar [aor'kar] vt to hang

ahorita [ao'rita] (fam: esp AM) adv right now

ahorrar [ao'rrar] vt (dinero) to save; (esfuerzos) to save, avoid; **ahorro** nm (acto) saving; **ahorros** nmpl (dinero) savings

ahuecar [awe'kar] vt to hollow (out); (voz) to deepen; **~se** vr to give o.s. airs

ahumar [au'mar] vt to smoke, cure; (llenar de humo) to fill with smoke ♦ vi to smoke; **~se** vr to fill with smoke

ahuyentar [aujen'tar] vt to drive off, frighten off; (fig) to dispel

airado, a [ai'raðo, a] adj angry

airar [ai'rar] vt to anger; **~se** vr to get angry

aire ['aire] nm air; (viento) wind; (corriente) draught; (MUS) tune; **~s** nmpl: **darse ~s** to give o.s. airs; **al ~ libre** in the open air; **~ acondicionado** air conditioning; **airearse** vr (persona) to go out for a breath of fresh air; **airoso, a** adj windy; draughty; (fig) graceful

aislado, a [ais'laðo, a] adj isolated; (incomunicado) cut-off; (ELEC) insulated

aislar [ais'lar] vt to isolate; (ELEC) to insulate

ajardinado, a [axarði'naðo, a] adj landscaped

ajedrez [axe'ðreθ] nm chess

ajeno, a [a'xeno, a] adj (que pertenece a otro) somebody else's; **~ a** foreign to

ajetreado, a [axetre'aðo, a] adj busy

ajetreo [axe'treo] nm bustle

ají [a'xi] (AM) nm chil(l)i, red pepper; (salsa) chil(l)i sauce

ajillo [a'xiλo] nm: **gambas al ~** garlic prawns

ajo ['axo] nm garlic

ajuar [a'xwar] nm household furnishings pl; (de novia) trousseau; (de niño) layette

ajustado, a [axus'taðo, a] adj (tornillo) tight; (cálculo) right; (ropa) tight(-fitting); (resultado) close

ajustar [axus'tar] vt (adaptar) to adjust; (encajar) to fit; (TEC) to engage; (IMPRENTA) to make up; (apretar) to tighten; (concertar) to agree (on); (reconciliar) to reconcile; (cuentas, deudas) to settle ♦ vi to fit; **~se** vr: **~se a** (precio etc) to be in keeping with, fit in with; **~ las cuentas a uno** to get even with sb

ajuste [a'xuste] nm adjustment; (COSTURA) fitting; (acuerdo) compromise; (de cuenta) settlement

al [al] (= **a + el**) ver **a**

ala ['ala] nf wing; (de sombrero) brim; (futbolista) winger; **~ delta** nf hang-glider

alabanza [ala'βanθa] nf praise

alabar [ala'βar] vt to praise

alacena [ala'θena] nf kitchen cupboard (BRIT), kitchen closet (US)

alacrán [ala'kran] nm scorpion

alambique [alam'bike] nm still

alambrada [alam'braða] nf wire fence; (red) wire netting

alambrado [alam'braðo] nm = **alambrada**

alambre [a'lambre] nm wire; ~ de púas barbed wire

alameda [ala'meða] nf (plantío) poplar grove; (lugar de paseo) avenue, boulevard

álamo ['alamo] nm poplar; ~ temblón aspen

alarde [a'larðe] nm show, display; hacer ~ de to boast of

alargador [alarɣa'ðor] nm (ELEC) extension lead

alargar [alar'ɣar] vt to lengthen, extend; (paso) to hasten; (brazo) to stretch out; (cuerda) to pay out; (conversación) to spin out; ~se vr to get longer

alarido [ala'riðo] nm shriek

alarma [a'larma] nf alarm

alarmar vt to alarm; ~se to get alarmed; **alarmante** [alar'mante] adj alarming

alba ['alβa] nf dawn

albacea [alβa'θea] nm/f executor/ executrix

albahaca [al'βaka] nf basil

Albania [al'βanja] nf Albania

albañil [alβa'ɲil] nm bricklayer; (cantero) mason

albarán [alβa'ran] nm (COM) delivery note, invoice

albaricoque [alβari'koke] nm apricot

albedrío [alβe'ðrio] nm: libre ~ free will

alberca [al'βerka] nf reservoir; (AM) swimming pool

albergar [alβer'ɣar] vt to shelter

albergue etc [al'βerɣe] vb ver **albergar** ♦ nm shelter, refuge; ~ juvenil youth hostel

albóndiga [al'βondiɣa] nf meatball

albornoz [alβor'noθ] nm (de los árabes) burnous; (para el baño) bathrobe

alborotar [alβoro'tar] vi to make a row ♦ vt to agitate, stir up; ~se vr to get excited; (mar) to get rough; **alboroto** nm row, uproar

alborozar [alβoro'θar] vt to gladden; ~se vr to rejoice

alborozo [alβo'roθo] nm joy

álbum ['alβum] (pl ~s, ~es) nm album; ~ de recortes scrapbook

alcachofa [alka'tʃofa] nf artichoke

alcalde, esa [al'kalde, esa] nm/f mayor(ess)

alcaldía [alkal'dia] nf mayoralty; (lugar) mayor's office

alcance etc [al'kanθe] vb ver **alcanzar** ♦ nm reach; (COM) adverse balance

alcantarilla [alkanta'riʎa] nf (de aguas cloacales) sewer; (en la calle) gutter

alcanzar [alkan'θar] vt (algo: con la mano, el pie) to reach; (alguien: en el camino etc) to catch up (with); (autobús) to catch; (suj: bala) to hit, strike ♦ vi (ser suficiente) to be enough; ~ a hacer to manage to do

alcaparra [alka'parra] nf caper

alcayata [alka'jata] nf hook

alcázar [al'kaθar] nm fortress; (NAUT) quarter-deck

alcoba [al'koβa] nf bedroom

alcohol [al'kol] nm alcohol; ~ metílico methylated spirits pl (BRIT), wood alcohol (US); **alcohólico, a** adj, nm/f alcoholic

alcoholímetro [alko'limetro] nm Breathalyser ® (BRIT), drunkometer (US)

alcoholismo [alko'lismo] nm alcoholism

alcornoque [alkor'noke] nm cork tree; (fam) idiot

alcurnia [al'kurnja] nf lineage
aldaba [al'daβa] nf (door) knocker
aldea [al'dea] nf village; **~no, a** adj village cpd ♦ nm/f villager
aleación [alea'θjon] nf alloy
aleatorio, a [alea'torjo, a] adj random
aleccionar [alekθjo'nar] vt to instruct; (adiestrar) to train
alegación [aleɣa'θjon] nf allegation
alegar [ale'ɣar] vt to claim; (JUR) to plead ♦ vi (AM) to argue
alegato [ale'ɣato] nm (JUR) allegation; (AM) argument
alegoría [aleɣo'ria] nf allegory
alegrar [ale'ɣrar] vt (causar alegría) to cheer (up); (fuego) to poke; (fiesta) to liven up; **~se** vr (fam) to get merry o tight; **~se de** to be glad about
alegre [a'leɣre] adj happy, cheerful; (fam) merry, tight; (chiste) risqué, blue; **alegría** nf happiness; merriment
alejamiento [alexa'mjento] nm removal; (distancia) remoteness
alejar [ale'xar] vt to remove; (fig) to estrange; **~se** vr to move away
alemán, ana [ale'man, ana] adj, nm/f German ♦ nm (LING) German
Alemania [ale'manja] nf:
  ~ Occidental/Oriental West/East Germany
alentador, a [alenta'ðor, a] adj encouraging
alentar [alen'tar] vt to encourage
alergia [a'lerxja] nf allergy
alero [a'lero] nm (de tejado) eaves pl; (de carruaje) mudguard
alerta [a'lerta] adj, nm alert
aleta [a'leta] nf (de pez) fin; (de ave) wing; (de foca, DEPORTE) flipper; (AUTO) mudguard
aletargar [aletar'ɣar] vt to make drowsy; (entumecer) to make numb; **~se** vr to grow drowsy; to become numb
aletear [alete'ar] vi to flutter
alevín [ale'βin] nm fry, young fish
alevosía [aleβo'sia] nf treachery

alfabeto [alfa'βeto] nm alphabet
alfalfa [al'falfa] nf alfalfa, lucerne
alfarería [alfare'ria] nf pottery; (tienda) pottery shop; **alfarero, a** nm/f potter
aléizar [al'feiθar] nm window-sill
alférez [al'fereθ] nm (MIL) second lieutenant; (NAUT) ensign
alfil [al'fil] nm (AJEDREZ) bishop
alfiler [alfi'ler] nm pin; (broche) clip
alfiletero [alfile'tero] nm needlecase
alfombra [al'fombra] nf carpet; (más pequeña) rug; **alfombrar** vt to carpet; **alfombrilla** nf rug, mat
alforja [al'forxa] nf saddlebag
algarabía [alɣara'βia] nf (fam) gibberish; (griterío) hullabaloo
algas ['alɣas] nfpl seaweed
álgebra ['alxeβra] nf algebra
álgido, a [al'xiðo, a] adj (momento etc) crucial, decisive
algo ['alɣo] pron something; anything ♦ adv somewhat, rather; **¿~ más?** anything else?; (en tienda) is that all?; **por ~ será** there must be some reason for it
algodón [alɣo'ðon] nm cotton; (planta) cotton plant; **~ de azúcar** candy floss (BRIT), cotton candy (US); **~ hidrófilo** cotton wool (BRIT), absorbent cotton (US)
algodonero, a [alɣoðo'nero, a] adj cotton cpd ♦ nm/f cotton grower ♦ nm cotton plant
alguacil [alɣwa'θil] nm bailiff; (TAUR) mounted official
alguien ['alɣjen] pron someone, somebody; (en frases interrogativas) anyone, anybody
alguno, a [al'ɣuno, a] adj (delante de nm: **algún**) some; (después de n): **no tiene talento** he has no talent, he doesn't have any talent ♦ pron (alguien) someone, somebody; **algún que otro libro** some book or other; **algún día iré** I'll go one o some day; **sin interés** without the slightest interest; **~ que otro** an occasional

one; **~s piensan** some (people) think
alhaja [a'laxa] *nf* jewel; *(tesoro)* precious object, treasure
alhelí [ale'li] *nm* wallflower, stock
aliado, a [a'ljaðo, a] *adj* allied
alianza [a'ljanθa] *nf* alliance; *(anillo)* wedding ring
aliar [a'ljar] *vt* to ally; **~se** *vr* to form an alliance
alias ['aljas] *adv* alias
alicates [ali'kates] *nmpl* pliers; **~ de uñas** nail clippers
aliciente [ali'θjente] *nm* incentive; *(atracción)* attraction
alienación [aljena'θjon] *nf* alienation
aliento [a'ljento] *nm* breath; *(respiración)* breathing; **sin ~** breathless
aligerar [alixe'rar] *vt* to lighten; *(reducir)* to shorten; *(aliviar)* to alleviate; *(mitigar)* to ease; *(paso)* to quicken
alijo [a'lixo] *nm* consignment
alimaña [ali'maɲa] *nf* pest
alimentación [alimenta'θjon] *nf* *(comida)* food; *(acción)* feeding; *(tienda)* grocer's (shop); **alimentador** *nm:* **alimentador de papel** sheet-feeder
alimentar [alimen'tar] *vt* to feed; *(nutrir)* to nourish; **~se** *vr* to feed
alimenticio, a [alimen'tiθjo, a] *adj* food *cpd*; *(nutritivo)* nourishing, nutritious
alimento [ali'mento] *nm* food; *(nutrición)* nourishment
alineación [alinea'θjon] *nf* alignment; *(DEPORTE)* line-up
alinear [aline'ar] *vt* to align; **~se** *vr* *(DEPORTE)* to line up; **~se en** to fall in with
aliñar [ali'ɲar] *vt* (CULIN) to season; **aliño** *nm* (CULIN) dressing
alioli [ali'oli] *nm* garlic mayonnaise
alisar [ali'sar] *vt* to smooth
aliso [a'liso] *nm* alder
alistarse [alis'tarse] *vr* to enlist; *(inscribirse)* to enrol

aliviar [ali'ßjar] *vt* *(carga)* to lighten; *(persona)* to relieve; *(dolor)* to relieve, alleviate
alivio [a'lißjo] *nm* alleviation, relief
aljibe [al'xiße] *nm* cistern
allá [a'ʎa] *adv* *(lugar)* there; *(por ahí)* over there; *(tiempo)* then; **~ abajo** down there; **más ~** further on; **más ~ de** beyond; **¡~ tú!** that's your problem!
allanamiento [aʎana'mjento] *nm:* **~ de morada** burglary
allanar [aʎa'nar] *vt* to flatten, level (out); *(igualar)* to smooth (out); *(fig)* to subdue; *(JUR)* to burgle, break into
allegado, a [aʎe'xaðo, a] *adj* near, close ♦ *nm/f* relation
allí [a'ʎi] *adv* there; **~ mismo** right there; **por ~** over there; *(por ese camino)* that way
alma ['alma] *nf* soul; *(persona)* person
almacén [alma'θen] *nm* *(depósito)* warehouse, store; *(MIL)* magazine; *(AM)* shop; **(grandes) almacenes** *nmpl* department store *sg*; **almacenaje** *nm* storage
almacenar [almaθe'nar] *vt* to store, put in storage; *(proveerse)* to stock up with; **almacenero** *nm* (AM) shopkeeper
almanaque [alma'nake] *nm* almanac
almeja [al'mexa] *nf* clam
almendra [al'mendra] *nf* almond; **almendro** *nm* almond tree
almíbar [al'mißar] *nm* syrup
almidón [almi'ðon] *nm* starch; **almidonar** *vt* to starch
almirante [almi'rante] *nm* admiral
almirez [almi'reθ] *nm* mortar
almizcle [al'miθkle] *nm* musk
almohada [almo'aða] *nf* pillow; *(funda)* pillowcase; **almohadilla** *nf* cushion; *(TEC)* pad; *(AM)* pincushion
almohadón [almoa'ðon] *nm* large pillow; bolster
almorranas [almo'rranas] *nfpl* piles, haemorrhoids

almorzar

almorzar [almor'θar] vt: ~ **una tortilla** to have an omelette for lunch ♦ vi to (have) lunch

almuerzo etc [al'mwerθo] vb ver **almorzar** ♦ nm lunch

alocado, a [alo'kaðo, a] adj crazy

alojamiento [aloxa'mjento] nm lodging(s) (pl); (viviendas) housing

alojar [alo'xar] vt to lodge; ~**se** vr to lodge, stay

alondra [a'londra] nf lark, skylark

alpargata [alpar'vata] nf rope-soled sandal, espadrille

Alpes ['alpes] nmpl: **los** ~ the Alps

alpinismo [alpi'nismo] nm mountaineering, climbing; **alpinista** nm/f mountaineer, climber

alpiste [al'piste] nm birdseed

alquilar [alki'lar] vt (suj: propietario: inmuebles) to let, rent (out); (: coche) to hire out; (: TV) to rent (out); (suj: alquilador: inmuebles, TV) to rent; (: coche) to hire; "**se alquila casa**" "house to let (BRIT) o for rent (US)"

alquiler [alki'ler] nm renting; letting; hiring; (arriendo) rent; hire charge; ~ **de automóviles** car hire; **de** ~ for hire

alquimia [al'kimja] nf alchemy

alquitrán [alki'tran] nm tar

alrededor [alreðe'ðor] adv around, about; ~ **de** around, about; **mirar a su** ~ to look (round) about one; ~**es** nmpl surroundings

alta ['alta] nf (certificate of) discharge; **dar de** ~ to discharge

altanería [altane'ria] nf haughtiness, arrogance; **altanero, a** adj arrogant, haughty

altar [al'tar] nm altar

altavoz [alta'βoθ] nm loudspeaker; (amplificador) amplifier

alteración [altera'θjon] nf alteration; (alboroto) disturbance

alterar [alte'rar] vt to alter; to disturb; ~**se** vr (persona) to get upset

altercado [alter'kaðo] nm argument

alternar [alter'nar] vt to alternate ♦ vi to alternate; (turnar) to take turns; ~**se** vr to alternate; to take turns; ~ **con** to mix with; **alternativa** nf alternative; (elección) choice; **alternativo, a** adj alternative; (alterno) alternating; **alterno, a** adj alternate; (ELEC) alternating

Alteza [al'teθa] nf (tratamiento) Highness

altibajos [alti'βaxos] nmpl ups and downs

altiplanicie [altipla'niθje] nf high plateau

altiplano [alti'plano] nm = **altiplanicie**

altisonante [altiso'nante] adj high-flown, high-sounding

altitud [alti'tuð] nf height; (AVIAT, GEO) altitude

altivez [alti'βeθ] nf haughtiness, arrogance; **altivo, a** adj haughty, arrogant

alto, a ['alto, a] adj high; (persona) tall; (sonido) high, sharp; (noble) high, lofty ♦ nm halt; (MUS) alto; (GEO) hill; (AM) pile ♦ adv (de sitio) high; (de sonido) loud, loudly ♦ excl halt!; **la pared tiene 2 metros de** ~ the wall is 2 metres high; **en alta mar** on the high seas; **en voz alta** in a loud voice; **las altas horas de la noche** the small o wee hours; **en lo** ~ at the top of; **pasar por** ~ to overlook

altoparlante [altopar'lante] (AM) nm loudspeaker

altruismo [altru'ismo] nm altruism

altura [al'tura] nf height; (NAUT) depth; (GEO) latitude; **la pared tiene 1.80 de** ~ the wall is 1 metre 80cm high; **a estas** ~**s** at this stage; **a estas** ~**s del año** at this time of the year

alubia [a'luβja] nf bean

alucinación [aluθina'θjon] nf hallucination

alucinar [aluθi'nar] vi to hallucinate ♦ vt to deceive; (fascinar) to fascinate

alud [a'luð] *nm* avalanche; (*fig*) flood
aludir [alu'ðir] *vi*: ~ **a** to allude to; **darse por aludido** to take the hint
alumbrado [alum'braðo] *nm* lighting; **alumbramiento** *nm* lighting; (*MED*) childbirth, delivery
alumbrar [alum'brar] *vt* to light (up) ♦ *vi* (*MED*) to give birth
aluminio [alu'minjo] *nm* aluminium (*BRIT*), aluminum (*US*)
alumno, a [a'lumno, a] *nm/f* pupil, student
alunizar [aluni'θar] *vi* to land on the moon
alusión [alu'sjon] *nf* allusion
alusivo, a [alu'siβo, a] *adj* allusive
aluvión [alu'βjon] *nm* alluvium; (*fig*) flood
alverja [al'βerxa] (*AM*) *nf* pea
alza [al'θa] *nf* rise; (*MIL*) sight
alzada [al'θaða] *nf* (*de caballos*) height; (*JUR*) appeal
alzamiento [alθa'mjento] *nm* (*rebelión*) rising
alzar [al'θar] *vt* to lift (up); (*precio, muro*) to raise; (*cuello de abrigo*) to turn up; (*AGR*) to gather in; (*IMPRENTA*) to gather; ~**se** *vr* to get up, rise; (*rebelarse*) to revolt; (*COM*) to go fraudulently bankrupt; (*JUR*) to appeal
ama ['ama] *nf* lady of the house; (*dueña*) owner; (*institutriz*) governess; (*madre adoptiva*) foster mother; ~ **de casa** housewife; ~ **de llaves** housekeeper
amabilidad [amaβili'ðað] *nf* kindness; (*simpatía*) niceness; **amable** *adj* kind; nice; **es usted muy amable** that's very kind of you
amaestrado, a [amaes'traðo, a] *adj* (*animal: en circo etc*) performing
amaestrar [amaes'trar] *vt* to train
amago [a'mayo] *nm* threat; (*gesto*) threatening gesture; (*MED*) symptom
amainar [amai'nar] *vi* (*viento*) to die down
amalgama [amal'yama] *nf* amalgam;

amalgamar *vt* to amalgamate; (*combinar*) to combine, mix
amamantar [amaman'tar] *vt* to suckle, nurse
amanecer [amane'θer] *vi* to dawn ♦ *nm* dawn; ~ **afiebrado** to wake up with a fever
amanerado, a [amane'raðo, a] *adj* affected
amansar [aman'sar] *vt* to tame; (*persona*) to subdue; ~**se** *vr* (*persona*) to calm down
amante [a'mante] *adj*: ~ **de** fond of ♦ *nm/f* lover
amapola [ama'pola] *nf* poppy
amar [a'mar] *vt* to love
amargado, a [amar'yaðo, a] *adj* bitter
amargar [amar'xar] *vt* to make bitter; (*fig*) to embitter; ~**se** *vr* to become embittered
amargo, a [a'maryo, a] *adj* bitter; **amargura** *nf* bitterness
amarillento, a [amari'ʎento, a] *adj* yellowish; (*tez*) sallow; **amarillo, a** *adj, nm* yellow
amarrar [ama'rrar] *vt* to moor; (*sujetar*) to tie up
amarras [a'marras] *nfpl*: **soltar** ~ to set sail
amasar [ama'sar] *vt* (*masa*) to knead; (*mezclar*) to mix, prepare; (*confeccionar*) to concoct; **amasijo** *nm* kneading; mixing; (*fig*) hotchpotch
amateur [ama'tur] *nm/f* amateur
amazona [ama'θona] *nf* horsewoman; **A~s** *nm*: **el A~s** the Amazon
ambages [am'baxes] *nmpl*: **sin** ~ in plain language
ámbar ['ambar] *nm* amber
ambición [ambi'θjon] *nf* ambition; **ambicionar** *vt* to aspire to; **ambicioso, a** *adj* ambitious
ambidextro, a [ambi'ðekstro, a] *adj* ambidextrous
ambientación [ambjenta'θjon] *nf* (*CINE, TEATRO etc*) setting; (*RADIO*) sound effects

ambiente [am'bjente] nm (tb fig) atmosphere; (medio) environment

ambigüedad [ambixwe'ðað] nf ambiguity; **ambiguo, a** adj ambiguous

ámbito ['ambito] nm (campo) field; (fig) scope

ambos, as ['ambos, as] adj pl, pron pl both

ambulancia [ambu'lanθja] nf ambulance

ambulante [ambu'lante] adj travelling cpd, itinerant

ambulatorio [ambula'torjo] nm state health-service clinic

amedrentar [ameðren'tar] vt to scare

amén [a'men] excl amen; ~ **de** besides

amenaza [ame'naθa] nf threat

amenazar [amena'θar] vt to threaten
♦ vi: ~ **con hacer** to threaten to do

amenidad [ameni'ðað] nf pleasantness

ameno, a [a'meno, a] adj pleasant

América [a'merika] nf America; ~ **del Norte/del Sur** North/South America; ~ **Central/Latina** Central/Latin America; **americana** nf coat, jacket; ver tb **americano; americano, a** adj, nm/f American

amerizar [ameri'θar] vi (avión) to land (on the sea)

ametralladora [ametraʎa'ðora] nf machine gun

amianto [a'mjanto] nm asbestos

amigable [ami'vaßle] adj friendly

amígdala [a'miɣðala] nf tonsil; **amigdalitis** nf tonsilitis

amigo, a [a'mixo, a] adj friendly
♦ nm/f friend; (amante) lover; **ser ~ de algo** to be fond of sth; **ser muy ~s** to be close friends

amilanar [amila'nar] vt to scare; ~**se** vr to be scared

aminorar [amino'rar] vt to diminish; (reducir) to reduce; ~ **la marcha** to slow down

amistad [amis'tað] nf friendship; ~**es** nfpl (amigos) friends; **amistoso, a** adj

friendly

amnesia [am'nesja] nf amnesia

amnistía [amnis'tia] nf amnesty

amo ['amo] nm owner; (jefe) boss

amodorrarse [amoðo'rrarse] vr to get sleepy

amoldar [amol'dar] vt to mould; (adaptar) to adapt

amonestación [amonesta'θjon] nf warning; **amonestaciones** nfpl (REL) marriage banns

amonestar [amones'tar] vt to warn; (REL) to publish the banns of

amontonar [amonto'nar] vt to collect, pile up; ~**se** vr to crowd together; (acumularse) to pile up

amor [a'mor] nm love; (amante) lover; **hacer el** ~ to make love; ~ **propio** self-respect

amoratado, a [amora'taðo, a] adj purple

amordazar [amorða'θar] vt to muzzle; (fig) to gag

amorfo, a [a'morfo, a] adj amorphous, shapeless

amoroso, a [amo'roso, a] adj affectionate, loving

amortajar [amorta'xar] vt to shroud

amortiguador [amortiɣwa'ðor] nm shock absorber; (parachoques) bumper; ~**es** nmpl (AUTO) suspension sg

amortiguar [amorti'ɣwar] vt to deaden; (ruido) to muffle; (color) to soften

amortización [amortiθa'θjon] nf (de deuda) repayment; (de bono) redemption

amotinar [amoti'nar] vt to stir up, incite (to riot); ~**se** vr to mutiny

amparar [ampa'rar] vt to protect; ~**se** vr to seek protection; (de la lluvia etc) to shelter; **amparo** nm help, protection; **al amparo de** under the protection of

amperio [am'perjo] nm ampère, amp

ampliación [amplja'θjon] nf enlargement; (extensión) extension

ampliar [am'pljar] vt to enlarge; to extend

amplificación [amplifika'θjon] nf enlargement; **amplificador** nm amplifier

amplificar [amplifi'kar] vt to amplify

amplio, a ['ampljo, a] adj spacious; (de falda etc) full; (extenso) extensive; (ancho) wide; **amplitud** nf spaciousness; extent; (fig) amplitude

ampolla [am'poʎa] nf blister; (MED) ampoule

ampuloso, a [ampu'loso, a] adj bombastic, pompous

amputar [ampu'tar] vt to cut off, amputate

amueblar [amwe'βlar] vt to furnish

amurallar [amura'ʎar] vt to wall up o in

anacronismo [anakro'nismo] nm anachronism

anales [a'nales] nmpl annals

analfabetismo [analfaβe'tismo] nm illiteracy; **analfabeto, a** adj, nm/f illiterate

analgésico [anal'xesiko] nm painkiller, analgesic

análisis [a'nalisis] nm inv analysis

analista [ana'lista] nm/f (gen) analyst

analizar [anali'θar] vt to analyse

analogía [analo'xia] nf analogy

analógico, a [ana'loxiko, a] adj (INFORM) analog; (reloj) analogue (BRIT), analog (US)

análogo, a [a'nalovo, a] adj analogous, similar

ananá(s) [ana'na(s)] (AM) nm pineapple

anaquel [ana'kel] nm shelf

anarquía [anar'kia] nf anarchy; **anarquismo** nm anarchism; **anarquista** nm/f anarchist

anatomía [anato'mia] nf anatomy

anca ['anka] nf rump, haunch; **~s** nfpl (fam) behind sg

ancho, a ['antʃo, a] adj wide; (falda) full; (fig) liberal ♦ nm width; (FERRO)

gauge; **ponerse ~** to get conceited; **estar a sus anchas** to be at one's ease

anchoa [an'tʃoa] nf anchovy

anchura [an'tʃura] nf width; (extensión) wideness

anciano, a [an'θjano, a] adj old, aged ♦ nm/f old man/woman; elder

ancla ['ankla] nf anchor; **~dero** nm anchorage; **anclar** vi to (drop) anchor

andadura [anda'ðura] nf gait; (de caballo) pace

Andalucía [andalu'θia] nf Andalusia; **andaluz, a** adj, nm/f Andalusian

andamiaje [anda'mjaxe] nm = andamio

andamio [an'damjo] nm scaffold(ing)

andar [an'dar] vt to go, cover, travel ♦ vi to go, walk, travel; (funcionar) to go, work; (estar) to be ♦ nm walk, gait, pace; **~se** vr to go away; **~ a pie/a caballo/en bicicleta** to go on foot/ on horseback/by bicycle; **~ haciendo algo** to be doing sth; **¡anda!** (sorpresa) go on!; **anda por o en los 40** he's about 40

andén [an'den] nm (FERRO) platform; (NAUT) quayside; (AM: de la calle) pavement (BRIT), sidewalk (US)

Andes ['andes] nmpl: **los ~** the Andes

Andorra [an'dorra] nf Andorra

andrajo [an'draxo] nm rag; **~so, a** adj ragged

anduve etc [an'duβe] vb ver **andar**

anécdota [a'nekðota] nf anecdote, story

anegar [ane'var] vt to flood; (ahogar) to drown; **~se** vr to drown; (hundirse) to sink

anejo, a [a'nexo, a] adj, nm = **anexo**

anemia [a'nemja] nf anaemia

anestesia [anes'tesja] nf (sustancia) anaesthetic; (proceso) anaesthesia

anexar [anek'sar] vt to annex; (documento) to attach; **anexión** nf annexation; **anexionamiento** nm annexation; **anexo, a** adj attached

♦ *nm* annexe

anfibio, a [an'fiβjo, a] *adj* amphibious ♦ *nm* amphibian

anfiteatro [anfite'atro] *nm* amphitheatre; (*TEATRO*) dress circle

anfitrión, ona [anfi'trjon, ona] *nm/f* host(ess)

ángel ['anxel] *nm* angel; ~ **de la guarda** guardian angel; **tener** ~ to be charming; **angelical** *adj*, **angélico, a** *adj* angelic(al)

angina [an'xina] *nf* (*MED*) inflammation of the throat; ~ **de pecho** angina; **tener ~s** to have tonsillitis

anglicano, a [angli'kano, a] *adj, nm/f* Anglican

anglosajón, ona [anglosa'xon, ona] *adj* Anglo-Saxon

angosto, a [an'gosto, a] *adj* narrow

anguila [an'gila] *nf* eel

angula [an'gula] *nf* elver, baby eel

ángulo ['angulo] *nm* angle; (*esquina*) corner; (*curva*) bend

angustia [an'gustja] *nf* anguish; **angustiar** *vt* to distress, grieve

anhelar [ane'lar] *vt* to be eager for; (*desear*) to long for, desire ♦ *vi* to pant, gasp; **anhelo** *nm* eagerness; desire

anidar [ani'ðar] *vi* to nest

anillo [a'niʎo] *nm* ring; ~ **de boda** wedding ring

animación [anima'θjon] *nf* liveliness; (*vitalidad*) life; (*actividad*) activity; bustle

animado, a [ani'maðo, a] *adj* lively; (*vivaz*) animated; **animador, a** *nm/f* (*TV*) host(ess), compère; (*DEPORTE*) cheerleader

animadversión [animaðβer'sjon] *nf* ill-will, antagonism

animal [ani'mal] *adj* animal; (*fig*) stupid ♦ *nm* animal; (*fig*) fool; (*bestia*) brute

animar [ani'mar] *vt* (*BIO*) to animate, give life to; (*fig*) to liven up, brighten up, cheer up; (*estimular*) to stimulate;

~**se** *vr* to cheer up; to feel encouraged; (*decidirse*) to make up one's mind

ánimo ['animo] *nm* (*alma*) soul; (*mente*) mind; (*valentía*) courage ♦ *excl* cheer up!

animoso, a [ani'moso, a] *adj* brave; (*vivo*) lively

aniquilar [aniki'lar] *vt* to annihilate, destroy

anís [a'nis] *nm* aniseed; (*licor*) anisette

aniversario [aniβer'sarjo] *nm* anniversary

anoche [a'notʃe] *adv* last night; **antes de ~** the night before last

anochecer [anotʃe'θer] *vi* to get dark ♦ *nm* nightfall, dark; **al ~** at nightfall

anodino, a [ano'ðino, a] *adj* dull, anodyne

anomalía [anoma'lia] *nf* anomaly

anonadado, a [anona'ðaðo, a] *adj*: **estar/quedar/sentirse** ~ to be overwhelmed o amazed

anonimato [anoni'mato] *nm* anonymity

anónimo, a [a'nonimo, a] *adj* anonymous; (*COM*) limited ♦ *nm* (*carta*) anonymous letter; (: *maliciosa*) poison-pen letter

anormal [anor'mal] *adj* abnormal

anotación [anota'θjon] *nf* note; annotation

anotar [ano'tar] *vt* to note down; (*comentar*) to annotate

anquilosamiento [ankilosa'mjento] *nm* (*fig*) paralysis; stagnation

anquilosarse [ankilo'sarse] *vr* (*fig: persona*) to get out of touch; (*método, costumbres*) to go out of date

ansia ['ansja] *nf* anxiety; (*añoranza*) yearning; **ansiar** *vt* to long for

ansiedad [ansje'ðað] *nf* anxiety

ansioso, a [an'sjoso, a] *adj* anxious; (*anhelante*) eager; ~ **de o por algo** greedy for sth

antagónico, a [anta'yoniko, a] *adj* antagonistic; (*opuesto*) contrasting; **antagonista** *nm/f* antagonist

antaño [an'taɲo] *adv* long ago, formerly

Antártico [an'tartiko] *nm:* **el ~** the Antarctic

ante ['ante] *prep* before, in the presence of; (*problema etc*) faced with ♦ *nm* (*piel*) suede; **~ todo** above all

anteanoche [antea'notʃe] *adv* the night before last

anteayer [antea'jer] *adv* the day before yesterday

antebrazo [ante'ßraθo] *nm* forearm

antecedente [anteθe'ðente] *adj* previous ♦ *nm* antecedent; **~s** *nmpl* (*JUR*): **~s penales** criminal record; (*procedencia*) background

anteceder [anteθe'ðer] *vt* to precede, go before

antecesor, a [anteθe'sor, a] *nm/f* predecessor

antedicho, a [ante'ðitʃo, a] *adj* aforementioned

antelación [antela'θjon] *nf:* **con ~** in advance

antemano [ante'mano]: **de ~** *adv* beforehand, in advance

antena [an'tena] *nf* antenna; (*de televisión etc*) aerial; **~ parabólica** satellite dish

anteojo [ante'oxo] *nm* eyeglass; **~s** *nmpl* (*AM*) glasses, spectacles

antepasados [antepa'saðos] *nmpl* ancestors

anteponer [antepo'ner] *vt* to place in front; (*fig*) to prefer

anteproyecto [antepro'jekto] *nm* preliminary sketch; (*fig*) blueprint

anterior [ante'rjor] *adj* preceding, previous; **~idad** *nf:* **con ~idad a** prior to, before

antes ['antes] *adv* (*con prioridad*) before ♦ *prep:* **~ de** before ♦ *conj:* **~ de ir/de que te vayas** before going/before you go; **~ bien** (but) rather; **dos días ~** two days before o previously; **no quiso venir ~** she didn't want to come any earlier; **tomo**

el avión ~ que el barco I take the plane rather than the boat; **que yo ~ que me;** **lo ~ posible** as soon as possible; **cuanto ~ mejor** the sooner the better

antiaéreo, a [antia'ereo, a] *adj* anti-aircraft

antibalas [anti'ßalas] *adj inv:* **chaleco ~** bullet-proof jacket

antibiótico [anti'ßjotiko] *nm* antibiotic

anticiclón [antiθi'klon] *nm* anticyclone

anticipación [antiθipa'θjon] *nf* anticipation; **con 10 minutos de ~** 10 minutes early

anticipado, a [antiθi'paðo, a] *adj* (*pago*) advance; **por ~** in advance

anticipar [antiθi'par] *vt* to anticipate; (*adelantar*) to bring forward; (*COM*) to advance; **~se** *vr:* **~se a su época** to be ahead of one's time

anticipo [anti'θipo] *nm* (*COM*) advance

anticonceptivo, a [antikonθep'tißo, a] *adj, nm* contraceptive

anticongelante [antikonxe'lante] *nm* antifreeze

anticuado, a [anti'kwaðo, a] *adj* out-of-date, old-fashioned; (*desusado*) obsolete

anticuario [anti'kwarjo] *nm* antique dealer

anticuerpo [anti'kwerpo] *nm* (*MED*) antibody

antídoto [an'tiðoto] *nm* antidote

antiestético, a [anties'tetiko, a] *adj* unsightly

antifaz [anti'faθ] *nm* mask; (*velo*) veil

antigualla [anti'ɣwaʎa] *nf* antique; (*reliquia*) relic

antiguamente [antiɣwa'mente] *adv* formerly; (*hace mucho tiempo*) long ago

antigüedad [antiɣwe'ðað] *nf* antiquity; (*artículo*) antique; (*rango*) seniority

antiguo, a [an'tiɣwo, a] *adj* old,

ancient; *(que fue)* former

Antillas [an'tiʎas] *nfpl*: **las ~** the West Indies

antílope [an'tilope] *nm* antelope

antinatural [antinatu'ral] *adj* unnatural

antipatía [antipa'tia] *nf* antipathy, dislike; **antipático, a** *adj* disagreeable, unpleasant

antirrobo [anti'rroβo] *adj inv (alarma etc)* anti-theft

antisemita [antise'mita] *adj* anti-Semitic ♦ *nm/f* anti-Semite

antiséptico, a [anti'septiko, a] *adj* antiseptic ♦ *nm* antiseptic

antítesis [an'titesis] *nf inv* antithesis

antojadizo, a [antoxa'ðiθo, a] *adj* capricious

antojarse [anto'xarse] *vr (desear)*: **se me antoja comprarlo** I have a mind to buy it; *(pensar)*: **se me antoja que** I have a feeling that

antojo [an'toxo] *nm* caprice, whim; *(rosa)* birthmark; *(lunar)* mole

antología [antolo'xia] *nf* anthology

antorcha [an'tortʃa] *nf* torch

antro ['antro] *nm* cavern

antropófago, a [antro'pofaxo, a] *adj, nm/f* cannibal

antropología [antropolo'xia] *nf* anthropology

anual [a'nwal] *adj* annual

anuario [a'nwarjo] *nm* yearbook

anudar [anu'ðar] *vt* to knot, tie; *(unir)* to join; **~se** *vr* to get tied up

anulación [anula'θjon] *nf* annulment; *(cancelación)* cancellation

anular [anu'lar] *vt (contrato)* to annul, cancel; *(ley)* to revoke, repeal; *(suscripción)* to cancel ♦ *nm* ring finger

Anunciación [anunθja'θjon] *nf (REL)* Annunciation

anunciante [anun'θjante] *nm/f (COM)* advertiser

anunciar [anun'θjar] *vt* to announce; *(proclamar)* to proclaim; *(COM)* to advertise

anuncio [a'nunθjo] *nm* announcement; *(señal)* sign; *(COM)* advertisement; *(cartel)* poster

anzuelo [an'θwelo] *nm* hook; *(para pescar)* fish hook

añadidura [aɲaði'ðura] *nf* addition, extra; **por ~** besides, in addition

añadir [aɲa'ðir] *vt* to add

añejo, a [a'ɲexo, a] *adj* old; *(vino)* mellow

añicos [a'ɲikos] *nmpl*: **hacer ~** to smash, shatter

añil [a'ɲil] *nm (BOT, color)* indigo

año ['aɲo] *nm* year; **¡Feliz A~ Nuevo!** Happy New Year!; **tener 15 ~s** to be 15 (years old); **los ~ 90** the nineties; **~ bisiesto/escolar** leap/school year; **el ~ que viene** next year

añoranza [aɲo'ranθa] *nf* nostalgia; *(anhelo)* longing

apabullar [apaβu'ʎar] *vt (tb fig)* to crush, squash

apacentar [apaθen'tar] *vt* to pasture, graze

apacible [apa'θiβle] *adj* gentle, mild

apaciguar [apaθi'ɣwar] *vt* to pacify, calm (down)

apadrinar [apaðri'nar] *vt* to sponsor, support; *(REL)* to be godfather to

apagado, a [apa'ɣaðo, a] *adj (volcán)* extinct; *(color)* dull; *(voz)* quiet; *(sonido)* muted, muffled; *(persona: apático)* listless; **estar ~** *(fuego, luz)* to be out; *(RADIO, TV etc)* to be off

apagar [apa'ɣar] *vt* to put out; *(ELEC, RADIO, TV)* to turn off; *(sonido)* to silence, muffle; *(sed)* to quench

apagón [apa'ɣon] *nm* blackout; power cut

apalabrar [apala'βrar] *vt* to agree to; *(contratar)* to engage

apalear [apale'ar] *vt* to beat, thrash

apañar [apa'ɲar] *vt* to pick up; *(asir)* to take hold of, grasp; *(reparar)* to mend, patch up; **~se** *vr* to manage, get along

aparador [apara'ðor] *nm* sideboard; *(AM: escaparate)* shop window

aparato [apa'rato] nm apparatus; (máquina) machine; (doméstico) appliance; (boato) ostentation; ~ de facsímil facsimile (machine), fax; ~ digestivo (ANAT) digestive system; ~so, a adj showy, ostentatious

aparcamiento [aparka'mjento] nm car park (BRIT), parking lot (US)

aparcar [apar'kar] vt, vi to park

aparear [apare'ar] vt (objetos) to pair, match; (animales) to mate; ~se vr to make a pair; to mate

aparecer [apare'θer] vi to appear; ~se vr to appear

aparejado, a [apare'xaðo, a] adj fit, suitable; llevar o traer ~ to involve; **aparejador, a** nm/f (ARQ) master builder

aparejo [apa'rexo] nm harness; rigging; (de poleas) block and tackle

aparentar [aparen'tar] vt (edad) to look; (fingir): ~ tristeza to pretend to be sad

aparente [apa'rente] adj apparent; (adecuado) suitable

aparezco etc vb ver **aparecer**

aparición [apari'θjon] nf appearance; (de libro) publication; (espectro) apparition

apariencia [apa'rjenθja] nf (outward) appearance; en ~ outwardly, seemingly

apartado, a [apar'taðo, a] adj separate; (lejano) remote ♦ nm (tipográfico) paragraph; ~ (de correos) post office box

apartamento [aparta'mento] nm apartment, flat (BRIT)

apartamiento [aparta'mjento] nm separation; (aislamiento) remoteness, isolation; (AM) apartment, flat (BRIT)

apartar [apar'tar] vt to separate; (quitar) to remove; ~se vr to separate, part; (irse) to move away; to keep away

aparte [a'parte] adv (separadamente) separately; (además) besides ♦ nm

aside; (tipográfico) new paragraph

aparthotel [aparto'tel] nm serviced apartments

apasionado, a [apasjo'naðo, a] adj passionate

apasionar [apasjo'nar] vt to excite; le apasiona el fútbol she's crazy about football; ~se vr to get excited

apatía [apa'tia] nf apathy

apático, a [a'patiko, a] adj apathetic

Apdo abr (= Apartado (de Correos)) PO Box

apeadero [apea'ðero] nm halt, stop, stopping place

apearse [ape'arse] vr (jinete) to dismount; (bajarse) to get down o out; (AUTO, FERRO) to get off o out

apechugar [apetʃu'var] vr: ~ con algo to face up to sth

apedrear [apeðre'ar] vt to stone

apegarse [ape'varse] vr: ~ a to become attached to; **apego** nm attachment, devotion

apelación [apela'θjon] nf appeal

apelar [ape'lar] vi to appeal; ~ a (fig) to resort to

apellidar [apeʎi'ðar] vt to call, name; ~se vr: se apellida Pérez her (sur)name's Pérez

apellido [ape'ʎiðo] nm surname

apelmazarse [apelma'θarse] vr (masa, arroz) to go hard; (prenda de tana) to shrink

apenar [ape'nar] vt to grieve, trouble; (AM: avergonzar) to embarrass; ~se vr to grieve; (AM) to be embarrassed

apenas [a'penas] adv scarcely, hardly ♦ conj as soon as, no sooner

apéndice [a'pendiθe] nm appendix; **apendicitis** nf appendicitis

aperitivo [aperi'tiβo] nm (bebida) aperitif; (comida) appetizer

apero [a'pero] nm (AGR) implement; ~s nmpl farm equipment sg

apertura [aper'tura] nf opening; (POL) liberalization

apesadumbrar [apesaðum'brar] vt to

grieve, sadden; **~se** vr to distress o.s.

apestar |apes'tar| vt to infect ♦ vi: **~ (a)** to stink (of)

apetecer |apete'θer| vt: ¿**te apetece un café?** do you fancy a (cup of) coffee?; **apetecible** adj desirable; (comida) appetizing

apetito |ape'tito| nm appetite; **~so, a** adj appetizing; (fig) tempting

apiadarse |apja'ðarse| vr: **~ de** to take pity on

ápice |'apiθe| nm whit, iota

apilar |api'lar| vt to pile o heap up; **~se** vr to pile up

apiñarse |api'narse| vr to crowd o press together

apio |'apjo| nm celery

apisonadora |apisona'ðora| nf steamroller

aplacar |apla'kar| vt to placate; **~se** vr to calm down

aplanar |apla'nar| vt to smooth, level; (allanar) to roll flat, flatten

aplastante |aplas'tante| adj overwhelming; (lógica) compelling

aplastar |aplas'tar| vt to squash (flat); (fig) to crush

aplatanarse |aplata'narse| vr to get lethargic

aplaudir |aplau'ðir| vt to applaud

aplauso |a'plauso| nm applause; (fig) approval, acclaim

aplazamiento |aplaθa'mjento| nm postponement

aplazar |apla'θar| vt to postpone, defer

aplicación |aplika'θjon| nf application; (esfuerzo) effort

aplicado, a |apli'kaðo, a| adj diligent, hard-working

aplicar |apli'kar| vt (ejecutar) to apply; **~se** vr to apply o.s.

aplique |a'plike| vb ver **aplicar** ♦ nm wall light

aplomo |a'plomo| nm aplomb, self-assurance

apocado, a |apo'kaðo, a| adj timid

apodar |apo'ðar| vt to nickname

apoderado |apoðe'raðo| nm agent, representative

apoderarse |apoðe'rarse| vr: **~ de** to take possession of

apodo |a'poðo| nm nickname

apogeo |apo'xeo| nm peak, summit

apolillarse |apoli'ʎarse| vr to get moth-eaten

apología |apolo'xia| nf eulogy; (defensa) defence

apoltronarse |apoltro'narse| vr to get lazy

apoplejía |apople'xia| nf apoplexy, stroke

apoquinar |apoki'nar| (fam) vt to fork out, cough up

aporrear |aporre'ar| vt to beat (up)

aportar |apor'tar| vt to contribute ♦ vi to reach port; **~se** vr (AM: llegar) to arrive, come

aposento |apo'sento| nm lodging; (habitación) room

aposta |a'posta| adv deliberately, on purpose

apostar |apos'tar| vt to bet, stake; (tropas etc) to station, post ♦ vi to bet

apóstol |a'postol| nm apostle

apóstrofo |a'postrofo| nm apostrophe

apoyar |apo'jar| vt to lean, rest; (fig) to support, back; **~se en** to lean on; **apoyo** nm (gen) support; backing, help

apreciable |apre'θjaβle| adj considerable; (fig) esteemed

apreciar |apre'θjar| vt to evaluate, assess; (COM) to appreciate, value; (persona) to respect; (tamaño) to gauge, assess; (detalles) to notice

aprecio |a'preθjo| nm valuation, estimate; (fig) appreciation

aprehender |apreen'der| vt to apprehend, detain

apremiante |apre'mjante| adj urgent, pressing

apremiar |apre'mjar| vt to compel, force ♦ vi to be urgent, press;

apremio nm urgency

aprender |apren'der| vt, vi to learn

aprendiz, a |apren'diθ, a| nm/f apprentice; (principiante) learner; ~ **de conductor** learner driver; ~**aje** nm apprenticeship

aprensión |apren'sjon| nm apprehension, fear; **aprensivo, a** adj apprehensive

apresar |apre'sar| vt to seize; (capturar) to capture

aprestar |apres'tar| vt to prepare, get ready; (TEC) to prime, size; ~**se** vr to get ready

apresurado, a |apresu'raðo, a| adj hurried, hasty; **apresuramiento** nm hurry, haste

apresurar |apresu'rar| vt to hurry, accelerate; ~**se** vr to hurry, make haste

apretado, a |apre'taðo, a| adj tight; (escritura) cramped

apretar |apre'tar| vt to squeeze; (TEC) to tighten; (presionar) to press together, pack ♦ vi to be too tight

apretón |apre'ton| nm squeeze; ~ **de manos** handshake

aprieto |a'prjeto| nm squeeze; (dificultad) difficulty; **estar en un ~** to be in a fix

aprisa |a'prisa| adv quickly, hurriedly

aprisionar |aprisjo'nar| vt to imprison

aprobación |aproßa'θjon| nf approval

aprobar |apro'ßar| vt to approve (of); (examen, materia) to pass ♦ vi to pass

apropiación |apropja'θjon| nf appropriation

apropiado, a |apro'pjaðo, a| adj appropriate

apropiarse |apro'pjarse| vr: ~ **de** to appropriate

aprovechado, a |aproße'tʃaðo, a| adj industrious, hard-working; (económico) thrifty; (pey) unscrupulous; **aprovechamiento** nm use; exploitation

aprovechar |aproße'tʃar| vt to use; (explotar) to exploit; (experiencia) to

profit from; (oferta, oportunidad) to take advantage of ♦ vi to progress, improve; ~**se** vr: ~**se de** to make use of; to take advantage of; **¡que aproveche!** enjoy your meal!

aproximación |aproksima'θjon| nf approximation; (de lotería) consolation prize; **aproximado, a** adj approximate

aproximar |aproksi'mar| vt to bring nearer; ~**se** vr to come near, approach

apruebo etc vb ver **aprobar**

aptitud |apti'tuð| nf aptitude

apto, a |a'pto, a| adj suitable

apuesta |a'pwesta| nf bet, wager

apuesto, a |a'pwesto, a| adj neat, elegant

apuntador |apunta'ðor| nm prompter

apuntalar |apunta'lar| vt to prop up

apuntar |apun'tar| vt (con arma) to aim at; (con dedo) to point at o to; (anotar) to note (down); (TEATRO) to prompt; ~**se** vr (DEPORTE: tanto, victoria) to score; (ESCOL) to enrol

apunte |a'punte| nm note

apuñalar |apuɲa'lar| vt to stab

apurado, a |apu'raðo, a| adj needy; (difícil) difficult; (peligroso) dangerous; (AM) hurried, rushed

apurar |apu'rar| vt (agotar) to drain; (recursos) to use up; (molestar) to annoy; ~**se** vr (preocuparse) to worry; (darse prisa) to hurry

apuro |a'puro| nm (aprieto) fix, jam; (escasez) want, hardship; (vergüenza) embarrassment; (AM) haste, urgency

aquejado, a |ake'xaðo, a| adj: ~ **de** (MED) afflicted by

aquél, aquélla |a'kel, a'keʎa| (pl **aquéllos, as**) pron that (one); (pl) those (ones)

aquel, aquella |a'kel, a'keʎa| (pl **aquellos, as**) adj that; (pl) those

aquello |a'keʎo| pron that, that business

aquí |a'ki| adv (lugar) here; (tiempo) now; ~ **arriba** up here; ~ **mismo**

right here; **~ yace** here lies; **de ~ a siete días** a week from now

aquietar [akje'tar] *vt* to quieten (down), calm (down)

ara ['ara] *nf:* **en ~s de** for the sake of

árabe ['araβe] *adj, nm/f* Arab ♦ *nm* (*LING*) Arabic

Arabia [a'raβja] *nf:* **~ Saudí** o **Saudita** Saudi Arabia

arado [a'raðo] *nm* plough

Aragón [ara'von] *nm* Aragon;
aragonés, esa *adj, nm/f* Aragonese

arancel [aran'θel] *nm* tariff, duty; **~ de aduanas** customs (duty)

arandela [aran'dela] *nf* (*TEC*) washer

araña [a'rana] *nf* (*ZOOL*) spider;
(*lámpara*) chandelier

arañar [ara'nar] *vt* to scratch

arañazo [ara'naθo] *nm* scratch

arar [a'rar] *vt* to plough, till

arbitraje [arβi'traxe] *nm* arbitration

arbitrar [arβi'trar] *vt* to arbitrate in;
(*DEPORTE*) to referee ♦ *vi* to arbitrate

arbitrariedad [arβitrarje'ðað] *nf*
arbitrariness; (*acto*) arbitrary act;
arbitrario, a *adj* arbitrary

arbitrio [ar'βitrjo] *nm* free will; (*JUR*)
adjudication, decision

árbitro ['arβitro] *nm* arbitrator;
(*DEPORTE*) referee; (*TENIS*) umpire

árbol ['arβol] *nm* (*BOT*) tree; (*NAUT*)
mast; (*TEC*) axle, shaft; **arbolado, a**
adj wooded; (*camino etc*) tree-lined
♦ *nm* woodland

arboleda [arβo'leða] *nf* grove,
plantation

arbusto [ar'βusto] *nm* bush, shrub

arca ['arka] *nf* chest, box

arcada [ar'kaða] *nf* arcade; (*de puente*)
arch, span; **~s** *nfpl* (*náuseas*) retching
sg

arcaico, a [ar'kaiko, a] *adj* archaic

arce ['arθe] *nm* maple tree

arcén [ar'θen] *nm* (*de autopista*) hard
shoulder; (*de carretera*) verge

archipiélago [artʃi'pjelaxo] *nm*
archipelago

archivador [artʃiβa'ðor] *nm* filing
cabinet

archivar [artʃi'βar] *vt* to file (away);
archivo *nm* file, archive(s) (*pl*)

arcilla [ar'θiʎa] *nf* clay

arco ['arko] *nm* arch; (*MAT*) arc; (*MIL,
MUS*) bow; **~ iris** rainbow

arder [ar'ðer] *vi* to burn; **estar que
arde** (*persona*) to fume

ardid [ar'ðið] *nm* ploy, trick

ardiente [ar'ðjente] *adj* burning,
ardent

ardilla [ar'ðiʎa] *nf* squirrel

ardor [ar'ðor] *nm* (*calor*) heat; (*fig*)
ardour; **~ de estómago** heartburn

arduo, a [a'rðwo, a] *adj* arduous

área ['area] *nf* area; (*DEPORTE*) penalty
area

arena [a'rena] *nf* sand; (*de una lucha*)
arena; **~ movedizas** quicksand *sg*

arenal [are'nal] *nm* (*arena movediza*)
quicksand

arengar [aren'gar] *vt* to harangue

arenisca [are'niska] *nf* sandstone;
(*cascajo*) grit

arenoso, a [are'noso, a] *adj* sandy

arenque [a'renke] *nm* herring

argamasa [arva'masa] *nf* mortar,
plaster

Argel [ar'xel] *n* Algiers; **Argelia** *nf*
Algeria; **argelino, a** *adj, nm/f* Algerian

Argentina [arxen'tina] *nf:* **(la) ~**
Argentina

argentino, a [arxen'tino, a] *adj*
Argentinian; (*de plata*) silvery ♦ *nm/f*
Argentinian

argolla [ar'xoʎa] *nf* (*large*) ring

argot [ar'vo] (*pl* **~s**) *nm* slang

argucia [ar'vuθja] *nf* subtlety, sophistry

argüir [ar'xwir] *vt* to deduce; (*discutir*)
to argue; (*indicar*) to indicate, imply;
(*censurar*) to reproach ♦ *vi* to argue

argumentación [arvumenta'θjon] *nf*
(line of) argument

argumentar [arvumen'tar] *vt, vi* to
argue

argumento [arvu'mento] *nm*

argument; (*razonamiento*) reasoning; (*de novela etc*) plot; (*CINE, TV*) storyline

aria ['arja] *nf* aria

aridez [ari'ðeθ] *nf* aridity, dryness

árido, a ['ariðo, a] *adj* arid, dry; **~s** *nmpl* (COM) dry goods

Aries ['arjes] *nm* Aries

ario, a ['arjo, a] *adj* Aryan

arisco, a [a'risko, a] *adj* surly; (*insociable*) unsociable

aristócrata [aris'tokrata] *nm/f* aristocrat

aritmética [arit'metika] *nf* arithmetic

arma ['arma] *nf* arm; **~s** *nfpl* arms; **~ blanca** blade, knife; (*espada*) sword; **~ de fuego** firearm; **~s cortas** small arms

armada [ar'maða] *nf* armada; (*flota*) fleet

armadillo [arma'ðiλo] *nm* armadillo

armado, a [ar'maðo, a] *adj* armed; (TEC) reinforced

armador [arma'ðor] *nm* (NAUT) shipowner

armadura [arma'ðura] *nf* (MIL) armour; (TEC) framework; (ZOOL) skeleton; (FÍSICA) armature

armamento [arma'mento] *nm* armament; (NAUT) fitting-out

armar [ar'mar] *vt* (*soldado*) to arm; (*máquina*) to assemble; (*navío*) to fit out; **~la, ~ un lío** to start a row, kick up a fuss

armario [ar'marjo] *nm* wardrobe; (*de cocina, baño*) cupboard

armatoste [arma'toste] *nm* (*mueble*) monstrosity; (*máquina*) contraption

armazón [arma'θon] *nf o m* body, chassis; (*de mueble etc*) frame; (ARQ) skeleton

armería [arme'ria] *nf* gunsmith's

armiño [ar'miɲo] *nm* stoat; (*piel*) ermine

armisticio [armis'tiθjo] *nm* armistice

armonía [armo'nia] *nf* harmony

armónica [ar'monika] *nf* harmonica

armonioso, a [armo'njoso, a] *adj* harmonious

armonizar [armoni'θar] *vt* to harmonize; (*diferencias*) to reconcile ♦ *vi*: **~ con** (*fig*) to be in keeping with; (*colores*) to tone in with, blend

arnés [ar'nes] *nm* armour; **arneses** *nmpl* (*de caballo etc*) harness *sg*

aro ['aro] *nm* ring; (*tejo*) quoit; (AM: *pendiente*) earring

aroma [a'roma] *nm* aroma, scent

aromático, a [aro'matiko, a] *adj* aromatic

arpa ['arpa] *nf* harp

arpía [ar'pia] *nf* shrew

arpillera [arpi'λera] *nf* sacking, sackcloth

arpón [ar'pon] *nm* harpoon

arquear [arke'ar] *vt* to arch, bend; **~se** *vr* to arch, bend

arqueología [arkeolo'xia] *nf* archaeology; **arqueólogo, a** *nm/f* archaeologist

arquero [ar'kero] *nm* archer, bowman

arquetipo [arke'tipo] *nm* archetype

arquitecto [arki'tekto] *nm* architect; **arquitectura** *nf* architecture

arrabal [arra'βal] *nm* suburb; (AM) slum; **~es** *nmpl* (*afueras*) outskirts

arraigado, a [arrai'ɣaðo, a] *adj* deep-rooted; (*fig*) established

arraigar [arrai'ɣar] *vt* to establish ♦ *vi* to take root; **~se** *vr* to take root; (*persona*) to settle

arrancar [arran'kar] *vt* (*sacar*) to extract, pull out; (*arrebatar*) to snatch (away); (INFORM) to boot; (*fig*) to extract ♦ *vi* (AUTO, *máquina*) to start; (*ponerse en marcha*) to get going; **~ de** to stem from

arranque *etc* [a'rranke] *vb ver* **arrancar** ♦ *nm* sudden start; (AUTO) start; (*fig*) fit, outburst

arrasar [arra'sar] *vt* (*aplanar*) to level, flatten; (*destruir*) to demolish

arrastrado, a [arras'traðo, a] *adj* poor, wretched; (AM) servile

arrastrar [arras'trar] *vt* to drag

(along); (fig) to drag down, degrade; (suj: agua, viento) to carry away ♦ vi to drag, trail on the ground; **~se** vr to crawl; (fig) to grovel; **llevar algo arrastrado** to drag sth along

arrastre [a'rrastre] nm drag, dragging

arre ['arre] excl gee up!

arrear [arre'ar] vt to drive on, urge on ♦ vi to hurry along

arrebatado, a [arreβa'taðo, a] adj rash, impetuous; (repentino) sudden, hasty

arrebatar [arreβa'tar] vt to snatch (away), seize; (fig) to captivate; **~se** vr to get carried away, get excited

arrebato [arre'βato] nm fit of rage, fury; (éxtasis) rapture

arrecife [arre'θife] nm (tb: ~ de coral) reef

arredrarse [arre'ðrarse] vr: ~ (ante algo) to be intimidated (by sth)

arreglado, a [arre'ɣlaðo, a] adj (ordenado) neat, orderly; (moderado) moderate, reasonable

arreglar [arre'ɣlar] vt (poner orden) to tidy up; (algo roto) to fix, repair; (problema) to solve; **~se** vr to reach an understanding; **arreglárselas** (fam) to get by, manage

arreglo [a'rreɣlo] nm settlement; (orden) order; (acuerdo) agreement; (MUS) arrangement, setting

arrellanarse [arreʎa'narse] vr: ~ en to sit back in/on

arremangar [arreman'gar] vt to roll up, turn up; **~se** vr to roll up one's sleeves

arremeter [arreme'ter] vi: ~ contra to attack, rush at

arrendamiento [arrenda'mjento] nm letting; (alquilar) leasing; (contrato) lease; (alquiler) rent; **arrendar** vt to let, lease; to rent; **arrendatario, a** nm/f tenant

arreos [a'rreos] nmpl (de caballo) harness sg, trappings

arrepentimiento [arrepenti'mjento] nm regret, repentance

arrepentirse [arrepen'tirse] vr to repent; ~ **de** to regret

arrestar [arres'tar] vt to arrest; (encarcelar) to imprison; **arresto** nm arrest; (MIL) detention; (audacia) boldness, daring; **arresto domiciliario** house arrest

arriar [a'rrjar] vt (velas) to haul down; (bandera) to lower, strike; (cable) to pay out

---

PALABRA CLAVE

---

arriba [a'rriβa] adv **1** (posición) above; **desde ~** from above; **~ de todo** at the very top, right on top; **Juan está ~** Juan is upstairs; **lo ~ mencionado** the aforementioned

2 (dirección): **calle ~** up the street

3: de ~ abajo from top to bottom; **mirar a uno de ~ abajo** to look sb up and down

4: para ~: de 5000 pesetas para ~ from 5000 pesetas up(wards)

♦ adj: **de ~:** el piso de ~ the upstairs flat (BRIT) o apartment; **la parte de ~** the top o upper part

♦ prep: ~ **de** (AM) above; ~ **de 200 dólares** more than 200 dollars

♦ excl: ¡~! up!; ¡manos ~! hands up!; ¡~ España! long live Spain!

arribar [arri'βar] vi to put into port; (llegar) to arrive

arribista [arri'βista] nm/f parvenu(e), upstart

arriendo etc [a'rrjendo] vb ver **arrendar** ♦ nm = **arrendamiento**

arriero [a'rrjero] nm muleteer

arriesgado, a [arrjes'ɣaðo, a] adj (peligroso) risky; (audaz) bold, daring

arriesgar [arrjes'ɣar] vt to risk; (poner en peligro) to endanger; **~se** vr to take a risk

arrimar [arri'mar] vt (acercar) to bring close; (poner de lado) to set aside; **~se** vr to come close o closer; **~se a** to lean on

arrinconar |arrinko'nar| vt (colocar) to put in a corner; (enemigo) to corner; (fig) to put on one side; (abandonar) to push aside

arrodillarse |arroði'ʎarse| vr to kneel (down)

arrogancia |arro'vanθja| nf arrogance; **arrogante** adj arrogant

arrojar |arro'xar| vt to throw, hurl; (humo) to emit, give out; (COM) to yield, produce; **~se** vr to throw o hurl o.s.

arrojo |a'rroxo| nm daring

arrollador, a |arroʎa'ðor, a| adj overwhelming

arrollar |arro'ʎar| vt (AUTO etc) to run over, knock down; (DEPORTE) to crush

arropar |arro'par| vt to cover, wrap up; **~se** vr to wrap o.s. up

arroyo |a'rrojo| nm stream; (de la calle) gutter

arroz |a'rroθ| nm rice; **~ con leche** rice pudding

arruga |a'rruxa| nf (de cara) wrinkle; (de vestido) crease

arrugar |arru'xar| vt to wrinkle; to crease; **~se** vr to get creased

arruinar |arrwi'nar| vt to ruin, wreck; **~se** vr to be ruined, go bankrupt

arrullar |arru'ʎar| vi to coo ♦ vt to lull to sleep

arsenal |arse'nal| nm naval dockyard; (MIL) arsenal

arsénico |ar'seniko| nm arsenic

arte |'arte| (gen m en sg y siempre f en pl) nm art; (maña) skill, guile; **~s** nfpl (bellas **~s**) arts

artefacto |arte'fakto| nm appliance

arteria |ar'terja| nf artery

artesanía |artesa'nia| nf craftsmanship; (artículos) handicrafts pl; **artesano, a** nm/f artisan, craftsman/ woman

ártico, a |'artiko, a| adj Arctic ♦ nm: **el A~** the Arctic

articulación |artikula'θjon| nf

articulation; (MED, TEC) joint;

articulado, a adj articulated; jointed

articular |artiku'lar| vt to articulate; to join together

artículo |ar'tikulo| nm article; (cosa) thing, article; **~s** nmpl (COM) goods

artífice |ar'tifiθe| nm/f (fig) architect

artificial |artifi'θjal| adj artificial

artificio |arti'fiθjo| nm art, skill; (astucia) cunning

artillería |artiʎe'ria| nf artillery

artillero |arti'ʎero| nm artilleryman, gunner

artilugio |arti'luxjo| nm gadget

artimaña |arti'mana| nf trap, snare; (astucia) cunning

artista |ar'tista| nm/f (pintor) artist, painter; (TEATRO) artist, artiste; **~ de cine** film actor/actress; **artístico, a** adj artistic

artritis |ar'tritis| nf arthritis

arveja |ar'βexa| nf (AM) pea

arzobispo |arθo'βispo| nm archbishop

as |as| nm ace

asa |'asa| nf handle; (fig) lever

asado |a'saðo| nm roast (meat); (AM: barbacoa) barbecue

asador |asa'ðor| nm spit

asadura |asa'ðura| nf entrails pl, offal

asalariado, a |asala'rjaðo, a| adj paid, salaried ♦ nm/f wage earner

asaltante |asal'tante| nm/f attacker

asaltar |asal'tar| vt to attack, assault; (fig) to assail; **asalto** nm attack, assault; (DEPORTE) round

asamblea |asam'blea| nf assembly; (reunión) meeting

asar |a'sar| vt to roast

asbesto |as'βesto| nm asbestos

ascendencia |asθen'denθja| nf ancestry; (AM) ascendancy; **de ~ francesa** of French origin

ascender |asθen'der| vi (subir) to ascend, rise; (ser promovido) to gain promotion ♦ vt to promote; **~ a** to amount to; **ascendiente** nm influence ♦ nm/f ancestor

ascensión [asθen'sjon] nf ascent; (REL): **la A~** the Ascension

ascenso [as'θenso] nm ascent; (promoción) promotion

ascensor [asθen'sor] nm lift (BRIT), elevator (US)

ascético, a [as'θetiko, a] adj ascetic

asco ['asko] nm: **¡qué ~!** how revolting o disgusting; **el ajo me da ~** I hate o loathe garlic; **estar hecho un ~** to be filthy

ascua ['askwa] nf ember; **estar en ~s** to be on tenterhooks

aseado, a [ase'aðo, a] adj clean; (arreglado) tidy; (pulcro) smart

asear [ase'ar] vt to clean, wash; to tidy (up)

asediar [ase'ðjar] vt (MIL) to besiege, lay siege to; (fig) to chase, pester; **asedio** nm siege; (COM) run

asegurado, a [aseɣu'raðo, a] adj insured

asegurador, a nm/f insurer

asegurar [aseɣu'rar] vt (consolidar) to secure, fasten; (dar garantía de) to guarantee; (preservar) to safeguard; (afirmar, dar por cierto) to assure, affirm; (tranquilizar) to reassure; (tomar un seguro) to insure; **~se** vr to assure o.s., make sure

asemejarse [aseme'xarse] vr to be alike; **~ a** to be like, resemble

asentado, a [asen'taðo, a] adj established, settled

asentar [asen'tar] vt (sentar) to seat, sit down; (poner) to place, establish; (alisar) to level, smooth down o out; (anotar) to note down ♦ vi to be suitable, suit

asentir [asen'tir] vi to assent, agree; **~ con la cabeza** to nod (one's head)

aseo [a'seo] nm cleanliness; **~s** nmpl (servicios) toilet sg (BRIT), cloakroom sg (BRIT), restroom sg (US)

aséptico, a [a'septiko, a] adj germ-free, free from infection

asequible [ase'kiβle] adj (precio)

reasonable; (meta) attainable; (persona) approachable

aserradero [aserra'ðero] nm sawmill; **aserrar** vt to saw

asesinar [asesi'nar] vt to murder; (POL) to assassinate; **asesinato** nm murder; assassination

asesino, a [ase'sino, a] nm/f murderer, killer; (POL) assassin

asesor, a [ase'sor, a] nm/f adviser, consultant

asesorar [aseso'rar] vt (JUR) to advise, give legal advice to; (COM) to act as consultant to; **~se** vr: **~se con o de** to take advice from, consult; **asesoría** nf (cargo) consultancy; (oficina) consultant's office

asestar [ases'tar] vt (golpe) to deal, strike

asfalto [as'falto] nm asphalt

asfixia [as'fiksja] nf asphyxia, suffocation

asfixiar [asfik'sjar] vt to asphyxiate, suffocate; **~se** vr to be asphyxiated, suffocate

asgo etc vb ver **asir**

así [a'si] adv (de esta manera) in this way, like this, thus; (aunque) although; (tan pronto como) as soon as; **~ que** so; **~ como** as well as; **~ y todo** even so; **¿no es ~?** isn't it?, didn't you? etc; **~ de grande** this big

Asia ['asja] nf Asia; **asiático, a** adj, nm/f Asian, Asiatic

asidero [asi'ðero] nm handle

asiduidad [asiðwi'ðað] nf assiduousness; **asiduo, a** adj assiduous; (frecuente) frequent ♦ nm/f regular (customer)

asiento [a'sjento] nm (mueble) seat, chair; (de coche, en tribunal etc) seat; (localidad) seat, place; (fundamento) site; **~ delantero/trasero** front/back seat

asignación [asiɣna'θjon] nf (atribución) assignment; (reparto) allocation; (sueldo) salary; **~ (semanal)**

pocket money

asignar |asix'nar| *vt* to assign, allocate

asignatura |asixna'tura| *nf* subject; course

asilado, a |asi'laðo, a| *nm/f* inmate; (POL) refugee

asilo |a'silo| *nm* (refugio) asylum, refuge; (establecimiento) home, institution; **~ político** political asylum

asimilación |asimila'θjon| *nf* assimilation

asimilar |asimi'lar| *vt* to assimilate

asimismo |asi'mismo| *adv* in the same way, likewise

asir |a'sir| *vt* to seize, grasp

asistencia |asis'tenθja| *nf* audience; (MED) attendance; (ayuda) assistance; **asistente** *nm/f* assistant; **los asistentes** those present; **asistente social** social worker

asistido, a |asis'tiðo, a| *adj:* **~ por ordenador** computer-assisted

asistir |asis'tir| *vt* to assist, help ♦ *vi:* **~ a** to attend, be present at

asma |'asma| *nf* asthma

asno |'asno| *nm* donkey; (fig) ass

asociación |asoθja'θjon| *nf* association; (COM) partnership; **asociado, a** *adj* associate ♦ *nm/f* associate; (COM) partner

asociar |aso'θjar| *vt* to associate

asolar |aso'lar| *vt* to destroy

asomar |aso'mar| *vt* to show, stick out ♦ *vi* to appear; **~se** *vr* to appear, show up; **~ la cabeza por la ventana** to put one's head out of the window

asombrar |asom'brar| *vt* to amaze, astonish; **~se** *vr* (sorprenderse) to be amazed; (asustarse) to get a fright; **asombro** *nm* amazement, astonishment; (susto) fright; **asombroso, a** *adj* astonishing, amazing

asomo |a'somo| *nm* hint, sign

aspa |'aspa| *nf* (cruz) cross; (de molino) sail; **en ~** X-shaped

aspaviento |aspa'βjento| *nm*

exaggerated display of feeling; (fam) fuss

aspecto |as'pekto| *nm* (apariencia) look, appearance; (fig) aspect

aspereza |aspe'reθa| *nf* roughness; (agrura) sourness; (de carácter) surliness; **áspero, a** *adj* rough; bitter; sour; harsh

aspersión |asper'sjon| *nf* sprinkling

aspiración |aspira'θjon| *nf* breath, inhalation; (MUS) short pause; **aspiraciones** *nfpl* (ambiciones) aspirations

aspirador |aspira'ðor| *nm* = **aspiradora**

aspiradora |aspira'ðora| *nf* vacuum cleaner, Hoover ®

aspirante |aspi'rante| *nm/f* (candidato) candidate; (DEPORTE) contender

aspirar |aspi'rar| *vt* to breathe in ♦ *vi:* **~ a** to aspire to

aspirina |aspi'rina| *nf* aspirin

asquear |aske'ar| *vt* to sicken ♦ *vi* to be sickening; **~se** *vr* to feel disgusted; **asqueroso, a** *adj* disgusting, sickening

asta |'asta| *nf* lance; (arpón) spear; (mango) shaft, handle; (ZOOL) horn; **a media ~** at half mast

asterisco |aste'risko| *nm* asterisk

astilla |as'tiʎa| *nf* splinter; (pedacito) chip; **~s** *nfpl* (leña) firewood *sg*

astillero |asti'ʎero| *nm* shipyard

astringente |astrin'xente| *adj, nm* astringent

astro |'astro| *nm* star

astrología |astrolo'xia| *nf* astrology; **astrólogo, a** *nm/f* astrologer

astronauta |astro'nauta| *nm/f* astronaut

astronave |astro'naße| *nm* spaceship

astronomía |astrono'mia| *nf* astronomy; **astrónomo, a** *nm/f* astronomer

astucia |as'tuθja| *nf* astuteness; (ardid) clever trick

asturiano, a |astu'rjano, a| *adj, nm/f*

Asturian

astuto, a [as'tuto, a] *adj* astute; (*taimado*) cunning

asumir [asu'mir] *vt* to assume

asunción [asun'θjon] *nf* assumption; (*REL*): **A~** Assumption

asunto [a'sunto] *nm* (*tema*) matter, subject; (*negocio*) business

asustar [asus'tar] *vt* to frighten; **~se** *vr* to be (*o* become) frightened

atacar [ata'kar] *vt* to attack

atadura [ata'ðura] *nf* bond, tie

atajar [ata'xar] *vt* (*enfermedad, mal*) to stop ♦ *vi* (*persona*) to take a short cut

atajo [a'taxo] *nm* short cut

atañer [ata'ɲer]: **~ a** to concern

ataque *etc* [a'take] *vb ver* **atacar** ♦ *nm* attack; **~ cardíaco** heart attack

atar [a'tar] *vt* to tie, tie up

atardecer [atarðe'θer] *vi* to get dark ♦ *nm* evening; (*crepúsculo*) dusk

atareado, a [atare'aðo, a] *adj* busy

atascar [atas'kar] *vt* to clog up; (*obstruir*) to jam; (*fig*) to hinder; **~se** *vr* to stall; (*cañería*) to get blocked up; **atasco** *nm* obstruction; (*AUTO*) traffic jam

ataúd [ata'uð] *nm* coffin

ataviar [ata'βjar] *vt* to deck, array; **~se** *vr* to dress up

atavío [ata'βio] *nm* attire, dress; **~s** *nmpl* finery *sg*

atemorizar [atemori'θar] *vt* to frighten, scare; **~se** *vr* to get scared

Atenas [a'tenas] *n* Athens

atención [aten'θjon] *nf* attention; (*bondad*) kindness ♦ *excl* (be) careful!, look out!

atender [aten'der] *vt* to attend to, look after ♦ *vi* to pay attention

atenerse [ate'nerse] *vr*: **~ a** to abide by, adhere to

atentado [aten'taðo] *nm* crime, illegal act; (*asalto*) assault; **~ contra la vida de uno** attempt on sb's life

atentamente [atenta'mente] *adv*: **Le saluda ~** Yours faithfully

atentar [aten'tar] *vi*: **~ a o contra** to commit an outrage against

atento, a [a'tento, a] *adj* attentive, observant; (*cortés*) polite, thoughtful

atenuante [ate'nwante] *adj* extenuating

atenuar [ate'nwar] *vt* (*disminuir*) to lessen, minimize

ateo, a [a'teo, a] *adj* atheistic ♦ *nm/f* atheist

aterciopelado, a [aterθjope'laðo, a] *adj* velvety

aterido, a [ate'riðo, a] *adj*: **~ de frío** frozen stiff

aterrador, a [aterra'ðor, a] *adj* frightening

aterrar [ate'rrar] *vt* to frighten; to terrify

aterrizaje [aterri'θaxe] *nm* landing

aterrizar [aterri'θar] *vi* to land

aterrorizar [aterrori'θar] *vt* to terrify

atesorar [ateso'rar] *vt* to hoard

atestado, a [ates'taðo, a] *adj* packed ♦ *nm* (*JUR*) affidavit

atestar [ates'tar] *vt* to pack, stuff; (*JUR*) to attest, testify to

atestiguar [atesti'ɣwar] *vt* to testify to, bear witness to

atiborrar [atiβo'rrar] *vt* to fill, stuff; **~se** *vr* to stuff o.s.

ático [a'tiko] *nm* attic; **~ de lujo** penthouse (flat (*BRIT*) *o* apartment)

atinado, a [ati'naðo, a] *adj* (*sensato*) wise; (*correcto*) right, correct

atinar [ati'nar] *vi* (*al disparar*): **~ al blanco** to hit the target; (*fig*) to be right

atisbar [atis'βar] *vt* to spy on; (*echar una ojeada*) to peep at

atizar [ati'θar] *vt* to poke; (*horno etc*) to stoke; (*fig*) to stir up, rouse

atlántico, a [at'lantiko, a] *adj* Atlantic ♦ *nm*: **el (océano) A~** the Atlantic (Ocean)

atlas [a'tlas] *nm* atlas

atleta [at'leta] *nm* athlete; **atlético, a** *adj* athletic; **atletismo** *nm* athletics *sg*

atmósfera [at'mosfera] *nf* atmosphere

atolladero [atoʎa'ðero] *nm* (*fig*) jam, fix

atolondramiento [atolondra'mjento] *nm* bewilderment; (*insensatez*) silliness

atómico, a [a'tomiko, a] *adj* atomic

atomizador [atomiθa'ðor] *nm* atomizer; (*de perfume*) spray

átomo ['atomo] *nm* atom

atónito, a [a'tonito, a] *adj* astonished, amazed

atontado, a [aton'taðo, a] *adj* stunned; (*bobo*) silly, daft

atontar [aton'tar] *vt* to stun; **~se** *vr* to become confused

atormentar [atormen'tar] *vt* to torture; (*molestar*) to torment; (*acosar*) to plague, harass

atornillar [atorni'ʎar] *vt* to screw on o down

atosigar [atosi'ɣar] *vt* to harass, pester

atracador, a [atraka'ðor, a] *nm/f* robber

atracar [atra'kar] *vt* (*NAUT*) to moor; (*robar*) to hold up, rob ♦ *vi* to moor; **~se** *vr*: **~se (de)** to stuff o.s. (with)

atracción [atrak'θjon] *nf* attraction

atraco [a'trako] *nm* holdup, robbery

atracón [atra'kon] *nm*: **darse** *o* **pegarse un ~ (de)** (*fam*) to stuff o.s. (with)

atractivo, a [atrak'tiβo, a] *adj* attractive ♦ *nm* appeal

atraer [atra'er] *vt* to attract

atragantarse [atraɣan'tarse] *vr*: **~ (con)** to choke (on); **se me ha atragantado el chico** I can't stand the boy

atrancar [atran'kar] *vt* (*puerta*) to bar, bolt

atrapar [atra'par] *vt* to trap; (*resfriado etc*) to catch

atrás [a'tras] *adv* (*movimiento*) back (-wards); (*lugar*) behind; (*tiempo*) previously; **ir hacia ~** to go back(wards); **ir a la zaga** to go to the rear; **estar ~** to be behind o at the back

atrasado, a [atra'saðo, a] *adj* slow; (*pago*) overdue, late; (*país*) backward

atrasar [atra'sar] *vi* to be slow; **~se** *vr* to remain behind; (*tren*) to be o run late; **atraso** *nm* slowness; lateness, delay; (*de país*) backwardness; **atrasos** *nmpl* (*COM*) arrears

atravesar [atraβe'sar] *vt* (*cruzar*) to cross (over); (*traspasar*) to pierce; to go through; (*poner al través*) to lay o put across; **~se** *vr* to come in between; (*intervenir*) to interfere

atravieso *etc vb ver* **atravesar**

atrayente [atra'jente] *adj* attractive

atreverse [atre'βerse] *vr* to dare; (*insolentarse*) to be insolent; **atrevido, a** *adj* daring; insolent; **atrevimiento** *nm* daring; insolence

atribución [atriβu'θjon] *nf*: **atribuciones** (*POL*) powers; (*ADMIN*) responsibilities

atribuir [atriβu'ir] *vt* to attribute; (*funciones*) to confer

atribular [atriβu'lar] *vt* to afflict, distress

atributo [atri'βuto] *nm* attribute

atril [a'tril] *nm* (*para libro*) lectern; (*MUS*) music stand

atrocidad [atroθi'ðað] *nf* atrocity, outrage

atropellar [atrope'ʎar] *vt* (*derribar*) to knock over o down; (*empujar*) to push (aside); (*AUTO*) to run over, run down; (*agraviar*) to insult; **~se** *vr* to act hastily; **atropello** *nm* (*AUTO*) accident; (*empujón*) push; (*agravio*) wrong; (*atrocidad*) outrage

atroz [a'troθ] *adj* atrocious, awful

ATS *nmf abr* (= *Ayudante Técnico Sanitario*) nurse

atto, a *abr* = **atento**

atuendo [a'twendo] *nm* attire

atún [a'tun] *nm* tuna

aturdir [atur'ðir] *vt* to stun; (*de ruido*) to deafen; (*fig*) to dumbfound, bewilder

atusar [atu'sar] *vt* to smooth (down)

audacia [au'ðaθja] *nf* boldness, audacity; **audaz** *adj* bold, audacious

audible [au'ðiβle] *adj* audible

audición [auði'θjon] *nf* hearing; (*TEATRO*) audition

audiencia [au'ðjenθja] *nf* audience; **A~** (*JUR*) High Court

audífono [au'ðifono] *nm* (*para sordos*) hearing aid

auditor [auði'tor] *nm* (*JUR*) judge advocate; (*COM*) auditor

auditorio [auði'torjo] *nm* audience; (*sala*) auditorium

auge ['auxe] *nm* boom; (*clímax*) climax

augurar [auxu'rar] *vt* to predict; (*presagiar*) to portend

augurio [au'vurjo] *nm* omen

aula ['aula] *nf* classroom; (*en universidad etc*) lecture room

aullar [au'ʎar] *vi* to howl, yell

aullido [au'ʎiðo] *nm* howl, yell

aumentar [aumen'tar] *vt* to increase; (*precios*) to put up; (*producción*) to step up; (*con microscopio, anteojos*) to magnify ♦ *vi* to increase, be on the increase; **~se** *vr* to increase, be on the increase; **aumento** *nm* increase; rise

aun [a'un] *adv* even; **~ así** even so; **~ más** even o yet more

aún [a'un] *adv:* **~ está aquí** he's still here; **~ no lo sabemos** we don't know yet; **¿no ha venido ~?** hasn't she come yet?

aunque [a'unke] *conj* though, although, even though

aúpa [a'upa] *excl* come on!

aureola [aure'ola] *nf* halo

auricular [auriku'lar] *nm* (*TEL*) earpiece, receiver; **~es** *nmpl* (*para escuchar música etc*) headphones

aurora [au'rora] *nf* dawn

auscultar [auskul'tar] *vt* (*MED: pecho*) to listen to, sound

ausencia [au'senθja] *nf* absence

ausentarse [ausen'tarse] *vr* to go away; (*por poco tiempo*) to go out

ausente [au'sente] *adj* absent

auspicios [aus'piθjos] *nmpl* auspices

austeridad [austeri'ðað] *nf* austerity; **austero, a** *adj* austere

austral [aus'tral] *adj* southern ♦ *nm* monetary unit of Argentina

Australia [aus'tralja] *nf* Australia; **australiano, a** *adj, nm/f* Australian

Austria ['austrja] *nf* Austria; **austríaco, a** *adj, nm/f* Austrian

auténtico, a [au'tentiko, a] *adj* authentic

auto ['auto] *nm* (*JUR*) edict, decree; (*: orden*) writ; (*AUTO*) car; **~s** *nmpl* (*JUR*) proceedings; (*: acta*) court record *sg*

autoadhesivo [autoaðe'siβo] *adj* self-adhesive; (*sobre*) self-sealing

autobiografía [autoβjoɣra'fia] *nf* autobiography

autobús [auto'βus] *nm* bus

autocar [auto'kar] *nm* coach (*BRIT*), (passenger) bus (*US*)

autóctono, a [au'toktono, a] *adj* native, indigenous

autodefensa [autoðe'fensa] *nf* self-defence

autodeterminación [autoðetermina'θjon] *nf* self-determination

autodidacta [autoði'ðakta] *adj* self-taught

autoescuela [autoes'kwela] *nf* driving school

autógrafo [au'toɣrafo] *nm* autograph

autómata [au'tomata] *nm* automaton

automático, a [auto'matiko, a] *adj* automatic ♦ *nm* press stud

automotor, triz [automo'tor, 'triθ] *adj* self-propelled ♦ *nm* diesel train

automóvil [auto'moβil] *nm* (*motor*) car (*BRIT*), automobile (*US*)

automovilismo *nm* (*actividad*) motoring; (*DEPORTE*) motor racing; **automovilista** *nm/f* motorist, driver; **automovilístico, a** *adj* (*industria*) motor *cpd*

autonomía [autono'mia] *nf* autonomy; **autónomo, a** (*ESP*),

autonómico, a (ESP) adj (POL)
autonomous

autopista |auto'pista| nf motorway
(BRIT), freeway (US); **~ de peaje** toll
road (BRIT), turnpike road (US)

autopsia |au'topsja| nf autopsy,
postmortem

autor, a |au'tor, a| nm/f author

autoridad |autori'ðað| nf authority;
autoritario, a adj authoritarian

autorización |autoriθa'θjon| nf
authorization; **autorizado, a** adj
authorized; (aprobado) approved

autorizar |autoriθ'ar| vt to authorize;
(aprobar) to approve

autorretrato |autorre'trato| nm self-
portrait

autoservicio |autoser'βiθjo| nm
(tienda) self-service shop (BRIT) o store
(US); (restaurante) self-service restaurant

autostop |auto'stop| nm hitch-hiking;
hacer ~ to hitch-hike; **~ista** nm/f
hitch-hiker

autosuficiencia |autosufi'θjenθja| nf
self-sufficiency

autovía |auto'βia| nf ≈ A-road (BRIT),
dual carriageway (BRIT), ≈ state
highway (US)

auxiliar |auksi'ljar| vt to help ♦ nm/f
assistant; **auxilio** nm assistance, help;
primeros auxilios first aid sg

Av abr (= Avenida) Av(e).

aval |a'βal| nm guarantee; (persona)
guarantor

avalancha |aβa'lantʃa| nf avalanche

avance |a'βanθe| nm advance; (pago)
advance payment; (CINE) trailer

avanzar |aβan'θar| vt, vi to advance

avaricia |aβa'riθja| nf avarice, greed;
avaricioso, a adj avaricious, greedy

avaro, a |a'βaro, a| adj miserly, mean
♦ nm/f miser

avasallar |aβasa'ʎar| vt to subdue,
subjugate

Avda abr (= Avenida) Av(e).

AVE |'aβe| nm abr (= Alta Velocidad
Española) ≈ bullet train

ave |'aβe| nf bird; **~ de rapiña** bird of
prey

avecinarse |aβeθi'narse| vr (tormenta,
fig) to be on the way

avellana |aβe'ʎana| nf hazelnut;
avellano nm hazel tree

avemaría |aβema'ria| nm Hail Mary,
Ave Maria

avena |a'βena| nf oats pl

avenida |aβe'niða| nf (calle) avenue

avenir |aβe'nir| vt to reconcile; **~se** vr
to come to an agreement, reach a
compromise

aventajado, a |aβenta'xaðo, a| adj
outstanding

aventajar |aβenta'xar| vt (sobrepasar)
to surpass, outstrip

aventura |aβen'tura| nf adventure;
aventurado, a adj risky; **aventurero,
a** adj adventurous

avergonzar |aβerɣon'θar| vt to
shame; (desconcertar) to embarrass;
~se vr to be ashamed; to be
embarrassed

avería |aβe'ria| nf (TEC) breakdown,
fault

averiado, a |aβe'rjaðo, a| adj broken
down; **"~"** "out of order"

averiguación |aβeriɣwa'θjon| nf
investigation; (descubrimiento)
ascertainment

averiguar |aβeri'ɣwar| vt to
investigate; (descubrir) to find out,
ascertain

aversión |aβer'sjon| nf aversion, dislike

avestruz |aβes'truθ| nm ostrich

aviación |aβja'θjon| nf aviation;
(fuerzas aéreas) air force

aviador, a |aβja'ðor, a| nm/f aviator,
airman/woman

avicultura |aβikul'tura| nf poultry
farming

avidez |aβi'ðeθ| nf avidity, eagerness;
ávido, a adj avid, eager

avinagrado, a |aβina'ɣraðo, a| adj
sour, acid

avión |a'βjon| nm aeroplane; (ave)

martin; **~ de reacción** jet (plane)
avioneta [aβjo'neta] nf light aircraft
avisar [aβi'sar] vt (advertir) to warn,
notify; (informar) to tell; (aconsejar) to
advise, counsel; **aviso** nm warning;
(noticia) notice
avispa [a'βispa] nf wasp
avispado, a [aβis'paðo, a] aj sharp,
clever
avispero [aβis'pero] nm wasp's nest
avispón [aβis'pon] nm hornet
avistar [aβis'tar] vt to sight, spot
avituallar [aβitwa'ʎar] vt to supply
with food
avivar [aβi'βar] vt to strengthen,
intensify; **~se** vr to revive, acquire new
life
axila [ak'sila] nf armpit
axioma [ak'sjoma] nm axiom
ay [ai] excl (dolor) owl, ouch!; (aflicción)
oh!, oh dear!; **¡~ de mí!** poor me!
aya ['aja] nf governess; (niñera) nanny
ayer [a'jer] adv, nm yesterday; **antes
de ~** the day before yesterday
ayote [a'jote] (AM) nm pumpkin
ayuda [a'juða] nf help, assistance ♦ nm
page; **ayudante, a** nm/f assistant,
helper; (ESCOL) assistant; (MIL) adjutant
ayudar [aju'ðar] vt to help, assist
ayunar [aju'nar] vi to fast; **ayunas**
nfpl: **estar en ayunas** to be fasting;
ayuno nm fast; fasting
ayuntamiento [ajunta'mjento] nm
(consejo) town o city council; (edificio)
town o city hall
azabache [aθa'βatʃe] nm jet
azada [a'θaða] nf hoe
azafata [aθa'fata] nf air stewardess
azafrán [aθa'fran] nm saffron
azahar [aθa'ar] nm orange/lemon
blossom
azar [a'θar] nm (casualidad) chance,
fate; (desgracia) misfortune, accident;
por ~ by chance; **al ~** at random
azoramiento [aθora'mjento] nm
alarm; (confusión) confusion
azorar [aθo'rar] vt to alarm; **~se** vr to

get alarmed
Azores [a'θores] nfpl: **las ~** the Azores
azotar [aθo'tar] vt to whip, beat;
(pegar) to spank; **azote** nm (látigo)
whip; (latigazo) lash, stroke; (en las
nalgas) spank; (calamidad) calamity
azotea [aθo'tea] nf (flat) roof
azteca [aθ'teka] adj, nm/f Aztec
azúcar [a'θukar] nm sugar;
azucarado, a adj sugary, sweet
azucarero, a [aθuka'rero, a] adj sugar
cpd ♦ nm sugar bowl
azucena [aθu'θena] nf white lily
azufre [a'θufre] nm sulphur
azul [a'θul] adj, nm blue; **~ marino**
navy blue
azulejo [aθu'lexo] nm tile
azuzar [aθu'θar] vt to incite, egg on

B, b

B.A. abr (= Buenos Aires) B.A.
baba ['baβa] nf spittle, saliva; **babear**
vi to drool, slaver
babero [ba'βero] nm bib
babor [ba'βor] nm port (side)
baboso, a [ba'βoso, a] (AM: fam) adj
silly
baca ['baka] nf (AUTO) luggage o roof
rack
bacalao [baka'lao] nm cod(fish)
bache ['batʃe] nm pothole, rut; (fig)
bad patch
bachillerato [batʃiʎe'rato] nm higher
secondary school course
bacteria [bak'terja] nf bacterium, germ
báculo ['bakulo] nm stick, staff
bagaje [ba'xaxe] nm baggage, luggage
Bahama [ba'ama]: **las (Islas) ~** nfpl
the Bahamas
bahía [ba'ia] nf bay
bailar [bai'lar] vt, vi to dance; **~ín, ina**
nm/f (ballet) dancer; **baile** nm dance;
(formal) ball
baja ['baxa] nf drop, fall; (MIL) casualty;
dar de ~ (soldado) to discharge;

(*empleado*) to dismiss

bajada [ba'xaða] nf descent; (*camino*) slope; (*de aguas*) ebb

bajar [ba'xar] vi to go down, come down; (*temperatura, precios*) to drop, fall ♦ vt (*cabeza*) to bow; (*escalera*) to go down, come down; (*precio, voz*) to lower; (*llevar abajo*) to take down; **~se** vr (*de coche*) to get out; (*de autobús, tren*) to get off; **~ de** (*coche*) to get out of; (*autobús, tren*) to get off

bajeza [ba'xeθa] nf baseness no pl; (*una ~*) vile deed

bajío [ba'xio] nm (AM) lowlands pl

bajo, a ['baxo, a] adj (*mueble, número, precio*) low; (*piso*) ground; (*de estatura*) small, short; (*color*) pale; (*sonido*) faint, soft, low; (*voz: en tono*) deep; (*metal*) base; (*humilde*) low, humble ♦ adv (*hablar*) softly, quietly; (*volar*) low ♦ prep under, below, underneath ♦ nm (MUS) bass; **~ la lluvia** in the rain

bajón [ba'xon] nm fall, drop

bakalao [baka'lao] (*fam*) nm rave (music)

bala ['bala] nf bullet

balance [ba'lanθe] nm (COM) balance; (: *libro*) balance sheet; (: *cuenta general*) stocktaking

balancear [balanθe'ar] vt to balance ♦ vi to swing (to and fro); (*vacilar*) to hesitate; **~se** vr to swing (to and fro); to hesitate; **balanceo** nm swinging

balanza [ba'lanθa] nf scales pl, balance; (ASTROLOGÍA): **B~** Libra; **~ comercial** balance of trade; **~ de pagos** balance of payments

balar [ba'lar] vi to bleat

balaustrada [balaus'traða] nf balustrade; (*pasamanos*) banisters pl

balazo [ba'laθo] nm (*golpe*) shot; (*herida*) bullet wound

balbucear [balβuθe'ar] vi, vt to stammer, stutter; **balbuceo** nm stammering, stuttering

balbucir [balβu'θir] vi, vt to stammer, stutter

balcón [bal'kon] nm balcony

balde ['balde] nm bucket, pail; **de ~** (for) free, for nothing; **en ~** in vain

baldío, a [bal'dio, a] adj uncultivated; (*terreno*) waste ♦ nm waste land

baldosa [bal'dosa] nf (*azulejo*) floor tile; (*grande*) flagstone; **baldosín** nm (small) tile

Baleares [bale'ares] nfpl: **las (Islas) ~** the Balearic Islands

balido [ba'liðo] nm bleat, bleating

baliza [ba'liθa] nf (AVIAT) beacon; (NAUT) buoy

ballena [ba'ʎena] nf whale

ballesta [ba'ʎesta] nf crossbow; (AUTO) spring

ballet [ba'le] (pl **~s**) nm ballet

balneario, a [balne'arjo, a] adj: **estación balnearia** (AM) (bathing) resort ♦ nm spa, health resort

balón [ba'lon] nm ball

baloncesto [balon'θesto] nm basketball

balonmano [balon'mano] nm handball

balonvolea [balombo'lea] nm volleyball

balsa ['balsa] nf raft; (BOT) balsa wood

bálsamo ['balsamo] nm balsam, balm

baluarte [ba'lwarte] nm bastion, bulwark

bambolear [bambole'ar] vi to swing, sway; (*silla*) to wobble; **~se** vr to swing, sway; to wobble; **bamboleo** nm swinging, swaying; wobbling

bambú [bam'bu] nm bamboo

banana [ba'nana] (AM) nf banana; **banano** (AM) nm banana tree

banca ['banka] nf (COM) banking

bancario, a [ban'karjo, a] adj banking cpd, bank cpd

bancarrota [banka'rrota] nf bankruptcy; **hacer ~** to go bankrupt

banco ['banko] nm bench; (ESCOL) desk; (COM) bank; (GEO) stratum; **~ de crédito/de ahorros** credit/savings bank; **~ de arena** sandbank; **~ de**

datos databank

banda ['banda] nf band; (pandilla)
gang; (NAUT) side, edge; **la
B~ Oriental** Uruguay; **~ sonora**
soundtrack

bandada [ban'daða] nf (de pájaros)
flock; (de peces) shoal

bandazo [ban'daθo] nm: **dar ~s**
to sway from side to side

bandeja [ban'dexa] nf tray

bandera [ban'dera] nf flag

banderilla [bande'riʎa] nf banderilla

banderín [bande'rin] nm pennant,
small flag

bandido [ban'diðo] nm bandit

bando ['bando] nm (edicto) edict,
proclamation; (facción) faction; **los ~s**
(REL) the banns

bandolera [bando'lera] nf: **llevar en
~** to wear across one's chest

bandolero [bando'lero] nm bandit,
brigand

banquero [ban'kero] nm banker

banqueta [ban'keta] nf stool; (AM: en
la calle) pavement (BRIT), sidewalk (US)

banquete [ban'kete] nm banquet;
(para convidados) formal dinner

banquillo [ban'kiʎo] nm (JUR) dock,
prisoner's bench; (banco) bench; (para
los pies) footstool

bañador [baɲa'ðor] nm swimming
costume (BRIT), bathing suit (US)

bañar [ba'ɲar] vt to bath, bathe;
(objeto) to dip; (de barniz) to coat; **~se**
vr (en el mar) to bathe, swim; (en la
bañera) to have a bath

bañera [ba'ɲera] nf bath(tub)

bañero, a [ba'ɲero, a] (AM) nm/f
lifeguard

bañista [ba'ɲista] nm/f bather

baño ['baɲo] nm (en bañera) bath; (en
río) dip, swim; (cuarto) bathroom;
(bañera) bath(tub); (capa) coating

baqueta [ba'keta] nf (MUS) drumstick

bar [bar] nm bar

barahúnda [bara'unda] nf uproar,
hubbub

baraja [ba'raxa] nf pack (of cards)

barajar [bara'xar] vt (naipes) to shuffle; (fig) to
jumble up

baranda [ba'randa] nf = **barandilla**

barandilla [baran'diʎa] nf rail, railing

baratija [bara'tixa] nf trinket

baratillo [bara'tiʎo] nm (tienda)
junkshop; (subasta) bargain sale;
(conjunto de cosas) secondhand goods
pl

barato, a [ba'rato, a] adj cheap ♦ adv
cheap, cheaply

baraúnda [bara'unda] nf =
barahúnda

barba ['barβa] nf (mentón) chin; (pelo)
beard

barbacoa [barβa'koa] nf (parrilla)
barbecue; (carne) barbecued meat

barbaridad [barβari'ðað] nf barbarity;
(acto) barbarism; (atrocidad) outrage;
una ~ (fam) loads; **¡qué ~!** (fam) how
awful!

barbarie [bar'βarje] nf barbarism,
savagery; (crueldad) barbarity

barbarismo [barβa'rismo] nm =
barbarie

bárbaro, a ['barβaro, a] adj barbarous,
cruel; (grosero) rough, uncouth ♦ nm/f
barbarian ♦ adv: **lo pasamos ~** (fam)
we had a great time; **¡qué ~!** (fam)
how marvellous!; **un éxito ~** (fam) a
terrific success; **es un tipo ~** (fam)
he's a great bloke

barbecho [bar'βetʃo] nm fallow land

barbero [bar'βero] nm barber,
hairdresser

barbilla [bar'βiʎa] nf chin, tip of the
chin

barbo ['barβo] nm barbel; **~ de mar**
red mullet

barbotear [barβote'ar] vt, vi to
mutter, mumble

barbudo, a [bar'βuðo, a] adj bearded

barca ['barka] nf (small) boat;
~ pesquera fishing boat; **~ de pasaje**
ferry; **~za** nf barge; **~za de
desembarco** landing craft

Barcelona [barθe'lona] *n* Barcelona

barcelonés, esa [barθelo'nes, esa] *adj* o from Barcelona

barco ['barko] *nm* boat; (*grande*) ship; ~ **de carga** cargo boat; ~ **de vela** sailing ship

baremo [ba'remo] *nm* (*MAT, fig*) scale

barítono [ba'ritono] *nm* baritone

barman ['barman] *nm* barman

Barna *n* = Barcelona

barniz [bar'niθ] *nm* varnish; (*en la loza*) glaze; (*fig*) veneer; ~**ar** *vt* to varnish; (*loza*) to glaze

barómetro [ba'rometro] *nm* barometer

barquero [bar'kero] *nm* boatman

barquillo [bar'kiʎo] *nm* cone, cornet

barra ['barra] *nf* bar, rod; (*de un bar, café*) bar; (*de pan*) French stick; (*palanca*) lever; ~ **de carmín** o **de labios** lipstick; ~ **libre** free bar

barraca [ba'rraka] *nf* hut, cabin

barranco [ba'rranko] *nm* ravine; (*fig*) difficulty

barrena [ba'rrena] *nf* drill; **barrenar** *vt* to drill (through), bore; **barreno** *nm* large drill

barrer [ba'rrer] *vt* to sweep; (*quitar*) to sweep away

barrera [ba'rrera] *nf* barrier

barriada [ba'rrjaða] *nf* quarter, district

barricada [barri'kaða] *nf* barricade

barrida [ba'rriða] *nf* sweep, sweeping

barrido [ba'rriðo] *nm* = **barrida**

barriga [ba'rriɣa] *nf* belly; (*panza*) paunch; **barrigón, ona** *adj* potbellied; **barrigudo, a** *adj* potbellied

barril [ba'rril] *nm* barrel, cask

barrio ['barrjo] *nm* (*vecindad*) area, neighborhood (*US*); (*en las afueras*) suburb; ~ **chino** red-light district

barro ['barro] *nm* (*lodo*) mud; (*objetos*) earthenware; (*MED*) pimple

barroco, a [ba'rroko, a] *adj, nm* baroque

barrote [ba'rrote] *nm* (*de ventana*) bar

barruntar [barrun'tar] *vt* (*conjeturar*) to guess; (*presentir*) to suspect; **barrunto** *nm* guess; suspicion

bartola [bar'tola]: **a la** ~ *adv*: **tirarse a la** ~ to take it easy, be lazy

bártulos ['bartulos] *nmpl* things, belongings

barullo [ba'ruʎo] *nm* row, uproar

basar [ba'sar] *vt* to base; ~**se** *vr*: ~**se en** to be based on

báscula ['baskula] *nf* (platform) scales

base ['base] *nf* base; **a** ~ **de** on the basis of; (*mediante*) by means of; ~ **de datos** (*INFORM*) database

básico, a ['basiko, a] *adj* basic

basílica [ba'silika] *nf* basilica

PALABRA CLAVE

bastante [bas'tante] *adj* **1** (*suficiente*) enough; ~ **dinero** enough o sufficient money; ~**s libros** enough books
2 (*valor intensivo*): ~ **gente** quite a lot of people; **tener** ~ **calor** to be rather hot

♦ *adv*: ~ **bueno/malo** quite good/ rather bad; ~ **rico** pretty rich; (*lo*) ~ **inteligente (como) para hacer algo** clever enough o sufficiently clever to do sth

---

bastar [bas'tar] *vi* to be enough o sufficient; ~**se** *vr* to be self-sufficient; ~ **para** to be enough to; **¡basta!** (that's) enough!

bastardilla [bastar'ðiʎa] *nf* italics

bastardo, a [bas'tarðo, a] *adj, nm/f* bastard

bastidor [basti'ðor] *nm* frame; (*de coche*) chassis; (*TEATRO*) wing; **entre** ~**es** (*fig*) behind the scenes

basto, a ['basto, a] *adj* coarse, rough; ~**s** *nmpl* (*NAIPES*) ≈ clubs

bastón [bas'ton] *nm* stick, staff; (*para pasear*) walking stick

bastoncillo [baston'θiʎo] *nm* cotton bud

basura [ba'sura] *nf* rubbish (*BRIT*), garbage (*US*)

basurero [basu'rero] nm (hombre) dustman (BRIT), garbage man (US); (lugar) dump; (cubo) (rubbish) bin (BRIT), trash can (US)

bata ['bata] nf (gen) dressing gown; (cubretodo) smock, overall; (MED, TEC etc) lab(oratory) coat

batalla [ba'taʎa] nf battle; **de ~** (fig) for everyday use

batallar [bata'ʎar] vi to fight

batallón [bata'ʎon] nm battalion

batata [ba'tata] nf sweet potato

batería [bate'ria] nf battery; (MUS) drums; **~ de cocina** kitchen utensils

batido, a [ba'tiðo, a] adj (camino) beaten, well-trodden ♦ nm (CULIN): **~ (de leche)** milk shake

batidora [bati'ðora] nf beater, mixer; **~ eléctrica** food mixer, blender

batir [ba'tir] vt to beat, strike; (vencer) to beat, defeat; (revolver) to beat, mix; **~se** vr to fight; **~ palmas** to clap, applaud

batuta [ba'tuta] nf baton; **llevar la ~** (fig) to be the boss, be in charge

baúl [ba'ul] nm trunk; (AUTO) boot (BRIT), trunk (US)

bautismo [bau'tismo] nm baptism, christening

bautizar [bauti'θar] vt to baptize, christen; (fam: diluir) to water down; **bautizo** nm baptism, christening

baya ['baja] nf berry

bayeta [ba'jeta] nf floorcloth

bayoneta [bajo'neta] nf bayonet

baza ['baθa] nf trick; **meter ~** to butt in

bazar [ba'θar] nm bazaar

bazofia [ba'θofja] nf trash

beato, a [be'ato, a] adj blessed; (piadoso) pious

bebé [be'ße] (pl **~s**) nm baby

bebedor, a [beße'ðor, a] adj hard-drinking

beber [be'ßer] vt, vi to drink

bebida [be'ßiða] nf drink; **bebido, a** adj drunk

beca ['beka] nf grant, scholarship

becario, a [be'karjo, a] nm/f scholarship holder, grant holder

bedel [be'ðel] nm (ESCOL) janitor; (UNIV) porter

béisbol ['beisßol] nm (DEPORTE) baseball

belén [be'len] nm (de navidad) nativity scene, crib; **B~** Bethlehem

belga ['belɣa] adj, nm/f Belgian

Bélgica ['belxika] nf Belgium

bélico, a ['beliko, a] adj (actitud) warlike; **belicoso, a** adj (guerrero) warlike; (agresivo) aggressive, bellicose

beligerante [belixe'rante] adj belligerent

belleza [be'ʎeθa] nf beauty

bello, a ['beʎo, a] adj beautiful, lovely; **Bellas Artes** Fine Art

bellota [be'ʎota] nf acorn

bemol [be'mol] nm (MUS) flat; **esto tiene ~es** (fam) this is a tough one

bencina [ben'θina] (AM) nf (gasolina) petrol (BRIT), gasoline (US)

bendecir [bende'θir] vt to bless

bendición [bendi'θjon] nf blessing

bendito, a [ben'dito, a] pp de **bendecir** ♦ adj holy; (afortunado) lucky; (feliz) happy; (sencillo) simple ♦ nm/f simple soul

beneficencia [benefi'θenθja] nf charity

beneficiar [benefi'θjar] vt to benefit, be of benefit to; **~se** vr to benefit, profit; **~io, a** nm/f beneficiary

beneficio [benefi'θjo] nm (bien) benefit, advantage; (ganancia) profit, gain; **~so, a** adj beneficial

benéfico, a [be'nefiko, a] adj charitable

beneplácito [bene'plaθito] nm approval, consent

benevolencia [beneßo'lenθja] nf benevolence, kindness; **benévolo, a** adj benevolent, kind

benigno, a [be'nixno, a] adj kind; (suave) mild; (MED: tumor) benign, non-malignant

berberecho [berβe'retʃo] nm (ZOOL, CULIN) cockle

berenjena [beren'xena] nf aubergine (BRIT), eggplant (US)

Berlín [ber'lin] n Berlin; **berlinés, esa** adj of o from Berlin ♦ nm/f Berliner

bermudas [ber'muðas] nfpl Bermuda shorts

berrear [berre'ar] vi to bellow, low

berrido [be'rriðo] nm bellow(ing)

berrinche [be'rrintʃe] (fam) nm temper, tantrum

berro ['berro] nm watercress

berza ['berθa] nf cabbage

besamel [besa'mel] nf (CULIN) white sauce, bechamel sauce

besar [be'sar] vt to kiss; (fig: tocar) to graze; **~se** vr to kiss (one another); **beso** nm kiss

bestia ['bestja] nf beast, animal; (fig) idiot; **~ de carga** beast of burden

bestial [bes'tjal] adj bestial; (fam) terrific; **~idad** nf bestiality; (fam) stupidity

besugo [be'suɣo] nm sea bream; (fam) idiot

besuquear [besuke'ar] vt to cover with kisses; **~se** vr to kiss and cuddle

betún [be'tun] nm shoe polish; (QUÍM) bitumen

biberón [biβe'ron] nm feeding bottle

Biblia ['biβlja] nf Bible

bibliografía [biβljoɣra'fia] nf bibliography

biblioteca [biβljo'teka] nf library; (mueble) bookshelves; **~ de consulta** reference library; **~rio, a** nm/f librarian

bicarbonato [bikarβo'nato] nm bicarbonate

bicho ['bitʃo] nm (animal) small animal; (sabandija) bug, insect; (TAUR) bull

bici ['biθi] (fam) nf bike

bicicleta [biθi'kleta] nf bicycle, cycle; **ir en ~** to cycle

bidé [bi'ðe] (pl **~s**) nm bidet

bidón [bi'ðon] nm (de aceite) drum; (de gasolina) can

─────────────────

bien [bjen] nm 1 (bienestar) good; **te lo digo por tu ~** I'm telling you for your own good; **el ~ y el mal** good and evil

2 (posesión): **~es** goods; **~es de consumo** consumer goods; **~es inmuebles** o **raíces/~es muebles** real estate sg/personal property sg

♦ adv 1 (de manera satisfactoria, correcta etc) well; **trabaja/come ~** she works/eats well; **contestó ~** he answered correctly; **me siento ~** I feel fine; **no me siento ~** I don't feel very well; **se está ~ aquí** it's nice here

2 (frases): **hiciste ~ en llamarme** you were right to call me

3 (valor intensivo) very; **un cuarto ~ caliente** a nice warm room; **~ se ve que ...** it's quite clear that ...

4: **estar ~**: **estoy muy ~ aquí** I feel very happy here; **está ~ que vengan** it's all right for them to come; **¡está ~! lo haré** oh all right, I'll do it

5 (de buena gana): **yo ~ que iría pero ...** I'd gladly go but ...

♦ excl **¡~!** (aprobación) O.K.!; **¡muy ~!** well done!

♦ adj inv (matiz despectivo): **niño ~** rich kid; **gente ~** posh people

♦ conj 1: **~ ... ~**: **en coche ~ en tren** either by car or by train

2: **no ~** (esp AM): **no ~ llegue te llamaré** as soon as I arrive I'll call you

3: **si ~** even though; ver tb **más**

─────────────────

bienal [bje'nal] adj biennial

bienaventurado, a [bjenaβentu'raðo, a] adj (feliz) happy, fortunate

bienestar [bjenes'tar] nm well-being, welfare

bienhechor, a [bjene'tʃor, a] adj beneficent ♦ nm/f benefactor/ benefactress

bienvenida [bjembe'niða] nf welcome; **dar la ~ a uno** to welcome sb

bienvenido [bjembe'niðo] excl welcome!

bife ['bife] (AM) nm steak

bifurcación [bifurka'θjon] nf fork

bifurcarse [bifur'karse] vr (camino, carretera, río) to fork

bigamia [bi'γamja] nf bigamy; **bígamo, a** adj bigamous ♦ nm/f bigamist

bigote [bi'γote] nm moustache; **bigotudo, a** adj with a big moustache

bikini [bi'kini] nm bikini; (CULIN) toasted ham and cheese sandwich

bilbaíno, a [bilβa'ino, a] adj from of Bilbao

bilingüe [bi'lingwe] adj bilingual

billar [bi'ʎar] nm billiards sg; (lugar) billiard hall; (mini-casino) amusement arcade; **~ americano** pool

billete [bi'ʎete] nm ticket; (de banco) (bank)note (BRIT), bill (US); (carta) note; **~ sencillo, a de ida solamente** single (BRIT) o one-way (US) ticket; **~ de ida y vuelta** return (BRIT) o round-trip (US) ticket; **~ de 20 libras** £20 note

billetera [biʎe'tera] nf wallet

billetero [biʎe'tero] nm = **billetera**

billón [bi'ʎon] nm billion

bimensual [bimen'swal] adj twice monthly

bimotor [bimo'tor] adj twin-engined ♦ nm twin-engined plane

bingo ['biŋgo] nm bingo

biodegradable [bioðeɣra'ðaβle] adj biodegradable

biografía [bioɣra'fia] nf biography; **biógrafo, a** nm/f biographer

biología [biolo'xia] nf biology; **biológico, a** adj biological; **biólogo, a** nm/f biologist

biombo ['bjombo] nm (folding) screen

biopsia [bi'opsja] nf biopsy

biquini [bi'kini] nm bikini

birlar [bir'lar] (fam) vt to pinch

Birmania [bir'manja] nf Burma

birria ['birrja] nf: **ser una ~** (película, libro) to be rubbish

bis [bis] excl encore! ♦ adv: **viven en el 27 ~** they live at 27a

bisabuelo, a [bisa'βwelo, a] nm/f great-grandfather/mother

bisagra [bi'saɣra] nf hinge

bisiesto [bi'sjesto] adj: **año ~** leap year

bisnieto, a [bis'njeto, a] nm/f great-grandson/daughter

bisonte [bi'sonte] nm bison

bisté [bis'te] nm = **bistec**

bistec [bis'tek] nm steak

bisturí [bistu'ri] nm scalpel

bisutería [bisute'ria] nf imitation o costume jewellery

bit [bit] nm (INFORM) bit

bizco, a ['biθko, a] adj cross-eyed

bizcocho [biθ'kotʃo] nm (CULIN) sponge cake

bizquear [biθke'ar] vi to squint

blanca ['blanka] nf (MUS) minim; **estar sin ~** to be broke; ver tb **blanco**

blanco, a ['blanko, a] adj white ♦ nm/f white man/woman, white ♦ nm (color) white; (en texto) blank; (MIL, fig) target; **en ~** blank; **noche en ~** sleepless night

blancura [blan'kura] nf whiteness

blandir [blan'dir] vt to brandish

blando, a ['blando, a] adj soft; (tierno) tender, gentle; (carácter) mild; (fam) cowardly; **blandura** nf softness; tenderness; mildness

blanquear [blanke'ar] vt to whiten; (fachada) to whitewash; (paño) to bleach ♦ vi to turn white; **blanquecino, a** adj whitish

blasfemar [blasfe'mar] vi to blaspheme, curse; **blasfemia** nf blasphemy

blasón [bla'son] nm coat of arms

bledo ['bleðo] nm: **me importa un ~** I couldn't care less

blindado, a [blin'daðo, a] *adj* (MIL) armour-plated; (*antibala*) bullet-proof; **coche** (ESP) o **carro** (AM) ~ armoured car

blindaje [blin'daxe] *nm* armour, armour-plating

bloc [blok] (*pl* ~**s**) *nm* writing pad

bloque ['bloke] *nm* block; (POL) bloc; ~ **de cilindros** cylinder block

bloquear [bloke'ar] *vt* to blockade; **bloqueo** *nm* blockade; (COM) freezing, blocking

blusa ['blusa] *nf* blouse

boato [bo'ato] *nm* show, ostentation

bobada [bo'βaða] *nf* foolish action; foolish statement; **decir ~s** to talk nonsense

bobería [boβe'ria] *nf* = **bobada**

bobina [bo'βina] *nf* (TEC) bobbin; (FOTO) spool; (ELEC) coil

bobo, a ['boβo, a] *adj* (*tonto*) daft, silly; (*cándido*) naïve ♦ *nm/f* fool, idiot ♦ *nm* (TEATRO) clown, funny man

boca ['boka] *nf* mouth; (*de crustáceo*) pincer; (*de cañón*) muzzle; (*entrada*) mouth, entrance; ~**s** *nfpl* (*de río*) mouth *sg*; ~ **abajo/arriba** face down/up; **se me hace agua la** ~ my mouth is watering

bocacalle [boka'kaʎe] *nf* (entrance to a) street; **la primera** ~ the first turning o street

bocadillo [boka'ðiʎo] *nm* sandwich

bocado [bo'kaðo] *nm* mouthful, bite; (*de caballo*) bridle; ~ **de Adán** Adam's apple

bocajarro [boka'xarro]: **a** ~ *adv* (*disparar, preguntar*) point-blank

bocanada [boka'naða] *nf* (*de vino*) mouthful, swallow; (*de aire*) gust, puff

bocata [bo'kata] (*fam*) *nm* sandwich

bocazas [bo'kaθas] (*fam*) *nm inv* bigmouth

boceto [bo'θeto] *nm* sketch, outline

bochorno [bo'tʃorno] *nm* (*vergüenza*) embarrassment; (*calor*): **hace** ~ it's very muggy; ~**so, a** *adj* muggy; embarrassing

bocina [bo'θina] *nf* (MUS) trumpet; (AUTO) horn; (*para hablar*) megaphone

boda ['boða] *nf* (*tb:* ~**s**) wedding, marriage; (*fiesta*) wedding reception; ~**s de plata/de oro** silver/golden wedding

bodega [bo'ðeɣa] *nf* (*de vino*) (wine) cellar; (*depósito*) storeroom; (*de barco*) hold

bodegón [boðe'xon] *nm* (ARTE) still life

bofe ['bofe] *nm* (*tb:* ~**s: de res**) lights

bofetada [bofe'taða] *nf* slap (in the face)

bofetón [bofe'ton] *nm* = **bofetada**

boga ['boɣa] *nf*: **en** ~ (*fig*) in vogue

bogar [bo'ɣar] *vi* (*remar*) to row; (*navegar*) to sail

bogavante [boɣa'βante] *nm* lobster

Bogotá [boɣo'ta] *n* Bogotá

bohemio, a [bo'emjo, a] *adj, nm/f* Bohemian

boicot [boi'kot] (*pl* ~**s**) *nm* boycott; ~**ear** *vt* to boycott; ~**eo** *nm* boycott

boina ['boina] *nf* beret

bola ['bola] *nf* ball; (*canica*) marble; (NAIPES) (grand) slam; (*betún*) shoe polish; (*mentira*) tale, story; ~**s** (AM) *nfpl* **bolas** *sg*; ~ **de billar** billiard ball; ~ **de nieve** snowball

bolchevique [boltʃe'βike] *adj, nm/f* Bolshevik

boleadoras [bolea'ðoras] (AM) *nfpl* **bolas** *sg*

bolera [bo'lera] *nf* skittle o bowling alley

boleta [bo'leta] (AM) *nf* (*billete*) ticket; (*permiso*) pass, permit

boletería [bolete'ria] (AM) *nf* ticket office

boletín [bole'tin] *nm* bulletin; (*periódico*) journal, review; ~ **de noticias** news bulletin

boleto [bo'leto] *nm* ticket

boli ['boli] (*fam*) *nm* Biro ®, pen

bolígrafo [bo'liɣrafo] *nm* ball-point

pen, Biro ®

bolívar [bo'liβar] nm monetary unit of Venezuela

Bolivia [bo'liβja] nf Bolivia; **boliviano, a** adj, nm/f Bolivian

bollería [boʎe'ria] nf cakes pl and pastries pl

bollo ['boʎo] nm (pan) roll; (bulto) bump, lump; (abolladura) dent

bolo ['bolo] nm skittle; (píldora) (large) pill; **(juego de) ~s** nmpl skittles sg

bolsa ['bolsa] nf bag; (AM) pocket; (ANAT) cavity, sac; (COM) stock exchange; (MINERÍA) pocket; **de ~** pocket cpd; **~ de agua caliente** hot water bottle; **~ de aire** air pocket; **~ de papel** paper bag; **~ de plástico** plastic bag

bolsillo [bol'siʎo] nm pocket; (cartera) purse; **de ~** pocket(-size)

bolsista [bol'sista] nm/f stockbroker

bolso ['bolso] nm (bolsa) bag; (de mujer) handbag

bomba ['bomba] nf (MIL) bomb; (TEC) pump ♦ (fam) adj: **noticia ~** bombshell ♦ (fam) adv: **pasarlo ~** to have a great time; **~ atómica/de humo/de efecto retardado** atomic/ smoke/time bomb

bombardear [bombarðe'ar] vt to bombard; (MIL) to bomb; **bombardeo** nm bombardment; bombing

bombardero [bombar'ðero] nm bomber

bombear [bombe'ar] vt (agua) to pump (out o up); **~se** vr to warp

bombero [bom'bero] nm fireman

bombilla [bom'biʎa] (ESP) nf (light) bulb

bombín [bom'bin] nm bowler hat

bombo ['bombo] nm (MUS) bass drum; (TEC) drum

bombón [bom'bon] nm chocolate

bombona [bom'bona] nf (de butano, oxígeno) cylinder

bonachón, ona [bona'tʃon, ona] adj good-natured, easy-going

bonanza [bo'nanθa] nf (NAUT) fair weather; (fig) bonanza; (MINERÍA) rich pocket o vein

bondad [bon'dað] nf goodness, kindness; **tenga la ~ de** (please) be good enough to; **~oso, a** adj good, kind

bonificación [bonifika'θjon] nf bonus

bonito, a [bo'nito, a] adj pretty; (agradable) nice ♦ nm (atún) tuna (fish)

bono ['bono] nm voucher; (FIN) bond

bonobús [bono'βus] (ESP) nm bus pass

bonoloto [bono'loto] nf state-run weekly lottery

boquerón [boke'ron] nm (pez) (kind of) anchovy; (agujero) large hole

boquete [bo'kete] nm gap, hole

boquiabierto, a [bokia'βjerto, a] adj: **quedar ~** to be amazed o flabbergasted

boquilla [bo'kiʎa] nf (para riego) nozzle; (para cigarro) cigarette holder; (MUS) mouthpiece

borbotón [borβo'ton] nm: **salir a borbotones** to gush out

borda ['borða] nf (NAUT) (ship's) rail; **tirar algo/caerse por la ~** to throw sth/fall overboard

bordado [bor'ðaðo] nm embroidery

bordar [bor'ðar] vt to embroider

borde ['borðe] nm edge, border; (de camino etc) side; (en la costura) hem; **al ~ de** (fig) on the verge o brink of; **ser ~** (ESP: fam) to be rude; **~ar** vt to border

bordillo [bor'ðiʎo] nm kerb (BRIT), curb (US)

bordo ['borðo] nm (NAUT) side; **a ~** on board

borinqueño, a [borin'kenjo, a] adj, nm/f Puerto Rican

borla ['borla] nf (adorno) tassel

borrachera [borra'tʃera] nf (ebriedad) drunkenness; (orgía) spree, binge

borracho, a [bo'rratʃo, a] adj drunk ♦ nm/f (habitual) drunkard, drunk; (temporal) drunk, drunk man/woman

borrador [borra'ðor] nm (escritura) first draft, rough sketch; (goma) rubber (BRIT), eraser

borrar [bo'rrar] vt to erase, rub out

borrasca [bo'rraska] nf storm

borrico, a [bo'rriko, a] nm/f donkey/ she-donkey; (fig) stupid man/woman

borrón [bo'rron] nm (mancha) stain

borroso, a [bo'rroso, a] adj vague, unclear; (escritura) illegible

bosque ['boske] nm wood; (grande) forest

bosquejar [boske'xar] vt to sketch; **bosquejo** nm sketch

bostezar [boste'θar] vi to yawn; **bostezo** nm yawn

bota ['bota] nf (calzado) boot; (para vino) leather wine bottle; **~s de agua**, **~s de goma** Wellingtons

botánica [bo'tanika] nf (ciencia) botany; ver tb **botánico**

botánico, a [bo'taniko, a] adj botanical ♦ nm/f botanist

botar [bo'tar] vt to throw, hurl; (NAUT) to launch; (AM) to throw out ♦ vi to bounce

bote ['bote] nm (salto) bounce; (golpe) thrust; (vasija) tin, can; (embarcación) boat; **de ~ en ~** packed, jammed full; **~ de la basura** (AM) dustbin (BRIT), trashcan (US); **~ salvavidas** lifeboat

botella [bo'teʎa] nf bottle; **botellín** nm small bottle

botica [bo'tika] nf chemist's (shop) (BRIT), pharmacy; **~rio, a** nm/f chemist (BRIT), pharmacist

botijo [bo'tixo] nm (earthenware) jug

botín [bo'tin] nm (calzado) half boot; (polaina) spat; (MIL) booty

botiquín [boti'kin] nm (armario) medicine cabinet; (portátil) first-aid kit

botón [bo'ton] nm button; (BOT) bud; **~ de oro** buttercup

botones [bo'tones] nm inv bellboy (BRIT), bellhop (US)

bóveda ['boßeða] nf (ARQ) vault

boxeador [boksea'ðor] nm boxer

boxear [bokse'ar] vi to box

boxeo [bok'seo] nm boxing

boya ['boja] nf (NAUT) buoy; (de caña) float

boyante [bo'jante] adj prosperous

bozal [bo'θal] nm (de caballo) halter; (de perro) muzzle

bracear [braθe'ar] vi (agitar los brazos) to wave one's arms

bracero [bra'θero] nm labourer; (en el campo) farmhand

bragas ['braɣas] nfpl (de mujer) panties, knickers (BRIT)

braguet a [bra'ɣeta] nf fly, flies pl

braille [breil] nm braille

bramar [bra'mar] vi to bellow, roar; **bramido** nm bellow, roar

brasa ['brasa] nf live o hot coal

brasero [bra'sero] nm brazier

Brasil [bra'sil] nm: **(el) ~** Brazil; **brasileño, a** adj, nm/f Brazilian

bravata [bra'ßata] nf boast

braveza [bra'ßeθa] nf (valor) bravery; (ferocidad) ferocity

bravío, a [bra'ßio, a] adj wild; (feroz) fierce

bravo, a ['braßo, a] adj (valiente) brave; (feroz) ferocious; (salvaje) wild; (mar etc) rough, stormy ♦ excl bravo!; **bravura** nf bravery; ferocity

braza ['braθa] nf fathom; **nadar a la ~** to swim (the) breast-stroke

brazada [bra'θaða] nf stroke

brazado [bra'θaðo] nm armful

brazalete [braθa'lete] nm (pulsera) bracelet; (banda) armband

brazo ['braθo] nm arm; (ZOOL) foreleg; (BOT) limb, branch; **luchar a ~ partido** to fight hand-to-hand; **ir cogidos del ~** to walk arm in arm

brea ['brea] nf pitch, tar

brebaje [bre'ßaxe] nm potion

brecha ['bretʃa] nf (hoyo, vacío) gap, opening; (MIL, fig) breach

brega ['breɣa] nf (lucha) struggle; (trabajo) hard work

breva ['breßa] nf early fig

breve ['breße] *adj* short, brief ♦ *nf*
(MUS) breve; **~dad** *nf* brevity, shortness
brezo ['breθo] *nm* heather
bribón, ona [bri'ßon, ona] *adj* idle,
lazy ♦ *nm/f* (pícaro) rascal, rogue
bricolaje [briko'laxe] *nm* do-it-
yourself, DIY
brida ['briða] *nf* bridle, rein; (TEC)
clamp; **a toda ~** at top speed
bridge [britʃ] *nm* bridge
brigada [bri'ɣaða] *nf* (unidad) brigade;
(trabajadores) squad, gang ♦ *nm* ≈
staff-sergeant, sergeant-major
brillante [bri'ʎante] *adj* brilliant ♦ *nm*
diamond
brillar [bri'ʎar] *vi* (tb fig) to shine;
(joyas) to sparkle
brillo ['briʎo] *nm* shine; (brillantez)
brilliance; (fig) splendour; **sacar ~ a** to
polish
brincar [brin'kar] *vi* to skip about, hop
about, jump about; **está que brinca**
he's hopping mad
brinco ['brinko] *nm* jump, leap
brindar [brin'dar] *vi*: **~ a o por** to
drink (a toast) to ♦ *vt* to offer, present
brindis ['brindis] *nm inv* toast
brío ['brio] *nm* spirit, dash; **brioso, a**
adj spirited, dashing
brisa ['brisa] *nf* breeze
británico, a [bri'taniko, a] *adj* British
♦ *nm/f* Briton, British person
brizna ['briθna] *nf* (de hierba, paja)
blade; (de tabaco) leaf
broca ['broka] *nf* (TEC) drill, bit
brocal [bro'kal] *nm* rim
brocha ['brotʃa] *nf* (large) paintbrush;
~ de afeitar shaving brush
broche ['brotʃe] *nm* brooch
broma ['broma] *nf* joke; **en ~** in fun,
as a joke; **~ pesada** practical joke;
bromear *vi* to joke
bromista [bro'mista] *adj* fond of
joking ♦ *nm/f* joker, wag
bronca ['bronka] *nf* row; **echar una
~ a uno** to tick sb off
bronce ['bronθe] *nm* bronze; **~ado, a**

adj bronze; (por el sol) tanned ♦ *nm*
(sun)tan; (TEC) bronzing
bronceador [bronθea'ðor] *nm* suntan
lotion
broncearse [bronθe'arse] *vr* to get a
suntan
bronco, a ['bronko, a] *adj* (manera)
rude, surly; (voz) harsh
bronquio ['bronkjo] *nm* (ANAT)
bronchial tube
bronquitis [bron'kitis] *nf inv*
bronchitis
brotar [bro'tar] *vi* (BOT) to sprout;
(aguas) to gush (forth); (MED) to break
out
brote ['brote] *nm* (BOT) shoot; (MED,
fig) outbreak
bruces ['bruθes]: **de ~** *adv*: **caer** *o* **dar
de ~** to fall headlong, fall flat
bruja ['bruxa] *nf* witch; **brujería** *nf*
witchcraft
brujo ['bruxo] *nm* wizard, magician
brújula ['bruxula] *nf* compass
bruma ['bruma] *nf* mist; **brumoso, a**
adj misty
bruñir [bru'ɲir] *vt* to polish
brusco, a ['brusko, a] *adj* (súbito)
sudden; (áspero) brusque
Bruselas [bru'selas] *n* Brussels
brutal [bru'tal] *adj* brutal
brutalidad [brutali'ðað] *nf* brutality
bruto, a ['bruto, a] *adj* (idiota) stupid;
(bestial) brutish; (peso) gross; **en ~**
raw, unworked
Bs.As. *abr* (= Buenos Aires) B.A.
bucal [bu'kal] *adj* oral; **por vía ~** orally
bucear [buθe'ar] *vi* to dive ♦ *vt* to
explore; **buceo** *nm* diving
bucle ['bukle] *nm* curl
budismo [bu'ðismo] *nm* Buddhism
buen [bwen] *adj m ver* **bueno**
buenamente [bwena'mente] *adv*
(fácilmente) easily; (voluntariamente)
willingly
buenaventura [bwenaßen'tura] *nf*
(suerte) good luck; (adivinación)
fortune

PALABRA CLAVE

bueno, a ['bweno, a] *adj* (*antes de nmsg*: **buen**) **1** (*excelente etc*) good; **es un libro ~, es un buen libro** it's a good book; **hace ~, hace buen tiempo** the weather is fine, it is fine; **el ~ de Paco** good old Paco; **fue muy ~ conmigo** he was very nice *o* kind to me

2 (*apropiado*): **ser ~ para** to be good for; **creo que vamos por buen camino** I think we're on the right track

3 (*irónico*): **le di un buen rapapolvo** I gave him a good *o* real ticking off; **¡buen conductor estás hecho!** some *o* a fine conductor you are!; **¡estaría ~ que ...!** a fine thing it would be if ...!

4 (*atractivo, sabroso*): **está ~ este bizcocho** this sponge is delicious; **Carmen está muy buena** Carmen is gorgeous

5 (*saludos*): **¡buen día!, ¡~s días!** (good) morning!; **¡buenas (tardes)!** (good) afternoon!; (*más tarde*) (good) evening!; **¡buenas noches!** good night!

6 (*otras locuciones*): **estar de buenas** to be in a good mood; **por las buenas o por las malas** by hook or by crook; **de buenas a primeras** all of a sudden

♦ *excl*: **¡~!** all right!; **~, ¿y qué?** well, so what?

Buenos Aires *nm* Buenos Aires
buey [bwei] *nm* ox
búfalo ['bufalo] *nm* buffalo
bufanda [bu'fanda] *nf* scarf
bufar [bu'far] *vi* to snort
bufete [bu'fete] *nm* (*despacho de abogado*) lawyer's office
buffer ['bufer] *nm* (*INFORM*) buffer
bufón [bu'fon] *nm* clown
buhardilla [buar'ðiʎa] *nf* attic

búho ['buo] *nm* owl; (*fig*) hermit, recluse
buhonero [buo'nero] *nm* pedlar
buitre ['bwitre] *nm* vulture
bujía [bu'xia] *nf* (*vela*) candle; (*ELEC*) candle (power); (*AUTO*) spark plug
bula ['bula] *nf* (*papal*) bull
bulbo ['bulβo] *nm* bulb
bulevar [bule'βar] *nm* boulevard
Bulgaria [bul'βarja] *nf* Bulgaria;
búlgaro, a *adj, nm/f* Bulgarian
bulla ['buʎa] *nf* (*ruido*) uproar; (*de gente*) crowd
bullicio [bu'ʎiθjo] *nm* (*ruido*) uproar; (*movimiento*) bustle
bullir [bu'ʎir] *vi* (*hervir*) to boil; (*burbujear*) to bubble
bulto ['bulto] *nm* (*paquete*) package; (*fardo*) bundle; (*tamaño*) size, bulkiness; (*MED*) swelling, lump; (*silueta*) vague shape
buñuelo [bu'ɲwelo] *nm* ≈ doughnut (*BRIT*), ≈ donut (*US*); (*fruta de sartén*) fritter
BUP [bup] *nm abr* (*ESP*: = *Bachillerato Unificado Polivalente*) *secondary education and leaving certificate for 14–17 age group*
buque ['buke] *nm* ship, vessel
burbuja [bur'βuxa] *nf* bubble;
burbujear *vi* to bubble
burdel [bur'ðel] *nm* brothel
burdo, a ['burðo, a] *adj* coarse, rough
burgués, esa [bur'ɣes, esa] *adj* middle-class, bourgeois; **burguesía** *nf* middle class, bourgeoisie
burla ['burla] *nf* (*mofa*) gibe; (*broma*) joke; (*engaño*) trick
burladero [burla'ðero] *nm* (*bullfighter's*) refuge
burlar [bur'lar] *vt* (*engañar*) to deceive ♦ *vi* to joke; **~se** *vr* to joke; **~se de** to make fun of
burlesco, a [bur'lesko, a] *adj* burlesque
burlón, ona [bur'lon, ona] *adj* mocking

burocracia [buro'kraθja] nf civil service

burócrata [bu'rokrata] nm/f civil servant

burrada [bu'rraða] nf: **decir/soltar ~s** to talk nonsense; **hacer ~s** to act stupid; **una ~** (*mucho*) a (hell of a) lot

burro, a ['burro, a] nm/f donkey/she-donkey; (*fig*) ass, idiot

bursátil [bur'satil] adj stock-exchange cpd

bus [bus] nm bus

busca ['buska] nf search, hunt ♦ nm (TEL) bleeper; **en ~ de** in search of

buscar [bus'kar] vt to look for, search for, seek ♦ vi to look, search, seek; **se busca secretaria** secretary wanted

busque etc vb ver **buscar**

búsqueda [ˈbuskeða] nf = **busca**

busto [ˈbusto] nm (ANAT, ARTE) bust

butaca [buˈtaka] nf armchair; (*de cine, teatro*) stall, seat

butano [buˈtano] nm butane (gas)

buzo [ˈbuθo] nm diver

buzón [buˈθon] nm (*en puerta*) letter box; (*en la calle*) pillar box

C, c

C. abr (= *centígrado*) C; (= *compañía*) Co.

c. abr (= *capítulo*) ch.

C/ abr (= *calle*) St

c.a. abr (= *corriente alterna*) AC

cabal [kaˈβal] adj (*exacto*) exact; (*correcto*) right, proper; (*acabado*) finished, complete; **~es** nmpl: **estar en sus ~es** to be in one's right mind

cábalas [ˈkaβalas] nfpl: **hacer ~** to guess

cabalgar [kaβalˈɣar] vt, vi to ride

cabalgata [kaβalˈɣata] nf procession

caballa [kaˈβaʎa] nf mackerel

caballeresco, a [kaβaʎeˈresko, a] adj noble, chivalrous

caballería [kaβaʎeˈria] nf mount; (MIL)

cavalry

caballeriza [kaβaʎeˈriθa] nf stable; **caballerizo** nm groom, stableman

caballero [kaβaˈʎero] nm gentleman; (*de la orden de caballería*) knight; (*trato directo*) sir

caballerosidad [kaβaʎerosiˈðað] nf chivalry

caballete [kaβaˈʎete] nm (ARTE) easel; (TEC) trestle

caballito [kaβaˈʎito] nm (*caballo pequeño*) small horse, pony; **~s** nmpl (*en verbena*) roundabout, merry-go-round

caballo [kaˈβaʎo] nm horse; (AJEDREZ) knight; (NAIPES) queen; **ir en ~** to ride; **~ de vapor** o **de fuerza** horsepower; **~ de carreras** racehorse

cabaña [kaˈβaɲa] nf (*casita*) hut, cabin

cabaré [kabaˈre] (*pl* **~s**) nm cabaret

cabaret [kabaˈre] (*pl* **~s**) nm cabaret

cabecear [kaβeθeˈar] vt, vi to nod

cabecera [kaβeˈθera] nf head; (IMPRENTA) headline

cabecilla [kaβeˈθiʎa] nm ringleader

cabellera [kaβeˈʎera] nf (head of) hair; (*de cometa*) tail

cabello [kaˈβeʎo] nm (*tb: ~s*) hair

caber [kaˈβer] vi (*entrar*) to fit, go; **caben 3 más** there's room for 3 more

cabestrillo [kaβesˈtriʎo] nm sling

cabestro [kaˈβestro] nm halter

cabeza [kaˈβeθa] nf head; (POL) chief, leader; **~ rapada** skinhead; **~da** nf (*golpe*) butt; **dar ~das** to nod off; **cabezón, ona** adj (*vino*) heady; (*fam: persona*) pig-headed

cabida [kaˈβiða] nf space

cabildo [kaˈβildo] nm (*de iglesia*) chapter; (POL) town council

cabina [kaˈβina] nf (*de camión*) cab; **~ telefónica** telephone box (BRIT) o booth

cabizbajo, a [kaβiθˈβaxo, a] adj crestfallen, dejected

cable [ˈkaβle] nm cable

cabo [ˈkaβo] nm (*de objeto*) end,

extremity; (MIL) corporal; (NAUT) rope, cable; (GEO) cape; **al ~ de 3 días** after 3 days

cabra ['kaβra] *nf* goat

cabré *etc vb ver* **caber**

cabrear [kaβre'ar] (*fam*) *vt* to bug; **~se** *vr* (*enfadarse*) to fly off the handle

cabrío, a [ka'βrio, a] *adj* goatish; **macho ~** (he-)goat, billy goat

cabriola [ka'βrjola] *nf* caper

cabritilla [kaβri'tiʎa] *nf* kid, kidskin

cabrito [ka'βrito] *nm* kid

cabrón [ka'βron] *nm* cuckold; (*fam*!) bastard (!)

caca ['kaka] (*fam*) *nf* pooh

cacahuete [kaka'wete] (*ESP*) *nm* peanut

cacao [ka'kao] *nm* cocoa; (*BOT*) cacao

cacarear [kakare'ar] *vi* (*persona*) to boast; (*gallina*) to crow

cacería [kaθe'ria] *nf* hunt

cacerola [kaθe'rola] *nf* pan, saucepan

cachalote [katʃa'lote] *nm* (*ZOOL*) sperm whale

cacharro [ka'tʃarro] *nm* earthenware pot; **~s** *nmpl* pots and pans

cachear [katʃe'ar] *vt* to search, frisk

cachemir [katʃe'mir] *nm* cashmere

cacheo [ka'tʃeo] *nm* searching, frisking

cachete [ka'tʃete] *nm* (*ANAT*) cheek; (*bofetada*) slap (in the face)

cachiporra [katʃi'porra] *nf* truncheon

cachivache [katʃi'βatʃe] *nm* (*trasto*) piece of junk; **~s** *nmpl* junk *sg*

cacho ['katʃo] *nm* (small) bit; (*AM: cuerno*) horn

cachondeo [katʃon'deo] (*fam*) *nm* farce, joke

cachondo, a [ka'tʃondo, a] *adj* (*ZOOL*) on heat; (*fam: sexualmente*) randy; (: *gracioso*) funny

cachorro, a [ka'tʃorro, a] *nm/f* (*perro*) pup, puppy; (*león*) cub

cacique [ka'θike] *nm* chief, local ruler; (*POL*) local party boss; **caciquismo** *nm* system of control by the local boss

caco ['kako] *nm* pickpocket

cacto ['kakto] *nm* cactus

cactus ['kaktus] *nm inv* cactus

cada ['kaða] *adj inv* each; (*antes de número*) every; **~ uno/a** each one, every one; **~ día** every day; **~ dos días** every other day; **~ una/a cada uno**, every one; **~ vez más/menos** more and more/less and less; **uno de ~ diez** one out of every ten

cadalso [ka'ðalso] *nm* scaffold

cadáver [ka'ðaβer] *nm* (dead) body, corpse

cadena [ka'ðena] *nf* chain; (*TV*) channel; **trabajo en ~** assembly line work; **~ perpetua** (*JUR*) life imprisonment

cadencia [ka'ðenθja] *nf* rhythm

cadera [ka'ðera] *nf* hip

cadete [ka'ðete] *nm* cadet

caducar [kaðu'kar] *vi* to expire; **caduco, a** *adj* expired; (*persona*) very old

caer [ka'er] *vi* to fall (down); **~se** *vr* to fall (down); **me cae bien/mal** I get on well with him/I can't stand him; **~ en la cuenta** to realize; **su cumpleaños cae en viernes** her birthday falls on a Friday

café [ka'fe] (*pl* **~s**) *nm* (*bebida, planta*) coffee; (*lugar*) café ♦ *adj* (*color*) brown; **~ con leche** white coffee; **~ solo** black coffee

cafetera [kafe'tera] *nf* coffee pot

cafetería [kafete'ria] *nf* (*gen*) café

cafetero, a [kafe'tero, a] *adj* coffee *cpd*; **ser muy ~** to be a coffee addict

cagar [ka'ɣar] (*fam*!) *vt* to bungle, mess up ♦ *vi* to have a shit (!)

caída [ka'iða] *nf* fall; (*declive*) slope; (*disminución*) fall, drop

caído, a [ka'iðo, a] *adj* drooping

caiga *etc vb ver* **caer**

caimán [kai'man] *nm* alligator

caja ['kaxa] *nf* box; (*para reloj*) case; (*de ascensor*) shaft; (*COM*) cashbox; (*donde se hacen los pagos*) cashdesk; (: *en supermercado*) checkout, till; **~ de**

ahorros savings bank; **~ de cambios** gearbox; **~ fuerte**, **~ de caudales** safe, strongbox

cajero, a [ka'xero, a] nm/f cashier; **~ automático** cash dispenser

cajetilla [kaxe'tiʎa] nf (de cigarrillos) packet

cajón [ka'xon] nm big box; (de mueble) drawer

cal [kal] nf lime

cala ['kala] nf (GEO) cove, inlet; (de barco) hold

calabacín [kalaβa'θin] nm (BOT) baby marrow; (: más pequeño) courgette (BRIT), zucchini (US)

calabaza [kala'βaθa] nf (BOT) pumpkin

calabozo [kala'βoθo] nm (cárcel) prison; (celda) cell

calada [ka'laða] nf (de cigarrillo) puff

calado, a [ka'laðo, a] adj (prenda) lace cpd ♦ nm (NAUT) draught

calamar [kala'mar] nm squid no pl

calambre [ka'lambre] nm (tb: ~s) cramp

calamidad [kalami'ðað] nf calamity, disaster

calar [ka'lar] vt to soak, drench; (penetrar) to pierce, penetrate; (comprender) to see through; (vela) to lower; **~se** vr (AUTO) to stall; **se las gafas** to stick one's glasses on

calavera [kala'βera] nf skull

calcar [kal'kar] vt (reproducir) to trace; (imitar) to copy

calcetín [kalθe'tin] nm sock

calcinar [kalθi'nar] vt to burn, blacken

calcio ['kalθjo] nm calcium

calcomanía [kalkoma'nia] nf transfer

calculador, a [kalkula'ðor, a] adj (persona) calculating

calculadora [kalkula'ðora] nf calculator

calcular [kalku'lar] vt (MAT) to calculate, compute; **~ que ...** to reckon that ...; **cálculo** nm calculation

caldear [kalde'ar] vt to warm (up), heat (up)

caldera [kal'dera] nf boiler

calderilla [kalde'riʎa] nf (moneda) small change

caldero [kal'dero] nm small boiler

caldo ['kaldo] nm stock; (consomé) consommé

calefacción [kalefak'θjon] nf heating; **~ central** central heating

calendario [kalen'darjo] nm calendar

calentador [kalenta'ðor] nm heater

calentamiento [kalenta'mjento] nm (DEPORTE) warm-up

calentar [kalen'tar] vt to heat (up); **~se** vr to heat up, warm up; (fig: discusión etc) to get heated

calentura [kalen'tura] nf (MED) fever, (high) temperature

calibrar [kali'βrar] vt to gauge, measure; **calibre** nm (de cañón) calibre, bore; (diámetro) diameter; (fig) calibre

calidad [kali'ðað] nf quality; **de ~** quality cpd; **en ~ de** in the capacity of, as

cálido, a ['kaliðo, a] adj hot; (fig) warm

caliente etc [ka'ljente] vb ver **calentar** ♦ adj hot; (fig) fiery; (disputa) heated; (fam: cachondo) randy

calificación [kalifika'θjon] nf qualification; (de alumno) grade, mark

calificar [kalifi'kar] vt to qualify; (alumno) to grade, mark; **~ de** to describe as

calima [ka'lima] nf (cerca del mar) mist

cáliz ['kaliθ] nm chalice

caliza [ka'liθa] nf limestone

calizo, a [ka'liθo, a] adj lime cpd

callado, a [ka'ʎaðo, a] adj quiet

callar [ka'ʎar] vt (asunto delicado) to keep quiet about, say nothing about; (persona, opinión) to silence ♦ vi to keep quiet, be silent; **~se** vr to keep quiet, be silent; **¡cállate!** be quiet!, shut up!

calle ['kaʎe] nf street; (DEPORTE) lane; **~ arriba/abajo** up/down the street;

~ de un solo sentido one-way street

calleja [ka'ʎexa] nf alley, narrow street; **callejear** vi to wander (about) the streets; **callejero, a** adj street cpd ♦ nm street map; **callejón** nm alley, passage; **callejón sin salida** cul-de-sac; **callejuela** nf side-street, alley

callista [ka'ʎista] nm/f chiropodist

callo [kaʎo] nm callus; (en el pie) corn; **~s** nmpl (CULIN) tripe sg

calma ['kalma] nf calm

calmante [kal'mante] nm sedative, tranquillizer

calmar [kal'mar] vt to calm, calm down ♦ vi (tempestad) to abate; (mente etc) to become calm

calmoso, a [kal'moso, a] adj calm, quiet

calor [ka'lor] nm heat; (agradable) warmth; **hace ~** it's hot; **tener ~** to be hot

caloría [kalo'ria] nf calorie

calumnia [ka'lumnja] nf calumny, slander; **calumnioso, a** adj slanderous

caluroso, a [kalu'roso, a] adj hot; (sin exceso) warm; (fig) enthusiastic

calva ['kalβa] nf bald patch; (en bosque) clearing

calvario [kal'βarjo] nm stations pl of the cross

calvicie [kal'βiθje] nf baldness

calvo, a ['kalβo, a] adj bald; (terreno) bare, barren; (tejido) threadbare

calza [kalθa] nf wedge, chock

calzada [kal'θaða] nf roadway, highway

calzado, a [kal'θaðo, a] adj shod ♦ nm footwear

calzador [kalθa'ðor] nm shoehorn

calzar [kal'θar] vt (zapatos etc) to wear; (un mueble) to put a wedge under; **~se** vr: **~se los zapatos** to put on one's shoes; **¿qué número calza?** what size do you take?

calzón [kal'θon] nm (tb: **calzones** nmpl) shorts; (AM: de hombre) (pants); (: de mujer) panties

calzoncillos [kalθon'θiʎos] nmpl underpants

cama ['kama] nf bed; **~ individual/de matrimonio** single/double bed

camafeo [kama'feo] nm cameo

camaleón [kamale'on] nm chameleon

cámara ['kamara] nf chamber; (habitación) room; (sala) hall; (CINE) cine camera; (fotográfica) camera; **~ de aire** inner tube; **~ de comercio** chamber of commerce; **~ frigorífica** cold-storage room

camarada [kama'raða] nm comrade, companion

camarera [kama'rera] nf (en restaurante) waitress; (en casa, hotel) maid

camarero [kama'rero] nm waiter

camarilla [kama'riʎa] nf clique

camarón [kama'ron] nm shrimp

camarote [kama'rote] nm cabin

cambiable [kam'bjaβle] adj (variable) changeable, variable; (intercambiable) interchangeable

cambiante [kam'bjante] adj variable

cambiar [kam'bjar] vt to change; (dinero) to exchange ♦ vi to change; **~se** vr (mudarse) to move; (de ropa) to change; **~ de idea** to change one's mind; **~ de ropa** to change (one's clothes)

cambio ['kambjo] nm change; (trueque) exchange; (COM) rate of exchange; (oficina) bureau de change; (dinero menudo) small change; **en ~** on the other hand; (en lugar de) instead; **~ de divisas** foreign exchange; **~ de velocidades** gear lever

camelar [kame'lar] vt to sweet-talk

camello [ka'meʎo] nm camel; (fam: traficante) pusher

camerino [kame'rino] nm dressing room

camilla [ka'miʎa] nf (MED) stretcher

caminante [kami'nante] nm/f traveller

caminar [kami'nar] vi (marchar) to walk, go ♦ vt (recorrer) to cover, travel

caminata [kami'nata] nf long walk; (por el campo) hike

camino [ka'mino] nm way, road; (sendero) track; **a medio ~** halfway (there); **en el ~** on the way, en route; **~ de** on the way to; **~ particular** private road

---
Camino de Santiago

The **Camino de Santiago** is a medieval pilgrim route stretching from the Pyrenees to Santiago de Compostela in north-west Spain, where tradition has it the body of the Apostle James is buried. Nowadays it is a popular tourist route as well as a religious one.

---

camión [ka'mjon] nm lorry (BRIT), truck (US); **~ cisterna** tanker; **camionero, a** nm/f lorry o truck driver

camioneta [kamjo'neta] nf van, light truck

camisa [ka'misa] nf shirt; (BOT) skin; **~ de fuerza** straitjacket; **camisería** nf outfitter's (shop)

camiseta [kami'seta] nf (prenda) tee-shirt; (: ropa interior) vest; (de deportista) top

camisón [kami'son] nm nightdress, nightgown

camorra [ka'morra] nf: **buscar ~** to look for trouble

campamento [kampa'mento] nm camp

campana [kam'pana] nf bell; **~ de cristal** bell jar; **~da** nf peal; **~rio** nm belfry

campanilla [kampa'niʎa] nf small bell

campaña [kam'paɲa] nf (MIL, POL) campaign

campechano, a [kampe'tʃano, a] adj (franco) open

campeón, ona [kampe'on, ona] nm/f champion; **campeonato** nm championship

campesino, a [kampe'sino, a] adj country cpd, rural; (gente) peasant cpd ♦ nm/f countryman/woman; (agricultor) farmer

campestre [kam'pestre] adj country cpd, rural

camping ['kampin] (pl ~s) nm camping; (lugar) campsite; **ir de** o **hacer ~** to go camping

campo ['kampo] nm (fuera de la ciudad) country, countryside; (AGR, ELEC) field; (de fútbol) pitch; (de golf) course; (MIL) camp; **~ de batalla** battlefield; **~ de deportes** sports ground, playing field

camposanto [kampo'santo] nm cemetery

camuflaje [kamu'flaxe] nm camouflage

cana ['kana] nf white o grey hair; **tener ~s** to be going grey

Canadá [kana'ða] nm Canada; **canadiense** adj, nm/f Canadian ♦ nf fur-lined jacket

canal [ka'nal] nm canal; (GEO) channel, strait; (de televisión) channel; (de tejado) gutter; **~ de Panamá** Panama Canal; **~izar** vt to channel

canalla [ka'naʎa] nf rabble, mob ♦ nm swine

canalón [kana'lon] nm (conducto vertical) drainpipe; (del tejado) gutter

canapé [kana'pe] (pl ~s) nm sofa, settee; (CULIN) canapé

Canarias [ka'narjas] nfpl: **(las Islas) ~** the Canary Islands, the Canaries

canario, a [ka'narjo, a] adj, nm/f (native) of the Canary Isles ♦ nm (ZOOL) canary

canasta [ka'nasta] nf (round) basket; **canastilla** nf small basket; (de niño) layette

canasto [ka'nasto] nm large basket

cancela [kan'θela] nf gate

cancelación [kanθela'θjon] nf cancellation

cancelar [kanθe'lar] vt to cancel; (una

deuda) to write off
cáncer ['kanθer] *nm* (MED) cancer; (ASTROLOGÍA): **C~** Cancer
cancha ['kantʃa] *nf* (de baloncesto, tenis etc) court; (AM: de fútbol) pitch
canciller [kanθi'ʎer] *nm* chancellor
canción [kan'θjon] *nf* song; **~ de cuna** lullaby; **cancionero** *nm* song book
candado [kan'daðo] *nm* padlock
candente [kan'dente] *adj* red-hot; (fig: tema) burning
candidato, a [kandi'ðato, a] *nm/f* candidate
candidez [kandi'ðeθ] *nf* (sencillez) simplicity; (simpleza) naiveté; **cándido, a** *adj* simple; naive
candil [kan'dil] *nm* oil lamp; **~ejas** *nfpl* (TEATRO) footlights
candor [kan'dor] *nm* (sinceridad) frankness; (inocencia) innocence
canela [ka'nela] *nf* cinnamon
canelones [kane'lones] *nmpl* cannelloni
cangrejo [kan'grexo] *nm* crab
canguro [kan'guro] *nm* kangaroo; **hacer de ~** to babysit
caníbal [ka'niβal] *adj, nm/f* cannibal
canica [ka'nika] *nf* marble
canijo, a [ka'nixo, a] *adj* frail, sickly
canino, a [ka'nino, a] *adj* canine ♦ *nm* canine (tooth)
canjear [kanxe'ar] *vt* to exchange
cano, a [ka'no, a] *adj* grey-haired, white-haired
canoa [ka'noa] *nf* canoe
canon ['kanon] *nm* canon; (pensión) rent; (COM) tax
canónigo [ka'noniνo] *nm* canon
canonizar [kanoni'θar] *vt* to canonize
canoso, a [ka'noso, a] *adj* grey-haired
cansado, a [kan'saðo, a] *adj* tired, weary; (tedioso) tedious, boring
cansancio [kan'sanθjo] *nm* tiredness, fatigue
cansar [kan'sar] *vt* (fatigar) to tire, tire out; (aburrir) to bore; (fastidiar) to

bother; **~se** *vr* to tire, get tired; (aburrirse) to get bored
cantábrico, a [kan'taβriko, a] *adj* Cantabrian; **mar C~** Bay of Biscay
cantante [kan'tante] *adj* singing ♦ *nm/f* singer
cantar [kan'tar] *vt* to sing ♦ *vi* to sing; (insecto) to chirp ♦ *nm* (acción) singing; (canción) song; (poema) poem
cántara ['kantara] *nf* large pitcher
cántaro ['kantaro] *nm* pitcher, jug; **llover a ~s** to rain cats and dogs
cante ['kante] *nm*: **~ jondo** flamenco singing
cantera [kan'tera] *nf* quarry
cantidad [kanti'ðað] *nf* quantity, amount
cantimplora [kantim'plora] *nf* (frasco) water bottle, canteen
cantina [kan'tina] *nf* canteen; (de estación) buffet
canto ['kanto] *nm* singing; (canción) song; (borde) edge, rim; (de un cuchillo) back; **~ rodado** boulder
cantor, a [kan'tor, a] *nm/f* singer
canturrear [kanturre'ar] *vi* to sing softly
canuto [ka'nuto] *nm* (tubo) small tube; (fam: droga) joint
caña ['kaŋa] *nf* (BOT: tallo) stem, stalk; (carrizo) reed; (vaso) tumbler; (de cerveza) glass of beer; (ANAT) shinbone; **~ de azúcar** sugar cane; **~ de pescar** fishing rod
cañada [ka'ŋaða] *nf* (entre dos montañas) gully, ravine; (camino) cattle track
cáñamo ['kaŋamo] *nm* hemp
cañería [kaŋe'ria] *nf* (tubo) pipe
caño ['kaŋo] *nm* (tubo) tube, pipe; (de albañal) sewer; (MUS) pipe; (de fuente) jet
cañón [ka'ŋon] *nm* (MIL) cannon; (de fusil) barrel; (GEO) canyon, gorge
caoba [ka'oβa] *nf* mahogany
caos ['kaos] *nm* chaos
cap. *abr* (= capítulo) ch.

capa ['kapa] nf cloak, cape; (GEO) layer, stratum; **so ~ de** under the pretext of; **~ de ozono** ozone layer

capacidad [kapaθi'ðað] nf (medida) capacity; (aptitud) capacity, ability

capacitar [kapaθi'tar] vt: **~ a algn para (hacer)** to enable sb to (do)

capar [ka'par] vt to castrate, geld

caparazón [kapara'θon] nm shell

capataz [kapa'taθ] nm foreman

capaz [ka'paθ] adj able, capable; (amplio) capacious, roomy

capcioso, a [kap'θjoso, a] adj wily, deceitful

capellán [kape'ʎan] nm chaplain; (sacerdote) priest

caperuza [kape'ruθa] nf hood

capicúa [kapi'kua] adj inv (número, fecha) reversible

capilla [ka'piʎa] nf chapel

capital [kapi'tal] adj capital ♦ nm (COM) capital ♦ nf (ciudad) capital; **~ social** share o authorized capital

capitalismo [kapita'lismo] nm capitalism; **capitalista** adj, nm/f capitalist

capitán [kapi'tan] nm captain

capitanear [kapitane'ar] vt to captain

capitulación [kapitula'θjon] nf (rendición) capitulation, surrender; (acuerdo) agreement, pact; **capitulaciones (matrimoniales)** nfpl marriage contract sg

capitular [kapitu'lar] vi to make an agreement

capítulo [ka'pitulo] nm chapter

capó [ka'po] nm (AUTO) bonnet

capón [ka'pon] nm (gallo) capon

capota [ka'pota] nf (de mujer) bonnet; (AUTO) hood (BRIT), top (US)

capote [ka'pote] nm (abrigo: de militar) greatcoat; (: de torero) cloak

capricho [ka'pritʃo] nm whim, caprice; **~so, a** adj capricious

Capricornio [kapri'kornjo] nm Capricorn

cápsula ['kapsula] nf capsule

captar [kap'tar] vt (comprender) to understand; (RADIO) to pick up; (atención, apoyo) to attract

captura [kap'tura] nf capture; (JUR) arrest; **capturar** vt to capture; to arrest

capucha [ka'putʃa] nf hood, cowl

capullo [ka'puɲo] nm (BOT) bud; (ZOOL) cocoon; (fam) idiot

caqui ['kaki] nm khaki

cara ['kara] nf (ANAT, de moneda) face; (de disco) side; (descaro) boldness; **~ a** facing; **de ~** opposite, facing; **dar la ~** to face the consequences; **¿~ o cruz?** heads or tails?; **¡qué ~ (más dura)!** what a nerve!

carabina [kara'ßina] nf carbine, rifle; (persona) chaperone

Caracas [ka'rakas] n Caracas

caracol [kara'kol] nm (ZOOL) snail; (concha) (sea) shell

carácter [ka'rakter] (pl **caracteres**) nm character; **tener buen/mal ~** to be good natured/bad tempered

característica [karakte'ristika] nf characteristic

característico, a [karakte'ristiko, a] adj characteristic

caracterizar [karakteri'θar] vt to characterize, typify

caradura [kara'ðura] nm/f: **es un ~** he's got a nerve

carajillo [kara'xiʎo] nm coffee with a dash of brandy

carajo [ka'raxo] (fam!) nm: **¡~!** shit! (!)

caramba [ka'ramba] excl good gracious!

carámbano [ka'rambano] nm icicle

caramelo [kara'melo] nm (dulce) sweet; (azúcar fundida) caramel

caravana [kara'ßana] nf caravan; (fig) group; (AUTO) tailback

carbón [kar'ßon] nm coal; **papel ~** carbon paper; **carboncillo** [-'niʎo] nm (ARTE) charcoal; **carbonero, a** nm/f coal merchant; **carbonilla** [-'niʎa] nf coal dust

carbonizar [karβoni'θar] vt to carbonize; (quemar) to char

carbono [kar'βono] nm carbon

carburador [karβura'ðor] nm carburettor

carburante [karβu'rante] nm (para motor) fuel

carcajada [karka'xaða] nf (loud) laugh, guffaw

cárcel [kar'θel] nf prison, jail; (TEC) clamp; **carcelero, a** adj prison cpd ♦ nm/f warder

carcoma [kar'koma] nf woodworm

carcomer [karko'mer] vt to bore into, eat into; (fig) to undermine; **~se** vr to become worm-eaten; (fig) to decay

cardar [kar'ðar] vt (pelo) to backcomb

cardenal [karðe'nal] nm (REL) cardinal; (MED) bruise

cardíaco, a [kar'ðiako, a] adj cardiac, heart cpd

cardinal [karði'nal] adj cardinal

cardo [kar'ðo] nm thistle

carearse [kare'arse] vr to come face to face

carecer [kare'θer] vi: ~ **de** to lack, be in need of

carencia [ka'renθja] nf lack; (escasez) shortage; (MED) deficiency

carente [ka'rente] adj: ~ **de** lacking in, devoid of

carestía [kares'tia] nf (escasez) scarcity, shortage; (COM) high cost

careta [ka'reta] nf mask

carga [karva] nf (peso, ELEC) load; (de barco) cargo, freight; (MIL) charge; (responsabilidad) duty, obligation

cargado, a [kar'vaðo, a] adj loaded; (ELEC) live; (café, té) strong; (cielo) overcast

cargamento [karva'mento] nm (acción) loading; (mercancías) load, cargo

cargar [kar'var] vt (barco, arma) to load; (ELEC) to charge; (COM: algo en cuenta) to charge; (INFORM) to load ♦ vi (MIL) to charge; (AUTO) to load (up);

~ **con** to pick up, carry away; (peso, fig) to shoulder, bear; **~se** (fam) vr (estropear) to break; (matar) to bump off

cargo ['karvo] nm (puesto) post, office; (responsabilidad) duty, obligation; (JUR) charge; **hacerse ~ de** to take charge of o responsibility for

carguero [kar'vero] nm freighter, cargo boat; (avión) freight plane

Caribe [ka'riβe] nm: **el ~** the Caribbean; **del ~** Caribbean

caribeño, a [kari'βeɲo, a] adj Caribbean

caricatura [karika'tura] nf caricature

caricia [ka'riθja] nf caress

caridad [kari'ðað] nf charity

caries ['karjes] nf inv tooth decay

cariño [ka'riɲo] nm affection, love; (caricia) caress; (en carta) love ...; **tener ~ a** to be fond of; **~so, a** adj affectionate

carisma [ka'risma] nm charisma

caritativo, a [karita'tiβo, a] adj charitable

cariz [ka'riθ] nm: **tener o tomar buen/mal ~** to look good/bad

carmesí [karme'si] adj, nm crimson

carmín [kar'min] nm lipstick

carnal [kar'nal] adj carnal; **primo ~** first cousin

carnaval [karna'βal] nm carnival

---

carnaval

Carnaval is the traditional period of fun, feasting and partying which takes place in the three days before the start of Lent ("Cuaresma"). Although in decline during the Franco years the carnival has grown in popularity recently in Spain. Cádiz and Tenerife are particularly well-known for their flamboyant celebrations with fancy-dress parties, parades and firework displays being the order of the day.

carne ['karne] *nf* flesh; (CULIN) meat;
~ **de cerdo/cordero/ternera/vaca**
pork/lamb/veal/beef; ~ **de gallina**
(*fig*): **se me pone la ~ de gallina
sólo verlo** I get the creeps just seeing
it

carné [kar'ne] (*pl* ~**s**) *nm*: ~ **de
conducir** driving licence (BRIT),
driver's license (US); ~ **de identidad**
identity card

carnero [kar'nero] *nm* sheep, ram;
(*carne*) mutton

carnet [kar'ne] (*pl* ~**s**) *nm* = **carné**

carnicería [karniθe'ria] *nf* butcher's
(shop); (*fig*: *matanza*) carnage,
slaughter

carnicero, a [karni'θero, a] *adj*
carnivorous ♦ *nm/f* (*tb fig*) butcher;
(*carnívoro*) carnivore

carnívoro, a [kar'niβoro, a] *adj*
carnivorous

carnoso, a [kar'noso, a] *adj* beefy, fat

caro, a ['karo, a] *adj* dear; (COM) dear,
expensive ♦ *adv* dear, dearly

carpa ['karpa] *nf* (*pez*) carp; (*de circo*)
big top; (AM: *de camping*) tent

carpeta [kar'peta] *nf* folder, file

carpintería [karpinte'ria] *nf* carpentry,
joinery; **carpintero** *nm* carpenter

carraspear [karraspe'ar] *vi* to clear
one's throat

carraspera [karras'pera] *nf* hoarseness

carrera [ka'rrera] *nf* (*acción*) run(ning);
(*espacio recorrido*) run; (*competición*)
race; (*trayecto*) course; (*profesión*)
career; (ESCOL) course

carreta [ka'rreta] *nf* wagon, cart

carrete [ka'rrete] *nm* reel, spool; (TEC)
coil

carretera [karre'tera] *nf* (main) road,
highway; ~ **de circunvalación** ring
road; ~ **nacional** ≈ A road (BRIT), ≈
state highway (US)

carretilla [karre'tiʎa] *nf* trolley; (AGR)
(wheel)barrow

carril [ka'rril] *nm* furrow; (*de autopista*)
lane; (FERRO) rail

carrillo [ka'rriʎo] *nm* (ANAT) cheek;
(TEC) pulley

carrito [ka'rrito] *nm* trolley

carro ['karro] *nm* cart, wagon; (MIL)
tank; (AM: *coche*) car

carrocería [karroθe'ria] *nf* bodywork,
coachwork

carroña [ka'rroɲa] *nf* carrion *no pl*

carroza [ka'rroθa] *nf* (*carruaje*)
coach

carrusel [karru'sel] *nm* merry-go-
round, roundabout

carta ['karta] *nf* letter; (CULIN) menu;
(*naipe*) card; (*mapa*) map; (JUR)
document; ~ **de ajuste** (TV) test card;
~ **de crédito** credit card;
~ **certificada** registered letter;
~ **marítima** chart; ~ **verde** (AUTO)
green card

cartabón [karta'βon] *nm* set square

cartel [kar'tel] *nm* (*anuncio*) poster,
placard; (ESCOL) wall chart; (COM)
cartel; ~**era** *nf* hoarding, billboard; (*en
periódico etc*) entertainments guide;
"en ~era" "showing"

cartera [kar'tera] *nf* (*de bolsillo*) wallet;
(*de colegial, cobrador*) satchel; (*de
señora*) handbag; (*para documentos*)
briefcase; (COM) portfolio; **ocupa la
~ de Agricultura** she is Minister of
Agriculture

carterista [karte'rista] *nm/f* pickpocket

cartero [kar'tero] *nm* postman

cartilla [kar'tiʎa] *nf* primer, first
reading book; ~ **de ahorros** savings
book

cartón [kar'ton] *nm* cardboard;
~ **piedra** papier-mâché

cartucho [kar'tutʃo] *nm* (MIL) cartridge

cartulina [kartu'lina] *nf* card

casa ['kasa] *nf* house; (*hogar*) home;
(COM) firm, company; **en ~** at home;
~ **consistorial** town hall; ~ **de
huéspedes** boarding house; ~ **de
socorro** first aid post

casado, a [ka'saðo, a] *adj* married
♦ *nm/f* married man/woman

casamiento [kasa'mjento] nm marriage, wedding

casar [ka'sar] vt to marry; (JUR) to quash, annul; **~se** vr to marry, get married

cascabel [kaska'βel] nm (small) bell

cascada [kas'kaða] nf waterfall

cascanueces [kaska'nweθes] nm inv nutcrackers pl

cascar [kas'kar] vt to crack, split, break (open); **~se** vr to crack, split, break (open)

cáscara ['kaskara] nf (de huevo, fruta seca) shell; (de fruta) skin; (de limón) peel

casco ['kasko] nm (de bombero, soldado) helmet; (NAUT: de barco) hull; (ZOOL: de caballo) hoof; (botella) empty bottle; (de ciudad): **el ~ antiguo** the old part; **el ~ urbano** the town centre; **los ~s azules** the UN peace-keeping force, the blue berets

cascote [kas'kote] nm rubble

caserío [kase'rio] nm hamlet; (casa) country house

casero, a [ka'sero, a] adj (pan etc) home-made ♦ nm/f (propietario) landlord/lady; **ser muy ~** to be home-loving; **"comida casera"** "home cooking"

caseta [ka'seta] nf hut; (para bañista) cubicle; (de feria) stall

casete [ka'sete] nm o f cassette

casi ['kasi] adv almost, nearly; **~ nada** hardly anything; **~ nunca** hardly ever, almost never; **~ te caes** you almost fell

casilla [ka'siʎa] nf (casita) hut, cabin; (AJEDREZ) square; (para cartas) pigeonhole; **casillero** nm (para cartas) pigeonholes pl

casino [ka'sino] nm club; (de juego) casino

caso ['kaso] nm case; **en ~ de ...** in case of ...; **en ~ de que ...** in case; **el ~ es que** the fact is that; **en ese ~** in that case; **hacer ~ a** to pay attention to; **hacer** o **venir al ~** to be relevant

caspa ['kaspa] nf dandruff

cassette [ka'sete] nm o f = **casete**

casta ['kasta] nf caste; (raza) breed; (linaje) lineage

castaña [kas'taɲa] nf chestnut

castañetear [kastaɲete'ar] vi (dientes) to chatter

castaño, a [kas'taɲo, a] adj chestnut (-coloured), brown ♦ nm chestnut tree

castañuelas [kasta'ɲwelas] nfpl castanets

castellano, a [kaste'ʎano, a] adj, nm/f Castilian ♦ nm (LING) Castilian, Spanish

castidad [kasti'ðað] nf chastity, purity

castigar [kasti'ɣar] vt to punish; (DEPORTE) to penalize; **castigo** nm punishment; (DEPORTE) penalty

Castilla [kas'tiʎa] nf Castille

castillo [kas'tiʎo] nm castle

castizo, a [kas'tiθo, a] adj (LING) pure

casto, a ['kasto, a] adj chaste, pure

castor [kas'tor] nm beaver

castrar [kas'trar] vt to castrate

castrense [kas'trense] adj (disciplina, vida) military

casual [ka'swal] adj chance, accidental; **~idad** nf chance, accident; (combinación de circunstancias) coincidence; **¡qué ~idad!** what a coincidence!

cataclismo [kata'klismo] nm cataclysm

catador, a [kata'ðor, a] nm/f wine taster

catalán, ana [kata'lan, ana] adj, nm/f Catalan ♦ nm (LING) Catalan

catalizador [kataliθa'ðor] nm catalyst; (AUT) catalytic convertor

catalogar [katalo'ɣar] vt to catalogue; **~ a algn (de)** (fig) to categorize sb (as)

catálogo [ka'taloɣo] nm catalogue

Cataluña [kata'luɲa] nf Catalonia

catar [ka'tar] vt to taste, sample

catarata [kata'rata] nf (GEO) waterfall;

(MED) cataract

catarro [ka'tarro] nm catarrh; (constipado) cold

catástrofe [ka'tastrofe] nf catastrophe

catear [kate'ar] (fam) vt (examen, alumno) to fail

cátedra ['kateðra] nf (UNIV) chair, professorship

catedral [kate'ðral] nf cathedral

catedrático, a [kate'ðratiko, a] nm/f professor

categoría [kateɣo'ria] nf category; (rango) rank, standing; (calidad) quality; **de ~** (hotel) top-class

categórico, a [kate'ɣoriko, a] adj categorical

cateto, a ['kateto, a] (pey) nm/f peasant

catolicismo [katoli'θismo] nm Catholicism

católico, a [ka'toliko, a] adj, nm/f Catholic

catorce [ka'torθe] num fourteen

cauce ['kauθe] nm (de río) riverbed; (fig) channel

caucho ['kautʃo] nm rubber; (AM: llanta) tyre

caución [kau'θjon] nf bail; **caucionar** vt (JUR) to bail, go bail for

caudal [kau'ðal] nm (de río) volume, flow; (fortuna) wealth; (abundancia) abundance; **~oso, a** adj (río) large

caudillo [kau'ðiʎo] nm leader, chief

causa ['kausa] nf cause; (razón) reason; (JUR) lawsuit, case; **a ~ de** because of

causar [kau'sar] vt to cause

cautela [kau'tela] nf caution, cautiousness; **cauteloso, a** adj cautious, wary

cautivar [kauti'βar] vt to capture; (atraer) to captivate

cautiverio [kauti'βerjo] nm captivity

cautividad [kautiβi'ðað] nf = cautiverio

cautivo, a [kau'tiβo, a] adj, nm/f captive

cauto, a ['kauto, a] adj cautious,

careful

cava ['kaβa] nm champagne-type wine

cavar [ka'βar] vt to dig

caverna [ka'βerna] nf cave, cavern

cavidad [kaβi'ðað] nf cavity

cavilar [kaβi'lar] vt to ponder

cayado [ka'jaðo] nm (de pastor) crook; (de obispo) crozier

cayendo etc vb ver **caer**

caza ['kaθa] nf (acción: gen) hunting; (: con fusil) shooting; (una ~) hunt, chase; (animales) game ♦ nm (AVIAT) fighter

cazador, a [kaθa'ðor, a] nm/f hunter; **cazadora** nf jacket

cazar [ka'θar] vt to hunt; (perseguir) to chase; (prender) to catch

cazo ['kaθo] nm saucepan

cazuela [ka'θwela] nf (vasija) pan; (guisado) casserole

CD abbr (= compact disc) CD

CD-ROM abbr m CD-ROM

CE nf abr (= Comunidad Europea) EC

cebada [θe'βaða] nf barley

cebar [θe'βar] vt (animal) to fatten (up); (anzuelo) to bait; (MIL, TEC) to prime

cebo ['θeβo] nm (para animales) feed, food; (para peces, fig) bait; (de arma) charge

cebolla [θe'βoʎa] nf onion; **cebolleta** nf spring onion; **cebollín** nm spring onion

cebra ['θeβra] nf zebra

cecear [θeθe'ar] vi to lisp; **ceceo** nm lisp

ceder [θe'ðer] vt to hand over, give up, part with ♦ vi (renunciar) to give in, yield; (disminuir) to diminish, decline; (romperse) to give way

cedro ['θeðro] nm cedar

cédula ['θeðula] nf certificate, document

cegar [θe'ɣar] vt to blind; (tubería etc) to block up, stop up ♦ vi to go blind; **~se** vr: **~se (de)** to be blinded (by)

ceguera [θe'ɣera] nf blindness

CEI *abbr* (= *Confederación de Estados Independientes*) CIS

ceja ['θexa] *nf* eyebrow

cejar [θe'xar] *vi* (*fig*) to back down

celador, a [θela'ðor, a] *nm/f* (*de edificio*) watchman; (*de museo etc*) attendant

celda ['θelda] *nf* cell

celebración [θeleβra'θjon] *nf* celebration

celebrar [θele'βrar] *vt* to celebrate; (*alabar*) to praise ♦ *vi* to be glad; **~se** *vr* to occur, take place

célebre ['θelebre] *adj* famous

celebridad [θeleβri'ðað] *nf* fame; (*persona*) celebrity

celeste [θe'leste] *adj* (*azul*) sky-blue

celestial [θeles'tjal] *adj* celestial, heavenly

celibato [θeli'βato] *nm* celibacy

célibe ['θeliβe] *adj, nm/f* celibate

celo¹ ['θelo] *nm* zeal; (*REL*) fervour; (*ZOOL*): **en ~** on heat; **~s** *nmpl* jealousy *sg*; **tener ~s** to be jealous

celo² ® ['θelo] *nm* Sellotape ®

celofán [θelo'fan] *nm* cellophane

celoso, a [θe'loso, a] *adj* jealous; (*trabajador*) zealous

celta ['θelta] *adj* Celtic ♦ *nm/f* Celt

célula ['θelula] *nf* cell; **~ solar** solar cell

celulitis [θelu'litis] *nf* cellulite

celuloide [θelu'loiðe] *nm* celluloid

cementerio [θemen'terjo] *nm* cemetery, graveyard

cemento [θe'mento] *nm* cement; (*hormigón*) concrete; (*AM: cola*) glue

cena ['θena] *nf* evening meal, dinner

cenagal [θena'xal] *nm* bog, quagmire

cenar [θe'nar] *vt* to have for dinner ♦ *vi* to have dinner

cenicero [θeni'θero] *nm* ashtray

cenit [θe'nit] *nm* zenith

ceniza [θe'niθa] *nf* ash, ashes *pl*

censo ['θenso] *nm* census; **~ electoral** electoral roll

censura [θen'sura] *nf* (*POL*) censorship

censurar [θensu'rar] *vt* (*idea*) to censure; (*cortar: película*) to censor

centella [θen'teʎa] *nf* spark

centellear [θenteʎe'ar] *vi* (*metal*) to gleam; (*estrella*) to twinkle; (*fig*) to sparkle

centenar [θente'nar] *nm* hundred

centenario, a [θente'narjo, a] *adj* centenary; hundred-year-old ♦ *nm* centenary

centeno [θen'teno] *nm* (*BOT*) rye

centésimo, a [θen'tesimo, a] *adj* hundredth

centígrado [θen'tixraðo] *adj* centigrade

centímetro [θen'timetro] *nm* centimetre (*BRIT*), centimeter (*US*)

céntimo ['θentimo] *nm* cent

centinela [θenti'nela] *nm* sentry, guard

centollo [θen'toʎo] *nm* spider crab

central [θen'tral] *adj* central ♦ *nf* head office; (*TEC*) plant; (*TEL*) exchange; **~ eléctrica** power station; **~ nuclear** nuclear power station; **~ telefónica** telephone exchange

centralita [θentra'lita] *nf* switchboard

centralizar [θentrali'θar] *vt* to centralize

centrar [θen'trar] *vt* to centre

céntrico, a ['θentriko, a] *adj* central

centrifugar [θentrifu'xar] *vt* to spin-dry

centrista [θen'trista] *adj* centre *cpd*

centro ['θentro] *nm* centre; **~ comercial** shopping centre; **~ juvenil** youth club

centroamericano, a [θentroameri'kano, a] *adj, nm/f* Central American

ceñido, a [θe'niðo, a] *adj* (*chaqueta, pantalón*) tight(-fitting)

ceñir [θe'nir] *vt* (*rodear*) to encircle, surround; (*ajustar*) to fit (tightly)

ceño ['θeno] *nm* frown, scowl; **fruncir el ~** to frown, knit one's brow

CEOE *nf abr* (*ESP*: = *Confederación*

Española de Organizaciones Empresariales) ≈ CBI (*BRIT*), employers' organization

cepillar [θepiˈʎar] vt to brush; (*madera*) to plane (down)

cepillo [θeˈpiʎo] nm brush; (*para madera*) plane; **~ de dientes** toothbrush

cera [ˈθera] nf wax

cerámica [θeˈramika] nf pottery; (*arte*) ceramics

cerca [ˈθerka] nf fence ♦ adv near, nearby, close; **~ de** near, close to

cercanías [θerkaˈnias] nfpl (*afueras*) outskirts, suburbs

cercano, a [θerˈkano, a] adj close, near

cercar [θerˈkar] vt to fence in; (*rodear*) to surround

cerciorar [θerθjoˈrar] vt (*asegurar*) to assure; **~se** vr (*asegurarse*) to make sure

cerco [ˈθerko] nm (*AGR*) enclosure; (*AM*) fence; (*MIL*) siege

cerdo a [ˈθerðo, a] nm/f pig/sow

cereal [θereˈal] nm cereal; **~es** nmpl cereals, grain sg

cerebro [θeˈreβro] nm brain; (*fig*) brains pl

ceremonia [θereˈmonja] nf ceremony; **ceremonial** adj, nm ceremonial; **ceremonioso, a** adj ceremonious

cereza [θeˈreθa] nf cherry

cerilla [θeˈriʎa] nf (*fósforo*) match

cernerse [θerˈnerse] vr to hover

cero [ˈθero] nm nothing, zero

cerrado, a [θeˈrraðo, a] adj closed, shut; (*con llave*) locked; (*tiempo*) cloudy, overcast; (*curva*) sharp; (*acento*) thick, broad

cerradura [θerraˈðura] nf (*acción*) closing; (*mecanismo*) lock

cerrajero [θerraˈxero] nm locksmith

cerrar [θeˈrrar] vt to close, shut; (*paso, carretera*) to close; (*grifo*) to turn off; (*cuenta, negocio*) to close ♦ vi to close, shut; (*la noche*) to come down; **~se** vr

to close, shut; **~ con llave** to lock; **~ un trato** to strike a bargain

cerro [ˈθerro] nm hill

cerrojo [θeˈrroxo] nm (*herramienta*) bolt; (*de puerta*) latch

certamen [θerˈtamen] nm competition, contest

certero, a [θerˈtero, a] adj (*gen*) accurate

certeza [θerˈteθa] nf certainty

certidumbre [θertiˈðumbre] nf = **certeza**

certificado [θertifiˈkaðo] nm certificate

certificar [θertifiˈkar] vt (*asegurar, atestar*) to certify

cervatillo [θerβaˈtiʎo] nm fawn

cervecería [θerβeθeˈria] nf (*fábrica*) brewery; (*bar*) public house, pub

cerveza [θerˈβeθa] nf beer

cesante [θeˈsante] adj redundant

cesar [θeˈsar] vi to cease, stop ♦ vt (*funcionario*) to remove from office

cesárea [θeˈsarea] nf (*MED*) Caesarean operation o section

cese [ˈθese] nm (*de trabajo*) dismissal; (*de pago*) suspension

césped [ˈθespeð] nm grass, lawn

cesta [ˈθesta] nf basket

cesto [ˈθesto] nm (large) basket, hamper

cetro [ˈθetro] nm sceptre

cfr abr (= *confróntese*) cf.

chabacano, a [tʃaβaˈkano, a] adj vulgar, coarse

chabola [tʃaˈβola] nf shack; **barrio de ~s** shanty town sg

chacal [tʃaˈkal] nm jackal

chacha [ˈtʃatʃa] (*fam*) nf maid

cháchara [ˈtʃatʃara] nf chatter; **estar de ~** to chatter away

chacra [ˈtʃakra] (*AM*) nf smallholding

chafar [tʃaˈfar] vt (*aplastar*) to crush; (*plan etc*) to ruin

chal [tʃal] nm shawl

chalado, a [tʃaˈlaðo, a] (*fam*) adj crazy

chalé [tʃaˈle] (*pl* **~s**) nm villa; ≈

detached house

chaleco [tʃa'leko] *nm* waistcoat, vest (*US*); ~ **salvavidas** life jacket

chalet [tʃa'le] (*pl* ~**s**) *nm* = **chalé**

champán [tʃam'pan] *nm* champagne

champaña [tʃam'paɲa] *nm* = **champán**

champiñón [tʃampi'ɲon] *nm* mushroom

champú [tʃam'pu] (*pl* **champúes**, **champús**) *nm* shampoo

chamuscar [tʃamus'kar] *vt* to scorch, sear, singe

chance [tʃanθe] (*AM*) *nm* chance

chancho, a ['tʃantʃo, a] (*AM*) *nm/f* pig

chanchullo [tʃan'tʃuʎo] (*fam*) *nm* fiddle

chandal [tʃan'dal] *nm* tracksuit

chantaje [tʃan'taxe] *nm* blackmail

chapa ['tʃapa] *nf* (*de metal*) plate, sheet; (*de madera*) board, panel; (*AM*: *AUTO*) number (*BRIT*) o license (*US*) plate; ~**do, a** *adj*: ~**do en oro** gold-plated

chaparrón [tʃapa'rron] *nm* downpour, cloudburst

chapotear [tʃapote'ar] *vi* to splash about

chapurrear [tʃapurre'ar] *vt* (*idioma*) to speak badly

chapuza [tʃa'puθa] *nf* botched job

chapuzón [tʃapu'θon] *nm*: **darse un ~** to go for a dip

chaqueta [tʃa'keta] *nf* jacket

chaquetón [tʃake'ton] *nm* long jacket

charca ['tʃarka] *nf* pond, pool

charco ['tʃarko] *nm* pool, puddle

charcutería [tʃarkute'ria] *nf* (*tienda*) shop selling chiefly pork meat products; (*productos*) cooked pork meats *pl*

charla ['tʃarla] *nf* talk, chat; (*conferencia*) lecture

charlar [tʃar'lar] *vi* to talk, chat

charlatán, ana [tʃarla'tan, ana] *nm/f* (*hablador*) chatterbox; (*estafador*) trickster

charol [tʃa'rol] *nm* varnish; (*cuero*)

patent leather

chascarrillo [tʃaska'rriʎo] (*fam*) *nm* funny story

chasco ['tʃasko] *nm* (*desengaño*) disappointment

chasis ['tʃasis] *nm inv* chassis

chasquear [tʃaske'ar] *vt* (*látigo*) to crack; (*lengua*) to click; **chasquido** *nm* crack; click

chatarra [tʃa'tarra] *nf* scrap (metal)

chato, a ['tʃato, a] *adj* flat; (*nariz*) snub

chaval, a [tʃa'βal, a] *nm/f* kid, lad/lass

checo, a ['tʃeko, a] *adj, nm/f* Czech

checo(e)slovaco, a [tʃeko(e)slo'βako, a] *adj, nm/f* Czech, Czechoslovak

Checo(e)slovaquia [tʃeko(e)slo'-βakja] *nf* Czechoslovakia

cheque ['tʃeke] *nm* cheque (*BRIT*), check (*US*); ~ **de viajero** traveller's cheque (*BRIT*), traveler's check (*US*)

chequeo [tʃe'keo] *nm* (*MED*) check-up; (*AUTO*) service

chequera [tʃe'kera] (*AM*) *nf* chequebook (*BRIT*), checkbook (*US*)

chicano, a [tʃi'kano, a] *adj, nm/f* chicano

chícharo ['tʃitʃaro] (*AM*) *nm* pea

chichón [tʃi'tʃon] *nm* bump, lump

chicle ['tʃikle] *nm* chewing gum

chico, a ['tʃiko, a] *adj* small, little ♦ *nm* (*niño*) child; (*muchacho*) boy/girl

chiflado, a [tʃi'flaðo, a] *adj* crazy

chiflar [tʃi'flar] *vt* to hiss, boo

Chile ['tʃile] *nm* Chile; **chileno, a** *adj, nm/f* Chilean

chile ['tʃile] *nm* chilli pepper

chillar [tʃi'ʎar] *vi* (*persona*) to yell, scream; (*animal salvaje*) to howl; (*cerdo*) to squeal

chillido [tʃi'ʎiðo] *nm* (*de persona*) yell, scream; (*de animal*) howl

chillón, ona [tʃi'ʎon, ona] *adj* (*niño*) noisy; (*color*) loud, gaudy

chimenea [tʃime'nea] *nf* chimney; (*hogar*) fireplace

China ['tʃina] nf: (la) ~ China

chinche ['tʃintʃe] nf (insecto) (bed)bug; (TEC) drawing pin (BRIT), thumbtack (US) ♦ nm/f nuisance, pest

chincheta [tʃin'tʃeta] nf drawing pin (BRIT), thumbtack (US)

chino, a ['tʃino, a] adj, nm/f Chinese ♦ nm (LING) Chinese

chipirón [tʃipi'ron] nm (ZOOL, CULIN) squid

Chipre ['tʃipre] nf Cyprus; **chipriota** adj, nm/f Cypriot

chiquillo, a [tʃi'kiʎo, a] nm/f (fam) kid

chirimoya [tʃiri'moja] nf custard apple

chiringuito [tʃirin'xito] nm small open-air bar

chiripa [tʃi'ripa] nf fluke

chirriar [tʃi'rrjar] vi to creak, squeak

chirrido [tʃi'rriðo] nm creak(ing), squeak(ing)

chis [tʃis] excl sh!

chisme ['tʃisme] nm (habladurías) piece of gossip; (fam: objeto) thingummyjig

chismoso, a [tʃis'moso, a] adj gossiping ♦ nm/f gossip

chispa ['tʃispa] nf spark; (fig) sparkle; (ingenio) wit; (fam) drunkenness

chispear [tʃispe'ar] vi (lloviznar) to drizzle

chisporrotear [tʃisporrote'ar] vi (fuego) to throw out sparks; (leña) to crackle; (aceite) to hiss, splutter

chiste ['tʃiste] nm joke, funny story

chistoso, a [tʃis'toso, a] adj funny, amusing

chivo, a ['tʃiβo, a] nm/f (billy-/nanny-) goat; ~ **expiatorio** scapegoat

chocante [tʃo'kante] adj startling; (extraño) odd; (ofensivo) shocking

chocar [tʃo'kar] vi (coches etc) to collide, crash ♦ vt to shock; (sorprender) to startle; ~ **con** to collide with; (fig) to run into, run up against; ¡chócala! (fam) put it there!

chochear [tʃotʃe'ar] vi to dodder, be senile

chocho, a ['tʃotʃo, a] adj doddering, senile; (fig) soft, doting

chocolate [tʃoko'late] adj, nm chocolate; **chocolatina** nf chocolate

chofer [tʃo'fer] nm = **chófer**

chófer ['tʃofer] nm driver

chollo ['tʃoʎo] nm (fam) bargain, snip

choque etc ['tʃoke] vb ver **chocar** ♦ nm (impacto) impact; (golpe) jolt; (AUTO) crash; (fig) conflict; ~ **frontal** head-on collision

chorizo [tʃo'riθo] nm hard pork sausage, (type of) salami

chorrada [tʃo'rraða] nf (fam) nm: ¡es una ~! that's crap! (!); **decir** ~s to talk crap (!)

chorrear [tʃorre'ar] vi to gush (out), spout (out); (gotear) to drip, trickle

chorro ['tʃorro] nm jet; (fig) stream

choza ['tʃoθa] nf hut, shack

chubasco [tʃu'Basko] nm squall

chubasquero [tʃuBas'kero] nm lightweight raincoat

chuchería [tʃutʃe'ria] nf trinket

chuleta [tʃu'leta] nf chop, cutlet

chulo ['tʃulo] nm (de prostituta) pimp

chupar [tʃu'par] vt to suck; (absorber) to absorb; ~**se** vr to grow thin

chupete [tʃu'pete] nm dummy (BRIT), pacifier (US)

chupito [tʃu'pito] nm (fam) shot

churro ['tʃurro] nm (type of) fritter

chusma ['tʃusma] nf rabble, mob

chutar [tʃu'tar] vi to shoot (at goal)

Cía abr = **compañía** Co.

cianuro [θja'nuro] nm cyanide

cicatriz [θika'triθ] nf scar; ~**arse** vr to heal (up), form a scar

ciclismo [θi'klismo] nm cycling

ciclista [θi'klista] adj cycle cpd ♦ nm/f cyclist

ciclo ['θiklo] nm cycle; ~**turismo** nm: **hacer** ~**turismo** to go on a cycling holiday

ciclón [θi'klon] *nm* cyclone

ciego, a ['θjeɣo, a] *adj* blind ♦ *nm/f* blind man/woman

cielo ['θjelo] *nm* sky; (*REL*) heaven; **¡~s!** good heavens!

ciempiés [θjem'pjes] *nm inv* centipede

cien [θjen] *num ver* **ciento**

ciénaga [θjenaγa] *nf* marsh, swamp

ciencia [θjenθja] *nf* science; **~s** *nfpl* (*ESCOL*) science *sg*; **~-ficción** *nf* science fiction

cieno [θjeno] *nm* mud, mire

científico, a [θjen'tifiko, a] *adj* scientific ♦ *nm/f* scientist

ciento [θjento] (*tb: cien*) *num* hundred; **pagar al 10 por** ~ to pay at 10 per cent

cierre *etc* ['θjerre] *vb ver* **cerrar** ♦ *nm* closing, shutting; (*con llave*) locking; ~ **de cremallera** zip (fastener)

cierro *etc vb ver* **cerrar**

cierto, a ['θjerto, a] *adj* sure, certain; (*un tal*) a certain; (*correcto*) right, correct; ~ **hombre** a certain man; **ciertas personas** certain *o* some people; **sí, es** ~ yes, that's correct

ciervo ['θjerβo] *nm* deer; (*macho*) stag

cierzo ['θjerθo] *nm* north wind

cifra ['θifra] *nf* number; (*secreta*) code

cifrar [θi'frar] *vt* to code, write in code

cigala [θi'ɣala] *nf* Norway lobster

cigarra [θi'ɣarra] *nf* cicada

cigarrillo [θiɣa'rriʎo] *nm* cigarette

cigarro [θi'ɣarro] *nm* cigarette; (*puro*) cigar

cigüeña [θi'ɣweɲa] *nf* stork

cilíndrico, a [θi'lindriko, a] *adj* cylindrical

cilindro [θi'lindro] *nm* cylinder

cima ['θima] *nf* (*de montaña*) top, peak; (*de árbol*) top; (*fig: fundar*) to sway

cimbrearse [θimbre'arse] *vr* to sway

cimentar [θimen'tar] *vt* to lay the foundations of; (*fig: fundar*) to found

cimiento [θi'mjento] *nm* foundation

cinc [θink] *nm* zinc

cincel [θin'θel] *nm* chisel; **~ar** *vt* to chisel

cinco ['θinko] *num* five

cincuenta [θin'kwenta] *num* fifty

cine ['θine] *nm* cinema

cineasta [θine'asta] *nm/f* film director

cinematográfico, a [θinemato'-ɣrafiko, a] *adj* cine-, film *cpd*

cínico, a ['θiniko, a] *adj* cynical ♦ *nm/f* cynic

cinismo [θi'nismo] *nm* cynicism

cinta ['θinta] *nf* band, strip; (*de tela*) ribbon; (*película*) reel; (*de máquina de escribir*) ribbon; ~ **adhesiva** sticky tape; ~ **de vídeo** videotape; ~ **magnetofónica** tape; ~ **métrica** tape measure

cintura [θin'tura] *nf* waist

cinturón [θintu'ron] *nm* belt; ~ **de seguridad** safety belt

ciprés [θi'pres] *nm* cypress (tree)

circo ['θirko] *nm* circus

circuito [θir'kwito] *nm* circuit

circulación [θirkula'θjon] *nf* circulation; (*AUTO*) traffic

circular [θirku'lar] *adj, nf* circular ♦ *vi, vt* to circulate ♦ *vi* (*AUTO*) to drive; **"circule por la derecha"** "keep to the right"

círculo ['θirkulo] *nm* circle; ~ **vicioso** vicious circle

circuncidar [θirkunθi'dar] *vt* to circumcise

circundar [θirkun'dar] *vt* to surround

circunferencia [θirkunfe'renθja] *nf* circumference

circunscribir [θirkunskri'βir] *vt* to circumscribe; **~se** *vr* to be limited

circunscripción [θirkunskrip'θjon] *nf* (*POL*) constituency

circunspecto, a [θirkuns'pekto, a] *adj* circumspect, cautious

circunstancia [θirkuns'tanθja] *nf* circumstance

cirio ['θirjo] *nm* (wax) candle

ciruela [θi'rwela] *nf* plum; ~ **pasa** prune

cirugía [θiru'xia] *nf* surgery;
~ **estética** o **plástica** plastic surgery

cirujano [θiru'xano] *nm* surgeon

cisne ['θisne] *nm* swan

cisterna [θis'terna] *nf* cistern, tank

cita ['θita] *nf* appointment, meeting;
(*de novios*) date; (*referencia*) quotation

citación [θita'θjon] *nf* (*JUR*) summons
sg

citar [θi'tar] *vt* (*gen*) to make an
appointment with; (*JUR*) to summons;
(*un autor, texto*) to quote; ~**se** *vr*: **se
citaron en el cine** they arranged to
meet at the cinema

cítricos ['θitrikos] *nmpl* citrus fruit/s

ciudad [θju'ðað] *nf* town; (*más grande*)
city; ~**anía** *nf* citizenship; ~**ano, a**
nm/f citizen

cívico, a ['θiβiko, a] *adj* civic

civil [θi'βil] *adj* civil ♦ *nm* (*guardia*)
policeman

civilización [θiβiliθa'θjon] *nf*
civilization

civilizar [θiβili'θar] *vt* to civilize

civismo [θi'βismo] *nm* public spirit

cizaña [θi'θaɲa] *nf* (*fig*) discord

cl. *abr* (= *centilitro*) cl.

clamar [kla'mar] *vt* to clamour for, cry
out for ♦ *vi* to cry out, clamour

clamor [kla'mor] *nm* clamour, protest

clandestino, a [klandes'tino, a] *adj*
clandestine; (*POL*) underground

clara ['klara] *nf* (*de huevo*) egg white

claraboya [klara'βoja] *nf* skylight

clarear [klare'ar] *vi* (*el día*) to dawn; (*el
cielo*) to clear up, brighten up; ~**se** *vr*
to be transparent

clarete [kla'rete] *nm* rosé (wine)

claridad [klari'ðað] *nf* (*del día*)
brightness; (*de estilo*) clarity

clarificar [klarifi'kar] *vt* to clarify

clarinete [klari'nete] *nm* clarinet

clarividencia [klariβi'ðenθja] *nf*
clairvoyance; (*fig*) far-sightedness

claro, a ['klaro, a] *adj* clear; (*luminoso*)
bright; (*color*) light; (*evidente*) clear,
evident; (*poco espeso*) thin ♦ *nm* (*en

bosque*) clearing ♦ *adv* clearly ♦ *excl*
(*tb:* ~ *que sí*) of course!

clase ['klase] *nf* class; ~ **alta/media/
obrera** upper/middle/working class;
~**s particulares** private lessons,
private tuition *sg*

clásico, a ['klasiko, a] *adj* classical

clasificación [klasifika'θjon] *nf*
classification; (*DEPORTE*) league (table)

clasificar [klasifi'kar] *vt* to classify

claudicar [klauði'kar] *vi* to give in

claustro ['klaustro] *nm* cloister

cláusula ['klausula] *nf* clause

clausura [klau'sura] *nf* closing, closure;
clausurar *vt* (*congreso etc*) to bring to
a close

clavar [kla'βar] *vt* (*clavo*) to hammer
in; (*cuchillo*) to stick, thrust

clave ['klaβe] *nf* key; (*MUS*) clef

clavel [kla'βel] *nm* carnation

clavícula [kla'βikula] *nf* collar bone

clavija [kla'βixa] *nf* peg, dowel, pin;
(*ELEC*) plug

clavo ['klaβo] *nm* (*de metal*) nail; (*BOT*)
clove

claxon ['klakson] (*pl* ~**s**) *nm* horn

clemencia [kle'menθja] *nf* mercy,
clemency

cleptómano, a [klep'tomano, a] *nm/f*
kleptomaniac

clérigo ['klerixo] *nm* priest

clero ['klero] *nm* clergy

cliché [kli'tʃe] *nm* cliché; (*FOTO*)
negative

cliente, a ['kljente, a] *nm/f* client,
customer

clientela [kljen'tela] *nf* clientele,
customers *pl*

clima ['klima] *nm* climate

climatizado, a [klimati'θaðo, a] *adj*
air-conditioned

clímax ['klimaks] *nm inv* climax

clínica ['klinika] *nf* clinic; (*particular*)
private hospital

clip [klip] (*pl* ~**s**) *nm* paper clip

clítoris ['klitoris] *nm inv* (*ANAT*) clitoris

cloaca [klo'aka] *nf* sewer

cloro |'kloro| nm chlorine

club |klub| (pl ~s o ~es) nm club; ~ **de jóvenes** youth club

cm abr (= centímetro, centímetros) cm

C.N.T. (ESP) abr = Confederación Nacional de Trabajo

coacción |koak'θjon| nf coercion, compulsion; **coaccionar** vt to coerce

coagular |koaɣu'lar| vt (leche, sangre) to clot; **~se** vr to clot; **coágulo** nm clot

coalición |koali'θjon| nf coalition

coartada |koar'taða| nf alibi

coartar |koar'tar| vt to limit, restrict

coba |'koβa| nf: **dar ~ a uno** to soft-soap sb

cobarde |ko'βarðe| adj cowardly ♦ nm coward; **cobardía** nf cowardice

cobaya |ko'βaja| nf guinea pig

cobertizo |koβer'tiθo| nm shelter

cobertura |koβer'tura| nf cover

cobija |ko'βixa| (AM) nf blanket

cobijar |koβi'xar| vt (cubrir) to cover; (proteger) to shelter; **cobijo** nm shelter

cobra |'koβra| nf cobra

cobrador, a |koβra'ðor, a| nm/f (de autobús) conductor/conductress; (de impuestos, gas) collector

cobrar |ko'βrar| vt (cheque) to cash; (sueldo) to collect, draw; (objeto) to recover; (precio) to charge; (deuda) to collect ♦ vi to be paid; **cóbrese al entregar** cash on delivery

cobre |'koβre| nm copper; **~s** nmpl (MUS) brass instruments

cobro |'koβro| nm (de cheque) cashing; **presentar al ~** to cash

cocaína |koka'ina| nf cocaine

cocción |kok'θjon| nf (CULIN) cooking; (en agua) boiling

cocear |koθe'ar| vi to kick

cocer |ko'θer| vt, vi to cook; (en agua) to boil; (en horno) to bake

coche |'kotʃe| nm (AUTO) car (BRIT), automobile (US); (de tren, de caballos) coach, carriage; (para niños) pram (BRIT), baby carriage (US); **ir en ~** to

drive; ~ **celular** Black Maria, prison van; ~ **de bomberos** fire engine; ~ **fúnebre** hearse; **coche-cama** (pl **coches-cama**) nm (FERRO) sleeping car, sleeper

cochera |ko'tʃera| nf garage; (de autobuses, trenes) depot

coche restaurante nm (pl **coches restaurante**) nm (FERRO) dining car, diner

cochinillo |kotʃi'niʎo| nm (CULIN) suckling pig, sucking pig

cochino, a |ko'tʃino, a| adj filthy, dirty ♦ nm/f pig

cocido |ko'θiðo| nm stew

cocina |ko'θina| nf kitchen; (aparato) cooker, stove; (acto) cookery; ~ **eléctrica/de gas** electric/gas cooker; ~ **francesa** French cuisine; **cocinar** vt, vi to cook

cocinero, a |koθi'nero, a| nm/f cook

coco |'koko| nm coconut

cocodrilo |koko'ðrilo| nm crocodile

cocotero |koko'tero| nm coconut palm

cóctel |'koktel| nm cocktail

codazo |ko'ðaθo| nm: **dar un ~ a uno** to nudge sb

codicia |ko'ðiθja| nf greed; **codiciar** vt to covet; **codicioso, a** adj covetous

código |'koðiɣo| nm code; ~ **de barras** bar code; ~ **civil** common law; ~ **de (la) circulación** highway code; ~ **postal** postcode

codillo |ko'ðiʎo| nm (ZOOL) knee; (TEC) elbow (joint)

codo |'koðo| nm (ANAT, de tubo) elbow; (ZOOL) knee

codorniz |koðor'niθ| nf quail

coerción |koer'θjon| nf coercion

coetáneo, a |koe'taneo, a| adj, nm/f contemporary

coexistir |koe(k)sis'tir| vi to coexist

cofradía |kofra'ðia| nf brotherhood, fraternity

cofre |'kofre| nm (de joyas) case; (de dinero) chest

coger [ko'xer] (*ESP*) *vt* to take (hold of); (*objeto caído*) to pick up; (*frutas*) to pick, harvest; (*resfriado, ladrón, pelota*) to catch ♦ *vi*: ~ **por el buen camino** to take the right road; ~**se** *vr* (*el dedo*) to catch; ~**se a algo** to get hold of sth

cogollo [ko'ɣoʎo] *nm* (*de lechuga*) heart

cogote [ko'ɣote] *nm* back o nape of the neck

cohabitar [koaßi'tar] *vi* to live together, cohabit

cohecho [ko'etʃo] *nm* (*acción*) bribery; (*soborno*) bribe

coherente [koe'rente] *adj* coherent

cohesión [koe'sjon] *nm* cohesion

cohete [ko'ete] *nm* rocket

cohibido, a [koi'ßiðo, a] *adj* (*PSICO*) inhibited; (*tímido*) shy

cohibir [koi'ßir] *vt* to restrain, restrict

coincidencia [koinθi'ðenθja] *nf* coincidence

coincidir [koinθi'ðir] *vi* (*en idea*) to coincide, agree; (*en lugar*) to coincide

coito ['koito] *nm* intercourse, coitus

coja *etc* vb ver **coger**

cojear [koxe'ar] *vi* (*persona*) to limp, hobble; (*mueble*) to wobble, rock

cojera [ko'xera] *nf* limp

cojín [ko'xin] *nm* cushion; **cojinete** *nm* (*TEC*) ball bearing

cojo, a *etc* [ˈkoxo, a] *vb ver* **coger** ♦ *adj* (*que no puede andar*) lame, crippled; (*mueble*) wobbly ♦ *nm/f* lame person, cripple

cojón [koˈxon] (*fam*) *nm*: **¡cojones!** shit! (*!*); **cojonudo, a** (*fam*) *adj* great, fantastic

col [kol] *nf* cabbage; ~**es de Bruselas** Brussels sprouts

cola ['kola] *nf* tail; (*de gente*) queue; (*lugar*) end, last place; (*para pegar*) glue, gum; **hacer** ~ to queue (up)

colaborador, a [kolaßoraˈðor, a] *nm/f* collaborator

colaborar [kolaßoˈrar] *vi* to collaborate

colada [koˈlaða] *nf*: **hacer la** ~ to do the washing

colador [kolaˈðor] *nm* (*de líquidos*) strainer; (*para verduras etc*) colander

colapso [koˈlapso] *nm* collapse; ~ **nervioso** nervous breakdown

colar [koˈlar] *vt* (*líquido*) to strain off; (*metal*) to cast ♦ *vi* to ooze, seep (through); ~**se** *vr* to jump the queue; ~**se en** to get into without paying; (*fiesta*) to gatecrash

colcha ['koltʃa] *nf* bedspread

colchón [kolˈtʃon] *nm* mattress; ~ **inflable** o **neumático** air bed, air mattress

colchoneta [koltʃoˈneta] *nf* (*en gimnasio*) mat; (*de playa*) air bed

colección [kolekˈθjon] *nf* collection; **coleccionar** *vt* to collect; **coleccionista** *nm/f* collector

colecta [koˈlekta] *nf* collection

colectivo, a [kolekˈtißo, a] *adj* collective, joint ♦ *nm* (*AM*) (small) bus

colega [koˈleɣa] *nm/f* colleague

colegial, a [koleˈxjal, a] *nm/f* schoolboy/girl

colegio [koˈlexjo] *nm* college; (*escuela*) school; (*de abogados etc*) association; ~ **electoral** polling station; ~ **mayor** hall of residence

---

A **colegio** *is normally a private primary or secondary school. In the state system it means a primary school although these are also called* **escuelas**. *State secondary schools are called* **institutos**.

---

colegir [koleˈxir] *vt* to infer, conclude

cólera [ˈkolera] *nf* (*ira*) anger; (*MED*) cholera; **colérico, a** [koˈleriko, a] *adj* irascible, bad-tempered

colesterol [kolesteˈrol] *nm* cholesterol

coleta [koˈleta] *nf* pigtail

colgante [kolˈvante] *adj* hanging ♦ *nm* (*joya*) pendant

colgar [kol'ɣar] vt to hang (up); (ropa) to hang out ♦ vi to hang; (TELEC) to hang up

cólico ['koliko] nm colic

coliflor [koli'flor] nf cauliflower

colilla [ko'liʎa] nf cigarette end, butt

colina [ko'lina] nf hill

colisión [koli'sjon] nf collision; ~ **de frente** head-on crash

collar [ko'ʎar] nm necklace; (de perro) collar

colmar [kol'mar] vt to fill to the brim; (fig) to fulfil, realize

colmena [kol'mena] nf beehive

colmillo [kol'miʎo] nm (diente) eye tooth; (de elefante) tusk; (de perro) fang

colmo ['kolmo] nm: ¡es el ~! it's the limit!

colocación [koloka'θjon] nf (acto) placing; (empleo) job, position

colocar [kolo'kar] vt to place, put, position; (dinero) to invest; (poner en empleo) to find a job for; ~**se** vr to get a job

Colombia [ko'lombja] nf Colombia; **colombiano, a** adj, nm/f Colombian

colonia [ko'lonja] nf colony; (de casas) housing estate; (agua de ~) cologne

colonización [koloniθa'θjon] nf colonization; **colonizador, a** [koloniθa'ðor, a] adj colonizing ♦ nm/f colonist, settler

colonizar [koloni'θar] vt to colonize

coloquio [ko'lokjo] nm conversation; (congreso) conference

color [ko'lor] nm colour

colorado, a [kolo'raðo, a] adj (rojo) red; (LAM: chiste) rude

colorante [kolo'rante] nm colouring

colorear [kolore'ar] vt to colour

colorete [kolo'rete] nm blusher

colorido [kolo'riðo] nm colouring

columna [ko'lumna] nf column; (pilar) pillar; (apoyo) support

columpiar [kolum'pjar] vt to swing; ~**se** vr to swing; **columpio** nm swing

coma ['koma] nf comma ♦ nm (MED) coma

comadre [ko'maðre] nf (madrina) godmother; (chismosa) gossip; **comadrona** nf midwife

comandancia [koman'danθja] nf command

comandante [koman'dante] nm commandant

comarca [ko'marka] nf region

comba ['komba] nf (curva) curve; (cuerda) skipping rope; **saltar a la ~** to skip

combar [kom'bar] vt to bend, curve

combate [kom'bate] nm fight; **combatiente** nm combatant

combatir [komba'tir] vt to fight, combat

combinación [kombina'θjon] nf combination; (QUÍM) compound; (prenda) slip

combinar [kombi'nar] vt to combine

combustible [kombus'tißle] nm fuel

combustión [kombus'tjon] nf combustion

comedia [ko'meðja] nf comedy; (TEATRO) play, drama

comediante [kome'ðjante] nm/f (comic) actor/actress

comedido, a [kome'ðiðo, a] adj moderate

comedor, a [kome'ðor, a] nm (habitación) dining room; (cantina) canteen

comensal [komen'sal] nm/f fellow guest (o diner)

comentar [komen'tar] vt to comment on

comentario [komen'tarjo] nm comment, remark; (literario) commentary; ~**s** nmpl (chismes) gossip sg

comentarista [komenta'rista] nm/f commentator

comenzar [komen'θar] vt, vi to begin, start; ~ **a hacer algo** to begin o start doing sth

comer [ko'mer] vt to eat; (DAMAS,

AJEDREZ) to take, capture ♦ vi to eat; (almorzar) to have lunch; **~se** vr to eat up

comercial [komer'θjal] adj commercial; (relativo al negocio) business cpd; **comercializar** vt (producto) to market; (pey) to commercialize

comerciante [komer'θjante] nm/f trader, merchant

comerciar [komer'θjar] vi to trade, do business

comercio [ko'merθjo] nm commerce, trade; (negocio) business; (fig) dealings pl

comestible [komes'tiβle] adj eatable, edible; **~s** nmpl food sg, foodstuffs

cometa [ko'meta] nm comet ♦ nf kite

cometer [kome'ter] vt to commit

cometido [kome'tiðo] nm task, assignment

comezón [kome'θon] nf itch, itching

cómic ['komik] nm comic

comicios [ko'miθjos] nmpl elections

cómico, a [ko'miko, a] adj comic(al) ♦ nm/f comedian

comida [ko'miða] nf (alimento) food; (almuerzo, cena) meal; (de mediodía) lunch

comidilla [komi'ðiʎa] nf: **ser la ~ de la ciudad** to be the talk of the town

comienzo etc [ko'mjenθo] vb ver **comenzar** ♦ nm beginning, start

comillas [ko'miʎas] nfpl quotation marks

comilona [komi'lona] (fam) nf blow-out

comino [ko'mino] nm: **(no) me importa un ~** I don't give a damn

comisaría [komisa'ria] nf (de policía) police station; (MIL) commissariat

comisario [komi'sarjo] nm (MIL etc) commissary; (POL) commissar

comisión [komi'sjon] nf commission

comité [komi'te] (pl **~s**) nm committee

comitiva [komi'tiβa] nf retinue

como ['komo] adv as; (tal ~) like; (aproximadamente) about, approximately ♦ conj (ya que, puesto que) as, since; ¡~ no! of course!; ~ **no lo haga hoy** unless he does it today; ~ **si** as if; **es tan alto ~ ancho** it is as high as it is wide

cómo ['komo] adv how?, why? ♦ excl what?, I beg your pardon? ♦ nm: **el ~ y el porqué** the whys and wherefores

cómoda ['komoða] nf chest of drawers

comodidad [komoði'ðað] nf comfort; **venga a su ~** come at your convenience

comodín [komo'ðin] nm joker

cómodo, a ['komoðo, a] adj comfortable; (práctico, de fácil uso) convenient

compact disc nm compact disk player

compacto, a [kom'pakto, a] adj compact

compadecer [kompaðe'θer] vt to pity, be sorry for; **~se** vr: **~se de** to pity, be sorry for

compadre [kom'paðre] nm (padrino) godfather; (amigo) friend, pal

compañero, a [kompa'ɲero, a] nm/f companion; (novio) boy/girlfriend; ~ **de clase** classmate

compañía [kompa'ɲia] nf company

comparación [kompara'θjon] nf comparison; **en ~ con** in comparison with

comparar [kompa'rar] vt to compare

comparecer [kompare'θer] vi to appear (in court)

comparsa [kom'parsa] nm/f (TEATRO) extra

compartimiento [komparti'mjento] nm (FERRO) compartment

compartir [kompar'tir] vt to share; (dinero, comida etc) to divide (up), share (out)

compás [kom'pas] nm (MUS) beat, rhythm; (MAT) compasses pl; (NAUT etc) compass

compasión [kompa'sjon] *nf* compassion, pity

compasivo, a [kompa'siβo, a] *adj* compassionate

compatibilidad [kompatiβili'ðað] *nf* compatibility

compatible [kompa'tiβle] *adj* compatible

compatriota [kompa'trjota] *nm/f* compatriot, fellow countryman/woman

compendiar [kompen'djar] *vt* to summarize; **compendio** *nm* summary

compenetrarse [kompene'trarse] *vr* to be in tune

compensación [kompensa'θjon] *nf* compensation

compensar [kompen'sar] *vt* to compensate

competencia [kompe'tenθja] *nf* (*incumbencia*) domain, field; (*JUR, habilidad*) competence; (*rivalidad*) competition

competente [kompe'tente] *adj* competent

competición [kompeti'θjon] *nf* competition

competir [kompe'tir] *vi* to compete

compilar [kompi'lar] *vt* to compile

complacencia [kompla'θenθja] *nf* (*placer*) pleasure; (*tolerancia excesiva*) complacency

complacer [kompla'θer] *vt* to please; **~se** *vr* to be pleased

complaciente [kompla'θjente] *adj* kind, obliging, helpful

complejo, a [kom'plexo, a] *adj, nm* complex

complementario, a [komplemen'tarjo, a] *adj* complementary

completar [komple'tar] *vt* to complete

completo, a [kom'pleto, a] *adj* (*perfecto*) perfect; (*lleno*) full ♦ *nm* full complement

complicado, a [kompli'kaðo, a] *adj*

complicated; **estar ~ en** to be mixed up in

cómplice ['kompliθe] *nm/f* accomplice

complot [kom'plo(t)] (*pl* **~s**) *nm* plot

componer [kompo'ner] *vt* (*MUS, LITERATURA, IMPRENTA*) to compose; (*algo roto*) to mend, repair; (*arreglar*) to arrange; **~se** *vr*: **~se de** to consist of; **componérselas para hacer algo** to manage to do sth

comportamiento [komporta'mjento] *nm* behaviour, conduct

comportarse [kompor'tarse] *vr* to behave

composición [komposi'θjon] *nf* composition

compositor, a [komposi'tor, a] *nm/f* composer

compostura [kompos'tura] *nf* (*actitud*) composure

compra ['kompra] *nf* purchase; **ir de ~s** to go shopping; **comprador, a** *nm/f* buyer, purchaser

comprar [kom'prar] *vt* to buy, purchase

comprender [kompren'der] *vt* to understand; (*incluir*) to comprise, include

comprensión [kompren'sjon] *nf* understanding; **comprensivo, a** *adj* (*actitud*) understanding

compresa [kom'presa] *nf*: **~ higiénica** sanitary towel (*BRIT*) o napkin (*US*)

comprimido, a [kompri'miðo, a] *adj* compressed ♦ *nm* (*MED*) pill, tablet

comprimir [kompri'mir] *vt* to compress

comprobante [kompro'βante] *nm* proof; (*COM*) voucher; **~ de recibo** receipt

comprobar [kompro'βar] *vt* to check; (*probar*) to prove; (*TEC*) to check, test

comprometer [komprome'ter] *vt* to compromise; (*poner en peligro*) to endanger; **~se** *vr* (*involucrarse*) to get involved

compromiso [kompro'miso] nm
(obligación) obligation; (cometido)
commitment; (convenio) agreement;
(apuro) awkward situation

compuesto, a [kom'pwesto, a] adj:
~ **de** composed of, made up of ♦ nm
compound

computador [komputa'ðor] nm
computer; ~ **central** mainframe
computer; ~ **personal** personal
computer

computadora [komputa'ðora] nf =
computador

cómputo ['komputo] nm calculation

comulgar [komul'ɣar] vi to receive
communion

común [ko'mun] adj common ♦ nm:
el ~ the community

comunicación [komunika'θjon] nf
communication; (informe) report

comunicado [komuni'kaðo] nm
announcement; ~ **de prensa** press
release

comunicar [komuni'kar] vt, vi to
communicate; ~**se** vr to communicate;
está comunicando (TEL) the line's
engaged (BRIT) o busy (US);
comunicativo, a adj communicative

comunidad [komuni'ðað] nf
community; ~ **autónoma** (POL)
autonomous region; **C~ Económica
Europea** European Economic
Community

comunión [komu'njon] nf
communion

comunismo [komu'nismo] nm
communism; **comunista** adj, nm/f
communist

PALABRA CLAVE

---

con [kon] prep **1** (medio, compañía)
with; **comer ~ cuchara** to eat with a
spoon; **pasear ~ uno** to go for a walk
with sb

2 (a pesar de): ~ **todo, merece
nuestros respetos** all the same, he
deserves our respect

3 (para ~): **es muy bueno para
~ los niños** he's very good with (the)
children

4 (+ infin): ~ **llegar tan tarde se
quedó sin comer** by arriving so late
he missed out on eating

♦ conj: ~ **que: que se suficiente ~ que
le escribas** it will be sufficient if you
write to her

conato [ko'nato] nm attempt; ~ **de
robo** attempted robbery

concebir [konθe'βir] vt, vi to conceive

conceder [konθe'ðer] vt to concede

concejal, a [konθe'xal, a] nm/f town
councillor

concentración [konθentra'θjon] nf
concentration

concentrar [konθen'trar] vt to
concentrate; ~**se** vr to concentrate

concepción [konθep'θjon] nf
conception

concepto [kon'θepto] nm concept

concernir [konθer'nir] vi to concern;
en lo que concierne a ... as far as ...
is concerned; **en lo que a mí
concierne** as far as I'm concerned

concertar [konθer'tar] vt (MUS) to
harmonize; (acordar: precio) to agree;
(: tratado) to conclude; (trato) to
arrange, fix up; (combinar: esfuerzos) to
coordinate ♦ vi to harmonize, be in
tune

concesión [konθe'sjon] nf concession

concesionario [konθesjo'narjo] nm
(licensed) dealer, agent

concha ['kontʃa] nf shell

conciencia [kon'θjenθja] nf
conscience; **tener/tomar ~ de** to be/
become aware of; **tener la ~ limpia/
tranquila** to have a clear conscience

concienciar [konθjen'θjar] vt to make
aware; ~**se** vr to become aware

concienzudo, a [konθjen'θuðo, a]
adj conscientious

concierto etc [kon'θjerto] vb ver
concertar ♦ nm concert; (obra)

concerto

conciliar [konθi'ljar] vt to reconcile

concilio [kon'θiljo] nm council

conciso, a [kon'θiso, a] adj concise

concluir [konklu'ir] vt, vi to conclude; **~se** vr to conclude

conclusión [konklu'sjon] nf conclusion

concluyente [konklu'jente] adj (prueba, información) conclusive

concordar [konkor'ðar] vt to reconcile ♦ vi to agree, tally

concordia [kon'korðja] nf harmony

concretar [konkre'tar] vt to make concrete, make more specific; **~se** vr to become more definite

concreto, a [kon'kreto, a] adj, nm (AM) concrete; **en ~** (en resumen) to sum up; (específicamente) specifically; **no hay nada en ~** there's nothing definite

concurrencia [konku'rrenθja] nf turnout

concurrido, a [konku'rriðo, a] adj (calle) busy; (local, reunión) crowded

concurrir [konku'rrir] vi (juntarse: ríos) to meet, come together; (: personas) to gather, meet

concursante [konkur'sante] nm/f competitor

concurso [kon'kurso] nm (de público) crowd; (ESCOL, DEPORTE, competencia) competition; (ayuda) help, cooperation

condal [kon'dal] adj: **la Ciudad C~** Barcelona

conde ['konde] nm count

condecoración [kondekora'θjon] nf (MIL) medal

condecorar [kondeko'rar] vt (MIL) to decorate

condena [kon'dena] nf sentence

condenación [kondena'θjon] nf condemnation; (REL) damnation

condenar [konde'nar] vt to condemn; (JUR) to convict; **~se** vr (REL) to be damned

condensar [konden'sar] vt to

condense

condesa [kon'desa] nf countess

condición [kondi'θjon] nf condition; **condicional** adj conditional

condicionar [kondiθjo'nar] vt (acondicionar) to condition; **~ algo a** to make sth conditional on

condimento [kondi'mento] nm seasoning

condolerse [kondo'lerse] vr to sympathize

condón [kon'don] nm condom

conducir [kondu'θir] vt to take, convey; (AUTO) to drive ♦ vi to drive; (fig) to lead; **~se** vr to behave

conducta [kon'dukta] nf conduct, behaviour

conducto [kon'dukto] nm pipe, tube; (fig) channel

conductor, a [konduk'tor, a] adj leading, guiding ♦ nm (FÍSICA) conductor; (de vehículo) driver

conduje etc vb ver **conducir**

conduzco etc vb ver **conducir**

conectado, a [konek'taðo, a] adj (INFORM) on-line

conectar [konek'tar] vt to connect (up); (enchufar) plug in

conejillo [kone'xiʎo] nm: **~ de Indias** (ZOOL) guinea pig

conejo [ko'nexo] nm rabbit

conexión [konek'sjon] nf connection

confección [confe(k)'θjon] nf preparation; (industria) clothing industry

confeccionar [konfekθjo'nar] vt to make (up)

confederación [konfeðera'θjon] nf confederation

conferencia [konfe'renθja] nf conference; (lección) lecture; (TEL) call

conferir [konfe'rir] vt to award

confesar [konfe'sar] vt to confess, admit

confesión [konfe'sjon] nf confession

confesionario [konfesjo'narjo] nm confessional

confeti [kon'feti] nm confetti

confiado, a [konfja'ðo, a] adj (crédulo) trusting; (seguro) confident

confianza [kon'fjanθa] nf trust; (seguridad) confidence; (familiaridad) intimacy, familiarity

confiar [kon'fjar] vt to entrust ♦ vi to trust

confidencia [konfi'ðenθja] nf confidence

confidencial [konfiðen'θjal] adj confidential

confidente [konfi'ðente] nm/f confidant/e; (policial) informer

configurar [konfixu'rar] vt to shape, form

confin [kon'fin] nm limit; **confines** nmpl confines, limits

confinar [konfi'nar] vi to confine; (desterrar) to banish

confirmar [konfir'mar] vt to confirm

confiscar [konfis'kar] vt to confiscate

confite [kon'fite] nm sweet (BRIT), candy (US)

confitería [konfite'ria] nf (tienda) confectioner's (shop)

confitura [konfi'tura] nf jam

conflictivo, a [konflik'tiβo, a] adj (asunto, propuesta) controversial; (país, situación) troubled

conflicto [kon'flikto] nm conflict; (fig) clash

confluir [kon'flwir] vi (ríos) to meet; (gente) to gather

conformar [konfor'mar] vt to shape, fashion ♦ vi to agree; **~se** vr to conform; (resignarse) to resign o.s.

conforme [kon'forme] adj (correspondiente): **~ con** in line with; (de acuerdo): **estar ~s (con algo)** to be in agreement (with sth) ♦ adv as ♦ excl agreed! ♦ prep: **~ a** in accordance with; **quedarse ~ (con algo)** to be satisfied (with sth)

conformidad [konformi'ðað] nf (semejanza) similarity; (acuerdo) agreement; **conformista** adj, nm/f

conformist

confortable [konfor'taβle] adj comfortable

confortar [konfor'tar] vt to comfort

confrontar [konfron'tar] vt to confront; (dos personas) to bring face to face; (cotejar) to compare

confundir [konfun'dir] vt (equivocar) to mistake, confuse; (turbar) to confuse; **~se** vr (turbarse) to get confused; (equivocarse) to make a mistake; (mezclarse) to mix

confusión [konfu'sjon] nf confusion

confuso, a [kon'fuso, a] adj confused

congelado, a [konxe'laðo, a] adj frozen; **~s** nmpl frozen food(s); **congelador** nm (aparato) freezer, deep freeze

congelar [konxe'lar] vt to freeze; **~se** vr (sangre, grasa) to congeal

congeniar [konxe'njar] vi to get on (BRIT) o along (US) well

congestión [konxes'tjon] nf congestion

congestionar [konxestjo'nar] vt to congest

congoja [kon'goxa] nf distress, grief

congraciarse [kongra'θjarse] vr to ingratiate o.s.

congratular [kongratu'lar] vt to congratulate

congregación [kongreɣa'θjon] nf congregation

congregar [kongre'ɣar] vt to gather together; **~se** vr to gather together

congresista [kongre'sista] nm/f delegate, congressman/woman

congreso [kon'greso] nm congress

congrio ['kongrjo] nm conger eel

conjetura [konxe'tura] nf guess; **conjeturar** vt to guess

conjugar [konxu'ɣar] vt to combine, fit together; (LING) to conjugate

conjunción [konxun'θjon] nf conjunction

conjunto, a [kon'xunto, a] adj joint, united ♦ nm whole; (MUS) band; **en ~**

as a whole
conjurar [konxu'rar] vt (REL) to
exorcise; (fig) to ward off ♦ vi to plot
conmemoración [konmemora'θjon]
nf commemoration
conmemorar [konmemo'rar] vt to
commemorate
conmigo [kon'miɣo] pron with me
conmoción [konmo'θjon] nf shock;
(fig) upheaval; ~ **cerebral** (MED)
concussion
conmovedor, a [konmoβe'ðor, a] adj
touching, moving; (emocionante)
exciting
conmover [konmo'βer] vt to shake,
disturb; (fig) to move
conmutador [konmuta'ðor] nm
switch; (AM: TEL: centralita)
switchboard; (: central) telephone
exchange
cono ['kono] nm cone
conocedor, a [konoθe'ðor, a] adj
expert, knowledgeable ♦ nm/f expert
conocer [kono'θer] vt to know; (por
primera vez) to meet, get to know;
(entender) to know about; (reconocer)
to recognize; **~se** vr (una persona) to
know o.s.; (dos personas) to (get to)
know each other
conocido, a [kono'θiðo, a] adj (well-)
known ♦ nm/f acquaintance
conocimiento [konoθi'mjento] nm
knowledge; (MED) consciousness; **~s**
nmpl (saber) knowledge sg
conozco etc vb ver **conocer**
conque ['konke] conj and so, so then
conquista [kon'kista] nf conquest;
conquistador, a [konkista'ðor, a] adj
conquering
♦ nm conqueror
conquistar [konkis'tar] vt to conquer
consagrar [konsa'ɣrar] vt (REL) to
consecrate; (fig) to devote
consciente [kons'θjente] adj
conscious
consecución [konseku'θjon] nf
acquisition; (de fin) attainment
consecuencia [konse'kwenθja] nf

consequence, outcome; (coherencia)
consistency
consecuente [konse'kwente] adj
consistent
consecutivo, a [konseku'tiβo, a] adj
consecutive
conseguir [konse'ɣir] vt to get,
obtain; (objetivo) to attain
consejero, a [konse'xero, a] nm/f
adviser, consultant; (POL) councillor
consejo [kon'sexo] nm advice; (POL)
council; ~ **de administración** (COM)
board of directors; ~ **de guerra** court
martial; ~ **de ministros** cabinet
meeting
consenso [kon'senso] nm consensus
consentimiento [konsenti'mjento]
nm consent
consentir [konsen'tir] vt (permitir,
tolerar) to consent to; (mimar) to
pamper, spoil; (aguantar) to put up
with ♦ vi to agree, consent; ~ **que
uno haga algo** to allow sb to do sth
conserje [kon'serxe] nm caretaker;
(portero) porter
conservación [konserβa'θjon] nf
conservation; (de alimentos, vida)
preservation
conservador, a [konserβa'ðor, a] adj
(POL) conservative ♦ nm/f conservative
conservante [konser'βante] nm
preservative
conservar [konser'βar] vt to conserve,
keep; (alimentos, vida) to preserve; **~se**
vr to survive
conservas [kon'serβas] nfpl canned
food(s) (pl)
conservatorio [konserβa'torjo] nm
(MUS) conservatoire, conservatory
considerable [konsiðe'raβle] adj
considerable
consideración [konsiðera'θjon] nf
consideration; (estimación) respect
considerado, a [konsiðe'raðo, a] adj
(atento) considerate; (respetado)
respected
considerar [konsiðe'rar] vt to consider

consigna [kon'siɣna] nf (*orden*) order, instruction; (*para equipajes*) left-luggage office

consigo *etc* [kon'siɣo] vb ver **conseguir ♦** pron (m) with him; (f) with her; (Vd) with you; (*reflexivo*) with o.s.

consiguiendo *etc* vb ver **conseguir**

consiguiente [konsi'ɣjente] adj consequent; **por ~** and so, therefore, consequently

consistente [konsis'tente] adj consistent; (*sólido*) solid, firm; (*válido*) sound

consistir [konsis'tir] vi: ~ en (*componerse de*) to consist of

consola [kon'sola] nf (*mueble*) console table; (*de videojuegos*) console

consolación [konsola'θjon] nf consolation

consolar [konso'lar] vt to console

consolidar [konsoli'ðar] vt to consolidate

consomé [konso'me] (pl **~s**) nm consommé, clear soup

consonante [konso'nante] adj consonant, harmonious ♦ nf consonant

consorcio [kon'sorθjo] nm consortium

conspiración [konspira'θjon] nf conspiracy

conspirador, a [konspira'ðor, a] nm/f conspirator

conspirar [konspi'rar] vi to conspire

constancia [kons'tanθja] nf constancy; **dejar ♦ de** to put on record

constante [kons'tante] adj, nf constant

constar [kons'tar] vi (*evidenciarse*) to be clear o evident; ~ **de** to consist of

constatar [konsta'tar] vt to verify

consternación [konsterna'θjon] nf consternation

constipado, a [konsti'paðo, a] adj: **estar ~** to have a cold ♦ nm cold

constitución [konstitu'θjon] nf constitution; **constitucional** adj constitutional

constituir [konstitu'ir] vt (*formar, componer*) to constitute, make up; (*fundar, erigir, ordenar*) to constitute, establish

constituyente [konstitu'jente] adj constituent

constreñir [konstre'ɲir] vt (*restringir*) to restrict

construcción [konstruk'θjon] nf construction, building

constructor, a [konstruk'tor, a] nm/f builder

construir [konstru'ir] vt to build, construct

construyendo *etc* vb ver **construir**

consuelo [kon'swelo] nm consolation, solace

cónsul ['konsul] nm consul; **consulado** nm consulate

consulta [kon'sulta] nf consultation; (MED): **horas de ~** surgery hours

consultar [konsul'tar] vt to consult

consultorio [konsul'torjo] nm (MED) surgery

consumar [konsu'mar] vt to complete, carry out; (*crimen*) to commit; (*sentencia*) to carry out

consumición [konsumi'θjon] nf consumption; (*bebida*) drink; (*comida*) food; ~ **mínima** cover charge

consumidor, a [konsumi'ðor, a] nm/f consumer

consumir [konsu'mir] vt to consume; **~se** vr to be consumed; (*persona*) to waste away

consumismo [konsu'mismo] nm consumerism

consumo [kon'sumo] nm consumption

contabilidad [kontaβili'ðað] nf accounting, book-keeping; (*profesión*) accountancy; **contable** nm/f accountant

contacto [kon'takto] nm contact; (AUTO) ignition

contado, a [kon'taðo, a] adj: **~s**

(*escasos*) numbered, scarce, few ♦ *nm*:
pagar al ~ to pay (in) cash

contador [konta'ðor] *nm* (*aparato*)
meter; (*AM*: *contante*) accountant

contagiar [konta'xjar] *vt* (*enfermedad*)
to pass on, transmit; (*persona*) to
infect; **~se** *vr* to become infected

contagio [kon'taxjo] *nm* infection;
contagioso, a *adj* infectious; (*fig*)
catching

contaminación [kontamina'θjon] *nf*
contamination; (*polución*) pollution

contaminar [kontami'nar] *vt* to
contaminate; (*aire, agua*) to pollute

contante [kon'tante] *adj*: **dinero ~ (y
sonante)** cash

contar [kon'tar] *vt* (*páginas, dinero*) to
count; (*anécdota, chiste etc*) to tell ♦ *vi*
to count; **~ con** to rely on, count on

contemplación [kontempla'θjon] *nf*
contemplation

contemplar [kontem'plar] *vt* to
contemplate; (*mirar*) to look at

contemporáneo, a
[kontempo'raneo, a] *adj, nm/f*
contemporary

contendiente [konten'djente] *nm/f*
contestant

contenedor [kontene'ðor] *nm*
container

contener [konte'ner] *vt* to contain,
hold; (*retener*) to hold back, contain;
~se *vr* to control o restrain o.s.

contenido, a [konte'niðo, a] *adj*
(*moderado*) restrained; (*risa etc*)
suppressed ♦ *nm* contents *pl*, content

contentar [konten'tar] *vt* (*satisfacer*)
to satisfy; (*complacer*) to please; **~se** *vr*
to be satisfied

contento, a [kon'tento, a] *adj* (*alegre*)
pleased; (*feliz*) happy

contestación [kontesta'θjon] *nf*
answer, reply

contestador [kontesta'ðor] *nm*:
~ automático answering machine

contestar [kontes'tar] *vt* to answer,
reply; (*JUR*) to corroborate, confirm

contexto [kon'te(k)sto] *nm* context

contienda [kon'tjenda] *nf* contest

contigo [kon'tiɣo] *pron* with you

contiguo, a [kon'tiɣwo, a] *adj*
adjacent, adjoining

continente [konti'nente] *adj, nm*
continent

contingencia [kontin'xenθja] *nf*
contingency; (*riesgo*) risk;
contingente *adj, nm* contingent

continuación [kontinwa'θjon] *nf*
continuation; **a ~** then, next

continuar [konti'nwar] *vt* to continue,
go on with ♦ *vi* to continue, go on;
~ hablando to continue talking o to
talk

continuidad [kontinwi'ðað] *nf*
continuity

continuo, a [kon'tinwo, a] *adj* (*sin
interrupción*) continuous; (*acción
perseverante*) continual

contorno [kon'torno] *nm* outline;
(*GEO*) contour; **~s** *nmpl* neighbourhood
sg, surrounding area *sg*

contorsión [kontor'sjon] *nf*
contortion

contra [kontra] *prep, ad* against ♦ *nm*
in con ♦ *nf*: **la C~** (*de Nicaragua*) the
Contras *pl*

contraataque [kontraa'take] *nm*
counter-attack

contrabajo [kontra'βaxo] *nm* double
bass

contrabandista [kontraβan'dista]
nm/f smuggler

contrabando [kontra'βando] *nm*
(*acción*) smuggling; (*mercancías*)
contraband

contracción [kontrak'θjon] *nf*
contraction

contracorriente [kontrako'rrjente]:
(a) ~ *adv* against the current

contradecir [kontraðe'θir] *vt* to
contradict

contradicción [kontraðik'θjon] *nf*
contradiction

contradictorio, a [kontraðik'torjo, a] *adj*

adj contradictory

contraer [kontra'er] *vt* to contract; (*limitar*) to restrict; **~se** *vr* to contract; (*limitarse*) to limit o.s.

contraluz [kontra'luθ] *nf*: **a ~** against the light

contrapartida [kontrapar'tiða] *nf*: **como ~ (de)** in return (for)

contrapelo [kontra'pelo]: **a ~** *adv* the wrong way

contrapesar [kontrape'sar] *vt* to counterbalance; (*fig*) to offset; **contrapeso** *nm* counterweight

contraportada [kontrapor'taða] *nf* (*de revista*) back cover

contraproducente [kontraproðu'θente] *adj* counterproductive

contrariar [kontra'rjar] *vt* (*oponerse*) to oppose; (*poner obstáculo*) to impede; (*enfadar*) to vex

contrariedad [kontrarje'ðað] *nf* (*obstáculo*) obstacle, setback; (*disgusto*) vexation, annoyance

contrario, a [kon'trarjo, a] *adj* contrary; (*persona*) opposed; (*sentido, lado*) opposite ♦ *nm/f* enemy, adversary; (*DEPORTE*) opponent; **al/por el ~** on the contrary; **de lo ~** otherwise

contrarreloj [kontrarre'lo] *nf* (*tb*: **prueba ~**) time trial

contrarrestar [kontrarres'tar] *vt* to counteract

contrasentido [kontrasen'tiðo] *nm*: **es un ~ que él ...** it doesn't make sense for him to ...

contraseña [kontra'seɲa] *nf* (*INFORM*) password

contrastar [kontras'tar] *vt, vi* to contrast

contraste [kon'traste] *nm* contrast

contratar [kontra'tar] *vt* (*firmar un acuerdo para*) to contract for; (*empleados, obreros*) to hire, engage; **~se** *vr* to sign on

contratiempo [kontra'tjempo] *nm*

setback

contratista [kontra'tista] *nm/f* contractor

contrato [kon'trato] *nm* contract

contravenir [kontraße'nir] *vi*: **~ a** to contravene, violate

contraventana [kontraßen'tana] *nf* shutter

contribución [kontrißu'θjon] *nf* (*municipal etc*) tax; (*ayuda*) contribution

contribuir [kontrißu'ir] *vt, vi* to contribute; (*COM*) to pay (in taxes)

contribuyente [kontrißu'jente] *nm/f* (*COM*) taxpayer; (*que ayuda*) contributor

contrincante [kontrin'kante] *nm* opponent

control [kon'trol] *nm* control; (*inspección*) inspection, check; **~ador, a** *nm/f* controller; **~ador aéreo** air-traffic controller

controlar [kontro'lar] *vt* to control; (*inspeccionar*) to inspect, check

controversia [kontro'ßersja] *nf* controversy

contundente [kontun'dente] *adj* (*instrumento*) blunt; (*argumento, derrota*) overwhelming

contusión [kontu'sjon] *nf* bruise

convalecencia [kombale'θenθja] *nf* convalescence

convalecer [kombale'θer] *vi* to convalesce, get better

convaleciente [kombale'θjente] *adj, nm/f* convalescent

convalidar [kombali'ðar] *vt* (*título*) to recognize

convencer [komben'θer] *vt* to convince

convencimiento [kombenθi'mjento] *nm* (*certidumbre*) conviction

convención [komben'θjon] *nf* convention

conveniencia [kombe'njenθja] *nf* suitability; (*conformidad*) agreement; (*utilidad, provecho*) usefulness; **~s** *nfpl* (*convenciones*) conventions; (*COM*) property sg

conveniente [kombe'njente] *adj* suitable; (*útil*) useful

convenio [kom'benjo] *nm* agreement, treaty

convenir [kombe'nir] *vi* (*estar de acuerdo*) to agree; (*venir bien*) to suit, be suitable

convento [kom'bento] *nm* convent

convenza *etc vb ver* **convencer**

converger [komber'xer] *vi* to converge

convergir [komber'xir] *vi* = **converger**

conversación [kombersa'θjon] *nf* conversation

conversar [komber'sar] *vi* to talk, converse

conversión [komber'sjon] *nf* conversion

convertir [komber'tir] *vt* to convert

convicción [kombik'θjon] *nf* conviction

convicto, a [kom'bikto, a] *adj* convicted

convidado, a [kombi'ðaðo, a] *nm/f* guest

convidar [kombi'ðar] *vt* to invite

convincente [kombin'θente] *adj* convincing

convite [kom'bite] *nm* invitation; (*banquete*) banquet

convivencia [kombi'βenθja] *nf* coexistence, living together

convivir [kombi'βir] *vi* to live together

convocar [kombo'kar] *vt* to summon, call (together)

convocatoria [komboka'torja] *nf* (*de oposiciones, elecciones*) notice; (*de huelga*) call

convulsión [kombul'sjon] *nf* convulsion

conyugal [konju'val] *adj* conjugal; **cónyuge** [ˈkonjuxe] *nm/f* spouse

coñac [koˈɲa(k)] (*pl* **~s**) *nm* cognac, brandy

coño [ˈkoɲo] (*fam!*) *excl* (*enfado*) shit! (*!*); (*sorpresa*) bloody hell! (*!*)

cooperación [koopera'θjon] *nf* cooperation

cooperar [koope'rar] *vi* to cooperate

cooperativa [koopera'tiβa] *nf* cooperative

coordinadora [koorðina'ðora] *nf* (*comité*) coordinating committee

coordinar [koorði'nar] *vt* to coordinate

copa [ˈkopa] *nf* cup; (*vaso*) glass; (*bebida*): (**tomar una**) **~** (to have a) drink; (*de árbol*) top; (*de sombrero*) crown; **~s** *nfpl* (*NAIPES*) ≈ hearts

copia [ˈkopja] *nf* copy; **~ de respaldo** *o* **seguridad** (*INFORM*) back-up copy; **copiar** *vt* to copy

copioso, a [ko'pjoso, a] *adj* copious, plentiful

copla [ˈkopla] *nf* verse; (*canción*) (popular) song

copo [ˈkopo] *nm*: **~ de nieve** snowflake; **~s de maíz** cornflakes

coqueta [ko'keta] *adj* flirtatious, coquettish; **coquetear** *vi* to flirt

coraje [ko'raxe] *nm* courage; (*ánimo*) spirit; (*ira*) anger

coral [ko'ral] *adj* choral ♦ *nf* (*MUS*) choir ♦ *nm* (*ZOOL*) coral

coraza [ko'raθa] *nf* (*armadura*) armour; (*blindaje*) armour-plating

corazón [kora'θon] *nm* heart

corazonada [koraθo'naða] *nf* impulse; (*presentimiento*) hunch

corbata [kor'βata] *nf* tie

corchete [kor'tʃete] *nm* catch, clasp

corcho [ˈkortʃo] *nm* cork; (*PESCA*) float

cordel [kor'ðel] *nm* cord, line

cordero [kor'ðero] *nm* lamb

cordial [kor'ðjal] *adj* cordial; **~idad** *nf* warmth, cordiality

cordillera [korði'ʎera] *nf* range (of mountains)

Córdoba [ˈkorðoβa] *n* Cordova

cordón [kor'ðon] *nm* (*cuerda*) cord, string; (*de zapatos*) lace; (*MIL etc*) cordon

cordura [kor'ðura] nf: **con ~** (*obrar, hablar*) sensibly

corneta [kor'neta] nf bugle

cornisa [kor'nisa] nf (*ARQ*) cornice

coro ['koro] nm chorus; (*conjunto de cantores*) choir

corona [ko'rona] nf crown; (*de flores*) garland; **coronación** nf coronation; **coronar** vt to crown

coronel [koro'nel] nm colonel

coronilla [koro'niʎa] nf (*ANAT*) crown (of the head)

corporación [korpora'θjon] nf corporation

corporal [korpo'ral] adj corporal, bodily

corpulento, a [korpu'lento a] adj (*persona*) heavily-built

corral [ko'rral] nm farmyard

correa [ko'rrea] nf strap; (*cinturón*) belt; (*de perro*) lead, leash

corrección [korrek'θjon] nf correction; (*reprensión*) rebuke; **correccional** nm reformatory

correcto, a [ko'rrekto a] adj correct; (*persona*) well-mannered

corredizo, a [korre'ðiθo a] adj (*puerta etc*) sliding

corredor, a [korre'ðor a] nm (*pasillo*) corridor; (*balcón corrido*) gallery; (*COM*) agent, broker ♦ nm/f (*DEPORTE*) runner

corregir [korre'xir] vt (*error*) to correct; **~se** vr to reform

correo [ko'rreo] nm post, mail; (*persona*) courier; **C~s** nmpl Post Office sg; **~ aéreo** airmail; **~ electrónico** electronic mail, e-mail

correr [ko'rrer] vt to run; (*cortinas*) to draw; (*cerrojo*) to shoot ♦ vi to run; (*líquido*) to run, flow; **~se** vr to slide, move; (*colores*) to run

correspondencia [korrespon'denθja] nf correspondence; (*FERRO*) connection

corresponder [korrespon'der] vi to correspond; (*convenir*) to be suitable; (*pertenecer*) to belong; (*concernir*) to

concern; **~se** vr (*por escrito*) to correspond; (*amarse*) to love one another

correspondiente [korrespon'djente] adj corresponding

corresponsal [korrespon'sal] nm/f correspondent

corrida [ko'rriða] nf (*de toros*) bullfight

corrido, a [ko'rriðo a] adj (*avergonzado*) abashed; **3 noches corridas** 3 nights running; **un kilo ~** a good kilo

corriente [ko'rrjente] adj (*agua*) running; (*dinero etc*) current; (*común*) ordinary, normal ♦ nf current ♦ nm current month; **~ eléctrica** electric current

corrija etc vb ver **corregir**

corrillo [ko'rriʎo] nm ring, circle (of people); (*fig*) clique

corro ['korro] nm ring, circle (of people)

corroborar [korroβo'rar] vt to corroborate

corroer [korro'er] vt to corrode; (*GEO*) to erode

corromper [korrom'per] vt (*madera*) to rot; (*fig*) to corrupt

corrosivo, a [korro'siβo a] adj corrosive

corrupción [korrup'θjon] nf rot, decay; (*fig*) corruption

corsé [kor'se] nm corset

cortacésped [korta'θespeð] nm lawn mower

cortado, a [kor'taðo a] adj (*gen*) cut; (*leche*) sour; (*tímido*) shy; (*avergonzado*) embarrassed ♦ nm coffee (with a little milk)

cortar [kor'tar] vt to cut; (*suministro*) to cut off; (*un pasaje*) to cut out ♦ vi to cut; **~se** vr (*avergonzarse*) to become embarrassed; (*leche*) to turn, curdle; **~se el pelo** to have one's hair cut

cortauñas [korta'uɲas] nm inv nail clippers pl

corte ['korte] nm cut, cutting; (*de tela*)

piece, length ♦ nf: **las C~s** the Spanish Parliament; **~ y confección** dressmaking; **~ de luz** power cut

cortejar [korte'xar] vt to court

cortejo [kor'texo] nm entourage; **~ fúnebre** funeral procession

cortés [kor'tes] adj courteous, polite

cortesía [korte'sia] nf courtesy

corteza [kor'teθa] nf (de árbol) bark; (de pan) crust

cortijo [kor'tixo] nm farm, farmhouse

cortina [kor'tina] nf curtain

corto, a ['korto, a] adj (breve) short; (tímido) bashful; **~ de luces** not very bright; **~ de vista** short-sighted; **estar ~ de fondos** to be short of funds; **~circuito** nm short circuit; **~metraje** nm (CINE) short

cosa ['kosa] nf thing; **~ de** about; **eso es ~ mía** that's my business

coscorrón [kosko'rron] nm bump on the head

cosecha [ko'setʃa] nf (AGR) harvest; (de vino) vintage

cosechar [kose'tʃar] vt to harvest, gather (in)

coser [ko'ser] vt to sew

cosmético, a [kos'metiko, a] adj, nm cosmetic

cosquillas [kos'kiʎas] nfpl: **hacer ~** to tickle; **tener ~** to be ticklish

costa ['kosta] nf (GEO) coast; **C~ Brava** Costa Brava; **C~ Cantábrica** Cantabrian Coast; **C~ del Sol** Costa del Sol; **a toda ~** at all costs

costado [kos'taðo] nm side

costar [kos'tar] vt (valer) to cost; **me cuesta hablarle** I find it hard to talk to him

Costa Rica nf Costa Rica; **costarricense** adj, nm/f Costa Rican; **costarriqueño, a** adj, nm/f Costa Rican

coste ['koste] nm = **costo**

costear [koste'ar] vt to pay for

costero, a [kos'tero, a] adj (pueblecito, camino) coastal

costilla [kos'tiʎa] nf rib; (CULIN) cutlet

costo ['kosto] nm cost, price; **~ de la vida** cost of living; **~so, a** adj costly, expensive

costra ['kostra] nf (corteza) crust; (MED) scab

costumbre [kos'tumbre] nf custom, habit

costura [kos'tura] nf sewing, needlework; (zurcido) seam

costurera [kostu'rera] nf dressmaker

costurero [kostu'rero] nm sewing box o case

cotejar [kote'xar] vt to compare

cotidiano, a [koti'ðjano, a] adj daily, day to day

cotilla [ko'tiʎa] nm/f (fam) gossip; **cotillear** vi to gossip; **cotilleo** nm gossip(ing)

cotización [kotiθa'θjon] nf (COM) quotation, price; (de club) dues pl

cotizar [koti'θar] vt (COM) to quote, price; **~se** vr: **~se a** to sell at, fetch; (BOLSA) to stand at, be quoted at

coto ['koto] nm (terreno cercado) enclosure; (de caza) reserve

cotorra [ko'torra] nf parrot

COU [kou] (ESP) nm abr (= Curso de Orientación Universitaria) 1 year course leading to final school-leaving certificate and university entrance examinations

coyote [ko'jote] nm coyote, prairie wolf

coyuntura [kojun'tura] nf juncture, occasion

coz [koθ] nf kick

crack nm (droga) crack

cráneo ['kraneo] nm skull, cranium

cráter ['krater] nm crater

creación [krea'θjon] nf creation

creador, a [krea'ðor, a] adj creative ♦ nm/f creator

crear [kre'ar] vt to create, make

crecer [kre'θer] vi to grow; (precio) to rise

creces ['kreθes] nf: **con ~** adv amply, fully

crecido, a [kre'θiðo, a] *adj* (*persona*, *planta*) full-grown; (*cantidad*) large
creciente [kre'θjente] *adj* growing; (*cantidad*) increasing; (*luna*) crescent ♦ *nm* crescent
crecimiento [kreθi'mjento] *nm* growth; (*aumento*) increase
credenciales [kreðen'θjales] *nfpl* credentials
crédito ['kreðito] *nm* credit
credo ['kreðo] *nm* creed
crédulo, a ['kreðulo, a] *adj* credulous
creencia [kre'enθja] *nf* belief
creer [kre'er] *vt, vi* to think, believe; **~se** *vr* to believe o.s. (to be); **~ en** to believe in; **¡ya lo creo!** I should think so!
creíble [kre'iβle] *adj* credible, believable
creído, a [kre'iðo, a] *adj* (*engreído*) conceited
crema ['krema] *nf* cream; **~ pastelera** (confectioner's) custard
cremallera [krema'ʎera] *nf* zip (fastener)
crematorio [krema'torjo] *nm* (*tb*: **horno ~**) crematorium
crepitar [krepi'tar] *vi* to crackle
crepúsculo [kre'puskulo] *nm* twilight, dusk
cresta ['kresta] *nf* (*GEO, ZOOL*) crest
creyendo *vb ver* **creer**
creyente [kre'jente] *nm/f* believer
creyó *etc vb ver* **creer**
crezco *etc vb ver* **crecer**
cria *etc* ['kria] *vb ver* **criar** ♦ *nf* (*de animales*) rearing, breeding; (*animal*) young; *ver tb* **crío**
criadero [kria'ðero] *nm* (*ZOOL*) breeding place
criado, a [kri'aðo, a] *nm* servant ♦ *nf* servant, maid
criador [kria'ðor] *nm* breeder
crianza [kri'anθa] *nf* rearing, breeding; (*fig*) breeding
criar [kri'ar] *vt* (*educar*) to bring up; (*producir*) to grow, produce; (*animales*)

to breed
criatura [kria'tura] *nf* creature; (*niño*) baby, (small) child
criba ['kriβa] *nf* sieve; **cribar** *vt* to sieve
crimen ['krimen] *nm* crime
criminal [krimi'nal] *adj, nm/f* criminal
crin [krin] *nf* (*tb*: **~es** *nfpl*) mane
crío, a ['krio, a] (*fam*) *nm/f* (*niño*) kid
crisis ['krisis] *nf inv* crisis; **~ nerviosa** nervous breakdown
crispar [kris'par] *vt* (*nervios*) to set on edge
cristal [kris'tal] *nm* crystal; (*de ventana*) glass, pane; (*lente*) lens; **~ino, a** *adj* crystalline; (*fig*) clear ♦ *nm* lens (of the eye); **~izar** *vt, vi* to crystallize
cristiandad [kristjan'dað] *nf* Christendom
cristianismo [kristja'nismo] *nm* Christianity
cristiano, a [kris'tjano, a] *adj, nm/f* Christian
Cristo ['kristo] *nm* Christ; (*crucifijo*) crucifix
criterio [kri'terjo] *nm* criterion; (*juicio*) judgement
crítica ['kritika] *nf* criticism; *ver tb* **crítico**
criticar [kriti'kar] *vt* to criticize
crítico, a ['kritiko, a] *adj* critical ♦ *nm/f* critic
Croacia *nf* Croatia
croar [kro'ar] *vi* to croak
cromo ['kromo] *nm* chrome
crónica ['kronika] *nf* chronicle, account
crónico, a ['kroniko, a] *adj* chronic
cronómetro [kro'nometro] *nm* stopwatch
croqueta [kro'keta] *nf* croquette
cruce *etc* ['kruθe] *vb ver* **cruzar** ♦ *nm* crossing; (*de carreteras*) crossroads
crucificar [kruθifi'kar] *vt* to crucify
crucifijo [kruθi'fixo] *nm* crucifix
crucigrama [kruθi'xrama] *nm* crossword (puzzle)

crudo, a ['kruðo, a] *adj* raw; (*no maduro*) unripe; (*petróleo*) crude; (*rudo, cruel*) cruel ♦ *nm* crude (oil)

cruel [krwel] *adj* cruel; **~dad** *nf* cruelty

crujido [kru'xiðo] *nm* (*de madera etc*) creak

crujiente [kru'xjente] *adj* (*galleta etc*) crunchy

crujir [kru'xir] *vi* (*madera etc*) to creak; (*dedos*) to crack; (*dientes*) to grind; (*nieve, arena*) to crunch

cruz [kruθ] *nf* cross; (*de moneda*) tails *sg*; **~ gamada** swastika

cruzada [kru'θaða] *nf* crusade

cruzado, a [kru'θaðo, a] *adj* crossed ♦ *nm* crusader

cruzar [kru'θar] *vt* to cross; **~se** *vr* (*líneas etc*) to cross; (*personas*) to pass each other

Cruz Roja *nf* Red Cross

cuaderno [kwa'ðerno] *nm* notebook; (*de escuela*) exercise book; (*NAUT*) logbook

cuadra ['kwaðra] *nf* (*caballeriza*) stable; (*AM*) block

cuadrado, a [kwa'ðraðo, a] *adj* square ♦ *nm* (*MAT*) square

cuadrar [kwa'ðrar] *vt* to square ♦ *vi*: **~ con** to square with, tally with; **~se** *vr* (*soldado*) to stand to attention

cuadrilátero [kwaðri'latero] *nm* (*DEPORTE*) boxing ring; (*GEOM*) quadrilateral

cuadrilla [kwa'ðriʎa] *nf* party, group

cuadro ['kwaðro] *nm* square; (*ARTE*) painting; (*TEATRO*) scene; (*diagrama*) chart; (*DEPORTE, MED*) team; **tela a ~s** checked (*BRIT*) o chequered (*US*) material

cuádruple ['kwaðruple] *adj* quadruple

cuajar [kwa'xar] *vt* (*leche*) to curdle; (*sangre*) to congeal; (*CULIN*) to set; **~se** *vr* to curdle; to congeal; to set; (*llenarse*) to fill up

cuajo ['kwaxo] *nm*: **de ~** (*arrancar*) by the roots; (*cortar*) completely

cual [kwal] *adv* like, as, ♦ *pron*: **el ~** *etc*

which; (*persona: sujeto*) who; (: *objeto*) whom ♦ *adj* such as; **cada ~** each one; **déjalo tal ~** leave it just as it is

cuál [kwal] *pron interr* which one

cualesquier(a) [kwales'kjer(a)] *pl de* **cualquier(a)**

cualidad [kwali'ðað] *nf* quality

cualquier [kwal'kjer] *adj ver* **cualquiera**

cualquiera [kwal'kjera] (*pl* **cualesquiera**) *adj* (*delante de nm y f:* **cualquier**) any ♦ *pron* anybody; **un coche ~ servirá** any car will do; **no es un hombre ~** he isn't just anybody; **cualquier día/libro** any day/book; **eso ~ lo sabe hacer** anybody can do that; **es un ~** he's a nobody

cuando ['kwando] *adv* when; (*aún si*) if, even if ♦ *conj* (*puesto que*) since ♦ *prep*: **yo, ~ niño ...** when I was a child ...; **~ no sea así** even if it is not so; **~ más** at (the) most; **~ menos** at least; **~ no** if not, otherwise; **de ~ en ~** from time to time

cuándo ['kwando] *adv* when; **¿desde ~?, ¿de ~ acá?** since when?

cuantía [kwan'tia] *nf* (*importe: de pérdidas, deuda, daños*) extent

cuantioso, a [kwan'tjoso, a] *adj* substantial

┌─────────────────────┐
│ *PALABRA CLAVE* │
└─────────────────────┘

cuanto, a ['kwanto, a] *adj* **1** (*todo*): **tiene todo ~ desea** he's got everything he wants; **le daremos ~s ejemplares necesite** we'll give him as many copies as o all the copies he needs; **~s hombres la ven** all the men who see her

2: **unos ~s: había unos ~s periodistas** there were a few journalists

3 (+ *más*): **~ más vino bebes peor te sentirás** the more wine you drink the worse you'll feel

♦ *pron*: **tiene ~ desea** he has

everything he wants; **tome ~/~s quiera** take as much/many as you want

♦ *adv:* **en ~: en ~ profesor** as a teacher; **en ~ a mí** as for me; *ver tb* **antes**

♦ *conj* **1: ~ más gana menos gasta** the more he earns the less he spends; **~ más joven más confiado** the younger you are the more trusting you are

2: en ~: en ~ llegue/llegué as soon as I arrive/arrived

---

cuánto, a ['kwanto, a] *adj* (*exclamación*) what a lot of; (*interr: sg*) how much?; (: *pl*) how many? ♦ *pron, adv* how; (*interr: sg*) how much?; (: *pl*) how many? **¡cuánta gente!** what a lot of people!; **¿~ cuesta?** how much does it cost?; **¿a ~s estamos?** what's the date?; **Señor no sé ~s** Mr. So-and-So

cuarenta [kwa'renta] *num* forty

cuarentena [kwaren'tena] *nf* quarantine

cuaresma [kwa'resma] *nf* Lent

cuarta ['kwarta] *nf* (*MAT*) quarter, fourth; (*palmo*) span

cuartel [kwar'tel] *nm* (*MIL*) barracks *pl*; **~ general** headquarters *pl*

cuarteto [kwar'teto] *nm* quartet

cuarto, a ['kwarto, a] *adj* fourth ♦ *nm* (*MAT*) quarter, fourth; (*habitación*) room; **~ de baño** bathroom; **~ de estar** living room; **~ de hora** quarter (of an) hour; **~ de kilo** quarter kilo

cuatro ['kwatro] *num* four

Cuba ['kußa] *nf* Cuba; **cubano, a** *adj, nm/f* Cuban

cuba ['kußa] *nf* cask, barrel

cubata [ku'ßata] *nm* (*fam*) large drink (*of rum and coke etc*)

cúbico, a ['kußiko, a] *adj* cubic

cubierta [ku'ßjerta] *nf* cover, covering; (*neumático*) tyre; (*NAUT*) deck

cubierto, a [ku'ßjerto, a] *pp de* **cubrir**

♦ *adj* covered ♦ *nm* cover; (*lugar en la mesa*) place; **~s** *nmpl* cutlery *sg*; **a ~** under cover

cubil [ku'ßil] *nm* den; **~ete** *nm* (*en juegos*) cup

cubito [ku'ßito] *nm:* **~ de hielo** ice-cube

cubo ['kußo] *nm* (*MATH*) cube; (*balde*) bucket, tub; (*TEC*) drum

cubrecama [kußre'kama] *nm* bedspread

cubrir [ku'ßrir] *vt* to cover; **~se** *vr* (*cielo*) to become overcast

cucaracha [kuka'ratʃa] *nf* cockroach

cuchara [ku'tʃara] *nf* spoon; (*TEC*) scoop; **~da** *nf* spoonful; **~dita** *nf* teaspoonful

cucharilla [kutʃa'riʎa] *nf* teaspoon

cucharón [kutʃa'ron] *nm* ladle

cuchichear [kutʃitʃe'ar] *vi* to whisper

cuchilla [ku'tʃiʎa] *nf* (*large*) knife; (*de arma blanca*) blade; **~ de afeitar** razor blade

cuchillo [ku'tʃiʎo] *nm* knife

cuchitril [kutʃi'tril] *nm* hovel

cuclillas [ku'kliʎas] *nfpl:* **en ~** squatting

cuco, a ['kuko, a] *adj* pretty; (*astuto*) sharp ♦ *nm* cuckoo

cucurucho [kuku'rutʃo] *nm* cornet

cuello ['kweʎo] *nm* (*ANAT*) neck; (*de vestido, camisa*) collar

cuenca ['kwenka] *nf* (*ANAT*) eye socket; (*GEO*) bowl, deep valley

cuenco ['kwenko] *nm* bowl

cuenta *etc* ['kwenta] *vb ver* **contar**

♦ *nf* (*cálculo*) count, counting; (*en café, restaurante*) bill (*BRIT*), check (*US*); (*COM*) account; (*de collar*) bead; **a fin de ~s** in the end; **caer en la ~** to catch on; **darse ~ de** to realize; **tener en ~** to bear in mind; **echar ~s** to take stock; **~ corriente/de ahorros** current/savings account; **~ atrás** countdown; **~kilómetros** *nm inv* milometer; (*de velocidad*) speedometer

cuento *etc* ['kwento] *vb ver* **contar**

♦ *nm* story

cuerda ['kwerða] *nf* rope; (*fina*) string; (*de reloj*) spring; **dar ~ a un reloj** to wind up a clock; **~ floja** tightrope

cuerdo, a ['kwerðo, a] *adj* sane; (*prudente*) wise, sensible

cuerno ['kwerno] *nm* horn

cuero ['kwero] *nm* leather; **en ~s** stark naked; **~ cabelludo** scalp

cuerpo ['kwerpo] *nm* body

cuervo ['kwerßo] *nm* crow

cuesta *etc* ['kwesta] *vb ver* **costar** ♦ *nf* slope; (*en camino etc*) hill; **~ arriba/ abajo** uphill/downhill; **a ~s** on one's back

cueste *etc vb ver* **costar**

cuestión [kwes'tjon] *nf* matter, question, issue

cueva ['kweßa] *nf* cave

cuidado [kwi'ðaðo] *nm* care, carefulness; (*preocupación*) care, worry ♦ *excl* careful!, look out!

cuidadoso, a [kwiða'ðoso, a] *adj* careful; (*preocupado*) anxious

cuidar [kwi'ðar] *vt* to care for; (*ocuparse de*) to take care of, look after ♦ *vi*: **~ de** to take care of, look after; **~se** *vt* to look after o.s.; **~se de hacer algo** to take care to do sth

culata [ku'lata] *nf* (*de fusil*) butt

culebra [ku'leßra] *nf* snake

culebrón [kule'ßron] *nm* (*fam*) (*TV*) soap(-opera)

culinario, a [kuli'narjo, a] *adj* culinary, cooking *cpd*

culminación [kulmina'θjon] *nf* culmination

culo ['kulo] *nm* bottom, backside; (*de vaso, botella*) bottom

culpa ['kulpa] *nf* fault; (*JUR*) guilt; **por ~ de** because of; **tener la ~ (de)** to be to blame (for); **~bilidad** *nf* guilt; **~ble** *adj* guilty ♦ *nm/f* culprit

culpar [kul'par] *vt* to blame; (*acusar*) to accuse

cultivar [kulti'ßar] *vt* to cultivate

cultivo [kul'tißo] *nm* (*acto*) cultivation; (*plantas*) crop

culto, a ['kulto, a] *adj* (*que tiene cultura*) cultured, educated ♦ *nm* (*homenaje*) worship; (*religión*) cult

cultura [kul'tura] *nf* culture

culturismo [kultu'rismo] *nm* body-building

cumbre ['kumbre] *nf* summit, top

cumpleaños [kumple'aɲos] *nm inv* birthday

cumplido, a [kum'pliðo, a] *adj* (*abundante*) plentiful; (*cortés*) courteous ♦ *nm* compliment; **visita de ~** courtesy call

cumplidor, a [kumpli'ðor, a] *adj* reliable

cumplimentar [kumplimen'tar] *vt* to congratulate

cumplimiento [kumpli'mjento] *nm* (*de un deber*) fulfilment; (*acabamiento*) completion

cumplir [kum'plir] *vt* (*orden*) to carry out, obey; (*promesa*) to carry out, fulfil; (*condena*) to serve ♦ *vi*: **~ con** (*deberes*) to carry out, fulfil; **~se** *vr* (*plazo*) to expire; **hoy cumple dieciocho años** he is eighteen today

cúmulo ['kumulo] *nm* heap

cuna ['kuna] *nf* cradle, cot

cundir [kun'dir] *vi* (*noticia, rumor, pánico*) to spread; (*rendir*) to go a long way

cuneta [ku'neta] *nf* ditch

cuña ['kuɲa] *nf* wedge

cuñado, a [ku'ɲaðo, a] *nm/f* brother-/ sister-in-law

cuota ['kwota] *nf* (*parte proporcional*) share; (*cotización*) fee, dues *pl*

cupe *etc vb ver* **caber**

cupiera *etc vb ver* **caber**

cupo ['kupo] *vb ver* **caber** ♦ *nm* quota

cupón [ku'pon] *nm* coupon

cúpula ['kupula] *nf* dome

cura ['kura] *nf* (*curación*) cure; (*método curativo*) treatment ♦ *nm* priest

curación [kura'θjon] *nf* cure; (*acción*) curing

curandero, a [kuran'dero, a] nm/f quack

curar [ku'rar] vt (MED: herida) to treat, dress; (: enfermo) to cure; (CULIN) to cure, salt; (cuero) to tan; ~se vr to get well, recover

curiosear [kurjose'ar] vt to glance at, look over ♦ vi to look round, wander round; (explorar) to poke about

curiosidad [kurjosi'ðað] nf curiosity

curioso, a [ku'rjoso, a] adj curious ♦ nm/f bystander, onlooker

currante [ku'rrante] (fam) nm/f worker

currar [ku'rrar] (fam) vi to work

currículo [ku'rrikulo] = **curriculum**

curriculum [ku'rrikulum] nm curriculum vitae

cursi ['kursi] (fam) adj affected

cursillo [kur'siλo] nm short course

cursiva [kur'siβa] nf italics pl

curso ['kurso] nm course; en ~ (año) current; (proceso) going on, under way

cursor [kur'sor] (INFORM) cursor

curtido, a [kur'tiðo, a] adj (cara etc) weather-beaten; (fig: persona) experienced

curtir [kur'tir] vt (cuero etc) to tan

curva ['kurβa] nf curve, bend

cúspide ['kuspiðe] nf (GEO) peak; (fig) top

custodia [kus'toðja] nf safekeeping; custody; **custodiar** (vt (conservar)) to take care of; (vigilar) to guard

cutis ['kutis] nm inv skin, complexion

cutre ['kutre] (fam) adj (lugar) grotty

cuyo, a ['kujo, a] pron (de quien) whose; (de que) whose, of which; en ~ caso in which case

C.V. abr (= caballos de vapor) H.P.

D, d

D. abr (= Don) Esq.

Da. abr = **Doña**

dádiva ['daðiβa] nf (donación) donation; (regalo) gift; **dadivoso, a**

adj generous

dado, a ['daðo, a] pp de **dar** ♦ nm die; ~s nmpl dice; ~ que given that

daltónico, a [dal'toniko, a] adj colour-blind

dama ['dama] nf (gen) lady; (AJEDREZ) queen; ~s nfpl (juego) draughts sg

damnificar [damnifi'kar] vt to harm; (persona) to injure

danés, esa [da'nes, esa] adj Danish ♦ nm/f Dane

danzar [dan'θar] vt, vi to dance

dañar [da'ɲar] vt (objeto) to damage; (persona) to hurt; ~se vr (objeto) to get damaged

dañino, a [da'ɲino, a] adj harmful

daño ['daɲo] nm (a un objeto) damage; (a una persona) harm, injury; ~s y perjuicios (JUR) damages; hacer ~ a to damage; (persona) to hurt, injure; **hacerse ~** to hurt o.s.

PALABRA CLAVE

dar [dar] vt 1 (gen) to give; (obra de teatro) to put on; (film) to show; (fiesta) to hold; ~ algo a uno to give sb sth o sth to sb; ~ de beber a uno to give sb a drink

2 (producir: intereses) to yield; (fruta) to produce

3 (locuciones + n): da gusto escucharle it's a pleasure to listen to him; ver tb paseo y otros sustantivos

4 (+ n: = perífrasis de verbo): me da asco it sickens me

5 (considerar): ~ algo por descontado/entendido to take sth for granted/as read; ~ algo por concluido to consider sth finished

6 (hora): el reloj dio las 6 the clock struck 6 (o'clock)

7: me da lo mismo it's all the same to me; ver tb igual, más

♦ vi 1: ~ con: dimos con él dos horas más tarde we came across him two hours later; al final di con la solución I eventually came up with

the answer
2: **~ en** (*blanco, suelo*) to hit; **el sol me da en la cara** the sun is shining (right) on my face
3: **~ de sí** (*zapatos etc*) to stretch, give
♦ **~ se** *vr* **1**: **~se por vencido** to give up
2 (*ocurrir*): **se han dado muchos casos** there have been a lot of cases
3: **~se a**: **se ha dado a la bebida** he's taken to drinking
4: **se me dan bien/mal las ciencias** I'm good/bad at science
5: **dárselas de experto** he fancies himself o poses as an expert

dardo [ˈdarðo] *nm* dart
datar [daˈtar] *vi*: **~ de** to date from
dátil [ˈdatil] *nm* date
dato [ˈdato] *nm* fact, piece of information; **~s personales** personal details
DC *abbr m* (= *disco compacto*) CD
dcha. *abr* (= *derecha*) r.h.
d. de J.C. *abr* (= *después de Jesucristo*) A.D.

PALABRA CLAVE

de [de] *prep* (*de*+ *el* = *del*) **1** (*posesión*) of; **la casa = Isabel/mis padres** Isabel's/my parents' house; **es ~ ellos** it's theirs
2 (*origen, distancia, con números*) from; **soy ~ Gijón** I'm from Gijón; **~ 8 a 20** from 8 to 20; **salir del cine** to go out o leave the cinema; **~ 2 en 2** by 2, 2 at a time
3 (*valor descriptivo*): **una copa ~ vino** a glass of wine; **la mesa = la cocina** the kitchen table; **un billete ~ 1000 pesetas** a 1000 peseta note; **un niño ~ tres años** a three-year-old (child); **una máquina ~ coser** a sewing machine; **ir vestido ~ gris** to be dressed in grey; **la niña del vestido azul** the girl in the blue dress; **trabaja**

~ profesora she works as a teacher; **~ lado** sideways; **~ atrás/delante** rear/front
4 (*hora, tiempo*): **a las 8 ~ la mañana** at 8 o'clock in the morning; **~ día/ noche** by day/night; **~ hoy en ocho días** a week from now; **~ niño era gordo** as a child he was fat
5 (*comparaciones*): **más/menos ~ cien personas** more/less than a hundred people; **el más caro ~ la tienda** the most expensive in the shop; **menos/más ~ lo pensado** less/more than expected
6 (*causa*): **del calor** from the heat; **~ puro tonto** out of sheer stupidity
7 (*tema*) about; **clases ~ inglés** English classes; **¿sabes algo ~ él?** do you know anything about him?; **un libro ~ física** a physics book
8 (*adj* + *de* + *infin*): **fácil ~ entender** easy to understand
9 (*oraciones pasivas*): **fue respetado ~ todos** he was loved by all
10 (*condicional* + *infin*) if; **~ ser posible** if possible; **~ no terminarlo hoy** if I *etc* don't finish it today

dé *vb ver* **dar**
deambular [deambuˈlar] *vi* to wander
debajo [deˈβaxo] *adv* underneath; **~ de** below, under; **por ~ de** beneath
debate [deˈβate] *nm* debate; **debatir** *vt* to debate
deber [deˈβer] *nm* duty ♦ *vt* to owe ♦ *vi*: **debe (de)** it must, it should; **~es** *nmpl* (ESCOL) homework; **debo hacerlo** I must do it; **debe de ir** he should go; **~se** *vr*: **~se a** to be owing o due to
debido, a [deˈβiðo, a] *adj* proper, just; **~ a** due to, because of
débil [ˈdeβil] *adj* (*persona, carácter*) weak; (*luz*) dim; **debilidad** *nf* weakness; dimness
debilitar [deβiliˈtar] *vt* to weaken; **~se** *vr* to grow weak

debutar [deβu'tar] vi to make one's debut

década ['dekaða] nf decade

decadencia [deka'ðenθja] nf (estado) decadence; (proceso) decline, decay

decaer [deka'er] vi (declinar) to decline; (debilitarse) to weaken

decaído, a [deka'iðo, a] adj: **estar ~** (abatido) to be down

decaimiento [dekai'mjento] nm (declinación) decline; (desaliento) discouragement; (MED: estado débil) weakness

decano, a [de'kano, a] nm/f (de universidad etc) dean

decapitar [dekapi'tar] vt to behead

decena [de'θena] nf: **una ~** ten (or so)

decencia [de'θenθja] nf decency

decente [de'θente] adj decent

decepción [deθep'θjon] nf disappointment

decepcionar [deθepθjo'nar] vt to disappoint

decidir [deθi'ðir] vt, vi to decide; **~se** vr: **~se a** to make up one's mind to

décimo, a ['deθimo, a] adj tenth ♦ nm tenth

decir [de'θir] vt to say; (contar) to tell; (hablar) to speak ♦ nm saying; **~se** vr: **se dice que** it is said that; **~ para o entre sí** to say to o.s.; **querer ~** to mean; **¡dígame!** (TEL) hello!; (en tienda) can I help you?

decisión [deθi'sjon] nf (resolución) decision; (firmeza) decisiveness

decisivo, a [deθi'siβo, a] adj decisive

declaración [deklara'θjon] nf (manifestación) statement; (de amor) declaration; **~ de ingresos o de la renta** o **fiscal** income-tax return

declarar [dekla'rar] vt to declare ♦ vi to declare; (JUR) to testify; **~se** vr to propose

declinar [dekli'nar] vt (gen) to decline; (JUR) to reject ♦ vi (el día) to draw to a close

declive [de'kliβe] nm (cuesta) slope;

(fig) decline

decodificador [dekoðifika'ðor] nm decoder

decolorarse [dekolo'rarse] vr to become discoloured

decoración [dekora'θjon] nf decoration

decorado [deko'raðo] nm (CINE, TEATRO) scenery, set

decorar [deko'rar] vt to decorate; **decorativo, a** adj ornamental, decorative

decoro [de'koro] nm (respeto) respect; (dignidad) decency; (recato) propriety; **~so, a** adj (decente) decent; (modesto) modest; (digno) proper

decrecer [dekre'θer] vi to decrease, diminish

decrépito, a [de'krepito, a] adj decrepit

decretar [dekre'tar] vt to decree; **decreto** nm decree

dedal [de'ðal] nm thimble

dedicación [deðika'θjon] nf dedication

dedicar [deði'kar] vt (libro) to dedicate; (tiempo, dinero) to devote; (palabras: decir, consagrar) to dedicate, devote; **dedicatoria** nf (de libro) dedication

dedo ['deðo] nm finger; **~ (del pie)** toe; **~ pulgar** thumb; **~ índice** index finger; **~ corazón** middle finger; **~ anular** ring finger; **~ meñique** little finger; **hacer ~** (fam) to hitch (a lift)

deducción [deðuk'θjon] nf deduction

deducir [deðu'θir] vt (concluir) to deduce, infer; (COM) to deduct

defecto [de'fekto] nm defect, flaw; **defectuoso, a** adj defective, faulty

defender [defen'der] vt to defend

defensa [de'fensa] nf defence ♦ nm (DEPORTE) defender, back; **defensivo, a** adj defensive; **a la defensiva** on the defensive

defensor, a [defen'sor, a] adj defending ♦ nm/f (abogado ~)

defending counsel; (*protector*) protector

deficiencia [defi'θjenθja] *nf* deficiency

deficiente [defi'θjente] *adj* (*defectuoso*) defective; **~ en** lacking o deficient in; **ser un ~ mental** to be mentally handicapped

déficit ['defiθit] (*pl* **~s**) *nm* deficit

definición [difini'θjon] *nf* definition

definir [defi'nir] *vt* (*determinar*) to determine, establish; (*decidir*) to define; (*aclarar*) to clarify; **definitivo, a** *adj* definitive; **en definitiva** definitively; (*en resumen*) in short

deformación [deforma'θjon] *nf* (*alteración*) deformation; (*RADIO etc*) distortion

deformar [defor'mar] *vt* (*gen*) to deform; **~se** *vr* to become deformed; **deforme** *adj* (*informe*) deformed; (*feo*) ugly; (*malhecho*) misshapen

defraudar [defrau'ðar] *vt* (*decepcionar*) to disappoint; (*estafar*) to defraud

defunción [defun'θjon] *nf* death, demise

degeneración [dexenera'θjon] *nf* (*de las células*) degeneration; (*moral*) degeneracy

degenerar [dexene'rar] *vi* to degenerate

degollar [deɣo'ʎar] *vt* to behead; (*fig*) to slaughter

degradar [deɣra'ðar] *vt* to debase, degrade; **~se** *vr* to demean o.s.

degustación [deɣusta'θjon] *nf* sampling, tasting

deificar [deifi'kar] *vt* to deify

dejadez [dexa'ðeθ] *nf* (*negligencia*) neglect; (*descuido*) untidiness, carelessness

dejar [de'xar] *vt* to leave; (*permitir*) to allow, let; (*abandonar*) to abandon, forsake; (*beneficios*) to produce, yield ♦ *vi*: **~ de** (*parar*) to stop; (*no hacer*) to fail to; **no dejes de comprar un billete** make sure you buy a ticket; **~ a un lado** to leave o set aside

dejo ['dexo] *nm* (*LING*) accent

del [del] (= **de+ el**) *ver* **de**

delantal [delan'tal] *nm* apron

delante [de'lante] *adv* in front, (*enfrente*) opposite; (*adelante*) ahead; **~ de** in front of, before

delantera [delan'tera] *nf* (*de vestido, casa etc*) front part; (*DEPORTE*) forward line; **llevar la ~ (a uno)** to be ahead (of sb)

delantero, a [delan'tero, a] *adj* front ♦ *nm* (*DEPORTE*) forward, striker

delatar [dela'tar] *vt* to inform on o against, betray; **delator, a** *nm/f* informer

delegación [deleɣa'θjon] *nf* (*acción, delegados*) delegation; (*COM: oficina*) office, branch; **~ de policía** police station

delegado, a [dele'ɣaðo, a] *nm/f* delegate; (*COM*) agent

delegar [dele'ɣar] *vt* to delegate

deletrear [deletre'ar] *vt* to spell (out)

deleznable [deleθ'naβle] *adj* brittle; (*excusa, idea*) feeble

delfín [del'fin] *nm* dolphin

delgadez [delɣa'ðeθ] *nf* thinness, slimness

delgado, a [del'ɣaðo, a] *adj* thin; (*persona*) slim, thin; (*tela etc*) light, delicate

deliberación [deliβera'θjon] *nf* deliberation

deliberar [deliβe'rar] *vt* to debate, discuss

delicadeza [delika'ðeθa] *nf* (*gen*) delicacy; (*refinamiento, sutileza*) refinement

delicado, a [deli'kaðo, a] *adj* (*gen*) delicate; (*sensible*) sensitive; (*quisquilloso*) touchy

delicia [de'liθja] *nf* delight

delicioso, a [deli'θjoso, a] *adj* (*gracioso*) delightful; (*exquisito*) delicious

delimitar [delimi'tar] *vt* (*funciones, responsabilidades*) to define

delincuencia |delin'kwenθja| nf delinquency; **delincuente** nm/f delinquent; (*criminal*) criminal

delineante |deline'ante| nm/f draughtsman/woman

delinear |deline'ar| vt (*dibujo*) to draw; (*fig, contornos*) to outline

delinquir |delin'kir| vi to commit an offence

delirante |deli'rante| adj delirious

delirar |deli'rar| vi to be delirious, rave

delirio |de'lirjo| nm (MED) delirium; (*palabras insensatas*) ravings pl

delito |de'lito| nm (gen) crime; (*infracción*) offence

delta |'delta| nm delta

demacrado, a |dema'krado, a| adj: **estar ~** to look pale and drawn, be wasted away

demagogo, a |dema'ɣoɣo, a| nm/f demagogue

demanda |de'manda| nf (*pedido*, COM) demand; (*petición*) request; (JUR) action, lawsuit

demandante |deman'dante| nm/f claimant

demandar |deman'dar| vt (gen) to demand; (JUR) to sue, file a lawsuit against

demarcación |demarka'θjon| nf (de terreno) demarcation

demás |de'mas| adj: **los ~ niños** the other children, the remaining children ♦ pron: **los/las ~** the others, the rest (of them); **lo ~** the rest (of it)

demasía |dema'sia| nf (*exceso*) excess, surplus; **comer en ~** to eat to excess

demasiado, a |dema'sjaðo, a| adj: **~ vino** too much wine ♦ adv (*antes de adj, adv*) too; (*libros*) too many books; **¡esto es ~!** that's the limit!; **hace ~ calor** it's too hot; **~ despacio** too slowly; **~s** too many

demencia |de'menθja| nf (*locura*) madness; **demente** nm/f lunatic ♦ adj mad, insane

democracia |demo'kraθja| nf democracy

demócrata |de'mokrata| nm/f democrat; **democrático, a** adj democratic

demoler |demo'ler| vt to demolish; **demolición** nf demolition

demonio |de'monjo| nm devil, demon; **¡~s!** hell!, damn!; **¿cómo ~s?** how the hell?

demora |de'mora| nf delay; **demorar** vt (*retardar*) to delay, hold back; (*detener*) to hold up ♦ vi to linger, stay on; **~se** vr to be delayed

demos vb ver **dar**

demostración |demostra'θjon| nf (MAT) proof; (de afecto) show, display

demostrar |demos'trar| vt (*probar*) to prove; (*mostrar*) to show; (*manifestar*) to demonstrate

demudado, a |demu'ðaðo, a| adj (*rostro*) pale

den vb ver **dar**

denegar |dene'var| vt (*rechazar*) to refuse; (JUR) to reject

denigrar |deni'vrar| vt (*desacreditar, infamar*) to denigrate; (*injuriar*) to insult

---

Denominación de Origen

The Denominación de Origen, abbreviated to D.O., is a prestigious classification awarded to food products such as wines, cheeses, sausages and hams which meet the stringent quality and production standards of the designated region. D.O. labels serve as a guarantee of quality.

---

denotar |deno'tar| vt to denote

densidad |densi'ðað| nf density; (fig) thickness

denso, a |'denso, a| adj dense; (*espeso, pastoso*) thick; (fig) heavy

dentadura |denta'ðura| nf (set of) teeth pl; **~ postiza** false teeth pl

dentera |den'tera| nf (*sensación desagradable*) shivers pl

dentífrico, a |den'tifriko, a| adj dental
♦ nm toothpaste

dentista |den'tista| nm/f dentist

dentro |'dentro| adv inside ♦ prep:
~ **de**, inside, within; **por** ~ (on the)
inside; **mirar por** ~ to look inside;
~ **de tres meses** within three months

denuncia |de'nunθja| nf (delación)
denunciation; (acusación) accusation;
(de accidente) report; **denunciar** vt to
report; (delatar) to inform on o against

departamento |departa'mento| nm
(sección administrativa) department,
section; (AM: apartamento) flat (BRIT),
apartment

dependencia |depen'denθja| nf
dependence; (POL) dependency; (COM)
office, section

depender |depen'der| vi: ~ **de** to
depend on

dependienta |depen'djenta| nf
saleswoman, shop assistant

dependiente |depen'djente| adj
dependent ♦ nm salesman, shop
assistant

depilar |depi'lar| vt (con cera) to wax;
(cejas) to pluck; **depilatorio** nm hair
remover

deplorable |deplo'raßle| adj
deplorable

deplorar |deplo'rar| vt to deplore

deponer |depo'ner| vt to lay down
♦ vi (JUR) to give evidence; (declarar) to
make a statement

deportar |depor'tar| vt to deport

deporte |de'porte| nm sport; **hacer** ~
to play sports; **deportista** adj sports
cpd ♦ nm/f sportsman/woman;
deportivo, a adj (club, periódico)
sports cpd ♦ nm sports car

depositar |deposi'tar| vt (dinero) to
deposit; (mercancías) to put away,
store; ~**se** vr to settle; ~**io, a** nm/f
trustee

depósito |de'posito| nm (gen) deposit;
(almacén) warehouse, store; (de agua,
gasolina etc) tank; ~ **de cadáveres**

mortuary

depreciar |depre'θjar| vt to
depreciate, reduce the value of; ~**se** vr
to depreciate, lose value

depredador, a |depreða'ðor, a| adj
predatory ♦ nm predator

depresión |depre'sjon| nf depression

deprimido, a |depri'miðo, a| adj
depressed

deprimir |depri'mir| vt to depress;
~**se** vr (persona) to become depressed

deprisa |de'prisa| adv quickly,
hurriedly

depuración |depura'θjon| nf
purification; (POL) purge

depurar |depu'rar| vt to purify;
(purgar) to purge

derecha |de'retʃa| nf right(-hand) side;
(POL) right; **a la** ~ (estar) on the right;
(torcer etc) (to the) right

derecho, a |de'retʃo, a| adj right,
right-hand ♦ nm (privilegio) right;
(lado) right(-hand) side; (leyes) law
♦ adv straight, directly; ~**s** nmpl (de
aduana) duty sg; (de autor) royalties;
tener ~ **a** to have a right to

deriva |de'riβa| nf: **ir** o **estar a la** ~ to
drift, be adrift

derivado |deri'βaðo| nm (COM) by-
product

derivar |deri'βar| vt to derive; (desviar)
to direct ♦ vi to derive, be derived;
(NAUT) to drift; ~**se** vr to derive, be
derived; to drift

derramamiento |derrama'mjento|
nm (dispersión) spilling; ~ **de sangre**
bloodshed

derramar |derra'mar| vt to spill;
(verter) to pour out; (esparcir) to
scatter; ~**se** vr to pour out;
~ **lágrimas** to weep

derrame |de'rrame| nm (de líquido)
spilling; (de sangre) shedding; (de tubo
etc) overflow; (pérdida) leakage; (MED)
discharge

derredor |derre'ðor| adv: **al** o **en** ~ de
around, about

derretido, a [derre'tiðo, a] adj melted; (metal) molten

derretir [derre'tir] vt (gen) to melt; (nieve) to thaw; **~se** vr to melt

derribar [derri'βar] vt to knock down; (construcción) to demolish; (persona, gobierno, político) to bring down

derrocar [derro'kar] vt (gobierno) to bring down, overthrow

derrochar [derro'tʃar] vt to squander; **derroche** nm (despilfarro) waste, squandering

derrota [de'rrota] nf (NAUT) course; (MIL, DEPORTE etc) defeat, rout; **derrotar** vt (gen) to defeat; **derrotero** nm (rumbo) course

derruir [derru'ir] vt (edificio) to demolish

derrumbar [derrum'bar] vt (edificio) to knock down; **~se** vr to collapse

derruyendo etc vb ver **derruir**

des vb ver **dar**

desabotonar [desaβoto'nar] vt to unbutton, undo; **~se** vr to come undone

desabrido, a [desa'βriðo, a] adj (comida) insipid, tasteless; (persona) rude, surly; (respuesta) sharp; (tiempo) unpleasant

desabrochar [desaβro'tʃar] vt (botones, broches) to undo, unfasten; **~se** vr (ropa etc) to come undone

desacato [desa'kato] nm (falta de respeto) disrespect; (JUR) contempt

desacertado, a [desaθer'taðo, a] adj (equivocado) mistaken; (inoportuno) unwise

desacierto [desa'θjerto] nm mistake, error

desaconsejado, a [desakonse'xaðo, a] adj ill-advised

desaconsejar [desakonse'xar] vt to advise against

desacreditar [desakreði'tar] vt (desprestigiar) to discredit, bring into disrepute; (denigrar) to run down

desacuerdo [desa'kwerðo] nm disagreement, discord

desafiar [desa'fjar] vt (retar) to challenge; (enfrentarse a) to defy

desafilado, a [desafi'laðo, a] adj blunt

desafinado, a [desafi'naðo, a] adj: **estar ~** to be out of tune

desafinar [desafi'nar] vi (al cantar) to be o go out of tune

desafío etc [desa'fio] vb ver **desafiar** ♦ nm (reto) challenge; (combate) duel; (resistencia) defiance

desaforado, a [desafo'raðo, a] adj (grito) ear-splitting; (comportamiento) outrageous

desafortunadamente [desafortunaða'mente] adv unfortunately

desafortunado, a [desafortu'naðo, a] adj (desgraciado) unfortunate, unlucky

desagradable [desaɣra'ðaβle] adj (fastidioso, enojoso) unpleasant; (irritante) disagreeable

desagradar [desaɣra'ðar] vi (disgustar) to displease; (molestar) to bother

desagradecido, a [desaɣraðe'θiðo, a] adj ungrateful

desagrado [desa'ɣraðo] nm (disgusto) displeasure; (contrariedad) dissatisfaction

desagraviar [desaɣra'βjar] vt to make amends to

desagüe [des'aɣwe] nm (de un líquido) drainage; (cañería) drainpipe; (salida) outlet, drain

desaguisado [desaɣi'saðo] nm outrage

desahogado, a [desao'ɣaðo, a] adj (holgado) comfortable; (espacioso) roomy, large

desahogar [desao'ɣar] vt (aliviar) to ease, relieve; (ira) to vent; **~se** vr (relajarse) to relax; (desfogarse) to let off steam

desahogo [desa'oɣo] nm (alivio) relief; (comodidad) comfort, ease

desahuciar [desau'θjar] vt (enfermo) to give up hope for; (inquilino) to evict;

desahucio nm eviction

desairar [desai'rar] vt (menospreciar) to slight, snub

desaire [des'aire] nm (menosprecio) slight; (falta de garbo) unattractiveness

desajustar [desaxus'tar] vt (desarreglar) to disarrange; (desconcertar) to throw off balance; **~se** vr to get out of order; (aflojarse) to loosen

desajuste [desa'xuste] nm (de máquina) disorder; (situación) imbalance

desalentador, a [desalenta'ðor, a] adj discouraging

desalentar [desalen'tar] vt (desanimar) to discourage

desaliento etc [desa'ljento] vb ver **desalentar** ♦ nm discouragement

desaliño [desa'liɲo] nm slovenliness

desalmado, a [desal'maðo, a] adj (cruel) cruel, heartless

desalojar [desalo'xar] vt (expulsar, echar) to eject; (abandonar) to move out of ♦ vi to move out

desamor [desa'mor] nm (frialdad) indifference; (odio) dislike

desamparado, a [desampa'raðo, a] adj (persona) helpless; (lugar: expuesto) exposed; (desierto) deserted

desamparar [desampa'rar] vt (abandonar) to desert, abandon; (JUR) to leave defenceless; (barco) to abandon

desandar [desan'dar] vt: **~ lo andado** o **el camino** to retrace one's steps

desangrar [desaŋ'grar] vt to bleed; (fig: persona) to bleed dry; **~se** vr to lose a lot of blood

desanimado, a [desani'maðo, a] adj (persona) downhearted; (espectáculo, fiesta) dull

desanimar [desani'mar] vt (desalentar) to discourage; (deprimir) to depress; **~se** vr to lose heart

desapacible [desapa'θiβle] adj (gen) unpleasant

desaparecer [desapare'θer] vi (gen) to disappear; (el sol, la luz) to vanish; **desaparecido, a** adj missing; **desaparición** nf disappearance

desapasionado, a [desapasjo'naðo, a] adj dispassionate, impartial

desapego [desa'pexo] nm (frialdad) coolness; (distancia) detachment

desapercibido, a [desaperθi'βiðo, a] adj (desprevenido) unprepared; **pasar ~** to go unnoticed

desaprensivo, a [desapren'siβo, a] adj unscrupulous

desaprobar [desapro'βar] vt (reprobar) to disapprove of; (condenar) to condemn; (no consentir) to reject

desaprovechado, a [desaproβe'tʃaðo, a] adj (oportunidad, tiempo) wasted; (estudiante) slack

desaprovechar [desaproβe'tʃar] vt to waste

desarmar [desar'mar] vt (MIL, fig) to disarm; (TEC) to take apart, dismantle; **desarme** nm disarmament

desarraigar [desarrai'xar] vt to uproot; **desarraigo** nm uprooting

desarreglar [desarre'xlar] vt (desordenar) to disarrange; (trastocar) to upset, disturb

desarreglo [desa'rrexlo] nm (de casa, persona) untidiness; (desorden) disorder

desarrollar [desarro'ʎar] vt (gen) to develop; **~se** vr to develop; (ocurrir) to take place; (FOTO) to develop; **desarrollo** nm development

desarticular [desartiku'lar] vt (hueso) to dislocate; (objeto) to take apart; (fig) to break up

desasir [desa'sir] vt to loosen

desasosegar [desasose'xar] vt (inquietar) to disturb, make uneasy; **~se** vr to become uneasy

desasosiego etc [desaso'sjexo] vb ver **desasosegar** ♦ nm (intranquilidad) uneasiness, restlessness; (ansiedad) anxiety

desastrado, a [desas'traðo, a] adj

(*desaliñado*) shabby; (*sucio*) dirty

desastre [de'sastre] *nm* disaster;
desastroso, a *adj* disastrous

desatado, a [desa'taðo, a] *adj*
(*desligado*) untied; (*violento*) violent,
wild

desatar [desa'tar] *vt* (*nudo*) to untie;
(*paquete*) to undo; (*separar*) to detach;
~se *vr* (*zapatos*) to come untied;
(*tormenta*) to break

desatascar [desatas'kar] *vt* (*cañería*) to
unblock, clear

desatender [desaten'der] *vt* (*no
prestar atención a*) to disregard;
(*abandonar*) to neglect

desatento, a [desa'tento, a] *adj*
(*distraído*) inattentive; (*descortés*)
discourteous

desatinado, a [desati'naðo, a] *adj*
foolish, silly; **desatino** *nm* (*idiotez*)
foolishness, folly; (*error*) blunder

desatornillar [desatorni'ʎar] *vt* to
unscrew

desatrancar [desatran'kar] *vt* (*puerta*)
to unbolt; (*cañería*) to clear, unblock

desautorizado, a [desautori'θaðo, a]
adj unauthorized

desautorizar [desautori'θar] *vt*
(*oficial*) to deprive of authority;
(*informe*) to deny

desavenencia [desaβe'nenθja] *nf*
(*desacuerdo*) disagreement;
(*discrepancia*) quarrel

desayunar [desaju'nar] *vi* to have
breakfast ♦ *vt* to have for breakfast;
desayuno *nm* breakfast

desazón [desa'θon] *nf* anxiety

desazonarse [desaθo'narse] *vr* to
worry, be anxious

desbandarse [desβan'darse] *vr* (MIL)
to disband; (*fig*) to flee in disorder

desbarajuste [desβara'xuste] *nm*
confusion, disorder

desbaratar [desβara'tar] *vt* (*deshacer,
destruir*) to ruin

desbloquear [desβloke'ar] *vt*
(*negociaciones, tráfico*) to get going

again; (COM: *cuenta*) to unfreeze

desbocado, a [desβo'kaðo, a] *adj*
(*caballo*) runaway

desbordar [desβor'ðar] *vt* (*sobrepasar*)
to go beyond; (*exceder*) to exceed; **~se**
vr (*río*) to overflow; (*entusiasmo*) to
erupt

descabalgar [deskaβal'ɣar] *vi* to
dismount

descabellado, a [deskaβe'ʎaðo, a]
adj (*disparatado*) wild, crazy

descafeinado, a [deskafei'naðo, a]
adj decaffeinated ♦ *nm* decaffeinated
coffee

descalabro [deska'laβro] *nm* blow;
(*desgracia*) misfortune

descalificar [deskalifi'kar] *vt* to
disqualify; (*desacreditar*) to discredit

descalzar [deskal'θar] *vt* (*zapato*) to
take off; **descalzo, a** *adj* barefoot(ed)

descambiar [deskam'bjar] *vt* to
exchange

descaminado, a [deskami'naðo, a]
adj (*equivocado*) on the wrong road;
(*fig*) misguided

descampado [deskam'paðo] *nm* open
space

descansado, a [deskan'saðo, a] *adj*
(*gen*) rested; (*que tranquiliza*) restful

descansar [deskan'sar] *vt* (*gen*) to rest
♦ *vi* to rest, have a rest; (*echarse*) to lie
down

descansillo [deskan'siʎo] *nm* (*de
escalera*) landing

descanso [des'kanso] *nm* (*reposo*) rest;
(*alivio*) relief; (*pausa*) break; (DEPORTE)
interval, half time

descapotable [deskapo'taβle] *nm* (tb:
coche ~) convertible

descarado, a [deska'raðo, a] *adj*
shameless; (*insolente*) cheeky

descarga [des'karɣa] *nf* (ARQ, ELEC,
MIL) discharge; (NAUT) unloading

descargar [deskar'ɣar] *vt* to unload;
(*golpe*) to let fly; **~se** *vr* to unburden
o.s.; **descargo** *nm* (COM) receipt; (JUR)
evidence

descaro [des'karo] nm nerve

descarriar [deska'rrjar] vt (descaminar) to misdirect; (fig) to lead astray; **~se** vr (perderse) to lose one's way; (separarse) to stray; (pervertirse) to err, go astray

descarrilamiento [deskarrila'mjento] nm (de tren) derailment

descarrilar [deskarri'lar] vi to be derailed

descartar [deskar'tar] vt (rechazar) to reject; (eliminar) to rule out; **~se** vr (NAIPES) to discard; **~se de** to shirk

descascarillado, a [deskaskari'ʎaðo, a] adj (paredes) peeling

descendencia [desθen'denθja] nf (origen) origin, descent; (hijos) offspring

descender [desθen'der] vt (bajar: escalera) to go down ♦ vi to descend; (temperatura, nivel) to fall, drop; **~ de** to be descended from

descendiente [desθen'djente] nm/f descendant

descenso [des'θenso] nm descent; (de temperatura) drop

descifrar [desθi'frar] vt to decipher; (mensaje) to decode

descolgar [deskol'ɣar] vt (bajar) to take down; (teléfono) to pick up; **~se** vr to let o.s. down

descolorido, a [deskolo'riðo, a] adj faded; (pálido) pale

descompasado, a [deskompa'saðo, a] adj (sin proporción) out of all proportion; (excesivo) excessive

descomponer [deskompo'ner] vt (desordenar) to disarrange, disturb; (TEC) to put out of order; (dividir) to break down (into parts); (fig) to provoke; **~se** vr (corromperse) to rot, decompose; (TEC) to break down

descomposición [deskomposi'θjon] nf (de un objeto) breakdown; (de fruta etc) decomposition; **~ de vientre** stomach upset, diarrhoea

descompuesto, a [deskom'pwesto, a] adj (corrompido) decomposed; (roto)

broken

descomunal [deskomu'nal] adj (enorme) huge

desconcertado, a [deskonθer'taðo, a] adj disconcerted, bewildered

desconcertar [deskonθer'tar] vt (confundir) to baffle; (incomodar) to upset, put out; **~se** vr (turbarse) to be upset

desconchado, a [deskon'tʃaðo, a] adj (pintura) peeling

desconcierto etc [deskon'θjerto] vb ver **desconcertar** ♦ nm (gen) disorder; (desorientación) uncertainty; (inquietud) uneasiness

desconectar [deskonek'tar] vt to disconnect

desconfianza [deskon'fjanθa] nf distrust

desconfiar [deskon'fjar] vi to be distrustful; **~ de** to distrust, suspect

descongelar [deskonxe'lar] vt to defrost; (COM, POL) to unfreeze

descongestionar [deskonxestjo'nar] vt (cabeza, tráfico) to clear

desconocer [deskono'θer] vt (ignorar) not to know, be ignorant of

desconocido, a [deskono'θiðo, a] adj unknown ♦ nm/f stranger

desconocimiento [deskonoθi'-mjento] nm (falta de conocimientos) ignorance

desconsiderado, a [deskonsiðe'raðo, a] adj inconsiderate; (insensible) thoughtless

desconsolar [deskonso'lar] vt to distress; **~se** vr to despair

desconsuelo etc [deskon'swelo] vb ver **desconsolar** ♦ nm (tristeza) distress; (desesperación) despair

descontado, a [deskon'taðo, a] adj: **dar por ~ (que)** to take (it) for granted (that)

descontar [deskon'tar] vt (deducir) to take away, deduct; (rebajar) to discount

descontento, a [deskon'tento, a] adj

dissatisfied ♦ *nm* dissatisfaction, discontent

descorazonar [deskoraθo'nar] *vt* to discourage, dishearten

descorchar [deskor'tʃar] *vt* to uncork

descorrer [desko'rrer] *vt* (*cortinas, cerrojo*) to draw back

descortés [deskor'tes] *adj* (*mal educado*) discourteous; (*grosero*) rude

descoser [desko'ser] *vt* to unstitch; **~se** *vr* to come apart (at the seams)

descosido, a [desko'siðo, a] *adj* (*COSTURA*) unstitched

descrédito [des'kreðito] *nm* discredit

descreído, a [deskre'iðo, a] *adj* (*incrédulo*) incredulous; (*falto de fe*) unbelieving

descremado, a [deskre'maðo, a] *adj* skimmed

describir [deskri'ßir] *vt* to describe; **descripción** [deskrip'θjon] *nf* description

descrito [des'krito] *pp de* **describir**

descuartizar [deskwarti'θar] *vt* (*animal*) to cut up

descubierto, a [desku'ßjerto, a] *pp de* **descubrir** ♦ *adj* uncovered, bare; (*persona*) bareheaded ♦ *nm* (*bancario*) overdraft; **al ~** in the open

descubrimiento [deskußri'mjento] *nm* (*hallazgo*) discovery; (*revelación*) revelation

descubrir [desku'ßrir] *vt* to discover, find; (*inaugurar*) to unveil; (*vislumbrar*) to detect; (*revelar*) to reveal, show; (*destapar*) to uncover; **~se** *vr* to reveal o.s.; (*quitarse sombrero*) to take off one's hat; (*confesar*) to confess

descuento *etc* [des'kwento] *vb ver* **descontar** ♦ *nm* discount

descuidado, a [deskwi'ðaðo, a] *adj* (*sin cuidado*) careless; (*desordenado*) untidy; (*olvidadizo*) forgetful; (*dejado*) neglected; (*desprevenido*) unprepared

descuidar [deskwi'ðar] *vt* (*dejar*) to neglect; (*olvidar*) to overlook; **~se** *vr* (*distraerse*) to be careless;

(*abandonarse*) to let o.s. go; (*desprevenirse*) to drop one's guard; **¡descuida!** don't worry!; **descuido** *nm* (*dejadez*) carelessness; (*olvido*) negligence

─────────────────────
PALABRA CLAVE
─────────────────────

desde ['desðe] *prep* **1** (*lugar*) from; **~ Burgos hasta mi casa hay 30 km** it's 30 kms from Burgos to my house

2 (*posición*): **hablaba ~ el balcón** she was speaking from the balcony

3 (*tiempo: + ad, n*): **~ ahora** from now on; **~ la boda** since the wedding; **~ niño** since I *etc* was a child; **~ 3 años atrás** since 3 years ago

4 (*tiempo: + vb, fecha*) since; for; **nos conocemos ~ 1992/~ hace 20 años** we've known each other since 1992/for 20 years; **no le veo ~ 1997/~ hace 5 años** I haven't seen him since 1997/for 5 years

5 (*gama*): **~ los más lujosos hasta los más económicos** from the most luxurious to the most reasonably priced

6: **~ luego (que no)** of course (not) ♦ *conj*: **~ que**: **~ que recuerdo** for as long as I can remember; **~ que llegó no ha salido** he hasn't been out since he arrived

desdecirse [desðe'θirse] *vr* to retract; **~ de** to go back on

desdén [des'ðen] *nm* scorn

desdeñar [desðe'nar] *vt* (*despreciar*) to scorn

desdicha [des'ðitʃa] *nf* (*desgracia*) misfortune; (*infelicidad*) unhappiness; **desdichado, a** *adj* (*sin suerte*) unlucky; (*infeliz*) unhappy

desdoblar [desðo'ßlar] *vt* (*extender*) to spread out; (*desplegar*) to unfold

desear [dese'ar] *vt* to want, desire, wish for

desecar [dese'kar] *vt* to dry up; **~se** *vr* to dry up

desechar [dese'tʃar] vt (basura) to throw out o away; (ideas) to reject, discard; **desechos** nmpl rubbish sg, waste sg

desembalar [desemba'lar] vt to unpack

desembarazar [desembara'θar] vt (desocupar) to clear; (desenredar) to free; **~se** vr: **~se de** to free o.s. of, get rid of

desembarcar [desembar'kar] vt (mercancías etc) to unload ♦ vi to disembark; **~se** vr to disembark

desembocadura [desemboka'ðura] nf (de río) mouth; (de calle) opening

desembocar [desembo'kar] vi (río) to flow into; (fig) to result in

desembolso [desem'bolso] nm payment

desembragar [desembra'ɣar] vi to declutch

desembrollar [desembro'ʎar] vt (madeja) to unravel; (asunto, malentendido) to sort out

desemejanza [deseme'xanθa] nf dissimilarity

desempaquetar [desempake'tar] vt (regalo) to unwrap; (mercancía) to unpack

desempatar [desempa'tar] vi to replay, hold a play-off; **desempate** nm (FÚTBOL) replay, play-off; (TENIS) tie-break(er)

desempeñar [desempe'nar] vt (cargo) to hold; (papel) to perform; (lo empeñado) to redeem; **~ un papel** (fig) to play a role

desempeño [desem'peno] nm redeeming; (de cargo) occupation

desempleado, a [desemple'aðo, a] nm/f unemployed person; **desempleo** nm unemployment

desempolvar [desempol'βar] vt (muebles etc) to dust; (lo olvidado) to revive

desencadenar [desenkaðe'nar] vt to unchain; (ira) to unleash; **~se** vr to

break loose; (tormenta) to burst; (guerra) to break out

desencajar [desenka'xar] vt (hueso) to dislocate; (mecanismo, pieza) to disconnect, disengage

desencanto [desen'kanto] nm disillusionment

desenchufar [desentʃu'far] vt to unplug

desenfadado, a [desenfa'ðaðo, a] adj (desenvuelto) uninhibited; (descarado) forward; **desenfado** nm (libertad) freedom; (comportamiento) free and easy manner; (descaro) forwardness

desenfocado, a [desenfo'kaðo, a] adj (FOTO) out of focus

desenfrenado, a [desenfre'naðo, a] adj (descontrolado) uncontrolled; (inmoderado) unbridled; **desenfreno** nm wildness; (de las pasiones) lack of self-control

desenganchar [desengan'tʃar] vt (gen) to unhook; (FERRO) to uncouple

desengañar [desenga'nar] vt to disillusion; **~se** vr to become disillusioned; **desengaño** nm disillusionment; (decepción) disappointment

desenlace [desen'laθe] nm outcome

desenmarañar [desenmara'nar] vt (fig) to unravel

desenmascarar [desenmaska'rar] vt to unmask

desenredar [desenre'ðar] vt (pelo) to untangle; (problema) to sort out

desenroscar [desenros'kar] vt to unscrew

desentenderse [desenten'derse] vr: **~ de** to pretend not to know about; (apartarse) to have nothing to do with

desenterrar [desente'rrar] vt to exhume; (tesoro, fig) to unearth, dig up

desentonar [desento'nar] vi (MUS) to sing (o play) out of tune; (color) to clash

desentrañar [desentra'nar] vt (misterio) to unravel

desentumecer |desentume'θer| vt (pierna etc) to stretch

desenvoltura |desenßol'tura| nf ease

desenvolver |desenßol'ßer| vt (paquete) to unwrap; (fig) to develop; **~se** vr (desarrollarse) to unfold, develop; (arreglárselas) to cope

deseo |de'seo| nm desire, wish; **~so, a** adj: **estar ~so de** to be anxious to

desequilibrado, a |desekili'ßraðo, a| adj unbalanced

desertar |deser'tar| vi to desert

desértico, a |de'sertiko, a| adj desert cpd

desesperación |desespera'θjon| nf (impaciencia) desperation, despair; (irritación) fury

desesperar |desespe'rar| vt to drive to despair; (exasperar) to drive to distraction ♦ vi: **~ de** to despair of; **~se** vr to despair, lose hope

desestabilizar |desestaßili'θar| vt to destabilize

desestimar |desesti'mar| vt (menospreciar) to have a low opinion of; (rechazar) to reject

desfachatez |desfatʃa'teθ| nf (insolencia) impudence; (descaro) rudeness

desfalco |des'falko| nm embezzlement

desfallecer |desfaʎe'θer| vi (perder las fuerzas) to become weak; (desvanecerse) to faint

desfasado, a |desfa'saðo, a| adj (anticuado) old-fashioned; **desfase** nm (diferencia) gap

desfavorable |desfaßo'raßle| adj unfavourable

desfigurar |desfiɣu'rar| vt (cara) to disfigure; (cuerpo) to deform

desfiladero |desfila'ðero| nm gorge

desfilar |desfi'lar| vi to parade; **desfile** nm procession

desfogarse |desfo'varse| vr (fig) to let off steam

desgajar |desva'xar| vt (arrancar) to tear off; (romper) to break off; **~se** vr

desgana |des'vana| nf (falta de apetito) loss of appetite; (apatía) unwillingness; **~do, a** adj: **estar ~do** (sin apetito) to have no appetite; (sin entusiasmo) to have lost interest

desgarrador, a |desvarra'ðor, a| adj (fig) heartrending

desgarrar |desva'rrar| vt to tear (up); (fig) to shatter; **desgarro** nm (en tela) tear; (aflicción) grief

desgastar |desvas'tar| vt (deteriorar) to wear away o down; (estropear) to spoil; **~se** vr to get worn out; **desgaste** nm wear (and tear)

desglosar |desvlo'sar| vt (factura) to break down

desgracia |des'vraθja| nf misfortune; (accidente) accident; (vergüenza) disgrace; (contratiempo) setback; **por ~** unfortunately

desgraciado, a |desvra'θjaðo, a| adj (sin suerte) unlucky, unfortunate; (miserable) wretched; (infeliz) miserable

desgravación |desvraßa'θjon| nf (COM): **~ fiscal** tax relief

desgravar |desvra'ßar| vt (impuestos) to reduce the tax o duty on

deshabitado, a |desaßi'taðo, a| adj uninhabited

deshacer |desa'θer| vt (casa) to break up; (TEC) to take apart; (enemigo) to defeat; (diluir) to melt; (contrato) to break; (intriga) to solve; **~se** vr (disolverse) to melt; (despedazarse) to come apart o undone; **~se de** to get rid of; **~se en lágrimas** to burst into tears

desharrapado, a |desarra'paðo, a| adj (persona) shabby

deshecho, a |des'etʃo, a| adj undone; (roto) smashed; (persona): **estar ~** to be shattered

desheredar |desere'ðar| vt to disinherit

deshidratar |desiðra'tar| vt to dehydrate

deshielo |des'jelo| nm thaw

deshonesto, a |deso'nesto, a| adj
indecent

deshonra |des'onra| nf (deshonor)
dishonour; (vergüenza) shame

deshora |de'sora|: **a ~** adv at the
wrong time

deshuesar |deswe'sar| vt (carne) to
bone; (fruta) to stone

desierto, a |de'sjerto, a| adj (casa,
calle, negocio) deserted ♦ nm desert

designar |desix'nar| vt (nombrar) to
designate; (indicar) to fix

designio |de'sixnjo| nm plan

desigual |desi'ywal| adj (terreno)
uneven; (lucha etc) unequal

desilusión |desilu'sjon| nf
disillusionment; (decepción)
disappointment; **desilusionar** vt to
disillusion; to disappoint;
desilusionarse vr to become
disillusioned

desinfectar |desinfek'tar| vt to
disinfect

desinflar |desin'flar| vt to deflate

desintegración |desinteɣra'θjon| nf
disintegration

desinterés |desinte'res| nm (desgana)
lack of interest; (altruismo)
unselfishness

desintoxicarse |desintoksi'karse| vr
(drogadicto) to undergo detoxification

desistir |desis'tir| vi (renunciar) to
stop, desist

desleal |desle'al| adj (infiel) disloyal;
(COM: competencia) unfair; **~tad** nf
disloyalty

desleír |desle'ir| vt (líquido) to dilute;
(sólido) to dissolve

deslenguado, a |deslen'gwaðo, a| adj
(grosero) foul-mouthed

desligar |desli'ɣar| vt (desatar) to
untie, undo; (separar) to separate; **~se**
vr (de un compromiso) to extricate o.s.

desliz |des'liθ| nm (fig) lapse; **~ar** vt to
slip, slide

deslucido, a |deslu'θiðo, a| adj dull;

(torpe) awkward, graceless;
(deslustrado) tarnished

deslumbrar |deslum'brar| vt to dazzle

desmadrarse |desma'ðrarse| (fam) vr
(descontrolarse) to run wild; (divertirse)
to let one's hair down; **desmadre**
(fam) nm (desorganización) chaos;
(jaleo) commotion

desmán |des'man| nm (exceso)
outrage; (abuso de poder) abuse

desmandarse |desman'darse| vr
(portarse mal) to behave badly;
(excederse) to get out of hand; (caballo)
to bolt

desmantelar |desmante'lar| vt
(deshacer) to dismantle; (casa) to strip

desmaquillador |desmakiʎa'ðor| nm
make-up remover

desmayar |desma'jar| vi to lose heart;
~se vr (MED) to faint; **desmayo** nm
(MED: acto) faint; (: estado)
unconsciousness

desmedido, a |desme'ðiðo, a| adj
excessive

desmejorar |desmexo'rar| vt (dañar)
to impair, spoil; (MED) to weaken

desmembrar |desmem'brar| vt (MED)
to dismember; (fig) to separate

desmemoriado, a |desmemo'rjaðo,
a| adj forgetful

desmentir |desmen'tir| vt (contradecir)
to contradict; (refutar) to deny

desmenuzar |desmenu'θar| vt
(deshacer) to crumble; (carne) to chop;
(examinar) to examine closely

desmerecer |desmere'θer| vt to be
unworthy of ♦ vi (deteriorarse) to
deteriorate

desmesurado, a |desmesu'raðo, a|
adj disproportionate

desmontable |desmon'taßle| adj (que
se quita: pieza) detachable; (que se
puede plegar etc) collapsible, folding

desmontar |desmon'tar| vt (deshacer)
to dismantle; (tierra) to level ♦ vi to
dismount

desmoralizar |desmorali'θar| vt to

demoralize

desmoronar [desmoro'nar] *vt* to wear away, erode; **~se** *vr* (*edificio, dique*) to collapse; (*economía*) to decline

desnatado, a [desna'taðo, a] *adj* skimmed

desnivel [desni'ßel] *nm* (*de terreno*) unevenness

desnudar [desnu'ðar] *vt* (*desvestir*) to undress; (*despojar*) to strip; **~se** *vr* (*desvestirse*) to get undressed; **desnudo, a** *adj* naked ♦ *nm/f* nude; **desnudo de** devoid or bereft of

desnutrición [desnutri'θjon] *nf* malnutrition; **desnutrido, a** *adj* undernourished

desobedecer [desoßeðe'θer] *vt, vi* to disobey; **desobediencia** *nf* disobedience

desocupado, a [desoku'paðo, a] *adj* at leisure; (*desempleado*) unemployed; (*deshabitado*) empty, vacant

desocupar [desoku'par] *vt* to vacate

desodorante [desoðo'rante] *nm* deodorant

desolación [desola'θjon] *nf* (*de lugar*) desolation; (*fig*) grief

desolar [deso'lar] *vt* to ruin, lay waste

desorbitado, a [desorßi'taðo, a] *adj* (*excesivo: ambición*) boundless; (*deseos*) excessive; (: *precio*) exorbitant

desorden [des'orðen] *nm* confusion; (*político*) disorder, unrest

desorganizar [desorɣani'θar] *vt* (*desordenar*) to disorganize; **desorganización** *nf* (*de persona*) disorganization; (*en empresa, oficina*) disorder, chaos

desorientar [desorjen'tar] *vt* (*extraviar*) to mislead; (*confundir, desconcertar*) to confuse; **~se** *vr* (*perderse*) to lose one's way

despabilado, a [despaßi'laðo, a] *adj* (*despierto*) wide-awake; (*fig*) alert, sharp

despabilar [despaßi'lar] *vt* (*el ingenio*) to sharpen ♦ *vi* to wake up; (*fig*) to get

a move on; **~se** *vr* to wake up; to get a move on

despachar [despa'tʃar] *vt* (*negocio*) to do, complete; (*enviar*) to send, dispatch; (*vender*) to sell, deal in; (*billete*) to issue; (*mandar ir*) to send away

despacho [des'patʃo] *nm* (*oficina*) office; (*de paquetes*) dispatch; (*venta*) sale; (*comunicación*) message

despacio [des'paθjo] *adv* slowly

desparpajo [despar'paxo] *nm* self-confidence; (*pey*) nerve

desparramar [despara'mar] *vt* (*esparcir*) to scatter; (*líquido*) to spill

despavorido, a [despaßo'riðo, a] *adj* terrified

despecho [des'petʃo] *nm* spite; **a ~ de** in spite of

despectivo, a [despek'tißo, a] *adj* (*despreciativo*) derogatory; (*LING*) pejorative

despedazar [despeðe'θar] *vt* to tear to pieces

despedida [despe'ðiða] *nf* (*adiós*) farewell; (*de obrero*) sacking

despedir [despe'ðir] *vt* (*visita*) to see off, show out; (*empleado*) to dismiss; (*inquilino*) to evict; (*objeto*) to hurl; (*olor etc*) to give out o off; **~se** *vr*: **~se de** to say goodbye to

despegar [despe'ɣar] *vt* to unstick ♦ *vi* (*avión*) to take off; **~se** *vr* to come loose, come unstuck; **despego** *nm* detachment

despegue *etc* [des'peɣe] *vb ver* **despegar** ♦ *nm* takeoff

despeinado, a [despei'naðo, a] *adj* dishevelled, unkempt

despejado, a [despe'xaðo, a] *adj* (*lugar*) clear, free; (*cielo*) clear; (*persona*) wide-awake, bright

despejar [despe'xar] *vt* (*gen*) to clear; (*misterio*) to clear up ♦ *vi* (*el tiempo*) to clear; **~se** *vr* (*tiempo, cielo*) to clear (up); (*misterio*) to become clearer; (*cabeza*) to clear

despellejar [despeʎeˈxar] vt (animal) to skin

despensa [desˈpensa] nf larder

despeñadero [despeɲaˈðero] nm (GEO) cliff, precipice

despeñarse [despeˈɲarse] vr to hurl o.s. down; (coche) to tumble over

desperdicio [desperˈðiθjo] nm (despilfarro) squandering; (basura) rubbish sg (BRIT), garbage sg (US); (residuos) waste sg

desperdigarse [desperðiˈɣarse] vr (rebaño, familia) to scatter, spread out; (granos de arroz, semillas) to scatter

desperezarse [despereˈθarse] vr to stretch

desperfecto [desperˈfekto] nm (deterioro) slight damage; (defecto) flaw, imperfection

despertador [despertaˈðor] nm alarm clock

despertar [desperˈtar] nm awakening ♦ vt (persona) to wake up; (recuerdos) to revive; (sentimiento) to arouse ♦ vi to awaken, wake up; ~se vr to awaken, wake up

despiadado, a [despjaˈðaðo, a] adj (ataque) merciless; (persona) heartless

despido etc [desˈpiðo] vb ver **despedir** ♦ nm dismissal, sacking

despierto, a etc [desˈpjerto, a] vb ver **despertar** ♦ adj awake; (fig) sharp, alert

despilfarro [despilˈfarro] nm (derroche) squandering; (lujo desmedido) extravagance

despistar [despisˈtar] vt to throw off the track o scent; (confundir) to mislead, confuse; ~se vr to take the wrong road; (confundirse) to become confused

despiste [desˈpiste] nm absent-mindedness; un ~ a mistake, slip

desplazamiento [desplaθaˈmjento] nm displacement

desplazar [desplaˈθar] vt to move;

(NAUT) to displace; (INFORM) to scroll; (fig) to oust; ~se vr (persona) to travel

desplegar [despleˈɣar] vt (tela, papel) to unfold, open out; (bandera) to unfurl; **despliegue** etc [desˈpleɣe] vb ver **desplegar** ♦ nm display

desplomarse [desploˈmarse] vr (edificio, gobierno, persona) to collapse

desplumar [despluˈmar] vt (ave) to pluck; (fam: estafar) to fleece

despoblado, a [despoˈßlaðo, a] adj (sin habitantes) uninhabited

despojar [despoˈxar] vt (alguien: de sus bienes) to divest of, deprive of; (casa) to strip, leave bare; (alguien: de su cargo) to strip of

despojo [desˈpoxo] nm (acto) plundering; (objetos) plunder, loot; ~s nmpl (de ave, res) offal sg

desposado, a [despoˈsaðo, a] adj, nm/f newly-wed

desposar [despoˈsar] vt to marry; ~se vr to get married

desposeer [desposeˈer] vt: ~ a uno de (puesto, autoridad) to strip sb of

déspota [ˈdespota] nm/f despot

despreciar [despreˈθjar] vt (desdeñar) to despise, scorn; (afrentar) to slight; **desprecio** nm scorn, contempt; slight

desprender [desprenˈder] vt (broche) to unfasten; (olor) to give off; ~se vr (botón: caerse) to fall off; (broche) to come unfastened; (olor, perfume) to be given off; ~se de algo que ... to draw from sth that ...

desprendimiento [desprendiˈmjento] nm (gen) loosening; (generosidad) disinterestedness; (de tierra, rocas) landslide

despreocupado, a [despreoku'paðo, a] adj (sin preocupación) unworried, nonchalant; (negligente) careless

despreocuparse [despreoku'parse] vr not to worry; ~ de to have no interest in

desprestigiar [despresti'xjar] vt (criticar) to run down; (desacreditar) to discredit

desprevenido, a [despreβeˈniðo, a] *adj* (*no preparado*) unprepared, unready

desproporcionado, a [desproporθjoˈnaðo, a] *adj* disproportionate, out of proportion

desprovisto, a [desproˈβisto, a] *adj*: ~ **de** devoid of

después [desˈpwes] *adv* afterwards, later; (*próximo paso*) next; ~ **de comer** after lunch; **un año** ~ a year later; ~ **se debatió el tema** next the matter was discussed; ~ **de corregido el texto** after the text had been corrected; ~ **de todo** after all

desquiciado, a [deskiˈθjaðo, a] *adj* deranged

desquite [desˈkite] *nm* (*satisfacción*) satisfaction; (*venganza*) revenge

destacar [destaˈkar] *vt* to emphasize, point up; (*MIL*) to detach, detail ♦ *vi* (*resaltarse*) to stand out; (*persona*) to be outstanding o exceptional; ~**se** *vr* to stand out; to be outstanding o exceptional

destajo [desˈtaxo] *nm*: **trabajar a** ~ to do piecework

destapar [destaˈpar] *vt* (*botella*) to open; (*cacerola*) to take the lid off; (*descubrir*) to uncover; ~**se** *vr* (*revelarse*) to reveal one's true character

destartalado, a [destartaˈlaðo, a] *adj* (*desordenado*) untidy; (*ruinoso*) tumbledown

destello [desˈteʎo] *nm* (*de estrella*) twinkle; (*de faro*) signal light

destemplado, a [destemˈplaðo, a] *adj* (*MUS*) out of tune; (*voz*) harsh; (*MED*) out of sorts; (*tiempo*) unpleasant, nasty

desteñir [desteˈɲir] *vt* to fade ♦ *vi* to fade; ~**se** *vr* to fade; **esta tela no desteñe** this fabric will not run

desternillarse [desterniˈʎarse] *vr*: ~ **de risa** to split one's sides laughing

desterrar [desteˈrrar] *vt* (*exilar*) to

exile; (*fig*) to banish, dismiss

destiempo [desˈtjempo]: **a** ~ *adv* out of turn

destierro *etc* [desˈtjerro] *vb ver* **desterrar** ♦ *nm* exile

destilar [destiˈlar] *vt* to distil; **destilería** *nf* distillery

destinar [destiˈnar] *vt* (*funcionario*) to appoint, assign; (*fondos*): ~ **(a)** to set aside (for)

destinatario, a [destinaˈtarjo, a] *nm/f* addressee

destino [desˈtino] *nm* (*suerte*) destiny; (*de avión, viajero*) destination

destituir [destituˈir] *vt* to dismiss

destornillador [destorniʎaˈðor] *nm* screwdriver

destornillar [destorniˈʎar] *vt* (*tornillo*) to unscrew; ~**se** *vr* to unscrew

destreza [desˈtreθa] *nf* (*habilidad*) skill; (*maña*) dexterity

destrozar [destroˈθar] *vt* (*romper*) to smash, break (up); (*estropear*) to ruin; (*nervios*) to shatter

destrozo [desˈtroθo] *nm* (*acción*) destruction; (*desastre*) smashing; ~**s** *nmpl* (*pedazos*) pieces; (*daños*) havoc *sg*

destrucción [destrukˈθjon] *nf* destruction

destruir [destruˈir] *vt* to destroy

desuso [deˈsuso] *nm* disuse; **caer en** ~ to become obsolete

desvalido, a [desβaˈliðo, a] *adj* (*desprotegido*) destitute; (*sin fuerzas*) helpless

desvalijar [desβaliˈxar] *vt* (*persona*) to rob; (*casa, tienda*) to burgle; (*coche*) to break into

desván [desˈβan] *nm* attic

desvanecer [desβaneˈθer] *vt* (*disipar*) to dispel; (*borrar*) to blur; ~**se** *vr* (*humo etc*) to vanish, disappear; (*color*) to fade; (*recuerdo, sonido*) to fade away; (*MED*) to pass out; (*duda*) to be dispelled

desvanecimiento [desβaneθiˈmjento| *nm* (*desaparición*) disappearance; (*de colores*) fading; (*evaporación*) evaporation; (*MED*) fainting fit

desvariar [desßa'rjar] *vi* (*enfermo*) to be delirious; **desvarío** *nm* delirium

desvelar [desße'lar] *vt* to keep awake; **~se** *vr* (*no poder dormir*) to stay awake; (*preocuparse*) to be vigilant o watchful

desvelos [des'ßelos] *nmpl* worrying *sg*

desvencijado, a [desßenθi'xaðo, a] *adj* (*silla*) rickety; (*máquina*) broken-down

desventaja [desßen'taxa] *nf* disadvantage

desventura [desßen'tura] *nf* misfortune

desvergonzado, a [desßerɣonˈθaðo, a] *adj* shameless

desvergüenza [desßerˈɣwenθa] *nf* (*descaro*) shamelessness; (*insolencia*) impudence; (*mala conducta*) effrontery

desvestir [desßes'tir] *vt* to undress; **~se** *vr* to undress

desviación [desßja'θjon] *nf* deviation; (*AUTO*) diversion, detour

desviar [des'ßjar] *vt* to turn aside; (*río*) to alter the course of; (*navío*) to divert, re-route; (*conversación*) to sidetrack; **~se** *vr* (*apartarse del camino*) to turn aside; (: *barco*) to go off course

desvío *etc* [des'ßio] *vb ver* **desviar** ♦ *nm* (*desviación*) detour, diversion; (*fig*) indifference

desvirtuar [desßir'twar] *vt* to distort

desvivirse [desßi'ßirse] *vr*: **~ por** (*anhelar*) to long for, crave for; (*hacer lo posible por*) to do one's utmost for

detallar [deta'ʎar] *vt* to detail

detalle [de'taʎe] *nm* detail; (*gesto*) gesture, token; **al ~** in detail; (*COM*) retail

detallista [deta'ʎista] *nm/f* (*COM*) retailer

detective [detek'tiße] *nm/f* detective

detener [dete'ner] *vt* (*gen*) to stop; (*JUR*) to arrest; (*objeto*) to keep; **~se** *vr*

to stop; (*demorarse*) to linger over, linger over

detenidamente [deteniða'mente] *adv* (*minuciosamente*) carefully; (*extensamente*) at great length

detenido, a [dete'niðo, a] *adj* (*arrestado*) under arrest ♦ *nm/f* person under arrest, prisoner

detenimiento [deteni'mjento] *nm*: **con ~** thoroughly; (*observar, considerar*) carefully

detergente [deter'xente] *nm* detergent

deteriorar [deterjo'rar] *vt* to spoil, damage; **~se** *vr* to deteriorate; **deterioro** *nm* deterioration

determinación [determina'θjon] *nf* (*empeño*) determination; (*decisión*) decision; **determinado, a** *adj* specific

determinar [determi'nar] *vt* (*plazo*) to fix; (*precio*) to settle; **~se** *vr* to decide

detestar [detes'tar] *vt* to detest

detractor, a [detrak'tor, a] *nm/f* slanderer, libeller

detrás [de'tras] *adv* behind; (*atrás*) at the back; **~ de** behind

detrimento [detri'mento] *nm*: **en ~ de** to the detriment of

deuda [ˈdeuða] *nf* debt

devaluación [deßalwa'θjon] *nf* devaluation

devastar [deßas'tar] *vt* (*destruir*) to devastate

devoción [deßo'θjon] *nf* devotion

devolución [deßolu'θjon] *nf* (*reenvío*) return, sending back; (*reembolso*) repayment; (*JUR*) devolution

devolver [deßol'ßer] *vt* to return; (*lo extraviado, lo prestado*) to give back; (*carta al correo*) to send back; (*COM*) to repay, refund ♦ *vi* (*vomitar*) to be sick

devorar [deßo'rar] *vt* to devour

devoto, a [de'ßoto, a] *adj* devout ♦ *nm/f* admirer

devuelto *pp de* **devolver**

devuelva *etc vb ver* **devolver**

di *vb ver* **dar**; **decir**

día ['dia] nm day; ¿qué ~ es? what's the date?; **estar/poner al ~** to be/keep up to date; **el ~ de hoy/de mañana** today/tomorrow; **al ~ siguiente** (on) the following day; **vivir al ~** to live from hand to mouth; **de ~** by day, in daylight; **en pleno ~** in full daylight; **D~ de Reyes** Epiphany; **~ festivo** (ESP) o **feriado** (AM) holiday; **~ libre** day off

diabetes [dja'βetes] nf diabetes

diablo ['djaβlo] nm devil; **diablura** nf prank

diadema [dja'ðema] nf tiara

diafragma [dja'fraɣma] nm diaphragm

diagnosis [djaɣ'nosis] nf inv diagnosis

diagnóstico [djaɣ'nostiko] nm = **diagnosis**

diagonal [djaɣo'nal] adj diagonal

diagrama [dja'ɣrama] nm diagram; **~ de flujo** flowchart

dial [djal] nm dial

dialecto [dja'lekto] nm dialect

dialogar [djalo'ɣar] vi: **~ con** (POL) to hold talks with

diálogo ['djaloɣo] nm dialogue

diamante [dja'mante] nm diamond

diana ['djana] nf (MIL) reveille; (de blanco) centre, bull's-eye

diapositiva [djaposi'tiβa] nf (FOTO) slide, transparency

diario, a ['djarjo, a] adj daily ♦ nm newspaper; **a ~** daily; **de ~** everyday

diarrea [dja'rrea] nf diarrhoea

dibujar [diβu'xar] vt to draw, sketch; **dibujo** nm drawing; **dibujos animados** cartoons

diccionario [dikθjo'narjo] nm dictionary

dice etc vb ver **decir**

dicho, a ['ditʃo, a] pp de **decir** ♦ adj: **en ~s países** in the aforementioned countries ♦ nm saying

dichoso, a [di'tʃoso, a] adj happy

diciembre [di'θjembre] nm December

dictado [dik'taðo] nm dictation

dictador [dikta'ðor] nm dictator;

dictadura nf dictatorship

dictamen [dik'tamen] nm (opinión) opinion; (juicio) judgment; (informe) report

dictar [dik'tar] vt (carta) to dictate; (JUR: sentencia) to pronounce; (decreto) to issue; (AM: clase) to give

didáctico, a [di'ðaktiko, a] adj educational

diecinueve [djeθi'nweβe] num nineteen

dieciocho [djeθi'otʃo] num eighteen

dieciséis [djeθi'seis] num sixteen

diecisiete [djeθi'sjete] num seventeen

diente ['djente] nm (ANAT, TEC) tooth; (ZOOL) fang; (: de elefante) tusk; (de ajo) clove; **hablar entre ~s** to mutter, mumble

diera etc vb ver **dar**

diesel ['disel] adj: **motor ~** diesel engine

diestro, a ['djestro, a] adj (derecho) right; (hábil) skilful

dieta ['djeta] nf diet; **dietética** nf: **tienda de dietética** health food shop; **dietético, a** adj diet (atr), dietary

diez [djeθ] num ten

diezmar [djeθ'mar] vt (población) to decimate

difamar [difa'mar] vt (JUR: hablando) to slander; (: por escrito) to libel

diferencia [dife'renθja] nf difference; **diferenciar** vt to differentiate between ♦ vi to differ; **diferenciarse** vr to differ, be different; (distinguirse) to distinguish o.s.

diferente [dife'rente] adj different

diferido [dife'riðo] nm: **en ~** (TV etc) recorded

difícil [di'fiθil] adj difficult

dificultad [difikul'taθ] nf difficulty; (problema) trouble

dificultar [difikul'tar] vt (complicar) to complicate, make difficult; (estorbar) to obstruct

difteria [dif'terja] nf diphtheria

difundir [difun'dir] vt (calor, luz) to diffuse; (RADIO, TV) to broadcast; ~ **una noticia** to spread a piece of news; **~se** vr to spread (out)

difunto, a [di'funto, a] adj dead, deceased ♦ nm/f deceased (person)

difusión [difu'sjon] nf (RADIO, TV) broadcasting

diga etc vb ver **decir**

digerir [dixe'rir] vt to digest; (fig) to absorb; **digestión** nf digestion; **digestivo, a** adj digestive

digital [dixi'tal] adj digital

dignarse [div'narse] vr to deign to

dignatario, a [divna'tarjo, a] nm/f dignitary

dignidad [divni'ðað] nf dignity

digno, a [di'vno, a] adj worthy

digo etc vb ver **decir**

dije etc vb ver **decir**

dilapidar [dilapi'ðar] vt (dinero, herencia) to squander, waste

dilatar [dila'tar] vt (cuerpo) to dilate; (prolongar) to prolong

dilema [di'lema] nm dilemma

diligencia [dili'xenθja] nf diligence; (ocupación) errand, job; **~s** nfpl (JUR) formalities; **diligente** adj diligent

diluir [dilu'ir] vt to dilute

diluvio [di'lußjo] nm deluge, flood

dimensión [dimen'sjon] nf dimension

diminuto, a [dimi'nuto, a] adj tiny, diminutive

dimitir [dimi'tir] vi to resign

dimos vb ver **dar**

Dinamarca [dina'marka] nf Denmark

dinámico, a [di'namiko, a] adj dynamic

dinamita [dina'mita] nf dynamite

dinamo ['dinamo] nf dynamo

dineral [dine'ral] nm large sum of money, fortune

dinero [di'nero] nm money; **~ contante, ~ efectivo** (ready) cash; **~ suelto** (loose) change

dio vb ver **dar**

dios [djos] nm god; **¡D~ mío!** (oh,)

my God!

diosa ['djosa] nf goddess

diploma [di'ploma] nm diploma

diplomacia [diplo'maθja] nf diplomacy; (fig) tact

diplomado, a [diplo'maðo, a] adj qualified

diplomático, a [diplo'matiko, a] adj diplomatic ♦ nm/f diplomat

diputación [diputa'θjon] nf (tb: ~ provincial) ≈ county council

diputado, a [dipu'taðo, a] nm/f delegate; (POL) ≈ member of parliament (BRIT), ≈ representative (US)

dique ['dike] nm dyke

diré etc vb ver **decir**

dirección [direk'θjon] nf direction; (señas) address; (AUTO) steering; (gerencia) management; (POL) leadership; **~ única/prohibida** one-way street/no entry

directa [di'rekta] nf (AUTO) top gear

directiva [direk'tißa] nf (DEP, tb: junta ~) board of directors

directo, a [di'rekto, a] adj direct; (RADIO, TV) live; **transmitir en ~** to broadcast live

director, a [direk'tor, a] adj leading ♦ nm/f director; (ESCOL) head(teacher) (BRIT), principal (US); (gerente) manager(ess); (PRENSA) editor; **~ de cine** film director; **~ general** managing director

dirigente [diri'xente] nm/f (POL) leader

dirigir [diri'xir] vt to direct; (carta) to address; (obra de teatro, film) to direct; (MUS) to conduct; (negocio) to manage; **~se** vr: **~se a** to go towards, make one's way towards; (hablar con) to speak to

dirija etc vb ver **dirigir**

discernir [disθer'nir] vt to discern

disciplina [disθi'plina] nf discipline

discípulo, a [dis'θipulo, a] nm/f disciple

disco ['disko] nm disc; (DEPORTE)

discus; (TEL) dial; (AUTO: semáforo) light; (MUS) record; (INFORM): ~ **flexible/rígido** floppy/hard disk; ~ **compacto/de larga duración** compact disc/long-playing record; ~ **de freno** brake disc

disconforme [diskon'forme] adj differing; **estar ~ (con)** to be in disagreement (with)

discordia [dis'korðja] nf discord

discoteca [disko'teka] nf disco(theque)

discreción [diskre'θjon] nf discretion; (reserva) prudence; **comer a ~** to eat as much as one wishes; **discrecional** adj (facultativo) discretionary

discrepancia [diskre'panθja] nf (diferencia) discrepancy; (desacuerdo) disagreement

discreto, a [dis'kreto, a] adj discreet

discriminación [diskrimina'θjon] nf discrimination

disculpa [dis'kulpa] nf excuse; (pedir perdón) apology; **pedir ~s a/por** to apologize to/for; **disculpar** vt to excuse, pardon; **disculparse** vr to excuse o.s.; to apologize

discurrir [disku'rrir] vi (pensar, reflexionar) to think, meditate; (el tiempo) to pass, go by

discurso [dis'kurso] nm speech

discusión [disku'sjon] nf (diálogo) discussion; (riña) argument

discutir [disku'tir] vt (debatir) to discuss; (pelear) to argue about; (contradecir) to argue against ♦ vi (debatir) to discuss; (pelearse) to argue

disecar [dise'kar] vt (conservar: animal) to stuff; (: planta) to dry

diseminar [disemi'nar] vt to disseminate, spread

diseñar [dise'ɲar] vt, vi to design

diseño [dise'ɲo] nm design

disfraz [dis'fraθ] nm (máscara) disguise; (excusa) pretext; **~ar** vt to disguise; **~arse** vr: **~arse de** to disguise o.s. as

disfrutar [disfru'tar] vt to enjoy ♦ vi to enjoy o.s.; ~ **de** to enjoy, possess

disgregarse [disɣre'ɣarse] vr (muchedumbre) to disperse

disgustar [disɣus'tar] vt (no gustar) to displease; (contrariar, enojar) to annoy, upset; **~se** vr (enfadarse) to get upset; (dos personas) to fall out

disgusto [dis'ɣusto] nm (contrariedad) annoyance; (tristeza) grief; (riña) quarrel

disidente [disi'ðente] nm dissident

disimular [disimu'lar] vt (ocultar) to hide, conceal ♦ vi to dissemble

disipar [disi'par] vt to dispel; (fortuna) to squander; **~se** vr (nubes) to vanish; (indisciplinarse) to dissipate

dislocarse [dislo'karse] vr (articulación) to sprain, dislocate

disminución [disminu'θjon] nf decrease, reduction

disminuido, a [disminu'iðo, a] nm/f: ~ **mental/físico** mentally/physically handicapped person

disminuir [disminu'ir] vt to decrease, diminish

disociarse [diso'θjarse] vr: ~ **(de)** to dissociate o.s. (from)

disolver [disol'ßer] vt (gen) to dissolve; **~se** vr to dissolve; (COM) to go into liquidation

dispar [dis'par] adj different

disparar [dispa'rar] vt, vi to shoot, fire

disparate [dispa'rate] nm (tontería) foolish remark; (error) blunder; **decir ~s** to talk nonsense

disparo [dis'paro] nm shot

dispensar [dispen'sar] vt to dispense; (disculpar) to excuse

dispersar [disper'sar] vt to disperse; **~se** vr to scatter

disponer [dispo'ner] vt (arreglar) to arrange; (ordenar) to put in order; (preparar) to prepare, get ready ♦ vi: ~ **de** to have, own; **~se** vr: **~se a** o **para hacer** to prepare to do

disponible [dispo'nißle] adj available

disposición [disposi'θjon] nf arrangement, disposition; (INFORM) layout; **a la ~ de** at the disposal of; **~ de ánimo** state of mind

dispositivo [disposi'tiβo] nm device, mechanism

dispuesto, a [dis'pwesto, a] pp de **disponer** ♦ adj (arreglado) arranged; (preparado) disposed

disputar [dispu'tar] vt (carrera) to compete in

disquete [dis'kete] nm floppy disk, diskette

distancia [dis'tanθja] nf distance

distanciar [distan'θjar] vt to space out; **~se** vr to become estranged

distante [dis'tante] adj distant

distar [dis'tar] vi: **dista 5km de aquí** it is 5km from here

diste vb ver **dar**

disteis ['disteis] vb ver **dar**

distensión [disten'sjon] nf (en las relaciones) relaxation; (POL) détente; (muscular) strain

distinción [distin'θjon] nf distinction; (elegancia) elegance; (honor) honour

distinguido, a [distin'giðo, a] adj distinguished

distinguir [distin'gir] vt to distinguish; (escoger) to single out; **~se** vr to be distinguished

distintivo [distin'tiβo] nm badge; (fig) characteristic

distinto, a [dis'tinto, a] adj different; (claro) clear

distracción [distrak'θjon] nf distraction; (pasatiempo) hobby, pastime; (olvido) absent-mindedness, distraction

distraer [distra'er] vt (atención) to distract; (divertir) to amuse; (fondos) to embezzle; **~se** vr (entretenerse) to amuse o.s.; (perder la concentración) to allow one's attention to wander

distraído, a [distra'iðo, a] adj (gen) absent-minded; (entretenido) amusing

distribuidor, a [distriβui'ðor, a] nm/f

distributor; **distribuidora** nf (COM) dealer, agent; (CINE) distributor

distribuir [distriβu'ir] vt to distribute

distrito [dis'trito] nm (sector, territorio) region; (barrio) district

disturbio [dis'turβjo] nm disturbance; (desorden) riot

disuadir [diswa'ðir] vt to dissuade

disuelto [di'swelto] pp de **disolver**

disyuntiva [disjun'tiβa] nf dilemma

DIU nm abr (= dispositivo intrauterino) IUD

diurno, a ['djurno, a] adj day cpd

divagar [diβa'var] vi (desviarse) to digress

diván [di'βan] nm divan

divergencia [diβer'xenθja] nf divergence

diversidad [diβersi'ðað] nf diversity, variety

diversificar [diβersifi'kar] vt to diversify

diversión [diβer'sjon] nf (gen) entertainment; (actividad) hobby, pastime

diverso, a [di'βerso, a] adj diverse; **~s libros** several books; **~s** nmpl sundries

divertido, a [diβer'tiðo, a] adj (chiste) amusing; (fiesta etc) enjoyable

divertir [diβer'tir] vt (entretener, recrear) to amuse; **~se** vr (pasarlo bien) to have a good time; (distraerse) to amuse o.s.

dividendos [diβi'ðendos] nmpl (COM) dividends

dividir [diβi'ðir] vt (gen) to divide; (distribuir) to distribute, share out

divierta etc vb ver **divertir**

divino, a [di'βino, a] adj divine

divirtiendo etc vb ver **divertir**

divisa [di'βisa] nf (emblema) emblem, badge; **~s** nfpl foreign exchange sg

divisar [diβi'sar] vt to make out, distinguish

división [diβi'sjon] nf (gen) division; (de partido) split; (de país) partition

divorciar [diβor'θjar] vt to divorce;

~se vr to get divorced; **divorcio** nm divorce

divulgar [diβul'var] vt (ideas) to spread; (secreto) to divulge

DNI (ESP) nm abr (= Documento Nacional de Identidad) national identity card

---

DNI

The **Documento Nacional de Identidad** is a Spanish ID card which must be carried at all times and produced on request for the police. It contains the holder's photo, fingerprints and personal details. It is also known as the DNI or "carnet de identidad".

Dña. abr (= doña) Mrs

do [do] nm (MUS) do, C

dobladillo [doβla'ðiʎo] nm (de vestido) hem; (de pantalón: vuelta) turn-up (BRIT), cuff (US)

doblar [do'βlar] vt to double; (papel) to fold; (caño) to bend; (la esquina) to turn, go round; (film) to dub ♦ vi to turn; (campana) to toll; **~se** vr (plegarse) to fold (up), crease; (encorvarse) to bend

doble ['doβle] adj double; (de dos aspectos) dual; (fig) two-faced ♦ nm double ♦ nm/f (TEATRO) double, stand-in; **~s** nmpl (DEPORTE) doubles sg; **con sentido ~** with a double meaning

doblegar [doβle'var] vt to fold, crease; **~se** vr to yield

doblez [do'βleθ] nm fold, hem ♦ nf insincerity, duplicity

doce ['doθe] num twelve; **~na** nf dozen

docente [do'θente] adj: **centro/personal ~** teaching establishment/staff

dócil ['doθil] adj (pasivo) docile; (obediente) obedient

docto, a ['dokto, a] adj: **~ en** instructed in

doctor, a [dok'tor, a] nm/f doctor

doctorado [dokto'raðo] nm doctorate

doctrina [dok'trina] nf doctrine, teaching

documentación [dokumenta'θjon] nf documentation, papers pl

documental [dokumen'tal] adj, nm documentary

documento [doku'mento] nm (certificado) document; **~ national de identidad** identity card

dólar ['dolar] nm dollar

doler [do'ler] vt, vi to hurt; (fig) to grieve; **~se** vr (de su situación) to grieve, feel sorry; (de las desgracias ajenas) to sympathize; **me duele el brazo** my arm hurts

dolor [do'lor] nm pain; (fig) grief, sorrow; **~ de cabeza** headache; **~ de estómago** stomachache

domar [do'mar] vt to tame

domesticar [domesti'kar] vt = **domar**

doméstico, a [do'mestiko, a] adj (vida, servicio) home; (tareas) household; (animal) tame, pet

domiciliación [domiθilia'θjon] nf: **~ de pagos** (COM) standing order

domicilio [domi'θiljo] nm home; **~ particular** private residence; **~ social** (COM) head office; **sin ~ fijo** of no fixed abode

dominante [domi'nante] adj dominant; (persona) domineering

dominar [domi'nar] vt (gen) to dominate; (idiomas) to be fluent in ♦ vi to dominate, prevail; **~se** vr to control o.s.

domingo [do'mingo] nm Sunday

dominio [do'minjo] nm (tierras) domain; (autoridad) power, authority; (de las pasiones) grip, hold; (de idiomas) command

don [don] nm (talento) gift; **~ Juan Gómez** Mr Juan Gómez, Juan Gómez Esq (BRIT)

Don/Doña

The term **don/doña** often abbreviated to D./Dña is placed before the first name as a mark of respect for an older or more senior person - eg Don Diego, Doña Inés. Although becoming rarer in Spain it is still used with names and surnames on official documents and formal correspondence - eg "Sr. D. Pedro Rodríguez Hernández", "Sra. Dña. Inés Rodríguez Hernández".

---

donaire [do'naire] *nm* charm

donar [do'nar] *vt* to donate

donativo [dona'tiβo] *nm* donation

doncella [don'θeʎa] *nf* (*criada*) maid

donde ['donde] *adv* where ♦ *prep:* **el coche está allí ~ el farol** the car is over there by the lamppost o where the lamppost is; **en ~** where, in which

dónde ['donde] *adv interrogativo* where?; **¿a ~ vas?** where are you going (to)?; **¿de ~ vienes?** where have you been?; **¿por ~?** where?, whereabouts?

dondequiera [donde'kjera] *adv* anywhere; **por ~** everywhere, all over the place ♦ *conj:* **~ que** wherever

doña ['dona] *nf:* **~ Alicia** Alicia; **~ Victoria Benito** Mrs Victoria Benito

dorado, a [do'raðo, a] *adj* (*color*) golden; (*TEC*) gilt

dormir [dor'mir] *vt:* **~ la siesta** to have an afternoon nap ♦ *vi* to sleep; **~se** *vr* to fall asleep

dormitar [dormi'tar] *vi* to doze

dormitorio [dormi'torjo] *nm* bedroom; **~ común** dormitory

dorsal [dor'sal] *nm* (*DEPORTE*) number

dorso ['dorso] *nm* (*de mano*) back; (*de hoja*) reverse

dos [dos] *num* two

dosis ['dosis] *nf inv* dose, dosage

dotado, a [do'taðo, a] *adj* gifted; **~ de** endowed with

dotar [do'tar] *vt* to endow; **dote** *nf* dowry; **dotes** *nfpl* (*talentos*) gifts

doy *vb ver* **dar**

dragar [dra'ɣar] *vt* (*río*) to dredge; (*minas*) to sweep

drama ['drama] *nm* drama

dramaturgo [drama'turɣo] *nm* dramatist, playwright

drástico, a ['drastiko, a] *adj* drastic

drenaje [dre'naxe] *nm* drainage

droga ['droɣa] *nf* drug

drogadicto, a [droɣa'ðikto, a] *nm/f* drug addict

droguería [droɣe'ria] *nf* hardware shop (*BRIT*) o store (*US*)

ducha ['dutʃa] *nf* (*baño*) shower; (*MED*) douche; **ducharse** *vr* to take a shower

duda ['duða] *nf* doubt; **dudar** *vi* to doubt; **dudoso, a** [du'ðoso, a] *adj* (*incierto*) hesitant; (*sospechoso*) doubtful

duela *etc vb ver* **doler**

duelo ['dwelo] *vb ver* **doler** ♦ *nm* (*combate*) duel; (*luto*) mourning

duende ['dwende] *nm* imp, goblin

dueño, a ['dweno, a] *nm/f* (*propietario*) owner; (*de pensión, taberna*) landlord/lady; (*empresario*) employer

duermo *etc vb ver* **dormir**

dulce ['dulθe] *adj* sweet ♦ *adv* gently, softly ♦ *nm* sweet

dulzura [dul'θura] *nf* sweetness; (*ternura*) gentleness

duna ['duna] *nf* (*GEO*) dune

dúo ['duo] *nm* duet

duplicar [dupli'kar] *vt* (*hacer el doble de*) to duplicate; **~se** *vr* to double

duque ['duke] *nm* duke; **~sa** *nf* duchess

duración [dura'θjon] *nf* (*de película, disco etc*) length; (*de pila etc*) life; (*curso: de acontecimientos etc*) duration

duradero, a [dura'ðero, a] *adj* (*tela etc*) hard-wearing; (*fe, paz*) lasting

durante [du'rante] *prep* during

durar [du'rar] *vi* to last; (*recuerdo*) to remain

durazno [du'raθno] (AM) nm (fruta) peach; (árbol) peach tree

durex ['dureks] (AM) nm (tira adhesiva) Sellotape ® (BRIT), Scotch tape ® (US)

dureza [du'reθa] nf (calidad) hardness

duro, a ['duro, a] adj hard; (carácter) tough ♦ adv hard ♦ nm (moneda) five peseta coin o pieza

E, e

E abr (= este) E

e [e] conj and

ebanista [eβa'nista] nm/f cabinetmaker

ébano ['eβano] nm ebony

ebrio, a ['eβrjo, a] adj drunk

ebullición [eβuʎi'θjon] nf boiling

eccema [ek'θema] nf (MED) eczema

echar [e'tʃar] vt to throw; (agua, vino) to pour (out); (empleado: despedir) to fire, sack; (hojas) to sprout; (cartas) to post; (humo) to emit, give out ♦ vi: ~ a correr/llorar to run off/burst into tears; ~se vr to lie down; ~ llave a to lock (up); ~ abajo (gobierno) to overthrow; (edificio) to demolish; ~ mano a to lay hands on; ~ una mano a uno (ayudar) to give sb a hand; ~ de menos to miss

eclesiástico, a [ekle'sjastiko, a] adj ecclesiastical

eclipse [e'klipse] nm eclipse

eco ['eko] nm echo; **tener ~** to catch on

ecología [ekolo'via] nf ecology; **ecológico, a** [eko'loxiko, a] adj (producto, método) environmentally-friendly; (agricultura) organic; **ecologista** adj ecological, environmental ♦ nm/f environmentalist

economato [ekono'mato] nm cooperative store

economía [ekono'mia] nf (sistema) economy; (carrera) economics

económico, a [eko'nomiko, a] adj (barato) cheap, economical;

(ahorrativo) thrifty; (COM: año etc) financial; (: situación) economic

economista [ekono'mista] nm/f economist

ECU [eku] nm ECU

ecuador [ekwa'ðor] nm equator; **(el) E~** Ecuador

ecuánime [e'kwanime] adj (carácter) level-headed; (estado) calm

ecuatoriano, a [ekwato'rjano, a] adj, nm/f Ecuadorian

ecuestre [e'kwestre] adj equestrian

eczema [ek'θema] nm = **eccema**

edad [e'ðað] nf age; **¿qué ~ tienes?** how old are you?; **tiene ocho años de ~** he is eight (years old); **de ~ mediana/avanzada** middle-aged/ advanced in years; **la E~ Media** the Middle Ages

edición [eði'θjon] nf (acto) publication; (ejemplar) edition

edificar [eðifi'kar] vt, vi to build

edificio [eði'fiθjo] nm building; (fig) edifice, structure

Edimburgo [eðim'burvo] nm Edinburgh

editar [eði'tar] vt (publicar) to publish; (preparar textos) to edit

editor, a [eði'tor, a] nm/f (que publica) publisher; (redactor) editor ♦ adj: **casa ~a** publishing house, publisher; **~ial** adj editorial ♦ nm leading article, editorial; **casa ~ial** publishing house, publisher

edredón [eðre'ðon] nm duvet

educación [eðuka'θjon] nf education; (crianza) upbringing; (modales) (good) manners pl

educado, a [eðu'kaðo, a] adj: **bien/ mal ~** well/badly behaved

educar [eðu'kar] vt to educate; (criar) to bring up; (voz) to train

EE. UU. nmpl abr (= Estados Unidos) US(A)

efectista [efek'tista] adj sensationalist

efectivamente [efektiβa'mente] adv (como respuesta) exactly, precisely;

(*verdaderamente*) really; (*de hecho*) in fact

efectivo, a [efek'tiβo, a] *adj* effective; (*real*) actual, real ♦ *nm*: **pagar en ~** to pay (in) cash; **hacer ~ un cheque** to cash a cheque

efecto [e'fekto] *nm* effect, result; **~s** *nmpl* (*~ personales*) effects; (*bienes*) goods; (*COM*) assets; **en ~** in fact; (*respuesta*) exactly, indeed; **~ invernadero** greenhouse effect

efectuar [efek'twar] *vt* to carry out; (*viaje*) to make

eficacia [efi'kaθja] *nf* (*de persona*) efficiency; (*de medicamento etc*) effectiveness

eficaz [efi'kaθ] *adj* (*persona*) efficient; (*acción*) effective

eficiente [efi'θjente] *adj* efficient

efusivo, a [efu'siβo, a] *adj* effusive; **mis más efusivas gracias** my warmest thanks

EGB (*ESP*) *nf abr* (*ESCOL*) = *Educación General Básica*

egipcio, a [e'xipθjo, a] *adj, nm/f* Egyptian

Egipto [e'xipto] *nm* Egypt

egoísmo [evo'ismo] *nm* egoism

egoísta [evo'ista] *adj* egotistical, selfish ♦ *nm/f* egoist

egregio, a [e'vrexjo, a] *adj* eminent, distinguished

Eire ['eire] *nm* Eire

ej. *abr* (= *ejemplo*) eg

eje ['exe] *nm* (*GEO, MAT*) axis; (*de rueda*) axle; (*de máquina*) shaft, spindle

ejecución [exeku'θjon] *nf* execution; (*cumplimiento*) fulfilment; (*MUS*) performance; (*JUR: embargo de deudor*) attachment

ejecutar [exeku'tar] *vt* to execute, carry out; (*matar*) to execute; (*cumplir*) to fulfil; (*MUS*) to perform; (*JUR: embargar*) to attach, distrain (on)

ejecutivo, a [exeku'tiβo, a] *adj* executive; **el (poder) ~** the executive (power)

ejemplar [exem'plar] *adj* exemplary ♦ *nm* example; (*ZOOL*) specimen; (*de libro*) copy; (*de periódico*) number, issue

ejemplo [e'xemplo] *nm* example; **por ~** for example

ejercer [exer'θer] *vt* to exercise; (*influencia*) to exert; (*un oficio*) to practise ♦ *vi* (*practicar*): **~ (de)** to practise (as)

ejercicio [exer'θiθjo] *nm* exercise; (*periodo*) tenure; **~ comercial** financial year

ejército [e'xerθito] *nm* army; **entrar en el ~** to join the army, join up

ejote [e'xote] (*AM*) *nm* green bean

┌─────────────────────┐
│ *PALABRA CLAVE* │
└─────────────────────┘

el [el] (*f* **la**, *pl* **los, las**, *neutro* **lo**) *art def* **1** the; **el libro/la mesa/los estudiantes** the book/table/students
2 (*con n abstracto: no se traduce*): **el amor/la juventud** love/youth
3 (*posesión: se traduce a menudo por adj posesivo*): **romperse el brazo** to break one's arm; **levantó la mano** he put his hand up; **se puso el sombrero** he put her hat on
4 (*valor descriptivo*): **tener la boca grande/los ojos azules** to have a big mouth/blue eyes
5 (*con días*) on; **me iré el viernes** I'll leave on Friday; **los domingos suelo ir a nadar** on Sundays I generally go swimming
6 (*lo + adj*): **lo difícil/caro** what is difficult/expensive; (= *cuán*): **no se da cuenta de lo pesado que es** he doesn't realize how boring he is
♦ *pron demos* **1**: **mi libro y el de usted** my book and yours; **las de Pepe son mejores** Pepe's are better; **no la(s) blanca(s) sino la(s) gris(es)** not the white one(s) but the grey one(s)
2: **lo de: lo de ayer** what happened yesterday; **lo de las facturas** that business about the invoices

♦ *pron relativo*: **el que** *etc* **1** (*indef*): **el (los) que quiera(n) que se vaya(n)** anyone who wants to can leave; **llévase el que más le guste** take the one you like best

2 (*def*): **el que compré ayer** the one I bought yesterday; **los que se van** those who leave

3: **lo que**: **lo que pienso yo/más me gusta** what I think/like most

♦ *conj*: **el que**: **el que lo diga** the fact that he says so; **el que sea tan vago me molesta** his being so lazy bothers me

♦ *excl*: **¡el susto que me diste!** what a fright you gave me!

♦ *pron personal* **1** (*persona*: *m*) him; (: *f*) her; (: *pl*) them; **lo/las veo** I can see him/them

2 (*animal, cosa*: *sg*) it; (: *pl*) them; **lo** (*o* **la**) **veo** I can see it; **los** (*o* **las**) **veo** I can see them

3: **lo** (*como sustituto de frase*): **no lo sabía** I didn't know; **ya lo entiendo** I understand now

él [el] *pron* (*persona*) he; (*cosa*) it; (*después de prep*: *persona*) him; (: *cosa*) it; **de ~** his

elaborar [elaβo'rar] *vt* (*producto*) to make, manufacture; (*preparar*) to prepare; (*madera, metal etc*) to work; (*proyecto etc*) to work on o out

elasticidad [elastiθi'ðað] *nf* elasticity

elástico, a [e'lastiko, a] *adj* elastic; (*flexible*) flexible ♦ *nm* elastic; (*un ~*) elastic band

elección [elek'θjon] *nf* election; (*selección*) choice, selection

electorado [elekto'raðo] *nm* electorate, voters *pl*

electricidad [elektriθi'ðað] *nf* electricity

electricista [elektri'θista] *nm/f* electrician

eléctrico, a [e'lektriko, a] *adj* electric

electro... [elektro] *prefijo* electro-;

~cardiograma *nm* electrocardiogram; **~cutar** *vt* to electrocute; **~do** *nm* electrode; **~domésticos** *nmpl* (electrical) household appliances; **~magnético, a** *adj* electromagnetic

electrónica [elek'tronika] *nf* electronics *sg*

electrónico, a [elek'troniko, a] *adj* electronic

elefante [ele'fante] *nm* elephant

elegancia [ele'xanθja] *nf* elegance, grace; (*estilo*) stylishness

elegante [ele'vante] *adj* elegant, graceful; (*estiloso*) stylish, fashionable

elegir [ele'xir] *vt* (*escoger*) to choose, select; (*optar*) to opt for; (*presidente*) to elect

elemental [elemen'tal] *adj* (*claro, obvio*) elementary; (*fundamental*) elemental, fundamental

elemento [ele'mento] *nm* element; (*fig*) ingredient; **~s** *nmpl* elements, rudiments

elepé [ele'pe] (*pl*: **elepés**) *nm* L.P.

elevación [eleβa'θjon] *nf* elevation; (*acto*) raising, lifting; (*de precios*) rise; (GEO *etc*) height, altitude

elevar [ele'βar] *vt* to raise, lift (up); (*precio*) to put up; **~se** *vr* (*edificio*) to rise; (*precios*) to go up

eligiendo *etc vb ver* **elegir**

elija *etc vb ver* **elegir**

eliminar [elimi'nar] *vt* to eliminate, remove

eliminatoria [elimina'torja] *nf* heat, preliminary (round)

elite [e'lite] *nf* elite

ella [e'ʎa] *pron* (*persona*) she; (*cosa*) it; (*después de prep*: *persona*) her; (: *cosa*) it; **de ~** hers

ellas [e'ʎas] *pron* (*personas y cosas*) they; (*después de prep*) them; **de ~** theirs

ello [e'ʎo] *pron* it

ellos [e'ʎos] *pron* they; (*después de prep*) them; **de ~** theirs

elocuencia [elo'kwenθja] *nf*

eloquence

elogiar [elo'xjar] vt to praise; **elogio** nm praise

elote [e'lote] (AM) nm corn on the cob

eludir [elu'ðir] vt to avoid

emanar [ema'nar] vi: ~ **de** to emanate from, come from; (derivar de) to originate in

emancipar [emanθi'par] vt to emancipate; ~**se** vr to become emancipated, free o.s.

embadurnar [embaður'nar] vt to smear

embajada [emba'xaða] nf embassy

embajador, a [embaxa'ðor, a] nm/f ambassador/ambassadress

embalaje [emba'laxe] nm packing

embalar [emba'lar] vt to parcel, wrap (up); ~**se** vr to go fast

embalsamar [embalsa'mar] vt to embalm

embalse [em'balse] nm (presa) dam; (lago) reservoir

embarazada [embara'ðaða] adj pregnant ♦ nf pregnant woman

embarazo [emba'raθo] nm (de mujer) pregnancy; (impedimento) obstacle, obstruction; (timidez) embarrassment; **embarazoso, a** adj awkward, embarrassing

embarcación [embarka'θjon] nf (barco) boat, craft; (acto) embarkation, boarding

embarcadero [embarka'ðero] nm pier, landing stage

embarcar [embar'kar] vt (cargamento) to ship, stow; (persona) to embark, put on board; ~**se** vr to embark, go on board

embargar [embar'var] vt (JUR) to seize, impound

embargo [em'barvo] nm (JUR) seizure; (COM, POL) embargo

embargue [em'barve] etc vb ver **embargar**

embarque etc [em'barke] vb ver **embarcar** ♦ nm shipment, loading

embaucar [embau'kar] vt to trick, fool

embeber [embe'ßer] vt (absorber) to absorb, soak up; (empapar) to saturate ♦ vi to shrink; ~**se** vr: ~**se en un libro** to be engrossed o absorbed in a book

embellecer [embeλe'θer] vt to embellish, beautify

embestida [embes'tiða] nf attack, onslaught; (carga) charge

embestir [embes'tir] vt to attack, assault; to charge, attack ♦ vi to attack

emblema [em'blema] nm emblem

embobado, a [embo'ßaðo, a] adj (atontado) stunned, bewildered

embolia [em'bolja] nf (MED) clot

émbolo ['embolo] nm (AUTO) piston

embolsar [embol'sar] vt to pocket, put in one's pocket

emborrachar [emborra'tʃar] vt to make drunk, intoxicate; ~**se** vr to get drunk

emboscada [embos'kaða] nf ambush

embotar [embo'tar] vt to blunt, dull; ~**se** vr (adormecerse) to go numb

embotellamiento [emboteλa'-mjento] nm (AUTO) traffic jam

embotellar [embote'λar] vt to bottle

embrague [em'braße] nm (tb: pedal de ~) clutch

embriagar [embrja'var] vt (emborrachar) to make drunk; ~**se** vr (emborracharse) to get drunk

embrión [em'brjon] nm embryo

embrollar [embro'λar] vt (el asunto) to confuse, complicate; (implicar) to involve, embroil; ~**se** vr (confundirse) to get into a muddle o mess

embrollo [em'broλo] nm (enredo) muddle, confusion; (aprieto) fix, jam

embrujado, a [embru'xaðo, a] adj bewitched; **casa embrujada** haunted house

embrutecer [embrute'θer] vt (atontar) to stupefy; ~**se** vr to be stupefied

embudo [em'buðo] nm funnel

embuste [em'buste] nm (mentira) lie;

~ro, a adj lying, deceitful ♦ nm/f (mentiroso) liar

embutido [embu'tiðo] nm (CULIN) sausage; (TEC) inlay

emergencia [emer'xenθja] nf emergency; (surgimiento) emergence

emerger [emer'xer] vi to emerge, appear

emigración [emiɣra'θjon] nf emigration; (de pájaros) migration

emigrar [emi'ɣrar] vi (personas) to emigrate; (pájaros) to migrate

eminencia [emi'nenθja] nf eminence; **eminente** adj eminent, distinguished; (elevado) high

emisario [emi'sarjo] nm emissary

emisión [emi'sjon] nf (acto) emission; (COM etc) issue; (RADIO, TV: acto) broadcasting; (: programa) broadcast, programme (BRIT), program (US)

emisora [emi'sora] nf radio o broadcasting station

emitir [emi'tir] vt (olor etc) to emit, give off; (moneda etc) to issue; (opinión) to express; (RADIO) to broadcast

emoción [emo'θjon] nf emotion; (excitación) excitement; (sentimiento) feeling

emocionante [emoθjo'nante] adj (excitante) exciting, thrilling

emocionar [emoθjo'nar] vt (excitar) to excite, thrill; (conmover) to move, touch; (impresionar) to impress

emotivo, a [emo'tiβo, a] adj emotional

empacar [empa'kar] vt (gen) to pack; (en caja) to bale, crate

empacho [em'patʃo] nm (MED) indigestion; (fig) embarrassment

empadronarse [empaðro'narse] vr (POL: como elector) to register

empalagoso, a [empala'ɣoso, a] adj cloying; (fig) tiresome

empalmar [empal'mar] vt to join, connect ♦ vi (dos caminos) to meet, join; **empalme** nm joint, connection;

junction; (de trenes) connection

empanada [empa'naða] nf pie, pasty

empantanarse [empanta'narse] vr to get swamped; (fig) to get bogged down

empañarse [empa'ɲarse] vr (cristales etc) to steam up

empapar [empa'par] vt (mojar) to soak, saturate; (absorber) to soak up, absorb; **~se** vr: **~se de** to soak up

empapelar [empape'lar] vt (paredes) to paper

empaquetar [empake'tar] vt to pack, parcel up

empastar [empas'tar] vt (embadurnar) to paste; (diente) to fill

empaste [em'paste] nm (de diente) filling

empatar [empa'tar] vi to draw, tie; **empate** nm draw, tie

empecé etc vb ver **empezar**

empedernido, a [empeðer'niðo, a] adj hard, heartless; (fumador) inveterate

empedrado, a [empe'ðraðo, a] adj paved ♦ nm paving

empeine [em'peine] nm (de pie, zapato) instep

empellón [empe'ʎon] nm push, shove

empeñado, a [empe'ɲaðo, a] adj (persona) determined; (objeto) pawned

empeñar [empe'ɲar] vt (objeto) to pawn, pledge; (persona) to compel; **~se** vr (endeudarse) to get into debt; **~se en** to be set on, be determined to

empeño [em'peɲo] nm (determinación, insistencia) determination, insistence; **casa de ~s** pawnshop

empeorar [empeo'rar] vt to make worse, worsen ♦ vi to get worse, deteriorate

empequeñecer [empekeɲe'θer] vt to dwarf; (minusvalorar) to belittle

emperador [empera'ðor] nm emperor; **emperatriz** nf empress

empezar [empe'θar] vt, vi to begin, start

empiece etc vb ver **empezar**

empiezo etc vb ver **empezar**

empinar [empi'nar] vt to raise; **~se** vr (persona) to stand on tiptoe; (animal) to rear up; (camino) to climb steeply

empírico, a [em'piriko, a] adj empirical

emplasto [em'plasto] nm (MED) plaster

emplazamiento [emplaθa'mjento] nm site, location; (JUR) summons

emplazar [empla'θar] vt (ubicar) to site, place, locate; (JUR) to summons; (convocar) to summon

empleado, a [emple'aðo, a] nm/f (gen) employee; (de banco etc) clerk

emplear [emple'ar] vt (usar) to use, employ; (dar trabajo a) to employ; **~se** vr (conseguir trabajo) to be employed; (ocuparse) to occupy o.s.

empleo [em'pleo] nm (puesto) job; (puestos: colectivamente) employment; (uso) use, employment

empobrecer [empoβre'θer] vt to impoverish; **~se** vr to become poor o impoverished

empollar [empo'ʎar] vt, vi to swot (up); **empollón, ona** (fam) nm/f swot

emporio [em'porjo] nm (AM: gran almacén) department store

empotrado, a [empo'traðo, a] adj (armario etc) built-in

emprender [empren'der] vt (empezar) to begin, embark on; (acometer) to tackle, take on

empresa [em'presa] nf (de espíritu etc) enterprise; (COM) company, firm; **~rio, a** nm/f (COM) businessman/woman

empréstito [em'prestito] nm (public) loan

empujar [empu'xar] vt to push, shove

empujón [empu'xon] nm push, shove

empuñar [empu'ɲar] vt (asir) to grasp, take (firm) hold of

emular [emu'lar] vt to emulate; (rivalizar) to rival

---

en [en] prep **1** (posición) in; (: sobre) on; **está ~ el cajón** it's in the drawer; **~ Argentina/La Paz** in Argentina/La Paz; **~ la oficina/el colegio** at the office/school; **está ~ el suelo/quinto piso** it's on the floor/the fifth floor

2 (dirección) into; **entró ~ el aula** she went into the classroom; **meter algo ~ el bolso** to put sth into one's bag

3 (tiempo) in; on; **~ 1605/3 semanas/invierno** in 1605/3 weeks/ winter; **~ (el mes de) enero** in (the month of) January; **~ aquella ocasión/época** on that occasion/at that time

4 (precio) for; **lo vendió ~ 20 dólares** he sold it for 20 dollars

5 (diferencia) by; **reducir/aumentar ~ una tercera parte/un 20 por ciento** to reduce/increase by a third/ 20 per cent

6 (manera): **~ avión/autobús** by plane/bus; **escrito ~ inglés** written in English

7 (después de vb que indica gastar etc) on; **han cobrado demasiado ~ dietas** they've charged too much to expenses; **se le va la mitad del sueldo ~ comida** he spends half his salary on food

8 (tema, ocupación): **experto ~ la materia** expert on the subject; **trabaja ~ la construcción** he works in the building industry

9 (adj + **~** + infin): **lento ~ reaccionar** slow to react

└──────────────────┘

enaguas [e'naɣwas] nfpl petticoat sg, underskirt sg

enajenación [enaxena'θjon] nf: **~ mental** mental derangement

enajenar [enaxe'nar] vt (volver loco) to drive mad

enamorado, a [enamo'raðo, a] adj in love ♦ nm/f lover

enamorar |enamo'rar| vt to win the love of; **~se** vr: **~se de alguien** to fall in love with sb

enano, a |e'nano, a| adj tiny ♦ nm/f dwarf

enardecer |enarðe'θer| vt (pasiones) to fire, inflame; (persona) to fill with enthusiasm; **~se** vr: **~se por** to get excited about; (entusiasmarse) to get enthusiastic about

encabezamiento |enkaβeθa'mjento| nm (de carta) heading; (de periódico) headline

encabezar |enkaβe'θar| vt (movimiento, revolución) to lead, head; (lista) to head, be at the top of; (carta) to put a heading to

encadenar |enkaðe'nar| vt to chain (together); (poner grilletes a) to shackle

encajar |enka'xar| vt (ajustar): **~ (en)** to fit (into); (fam: golpe) to take ♦ vi to fit (well); (fig: corresponder a) to match; **~se** vr: **~se en un sillón** to squeeze into a chair

encaje |en'kaxe| nm (labor) lace

encalar |enka'lar| vt (pared) to whitewash

encallar |enka'ʎar| vi (NAUT) to run aground

encaminar |enkami'nar| vt to direct, send; **~se** vr: **~se a** to set out for

encantado, a |enkan'taðo, a| adj (hechizado) bewitched; (muy contento) delighted; **¡~!** how do you do, pleased to meet you

encantador, a |enkanta'ðor, a| adj charming, lovely ♦ nm/f magician, enchanter/enchantress

encantar |enkan'tar| vt (agradar) to charm, delight; (hechizar) to bewitch, cast a spell on; **me encanta eso** I love that; **encanto** nm (hechizo) spell, charm; (fig) charm, delight

encarcelar |enkarθe'lar| vt to imprison, jail

encarecer |enkare'θer| vt to put up the price of; **~se** vr to get dearer

encarecimiento |enkareθi'mjento| nm price increase

encargado, a |enkar'γaðo, a| adj in charge ♦ nm/f agent, representative; (responsable) responsible

encargar |enkar'γar| vt to entrust; (recomendar) to recommend; **~se** vr: **~se de** to look after, take charge of

encargo |en'karγo| nm (tarea) assignment, job; (responsabilidad) responsibility; (COM) order

encariñarse |enkari'ɲarse| vr: **~ con** to grow fond of, get attached to

encarnación |enkarna'θjon| nf incarnation, embodiment

encarnizado, a |enkarni'θaðo, a| adj (lucha) bloody, fierce

encarrilar |enkarri'lar| vt (tren) to put back on the rails; (fig) to correct, put on the right track

encasillar |enkasi'ʎar| vt (tb fig) to pigeonhole; (actor) to typecast

encauzar |enkau'θar| vt to channel

encendedor |enθende'ðor| nm lighter

encender |enθen'der| vt (con fuego) to light; (luz, radio) to put on, switch on; (avivar: pasiones) to inflame; **~se** vr to catch fire; (excitarse) to get excited; (de cólera) to flare up; (el rostro) to blush

encendido |enθen'diðo| nm (AUTO) ignition

encerado |enθe'raðo| nm (ESCOL) blackboard

encerrar |enθe'rrar| vt (confinar) to shut in, shut up; (comprender, incluir) to include, contain

encharcado, a |entʃar'kaðo, a| adj (terreno) flooded

encharcarse |entʃar'karse| vr to get flooded

enchufado, a |entʃu'faðo, a| (fam) nm/f well-connected person

enchufar |entʃu'far| vt (ELEC) to plug in; (TEC) to connect, fit together; **enchufe** nm (ELEC: clavija) plug;

(: *toma*) socket; (*de dos tubos*) joint, connection; (*fam: influencia*) contact, connection; (: *puesto*) cushy job

encía [en'θia] nf gum

encienda etc vb ver **encender**

encierro etc [en'θjerro] vb ver **encerrar ♦** nm shutting in, shutting up; (*calabozo*) prison

encima [en'θima] adv (*sobre*) above, over; (*además*) besides; **~ de** (*en*) on, on top of; (*sobre*) above, over; (*además de*) besides, on top of; **por ~ de** over; **¿llevas dinero ~?** have you (got) any money on you?; **se me vino ~** it took me by surprise

encina [en'θina] nf holm oak

encinta [en'θinta] adj pregnant

enclenque [en'klenke] adj weak, sickly

encoger [enko'xer] vt to shrink, contract; **~se** vr to shrink, contract; (*fig*) to cringe; **~se de hombros** to shrug one's shoulders

encolar [enko'lar] vt (*engomar*) to glue, paste; (*pegar*) to stick down

encolerizar [enkoleri'θar] vt to anger, provoke; **~se** vr to get angry

encomendar [enkomen'dar] vt to entrust, commend; **~se** vr: **~se a** to put one's trust in

encomiar [enko'mjar] vt to praise, pay tribute to

encomienda etc [enko'mjenda] vb ver **encomendar ♦** nm (*encargo*) charge, commission; (*elogio*) tribute; **~ postal** (AM) parcel post

encontrado, a [enkon'traðo, a] adj (*contrario*) contrary, conflicting

encontrar [enkon'trar] vt (*hallar*) to find; (*inesperadamente*) to meet, run into; **~se** vr to meet (each other); (*situarse*) to be (situated); **~se con** to meet; **~se bien (de salud)** to feel well

encrespar [enkres'par] vt (*cabellos*) to curl; (*fig*) to anger, irritate; **~se** vr (*el mar*) to get rough; (*fig*) to get cross, get irritated

encrucijada [enkruθi'xaða] nf crossroads sg

encuadernación [enkwaðerna'θjon] nf binding

encuadernador, a [enkwaðerna'ðor, a] nm/f bookbinder

encuadrar [enkwa'ðrar] vt (*retrato*) to frame; (*ajustar*) to fit, insert; (*contener*) to contain

encubrir [enku'ßrir] vt (*ocultar*) to hide, conceal; (*criminal*) to harbour, shelter

encuentro etc [en'kwentro] vb ver **encontrar ♦** nm (*de personas*) meeting; (AUTO etc) collision, crash; (DEPORTE) match, game; (MIL) encounter

encuesta [en'kwesta] nf inquiry, investigation; (*sondeo*) (public) opinion poll; **~ judicial** post mortem

encumbrar [enkum'brar] vt (*persona*) to exalt

endeble [en'deßle] adj (*argumento, excusa, persona*) weak

endémico, a [en'demiko, a] adj (MED) endemic; (*fig*) rife, chronic

endemoniado, a [endemo'njaðo, a] adj possessed (of the devil); (*travieso*) devilish

enderezar [endere'θar] vt (*poner derecho*) to straighten (out); (: *verticalmente*) to set upright; (*situación*) to straighten o sort out; (*dirigir*) to direct; **~se** vr (*persona sentada*) to straighten up

endeudarse [endeu'ðarse] vr to get into debt

endiablado, a [endja'ßlaðo, a] adj devilish, diabolical; (*travieso*) mischievous

endilgar [endil'var] (*fam*) vt: **~le algo a uno** to lumber sb with sth; **~le un sermón a uno** to lecture sb

endiñar [endi'nar] (*fam*) vt (*bofetón*) to land, belt

endosar [endo'sar] vt (*cheque etc*) to endorse

endulzar [endul'θar] vt to sweeten; (suavizar) to soften

endurecer [endure'θer] vt to harden; **~se** vr to harden, grow hard

enema [e'nema] nm (MED) enema

enemigo, a [ene'mixo, a] adj enemy, hostile ♦ nm/f enemy

enemistad [enemis'tað] nf enmity

enemistar [enemis'tar] vt to make enemies of, cause a rift between; **~se** vr to become enemies; (amigos) to fall out

energía [ener'xia] nf (vigor) energy, drive; (empuje) push; (TEC, ELEC) energy, power; **~ eólica** wind power; **~ solar** solar energy/power

enérgico, a [e'nerxiko, a] adj (gen) energetic; (voz, modales) forceful

energúmeno [ener'vumeno, a] nm/f (fig) madman/woman

enero [e'nero] nm January

enfadado, a [enfa'ðaðo, a] adj angry, annoyed

enfadar [enfa'ðar] vt to anger, annoy; **~se** vr to get angry o annoyed

enfado [en'faðo] nm (enojo) anger, annoyance; (disgusto) trouble, bother

énfasis ['enfasis] nm emphasis, stress

enfático, a [en'fatiko, a] adj emphatic

enfermar [enfer'mar] vt to make ill ♦ vi to fall ill, be taken ill

enfermedad [enferme'ðað] nf illness; **~ venérea** venereal disease

enfermera [enfer'mera] nf nurse

enfermería [enferme'ria] nf infirmary; (de colegio etc) sick bay

enfermero [enfer'mero] nm (male) nurse

enfermizo, a [enfer'miθo, a] adj (persona) sickly, unhealthy; (fig) unhealthy

enfermo, a [en'fermo, a] adj ill, sick ♦ nm/f invalid, sick person; (en hospital) patient

enflaquecer [enflake'θer] vt (adelgazar) to make thin; (debilitar) to weaken

enfocar [enfo'kar] vt (foto etc) to focus; (problema etc) to approach

enfoque etc [en'foke] vb ver **enfocar** ♦ nm focus.

enfrascarse [enfras'karse] vr: **~ en algo** to bury o.s. in sth

enfrentar [enfren'tar] vt (peligro) to face (up to), confront; (oponer) to bring face to face; **~se** vr (dos personas) to face o confront each other; (DEPORTE: dos equipos) to meet; **~se a** o **con** to face up to, confront

enfrente [en'frente] adv opposite; **la casa de ~** the house opposite, the house across the street; **~ de** opposite, facing

enfriamiento [enfria'mjento] nm chilling, refrigeration; (MED) cold, chill

enfriar [enfri'ar] vt (alimentos) to cool, chill; (algo caliente) to cool down; **~se** vr to cool down; (MED) to catch a chill; (amistad) to cool

enfurecer [enfure'θer] vt to enrage, madden; **~se** vr to become furious, fly into a rage; (mar) to get rough

engalanar [engala'nar] vt (adornar) to adorn; (ciudad) to decorate; **~se** vr to get dressed up

enganchar [engan'tʃar] vt to hook; (dos vagones) to hitch up; (TEC) to couple, connect; (MIL) to recruit; **~se** vr (MIL) to enlist, join up

enganche [en'gantʃe] nm hook; (TEC) coupling, connection; (acto) hooking (up); (MIL) recruitment, enlistment; (AM: depósito) deposit

engañar [enga'ɲar] vt to deceive; (estafar) to cheat, swindle; **~se** vr (equivocarse) to be wrong; (disimular la verdad) to deceive o.s.

engaño [en'gaɲo] nm deceit; (estafa) trick, swindle; (error) mistake, misunderstanding; (ilusión) delusion; **~so, a** adj (tramposo) crooked; (mentiroso) dishonest, deceitful; (aspecto) deceptive; (consejo) misleading

engarzar [engar'θar] vt (joya) to set, mount; (fig) to link, connect

engatusar [engatu'sar] (fam) vt to coax

engendrar [enxen'drar] vt to breed; (procrear) to beget; (causar) to cause, produce; **engendro** nm (BIO) foetus; (fig) monstrosity

englobar [englo'Bar] vt to include, comprise

engordar [engor'ðar] vt to fatten ♦ vi to get fat, put on weight

engorroso, a [engo'rroso, a] adj bothersome, trying

engranaje [engra'naxe] nm (AUTO) gear

engrandecer [engrande'θer] vt to enlarge, magnify; (alabar) to praise, speak highly of; (exagerar) to exaggerate

engrasar [engra'sar] vt (TEC: poner grasa) to grease; (: lubricar) to lubricate, oil; (manchar) to make greasy

engreído, a [engre'iðo, a] adj vain, conceited

engrosar [engro'sar] vt (ensanchar) to enlarge; (aumentar) to increase; (hinchar) to swell

enhebrar [ene'βrar] vt to thread

enhorabuena [enora'βwena] excl ¡~! congratulations! ♦ nf: **dar la ~ a** to congratulate

enigma [e'niɣma] nm enigma; (problema) puzzle; (misterio) mystery

enjabonar [enxaβo'nar] vt to soap; (fam: adular) to soft-soap

enjambre [en'xambre] nm swarm

enjaular [enxau'lar] vt (put in a) cage; (fam) to jail, lock up

enjuagar [enxwa'ɣar] vt (ropa) to rinse (out)

enjuague etc [en'xwaɣe] vb ver **enjuagar** ♦ nm (MED) mouthwash; (de ropa) rinse, rinsing

enjugar [enxu'ɣar] vt to wipe (off); (lágrimas) to dry; (déficit) to wipe out

enjuiciar [enxwi'θjar] vt (JUR: procesar) to prosecute, try; (fig) to judge

enjuto, a [en'xuto, a] adj (flaco) lean, skinny

enlace [en'laθe] nm link, connection; (relación) relationship; (tb: ~ matrimonial) marriage; (de carretera, trenes) connection; ~ **sindical** shop steward

enlatado, a [enla'taðo, a] adj (comida, productos) tinned, canned

enlazar [enla'θar] vt (unir con lazos) to bind together; (atar) to tie; (conectar) to link, connect; (AM) to lasso

enlodar [enlo'ðar] vt to cover in mud; (fig: manchar) to stain; (: rebajar) to debase

enloquecer [enloke'θer] vt to drive mad ♦ vi to go mad; ~**se** vr to go mad

enlutado, a [enlu'taðo, a] adj (persona) in mourning

enmarañar [enmara'nar] vt (enredar) to tangle (up), entangle; (complicar) to complicate; (confundir) to confuse; ~**se** vr (enredarse) to become entangled; (confundirse) to get confused

enmarcar [enmar'kar] vt (cuadro) to frame

enmascarar [enmaska'rar] vt to mask; ~**se** vr to put on a mask

enmendar [enmen'dar] vt to emend, correct; (constitución etc) to amend; (comportamiento) to reform; ~**se** vr to reform, mend one's ways; **enmienda** nf correction; amendment; reform

enmohecerse [enmoe'θerse] vr (metal) to rust, go rusty; (muro, plantas) to get mouldy

enmudecer [enmuðe'θer] vi (perder el habla) to fall silent; (guardar silencio) to remain silent

ennegrecer [ennexre'θer] vt (poner negro) to blacken; (oscurecer) to darken; ~**se** vr to turn black; (oscurecerse) to get dark, darken

ennoblecer [ennoβle'θer] vt to ennoble

enojar [eno'xar] vt (encolerizar) to

anger; (*disgustar*) to annoy, upset; **~se** *vr* to get angry; to get annoyed

enojo [e'noxo] *nm* (*cólera*) anger; (*irritación*) annoyance; **~so, a** *adj* annoying

enorgullecerse [enorɣuʎe'θerse] *vr* to be proud; **~ de** to pride o.s. on, be proud of

enorme [e'norme] *adj* enormous, huge; (*fig*) monstrous; **enormidad** *nf* hugeness, immensity

enrarecido, a [enrare'θiðo, a] *adj* (*atmósfera, aire*) rarefied

enredadera [enreða'ðera] *nf* (*BOT*) creeper, climbing plant

enredar [enre'ðar] *vt* (*cables, hilos etc*) to tangle (up), entangle; (*situación*) to complicate, confuse; (*sembrar cizaña*) to sow discord among o between; (*implicar*) to embroil, implicate; **~se** *vr* to get entangled, get tangled (up); (*situación*) to get complicated; (*persona*) to get embroiled; (*AM: fam*) to meddle

enredo [en'reðo] *nm* (*maraña*) tangle; (*confusión*) mix-up, confusion; (*intriga*) intrigue

enrejado [enre'xaðo] *nm* fence, railings *pl*

enrevesado, a [enreβe'saðo, a] *adj* (*asunto*) complicated, involved

enriquecer [enrike'θer] *vt* to make rich, enrich; **~se** *vr* to get rich

enrojecer [enroxe'θer] *vt* to redden ♦ *vi* (*persona*) to blush; **~se** *vr* to blush

enrolar [enro'lar] *vt* (*MIL*) to enlist; (*reclutar*) to recruit; **~se** *vr* (*MIL*) to join up; (*afiliarse*) to enrol

enrollar [enro'ʎar] *vt* to roll (up), wind (up)

enroscar [enros'kar] *vt* (*torcer, doblar*) to coil (round), wind; (*tornillo, rosca*) to screw in; **~se** *vr* to coil, wind

ensalada [ensa'laða] *nf* salad; **ensaladilla (rusa)** *nf* Russian salad

ensalzar [ensal'θar] *vt* (*alabar*) to praise, extol; (*exaltar*) to exalt

ensamblaje [ensam'blaxe] *nm* assembly; (*TEC*) joint

ensanchar [ensan'tʃar] *vt* (*hacer más ancho*) to widen; (*agrandar*) to enlarge, expand; (*COSTURA*) to let out; **~se** *vr* to get wider, expand; **ensanche** *nm* (*de calle*) widening

ensangrentar [ensangren'tar] *vt* to stain with blood

ensañar [ensa'ɲar] *vt* to enrage; **~se** *vr*: **~se con** to treat brutally

ensartar [ensar'tar] *vt* (*cuentas, perlas etc*) to string (together)

ensayar [ensa'jar] *vt* to test, try (out); (*TEATRO*) to rehearse

ensayo [en'sajo] *nm* test, trial; (*QUÍM*) experiment; (*TEATRO*) rehearsal; (*DEPORTE*) try; (*ESCOL, LITERATURA*) essay

enseguida [ense'ɣiða] *adv* at once, right away

ensenada [ense'naða] *nf* inlet, cove

enseñanza [ense'ɲanθa] *nf* (*educación*) education; (*acción*) teaching; (*doctrina*) teaching, doctrine

enseñar [ense'ɲar] *vt* (*educar*) to teach; (*mostrar, señalar*) to show

enseres [en'seres] *nmpl* belongings

ensillar [ensi'ʎar] *vt* to saddle (up)

ensimismarse [ensimis'marse] *vr* (*abstraerse*) to become lost in thought; (*AM*) to become conceited

ensombrecer [ensombre'θer] *vt* to darken, cast a shadow over; (*fig*) to overshadow, put in the shade

ensordecer [ensorðe'θer] *vt* to deafen ♦ *vi* to go deaf

ensortijado, a [ensorti'xaðo, a] *adj* (*pelo*) curly

ensuciar [ensu'θjar] *vt* (*manchar*) to dirty, soil; (*fig*) to defile; **~se** *vr* to get dirty; (*niño*) to wet o.s.

ensueño [en'sweno] *nm* (*sueño*) dream, fantasy; (*ilusión*) illusion; (*soñando despierto*) daydream

entablar [enta'βlar] *vt* (*recubrir*) to board (up); (*AJEDREZ, DAMAS*) to set up; (*conversación*) to strike up; (*JUR*) to file

♦ *vi* to draw

entablillar |entaβli'ʎar| *vt* (MED) to (put in a) splint

entallar |enta'ʎar| *vt* (traje) to tailor ♦ *vi*: **el traje entalla bien** the suit fits well

ente |'ente| *nm* (organización) body, organization; (fam: persona) odd character

entender |enten'der| *vt* (comprender) to understand; (darse cuenta) to realize ♦ *vi* to understand; (creer) to think, believe; **~se** *vr* (comprenderse) to be understood; (2 personas) to get on together; (ponerse de acuerdo) to agree, reach an agreement; **~ de** to know all about; **~ algo de** to know a little about; **~ en** to deal with, have to do with; **~se mal** (2 personas) to get on badly

entendido, a |enten'diðo, a| *adj* (comprendido) understood; (hábil) skilled; (inteligente) knowledgeable ♦ *nm/f* (experto) expert ♦ *excl* agreed!; **entendimiento** *nm* (comprensión) understanding; (inteligencia) mind, intellect; (juicio) judgement

enterado, a |ente'raðo, a| *adj* well-informed; **estar ~ de** to know about, be aware of

enteramente |entera'mente| *adv* entirely, completely

enterar |ente'rar| *vt* (informar) to inform, tell; **~se** *vr* to find out, get to know

entereza |ente're θa| *nf* (totalidad) entirety; (fig: carácter) strength of mind; (: honradez) integrity

enternecer |enterne'θer| *vt* (ablandar) to soften; (apiadar) to touch, move; **~se** *vr* to be touched, be moved

entero, a |en'tero, a| *adj* (total) whole, entire; (fig: honesto) honest; (: firme) firm, resolute ♦ *nm* (COM: punto) point; (AM: pago) payment

enterrador |enterra'ðor| *nm* gravedigger

enterrar |ente'rrar| *vt* to bury

entibiar |enti'βjar| *vt* (enfriar) to cool; (calentar) to warm; **~se** *vr* (fig) to cool

entidad |enti'ðað| *nf* (empresa) firm, company; (organismo) body; (sociedad) society; (FILOSOFÍA) entity

entiendo *etc vb ver* **entender**

entierro |en'tjerro| *nm* (acción) burial; (funeral) funeral

entonación |entona'θjon| *nf* (LING) intonation

entonar |ento'nar| *vt* (canción) to intone; (colores) to tone; (MED) to tone up ♦ *vi* to be in tune

entonces |en'tonθes| *adv* then, at that time; **desde ~** since then; **en aquel ~** at that time; **(pues) ~** and so

entornar |entor'nar| *vt* (puerta, ventana) to half close, leave ajar; (los ojos) to screw up

entorpecer |entorpe'θer| *vt* (entendimiento) to dull; (impedir) to obstruct, hinder; (: tránsito) to slow down, delay

entrada |en'traða| *nf* (acción) entry, access; (sitio) entrance, way in; (INFORM) input; (COM) receipts *pl*, takings *pl*; (CULIN) starter; (DEPORTE) innings *sg*; (TEATRO) house, audience; (billete) ticket; (COM): **~s y salidas** income and expenditure; (TEC): **~ de aire** air intake *o* inlet; **de ~** from the outset

entrado, a |en'traðo, a| *adj*: **~ en años** elderly; **una vez ~ el verano** in the summer(time), when summer comes

entramparse |entram'parse| *vr* to get into debt

entrante |en'trante| *adj* next, coming; **mes/año ~** next month/year; **~s** *nmpl* starters

entraña |en'traɲa| *nf* (fig: centro) heart, core; (raíz) root; **~s** *nfpl* (ANAT) entrails; (fig) heart; **sin ~s** (fig) heartless; **entrañable** *adj* close, intimate; **entrañar** *vt* to entail

entrar [en'trar] vt (*introducir*) to bring in; (*INFORM*) to input ♦ vi (*meterse*) to go in, come in, enter; (*comenzar*): ~ **diciendo** to begin by saying; **hacer** ~ to show in; **no me entra** I can't get the hang of it

entre ['entre] prep (*dos*) between; (*más de dos*) among(st)

entreabrir [entrea'βrir] vt to half-open, open halfway

entrecejo [entre'θexo] nm: **fruncir el** ~ to frown

entrecortado, a [entrekor'taðo, a] adj (*respiración*) difficult; (*habla*) faltering

entredicho [entre'ðitʃo] nm (*JUR*) injunction; **poner en** ~ to cast doubt on; **estar en** ~ to be in doubt

entrega [en'treγa] nf (*de mercancías*) delivery; (*de novela etc*) instalment

entregar [entre'γar] vt (*dar*) to hand (over), deliver; ~**se** vr (*rendirse*) to surrender, give in, submit; (*dedicarse*) to devote o.s.

entrelazar [entrela'θar] vt to entwine

entremeses [entre'meses] nmpl hors d'oeuvres

entremeter [entreme'ter] vt to insert, put in; ~**se** vr to meddle, interfere; **entremetido, a** adj meddling, interfering

entremezclar [entremeθ'klar] vt to intermingle; ~**se** vr to intermingle

entrenador, a [entrena'ðor, a] nm/f trainer, coach

entrenarse [entre'narse] vr to train

entrepierna [entre'pjerna] nf crotch

entresacar [entresa'kar] vt to pick out, select

entresuelo [entre'swelo] nm mezzanine

entretanto [entre'tanto] adv meanwhile, meantime

entretejer [entrete'xer] vt to interweave

entretener [entrete'ner] vt (*divertir*) to entertain, amuse; (*detener*) to hold up,

delay; ~**se** vr (*divertirse*) to amuse o.s.; (*retrasarse*) to delay, linger;
entretenido, a adj entertaining, amusing; **entretenimiento** nm entertainment, amusement

entrever [entre'βer] vt to glimpse, catch a glimpse of

entrevista [entre'βista] nf interview; **entrevistar** vt to interview; **entrevistarse** vr to have an interview

entristecer [entriste'θer] vt to sadden, grieve; ~**se** vr to grow sad

entrometerse [entrome'terse] vr: ~ **(en)** to interfere (in o with)

entroncar [entron'kar] vi to be connected o related

entumecer [entume'θer] vt to numb, benumb; ~**se** vr (*por el frío*) to go o become numb; **entumecido, a** adj numb, stiff

enturbiar [entur'βjar] vt (*el agua*) to make cloudy; (*fig*) to confuse; ~**se** vr (*oscurecerse*) to become cloudy; (*fig*) to get confused, become obscure

entusiasmar [entusjas'mar] vt to excite, fill with enthusiasm; (*gustar mucho*) to delight; ~**se** vr: ~**se con** o **por** to get enthusiastic o excited about

entusiasmo [entu'sjasmo] nm enthusiasm; (*excitación*) excitement

entusiasta [entu'sjasta] adj enthusiastic ♦ nm/f enthusiast

enumerar [enume'rar] vt to enumerate

enunciación [enunθja'θjon] nf enunciation

enunciado [enun'θjaðo] nm enunciation

envainar [embai'nar] vt to sheathe

envalentonar [embalento'nar] vt to give courage to; ~**se** vr (*pey: jactarse*) to boast, brag

envanecer [embane'θer] vt to make conceited; ~**se** vr to grow conceited

envasar [emba'sar] vt (*empaquetar*) to pack, wrap; (*enfrascar*) to bottle; (*enlatar*) to can; (*embolsar*) to pocket

envase |em'base| nm (en paquete)
packing, wrapping; (en botella)
bottling; (en lata) canning; (recipiente)
container; (paquete) package; (botella)
bottle; (lata) tin (BRIT), can

envejecer |embexe'θer| vt to make
old, age ♦ vi (volverse viejo) to grow
old; (parecer viejo) to age; ~se vr to
grow old; to age

envenenar |embene'nar| vt to poison;
(fig) to embitter

envergadura |emberva'δura| nf (fig)
scope, compass

envés |em'bes| nm (de tela) back,
wrong side

enviar |em'bjar| vt to send

enviciarse |embi'θjarse| vr: ~ (con) to
get addicted (to)

envidia |em'biδja| nf envy; **tener ~ a**
to envy, be jealous of; **envidiar** vt to
envy

envío |em'bio| nm (acción) sending;
(de mercancías) consignment; (de
dinero) remittance

enviudar |embju'δar| vi to be
widowed

envoltura |embol'tura| nf (cobertura)
cover; (embalaje) wrapper, wrapping;
envoltorio nm package

envolver |embol'βer| vt to wrap (up);
(cubrir) to cover; (enemigo) to
surround; (implicar) to involve,
implicate

envuelto |em'bwelto| pp de **envolver**

enyesar |enje'sar| vt (pared) to plaster;
(MED) to put in plaster

enzarzarse |enθar'θarse| vr: ~ **en**
(pelea) to get mixed up in; (disputa) to
get involved in

épica |'epika| nf epic

épico, a |'epiko, a| adj epic

epidemia |epi'δemja| nf epidemic

epilepsia |epi'lepsja| nf epilepsy

epílogo |e'pilovo| nm epilogue

episodio |epi'soδjo| nm episode

epístola |e'pistola| nf epistle

época |'epoka| nf period, time;

(HISTORIA) age, epoch; **hacer ~** to be
epoch-making

equilibrar |ekili'ßrar| vt to balance;
equilibrio nm balance, equilibrium;
equilibrista nm/f (funámbulo)
tightrope walker; (acróbata) acrobat

equipaje |eki'paxe| nm luggage;
(avíos): ~ **de mano** hand luggage

equipar |eki'par| vt (proveer) to equip

equipararse |ekipa'rarse| vr: ~ **con** to
be on a level with

equipo |e'kipo| nm (conjunto de cosas)
equipment; (DEPORTE) team; (de
obreros) shift

equis |'ekis| nf inv (the letter) X

equitación |ekita'θjon| nf horse riding

equitativo, a |ekita'tißo, a| adj
equitable, fair

equivalente |ekißa'lente| adj, nm
equivalent

equivaler |ekißa'ler| vi to be
equivalent o equal

equivocación |ekißoka'θjon| nf
mistake, error

equivocado, a |ekißo'kaδo, a| adj
wrong, mistaken

equivocarse |ekißo'karse| vr to be
wrong, make a mistake; ~ **de camino**
to take the wrong road

equívoco, a |e'kißoko, a| adj (dudoso)
suspect; (ambiguo) ambiguous ♦ nm
ambiguity; (malentendido)
misunderstanding

era |'era| vb ver **ser** ♦ nf era, age

erais vb ver **ser**

éramos vb ver **ser**

eran vb ver **ser**

erario |e'rarjo| nm exchequer (BRIT),
treasury

eras vb ver **ser**

erección |erek'θjon| nf erection

eres vb ver **ser**

erguir |er'xir| vt to raise, lift; (poner
derecho) to straighten; ~se vr to
straighten up

erigir |eri'xir| vt to erect, build; ~se vr:
~se **en** to set o.s. up as

erizarse [eri'θarse] vr (*pelo: de perro*) to bristle; (: *de persona*) to stand on end

erizo [e'riθo] nm (ZOOL) hedgehog; **~ de mar** sea-urchin

ermita [er'mita] nf hermitage

ermitaño, a [ermi'taɲo, a] nm/f hermit

erosión [ero'sjon] nf erosion

erosionar [erosjo'nar] vt to erode

erótico, a [e'rotiko, a] adj erotic; **erotismo** nm eroticism

erradicar [erraði'kar] vt to eradicate

errante [e'rrante] adj wandering, errant

errar [e'rrar] vi (*vagar*) to wander, roam; (*equivocarse*) to be mistaken ♦ vt: **~ el camino** to take the wrong road; **~ el tiro** to miss

erróneo, a [e'rroneo, a] adj (*equivocado*) wrong, mistaken

error [e'rror] nm error, mistake; (INFORM) bug; **~ de imprenta** misprint

eructar [eruk'tar] vt to belch, burp

erudito, a [eru'ðito, a] adj erudite, learned

erupción [erup'θjon] nf eruption; (MED) rash

es vb ver **ser**

esa ['esa] (pl **esas**) adj demos ver **ese**

ésa ['esa] (pl **ésas**) pron ver **ése**

esbelto, a [es'ßelto, a] adj slim, slender

esbozo [es'ßoθo] nm sketch, outline

escabeche [eska'ßetʃe] nm brine; (*de aceitunas etc*) pickle; **en ~** pickled

escabroso, a [eska'ßroso, a] adj (*accidentado*) rough, uneven; (*fig*) tough, difficult; (: *atrevido*) risqué

escabullirse [eskaßu'ʎirse] vr to slip away, to clear out

escafandra [eska'fandra] nf (*buzo*) diving suit; (~ *espacial*) space suit

escala [es'kala] nf (*proporción, MUS*) scale; (*de mano*) ladder; (AVIAT) stopover; **hacer ~ en** to stop o call in

escalafón [eskala'fon] nm (*escala de salarios*) salary scale, wage scale

escalar [eska'lar] vt to climb, scale

escalera [eska'lera] nf stairs pl, staircase; (*escala*) ladder; (NAIPES) run; **~ mecánica** (*escalator*); **~ de caracol** spiral staircase

escalfar [eskal'far] vt (*huevos*) to poach

escalinata [eskali'nata] nf staircase

escalofriante [eskalo'frjante] adj chilling

escalofrío [eskalo'frio] nm (MED) chill; **~s** nmpl (fig) shivers

escalón [eska'lon] nm step, stair; (*de escalera*) rung

escalope [eska'lope] nm (CULIN) escalope

escama [es'kama] nf (*de pez, serpiente*) scale; (*de jabón*) flake; (fig) resentment

escamar [eska'mar] vt (fig) to make wary o suspicious

escamotear [eskamote'ar] vt (*robar*) to lift, swipe; (*hacer desaparecer*) to make disappear

escampar [eskam'par] vb impers to stop raining

escandalizar [eskandali'θar] vt to scandalize, shock; **~se** vr to be shocked; (*ofenderse*) to be offended

escándalo [es'kandalo] nm scandal; (*alboroto, tumulto*) row, uproar; **escandaloso, a** adj scandalous, shocking

escandinavo, a [eskandi'naßo, a] adj, nm/f Scandinavian

escaño [es'kaɲo] nm bench; (POL) seat

escapar [eska'par] vi (*gen*) to escape, run away; (DEPORTE) to break away; **~se** vr to escape, get away; (*agua, gas*) to leak (out)

escaparate [eskapa'rate] nm shop window

escape [es'kape] nm (*de agua, gas*) leak; (*de motor*) exhaust

escarabajo [eskara'ßaxo] nm beetle

escaramuza [eskara'muθa] nf skirmish

escarbar [eskar'ßar] vt (tierra) to scratch

escarceos [eskar'θeos] nmpl (fig): **en mis ~ con la política ...** in my dealings with politics ...; **~ amorosos** love affairs

escarcha [es'kartʃa] nf frost

escarchado, a [eskar'tʃaðo, a] adj (CULIN: fruta) crystallized

escarlata [eskar'lata] adj inv scarlet; **escarlatina** nf scarlet fever

escarmentar [eskarmen'tar] vt to punish severely ♦ vi to learn one's lesson

escarmiento etc [eskar'mjento] vb ver **escarmentar** ♦ nm (ejemplo) lesson; (castigo) punishment

escarnio [es'karnjo] nm mockery; (injuria) insult

escarola [eska'rola] nf endive

escarpado, a [eskar'paðo, a] adj (pendiente) sheer, steep; (rocas) craggy

escasear [eskase'ar] vi to be scarce

escasez [eska'seθ] nf (falta) shortage, scarcity; (pobreza) poverty

escaso, a [es'kaso, a] adj (poco) scarce; (raro) rare; (ralo) thin, sparse; (limitado) limited

escatimar [eskati'mar] vt to skimp (on), be sparing with

escayola [eska'jola] nf plaster

escena [es'θena] nf scene

escenario [esθe'narjo] nm (TEATRO) stage; (CINE) set; (fig) scene; **escenografía** nf set design

escepticismo [esθepti'θismo] nm scepticism; **escéptico, a** adj sceptical ♦ nm/f sceptic

escisión [esθi'sjon] nf (de partido, secta) split

esclarecer [esklare'θer] vt (misterio, problema) to shed light on

esclavitud [esklaßi'tuð] nf slavery

esclavizar [esklaßi'θar] vt to enslave

esclavo, a [es'klaßo, a] nm/f slave

esclusa [es'klusa] nf (de canal) lock; (compuerta) floodgate

escoba [es'koßa] nf broom; **escobilla** nf brush

escocer [esko'θer] vi to burn, sting; **~se** vr to chafe, get chafed

escocés, esa [esko'θes, esa] adj Scottish ♦ nm/f Scotsman/woman, Scot

Escocia [es'koθja] nf Scotland

escoger [esko'xer] vt to choose, pick, select; **escogido, a** adj chosen, selected

escolar [esko'lar] adj school cpd ♦ nm/f schoolboy/girl, pupil

escollo [es'koʎo] nm (obstáculo) pitfall

escolta [es'kolta] nf escort; **escoltar** vt to escort

escombros [es'kombros] nmpl (basura) rubbish sg; (restos) debris sg

esconder [eskon'der] vt to hide, conceal; **~se** vr to hide; **escondidas** (AM) nfpl: **a escondidas** secretly; **escondite** nm hiding place; (juego) hide-and-seek; **escondrijo** nm hiding place, hideout

escopeta [esko'peta] nf shotgun

escoria [es'korja] nf (de alto horno) slag; (fig) scum, dregs pl

Escorpio [es'korpjo] nm Scorpio

escorpión [eskor'pjon] nm scorpion

escotado, a [esko'taðo, a] adj low-cut

escote [es'kote] nm (de vestido) low neck; **pagar a ~** to share the expenses

escotilla [esko'tiʎa] nf (NAUT) hatch(way)

escozor [esko'θor] nm (dolor) sting(ing)

escribir [eskri'ßir] vt, vi to write; **~ a máquina** to type; **¿cómo se escribe?** how do you spell it?

escrito, a [es'krito, a] pp de **escribir** ♦ nm (documento) document; (manuscrito) text, manuscript; **por ~** in writing

escritor, a [eskri'tor, a] nm/f writer

escritorio [eskri'torjo] nm desk

escritura [eskri'tura] nf (acción) writing; (caligrafía) (hand)writing; (JUR: documento) deed

escrúpulo [es'krupulo] nm scruple; (*minuciosidad*) scrupulousness; **escrupuloso, a** adj scrupulous

escrutar [eskru'tar] vt to scrutinize, examine; (*votos*) to count

escrutinio [eskru'tinjo] nm (*examen atento*) scrutiny; (POL: *recuento de votos*) count(ing)

escuadra [es'kwaðra] nf (MIL etc) squad; (NAUT) squadron; (*de coches etc*) fleet; **escuadrilla** nf (*de aviones*) squadron; (AM: *de obreros*) gang

escuadrón [eskwa'ðron] nm squadron

escuálido, a [es'kwaliðo, a] adj skinny, scraggy; (*sucio*) squalid

escuchar [esku'tʃar] vt to listen to ♦ vi to listen

escudilla [esku'ðiʎa] nf bowl, basin

escudo [es'kuðo] nm shield

escudriñar [eskuðri'nar] vt (*examinar*) to investigate, scrutinize; (*mirar de lejos*) to scan

escuela [es'kwela] nf school; ~ **de artes y oficios** (ESP) ≈ technical college; ~ **normal** teacher training college

escueto, a [es'kweto, a] adj plain; (*estilo*) simple

escuincle [es'kwinkle] (AM: fam) nm/f kid

esculpir [eskul'pir] vt to sculpt; (*grabar*) to engrave; (*tallar*) to carve; **escultor, a** nm/f sculptor/tress; **escultura** nf sculpture

escupidera [eskupi'ðera] nf spittoon

escupir [esku'pir] vt, vi to spit (out)

escurreplatos [eskurre'platos] nm inv plate rack

escurridizo, a [eskurri'ðiθo, a] adj slippery

escurridor [eskurri'ðor] nm colander

escurrir [esku'rrir] vt (*ropa*) to wring out; (*verduras, platos*) to strain ♦ vi (*líquidos*) to drip; **~se** vr (*secarse*) to drain; (*resbalarse*) to slip, slide; (*escaparse*) to slip away

ese [e'se] (f **esa**, pl **esos, esas**) adj

demos (sg) that; (pl) those

ése [e'se] (f **ésa**, pl **ésos, ésas**) pron (sg) that (one); (pl) those (ones); ~ ... **éste** ... the former ... the latter ...; **no me vengas con ésas** don't give me any more of that nonsense

esencia [e'senθja] nf essence; **esencial** adj essential

esfera [es'fera] nf sphere; (*de reloj*) face; **esférico, a** adj spherical

esforzarse [esfor'θarse] vr to exert o.s., make an effort

esfuerzo etc [es'fwerθo] vb ver **esforzar** ♦ nm effort

esfumarse [esfu'marse] vr (*apoyo, esperanzas*) to fade away

esgrima [es'γrima] nf fencing

esgrimir [esγri'mir] vt (*arma*) to brandish; (*argumento*) to use

esguince [es'γinθe] nm (MED) sprain

eslabón [esla'βon] nm link

eslip [ez'lip] nm pants pl (BRIT), briefs pl

eslovaco, a [eslo'βako, a] adj, nm/f Slovak, Slovakian ♦ nm (LING) Slovak, Slovakian

Eslovaquia [eslo'βakja] nf Slovakia

esmaltar [esmal'tar] vt to enamel; **esmalte** nm enamel; **esmalte de uñas** nail varnish o polish

esmerado, a [esme'raðo, a] adj careful, neat

esmeralda [esme'ralda] nf emerald

esmerarse [esme'rarse] vr (*aplicarse*) to take great pains, exercise great care; (*afanarse*) to work hard

esmero [es'mero] nm (*great*) care

esnob [es'nob] (pl ~**s**) adj (*persona*) snobbish ♦ nm/f snob; ~**ismo** nm snobbery

eso [e'so] pron that, that thing o matter; ~ **de** su coche that business about his car; ~ **de ir al cine** all that about going to the cinema; **a ~ de las cinco** at about five o'clock; **en ~** thereupon, at that point; ~ **es** that's it; ¡~ **sí que es vida!** now that is really living!; **por ~ te lo dije** that's why I told you; **y ~ que llovía** in spite of the fact it was raining

esos ['esos] adj demos ver **ese**

ésos ['esos] pron ver **ése**

espabilar etc [espaβi'lar] = **despabilar** etc

espacial [espa'θjal] adj (del espacio) space cpd

espaciar [espa'θjar] vt to space (out)

espacio [es'paθjo] nm space; (MUS) interval; (RADIO, TV) programme (BRIT), program (US); **el ~** space; **~so, a** adj spacious, roomy

espada [es'paða] nf sword; **~s** nfpl (NAIPES) spades

espaguetis [espa'xetis] nmpl spaghetti sg

espalda [es'palda] nf (gen) back; **~s** nfpl (hombros) shoulders; **a ~s de uno** behind sb's back; **tenderse de ~s** to lie (down) on one's back; **volver la ~ a alguien** to cold-shoulder sb

espantajo [espan'taxo] nm = **espantapájaros**

espantapájaros [espanta'paxaros] nm inv scarecrow

espantar [espan'tar] vt (asustar) to frighten, scare; (ahuyentar) to frighten off; (asombrar) to horrify, appal; **~se** vr to get frightened o scared; to be appalled

espanto [es'panto] nm (susto) fright; (terror) terror; (asombro) astonishment; **~so, a** adj frightening; terrifying; astonishing

España [es'paɲa] nf Spain; **español, a** adj Spanish ♦ nm/f Spaniard ♦ nm (LING) Spanish

esparadrapo [espara'ðrapo] nm (sticking) plaster (BRIT), adhesive tape (US)

esparcimiento [esparθi'mjento] nm (dispersión) spreading; (diseminación) scattering; (fig) cheerfulness

esparcir [espar'θir] vt to spread; (diseminar) to scatter; **~se** vr to spread (out); to scatter; (divertirse) to enjoy

o.s.

espárrago [es'parraxo] nm asparagus

esparto [es'parto] nm esparto (grass)

espasmo [es'pasmo] nm spasm

espátula [es'patula] nf spatula

especia [es'peθja] nf spice

especial [espe'θjal] adj special; **~idad** nf speciality (BRIT), specialty (US)

especie [es'peθje] nf (BIO) species; (clase) kind, sort; **en ~** in kind

especificar [espeθifi'kar] vt to specify; **específico, a** adj specific

espécimen [es'peθimen] (pl **especímenes**) nm specimen

espectáculo [espek'takulo] nm (gen) spectacle; (TEATRO etc) show

espectador, a [espekta'ðor, a] nm/f spectator

espectro [es'pektro] nm ghost; (fig) spectre

especular [espeku'lar] vt, vi to speculate

espejismo [espe'xismo] nm mirage

espejo [es'pexo] nm mirror; **~ retrovisor** rear-view mirror

espeluznante [espeluθ'nante] adj horrifying, hair-raising

espera [es'pera] nf (pausa, intervalo) wait; (JUR: plazo) respite; **en ~ de** waiting for; (con expectativa) expecting

esperanza [espe'ranθa] nf (confianza) hope; (expectativa) expectation; **hay pocas ~s de que venga** there is little prospect of his coming

esperar [espe'rar] vt (aguardar) to wait for; (tener expectativa de) to expect; (desear) to hope for ♦ vi to wait; to expect; to hope

esperma [es'perma] nf sperm

espesar [espe'sar] vt to thicken; **~se** vr to thicken, get thicker

espeso, a [es'peso, a] adj thick; **espesor** nm thickness

espía [es'pia] nm/f spy; **espiar** vt (observar) to spy on

espiga [es'pixa] nf (BOT: de trigo etc) ear

espigón [espi'ɣon] nm (BOT) ear; (NAUT) breakwater

espina [es'pina] nf thorn; (de pez) bone; ~ **dorsal** (ANAT) spine

espinaca [espi'naka] nf spinach

espinazo [espi'naθo] nm spine, backbone

espinilla [espi'niʎa] nf (ANAT: tibia) shin(bone); (grano) blackhead

espinoso, a [espi'noso, a] adj (planta) thorny, prickly; (asunto) difficult

espionaje [espjo'naxe] nm spying, espionage

espiral [espi'ral] adj, nf spiral

espirar [espi'rar] vt to breathe out, exhale

espiritista [espiri'tista] adj, nm/f spiritualist

espíritu [es'piritu] nm spirit; **espiritual** adj spiritual

espita [es'pita] nf tap

espléndido, a [es'plendiðo, a] adj (magnífico) magnificent, splendid; (generoso) generous

esplendor [esplen'dor] nm splendour

espolear [espole'ar] vt to spur on

espoleta [espo'leta] nf (de bomba) fuse

espolón [espo'lon] nm sea wall

espolvorear [espolβore'ar] vt to dust, sprinkle

esponja [es'ponxa] nf sponge; (fig) sponger; **esponjoso, a** adj spongy

espontaneidad [espontanei'ðað] nf spontaneity; **espontáneo, a** adj spontaneous

esposa [es'posa] nf wife; **~s** nfpl handcuffs; **esposar** vt to handcuff

esposo [es'poso] nm husband

espray [es'prai] nm spray

espuela [es'pwela] nf spur

espuma [es'puma] nf foam; (de cerveza) froth, head; (de jabón) lather; **espumadera** nf (utensilio) skimmer; **espumoso, a** adj frothy, foamy; (vino) sparkling

esqueleto [eske'leto] nm skeleton

esquema [es'kema] nm (diagrama)

diagram; (dibujo) plan; (FILOSOFÍA) schema

esquí [es'ki] (pl **~s**) nm (objeto) ski; (DEPORTE) skiing; **~ acuático** water-skiing; **esquiar** vi to ski

esquilar [eski'lar] vt to shear

esquimal [eski'mal] adj, nm/f Eskimo

esquina [es'kina] nf corner

esquinazo [eski'naθo] nm: **dar ~ a algn** to give sb the slip

esquirol [eski'rol] nm blackleg

esquivar [eski'βar] vt to avoid

esquivo, a [es'kiβo, a] adj evasive; (tímido) reserved; (huraño) unsociable

esta ['esta] adj demos ver **este²**

está vb ver **estar**

ésta ['esta] pron ver **éste**

estabilidad [estaβili'ðað] nf stability; **estable** adj stable

establecer [estaβle'θer] vt to establish; **~se** vr to establish o.s.; (echar raíces) to settle (down); **establecimiento** nm establishment

establo [es'taβlo] nm (AGR) stable

estaca [es'taka] nf stake, post; (de tienda de campaña) peg

estacada [esta'kaða] nf (cerca) fence, fencing; (palenque) stockade

estación [esta'θjon] nf station; (del año) season; **~ de autobuses** bus station; **~ balnearia** seaside resort; **~ de servicio** service station

estacionamiento [estaθjona'mjento] nm (AUTO) parking; (MIL) stationing

estacionar [estaθjo'nar] vt (AUTO) to park; (MIL) to station; **~io, a** adj stationary; (COM: mercado) slack

estadio [es'taðjo] nm (fase) stage, phase; (DEPORTE) stadium

estadista [esta'ðista] nm (POL) statesman; (ESTADÍSTICA) statistician

estadística [esta'ðistika] nf figure, statistic; (ciencia) statistics sg

estado [es'taðo] nm (POL: condición) state; **~ de ánimo** state of mind; **~ de cuenta** bank statement; **~ de sitio** state of siege; **~ civil** marital status;

~ **mayor** staff; **estar en** ~ to be
pregnant; **(los) E~s Unidos** nmpl the
United States (los) (of America) sg
estadounidense [estaðouni'ðense]
adj United States cpd, American ♦ nm/f
American

estafa [es'tafa] nf swindle, trick;
estafar vt to swindle, defraud
estafeta [esta'feta] nf (oficina de
correos) post office; ~ **diplomática**
diplomatic bag
estáis vb ver **estar**
estallar [esta'ʎar] vi to burst; (bomba)
to explode, go off; (epidemia, guerra,
rebelión) to break out; ~ **en llanto** to
burst into tears; **estallido** nm
explosion; (fig) outbreak
estampa [es'tampa] nf print,
engraving
estampado, a [estam'paðo, a] adj
printed ♦ nm (impresión: acción)
printing; (: efecto) print; (marca)
stamping
estampar [estam'par] vt (imprimir) to
print; (marcar) to stamp; (metal) to
engrave; (poner sello en) to stamp; (fig)
to stamp, imprint
estampida [estam'piða] nf stampede
estampido [estam'piðo] nm bang,
report
están vb ver **estar**
estancado, a [estan'kaðo, a] adj
stagnant
estancar [estan'kar] vt (aguas) to hold
up, hold back; (COM) to monopolize;
(fig) to block, hold up; **~se** vr to
stagnate
estancia [es'tanθja] nf (permanencia)
stay; (sala) room; (AM) farm, ranch;
estanciero (AM) nm farmer, rancher
estanco, a [es'tanko, a] adj watertight
♦ nm tobacconist's (shop), cigar store
(US)

Estanco

Cigarettes, tobacco, postage stamps
and official forms ar. all sold under

state monopoly in shops called an
estanco. Although tobacco products
can also be bought in bars and
quioscos they are generally more
expensive.

---

estándar [es'tandar] adj, nm standard;
estandarizar vt to standardize
estandarte [estan'darte] nm banner,
standard
estanque [es'tanke] nm (lago) pool,
pond; (AGR) reservoir
estanquero, a [estan'kero, a] nm/f
tobacconist
estante [es'tante] nm (armario) rack,
stand; (biblioteca) bookcase; (anaquel)
shelf; (AM) prop; **estantería** nf
shelving, shelves pl
estaño [es'taɲo] nm tin

PALABRA CLAVE

estar [es'tar] vi **1** (posición) to be; **está
en la plaza** it's in the square; ¿**está
Juan?** is Juan in?; **estamos a 30 km
de Junín** we're 30 kms from Junín
2 (+ adj: estado) to be; ~ **enfermo** to
be ill; **está muy elegante** he's
looking very smart; ¿**cómo estás?**
how are you keeping?
3 (+ gerundio) to be; **estoy leyendo**
I'm reading
4 (uso pasivo): **está condenado a
muerte** he's been condemned to
death; **está envasado en ...** it's
packed in ...
5 (con fechas): ¿**a cuántos estamos?**
what's the date today?; **estamos a 5
de mayo** it's the 5th of May
6 (locuciones): ¿**estamos?** (¿de
acuerdo?) okay?; (¿listo?) ready?; **¡ya
está bien!** that's enough!
7: ~ **de**: ~ **de vacaciones/viaje** to be
on holiday/away o on a trip; **está de
camarero** he's working as a waiter
8: ~ **para**: **está para salir** he's about
to leave; **no estoy para bromas** I'm
not in the mood for jokes

9: ~ por (propuesta etc) to be in favour of; (persona etc) to support, side with; **está por limpiar** it still has to be cleaned

10: ~ sin: ~ sin dinero to have no money; **está sin terminar** it isn't finished yet

♦ **~se** vr: **se estuvo en la cama toda la tarde** he stayed in bed all afternoon

---

estas ['estas] adj demos ver **este²**

éstas ['estas] pron ver **éste**

estatal [esta'tal] adj state cpd

estático, a [es'tatiko, a] adj static

estatua [es'tatwa] nf statue

estatura [esta'tura] nf stature, height

estatuto [esta'tuto] nm (JUR) statute; (de ciudad) bye-law; (de comité) rule

este¹ ['este] nm east

este² ['este] (f **esta**, pl **estos**, **estas**) adj demos (sg) this; (pl) these

esté etc vb ver **estar**

éste ['este] (f **ésta**, pl **éstos**, **éstas**) pron (sg) this (one); (pl) these (ones); **ése ... ~ ...** the former ... the latter ....

estelar [este'lar] adj (ASTRO) stellar; (actuación, reparto) star (atr)

estén etc vb ver **estar**

estepa [es'tepa] nf (GEO) steppe

estera [es'tera] nf mat(ting)

estéreo [es'tereo] adj inv, nm stereo; **estereotipo** nm stereotype

estéril [es'teril] adj sterile, barren; (fig) vain, futile; **esterilizar** vt to sterilize

esterlina [ester'lina] adj: **libra ~** pound sterling

estés etc vb ver **estar**

estética [es'tetika] nf aesthetics sg

estético, a [es'tetiko, a] adj aesthetic

estibador [estiβa'ðor] nm stevedore, docker

estiércol [es'tjerkol] nm dung, manure

estigma [es'tiɣma] nm stigma

estilarse [esti'larse] vr to be in fashion

estilo [es'tilo] nm style; (TEC) stylus; (NATACIÓN) stroke; **algo por el ~**

something along those lines

estima [es'tima] nf esteem, respect

estimación [estima'θjon] nf (evaluación) estimation; (aprecio, afecto) esteem, regard

estimar [esti'mar] vt (evaluar) to estimate; (valorar) to value; (apreciar) to esteem, respect; (pensar, considerar) to think, reckon

estimulante [estimu'lante] adj stimulating ♦ nm stimulant

estimular [estimu'lar] vt to stimulate; (excitar) to excite

estímulo [es'timulo] nm stimulus; (ánimo) encouragement

estipulación [estipula'θjon] nf stipulation, condition

estipular [estipu'lar] vt to stipulate

estirado, a [esti'raðo, a] adj (tenso) (stretched o drawn) tight; (fig: persona) stiff, pompous

estirar [esti'rar] vt to stretch; (dinero, suma etc) to stretch out; **~se** vr to stretch

estirón [esti'ron] nm pull, tug; (crecimiento) spurt, sudden growth; **dar un ~** (niño) to shoot up

estirpe [es'tirpe] nf stock, lineage

estival [esti'βal] adj summer cpd

esto ['esto] pron this, this thing o matter; **~ de la boda** this business about the wedding

Estocolmo [esto'kolmo] nm Stockholm

estofado [esto'faðo] nm stew

estofar [esto'far] vt to stew

estómago [es'tomaxo] nm stomach; **tener ~** to be thick-skinned

estorbar [estor'βar] vt to hinder, obstruct; (molestar) to bother, disturb ♦ vi to be in the way; **estorbo** nm (molestia) bother, nuisance; (obstáculo) hindrance, obstacle

estornudar [estornu'ðar] vi to sneeze

estos ['estos] adj demos ver **este²**

éstos ['estos] pron ver **éste**

estoy vb ver **estar**

estrado [es'traðo] *nm* platform

estrafalario, a [estrafa'larjo, a] *adj* odd, eccentric

estrago [es'trayo] *nm* ruin, destruction; **hacer ~s en** to wreak havoc among

estragón [estra'yon] *nm* tarragon

estrambótico, a [estram'botiko, a] *adj* (*persona*) eccentric; (*peinado, ropa*) outlandish

estrangulador, a [estrangula'ðor, a] *nm/f* strangler ♦ *nm* (TEC) throttle; (AUTO) choke

estrangular [estrangu'lar] *vt* (*persona*) to strangle; (MED) to strangulate

estratagema [estrata'xema] *nf* (MIL) stratagem; (*astucia*) cunning

estrategia [estra'texja] *nf* strategy; **estratégico, a** *adj* strategic

estrato [es'trato] *nm* stratum, layer

estrechamente [estretʃa'mente] *adv* (*íntimamente*) closely, intimately; (*pobremente: vivir*) poorly

estrechar [estre'tʃar] *vt* (*reducir*) to narrow; (COSTURA) to take in; (*abrazar*) to hug, embrace; **~se** *vr* (*reducirse*) to narrow, grow narrow; (*abrazarse*) to embrace; **~ la mano** to shake hands

estrechez [estre'tʃeθ] *nf* narrowness; (*de ropa*) tightness; **estrecheces** *nfpl* (*dificultades económicas*) financial difficulties

estrecho, a [es'tretʃo, a] *adj* narrow; (*apretado*) tight; (*íntimo*) close, intimate; (*miserable*) mean ♦ *nm* strait; **~ de miras** narrow-minded

estrella [es'treʎa] *nf* star; **~ de mar** (ZOOL) starfish; **~ fugaz** shooting star; **estrellado, a** *adj* (*forma*) star-shaped; (*cielo*) starry

estrellar [estre'ʎar] *vt* (*hacer añicos*) to smash (to pieces); (*huevos*) to fry; **~se** *vr* to smash; (*chocarse*) to crash; (*fracasar*) to fail

estremecer [estreme'θer] *vt* to shake; **~se** *vr* to shake, tremble; **estremecimiento** *nm* (*temblor*) trembling, shaking

estrenar [estre'nar] *vt* (*vestido*) to wear for the first time; (*casa*) to move into; (*película, obra de teatro*) to premiere; **~se** *vr* (*persona*) to make one's début; **estreno** (CINE etc) première

estreñido, a [estre'ɲiðo, a] *adj* constipated

estreñimiento [estreɲi'mjento] *nm* constipation

estrépito [es'trepito] *nm* noise, racket; (*fig*) fuss; **estrepitoso, a** *adj* noisy; (*fiesta*) rowdy

estría [es'tria] *nf* groove

estribación [estriβa'θjon] *nf* (GEO) spur, foothill

estribar [estri'βar] *vi*: **~ en** to lie on

estribillo [estri'βiʎo] *nm* (LITERATURA) refrain; (MUS) chorus

estribo [es'triβo] *nm* (*de jinete*) stirrup; (*de coche, tren*) step; (*de puente*) support; (GEO) spur; **perder los ~s** to fly off the handle

estribor [estri'βor] *nm* (NAUT) starboard

estricto, a [es'trikto, a] *adj* (*riguroso*) strict; (*severo*) severe

estridente [estri'ðente] *adj* (*color*) loud; (*voz*) raucous

estropajo [estro'paxo] *nm* scourer

estropear [estrope'ar] *vt* to spoil; (*dañar*) to damage; **~se** *vr* (*objeto*) to get damaged; (*persona: la piel etc*) to be ruined

estructura [estruk'tura] *nf* structure

estruendo [es'trwendo] *nm* (*ruido*) racket, din; (*fig: alboroto*) uproar, turmoil

estrujar [estru'xar] *vt* (*apretar*) to squeeze; (*aplastar*) to crush; (*fig*) to drain, bleed

estuario [es'twarjo] *nm* estuary

estuche [es'tutʃe] *nm* box, case

estudiante [estu'ðjante] *nm/f* student; **estudiantil** *adj* student *cpd*

estudiar [estu'ðjar] *vt* to study

estudio [es'tuðjo] *nm* study; (CINE,

ARTE, RADIO) studio; **~s** *nmpl* studies; (*erudición*) learning *sg*; **~so, a** *adj* studious

estufa [es'tufa] *nf* heater, fire

estupefaciente [estupefa'θjente] *nm* drug, narcotic

estupefacto, a [estupe'fakto, a] *adj* speechless, thunderstruck

estupendo, a [estu'pendo, a] *adj* wonderful, terrific; (*fam*) great; **¡~!** that's great!, fantastic!

estupidez [estupi'ðeθ] *nf* (*torpeza*) stupidity; (*acto*) stupid thing (to do)

estúpido, a [es'tupiðo, a] *adj* stupid, silly

estupor [estu'por] *nm* stupor; (*fig*) astonishment, amazement

estuve *etc vb ver* **estar**

esvástica [es'βastika] *nf* swastika

ETA ['eta] (*ESP*) *nf abr* (= *Euskadi ta Askatasuna*) ETA

etapa [e'tapa] *nf* (*de viaje*) stage; (*DEPORTE*) leg; (*parada*) stopping place; (*fase*) stage, phase

etarra [e'tarra] *nm/f* member of ETA

etc. *abr* (= *etcétera*) etc

etcétera [et'θetera] *adv* etcetera

eternidad [eterni'ðaô] *nf* eternity; **eterno, a** *adj* eternal, everlasting

ética ['etika] *nf* ethics *pl*

ético, a [a ['etiko, a] *adj* ethical

etiqueta [eti'keta] *nf* (*modales*) etiquette; (*rótulo*) label, tag

Eucaristía [eukaris'tia] *nf* Eucharist

eufemismo [eufe'mismo] *nm* euphemism

euforia [eu'forja] *nf* euphoria

eurodiputado, a [euroðipu'taðo, a] *nm/f* Euro MP, MEP

Europa [eu'ropa] *nf* Europe; **europeo, a** *adj, nm/f* European

Euskadi [eus'kaði] *nm* the Basque Country o Provinces *pl*

euskera [eus'kera] *nm* (*LING*) Basque

evacuación [eβakwa'θjon] *nf* evacuation

evacuar [eβa'kwar] *vt* to evacuate

evadir [eβa'ðir] *vt* to evade, avoid; **~se** *vr* to escape

evaluar [eβa'lwar] *vt* to evaluate

evangelio [eβan'xeljo] *nm* gospel

evaporar [eβapo'rar] *vt* to evaporate; **~se** *vr* to vanish

evasión [eβa'sjon] *nf* escape, flight; (*fig*) evasion; **~ de capitales** flight of capital

evasiva [eβa'siβa] *nf* (*pretexto*) excuse

evasivo, a [eβa'siβo, a] *adj* evasive, non-committal

evento [e'βento] *nm* event

eventual [eβen'twal] *adj* possible, conditional (upon circumstances); (*trabajador*) casual, temporary

evidencia [eβi'ðenθja] *nf* evidence, proof; **evidenciar** *vt* (*hacer patente*) to make evident; (*probar*) to prove; show; **evidenciarse** *vr* to be evident

evidente [eβi'ðente] *adj* obvious, clear, evident

evitar [eβi'tar] *vt* (*evadir*) to avoid; (*impedir*) to prevent

evocar [eβo'kar] *vt* to evoke, call forth

evolución [eβolu'θjon] *nf* (*desarrollo*) evolution, development; (*cambio*) change; (*MIL*) manoeuvre; **evolucionar** *vi* to evolve; to manoeuvre

ex [eks] *adj* ex-; **el ~ ministro** the former minister, the ex-minister

exacerbar [eksaθer'βar] *vt* to irritate, annoy

exactamente [eksakta'mente] *adv* exactly

exactitud [eksakti'tuð] *nf* exactness; (*precisión*) accuracy; (*puntualidad*) punctuality; **exacto, a** *adj* exact; accurate; punctual; **¡exacto!** exactly!

exageración [eksaxera'θjon] *nf* exaggeration

exagerar [eksaxe'rar] *vt, vi* to exaggerate

exaltado, a [eksal'taðo, a] *adj* (*apasionado*) over-excited, worked-up; (*POL*) extreme

exaltar [eksal'tar] vt to exalt, glorify; **~se** vr (excitarse) to get excited o worked-up

examen [ek'samen] nm examination

examinar [eksami'nar] vt to examine; **~se** vr to be examined, take an examination

exasperar [eksaspe'rar] vt to exasperate; **~se** vr to get exasperated, lose patience

Exca. abr = **Excelencia**

excavadora [ekskaβa'ðora] nf excavator

excavar [ekska'ßar] vt to excavate

excedencia [eksθe'ðenθja] nf: **estar en ~** to be on leave; **pedir** o **solicitar la ~** to ask for leave

excedente [eksθe'ðente] adj, nm excess, surplus

exceder [eksθe'ðer] vt to exceed, surpass; **~se** vr (extralimitarse) to go too far

excelencia [eksθe'lenθja] nf excellence; **E~** Excellency; **excelente** adj excellent

excentricidad [eksθentriθi'ðað] nf eccentricity; **excéntrico, a** adj, nm/f eccentric

excepción [eksθep'θjon] nf exception; **excepcional** adj exceptional

excepto [eks'θepto] adv excepting, except (for)

exceptuar [eksθep'twar] vt to except, exclude

excesivo, a [eksθe'siβo, a] adj excessive

exceso [eks'θeso] nm (gen) excess; (COM) surplus; **~ de equipaje/peso** excess luggage/weight

excitación [eksθita'θjon] nf (sensación) excitement; (acción) excitation

excitado, a [eksθi'taðo, a] adj excited; (emociones) aroused

excitar [eksθi'tar] vt to excite; (incitar) to urge; **~se** vr to get excited

exclamación [eksklama'θjon] nf exclamation

exclamar [ekskla'mar] vi to exclaim

excluir [eksklu'ir] vt to exclude; (dejar fuera) to shut out; (descartar) to reject; **exclusión** nf exclusion

exclusiva [eksklu'siβa] nf (PRENSA) exclusive, scoop; (COM) sole right

exclusivo, a [eksklu'siβo, a] adj exclusive; **derecho ~** sole o exclusive right

Excmo. abr = **excelentísimo**

excomulgar [ekskomul'var] vt (REL) to excommunicate

excomunión [ekskomu'njon] nf excommunication

excursión [ekskur'sjon] nf excursion, outing; **excursionista** nm/f (turista) sightseer

excusa [eks'kusa] nf excuse; (disculpa) apology

excusar [eksku'sar] vt to excuse; **~se** vr (disculparse) to apologize

exhalar [eksa'lar] vt to exhale, breathe out; (olor etc) to give off; (suspiro) to breathe, heave

exhaustivo, a [eksaus'tiβo, a] adj (análisis) thorough; (estudio) exhaustive

exhausto, a [ek'sausto, a] adj exhausted

exhibición [eksiβi'θjon] nf exhibition, display, show

exhibir [eksi'ßir] vt to exhibit, display, show

exhortar [eksor'tar] vt: **~ a** to exhort to

exigencia [eksi'xenθja] nf demand, requirement; **exigente** adj demanding

exigir [eksi'xir] vt (gen) to demand, require; **~ el pago** to demand payment

exiliado, a [eksi'ljaðo, a] adj exiled ♦ nm/f exile

exilio [ek'siljo] nm exile

eximir [eksi'mir] vt to exempt

existencia [eksis'tenθja] nf existence; **~s** nfpl stock(s) (pl)

existir [eksis'tir] vi to exist, be

éxito ['eksito] nm (triunfo) success; (MUS etc) hit; **tener ~** to be successful

exonerar [ekson'e'rar] vt to exonerate; **~ de una obligación** to free from an obligation

exorbitante [eksorßi'tante] adj (precio) exorbitant; (cantidad) excessive

exorcizar [eksorθi'θar] vt to exorcize

exótico, a [ek'sotiko, a] adj exotic

expandir [ekspan'dir] vt to expand

expansión [ekspan'sjon] nf expansion

expansivo, a [ekspan'sißo, a] adj: **onda ~a** shock wave

expatriarse [ekspa'trjarse] vr to emigrate; (POL) to go into exile

expectativa [ekspekta'tißa] nf (espera) expectation; (perspectiva) prospect

expedición [ekspeði'θjon] nf (excursión) expedition

expediente [ekspe'ðjente] nm expedient; (JUR: procedimento) action, proceedings pl; (: papeles) dossier, file, record

expedir [ekspe'ðir] vt (despachar) to send, forward; (pasaporte) to issue

expendedor, a [ekspende'ðor, a] nm/f (vendedor) dealer

expensas [eks'pensas] nfpl: **a ~ de** at the expense of

experiencia [ekspe'rjenθja] nf experience

experimentado, a [eksperimen'taðo, a] adj experienced

experimentar [eksperimen'tar] vt (en laboratorio) to experiment with; (probar) to test, try out; (notar, observar) to experience; (deterioro, pérdida) to suffer; **experimento** nm experiment

experto, a [eks'perto, a] adj expert, skilled ♦ nm/f expert

expiar [ekspi'ar] vt to atone for

expirar [ekspi'rar] vi to expire

explanada [eskpla'naða] nf (llano) plain

explayarse [ekspla'jarse] vr (en discurso) to speak at length; **~ con**

uno to confide in sb

explicación [eksplika'θjon] nf explanation

explicar [ekspli'kar] vt to explain; **~se** vr to explain (o.s.)

explícito, a [eks'pliθito, a] adj explicit

explique etc vb ver **explicar**

explorador, a [eksplora'ðor, a] nm/f (pionero) explorer; (MIL) scout ♦ nm (MED) probe; (TEC) (radar) scanner

explorar [eksplo'rar] vt to explore; (MED) to probe; (radar) to scan

explosión [eksplo'sjon] nf explosion; **explosivo, a** adj explosive

explotación [eksplota'θjon] nf exploitation; (de planta etc) running

explotar [eksplo'tar] vt to exploit; to run, operate ♦ vi to explode

exponer [ekspo'ner] vt to expose; (cuadro) to display; (vida) to risk; (idea) to explain; **~se** vr: **~se a (hacer) algo** to run the risk of (doing) sth

exportación [eksporta'θjon] nf (acción) export; (mercancías) exports pl

exportar [ekspor'tar] vt to export

exposición [eksposi'θjon] nf (gen) exposure; (de arte) show, exhibition; (explicación) explanation; (declaración) account, statement

expresamente [ekspresa'mente] adv (decir) clearly; (a propósito) expressly

expresar [ekspre'sar] vt to express; **expresión** nf expression

expresivo, a [ekspre'sißo, a] adj (persona, gesto, palabras) expressive; (cariñoso) affectionate

expreso, a [eks'preso, a] pp de **expresar** ♦ adj (explícito) express; (claro) clear, definite; (tren) fast ♦ adv: **mandar ~** to send by express (delivery)

express [eks'pres] (AM) adv: **enviar algo ~** to send sth special delivery

exprimidor [eksprimi'ðor] nm squeezer

exprimir [ekspri'mir] vt (fruta) to squeeze; (zumo) to squeeze out

expropiar [ekspro'pjar] vt to expropriate

expuesto, a [eks'pwesto, a] pp de **exponer** ♦ adj exposed; (cuadro etc) on show, on display

expulsar [ekspul'sar] vt (echar) to eject, throw out; (alumno) to expel; (despedir) to sack, fire; (DEPORTE) to send off; **expulsión** nf expulsion; sending-off

exquisito, a [ekski'sito, a] adj exquisite; (comida) delicious

éxtasis ['ekstasis] nm ecstasy

extender [eksten'der] vt to extend; (los brazos) to stretch out, hold out; (mapa, tela) to spread (out), open (out); (mantequilla) to spread; (certificado) to issue; (cheque, recibo) to make out; (documento) to draw up; **~se** vr (gen) to extend; (persona: en el suelo) to stretch out; (epidemia) to spread; **extendido, a** adj (abierto) spread out, open; (brazos) outstretched; (costumbre) widespread

extensión [eksten'sjon] nf (de terreno, mar) expanse, stretch; (de tiempo) length, duration; (TEL) extension; **en toda la ~ de la palabra** in every sense of the word

extenso, a [eks'tenso, a] adj extensive

extenuar [ekste'nwar] vt (debilitar) to weaken

exterior [ekste'rjor] adj (de fuera) external; (afuera) outside, exterior; (apariencia) outward; (deuda, relaciones) foreign ♦ nm (gen) exterior, outside; (aspecto) outward appearance; (DEPORTE) wing(er); (países extranjeros) abroad; **en el ~** abroad; **al ~** outwardly, on the surface

exterminar [ekstermi'nar] vt to exterminate; **exterminio** nm extermination

externo, a [eks'terno, a] adj (exterior) external, outside; (superficial) outward ♦ nm/f day pupil

extinguir [ekstin'gir] vt (fuego) to extinguish, put out; (raza, población) to wipe out; **~se** vr (fuego) to go out; (BIO) to die out, become extinct

extinto, a [eks'tinto, a] adj extinct

extintor [ekstin'tor] nm (fire) extinguisher

extirpar [ekstir'par] vt (MED) to remove (surgically)

extorsión [ekstor'sjon] nf extorsion

extra ['ekstra] adj inv (tiempo) extra; (chocolate, vino) good-quality ♦ nm/f extra ♦ nm extra; (bono) bonus

extracción [ekstrak'θjon] nf extraction; (en lotería) draw

extracto [eks'trakto] nm extract

extradición [ekstraði'θjon] nf extradition

extraer [ekstra'er] vt to extract, take out

extraescolar [ekstraesko'lar] adj: **actividad ~** extracurricular activity

extralimitarse [ekstralimi'tarse] vr to go too far

extranjero, a [ekstran'xero, a] adj foreign ♦ nm/f foreigner ♦ nm foreign countries pl; **en el ~** abroad

extrañar [ekstra'ɲar] vt (sorprender) to find strange o odd; (echar de menos) to miss; **~se** vr (sorprenderse) to be amazed, be surprised

extrañeza [ekstra'ɲeθa] nf (rareza) strangeness, oddness; (asombro) amazement, surprise

extraño, a [eks'traɲo, a] adj (extranjero) foreign; (raro, sorprendente) strange, odd

extraordinario, a [ekstraorði'narjo, a] adj extraordinary; (edición, número) special ♦ nm (de periódico) special edition; **horas extraordinarias** overtime sg

extrarradio [ekstra'rraðjo] nm suburbs

extravagancia [ekstraβa'γanθja] nf oddness; outlandishness

extravagante [ekstraβa'γante] adj (excéntrico) eccentric; (estrafalario) outlandish

extraviado, a [ekstra'βjaðo, a] adj

lost, missing

extraviar [ekstra'βjar] vt (persona: desorientar) to mislead, misdirect; (perder) to lose, misplace; **~se** vr to lose one's way, get lost; **extravío** nm loss; (fig) deviation

extremar [ekstre'mar] vt to carry to extremes; **~se** vr to do one's utmost, make every effort

extremaunción [ekstremaun'θjon] nf extreme unction

extremidad [ekstremi'ðað] nf (punta) extremity; **~es** nfpl (ANAT) extremities

extremo, a [eks'tremo, a] adj extreme; (último) last ♦ nm end; (límite, grado sumo) extreme; **en último ~** as a last resort

extrovertido, a [ekstroβer'tiðo, a] adj, nm/f extrovert

exuberancia [eksuβe'ranθja] nf exuberance; **exuberante** adj exuberant; (fig) luxuriant, lush

eyacular [ejaku'lar] vt, vi to ejaculate

F, f

f.a.b. abr (= franco a bordo) f.o.b.

fabada [fa'βaða] nf bean and sausage stew

fábrica ['faβrika] nf factory; **marca de ~** trademark; **precio de ~** factory price

fabricación [faβrika'θjon] nf (manufactura) manufacture; (producción) production; **de ~ casera** home-made; **~ en serie** mass production

fabricante [faβri'kante] nm/f manufacturer

fabricar [faβri'kar] vt (manufacturar) to manufacture, make; (construir) to build; (cuento) to fabricate, devise

fábula ['faβula] nf (cuento) fable; (chisme) rumour; (mentira) fib

fabuloso, a [faβu'loso, a] adj (oportunidad, tiempo) fabulous, great

facción [fak'θjon] nf (POL) faction;

facciones nfpl (del rostro) features

faceta [fa'θeta] nf facet

facha ['fatʃa] (fam) nf (aspecto) look; (cara) face

fachada [fa'tʃaða] nf (ARQ) façade, front

fácil [faθil] adj (simple) easy; (probable) likely

facilidad [faθili'ðað] nf (capacidad) ease; (sencillez) simplicity; (de palabra) fluency; **~es** nfpl facilities

facilitar [faθili'tar] vt (hacer fácil) to make easy; (proporcionar) to provide

fácilmente [faθil'mente] adv easily

facsímil [fak'simil] nm facsimile, fax

factible [fak'tiβle] adj feasible

factor [fak'tor] nm factor

factura [fak'tura] nf (cuenta) bill; **facturación** nf (de equipaje) check-in; **facturar** vt (COM) to invoice, charge for; (equipaje) to check in

facultad [fakul'tað] nf (aptitud, ESCOL etc) faculty; (poder) power

faena [fa'ena] nf (trabajo) work; (quehacer) task, job

faisán [fai'san] nm pheasant

faja ['faxa] nf (para la cintura) sash; (de mujer) corset; (de tierra) strip

fajo ['faxo] nm (de papeles) bundle; (de billetes) wad

falacia [fa'laθja] nf fallacy

falda ['falda] nf (prenda de vestir) skirt

falla ['faʎa] nf (defecto) fault, flaw

fallar [fa'ʎar] vt (JUR) to pronounce sentence on ♦ vi (memoria) to fail; (motor) to miss

---

Fallas

In the week of 19 March (the feast of San José), Valencia honours its patron saint with a spectacular fiesta called **Las Fallas**. The Fallas are huge papier-mâché, cardboard and wooden sculptures which are built by competing teams throughout the year. They depict politicians and well-known public figures and are thrown onto bonfires and set alight once a jury has judged them - only the best sculpture escapes the flames.

fallecer [faʎe'θer] vi to pass away, die; **fallecimiento** nm decease, demise

fallido, a [fa'ʎiðo, a] adj (gen) frustrated, unsuccessful

fallo ['faʎo] nm (JUR) verdict, ruling; (fracaso) failure; **~ cardíaco** heart failure

falsedad [false'ðað] nf falseness; (hipocresía) hypocrisy; (mentira) falsehood

falsificar [falsifi'kar] vt (firma etc) to forge; (moneda) to counterfeit

falso, a ['falso, a] adj false; (documento, moneda etc) fake; **en ~** falsely

falta ['falta] nf (defecto) fault, flaw; (privación) lack, want; (ausencia) absence; (carencia) shortage; (equivocación) mistake; (DEPORTE) foul; **echar en ~** to miss; **hacer ~ hacer algo** to be necessary to do sth; **me hace ~ una pluma** I need a pen; **~ de educación** bad manners sg

faltar [fal'tar] vi (escasear) to be lacking, be wanting; (ausentarse) to be absent, be missing; **faltan 2 horas para llegar** there are 2 hours to go till arrival; **~ al respeto a uno** to be disrespectful to sb; **¡no faltaba más!** (no hay de qué) don't mention it

fama ['fama] nf (renombre) fame; (reputación) reputation

famélico, a [fa'meliko, a] adj starving

familia [fa'milja] nf family; **~ política** in-laws pl

familiar [fami'ljar] adj (relativo a la familia) family cpd; (conocido, informal) familiar ♦ nm relative, relation; **~idad** nf (gen) familiarity; (informalidad) homeliness; **~izarse** vr: **~izarse con** to familiarize o.s. with

famoso, a [fa'moso, a] adj (renombrado) famous

fanático, a [fa'natiko, a] adj fanatical ♦ nm/f fanatic; (CINE, DEPORTE) fan; **fanatismo** nm fanaticism

fanfarrón, ona [fanfa'rron, ona] adj boastful

fango ['fango] nm mud; **~so, a** adj muddy

fantasía [fanta'sia] nf fantasy, imagination; **joyas de ~** imitation jewellery sg

fantasma [fan'tasma] nm (espectro) ghost, apparition; (fanfarrón) show-off

fantástico, a [fan'tastiko, a] adj fantastic

farmacéutico, a [farma'θeutiko, a] adj pharmaceutical ♦ nm/f chemist (BRIT), pharmacist

farmacia [far'maθja] nf chemist's (shop) (BRIT), pharmacy; **~ de turno** duty chemist; **~ de guardia** all-night chemist

fármaco [farmako] nm drug

faro ['faro] nm (NAUT: torre) lighthouse; (AUTO) headlamp; **~s antiniebla** fog lamps; **~s delanteros/traseros** headlights/rear lights

farol [fa'rol] nm lantern, lamp

farola [fa'rola] nf street lamp (BRIT) o light (US)

farsa ['farsa] nf (gen) farce

farsante [far'sante] nm/f fraud, fake

fascículo [fas'θikulo] nm (de revista) part, instalment

fascinar [fasθi'nar] vt (gen) to fascinate

fascismo [fas'θismo] nm fascism; **fascista** adj, nm/f fascist

fase ['fase] nf phase

fastidiar [fasti'ðjar] vt (molestar) to annoy, bother; (estropear) to spoil; **~se** vr: **¡que se fastidie!** (fam) he'll just have to put up with it!

fastidio [fas'tiðjo] nm (molestia) annoyance; **~so, a** adj (molesto) annoying

fastuoso, a [fas'twoso, a] adj (banquete, boda) lavish; (acto) pompous

fatal |fa'tal| adj (gen) fatal; (desgraciado) ill-fated; (fam: malo, pésimo) awful; **~idad** nf (destino) fate; (mala suerte) misfortune

fatiga |fa'tiɣa| nf (cansancio) fatigue, weariness

fatigar |fati'ɣar| vt to tire, weary; **~se** vr to get tired

fatigoso, a |fati'ɣoso, a| adj (cansador) tiring

fatuo, a |'fatwo, a| adj (vano) fatuous; (presuntuoso) conceited

favor |fa'ɓor| nm favour; **estar a ~ de** to be in favour of; **haga el ~ de...** would you be so good as to..., kindly...; **por ~** please; **~able** adj favourable

favorecer |faɓore'θer| vt to favour; (vestido etc) to become, flatter; **este peinado le favorece** this hairstyle suits him

favorito, a |faɓo'rito, a| adj, nm/f favourite

fax |faks| nm inv fax; **mandar por ~** to fax

faz |faθ| nf face; **la ~ de la tierra** the face of the earth

fe |fe| nf (REL) faith; (documento) certificate; **prestar ~ a** to believe, credit; **actuar con buena/mala ~** to act in good/bad faith; **dar ~ de** to bear witness to

fealdad |feal'dað| nf ugliness

febrero |fe'ɓrero| nm February

febril |fe'ɓril| adj (fig: actividad) hectic; (mente, mirada) feverish

fecha |'fetʃa| nf date; **~ de caducidad** (de producto alimenticio) sell-by date; (de contrato etc) expiry date; **con ~ adelantada** postdated; **en ~ próxima** soon; **hasta la ~** to date, so far; **poner ~** to date; **fechar** vt to date

fecundar |fekun'dar| vt (generar) to fertilize, make fertile; **fecundo, a** adj (fértil) fertile; (fig) prolific; (productivo)

productive

federación |feðera'θjon| nf federation

felicidad |feliθi'ðað| nf happiness; **~es** nfpl (felicitaciones) best wishes, congratulations

felicitación |feliθita'θjon| nf: **¡felicitaciones!** congratulations!

felicitar |feliθi'tar| vt to congratulate

feligrés, esa |feli'ɣres, esa| nm/f parishioner

feliz |fe'liθ| adj happy

felpudo |fel'puðo| nm doormat

femenino, a |feme'nino, a| adj, nm feminine

feminista |femi'nista| adj, nm/f feminist

fenómeno |fe'nomeno| nm phenomenon; (fig) freak, accident ♦ adj great ♦ excl great!, marvellous!; **fenomenal** adj = **fenómeno**

feo, a |'feo, a| adj (gen) ugly; (desagradable) bad, nasty

féretro |'feretro| nm (ataúd) coffin; (sarcófago) bier

feria |'ferja| nf (gen) fair; (descanso) holiday, rest day; (AM: mercado) village market; (: cambio) loose o small change

fermentar |fermen'tar| vi to ferment

ferocidad |feroθi'ðað| nf fierceness, ferocity

feroz |fe'roθ| adj (cruel) cruel; (salvaje) fierce

férreo, a |'ferreo, a| adj iron

ferretería |ferrete'ria| nf (tienda) ironmonger's (shop) (BRIT), hardware store

ferrocarril |ferroka'rril| nm railway

ferroviario, a |ferro'ɓjarjo, a| adj rail cpd

fértil |'fertil| adj (productivo) fertile; (rico) rich; **fertilidad** nf (gen) fertility; (productividad) fruitfulness

ferviente |fer'ɓjente| adj fervent

fervor |fer'ɓor| nm fervour; **~oso, a** adj fervent

festejar |feste'xar| vt (celebrar) to

celebrate

festejo [fes'texo] *nm* celebration; **festejos** *nmpl (fiestas)* festivals

festín [fes'tin] *nm* feast, banquet

festival [festi'βal] *nm* festival

festividad [festiβi'ðað] *nf* festivity

festivo, a [fes'tiβo, a] *adj (de fiesta)* festive; *(CINE, LITERATURA)* humorous; **día ~** holiday

fétido, a ['fetiðo, a] *adj* foul-smelling

feto ['feto] *nm* foetus

fiable ['fjaβle] *adj (persona)* trustworthy; *(máquina)* reliable

fiador, a [fja'ðor, a] *nm/f (JUR)* surety, guarantor; *(COM)* backer; **salir ~ por uno** to stand bail for sb

fiambre ['fjambre] *nm* cold meat

fianza ['fjanθa] *nf* surety; *(JUR)*: **libertad bajo ~** release on bail

fiar [fi'ar] *vt (salir garante de)* to guarantee; *(vender a crédito)* to sell on credit; *(secreto)* to confide (to) ♦ *vi* to trust; **~se** *vr* to trust (in), rely on; **~se de uno** to rely on sb

fibra ['fiβra] *nf* fibre; **~ óptica** optical fibre

ficción [fik'θjon] *nf* fiction

ficha ['fitʃa] *nf (TEL)* token; *(en juegos)* counter, marker; *(tarjeta)* (index) card; **fichar** *vt (archivar)* to file, index; *(DEPORTE)* to sign; **estar fichado** to have a record; **fichero** *nm* box file; *(INFORM)* file

ficticio, a [fik'tiθjo, a] *adj (imaginario)* fictitious; *(falso)* fabricated

fidelidad [fiðeli'ðað] *nf (lealtad)* fidelity, loyalty; **alta ~** high fidelity, hi-fi

fideos [fi'ðeos] *nmpl* noodles

fiebre ['fjeβre] *nf (MED)* fever; *(fig)* fever, excitement; **~ amarilla/del heno** yellow/hay fever; **~ palúdica** malaria; **tener ~** to have a temperature

fiel [fjel] *adj (leal)* faithful, loyal; *(fiable)* reliable; *(exacto)* accurate, faithful ♦ *nm*: **los ~es** the faithful

fieltro ['fjeltro] *nm* felt

fiera ['fjera] *nf (animal feroz)* wild animal o beast; *(fig)* dragon; *ver tb* **fiero**

fiero, a ['fjero, a] *adj (cruel)* cruel; *(feroz)* fierce; *(duro)* harsh

fiesta ['fjesta] *nf* party; *(de pueblo)* festival; *(vacaciones, tb: ~s)* holiday *sg*; *(REL)*: **~ de guardar** day of obligation

---
Fiestas

Fiestas *can be official public holidays or holidays set by each autonomous region, many of which coincide with religious festivals. There are also many* **fiestas** *all over Spain for a local patron saint or the Virgin Mary. These often last several days and can include religious processions, carnival parades, bullfights and dancing.*

---

figura [fi'ɣura] *nf (gen)* figure; *(forma, imagen)* shape, form; *(NAIPES)* face card

figurar [fiɣu'rar] *vt (representar)* to represent; *(fingir)* to figure ♦ *vi* to figure; **~se** *vr (imaginarse)* to imagine; *(suponer)* to suppose

fijador [fixa'ðor] *nm (FOTO etc)* fixative; *(de pelo)* gel

fijar [fi'xar] *vt (gen)* to fix; *(estampilla)* to affix, stick (on); **~se** *vr*: **~se en** to notice

fijo, a ['fixo, a] *adj (gen)* fixed; *(firme)* firm; *(permanente)* permanent ♦ *adv*: **mirar ~** to stare

fila ['fila] *nf* row; *(MIL)* rank; **ponerse en ~** to line up, get into line

filántropo, a [fi'lantropo, a] *nm/f* philanthropist

filatelia [fila'telja] *nf* philately, stamp collecting

filete [fi'lete] *nm (carne)* fillet steak; *(pescado)* fillet

filiación [filja'θjon] *nf (POL)* affiliation

filial [fi'ljal] *adj* filial ♦ *nf* subsidiary

Filipinas [fili'pinas] *nfpl*: **las ~** the Philippines; **filipino, a** *adj, nm/f*

Philippine
filmar [fil'mar] *vt* to film, shoot
filo ['filo] *nm* (*gen*) edge; **sacar ~ a** to sharpen; **al ~ del mediodía** at about midday; **de doble ~** double-edged
filón [fi'lon] *nm* (MINERÍA) vein, lode; (*fig*) goldmine
filosofía [filoso'fia] *nf* philosophy; **filósofo, a** *nm/f* philosopher
filtrar [fil'trar] *vt, vi* to filter, strain; **~se** *vr* to filter; **filtro** *nm* (TEC, *utensilio*) filter
fin [fin] *nm* end; (*objetivo*) aim, purpose; **al ~ y al cabo** when all's said and done; **a ~ de** in order to; **por ~** finally; **en ~** in short; **~ de semana** weekend
final [fi'nal] *adj* final ♦ *nm* end, conclusion ♦ *nf* final; **~idad** *nf* (*propósito*) purpose, intention; **~ista** *nm/f* finalist; **~izar** *vt* to end, finish; (INFORM) to log out o off ♦ *vi* to end, come to an end
financiar [finan'θjar] *vt* to finance; **financiero, a** *adj* financial ♦ *nm/f* financier
finca ['finka] *nf* (*bien inmueble*) property, land; (*casa de ccmpo*) country house; (AM) farm
fingir [fin'xir] *vt* (*simular*) to simulate, feign ♦ *vi* (*aparentar*) to pretend
finlandés, esa [finlan'des, esa] *adj* Finnish ♦ *nm/f* Finn ♦ *nm* (LING) Finnish
Finlandia [fin'landja] *nf* Finland
fino, a ['fino, a] *adj* fine; (*delgado*) slender; (*de buenas maneras*) polite, refined; (*jerez*) fino, dry
firma ['firma] *nf* signature; (COM) firm, company
firmamento [firma'mento] *nm* firmament
firmar [fir'mar] *vt* to sign
firme ['firme] *adj* firm; (*estable*) stable; (*sólido*) solid; (*constante*) steady; (*decidido*) resolute ♦ *nm* road (surface); **~mente** *adv* firmly; **~za** *nf* firmness; (*constancia*) steadiness; (*solidez*) solidity

fiscal [fis'kal] *adj* fiscal ♦ *nm/f* public prosecutor; **año ~** tax o fiscal year
fisco ['fisko] *nm* (*hacienda*) treasury, exchequer (BRIT)
fisgar [fis'xar] *vt* to pry into
fisgonear [fisɣone'ar] *vt* to poke one's nose into ♦ *vi* to pry, spy
física [fi'sika] *nf* physics *sg*; *ver tb* **físico**
físico, a ['fisiko, a] *adj* physical ♦ *nm* physique ♦ *nm/f* physicist
fisura [fi'sura] *nf* crack; (MED) fracture
flác(c)ido, a ['fla(k)θiðo, a] *adj* flabby
flaco, a ['flako, a] *adj* (*muy delgado*) skinny, thin; (*débil*) weak, feeble
flagrante [fla'ɣrante] *adj* flagrant
flamante [fla'mante] (*fam*) *adj* brilliant; (*nuevo*) brand-new
flamenco, a [fla'menko, a] *adj* (*de Flandes*) Flemish; (*baile, música*) flamenco ♦ *nm* (*baile, música*) flamenco
flan [flan] *nm* creme caramel
flaqueza [fla'keθa] *nf* (*delgadez*) thinness, leanness; (*fig*) weakness
flash [flaʃ] (*pl* **~s** o **~es**) *nm* (FOTO) flash
flauta ['flauta] *nf* (MUS) flute
flecha ['fletʃa] *nf* arrow
flechazo [fle'tʃaθo] *nm* love at first sight
fleco ['fleko] *nm* fringe
flema ['flema] *nm* phlegm
flequillo [fle'kiʎo] *nm* (*pelo*) fringe
flexible [flek'siβle] *adj* flexible
flexión [flek'sjon] *nf* press-up
flexo ['flekso] *nm* adjustable table-lamp
flojera [flo'xera] (AM: *fam*) *nf*: **me da ~** I can't be bothered
flojo, a ['floxo, a] *adj* (*gen*) loose; (*sin fuerzas*) limp; (*débil*) weak
flor [flor] *nf* flower; **a ~ de** on the surface of; **~ecer** *vi* (BOT) to flower, bloom; (*fig*) to flourish; **~eciente** *adj* (BOT) in flower, flowering; (*fig*) thriving; **~ero** *nm* vase; **~istería** *nf* florist's (shop)

flota ['flota] nf fleet
flotador [flota'ðor] nm (gen) float; (para nadar) rubber ring
flotar [flo'tar] vi (gen) to float; **flote** nm: **a flote** afloat; **salir a flote** (fig) to get back on one's feet
fluctuar [fluk'twar] vi (oscilar) to fluctuate
fluidez [flui'ðeθ] nf fluidity; (fig) fluency
fluído, a [flu'iðo, a] adj, nm fluid
fluir [flu'ir] vi to flow
flujo ['fluxo] nm flow; **~ y reflujo** ebb and flow
flúor ['fluor] nm fluoride
fluvial [fluβi'al] adj (navegación, cuenca) fluvial, river cpd
foca ['foka] nf seal
foco ['foko] nm focus; (ELEC) floodlight; (AM) (light) bulb
fofo, a ['fofo, a] adj soft, spongy; (carnes) flabby
fogata [fo'vata] nf bonfire
fogón [fo'von] nm (de cocina) ring, burner
fogoso, a [fo'voso, a] adj spirited
folio ['foljo] nm folio, page
follaje [fo'ʎaxe] nm foliage
folletín [foʎe'tin] nm newspaper serial
folleto [fo'ʎeto] nm (POL) pamphlet
follón [fo'ʎon] (fam) nm (lío) mess; (conmoción) fuss; **armar un ~** to kick up a row
fomentar [fomen'tar] vt (MED) to foment; **fomento** nm (promoción) promotion
fonda ['fonda] nf inn
fondo ['fondo] nm (de mar) bottom; (de coche, sala) back; (ARTE etc) background; (reserva) fund; **~s** nmpl (COM) funds, resources; **una investigación a ~** a thorough investigation; **en el ~** at bottom, deep down
fontanería [fontane'ria] nf plumbing; **fontanero, a** nm/f plumber
footing ['futin] nm jogging; **hacer ~**

to jog, go jogging
forastero, a [foras'tero, a] nm/f stranger
forcejear [forθexe'ar] vi (luchar) to struggle
forense [fo'rense] nm/f pathologist
forjar [for'xar] vt to forge
forma ['forma] nf (figura) form, shape; (MED) fitness; (método) way, means; **las ~s** the conventions; **estar en ~** to be fit
formación [forma'θjon] nf (gen) formation; (educación) education; **~ profesional** vocational training
formal [for'mal] adj (gen) formal; (fig: serio) serious; (: de fiar) reliable; **~idad** nf formality; seriousness; **~izar** vt (JUR) to formalize; (situación) to put in order, regularize; **~izarse** vr (situación) to be put in order, be regularized
formar [for'mar] vt (componer) to form, shape; (constituir) to make up, constitute; (ESCOL) to train, educate; **~se** vr (ESCOL) to be trained, educated; (cobrar forma) to form, take form; (desarrollarse) to develop
formatear [formate'ar] vt to format
formativo, a [forma'tiβo, a] adj (lecturas, años) formative
formato [for'mato] nm format
formidable [formi'ðaβle] adj (temible) formidable; (estupendo) tremendous
fórmula ['formula] nf formula
formular [formu'lar] vt (queja) to make, lodge; (petición) to draw up; (pregunta) to pose
formulario [formu'larjo] nm form
fornido, a [for'niðo, a] adj well-built
forrar [fo'rrar] vt (abrigo) to line; (libro) to cover; **forro** nm (de cuaderno) cover; (COSTURA) lining; (de sillón) upholstery
fortalecer [fortale'θer] vt to strengthen
fortaleza [forta'leθa] nf (MIL) fortress, stronghold; (fuerza) strength; (determinación) resolution

fortuito, a [for'twito, a] *adj* accidental

fortuna [for'tuna] *nf* (*suerte*) fortune, (good) luck; (*riqueza*) fortune, wealth

forzar [for'θar] *vt* (*puerta*) to force (open); (*compeler*) to compel

forzoso, a [for'θoso, a] *adj* necessary

fosa ['fosa] *nf* (*sepultura*) grave; (*en tierra*) pit; **~s nasales** nostrils

fósforo ['fosforo] *nm* (*QUÍM*) phosphorus; (*cerilla*) match

foso ['foso] *nm* ditch; (*TEATRO*) pit; (*AUTO*): **~ de reconocimiento** inspection pit

foto ['foto] *nf* photo, snap(shot); **sacar una ~** to take a photo o picture

fotocopia [foto'kopja] *nf* photocopy; **fotocopiadora** *nf* photocopier; **fotocopiar** *vt* to photocopy

fotografía [fotoɣra'fia] *nf* (*ARTE*) photography; (*una ~*) photograph; **fotografiar** *vt* to photograph

fotógrafo, a [fo'toɣrafo, a] *nm/f* photographer

fracasar [fraka'sar] *vi* (*gen*) to fail

fracaso [fra'kaso] *nm* failure

fracción [frak'θjon] *nf* fraction; **fraccionamiento** (*AM*) *nm* housing estate

fractura [frak'tura] *nf* fracture, break

fragancia [fra'ɣanθja] *nf* (*olor*) fragrance, perfume

frágil ['fraxil] *adj* (*débil*) fragile; (*COM*) breakable

fragmento [fraɣ'mento] *nm* (*pedazo*) fragment

fragua ['fraɣwa] *nf* forge; **fraguar** *vt* to forge; (*fig*) to concoct ♦ *vi* to harden

fraile ['fraile] *nm* (*REL*) friar; (: *monje*) monk

frambuesa [fram'bwesa] *nf* raspberry

francamente [franka'mente] *adv* (*hablar, decir*) frankly; (*realmente*) really

francés, esa [fran'θes, esa] *adj* French ♦ *nm/f* Frenchman/woman ♦ *nm* (*LING*) French

Francia ['franθja] *nf* France

franco, a ['franko, a] *adj* (*cándido*)

frank, open; (*COM: exento*) free ♦ *nm* (*moneda*) franc

francotirador, a [frankotira'ðor, a] *nm/f* sniper

franela [fra'nela] *nf* flannel

franja ['franxa] *nf* fringe

franquear [franke'ar] *vt* (*camino*) to clear; (*carta, paquete postal*) to frank, stamp; (*obstáculo*) to overcome

franqueo [fran'keo] *nm* postage

franqueza [fran'keθa] *nf* (*candor*) frankness

frasco ['frasko] *nm* bottle, flask; **~ al vacío** (*vacuum*) flask

frase ['frase] *nf* sentence; **~ hecha** set phrase; (*pey*) stock phrase

fraterno, a [fra'terno, a] *adj* brotherly, fraternal

fraude ['frauðe] *nm* (*cualidad*) dishonesty; (*acto*) fraud; **fraudulento, a** *adj* fraudulent

frazada [fra'saða] (*AM*) *nf* blanket

frecuencia [fre'kwenθja] *nf* frequency; **con ~** frequently, often

frecuentar [frekwen'tar] *vt* to frequent

fregadero [freɣa'ðero] *nm* (kitchen) sink

fregar [fre'ɣar] *vt* (*trotar*) to scrub; (*platos*) to wash (up); (*AM*) to annoy

fregona [fre'ɣona] *nf* mop

freir [fre'ir] *vt* to fry

frenar [fre'nar] *vt* to brake; (*fig*) to check

frenazo [fre'naθo] *nm*: **dar un ~** to brake sharply

frenesí [frene'si] *nm* frenzy; **frenético, a** *adj* frantic

freno ['freno] *nm* (*TEC, AUTO*) brake; (*de cabalgadura*) bit; (*fig*) check

frente ['frente] *nm* (*ARQ, POL*) front; (*de objeto*) front part ♦ *nf* forehead, brow; **~ a** in front of; **en situación opuesta de**) opposite; **al ~ de** (*fig*) at the head of; **chocar de ~** to crash head-on; **hacer ~ a** to face up to

fresa ['fresa] (*ESP*) *nf* strawberry

fresco, a ['fresko, a] *adj* (*nuevo*) fresh;

(*frío*) cool; (*descarado*) cheeky ♦ *nm*
(*aire*) fresh air; (*ARTE*) fresco; (*AM: jugo*)
fruit drink ♦ *nm/f* (*fam*): **ser un ~** to
have a nerve; **tomar el ~** to get some
fresh air; **frescura** *nf* freshness;
(*descaro*) cheek, nerve

frialdad [frial'daθ] *nf* (*gen*) coldness;
(*indiferencia*) indifference

fricción [frik'θjon] *nf* (*gen*) friction;
(*acto*) rub(bing); (*MED*) massage

frigidez [frixi'δeθ] *nf* frigidity

frigorífico [friɣo'rifiko] *nm* refrigerator

frijol [fri'xol] *nm* kidney bean

frío, a *etc* [fri'o, a] *vb ver* **freír** ♦ *adj*
cold; (*indiferente*) indifferent ♦ *nm* cold;
indifference; **hace ~** it's cold; **tener ~**
to be cold

frito, a [fri'to, a] *adj* fried; **me trae
~ ese hombre** I'm sick and tired of
that man; **fritos** *nmpl* fried food

frívolo, a [fri'βolo, a] *adj* frivolous

frontal [fron'tal] *adj* frontal; **choque ~**
head-on collision

frontera [fron'tera] *nf* frontier;
fronterizo, a *adj* frontier *cpd*;
(*contiguo*) bordering

frontón [fron'ton] *nm* (*DEPORTE:
cancha*) pelota court; (: *juego*) pelota

frotar [fro'tar] *vt* to rub; **~se** *vr*: **~se
las manos** to rub one's hands

fructífero, a [fruk'tifero, a] *adj* fruitful

fruncir [frun'θir] *vt* to pleat; **~ el ceño** to knit
(*COSTURA*) to pleat; **~ el ceño** to knit
one's brow

frustrar [frus'trar] *vt* to frustrate

fruta [fruta] *nf* fruit; **frutería** *nf* fruit
shop; **frutero, a** *adj* fruit *cpd* ♦ *nm/f*
fruiterer ♦ *nm* fruit bowl

frutilla [fru'tiʎa] (*AM*) *nf* strawberry

fruto [fruto] *nm* fruit; (*fig: resultado*)
result; (: *beneficio*) benefit; **~s secos**
nuts; (*pasas etc*) dried fruit *sg*

fue *vb ver* **ser**; **ir**

fuego [fweɣo] *nm* (*gen*) fire; **a
~ lento** on a low heat; **¿tienes ~?**
have you (got) a light?; **~s artificiales
o de artificio** fireworks

fuente ['fwente] *nf* fountain;
(*manantial, fig*) spring; (*origen*) source;
(*plato*) large dish

fuera *etc* ['fwera] *vb ver* **ser, ir** ♦ *adv*
out(side); (*en otra parte*) away;
(*excepto, salvo*) except, save ♦ *prep*:
~ de outside; (*fig*) besides; **~ de sí**
beside o.s.; **por ~** (on the) outside

fuera-borda [fwera'βorδa] *nm*
speedboat

fuerte ['fwerte] *adj* strong; (*golpe*)
hard; (*ruido*) loud; (*comida*) rich;
(*lluvia*) heavy; (*dolor*) intense ♦ *adv*
strongly; hard; loud(ly)

fuerza *etc* ['fwerθa] *vb ver* **forzar** ♦ *nf*
(*fortaleza*) strength; (*TEC, ELEC*) power;
(*coacción*) force; (*MIL: tb: ~s*) forces *pl*;
a ~ de by dint of; **cobrar ~s** to
recover one's strength; **tener ~s para**
to have the strength to; **a la ~** forcibly,
by force; **por ~** of necessity; **~ de
voluntad** willpower

fuga ['fuɣa] *nf* (*huida*) flight, escape;
(*de gas etc*) leak

fugarse [fu'xarse] *vr* to flee, escape

fugaz [fu'ɣaθ] *adj* fleeting

fugitivo, a [fuxi'tiβo, a] *adj, nm/f*
fugitive

fui *vb ver* **ser; ir**

fulano, a [fu'lano, a] *nm/f* so-and-so,
what's-his-name/what's-her-name

fulminante [fulmi'nante] *adj* (*fig:
mirada*) fierce; (*MED: enfermedad,
ataque*) sudden; (*fam: éxito, golpe*)
sudden

fumador, a [fuma'δor, a] *nm/f* smoker

fumar [fu'mar] *vt, vi* to smoke; **~ en
pipa** to smoke a pipe

función [fun'θjon] *nf* function; (*en
trabajo*) duties *pl*; (*espectáculo*) show;
entrar en funciones to take up one's
duties

funcionar [funθjo'nar] *vi* (*gen*) to
function; (*máquina*) to work; **"no
funciona"** "out of order"

funcionario, a [funθjo'narjo, a] *nm/f*
civil servant

funda ['funda] nf (gen) cover; (de almohada) pillowcase

fundación [funda'θjon] nf foundation

fundamental [fundamen'tal] adj fundamental, basic

fundamentar [fundamen'tar] vt (poner base) to lay the foundations of; (establecer) to found; (fig) to base; **fundamento** nm (base) foundation

fundar [fun'dar] vt to found; **~se** vr: **~se en** to be founded on

fundición [fundi'θjon] nf fusing; (fábrica) foundry

fundir [fun'dir] vt (gen) to fuse; (metal) to smelt, melt down; (nieve etc) to melt; (COM) to merge; (estatua) to cast; **~se** vr (colores etc) to merge, blend; (unirse) to fuse together; (ELEC: fusible, lámpara etc) to fuse, blow; (nieve etc) to melt

fúnebre ['funeβre] adj funeral cpd, funereal

funeral [fune'ral] nm funeral; **funeraria** nf undertaker's

funesto, a [fu'nesto, a] adj (día) ill-fated; (decisión) fatal

furgón [fur'xon] nm wagon; **furgoneta** nf (AUTO, COM) (transit) van (BRIT), pick-up (truck) (US)

furia ['furja] nf (ira) fury; (violencia) violence; **furibundo, a** adj furious; **furioso, a** adj (iracundo) furious; (violento) violent; **furor** nm (cólera) rage

furtivo, a [fur'tiβo, a] adj furtive ♦ nm poacher

fusible [fu'siβle] nm fuse

fusil [fu'sil] nm rifle; **~ar** vt to shoot

fusión [fu'sjon] nf (gen) melting; (unión) fusion; (COM) merger

fútbol ['futβol] nm football; **futbolín** nm table football; **futbolista** nm footballer

futuro, a [fu'turo, a] adj, nm future

G, g

gabardina [gaβar'ðina] nf raincoat, gabardine

gabinete [gaβi'nete] nm (POL) cabinet; (estudio) study; (de abogados etc) office

gaceta [ga'θeta] nf gazette

gachas ['gatʃas] nfpl porridge sg

gafas ['gafas] nfpl glasses; **~ de sol** sunglasses

gafe ['gafe] nm jinx

gaita ['gaita] nf bagpipes pl

gajes ['gaxes] nmpl: **los ~ del oficio** occupational hazards

gajo ['gaxo] nm (de naranja) segment

gala ['gala] nf (traje de etiqueta) full dress; **~s** nfpl (ropa) finery sg; **estar de ~** to be in one's best clothes; **hacer ~ de** to display

galante [ga'lante] adj gallant; **galantería** (caballerosidad) gallantry; (cumplido) politeness; (comentario) compliment

galápago [ga'lapaxo] nm (ZOOL) turtle

galardón [galar'ðon] nm award, prize

galaxia [ga'laksja] nf galaxy

galera [ga'lera] nf (nave) galley; (carro) wagon; (IMPRENTA) galley

galería [gale'ria] nf (gen) gallery; (balcón) veranda(h); (pasillo) corridor

Gales ['gales] nm (tb: País de ~) Wales; **galés, esa** adj Welsh ♦ nm/f Welshman/woman ♦ nm (LING) Welsh

galgo, a ['galxo, a] nm/f greyhound

galimatías [galima'tias] nmpl (lenguaje) gibberish sg, nonsense sg

gallardía [gaʎar'ðia] nf (valor) bravery

gallego, a [ga'ʎexo, a] adj, nm/f Galician

galleta [ga'ʎeta] nf biscuit (BRIT), cookie (US)

gallina [ga'ʎina] nf hen ♦ nm/f (fam: cobarde) chicken; **gallinero** nm henhouse; (TEATRO) top gallery

gallo ['gaʎo] nm cock, rooster

galón [ga'lon] nm (MIL) stripe; (COSTURA) braid; (medida) gallon

galopar [galo'par] vi to gallop

gama ['gama] nf (fig) range

gamba ['gamba] nf prawn (BRIT), shrimp (US)

gamberro, a [gam'berro, a] nm/f hooligan, lout

gamuza [ga'muθa] nf chamois

gana ['gana] nf (deseo) desire, wish; (apetito) appetite; (voluntad) will; (añoranza) longing; **de buena ~** willingly; **de mala ~** reluctantly; **me da ~s de** I feel like, I want to; **no me da la ~** I don't feel like it; **tener ~s de** to feel like

ganadería [ganaðe'ria] nf (ganado) livestock; (ganado vacuno) cattle pl; (cría, comercio) cattle raising

ganado [ga'naðo] nm livestock; **~ lanar** sheep pl; **~ mayor** cattle pl; **~ porcino** pigs pl

ganador, a [gana'ðor, a] adj winning
♦ nm/f winner

ganancia [ga'nanθja] nf (lo ganado) gain; (aumento) increase; (beneficio) profit; **~s** nfpl (ingresos) earnings; (beneficios) profit sg, winnings

ganar [ga'nar] vt (obtener) to get, obtain; (sacar ventaja) to gain; (salario etc) to earn; (DEPORTE, premio) to win; (derrotar a) to beat; (alcanzar) to reach ♦ vi (DEPORTE) to win; **~se** vr: **~se la vida** to earn one's living

ganchillo [gan't∫iʎo] nm crochet

gancho ['gant∫o] nm (gen) hook; (colgador) hanger

gandul, a [gan'dul, a] adj, nm/f good-for-nothing, layabout

ganga ['ganga] nf bargain

gangrena [gan'grena] nf gangrene

ganso, a ['ganso, a] nm/f (ZOOL) goose; (fam) idiot

ganzúa [gan'θua] nf skeleton key

garabatear [garaβate'ar] vi, vt (al escribir) to scribble, scrawl

garabato [gara'βato] nm (escritura)

scrawl, scribble

garaje [ga'raxe] nm garage

garante [ga'rante] adj responsible
♦ nm/f guarantor

garantía [garan'tia] nf guarantee

garantizar [garanti'θar] vt to guarantee

garbanzo [gar'βanθo] nm chickpea (BRIT), garbanzo (US)

garbo [garβo] nm grace, elegance

garfio [garfjo] nm grappling iron

garganta [gar'xanta] nf (ANAT) throat; (de botella) neck; **gargantilla** nf necklace

gárgaras ['garxaras] nfpl: **hacer ~** to gargle

garita [ga'rita] nf cabin, hut; (MIL) sentry box

garra ['garra] nf (de gato, TEC) claw; (de ave) talon; (fam: mano) hand, paw

garrafa [ga'rrafa] nf carafe, decanter

garrapata [garra'pata] nf tick

garrote [ga'rrote] nm (palo) stick; (porra) cudgel; (suplicio) garrotte

garza ['garθa] nf heron

gas [gas] nm gas

gasa ['gasa] nf gauze

gaseosa [gase'osa] nf lemonade

gaseoso, a [gase'oso, a] adj gassy, fizzy

gasoil [ga'soil] nm diesel (oil)

gasóleo [ga'soleo] nm = **gasoil**

gasolina [gaso'lina] nf petrol, gas(oline) (US); **gasolinera** nf petrol (BRIT) o gas (US) station

gastado, a [gas'taðo, a] adj (dinero) spent; (ropa) worn out; (usado: frase etc) trite

gastar [gas'tar] vt (dinero, tiempo) to spend; (fuerzas) to use up; (desperdiciar) to waste; (llevar) to wear; **~se** vr to wear out; (estropearse) to waste; **~ bromas** to crack jokes; **¿qué número gastas?** what size (shoe) do you take?

gasto ['gasto] nm (desembolso) expenditure, spending; (consumo, uso) use; **~s** nmpl (desembolsos) expenses; (cargos) charges, costs

gastronomía [gastrono'mia] nf gastronomy

gatear [gate'ar] vi (andar a gatas) to go on all fours

gatillo [ga'tiʎo] nm (de arma de fuego) trigger; (de dentista) forceps

gato, a ['gato, a] nm/f cat ♦ nm (TEC) jack; **andar a gatas** to go on all fours

gaviota [ga'βjota] nf seagull

gay [ge] adj inv, nm gay, homosexual

gazpacho [gaθ'patʃo] nm gazpacho

gel [xel] nm (tb: **~ de baño/ducha**) gel

gelatina [xela'tina] nf jelly; (polvos etc) gelatine

gema ['xema] nf gem

gemelo, a [xe'melo, a] adj, nm/f twin; **~s** nmpl (de camisa) cufflinks; (prismáticos) field glasses, binoculars

gemido [xe'miðo] nm (quejido) moan, groan; (aullido) howl

Géminis ['xeminis] nm Gemini

gemir [xe'mir] vi (quejarse) to moan, groan; (aullar) to howl

generación [xenera'θjon] nf generation

general [xene'ral] adj general ♦ nm general; **por lo o en ~** in general; **G~itat** nf Catalan parliament; **~izar** vt to generalize; **~izarse** vr to become generalized, spread; **~mente** adv generally

generar [xene'rar] vt to generate

género ['xenero] nm (clase) kind, sort; (tipo) type; (BIO) genus; (LING) gender; (COM) material; **~ humano** human race

generosidad [xenerosi'ðað] nf generosity; **generoso, a** adj generous

genial [xe'njal] adj inspired; (idea) brilliant; (afable) genial

genio ['xenjo] nm (carácter) nature, disposition; (humor) temper; (facultad creadora) genius; **de mal ~** bad-tempered

genital [xeni'tal] adj genital; **genitales** nmpl genitals

gente ['xente] nf (personas) people pl; (parientes) relatives pl

gentil [xen'til] adj (elegante) graceful; (encantador) charming; **~eza** nf grace; charm; (cortesía) courtesy

gentío [xen'tio] nm crowd, throng

genuino, a [xe'nwino, a] adj genuine

geografía [xeoɣra'fia] nf geography

geología [xeolo'xia] nf geology

geometría [xeome'tria] nf geometry

gerencia [xe'renθja] nf management; **gerente** nm (supervisor) manager; (jefe) director

geriatría [xeria'tria] nf (MED) geriatrics sg

germen ['xermen] nm germ

germinar [xermi'nar] vi to germinate

gesticular [xestiku'lar] vi to gesticulate; (hacer muecas) to grimace; **gesticulación** nf gesticulation; (mueca) grimace

gestión [xes'tjon] nf management; (diligencia, acción) negotiation; **gestionar** vt (lograr) to try to arrange; (dirigir) to manage

gesto ['xesto] nm (mueca) grimace; (ademán) gesture

Gibraltar [xiβral'tar] nm Gibraltar; **gibraltareño, a** adj, nm/f Gibraltarian

gigante [xi'γante] adj, nm/f giant; **gigantesco, a** adj gigantic

gilipollas [xili'poʎas] (fam) adj inv daft ♦ nm/f inv wally

gimnasia [xim'nasja] nf gymnastics pl; **gimnasio** nm gymnasium; **gimnasta** nm/f gymnast

gimotear [ximote'ar] vi to whine, whimper

ginebra [xi'neβra] nf gin

ginecólogo, a [xine'koloɣo, a] nm/f gynaecologist

gira ['xira] nf tour, trip

girar [xi'rar] vi (dar la vuelta) to turn (around); (: rápidamente) to spin; (COM: giro postal) to draw; (: letra de cambio) to issue ♦ vi to turn (round); (*rápido*) to spin

girasol [xira'sol] nm sunflower

giratorio, a [xira'torjo, a] adj revolving

giro ['xiro] nm (*movimiento*) turn, revolution; (*LING*) expression; (*COM*) draft; **~ bancario/postal** bank giro/postal order

gis [xis] (*AM*) nm chalk

gitano, a [xi'tano, a] adj, nm/f gypsy

glacial [gla'θjal] adj icy, freezing

glaciar [gla'θjar] nm glacier

glándula ['glandula] nf gland

global [glo'βal] adj global

globo ['gloβo] nm (*esfera*) globe, sphere; (*aerostato, juguete*) balloon

glóbulo ['gloβulo] nm globule; (*ANAT*) corpuscle

gloria ['glorja] nf glory

glorieta [glo'rjeta] nf (*de jardín*) bower, arbour; (*plazoleta*) roundabout (*BRIT*), traffic circle (*US*)

glorificar [glorifi'kar] vt (*enaltecer*) to glorify, praise

glorioso, a [glo'rjoso, a] adj glorious

glotón, ona [glo'ton, ona] adj gluttonous, greedy ♦ nm/f glutton

glucosa [glu'kosa] nf glucose

gobernador, a [goβerna'ðor, a] adj governing ♦ nm/f governor; **gobernante** adj governing

gobernar [goβer'nar] vt (*dirigir*) to guide, direct; (*POL*) to rule, govern ♦ vi to govern; (*NAUT*) to steer

gobierno etc [go'βjerno] vb ver **gobernar** ♦ nm (*POL*) government; (*dirección*) guidance, direction; (*NAUT*) steering

goce etc ['goθe] vb ver **gozar** ♦ nm enjoyment

gol [gol] nm goal

golf [golf] nm golf

golfa ['golfa] (*fam!*) nf (*mujer*) slut, whore

golfo ['golfo, a] nm (*GEO*) gulf ♦ nm/f (*fam: niño*) urchin; (*gamberro*) lout

golondrina [golon'drina] nf swallow

golosina [golo'sina] nf (*dulce*) sweet; **goloso, a** adj sweet-toothed

golpe ['golpe] nm blow; (*de puño*) punch; (*de mano*) smack; (*de remo*) stroke; (*fig: choque*) clash; **no dar ~** to be good idle; **de un ~** with one blow; **de ~** suddenly; **~ (de estado)** coup (d'état); **golpear** vt, vi to strike, knock; (*asestar*) to beat; (*de puño*) to punch; (*golpetear*) to tap

goma ['goma] nf (*caucho*) rubber; (*elástico*) elastic; (*una ~*) elastic band; **~ espuma** foam rubber; **~ de pegar** gum, glue; **~ de borrar** eraser, rubber (*BRIT*)

gomina [go'mina] nf hair gel

gordo, a ['gorðo, a] adj (*gen*) fat; (*fam*) enormous; **el (premio) ~** (*en lotería*) first prize; **gordura** nf fat; (*corpulencia*) fatness, stoutness

gorila [go'rila] nm gorilla

gorjear [gorxe'ar] vi to twitter, chirp

gorra ['gorra] nf cap; (*de niño*) bonnet; (*militar*) bearskin; **entrar de ~** (*fam*) to gatecrash; **ir de ~** to sponge

gorrión [go'rrjon] nm sparrow

gorro ['gorro] nm (*gen*) cap; (*de niño, mujer*) bonnet

gorrón, ona [go'rron, ona] nm/f scrounger; **gorronear** (*fam*) vi to scrounge

gota ['gota] nf (*gen*) drop; (*de sudor*) bead; (*MED*) gout; **gotear** vi to drip; (*lloviznar*) to drizzle; **gotera** nf leak

gozar [go'θar] vi to enjoy o.s.; **~ de** (*disfrutar*) to enjoy; (*poseer*) to possess

gozne ['goθne] nm hinge

gozo ['goθo] nm (*alegría*) joy; (*placer*) pleasure

gr. abr (= *gramo, gramos*) g

grabación [graβa'θjon] nf recording

grabado [gra'βaðo] nm print, engraving

grabadora [graβa'ðora] nf tape-recorder

grabar [gra'ßar] vt to engrave; (discos, cintas) to record

gracia ['graθja] nf (encanto) grace, gracefulness; (humor) humour, wit; ¡**(muchas) ~s!** thanks (very much)!; **~s a** thanks to; **tener ~** (chiste etc) to be funny; **no me hace ~** I am not keen; **gracioso, a** adj (divertido) funny, amusing; (cómico) comic
♦ nm/f (TEATRO) comic character

grada ['graða] nf (de escalera) step; (de anfiteatro) tier, row; **~s** nfpl (DEPORTE: de estadio) terraces

gradería [graðe'ria] nf (gradas) (flight of) steps pl; (de anfiteatro) tiers pl, rows pl; (DEPORTE: de estadio) terraces pl; **~ cubierta** covered stand

grado ['graðo] nm degree; (de aceite, vino) grade; (grada) step; (MIL) rank; **de buen ~** willingly

graduación [graðwa'θjon] nf (del alcohol) proof, strength; (ESCOL) graduation; (MIL) rank

gradual [gra'ðwal] adj gradual

graduar [gra'ðwar] vt (gen) to graduate; (MIL) to commission; **~se** vr to graduate; **~se la vista** to have one's eyes tested

gráfica ['grafika] nf graph

gráfico, a ['grafiko, a] adj graphic
♦ nm diagram; **~s** nmpl (INFORM) graphics

grajo ['graxo] nm rook

Gral abr (= General) Gen.

gramática [gra'matika] nf grammar

gramo ['gramo] nm gramme (BRIT), gram (US)

gran [gran] adj ver **grande**

grana ['grana] nf (color, tela) scarlet

granada [gra'naða] nf pomegranate; (MIL) grenade

granate [gra'nate] adj deep red

Gran Bretaña [-bre'taɲa] nf Great Britain

grande ['grande] (antes de nmsg: **gran**) adj (de tamaño) big, large; (alto) tall; (distinguido) great; (impresionante)

grand ♦ nm grandee; **grandeza** nf greatness

grandioso, a [gran'djoso, a] adj magnificent, grand

granel [gra'nel]: **a ~** adv (COM) in bulk

granero [gra'nero] nm granary, barn

granito [gra'nito] nm (AGR) small grain; (roca) granite

granizado [grani'θaðo] nm iced drink

granizar [grani'θar] vi to hail; **granizo** nm hail

granja ['granxa] nf (gen) farm; **granjear** vt to win, gain; **granjearse** vr to win, gain; **granjero, a** nm/f farmer

grano ['grano] nm grain; (semilla) seed; (de café) bean; (MED) pimple, spot

granuja [gra'nuxa] nm/f rogue; (golfillo) urchin

grapa ['grapa] nf staple; (TEC) clamp; **grapadora** nf stapler

grasa ['grasa] nf (gen) grease; (de cocinar) fat, lard; (sebo) suet; (mugre) filth; **grasiento, a** adj greasy; (de aceite) oily; **graso, a** adj (leche, queso, carne) fatty; (pelo, piel) greasy

gratificación [gratifika'θjon] nf (bono) bonus; (recompensa) reward

gratificar [gratifi'kar] vt to reward

gratinar [grati'nar] vt to cook au gratin

gratis ['gratis] adv free

gratitud [grati'tuð] nf gratitude

grato, a ['grato, a] adj (agradable) pleasant, agreeable

gratuito, a [gra'twito, a] adj (gratis) free; (sin razón) gratuitous

gravamen [gra'ßamen] nm (impuesto) tax

gravar [gra'ßar] vt to tax

grave ['graße] adj heavy; (serio) grave, serious; **~dad** nf gravity

gravilla [gra'ßiʎa] nf gravel

gravitar [graßi'tar] vi to gravitate; **~ sobre** to rest on

graznar [graθ'nar] vi (cuervo) to squawk; (pato) to quack; (hablar ronco) to croak

Grecia ['greθja] nf Greece

gremio ['gremjo] nm trade, industry

greña ['greɲa] nf (cabellos) shock of hair

gresca ['greska] nf uproar

griego, a ['grjeɣo, a] adj, nm/f Greek

grieta ['grjeta] nf crack

grifo ['grifo] nm tap; (AM: AUTO) petrol (BRIT) o gas (US) station

grilletes [gri'ʎetes] nmpl fetters

grillo ['griʎo] nm (ZOOL) cricket

gripe ['gripe] nf flu, influenza

gris [gris] adj (color) grey

gritar [gri'tar] vt, vi to shout, yell; **grito** nm shout, yell; (de horror) scream

grosella [gro'seʎa] nf (red)currant; **~ negra** blackcurrant

grosería [grose'ria] nf (actitud) rudeness; (comentario) vulgar comment; **grosero, a** adj (poco cortés) rude, bad-mannered; (ordinario) vulgar, crude

grosor [gro'sor] nm thickness

grotesco, a [gro'tesko, a] adj grotesque

grúa ['grua] nf (TEC) crane; (de petróleo) derrick

grueso, a ['grweso, a] adj thick; (persona) stout ♦ nm bulk; **el ~ de** the bulk of

grulla ['gruʎa] nf crane

grumo ['grumo] nm clot, lump

gruñido [gru'ɲiðo] nm grunt; (de persona) grumble

gruñir [gru'ɲir] vi (animal) to growl; (persona) to grumble

grupa ['grupa] nf (ZOOL) rump

grupo ['grupo] nm group; (TEC) unit, set

gruta ['gruta] nf grotto

guadaña [gwa'ðaɲa] nf scythe

guagua ['gwaxwa] (AM) nf (niño) baby; (bus) bus

guante ['gwante] nm glove; **~ra** nf glove compartment

guapo, a ['gwapo, a] adj good-looking, attractive; (elegante) smart

guarda ['gwarða] nm/f (persona) guard, keeper ♦ nf (acto) custody; (custodia) custody; **~bosques** nm inv gamekeeper; **~costas** nm inv coastguard vessel ♦ nm/f guardian, protector; **~espaldas** nm/f inv bodyguard; **~meta** nm/f goalkeeper; **guardar** vt (gen) to keep; (vigilar) to guard, watch over; (dinero: ahorrar) to save; **guardarse** vr (preservarse) to protect o.s.; (evitar) to avoid; **guardar cama** to stay in bed; **~rropa** nm (armario) wardrobe; (en establecimiento público) cloakroom

guardería [gwarðe'ria] nf nursery

guardia ['gwarðja] nf (MIL) guard; (cuidado) care, custody ♦ nm/f guard; (policía) policeman/woman; **estar de ~** to be on guard; **montar ~** to mount guard; **G~ Civil** Civil Guard; **G~ Nacional** National Guard

guardián, ana [gwar'ðjan, ana] nm/f (gen) guardian, keeper

guarecer [gware'θer] vt (proteger) to protect; (abrigar) to shelter; **~se** vr to take refuge

guarida [gwa'riða] nf (de animal) den, lair; (refugio) refuge

guarnecer [gwarne'θer] vt (equipar) to provide; (adornar) to adorn; (TEC) to reinforce; **guarnición** nf (de vestimenta) trimming; (de piedra) mount; (CULIN) garnish; (arneses) harness; (MIL) garrison

guarro, a ['gwarro, a] nm/f pig

guasa ['gwasa] nf joke; **guasón, ona** adj (bromista) joking ♦ nm/f wit; joker

Guatemala [gwate'mala] nf Guatemala

guay [gwai] (fam) adj super, great

gubernativo, a [gußerna'tißo, a] adj governmental

guerra ['gerra] nf war; **~ civil** civil war; **~ fría** cold war; **dar ~** to annoy; **guerrear** vi to wage war; **guerrero, a**

adj fighting; (*carácter*) warlike ♦ *nm/f* warrior

guerrilla [geˈrriʎa] *nf* guerrilla warfare; (*tropas*) guerrilla band o group

guía *etc* [ˈgia] *vb ver* **guiar** ♦ *nm/f* (*persona*) guide ♦ *nf* (*libro*) guidebook; ~ **de ferrocarriles** railway timetable; ~ **telefónica** telephone directory

guiar [giˈar] *vt* to guide, direct; (*AUTO*) to steer; ~**se** *vr*: ~**se por** to be guided by

guijarro [giˈxarro] *nm* pebble

guillotina [giʎoˈtina] *nf* guillotine

guinda [ˈginda] *nf* morello cherry

guindilla [ginˈdiʎa] *nf* chilli pepper

guiñapo [giˈɲapo] *nm* (*harapo*) rag; (*persona*) reprobate, rogue

guiñar [giˈɲar] *vt* to wink

guión [giˈon] *nm* (*LING*) hyphen, dash; (*CINE*) script; **guionista** *nm/f* scriptwriter

guiri [ˈgiri] (*fam: pey*) *nm/f* foreigner

guirnalda [girˈnalda] *nf* garland

guisado [giˈsaðo] *nm* stew

guisante [giˈsante] *nm* pea

guisar [giˈsar] *vt, vi* to cook; **guiso** *nm* cooked dish

guitarra [giˈtarra] *nf* guitar

gula [ˈgula] *nf* gluttony, greed

gusano [guˈsano] *nm* worm; (*lombriz*) earthworm

gustar [gusˈtar] *vt* to taste, sample ♦ *vi* to please, be pleasing; ~ **de algo** to like o enjoy sth; **me gustan las uvas** I like grapes; **le gusta nadar** she likes o enjoys swimming

gusto [ˈgusto] *nm* (*sentido, sabor*) taste; (*placer*) pleasure; **tiene ~ a menta** it tastes of mint; **tener buen ~** to have good taste; **sentirse a ~** to feel at ease; **mucho ~ (en conocerle)** pleased to meet you; **el ~ es mío** the pleasure is mine; **con ~** willingly, gladly; ~**so, a** *adj* (*sabroso*) tasty; (*agradable*) pleasant

H, h

ha *vb ver* **haber**

haba [ˈaβa] *nf* bean

Habana [aˈβana] *nf*: **la ~** Havana

habano [aˈβano] *nm* Havana cigar

habéis *vb ver* **haber**

PALABRA CLAVE

haber [aˈβer] *vb aux* **1** (*tiempos compuestos*) to have; **había comido** I had eaten; **antes/después de ~lo visto** before seeing/after seeing o having seen it

2: **¡~lo dicho antes!** you should have said so before!

3: ~ **de**: **he de hacerlo** I have to do it; **ha de llegar mañana** it should arrive tomorrow

♦ *vb impers* **1** (*existencia: sg*) there is; (*: pl*) there are; **hay un hermano/dos hermanos** there is one brother/there are two brothers; **¿cuánto hay de aquí a Sucre?** how far is it from here to Sucre?

2 (*obligación*): **hay que hacer algo** something must be done; **hay que apuntarlo para acordarse** you have to write it down to remember

3: **¡hay que ver!** well I never!

4: **¡no hay de o por (*AM*) qué!** don't mention it!, not at all

5: **¿qué hay?** (*¿qué pasa?*) what's up?, what's the matter?; (*¿qué tal?*) how's it going?

♦ ~**se** *vr*: **habérselas con uno** to have it out with sb

♦ *vt*: **he aquí unas sugerencias** here are some suggestions; **no hay cintas blancas pero sí las hay rojas** there aren't any white ribbons but there are some red ones

♦ *nm* (*en cuenta*) credit side; ~**es** *nmpl* assets; **¿cuánto tengo en el ~?** how much do I have in my account?; **tiene** varias novelas en su ~ he has several novels to his credit

habichuela [aβi'tʃwela] nf kidney bean

hábil ['aβil] adj (listo) clever, smart; (capaz) fit, capable; (experto) expert; **día** ~ working day; **habilidad** nf skill, ability

habilitar [aβili'tar] vt (capacitar) to enable; (dar instrumentos) to equip; (financiar) to finance

hábilmente [aβil'mente] adv skilfully, expertly

habitación [aβita'θjon] nf (cuarto) room; (BIO: morada) habitat; ~ **sencilla** o **individual** single room; ~ **doble** o **de matrimonio** double room

habitante [aβi'tante] nm/f inhabitant

habitar [aβi'tar] vt (residir en) to inhabit; (ocupar) to occupy ♦ vi to live

hábito ['aβito] nm habit

habitual [aβi'twal] adj usual

habituar [aβi'twar] vt to accustom; ~**se** vr: ~**se a** to get used to

habla ['aβla] nf (capacidad de hablar) speech; (idioma) language; (dialecto) dialect; **perder el** ~ to become speechless; **de** ~ **francesa** French-speaking; **estar al** ~ to be in contact; (TEL) to be on the line; **¡González al** ~! (TEL) González speaking!

hablador, a [aβla'ðor, a] adj talkative ♦ nm/f chatterbox

habladuría [aβlaðu'ria] nf rumour; ~**s** nfpl gossip sg

hablante [a'βlante] adj speaking ♦ nm/f speaker

hablar [a'βlar] vt to speak, talk ♦ vi to speak; ~**se** vr to speak to each other; ~ **con** to speak to; ~ **de** to speak of o about; "**se habla inglés**" "English spoken here"; **¡ni** ~! it's out of the question!

habré etc vb ver **haber**

hacendoso, a [aθen'doso, a] adj industrious

hacer [a'θer] vt **1** (fabricar, producir) to make; (construir) to build; ~ **una película/un ruido** to make a film/noise; **el guisado lo hice yo** I made o cooked the stew

2 (ejecutar: trabajo etc) to do; ~ **la colada** to do the washing; ~ **la comida** to do the cooking; **¿qué haces?** what are you doing?; ~ **el malo** o **el papel del malo** (TEATRO) to play the villain

3 (estudios, algunos deportes) to do; ~ **español/económicas** to do o study Spanish/economics; ~ **yoga/gimnasia** to do yoga/go to gym

4 (transformar, incidir en): **esto lo hará más difícil** this will make it more difficult; **salir te hará sentir mejor** going out will make you feel better

5 (cálculo): **2 y 2 hacen 4** 2 and 2 make 4; **éste hace 100** this one makes 100

6 (+ sub): **esto hará que ganemos** this will make us win; **harás que no quiera venir** you'll stop him wanting to come

7 (como sustituto de vb) to do; **él bebió y yo hice lo mismo** he drank and I did likewise

8: **no hace más que criticar** all he does is criticize

♦ vb semi-aux: **hacer** + infin **1** (directo): **les hice venir** I made o had them come; ~ **trabajar a los demás** to get others to work

2 (por intermedio de otros): ~ **reparar algo** to get sth repaired

♦ vi **1**: **haz como que no lo sabes** act as if you don't know

2 (ser apropiado): **si os hace** if it's alright with you

3: ~ **de**: ~ **de madre para uno** to be like a mother to sb; (TEATRO): ~ **de Otelo** to play Othello

♦ vb impers **1**: **hace calor/frío** it's
hot/cold; ver tb **bueno**; **sol**; **tiempo**
2 (tiempo): **hace 3 años** 3 years ago;
hace un mes que voy/no voy I've
been going/I haven't been for a month
3: **¿cómo has hecho para llegar
tan rápido?** how did you manage to
get here so quickly?
♦ **~se** vr **1** (volverse) to become; **se
hicieron amigos** they became friends
2 (acostumbrarse): **~se a** to get used
to
3: **se hace con huevos y leche** it's
made out of eggs and milk; **eso no se
hace** that's not done
4 (obtener): **~se de** o **con algo** to get
hold of sth
5 (fingirse): **~se el sueco** to turn a
deaf ear

hacha ['atʃa] nf axe; (antorcha) torch
hachís [a'tʃis] nm hashish
hacia ['aθja] prep (en dirección de)
towards; (cerca de) near; (actitud)
towards; **~ arriba/abajo** up(wards)/
down(wards); **~ mediodía** about noon
hacienda [a'θjenda] nf (propiedad)
property; (finca) farm; (AM) ranch;
~ pública public finance; **(Ministerio
de) H~** Exchequer (BRIT), Treasury
Department (US)
hada ['aða] nf fairy
hago etc vb ver **hacer**
Haití [ai'ti] nm Haiti
halagar [ala'ɣar] vt to flatter
halago [a'laɣo] nm flattery;
halagüeño, a adj flattering
halcón [al'kon] nm falcon, hawk
hallar [a'ʎar] vt (gen) to find;
(descubrir) to discover; (toparse con)
to run into; **~se** vr to be (situated);
hallazgo nm discovery; (cosa) find
halterofilia [altero'filja] nf
weightlifting
hamaca [a'maka] nf hammock
hambre ['ambre] nf hunger; (plaga)
famine; (deseo) longing; **tener ~** to be

hungry; **hambriento, a** adj hungry,
starving
hamburguesa [ambur'ɣesa] nf
hamburger; **hamburguesería** nf
burger bar
han vb ver **haber**
harapiento, a [ara'pjento, a] adj
tattered, in rags
harapos [a'rapos] nmpl rags
haré etc vb ver **hacer**
harina [a'rina] nf flour
hartar [ar'tar] vt to satiate, glut; (fig)
to tire, sicken; **~se** vr (de comida) to fill
o.s., gorge o.s.; (cansarse) to get fed
up (de with); **hartazgo** nm surfeit,
glut; **harto, a** adj (lleno) full; (cansado)
fed up ♦ adv (bastante) enough; (muy)
very; **estar harto de** to be fed up
with
has vb ver **haber**
hasta ['asta] adv even ♦ prep
(alcanzando a) as far as; up to; down
to; (de tiempo: a tal hora) till, until;
(antes de) before ♦ conj: **~ que** until;
~ luego/el sábado see you soon/on
Saturday
hastiar [as'tjar] vt (gen) to weary;
(aburrir) to bore; **~se** vr: **~se de** to get
fed up with; **hastío** nm weariness;
boredom
hatillo [a'tiʎo] nm belongings pl, kit;
(montón) bundle, heap
hay vb ver **haber**
Haya ['aja] nf: **la ~** The Hague
haya etc ['aja] vb ver **haber** ♦ nf beech
tree
haz [aθ] vb ver **hacer** ♦ nm (de luz)
beam
hazaña [a'θaɲa] nf feat, exploit
hazmerreír [aθmerre'ir] nm inv
laughing stock
he vb ver **haber**
hebilla [e'βiʎa] nf buckle, clasp
hebra ['eβra] nf thread; (BOT: fibra)
fibre, grain
hebreo, a [e'βreo, a] adj, nm/f Hebrew
♦ nm (LING) Hebrew

hechizar [etʃi'θar] *vt* to cast a spell on, bewitch

hechizo [e'tʃiθo] *nm* witchcraft, magic; (*acto de magia*) spell, charm

hecho, a ['etʃo, a] *pp de* **hacer ♦** *adj* (*carne*) done; (*COSTURA*) ready-to-wear **♦** *nm* deed, act; (*dato*) fact; (*cuestión*) matter; (*suceso*) event **♦** *excl* agreed!, done!; **¡bien ~!** well done!; **de ~** in fact, as a matter of fact

hechura [e'tʃura] *nf* (*forma*) form, shape; (*de persona*) build

hectárea [ek'tarea] *nf* hectare

heder [e'ðer] *vi* to stink, smell

hediondo, a [e'ðjondo, a] *adj* stinking

hedor [e'ðor] *nm* stench

helada [e'laða] *nf* frost

heladera [ela'ðera] (*AM*) *nf* (*refrigerador*) refrigerator

helado, a [e'laðo, a] *adj* frozen; (*glacial*) icy; (*fig*) chilly, cold **♦** *nm* ice cream

helar [e'lar] *vt* to freeze, ice (up); (*dejar atónito*) to amaze; (*desalentar*) to discourage **♦** *vi* to freeze; **~se** *vr* to freeze

helecho [e'letʃo] *nm* fern

hélice ['eliθe] *nf* (*TEC*) propeller

helicóptero [eli'koptero] *nm* helicopter

hembra ['embra] *nf* (*BOT, ZOOL*) female; (*mujer*) woman; (*TEC*) nut

hemorragia [emo'rraxja] *nf* haemorrhage

hemorroides [emo'rroiðes] *nfpl* haemorrhoids, piles

hemos *vb ver* **haber**

hendidura [endi'ðura] *nf* crack, split

heno ['eno] *nm* hay

herbicida [erβi'θiða] *nm* weedkiller

heredad [ere'ðað] *nf* landed property; (*granja*) farm

heredar [ere'ðar] *vt* to inherit; **heredero, a** *nm/f* heir(ess)

hereje [e'rexe] *nm/f* heretic

herencia [e'renθja] *nf* inheritance

herida [e'riða] *nf* wound, injury; *ver tb*

herido

herido, a [e'riðo, a] *adj* injured, wounded **♦** *nm/f* casualty

herir [e'rir] *vt* to wound, injure; (*fig*) to offend

hermanastro, a [erma'nastro, a] *nm/f* stepbrother/sister

hermandad [erman'dað] *nf* brotherhood

hermano, a [er'mano, a] *nm/f* brother/sister; **~ gemelo** twin brother; **hermana gemela** twin sister; **~ político** brother-in-law; **hermana política** sister-in-law

hermético, a [er'metiko, a] *adj* hermetic; (*fig*) watertight

hermoso, a [er'moso, a] *adj* beautiful, lovely; (*estupendo*) splendid; (*guapo*) handsome; **hermosura** *nf* beauty

hernia ['ernja] *nf* hernia

héroe ['eroe] *nm* hero

heroína [ero'ina] *nf* (*mujer*) heroine; (*droga*) heroin

heroísmo [ero'ismo] *nm* heroism

herradura [erra'ðura] *nf* horseshoe

herramienta [erra'mjenta] *nf* tool

herrero [e'rrero] *nm* blacksmith

herrumbre [e'rrumbre] *nf* rust

hervidero [erβi'ðero] *nm* (*fig*) swarm; (*POL etc*) hotbed

hervir [er'βir] *vi* to boil; (*burbujear*) to bubble; (*fig*): **~ de** to teem with; **~ a fuego lento** to simmer; **hervor** *nm* boiling; (*fig*) ardour, fervour

heterosexual [eterosek'swal] *adj* heterosexual

hice *etc vb ver* **hacer**

hidratante [iðra'tante] *adj*: **crema ~** moisturizing cream, moisturizer; **hidratar** *vt* (*piel*) to moisturize; **hidrato** *nm*: **hidratos de carbono** carbohydrates

hidráulica [i'ðraulika] *nf* hydraulics *sg*

hidráulico, a [i'ðrauliko, a] *adj* hydraulic

hidro... [iðro] *prefijo* hydro..., water-...; **~eléctrico, a** *adj* hydroelectric;

~fobia nf hydrophobia, rabies;
hidrógeno nm hydrogen

hiedra ['jeðra] nf ivy

hiel [jel] nf gall, bile; (fig) bitterness

hiela etc vb ver **helar**

hielo ['jelo] nm (gen) ice; (escarcha)
frost; (fig) coldness, reserve

hiena ['jena] nf hyena

hierba ['jerβa] nf (pasto) grass; (CULIN,
MED: planta) herb; **mala ~** weed; (fig)
evil influence; **~buena** nf mint

hierro ['jerro] nm (metal) iron; (objeto)
iron object

hígado ['iɣaðo] nm liver

higiene [i'xjene] nf hygiene;
higiénico, a adj hygienic

higo ['iɣo] nm fig; **higuera** nf fig tree

hijastro, a [i'xastro, a] nm/f stepson/
daughter

hijo, a ['ixo, a] nm/f son/daughter,
child; **~s** nmpl children, sons and
daughters; **~ de papá/mamá**
daddy's/mummy's boy; **~ de puta**
(fam!) bastard (!), son of a bitch (!)

hilar [i'lar] vt to spin; **~ fino** to split
hairs

hilera [i'lera] nf row, file

hilo ['ilo] nm thread; (BOT) fibre;
(metal) wire; (de agua) trickle, thin
stream

hilvanar [ilβa'nar] vt (COSTURA) to tack
(BRIT), baste (US); (fig) to do hurriedly

himno ['imno] nm hymn; **~ nacional**
national anthem

hincapié [inka'pje] nm: **hacer ~ en** to
emphasize

hincar [in'kar] vt to drive (in), thrust
(in); **~se** vr: **~se de rodillas** to kneel
down

hincha ['intʃa] (fam) nm/f fan

hinchado, a [in'tʃaðo, a] adj (gen)
swollen; (persona) pompous

hinchar [in'tʃar] vt (gen) to swell;
(inflar) to blow up, inflate; (fig) to
exaggerate; **~se** vr (inflarse) to swell
up; (fam: de comer) to stuff o.s.;

hinchazón nf (MED) swelling; (altivez)
arrogance

hinojo [i'noxo] nm fennel

hipermercado [ipermer'kaðo] nm
hypermarket, superstore

hípico, a ['ipiko, a] adj horse cpd

hipnotismo [ipno'tismo] nm
hypnotism; **hipnotizar** vt to hypnotize

hipo ['ipo] nm hiccups pl

hipocresía [ipokre'sia] nf hypocrisy;
hipócrita adj hypocritical ♦ nm/f
hypocrite

hipódromo [i'poðromo] nm racetrack

hipopótamo [ipo'potamo] nm
hippopotamus

hipoteca [ipo'teka] nf mortgage

hipótesis [i'potesis] nf inv hypothesis

hiriente [i'rjente] adj offensive,
wounding

hispánico, a [is'paniko, a] adj
Hispanic

hispano, a [is'pano, a] adj Hispanic,
Spanish, Hispano- ♦ nm/f Spaniard;
H~américa nf Latin America;
~americano, a adj, nm/f Latin
American

histeria [is'terja] nf hysteria

historia [is'torja] nf history; (cuento)
story, tale; **~s** nfpl (chismes) gossip sg;
dejarse de ~s to come to the point;
pasar a la ~ to go down in history;
~dor, a nm/f historian; **historial** nm
(profesional) curriculum vitae, C.V.;
(MED) case history; **histórico, a** adj
historical; (memorable) historic

historieta [isto'rjeta] nf tale, anecdote;
(dibujos) comic strip

hito ['ito] nm (fig) landmark

hizo vb ver **hacer**

Hnos abr (= Hermanos) Bros.

hocico [o'θiko] nm snout

hockey ['xoki] nm hockey; **~ sobre
hielo** ice hockey

hogar [o'ɣar] nm fireplace, hearth;
(casa) home; (vida familiar) home life;
~eño, a adj home cpd; (persona)
home-loving

hoguera [o'ɣera] nf (gen) bonfire

hoja ['oxa] nf (gen) leaf; (de flor) petal; (de papel) sheet; (página) page; **~ de afeitar** razor blade

hojalata [oxa'lata] nf tin(plate)

hojaldre [o'xaldre] nm (CULIN) puff pastry

hojear [oxe'ar] vt to leaf through, turn the pages of

hola ['ola] excl hello!

Holanda [o'landa] nf Holland; **holandés, esa** adj Dutch ♦ nm/f Dutchman/woman ♦ nm (LING) Dutch

holgado, a [ol'xaðo, a] adj (ropa) loose, baggy; (rico) comfortable

holgar [ol'xar] vi (descansar) to rest; (sobrar) to be superfluous; **huelga decir que** it goes without saying that

holgazán, ana [olxa'θan, ana] adj idle, lazy ♦ nm/f loafer

holgura [ol'xura] nf looseness, bagginess; (TEC) play, free movement; (vida) comfortable living

hollín [o'ʎin] nm soot

hombre ['ombre] nm (gen) man; (raza humana): **el ~** man(kind) ♦ excl ¡sí ~! (claro) of course!; (para énfasis) man, old boy; **~ de negocios** businessman; **~ de pro** honest man; **~-rana** frogman

hombrera [om'brera] nf shoulder strap

hombro ['ombro] nm shoulder

hombruno, a [om'bruno, a] adj mannish

homenaje [ome'naxe] nm (gen) homage; (tributo) tribute

homicida [omi'θiða] adj homicidal ♦ nm/f murderer; **homicidio** nm murder, homicide

homologar [omolo'ðar] vt (COM: productos, tamaños) to standardize; **homólogo, a** adj: **su** etc **homólogo** his etc counterpart o opposite number

homosexual [omosek'swal] adj, nm/f homosexual

hondo, a ['ondo, a] adj deep; **lo ~** the depth(s) (pl), the bottom; **~nada** nf

hollow, depression; (cañón) ravine

Honduras [on'duras] nf Honduras

hondureño, a [ondu'reno, a] adj, nm/f Honduran

honestidad [onesti'ðað] nf purity, chastity; (decencia) decency; **honesto, a** adj chaste; decent, honest; (justo) just

hongo ['ongo] nm (BOT: gen) fungus; (: comestible) mushroom; (: venenoso) toadstool

honor [o'nor] nm (gen) honour; **en ~ a la verdad** to be fair; **~able** adj honourable

honorario, a [ono'rarjo, a] adj honorary; **~s** nmpl fees

honra ['onra] nf (gen) honour; (renombre) good name; **~dez** nf honesty; (de persona) integrity; **~do, a** adj honest, upright

honrar [on'rar] vt to honour; **~se** vr: **~se con algo/de hacer algo** to be honoured by sth/to do sth

honroso, a [on'roso, a] adj (honrado) honourable; (respetado) respectable

hora ['ora] nf (una ~) hour; (tiempo) time; **¿qué ~ es?** what time is it?; **¿a qué ~?** at what time?; **media ~** half an hour; **a la ~ de recreo** at playtime; **a primera ~** first thing (in the morning); **a última ~** at the last moment; **a altas ~s** in the small hours; **¡a buena ~!** about time, too!; **dar la ~** to strike the hour; **~s de oficina/de trabajo** office/working hours; **~s de visita** visiting times; **~s extras o extraordinarias** overtime sg; **~s punta** rush hours

horadar [ora'ðar] vt to drill, bore

horario, a [o'rarjo, a] adj hourly, hour cpd ♦ nm timetable; **~ comercial** business hours pl

horca ['orka] nf gallows sg

horcajadas [orka'xaðas]: **a ~** adv astride

horchata [or'tʃata] nf cold drink made from tiger nuts and water, tiger nut milk

horizontal [oriθon'tal] adj horizontal

horizonte [ori'θonte] nm horizon

horma ['orma] nf mould

hormiga [or'miɣa] nf ant; **~s** nfpl (MED) pins and needles

hormigón [ormi'ɣon] nm concrete; **~ armado/pretensado** reinforced/prestressed concrete

hormigueo [ormi'ɣeo] nm (comezón) itch

hormona [or'mona] nf hormone

hornada [or'naða] nf batch (of loaves etc)

hornillo [or'niʎo] nm (cocina) portable stove

horno ['orno] nm (CULIN) oven; (TEC) furnace; **alto ~** blast furnace

horóscopo [o'roskopo] nm horoscope

horquilla [or'kiʎa] nf hairpin; (AGR) pitchfork

horrendo, a [o'rrendo, a] adj horrendous, frightful

horrible [o'rriβle] adj horrible, dreadful

horripilante [orripi'lante] adj hair-raising, horrifying

horror [o'rror] nm horror, dread; (atrocidad) atrocity; **¡qué ~!** (fam) how awful!; **~izar** vt to horrify, frighten; **~izarse** vr to be horrified; **~oso, a** adj horrifying, ghastly

hortaliza [orta'liθa] nf vegetable

hortelano, a [orte'lano, a] nm/f (market) gardener

hortera [or'tera] (fam) adj tacky

hosco, a ['osko, a] adj sullen, gloomy

hospedar [ospe'ðar] vt to put up; **~se** vr to stay, lodge

hospital [ospi'tal] nm hospital

hospitalario, a [ospita'larjo, a] adj (acogedor) hospitable; **hospitalidad** nf hospitality

hostal [os'tal] nm small hotel

hostelería [ostele'ria] nf hotel business o trade

hostia ['ostja] nf (REL) host, consecrated wafer; (fam!: golpe) whack, punch ♦ excl (fam!): **¡~(s)!** damn!

hostigar [osti'ɣar] vt to whip; (fig) to harass, pester

hostil [os'til] adj hostile; **~idad** nf hostility

hotel [o'tel] nm hotel; **~ero, a** adj hotel cpd ♦ nm/f hotelier

Hotel

In Spain you can choose from the following categories of accommodation, in descending order of quality and price: **hotel** (from 5 stars to 1), **hostal**, **pensión**, **casa de huéspedes**, **fonda**. The State also runs luxury hotels called **paradores**, which are usually sited in places of particular historical interest and are often historic buildings themselves.

hoy [oi] adv (este día) today; (la actualidad) now(adays) ♦ nm present time; **~ (en) día** now(adays)

hoyo ['ojo] nm hole, pit; **hoyuelo** nm dimple

hoz [oθ] nf sickle

hube etc vb ver **haber**

hucha ['utʃa] nf money box

hueco, a ['weko, a] adj (vacío) hollow, empty; (resonante) booming ♦ nm hollow, cavity

huelga etc ['welɣa] vb ver **holgar** ♦ nf strike; **declararse en ~** to go on strike, come out on strike; **~ de hambre** hunger strike

huelguista [wel'ɣista] nm/f striker

huella ['weʎa] nf (pisada) tread; (marca del paso) footprint, footstep; (: de animal, máquina) track; **~ digital** fingerprint

huelo etc vb ver **oler**

huérfano, a ['werfano, a] adj orphan(ed) ♦ nm/f orphan

huerta ['werta] nf market garden; (en Murcia y Valencia) irrigated region

huerto ['werto] nm kitchen garden; (de árboles frutales) orchard

hueso ['weso] nm (ANAT) bone; (de fruta) stone

huésped, a ['wespeð, a] nm/f guest

huesudo, a [we'suðo, a] adj bony, big-boned

hueva ['weßa] nf roe

huevera [we'ßera] nf eggcup

huevo ['weßo] nm egg; ~ **duro/ escalfado/frito** (ESP) o **estrellado** (AM)/**pasado por agua** hard-boiled/ poached/fried/soft-boiled egg; ~**s revueltos** scrambled eggs

huida [u'iða] nf escape, flight

huidizo, a [ui'ðiðo, a] adj shy

huir [u'ir] vi (escapar) to flee, escape; (evitar) to avoid; ~**se** vr (escaparse) to escape

hule ['ule] nm oilskin

humanidad [umani'ðað] nf (género humano) man(kind); (cualidad) humanity

humanitario, a [umani'tarjo, a] adj humanitarian

humano, a [u'mano, a] adj (gen) human; (humanitario) humane ♦ nm human; **ser** ~ human being

humareda [uma'reða] nf cloud of smoke

humedad [ume'ðað] nf (del clima) humidity; (de pared etc) dampness; **a prueba de** ~ damp-proof;

humedecer vt to moisten, wet; **humedecerse** vr to get wet

húmedo, a ['umeðo, a] adj (mojado) damp, wet; (tiempo etc) humid

humildad [umil'ðað] nf humility, humbleness; **humilde** adj humble, modest

humillación [umiʎa'θjon] nf humiliation; **humillante** adj humiliating

humillar [umi'ʎar] vt to humiliate; ~**se** vr to humble o.s., grovel

humo ['umo] nm (de fuego) smoke; (gas nocivo) fumes pl; (vapor) steam, vapour; ~**s** nmpl (fig) conceit sg

humor [u'mor] nm (disposición) mood,

temper; (lo que divierte) humour; **de buen/mal** ~ in a good/bad mood; ~**ista** nm/f comic; ~**ístico, a** adj funny, humorous

hundimiento [undi'mjento] nm (gen) sinking; (colapso) collapse

hundir [un'dir] vt to sink; (edificio, plan) to ruin, destroy; ~**se** vr to sink, collapse

húngaro, a ['ungaro, a] adj, nm/f Hungarian

Hungría [un'gria] nf Hungary

huracán [ura'kan] nm hurricane

huraño, a [u'raɲo, a] adj (antisocial) unsociable

hurgar [ur'xar] vt to poke, jab; (remover) to stir (up); ~**se** vr: ~**se (las narices)** to pick one's nose

hurón, ona [u'ron, ona] nm (ZOOL) ferret

hurtadillas [urta'ðiʎas]: **a** ~ adv stealthily, on the sly

hurtar [ur'tar] vt to steal; **hurto** nm theft, stealing

husmear [usme'ar] vt (oler) to sniff out, scent; (fam) to pry into

huyo etc vb ver **huir**

I, i

iba etc vb ver **ir**

ibérico, a [i'ßeriko, a] adj Iberian

iberoamericano, a [ißeroameri'kano, a] adj, nm/f Latin American

Ibiza [i'ßiθa] nf Ibiza

iceberg [iθe'ßer] nm iceberg

icono [i'kono] nm ikon, icon

iconoclasta [ikono'klasta] adj iconoclastic ♦ nm/f iconoclast

ictericia [ikte'riθja] nf jaundice

I + D abr (= Investigación y Desarrollo) R & D

ida ['iða] nf going, departure; ~ **y vuelta** round trip, return

idea [i'ðea] nf idea; **no tengo la menor** ~ I haven't a clue

ideal [iðe'al] *adj, nm* ideal; **~ista** *nm/f* idealist; **~izar** *vt* to idealize

idear [iðe'ar] *vt* to think up; *(aparato)* to invent; *(viaje)* to plan

ídem ['iðem] *pron* ditto

idéntico, a [i'ðentiko, a] *adj* identical

identidad [iðenti'ðað] *nf* identity

identificación [iðentifika'θjon] *nf* identification

identificar [iðentifi'kar] *vt* to identify; **~se** *vr*: **~se con** to identify with

ideología [iðeolo'xia] *nf* ideology

idilio [i'ðiljo] *nm* love-affair

idioma [i'ðjoma] *nm* (*gen*) language

idiota [i'ðjota] *adj* idiotic ♦ *nm/f* idiot; **idiotez** *nf* idiocy

ídolo ['iðolo] *nm* (*tb: fig*) idol

idóneo, a [i'ðoneo, a] *adj* suitable

iglesia [i'ɣlesja] *nf* church

ignorancia [iɣno'ranθja] *nf* ignorance; **ignorante** *adj* ignorant, uninformed ♦ *nm/f* ignoramus

ignorar [iɣno'rar] *vt* not to know, be ignorant of; *(no hacer caso a)* to ignore

igual [i'ɣwal] *adj* (*gen*) equal; *(similar)* like, similar; *(mismo)* (the) same; *(constante)* constant; *(temperatura)* even ♦ *nm/f* equal; **~ que** like, the same as; **me da o es ~** I don't care; **son ~es** they're the same; **al ~ que** *prep, conj* like, just like

igualada [iɣwa'laða] *nf* equaliser

igualar [iɣwa'lar] *vt* (*gen*) to equalize, make equal; *(allanar, nivelar)* to level (off), even (out); **~se** *vr* (*platos de balanza*) to balance out

igualdad [iɣwal'ðað] *nf* equality; *(similaridad)* sameness; *(uniformidad)* uniformity

igualmente [iɣwal'mente] *adv* equally; *(también)* also, likewise ♦ *excl* the same to you!

ikurriña [iku'rrina] *nf* Basque flag

ilegal [ile'val] *adj* illegal

ilegítimo, a [ile'xitimo, a] *adj* illegitimate

ileso, a [i'leso, a] *adj* unhurt

ilícito, a [i'liθito] *adj* illicit

ilimitado, a [ilimi'taðo, a] *adj* unlimited

ilógico, a [i'loxiko, a] *adj* illogical

iluminación [ilumina'θjon] *nf* illumination; *(alumbrado)* lighting

iluminar [ilumi'nar] *vt* to illuminate, light (up); *(fig)* to enlighten

ilusión [ilu'sjon] *nf* illusion; *(quimera)* delusion; *(esperanza)* hope; **hacerse ilusiones** to build up one's hopes; **ilusionado, a** *adj* excited; **ilusionar** *vi*: **le ilusiona ir de vacaciones** he's looking forward to going on holiday; **ilusionarse** *vr*: **ilusionarse (con)** to get excited about

ilusionista [ilusjo'nista] *nm/f* conjurer

iluso, a [i'luso, a] *adj* easily deceived ♦ *nm/f* dreamer

ilusorio, a [ilu'sorjo, a] *adj* (*de ilusión*) illusory, deceptive; *(esperanza)* vain

ilustración [ilustra'θjon] *nf* illustration; *(saber)* learning, erudition; **la I~** the Enlightenment; **ilustrado, a** *adj* illustrated; learned

ilustrar [ilus'trar] *vt* to illustrate; *(instruir)* to instruct; *(explicar)* to explain, make clear; **~se** *vr* to acquire knowledge

ilustre [i'lustre] *adj* famous, illustrious

imagen [i'maxen] *nf* (*gen*) image; *(dibujo)* picture

imaginación [imaxina'θjon] *nf* imagination

imaginar [imaxi'nar] *vt* (*gen*) to imagine; *(idear)* to think up; *(suponer)* to suppose; **~se** *vr* to imagine; **~io, a** *adj* imaginary; **imaginativo, a** *adj* imaginative

imán [i'man] *nm* magnet

imbécil [im'beθil] *nm/f* imbecile, idiot

imitación [imita'θjon] *nf* imitation

imitar [imi'tar] *vt* to imitate; *(parodiar, remedar)* to mimic, ape

impaciencia [impa'θjenθja] *nf* impatience; **impaciente** *adj* impatient; *(nervioso)* anxious

impacto [im'pakto] *nm* impact

impar [im'par] *adj* odd

imparcial [impar'θjal] *adj* impartial, fair

impartir [impar'tir] *vt* to impart, give

impasible [impa'sißle] *adj* impassive

impecable [impe'kaßle] *adj* impeccable

impedimento [impeði'mento] *nm* impediment, obstacle

impedir [impe'ðir] *vt* (*obstruir*) to impede, obstruct; (*estorbar*) to prevent

impenetrable [impene'traßle] *adj* impenetrable; (*fig*) incomprehensible

imperar [impe'rar] *vi* (*reinar*) to rule, reign; (*fig*) to prevail, reign; (*precio*) to be current

imperativo, a [impera'tiβo, a] *adj* (*urgente*, *LING*) imperative

imperceptible [imperθep'tißle] *adj* imperceptible

imperdible [imper'ðißle] *nm* safety pin

imperdonable [imperðo'naßle] *adj* unforgivable, inexcusable

imperfección [imperfek'θjon] *nf* imperfection

imperfecto, a [imper'fekto, a] *adj* imperfect

imperial [impe'rjal] *adj* imperial; **~ismo** *nm* imperialism

imperio [im'perjo] *nm* empire; (*autoridad*) rule, authority; (*fig*) pride, haughtiness; **~so, a** *adj* imperious; (*urgente*) urgent; (*imperativo*) imperative

impermeable [imperme'aßle] *adj* waterproof ♦ *nm* raincoat, mac (*BRIT*)

impersonal [imperso'nal] *adj* impersonal

impertinencia [imperti'nenθja] *nf* impertinence; **impertinente** *adj* impertinent

imperturbable [impertur'ßaßle] *adj* imperturbable

ímpetu ['impetu] *nm* (*impulso*) impetus, impulse; (*impetuosidad*)

impetuosity; (*violencia*) violence

impetuoso, a [impe'twoso, a] *adj* impetuous; (*río*) rushing; (*acto*) hasty

impío, a [im'pio, a] *adj* impious, ungodly

implacable [impla'kaßle] *adj* implacable

implantar [implan'tar] *vt* to introduce

implicar [impli'kar] *vt* to involve; (*entrañar*) to imply

implícito, a [im'pliθito, a] *adj* (*tácito*) implicit; (*sobreentendido*) implied

implorar [implo'rar] *vt* to beg, implore

imponente [impo'nente] *adj* (*impresionante*) impressive, imposing; (*solemne*) grand

imponer [impo'ner] *vt* (*gen*) to impose; (*exigir*) to exact; **~se** *vr* to assert o.s.; (*prevalecer*) to prevail; **imponible** *adj* (*COM*) taxable

impopular [impopu'lar] *adj* unpopular

importación [importa'θjon] *nf* (*acto*) importing; (*mercancías*) imports *pl*

importancia [impor'tanθja] *nf* importance; (*valor*) value, significance; (*extensión*) size, magnitude; **importante** *adj* important; valuable, significant

importar [impor'tar] *vt* (*del extranjero*) to import; (*costar*) to amount to ♦ *vi* to be important, matter; **me importa un rábano** I couldn't care less; **no importa** it doesn't matter; **¿le importa que fume?** do you mind if I smoke?

importe [im'porte] *nm* (*total*) amount; (*valor*) value

importunar [importu'nar] *vt* to bother, pester

imposibilidad [imposißili'ðað] *nf* impossibility; **imposibilitar** *vt* to make impossible, prevent

imposible [impo'sißle] *adj* (*gen*) impossible; (*insoportable*) unbearable, intolerable

imposición [imposi'θjon] *nf*

imposition; (COM: **impuesto**) tax;
(: *inversión*) deposit
impostor, a [impos'tor, a] nm/f
impostor
impotencia [impo'tenθja] nf
impotence; **impotente** adj impotent
impracticable [imprakti'kaβle] adj
(*irrealizable*) impracticable;
(*intransitable*) impassable
impreciso, a [impre'θiso, a] adj
imprecise, vague
impregnar [impreɣ'nar] vt to
impregnate; **~se** vr to become
impregnated
imprenta [im'prenta] nf (*acto*)
printing; (*aparato*) press; (*casa*)
printer's; (*letra*) print
imprescindible [impresθin'diβle] adj
essential, vital
impresión [impre'sjon] nf (*gen*)
impression; (IMPRENTA) printing;
(*edición*) edition; (FOTO) print; (*marca*)
imprint; **~ digital** fingerprint
impresionable [impresjo'naβle] adj
(*sensible*) impressionable
impresionante [impresjo'nante] adj
impressive; (*tremendo*) tremendous;
(*maravilloso*) great, marvellous
impresionar [impresjo'nar] vt
(*conmover*) to move; (*afectar*) to
impress, strike; (*película fotográfica*) to
expose; **~se** vr to be impressed;
(*conmoverse*) to be moved
impreso, a [im'preso, a] pp de
imprimir ♦ adj printed; **~s** nmpl
printed matter; **impresora** nf printer
imprevisto, a [impre'βisto, a] adj
(*gen*) unforeseen; (*inesperado*)
unexpected
imprimir [impri'mir] vt to imprint,
impress, stamp; (*textos*) to print;
(INFORM) to output, print out
improbable [impro'βaβle] adj
improbable; (*inverosímil*) unlikely
improcedente [improθe'δente] adj
inappropriate
improductivo, a [improδuk'tiβo, a]

adj unproductive
improperio [impro'perjo] nm insult
impropio, a [im'propjo, a] adj
improper
improvisado, a [improβi'saδo, a] adj
improvised
improvisar [improβi'sar] vt to
improvise
improviso, a [impro'βiso, a] adj: **de
~** unexpectedly, suddenly
imprudencia [impru'δenθja] nf
imprudence; (*indiscreción*) indiscretion;
(*descuido*) carelessness; **imprudente**
adj unwise, imprudent; (*indiscreto*)
indiscreet
impúdico, a [im'puδiko, a] adj
shameless; (*lujurioso*) lecherous
impuesto, a [im'pwesto, a] adj
imposed ♦ nm tax; **~ sobre el valor
añadido** value added tax
impugnar [impuɣ'nar] vt to oppose,
contest; (*refutar*) to refute, impugn
impulsar [impul'sar] vt to drive; (*
promover*) to promote, stimulate
impulsivo, a [impul'siβo, a] adj
impulsive; **impulso** nm impulse;
(*fuerza, empuje*) thrust, drive; (*fig:
sentimiento*) urge, impulse
impune [im'pune] adj unpunished
impureza [impu'reθa] nf impurity;
impuro, a [im'puro, a] adj impure
imputar [impu'tar] vt to attribute
inacabable [inaka'βaβle] adj (*infinito*)
endless; (*interminable*) interminable
inaccesible [inakθe'siβle] adj
inaccessible
inacción [inak'θjon] nf inactivity
inaceptable [inaθep'taβle] adj
unacceptable
inactividad [inaktiβi'δaδ] nf inactivity;
(COM) dullness; **inactivo, a** adj
inactive
inadecuado, a [inaδe'kwaδo, a] adj
(*insuficiente*) inadequate; (*inapto*)
unsuitable
inadmisible [inaδmi'siβle] adj
inadmissible

inadvertido, a [inaðβer'tiðo, a] adj (no visto) unnoticed

inagotable [inaɣo'taβle] adj inexhaustible

inaguantable [inaɣwan'taβle] adj unbearable

inalterable [inalte'raβle] adj immutable, unchangeable

inanición [inani'θjon] nf starvation

inanimado, a [inani'maðo, a] adj inanimate

inapreciable [inapre'θjaβle] adj (cantidad, diferencia) imperceptible; (ayuda, servicio) invaluable

inaudito, a [inau'ðito, a] adj unheard-of

inauguración [inauɣura'θjon] nf inauguration; opening

inaugurar [inauɣu'rar] vt to inaugurate; (exposición) to open

inca ['inka] nm/f Inca

incalculable [inkalku'laβle] adj incalculable

incandescente [inkandes'θente] adj incandescent

incansable [inkan'saβle] adj tireless, untiring

incapacidad [inkapaθi'ðað] nf incapacity; (incompetencia) incompetence; ~ física/mental physical/mental disability

incapacitar [inkapaθi'tar] vt (inhabilitar) to incapacitate, render unfit; (descalificar) to disqualify

incapaz [inka'paθ] adj incapable

incautación [inkauta'θjon] nf confiscation

incautarse [inkau'tarse] vr: ~ de to seize, confiscate

incauto, a [in'kauto, a] adj (imprudente) incautious, unwary

incendiar [inθen'djar] vt to set fire to; (fig) to inflame; ~se vr to catch fire; ~io, a adj incendiary

incendio [in'θendjo] nm fire

incentivo [inθen'tiβo] nm incentive

incertidumbre [inθerti'ðumbre] nf (inseguridad) uncertainty; (duda) doubt

incesante [inθe'sante] adj incessant

incesto [in'θesto] nm incest

incidencia [inθi'ðenθja] nf (MAT) incidence

incidente [inθi'ðente] nm incident

incidir [inθi'ðir] vi (influir) to influence; (afectar) to affect; ~ en un error to fall into error

incienso [in'θjenso] nm incense

incierto, a [in'θjerto, a] adj uncertain

incineración [inθinera'θjon] nf incineration; (de cadáveres) cremation

incinerar [inθine'rar] vt to burn; (cadáveres) to cremate

incipiente [inθi'pjente] adj incipient

incisión [inθi'sjon] nf incision

incisivo, a [inθi'siβo, a] adj sharp, cutting; (fig) incisive

incitar [inθi'tar] vt to incite, rouse

inclemencia [inkle'menθja] nf (severidad) harshness, severity; (del tiempo) inclemency

inclinación [inklina'θjon] nf (gen) inclination; (de tierras) slope, incline; (de cabeza) nod, bow; (fig) leaning, bent

inclinar [inkli'nar] vt to incline; (cabeza) to nod, bow ♦ vi to lean, slope; ~se vr to bow; (encorvarse) to stoop; ~se a (parecerse a) to take after, resemble; ~se ante to bow down to; **me inclino a pensar que** I'm inclined to think that

incluir [inklu'ir] vt to include; (incorporar) to incorporate; (meter) to enclose

inclusive [inklu'siβe] adv inclusive ♦ prep including

incluso [in'kluso] adv even

incógnita [in'koɣnita] nf (MAT) unknown quantity

incógnito [in'koɣnito] nm: de ~ incognito

incoherente [inkoe'rente] adj incoherent

incoloro, a [inko'loro, a] adj

colourless

incólume [in'kolume] adj unhurt, unharmed

incomodar [inkomo'ðar] vt to inconvenience; (molestar) to bother, trouble; (fastidiar) to annoy; ~se vr to put o.s. out; (fastidiarse) to get annoyed

incomodidad [inkomoði'ðað] nf inconvenience; (fastidio, enojo) annoyance; (de vivienda) discomfort

incómodo, a [in'komoðo, a] adj (incofortable) uncomfortable; (molesto) annoying; (inconveniente) inconvenient

incomparable [inkompa'raßle] adj incomparable

incompatible [inkompa'tißle] adj incompatible

incompetencia [inkompe'tenθja] nf incompetence; **incompetente** adj incompetent

incompleto, a [inkom'pleto, a] adj incomplete, unfinished

incomprensible [inkompren'sißle] adj incomprehensible

incomunicado, a [inkomuni'kaðo, a] adj (aislado) cut off, isolated; (confinado) in solitary confinement

inconcebible [inkonθe'ßißle] adj inconceivable

incondicional [inkondiθjo'nal] adj unconditional; (apoyo) wholehearted; (partidario) staunch

inconexo, a [inko'nekso, a] adj (gen) unconnected; (desunido) disconnected

inconfundible [inkonfun'dißle] adj unmistakable

incongruente [inkon'grwente] adj incongruous

inconsciencia [inkons'θjenθja] nf unconsciousness; (fig) thoughtlessness; **inconsciente** adj unconscious; thoughtless

inconsecuente [inkonse'kwente] adj inconsistent

inconsiderado, a [inkonsiðe'raðo, a] adj inconsiderate

inconsistente [inkonsis'tente] adj weak; (tela) flimsy

inconstancia [inkon'stanθja] nf inconstancy; (inestabilidad) unsteadiness; **inconstante** adj inconstant

incontable [inkon'taßle] adj countless, innumerable

incontestable [inkontes'taßle] adj unanswerable; (innegable) undeniable

incontinencia [inkonti'nenθja] nf incontinence

inconveniencia [inkombe'njenθja] nf unsuitability, inappropriateness; (descortesía) impoliteness; **inconveniente** adj unsuitable; impolite ♦ nm obstacle; (desventaja) disadvantage; **el inconveniente es que** ... the trouble is that ...

incordiar [inkor'ðjar] (fam) vt to bug, annoy

incorporación [inkorpora'θjon] nf incorporation

incorporar [inkorpo'rar] vt to incorporate; ~se vr to sit up

incorrección [inkorrek'θjon] nf (gen) incorrectness, inaccuracy; (descortesía) bad-mannered behaviour; **incorrecto, a** adj (gen) incorrect, wrong; (comportamiento) bad-mannered

incorregible [inkorre'xißle] adj incorrigible

incredulidad [inkreðuli'ðað] nf incredulity; (escepticismo) scepticism; **incrédulo, a** adj incredulous, unbelieving; sceptical

increíble [inkre'ißle] adj incredible

incremento [inkre'mento] nm increment; (aumento) rise, increase

increpar [inkre'par] vt to reprimand

incruento, a [in'krwento, a] adj bloodless

incrustar [inkrus'tar] vt to incrust; (piedras: en joya) to inlay

incubar [inku'ßar] vt to incubate

inculcar [inkul'kar] vt to inculcate

inculpar [inkul'par] vt (acusar) to

accuse; (*achacar, atribuir*) to charge, blame

inculto, a [in'kulto, a] *adj* (*persona*) uneducated; (*grosero*) uncouth ♦ *nm/f* ignoramus

incumplimiento [inkumpli'mjento] *nm* non-fulfilment; ~ **de contrato** breach of contract

incurrir [inku'rrir] *vi*: ~ **en** to incur; (*crimen*) to commit; ~ **en un error** to make a mistake

indagación [indaɣa'θjon] *nf* investigation; (*búsqueda*) search; (*JUR*) inquest

indagar [inda'ɣar] *vt* to investigate; to search; (*averiguar*) to ascertain

indecente [inde'θente] *adj* indecent, improper; (*lascivo*) obscene

indecible [inde'θiβle] *adj* unspeakable; (*indescriptible*) indescribable

indeciso, a [inde'θiso, a] *adj* (*por decidir*) undecided; (*vacilante*) hesitant

indefenso, a [inde'fenso, a] *adj* defenceless

indefinido, a [indefi'niðo, a] *adj* indefinite; (*vago*) vague, undefined

indeleble [inde'leβle] *adj* indelible

indemne [in'demne] *adj* (*objeto*) undamaged; (*persona*) unharmed, unhurt

indemnizar [indemni'θar] *vt* to indemnify; (*compensar*) to compensate

independencia [indepen'denθja] *nf* independence

independiente [indepen'djente] *adj* (*libre*) independent; (*autónomo*) self-sufficient

indeterminado, a [indetermi'naðo, a] *adj* indefinite; (*desconocido*) indeterminate

India ['indja] *nf*: **la ~** India

indicación [indika'θjon] *nf* indication; (*señal*) sign; (*sugerencia*) suggestion, hint

indicado, a [indi'kaðo, a] *adj* (*momento, método*) right; (*tratamiento*) appropriate; (*solución*) likely

indicador [indika'ðor] *nm* indicator; (*TEC*) gauge, meter

indicar [indi'kar] *vt* (*mostrar*) to indicate, show; (*termómetro etc*) to read, register; (*señalar*) to point to

índice ['indiθe] *nm* index; (*catálogo*) catalogue; (*ANAT*) index finger, forefinger

indicio [in'diθjo] *nm* indication, sign; (*en pesquisa etc*) clue

indiferencia [indife'renθja] *nf* indifference; (*apatía*) apathy; **indiferente** *adj* indifferent

indígena [in'dixena] *adj* indigenous, native ♦ *nm/f* native

indigencia [indi'xenθja] *nf* poverty, need

indigestión [indixes'tjon] *nf* indigestion

indigesto, a [indi'xesto, a] *adj* (*alimento*) indigestible; (*fig*) turgid

indignación [indiɣna'θjon] *nf* indignation

indignar [indiɣ'nar] *vt* to anger, make indignant; **~se** *vr*: **~se por** to get indignant about

indigno, a [in'diɣno, a] *adj* (*despreciable*) low, contemptible; (*inmerecido*) unworthy

indio, a ['indjo, a] *adj, nm/f* Indian

indirecta [indi'rekta] *nf* insinuation, innuendo; (*sugerencia*) hint

indirecto, a [indi'rekto, a] *adj* indirect

indiscreción [indiskre'θjon] *nf* (*imprudencia*) indiscretion; (*irreflexión*) tactlessness; (*acto*) gaffe, faux pas

indiscreto, a [indis'kreto, a] *adj* indiscreet

indiscriminado, a [indiskrimi'naðo, a] *adj* indiscriminate

indiscutible [indisku'tiβle] *adj* indisputable, unquestionable

indispensable [indispen'saβle] *adj* indispensable, essential

indisponer [indispo'ner] *vt* to spoil, upset; (*salud*) to make ill; **~se** *vr* to fall ill; **~se con uno** to fall out with sb

indisposición [indisposi'θjon] nf indisposition

indispuesto, a [indis'pwesto, a] adj (enfermo) unwell, indisposed

indistinto, a [indis'tinto, a] adj indistinct; (vago) vague

individual [indiβi'ðwal] adj individual; (habitación) single ♦ nm (DEPORTE) singles sg

individuo, a [indi'βiðwo, a] adj, nm individual

índole ['indole] nf (naturaleza) nature; (clase) sort, kind

indómito, a [in'domito, a] adj indomitable

inducir [indu'θir] vt to induce; (inferir) to infer; (persuadir) to persuade

indudable [indu'ðaβle] adj undoubted; (incuestionable) unquestionable

indulgencia [indul'xenθja] nf indulgence

indultar [indul'tar] vt (perdonar) to pardon, reprieve; (librar de pago) to exempt; **indulto** nm pardon; exemption

industria [in'dustrja] nf industry; (habilidad) skill; **industrial** adj industrial ♦ nm industrialist

inédito, a [in'eðito, a] adj (texto) unpublished; (nuevo) new

inefable [ine'faβle] adj ineffable, indescribable

ineficaz [inefi'kaθ] adj (inútil) ineffective; (ineficiente) inefficient

ineludible [inelu'ðiβle] adj inescapable, unavoidable

ineptitud [inepti'tuð] nf ineptitude, incompetence; **inepto, a** adj inept, incompetent

inequívoco, a [ine'kiβoko, a] adj unequivocal; (inconfundible) unmistakable

inercia [in'erθja] nf inertia; (pasividad) passivity

inerme [in'erme] adj (sin armas) unarmed; (indefenso) defenceless

inerte [in'erte] adj inert; (inmóvil) motionless

inesperado, a [inespe'raðo, a] adj unexpected, unforeseen

inestable [ines'taβle] adj unstable

inevitable [ineβi'taβle] adj inevitable

inexactitud [ineksakti'tuð] nf inaccuracy; **inexacto, a** adj inaccurate; (falso) untrue

inexperto, a [inek'sperto, a] adj (novato) inexperienced

infalible [infa'liβle] adj infallible; (plan) foolproof

infame [in'fame] adj infamous; (horrible) dreadful; **infamia** nf infamy; (deshonra) disgrace

infancia [in'fanθja] nf infancy, childhood

infantería [infante'ria] nf infantry

infantil [infan'til] adj (pueril, aniñado) infantile; (cándido) childlike; (literatura, ropa etc) children's

infarto [in'farto] nm (tb: ~ de miocardio) heart attack

infatigable [infati'βaβle] adj tireless, untiring

infección [infek'θjon] nf infection; **infeccioso, a** adj infectious

infectar [infek'tar] vt to infect; **~se** vr to become infected

infeliz [infe'liθ] adj unhappy, wretched ♦ nm/f wretch

inferior [infe'rjor] adj inferior; (situación) lower ♦ nm/f inferior, subordinate

inferir [infe'rir] vt (deducir) to infer, deduce; (causar) to cause

infestar [infes'tar] vt to infest

infidelidad [infiðeli'ðað] nf (gen) infidelity, unfaithfulness

infiel [in'fjel] adj unfaithful, disloyal; (erróneo) inaccurate ♦ nm/f infidel, unbeliever

infierno [in'fjerno] nm hell

infiltrarse [infil'trarse] vr: **~ en** to infiltrate in(to); (persona) to work one's way in(to)

ínfimo, a ['infimo, a] *adj* (*más bajo*) lowest; (*despreciable*) vile, mean

infinidad [infini'ðað] *nf* infinity; (*abundancia*) great quantity

infinito, a [infi'nito, a] *adj, nm* infinite

inflación [infla'θjon] *nf* (*hinchazón*) swelling; (*monetaria*) inflation; (*fig*) conceit; **inflacionario, a** *adj* inflationary

inflamar [infla'mar] *vt* (MED, *fig*) to inflame; **~se** *vr* to catch fire; to become inflamed

inflar [in'flar] *vt* (*hinchar*) to inflate, blow up; (*fig*) to exaggerate; **~se** *vr* to swell (up); (*fig*) to get conceited

inflexible [inflek'siβle] *adj* inflexible; (*fig*) unbending

infligir [infli'xir] *vt* to inflict

influencia [influ'enθja] *nf* influence; **influenciar** *vt* to influence

influir [influ'ir] *vt* to influence

influjo [in'fluxo] *nm* influence

influya *etc vb ver* **influir**

influyente [influ'jente] *adj* influential

información [informa'θjon] *nf* information; (*noticias*) news *sg*; (JUR) inquiry; **I~** (*oficina*) Information Office; (*mostrador*) Information Desk; (TEL) Directory Enquiries

informal [infor'mal] *adj* (*gen*) informal

informar [infor'mar] *vt* (*gen*) to inform; (*revelar*) to reveal, make known ♦ *vi* (JUR) to plead; (*denunciar*) to inform; (*dar cuenta de*) to report on; **~se** *vr* to find out; **~se de** to inquire into

informática [infor'matika] *nf* computer science, information technology

informe [in'forme] *adj* shapeless ♦ *nm* report

infortunio [infor'tunjo] *nm* misfortune

infracción [infrak'θjon] *nf* infraction, infringement

infranqueable [infranke'aßle] *adj* impassable; (*fig*) insurmountable

infravalorar [infrabalo'rar] *vt* to undervalue, underestimate

infringir [infrin'xir] *vt* to infringe, contravene

infructuoso, a [infruk'twoso, a] *adj* fruitless, unsuccessful

infundado, a [infun'dado, a] *adj* groundless, unfounded

infundir [infun'dir] *vt* to infuse, instil

infusión [infu'sjon] *nf* infusion; **~ de manzanilla** camomile tea

ingeniar [inxe'njar] *vt* to think up, devise; **~se** *vr*: **~se para** to manage to

ingeniería [inxenje'ria] *nf* engineering; **~ genética** genetic engineering; **ingeniero, a** *nm/f* engineer; **ingeniero de caminos/de sonido** civil engineer/sound engineer

ingenio [in'xenjo] *nm* (*talento*) talent; (*agudeza*) wit; (*habilidad*) ingenuity, inventiveness; **~ azucarero** (AM) sugar refinery

ingenioso, a [inxe'njoso, a] *adj* ingenious, clever; (*divertido*) witty

ingenuidad [inxenwi'ðað] *nf* ingenuousness; (*sencillez*) simplicity; **ingenuo, a** *adj* ingenuous

ingerir [inxe'rir] *vt* to ingest; (*tragar*) to swallow; (*consumir*) to consume

Inglaterra [ingla'terra] *nf* England

ingle ['ingle] *nf* groin

inglés, esa [in'gles, esa] *adj* English ♦ *nm/f* Englishman/woman ♦ *nm* (LING) English

ingratitud [ingrati'tuð] *nf* ingratitude; **ingrato, a** *adj* (*gen*) ungrateful

ingrediente [ingre'ðjente] *nm* ingredient

ingresar [ingre'sar] *vt* (*dinero*) to deposit ♦ *vi* to come in; **~ en un club** to join a club; **~ en el hospital** to go into hospital

ingreso [in'greso] *nm* (*entrada*) entry; (: *en hospital etc*) admission; **~s** *nmpl* (*dinero*) income *sg*; (: COM) takings *pl*

inhabitable [inaßi'taßle] *adj* uninhabitable

inhalar [ina'lar] *vt* to inhale

inherente [ine'rente] adj inherent

inhibir [ini'ßir] vt to inhibit

inhóspito, a [i'nospito, a] adj (región, paisaje) inhospitable

inhumano, a [inu'mano, a] adj inhuman

inicial [ini'θjal] adj, nf initial

iniciar [ini'θjar] vt (persona) to initiate; (empezar) to begin, commence; (conversación) to start up

iniciativa [iniθja'tißa] nf initiative; **la ~ privada** private enterprise

ininterrumpido, a [ininterrum'piðo, a] adj uninterrupted

injerencia [inxe'renθja] nf interference

injertar [inxer'tar] vt to graft; **injerto** nm graft

injuria [in'xurja] nf (agravio, ofensa) offence; (insulto) insult; **injuriar** vt to insult; **injurioso, a** adj offensive; insulting

injusticia [inxus'tiθja] nf injustice

injusto, a [in'xusto, a] adj unjust, unfair

inmadurez [inmaðu'reθ] nf immaturity

inmediaciones [inmeðja'θjones] nfpl neighbourhood sg, environs

inmediato, a [inme'ðjato, a] adj immediate; (contiguo) adjoining; (rápido) prompt; (próximo) neighbouring, next; **de ~** immediately

inmejorable [inmexo'raßle] adj unsurpassable; (precio) unbeatable

inmenso, a [in'menso, a] adj immense, huge

inmerecido, a [inmere'θiðo, a] adj undeserved

inmigración [inmiɣra'θjon] nf immigration

inmiscuirse [inmisku'irse] vr to interfere, meddle

inmobiliaria [inmoßi'ljarja] nf estate agency

inmobiliario, a [inmoßi'ljarjo, a] adj real-estate cpd, property cpd

inmolar [inmo'lar] vt to immolate,

sacrifice

inmoral [inmo'ral] adj immoral

inmortal [inmor'tal] adj immortal; **~izar** vt to immortalize

inmóvil [in'moßil] adj immobile

inmueble [in'mweßle] adj: **bienes ~s** real estate, landed property ♦ nm property

inmundicia [inmun'diθja] nf filth; **inmundo, a** adj filthy

inmune [in'mune] adj: **~ (a)** (MED) immune (to)

inmunidad [inmuni'ðað] nf immunity

inmutarse [inmu'tarse] vr to turn pale; **no se inmutó** he didn't turn a hair

innato, a [in'nato, a] adj innate

innecesario, a [inneθe'sarjo, a] adj unnecessary

innoble [in'noßle] adj ignoble

innovación [innoßa'θjon] nf innovation

innovar [inno'ßar] vt to introduce

inocencia [ino'θenθja] nf innocence

inocentada [inoθen'taða] nf practical joke

inocente [ino'θente] adj (ingenuo) naive, innocent; (inculpable) innocent; (sin malicia) harmless ♦ nm/f simpleton

Día de los Santos Inocentes

The 28th December, **el día de los (Santos) Inocentes,** is when the Church commemorates the story of Herod's slaughter of the innocent children of Judaea. On this day Spaniards play **inocentadas** (practical jokes) on each other, much like our April Fool's Day pranks.

inodoro [ino'ðoro] nm toilet, lavatory (BRIT)

inofensivo, a [inofen'sißo, a] adj inoffensive, harmless

inolvidable [inolßi'ðaßle] adj unforgettable

inopinado, a [inopi'naðo, a] adj

unexpected

inoportuno, a [inopor'tuno, a] *adj* untimely; (*molesto*) inconvenient

inoxidable [inoksi'ðaβle] *adj*: **acero ~** stainless steel

inquebrantable [inkeβran'taβle] *adj* unbreakable

inquietar [inkje'tar] *vt* to worry, trouble; **~se** *vr* to worry, get upset; **inquieto, a** *adj* anxious, worried; **inquietud** *nf* anxiety, worry

inquilino, a [inki'lino, a] *nm/f* tenant

inquirir [inki'rir] *vt* to enquire into, investigate

insaciable [insa'θjaβle] *adj* insatiable

insalubre [insa'luβre] *adj* unhealthy

inscribir [inskri'βir] *vt* to inscribe; **~ a uno en** (*lista*) to put sb on; (*censo*) to register sb on

inscripción [inskrip'θjon] *nf* inscription; (*ESCOL etc*) enrolment; (*censo*) registration

insecticida [insekti'θiða] *nm* insecticide

insecto [in'sekto] *nm* insect

inseguridad [inseyuri'ðað] *nf* insecurity

inseguro, a [inse'yuro, a] *adj* insecure; (*inconstante*) unsteady; (*incierto*) uncertain

insensatez [insensa'tez] *nf* foolishness, stupidity

insensato, a [insen'sato, a] *adj* foolish, stupid

insensibilidad [insensiβili'ðað] *nf* (*gen*) insensitivity; (*dureza de corazón*) callousness

insensible [insen'siβle] *adj* (*gen*) insensitive; (*movimiento*) imperceptible; (*sin sentido*) numb

insertar [inser'tar] *vt* to insert

inservible [inser'βiβle] *adj* useless

insidioso, a [insi'ðjoso, a] *adj* insidious

insignia [in'siynja] *nf* (*señal distintiva*) badge; (*estandarte*) flag

insignificante [insiynifi'kante] *adj* insignificant

insinuar [insi'nwar] *vt* to insinuate,

imply

insípido, a [in'sipiðo, a] *adj* insipid

insistencia [insis'tenθja] *nf* insistence

insistir [insis'tir] *vi* to insist; **~ en algo** to insist on sth; (*enfatizar*) to stress sth

insolación [insola'θjon] *nf* (*MED*) sunstroke

insolencia [inso'lenθja] *nf* insolence; **insolente** *adj* insolent

insólito, a [in'solito, a] *adj* unusual

insoluble [inso'luβle] *adj* insoluble

insolvencia [insol'βenθja] *nf* insolvency

insomnio [in'somnjo] *nm* insomnia

insondable [inson'daβle] *adj* bottomless; (*fig*) impenetrable

insonorizado, a [insonori'θaðo, a] *adj* (*cuarto etc*) soundproof

insoportable [insopor'taβle] *adj* unbearable

insospechado, a [insospe't∫aðo, a] *adj* (*inesperado*) unexpected

inspección [inspek'θjon] *nf* inspection, check; **inspeccionar** *vt* (*examinar*) to inspect, examine; (*controlar*) to check

inspector, a [inspek'tor, a] *nm/f* inspector

inspiración [inspira'θjon] *nf* inspiration

inspirar [inspi'rar] *vt* to inspire; (*MED*) to inhale; **~se** *vr*: **~se en** to be inspired by

instalación [instala'θjon] *nf* (*equipo*) fittings *pl*, equipment; **~ eléctrica** wiring

instalar [insta'lar] *vt* (*establecer*) to install; (*erguir*) to set up, erect; **~se** *vr* to establish o.s.; (*en una vivienda*) to move into

instancia [ins'tanθja] *nf* (*JUR*) petition; (*ruego*) request; **en última ~** as a last resort

instantánea [instan'tanea] *nf* snap(shot)

instantáneo, a [instan'taneo, a] *adj* instantaneous; **café ~** instant coffee

instante [ins'tante] nm instant, moment

instar [ins'tar] vt to press, urge

instaurar [instau'rar] vt (costumbre) to establish; (normas, sistema) to bring in, introduce; (gobierno) to instal

instigar [insti'var] vt to instigate

instinto [ins'tinto] nm instinct; **por ~** instinctively

institución [institu'θjon] nf institution, establishment

instituir [institu'ir] vt to establish; (fundar) to found; **instituto** nm (gen) institute; (ESP: ESCOL) ≈ comprehensive (BRIT) o high (US) school

institutriz [institu'triθ] nf governess

instrucción [instruk'θjon] nf instruction

instructivo, a [instruk'tiβo, a] adj instructive

instruir [instru'ir] vt (gen) to instruct; (enseñar) to teach, educate

instrumento [instru'mento] nm (gen) instrument; (herramienta) tool, implement

insubordinarse [insuβorði'narse] vr to rebel

insuficiencia [insufi'θjenθja] nf (carencia) lack; (inadecuación) inadequacy; **insuficiente** adj (gen) insufficient; (ESCOL: calificación) unsatisfactory

insufrible [insu'friβle] adj insufferable

insular [insu'lar] adj insular

insultar [insul'tar] vt to insult; **insulto** nm insult

insumiso, a [insu'miso, a] nm/f (POL) person who refuses to do military service or its substitute, community service

insuperable [insupe'raβle] adj (excelente) unsurpassable; (problema etc) insurmountable

insurgente [insur'xente] adj, nm/f insurgent

insurrección [insurrek'θjon] nf insurrection, rebellion

intachable [inta'tʃaβle] adj irreproachable

intacto, a [in'takto, a] adj intact

integral [inte'vral] adj integral; (completo) complete; **pan ~** wholemeal (BRIT) o wholewheat (US) bread

integrar [inte'vrar] vt to make up, compose; (MAT, fig) to integrate

integridad [intexri'ðað] nf wholeness; (carácter) integrity; **íntegro, a** adj whole, entire; (honrado) honest

intelectual [intelek'twal] adj, nm/f intellectual

inteligencia [inteli'xenθja] nf intelligence; (ingenio) ability; **inteligente** adj intelligent

inteligible [inteli'xiβle] adj intelligible

intemperie [intem'perje] nf: **a la ~** out in the open, exposed to the elements

intempestivo, a [intempes'tiβo, a] adj untimely

intención [inten'θjon] nf (gen) intention, purpose; **con segundas intenciones** maliciously; **con ~** deliberately

intencionado, a [intenθjo'naðo, a] adj deliberate; **bien ~** well-meaning; **mal ~** ill-disposed, hostile

intensidad [intensi'ðað] nf (gen) intensity; (ELEC, TEC) strength; **llover con ~** to rain hard

intenso, a [in'tenso, a] adj intense; (sentimiento) profound, deep

intentar [inten'tar] vt (tratar) to try, attempt; **intento** nm attempt

interactivo, a [interak'tiβo, a] adj (INFORM) interactive

intercalar [interka'lar] vt to insert

intercambio [inter'kambjo] nm exchange, swap

interceder [interθe'ðer] vi to intercede

interceptar [interθep'tar] vt to intercept

intercesión [interθe'sjon] nf intercession

interés [inte'res] nm (gen) interest; (parte) share, part; (pey) self-interest;

intereses creados vested interests
interesado, a [intere'saðo, a] *adj* interested; *(prejuiciado)* prejudiced; *(pey)* mercenary, self-seeking
interesante [intere'sante] *adj* interesting
interesar [intere'sar] *vt* to interest, be of interest to; **~se** *vr*: **~se en** o **por** to take an interest in
interferir [interfe'rir] *vt* to interfere with; *(TEL)* to jam ♦ *vi* to interfere
interfono [inter'fono] *nm* intercom
interino, a [inte'rino, a] *adj* temporary ♦ *nm/f* temporary holder of a post; *(MED)* locum; *(ESCOL)* supply teacher
interior [inte'rjor] *adj* inner, inside; *(COM)* domestic, internal ♦ *nm* interior, inside; *(fig)* soul, mind; **Ministerio del I~** ≈ Home Office *(BRIT)*, ≈ Department of the Interior *(US)*
interjección [interxek'θjon] *nf* interjection
interlocutor, a [interloku'tor, a] *nm/f* speaker
intermediario, a [interme'ðjarjo, a] *nm/f* intermediary
intermedio, a [inter'meðjo, a] *adj* intermediate ♦ *nm* interval
interminable [intermi'naßle] *adj* endless
intermitente [intermi'tente] *adj* intermittent ♦ *nm* *(AUTO)* indicator
internacional [internaθjo'nal] *adj* international
internado [inter'naðo] *nm* boarding school
internar [inter'nar] *vt* to intern; *(en un manicomio)* to commit; **~se** *vr* *(penetrar)* to penetrate
interno, a [inter'no, a] *adj* internal, interior; *(POL etc)* domestic ♦ *nm/f* *(alumno)* boarder
interponer [interpo'ner] *vt* to interpose, put in; **~se** *vr* to intervene
interpretación [interpreta'θjon] *nf* interpretation

interpretar [interpre'tar] *vt* to interpret; *(TEATRO, MUS)* to perform, play; **intérprete** *nm/f* *(LING)* interpreter, translator; *(MUS, TEATRO)* performer, artist(e)
interrogación [interroɣa'θjon] *nf* interrogation; *(LING: tb: signo de ~)* question mark
interrogar [interro'ɣar] *vt* to interrogate, question
interrumpir [interrum'pir] *vt* to interrupt
interrupción [interrup'θjon] *nf* interruption
interruptor [interrup'tor] *nm* *(ELEC)* switch
intersección [intersek'θjon] *nf* intersection
interurbano, a [interur'ßano, a] *adj*: **llamada interurbana** long-distance call
intervalo [inter'ßalo] *nm* interval; *(descanso)* break; **a ~s** at intervals, every now and then
intervenir [interße'nir] *vt* *(controlar)* to control, supervise; *(MED)* to operate on ♦ *vi* *(participar)* to take part, participate; *(mediar)* to intervene
interventor, a [interßen'tor, a] *nm/f* inspector; *(COM)* auditor
intestino [intes'tino] *nm* intestine
intimar [inti'mar] *vi* to become friendly
intimidad [intimi'ðað] *nf* intimacy; *(familiaridad)* familiarity; *(vida privada)* private life; *(JUR)* privacy
íntimo, a ['intimo, a] *adj* intimate
intolerable [intole'raßle] *adj* intolerable, unbearable
intoxicación [intoksika'θjon] *nf* poisoning
intranquilizarse [intrankili'θarse] *vr* to get worried o anxious; **intranquilo, a** *adj* worried
intransigente [intransi'xente] *adj* intransigent
intransitable [intransi'taßle] *adj*

intrépido 168 **ir**

impassable
intrépido, a [in'trepiðo, a] adj
intrepid
intriga [in'triɣa] nf intrigue; (plan)
plot; **intrigar** vt, vi to intrigue
intrincado, a [intriŋ'kaðo, a] adj
intricate
intrínseco, a [in'trinseko, a] adj
intrinsic
introducción [introðuk'θjon] nf
introduction
introducir [introðu'θir] vt (gen) to
introduce; (moneda etc) to insert;
(INFORM) to input, enter
intromisión [intromi'sjon] nf
interference, meddling
introvertido, a [introβer'tiðo, a] adj,
nm/f introvert
intruso, a [in'truso, a] adj intrusive
♦ nm/f intruder
intuición [intwi'θjon] nf intuition
inundación [inunda'θjon] nf
flood(ing); **inundar** vt to flood; (fig) to
swamp, inundate
inusitado, a [inusi'taðo, a] adj
unusual, rare
inútil [in'util] adj useless; (esfuerzo)
vain, fruitless; **inutilidad** nf uselessness
inutilizar [inutili'θar] vt to make o
render useless; **~se** vr to become
useless
invadir [imba'ðir] vt to invade
inválido, a [im'baliðo, a] adj invalid
♦ nm/f invalid
invariable [imba'rjaβle] adj invariable
invasión [imba'sjon] nf invasion
invasor, a [imba'sor, a] adj invading
♦ nm/f invader
invención [imben'θjon] nf invention
inventar [imben'tar] vt to invent
inventario [imben'tarjo] nm inventory
inventiva [imben'tiβa] nf
inventiveness
invento [im'bento] nm invention
inventor, a [imben'tor, a] nm/f
inventor
invernadero [imberna'ðero] nm

greenhouse
inverosímil [imbero'simil] adj
implausible
inversión [imber'sjon] nf (COM)
investment
inverso, a [im'berso, a] adj inverse,
opposite; **en el orden ~** in reverse
order; **a la inversa** inversely, the other
way round
inversor, a [imber'sor, a] nm/f (COM)
investor
invertir [imber'tir] vt (COM) to invest;
(volcar) to turn upside down; (tiempo
etc) to spend
investigación [imbestiɣa'θjon] nf
investigation; (ESCOL) research; **~ de
mercado** market research
investigar [imbesti'ɣar] vt to
investigate; (ESCOL) to do research into
invierno [im'bjerno] nm winter
invisible [imbi'siβle] adj invisible
invitado, a [imbi'taðo, a] nm/f guest
invitar [imbi'tar] vt to invite; (incitar)
to entice; (pagar) to buy, pay for
invocar [imbo'kar] vt to invoke, call on
involucrar [imbolu'krar]: **~ en** to
involve in; **~se** vr (persona): **~ en** to
get mixed up in
involuntario, a [imbolun'tarjo, a] adj
(movimiento, gesto) involuntary; (error)
unintentional
inyección [injek'θjon] nf injection
inyectar [injek'tar] vt to inject

┌─────────────────┐
│ **PALABRA CLAVE** │
└─────────────────┘

ir [ir] vi 1 to go; (a pie) to walk; (viajar)
to travel; **~ caminando** to walk; **fui
en tren** I went o travelled by train;
¡(ahora) voy! (I'm just) coming!
2: **~ (a) por: ~ (a) por el médico** to
fetch the doctor
3 (progresar: persona, cosa) to go; **el
trabajo va muy bien** work is going
very well; **¿cómo te va?** how are
things going?; **me va muy bien** I'm
getting on very well; **le fue fatal** it
went awfully badly for him

4 (*funcionar*): **el coche no va muy bien** the car isn't running very well
5: **te va estupendamente ese color** that colour suits you fantastically well
6 (*locuciones*): **¿vino? - ¡que va!** did he come? - of course not!; **vamos, no llores** come on, don't cry; **¡vaya coche!** what a car!, that's some car!
7: **no vaya a ser: tienes que correr, no vaya a ser que pierdas el tren** you'll have to run so as not to miss the train
8 (+ *pp*): **iba vestido muy bien** he was very well dressed
9: **no me** *etc* **va ni me viene** I *etc* don't care
♦ *vb aux* **1**: **~ a: voy/iba a hacerlo hoy** I am/was going to do it today
2 (+ *gerundio*): **iba anocheciendo** it was getting dark; **todo se me iba aclarando** everything was gradually becoming clearer to me
3 (+ *pp* = *pasivo*): **van vendidos 300 ejemplares** 300 copies have been sold so far
♦ **~se** *vr* **1**: **¿por dónde se va al zoológico?** which is the way to the zoo?
2 (*marcharse*) to leave; **ya se habrán ido** they must already have left o gone

ira [ˈira] *nf* anger, rage
Irak [iˈrak] *nm* = **Iraq**
Irán [iˈran] *nm* Iran; **iraní** *adj, nm/f* Iranian
Iraq [iˈrak] *nm* Iraq; **iraquí** *adj, nm/f* Iraqui
iris [ˈiris] *nm inv* (*tb*: **arco ~**) rainbow; (*ANAT*) iris
Irlanda [irˈlanda] *nf* Ireland; **irlandés, esa** *adj* Irish ♦ *nm/f* Irishman/woman; **los irlandeses** the Irish
ironía [iroˈnia] *nf* irony; **irónico, a** *adj* ironic(al)
IRPF [iˈerre ˈpe ˈefe] *n abr* (=*Impuesto sobre la Renta de las Personas Físicas*) (personal) income tax

irreal [irreˈal] *adj* unreal
irrecuperable [irrekupeˈraβle] *adj* irrecoverable, irretrievable
irreflexión [irreflekˈsjon] *nf* thoughtlessness
irregular [irreɣuˈlar] *adj* (*gen*) irregular; (*situación*) abnormal
irremediable [irremeˈðjaβle] *adj* irremediable; (*vicio*) incurable
irreparable [irrepaˈraβle] *adj* (*daños*) irreparable; (*pérdida*) irrecoverable
irresoluto, a [irresoˈluto, a] *adj* irresolute, hesitant
irrespetuoso, a [irrespeˈtwoso, a] *adj* disrespectful
irresponsable [irresponˈsaβle] *adj* irresponsible
irreversible [irreβerˈsible] *adj* irreversible
irrigar [irriˈɣar] *vt* to irrigate
irrisorio, a [irriˈsorjo, a] *adj* derisory, ridiculous
irritar [irriˈtar] *vt* to irritate, annoy
irrupción [irrupˈθjon] *nf* irruption; (*invasión*) invasion
isla [ˈisla] *nf* island
islandés, esa [islanˈdes, esa] *adj* Icelandic ♦ *nm/f* Icelander
Islandia [isˈlandja] *nf* Iceland
isleño, a [isˈleɲo, a] *adj* island *cpd* ♦ *nm/f* islander
Israel [israˈel] *nm* Israel; **israelí** *adj, nm/f* Israeli
istmo [ˈistmo] *nm* isthmus
Italia [iˈtalja] *nf* Italy; **italiano, a** *adj, nm/f* Italy; **italiano, a** *adj, nm/f* Italian
itinerario [itineˈrarjo] *nm* itinerary, route
IVA [ˈiβa] *nm abr* (= *impuesto sobre el valor añadido*) VAT
izar [iˈθar] *vt* to hoist
izdo, a *abr* (= *izquierdo, a*) l.
izquierda [iθˈkjerda] *nf* left; (*POL*) left (wing); **a la ~** (*estar*) on the left; (*torcer etc*) to the) left
izquierdista [iθkjerˈðista] *nm/f* left-winger, leftist

izquierdo, a [iθ'kjerðo, a] *adj* left

J, j

jabalí [xaβa'li] *nm* wild boar
jabalina [xaβa'lina] *nf* javelin
jabón [xa'βon] *nm* soap; **jabonar** *vt* to soap
jaca ['xaka] *nf* pony
jacinto [xa'θinto] *nm* hyacinth
jactarse [xak'tarse] *vr* to boast, brag
jadear [xaðe'ar] *vi* to pant, gasp for breath; **jadeo** *nm* panting, gasping
jaguar [xa'ɣwar] *nm* jaguar
jalea [xa'lea] *nf* jelly
jaleo [xa'leo] *nm* racket, uproar; **armar un ~** to kick up a racket
jalón [xa'lon] (*AM*) *nm* tug
jamás [xa'mas] *adv* never
jamón [xa'mon] *nm* ham; **~ dulce**, **~ de York** cooked ham; **~ serrano** cured ham
Japón [xa'pon] *nm*: **el ~** Japan; **japonés, esa** *adj*, *nm/f* Japanese ♦ *nm* (*LING*) Japanese
jaque ['xake] *nm*: **~ mate** checkmate
jaqueca [xa'keka] *nf* (very bad) headache, migraine
jarabe [xa'raβe] *nm* syrup
jarcia ['xarθja] *nf* (*NAUT*) ropes *pl*, rigging
jardín [xar'ðin] *nm* garden; **~ de infancia** (*ESP*) o **de niños** (*AM*) nursery (school); **jardinería** *nf* gardening; **jardinero, a** *nm/f* gardener
jarra ['xarra] *nf* jar; (*jarro*) jug
jarro ['xarro] *nm* jug
jarrón [xa'rron] *nm* vase
jaula ['xaula] *nf* cage
jauría [xau'ria] *nf* pack of hounds
jazmín [xaθ'min] *nm* jasmine
J. C. *abr* (= *Jesucristo*) J.C.
jefa ['xefa] *nf ver* **jefe**
jefatura [xefa'tura] *nf*: **~ de policía** police headquarters *sg*

jefe, a ['xefe, a] *nm/f* (*gen*) chief, head; (*patrón*) boss; **~ de cocina** chef; **~ de estación** stationmaster; **~ de estado** head of state
jengibre [xen'xiβre] *nm* ginger
jeque ['xeke] *nm* sheik
jerarquía [xerar'kia] *nf* (*orden*) hierarchy; (*rango*) rank; **jerárquico, a** *adj* hierarchic(al)
jerez [xe'reθ] *nm* sherry
jerga ['xerɣa] *nf* jargon
jeringa [xe'ringa] *nf* syringe; (*AM*) annoyance, bother; **~ de engrase** grease gun; **jeringar** *vt* (*fam*) to annoy, bother; **jeringuilla** *nf* syringe
jeroglífico [xero'vlifiko] *nm* hieroglyphic
jersey [xer'sei] (*pl* **~s**) *nm* jersey, pullover, jumper
Jerusalén [xerusa'len] *n* Jerusalem
Jesucristo [xesu'kristo] *nm* Jesus Christ
jesuita [xe'swita] *adj*, *nm* Jesuit
Jesús [xe'sus] *nm* Jesus; **¡~!** good heavens!; (*al estornudar*) bless you!
jinete, a [xi'nete, a] *nm/f* horseman/ woman, rider
jipijapa [xipi'xapa] (*AM*) *nm* straw hat
jirafa [xi'rafa] *nf* giraffe
jirón [xi'ron] *nm* rag, shred
jocoso, a [xo'koso, a] *adj* humorous, jocular
joder [xo'ðer] (*fam!*) *vt*, *vi* to fuck(!)
jofaina [xo'faina] *nf* washbasin
jornada [xor'naða] *nf* (*viaje de un día*) day's journey; (*camino o viaje entero*) journey; (*día de trabajo*) working day
jornal [xor'nal] *nm* (day's) wage; **~ero** *nm* (day) labourer
joroba [xo'roβa] *nf* hump, hunched back; **~do, a** *adj* hunchbacked ♦ *nm/f* hunchback
jota ['xota] *nf* (the letter) J; (*danza*) Aragonese dance; **no saber ni ~** to have no idea
joven ['xoβen] (*pl* **jóvenes**) *adj* young

♦ *nm* young man, youth ♦ *nf* young woman, girl

jovial [xo'βjal] *adj* cheerful, jolly

joya ['xoja] *nf* jewel, gem; (*fig: persona*) gem; **joyería** *nf* (*joyas*) jewellery; (*tienda*) jeweller's (shop); **joyero** *nm* (*persona*) jeweller; (*caja*) jewel case

juanete [xwa'nete] *nm* (*del pie*) bunion

jubilación [xuβila'θjon] *nf* (*retiro*) retirement

jubilado, a [xuβi'laðo, a] *adj* retired ♦ *nm/f* pensioner (*BRIT*), senior citizen

jubilar [xuβi'lar] *vt* to pension off, retire; (*fam*) to discard; ~**se** *vr* to retire

júbilo ['xuβilo] *nm* joy, rejoicing; **jubiloso, a** *adj* jubilant

judía [xu'ðia] *nf* (*CULIN*) bean; ~ **verde** French bean; *ver tb* **judío**

judicial [xuði'θjal] *adj* judicial

judío, a [xu'ðio, a] *adj* Jewish ♦ *nm/f* Jew(ess)

judo ['juðo] *nm* judo

juego *etc* ['xwexo] *vb ver* **jugar** ♦ *nm* (*gen*) play; (*pasatiempo, partido*) game; (*en casino*) gambling; (*conjunto*) set; **fuera de** ~ (*DEPORTE: persona*) offside; (*: pelota*) out of play; **J~s Olímpicos** Olympic Games

juerga ['xwerγa] *nf* binge; (*fiesta*) party; **ir de** ~ to go out on a binge

jueves ['xweβes] *nm inv* Thursday

juez [xweθ] *nm/f* judge; ~ **de línea** linesman; ~ **de salida** starter

jugada [xu'xaða] *nf* play; **buena** ~ good move/shot/stroke *etc*

jugador, a [xuxa'ðor, a] *nm/f* player; (*en casino*) gambler

jugar [xu'xar] *vt, vi* to play; (*en casino*) to gamble; (*apostar*) to bet; ~ **al fútbol** to play football

juglar [xu'xlar] *nm* minstrel

jugo ['xuxo] *nm* (*BOT*) juice; (*fig*) essence, substance; ~ **de fruta** (*AM*) fruit juice; ~**so, a** *adj* juicy; (*fig*) substantial, important

juguete [xu'xete] *nm* toy; ~**ar** *vi* to play; ~**ría** *nf* toyshop

juguetón, ona [xuxe'ton, ona] *adj* playful

juicio [xwiθjo] *nm* judgement; (*razón*) sanity, reason; (*opinión*) opinion; ~**so, a** *adj* wise, sensible

julio ['xuljo] *nm* July

junco ['xunko] *nm* rush, reed

jungla ['xungla] *nf* jungle

junio ['xunjo] *nm* June

junta ['xunta] *nf* (*asamblea*) meeting, assembly; (*comité, consejo*) board, council, committee; (*TEC*) joint

juntar [xun'tar] *vt* to join, unite; (*maquinaria*) to assemble, put together; (*dinero*) to collect; ~**se** *vr* to join, meet; (*reunirse: personas*) to meet, assemble; (*arrimarse*) to approach, draw closer; ~**se con uno** to join sb

junto, a ['xunto, a] *adj* joined; (*unido*) united; (*anexo*) near, close; (*contiguo, próximo*) next, adjacent ♦ *adv*: **todo** ~ all at once; ~**s** together; ~ **a** near (to), next to

jurado [xu'raðo] *nm* (*JUR: individuo*) juror; (: *grupo*) jury; (*de concurso: grupo*) panel of (judges); (: *individuo*) member of a panel

juramento [xura'mento] *nm* oath; (*maldición*) oath, curse; **prestar** ~ to take the oath; **tomar** ~ **a** to swear in, administer the oath to

jurar [xu'rar] *vt, vi* to swear; ~ **en falso** to commit perjury; **jurárselas a uno** to have it in for sb

jurídico, a [xu'riðiko, a] *adj* legal

jurisdicción [xurisðik'θjon] *nf* (*poder, autoridad*) jurisdiction; (*territorio*) district

jurisprudencia [xurispru'ðenθja] *nf* jurisprudence

jurista [xu'rista] *nm/f* jurist

justamente [xusta'mente] *adv* justly, fairly; (*precisamente*) just, exactly

justicia [xus'tiθja] *nf* justice; (*equidad*) fairness, justice; **justiciero, a** *adj* just, righteous

justificación [xustifika'θjon] *nf* justification; **justificar** vt to justify

justo, a [ˈxusto, a] adj (equitativo) just, fair, right; (preciso) exact, correct; (ajustado) tight ♦ adv (precisamente) exactly, precisely; (AM: apenas a tiempo) just in time

juvenil [xuβeˈnil] adj youthful

juventud [xuβenˈtuð] nf (adolescencia) youth; (jóvenes) young people pl

juzgado [xuθˈɣaðo] nm tribunal; (JUR) court

juzgar [xuθˈɣar] vt to judge; **a ~ por ...** to judge by ..., judging by ...

K, k

kg abr (= kilogramo) kg

kilo [ˈkilo] nm kilo ♦ pref: **~gramo** nm kilogramme; **~metraje** nm distance in kilometres, ≈ mileage; **kilómetro** nm kilometre; **~vatio** nm kilowatt

kiosco [ˈkjosko] nm = **quiosco**

km abr (= kilómetro) km

kv abr (= kilovatio) kw

L, l

l abr (= litro) l

la [la] art def the ♦ pron her; (Ud.) you; (cosa) it ♦ nm (MUS) la; **~ del sombrero rojo** the girl in the red hat; tb ver **el**

laberinto [laβeˈrinto] nm labyrinth

labia [ˈlaβja] nf fluency; (pey) glib tongue

labio [ˈlaβjo] nm lip

labor [laˈβor] nf labour; (AGR) farm work; (tarea) job, task; (COSTURA) needlework; **~able** adj (AGR) workable; **día ~able** working day; **~al** adj (accidente) at work; (jornada) working

laboratorio [laβoraˈtorjo] nm laboratory

laborioso, a [laβoˈrjoso, a] adj (persona) hard-working; (trabajo) tough

laborista [laβoˈrista] adj: **Partido L~** Labour Party

labrado, a [laˈβraðo, a] adj worked; (madera) carved; (metal) wrought

labrador, a [laβraˈðor, a] adj farming cpd ♦ nm/f farmer

labranza [laˈβranθa] nf (AGR) cultivation

labrar [laˈβrar] vt (gen) to work; (madera etc) to carve; (fig) to cause, bring about

labriego, a [laˈβrjeɣo, a] nm/f peasant

laca [ˈlaka] nf lacquer

lacayo [laˈkajo] nm lackey

lacio, a [ˈlaθjo, a] adj (pelo) lank, straight

lacón [laˈkon] nm shoulder of pork

lacónico, a [laˈkoniko, a] adj laconic

lacra [ˈlakra] nf (fig) blot; **lacrar** vt (cerrar) to seal (with sealing wax); **lacre** nm sealing wax

lactancia [lakˈtanθja] nf lactation

lactar [lakˈtar] vt, vi to suckle

lácteo, a [ˈlakteo, a] adj: **productos ~s** dairy products

ladear [laðeˈar] vt to tip, tilt ♦ vi to tilt; **~se** vr to lean

ladera [laˈðera] nf slope

lado [ˈlaðo] nm (gen) side; (fig) protection; (MIL) flank; **al ~ de** beside; **poner de ~** to put on its side; **poner a un ~** to put aside; **por todos ~s** on all sides, all round (BRIT)

ladrar [laˈðrar] vi to bark; **ladrido** nm bark, barking

ladrillo [laˈðriʎo] nm (gen) brick; (azulejo) tile

ladrón, ona [laˈðron, ona] nm/f thief

lagartija [laɣarˈtixa] nf (ZOOL) (small) lizard

lagarto [laˈɣarto] nm (ZOOL) lizard

lago [ˈlaɣo] nm lake

lágrima [ˈlaɣrima] nf tear

laguna [laˈɣuna] nf (lago) lagoon; (hueco) gap

laico, a [ˈlaiko, a] adj lay

lamentable [lamenˈtaβle] adj

lamentable, regrettable; (*miserable*) pitiful

lamentar |lamen'tar| *vt* (*sentir*) to regret; (*deplorar*) to lament; **lo lamento mucho** I'm very sorry; **~se a** (*AM*) to start to

lamer |la'mer| *vt* to lick

lámina ['lamina] *nf* (*plancha delgada*) sheet; (*para estampar, estampa*) plate

lámpara ['lampara] *nf* lamp; **~ de alcohol/gas** spirit/gas lamp; **~ de pie** standard lamp

lamparón |lampa'ron| *nm* grease spot

lana ['lana] *nf* wool

lancha ['lantʃa] *nf* launch; **~ de pesca** fishing boat; **~ salvavidas/torpedera** lifeboat/torpedo boat

langosta |lan'gosta| *nf* (*crustáceo*) lobster; (: *de río*) crayfish; **langostino** *nm* Dublin Bay prawn

languidecer |langiðe'θer| *vi* to languish; **languidez** *nf* languor; **lánguido, a** *adj* (*gen*) languid; (*sin energía*) listless

lanilla |la'niʎa| *nf* nap

lanza ['lanθa] *nf* (*arma*) lance, spear

lanzamiento |lanθa'mjento| *nm* (*gen*) throwing; (*NAUT, COM*) launch, launching; **~ de peso** putting the shot

lanzar |lan'θar| *vt* (*gen*) to throw; (*DEPORTE: pelota*) to bowl; (*NAUT, COM*) to launch; (*JUR*) to evict; **~se** *vr* to throw o.s.

lapa ['lapa] *nf* limpet

lapicero |lapi'θero| *nm* pencil; (*AM: bolígrafo*) Biro ®

lápida ['lapiða] *nf* stone; **~ mortuoria** headstone; **~ conmemorativa** memorial stone; **lapidario, a** *adj, nm* lapidary

lápiz ['lapiθ] *nm* pencil; **~ de color** coloured pencil; **~ de labios** lipstick

lapón, ona |la'pon, ona| *nm/f* Laplander, Lapp

lapso ['lapso] *nm* (*de tiempo*) interval; (*error*) error

lapsus ['lapsus] *nm inv* error, mistake

largar |lar'var| *vt* (*soltar*) to release; (*aflojar*) to loosen; (*lanzar*) to launch; (*fam*) to let fly; (*velas*) to unfurl; (*AM*) to throw; **~se** *vr* (*fam*) to beat it; **~se a** (*AM*) to start to

largo, a ['larvo, a] *adj* (*longitud*) long; (*tiempo*) lengthy ♦ *nm* length; (*MUS*) largo; **dos años ~s** two long years; **tiene 9 metros de ~** it is 9 metres long; **a lo ~ de** along; (*tiempo*) all through, throughout; **~metraje** *nm* feature film

laringe |la'rinxe| *nf* larynx; **laringitis** *nf* laryngitis

larva ['larβa] *nf* larva

las [las] *art del* the ♦ *pron* them; **~ que cantan** the ones/women/girls who sing; *tb ver* **el**

lascivo, a |las'θiβo, a| *adj* lewd

láser ['laser] *nm* laser

lástima ['lastima] *nf* (*pena*) pity; **dar ~** to be pitiful; **es una ~ que** it's a pity that; **¡qué ~!** what a pity!; **ella está hecha una ~** she looks pitiful

lastimar |lasti'mar| *vt* (*herir*) to wound; (*ofender*) to offend; **~se** *vr* to hurt o.s.; **lastimero, a** *adj* pitiful, pathetic

lastre ['lastre] *nm* (*TEC, NAUT*) ballast; (*fig*) dead weight

lata ['lata] *nf* (*metal*) tin; (*caja*) tin (*BRIT*), can; (*fam*) nuisance; **en ~** tinned (*BRIT*), canned; **dar (la) ~** to be a nuisance

latente |la'tente| *adj* latent

lateral |late'ral| *adj* side *cpd*, lateral ♦ *nm* (*TEATRO*) wings

latido |la'tiðo| *nm* (*del corazón*) beat

latifundio |lati'fundjo| *nm* large estate; **latifundista** *nm/f* owner of a large estate

latigazo |lati'xaθo| *nm* (*golpe*) lash; (*sonido*) crack

látigo ['latixo] *nm* whip

latín |la'tin| *nm* Latin

latino, a |la'tino, a| *adj* Latin; **~americano, a** *adj, nm/f* Latin-

American

latir [la'tir] vi (corazón, pulso) to beat
latitud [lati'tuð] nf (GEO) latitude
latón [la'ton] nm brass
latoso, a [la'toso, a] adj (molesto) annoying; (aburrido) boring
laúd [la'uð] nm lute
laurel [lau'rel] nm (BOT) laurel; (CULIN) bay
lava ['laβa] nf lava
lavabo [la'βaβo] nm (pila) washbasin; (tb: ~s) toilet
lavado [la'βaðo] nm washing; (de ropa) laundry; (ARTE) wash; ~ **de cerebro** brainwashing; ~ **en seco** dry-cleaning
lavadora [laβa'ðora] nf washing machine
lavanda [la'βanda] nf lavender
lavandería [laβande'ria] nf laundry; (automática) launderette
lavaplatos [laβa'platos] nm inv dishwasher
lavar [la'βar] vt to wash; (borrar) to wipe away; ~se vr to wash o.s.; ~se las manos to wash one's hands; ~se los dientes to brush one's teeth; ~ y marcar (pelo) to shampoo and set; ~ en seco to dry-clean; ~ los platos to wash the dishes
lavavajillas [laβaβa'xiʎas] nm inv dishwasher
laxante [lak'sante] nm laxative
lazada [la'θaða] nf bow
lazarillo [laθa'riʎo] nm: **perro ~** guide dog
lazo ['laθo] nm knot; (lazada) bow; (para animales) lasso; (trampa) snare; (vínculo) tie
le [le] pron (directo) him (o her); (: usted) you; (indirecto) to him (o her o it); (: usted) to you
leal [le'al] adj loyal; ~**tad** nf loyalty
lección [lek'θjon] nf lesson
leche ['letʃe] nf milk; **tiene mala ~** (fam!) he's a swine (!); ~ **condensada/en polvo** condensed/powdered milk; ~ **desnatada** skimmed milk; ~**ra**

nf (vendedora) milkmaid; (recipiente) (milk) churn; (AM) cow; ~**ro, a** adj dairy
lecho ['letʃo] nm (cama, de río) bed; (GEO) layer
lechón [le'tʃon] nm sucking (BRIT) o suckling (US) pig
lechoso, a [le'tʃoso, a] adj milky
lechuga [le'tʃuɣa] nf lettuce
lechuza [le'tʃuθa] nf owl
lector, a [lek'tor, a] nm/f reader ♦ nm: ~ **de discos compactos** CD player
lectura [lek'tura] nf reading
leer [le'er] vt to read
legado [le'ɣaðo] nm (don) bequest; (herencia) legacy; (enviado) legate
legajo [le'ɣaxo] nm file
legal [le'ɣal] adj (gen) legal; (persona) trustworthy; ~**idad** nf legality
legalizar [leɣali'θar] vt to legalize; (documento) to authenticate
legaña [le'ɣaɲa] nf sleep (in eyes)
legar [le'ɣar] vt to bequeath, leave
legendario, a [lexen'darjo, a] adj legendary
legión [le'xjon] nf legion; **legionario, a** adj legionary ♦ nm legionnaire
legislación [lexisla'θjon] nf legislation
legislar [lexis'lar] vi to legislate
legislatura [lexisla'tura] nf (POL) period of office
legitimar [lexiti'mar] vt to legitimize; **legítimo, a** adj (genuino) authentic; (legal) legitimate
lego, a ['leɣo, a] adj (REL) secular; (ignorante) ignorant ♦ nm layman
legua ['leɣwa] nf league
legumbres [le'ɣumbres] nfpl pulses
leído, a [le'iðo, a] adj well-read
lejanía [lexa'nia] nf distance; **lejano, a** adj far-off; (en el tiempo) distant; (fig) remote
lejía [le'xia] nf bleach
lejos ['lexos] adv far, far away; **a lo ~** in the distance; **de** o **desde ~** from afar; ~ **de** far from
lelo, a ['lelo, a] adj silly ♦ nm/f idiot

lema ['lema] nm motto; (POL) slogan
lencería [lenθe'ria] nf linen, drapery
lengua ['lengwa] nf tongue; (LING) language; **morderse la ~** to hold one's tongue
lenguado [len'gwaðo] nm sole
lenguaje [len'gwaxe] nm language
lengüeta [len'gweta] nf (ANAT) epiglottis; (zapatos) tongue; (MUS) reed
lente ['lente] nf lens; (lupa) magnifying glass; **~s** nfpl (gafas) glasses; **~s de contacto** contact lenses
lenteja [len'texa] nf lentil; **lentejuela** nf sequin
lentilla [len'tiʎa] nf contact lens
lentitud [lenti'tuð] nf slowness; **con ~** slowly
lento, a ['lento, a] adj slow
leña ['leɲa] nf firewood; **~dor, a** nm/f woodcutter
leño ['leɲo] nm (trozo de árbol) log; (madera) timber; (fig) blockhead
Leo ['leo] nm Leo
león [le'on] nm lion; **~ marino** sea lion
leopardo [leo'parðo] nm leopard
leotardos [leo'tarðos] nmpl tights
lepra ['lepra] nf leprosy; **leproso, a** nm/f leper
lerdo, a ['lerðo, a] adj (lento) slow; (patoso) clumsy
les [les] pron (directo) them; (: ustedes) you; (indirecto) to them; (: ustedes) to you
lesbiana [les'βjana] adj, nf lesbian
lesión [le'sjon] nf wound, lesion; (DEPORTE) injury; **lesionado, a** adj injured ♦ nm/f injured person
letal [le'tal] adj lethal
letanía [leta'nia] nf litany
letargo [le'tarɣo] nm lethargy
letra ['letra] nf letter; (escritura) handwriting; (MUS) lyrics pl; **~ de cambio** bill of exchange; **~ de imprenta** print; **~do, a** adj learned ♦ nm/f lawyer; **letrero** nm (cartel) sign; (etiqueta) label
letrina [le'trina] nf latrine

leucemia [leu'θemja] nf leukaemia
levadizo [leβa'ðiθo] adj: **puente ~** drawbridge
levadura [leβa'ðura] nf (para el pan) yeast; (de la cerveza) brewer's yeast
levantamiento [leβanta'mjento] nm raising, lifting; (rebelión) revolt, uprising; **~ de pesos** weight-lifting
levantar [leβan'tar] vt (gen) to raise; (del suelo) to pick up; (hacia arriba) to lift (up); (plan) to make, draw up; (mesa) to clear; (campamento) to strike; (fig) to cheer up, hearten; **~se** vr to get up; (enderezarse) to straighten up; (rebelarse) to rebel; **~ el ánimo** to cheer up
levante [le'βante] nm east coast; **el L~** region of Spain extending from Castellón to Murcia
levar [le'βar] vt to weigh
leve [le'βe] adj light; (fig) trivial; **~dad** nf lightness
levita [le'βita] nf frock coat
léxico ['leksiko] nm (vocabulario) vocabulary
ley [lei] nf (gen) law; (metal) standard
leyenda [le'jenda] nf legend
leyó etc vb ver **leer**
liar [li'ar] vt to tie (up); (unir) to bind; (envolver) to wrap (up); (enredar) to confuse; (cigarrillo) to roll; **~se** vr (fam) to get involved; **~se a palos** to get involved in a fight
Líbano ['liβano] nm: **el ~** (the) Lebanon
libelo [li'βelo] nm satire, lampoon
libélula [li'βelula] nf dragonfly
liberación [liβera'θjon] nf liberation; (de la cárcel) release
liberal [liβe'ral] adj, nm/f liberal; **~idad** nf liberality, generosity
liberar [liβe'rar] vt to liberate
libertad [liβer'tað] nf liberty, freedom; **~ de culto/de prensa/de comercio** freedom of worship/of the press/of trade; **~ condicional** probation; **~ bajo palabra** parole; **~ bajo fianza**

bail

libertar [liβer'tar] vt (*preso*) to set free; (*de una obligación*) to release; (*eximir*) to exempt

libertino, a [liβer'tino, a] adj permissive ♦ nm/f permissive person

libra ['liβra] nf pound; (ASTROLOGÍA): **L~** Libra; **~ esterlina** pound sterling

librar [li'βrar] vt (*de peligro*) to save; (*batalla*) to wage, fight; (*de impuestos*) to exempt; (*cheque*) to make out; (JUR) to exempt; **~se** vr: **~se de** to escape from, free o.s. from

libre ['liβre] adj free; (*lugar*) unoccupied; (*asiento*) vacant; (*de deudas*) free of debts; **~ de impuestos** free of tax; **~ tiro ~** free kick; **los 100 metros ~** the 100 metres free-style (race); **al aire ~** in the open air

librería [liβre'ria] nf (*tienda*) bookshop; **librero, a** nm/f bookseller

libreta [li'βreta] nf notebook; **~ de ahorros** savings book

libro ['liβro] nm book; **~ de bolsillo** paperback; **~ de caja** cashbook; **~ de cheques** chequebook (BRIT), checkbook (US); **~ de texto** textbook

Lic. abr = **licenciado, a**

licencia [li'θenθja] nf (*gen*) licence; (*permiso*) permission; **~ por enfermedad** sick leave; **~ de caza** game licence; **~do, a** adj licensed ♦ nm/f graduate; **licenciar** vt (*empleado*) to dismiss; (*permitir*) to permit, allow; (*soldado*) to discharge; (*estudiante*) to confer a degree upon; **licenciarse** vr: **licenciarse en letras** to graduate in arts

licencioso, a [liθen'θjoso, a] adj licentious

licitar [liθi'tar] vt to bid for; (AM) to sell by auction

lícito, a ['liθito, a] adj (*legal*) lawful; (*justo*) fair, just; (*permisible*) permissible

licor [li'kor] nm spirits pl (BRIT), liquor (US); (*de frutas etc*) liqueur

licuadora [likwa'ðora] nf blender

licuar [li'kwar] vt to liquidize

líder ['liðer] nm/f leader; **liderato** nm leadership; **liderazgo** nm leadership

lidia ['liðja] nf bullfighting; (*una ~*) bullfight; **toros de ~** fighting bulls; **lidiar** vt, vi to fight

liebre ['ljeβre] nf hare

lienzo ['ljenθo] nm linen; (ARTE) canvas; (ARQ) wall

liga ['liɣa] nf (*de medias*) garter, suspender; (AM: *gomita*) rubber band; (*confederación*) league

ligadura [liɣa'ðura] nf bond, tie; (MED, MUS) ligature

ligamento [liɣa'mento] nm ligament

ligar [li'ɣar] vt (*atar*) to tie; (*unir*) to join; (MED) to bind up; (MUS) to slur ♦ vi to mix, blend; (*fam*): (**él**) **liga mucho** he pulls a lot of women; **~se** vr to commit o.s.

ligereza [lixe'reθa] nf lightness; (*rapidez*) swiftness; (*agilidad*) agility; (*superficialidad*) flippancy

ligero, a [li'xero, a] adj (*de peso*) light; (*tela*) thin; (*rápido*) swift, quick; (*ágil*) agile, nimble; (*de importancia*) slight; (*de carácter*) flippant, superficial ♦ adv: **a la ligera** superficially

liguero [li'ɣero] nm suspender (BRIT) or garter (US) belt

lija ['lixa] nf (ZOOL) dogfish; (*tb: papel de ~*) sandpaper

lila ['lila] nf lilac

lima ['lima] nf file; (BOT) lime; **~ de uñas** nailfile; **limar** vt to file

limitación [limita'θjon] nf limitation, limit; **~ de velocidad** speed limit

limitar [limi'tar] vt to limit; (*reducir*) to reduce, cut down ♦ vi: **~ con** to border on; **~se** vr: **~se a** to limit o.s. to

límite ['limite] nm (*gen*) limit; (*fin*) end; (*frontera*) border; **~ de velocidad** speed limit

limítrofe [li'mitrofe] adj neighbouring

limón [li'mon] nm lemon ♦ adj:

amarillo ~ lemon-yellow; **limonada** nf lemonade

limosna [li'mosna] nf alms pl; **vivir de ~** to live on charity

limpiaparabrisas [limpjapara'βrisas] nm inv windscreen (BRIT) o windshield (US) wiper

limpiar [lim'pjar] vt to clean; (con trapo) to wipe; (quitar) to wipe away; (zapatos) to shine, polish; (fig) to clean up

limpieza [lim'pjeθa] nf (estado) cleanliness; (acto) cleaning; (: de las calles) cleansing; (: de zapatos) polishing; (habilidad) skill; (fig: POLICÍA) clean-up; (pureza) purity; (MIL): **operación de ~** mopping-up operation; **~ en seco** dry cleaning

limpio, a ['limpjo, a] adj clean; (moralmente) pure; (COM) clear, net; (fam) honest ♦ adv: **jugar ~** to play fair; **pasar a** (ESP) **o en** (AM) **~** to make a clean copy

linaje [li'naxe] nm lineage, family

lince [li'nθe] nm lynx

linchar [lin'tʃar] vt to lynch

lindar [lin'dar] vi to adjoin; **~ con** to border on; **linde** nm o f boundary; **lindero, a** adj adjoining ♦ nm boundary

lindo, a ['lindo, a] adj pretty, lovely ♦ adv: **nos divertimos de lo ~** we had a marvellous time; **canta muy ~** (AM) he sings beautifully

línea ['linea] nf (gen) line; **en ~** (INFORM) on line; **~ aérea** airline; **~ de meta** goal line; (de carrera) finishing line; **~ recta** straight line

lingote [lin'gote] nm ingot

lingüista [lin'gwista] nm/f linguist; **lingüística** nf linguistics sg

lino ['lino] nm linen; (BOT) flax

linóleo [li'noleo] nm lino, linoleum

linterna [lin'terna] nf torch (BRIT), flashlight (US)

lío ['lio] nm bundle; (fam) fuss; (desorden) muddle, mess; **armar un ~** to make a fuss

liquen ['liken] nm lichen

liquidación [likiða'θjon] nf liquidation; **venta de ~** clearance sale

liquidar [liki'ðar] vt (mercancías) to liquidate; (deudas) to pay off; (empresa) to wind up

líquido, a ['likiðo, a] adj liquid; (ganancia) net ♦ nm liquid; **~ imponible** net taxable income

lira ['lira] nf (MUS) lyre; (moneda) lira

lírico, a ['liriko, a] adj lyrical

lirio ['lirjo] nm (BOT) iris

lirón [li'ron] nm (ZOOL) dormouse; (fig) sleepyhead

Lisboa [lis'βoa] n Lisbon

lisiado, a [li'sjaðo, a] adj injured ♦ nm/f cripple

lisiar [li'sjar] vt to maim; **~se** vr to injure o.s.

liso, a ['liso, a] adj (terreno) flat; (cabello) straight; (superficie) even; (tela) plain

lisonja [li'sonxa] nf flattery

lista ['lista] nf list; (de alumnos) school register; (de libros) catalogue; (de platos) menu; (de precios) price list; **pasar ~** to call the roll; **~ de correos** poste restante; **~ de espera** waiting list; **tela de ~** striped material; **listín** nm: **~ (telefónico)** telephone directory

listo, a ['listo, a] adj (perspicaz) smart, clever; (preparado) ready

listón [lis'ton] nm (de madera, metal) strip

litera [li'tera] nf (en barco, tren) berth; (en dormitorio) bunk, bunk bed

literal [lite'ral] adj literal

literario, a [lite'rarjo, a] adj literary

literato, a [lite'rato, a] adj literary ♦ nm/f writer

literatura [litera'tura] nf literature

litigar [liti'ɣar] vt to fight ♦ vi (JUR) to go to law; (fig) to dispute, argue

litigio [li'tixjo] nm (JUR) lawsuit; (fig): **en ~ con** in dispute with

litografía [litoɣra'fia] nf lithography;

(una ~) lithograph

litoral [lito'ral] adj coastal ♦ nm coast, seaboard

litro ['litro] nm litre

liviano, a [li'βjano, a] adj (cosa, objeto) trivial

lívido, a ['liβiðo, a] adj livid

llaga ['ʎaɣa] nf wound

llama ['ʎama] nf flame; (ZOOL.) llama

llamada [ʎa'maða] nf call; ~ **al orden** call to order; ~ **a pie de página** reference note

llamamiento [ʎama'mjento] nm call

llamar [ʎa'mar] vt to call; (atención) to attract ♦ vi (por teléfono) to telephone; (a la puerta) to knock (o ring); (por señas) to beckon; (MIL) to call up; ~**se** vr to be called, be named; **¿cómo se llama usted?** what's your name?

llamarada [ʎama'raða] nf (llamas) blaze; (rubor) flush

llamativo, a [ʎama'tiβo, a] adj showy; (color) loud

llano, a ['ʎano, a] adj (superficie) flat; (persona) straightforward; (estilo) clear ♦ nm plain, flat ground

llanta ['ʎanta] nf (wheel) rim; (AM:): ~ **(de goma)** tyre; (: cámara) inner (tube)

llanto ['ʎanto] nm weeping

llanura [ʎa'nura] nf plain

llave ['ʎaβe] nf key; (del agua) tap; (MECÁNICA) spanner; (de la luz) switch; (MUS) key; ~ **inglesa** monkey wrench; ~ **maestra** master key; ~ **de contacto** (AUTO) ignition key; ~ **de paso** stopcock; **echar la ~ a** to lock up; ~**ro** nm keyring

llegada [ʎe'ɣaða] nf arrival

llegar [ʎe'ɣar] vi to arrive; (alcanzar) to reach; (bastar) to be enough; ~**se** vr: ~**se a** to approach; ~ **a** to manage to, succeed in; ~ **a saber** to find out; ~ **a ser** to become; ~ **a las manos de** to come into the hands of

llenar [ʎe'nar] vt to fill; (espacio) to cover; (formulario) to fill in o up; (fig)

to heap

lleno, a ['ʎeno, a] adj full, filled; (repleto) full up ♦ nm (TEATRO) full house; **dar de ~ contra un muro** to hit a wall head-on

llevadero, a [ʎeβa'ðero, a] adj bearable, tolerable

llevar [ʎe'βar] vt to take; (ropa) to wear; (cargar) to carry; (quitar) to take away; (en coche) to drive; (transportar) to transport; (traer: dinero) to carry; (conducir) to lead; (MAT) to carry ♦ vi (suj: camino etc): ~ **a** to lead to; ~**se** vr to carry off, take away; **llevamos dos días aquí** we have been here for two days; **él me lleva 2 años** he's 2 years older than me; (COM): ~ **los libros** to keep the books; ~**se bien** to get on well (together)

llorar [ʎo'rar] vt, vi to cry, weep; ~ **de risa** to cry with laughter

lloriquear [ʎorike'ar] vi to snivel, whimper

lloro ['ʎoro] nm crying, weeping

llorón, ona adj tearful ♦ nm/f cry-baby; ~**so, a** adj (gen) weeping, tearful; (triste) sad, sorrowful

llover [ʎo'βer] vi to rain

llovizna [ʎo'βiθna] nf drizzle; **lloviznar** vi to drizzle

llueve etc vb ver **llover**

lluvia ['ʎuβja] nf rain; ~ **radioactiva** (radioactive) fallout; **lluvioso, a** adj rainy

lo [lo] art def: ~ **bello** the beautiful, what is beautiful, that which is beautiful ♦ pron (persona) him; (cosa) it; tb ver **el**

loable [lo'aβle] adj praiseworthy; **loar** vt to praise

lobo ['loβo] nm wolf; ~ **de mar** (fig) sea dog; ~ **marino** seal

lóbrego, a ['loβreɣo, a] adj dark; (fig) gloomy

lóbulo ['loβulo] nm lobe

local [lo'kal] adj local ♦ nm place, site; (oficinas) premises pl; ~**idad** nf (barrio) locality; (*lugar*) location; (*TEATRO*) seat, ticket; **~izar** *vt* (*ubicar*) to locate, find; (*restringir*) to localize; (*situar*) to place

loción [lo'θjon] *nf* lotion

loco, a ['loko, a] *adj* mad ♦ *nm/f* lunatic, mad person

locomotora [lokomo'tora] *nf* engine, locomotive

locuaz [lo'kwaθ] *adj* loquacious

locución [loku'θjon] *nf* expression

locura [lo'kura] *nf* madness; (*acto*) crazy act

locutor, a [loku'tor, a] *nm/f* (*RADIO*) announcer; (*comentarista*) commentator; (*TV*) newsreader

locutorio [loku'torjo] *nm* (*en telefónica*) telephone booth

lodo ['loðo] *nm* mud

lógica ['loxika] *nf* logic

lógico, a ['loxiko, a] *adj* logical

logística [lo'xistika] *nf* logistics *sg*

logotipo [loðo'tipo] *nm* logo

logrado, a [lo'ðraðo, a] *adj* (*interpretación, reproducción*) polished, excellent

lograr [lo'ɣrar] *vt* to achieve; (*obtener*) to get, obtain; **~ hacer** to manage to do; **~ que uno venga** to manage to get sb to come

logro ['loɣro] *nm* achievement, success

loma ['loma] *nf* hillock (*BRIT*), small hill

lombriz [lom'briθ] *nf* worm

lomo ['lomo] *nm* (*de animal*) back; (*CULIN: de cerdo*) pork loin; (*: de vaca*) rib steak; (*de libro*) spine

lona ['lona] *nf* canvas

loncha ['lontʃa] *nf* = **lonja**

lonche ['lontʃe] (*AM*) *nm* lunch; **~ría** (*AM*) *nf* snack bar, diner (*US*)

Londres ['londres] *n* London

longaniza [longa'niθa] *nf* pork sausage

longitud [lonxi'tuð] *nf* length; (*GEO*) longitude; **tener 3 metros de ~** to be 3 metres long; **~ de onda** wavelength

lonja ['lonxa] *nf* slice; (*de tocino*) rasher; **~ de pescado** fish market

loro ['loro] *nm* parrot

los [los] *art def the* ♦ *pron* them; (*ustedes*) you; **mis libros y ~ tuyos** my books and yours; *tb ver* **el**

losa ['losa] *nf* stone; **~ sepulcral** gravestone

lote ['lote] *nm* portion; (*COM*) lot

lotería [lote'ria] *nf* lottery; (*juego*) lotto

loza ['loθa] *nf* crockery

lubina [lu'ßina] *nf* sea bass

lubricante [lußri'kante] *nm* lubricant

lubricar [lußri'kar] *vt* to lubricate

lucha ['lutʃa] *nf* fight, struggle; **~ de clases** class struggle; **~ libre** wrestling; **luchar** *vi* to fight

lucidez [luθi'ðeθ] *nf* lucidity

lúcido, a ['luθiðo, a] *adj* (*persona*) lucid; (*mente*) logical; (*idea*) crystal-clear

luciérnaga [lu'θjernaɣa] *nf* glow-worm

lucir [lu'θir] *vt* to illuminate, light (up); (*ostentar*) to show off ♦ *vi* (*brillar*) to shine; **~se** *vr* (*irónico*) to make a fool of o.s.

lucro ['lukro] *nm* profit, gain

lúdico, a ['ludiko, a] *adj* (*aspecto, actividad*) play *cpd*

luego ['lweɣo] *adv* (*después*) next; (*más tarde*) later, afterwards

lugar [lu'ɣar] *nm* place; (*sitio*) spot; **en ~ de** instead of; **hacer ~** to make room; **fuera de ~** out of place; **tener ~** to take place; **~ común** commonplace

lugareño, a [luɣaˈreɲo, a] adj village cpd ♦ nm/f villager

lugarteniente [luɣarteˈnjente] nm deputy

lúgubre [ˈluɣuβre] adj mournful

lujo [ˈluxo] nm luxury; (fig) profusion, abundance; **~so, a** adj luxurious

lujuria [luˈxurja] nf lust

lumbre [ˈlumbre] nf fire; (para cigarrillo) light

lumbrera [lumˈbrera] nf luminary

luminoso, a [lumiˈnoso, a] adj luminous, shining

luna [ˈluna] nf moon; (de un espejo) glass; (de gafas) lens; (fig) crescent; **~ llena/nueva** full/new moon; **estar en la ~** to have one's head in the clouds; **~ de miel** honeymoon

lunar [luˈnar] adj lunar ♦ nm (ANAT) mole; **tela de ~es** spotted material

lunes [ˈlunes] nm inv Monday

lupa [ˈlupa] nf magnifying glass

lustrar [lusˈtrar] vt (mueble) to polish; (zapatos) to shine; **lustre** nm polish; (fig) lustre; **dar lustre a** to polish; **lustroso, a** adj shining

luto [ˈluto] nm mourning; **llevar el o vestirse de ~** to be in mourning

Luxemburgo [luksemˈburɣo] nm Luxembourg

luz [luθ] (pl **luces**) nf light; **dar a ~ un niño** to give birth to a child; **sacar a la ~** to bring to light; **dar o encender** (ESP) o **prender** (AM)/**apagar la ~** to switch the light on/off; **a todas luces** by any reckoning; **tener pocas luces** to be dim o stupid; **~ roja/verde** red/green light; **~ de freno** brake light; **luces de tráfico** traffic lights; **traje de luces** bullfighter's costume

M, m

m abr (= metro) m; (= minuto) m

macarrones [makaˈrrones] nmpl macaroni sg

macedonia [maθeˈðonja] nf: **~ de frutas** fruit salad

macerar [maθeˈrar] vt to macerate

maceta [maˈθeta] nf (de flores) pot of flowers; (para plantas) flowerpot

machacar [matʃaˈkar] vt to crush, pound ♦ vi (insistir) to go on, keep on

machete [maˈtʃete] (AM) nm machete, (large) knife

machismo [maˈtʃismo] nm male chauvinism; **machista** adj, nm sexist

macho [ˈmatʃo] adj male; (fig) virile ♦ nm male; (fig) he-man

macizo, a [maˈθiθo, a] adj (grande) massive; (fuerte, sólido) solid ♦ nm mass, chunk

madeja [maˈðexa] nf (de lana) skein, hank; (de pelo) mass, mop

madera [maˈðera] nf wood; (fig) nature, character; **una ~** a piece of wood

madero [maˈðero] nm beam

madrastra [maˈðrastra] nf stepmother

madre [ˈmaðre] adj mother cpd; (AM) tremendous ♦ nf mother; (de vino etc) dregs pl; **~ política/soltera** mother-in-law/unmarried mother

Madrid [maˈðrið] n Madrid

madriguera [maðriˈɣera] nf burrow

madrileño, a [maðriˈleɲo, a] adj of o from Madrid ♦ nm/f native of Madrid

madrina [maˈðrina] nf godmother; (ARQ) prop, shore; (TEC) brace; (de boda) bridesmaid

madrugada [maðruˈɣaða] nf early morning; (alba) dawn, daybreak

madrugador, a [maðruɣaˈðor, a] adj early-rising

madrugar [maðruˈɣar] vi to get up early; (fig) to get ahead

madurar [maðuˈrar] vt, vi (fruta) to ripen; (fig) to mature; **madurez** nf ripeness; maturity; **maduro, a** adj ripe; mature

maestra [maˈestra] nf ver **maestro**

maestría [maesˈtria] nf mastery; (habilidad) skill, expertise

maestro, a [ma'estro, a] *adj* masterly; (*principal*) main ♦ *nm/f* master/mistress; (*profesor*) teacher ♦ *nm* (*autoridad*) authority; (*MUS*) maestro; (*AM*) skilled workman; **~ albañil** master mason

magdalena [mayða'lena] *nf* fairy cake

magia ['maxja] *nf* magic; **mágico, a** *adj* magic(al) ♦ *nm/f* magician

magisterio [maxis'terjo] *nm* (*enseñanza*) teaching; (*profesión*) teaching profession; (*maestros*) teachers *pl*

magistrado [maxis'traðo] *nm* magistrate

magistral [maxis'tral] *adj* magisterial; (*fig*) masterly

magnánimo, a [may'nanimo, a] *adj* magnanimous

magnate [may'nate] *nm* magnate, tycoon

magnético, a [may'netiko, a] *adj* magnetic; **magnetizar** *vt* to magnetize

magnetofón [maɣneto'fon] *nm* tape recorder; **magnetofónico, a** *adj*: **cinta magnetofónica** recording tape

magnetófono [maɣne'tofono] *nm* = **magnetofón**

magnífico, a [maɣ'nifiko, a] *adj* splendid, magnificent

magnitud [maɣni'tuð] *nf* magnitude

mago, a ['mayo, a] *nm/f* magician; **los Reyes M~s** the Magi, the Three Wise Men

magro, a ['mayro, a] *adj* (*carne*) lean

maguey [ma'vei] *nm* agave

magullar [mayu'ʎar] *vt* (*amoratar*) to bruise; (*dañar*) to damage

mahometano, a [maome'tano, a] *adj* Mohammedan

mahonesa [mao'nesa] *nf* mayonnaise

maíz [ma'iθ] *nm* maize (*BRIT*), corn (*US*); sweet corn

majadero, a [maxa'ðero, a] *adj* silly, stupid

majestad [maxes'tað] *nf* majesty; **majestuoso, a** *adj* majestic

majo, a ['maxo, a] *adj* nice; (*guapo*) attractive, good-looking; (*elegante*) smart

mal [mal] *adv* badly; (*equivocadamente*) wrongly ♦ *adj* = **malo** ♦ *nm* evil; (*desgracia*) misfortune; (*daño*) harm, damage; (*MED*) illness; **~ que bien** rightly or wrongly; **ir de ~ en peor** to get worse and worse

malabarismo [malaβa'rismo] *nm* juggling; **malabarista** *nm/f* juggler

malaria [ma'larja] *nf* malaria

malcriado, a [mal'krjaðo, a] *adj* spoiled

maldad [mal'dað] *nf* evil, wickedness

maldecir [malde'θir] *vt* to curse ♦ *vi*: **~ de** to speak ill of

maldición [maldi'θjon] *nf* curse

maldito, a [mal'dito, a] *adj* (*condenado*) damned; (*perverso*) wicked; **¡~ sea!** damn it!

maleante [male'ante] *nm/f* criminal, crook

maledicencia [maleði'θenθja] *nf* slander, scandal

maleducado, a [maleðu'kaðo, a] *adj* bad-mannered, rude

malentendido [malenten'diðo] *nm* misunderstanding

malestar [males'tar] *nm* (*gen*) discomfort; (*fig: inquietud*) uneasiness; (*POL*) unrest

maleta [ma'leta] *nf* case, suitcase; (*AUTO*) boot (*BRIT*), trunk (*US*); **hacer las ~s** to pack; **maletera** (*AM*) *nf*, **maletero** *nm* (*AUTO*) boot (*BRIT*), trunk (*US*); **maletín** *nm* small case, bag

malévolo, a [ma'leβolo, a] *adj* malicious, spiteful

maleza [ma'leθa] *nf* (*hierbas malas*) weeds *pl*; (*arbustos*) thicket

malgastar [malvas'tar] *vt* (*tiempo, dinero*) to waste; (*salud*) to ruin

malhechor [male'tʃor, a] *nm/f* delinquent

malhumorado, a [malumo'raðo, a] *adj* bad-tempered

malicia [ma'liθja] nf (maldad) wickedness; (astucia) slyness, guile; (mala intención) malice, spite; (carácter travieso) mischievousness; **malicioso, a** adj wicked, evil; sly, crafty; malicious, spiteful; mischievous

maligno, a [ma'liɣno, a] adj evil; (malévolo) malicious; (MED) malignant

malla ['maʎa] nf mesh; (de baño) swimsuit; (de ballet, gimnasia) leotard; **~s** nfpl tights; **~ de alambre** wire mesh

Mallorca [ma'ʎorka] nf Majorca

malo, a ['malo, a] adj bad; (falso) false ♦ nm/f villain; **estar ~** to be ill

malograr [malo'ɣrar] vt to spoil; (plan) to upset; (ocasión) to waste; **~se** vr (plan etc) to fail, come to grief; (persona) to die before one's time

malparado, a [malpa'raðo, a] adj: **salir ~** to come off badly

malpensado, a [malpen'saðo, a] adj nasty

malsano, a [mal'sano, a] adj unhealthy

malteada [malte'aða] (AM) nf milk shake

maltratar [maltra'tar] vt to ill-treat, mistreat

maltrecho, a [mal'tretʃo, a] adj battered, damaged

malvado, a [mal'βaðo, a] adj evil, villainous

malversar [malβer'sar] vt to embezzle, misappropriate

Malvinas [mal'βinas]: **Islas ~** nfpl Falkland Islands

malvivir [malβi'βir] vi to live poorly

mama ['mama] nf (de animal) teat; (de mujer) breast

mamá [ma'ma] (pl **~s**) (fam) nf mum, mummy

mamar [ma'mar] vt, vi to suck

mamarracho [mama'rratʃo] nm sight, mess

mamífero [ma'mifero] nm mammal

mampara [mam'para] nf (entre habitaciones) partition; (biombo) screen

mampostería [mamposte'ria] nf masonry

manada [ma'naða] nf (ZOOL) herd; (: de leones) pride; (: de lobos) pack

manantial [manan'tjal] nm spring

manar [ma'nar] vi to run, flow

mancha ['mantʃa] nf stain, mark; (ZOOL) patch; **manchar** vt (gen) to stain, mark; (ensuciar) to soil, dirty

manchego, a [man'tʃeɣo, a] adj of o from La Mancha

manco, a ['manko, a] adj (de un brazo) one-armed; (de una mano) one-handed; (fig) defective, faulty

mancomunar [mankomu'nar] vt to unite, bring together; (recursos) to pool; (JUR) to make jointly responsible; **mancomunidad** nf union, association; (comunidad) community; (JUR) joint responsibility

mandamiento [manda'mjento] nm (orden) order, command; (REL) commandment; **~ judicial** warrant

mandar [man'dar] vt (ordenar) to order; (dirigir) to lead, command; (enviar) to send; (pedir) to order, ask for ♦ vi to be in charge; (pey) to be bossy; **¿mande?** pardon?, excuse me?; **~ hacer un traje** to have a suit made

mandarina [manda'rina] nf tangerine, mandarin (orange)

mandato [man'dato] nm (orden) order; (POL: periodo) term of office; (: territorio) mandate; **~ judicial** (search) warrant

mandíbula [man'diβula] nf jaw

mandil [man'dil] nm apron

mando ['mando] nm (MIL) command; (de país) rule; (el primer lugar) lead; (POL) term of office; (TEC) control; **~ a la izquierda** left-hand drive

mandón, ona [man'don, ona] adj bossy, domineering

manejable [mane'xaβle] adj manageable

manejar [mane'xar] vt to manage;

(*máquina*) to work, operate; (*caballo etc*) to handle; (*casa*) to run, manage; (*AM: AUTO*) to drive; **~se** *vr* (*comportarse*) to act, behave; (*arreglárselas*) to manage; **manejo** *nm* management; handling; running; driving; (*facilidad de trato*) ease, confidence; **manejos** *nmpl* (*intrigas*) intrigues

manera [ma'nera] *nf* way, manner, fashion; **~s** *nfpl* (*modales*) manners; **su ~ de ser** the way he is; (*aire*) his manner; **de ninguna ~** no way, by no means; **de otra ~** otherwise; **de todas ~s** at any rate; **no hay ~ de persuadirle** there's no way of convincing him

manga ['manga] *nf* (*de camisa*) sleeve; (*de riego*) hose

mangar [man'gar] (*fam*) *vt* to pinch, nick

mango ['mango] *nm* handle; (*BOT*) mango

mangonear [mangone'ar] *vi* (*meterse*) to meddle, interfere; (*ser mandón*) to boss people about

manguera [man'gera] *nf* hose

manía [ma'nia] *nf* (*MED*) mania; (*fig: moda*) rage, craze; (*disgusto*) dislike; (*malicia*) spite; **maníaco, a** *adj* maniac(al) ♦ *nm/f* maniac

maniatar [manja'tar] *vt* to tie the hands of

maniático, a [ma'njatiko, a] *adj* maniac(al) ♦ *nm/f* maniac

manicomio [mani'komjo] *nm* mental hospital (*BRIT*), insane asylum (*US*)

manifestación [manifesta'θjon] *nf* (*declaración*) statement, declaration; (*de emoción*) show, display; (*POL: desfile*) demonstration; (*: concentración*) mass meeting

manifestar [manifes'tar] *vt* to show, manifest; (*declarar*) to state, declare; **manifiesto, a** *adj* clear, manifest ♦ *nm* manifesto

manillar [mani'ʎar] *nm* handlebars *pl*

maniobra [ma'njoβra] *nf* manœuvre; **~s** *nfpl* (*MIL*) manœuvres; **maniobrar** *vt* to manœuvre

manipulación [manipula'θjon] *nf* manipulation

manipular [manipu'lar] *vt* to manipulate; (*manejar*) to handle

maniquí [mani'ki] *nm* dummy ♦ *nm/f* model

manirroto, a [mani'rroto, a] *adj* lavish, extravagant ♦ *nm/f* spendthrift

manivela [mani'βela] *nf* crank

manjar [man'xar] *nm* (tasty) dish

mano ['mano] *nf* hand; (*ZOOL*) foot, paw; (*de pintura*) coat; (*serie*) lot, series; **a ~** by hand; **a ~ derecha/izquierda** on the right(-hand side)/left(-hand side); **de primera ~** (at) first hand; **de segunda ~** (at) second hand; **robo a ~ armada** armed robbery; **~ de obra** labour, manpower; **estrechar la ~ a uno** to shake sb's hand

manojo [ma'noxo] *nm* handful, bunch; **~ de llaves** bunch of keys

manopla [ma'nopla] *nf* mitten

manoseado, a [manose'aðo, a] *adj* well-worn

manosear [manose'ar] *vt* (*tocar*) to handle, touch; (*desordenar*) to mess up, rumple; (*insistir en*) to overwork; (*AM*) to caress, fondle

manotazo [mano'taθo] *nm* slap, smack

mansalva [man'salβa]: **a ~** *adv* indiscriminately

mansedumbre [manse'ðumbre] *nf* gentleness, meekness

mansión [man'sjon] *nf* mansion

manso, a ['manso, a] *adj* gentle, mild; (*animal*) tame

manta ['manta] *nf* blanket; (*AM: poncho*) poncho

manteca [man'teka] *nf* fat; (*AM*) butter; **~ de cacahuete/cacao** peanut/cocoa butter; **~ de cerdo** lard

mantecado [mante'kaðo] (*AM*) *nm* ice

cream

mantel [man'tel] nm tablecloth

mantendré etc vb ver **mantener**

mantener [mante'ner] vt to support, maintain; (alimentar) to sustain; (conservar) to keep; (TEC) to maintain, service; **~se** vr (seguir de pie) to be still standing; (no ceder) to hold one's ground; (subsistir) to sustain o.s., keep going; **mantenimiento** nm maintenance; sustenance; (sustento) support

mantequilla [mante'kiʎa] nf butter

mantilla [man'tiʎa] nf mantilla; **~s** nfpl (de bebé) baby clothes

manto ['manto] nm (capa) cloak; (de ceremonia) robe, gown

mantuve etc vb ver **mantener**

manual [ma'nwal] adj manual ♦ nm manual, handbook

manufactura [manufak'tura] nf manufacture; (fábrica) factory; **manufacturado, a** adj (producto) manufactured

manuscrito, a [manus'krito, a] adj handwritten ♦ nm manuscript

manutención [manuten'θjon] nf maintenance; (sustento) support

manzana [man'θana] nf apple; (ARQ) block (of houses)

manzanilla [manθa'niʎa] nf (planta) camomile; (infusión) camomile tea

manzano [man'θano] nm apple tree

maña ['maɲa] nf (gen) skill, dexterity; (pey) guile; (destreza) trick, knack

mañana [ma'ɲana] adv tomorrow ♦ nm future ♦ nf morning; de o por la ~ in the morning; ¡hasta ~! I see you tomorrow!; ~ por la ~ tomorrow morning

mañoso, a [ma'ɲoso, a] adj (hábil) skilful; (astuto) smart, clever

mapa ['mapa] nm map

maqueta [ma'keta] nf (scale) model

maquillaje [maki'ʎaxe] nm make-up; (acto) making up

maquillar [maki'ʎar] vt to make up;

~se vr to put on (some) make-up

máquina ['makina] nf machine; (de tren) locomotive, engine; (FOTO) camera; (AM: coche) car; (fig) machinery; **escrito a ~** typewritten; **~ de escribir** typewriter; **~ de coser/lavar** sewing/washing machine

maquinación [makina'θjon] nf machination, plot

maquinal [maki'nal] adj (fig) mechanical, automatic

maquinaria [maki'narja] nf (máquinas) machinery; (mecanismo) mechanism, works pl

maquinilla [maki'niʎa] nf: **~ de afeitar** razor

maquinista [maki'nista] nm/f (de tren) engine driver; (TEC) operator; (NAUT) engineer

mar [mar] nm o f sea; **~ adentro** o **afuera** out at sea; **en alta ~** on the high seas; **la ~ de** (fam) lots of; **el M~ Negro/Báltico** the Black/Baltic Sea

maraña [ma'raɲa] nf (maleza) thicket; (confusión) tangle

maravilla [mara'βiʎa] nf marvel, wonder; (BOT) marigold; **maravillar** vt to astonish, amaze; **maravillarse** vr to be astonished, be amazed; **maravilloso, a** adj wonderful, marvellous

marca ['marka] nf (gen) mark; (sello) stamp; (COM) make, brand; **de ~** excellent, outstanding; **~ de fábrica** trademark; **~ registrada** registered trademark

marcado, a [mar'kaðo, a] adj marked, strong

marcador [marka'ðor] nm (DEPORTE) scoreboard; (: persona) scorer

marcapasos [marka'pasos] nm inv pacemaker

marcar [mar'kar] vt (gen) to mark; (número de teléfono) to dial; (gol) to score; (números) to record, keep a tally of; (pelo) to set ♦ vi (DEPORTE) to score;

(TEL) to dial

marcha ['martʃa] nf march; (TEC) running, working; (AUTO) gear; (velocidad) speed; (fig) progress; (dirección) course; **poner en ~** to put into gear; (fig) to set in motion, get going; **dar ~ atrás** to reverse, put into reverse; **estar en ~** to be under way, be in motion

marchar [mar'tʃar] vi (ir) to go; (funcionar) to work, go; **~se** vr to go away, leave

marchitar [martʃi'tar] vt to wither, dry up; **~se** vr (BOT) to wither; (fig) to fade away; **marchito, a** adj withered, faded; (fig) in decline

marcial [mar'θjal] adj martial, military

marciano, a [mar'θjano, a] adj, nm/f Martian

marco ['marko] nm frame; (moneda) mark; (fig) framework

marea [ma'rea] nf tide

marear [mare'ar] vt (fig) to annoy, upset; (MED): **~ a uno** to make sb feel sick; **~se** vr (tener náuseas) to feel sick; (desvanecerse) to feel faint; (aturdirse) to feel dizzy; (fam: emborracharse) to get tipsy

maremoto [mare'moto] nm tidal wave

mareo [ma'reo] nm (náusea) sick feeling; (en viaje) travel sickness; (aturdimiento) dizziness; (fam: lata) nuisance

marfil [mar'fil] nm ivory

margarina [marxa'rina] nf margarine

margarita [marxa'rita] nf (BOT) daisy; (rueda) ~ daisywheel

margen ['marxen] nm (borde) edge, border; (fig) margin, space ♦ nf (de río etc) bank; **dar ~ para** to give an opportunity for; **mantenerse al ~** to keep out (of things)

marginar [marxi'nar] vt (socialmente) to marginalize, ostracize

marica [ma'rika] (fam) nm sissy

maricón [mari'kon] (fam) nm queer

marido [ma'riðo] nm husband

marihuana [mari'wana] nf marijuana, cannabis

marina [ma'rina] nf navy; **~ mercante** merchant navy

marinero, a [mari'nero, a] adj sea cpd ♦ nm sailor, seaman

marino, a [ma'rino, a] adj sea cpd, marine ♦ nm sailor

marioneta [marjo'neta] nf puppet

mariposa [mari'posa] nf butterfly

mariquita [mari'kita] nf ladybird (BRIT), ladybug (US)

mariscos [ma'riskos] nmpl shellfish inv, seafood's

marítimo, a [ma'ritimo, a] adj sea cpd, maritime

mármol ['marmol] nm marble

marqués, esa [mar'kes, esa] nm/f marquis/marchioness

marrón [ma'rron] adj brown

marroquí [marro'ki] adj, nm/f Moroccan ♦ nm Morocco (leather)

Marruecos [ma'rrwekos] nm Morocco

martes ['martes] nm inv Tuesday

| Martes y Trece |

According to Spanish superstition Tuesday is an unlucky day, even more so if it falls on the 13th of the month.

martillo [mar'tiʎo] nm hammer; **~ neumático** pneumatic drill (BRIT), jackhammer

mártir [ˈmartir] nm/f martyr; **martirio** nm martyrdom; (fig) torture, torment

marxismo [mark'sismo] nm Marxism; **marxista** adj, nm/f Marxist

marzo [ˈmarθo] nm March

| PALABRA CLAVE |

más [mas] adj, adv **1**: **~ (que, de)** (compar) more (than), ...+ er (than); **~ grande/inteligente** bigger/more intelligent; **trabaja ~ (que yo)** he

works more (than me); *ver tb* **cada**
2 (*superl*): **el ~** the most, ...+ **est**; **el ~ grande/inteligente (de)** the biggest/most intelligent (in)
3 (*negativo*): **no tengo ~ dinero** I haven't got any more money; **no viene ~ por aquí** he doesn't come round here any more
4 (*adicional*): **no le veo ~ solución que ...** I see no other solution than to ...; **¿quién ~?** anybody else?
5 (+ *adj*: *valor intensivo*): **¡qué perro ~ sucio!** what a filthy dog!; **¡es ~ tonto!** he's so stupid!
6 (*locuciones*): **~ o menos** more or less; **los ~** most people; **es ~** furthermore; **~ bien** rather; **¡qué ~ da!** what does it matter!; **ver más**
7 *por ~*: **por ~ que te esfuerces** no matter how hard you try; **por ~ que quisiera ...** much as I should like to ...
8 *de ~*: **veo que aquí estoy de ~** I can see I'm not needed here; **tenemos uno de ~** we've got one extra
♦ *prep*: **2 ~ 2 son 4** 2 and o plus 2 are 4
♦ *nm inv*: **este trabajo tiene sus ~ y sus menos** this job's got its good points and its bad points

mas |mas| *conj* but
masa |'masa| *nf* (*mezcla*) dough; (*volumen*) volume, mass; (*FÍSICA*) mass; **en ~** en masse; **las ~s** (*POL*) the masses
masacre |ma'sakre| *nf* massacre
masaje |ma'saxe| *nm* massage
máscara |'maskara| *nf* mask; **mascarilla** *nf* (*de belleza*, *MED*) mask
masculino, a |masku'lino, a| *adj* masculine; (*BIO*) male
masía |ma'sia| *nf* farmhouse
masificación |masifika'θjon| *nf* overcrowding
masivo, a |ma'siβo, a| *adj* mass *cpd*
masón |ma'son| *nm* (free)mason

masoquista |maso'kista| *nm/f* masochist
masticar |masti'kar| *vt* to chew
mástil |'mastil| *nm* (*de navío*) mast; (*de guitarra*) neck
mastín |mas'tin| *nm* mastiff
masturbación |masturβa'θjon| *nf* masturbation
masturbarse |mastur'βarse| *vr* to masturbate
mata |'mata| *nf* (*arbusto*) bush, shrub; (*de hierba*) tuft
matadero |mata'ðero| *nm* slaughterhouse, abattoir
matador, a |mata'ðor, a| *adj* killing ♦ *nm/f* killer ♦ *nm* (*TAUR*) matador, bullfighter
matamoscas |mata'moskas| *nm inv* (*palo*) fly swat
matanza |ma'tanθa| *nf* slaughter
matar |ma'tar| *vt*, *vi* to kill; **~se** *vr* (*suicidarse*) to kill o.s., commit suicide; (*morir*) to get killed; **~ el hambre** to stave off hunger
matasellos |mata'seʎos| *nm inv* postmark
mate |'mate| *adj* matt ♦ *nm* (*en ajedrez*) (check)mate; (*AM*: *hierba*) maté; (: *vasija*) gourd
matemáticas |mate'matikas| *nfpl* mathematics; **matemático, a** *adj* mathematical ♦ *nm/f* mathematician
materia |ma'terja| *nf* (*gen*) matter; (*TEC*) material; (*ESCOL*) subject; **en ~ de** on the subject of; **~ prima** raw material; **material** *adj* material ♦ *nm* material; (*TEC*) equipment;
materialismo *nm* materialism;
materialista *adj* materialist(ic);
materialmente *adv* materially; (*fig*) absolutely
maternal |mater'nal| *adj* motherly, maternal
maternidad |materni'ðað| *nf* motherhood, maternity; **materno, a** *adj* maternal; (*lengua*) mother *cpd*
matinal |mati'nal| *adj* morning *cpd*

matiz [ma'tiθ] *nm* shade; **~ar** *vt*
(*variar*) to vary; (*ARTE*) to blend; **~ar**
de to tinge with

matón [ma'ton] *nm* bully

matorral [mato'rral] *nm* thicket

matraca [ma'traka] *nf* rattle

matrícula [ma'trikula] *nf* (*registro*)
register; (*AUTO*) registration number;
(: *placa*) number plate; **matricular** *vt*
to register, enrol

matrimonial [matrimo'njal] *adj*
matrimonial

matrimonio [matri'monjo] *nm*
(*pareja*) (married) couple; (*unión*)
marriage

matriz [ma'triθ] *nf* (*ANAT*) womb;
(*TEC*) mould; **casa ~** (*COM*) head office

matrona [ma'trona] *nf* (*persona de
edad*) matron; (*comadrona*) midwife

maullar [mau'ʎar] *vi* to mew, miaow

maxilar [maksi'lar] *nm* jaw(bone)

máxima ['maksima] *nf* maxim

máxime ['maksime] *adv* especially

máximo, a ['maksimo, a] *adj*
maximum; (*más alto*) highest; (*más
grande*) greatest ♦ *nm* maximum

mayo ['majo] *nm* May

mayonesa [majo'nesa] *nf* mayonnaise

mayor [ma'jor] *adj* main, chief;
(*adulto*) adult; (*de edad avanzada*)
elderly; (*MUS*) major; (*compar. de
tamaño*) bigger; (: *de edad*) older;
(*superl: de tamaño*) biggest; (: *de edad*)
oldest ♦ *nm* (*adulto*) adult; **al por ~**
wholesale; **~ de edad** adult; **~es** *nmpl*
(*antepasados*) ancestors

mayoral [majo'ral] *nm* foreman

mayordomo [major'ðomo] *nm* butler

mayoría [majo'ria] *nf* majority, greater
part

mayorista [majo'rista] *nm/f*
wholesaler

mayoritario, a [majori'tarjo, a] *adj*
majority *cpd*

mayúscula [ma'juskula] *nf* capital
letter

mayúsculo, a [ma'juskulo, a] *adj* (*fig*)

big, tremendous

mazapán [maθa'pan] *nm* marzipan

mazo ['maθo] *nm* (*martillo*) mallet; (*de
flores*) bunch; (*DEPORTE*) bat

me [me] *pron* (*directo*) me; (*indirecto*)
(to) me; (*reflexivo*) (to) myself;
¡dámelo! give it to me!

mear [me'ar] (*fam*) *vi* to pee, piss (*!*)

mecánica [me'kanika] *nf* (*ESCOL*)
mechanics *sg*; (*mecanismo*) mechanism;
ver tb **mecánico**

mecánico, a [me'kaniko, a] *adj*
mechanical ♦ *nm/f* mechanic

mecanismo [meka'nismo] *nm*
mechanism; (*marcha*) gear

mecanografía [mekanoɣra'fia] *nf*
typewriting; **mecanógrafo, a** *nm/f*
typist

mecate [me'kate] (*AM*) *nm* rope

mecedora [meθe'ðora] *nf* rocking
chair

mecer [me'θer] *vt* (*cuna*) to rock; **~se**
vr to rock; (*ramo*) to sway

mecha ['metʃa] *nf* (*de vela*) wick; (*de
bomba*) fuse

mechero [me'tʃero] *nm* (*cigarette*)
lighter

mechón [me'tʃon] *nm* (*gen*) tuft; (*de
pelo*) lock

medalla [me'ðaʎa] *nf* medal

media ['meðja] *nf* (*ESP*) stocking; (*AM*)
sock; (*promedio*) average

mediado, a [me'ðjaðo, a] *adj* half-full;
(*trabajo*) half-completed; **a ~s de** in
the middle of, halfway through

mediano, a [me'ðjano, a] *adj* (*regular*)
medium, average; (*mediocre*) mediocre

medianoche [meðja'notʃe] *nf*
midnight

mediante [me'ðjante] *adv* by (means
of), through

mediar [me'ðjar] *vi* (*interceder*) to
mediate, intervene

medicación [meðika'θjon] *nf*
medication, treatment

medicamento [meðika'mento] *nm*
medicine, drug

medicina [meði'θina] *nf* medicine
medición [meði'θjon] *nf* measurement
médico, a ['meðiko, a] *adj* medical ♦ *nm/f* doctor
medida [me'ðiða] *nf* measure; *(medición)* measurement; *(prudencia)* moderation, prudence; **en cierta/gran ~** up to a point/to a great extent; **un traje a la ~** made-to-measure suit; **~ de cuello** collar size; **a ~ de** in proportion to; *(de acuerdo con)* in keeping with; **a ~ que** *(conforme)* as
medio, a ['meðjo, a] *adj* half (a); *(punto)* mid, middle; *(promedio)* average ♦ *adv* half ♦ *nm (centro)* middle, centre; *(promedio)* average; *(método)* means, way; *(ambiente)* environment; **~s** *nmpl* means, resources; **~ litro** half a litre; **las tres y media** half past three; **medio ambiente** environment; **M~ Oriente** Middle East; **a ~ terminar** half finished; **pagar a medias** to share the cost; **~ambiental** *adj (política, efectos)* environmental
mediocre [me'ðjokre] *adj* mediocre
mediodía [meðjo'ðia] *nm* midday, noon
medir [me'ðir] *vt, vi (gen)* to measure
meditar [meði'tar] *vt* to ponder, think over, meditate on; *(planear)* to think out
mediterráneo, a [meðite'rraneo, a] *adj* Mediterranean ♦ *nm*: **el M~** the Mediterranean (Sea)
médula ['meðula] *nf (ANAT)* marrow; **~ espinal** spinal cord
medusa [me'ðusa] *(ESP) nf* jellyfish
megafonía [meɣafo'nia] *nf* public address system, PA system; **megáfono** *nm* megaphone
megalómano, a [meɣa'lomano, a] *nm/f* megalomaniac
mejicano, a [mexi'kano, a] *adj, nm/f* Mexican
Méjico ['mexiko] *nm* Mexico

mejilla [me'xiʎa] *nf* cheek
mejillón [mexi'ʎon] *nm* mussel
mejor [me'xor] *adj, adv (compar)* better; *(superl)* best; **a lo ~** probably; *(quizá)* maybe; **~ dicho** rather; **tanto ~** so much the better
mejora [me'xora] *nf* improvement; **mejorar** *vt* to improve, make better ♦ *vi* to improve, get better; **mejorarse** *vr* to improve, get better
melancólico, a [melan'koliko, a] *adj (triste)* sad, melancholy; *(soñador)* dreamy
melena [me'lena] *nf (de persona)* long hair; *(ZOOL)* mane
mellizo, a [me'ʎiθo, a] *adj, nm/f* twin; **~s** *nmpl (AM)* cufflinks
melocotón [meloko'ton] *(ESP) nm* peach
melodía [melo'ðia] *nf* melody, tune
melodrama [melo'ðrama] *nm* melodrama; **melodramático, a** *adj* melodramatic
melón [me'lon] *nm* melon
membrete [mem'brete] *nm* letterhead
membrillo [mem'briʎo] *nm* quince; **carne de ~** quince jelly
memorable [memo'raßle] *adj* memorable
memoria [me'morja] *nf (gen)* memory; **~s** *nfpl (de autor)* memoirs; **memorizar** *vt* to memorize
menaje [me'naxe] *nm*: **~ de cocina** kitchenware
mencionar [menθjo'nar] *vt* to mention
mendigar [mendi'var] *vt* to beg (for)
mendigo, a [men'diɣo, a] *nm/f* beggar
mendrugo [men'druɣo] *nm* crust
menear [mene'ar] *vt* to move; **~se** *vr* to shake; *(balancearse)* to sway; *(moverse)* to move; *(fig)* to get a move on
menestra [me'nestra] *nf*: **~ de verduras** vegetable stew
menguante [men'gwante] *adj*

decreasing, diminishing

menguar [men'gwar] vt to lessen, diminish ♦ vi to diminish, decrease

menopausia [meno'pausja] nf menopause

menor [me'nor] adj (más pequeño: compar) smaller; (: superl) smallest; (más joven: compar) younger; (: superl) youngest; (MUS) minor ♦ nm/f (joven) young person, juvenile; **no tengo la ~ idea** I haven't the faintest idea; **al por ~** retail; **~ de edad** person under age

Menorca [me'norka] nf Minorca

PALABRA CLAVE

menos [menos] adj 1: **~ (que, de)** (compar: cantidad) less (than); (: número) fewer (than); **con ~ entusiasmo** with less enthusiasm; **~ gente** fewer people; ver tb **cada**

2 (superl): **es el que ~ culpa tiene** he is the least to blame

♦ adv 1 (compar): **~ (que, de)** less (than); **me gusta ~ que el otro** I like it less than the other one

2 (superl): **es el ~ listo (de su clase)** he's the least bright in his class; **de todas ellas es la que ~ me agrada** out of all of them she's the one I like least; **(por) lo ~** at (the very) least

3 (locuciones): **no quiero verle ni ~ visitarle** I don't want to see him let alone visit him; **tenemos 7 de ~** we're seven short

♦ prep except; (cifras) minus; **todos ~ él** everyone except (for) him; **5 ~ 2** 5 minus 2

♦ conj: **a ~ que: a ~ que venga mañana** unless he comes tomorrow

menospreciar [menospre'θjar] vt to underrate, undervalue; (despreciar) to scorn, despise

mensaje [men'saxe] nm message; **~ro, a** nm/f messenger

menstruación [menstrua'θjon] nf menstruation

menstruar [mens'trwar] vi to menstruate

mensual [men'swal] adj monthly; **1000 ptas ~es** 1000 ptas a month; **~idad** nf (salario) monthly salary; (COM) monthly payment, monthly instalment

menta ['menta] nf mint

mental [men'tal] adj mental; **~idad** nf mentality; **~izar** vt (sensibilizar) to make aware; (convencer) to convince; (padres) to prepare (mentally); **~izarse** vr (concienciarse) to become aware; **~izarse (de)** to get used to the idea (of); **~izarse de que ...** (convencerse) to get it into one's head that ...

mentar [men'tar] vt to mention, name

mente ['mente] nf mind

mentir [men'tir] vi to lie

mentira [men'tira] nf (una ~) lie; (acto) lying; (invención) fiction; **parece ~ que ...** it seems incredible that ..., I can't believe that ...

mentiroso, a [menti'roso, a] adj lying ♦ nm/f liar

menú [me'nu] (pl **~s**) nm menu; (AM) set meal; **del día** set menu

menudo, a [me'nuðo, a] adj (pequeño) small, tiny; (sin importancia) petty, insignificant; **¡~ negocio!** (fam) some deal!; **a ~** often, frequently

meñique [me'ɲike] nm little finger

meollo [me'oʎo] nm (fig) core

mercado [mer'kaðo] nm market

mercancía [merkan'θia] nf commodity; **~s** nfpl goods, merchandise sg

mercantil [merkan'til] adj mercantile, commercial

mercenario, a [merθe'narjo, a] adj, nm mercenary

mercería [merθe'ria] nf haberdashery (BRIT), notions (US); (tienda) haberdasher's (BRIT), notions store (US); (AM) drapery

mercurio [mer'kurjo] nm mercury

merecer |mere'θer| vt to deserve, merit ♦ vi to be deserving, be worthy; **merece la pena** it's worthwhile; **merecido, a** adj (well) deserved; **llevar su merecido** to get one's deserts

merendar |meren'dar| vt to have for tea ♦ vi to have tea; (en el campo) to have a picnic; **merendero** nm open-air cafe

merengue |me'renge| nm meringue

meridiano |meri'ðjano| nm (GEO) meridian

merienda |me'rjenda| nf (light) tea, afternoon snack; (de campo) picnic

mérito |'merito| nm merit; (valor) worth, value

merluza |mer'luθa| nf hake

merma |'merma| nf decrease; (pérdida) wastage; **mermar** vt to reduce, lessen ♦ vi to decrease, dwindle

mermelada |merme'laða| nf jam

mero, a |'mero, a| adj mere; (AM: fam) very

merodear |meroðe'ar| vi: ~ **por** to prowl about

mes |mes| nm month

mesa |'mesa| nf table; (de trabajo) desk; (GEO) plateau; ~ **directiva** board; ~ **redonda** (reunión) round table; **poner/quitar la** ~ to lay/clear the table; **mesero, a** (AM) nm/f waiter/waitress

meseta |me'seta| nf (GEO) meseta, tableland

mesilla |me'siʎa| nf: ~ **(de noche)** bedside table

mesón |me'son| nm inn

mestizo, a |mes'tiθo, a| adj half-caste, of mixed race ♦ nm/f half-caste

mesura |me'sura| nf moderation, restraint

meta |'meta| nf goal; (de carrera) finish

metabolismo |metaβo'lismo| nm metabolism

metáfora |me'tafora| nf metaphor

metal |me'tal| nm (materia) metal;

(MUS) brass; **metálico, a** adj metallic; (de metal) metal ♦ nm (dinero contante) cash

metalurgia |meta'lurxja| nf metallurgy

meteoro |mete'oro| nm meteor; **~logía** nf meteorology

meter |me'ter| vt (colocar) to put, place; (introducir) to put in, insert; (involucrar) to involve; (causar) to make, cause; **~se** vr: **~se en** to go into, enter; (fig) to interfere in, meddle in; **~se a** to start; **~se a escritor** to become a writer; **~se con uno** to provoke sb, pick a quarrel with sb

meticuloso, a |metiku'loso, a| adj meticulous, thorough

metódico, a |me'toðiko, a| adj methodical

método |'metoðo| nm method

metralleta |metra'ʎeta| nf sub-machine-gun

métrico, a |'metriko, a| adj metric

metro |'metro| nm metre; (tren) underground (BRIT), subway (US)

México |'mexiko| nm Mexico; **Ciudad de ~** Mexico City

mezcla |'meθkla| nf mixture; **mezclar** vt to mix (up); **mezclarse** vr to mix, mingle; **mezclarse en** to get mixed up in, get involved in

mezquino, a |meθ'kino, a| adj mean

mezquita |meθ'kita| nf mosque

mg. abr (= miligramo) mg

mi |mi| adj pos my ♦ nm (MUS) E

mí |mi| pron me; myself

mía |'mia| pron ver **mío**

miaja |'mjaxa| nf crumb

michelín |mitʃe'lin| (fam) nm (de grasa) spare tyre

micro |'mikro| nm minibus

microbio |mi'kroβjo| nm microbe

micrófono |mi'krofono| nm microphone

microondas |mikro'ondas| nm inv (tb: horno ~) microwave (oven)

microscopio |mikro'skopjo| nm

microscope

miedo |'mjeðo| nm fear; (nerviosismo) apprehension, nervousness; **tener ~ to be afraid; de ~** wonderful, marvellous; **hace un frío de ~** (fam) it's terribly cold; **~so, a** adj fearful, timid

miel |mjel| nf honey

miembro |'mjembro| nm limb; (socio) member; **~ viril** penis

mientras |'mjentras| conj while; (duración) as long as ♦ adv meanwhile; **~ tanto** meanwhile; **~ más tiene, más quiere** the more he has, the more he wants

miércoles |'mjerkoles| nm inv Wednesday

mierda |'mjerða| (fam!) nf shit (!)

miga |'miva| nf crumb; (fig: meollo) essence; **hacer buenas ~s** (fam) to get on well

migración |mivra'θjon| nf migration

mil |mil| num thousand; **dos ~ libras** two thousand pounds

milagro |mi'lavro| nm miracle; **~so, a** adj miraculous

milésima |mi'lesima| nf (de segundo) thousandth

mili |'mili| (fam) nf: **hacer la ~** to do one's military service

milicia |mi'liθja| nf militia; (servicio militar) military service

milímetro |mi'limetro| nm millimetre

militante |mili'tante| adj militant

militar |mili'tar| adj military ♦ nm/f soldier ♦ vi (MIL) to serve; (en un partido) to be a member

milla |'miʎa| nf mile

millar |mi'ʎar| nm thousand

millón |mi'ʎon| num million; **millonario, a** nm/f millionaire

mimar |mi'mar| vt to spoil, pamper

mimbre |'mimbre| nf wicker

mímica |'mimika| nf (para comunicarse) sign language; (imitación) mimicry

mimo |'mimo| nm (caricia) caress; (de niño) spoiling; (TEATRO) mime; (: actor)

mime artist

mina |'mina| nf mine; **minar** vt to mine; (fig) to undermine

mineral |mine'ral| adj mineral ♦ nm (GEO) mineral; (mena) ore

minero, a |mi'nero, a| adj mining cpd ♦ nm/f miner

miniatura |minja'tura| adj inv, nf miniature

minifalda |mini'falda| nf miniskirt

mínimo, a |'minimo, a| adj, nm minimum

minino, a |mi'nino, a| (fam) nm/f puss, pussy

ministerio |minis'terjo| nm Ministry; **M~ de Hacienda/de Asuntos Exteriores** Treasury (BRIT), Treasury Department (US)/Foreign Office (BRIT), State Department (US)

ministro, a |mi'nistro, a| nm/f minister

minoría |mino'ria| nf minority

minucioso, a |minu'θjoso, a| adj thorough, meticulous; (prolijo) very detailed

minúscula |mi'nuskula| nf small letter

minúsculo, a |mi'nuskulo, a| adj tiny, minute

minusválido, a |minus'βaliðo, a| adj (physically) handicapped ♦ nm/f (physically) handicapped person

minuta |mi'nuta| nf (de comida) menu

minutero |minu'tero| nm minute hand

minuto |mi'nuto| nm minute

mío, a |'mio, a| pron: **el ~/la mía** mine; **un amigo ~** a friend of mine; **lo ~** what is mine

miope |mi'ope| adj short-sighted

mira |'mira| nf (de arma) sight(s) (pl); (fig) aim, intention

mirada |mi'raða| nf look, glance; (expresión) look, expression; **clavar la ~ en** to stare at; **echar una ~ a** to glance at

mirado, a |mi'raðo, a| adj (sensato) sensible; (considerado) considerate;

bien/mal ~ well/not well thought of; **bien** ~ all things considered

mirador [mira'ðor] nm viewpoint, vantage point

mirar [mi'rar] vt to look at; (observar) to watch; (considerar) to consider, think over; (vigilar, cuidar) to watch, look after ♦ vi to look; (ARQ) to face; **~se** vr (dos personas) to look at each other; ~ **bien/mal** to think highly of/ have a poor opinion of; **~se al espejo** to look at o.s. in the mirror

mirilla [mi'riʎa] nf spyhole, peephole

mirlo ['mirlo] nm blackbird

misa ['misa] nf mass

miserable [mise'raßle] adj (avaro) mean, stingy; (nimio) miserable, paltry; (lugar) squalid; (fam) vile, despicable ♦ nm/f (malvado) rogue

miseria [mi'serja] nf (pobreza) poverty; (tacañería) meanness, stinginess; (condiciones) squalor; **una ~** a pittance

misericordia [miseri'korðja] nf (compasión) compassion, pity; (piedad) mercy

misil [mi'sil] nm missile

misión [mi'sjon] nf mission; **misionero, a** nm/f missionary

mismo, a ['mismo, a] adj (semejante) same; (después de pron) -self; (para énfasis) very ♦ adv: **aquí/hoy** ~ right here/this very day; **ahora** ~ right now ♦ conj: **lo** ~ **que** just like, just as; **el** ~ **traje** the same suit; **en ese** ~ **momento** at that very moment; **vino el** ~ **Ministro** the minister himself came; **yo** ~ **lo vi** I saw it myself; **lo** ~ the same (thing); **da lo** ~ it's all the same; **quedamos en las mismas** we're no further forward; **por lo** ~ for the same reason

misterio [mis'terjo] nm mystery; **~so, a** adj mysterious

mitad [mi'tað] nf (medio) half; (centro) middle; **a** ~ **de precio** (a) half-price; **en** o **a** ~ **del camino** halfway along the road; **cortar por la** ~ to cut through the middle

mitigar [miti'var] vt to mitigate; (dolor) to ease; (sed) to quench

mitin ['mitin] (pl **mítines**) nm meeting

mito ['mito] nm myth

mixto, a ['miksto, a] adj mixed

ml. abr (= mililitro) ml

mm. abr (= milímetro) mm

mobiliario [moßi'ljarjo] nm furniture

mochila [mo'tʃila] nf rucksack (BRIT), back-pack

moción [mo'θjon] nf motion

moco ['moko] nm mucus; **~s** nmpl (fam) snot; **limpiarse los ~s de la nariz** (fam) to wipe one's nose

moda ['moða] nf fashion; (estilo) style; **a la** o **de** ~ in fashion, fashionable; **pasado de** ~ out of fashion

modales [mo'ðales] nmpl manners

modalidad [moðali'ðað] nf kind, variety

modelar [moðe'lar] vt to model

modelo [mo'ðelo] adj inv, nm/f model

módem ['moðem] nm (INFORM) modem

moderado, a [moðe'raðo, a] adj moderate

moderar [moðe'rar] vt to moderate; (violencia) to restrain, control; (velocidad) to reduce; **~se** vr to restrain o.s., control o.s.

modernizar [moðerni'θar] vt to modernize

moderno, a [mo'ðerno, a] adj modern; (actual) present-day

modestia [mo'ðestja] nf modesty; **modesto, a** adj modest

módico, a ['moðiko, a] adj moderate, reasonable

modificar [moðifi'kar] vt to modify

modista, a [mo'ðista, a] nm/f (diseñador) couturier, designer; (que confecciona) dressmaker

modo ['moðo] nm way, manner; (MUS) mode; **~s** nmpl manners; **de ningún** ~ in no way; **de todos ~s** at any rate;

~ de empleo directions pl (for use)

modorra [mo'ðorra] nf drowsiness

mofa ['mofa] nf: **hacer ~ de** to mock; **mofarse** vr: **mofarse de** to mock, scoff at

mogollón [moɣo'ʎon] (fam) adv a hell of a lot

moho ['moo] nm mould, mildew; (en metal) rust; **~so, a** adj mouldy; rusty

mojar [mo'xar] vt to wet; (humedecer) to damp(en), moisten; (calar) to soak; **~se** vr to get wet

mojón [mo'xon] nm boundary stone

molde ['molde] nm mould; (COSTURA) pattern; (fig) model; **~ado** nm soft perm; **~ar** vt to mould

mole ['mole] nf mass, bulk; (edificio) pile

moler [mo'ler] vt to grind, crush

molestar [moles'tar] vt to bother; (fastidiar) to annoy; (incomodar) to inconvenience, put out ♦ vi to be a nuisance; **~se** vr to bother; (incomodarse) to go to trouble; (ofenderse) to take offence; **¿(no) te molesta si ...?** do you mind if ...?

molestia [mo'lestja] nf bother, trouble; (incomodidad) inconvenience; (MED) discomfort; **es una ~** it's a nuisance; **molesto, a** adj (que fastidia) annoying; (incómodo) inconvenient; (inquieto) uncomfortable, ill at ease; (enfadado) annoyed

molido, a [mo'liðo, a] adj: **estar ~** (fig) to be exhausted o dead beat

molinillo [moli'niʎo] nm: **~ de carne/café** mincer/coffee grinder

molino [mo'lino] nm (edificio) mill; (máquina) grinder

momentáneo, a [momen'taneo, a] adj momentary

momento [mo'mento] nm moment; **de ~** at the moment, for the moment

momia ['momja] nf mummy

monarca [mo'narka] nm/f monarch, ruler; **monarquía** nf monarchy; **monárquico, a** nm/f royalist,

monarchist

monasterio [monas'terjo] nm monastery

mondar [mon'dar] vt to peel; **~se** vr: **~se de risa** (fam) to split one's sides laughing

moneda [mo'neða] nf (tipo de dinero) currency, money; (pieza) coin; **una ~ de 5 pesetas** a 5 peseta piece; **monedero** nm purse; **monetario, a** adj monetary, financial

monitor [moni'tor, a] nm/f instructor, coach ♦ nm (TV) set; (INFORM) monitor

monja ['monxa] nf nun

monje ['monxe] nm monk

mono, a ['mono, a] adj (bonito) lovely, pretty; (gracioso) nice, charming ♦ nm/f monkey, ape ♦ nm dungarees pl; (overoles) overalls pl

monopatín [monopa'tin] nm skateboard

monopolio [mono'poljo] nm monopoly; **monopolizar** vt to monopolize

monotonía [monoto'nia] nf (sonido) monotone; (fig) monotony

monótono, a [mo'notono, a] adj monotonous

monstruo ['monstrwo] nm monster ♦ adj inv fantastic; **~so, a** adj monstrous

montaje [mon'taxe] nm assembly; (TEATRO) décor; (CINE) montage

montaña [mon'taɲa] nf (monte) mountain; (sierra) mountains pl, mountainous area; (AM: selva) forest; **~ rusa** roller coaster; **montañero, a** nm/f mountaineer; **montañés, esa** nm/f highlander; **montañismo** nm mountaineering

montar [mon'tar] vt (subir a) to mount, get on; (TEC) to assemble, put together; (negocio) to set up; (arma) to cock; (colocar) to lift on to; (CULIN) to beat ♦ vi to mount, get on; (sobresalir) to overlap; **~ en cólera** to get angry;

~ **a caballo** to ride, go horseriding

monte ['monte] nm (montaña)
mountain; (bosque) woodland; (área sin
cultivar) wild area, wild country;
M~ de Piedad pawnshop

montón [mon'ton] nm heap, pile;
(fig): **un ~ de** heaps of, lots of

monumento [monu'mento] nm
monument

monzón [mon'θon] nm monsoon

moño ['mono] nm bun

moqueta [mo'keta] nf fitted carpet

mora ['mora] nf blackberry; ver tb
moro

morada [mo'raða] nf (casa) dwelling,
abode

morado, a [mo'raðo, a] adj purple,
violet ♦ nm bruise

moral [mo'ral] adj moral ♦ nf (ética)
ethics pl; (moralidad) morals pl,
morality; (ánimo) morale

moraleja [mora'lexa] nf moral

moralidad [morali'ðað] nf morals pl,
morality

morboso, a [mor'ßoso, a] adj morbid

morcilla [mor'θiʎa] nf blood sausage,
≈ black pudding (BRIT)

mordaz [mor'ðaθ] adj (crítica) biting,
scathing

mordaza [mor'ðaθa] nf (para la boca)
gag; (TEC) clamp

morder [mor'ðer] vt to bite; (fig:
consumir) to eat away, eat into;
mordisco nm bite

moreno, a [mo'reno, a] adj (color)
(dark) brown; (de tez) dark; (de pelo ~)
dark-haired; (negro) black

morfina [mor'fina] nf morphine

moribundo, a [mori'ßundo, a] adj
dying

morir [mo'rir] vi to die; (fuego) to die
down; (luz) to go out; **~se** vr to die;
(fig) to be dying; **murió en un
accidente** he was killed in an
accident; **~se por algo** to be dying
for sth

moro, a ['moro, a] adj Moorish ♦ nm/f

Moor

moroso, a [mo'roso, a] nm/f bad
debtor, defaulter

morral [mo'rral] nm haversack

morro ['morro] nm (ZOOL) snout, nose;
(AUTO, AVIAT) nose

morsa ['morsa] nf walrus

mortadela [morta'ðela] nf mortadella

mortaja [mor'taxa] nf shroud

mortal [mor'tal] adj mortal; (golpe)
deadly; **~idad** nf mortality

mortero [mor'tero] nm mortar

mortífero, a [mor'tifero, a] adj
deadly, lethal

mortificar [mortifi'kar] vt to mortify

mosca ['moska] nf fly

Moscú [mos'ku] n Moscow

mosquearse [moske'arse] vr
(enojarse) to get cross; (ofenderse) to
take offence

mosquitero [moski'tero] nm
mosquito net

mosquito [mos'kito] nm mosquito

mostaza [mos'taθa] nf mustard

mosto ['mosto] nm (unfermented)
grape juice

mostrador [mostra'ðor] nm (de
tienda) counter; (de café) bar

mostrar [mos'trar] vt to show;
(exhibir) to display, exhibit; (explicar) to
explain; **~se** vr: **~se amable** to be
kind; to prove to be kind; **no se
muestra muy inteligente** he doesn't
seem (to be) very intelligent

mota ['mota] nf speck, tiny piece; (en
diseño) dot

mote ['mote] nm nickname

motín [mo'tin] nm (del pueblo) revolt,
rising; (del ejército) mutiny

motivar [moti'ßar] vt (causar) to
cause, motivate; (explicar) to explain,
justify; **motivo** nm motive, reason

moto ['moto] nf (fam) = **motocicleta**

motocicleta [motoθi'kleta] nf
motorbike (BRIT), motorcycle

motor [mo'tor] nm motor, engine; ~ **a
chorro** o **de reacción/de explosión**

jet engine/internal combustion engine

motora [mo'tora] *nf* motorboat

movedizo, a [moβe'ðiθo, a] *adj ver* **arena**

mover [mo'βer] *vt* to move; (*cabeza*) to shake; (*accionar*) to drive; (*fig*) to cause, provoke; **~se** *vr* to move; (*fig*) to get a move on

móvil ['moβil] *adj* mobile; (*pieza de máquina*) moving; (*mueble*) movable ♦ *nm* motive; **movilidad** *nf* mobility; **movilizar** *vt* to mobilize

movimiento [moβi'mjento] *nm* movement; (*TEC*) motion; (*actividad*) activity

mozo, a ['moθo, a] *adj* (*joven*) young ♦ *nm/f* youth, young man/girl

muchacho, a [mu'tʃatʃo, a] *nm/f* (*niño*) boy/girl; (*criado*) servant; (*criada*) maid

muchedumbre [mutʃe'ðumbre] *nf* crowd

PALABRA CLAVE

mucho, a ['mutʃo, a] *adj* **1** (*cantidad*) a lot of, much; (*número*) lots of, a lot of, many; **~ dinero** a lot of money; **hace ~ calor** it's very hot; **muchas amigas** lots o a lot of friends

2 (*sg: grande*): **ésta es mucha casa para él** this house is much too big for him

♦ *pron*: **tengo ~** I've got a lot to do; **~s dicen que ...** a lot of people say that ...; *ver tb* **tener**

♦ *adv* **1**: **me gusta ~** I like it a lot; **lo siento ~** I'm very sorry; **come ~** he eats a lot; **¿te vas a quedar ~?** are you going to be staying long?

2 (*respuesta*) very; **¿estás cansado? – ¡~!** are you tired? – very!

3 (*locuciones*): **como ~** at the most; **con ~: el mejor con ~** by far the best; **ni ~ menos: no es rico ni ~ menos** he's far from being rich

4: **por ~ que: por ~ que lo creas** no

---

matter how o however much you believe her

---

muda ['muða] *nf* change of clothes

mudanza [mu'ðanθa] *nf* (*de casa*) move

mudar [mu'ðar] *vt* to change; (*ZOOL*) to shed ♦ *vi* to change; **~se** *vr* (*la ropa*) to change; **~se de casa** to move house

mudo, a ['muðo, a] *adj* dumb; (*callado, CINE*) silent

mueble ['mweβle] *nm* piece of furniture; **~s** *nmpl* furniture *sg*

mueca ['mweka] *nf* face, grimace; **hacer ~s a** to make faces at

muela ['mwela] *nf* (back) tooth

muelle ['mweʎe] *nm* spring; (*NAUT*) wharf; (*malecón*) pier

muero *etc vb ver* **morir**

muerte ['mwerte] *nf* death; (*homicidio*) murder; **dar ~ a** to kill

muerto, a ['mwerto, a] *pp de* **morir** ♦ *adj* dead ♦ *nm/f* dead man/woman; (*difunto*) deceased; (*cadáver*) corpse; **estar ~ de cansancio** to be dead tired

muestra ['mwestra] *nf* (*señal*) indication, sign; (*demostración*) demonstration; (*prueba*) proof; (*estadística*) sample; (*modelo*) model, pattern; (*testimonio*) token

muestreo [mwes'treo] *nm* sample, sampling

muestro *etc vb ver* **mostrar**

muevo *etc vb ver* **mover**

mugir [mu'xir] *vi* (*vaca*) to moo

mugre ['muɣre] *nf* dirt, filth; **mugriento, a** *adj* dirty, filthy

mujer [mu'xer] *nf* woman; (*esposa*) wife; **~iego** *nm* womanizer

mula ['mula] *nf* mule

muleta [mu'leta] *nf* (*para andar*) crutch; (*TAUR*) stick with red cape attached

mullido, a [mu'ʎiðo, a] *adj* (*cama*) soft; (*hierba*) soft, springy

multa ['multa] nf fine; **poner una ~ a** to fine; **multar** vt to fine

multicines [multi'θines] nmpl multiscreen cinema

multinacional [multinaθjo'nal] nf multinational

múltiple ['multiple] adj multiple; (fig) many, numerous

multiplicar [multipli'kar] vt (MAT) to multiply; (fig) to increase; **~se** vr (BIO) to multiply; (fig) to be everywhere at once

multitud [multi'tuð] nf (muchedumbre) crowd; **~ de** lots of

mundano, a [mun'dano, a] adj worldly

mundial [mun'djal] adj world-wide, universal; (guerra, récord) world cpd

mundo ['mundo] nm world; **todo el ~** everybody; **tener ~** to be experienced, know one's way around

munición [muni'θjon] nf ammunition

municipal [muniθi'pal] adj municipal, local

municipio [muni'θipjo] nm (ayuntamiento) town council, corporation; (territorio administrativo) town, municipality

muñeca [mu'neka] nf (ANAT) wrist; (juguete) doll

muñeco [mu'neko] nm (figura) figure; (marioneta) puppet; (fig) puppet, pawn

mural [mu'ral] adj mural, wall cpd
♦ nm mural

muralla [mu'raʎa] nf (city) wall(s) (pl)

murciélago [mur'θjelaxo] nm bat

murmullo [mur'muʎo] nm murmur(ing); (cuchicheo) whispering

murmuración [murmura'θjon] nf gossip; **murmurar** vi to murmur, whisper; (cotillear) to gossip

muro ['muro] nm wall

muscular [musku'lar] adj muscular

músculo ['muskulo] nm muscle

museo [mu'seo] nm museum; **~ de arte** art gallery

musgo ['musxo] nm moss

música ['musika] nf music; ver tb **músico**

músico, a ['musiko, a] adj musical
♦ nm/f musician

muslo ['muslo] nm thigh

mustio, a ['mustjo, a] adj (persona) depressed, gloomy; (planta) faded, withered

musulmán, ana [musul'man, ana] nm/f Moslem

mutación [muta'θjon] nf (BIO) mutation; (cambio) (sudden) change

mutilar [muti'lar] vt to mutilate; (a una persona) to maim

mutismo [mu'tismo] nm (de persona) uncommunicativeness; (de autoridades) silence

mutuamente [mutwa'mente] adv mutually

mutuo, a ['mutwo, a] adj mutual

muy [mwi] adv very; (demasiado) too; **M~ Señor mío** Dear Sir; **~ de noche** very late at night; **eso es ~ de él** that's just like him

N, n

N abr (= norte) N

nabo ['naβo] nm turnip

nácar ['nakar] nm mother-of-pearl

nacer [na'θer] vi to be born; (de huevo) to hatch; (vegetal) to sprout; (río) to rise; **nací en Barcelona** I was born in Barcelona; **nació una sospecha en su mente** a suspicion formed in her mind; **nacido, a** adj born; **recién nacido** newborn; **naciente** adj new, emerging; (sol) rising; **nacimiento** nm birth; (de Navidad) Nativity; (de río) source

nación [na'θjon] nf nation; **nacional** adj national; **nacionalismo** nm nationalism; **nacionalista** nm/f nationalist; **nacionalizar** vt to nationalize; **nacionalizarse** vr (persona) to become naturalized

nada ['naða] *pron* nothing ♦ *adv* not at all, in no way; **no decir ~** to say nothing, not to say anything; **~ más** nothing else; **de ~** don't mention it

nadador, a [naða'ðor, a] *nm/f* swimmer

nadar [na'ðar] *vi* to swim

nadie ['naðje] *pron* nobody, no-one; **~ habló** nobody spoke; **no había ~** there was nobody there, there wasn't anybody there

nado ['naðo]: **a ~** *adv*: **pasar a ~** to swim across

nafta ['nafta] (*AM*) *nf* petrol (*BRIT*), gas (*US*)

naipe ['naipe] *nm* (playing card); **~s** *nmpl* cards

nalgas ['nalɣas] *nfpl* buttocks

nana ['nana] *nf* lullaby

naranja [na'ranxa] *adj inv, nf* orange; **media ~** (*fam*) better half; **naranjada** *nf* orangeade; **naranjo** *nm* orange tree

narciso [nar'θiso] *nm* narcissus

narcótico, a [nar'kotiko, a] *adj, nm* narcotic; **narcotizar** *vt* to drug; **narcotráfico** *nm* drug trafficking o running

nardo ['narðo] *nm* lily

narigudo, a [nari'ɣuðo, a] *adj* big-nosed

nariz [na'riθ] *nf* nose

narración [narra'θjon] *nf* narration; **narrador, a** *nm/f* narrator

narrar [na'rrar] *vt* to narrate, recount; **narrativa** *nf* narrative

nata ['nata] *nf* cream

natación [nata'θjon] *nf* swimming

natal [na'tal] *adj*: **ciudad ~** home town; **~idad** *nf* birth rate

natillas [na'tiʎas] *nfpl* custard *sg*

nativo, a [na'tißo, a] *adj, nm/f* native

nato, a ['nato, a] *adj* born; **un músico ~** a born musician

natural [natu'ral] *adj* natural; (*fruta etc*) fresh ♦ *nm/f* native ♦ *nm* (*disposición*) nature

naturaleza [natura'leθa] *nf* nature;

(*género*) nature, kind; **~ muerta** still life

naturalidad [naturali'ðað] *nf* naturalness

naturalmente [natural'mente] *adv* (*de modo natural*) in a natural way; **¡~!** of course!

naufragar [naufra'ɣar] *vi* to sink; **naufragio** *nm* shipwreck; **náufrago, a** *nm/f* castaway, shipwrecked person

nauseabundo, a [nausea'ßundo, a] *adj* nauseating, sickening

náuseas ['nauseas] *nfpl* nausea *sg*; **me da ~** it makes me feel sick

náutico, a ['nautiko, a] *adj* nautical

navaja [na'ßaxa] *nf* knife; (*de barbero, peluquero*) razor

naval [na'ßal] *adj* naval

Navarra [na'ßarra] *n* Navarre

nave [na'ße] *nf* (*barco*) ship, vessel; (*ARQ*) nave; **~ espacial** spaceship

navegación [naßeʁa'θjon] *nf* navigation; (*viaje*) sea journey; **~ aérea** air traffic; **~ costera** coastal shipping; **navegante** *nm/f* navigator; **navegar** *vi* (*barco*) to sail; (*avión*) to fly

navidad [naßi'ðað] *nf* Christmas; **~es** *nfpl* Christmas time; **Feliz N~** Merry Christmas; **navideño, a** *adj* Christmas *cpd*

navío [na'ßio] *nm* ship

nazca *etc vb ver* **nacer**

nazi ['naθi] *adj, nm/f* Nazi

NE *abr* (= *nor(d)este*) NE

neblina [ne'ßlina] *nf* mist

nebulosa [neßu'losa] *nf* nebula

necesario, a [neθe'sarjo, a] *adj* necessary

neceser [neθe'ser] *nm* toilet bag; (*bolsa grande*) holdall

necesidad [neθesi'ðað] *nf* need; (*lo inevitable*) necessity; (*miseria*) poverty, need; **en caso de ~** in case of need o emergency; **hacer sus ~es** to relieve o.s.

necesitado, a [neθesi'taðo, a] *adj* needy, poor; **~ de** in need of

necesitar [neθesi'tar] *vt* to need, require

necio, a ['neθjo, a] *adj* foolish

necrópolis [ne'kropolis] *nf inv* cemetery

nectarina [nekta'rina] *nf* nectarine

nefasto, a [ne'fasto, a] *adj* ill-fated, unlucky

negación [neɣa'θjon] *nf* negation; (*rechazo*) refusal, denial

negar [ne'ɣar] *vt* (*renegar, rechazar*) to refuse; (*prohibir*) to refuse, deny; (*desmentir*) to deny; **~se** *vr*: **~se a** to refuse to

negativa [neɣa'tißa] *nf* negative; (*rechazo*) refusal, denial

negativo, a [neɣa'tißo, a] *adj, nm* negative

negligencia [neɣli'xenθja] *nf* negligence; **negligente** *adj* negligent

negociado [neɣo'θjaðo] *nm* department, section

negociante [neɣo'θjante] *nm/f* businessman/woman

negociar [neɣo'θjar] *vt, vi* to negotiate; **~ en** to deal in, trade in

negocio [ne'ɣoθjo] *nm* (*COM*) business; (*asunto*) affair, business; (*operación comercial*) deal, transaction; (*AM*) firm; (*lugar*) place of business; **los ~s** business *sg*; **hacer ~** to do business

negra ['neɣra] *nf* (*MUS*) crotchet; *ver tb* **negro**

negro, a ['neɣro, a] *adj* black; (*suerte*) awful ♦ *nm* black ♦ *nm/f* black man/woman

nene, a ['nene, a] *nm/f* baby, small child

nenúfar [ne'nufar] *nm* water lily

neologismo [neolo'xismo] *nm* neologism

neón [ne'on] *nm*: **luces/lámpara de ~** neon lights/lamp

neoyorquino, a [neojor'kino, a] *adj* (of) New York

nervio ['nerßjo] *nm* nerve; **nerviosismo** *nm* nervousness, nerves

pl; **~so, a** *adj* nervous

neto, a ['neto, a] *adj* net

neumático, a [neu'matiko, a] *adj* pneumatic ♦ *nm* (*ESP*) tyre (*BRIT*), tire (*US*); **~ de recambio** spare tyre

neurasténico, a [neuras'teniko, a] *adj* (*fig*) hysterical

neurólogo, a [neu'rolovo, a] *nm/f* neurologist

neurona [neu'rona] *nf* nerve cell

neutral [neu'tral] *adj* neutral; **~izar** *vt* to neutralize; (*contrarrestar*) to counteract

neutro, a ['neutro, a] *adj* (*BIO*, *LING*) neuter

neutrón [neu'tron] *nm* neutron

nevada [ne'ßaða] *nf* snowstorm; (*caída de nieve*) snowfall

nevar [ne'ßar] *vi* to snow

nevera [ne'ßera] *nf* (*ESP*) refrigerator (*BRIT*), icebox (*US*)

nevería [neße'ria] *nf* (*AM*) ice-cream parlour

nexo ['nekso] *nm* link, connection

ni [ni] *conj* nor, neither; (*tb*: **~ siquiera**) not ... even; **~ aunque que** not even if; **~ blanco ~ negro** neither white nor black

Nicaragua [nika'raɣwa] *nf* Nicaragua; **nicaragüense** *adj, nm/f* Nicaraguan

nicho ['nitʃo] *nm* niche

nicotina [niko'tina] *nf* nicotine

nido ['niðo] *nm* nest

niebla ['njeßla] *nf* fog; (*neblina*) mist

niego *etc vb ver* **negar**

nieto, a ['njeto, a] *nm/f* grandson/daughter; **~s** *nmpl* grandchildren

nieve *etc* ['njeße] *vb ver* **nevar** ♦ *nf* snow; (*AM*) icecream

N.I.F. *nm abr* (= *Número de Identificación Fiscal*) *personal identification number used for financial and tax purposes*

nimiedad [nimje'ðað] *nf* triviality

nimio, a ['nimjo, a] *adj* trivial, insignificant

ninfa ['ninfa] *nf* nymph

ningún [niŋ'gun] adj ver **ninguno**

ninguno, a [niŋ'guno, a] (delante de nm: **ningún**) adj no ♦ pron (nadie) nobody; (ni uno) none, not one; (ni uno ni otro) neither; **de ninguna manera** by no means, not at all

niña ['niɲa] nf (ANAT) pupil; ver tb **niño**

niñera [ni'ɲera] nf nursemaid, nanny; **niñería** nf childish act

niñez [ni'ɲeθ] nf childhood; (infancia) infancy

niño, a ['niɲo, a] adj (joven) young; (inmaduro) immature ♦ nm/f child, boy/girl

nipón, ona [ni'pon, ona] adj, nm/f Japanese

níquel ['nikel] nm nickel; **niquelar** vt (TEC) to nickel-plate

níspero ['nispero] nm medlar

nitidez [niti'ðeθ] nf (claridad) clarity; (: de imagen) sharpness; **nítido, a** adj clear; sharp

nitrato [ni'trato] nm nitrate

nitrógeno [ni'troxeno] nm nitrogen

nivel [ni'βel] nm (GEO) level; (norma) level, standard; (altura) height; **~ de aceite** oil level; **~ de aire** spirit level; **~ de vida** standard of living; **~ar** vt to level out; (fig) to even up; (COM) to balance

NN. UU. nfpl abr (= Naciones Unidas) UN sg

no [no] adv no; not; (con verbo) not ♦ excl no!; **~ tengo nada** I don't have anything, I have nothing; **~ es el mío** it's not mine; **ahora ~** not now; **¿~ lo sabes?** don't you know?; **~ mucho** not much; **~ bien termine, le entregaré** as soon as I finish I'll hand it over; **~ más: ayer ~ más** just yesterday; **¡pase ~ más!** come in!; **¡a que ~ sabes?** I bet you don't know!; **¡cómo ~!** of course!; **los países ~ alineados** the non-aligned countries; **la ~ intervención** non-intervention

noble ['noβle] adj, nm/f noble; **~za** nf nobility

noche ['notʃe] nf night, night-time; (la tarde) evening; **de ~, por la ~** at night; **es de ~** it's dark

Noche de San Juan

The **Noche de San Juan** on the 24th June is a **fiesta** coinciding with the summer solstice and which has taken the place of other ancient pagan festivals. Traditionally fire plays a major part in these festivities with celebrations and dancing taking place around bonfires in towns and villages across the country.

nochebuena [notʃe'βwena] nf Christmas Eve

Nochebuena

Traditional Christmas celebrations in Spanish-speaking countries mainly take place on the night of **Nochebuena**, Christmas Eve. Families gather together for a large meal and the more religiously inclined attend Midnight Mass. While presents are traditionally given by **los Reyes Magos** on the 6th January, more and more people are exchanging gifts on Christmas Eve.

nochevieja [notʃe'βjexa] nf New Year's Eve

noción [no'θjon] nf notion

nocivo, a [no'θiβo, a] adj harmful

noctámbulo, a [nok'tambulo, a] nm/f sleepwalker

nocturno, a [nok'turno, a] adj (de la noche) nocturnal, night cpd; (de la tarde) evening cpd ♦ nm nocturne

nodriza [no'ðriθa] nf wet nurse; **buque o nave ~** supply ship

nogal [no'xal] nm walnut tree

nómada [no'maða] adj nomadic ♦ nm/f nomad

nombramiento [nombra'mjento] *nm* naming; (*a un empleo*) appointment

nombrar [nom'brar] *vt* (*designar*) to name; (*mencionar*) to mention; (*dar puesto a*) to appoint

nombre ['nombre] *nm* name; (*sustantivo*) noun; ~ **y apellidos** name in full; ~ **común/propio** common/ proper noun; ~ **de pila/de soltera** Christian/maiden name; **poner ~ a** to call, name

nómina ['nomina] *nf* (*lista*) payroll; (*hoja*) payslip

nominal [nomi'nal] *adj* nominal

nominar [nomi'nar] *vt* to nominate

nominativo, a [nomina'tiβo, a] *adj* (*COM*): **cheque ~ a X** cheque made out to X

nono, a ['nono, a] *adj* ninth

nordeste [nor'ðeste] *adj* north-east, north-eastern, north-easterly ♦ *nm* north-east

nórdico, a ['norðiko, a] *adj* Nordic

noreste [no'reste] *adj, nm* = **nordeste**

noria ['norja] *nf* (*AGR*) waterwheel; (*de carnaval*) big (*BRIT*) o ferris (*US*) wheel

norma ['norma] *nf* rule (of thumb)

normal [nor'mal] *adj* (*corriente*) normal; (*habitual*) usual, natural; **~idad** *nf* normality; **restablecer la ~idad** to restore order; **~izar** *vt* (*reglamentar*) to normalize; (*TEC*) to standardize; **~izarse** *vr* to return to normal; **~mente** *adv* normally

normando, a [nor'mando, a] *adj, nm/f* Norman

normativa [norma'tiβa] *nf* (set of) rules *pl*, regulations *pl*

noroeste [noro'este] *adj* north-west, north-western, north-westerly ♦ *nm* north-west

norte ['norte] *adj* north, northern, northerly ♦ *nm* north; (*fig*) guide

norteamericano, a [norteameri'kano, a] *adj, nm/f* (North) American

Noruega [no'rweɣa] *nf* Norway

noruego, a [no'rweɣo, a] *adj, nm/f* Norwegian

nos [nos] *pron* (*directo*) us; (*indirecto*) us; to us; for us; from us; (*reflexivo*) (to) ourselves; (*recíproco*) (to) each other; ~ **levantamos a las 7** we get up at 7

nosotros, as [no'sotros, as] *pron* (*sujeto*) we; (*después de prep*) us

nostalgia [nos'talxja] *nf* nostalgia

nota ['nota] *nf* note; (*ESCOL*) mark

notable [no'taβle] *adj* notable; (*ESCOL*) outstanding

notar [no'tar] *vt* to notice, note; **~se** *vr* to be obvious; **se nota que ...** one observes that ...

notarial [nota'rjal] *adj*: **acta ~** affidavit

notario [no'tarjo] *nm* notary

noticia [no'tiθja] *nf* (*información*) piece of news; **las ~s** the news *sg*; **tener ~s de alguien** to hear from sb

noticiero [noti'θjero] (*AM*) *nm* news bulletin

notificación [notifika'θjon] *nf* notification; **notificar** *vt* to notify, inform

notoriedad [notorje'ðað] *nf* fame, renown; **notorio, a** *adj* (*público*) well-known; (*evidente*) obvious

novato, a [no'βato, a] *adj* inexperienced ♦ *nm/f* beginner, novice

novecientos, as [noβe'θjentos, as] *num* nine hundred

novedad [noβe'ðað] *nf* (*calidad de nuevo*) newness; (*noticia*) piece of news; (*cambio*) change, (new) development

novel [no'βel] *adj* new; (*inexperto*) inexperienced ♦ *nm/f* beginner

novela [no'βela] *nf* novel

noveno, a [no'βeno, a] *adj* ninth

noventa [no'βenta] *num* ninety

novia ['noβja] *nf ver* **novio**

noviazgo [no'βjaθɣo] *nm* engagement

novicio, a [no'βiθjo, a] *nm/f* novice

noviembre [no'βjembre] *nm* November

novillada [noβi'ʎaða] nf (TAUR) bullfight with young bulls; **novillero** nm novice bullfighter; **novillo** nm young bull, bullock; **hacer novillos** (fam) to play truant

novio, a ['noβjo, a] nm/f boyfriend/ girlfriend; (prometido) fiancé/fiancée; (recién casado) bridegroom/bride; **los ~s** the newly-weds

nubarrón [nuβa'rron] nm storm cloud

nube ['nuβe] nf cloud

nublado, a [nu'βlaðo, a] adj cloudy; **nublarse** vr to grow dark

nubosidad [nuβosi'ðað] nf cloudiness; **había mucha ~** it was very cloudy

nuca ['nuka] nf nape of the neck

nuclear [nukle'ar] adj nuclear

núcleo ['nukleo] nm (centro) core; (FÍSICA) nucleus

nudillo [nu'ðiʎo] nm knuckle

nudista [nu'ðista] adj nudist

nudo ['nuðo] nm knot; **~so, a** adj knotty

nuera ['nwera] nf daughter-in-law

nuestro, a ['nwestro, a] adj pos our ♦ pron ours; **~ padre** our father; **un amigo ~** a friend of ours; **es el ~** it's ours

nueva ['nweβa] nf piece of news

nuevamente [nweβa'mente] adv (otra vez) again; (de nuevo) anew

Nueva York [-'jɔrk] n New York

Nueva Zelanda [-θe'landa] nf New Zealand

nueve ['nweβe] num nine

nuevo, a ['nweβo, a] adj (gen) new; **de ~** again

nuez [nweθ] nf walnut; **~ de Adán** Adam's apple; **~ moscada** nutmeg

nulidad [nuli'ðað] nf (incapacidad) incompetence; (abolición) nullity

nulo, a ['nulo, a] adj (inepto, torpe) useless; (inválido) (null and void); (DEPORTE) drawn, tied

núm. abr (= número) no

numeración [numera'θjon] nf (cifras) numbers pl; (arábiga, romana etc) numerals pl

numeral [nume'ral] nm numeral

numerar [nume'rar] vt to number

número ['numero] nm (gen) number; (tamaño: de zapato) size; (ejemplar: de diario) number, issue; **sin ~** numberless, unnumbered; **~ de matrícula/de teléfono** registration/ telephone number; **~ atrasado** back number

numeroso, a [nume'roso, a] adj numerous

nunca ['nunka] adv (jamás) never; **~ lo pensé** I never thought it; **no viene ~** he never comes; **~ más** never again; **más que ~** more than ever

nupcias ['nupθjas] nfpl wedding sg, nuptials

nutria ['nutrja] nf otter

nutrición [nutri'θjon] nf nutrition

nutrido, a [nu'triðo, a] adj (alimentado) nourished; (fig: grande) large; (abundante) abundant

nutrir [nu'trir] vt (alimentar) to nourish; (dar de comer) to feed; (fig) to strengthen; **nutritivo, a** adj nourishing, nutritious

nylon [ni'lon] nm nylon

Ñ ñ

ñato, a ['nato, a] (AM) adj snub-nosed

ñoñería [none'ria] nf insipidness

ñoño, a ['nono, a] adj (AM: tonto) silly, stupid; (soso) insipid; (persona) spineless

O, o

O abr (= oeste) W

o [o] conj or

o/ abr (= orden) o.

oasis [o'asis] nm inv oasis

obcecarse [oβθe'karse] vr to get o

become stubborn

obedecer [oβeðe'θer] vt to obey;
obediencia nf obedience; **obediente**
adj obedient

obertura [oβer'tura] nf overture

obesidad [oβesi'ðað] nf obesity;
obeso, a adj obese

obispo [o'βispo] nm bishop

objeción [oβxe'θjon] nf objection;
poner objeciones to raise objections

objetar [oβxe'tar] vt, vi to object

objetivo, a [oβxe'tiβo, a] adj, nm
objective

objeto [oβ'xeto] nm (cosa) object; (fin)
aim

objetor, a [oβxe'tor, a] nm/f objector

oblicuo, a [o'βlikwo, a] adj oblique;
(mirada) sidelong

obligación [oβliɣa'θjon] nf obligation;
(COM) bond

obligar [oβli'ɣar] vt to force; **~se** vr to
bind o.s.; **obligatorio, a** adj
compulsory, obligatory

oboe [o'βoe] nm oboe

obra ['oβra] nf work; (ARQ)
construction, building; (TEATRO) play;
~ maestra masterpiece; **~s públicas**
public works; **por ~ de** thanks to (the
efforts of); **obrar** vt to work; (tener
efecto) to have an effect on ♦ vi to act,
behave; (tener efecto) to have an effect;
la carta obra en su poder the letter
is in his/her possession

obrero, a [o'βrero, a] adj (clase)
working; (movimiento) labour cpd
♦ nm/f (gen) worker; (sin oficio)
labourer

obscenidad [oβsθeni'ðað] nf
obscenity; **obsceno, a** adj obscene

obscu... = oscu...

obsequiar [oβse'kjar] vt (ofrecer) to
present with; (agasajar) to make a fuss
of, lavish attention on; **obsequio** nm
(regalo) gift; (cortesía) courtesy,
attention

observación [oβserβa'θjon] nf
observation; (reflexión) remark

observador, a [oβserβa'ðor, a] nm/f
observer

observar [oβser'βar] vt to observe;
(anotar) to notice; **~se** vr to keep to,
observe

obsesión [oβse'sjon] nf obsession;
obsesivo, a adj obsessive

obsoleto, a [oβso'leto, a] adj obsolete

obstáculo [oβs'takulo] nm obstacle;
(impedimento) hindrance, drawback

obstante [oβs'tante]: **no ~** adv
nevertheless

obstinado, a [oβsti'naðo, a] adj
obstinate, stubborn

obstinarse [oβsti'narse] vr to be
obstinate; **~ en** to persist in

obstrucción [oβstruk'θjon] nf
obstruction; **obstruir** vt to obstruct

obtener [oβte'ner] vt (gen) to obtain;
(premio) to win

obturador [oβtura'ðor] nm (FOTO)
shutter

obvio, a ['oβßjo, a] adj obvious

oca ['oka] nf (animal) goose; (juego)
≈ snakes and ladders

ocasión [oka'sjon] nf (oportunidad)
opportunity, chance; (momento)
occasion, time; (causa) cause; **de ~**
secondhand; **ocasionar** vt to cause

ocaso [o'kaso] nm (fig) decline

occidente [okθi'ðente] nm west

OCDE nf abr (= Organización de
Cooperación y Desarrollo Económico)
OECD

océano [o'θeano] nm ocean; **el
~ índico** the Indian Ocean

ochenta [o'tʃenta] num eighty

ocho ['otʃo] num eight; **~ días** a week

ocio [o'θjo] nm (tiempo) leisure; (pey)
idleness; **~so, a** adj (inactivo) idle;
(inútil) useless

octavilla [okta'viʎa] nf leaflet,
pamphlet

octavo, a [ok'taβo, a] adj eighth

octubre [ok'tuβre] nm October

ocular [oku'lar] adj ocular, eye cpd;
testigo ~ eyewitness

oculista [oku'lista] nm/f oculist
ocultar [okul'tar] vt (esconder) to hide; (callar) to conceal; **oculto, a** adj hidden; (fig) secret
ocupación [okupa'θjon] nf occupation
ocupado, a [oku'paðo, a] adj (persona) busy; (plaza) occupied, taken; (teléfono) engaged; **ocupar** vt (gen) to occupy; **ocuparse** vr: **ocuparse de o en** (gen) to concern o.s. with; (cuidar) to look after
ocurrencia [oku'rrenθja] nf (idea) bright idea
ocurrir [oku'rrir] vi to happen; **~se** vr: **se me ocurrió que ...** it occurred to me that ...
odiar [o'ðjar] vt to hate; **odio** nm hate, hatred; **odioso, a** adj (gen) hateful; (malo) nasty
odontólogo, a [oðon'toloɣo, a] nm/f dentist, dental surgeon
OEA nf abr (= Organización de Estados Americanos) OAS
oeste [o'este] nm west; **una película del ~** a western
ofender [ofen'der] vt (agraviar) to offend; (insultar) to insult; **~se** vr to take offence; **ofensa** nf offence; **ofensiva** nf offensive; **ofensivo, a** adj offensive
oferta [o'ferta] nf offer; (propuesta) proposal; **la ~ y la demanda** supply and demand; **artículos en ~** goods on offer
oficial [ofi'θjal] adj official ♦ nm (MIL) officer
oficina [ofi'θina] nf office; **~ de correos** post office; **~ de turismo** tourist office; **oficinista** nm/f clerk
oficio [o'fiθjo] nm (profesión) profession; (puesto) post; (REL) service; **ser del ~** to be on old hand; **tener mucho ~** to have a lot of experience; **~ de difuntos** funeral service
oficioso, a [ofi'θjoso, a] adj (pey) (no oficial) unofficial, informal
ofimática [ofi'matika] nf office

automation
ofrecer [ofre'θer] vt (dar) to offer; (proponer) to propose; **~se** vr (persona) to offer o.s., volunteer; (situación) to present itself; **¿qué se le ofrece?, ¿se le ofrece algo?** what can I do for you?, can I get you anything?
ofrecimiento [ofreθi'mjento] nm offer
oftalmólogo, a [oftal'moloɣo, a] nm/f ophthalmologist
ofuscar [ofus'kar] vt (por pasión) to blind; (por luz) to dazzle
oída [o'iða] nf: **de ~s** by hearsay
oído [o'iðo] nm (ANAT) ear; (sentido) hearing
oigo etc vb ver **oír**
oír [o'ir] vt (gen) to hear; (atender a) to listen to; **¡oiga!** listen!; **~ misa** to attend mass
OIT nf abr (= Organización Internacional del Trabajo) ILO
ojal [o'xal] nm buttonhole
ojalá [oxa'la] excl if only (it were so)!, some hope! ♦ conj if only ...!, would that ...!; **~ (que) venga hoy** I hope he comes today
ojeada [oxe'aða] nf glance
ojera [o'xera] nf: **tener ~s** to have bags under one's eyes
ojeriza [oxe'riθa] nf ill-will
ojeroso, a [oxe'roso, a] adj haggard
ojo ['oxo] nm eye; (de puente) span; (de cerradura) keyhole ♦ excl careful!; **tener ~ para** to have an eye for; **~ de buey** porthole
okupa [o'kupa] (fam) nm/f squatter
ola ['ola] nf wave
olé [o'le] excl bravo!, olé!
oleada [ole'aða] nf big wave, swell; (fig) wave
oleaje [ole'axe] nm swell
óleo ['oleo] nm oil; **oleoducto** nm (oil) pipeline
oler [o'ler] vt (gen) to smell; (inquirir) to pry into; (fig: sospechar) to sniff out ♦ vi to smell; **~ a** to smell of
olfatear [olfate'ar] vt to smell; (inquirir)

to pry into; **olfato** nm sense of smell

oligarquía [oliɣar'kia] nf oligarchy

olimpiada [olim'piaða] nf: **las O~s** the Olympics; **olímpico, a** [o'limpiko, a] adj Olympic

oliva [o'liβa] nf (aceituna) olive; **aceite de ~** olive oil; **olivo** nm olive tree

olla ['oʎa] nf pan; (comida) stew; **~ a presión** o **exprés** pressure cooker; **~ podrida** type of Spanish stew

olmo ['olmo] nm elm (tree)

olor [o'lor] nm smell; **~oso, a** adj scented

olvidar [olβi'ðar] vt to forget; (omitir) to omit; **~se** vr (fig) to forget o.s.; **se me olvidó** I forgot

olvido [ol'βiðo] nm oblivion; (despiste) forgetfulness

ombligo [om'bliɣo] nm navel

omisión [omi'sjon] nf (abstención) omission; (descuido) neglect

omiso, a [o'miso, a] adj: **hacer caso ~ de** to ignore, pass over

omitir [omi'tir] vt to omit

omnipotente [omnipo'tente] adj omnipotent

omóplato [o'moplato] nm shoulder blade

OMS nf abr (= Organización Mundial de la Salud) WHO

once ['onθe] num eleven; **~s** (AM) tea break

onda ['onda] nf wave; **~ corta/larga/media** short/long/medium wave; **ondear** vt, vi to wave; (tener ondas) to be wavy; (agua) to ripple; **ondearse** vr to swing, sway

ondulación [ondula'θjon] nf undulation; **ondulado, a** adj wavy

ondular [ondu'lar] vt (el pelo) to wave ♦ vi to undulate; **~se** vr to undulate

ONG nf abr (= organización no gubernamental) NGO

ONU ['onu] nf abr (= Organización de las Naciones Unidas) UNO

opaco, a [o'pako, a] adj opaque

opción [op'θjon] nf (gen) option;

(derecho) right, option

OPEP ['opep] nf abr (= Organización de Países Exportadores de Petróleo) OPEC

ópera ['opera] nf opera; **~ bufa** o **cómica** comic opera

operación [opera'θjon] nf (gen) operation; (COM) transaction, deal

operador, a [opera'ðor, a] nm/f operator; (CINE: proyección) projectionist; (: rodaje) cameraman

operar [ope'rar] vt (producir) to produce, bring about; (MED) to operate on ♦ vi (COM) to operate, deal; **~se** vr to occur; (MED) to have an operation

opereta [ope'reta] nf operetta

opinar [opi'nar] vt to think ♦ vi to give one's opinion; **opinión** nf (creencia) belief; (criterio) opinion

opio ['opjo] nm opium

oponente [opo'nente] nm/f opponent

oponer [opo'ner] vt (resistencia) to put up, offer; (objetar) to object; (estar frente a frente) to be opposed; (dos personas) to oppose each other; **~ A a B** to set A against B; **me opongo a pensar que ...** I refuse to believe o think that ...

oportunidad [oportuni'ðað] nf (ocasión) opportunity; (posibilidad) chance

oportuno, a [opor'tuno, a] adj (en su tiempo) opportune, timely; (respuesta) suitable; **en el momento ~** at the right moment

oposición [oposi'θjon] nf opposition; **oposiciones** nfpl (ESCOL) public examinations

opositor, a [oposi'tor, a] nm/f (adversario) opponent; (candidato): **~ a (a)** candidate for

opresión [opre'sjon] nf oppression; **opresivo, a** adj oppressive; **opresor, a** nm/f oppressor

oprimir [opri'mir] vt to squeeze; (fig) to oppress

optar [op'tar] vi (elegir) to choose; **~**

por to opt for; **optativo, a** adj optional

óptico, a ['optiko, a] adj optic(al) ♦ nm/f optician; **óptica** nf optician's (shop); **desde esta óptica** from this point of view

optimismo [opti'mismo] nm optimism; **optimista** nm/f optimist

óptimo, a ['optimo, a] adj (el mejor) very best

opuesto, a [o'pwesto, a] adj (contrario) opposite; (antagónico) opposing

opulencia [opu'lenθja] nf opulence; **opulento, a** adj opulent

oración [ora'θjon] nf (REL) prayer; (LING) sentence

orador, a [ora'ðor, a] nm/f (conferenciante) speaker, orator

oral [o'ral] adj oral

orangután [orangu'tan] nm orangutan

orar [o'rar] vi to pray

oratoria [ora'torja] nf oratory

órbita ['orβita] nf orbit

orden ['orðen] nm (gen) order ♦ nf (gen) order; (INFORM) command; **~ del día** agenda; **de primer ~** first-rate; **en ~ de prioridad** in order of priority

ordenado, a [orðe'naðo, a] adj (metódico) methodical; (arreglado) orderly

ordenador [orðena'ðor] nm computer; **~ central** mainframe computer

ordenanza [orðe'nanθa] nf ordinance

ordenar [orðe'nar] vt (mandar) to order; (poner orden) to put in order, arrange; **~se** vr (REL) to be ordained

ordeñar [orðe'ɲar] vt to milk

ordinario, a [orði'narjo, a] adj (común) ordinary, usual; (vulgar) vulgar, common

orégano [o'reɣano] nm oregano

oreja [o'rexa] nf ear; (MECÁNICA) lug, flange

orfanato [orfa'nato] nm orphanage

orfandad [orfan'dað] nf orphanhood

orfebrería [orfeβre'ria] nf gold/silver work

orgánico, a [or'ɣaniko, a] adj organic

organigrama [orɣani'ɣrama] nm flow chart

organismo [orɣa'nismo] nm (BIO) organism; (POL) organization

organización [orɣaniθa'θjon] nf organization; **organizar** vt to organize

órgano ['orɣano] nm organ

orgasmo [or'ɣasmo] nm orgasm

orgía [or'xia] nf orgy

orgullo [or'ɣuʎo] nm pride; **orgulloso, a** adj (gen) proud; (altanero) haughty

orientación [orjenta'θjon] nf (posición) position; (dirección) direction

oriental [orjen'tal] adj eastern; (del Lejano Oriente) oriental

orientar [orjen'tar] vt (situar) to orientate; (señalar) to point; (dirigir) to direct; (guiar) to guide; **~se** vr to get one's bearings

oriente [o'rjente] nm east; **Cercano/Medio/Lejano O~** Near/Middle/Far East

origen [o'rixen] nm origin

original [orixi'nal] adj (nuevo) original; (extraño) odd, strange; **~idad** nf originality

originar [orixi'nar] vt to start, cause; **~se** vr to originate; **~io, a** adj original; **~io de** native of

orilla [o'riʎa] nf (borde) border; (de río) bank; (de bosque, tela) edge; (de mar) shore

orina [o'rina] nf urine; **orinal** nm (chamber) pot; **orinar** vi to urinate; **orinarse** vr to wet o.s.; **orines** nmpl urine

oriundo, a [o'rjundo, a] adj: **~ de** native of

ornitología [ornitolo'xia] nf ornithology, bird-watching

oro ['oro] nm gold; **~s** nmpl (NAIPES) hearts

oropel [oro'pel] nm tinsel

orquesta [or'kesta] nf orchestra; **~ de cámara/sinfónica** chamber/ symphony orchestra

orquídea [or'kiðea] nf orchid

ortiga [or'tiɣa] nf nettle

ortodoxo, a [orto'ðokso, a] adj orthodox

ortografía [ortoɣra'fia] nf spelling

ortopedia [orto'peðja] nf orthopaedics sg; **ortopédico, a** adj orthopaedic

oruga [o'ruɣa] nf caterpillar

orzuelo [or'θwelo] nm stye

os [os] pron (gen) you; (a vosotros) to you

osa ['osa] nf (she-)bear; **O~ Mayor/ Menor** Great/Little Bear

osadía [osa'ðia] nf daring

osar [o'sar] vi to dare

oscilación [osθila'θjon] nf (movimiento) oscillation; (fluctuación) fluctuation

oscilar [osθi'lar] vi to oscillate; to fluctuate

oscurecer [oskure'θer] vt to darken
♦ vi to grow dark; **~se** vr to grow o get dark

oscuridad [oskuri'ðað] nf obscurity; (tinieblas) darkness

oscuro, a [os'kuro, a] adj dark; (fig) obscure; **a oscuras** in the dark

óseo, a ['oseo, a] adj bony

oso ['oso] nm bear; **~ de peluche** teddy bear; **~ hormiguero** anteater

ostentación [ostenta'θjon] nf (gen) ostentation; (acto) display

ostentar [osten'tar] vt (gen) to show; (pey) to flaunt, show off; (poseer) to have, possess

ostra ['ostra] nf oyster

OTAN ['otan] nf abr (= Organización del Tratado del Atlántico Norte) NATO

otear [ote'ar] vt to observe; (fig) to look into

otitis [o'titis] nf earache

otoñal [oto'ɲal] adj autumnal

otoño [o'toɲo] nm autumn

otorgar [otor'xar] vt (conceder) to concede; (dar) to grant

otorrino, a [oto'rrino, a], **otorrinolaringólogo, a** [otorrinolarin'goloɣo, a], nm/f ear, nose and throat specialist

---

PALABRA CLAVE

otro, a ['otro, a] adj **1** (distinto: sg) another; (: pl) other; **con ~s amigos** with other o different friends

2 (adicional): **tráigame ~ café (más), por favor** can I have another coffee please; **~s 10 días más** another ten days

♦ pron **1**: **el ~** the other one; **(los) ~s** (the) others; **de ~** somebody else's; **que lo haga ~** let somebody else do it

2 (recíproco): **se odian (la) una a (la) otra** they hate one another o each other

3: **~ tanto**: **comer ~ tanto** to eat the same o as much again; **recibió una decena de telegramas y otras tantas llamadas** he got about ten telegrams and as many calls

---

ovación [oβa'θjon] nf ovation

oval [o'βal] adj oval; **~ado, a** adj oval; **óvalo** nm oval

ovario [o'βarjo] nm ovary

oveja [o'βexa] nf sheep

overol [oβe'rol] (AM) nm overalls pl

ovillo [o'βiλo] nm (de lana) ball of wool; **hacerse un ~** to curl up

OVNI ['oβni] nm abr (= objeto volante no identificado) UFO

ovulación [oβula'θjon] nf ovulation; **óvulo** nm ovum

oxidación [oksiða'θjon] nf rusting

oxidar [oksi'ðar] vt to rust; **~se** vr to go rusty

óxido ['oksiðo] nm oxide

oxigenado, a [oksixe'naðo, a] adj (QUÍM) oxygenated; (pelo) bleached

oxígeno [ok'sixeno] nm oxygen

oyente [o'jente] nm/f listener, hearer

oyes etc vb ver **oír**

ozono [o'θono] nm ozone

P, p

P abr (= padre) Fr.

pabellón [paβe'ʎon] nm bell tent; (ARQ) pavilion; (de hospital etc) block, section; (bandera) flag

pacer [pa'θer] vi to graze

paciencia [pa'θjenθja] nf patience

paciente [pa'θjente] adj, nm/f patient

pacificación [paθifika'θjon] nf pacification

pacificar [paθifi'kar] vt to pacify; (tranquilizar) to calm

pacífico, a [pa'θifiko, a] adj (persona) peaceable; (existencia) peaceful; **el** (océano) **P~** the Pacific (Ocean)

pacifismo [paθi'fismo] nm pacifism; **pacifista** nm/f pacifist

pacotilla [pako'tiʎa] nf: **de ~** (actor, escritor) third-rate; (mueble etc) cheap

pactar [pak'tar] vt to agree to o on ♦ vi to come to an agreement

pacto ['pakto] nm (tratado) pact; (acuerdo) agreement

padecer [paðe'θer] vt (sufrir) to suffer; (soportar) to endure, put up with; **padecimiento** nm suffering

padrastro [pa'ðrastro] nm stepfather

padre ['paðre] nm father ♦ adj (fam): **un éxito ~** a tremendous success; **~s** nmpl parents

padrino [pa'ðrino] nm (REL) godfather; (tb: ~ **de boda**) best man; (fig) sponsor, patron; **~s** nmpl godparents

padrón [pa'ðron] nm (censo) census, roll

paella [pa'eʎa] nf paella, dish of rice with meat, shellfish etc

paga ['paxa] nf (pago) payment; (sueldo) pay, wages pl

pagano, a [pa'xano, a] adj, nm/f pagan, heathen

pagar [pa'xar] vt to pay; (las compras, crimen) to pay for; (fig: favor) to repay ♦ vi to pay; **~ al contado/a plazos** to pay (in) cash/in instalments

pagaré [paxa're] nm I.O.U.

página ['paxina] nf page

pago ['paxo] nm (dinero) payment; **~ anticipado/a cuenta/contra reembolso/en especie** advance payment/payment on account/cash on delivery/payment in kind; **en ~ de** in return for

pág(s). abr (= página(s)) p(p).

pague etc vb ver **pagar**

país [pa'is] nm (gen) country; (región) land; **los P~es Bajos** the Low Countries; **el P~ Vasco** the Basque Country

paisaje [pai'saxe] nm landscape, scenery

paisano, a [pai'sano, a] adj of the same country ♦ nm/f (compatriota) fellow countryman/woman; **vestir de ~** (soldado) to be in civvies; (guardia) to be in plain clothes

paja ['paxa] nf straw; (fig) rubbish (BRIT), trash (US)

pajarita [paxa'rita] nf (corbata) bow tie

pájaro ['paxaro] nm bird; **~ carpintero** woodpecker

pajita [pa'xita] nf (drinking) straw

pala ['pala] nf spade, shovel; (raqueta etc) bat; (: de tenis) racquet; (CULIN) slice; **~ matamoscas** fly swat

palabra [pa'laβra] nf word; (facultad) (power of) speech; (derecho de hablar) right to speak; **tomar la ~** (en mitin) to take the floor

palabrota [pala'βrota] nf swearword

palacio [pa'laθjo] nm palace; (mansión) mansion, large house; **~ de justicia** courthouse; **~ municipal** town/city hall

paladar [pala'ðar] nm palate; **paladear** vt to taste

palanca [pa'laŋka] nf lever; (fig) pull, influence

palangana [palaŋ'gana] nf washbasin

palco ['palko] nm box

Palestina [pales'tina] nf Palestine; **palestino, a** nm/f Palestinian

paleta [pa'leta] nf (de pintor) palette; (de albañil) trowel; (de ping-pong) bat; (AM) ice lolly

paleto, a [pa'leto, a] (fam, pey) nm/f yokel

paliar [pa'ljar] vt (mitigar) to mitigate, alleviate; **paliativo** nm palliative

palidecer [paliðe'θer] vi to turn pale; **palidez** nf paleness; **pálido, a** adj pale

palillo [pa'liʎo] nm (mondadientes) toothpick; (para comer) chopstick

paliza [pa'liθa] nf beating, thrashing

palma ['palma] nf (ANAT) palm; (árbol) palm tree; **batir** o **dar ~s** to clap, applaud; **~da** nf slap; **~das** nfpl clapping sg, applause sg

palmar [pal'mar] (fam) vi (tb: **~la**) to die, kick the bucket

palmear [palme'ar] vt to clap

palmera [pal'mera] nf (BOT) palm tree

palmo ['palmo] nm (medida) span; (fig) small amount; **~ a ~** inch by inch

palo ['palo] nm stick; (poste) post; (de tienda de campaña) pole; (mango) handle, shaft; (golpe) blow, hit; (de golf) club; (de béisbol) bat; (NAUT) mast; (NAIPES) suit

paloma [pa'loma] nf dove, pigeon

palomitas [palo'mitas] nfpl popcorn sg

palpar [pal'par] vt to touch, feel

palpitación [palpita'θjon] nf palpitation

palpitante [palpi'tante] adj palpitating; (fig) burning

palpitar [palpi'tar] vi to palpitate; (latir) to beat

palta ['palta] (AM) nf avocado (pear)

paludismo [palu'ðismo] nm malaria

pamela [pa'mela] nf picture hat, sun hat

pampa ['pampa] (AM) nf pampas, prairie

pan [pan] nm bread; (una barra) loaf; **~ integral** wholemeal (BRIT) o wholewheat (US) bread; **~ rallado** breadcrumbs pl

pana ['pana] nf corduroy

panadería [panaðe'ria] nf baker's (shop); **panadero, a** nm/f baker

Panamá [pana'ma] nm Panama; **panameño, a** adj Panamanian

pancarta [paŋ'karta] nf placard, banner

panda ['panda] nm (ZOOL) panda

pandereta [pande'reta] nf tambourine

pandilla [pan'diʎa] nf set, group; (de criminales) gang; (pey: camarilla) clique

panecillo [pane'θiʎo] nm (bread) roll

panel [pa'nel] nm panel; **~ solar** solar panel

panfleto [pan'fleto] nm pamphlet

pánico ['paniko] nm panic

panorama [pano'rama] nm panorama; (vista) view

pantalla [pan'taʎa] nf (de cine) screen; (de lámpara) lampshade

pantalón [panta'lon] nm trousers; **pantalones** nmpl trousers

pantano [pan'tano] nm (ciénaga) marsh, swamp; (depósito: de agua) reservoir; (fig) jam, difficulty

panteón [pante'on] nm: **~ familiar** family tomb

pantera [pan'tera] nf panther

pantí(e)s ['pantis] nmpl tights

pantomima [panto'mima] nf pantomime

pantorrilla [panto'rriʎa] nf calf (of the leg)

pantufla [pan'tufla] nf slipper

panty(s) ['panti(s)] nm(pl) tights

panza ['panθa] nf belly, paunch

pañal [pa'ɲal] nm nappy (BRIT), diaper (US); **~es** nmpl (fig) early stages, infancy sg

paño ['paɲo] nm (tela) cloth; (pedazo

de tela) (piece of) cloth; (*trapo*) duster,
rag; ~ **higiénico** sanitary towel; ~**s
menores** underclothes

pañuelo |pa'ɲwelo| *nm* handkerchief,
hanky (*fam*); (*para la cabeza*)
(head)scarf

papa |'papa| *nm*: **el P~** the Pope ♦ *nf*
(*AM*) potato

papá |pa'pa| (*pl* ~**s**) (*fam*) *nm* dad(dy),
pa (*US*)

papada |pa'paða| *nf* double chin

papagayo |papa'yajo| *nm* parrot

papanatas |papa'natas| (*fam*) *nm inv*
simpleton

paparrucha |papa'rrutʃa| *nf* piece of
nonsense

papaya |pa'paja| *nf* papaya

papear |pa'pear| (*fam*) *vt, vi* to scoff

papel |pa'pel| *nm* paper; (*hoja de* ~)
sheet of paper; (*TEATRO, fig*) role; ~ **de
calco/carbón/de cartas** tracing
paper/carbon paper/stationery; ~ **de
envolver/pintado** wrapping paper/
wallpaper; ~ **de aluminio/higiénico**
aluminium (*BRIT*) o aluminum (*US*) foil/
toilet paper; ~ **de estaño** o **plata**
tinfoil; ~ **de lija** sandpaper; ~
moneda paper money; ~ **secante**
blotting paper

papeleo |pape'leo| *nm* red tape

papelera |pape'lera| *nf* wastepaper
basket; (*en la calle*) litter bin

papelería |papele'ria| *nf* stationer's
(shop)

papeleta |pape'leta| *nf* (*POL*) ballot
paper; (*ESCOL*) report

paperas |pa'peras| *nfpl* mumps *sg*

papilla |pa'piʎa| *nf* (*para niños*) baby
food

paquete |pa'kete| *nm* (*de cigarrillos
etc*) packet; (*CORREOS etc*) parcel; (*:
AM*) package tour; (*: fam*) nuisance

par |par| *adj* (*igual*) like, equal; (*MAT*)
even ♦ *nm* equal; (*de guantes*) pair; (*de
veces*) couple; (*POL*) peer; (*GOLF, COM*)
par; **abrir de ~ en ~** to open wide

para |'para| *prep* for; **no es ~ comer**

it's not for eating; **decir ~ sí** to say to
o.s.; ¿~ **qué lo quieres?** what do you
want it for?; **se casaron ~ separarse
otra vez** they married only to separate
again; **lo tendré ~ mañana** I'll have it
(for) tomorrow; **ir ~ casa** to go home,
head for home; ~ **profesor es muy
estúpido** he's very stupid for a
teacher; ¿**quién es usted ~ gritar
así?** who are you to shout like that?;
tengo bastante ~ vivir I have
enough to live on; *ver tb* **con**

parabién |para'ßjen| *nm*
congratulations *pl*

parábola |pa'raßola| *nf* parable; (*MAT*)
parabola; **parabólica** *nf* (*tb: antena* ~)
satellite dish

parabrisas |para'ßrisas| *nm inv*
windscreen (*BRIT*), windshield (*US*)

paracaídas |paraka'iðas| *nm inv*
parachute; **paracaidista** *nm/f*
parachutist; (*MIL*) paratrooper

parachoques |para'tʃokes| *nm inv*
(*AUTO*) bumper; (*MECÁNICA etc*) shock
absorber

parada |pa'raða| *nf* stop; (*acto*)
stopping; (*lugar*) stopping place; ~ **de
autobús** bus stop

paradero |para'ðero| *nm* stopping-
place; (*situación*) whereabouts

parado, a |pa'raðo, a| *adj* (*persona*)
motionless, standing still; (*fábrica*)
closed, at a standstill; (*coche*) stopped;
(*AM*) standing (up); (*sin empleo*)
unemployed, idle

paradoja |para'ðoxa| *nf* paradox

parador |para'ðor| *nm* parador, state-
run hotel

paráfrasis |pa'rafrasis| *nf inv*
paraphrase

paraguas |pa'raywas| *nm inv* umbrella

Paraguay |para'ywai| *nm*: **el** ~
Paraguay; **paraguayo, a** *adj, nm/f*
Paraguayan

paraíso |para'iso| *nm* paradise, heaven

paraje |pa'raxe| *nm* place, spot

paralelo, a [para'lelo, a] *adj* parallel

parálisis [pa'ralisis] *nf inv* paralysis; **paralítico, a** *adj, nm/f* paralytic

paralizar |para'li'θar| *vt* to paralyse; **~se** *vr* to become paralysed; (*fig*) to come to a standstill

paramilitar [paramili'tar] *adj* paramilitary

páramo ['paramo] *nm* bleak plateau

parangón [paran'gon] *nm*: **sin ~** incomparable

paranoico, a [para'noiko, a] *nm/f* paranoiac

parapente [para'pente] *nm* (*deporte*) paragliding; (*aparato*) paraglider

parapléjico, a [para'plexiko, a] *adj, nm/f* paraplegic

parar [pa'rar] *vt* to stop; (*golpe*) to ward off ♦ *vi* to stop; **~se** *vr* to stop; (*AM*) to stand up; **ha parado de llover** it has stopped raining; **van a ir a ~ a comisaría** they're going to end up in the police station; **~se en** to pay attention to

pararrayos [para'rrajos] *nm inv* lightning conductor

parásito, a [pa'rasito, a] *nm/f* parasite

parcela [par'θela] *nf* plot, piece of ground

parche ['partʃe] *nm* (*gen*) patch

parchís [par'tʃis] *nm* ludo

parcial [par'θjal] *adj* (*pago*) part-; (*eclipse*) partial; (*JUR*) prejudiced, biased; (*POL*) partisan; **~idad** *nf* prejudice, bias

pardillo, a [par'ðiʎo, a] (*pey*) *adj* yokel

parecer [pare'θer] *nm* (*opinión*) opinion, view; (*aspecto*) looks *pl* ♦ *vi* (*tener apariencia*) to seem, look; (*asemejarse*) to look o seem like; (*aparecer, llegar*) to appear; **~se** *vr* to look alike, resemble each other; **~se a** to look like, resemble; **según parece** evidently, apparently; **me parece que** I think (that), it seems to me that

parecido, a [pare'θiðo, a] *adj* similar ♦ *nm* similarity, likeness, resemblance;

bien ~ good-looking, nice-looking

pared [pa'reð] *nf* wall

pareja [pa'rexa] *nf* (*par*) pair; (*dos personas*) couple; (*otro: de un par*) other one (of a pair); (*persona*) partner

parentela [paren'tela] *nf* relations *pl*

parentesco [paren'tesko] *nm* relationship

paréntesis [pa'rentesis] *nm inv* parenthesis; (*en escrito*) bracket

parezco *etc vb ver* **parecer**

pariente, a [pa'rjente, a] *nm/f* relative, relation

parir [pa'rir] *vt* to give birth to ♦ *vi* (*mujer*) to give birth, have a baby

París [pa'ris] *n* Paris

parking ['parkin] *nm* car park (*BRIT*), parking lot (*US*)

parlamentar [parlamen'tar] *vi* to parley

parlamentario, a [parlamen'tarjo, a] *adj* parliamentary ♦ *nm/f* member of parliament

parlamento [parla'mento] *nm* parliament

parlanchín, ina [parlan'tʃin, ina] *adj* indiscreet ♦ *nm/f* chatterbox

parlar [par'lar] *vi* to chatter (away)

paro ['paro] *nm* (*huelga*) stoppage (of work), strike; (*desempleo*) unemployment; **subsidio de ~** unemployment benefit

parodia [pa'roðja] *nf* parody; **parodiar** *vt* to parody

parpadear [parpaðe'ar] *vi* (*ojos*) to blink; (*luz*) to flicker

párpado ['parpaðo] *nm* eyelid

parque ['parke] *nm* (*lugar verde*) park; **~ de atracciones/infantil/zoológico** fairground/playground/zoo

parqué [par'ke] *nm* parquet (flooring)

parquímetro [par'kimetro] *nm* parking meter

parra ['parra] *nf* (*grape*)vine

párrafo ['parrafo] *nm* paragraph; **echar un ~** (*fam*) to have a chat

parranda [pa'rranda] (*fam*) *nf* spree,

binge
parrilla [pa'rriʎa] nf (CULIN) grill; (de
coche) grille; **(carne a la)** ~ barbecue;
~da nf barbecue
párroco ['parroko] nm parish priest
parroquia [pa'rrokja] nf parish;
(iglesia) parish church; (com) clientele,
customers pl; **~no,** a nm/f parishioner,
client, customer
parsimonia [parsi'monja] nf
calmness, level-headedness
parte ['parte] nm message; (informe)
report ♦ nf part; (lado, cara) side; (de
reparto) share; (JUR) party; **en alguna**
~ **de Europa** somewhere in Europe;
en/por todas ~s everywhere; **en**
gran ~ to a large extent; **la mayor**
~ **de los españoles** most Spaniards;
de un tiempo a esta ~ for some
time past; **de** ~ **de alguien** on sb's
behalf; **¿de** ~ **de quién?** (TEL) who is
speaking?; **por** ~ **de** on the part of; **yo**
por mí ~ I for my part; **por otra** ~ on
the other hand; **dar** ~ to inform;
tomar ~ to take part
partición [parti'θjon] nf division,
sharing-out; (POL) partition
participación [partiθipa'θjon] nf
(acto) participation, taking part; (parte,
COM) share; (de lotería) shared prize;
(aviso) notice, notification
participante [partiθi'pante] nm/f
participant
participar [partiθi'par] vt to notify,
inform ♦ vi to take part, participate
partícipe [par'tiθipe] nm/f participant
particular [partiku'lar] adj (especial)
particular, special; (individual, personal)
private, personal ♦ nm (punto, asunto)
particular, point; (individuo) individual;
tiene coche ~ he has a car of his own
partida [par'tiða] nf (salida) departure;
(COM) entry, item; (juego) game; (grupo
de personas) band, group; **mala** ~
dirty trick; ~ **de nacimiento /**
matrimonio / defunción birth/
marriage/death certificate

partidario, a [parti'ðarjo, a] adj
partisan ♦ nm/f supporter, follower
partido [par'tiðo] nm (POL) party;
(DEPORTE) game, match; **sacar** ~ **de** to
profit o benefit from; **tomar** ~ to take
sides
partir [par'tir] vt (dividir) to split,
divide; (compartir, distribuir) to share
(out), distribute; (romper) to break
open, split open; (rebanada) to cut
(off) ♦ vi (ponerse en camino) to set off
o out; (comenzar) to start (off o out);
~**se** vr to crack o split o break (in two
etc); **a** ~ **de** (starting) from
partitura [parti'tura] nf (MUS) score
parto ['parto] nm birth; (fig) product,
creation; **estar de** ~ to be in labour
pasa ['pasa] nf raisin; ~ **de Corinto/de**
Esmira currant/sultana
pasada [pa'saða] nf passing, passage;
de ~ in passing, incidentally; **una**
mala ~ a dirty trick
pasadizo [pasa'ðiθo] nm (pasillo)
passage, corridor; (callejuela) alley
pasado, a [pa'saðo, a] adj past; (malo:
comida, fruta) bad; (muy cocido)
overdone; (anticuado) out of date ♦ nm
past; ~ **mañana** the day after
tomorrow; **el mes** ~ last month
pasador [pasa'ðor] nm (cerrojo) bolt;
(de pelo) hair slide; (horquilla) grip
pasaje [pa'saxe] nm passage; (pago de
viaje) fare; (los pasajeros) passengers pl;
(pasillo) passageway
pasajero, a [pasa'xero, a] adj passing;
(situación, estado) temporary; (amor,
enfermedad) brief ♦ nm/f passenger
pasamontañas [pasamon'taɲas] nm
inv balaclava helmet
pasaporte [pasa'porte] nm passport
pasar [pa'sar] vt to pass; (tiempo) to
spend; (desgracias) to suffer, endure;
(noticia) to give, pass on; (río) to cross;
(barrera) to pass through; (falta) to
overlook, tolerate; (contrincante) to
surpass, do better than; (coche) to
overtake; (CINE) to show; (enfermedad)

to give, infect with ♦ vi (gen) to pass; (terminarse) to be over; (ocurrir) to happen; **~se** vr (flores) to fade; (comida) to go bad o off; (fig) to overdo it, go too far; **~ de** to go beyond, exceed; **~ por** (AM) to fetch; **~lo bien/mal** to have a good/bad time; **¡pase!** come in!; **hacer ~** to show in; **~se al enemigo** to go over to the enemy; **se me pasó** I forgot; **no se le pasa nada** he misses nothing; **pase lo que pase** come what may; **¿qué pasa?** what's going on?, what's up?; **¿qué te pasa?** what's wrong?

pasarela [pasa'rela] nf footbridge; (en barco) gangway

pasatiempo [pasa'tjempo] nm pastime, hobby

Pascua ['paskwa] nf: **~ de (Resurrección)** Easter; **~ de Navidad** Christmas; **~s** nfpl Christmas (time); **¡felices ~s!** Merry Christmas!

pase ['pase] nm pass; (CINE) performance, showing

pasear [pase'ar] vt to take for a walk; (exhibir) to parade, show off ♦ vi to walk, go for a walk; **~se** vr to walk, go for a walk; **paseo** nm (avenida) avenue; (distancia corta) walk, stroll; **dar un** o **ir de paseo** to go for a walk

pasillo [pa'siʎo] nm passage, corridor

pasión [pa'sjon] nf passion

pasivo, a [pa'siβo, a] adj passive; (inactivo) inactive ♦ nm (COM) liabilities pl, debts pl

pasmar [pas'mar] vt (asombrar) to amaze, astonish; **pasmo** nm amazement, astonishment; (resfriado) chill; (fig) wonder, marvel; **pasmoso, a** adj amazing, astonishing

paso, a [paso, a] adj dried ♦ nm step; (modo de andar) walk; (huella) footprint; (rapidez) speed, pace, rate; (camino accesible) way through, passage; (cruce) crossing; (pasaje)

passing, passage; (GEO) pass; (estrecho) strait; **~ a nivel** (FERRO) level-crossing; **~ de peatones** pedestrian crossing; **a ese ~** (fig) at that rate; **salir al ~ de** o **a** to waylay; **estar de ~** to be passing through; **~ elevado** flyover; **prohibido el ~** no entry; **ceda el ~** give way

pasota [pa'sota] adj, nm/f ≈ dropout; **ser un (tipo) ~** to be a bit of a dropout; (ser indiferente) not to care about anything

pasta ['pasta] nf paste; (CULIN: masa) dough; (: de bizcochos etc) pastry; (fam) dough; **~s** nfpl (bizcochos) pastries, small cakes; (fideos, espaguetis etc) pasta; **~ de dientes** o **dentífrica** toothpaste

pastar [pas'tar] vt, vi to graze

pastel [pas'tel] nm (dulce) cake; (ARTE) pastel; **~ de carne** meat pie; **~ería** nf cake shop

pasteurizado, a [pasteuri'θaðo, a] adj pasteurized

pastilla [pas'tiʎa] nf (de jabón, chocolate) bar; (píldora) tablet, pill

pasto ['pasto] nm (hierba) grass; (lugar) pasture, field

pastor, a [pas'tor, a] nm/f shepherd/ ess ♦ nm (REL) clergyman, pastor; **~ alemán** Alsatian

pata ['pata] nf (pierna) leg; (pie) foot; (de muebles) leg; **~s arriba** upside down; **metedura de ~** (fam) gaffe; **meter la ~** (fam) to put one's foot in it; (TEC): **~ de cabra** crowbar; **tener buena/mala ~** to be lucky/unlucky; **~da** nf kick; (en el suelo) stamp

patalear [patale'ar] vi (en el suelo) to stamp one's feet

patata [pa'tata] nf potato; **~s fritas** chips, French fries; (de bolsa) crisps

paté [pa'te] nm pâté

patear [pate'ar] vt (pisar) to stamp on, trample (on); (pegar con el pie) to kick ♦ vi to stamp (with rage), stamp one's feet

patentar [paten'tar] vt to patent

patente [pa'tente] adj obvious, evident; (COM) patent ♦ nf patent

paternal [pater'nal] adj fatherly, paternal; **paterno, a** adj paternal

patético, a [pa'tetiko, a] adj pathetic, moving

patilla [pa'tiʎa] nf (de gafas) side(piece); ~s nfpl sideburns

patín [pa'tin] nm skate; (de trineo) runner; **patinaje** nm skating; **patinar** vi to skate; (resbalarse) to skid, slip; (fam) to slip up, blunder

patio ['patjo] nm (de casa) patio, courtyard; ~ **de recreo** playground

pato ['pato] nm duck; **pagar el ~** (fam) to take the blame, carry the can

patológico, a [pato'loxiko, a] adj pathological

patoso, a [pa'toso, a] (fam) adj clumsy

patraña [pa'traɲa] nf story, fib

patria ['patrja] nf native land, mother country

patrimonio [patri'monjo] nm inheritance; (fig) heritage

patriota [pa'trjota] nmf patriot; **patriotismo** nm patriotism

patrocinar [patroθi'nar] vt to sponsor; **patrocinio** nm sponsorship

patrón, ona [pa'tron, ona] nm/f (jefe) boss, chief, master/mistress; (propietario) landlord/lady; (REL) patron saint ♦ nm (TEC, COSTURA) pattern

patronal [patro'nal] adj: **la clase ~** management

patronato [patro'nato] nm sponsorship; (acto) patronage; (fundación benéfica) trust, foundation

patrulla [pa'truʎa] nf patrol

pausa ['pausa] nf pause, break

pausado, a [pau'saðo, a] adj slow, deliberate

pauta ['pauta] nf line, guide line

pavimento [paßi'mento] nm (con losas) pavement, paving

pavo ['paßo] nm turkey; ~ **real** peacock

pavor [pa'ßor] nm dread, terror

payaso, a [pa'jaso, a] nm/f clown

payo, a ['pajo, a] nm/f non-gipsy

paz [paθ] nf peace; (tranquilidad) peacefulness, tranquillity; **hacer las paces** to make peace; (fig) to make up

pazo ['paθo] nm country house

P.D. abr (= posdata) P.S., p.s.

peaje [pe'axe] nm toll

peatón [pea'ton] nm pedestrian

peca ['peka] nf freckle

pecado [pe'kaðo] nm sin; **pecador, a** adj sinful ♦ nm/f sinner

pecaminoso, a [pekami'noso, a] adj sinful

pecar [pe'kar] vi (REL) to sin; **peca de generoso** he is generous to a fault

pecera [pe'θera] nf fish tank; (redondo) goldfish bowl

pecho ['petʃo] nm (ANAT) chest; (de mujer) breast; **dar el ~ a** to breast-feed; **tomar algo a ~** to take sth to heart

pechuga [pe'tʃuʎa] nf breast

peculiar [peku'ljar] adj special, peculiar; (característico) typical, characteristic; ~**idad** nf peculiarity; special feature, characteristic

pedal [pe'ðal] nm pedal; ~**ear** vi to pedal

pedante [pe'ðante] adj pedantic ♦ nm/f pedant; ~**ría** nf pedantry

pedazo [pe'ðaθo] nm piece, bit; **hacerse ~s** to smash, shatter

pedernal [peðer'nal] nm flint

pediatra [pe'ðjatra] nm/f paediatrician

pedido [pe'ðiðo] nm (COM) order; (petición) request

pedir [pe'ðir] vt to ask for, request; (comida, COM: mandar) to order; (necesitar) to need, demand, require ♦ vi to ask; **me pidió que cerrara la puerta** he asked me to shut the door; **¿cuánto piden por el coche?** how much are they asking for the car?

pedo ['peðo] nm (fam!) fart

pega ['pexa] nf snag; **poner ~s (a)** to

complain (about)

pegadizo, a [peɣaˈðiθo, a] adj (MUS) catchy

pegajoso, a [peɣaˈxoso, a] adj sticky, adhesive

pegamento [peɣaˈmento] nm gum, glue

pegar [peˈɣar] vt (papel, sellos) to stick (on); (cartel) to stick up; (coser) to sew (on); (unir: partes) to join, fix together; (MED) to give, infect with; (dar: golpe) to give, deal ♦ vi (adherirse) to stick, adhere; (ir juntos: colores) to match, go together; (golpear) to hit; (quemar: el sol) to strike hot, burn (fig); **~se** vr (gen) to stick; (dos personas) to hit each other, fight; (fam): **~ un grito** to let out a yell; **~ un salto** to jump (with fright); **~ en** to touch; **~se un tiro** to shoot o.s.

pegatina [peɣaˈtina] nf sticker

pegote [peˈɣote] nm (fam) eyesore, sight

peinado [peiˈnaðo] nm hairstyle

peinar [peiˈnar] vt to comb; (hacer estilo) to style; **~se** vr to comb one's hair

peine [ˈpeine] nm comb; **~ta** nf ornamental comb

p.ej. abr (= por ejemplo) e.g.

Pekín [peˈkin] n Pekin(g)

pelado, a [peˈlaðo, a] adj (fruta, patata etc) peeled; (cabeza) shorn; (campo, fig) bare; (fam: sin dinero) broke

pelaje [peˈlaxe] nm (ZOOL) fur, coat; (fig) appearance

pelar [peˈlar] vt (fruta, patatas etc) to peel; (cortar el pelo a) to cut the hair of; (quitar la piel: animal) to skin; **~se** vr (la piel) to peel off; **voy a ~me** I'm going to get my hair cut

peldaño [pelˈdaɲo] nm step

pelea [peˈlea] nf (lucha) fight; (discusión) quarrel, row

peleado, a [peˈleaðo, a] adj: **estar ~ (con uno)** to have fallen out (with sb)

pelear [peleˈar] vi to fight; **~se** vr to fight; (reñirse) to fall out, quarrel

peletería [peleteˈria] nf furrier's, fur shop

pelícano [peˈlikano] nm pelican

película [peˈlikula] nf film; (cobertura ligera) thin covering; (FOTO: rollo) roll o reel of film

peligro [peˈliɣro] nm danger; (riesgo) risk; **correr ~ de** to run the risk of; **~so, a** adj dangerous; risky

pelirrojo, a [peliˈrroxo, a] adj red-haired, red-headed ♦ nm/f redhead

pellejo [peˈʎexo] nm (de animal) skin, hide

pellizcar [peʎiθˈkar] vt to pinch, nip

pelma [ˈpelma] (fam) nm/f pain (in the neck)

pelmazo [pelˈmaθo] (fam) nm = **pelma**

pelo [ˈpelo] nm (cabellos) hair; (de barba, bigote) whisker; (de animal: pellejo) hair, fur, coat; **al ~** just right; **venir al ~** to be exactly what one needs; **un hombre de ~ en pecho** a brave man; **por los ~s** by the skin of one's teeth; **no tener ~s en la lengua** to be outspoken, not mince words; **tomar el ~ a uno** to pull sb's leg

pelota [peˈlota] nf ball; **en ~** stark naked; **hacer la ~ (a uno)** (fam) to creep (to sb); **~ vasca** pelota

pelotari [peloˈtari] nm pelota player

pelotón [peloˈton] nm (MIL) squad, detachment

peluca [peˈluka] nf wig

peluche [peˈlutʃe] nm: **oso/muñeco de ~** teddy bear/soft toy

peludo, a [peˈluðo, a] adj hairy, shaggy

peluquería [pelukeˈria] nf hairdresser's; **peluquero, a** nm/f hairdresser

pelusa [peˈlusa] nf (BOT) down; (en tela) fluff

pena [ˈpena] nf (congoja) grief,

sadness; (*remordimiento*) regret;
(*dificultad*) trouble; (*dolor*) pain; (*JUR*)
sentence; **merecer** o **valer la ~** to be
worthwhile; **a duras ~s** with great
difficulty; **~ de muerte** death penalty;
~ pecuniaria fine; **¡qué ~!** what a
shame!

penal [pe'nal] *adj* penal ♦ *nm* (*cárcel*)
prison

penalidad [penali'ðað] *nf* (*problema,
dificultad*) trouble, hardship; (*JUR*)
penalty, punishment; **~es** *nfpl* trouble,
hardship

penalti, penalty [pe'nalti] (*pl* **~s** o
~es) *nm* penalty (kick)

pendiente [pen'djente] *adj* pending,
unsettled ♦ *nm* earring ♦ *nf* hill, slope

pene ['pene] *nm* penis

penetración [penetra'θjon] *nf* (*acto*)
penetration; (*agudeza*) sharpness,
insight

penetrante [pene'trante] *adj* (*herida*)
deep; (*persona, arma*) sharp; (*sonido*)
penetrating, piercing; (*mirada*)
searching; (*viento, ironía*) biting

penetrar [pene'trar] *vt* to penetrate,
pierce; (*entender*) to grasp ♦ *vi* to
penetrate, go in; (*entrar*) to enter, go
in; (*líquido*) to soak in; (*fig*) to pierce

penicilina [peniθi'lina] *nf* penicillin

península [pe'ninsula] *nf* peninsula;
peninsular *adj* peninsular

penique [pe'nike] *nm* penny

penitencia [peni'tenθja] *nf* penance

penoso, a [pe'noso, a] *adj*
(*lamentable*) distressing; (*difícil*)
arduous, difficult

pensador, a [pensa'ðor, a] *nm/f*
thinker

pensamiento [pensa'mjento] *nm*
thought; (*mente*) mind; (*idea*) idea

pensar [pen'sar] *vt* to think;
(*considerar*) to think over, think out;
(*proponerse*) to intend, plan;
(*imaginarse*) to think up, invent ♦ *vi* to
think; **~ en** to aim at, aspire to;
pensativo, a *adj* thoughtful, pensive

pensión [pen'sjon] *nf* (*casa*) boarding
o guest house; (*dinero*) pension; (*cama
y comida*) board and lodging;
~ completa full board; **media ~** half-
board; **pensionista** *nm/f* (*jubilado*)
(old-age) pensioner; (*huésped*) lodger

penúltimo, a [pe'nultimo, a] *adj*
penultimate, last but one

penumbra [pe'numbra] *nf* half-light

penuria [pe'nurja] *nf* shortage, want

peña ['peɲa] *nf* (*roca*) rock; (*cuesta*)
cliff, crag; (*grupo*) group, circle; (*AM:
club*) folk club

peñasco [pe'ɲasko] *nm* large rock,
boulder

peñón [pe'ɲon] *nm* wall of rock; **el P~**
the Rock (of Gibraltar)

peón [pe'on] *nm* labourer; (*AM*) farm
labourer, farmhand; (*AJEDREZ*) pawn

peonza [pe'onθa] *nf* spinning top

peor [pe'or] *adj* (*comparativo*) worse;
(*superlativo*) worst ♦ *adv* worse; worst;
de mal en ~ from bad to worse

pepinillo [pepi'niʎo] *nm* gherkin

pepino [pe'pino] *nm* cucumber; (**no**)
me importa un ~ I don't care one bit

pepita [pe'pita] *nf* (*BOT*) pip; (*MINERÍA*)
nugget

pepito [pe'pito] *nm*: **~ (de ternera)**
steak sandwich

pequeñez [peke'neθ] *nf* smallness,
littleness; (*trivialidad*) trifle, triviality

pequeño, a [pe'keɲo, a] *adj* small,
little

pera ['pera] *nf* pear; **peral** *nm* pear
tree

percance [per'kanθe] *nm* setback,
misfortune

percatarse [perka'tarse] *vr*: **~ de** to
notice, take note of

percebe [per'θeβe] *nm* barnacle

percepción [perθep'θjon] *nf* (*vista*)
perception; (*idea*) notion, idea

percha ['pertʃa] *nf* (*coat*)hanger;
(*ganchos*) coat hooks *pl*; (*de ave*) perch

percibir [perθi'βir] *vt* to perceive,
notice; (*COM*) to earn, get

percusión [perku'sjon] nf percussion
perdedor, a [perðe'ðor, a] adj losing
♦ nm/f loser
perder [per'ðer] vt to lose; (tiempo,
palabras) to waste; (oportunidad) to
lose, miss; (tren) to miss ♦ vi to lose;
~se vr (extraviarse) to get lost;
(desaparecer) to disappear, be lost to
view; (arruinarse) to be ruined; **echar
a ~** (comida) to spoil, ruin;
(oportunidad) to waste
perdición [perði'θjon] nf perdition,
ruin
pérdida ['perðiða] nf loss; (de tiempo)
waste; **~s** nfpl (COM) losses
perdido, a [per'ðiðo, a] adj lost
perdiz [per'ðiθ] nf partridge
perdón [per'ðon] nm (disculpa)
pardon, forgiveness; (clemencia) mercy;
¡**~!** sorry!, I beg your pardon!;
perdonar vt to pardon, forgive; (la
vida) to spare; (excusar) to exempt,
excuse; ¡**perdone (usted)!** sorry!, I
beg your pardon!
perdurar [perðu'rar] vi (resistir) to last,
endure; (seguir existiendo) to stand, still
exist
perecedero, a [pereθe'ðero, a] adj
perishable
perecer [pere'θer] vi to perish, die
peregrinación [pereɣrina'θjon] nf
(REL) pilgrimage
peregrino, a [pere'ɣrino, a] adj (idea)
strange, absurd ♦ nm/f pilgrim
perejil [pere'xil] nm parsley
perenne [pe'renne] adj everlasting,
perennial
pereza [pe'reθa] nf laziness, idleness;
perezoso, a adj lazy, idle
perfección [perfek'θjon] nf perfection;
perfeccionar vt to perfect; (mejorar)
to improve; (acabar) to complete,
finish
perfectamente [perfekta'mente] adv
perfectly
perfecto, a [per'fekto, a] adj perfect;
(total) complete

perfil [per'fil] nm profile; (contorno)
silhouette, outline; (ARQ) (cross)
section; **~es** nmpl features; **~ar** vt
(trazar) to outline; (fig) to shape, give
character to
perforación [perfora'θjon] nf
perforation; (con taladro) drilling;
perforadora nf punch
perforar [perfo'rar] vt to perforate;
(agujero) to drill, bore; (papel) to
punch a hole in ♦ vi to drill, bore
perfume [per'fume] nm perfume,
scent
pericia [pe'riθja] nf skill, expertise
periferia [peri'ferja] nf periphery; (de
ciudad) outskirts pl
periférico [peri'feriko] (AM) nm ring
road (BRIT), beltway (US)
perímetro [pe'rimetro] nm perimeter
periódico, a [pe'rjoðiko, a] adj
periodic(al) ♦ nm newspaper
periodismo [perjo'ðismo] nm
journalism; **periodista** nm/f journalist
periodo [pe'rjoðo] nm period
período [pe'rioðo] nm = **periodo**
periquito [peri'kito] nm budgerigar,
budgie
perito, a [pe'rito, a] adj (experto)
expert; (diestro) skilled, skilful ♦ nm/f
expert; skilled worker; (técnico)
technician
perjudicar [perxuði'kar] vt (gen) to
damage, harm; **perjudicial** adj
damaging, harmful; (en detrimento)
detrimental; **perjuicio** nm damage,
harm
perjurar [perxu'rar] vi to commit
perjury
perla ['perla] nf pearl; **me viene de
~s** it suits me fine
permanecer [permane'θer] vi
(quedarse) to stay, remain; (seguir) to
continue to be
permanencia [perma'nenθja] nf
permanence; (estancia) stay
permanente [perma'nente] adj
permanent, constant ♦ nf perm

permiso [per'miso] nm permission; (licencia) permit, licence; **con ~** excuse me; **estar de ~** (MIL) to be on leave; **~ de conducir** driving licence (BRIT), driver's license (US)

permitir [permi'tir] vt to permit, allow

pernera [per'nera] nf trouser leg

pernicioso, a [perni'θjoso, a] adj pernicious

pero ['pero] conj but; (aún) yet ♦ nm (defecto) flaw, defect; (reparo) objection

perpendicular [perpendiku'lar] adj perpendicular

perpetrar [perpe'trar] vt to perpetrate

perpetuar [perpe'twar] vt to perpetuate; **perpetuo, a** adj perpetual

perplejo, a [per'plexo, a] adj perplexed, bewildered

perra ['perra] nf (ZOOL) bitch; **estar sin una ~** to be flat broke

perrera [pe'rrera] nf kennel

perrito [pe'rrito] nm: **~ caliente** hot dog

perro ['perro] nm dog

persa ['persa] adj, nm/f Persian

persecución [perseku'θjon] nf pursuit, chase; (REL, POL) persecution

perseguir [perse'xir] vt to pursue, hunt; (cortejar) to chase after; (molestar) to pester, annoy; (REL, POL) to persecute

perseverante [perseβe'rante] adj persevering, persistent

perseverar [perseβe'rar] vi to persevere, persist

persiana [per'sjana] nf (Venetian) blind

persignarse [persix'narse] vr to cross o.s.

persistente [persis'tente] adj persistent

persistir [persis'tir] vi to persist

persona [per'sona] nf person; **~ mayor** elderly person

personaje [perso'naxe] nm important person, celebrity; (TEATRO etc) character

personal [perso'nal] adj (particular) personal; (para una persona) single, for one person ♦ nm personnel, staff; **~idad** nf personality

personarse [perso'narse] vr to appear in person

personificar [personifi'kar] vt to personify

perspectiva [perspek'tiβa] nf perspective; (vista, panorama) view, panorama; (posibilidad futura) outlook, prospect

perspicacia [perspi'kaθja] nf discernment, perspicacity

perspicaz [perspi'kaθ] adj shrewd

persuadir [perswa'ðir] vt (gen) to persuade; (convencer) to convince; **~se** vr to become convinced; **persuasión** nf persuasion; **persuasivo, a** adj persuasive; convincing

pertenecer [pertene'θer] vi to belong; (fig) to concern; **perteneciente** adj: **perteneciente a** belonging to; **pertenencia** nf ownership; **pertenencias** nfpl (bienes) possessions, property sg

pertenezca etc vb ver **pertenecer**

pértiga ['pertiva] nf: **salto de ~** pole vault

pertinente [perti'nente] adj relevant, pertinent; (apropiado) appropriate; **~ a** concerning, relevant to

perturbación [perturβa'θjon] nf (POL) disturbance; (MED) upset, disturbance

perturbado, a [pertur'βaðo, a] adj mentally unbalanced

perturbar [pertur'βar] vt (el orden) to disturb; (MED) to upset, disturb; (mentalmente) to perturb

Perú [pe'ru] nm: **el ~** Peru; **peruano, a** adj, nm/f Peruvian

perversión [perβer'sjon] nf perversion; **perverso, a** adj perverse; (depravado) depraved

pervertido, a [perβer'tiðo, a] adj perverted ♦ nm/f pervert

pervertir [perßer'tir] vt to pervert, corrupt

pesa ['pesa] nf weight; (DEPORTE) shot

pesadez [pesa'ðeθ] nf (peso) heaviness; (lentitud) slowness; (aburrimiento) tediousness

pesadilla [pesa'ðiʎa] nf nightmare, bad dream

pesado, a [pe'saðo, a] adj heavy; (lento) slow; (difícil, duro) tough, hard; (aburrido) boring, tedious; (tiempo) sultry

pésame ['pesame] nm expression of condolence, message of sympathy; **dar el ~** to express one's condolences

pesar [pe'sar] vt to weigh ♦ vi to weigh; (ser pesado) to weigh a lot, be heavy; (fig: opinión) to carry weight; **no pesa mucho** it is not very heavy ♦ nm (arrepentimiento) regret; (pena) grief, sorrow; **a ~ de** o **pese a** (que) in spite of, despite

pesca ['peska] nf (acto) fishing; (lo pescado) catch; **ir de ~** to go fishing

pescadería [peskaðe'ria] nf fish shop, fishmonger's (BRIT)

pescadilla [peska'ðiʎa] nf whiting

pescado [pes'kaðo] nm fish

pescador, a [peska'ðor, a] nm/f fisherman/woman

pescar [pes'kar] vt (tomar) to catch; (intentar tomar) to fish for; (conseguir: trabajo) to manage to get ♦ vi to fish, go fishing

pescuezo [pes'kweθo] nm neck

pesebre [pe'seßre] nm manger

peseta [pe'seta] nf peseta

pesimista [pesi'mista] adj pessimistic ♦ nm/f pessimist

pésimo, a ['pesimo, a] adj awful, dreadful

peso ['peso] nm weight; (balanza) scales pl; (moneda) peso; ~ **bruto/neto** gross/net weight; **vender al ~** to sell by weight

pesquero, a [pes'kero, a] adj fishing cpd

pesquisa [pes'kisa] nf inquiry

pestaña [pes'taɲa] nf (ANAT) eyelash; (borde) rim; **pestañear** vi to blink

peste ['peste] nf plague; (mal olor) stink, stench

pesticida [pesti'θiða] nm pesticide

pestillo [pes'tiʎo] nm (cerrojo) bolt; (picaporte) doorhandle

petaca [pe'taka] nf (de cigarros) cigarette case; (de pipa) tobacco pouch; (AM: maleta) suitcase

pétalo ['petalo] nm petal

petardo [pe'tarðo] nm firework, firecracker

petición [peti'θjon] nf (pedido) request, plea; (memorial) petition; (JUR) plea

petrificar [petrifi'kar] vt to petrify

petróleo [pe'troleo] nm oil, petroleum; **petrolero, a** adj petroleum cpd ♦ nm (oil) tanker

peyorativo, a [pejora'tißo, a] adj pejorative

pez [peθ] nm fish

pezón [pe'θon] nm teat, nipple

pezuña [pe'θuɲa] nf hoof

piadoso, a [pja'ðoso, a] adj (devoto) pious, devout; (misericordioso) kind, merciful

pianista [pja'nista] nm/f pianist

piano ['pjano] nm piano

piar [pjar] vi to cheep

pibe, a ['piße, a] (AM) nm/f boy/girl

picadero [pika'ðero] nm riding school

picadillo [pika'ðiʎo] nm mince, minced meat

picado, a [pi'kaðo, a] adj pricked, punctured; (CULIN) minced, chopped; (mar) choppy; (diente) bad; (tabaco) cut; (enfadado) cross

picador [pika'ðor] nm (TAUR) picador; (minero) faceworker

picadura [pika'ðura] nf (pinchazo) puncture; (de abeja) sting; (de mosquito) bite; (tabaco picado) cut tobacco

picante [pi'kante] adj hot; (comentario) racy, spicy

picaporte [pika'porte] nm (manija) doorhandle; (pestillo) latch

picar [pi'kar] vt (agujerear, perforar) to prick, puncture; (abeja) to sting; (mosquito, serpiente) to bite; (CULIN) to mince, chop; (incitar) to incite, goad; (dañar, irritar) to annoy, bother; (quemar: lengua) to burn, sting ♦ vi (pez) to bite, take the bait; (sol) to burn, scorch; (abeja, MED) to sting; (mosquito) to bite; ~se vr (agriarse) to turn sour, go off; (ofenderse) to take offence

picardía [pikar'ðia] nf villainy; (astucia) slyness, craftiness; (una ~) dirty trick; (palabra) rude/bad word o expression

pícaro, a ['pikaro, a] adj (malicioso) villainous; (travieso) mischievous ♦ nm (astuto) crafty sort; (sinvergüenza) rascal, scoundrel

pichón [pi'tʃon] nm young pigeon

pico ['piko] nm (de ave) beak; (punta) sharp point; (TEC) pick, pickaxe; (GEO) peak, summit; **y ~** and a bit

picor [pi'kor] nm itch

picotear [pikote'ar] vt to peck ♦ vi to nibble, pick

picudo, a [pi'kuðo, a] adj pointed, with a point

pidió etc vb ver **pedir**

pido etc vb ver **pedir**

pie [pje] (pl ~s) nm foot; (fig: motivo) motive, basis; (: fundamento) foothold; **ir a ~** to go on foot, walk; **estar de ~** to be standing (up); **ponerse de ~** to stand up; **de ~s a cabeza** from top to bottom; **al ~ de la letra** (citar) literally, verbatim; (copiar) exactly, word for word; **en ~ de guerra** on a war footing; **dar ~ a** to give cause for; **hacer ~** (en el agua) to touch the bottom

piedad [pje'ðað] nf (lástima) pity, compassion; (clemencia) mercy; (devoción) piety, devotion

piedra ['pjeðra] nf stone; (roca) rock; (de mechero) flint; (METEOROLOGÍA) hailstone

piel [pjel] nf (ANAT) skin; (ZOOL) skin, hide, fur; (cuero) leather; (BOT) skin, peel

pienso etc vb ver **pensar**

pierdo etc vb ver **perder**

pierna ['pjerna] nf leg

pieza ['pjeθa] nf piece; (habitación) room; **~ de recambio** o **repuesto** spare (part)

pigmeo, a [pix'meo, a] adj, nm/f pigmy

pijama [pi'xama] nm pyjamas pl

pila ['pila] nf (ELEC) battery; (montón) heap, pile; (lavabo) sink

píldora ['pilðora] nf pill; **la ~** (anticonceptiva) the (contraceptive) pill

pileta [pi'leta] nf basin, bowl; (AM) swimming pool

pillaje [pi'ʎaxe] nm pillage, plunder

pillar [pi'ʎar] vt (saquear) to pillage, plunder; (fam: coger) to catch; (: agarrar) to grasp, seize; (: entender) to grasp, catch on to; **~se** vr: **~se un dedo con la puerta** to catch one's finger in the door

pillo, a ['piʎo, a] adj villainous; (astuto) sly, crafty ♦ nm/f rascal, rogue, scoundrel

piloto [pi'loto] nm pilot; (de aparato) (pilot) light; (AUTO: luz) tail o rear light; (: conductor) driver

pimentón [pimen'ton] nm paprika

pimienta [pi'mjenta] nf pepper

pimiento [pi'mjento] nm pepper, pimiento

pin [pin] (pl pins) nm badge

pinacoteca [pinako'teka] nf art gallery

pinar [pi'nar] nm pine forest (BRIT), pine grove (US)

pincel [pin'θel] nm paintbrush

pinchadiscos [pintʃa'ðiskos] nm/f inv disc-jockey, DJ

pinchar [pin'tʃar] vt (perforar) to prick,

pierce; (*neumático*) to puncture; (*fig*) to prod

pinchazo [pin'tʃaθo] *nm* (*perforación*) prick; (*de neumático*) puncture; (*fig*) prod

pincho ['pintʃo] *nm* savoury (snack); ~ **moruno** shish kebab; ~ **de tortilla** small slice of omelette

ping-pong ['pin'pon] *nm* table tennis

pingüino [pin'gwino] *nm* penguin

pino ['pino] *nm* pine (tree)

pinta ['pinta] *nf* spot; (*de líquidos*) spot, drop; (*aspecto*) appearance, look(s) (*pl*); ~**do, a** *adj* spotted; (*de colores*) colourful; ~**das** *nfpl* graffiti *sg*

pintar [pin'tar] *vt* to paint ♦ *vi* to paint; (*fam*) to count, be important; ~**se** *vr* to put on make-up

pintor, a [pin'tor, a] *nm/f* painter

pintoresco, a [pinto'resko, a] *adj* picturesque

pintura [pin'tura] *nf* painting; ~ **a la acuarela** watercolour; ~ **al óleo** oil painting

pinza ['pinθa] *nf* (*ZOOL*) claw; (*para colgar ropa*) clothes peg; (*TEC*) pincers *pl*; ~**s** *nfpl* (*para depilar etc*) tweezers *pl*

piña ['pina] *nf* (*fruto del pino*) pine cone; (*fruta*) pineapple; (*fig*) group

piñón [pi'non] *nm* (*fruta*) pine nut; (*TEC*) pinion

pío, a ['pio, a] *adj* (*devoto*) pious, devout; (*misericordioso*) merciful

piojo ['pjoxo] *nm* louse

pionero, a [pjo'nero, a] *adj* pioneering ♦ *nm/f* pioneer

pipa ['pipa] *nf* pipe; ~**s** *nfpl* (*BOT*) (edible) sunflower seeds

pipí [pi'pi] (*fam*) *nm*: **hacer** ~ to have a wee(-wee) (*BRIT*), have to go (wee-wee) (*US*)

pique ['pike] *nm* (*resentimiento*) pique, resentment; (*rivalidad*) rivalry, competition; **irse a** ~ to sink; (*esperanza, familia*) to be ruined

piqueta [pi'keta] *nf* pick(axe)

piquete [pi'kete] *nm* (*MIL*) squad,

party; (*de obreros*) picket

pirado, a [pi'raðo, a] (*fam*) *adj* round the bend ♦ *nm/f* nutter

piragua [pi'rawa] *nf* canoe; **piragüismo** *nm* canoeing

pirámide [pi'ramiðe] *nf* pyramid

pirata [pi'rata] *adj, nm* pirate ♦ *nm/f*: ~ **informático/a** hacker

Pirineo(s) [piri'neo(s)] *nm(pl)* Pyrenees *pl*

pirómano, a [pi'romano, a] *nm/f* (*MED, JUR*) arsonist

piropo [pi'ropo] *nm* compliment, (piece of) flattery

pirueta [pi'rweta] *nf* pirouette

pis [pis] (*fam*) *nm* pee, piss; **hacer** ~ to have a pee; (*para niños*) to wee-wee

pisada [pi'saða] *nf* (*paso*) footstep; (*huella*) footprint

pisar [pi'sar] *vt* (*caminar sobre*) to walk on, tread on; (*apretar con el pie*) to press; (*fig*) to trample on, walk all over ♦ *vi* to tread, step, walk

piscina [pis'θina] *nf* swimming pool

Piscis ['pisθis] *nm* Pisces

piso ['piso] *nm* (*suelo, planta*) floor; (*apartamento*) flat (*BRIT*), apartment; **primer** ~ (*ESP*) first floor; (*AM*) ground floor

pisotear [pisote'ar] *vt* to trample (on *o* underfoot)

pista ['pista] *nf* track, trail; (*indicio*) clue; ~ **de aterrizaje** runway; ~ **de baile** dance floor; ~ **de hielo** ice rink; ~ **de tenis** tennis court

pistola [pis'tola] *nf* pistol; (*TEC*) spray-gun; **pistolero, a** *nm/f* gunman/woman, gangster

pistón [pis'ton] *nm* (*TEC*) piston; (*MUS*) key

pitar [pi'tar] *vt* (*silbato*) to blow; (*rechiflar*) to whistle at, boo ♦ *vi* to whistle; (*AUTO*) to sound *o* toot one's horn; (*AM*) to smoke

pitillo [pi'tiʎo] *nm* cigarette

pito ['pito] *nm* whistle; (*de coche*) horn

pitón [pi'ton] *nm* (*ZOOL*) python

pitonisa [pito'nisa] nf fortune-teller

pitorreo [pito'rreo] nm joke; **estar de ~** to be joking

pizarra [pi'θarra] nf (piedra) slate; (encerado) blackboard

pizca ['piθka] nf pinch, spot; (fig) spot, speck; **ni ~** not a bit

placa ['plaka] nf plate; (distintivo) badge, insignia; **~ de matrícula** number plate

placentero, a [plaθen'tero, a] adj pleasant, agreeable

placer [pla'θer] nm pleasure ♦ vt to please

plácido, a ['plaθiðo, a] adj placid

plaga ['plaɣa] nf plague; (MED) plague; (abundancia) abundance; **plagar** vt to infest, plague; (llenar) to fill

plagio ['plaxjo] nm plagiarism

plan [plan] nm (esquema, proyecto) plan; (idea, intento) idea, intention; **tener ~** (fam) to have a date; **tener un ~** (fam) to have an affair; **en ~ económico** (fam) on the cheap; **vamos en ~ de turismo** we're going as tourists; **si te pones en ese ~ ...** if that's your attitude ...

plana ['plana] nf sheet (of paper), page; (TEC) trowel; **en primera ~** on the front page; **~ mayor** staff

plancha ['plantʃa] nf (para planchar) iron; (rótulo) plate, sheet; (NAUT) gangway; **a la ~** (CULIN) grilled; **~do** nm ironing; **planchar** vt to iron ♦ vi to do the ironing

planeador [planea'ðor] nm glider

planear [plane'ar] vt to plan ♦ vi to glide

planeta [pla'neta] nm planet

planicie [pla'niθje] nf plain

planificación [planifika'θjon] nf planning; **~ familiar** family planning

plano, a ['plano, a] adj flat, level, even ♦ nm (MAT, TEC) plane; (FOTO) shot; (ARQ) plan; (GEO) map; (de ciudad) map, street plan; **primer ~** close-up; **caer de ~** to fall flat

planta ['planta] nf (BOT, TEC) plant; (ANAT) sole of the foot, foot; (piso) floor; (AM: personal) staff; **~ baja** ground floor

plantación [planta'θjon] nf (AGR) plantation; (acto) planting

plantar [plan'tar] vt (BOT) to plant; (levantar) to erect, set up; **~se** vr to stand firm; **~ a uno en la calle** to throw sb out; **dejar plantado a uno** (fam) to stand sb up

plantear [plante'ar] vt (problema) to pose; (dificultad) to raise

plantilla [plan'tiʎa] nf (de zapato) insole; (personal) personnel; **ser de ~** to be on the staff

plantón [plan'ton] nm (MIL) guard, sentry; (fam) long wait; **dar (un) ~ a uno** to stand sb up

plasmar [plas'mar] vt (dar forma) to mould, shape; (representar) to represent; **~se** vr: **~se en** to take the form of

plasta ['plasta] (fam) adj inv boring ♦ nm/f bore

plástico, a ['plastiko, a] adj plastic ♦ nm plastic

Plastilina ® [plasti'lina] nf Plasticina ®

plata ['plata] nf (metal) silver; (cosas hechas de ~) silverware; (AM) cash, dough; **hablar en ~** to speak bluntly o frankly

plataforma [plata'forma] nf platform; **~ de lanzamiento/perforación** launch(ing) pad/drilling rig

plátano ['platano] nm (fruta) banana; (árbol) plane tree; banana tree

platea [pla'tea] nf (TEATRO) pit

plateado, a [plate'aðo, a] adj silver; (TEC) silver-plated

plática ['platika] nf talk, chat; **platicar** vi to talk, chat

platillo [pla'tiʎo] nm saucer; **~s** nmpl (MUS) cymbals; **~ volador** o **volante** flying saucer

platino [pla'tino] nm platinum; **~s**

nmpl (AUTO) contact points

plato ['plato] *nm* plate, dish; *(parte de comida)* course; *(comida)* dish;
~ **combinado** set main course *(served on one plate)*; ~ **fuerte** main course;
primer ~ first course

playa ['plaja] *nf* beach; *(costa)* seaside;
~ **de estacionamiento** (AM) car park

playera [pla'jera] *nf* (AM: *camiseta*) T-shirt; ~**s** *nfpl* (*zapatos*) canvas shoes

plaza ['plaθa] *nf* square; *(mercado)* market(place); *(sitio)* room, space; *(en vehículo)* seat, place; *(colocación)* post, job; ~ **de toros** bullring

plazo ['plaθo] *nm* (*lapso de tiempo*) time, period; *(fecha de vencimiento)* expiry date; *(pago parcial)* instalment;
a corto/largo ~ short-/long-term;
comprar algo a ~**s** to buy sth on hire purchase (BRIT) o on time (US)

plazoleta [plaθo'leta] *nf* small square

pleamar [plea'mar] *nf* high tide

plebe ['pleβe] *nf*: **la** ~ the common people *pl*, the masses *pl*; (*pey*) the plebs *pl*; ~**yo, a** *adj* plebeian; *(pey)* coarse, common

plebiscito [pleβis'θito] *nm* plebiscite

plegable [ple'βaβle] *adj* collapsible; *(silla)* folding

plegar [ple'βar] *vt* (*doblar*) to fold, bend; *(COSTURA)* to pleat; ~**se** *vr* to yield, submit

pleito ['pleito] *nm* (JUR) lawsuit, case; *(fig)* dispute, feud

plenilunio [pleni'lunjo] *nm* full moon

plenitud [pleni'tuð] *nf* plenitude, fullness; *(abundancia)* abundance

pleno, a ['pleno, a] *adj* full; *(completo)* complete ♦ *nm* plenum; **en** ~ **día** in broad daylight; **en** ~ **verano** at the height of summer; **en plena cara** full in the face

pliego *etc* ['pljeɣo] *vb ver* **plegar** ♦ *nm* (*hoja*) sheet (of paper); *(carta)* sealed letter/document; ~ **de condiciones** details *pl*, specifications *pl*

pliegue *etc* ['pljeɣe] *vb ver* **plegar**

♦ *nm* fold, crease; *(de vestido)* pleat

plomero [plo'mero] *nm* (AM) plumber

plomo ['plomo] *nm* (*metal*) lead; (ELEC) fuse; **sin** ~ unleaded

pluma ['pluma] *nf* feather; *(para escribir)*: ~ **(estilográfica)** ink pen;
~ **fuente** (AM) fountain pen

plumero [plu'mero] *nm* (*para el polvo*) feather duster

plumón [plu'mon] *nm* (*de ave*) down; (AM: *fino*) felt-tip pen; (:: *ancho*) marker

plural [plu'ral] *adj* plural; ~**idad** *nf* plurality

pluriempleo [pluriem'pleo] *nm* having more than one job

plus [plus] *nm* bonus; ~**valía** *nf* (COM) appreciation

población [poβla'θjon] *nf* population; *(pueblo, ciudad)* town, city

poblado, a [po'βlaðo, a] *adj* inhabited ♦ *nm* (*aldea*) village; *(pueblo)* (small) town; **densamente** ~ densely populated

poblador, a [poβla'ðor, a] *nm/f* settler, colonist

poblar [po'βlar] *vt* (*colonizar*) to colonize; *(fundar)* to found; *(habitar)* to inhabit

pobre ['poβre] *adj* poor ♦ *nm/f* poor person; ~**za** *nf* poverty

pocilga [po'θilɣa] *nf* pigsty

pócima ['poθima] *nf* = **poción**

PALABRA CLAVE

---

poco, a ['poko, a] *adj* **1** (*sg*) little, not much; ~ **tiempo** little o not much time; **de** ~ **interés** of little interest, not very interesting; **poca cosa** not much

2 (*pl*) few, not many; **unos** ~**s** a few, some; ~**s niños comen lo que les conviene** few children eat what they should eat

♦ *adv* **1** little, not much; **cuesta** ~ it doesn't cost much

2 (+ *adj*: = *negativo, antónimo*):
~ **amable/inteligente** not very nice/

intelligent
3: por ~ me caigo I almost fell
4: a ~: a ~ de haberse casado shortly after getting married
5: ~ a ~ little by little

♦ *nm* a little, a bit; **un ~ triste/de dinero** a little sad/money

podar [po'ðar] *vt* to prune

___PALABRA CLAVE___

poder [po'ðer] *vi* **1** (*capacidad*) can, be able to; **no puedo hacerlo** I can't do it, I'm unable to do it
2 (*permiso*) can, may, be allowed to; **¿se puede?** may I (o we)?; **puedes irte ahora** you may go now; **no se puede fumar en este hospital** smoking is not allowed in this hospital
3 (*posibilidad*) may, might, could; **puede llegar mañana** he may *o* might arrive tomorrow; **pudiste haberte hecho daño** you might *o* could have hurt yourself; **¡podías habérmelo dicho antes!** you might have told me before!
4: puede ser: **puede ser** perhaps; **puede ser que lo sepa Tomás** Tomás may *o* might know
5: ¡no puedo más! I've had enough!; **no pude menos que dejarlo** I couldn't help but leave it; **es tonto a más no ~** he's as stupid as they come
6: ~ con: **no puedo con este crío** this kid's too much for me

♦ *nm* power; **~ adquisitivo** purchasing power; **detentar** *o* **ocupar** *o* **estar en el ~** to be in power

poderoso, a [poðe'roso, a] *adj* (*político, país*) powerful
podio ['poðjo] *nm* (*DEPORTE*) podium
podium ['poðjum] = **podio**
podrido, a [po'ðriðo, a] *adj* rotten, bad; (*fig*) rotten, corrupt
podrir [po'ðrir] = **pudrir**
poema [po'ema] *nm* poem

poesía [poe'sia] *nf* poetry
poeta [po'eta] *nm/f* poet; **poético, a** *adj* poetic(al)
poetisa [poe'tisa] *nf* (woman) poet
póker ['poker] *nm* poker
polaco, a [po'lako, a] *adj* Polish
♦ *nm/f* Pole

polar [po'lar] *adj* polar; **~idad** *nf* polarity; **~izarse** *vr* to polarize
polea [po'lea] *nf* pulley
polémica [po'lemika] *nf* polemics *sg*; (*una ~*) controversy, polemic
polen ['polen] *nm* pollen
policía [poli'θia] *nm/f* policeman/ woman ♦ *nf* police; **~co, a** *adj* police *cpd*; **novela policíaca** detective story; **policial** *adj* police *cpd*
polideportivo [poliðepor'tiβo] *nm* sports centre *o* complex
poligamia [poli'vamja] *nf* polygamy
polígono [po'liyono] *nm* (*MAT*) polygon; **~ industrial** industrial estate
polilla [po'liʎa] *nf* moth
polio ['poljo] *nf* polio
política [po'litika] *nf* politics *sg*; (*económica, agraria etc*) policy; *ver tb* **político**
político, a [po'litiko, a] *adj* political; (*discreto*) tactful; (*de familia*) -in-law
♦ *nm/f* politician; **padre ~** father-in-law
póliza ['poliθa] *nf* certificate, voucher; (*impuesto*) tax stamp; **~ de seguros** insurance policy
polizón [poli'θon] *nm* stowaway
pollera [po'ʎera] *nf* (*AM*) skirt
pollería [poʎe'ria] *nf* poulterer's (shop)
pollo ['poʎo] *nm* chicken
polo ['polo] *nm* (*GEO, ELEC*) pole; (*helado*) ice lolly; (*DEPORTE*) polo; (*suéter*) polo-neck; **~ Norte/Sur** North/South Pole
Polonia [po'lonja] *nf* Poland
poltrona [pol'trona] *nf* easy chair
polución [polu'θjon] *nf* pollution
polvera [pol'βera] *nf* powder compact
polvo ['polβo] *nm* dust; (*QUÍM, CULIN,*

MED) powder; **~s** nfpl (maquillaje) powder sg; **quitar el ~** to dust; **~ de talco** talcum powder; **estar hecho ~** (fam) to be worn out o exhausted

pólvora ['polβora] nf gunpowder; (fuegos artificiales) fireworks pl

polvoriento a [polβo'rjento, a] adj (superficie) dusty; (sustancia) powdery

pomada [po'maða] nf cream, ointment

pomelo [po'melo] nm grapefruit

pómez ['pomeθ] nf: **piedra ~** pumice stone

pomo ['pomo] nm doorknob

pompa ['pompa] nf (burbuja) bubble; (bomba) pump; (esplendor) pomp, splendour; **pomposo, a** adj splendid, magnificent; (pey) pompous

pómulo ['pomulo] nm cheekbone

pon [pon] vb ver **poner**

ponche ['pontʃe] nm punch

poncho ['pontʃo] nm poncho

ponderar [ponde'rar] vt (considerar) to weigh up, consider; (elogiar) to praise highly, speak in praise of

pondré etc vb ver **poner**

---PALABRA CLAVE---

poner [po'ner] vt **1** (colocar) to put; (telegrama) to send; (obra de teatro) to put on; (película) to show; **ponlo más fuerte** turn it up; **¿qué ponen en el Excelsior?** what's on at the Excelsior?
2 (tienda) to open; (instalar: gas etc) to put in; (radio, TV) to switch o turn on
3 (suponer): **pongamos que ...** let's suppose that ...
4 (contribuir): **el gobierno ha puesto otro millón** the government has contributed another million
5 (TELEC): **póngame con el Sr. López** can you put me through to Mr. López?
6: **~ de:** **le han puesto de director general** they've appointed him general manager
7 (+ adj) to make; **me estás**

poniendo nerviosa you're making me nervous
8 (dar nombre): **al hijo le pusieron Diego** they called their son Diego
♦ vi (gallina) to lay
♦ **~se** vr **1** (colocarse): **se puso a mi lado** he came and stood beside me; **tú ponte en esa silla** you go and sit on that chair
2 (vestido, cosméticos) to put on; **¿por qué no te pones el vestido nuevo?** why don't you put on o wear your new dress?
3 (+ adj) to turn; to get; become; **se puso muy serio** he got very serious; **después de lavarla la tela se puso azul** after washing it the material turned blue
4: **~se a:** **se puso a llorar** he started to cry; **tienes que ~te a estudiar** you must get down to studying
5: **~se a bien con uno** to make it up with sb; **~se a mal con uno** to get on the wrong side of sb

pongo etc vb ver **poner**

poniente [po'njente] nm (occidente) west; (viento) west wind

pontífice [pon'tifiθe] nm pope, pontiff

popa ['popa] nf stern

popular [popu'lar] adj popular; (cultura) of the people, folk cpd; **~idad** nf popularity; **~izarse** vr to become popular

---PALABRA CLAVE---

por [por] prep **1** (objetivo) for; **luchar ~ la patria** to fight for one's country
2 (+ infin): **~ no llegar tarde** so as not to arrive late; **~ citar unos ejemplos** to give a few examples
3 (causa) out of, because of; **~ escasez de fondos** through o for lack of funds
4 (tiempo): **~ la mañana/noche** in the morning/at night; **se queda ~ una semana** she's staying (for) a

week
5 (*lugar*): **pasar ~ Madrid** to pass
through Madrid; **ir a Guayaquil
~ Quito** to go to Guayaquil via Quito;
caminar ~ la calle to walk along the
street; *ver tb* **todo**
6 (*cambio, precio*): **te doy uno nuevo
~ el que tienes** I'll give you a new
one (in return) for the one you've got
7 (*valor distributivo*): **550 pesetas
~ hora/cabeza** 550 pesetas an o per
hour/a o per head
8 (*modo, medio*) **y: ~ correo/avión**
by post/air; **día ~ día** day by day;
entrar ~ la entrada principal to go
in through the main entrance
9: **10 ~ 10 son 100** 10 times 10 is
100
10 (*en lugar de*): **vino él ~ su jefe** he
came instead of his boss
11: **~ mí que revienten** as far as I'm
concerned they can drop dead
12: **¿~ qué?** why?; **¿~ qué no?** why
not?

porcelana [porθe'lana] *nf* porcelain;
(*china*) china
porcentaje [porθen'taxe] *nm*
percentage
porción [por'θjon] *nf* (*parte*) portion,
share; (*cantidad*) quantity, amount
pordiosero, a [porðjo'sero, a] *nm/f*
beggar
porfiar [por'fjar] *vi* to persist, insist;
(*disputar*) to argue stubbornly
pormenor [porme'nor] *nm* detail,
particular
pornografía [pornovra'fia] *nf*
pornography
poro ['poro] *nm* pore; **~so, a** *adj*
porous
porque ['porke] *conj* (*a causa de*)
because; (*ya que*) since; (*con el fin de*)
so that, in order that
porqué [por'ke] *nm* reason, cause
porquería [porke'ria] *nf* (*suciedad*)
filth, dirt; (*acción*) dirty trick; (*objeto*)

small thing, trifle; (*fig*) rubbish
porra ['porra] *nf* (*arma*) stick, club
porrazo [po'rraθo] *nm* blow, bump
porro ['porro] (*fam*) *nm* (*droga*) joint
(*fam*)
porrón [po'rron] *nm* glass wine jar with
a long spout
portaaviones [porta'(a)ßjones] *nm
inv* aircraft carrier
portada [por'taða] *nf* (*de revista*) cover
portador, a [porta'ðor, a] *nm/f* carrier,
bearer; (*COM*) bearer, payee
portaequipajes [portaeki'paxes] *nm
inv* (*AUTO: maletero*) boot; (: *baca*)
luggage rack
portal [por'tal] *nm* (*entrada*) vestibule,
hall; (*portada*) porch, doorway; (*puerta
de entrada*) main door
portamaletas [portama'letas] *nm inv*
(*AUTO: maletero*) boot; (: *baca*) roof
rack
portarse [por'tarse] *vr* to behave,
conduct o.s.
portátil [por'tatil] *adj* portable
portavoz [porta'ßoθ] *nm/f*
spokesman/woman
portazo [por'taθo] *nm*: **dar un ~** to
slam the door
porte ['porte] *nm* (*COM*) transport;
(*precio*) transport charges *pl*
portento [por'tento] *nm* marvel,
wonder; **~so, a** *adj* marvellous,
extraordinary
porteño, a [por'teɲo, a] *adj* of o from
Buenos Aires
portería [porte'ria] *nf* (*oficina*) porter's
office; (*DEPORTE*) goal
portero, a [por'tero, a] *nm/f* porter;
(*conserje*) caretaker; (*ujier*) doorman;
(*DEPORTE*) goalkeeper; **~ automático**
intercom
pórtico ['portiko] *nm* (*patio*) portico,
porch; (*fig*) gateway; (*arcada*) arcade
portorriqueño, a [portorri'keɲo, a]
adj Puerto Rican
Portugal [portu'val] *nm* Portugal
portugués, esa *adj*, *nm/f* Portuguese

♦ nm (LING) Portuguese

porvenir [porβe'nir] nm future

pos [pos] prep: **en ~ de** after, in pursuit of

posada [po'saða] nf (refugio) shelter, lodging; (mesón) guest house; **dar ~ a** to give shelter to, take in

posaderas [posa'ðeras] nfpl backside sg, buttocks

posar [po'sar] vt (en el suelo) to lay down, put down; (la mano) to place, put gently ♦ vi (modelo) to sit, pose; **~se** vr to settle; (pájaro) to perch; (avión) to land, come down

posavasos [posa'basos] nm inv coaster; (para cerveza) beermat

posdata [pos'ðata] nf postscript

pose ['pose] nf pose

poseedor, a [posee'ðor, a] nm/f owner, possessor; (de récord, puesto) holder

poseer [pose'er] vt to possess, own; (ventaja) to enjoy; (récord, puesto) to hold

posesión [pose'sjon] nf possession; **posesionarse** vr: **posesionarse de** to take possession of, take over

posesivo, a [pose'siβo, a] adj possessive

posgrado [pos'graðo] nm: **curso de ~** postgraduate course

posibilidad [posiβili'ðað] nf possibility; (oportunidad) chance; **posibilitar** vt to make possible; (hacer realizable) to make feasible

posible [po'siβle] adj possible; (realizable) feasible; **de ser ~** if possible; **en lo ~** as far as possible

posición [posi'θjon] nf position; (rango social) status

positivo, a [posi'tiβo, a] adj positive

poso ['poso] nm sediment; (heces) dregs pl

posponer [pospo'ner] vt (relegar) to put behind/below; (aplazar) to postpone

posta ['posta] nf: **a ~** deliberately, on

purpose

postal [pos'tal] adj postal ♦ nf postcard

poste ['poste] nm (de telégrafos etc) post, pole; (columna) pillar

póster ['poster] (pl **pósteres, pósters**) nm poster

postergar [poster'var] vt to postpone, delay

posteridad [posteri'ðað] nf posterity

posterior [poste'rjor] adj back, rear; (siguiente) following, subsequent; (más tarde) later; **~idad** nf: **con ~idad** later, subsequently

postgrado [post'graðo] nm = **posgrado**

postizo, a [pos'tiθo, a] adj false, artificial ♦ nm hairpiece

postor, a [pos'tor, a] nm/f bidder

postre ['postre] nm sweet, dessert

postrero, a [pos'trero, a] (delante de nmsg: **postrer**) adj (último) last; (que viene detrás) rear

postulado [postu'laðo] nm postulate

póstumo, a ['postumo, a] adj posthumous

postura [pos'tura] nf (del cuerpo) posture, position; (fig) attitude, position

potable [po'taβle] adj drinkable; **agua ~** drinking water

potaje [po'taxe] nm thick vegetable soup

pote ['pote] nm pot, jar

potencia [po'tenθja] nf power; **~l** [poten'θjal] adj, nm potential; **~r** vt to boost

potente [po'tente] adj powerful

potro, a ['potro, a] nm/f (ZOOL) colt/filly ♦ nm (de gimnasia) vaulting horse

pozo ['poθo] nm well; (de río) deep pool; (de mina) shaft

P.P. abr (= porte pagado) CP

práctica ['praktika] nf practice; (método) method; (arte, capacidad) skill; **en la ~** in practice

practicable [prakti'kaβle] adj

practicable; (*camino*) passable

practicante |prakti'kante| nm/f (MED: *ayudante de doctor*) medical assistant; (*: enfermero*) nurse; (*quien practica algo*) practitioner ♦ *adj* practising

practicar |prakti'kar| vt to practise; (DEPORTE) to play; (*realizar*) to carry out, perform

práctico, a |'praktiko, a| *adj* practical; (*instruido: persona*) skilled, expert

practique etc vb ver **practicar**

pradera |pra'ðera| nf meadow; (US etc) prairie

prado |'praðo| nm (*campo*) meadow, field; (*pastizal*) pasture

Praga |'praxa| n Prague

pragmático, a |prax'matiko, a| *adj* pragmatic

preámbulo |pre'ambulo| nm preamble, introduction

precario, a |pre'karjo, a| *adj* precarious

precaución |prekau'θjon| nf (*medida preventiva*) preventive measure, precaution; (*prudencia*) caution, wariness

precaver |preka'ßer| vt to guard against; (*impedir*) to forestall; **~se** vr: **~se de** o **contra algo** to (be on one's) guard against sth; **precavido, a** *adj* cautious, wary

precedente |preθe'ðente| *adj* preceding; (*anterior*) former ♦ nm precedent

preceder |preθe'ðer| vt, vi to precede, go before, come before

precepto |pre'θepto| nm precept

preciado, a |pre'θjaðo, a| *adj* (*estimado*) esteemed, valuable

preciarse |pre'θjarse| vr to boast; **~se de** to pride o.s. on, boast of being

precinto |pre'θinto| nm (tb: **~ de garantía**) seal

precio |'preθjo| nm price; (*costo*) cost; (*valor*) value, worth; (*de viaje*) fare; **~ al contado/de coste/de oportunidad** cash/cost/bargain price; **~ al detalle** o

al por menor retail price; **~ tope** top price

preciosidad |preθjosi'ðað| nf (*valor*) (high) value, (great) worth; (*encanto*) charm; (*cosa bonita*) beautiful thing; **es una ~** it's lovely, it's really beautiful

precioso, a |pre'θjoso, a| *adj* precious; (*de mucho valor*) valuable; (*fam*) lovely, beautiful

precipicio |preθi'piθjo| nm cliff, precipice; (*fig*) abyss

precipitación |preθipita'θjon| nf haste; (*lluvia*) rainfall

precipitado, a |preθipi'taðo, a| *adj* (*conducta*) hasty, rash; (*salida*) hasty, sudden

precipitar |preθipi'tar| vt (*arrojar*) to hurl down, throw; (*apresurar*) to hasten; (*acelerar*) to speed up, accelerate; **~se** vr to throw o.s.; (*apresurarse*) to rush; (*actuar sin pensar*) to act rashly

precisamente |preθisa'mente| *adv* precisely; (*exactamente*) precisely, exactly

precisar |preθi'sar| vt (*necesitar*) to need, require; (*fijar*) to determine exactly, fix; (*especificar*) to specify

precisión |preθi'sjon| nf (*exactitud*) precision

preciso, a |pre'θiso, a| *adj* (*exacto*) precise; (*necesario*) necessary, essential

preconcebido, a |prekonθe'ßiðo, a| *adj* preconceived

precoz |pre'koθ| *adj* (*persona*) precocious; (*calvicie etc*) premature

precursor, a |prekur'sor, a| nm/f predecessor, forerunner

predecir |preðe'θir| vt to predict, forecast

predestinado, a |preðesti'naðo, a| *adj* predestined

predicar |preði'kar| vt, vi to preach

predicción |preðik'θjon| nf prediction

predilecto, a |preði'lekto, a| *adj* favourite

predisponer |preðispo'ner| vt to

predispose; (*pey*) to prejudice;
predisposición *nf* inclination;
prejudice, bias

predominante [preðomi'nante] *adj*
predominant

predominar [preðomi'nar] *vt* to
dominate ♦ *vi* to predominate;
(*prevalecer*) to prevail; **predominio**
nm predominance; prevalence

preescolar [pre(e)sko'lar] *adj*
preschool

prefabricado, a [prefaßri'kaðo, a] *adj*
prefabricated

prefacio [pre'faθjo] *nm* preface

preferencia [prefe'renθja] *nf*
preference; **de ~** preferably, for
preference

preferible [prefe'rißle] *adj* preferable

preferir [prefe'rir] *vt* to prefer

prefiero *etc vb ver* **preferir**

prefijo [pre'fixo] *nm* (*TELEC*: *dialling*)
code

pregonar [prevo'nar] *vt* to proclaim,
announce

pregunta [pre'vunta] *nf* question;
hacer una ~ to ask a question

preguntar [prevun'tar] *vt* to ask;
(*cuestionar*) to question ♦ *vi* to ask; **~se**
vr to wonder; **~ por alguien** to ask for
sb

preguntón, ona [prevun'ton, ona]
adj inquisitive

prehistórico, a [preis'toriko, a] *adj*
prehistoric

prejuicio [pre'xwiθjo] *nm* (*acto*)
prejudgement; (*idea preconcebida*)
preconception; (*parcialidad*) prejudice,
bias

preliminar [prelimi'nar] *adj*
preliminary

preludio [pre'luðjo] *nm* prelude

prematuro, a [prema'turo, a] *adj*
premature

premeditación [premeðita'θjon] *nf*
premeditation

premeditar [premeði'tar] *vt* to
premeditate

premiar [pre'mjar] *vt* to reward; (*en
un concurso*) to give a prize to

premio ['premjo] *nm* reward; prize;
(*COM*) premium

premonición [premoni'θjon] *nf*
premonition

prenatal [prena'tal] *adj* antenatal,
prenatal

prenda ['prenda] *nf* (*ropa*) garment,
article of clothing; (*garantía*) pledge;
~s *nfpl* (*talentos*) talents, gifts

prendedor [prende'ðor] *nm* brooch

prender [pren'der] *vt* (*captar*) to catch,
capture; (*detener*) to arrest; (*COSTURA*)
to pin, attach; (*sujetar*) to fasten ♦ *vi* to
catch; (*arraigar*) to take root; **~se** *vr*
(*encenderse*) to catch fire

prendido, a [pren'diðo, a] (*AM*) *adj*
(*luz etc*) on

prensa ['prensa] *nf* press; **la ~** the
press; **prensar** *vt* to press

preñado, a [pre'naðo, a] *adj*
pregnant; **~ de** pregnant with, full of

preocupación [preokupa'θjon] *nf*
worry, concern; (*ansiedad*) anxiety

preocupado, a [preoku'paðo, a] *adj*
worried, concerned; (*ansioso*) anxious

preocupar [preoku'par] *vt* to worry;
~se *vr* to worry; **~se de algo** (*hacerse
cargo*) to take care of sth

preparación [prepara'θjon] *nf* (*acto*)
preparation; (*estado*) readiness;
(*entrenamiento*) training

preparado, a [prepa'raðo, a] *adj*
(*dispuesto*) prepared; (*CULIN*) ready (to
serve) ♦ *nm* preparation

preparar [prepa'rar] *vt* (*disponer*) to
prepare, get ready; (*TEC*: *tratar*) to
prepare, process; (*entrenar*) to teach,
train; **~se** *vr*: **~se a** *o* **para** to prepare
to *o* for, get ready to *o* for;
preparativo, a *adj* preparatory,
preliminary; **preparativos** *nmpl*
preparations; **preparatoria** (*AM*) *nf*
sixth-form college (*BRIT*), senior high
school (*US*)

prerrogativa [prerrova'tißa] *nf*

presa ['presa] nf (cosa apresada) catch; (víctima) victim; (de animal) prey; (de agua) dam

presagiar [presa'xjar] vt to presage, forebode; **presagio** nm omen

prescindir [presθin'dir] vi: ~ de (privarse de) to do without, go without; (descartar) to dispense with

prescribir [preskri'βir] vt to prescribe; **prescripción** nf prescription

presencia [pre'senθja] nf presence; **presencial** adj: **testigo presencial** eyewitness; **presenciar** vt to be present at; (asistir a) to attend; (ver) to see, witness

presentación [presenta'θjon] nf presentation; (introducción) introduction

presentador, a [presenta'ðor, a] nm/f presenter, compère

presentar [presen'tar] vt to present; (ofrecer) to offer; (mostrar) to show, display; (a una persona) to introduce; ~**se** vr (llegar inesperadamente) to appear, turn up; (ofrecerse como candidato) to run, stand; (aparecer) to show, appear; (solicitar empleo) to apply

presente [pre'sente] adj present ♦ nm present; **hacer** ~ to state, declare; **tener** ~ to remember, bear in mind

presentimiento [presenti'mjento] nm premonition, presentiment

presentir [presen'tir] vt to have a premonition of

preservación [preserßa'θjon] nf protection, preservation

preservar [preser'ßar] vt to protect, preserve; **preservativo** nm sheath, condom

presidencia [presi'ðenθja] nf presidency; (de comité) chairmanship

presidente [presi'ðente] nm/f president; (de comité) chairman/ woman

presidiario [presi'ðjarjo] nm convict

presidio [presi'ðjo] nm prison, penitentiary

presidir [presi'ðir] vt (dirigir) to preside at, preside over; (: comité) to take the chair at; (dominar) to dominate, rule ♦ vi to preside; to take the chair

presión [pre'sjon] nf pressure; **presionar** vt to press; (fig) to press, put pressure on ♦ vi: **presionar para** to press for

preso, a [preso, a] nm/f prisoner; **tomar** o **llevar** ~ a uno to arrest sb, take sb prisoner

prestación [presta'θjon] nf service; (subsidio) benefit; **prestaciones** nfpl (TEC, AUT) performance features

prestado, a [presta'ðo, a] adj on loan; **pedir** ~ to borrow

prestamista [presta'mista] nm/f moneylender

préstamo ['prestamo] nm loan; ~ **hipotecario** mortgage

prestar [pres'tar] vt to lend, loan; (atención) to pay; (ayuda) to give

presteza [pres'teθa] nf speed, promptness

prestigio [pres'tixjo] nm prestige; ~**so, a** adj (honorable) prestigious; (famoso, renombrado) renowned, famous

presumido, a [presu'miðo, a] adj (persona) vain

presumir [presu'mir] vt to presume ♦ vi (tener aires) to be conceited; **según cabe** ~ as may be presumed, presumably; **presunción** nf presumption; **presunto, a** adj (supuesto) supposed, presumed; (así llamado) so-called; **presuntuoso, a** adj conceited, presumptuous

presuponer [presupo'ner] vt to presuppose

presupuesto [presu'pwesto] pp de **presuponer** ♦ nm (FINANZAS) budget; (estimación: de costo) estimate

pretencioso, a [preten'θjoso, a] adj pretentious

pretender [preten'der] vt (intentar) to
try to, seek to; (reivindicar) to claim;
(buscar) to seek, try for; (cortejar) to
woo, court; ~ que to expect that;
pretendiente nm/f (amante) suitor;
(al trono) pretender; **pretensión** nf
(aspiración) aspiration; (reivindicación)
claim; (orgullo) pretension

pretexto [pre'teksto] nm pretext;
(excusa) excuse

prevalecer [preβale'θer] vi to prevail

prevención [preβen'θjon] nf
prevention; (precaución) precaution

prevenido, a [preβe'niðo, a] adj
prepared, ready; (cauteloso) cautious

prevenir [preβe'nir] vt (impedir) to
prevent; (predisponer) to prejudice,
bias; (avisar) to warn; (preparar) to
prepare, get ready; ~se vr to get
ready, prepare; ~se contra to take
precautions against; **preventivo, a** adj
preventive, precautionary

prever [pre'βer] vt to foresee

previo, a ['preβjo, a] adj (anterior)
previous; (preliminar) preliminary
♦ prep: ~ acuerdo de los otros
subject to the agreement of the others

previsión [preβi'sjon] nf (perspicacia)
foresight; (predicción) forecast;
previsto, a anticipated, forecast

prima ['prima] nf (COM) bonus; ~ de
seguro insurance premium; ver tb
primo

primacía [prima'θia] nf primacy

primario, a [pri'marjo, a] adj primary

primavera [prima'βera] nf
spring(-time)

primera [pri'mera] nf (AUTO) first gear;
(FERRO: tb: ~ clase) first class; **de ~**
(fam) first-class, first-rate

primero, a [pri'mero, a] adj (delante de
nmsg: primer) adj first; (principal)
prime ♦ adv first; (más bien) sooner,
rather; **primera plana** front page

primicia [pri'miθja] nf (tb:
~ informativa) scoop

primitivo, a [primi'tiβo, a] adj

primitive; (original) original

primo, a ['primo, a] adj prime ♦ nm/f
cousin; (fam) fool, idiot; ~ hermano
first cousin; **materias primas** raw
materials

primogénito, a [primo'xenito, a] adj
first-born

primordial [primor'ðjal] adj basic,
fundamental

primoroso, a [primo'roso, a] adj
exquisite, delicate

princesa [prin'θesa] nf princess

principal [prinθi'pal] adj principal,
main ♦ nm (jefe) chief, principal

príncipe ['prinθipe] nm prince

principiante [prinθi'pjante] nm/f
beginner

principio [prin'θipjo] nm (comienzo)
beginning, start; (origen) origin;
(primera etapa) rudiment, basic idea;
(moral) principle; a ~s de at the
beginning of

pringoso, a [prin'γoso, a] adj
(grasiento) greasy; (pegajoso) sticky

pringue ['pringe] nm (grasa) grease,
fat, dripping

prioridad [priori'ðað] nf priority

prisa ['prisa] nf (apresuramiento) hurry,
haste; (rapidez) speed; (urgencia) (sense
of) urgency; a o de ~ quickly; correr
~ to be urgent; darse ~ to hurry up;
estar de o tener ~ to be in a hurry

prisión [pri'sjon] nf (cárcel) prison;
(período de cárcel) imprisonment;
prisionero, a nm/f prisoner

prismáticos [pris'matikos] nmpl
binoculars

privación [priβa'θjon] nf deprivation;
(falta) want, privation

privado, a [pri'βaðo, a] adj private

privar [pri'βar] vt to deprive;
privativo, a adj exclusive

privilegiado, a [priβile'xjaðo, a] adj
privileged; (memoria) very good

privilegiar [priβile'xjar] vt to grant a
privilege to; (favorecer) to favour

privilegio [priβi'lexjo] nm privilege;

(concesión) concession

pro [pro] nm o f profit, advantage
♦ prep: **asociación ~ ciegos**
association for the blind ♦ prefijo:
~ soviético/americano pro-Soviet/
American; **en ~ de** on behalf of, for;
los ~s y los contras the pros and
cons

proa ['proa] nf bow, prow; **de ~** bow
cpd, fore

probabilidad [proβaβili'ðað] nf
probability, likelihood; (oportunidad,
posibilidad) chance, prospect;
probable adj probable, likely

probador [proβa'ðor] nm (en tienda)
fitting room

probar [pro'βar] vt (demostrar) to
prove; (someter a prueba) to test, try
out; (ropa) to try on; (comida) to taste
♦ vi to try; **~se un traje** to try on a
suit

probeta [pro'βeta] nf test tube

problema [pro'βlema] nm problem

procedente [proθe'ðente] adj
(razonable) reasonable; (conforme a
derecho) proper, fitting; **~ de** coming
from, originating in

proceder [proθe'ðer] vi (avanzar) to
proceed; (actuar) to act; (ser correcto)
to be right (and proper), be fitting
♦ nm (comportamiento) behaviour,
conduct; **~ de** to come from, originate
in; **procedimiento** nm procedure;
(proceso) process; (método) means pl,
method

procesado, a [proθe'saðo, a] nm/f
accused

procesador [proθesa'ðor] nm: **~ de
textos** word processor

procesar [proθe'sar] vt to try, put on
trial

procesión [proθe'sjon] nf procession

proceso [pro'θeso] nm process; (JUR)
trial

proclamar [prokla'mar] vt to proclaim

procreación [prokrea'θjon] nf
procreation

procrear [prokre'ar] vt, vi to procreate

procurador, a [prokura'ðor, a] nm/f
attorney

procurar [proku'rar] vt (intentar) to
try, endeavour; (conseguir) to get,
obtain; (asegurar) to secure; (producir)
to produce

prodigio [pro'ðixjo] nm prodigy;
(milagro) wonder, marvel; **~so, a** adj
prodigious, marvellous

pródigo, a ['proðiyo, a] adj: **hijo ~**
prodigal son

producción [proðuk'θjon] nf (gen)
production; (producto) output; **~ en
serie** mass production

producir [proðu'θir] vt to produce;
(causar) to cause, bring about; **~se** vr
(cambio) to come about; (accidente) to
take place; (problema etc) to arise;
(hacerse) to be produced, be made;
(estallar) to break out

productividad [proðuktiβi'ðað] nf
productivity; **productivo, a** adj
productive; (provechoso) profitable

producto [pro'ðukto] nm product

productor, a [proðuk'tor, a] adj
productive, producing ♦ nm/f producer

proeza [pro'eθa] nf exploit, feat

profanar [profa'nar] vt to desecrate,
profane; **profano, a** adj profane
♦ nm/f layman/woman

profecía [profe'θia] nf prophecy

proferir [profe'rir] vt (palabra, sonido)
to utter; (injuria) to hurl, let fly

profesión [profe'sjon] nf profession;
profesional adj professional

profesor, a [profe'sor, a] nm/f
teacher; **~ado** nm teaching profession

profeta [pro'feta] nm/f prophet;
profetizar vt, vi to prophesy

prófugo, a ['profuyo, a] nm/f fugitive;
(MIL: desertor) deserter

profundidad [profundi'ðað] nf depth;
profundizar vi: **profundizar en** to
go deeply into; **profundo, a** adj deep;
(misterio, pensador) profound

progenitor [proxeni'tor] nm ancestor;

~es nmpl (padres) parents
programa [pro'ɣrama] nm
programme (BRIT), program (US);
~ción nf programming; **~dor, a** nm/f
programmer; **programar** vt to
program
progresar [proɣre'sar] vi to progress,
make progress; **progresista** adj, nm/f
progressive; **progresivo, a** adj
progressive; (gradual) gradual;
(continuo) continuous; **progreso** nm
progress
prohibición [proiβi'θjon] nf
prohibition, ban
prohibir [proi'βir] vt to prohibit, ban,
forbid; **se prohibe fumar, prohibido
fumar** no smoking; **"prohibido el
paso"** "no entry"
prójimo, a [ˈproximo, a] nm/f fellow
man; (vecino) neighbour
proletariado [proleta'rjaðo] nm
proletariat
proletario, a [prole'tarjo, a] adj, nm/f
proletarian
proliferación [prolifera'θjon] nf
proliferation
proliferar [prolife'rar] vi to proliferate;
prolífico, a adj prolific
prólogo [ˈproloxo] nm prologue
prolongación [prolonga'θjon] nf
extension; **prolongado, a** adj (largo)
long; (alargado) lengthy
prolongar [prolon'ɣar] vt to extend;
(reunión etc) to prolong; (calle, tubo) to
extend
promedio [pro'meðjo] nm average;
(de distancia) middle, mid-point
promesa [pro'mesa] nf promise
prometer [prome'ter] vt to promise
♦ vi to show promise; **~se** vr (novios)
to get engaged; **prometido, a** adj
promised; engaged ♦ nm/f fiancé/
fiancée
prominente [promi'nente] adj
prominent
promiscuo, a [pro'miskwo, a] adj
promiscuous

promoción [promo'θjon] nf
promotion
promotor [promo'tor] nm promoter;
(instigador) instigator
promover [promo'βer] vt to promote;
(causar) to cause; (instigar) to instigate,
stir up
promulgar [promul'ɣar] vt to
promulgate; (anunciar) to proclaim
pronombre [pro'nombre] nm
pronoun
pronosticar [pronosti'kar] vt to
predict, foretell, forecast; **pronóstico**
nm prediction, forecast; **pronóstico
del tiempo** weather forecast
pronto, a [ˈpronto, a] adj (rápido)
prompt, quick; (preparado) ready ♦ adv
quickly, promptly; (en seguida) at once,
right away; (dentro de poco) soon;
(temprano) early ♦ nm: **tener ~ de
enojo** to be quick-tempered; **de ~**
suddenly; **por lo ~** meanwhile, for the
present
pronunciación [pronunθja'θjon] nf
pronunciation
pronunciar [pronun'θjar] vt to
pronounce; (discurso) to make, deliver;
~se vr to revolt, rebel; (declararse) to
declare o.s.
propagación [propaɣa'θjon] nf
propagation
propaganda [propa'ɣanda] nf
(política) propaganda; (comercial)
advertising
propagar [propa'ɣar] vt to propagate
propensión [propen'sjon] nf
inclination, propensity; **propenso, a**
adj inclined to; **ser propenso a** to be
inclined to, have a tendency to
propicio, a [pro'piθjo, a] adj
favourable, propitious
propiedad [propje'ðað] nf property;
(posesión) possession, ownership;
~ particular private property
propietario, a [propje'tarjo, a] nm/f
owner, proprietor
propina [pro'pina] nf tip

propio, a ['propjo, a] adj own, of one's own; (característico) characteristic, typical; (debido) proper; (mismo) selfsame, very; **el ~ ministro** the minister himself; **¿tienes casa propia?** have you a house of your own?

proponer [propo'ner] vt to propose, put forward; (persona) to pose; **~se** vr to propose, intend

proporción [propor'θjon] nf proportion; (MAT) ratio; **proporciones** nfpl (dimensiones) dimensions; (fig) size sg; **proporcionado, a** adj proportionate; (regular) medium, middling; (justo) just right; **proporcionar** vt (dar) to give, supply, provide

proposición [proposi'θjon] nf proposition; (propuesta) proposal

propósito [pro'posito] nm purpose; (intento) aim, intention ♦ adv: **a ~ by** the way, incidentally; (a posta) on purpose, deliberately; **a ~ de** about, with regard to

propuesta [pro'pwesta] vb ver **proponer** ♦ nf proposal

propulsar [propul'sar] vt to drive, propel; (fig) to promote, encourage; **propulsión** nf propulsion; **propulsión a chorro o por reacción** jet propulsion

prórroga ['prorroxa] nf extension; (JUR) stay; (COM) deferment; (DEPORTE) extra time; **prorrogar** vt (período) to extend; (decisión) to defer, postpone

prorrumpir [prorrum'pir] vi to burst forth, break out

prosa ['prosa] nf prose

proscrito, a [pro'skrito, a] adj banned

proseguir [prose'xir] vt to continue, carry on ♦ vi to continue, go on

prospección [prospek'θjon] nf exploration; (del oro) prospecting

prospecto [pros'pekto] nm prospectus

prosperar [prospe'rar] vi to prosper, thrive, flourish; **prosperidad** nf

prosperity; (éxito) success; **próspero, a** adj prosperous, flourishing; (que tiene éxito) successful

prostíbulo [pros'tiβulo] nm brothel (BRIT), house of prostitution (US)

prostitución [prostitu'θjon] nf prostitution

prostituir [prosti'twir] vt to prostitute; **~se** vr to prostitute o.s., become a prostitute

prostituta [prosti'tuta] nf prostitute

protagonista [protaxo'nista] nm/f protagonist

protagonizar [protaxoni'θar] vt to take the chief rôle in

protección [protek'θjon] nf protection

protector, a [protek'tor, a] adj protective, protecting ♦ nm/f protector

proteger [prote'xer] vt to protect; **protegido, a** nm/f protégé/protégée

proteína [prote'ina] nf protein

protesta [pro'testa] nf protest; (declaración) protestation

protestante [protes'tante] adj Protestant

protestar [protes'tar] vt to protest, declare ♦ vi to protest

protocolo [proto'kolo] nm protocol

prototipo [proto'tipo] nm prototype

prov. abr (= provincia) prov

provecho [pro'βetʃo] nm advantage, benefit; (FINANZAS) profit; **¡buen ~!** bon appétit!; **en ~ de** to the benefit of; **sacar ~ de** to benefit from, profit by

proveer [proβe'er] vt to provide, supply ♦ vi: **~ a** to provide for

provenir [proβe'nir] vi: **~ de** to come from, stem from

proverbio [pro'βerβjo] nm proverb

providencia [proβi'ðenθja] nf providence

provincia [pro'βinθja] nf province; **~no, a** adj provincial; (del campo) country cpd

provisión [proβi'sjon] nf provision; (abastecimiento) provision, supply;

(*medida*) measure, step

provisional [proβisjo'nal] *adj* provisional

provocación [proβoka'θjon] *nf* provocation

provocar [proβo'kar] *vt* to provoke; (*alentar*) to tempt, invite; (*causar*) to bring about, lead to; (*promover*) to promote; (*estimular*) to rouse, stimulate; ¿**te provoca un café?** (*AM*) would you like a coffee?;

provocativo, a *adj* provocative

próximamente [proksima'mente] *adv* shortly, soon

proximidad [proksimi'ðað] *nf* closeness, proximity; **próximo, a** *adj* near, close; (*vecino*) neighbouring; (*siguiente*) next

proyectar [projek'tar] *vt* (*objeto*) to hurl, throw; (*luz*) to cast, shed; (*CINE*) to screen, show; (*planear*) to plan

proyectil [projek'til] *nm* projectile, missile

proyecto [pro'jekto] *nm* plan; (*estimación de costo*) detailed estimate

proyector [projek'tor] *nm* (*CINE*) projector

prudencia [pru'ðenθja] *nf* (*sabiduría*) wisdom; (*cuidado*) care; **prudente** *adj* sensible, wise; (*conductor*) careful

prueba *etc* ['prweβa] *vb ver* **probar**
♦ *nf* proof; (*ensayo*) test, trial; (*degustación*) tasting, sampling; (*de ropa*) fitting; **a ~** on trial; **a ~ de** proof against; **a ~ de agua/fuego** waterproof/fireproof; **someter a ~** to put to the test

prurito [pru'rito] *nm* itch; (*de bebé*) nappy (*BRIT*) *o* diaper (*US*) rash

psico... [siko] *prefijo* psycho...;
~análisis *nm inv* psychoanalysis;
~logía *nf* psychology; **~lógico, a** *adj* psychological; **psicólogo, a** *nm/f* psychologist; **psicópata** *nm/f* psychopath; **~sis** *nf inv* psychosis

psiquiatra [si'kjatra] *nm/f* psychiatrist; **psiquiátrico, a** *adj* psychiatric

psíquico, a ['sikiko, a] *adj* psychic(al)

PSOE [pe'soe] *nm abr* = **Partido Socialista Obrero Español**

pta(s) *abr* = **peseta(s)**

pts *abr* = **pesetas**

púa ['pua] *nf* (*BOT, ZOOL*) prickle, spine; (*para guitarra*) plectrum (*BRIT*), pick (*US*); **alambre de ~** barbed wire

pubertad [pußer'tað] *nf* puberty

publicación [pußlika'θjon] *nf* publication

publicar [pußli'kar] *vt* (*editar*) to publish; (*hacer público*) to publicize; (*divulgar*) to make public, divulge

publicidad [pußliθi'ðað] *nf* publicity; (*COM: propaganda*) advertising; **publicitario, a** *adj* publicity *cpd*; advertising *cpd*

público, a ['pußliko, a] *adj* public
♦ *nm* public; (*TEATRO etc*) audience

puchero [pu'tʃero] *nm* (*CULIN: guiso*) stew; (: *olla*) cooking pot; **hacer ~s** to pout

pude *etc vb ver* **poder**

púdico, a ['puðiko, a] *adj* modest

pudiente [pu'ðjente] *adj* (*rico*) wealthy, well-to-do

pudiera *etc vb ver* **poder**

pudor [pu'ðor] *nm* modesty

pudrir [pu'ðrir] *vt* to rot; **~se** *vr* to rot, decay

pueblo ['pweßlo] *nm* people; (*nación*) nation; (*aldea*) village

puedo *etc vb ver* **poder**

puente ['pwente] *nm* bridge; **hacer ~** (*inf*) to take extra days off work between 2 public holidays; to take a long weekend; **~ aéreo** shuttle service; **~ colgante** suspension bridge

---

hacer puente

When a public holiday in Spain falls on a Tuesday or Thursday it is common practice for employers to make the Monday or Friday a holiday as well and to give everyone a four-day weekend. This is known as **hacer** puente. *When a named public holiday such as the Día de la Constitución falls on a Tuesday or Thursday, people refer to the whole holiday period as e.g. the puente de la Constitución.*

puerco, a ['pwerko, a] *nm/f* pig/sow ♦ *adj* (*sucio*) dirty, filthy; (*obsceno*) disgusting; ~ **de mar** porpoise; ~ **marino** dolphin

pueril [pwe'ril] *adj* childish

puerro ['pwerro] *nm* leek

puerta ['pwerta] *nf* door; (*de jardín*) gate; (*portal*) doorway; (*fig*) gateway; (*portería*) goal; **a la** ~ at the door; **a** ~ **cerrada** behind closed doors; ~ **giratoria** revolving door

puerto ['pwerto] *nm* port; (*paso*) pass; (*fig*) haven, refuge

Puerto Rico [pwerto'riko] *nm* Puerto Rico; **puertorriqueño, a** *adj, nm/f* Puerto Rican

pues [pwes] *adv* (*entonces*) then; (*bueno*) well, well then; (*así que*) so ♦ *conj* (*ya que*) since; **¡~!** (*sí*) yes!, certainly!

puesta ['pwesta] *nf* (*apuesta*) bet, stake; ~ **en marcha** starting; ~ **del sol** sunset

puesto, a ['pwesto, a] *pp de* **poner** ♦ *adj:* **tener algo ~** to have sth on, be wearing sth ♦ *nm* (*lugar, posición*) place; (*trabajo*) post, job; (*COM*) stall ♦ *conj:* ~ **que** since, as

púgil ['puxil] *nm* boxer

pugna ['puxna] *nf* battle, conflict; **pugnar** *vi* (*luchar*) to struggle, fight; (*pelear*) to fight

pujar [pu'xar] *vi* (*en subasta*) to bid; (*esforzarse*) to struggle, strain

pulcro, a ['pulkro, a] *adj* neat, tidy

pulga ['pulxa] *nf* flea

pulgada [pul'xaða] *nf* inch

pulgar [pul'xar] *nm* thumb

pulir [pu'lir] *vt* to polish; (*alisar*) to smooth; (*fig*) to polish up, touch up

pulla ['puʎa] *nf* cutting remark

pulmón [pul'mon] *nm* lung; **pulmonía** *nf* pneumonia

pulpa ['pulpa] *nf* pulp; (*de fruta*) flesh, soft part

pulpería [pulpe'ria] (*AM*) *nf* (*tienda*) small grocery store

púlpito ['pulpito] *nm* pulpit

pulpo ['pulpo] *nm* octopus

pulsación [pulsa'θjon] *nf* beat; **pulsaciones** pulse rate

pulsar [pul'sar] *vt* (*tecla*) to touch, tap; (*MUS*) to play; (*botón*) to press, push ♦ *vi* to pulsate; (*latir*) to beat, throb; (*MED*): ~ **a uno** to take sb's pulse

pulsera [pul'sera] *nf* bracelet

pulso ['pulso] *nm* (*ANAT*) pulse; (*fuerza*) strength; (*firmeza*) steadiness, steady hand

pulverizador [pulβeriθa'ðor] *nm* spray, spray gun

pulverizar [pulβeri'θar] *vt* to pulverize; (*líquido*) to spray

puna ['puna] (*AM*) *nf* mountain sickness

punitivo, a [puni'tiβo, a] *adj* punitive

punta ['punta] *nf* point, tip; (*extremidad*) end; (*fig*) touch, trace; **horas ~s** peak hours, rush hours; **sacar ~ a** to sharpen

puntada [pun'taða] *nf* (*COSTURA*) stitch

puntal [pun'tal] *nm* prop, support

puntapié [punta'pje] *nm* kick

puntear [punte'ar] *vt* to tick, mark

puntería [punte'ria] *nf* (*de arma*) aim, aiming; (*destreza*) marksmanship

puntero, a [pun'tero, a] *adj* leading ♦ *nm* (*palo*) pointer

puntiagudo, a [puntja'xuðo, a] *adj* sharp, pointed

puntilla [pun'tiʎa] *nf* (*encaje*) lace edging o trim; (*andar*) **de ~s** (to walk) on tiptoe

punto ['punto] *nm* (*gen*) point; (*señal diminuta*) spot, dot; (*COSTURA, MED*) stitch; (*lugar*) spot, place; (*momento*) point, moment; **a ~** ready; **estar a** ~ **de** to be on the point of o about to;

en ~ on the dot; ~ **muerto** dead centre; (AUTO) neutral (gear); ~ **final** full stop (BRIT), period (US); ~ **y coma** semicolon; ~ **de interrogación** question mark; ~ **de vista** point of view, viewpoint; **hacer** ~ (tejer) to knit
puntuación [puntwa'θjon] nf punctuation; (puntos: en examen) mark(s) (pl); (: DEPORTE) score
puntual [pun'twal] adj (a tiempo) punctual; (exacto) exact, accurate; ~**idad** nf punctuality; exactness, accuracy; ~**izar** vt to fix, specify
puntuar [pun'twar] vi (DEPORTE) to score, count
punzada [pun'θaða] nf (de dolor) twinge
punzante [pun'θante] adj (dolor) shooting, sharp; (herramienta) sharp; **punzar** vt to prick, pierce ♦ vi to shoot, stab
puñado [pu'naðo] nm handful
puñal [pu'nal] nm dagger; ~**ada** nf stab
puñetazo [pune'taθo] nm punch
puño ['puno] nm (ANAT) fist; (cantidad) fistful, handful; (COSTURA) cuff; (de herramienta) handle
pupila [pu'pila] nf pupil
pupitre [pu'pitre] nm desk
puré [pu're] nm puree; (sopa) (thick) soup; ~ **de patatas** mashed potatoes
pureza [pu'reθa] nf purity
purga ['purɣa] nf purge; **purgante** adj, nm purgative; **purgar** vt to purge
purgatorio [purɣa'torjo] nm purgatory
purificar [purifi'kar] vt to purify; (refinar) to refine
puritano, a [puri'tano, a] adj (actitud) puritanical; (iglesia, tradición) puritan ♦ nm/f puritan
puro, a ['puro, a] adj (puro; verdad) simple, plain ♦ adv: **de** ~ **cansado** out of sheer tiredness ♦ nm cigar
púrpura ['purpura] nf purple; **purpúreo, a** adj purple

pus [pus] nm pus
puse etc vb ver **poner**
pusiera etc vb ver **poner**
pústula ['pustula] nf pimple, sore
puta ['puta] (fam!) nf whore, prostitute
putrefacción [putrefak'θjon] nf rotting, putrefaction
PVP abr (ESP: = precio venta al público) RRP
pyme, PYME ['pime] nf abr (= Pequeña y Mediana Empresa) SME

Q, q

PALABRA CLAVE

que [ke] conj **1** (con oración subordinada: muchas veces no se traduce) that; **dijo** ~ **vendría** he said (that) he would come; **espero** ~ **lo encuentres** I hope (that) you find it; **ver tb el**
2 (en oración independiente): ¡~ **entre!** send him in; ¡~ **se mejore tu padre!** I hope your father gets better
3 (enfático): ¿**me quieres?** – ¡~ **sí!** do you love me? – of course!
4 (consecutivo: muchas veces no se traduce): **es tan grande** ~ **no lo puedo levantar** it's so big (that) I can't lift it
5 (comparaciones) than; **yo** ~ **tú/él** if I were you/him; **ver tb más; menos; mismo**
6 (valor disyuntivo): ~ **le guste o no** whether he likes it or not; ~ **venga o** ~ **no venga** whether he comes or not
7 (porque): **no puedo, ~ tengo** ~ **quedarme en casa** I can't, I've got to stay in

♦ pron **1** (cosa) that, which; (+ prep) which; **el sombrero** ~ **te compraste** the hat (that o which) you bought; **la cama en** ~ **dormí** the bed (that o which) I slept in
2 (persona: suj) that, who; (: objeto)

that, whom; **el amigo ~ me
acompañó al museo** the friend that
o who went to the museum with me:
la chica ~ invité the girl (that o
whom) I invited

qué [ke] *adj* what?, which? ♦ *pron*
what?; **¡~ divertido!** how funny!;
¿~ edad tienes? how old are you?;
¿de ~ me hablas? what are you
saying to me?; **¿~ tal?** how are you?,
how are things?; **¿~ hay (de nuevo)?**
what's new?

quebradizo, a [keβra'ðiθo, a] *adj*
fragile; (*persona*) frail

quebrado, a [ke'βraðo, a] *adj* (*roto*)
broken ♦ *nm/f* bankrupt ♦ *nm* (*MAT*)
fraction

quebrantar [keβran'tar] *vt* (*infringir*)
to violate, transgress; **~se** *vr* (*persona*)
to fail in health

quebranto [ke'βranto] *nm* damage,
harm; (*dolor*) grief, pain

quebrar [ke'βrar] *vt* to break, smash
♦ *vi* to go bankrupt; **~se** *vr* to break,
get broken; (*MED*) to be ruptured

quedar [ke'ðar] *vi* to stay, remain;
(*encontrarse: sitio*) to be; (*haber aún*)
to remain, be left; **~se** *vr* to remain, stay
(behind); **~se (con) algo** to keep sth;
~ en (*acordar*) to agree on/to; **~ en
nada** to come to nothing; **~ por
hacer** to be still to be done; **~ ciego/
mudo** to be left blind/dumb; **no te
queda bien ese vestido** that dress
doesn't suit you; **eso queda muy
lejos** that's a long way (away);
quedamos a las seis we agreed to
meet at six

quedo, a ['keðo, a] *adj* still ♦ *adv*
softly, gently

quehacer [kea'θer] *nm* task, job; **~es
(domésticos)** *nmpl* household chores

queja ['kexa] *nf* complaint; **quejarse**
vr (*enfermo*) to moan, groan; (*protestar*)
to complain; **quejarse de que** to
complain (about the fact) that;

quejido *nm* moan

quemado, a [ke'maðo, a] *adj* burnt

quemadura [kema'ðura] *nf* burn,
scald

quemar [ke'mar] *vt* to burn; (*fig:
malgastar*) to burn up, squander ♦ *vi* to
be burning hot; **~se** *vr* (*consumirse*) to
burn (up); (*del sol*) to get sunburn

quemarropa [kema'rropa]: **a ~** *adv*
point-blank

quepo *etc vb ver* **caber**

querella [ke'reʎa] *nf* (*JUR*) charge;
(*disputa*) dispute; **~rse** *vr* (*JUR*) to file a
complaint

PALABRA CLAVE

---

querer [ke'rer] *vt* **1** (*desear*) to want;
quiero más dinero I want more
money; **quisiera** o **querría un té** I'd
like a tea; **sin ~** unintentionally;
quiero ayudar/que vayas I want to
help/you to go

2 (*preguntas: para pedir algo*): **¿quiere
abrir la ventana?** could you open the
window?; **¿quieres echarme una
mano?** can you give me a hand?

3 (*amar*) to love; (*tener cariño a*) to be
fond of; **quiere mucho a sus hijos**
he's very fond of his children

4 (*requerir*): **esta planta quiere más
luz** this plant needs more light

**5: le pedí que me dejara ir pero no
quiso** I asked him to let me go but he
refused

querido, a [ke'riðo, a] *adj* dear ♦ *nm/f*
darling; (*amante*) lover

queso ['keso] *nm* cheese

quicio ['kiθjo] *nm* hinge; **sacar a uno
de ~** to get on sb's nerves

quiebra ['kjeβra] *nf* break, split; (*COM*)
bankruptcy; (*ECON*) slump

quiebro ['kjeβro] *nm* (*del cuerpo*)
swerve

quien [kjen] *pron* who; **hay ~ piensa
que** there are those who think that;
no hay ~ lo haga no-one will do it

quién [kjen] *pron* who, whom; **¿~ es?** who's there?

quienquiera [kjen'kjera] (*pl* **quienesquiera**) *pron* whoever

quiero *etc vb ver* **querer**

quieto, a ['kjeto, a] *adj* still; (*carácter*) placid; **quietud** *nf* stillness

quilate [ki'late] *nm* carat

quilla ['kiʎa] *nf* keel

quimera [ki'mera] *nf* chimera; **quimérico, a** *adj* fantastic

químico, a ['kimiko, a] *adj* chemical ♦ *nm/f* chemist ♦ *nf* chemistry

quincalla [kin'kaʎa] *nf* hardware, ironmongery (*BRIT*)

quince [kinθe] *num* fifteen; **~ días** a fortnight; **~añero, a** *nm/f* teenager; **~na** *nf* fortnight; (*pago*) fortnightly pay; **~nal** *adj* fortnightly

quiniela [ki'njela] *nf* football pools *pl*; **~s** *nfpl* (*impreso*) pools coupon *sg*

quinientos, as [ki'njentos, as] *adj, num* five hundred

quinina [ki'nina] *nf* quinine

quinto, a ['kinto, a] *adj* fifth ♦ *nf* country house; (*MIL*) call-up, draft

quiosco ['kjosko] *nm* (*de música*) bandstand; (*de periódicos*) news stand

quirófano [ki'rofano] *nm* operating theatre

quirúrgico, a [ki'rurxiko, a] *adj* surgical

quise *etc vb ver* **querer**

quisiera *etc vb ver* **querer**

quisquilloso, a [kiski'ʎoso, a] *adj* (*susceptible*) touchy; (*meticuloso*) pernickety

quiste ['kiste] *nm* cyst

quitaesmalte [kitaes'malte] *nm* nail-polish remover

quitamanchas [kita'mantʃas] *nm inv* stain remover

quitanieves [kita'njeßes] *nm inv* snowplough (*BRIT*), snowplow (*US*)

quitar [ki'tar] *vt* to remove, take away; (*ropa*) to take off; (*dolor*) to relieve; **¡quita de ahí!** get away!; **~se** *vr* to

withdraw; (*ropa*) to take off; **se quitó el sombrero** he took off his hat

quite ['kite] *nm* (*esgrima*) parry; (*evasión*) dodge

Quito ['kito] *n* Quito

quizá(s) [ki'θa(s)] *adv* perhaps, maybe

R, r

rábano ['raßano] *nm* radish; **me importa un ~** I don't give a damn

rabia ['raßja] *nf* (*MED*) rabies *sg*; (*ira*) fury, rage; **rabiar** *vi* to have rabies; to rage, be furious; **rabiar por algo** to long for sth

rabieta [ra'ßjeta] *nf* tantrum, fit of temper

rabino [ra'ßino] *nm* rabbi

rabioso, a [ra'ßjoso, a] *adj* rabid; (*fig*) furious

rabo ['raßo] *nm* tail

racha ['ratʃa] *nf* gust of wind: **buena/ mala ~** spell of good/bad luck

racial [ra'θjal] *adj* racial, race *cpd*

racimo [ra'θimo] *nm* bunch

raciocinio [raθjo'θinjo] *nm* reason

ración [ra'θjon] *nf* portion; **raciones** *nfpl* rations

racional [raθjo'nal] *adj* (*razonable*) reasonable; (*lógico*) rational; **~izar** *vt* to rationalize

racionar [raθjo'nar] *vt* to ration (out)

racismo [ra'θismo] *nm* racism; **racista** *adj, nm/f* racist

radar [ra'ðar] *nm* radar

radiactivo, a [raðiak'tißo, a] *adj* = **radioactivo**

radiador [raðja'ðor] *nm* radiator

radiante [ra'ðjante] *adj* radiant

radical [raði'kal] *adj, nm/f* radical

radicar [raði'kar] *vi*: **~ en** (*dificultad, problema*) to lie in; (*solución*) to consist in; **~se** *vr* to establish o.s., put down (one's) roots

radio ['raðjo] *nf* radio; (*aparato*) radio (set) ♦ *nm* (*MAT*) radius; (*QUIM*) radium;

~actividad nf radioactivity; **~activo, a** adj radioactive; **~difusión** nf broadcasting; **~emisora** nf transmitter, radio station; **~escucha** nm/f listener; **~grafía** nf X-ray; **~grafiar** vt to X-ray; **~terapia** nf radiotherapy; **~yente** nm/f listener

ráfaga ['rafaxa] nf gust; (de luz) flash; (de tiros) burst

raído, a [ra'iðo, a] adj (ropa) threadbare

raigambre [rai'xambre] nf (BOT) roots pl; (fig) tradition

raíz [ra'iθ] nf root; **~ cuadrada** square root; **a ~ de** as a result of

raja ['raxa] nf (de melón etc) slice; (grieta) crack; **rajar** vt to split; (fam) to slash; **rajarse** vr to split, crack; **rajarse de** to back out of

rajatabla [raxa'taßla]: **a ~** adv (estrictamente) strictly, to the letter

rallador [raʎa'ðor] nm grater

rallar [ra'ʎar] vt to grate

rama ['rama] nf branch; **~je** nm branches pl, foliage; **ramal** nm (de cuerda) strand; (FERRO) branch line (BRIT); (AUTO) branch (road) (BRIT)

rambla ['rambla] nf (avenida) avenue

ramificación [ramifika'θjon] nf ramification

ramificarse [ramifi'karse] vr to branch out

ramillete [rami'ʎete] nm bouquet

ramo ['ramo] nm branch; (sección) department, section

rampa ['rampa] nf ramp

ramplón, ona [ram'plon, ona] adj uncouth, coarse

rana ['rana] nf frog; **salto de ~** leapfrog

ranchero [ran'tʃero] nm (AM) rancher; smallholder

rancho ['rantʃo] nm (grande) ranch; (pequeño) small farm

rancio, a ['ranθjo, a] adj (comestibles) rancid; (vino) aged, mellow; (fig) ancient

rango ['rango] nm rank, standing

ranura [ra'nura] nf groove; (de teléfono etc) slot

rapar [ra'par] vt to shave; (los cabellos) to crop

rapaz [ra'paθ] (nf: **rapaza**) nm/f young boy/girl ♦ adj (ZOOL) predatory

rape ['rape] nm (pez) monkfish; **al ~** cropped

rapé [ra'pe] nm snuff

rapidez [rapi'ðeθ] nf speed, rapidity; **rápido, a** adj fast, quick ♦ adv quickly ♦ nm (FERRO) express; **rápidos** nmpl rapids

rapiña [ra'piɲa] nm robbery; **ave de ~** bird of prey

raptar [rap'tar] vt to kidnap; **rapto** nm kidnapping; (impulso) sudden impulse; (éxtasis) ecstasy, rapture

raqueta [ra'keta] nf racquet

raquítico, a [ra'kitiko, a] adj stunted; (fig) poor, inadequate; **raquitismo** nm rickets sg

rareza [ra'reθa] nf rarity; (fig) eccentricity

raro, a ['raro, a] adj (poco común) rare; (extraño) odd, strange; (excepcional) remarkable

ras [ras] nm: **a ~ de** level with; **a ~ de tierra** at ground level

rasar [ra'sar] vt (igualar) to level

rascacielos [raska'θjelos] nm inv skyscraper

rascar [ras'kar] vt (con las uñas etc) to scratch; (raspar) to scrape; **~se** vr to scratch (o.s.)

rasgar [ras'xar] vt to tear, rip (up)

rasgo ['rasxo] nm (con pluma) stroke; **~s** nmpl (facciones) features, characteristics; **a grandes ~s** in outline, broadly

rasguñar [rasxu'ɲar] vt to scratch; **rasguño** nm scratch

raso, a ['raso, a] adj (liso) flat, level; (a baja altura) very low ♦ nm satin; **cielo ~** clear sky

raspadura [raspa'ðura] nf (acto)

scrape, scraping; (marca) scratch; **~s** nfpl (de papel etc) scrapings

raspar [ras'par] vt to scrape; (arañar) to scratch; (limar) to file

rastra ['rastra] nf (AGR) rake; **a ~s** by dragging; (fig) unwillingly

rastreador [rastrea'ðor] nm tracker; **~ de minas** minesweeper

rastrear [rastre'ar] vt (seguir) to track

rastrero, a [ras'trero, a] adj (BOT, ZOOL) creeping; (fig) despicable, mean

rastrillo [ras'triʎo] nm rake

rastro ['rastro] nm (AGR) rake; (pista) track, trail; (vestigio) trace; **el R~** the Madrid fleamarket

rastrojo [ras'troxo] nm stubble

rasurador [rasura'ðor] (AM) nm electric shaver

rasuradora [rasura'ðora] (AM) nf = **rasurador**

rasurarse [rasu'rarse] vr to shave

rata ['rata] nf rat

ratear [rate'ar] vt (robar) to steal

ratero, a [ra'tero, a] adj light-fingered ♦ nm/f (carterista) pickpocket; (AM: de casas) burglar

ratificar [ratifi'kar] vt to ratify

rato ['rato] nm while, short time; **a ~s** from time to time; **hay para ~** there's still a long way to go; **al poco ~** soon afterwards; **pasar el ~** to kill time; **pasar un buen/mal ~** to have a good/rough time; **en mis ~s libres** in my spare time

ratón [ra'ton] nm mouse; **ratonera** nf mousetrap

raudal [rau'ðal] nm torrent; **a ~es** in abundance

raya ['raja] nf (línea) (marca) scratch; (en tela) stripe; (de pelo) parting; (límite) boundary; (pez) ray; (puntuación) dash; **a ~s** striped; **pasarse de la ~** to go too far; **tener a ~** to keep in check; **rayar** vt to line; to scratch; (subrayar) to underline ♦ vi: **rayar en o con** to border on

rayo ['rajo] nm (del sol) ray, beam; (de luz) shaft; (en una tormenta) (flash of) lightning; **~s X** X-rays

raza ['raθa] nf race; **~ humana** human race

razón [ra'θon] nf reason; (justicia) right, justice; (razonamiento) reasoning; (motivo) reason, motive; (MAT) ratio; **a ~ de 10 cada día** at the rate of 10 a day; **"~: ..."** "inquiries to ..."; **en ~ de** with regard to; **dar ~ a uno** to agree that sb is right; **tener ~** to be right; **~ directa/inversa** direct/inverse proportion; **~ de ser** raison d'être; **razonable** adj reasonable; (justo, moderado) fair; **razonamiento** nm (juicio) judg(e)ment; (argumento) reasoning; **razonar** vt, vi to reason, argue

reacción [reak'θjon] nf reaction; **avión a ~** jet plane; **~ en cadena** chain reaction; **reaccionar** vi to react; **reaccionario, a** adj reactionary

reacio, a [re'aθjo, a] adj stubborn

reactivar [reakti'βar] vt to revitalize

reactor [reak'tor] nm reactor

readaptación [reaðapta'θjon] nf: **~ profesional** industrial retraining

reajuste [rea'xuste] nm readjustment

real [re'al] adj real; (del rey, fig) royal

realce [re'alθe] nm (lustre, fig) splendour; **poner de ~** to emphasize

realidad [reali'ðað] nf reality, fact; (verdad) truth

realista [rea'lista] nm/f realist

realización [realiθa'θjon] nf fulfilment

realizador, a [realiθa'ðor, a] nm/f film-maker

realizar [reali'θar] vt (objetivo) to achieve; (plan) to carry out; (viaje) to make, undertake; **~se** vr to come about, come true

realmente [real'mente] adv really, actually

realquilar [realki'lar] vt to sublet

realzar [real'θar] vt to enhance; (acentuar) to highlight

reanimar [reani'mar] vt to revive;

(*alentar*) to encourage; **~se** *vr* to revive

reanudar |reanu'ðar| *vt* (*renovar*) to renew; (*historia, viaje*) to resume

reaparición |reapari'θjon| *nf* reappearance

rearme |re'arme| *nm* rearmament

rebaja |re'ßaxa| *nf* (COM) reduction; (: *descuento*) discount; **~s** *nfpl* (COM) sale; **rebajar** *vt* (*bajar*) to lower; (*reducir*) to reduce; (*disminuir*) to lessen; (*humillar*) to humble

rebanada |reßa'naða| *nf* slice

rebañar |reßa'ɲar| *vt* (*comida*) to scrape up; (*plato*) to scrape clean

rebaño |re'ßaɲo| *nm* herd; (*de ovejas*) flock

rebasar |reßa'sar| *vt* (*tb*: **~ de**) to exceed

rebatir |reßa'tir| *vt* to refute

rebeca |re'ßeka| *nf* cardigan

rebelarse |reße'larse| *vr* to rebel, revolt

rebelde |re'ßelde| *adj* rebellious; (*niño*) unruly ♦ *nm/f* rebel; **rebeldía** *nf* rebelliousness; (*desobediencia*) disobedience

rebelión |reße'ljon| *nf* rebellion

reblandecer |reßlande'θer| *vt* to soften

rebobinar |reßoßi'nar| *vt* (*cinta, película de vídeo*) to rewind

rebosante |reßo'sante| *adj* overflowing

rebosar |reßo'sar| *vi* (*líquido, recipiente*) to overflow; (*abundar*) to abound, be plentiful

rebotar |reßo'tar| *vt* to bounce; (*rechazar*) to repel ♦ *vi* (*pelota*) to bounce; (*bala*) to ricochet; **rebote** *nm* rebound; **de rebote** on the rebound

rebozado, a |reßo'θaðo, a| *adj* fried in batter o breadcrumbs

rebozar |reßo'θar| *vt* to wrap up; (CULIN) to fry in batter o breadcrumbs

rebuscado, a |reßus'kaðo, a| *adj* (*amanerado*) affected; (*palabra*) recherché; (*idea*) far-fetched

rebuscar |reßus'kar| *vi*: **~ (en/por)** to search carefully (in/for)

rebuznar |reßuθ'nar| *vi* to bray

recado |re'kaðo| *nm* (*mensaje*) message; (*encargo*) errand; **tomar un ~** (TEL) to take a message

recaer |reka'er| *vi* to relapse; **~ en** to fall to o on; (*criminal etc*) to fall back into, relapse into; **recaída** *nf* relapse

recalcar |rekal'kar| *vt* (*fig*) to stress, emphasize

recalcitrante |rekalθi'trante| *adj* recalcitrant

recalentar |rekalen'tar| *vt* (*volver a calentar*) to reheat; (*calentar demasiado*) to overheat

recámara |re'kamara| (AM) *nf* bedroom

recambio |re'kambjo| *nm* spare; (*de pluma*) refill

recapacitar |rekapaθi'tar| *vi* to reflect

recargado, a |rekar'xaðo, a| *adj* overloaded

recargar |rekar'xar| *vt* to overload; (*batería*) to recharge; **recargo** *nm* surcharge; (*aumento*) increase

recatado, a |reka'taðo, a| *adj* (*modesto*) modest, demure; (*prudente*) cautious

recato |re'kato| *nm* (*modestia*) modesty, demureness; (*cautela*) caution

recaudación |rekauða'θjon| *nf* (*acción*) collection; (*cantidad*) takings *pl*; (*en deporte*) gate; **recaudador, a** *nm/f* tax collector

recelar |reθe'lar| *vt*: **~ que** (*sospechar*) to suspect that; (*temer*) to fear that ♦ *vi*: **~ de** to distrust; **recelo** *nm* distrust, suspicion; **receloso, a** *adj* distrustful, suspicious

recepción |reθep'θjon| *nf* reception; **recepcionista** *nm/f* receptionist

receptáculo |reθep'takulo| *nm* receptacle

receptivo, a |reθep'tißo, a| *adj* receptive

receptor, a |reθep'tor, a| *nm/f*

recipient ♦ *nm* (*TEL*) receiver

recesión [reθe'sjon] *nf* (*COM*) recession

receta [re'θeta] *nf* (*CULIN*) recipe; (*MED*) prescription

rechazar [retʃa'θar] *vt* to reject; (*oferta*) to turn down; (*ataque*) to repel

rechazo [re'tʃaθo] *nm* rejection

rechifla [re'tʃifla] *nf* hissing, booing; (*fig*) derision

rechinar [retʃi'nar] *vi* to creak; (*dientes*) to grind

rechistar [retʃis'tar] *vi*: **sin ~** without a murmur

rechoncho, a [re'tʃontʃo, a] (*fam*) *adj* thickset (*BRIT*), heavy-set (*US*)

rechupete [retʃu'pete]: **de ~** (*comida*) delicious, scrumptious

recibidor, a [reθiβi'ðor, a] *nm* entrance hall

recibimiento [reθiβi'mjento] *nm* reception, welcome

recibir [reθi'βir] *vt* to receive; (*dar la bienvenida*) to welcome ♦ *vi* to entertain; **~se** *vr*: **~se de** to qualify as; **recibo** *nm* receipt

reciclar [reθi'klar] *vt* to recycle

recién [re'θjen] *adv* recently, newly; **los ~ casados** the newly-weds; **el ~ llegado** the newcomer; **el ~ nacido** the newborn child

reciente [re'θjente] *adj* recent; (*fresco*) fresh; **~mente** *adv* recently

recinto [re'θinto] *nm* enclosure; (*área*) area, place

recio, a ['reθjo, a] *adj* strong; tough; (*voz*) loud ♦ *adv* hard; loud(ly)

recipiente [reθi'pjente] *nm* receptacle

reciprocidad [reθiproθi'ðað] *nf* reciprocity; **recíproco, a** *adj* reciprocal

recital [reθi'tal] *nm* (*MUS*) recital; (*LITERATURA*) reading

recitar [reθi'tar] *vt* to recite

reclamación [reklama'θjon] *nf* claim, demand; (*queja*) complaint

reclamar [rekla'mar] *vt* to claim, demand ♦ *vi*: **~ contra** to complain about; **~ a uno en justicia** to take sb

to court; **reclamo** *nm* (*anuncio*) advertisement; (*tentación*) attraction

reclinar [rekli'nar] *vt* to recline, lean; **~se** *vr* to lean back

recluir [reklu'ir] *vt* to intern, confine

reclusión [reklu'sjon] *nf* (*prisión*) prison; (*refugio*) seclusion; **~ perpetua** life imprisonment

recluta [re'kluta] *nm/f* recruit ♦ *vt* recruitment; **reclutar** *vt* (*datos*) to collect; (*dinero*) to collect up; **~miento** [rekluta'mjento] *nm* recruitment

recobrar [reko'βrar] *vt* (*salud*) to recover; (*rescatar*) to get back; **~se** *vr* to recover

recodo [re'koðo] *nm* (*de río, camino*) bend

recogedor [rekoxe'ðor] *nm* dustpan

recoger [reko'xer] *vt* to collect; (*AGR*) to harvest; (*levantar*) to pick up; (*juntar*) to gather; (*pasar a buscar*) to come for, get; (*dar asilo*) to give shelter to; (*falda*) to gather up; (*pelo*) to put up; **~se** *vr* (*retirarse*) to retire; **recogido, a** *adj* (*lugar*) quiet, secluded; (*pequeño*) small ♦ *nf* (*CORREOS*) collection; (*AGR*) harvest

recolección [rekolek'θjon] *nf* (*AGR*) harvesting; (*colecta*) collection

recomendación [rekomenda'θjon] *nf* (*sugerencia*) suggestion, recommendation; (*referencia*) reference

recomendar [rekomen'dar] *vt* to suggest, recommend; (*confiar*) to entrust

recompensa [rekom'pensa] *nf* reward, recompense; **recompensar** *vt* to reward, recompense

recomponer [rekompo'ner] *vt* to mend

reconciliación [rekonθilja'θjon] *nf* reconciliation

reconciliar [rekonθi'ljar] *vt* to reconcile; **~se** *vr* to become reconciled

recóndito, a [re'kondito, a] *adj* (*lugar*) hidden, secret

reconfortar [rekonfor'tar] *vt* to

comfort

reconocer [rekono'θer] vt to recognize; (registrar) to search; (MED) to examine; **reconocido, a** adj recognized; (agradecido) grateful; **reconocimiento** nm recognition; search; examination; gratitude; (confesión) admission

reconquista [rekon'kista] nf reconquest; **la R~** the Reconquest (of Spain)

reconstituyente [rekonstitu'jente] nm tonic

reconstruir [rekonstru'ir] vt to reconstruct

reconversión [rekonßer'sjon] nf: **~ industrial** industrial rationalization

recopilación [rekopila'θjon] nf (resumen) summary; (compilación) compilation; **recopilar** vt to compile

récord ['rekorð] (pl **~s**) adj inv, nm record

recordar [rekor'ðar] vt (acordarse de) to remember; (acordar a otro) to remind ♦ vi to remember

recorrer [reko'rrer] vt (país) to cross, travel through; (distancia) to cover; (registrar) to search; (repasar) to look over; **recorrido** nm run, journey; **tren de largo recorrido** main-line train

recortado, a [rekor'taðo, a] adj uneven, irregular

recortar [rekor'tar] vt to cut out; **recorte** nm (acción, de prensa) cutting; (de telas, chapas) trimming; **recorte presupuestario** budget cut

recostado, a [rekos'taðo, a] adj leaning; **estar ~** to be lying down

recostar [rekos'tar] vt to lean; **~se** vr to lie down

recoveco [reko'ßeko] nm (de camino, río etc) bend; (en casa) cubby hole

recreación [rekrea'θjon] nf recreation

recrear [rekre'ar] vt (entretener) to entertain; (volver a crear) to recreate; **recreativo, a** adj recreational; **recreo** nm recreation; (ESCOL) break, playtime

recriminar [rekrimi'nar] vt to reproach ♦ vi to recriminate; **~se** vr to reproach each other

recrudecer [rekruðe'θer] vt, vi to worsen; **~se** vr to worsen

recrudecimiento [rekruðeθi'mjento] nm upsurge

recta ['rekta] nf straight line

rectángulo, a [rek'tangulo, a] adj rectangular ♦ nm rectangle

rectificar [rektifi'kar] vt to rectify; (volverse recto) to straighten ♦ vi to correct o.s.

rectitud [rekti'tuð] nf straightness; (fig) rectitude

recto, a ['rekto, a] adj straight; (persona) honest, upright ♦ nm rectum

rector, a [rek'tor, a] adj governing

recuadro [re'kwaðro] nm box; (TIPOGRAFÍA) inset

recubrir [reku'ßrir] vt: **~ (con)** (pintura, crema) to cover (with)

recuento [re'kwento] nm inventory; **hacer el ~ de** to count o reckon up

recuerdo [re'kwerðo] nm souvenir; **~s** nmpl (memorias) memories; **¡~s a tu madre!** give my regards to your mother!

recular [reku'lar] vi to back down

recuperable [rekupe'raßle] adj recoverable

recuperación [rekupera'θjon] nf recovery

recuperar [rekupe'rar] vt to recover; (tiempo) to make up; **~se** vr to recuperate

recurrir [reku'rrir] vi (JUR) to appeal; **~ a** to resort to; (persona) to turn to; **recurso** nm resort; (medios) means pl, resources pl; (JUR) appeal

recusar [reku'sar] vt to reject, refuse

red [reð] nf net, mesh; (FERRO etc) network; (trampa) trap

redacción [reðak'θjon] nf (acción) editing; (personal) editorial staff; (ESCOL) essay, composition

redactar [reðak'tar] vt to draw up,

draft; (periódico) to edit
redactor, a [reðak'tor, a] nm/f editor
redada [re'ðaða] nf: **~ policial** police raid, round-up
rededor [reðe'ðor] nm: **al o en ~** around, round about
redención [reðen'θjon] nf redemption
redicho, a [re'ðitʃo, a] adj affected
redil [re'ðil] nm sheepfold
redimir [reði'mir] vt to redeem
rédito ['reðito] nm interest, yield
redoblar [reðo'βlar] vt to redouble
♦ vi (tambor) to roll
redomado, a [reðo'maðo, a] adj (astuto) sly, crafty; (perfecto) utter
redonda [re'ðonda] nf: **a la ~** around, round about
redondear [reðonde'ar] vt to round, round off
redondel [reðon'del] nm (círculo) circle; (TAUR) bullring, arena
redondo, a [re'ðondo, a] adj (circular) round; (completo) complete
reducción [reðuk'θjon] nf reduction
reducido, a [reðu'θiðo, a] adj reduced; (limitado) limited; (pequeño) small
reducir [reðu'θir] vt to reduce; to limit; **~se** vr to diminish
redundancia [reðun'danθja] nf redundancy
reembolsar [re(e)mbol'sar] vt (persona) to reimburse; (dinero) to repay, pay back; (depósito) to refund; **reembolso** nm reimbursement; refund
reemplazar [re(e)mpla'θar] vt to replace; **reemplazo** nm replacement; **de reemplazo** (MIL) reserve
reencuentro [re(e)n'kwentro] nm reunion
referencia [refe'renθja] nf reference; **con ~ a** with reference to
referéndum [refe'rendum] (pl **~s**) nm referendum
referente [refe'rente] adj: **~ a** concerning, relating to

referir [refe'rir] vt (contar) to tell, recount; (relacionar) to refer, relate; **~se** vr: **~se a** to refer to
refilón [refi'lon]: **de ~** adv obliquely
refinado, a [refi'naðo, a] adj refined
refinamiento [refina'mjento] nm refinement
refinar [refi'nar] vt to refine; **refinería** nf refinery
reflejar [refle'xar] vt to reflect; **reflejo, a** adj reflected; (movimiento) reflex ♦ nm reflection; (ANAT) reflex
reflexión [reflek'sjon] nf reflection; **reflexionar** vt to reflect on ♦ vi to reflect; (detenerse) to pause (to think)
reflexivo, a [reflek'siβo, a] adj thoughtful; (LING) reflexive
reflujo [re'fluxo] nm ebb
reforma [re'forma] nf reform; (ARQ etc) repair; **~ agraria** agrarian reform
reformar [refor'mar] vt to reform; (modificar) to change, alter; (ARQ) to repair; **~se** vr to mend one's ways
reformatorio [reforma'torjo] nm reformatory
reforzar [refor'θar] vt to strengthen; (ARQ) to reinforce; (fig) to encourage
refractario, a [refrak'tarjo, a] adj (TEC) heat-resistant
refrán [re'fran] nm proverb, saying
refregar [refre'xar] vt to scrub
refrenar [refre'nar] vt to check, restrain
refrendar [refren'dar] vt (firma) to endorse, countersign; (ley) to approve
refrescante [refres'kante] adj refreshing, cooling
refrescar [refres'kar] vt to refresh ♦ vi to cool down; **~se** vr to get cooler; (tomar aire fresco) to go out for a breath of fresh air; (beber) to have a drink
refresco [re'fresko] nm soft drink, cool drink; **~-s** "refreshments"
refriega [re'frjexa] nf scuffle, brawl
refrigeración [refrixera'θjon] nf refrigeration; (de sala) air-conditioning

refrigerador |refrixera'ðor| nm refrigerator (BRIT), icebox (US)

refrigerar |refrixe'rar| vt to refrigerate; (sala) to air-condition

refuerzo |re'fwerθo| nm reinforcement; (TEC) support

refugiado, a |refu'xjaðo, a| nm/f refugee

refugiarse |refu'xjarse| vr to take refuge, shelter

refugio |re'fuxjo| nm refuge; (protección) shelter

refunfuñar |refunfu'nar| vi to grunt, growl; (quejarse) to grumble

refutar |refu'tar| vt to refute

regadera |rexa'ðera| nf watering can

regadío |rexa'ðio| nm irrigated land

regalado, a |rexa'laðo, a| adj comfortable, luxurious; (gratis) free, for nothing

regalar |rexa'lar| vt (dar) to give (as a present); (entregar) to give away; (mimar) to pamper, make a fuss of

regaliz |rexa'liθ| nm liquorice

regalo |re'xalo| nm (obsequio) gift, present; (gusto) pleasure

regañadientes |rexana'ðjentes|: **a ~** adv reluctantly

regañar |rexa'nar| vt to scold ♦ vi to grumble; **regañón, ona** adj nagging

regar |re'xar| vt to water, irrigate; (fig) to scatter, sprinkle

regatear |rexate'ar| vt (COM) to bargain over; (escatimar) to be mean with ♦ vi to bargain, haggle; (DEPORTE) to dribble; **regateo** nm bargaining; dribbling; (del cuerpo) swerve, dodge

regazo |re'xaθo| nm lap

regeneración |rexenera'θjon| nf regeneration

regenerar |rexene'rar| vt to regenerate

regentar |rexen'tar| vt to direct, manage; **regente** nm (COM) manager; (POL) regent

régimen |'reximen| (pl **regímenes**) nm regime; (MED) diet

regimiento |rexi'mjento| nm regiment

regio, a |'rexjo, a| adj royal, regal; (fig: suntuoso) splendid; (AM: fam) great, terrific

región |re'xjon| nf region

regir |re'xir| vt (gobernar) to govern, rule; (dirigir) to manage, run ♦ vi to apply, be in force

registrar |rexis'trar| vt (buscar) to search; (: en cajón) to look through; (inspeccionar) to inspect; (anotar) to register, record; (INFORM) to log; **~se** vr to register; (ocurrir) to happen

registro |re'xistro| nm (acto) registration; (MUS, libro) register; (inspección) inspection, search; **~ civil** registry office

regla |'rexla| nf (ley) rule, regulation; (de medir) ruler, rule; (MED: período) period

reglamentación |rexlamenta'θjon| nf (acto) regulation; (reglas) rules pl

reglamentar |rexlamen'tar| vt to regulate; **reglamentario, a** adj statutory; **reglamento** nm rules pl, regulations pl

regocijarse |rexoθi'xarse| vr: **~ de** to rejoice, be happy about; **regocijo** nm joy, happiness

regodearse |rexoðe'arse| vr to be glad, be delighted; **regodeo** nm delight

regresar |rexre'sar| vi to come back, go back, return; **regresivo, a** adj backward; (fig) regressive; **regreso** nm return

reguero |re'xero| nm (de sangre etc) trickle; (de humo) trail

regulador |rexula'ðor| nm regulator; (de radio etc) knob, control

regular |rexu'lar| adj regular; (normal) normal, usual; (común) ordinary; (organizado) regular, orderly; (mediano) average; (fam) not bad, so-so ♦ adv so-so, alright ♦ vt (controlar) to control, regulate; (TEC) to adjust; **por lo ~** as a rule; **~idad** nf regularity; **~izar** vt to regularize

regusto [re'ɣusto] nm aftertaste

rehabilitación [reaßilita'θjon] nf rehabilitation; (ARQ) restoration

rehabilitar [reaßili'tar] vt to rehabilitate; (ARQ) to restore; (reintegrar) to reinstate

rehacer [rea'θer] vt (reparar) to mend, repair; (volver a hacer) to redo, repeat; **~se** vr (MED) to recover

rehén [re'en] nm hostage

rehuir [reu'ir] vt to avoid, shun

rehusar [reu'sar] vt, vi to refuse

reina ['reina] nf queen; **~do** nm reign

reinante [rei'nante] adj (fig) prevailing

reinar [rei'nar] vi to reign

reincidir [reinθi'ðir] vi to relapse

reincorporarse [reinkorpo'rarse] vr: **~ a** to rejoin

reino ['reino] nm kingdom; **el R~ Unido** the United Kingdom

reintegrar [reinte'ɣrar] vt (reconstituir) to reconstruct; (persona) to reinstate; (dinero) to refund, pay back; **~se** vr: **~se a** to return to

reír [re'ir] vi to laugh; **~se** vr to laugh; **~se de** to laugh at

reiterar [reite'rar] vt to reiterate

reivindicación [reißindika'θjon] nf (demanda) claim, demand; (justificación) vindication

reivindicar [reißindi'kar] vt to claim

reja ['rexa] nf (de ventana) grille, bars pl; (en la calle) grating

rejilla [re'xiʎa] nf grating, grille; (muebles) wickerwork; (de ventilación) vent; (de coche etc) luggage rack

rejoneador [rexonea'ðor] nm mounted bullfighter

rejuvenecer [rexußene'θer] vt, vi to rejuvenate

relación [rela'θjon] nf relation, relationship; (MAT) ratio; (narración) report; **relaciones públicas** public relations; **con ~ a, en ~ con** in relation to; **relacionar** vt to relate,

connect; **relacionarse** vr to be connected, be linked

relajación [relaxa'θjon] nf relaxation

relajado, a [rela'xaðo, a] adj (disoluto) loose; (cómodo) relaxed; (MED) ruptured

relajar [rela'xar] vt to relax; **~se** vr to relax

relamerse [rela'merse] vr to lick one's lips

relamido, a [rela'miðo, a] adj (pulcro) overdressed; (afectado) affected

relámpago [re'lampaɣo] nm flash of lightning; **visita/huelga ~** lightning visit/strike; **relampaguear** vi to flash

relatar [rela'tar] vt to tell, relate

relativo, a [rela'tißo, a] adj relative; **en lo ~ a** concerning

relato [re'lato] nm (narración) story, tale

relegar [rele'ɣar] vt to relegate

relevante [rele'ßante] adj eminent, outstanding

relevar [rele'ßar] vt (sustituir) to relieve; **~se** vr to relay; **~ a uno de un cargo** to relieve sb of his post

relevo [re'leßo] nm relief; **carrera de ~s** relay race

relieve [re'ljeße] nm (ARTE, TEC) relief; (fig) prominence, importance; **bajo ~** bas-relief

religión [reli'xjon] nf religion; **religioso, a** adj religious ♦ nm/f monk/nun

relinchar [relin'tʃar] vi to neigh; **relincho** nm neigh; (acto) neighing

reliquia [re'likja] nf relic; **~ de familia** heirloom

rellano [re'ʎano] nm (ARQ) landing

rellenar [reʎe'nar] vt (llenar) to fill up; (CULIN) to stuff; (COSTURA) to pad; **relleno, a** adj full up; stuffed ♦ nm stuffing; (de tapicería) padding

reloj [re'lo(x)] nm clock; **~ (de pulsera)** wristwatch; **~ despertador** alarm (clock); **poner el ~** to set one's watch (o the clock); **~ero, a** nm/f clockmaker; watchmaker

reluciente [relu'θjente] adj brilliant, shining

relucir [relu'θir] vi to shine; (fig) to excel

relumbrar [relum'brar] vi to dazzle, shine brilliantly

remachar [rema'tʃar] vt to rivet; (fig) to hammer home, drive home; **remache** nm rivet

remanente [rema'nente] nm remainder; (COM) balance; (de producto) surplus

remangar [reman'gar] vt to roll up

remanso [re'manso] nm pool

remar [re'mar] vi to row

rematado, a [rema'taðo, a] adj complete, utter

rematar [rema'tar] vt to finish off; (COM) to sell off cheap ♦ vi to end, finish off; (DEPORTE) to shoot

remate [re'mate] nm end, finish; (punta) tip; (DEPORTE) shot; (ARQ) top; **de** o **para** to crown it all (BRIT), to top it off

remedar [reme'ðar] vt to imitate

remediar [reme'ðjar] vt to remedy; (subsanar) to make good, repair; (evitar) to avoid

remedio [re'meðjo] nm remedy; (alivio) relief, help; (JUR) recourse, remedy; **poner ~ a** to correct, stop; **no tener más ~** to have no alternative; **¡qué ~!** there's no choice!; **sin ~** hopeless

remedo [re'meðo] nm imitation; (pey) parody

remendar [remen'dar] vt to repair; (con parche) to patch

remesa [re'mesa] nf remittance; (COM) shipment

remiendo [re'mjendo] nm mend; (con parche) patch; (cosido) darn

remilgado, a [remil'xaðo, a] adj prim; (afectado) affected

remilgo [re'milxo] nm primness; (afectación) affectation

reminiscencia [reminis'θenθja] nf reminiscence

remiso, a [re'miso, a] adj slack, slow

remite [re'mite] nm (en sobre) name and address of sender

remitir [remi'tir] vt to remit, send ♦ vi (en carta): **remite: X** sender: X; **remitente** nm/f sender

remo ['remo] nm (de barco) oar; (DEPORTE) rowing

remojar [remo'xar] vt to steep, soak; (galleta etc) to dip, dunk

remojo [re'moxo] nm: **dejar la ropa en ~** to leave clothes to soak

remolacha [remo'latʃa] nf beet, beetroot

remolcador [remolka'ðor] nm (NAUT) tug; (AUTO) breakdown lorry

remolcar [remol'kar] vt to tow

remolino [remo'lino] nm eddy; (de agua) whirlpool; (de viento) whirlwind; (de gente) crowd

remolque [re'molke] nm tow, towing; (cuerda) towrope; **llevar a ~** to tow

remontar [remon'tar] vt to mend; **~se** vr to soar; **~se a** (COM) to amount to; **~ el vuelo** to soar

remorder [remor'ðer] vt to distress, disturb; **~le la conciencia a uno** to have a guilty conscience; **remordimiento** nm remorse

remoto, a [re'moto, a] adj remote

remover [remo'ßer] vt to stir; (tierra) to turn over; (objetos) to move round

remozar [remo'θar] vt (ARQ) to refurbish

remuneración [remunera'θjon] nf remuneration

remunerar [remune'rar] vt to remunerate; (premiar) to reward

renacer [rena'θer] vi to be reborn; (fig) to revive; **renacimiento** nm rebirth; **el Renacimiento** the Renaissance

renacuajo [rena'kwaxo] nm (ZOOL) tadpole

renal [re'nal] adj renal, kidney cpd

rencilla [ren'θiʎa] nf quarrel

rencor [reŋ'kor] nm rancour, bitterness; **~oso, a** adj spiteful

rendición [rendi'θjon] nf surrender

rendido, a [ren'diðo, a] adj (sumiso) submissive; (cansado) worn-out, exhausted

rendija [ren'dixa] nf (hendedura) crack, cleft

rendimiento [rendi'mjento] nm (producción) output; (TEC, COM) efficiency

rendir [ren'dir] vt (vencer) to defeat; (producir) to produce; (dar beneficio) to yield; (agotar) to exhaust ♦ vi to pay; **~se** vr (someterse) to surrender; (cansarse) to wear o.s. out; **~ homenaje** o **culto a** to pay homage to

renegar [rene'var] vi (renunciar) to renounce; (blasfemar) to blaspheme; (quejarse) to complain

RENFE ['renfe] nf abr (= Red Nacional de los Ferrocarriles Españoles) ≈ BR (BRIT)

renglón [reŋ'glon] nm (línea) line; (COM) item, article; **a ~ seguido** immediately after

renombrado, a [renom'braðo, a] adj renowned

renombre [re'nombre] nm renown

renovación [renoßa'θjon] nf (de contrato) renewal; (ARQ) renovation

renovar [reno'ßar] vt to renew; (ARQ) to renovate

renta ['renta] nf (ingresos) income; (beneficio) profit; (alquiler) rent; **~ vitalicia** annuity; **rentable** adj profitable; **rentar** vt to produce, yield

renuncia [re'nunθja] nf resignation

renunciar [renun'θjar] vt to renounce; (tabaco, alcohol etc): **~ a** to give up; (oferta, oportunidad) to turn down; (puesto) to resign

reñido, a [re'niðo, a] adj (batalla) bitter, hard-fought; **estar ~ con uno** to be on bad terms with sb

reñir [re'nir] vt (regañar) to scold ♦ vi

(estar peleado) to quarrel, fall out; (combatir) to fight

reo ['reo] nm/f culprit, offender; **~ de muerte** prisoner condemned to death

reojo [re'oxo]: **de ~** adv out of the corner of one's eye

reparación [repara'θjon] nf (acto) mending, repairing; (TEC) repair; (fig) amends, reparation

reparar [repa'rar] vt to repair; (fig) to make amends for; (observar) to observe ♦ vi: **~ en** (darse cuenta de) to notice; (prestar atención a) to pay attention to

reparo [re'paro] nm (advertencia) observation; (duda) doubt; (dificultad) difficulty; **poner ~s (a)** to raise objections (to)

repartición [reparti'θjon] nf distribution; (división) division; **repartidor, a** nm/f distributor

repartir [repar'tir] vt to distribute, share out; (CORREOS) to deliver; **reparto** nm (distribución) distribution; delivery; (TEATRO, CINE) cast; (AM: urbanización) housing estate (BRIT), real estate development (US)

repasar [repa'sar] vt (ESCOL) to revise; (MECÁNICA) to check, overhaul; (COSTURA) to mend; **repaso** nm revision; overhaul, checkup; mending

repatriar [repa'trjar] vt to repatriate

repecho [re'petʃo] nm steep incline

repelente [repe'lente] adj repellent, repulsive

repeler [repe'ler] vt to repel

repensar [repen'sar] vt to reconsider

repente [re'pente] nm: **de ~** suddenly; **~ de ira** fit of anger

repentino, a [repen'tino, a] adj sudden

repercusión [reperku'sjon] nf repercussion

repercutir [reperku'tir] vi (objeto) to rebound; (sonido) to echo; **~ en** (fig) to have repercussions on

repertorio [reper'torjo] nm list; (TEATRO) repertoire

repetición [repeti'θjon] nf repetition

repetir [repe'tir] vt to repeat; (plato) to have a second helping of ♦ vi to repeat; (sabor) to come back; ~se vr (volver sobre un tema) to repeat o.s.

repetitivo, a [repeti'tiβo, a] adj repetitive, repetitious

repicar [repi'kar] vt (campanas) to ring

repique [re'pike] nm pealing, ringing; ~teo nm pealing; (de tambor) drumming

repisa [re'pisa] nf ledge, shelf; (de ventana) windowsill; ~ de chimenea mantelpiece

repito etc vb ver **repetir**

replantearse [replante'arse] vr: ~ un problema to reconsider a problem

replegarse [reple'varse] vr to fall back, retreat

repleto, a [re'pleto, a] adj replete, full up

réplica ['replika] nf answer; (ARTE) replica

replicar [repli'kar] vi to answer; (objetar) to argue, answer back

repliegue [re'pljeve] nm (MIL) withdrawal

repoblación [repoβla'θjon] nf repopulation; (de río) restocking; ~ forestal reafforestation

repoblar [repo'βlar] vt to repopulate; (con árboles) to reafforest

repollo [re'poʎo] nm cabbage

reponer [repo'ner] vt to replace, put back; (TEATRO) to revive; ~se vr to recover; ~ que to reply that

reportaje [repor'taxe] nm report, article

reportero, a [repor'tero, a] nm/f reporter

reposacabezas [reposaka'βeθas] nm inv headrest

reposado, a [repo'saðo, a] adj (descansado) restful; (tranquilo) calm

reposar [repo'sar] vi to rest, repose

reposición [reposi'θjon] nf replacement; (CINE) remake

reposo [re'poso] nm rest

repostar [repos'tar] vt to replenish; (AUTO) to fill up (with petrol (BRIT) o gasoline (US))

repostería [reposte'ria] nf confectioner's (shop); **repostero, a** nm/f confectioner

reprender [repren'der] vt to reprimand

represa [re'presa] nf dam; (lago artificial) lake, pool

represalia [repre'salja] nf reprisal

representación [representa'θjon] nf representation; (TEATRO) performance; **representante** nm/f representative; performer

representar [represen'tar] vt to represent; (TEATRO) to perform; (edad) to look; ~se vr to imagine; **representativo, a** adj representative

represión [repre'sjon] nf repression

reprimenda [repri'menda] nf reprimand, rebuke

reprimir [repri'mir] vt to repress

reprobar [repro'βar] vt to censure, reprove

reprochar [repro'tʃar] vt to reproach; **reproche** nm reproach

reproducción [reproðuk'θjon] nf reproduction

reproducir [reproðu'θir] vt to reproduce; ~se vr to breed; (situación) to recur

reproductor, a [reproðuk'tor, a] adj reproductive

reptil [rep'til] nm reptile

república [re'puβlika] nf republic; R~ Dominicana Dominican Republic; **republicano, a** adj, nm/f republican

repudiar [repu'ðjar] vt to repudiate; (fe) to renounce

repuesto [re'pwesto] nm (pieza de recambio) spare (part); (abastecimiento) supply; **rueda de ~** spare wheel

repugnancia [repuɣ'nanθja] nf repugnance; **repugnante** adj repugnant, repulsive

repugnar [repuɣ'nar] vt to disgust

repulsa [re'pulsa] nf rebuff

repulsión [repul'sjon] nf repulsion, aversion; **repulsivo, a** adj repulsive

reputación [reputa'θjon] nf reputation

requemado, a [reke'maðo, a] adj (quemado) scorched; (bronceado) tanned

requerimiento [rekeri'mjento] nm request; (JUR) summons

requerir [reke'rir] vt (pedir) to ask, request; (exigir) to require; (llamar) to send for, summon

requesón [reke'son] nm cottage cheese

requete... [re'kete] prefijo extremely

réquiem ['rekjem] (pl ~s) nm requiem

requisito [reki'sito] nm requirement, requisite

res [res] nf beast, animal

resaca [re'saka] nf (en el mar) undertow, undercurrent; (fam) hangover

resaltar [resal'tar] vi to project, stick out; (fig) to stand out

resarcir [resar'θir] vt to compensate; **~se** vr to make up for

resbaladizo, a [resβala'ðiθo, a] adj slippery

resbalar [resβa'lar] vi to slip, slide; (fig) to slip (up); **~se** vr to slip, slide; to slip (up); **resbalón** nm (acción) slip

rescatar [reska'tar] vt (salvar) to save, rescue; (objeto) to get back, recover; (cautivos) to ransom

rescate [res'kate] nm rescue; (de objeto) recovery; **pagar un ~** to pay a ransom

rescindir [resθin'dir] vt to rescind

rescisión [resθi'sjon] nf cancellation

rescoldo [res'koldo] nm embers pl

resecar [rese'kar] vt to dry thoroughly; (MED) to cut out, remove; **~se** vr to dry up

reseco, a [re'seko, a] adj very dry; (fig) skinny

resentido, a [resen'tiðo, a] adj resentful

resentimiento [resenti'mjento] nm resentment, bitterness

resentirse [resen'tirse] vr (debilitarse: persona) to suffer; **~ de** (consecuencias) to feel the effects of; **~ de (o por) algo** to resent sth, be bitter about sth

reseña [re'seɲa] nf (cuenta) account; (informe) report; (LITERATURA) review

reseñar [rese'ɲar] vt to describe; (LITERATURA) to review

reserva [re'serβa] nf reserve; (reservación) reservation; **a ~ de que ... unless ...; con toda ~** in strictest confidence

reservado, a [reser'βaðo, a] adj reserved; (retraído) cold, distant ♦ nm private room

reservar [reser'βar] vt (guardar) to keep; (habitación, entrada) to reserve; **~se** vr (persona) to save o.s.; (callar) to keep to o.s.

resfriado [resfri'aðo] nm cold; **resfriarse** vr to cool; (MED) to catch (a) cold

resguardar [resɣwar'ðar] vt to protect, shield; **~se** vr: **~se de** to guard against; **resguardo** nm defence; (vale) voucher; (recibo) receipt, slip

residencia [resi'ðenθja] nf residence; **~l** nf (urbanización) housing estate

residente [resi'ðente] adj, nm/f resident

residir [resi'ðir] vi to reside, live; **~ en** to reside in, lie in

residuo [re'siðwo] nm residue

resignación [resiɣna'θjon] nf resignation; **resignarse** vr: **resignarse a o con** to resign o.s. to, be resigned to

resina [re'sina] nf resin

resistencia [resis'tenθja] nf (dureza) endurance, strength; (oposición, ELEC) resistance; **resistente** adj strong, hardy; resistant

resistir [resis'tir] vt (soportar) to bear;

(*oponerse a*) to resist, oppose; (*aguantar*) to put up with ♦ *vi* to resist; (*aguantar*) to last, endure; **~se** *vr:* **~se a** to refuse to, resist

resolución [resolu'θjon] *nf* resolution; (*decisión*) decision; **resoluto, a** *adj* resolute

resolver [resol'ßer] *vt* to resolve; (*solucionar*) to solve, resolve; (*decidir*) to decide, settle; **~se** *vr* to make up one's mind

resonancia [reso'nanθja] *nf* (*del sonido*) resonance; (*repercusión*) repercussion

resonar [reso'nar] *vi* to ring, echo

resoplar [reso'plar] *vi* to snort; **resoplido** *nm* heavy breathing

resorte [re'sorte] *nm* spring; (*fig*) lever

respaldar [respal'dar] *vt* to back (up), support; **~se** *vr* to lean back; **~se con** *o* **en** (*fig*) to take one's stand on; **respaldo** *nm* (*de sillón*) back; (*fig*) support, backing

respectivo, a [respek'tißo, a] *adj* respective; **en lo ~ a** with regard to

respecto [res'pekto] *nm*: **al ~** on this matter; **con ~ a, ~ de** with regard to, in relation to

respetable [respe'taßle] *adj* respectable

respetar [respe'tar] *vt* to respect; **respeto** *nm* respect; (*acatamiento*) deference; **respetos** *nmpl* respects; **respetuoso, a** *adj* respectful

respingo [res'pingo] *nm* start, jump

respiración [respira'θjon] *nf* breathing; (*MED*) respiration; (*ventilación*) ventilation

respirar [respi'rar] *vi* to breathe; **respiratorio, a** *adj* respiratory; **respiro** *nm* breathing; (*fig: descanso*) respite

resplandecer [resplande'θer] *vi* to shine; **resplandeciente** *adj* resplendent, shining; **resplandor** *nm* brilliance, brightness; (*de luz, fuego*) blaze

responder [respon'der] *vt* to answer ♦ *vi* to answer; (*fig*) to respond; (*pey*) to answer back; **~ de** *o* **por** to answer for; **respondón, ona** *adj* cheeky

responsabilidad [responsaßili'ðað] *nf* responsibility

responsabilizarse [responsaßili-'θarse] *vr* to make o.s. responsible, take charge

responsable [respon'saßle] *adj* responsible

respuesta [res'pwesta] *nf* answer, reply

resquebrajar [reskeßra'xar] *vt* to crack, split; **~se** *vr* to crack, split

resquemor [reske'mor] *nm* resentment

resquicio [res'kiθjo] *nm* chink; (*hendedura*) crack

resta ['resta] *nf* (*MAT*) remainder

restablecer [restaßle'θer] *vt* to re-establish, restore; **~se** *vr* to recover

restallar [resta'ʎar] *vi* to crack

restante [res'tante] *adj* remaining; **lo ~** the remainder

restar [res'tar] *vt* (*MAT*) to subtract; (*fig*) to take away ♦ *vi* to remain, be left

restauración [restaura'θjon] *nf* restoration

restaurante [restau'rante] *nm* restaurant

restaurar [restau'rar] *vt* to restore

restitución [restitu'θjon] *nf* return, restitution

restituir [restitu'ir] *vt* (*devolver*) to return, give back; (*rehabilitar*) to restore

resto ['resto] *nm* (*residuo*) rest, remainder; (*apuesta*) stake; **~s** *nmpl* remains

restregar [restre'var] *vt* to scrub, rub

restricción [restrik'θjon] *nf* restriction

restrictivo, a [restrik'tißo, a] *adj* restrictive

restringir [restrin'xir] *vt* to restrict, limit

resucitar [resuθi'tar] vt, vi to resuscitate, revive

resuello [re'sweʎo] nm (aliento) breath; **estar sin ~** to be breathless

resuelto, a [re'swelto, a] pp de **resolver** ♦ adj resolute, determined

resultado [resul'taðo] nm result; (conclusión) outcome; **resultante** adj resulting, resultant

resultar [resul'tar] vi (ser) to be; (llegar a ser) to turn out to be; (salir bien) to turn out well; (COM) to amount to; **~ de** to stem from; **me resulta difícil hacerlo** it's difficult for me to do it

resumen [re'sumen] (pl **resúmenes**) nm summary, résumé; **en ~** in short

resumir [resu'mir] vt to sum up; (cortar) to abridge, cut down; (condensar) to summarize

resurgir [resur'xir] vi (reaparecer) to reappear

resurrección [resurre(k)'θjon] nf resurrection

retablo [re'taßlo] nm altarpiece

retaguardia [reta'ɣwarðja] nf rearguard

retahíla [reta'ila] nf series, string

retal [re'tal] nm remnant

retar [re'tar] vt to challenge; (desafiar) to defy, dare

retardar [retar'ðar] vt (demorar) to delay; (hacer más lento) to slow down; (retener) to hold back

retazo [re'taθo] nm snippet (BRIT), fragment

retener [rete'ner] vt (intereses) to withhold

reticente [reti'θente] adj (tono) insinuating; (postura) reluctant; **ser ~ a hacer algo** to be reluctant o unwilling to do sth

retina [re'tina] nf retina

retintín [retin'tin] nm jangle, jingle

retirada [reti'raða] nf (MIL, refugio) retreat; (de dinero) withdrawal; (de embajador) recall; **retirado, a** adj (lugar) remote; (vida) quiet; (jubilado) retired

retirar [reti'rar] vt to withdraw; (quitar) to remove; (jubilar) to retire, pension off; **~se** vr to retreat, withdraw; to retire; (acostarse) to retire, go to bed; **retiro** nm retreat; retirement; (pago) pension

reto ['reto] nm dare, challenge

retocar [reto'kar] vt (fotografía) to touch up, retouch

retoño [re'tojno] nm sprout, shoot; (fig) offspring, child

retoque [re'toke] nm retouching

retorcer [retor'θer] vt to twist; (manos, lavado) to wring; **~se** vr to become twisted; (mover el cuerpo) to writhe

retorcido, a [retor'θiðo, a] adj (persona) devious

retórica [re'torika] nf rhetoric; (pey) affectedness; **retórico, a** adj rhetorical

retornar [retor'nar] vt to return, give back ♦ vi to return, go/come back; **retorno** nm return

retortijón [retorti'xon] nm twist, twisting

retozar [reto'θar] vi (juguetear) to frolic, romp; (saltar) to gambol; **retozón, ona** adj playful

retracción [retrak'θjon] nf retraction

retractarse [retrak'tarse] vr to retract; **me retracto** I take that back

retraerse [retra'erse] vr to retreat, withdraw; **retraído, a** adj shy, retiring; **retraimiento** nm retirement; (timidez) shyness

retransmisión [retransmi'sjon] nf repeat (broadcast)

retransmitir [retransmi'tir] vt (mensaje) to relay; (TV etc) to repeat, retransmit; (: en vivo) to broadcast live

retrasado, a [retra'saðo, a] adj late; (MED) mentally retarded; (país etc) backward, underdeveloped

retrasar [retra'sar] vt (demorar) to postpone, put off; (retardar) to slow down ♦ vi (atrasarse) to be late; (reloj) to be slow; (producción) to fall off;

(*quedarse atrás*) to lag behind; **~se** *vr* to be late; to be slow; to fall (off); to lag behind

retraso [re'traso] *nm* (*demora*) delay; (*lentitud*) slowness; (*tardanza*) lateness; (*atraso*) backwardness; **~s** (*FINANZAS*) *nmpl* arrears; **llegar con ~** to arrive late; **~ mental** mental deficiency

retratar [retra'tar] *vt* (*ARTE*) to paint the portrait of; (*fotografiar*) to photograph; (*fig*) to depict, describe; **~se** *vr* to have one's portrait painted; to have one's photograph taken; **retrato** *nm* portrait; (*fig*) likeness; **retrato-robot** *nm* Identikit ® picture

retreta [re'treta] *nf* retreat

retrete [re'trete] *nm* toilet

retribución [retriβu'θjon] *nf* (*recompensa*) reward; (*pago*) pay, payment

retribuir [retri'βwir] *vt* (*recompensar*) to reward; (*pagar*) to pay

retro... [retro] *prefijo* retro...

retroactivo, a [retroak'tiβo, a] *adj* retroactive, retrospective

retroceder [retroθe'ðer] *vi* (*echarse atrás*) to move back(wards); (*fig*) to back down

retroceso [retro'θeso] *nm* backward movement; (*MED*) relapse; (*fig*) backing down

retrógrado, a [re'troɣraðo, a] *adj* retrograde, retrogressive; (*POL*) reactionary

retrospectivo, a [retrospek'tiβo, a] *adj* retrospective

retrovisor [retroβi'sor] *nm* (*tb: espejo ~*) rear-view mirror

retumbar [retum'bar] *vi* to echo, resound

reúma [re'uma], **reuma** ['reuma] *nm* rheumatism

reumatismo [reuma'tismo] *nm* = **reúma**

reunificar [reunifi'kar] *vt* to reunify

reunión [reu'njon] *nf* (*asamblea*) meeting; (*fiesta*) party

reunir [reu'nir] *vt* (*juntar*) to reunite, join (together); (*recoger*) to gather (together); (*personas*) to get together; (*cualidades*) to combine; **~se** *vr* (*personas: en asamblea*) to meet, gather

revalidar [reβali'ðar] *vt* (*ratificar*) to confirm, ratify

revalorizar [reβalori'θar] *vt* to revalue, reassess

revancha [re'βantʃa] *nf* revenge

revelación [reβela'θjon] *nf* revelation

revelado [reβe'laðo] *nm* developing

revelar [reβe'lar] *vt* to reveal; (*FOTO*) to develop

reventa [re'βenta] *nf* (*de entradas: para concierto*) touting

reventar [reβen'tar] *vt* to burst, explode

reventón [reβen'ton] *nm* (*AUTO*) blow-out (*BRIT*), flat (*US*)

reverencia [reβe'renθja] *nf* reverence; **reverenciar** *vt* to revere

reverendo, a [reβe'rendo, a] *adj* reverend

reverente [reβe'rente] *adj* reverent

reversible [reβer'siβle] *adj* (*prenda*) reversible

reverso [re'βerso] *nm* back, other side; (*de moneda*) reverse

revertir [reβer'tir] *vi* to revert

revés [re'βes] *nm* back, wrong side; (*fig*) reverse, setback; (*DEPORTE*) backhand; **al ~** the wrong way round; (*de arriba abajo*) upside down; (*ropa*) inside out; **volver algo del ~** to turn sth round; (*ropa*) to turn sth inside out

revestir [reβes'tir] *vt* (*cubrir*) to cover, coat

revisar [reβi'sar] *vt* (*examinar*) to check; (*texto etc*) to revise; **revisión** *nf* revision

revisor, a [reβi'sor, a] *nm/f* inspector; (*FERRO*) ticket collector

revista [re'βista] *nf* magazine, review; (*TEATRO*) revue; (*inspección*) inspection; **pasar ~ a** to review, inspect

revivir [reßi'ßir] vi to revive

revocación [reßoka'θjon] nf repeal

revocar [reßo'kar] vt to revoke

revolcarse [reßol'karse] vr to roll about

revolotear [reßolote'ar] vi to flutter

revoltijo [reßol'tixo] nm mess, jumble

revoltoso, a [reßol'toso, a] adj (travieso) naughty, unruly

revolución [reßolu'θjon] nf revolution; **revolucionar** vt to revolutionize; **revolucionario, a** adj, nm/f revolutionary

revolver [reßol'ßer] vt (desordenar) to disturb, mess up; (mover) to move about ♦ vi: ~ **en** to go through, rummage (about) in; **~se** vr (volver contra) to turn on ♦ against

revólver [re'ßolßer] nm revolver

revuelo [re'ßwelo] nm fluttering; (fig) commotion

revuelta [re'ßwelta] nf (motín) revolt; (agitación) commotion

revuelto, a [re'ßwelto, a] pp de **revolver** ♦ adj (mezclado) mixed-up, in disorder

rey [rei] nm king; **Día de R~es** Twelfth Night

Reyes Magos

On the night before the 6th January (the Epiphany), children go to bed expecting los Reyes Magos (the Three Wise Men) to bring them presents. Twelfth Night processions, known as cabalgatas, take place that evening when 3 people dressed as los Reyes Magos arrive in the town by land or sea to the delight of the children.

reyerta [re'jerta] nf quarrel, brawl

rezagado, a [reθa'xaðo, a] nm/f straggler

rezagar [reθa'xar] vt (dejar atrás) to leave behind; (retrasar) to delay, postpone

rezar [re'θar] vi to pray; ~ **con** (fam) to concern, have to do with; **rezo** nm prayer

rezongar [reθon'gar] vi to grumble

rezumar [reθu'mar] vt to ooze

ría ['ria] nf estuary

riada [ri'aða] nf flood

ribera [ri'ßera] nf (de río) bank; (: área) riverside

ribete [ri'ßete] nm (de vestido) border; (fig) addition; **~ar** vt to edge, border

ricino [ri'θino] nm: **aceite de ~** castor oil

rico, a ['riko, a] adj rich; (adinerado) wealthy, rich; (lujoso) luxurious; (comida) delicious; (niño) lovely, cute ♦ nm/f rich person

rictus ['riktus] nm (mueca) sneer, grin

ridiculez [riðiku'leθ] nf absurdity

ridiculizar [riðikuli'θar] vt to ridicule

ridículo, a [ri'ðikulo, a] adj ridiculous; **hacer el ~** to make a fool of o.s.; **poner a uno en ~** to make a fool of sb

riego ['rjexo] nm (aspersión) watering; (irrigación) irrigation

riel [rjel] nm rail

rienda ['rjenda] nf rein; **dar ~ suelta a** to give free rein to

riesgo ['rjesxo] nm risk; **correr el ~ de** to run the risk of

rifa ['rifa] nf (lotería) raffle; **rifar** vt to raffle

rifle ['rifle] nm rifle

rigidez [rixi'ðeθ] nf rigidity, stiffness; (fig) strictness; **rígido, a** adj rigid, stiff; strict, inflexible

rigor [ri'vor] nm strictness, rigour; (inclemencia) harshness; **de ~** de rigueur, essential; **riguroso, a** adj rigorous; harsh; (severo) severe

rimar [ri'mar] vi to rhyme

rimbombante [rimbom'bante] adj pompous

rímel ['rimel] nm mascara

rímmel ['rimel] nm = rímel

rincón [rin'kon] nm corner (inside)

rinoceronte [rinoθe'ronte] nm rhinoceros

riña ['riɲa] nf (disputa) argument; (pelea) brawl

riñón [ri'ɲon] nm kidney

río etc ['rio] vb ver **reír** ♦ nm river; (fig) torrent, stream; ~ **abajo/arriba** downstream/upstream; ~ **de la Plata** River Plate

rioja [ri'oxa] nm (vino) rioja (wine)

rioplatense [riopla'tense] adj of o from the River Plate region

riqueza [ri'keθa] nf wealth, riches pl; (cualidad) richness

risa ['risa] nf laughter; (una ~) laugh; **¡qué ~!** what a laugh!

risco ['risko] nm crag, cliff

risible [ri'siβle] adj ludicrous, laughable

risotada [riso'taða] nf guffaw, loud laugh

ristra ['ristra] nf string

risueño, a [ri'sweɲo, a] adj (sonriente) smiling; (contento) cheerful

ritmo ['ritmo] nm rhythm; **a ~ lento** slowly; **trabajar a ~ lento** to go slow

rito ['rito] nm rite

ritual [ri'twal] adj, nm ritual

rival [ri'βal] adj, nm/f rival; **~idad** nf rivalry; **~izar** vi: **~izar con** to rival, vie with

rizado, a [ri'θaðo, a] adj curly ♦ nm curls pl

rizar [ri'θar] vt to curl; **~se** vr (pelo) to curl; (agua) to ripple; **rizo** nm curl; ripple

RNE nf abr = **Radio Nacional de España**

robar [ro'βar] vt to rob; (casa etc) to steal; (casa etc) to break into; (NAIPES) to draw

roble ['roβle] nm oak; **~dal** nm oakwood

robo ['roβo] nm robbery, theft

robot [ro'βot] nm robot; ~ **(de cocina)** food processor

robustecer [roβuste'θer] vt to strengthen

robusto, a [ro'βusto, a] adj robust, strong

roca ['roka] nf rock

roce ['roθe] nm (caricia) brush; (TEC) friction; (en la piel) graze; **tener ~ con** to be in close contact with

rociar [ro'θjar] vt to spray

rocín [ro'θin] nm nag, hack

rocío [ro'θio] nm dew

rocoso, a [ro'koso, a] adj rocky

rodaballo [roða'βaʎo] nm turbot

rodado, a [ro'ðaðo, a] adj (con ruedas) wheeled

rodaja [ro'ðaxa] nf slice

rodaje [ro'ðaxe] nm (CINE) shooting, filming; (AUTO): **en ~** running in

rodar [ro'ðar] vt (vehículo) to wheel (along); (escalera) to roll down; (viajar por) to travel over ♦ vi to roll; (coche) to go, run; (CINE) to shoot, film

rodear [roðe'ar] vt to surround ♦ vi to go round; **~se** vr: **~se de amigos** to surround o.s. with friends

rodeo [ro'ðeo] nm (ruta indirecta) detour; (evasión) evasion; (AM) rodeo; **hablar sin ~s** to come to the point, speak plainly

rodilla [ro'ðiʎa] nf knee; **de ~s** kneeling; **ponerse de ~s** to kneel (down)

rodillo [ro'ðiʎo] nm roller; (CULIN) rolling-pin

roedor, a [roe'ðor, a] adj gnawing ♦ nm rodent

roer [ro'er] vt (masticar) to gnaw; (corroer, fig) to corrode

rogar [ro'var] vt, vi (pedir) to ask for; (suplicar) to beg, plead; **se ruega no fumar** please do not smoke

rojizo, a [ro'xiθo, a] adj reddish

rojo, a ['roxo, a] adj, nm red; **al ~ vivo** red-hot

rol [rol] nm list, roll; (papel) role

rollizo, a [ro'ʎiθo, a] adj (objeto) cylindrical; (persona) plump

rollito [ro'ʎito] nm: ~ **de primavera** spring roll

rollo ['roʎo] nm roll; (de cuerda) coil; (madera) log; (fam) bore; ¡qué ~! what a carry-on!

Roma ['roma] n Rome

romance [ro'manθe] nm (amoroso) romance; (LITERATURA) ballad

romano, a [ro'mano, a] adj, nm/f Roman; a la romana in batter

romanticismo [romanti'θismo] nm romanticism

romántico, a [ro'mantiko, a] adj romantic

rombo ['rombo] nm (GEOM) rhombus

romería [rome'ria] nf (REL) pilgrimage; (excursión) trip, outing

Romería

Originally a pilgrimage to a shrine or church to express devotion to the Virgin Mary or a local Saint, the romería *has also become a rural festival which accompanies the pilgrimage. People come from all over to attend, bringing their own food and drink, and spend the day in celebration.*

romero, a [ro'mero, a] nm/f pilgrim ♦ nm rosemary

romo, a ['romo, a] adj blunt; (fig) dull

rompecabezas [rompeka'βeθas] nm inv riddle, puzzle; (juego) jigsaw (puzzle)

rompeolas [rompe'olas] nm inv breakwater

romper [rom'per] vt to break; (hacer pedazos) to smash; (papel, tela etc) to tear, rip ♦ vi (olas) to break; (sol, diente) to break through; ~ un contrato to break a contract; ~ a (empezar a) to start (suddenly); ~ a llorar to burst into tears; ~ con uno to fall out with sb

ron [ron] nm rum

roncar [ron'kar] vi to snore

ronco, a ['ronko, a] adj (afónico) hoarse; (áspero) raucous

ronda ['ronda] nf (gen) round; (patrulla) patrol; rondar vt to patrol ♦ vi to patrol; (fig) to prowl round

ronquido [ron'kiðo] nm snore, snoring

ronronear [ronrone'ar] vi to purr; **ronroneo** nm purr

roña ['rona] nf (VETERINARIA) mange; (mugre) dirt, grime; (óxido) rust

roñoso, a [ro'noso, a] adj (mugriento) filthy; (tacaño) mean

ropa ['ropa] nf clothes pl, clothing; ~ blanca linen; ~ de cama bed linen; ~ interior underwear; ~ para lavar washing; ~je nm gown, robes pl

ropero [ro'pero] nm linen cupboard; (guardarropa) wardrobe

rosa ['rosa] adj pink ♦ nf rose; ~ de los vientos the compass

rosado, a [ro'saðo, a] adj pink ♦ nm rosé

rosal [ro'sal] nm rosebush

rosario [ro'sarjo] nm (REL) rosary; rezar el ~ to say the rosary

rosca ['roska] nf (de tornillo) thread; (de humo) coil, spiral; (pan, postre) ring-shaped roll/pastry

rosetón [rose'ton] nm rosette; (ARQ) rose window

rosquilla [ros'kiʎa] nf doughnut-shaped fritter

rostro ['rostro] nm (cara) face

rotación [rota'θjon] nf rotation; ~ de cultivos crop rotation

rotativo, a [rota'tiβo, a] adj rotary

roto, a ['roto, a] pp de romper ♦ adj broken

rotonda [ro'tonda] nf roundabout

rótula ['rotula] nf kneecap; (TEC) ball-and-socket joint

rotulador [rotula'ðor] nm felt-tip pen

rotular [rotu'lar] vt (carta, documento) to head, entitle; (objeto) to label; **rótulo** nm heading, title; label; (letrero) sign

rotundamente [rotunda'mente] adv (negar) flatly; (responder, afirmar) emphatically; **rotundo, a** adj round;

(*enfático*) emphatic

rotura [ro'tura] *nf* (*acto*) breaking; (*MED*) fracture

roturar [rotu'rar] *vt* to plough

rozadura [roθa'ðura] *nf* abrasion, graze

rozar [ro'θar] *vt* (*frotar*) to rub; (*arañar*) to scratch; (*tocar ligeramente*) to shave, touch lightly; **~se** *vr* to rub (together); **~se con** (*fam*) to rub shoulders with

rte. *abr* (= *remite, remitente*) sender

RTVE *nf abr* = **Radiotelevisión Española**

rubí [ru'βi] *nm* ruby; (*de reloj*) jewel

rubio, a [ruβjo, a] *adj* fair-haired, blond(e) ♦ *nm/f* blond/blonde; **tabaco ~** Virginia tobacco

rubor [ru'βor] *nm* (*sonrojo*) blush; (*timidez*) bashfulness; **~izarse** *vr* to blush

rúbrica ['ruβrika] *nf* (*de la firma*) flourish; **rubricar** *vt* (*firmar*) to sign with a flourish; (*concluir*) to sign and seal

rudimentario, a [ruðimen'tarjo, a] *adj* rudimentary; **rudimento** *nm* rudiment

rudo, a ['ruðo, a] *adj* (*sin pulir*) unpolished; (*grosero*) coarse; (*violento*) violent; (*sencillo*) simple

rueda ['rweða] *nf* wheel; (*círculo*) ring, circle; (*rodaja*) slice, round; **~ delantera/trasera/de repuesto** front/back/spare wheel; **~ de prensa** press conference

ruedo [r'weðo] *nm* (*círculo*) circle; (*TAUR*) arena, bullring

ruego *etc* ['rwexo] *vb ver* **rogar** ♦ *nm* request

rufián [ru'fjan] *nm* scoundrel

rugby ['ruxβi] *nm* rugby

rugido [ru'xiðo] *nm* roar

rugir [ru'xir] *vi* to roar

rugoso, a [ru'xoso, a] *adj* (*arrugado*) wrinkled; (*áspero*) rough; (*desigual*) ridged

ruido ['rwiðo] *nm* noise; (*sonido*)

sound; (*alboroto*) racket, row; (*escándalo*) commotion, rumpus; **~so, a** *adj* noisy, loud; (*fig*) sensational

ruin [rwin] *adj* contemptible, mean

ruina ['rwina] *nf* ruin; (*colapso*) collapse; (*de persona*) ruin, downfall

ruindad [rwin'daθ] *nf* lowness, meanness; (*acto*) low o mean act

ruinoso, a [rwi'noso, a] *adj* ruinous; (*destartalado*) dilapidated, tumbledown; (*COM*) disastrous

ruiseñor [rwise'ɲor] *nm* nightingale

ruleta [ru'leta] *nf* roulette

rulo ['rulo] *nm* (*para el pelo*) curler

Rumanía [ruma'nia] *nf* Rumania

rumba ['rumba] *nf* rumba

rumbo ['rumbo] *nm* (*ruta*) route, direction; (*ángulo de dirección*) course, bearing; (*fig*) course of events; **ir con ~ a** to be heading for

rumboso, a [rum'boso, a] *adj* generous

rumiante [ru'mjante] *nm* ruminant

rumiar [ru'mjar] *vt* to chew; (*fig*) to chew over ♦ *vi* to chew the cud

rumor [ru'mor] *nm* (*ruido sordo*) low sound; (*murmuración*) murmur, buzz

rumorearse *vr*: **se rumorea que** it is rumoured that

runrún [run'run] *nm* (*voces*) murmur, sound of voices; (*fig*) rumour

rupestre [ru'pestre] *adj* rock *cpd*

ruptura [rup'tura] *nf* rupture

rural [ru'ral] *adj* rural

Rusia ['rusja] *nf* Russia; **ruso, a** *adj, nm/f* Russian

rústica [rustika] *nf*: **libro en ~** paperback (book); *ver tb* **rústico**

rústico, a [rustiko, a] *adj* rustic; (*ordinario*) coarse, uncouth ♦ *nm/f* yokel

ruta ['ruta] *nf* route

rutina [ru'tina] *nf* routine; **~rio, a** *adj* routine

S, s

S abr (= santo, a) St; (= sur) S
s. abr (= siglo) C.; (= siguiente) foll
S.A. abr (= Sociedad Anónima) Ltd.
(BRIT), Inc. (US)
sábado [ˈsaβaðo] nm Saturday
sábana [ˈsaβana] nf sheet
sabandija [saβanˈdixa] nf bug, insect
sabañón [saβaˈɲon] nm chilblain
saber [saˈβer] vt to know; (llegar a
conocer) to find out, learn; (tener
capacidad a) to know how to ♦ vi: ~ a
to taste of, taste like ♦ nm knowledge,
learning; **a ~** namely; **¿sabes
conducir/nadar?** can you drive/
swim?; **¿sabes francés?** do you speak
French?; **~ de memoria** to know by
heart; **hacer ~ algo a uno** to inform
sb of sth, let sb know sth
sabiduría [saβiðuˈria] nf
(conocimientos) wisdom; (instrucción)
learning
sabiendas [saˈβjendas]: **a ~** adv
knowingly
sabio, a [ˈsaβjo,a] adj (docto) learned;
(prudente) wise, sensible
sabor [saˈβor] nm taste, flavour; **~ear**
vt to taste, savour; (fig) to relish
sabotaje [saβoˈtaxe] nm sabotage
saboteador, a [saβotea'ðor, a] nm/f
saboteur
sabotear [saβoteˈar] vt to sabotage
sabré etc vb ver **saber**
sabroso, a [saˈβroso, a] adj tasty; (fig:
fam) racy, salty
sacacorchos [saka'kortʃos] nm inv
corkscrew
sacapuntas [saka'puntas] nm inv
pencil sharpener
sacar [saˈkar] vt to take out; (fig:
extraer) to get (out); (quitar) to
remove, get out; (hacer salir) to bring
out; (conclusión) to draw; (novela etc)
to publish, bring out; (ropa) to take off;

(obra) to make; (premio) to receive;
(entradas) to get; (TENIS) to serve;
~ adelante (niño) to bring up;
(negocio) to carry on, go on with; **~ a
uno a bailar** to get sb up to dance;
~ una foto to take a photo; **~ la
lengua** to stick out one's tongue;
~ buenas/malas notas to get good/
bad marks
sacarina [sakaˈrina] nf saccharin(e)
sacerdote [saθerˈðote] nm priest
saciar [saˈθjar] vt (hambre, sed) to
satisfy; **~se** vr (de comida) to get full
up; **comer hasta ~se** to eat one's fill
saco [ˈsako] nm bag; (grande) sack; (su
contenido) bagful; (AM) jacket; **~ de
dormir** sleeping bag
sacramento [sakraˈmento] nm
sacrament
sacrificar [sakrifiˈkar] vt to sacrifice;
sacrificio nm sacrifice
sacrilegio [sakriˈlexjo] nm sacrilege;
sacrílego, a adj sacrilegious
sacristía [sakrisˈtia] nf sacristy
sacro, a [ˈsakro, a] adj sacred
sacudida [sakuˈðiða] nf (agitación)
shake, shaking; (sacudimiento) jolt,
bump; **~ eléctrica** electric shock
sacudir [sakuˈðir] vt to shake; (golpear)
to hit
sádico, a [ˈsaðiko, a] adj sadistic
♦ nm/f sadist; **sadismo** nm sadism
saeta [saˈeta] nf (flecha) arrow
sagacidad [sayaθiˈðað] nf shrewdness,
cleverness; **sagaz** adj shrewd, clever
sagitario [saxiˈtarjo] nm Sagittarius
sagrado, a [saˈɣraðo, a] adj sacred,
holy
Sáhara [ˈsaara] nm: **el ~** the Sahara
(desert)
sal [sal] vb ver **salir** ♦ nf salt
sala [ˈsala] nf room; (~ de estar) living
room; (TEATRO) house, auditorium; (de
hospital) ward; **~ de apelación** court;
~ de espera waiting room; **~ de
estar** living room; **~ de fiestas** dance
hall

salado, a [sa'laðo, a] adj salty; (fig)
witty, amusing; **agua salada** salt
water

salar [sa'lar] vt to salt, add salt to

salarial [sala'rjal] adj (aumento,
revisión) wage cpd

salario [sa'larjo] nm wage, pay

salchicha [sal'tʃitʃa] nf (pork) sausage;
salchichón nm (salami-type) sausage

saldar [sal'dar] vt to pay; (vender) to
sell off; (fig) to settle, resolve; **saldo**
nm (pago) settlement; (de una cuenta)
balance; (lo restante) remnant(s) (pl),
remainder; **saldos** nmpl (en tienda)
sale

saldré etc vb ver **salir**

salero [sa'lero] nm salt cellar

salgo etc vb ver **salir**

salida [sa'liða] nf (puerta etc) exit, way
out; (acto) leaving, going out; (de tren,
AVIAT) departure; (TEC) output,
production; (fig) way out; (COM)
opening; (GEO, válvula) outlet; (de gas)
leak; **calle sin ~** cul-de-sac; **~ de
incendios** fire escape

saliente [sa'ljente] adj (ARQ)
projecting; (sol) rising; (fig) outstanding

PALABRA CLAVE

salir [sa'lir] vi **1** (partir: tb: **~ de**) to
leave; **Juan ha salido** Juan is out;
salió de la cocina he came out of the
kitchen

2 (aparecer) to appear; (disco, libro) to
come out; **anoche salió en la tele**
she appeared o was on TV last night;
salió en todos los periódicos it was
in all the papers

3 (resultar): **la muchacha nos salió
muy trabajadora** the girl turned out
to be a very hard worker; **la comida
te ha salido exquisita** the food was
delicious; **sale muy caro** it's very
expensive

4: **~le a uno algo: la entrevista que
hice me salió bien/mal** the
interview I did went o turned out well/

badly

5: **~ adelante: no sé como haré
para ~ adelante** I don't know how I'll
get by

♦ **~se** vr (líquido) to spill; (animal) to
escape

---

saliva [sa'liβa] nf saliva

salmo ['salmo] nm psalm

salmón [sal'mon] nm salmon

salmonete [salmo'nete] nm red
mullet

salmuera [sal'mwera] nf pickle, brine

salón [sa'lon] nm (de casa) living
room, lounge; (muebles) lounge suite;
~ de belleza beauty parlour; **~ de
baile** dance hall

salpicadero [salpika'ðero] nm (AUTO)
dashboard

salpicar [salpi'kar] vt (rociar) to
sprinkle, spatter; (esparcir) to scatter

salpicón [salpi'kon] nm: **~ de
mariscos** seafood salad

salsa ['salsa] nf sauce; (con carne
asada) gravy; (fig) spice

saltamontes [salta'montes] nm inv
grasshopper

saltar [sal'tar] vt to jump (over), leap
(over); (dejar de lado) to skip, miss out
♦ vi to jump, leap; (pelota) to bounce;
(al aire) to fly up; (quebrarse) to break;
(al agua) to dive; (fig) to explode, blow
up

salto ['salto] nm jump, leap; (al agua)
dive; **~ de agua** waterfall; **~ de altura**
high jump

saltón, ona [sal'ton, ona] adj (ojos)
bulging, popping; (dientes) protrud-
ing

salud [sa'luð] nf health; **¡(a su) ~!**
cheers!, good health!; **~able** adj (de
buena ~) healthy; (provechoso) good,
beneficial

saludar [salu'ðar] vt to greet; (MIL) to
salute; **saludo** nm greeting;
"saludos" (en carta) "best wishes",
"regards"

salva ['salßa] *nf*: **~ de aplausos**
ovation
salvación [salßa'θjon] *nf* salvation;
(*rescate*) rescue
salvado [sal'ßaðo] *nm* bran
salvaguardar [salßaɣwar'ðar] *vt* to
safeguard
salvajada [salßa'xaða] *nf* atrocity
salvaje [sal'ßaxe] *adj* wild; (*tribu*)
savage; **salvajismo** *nm* savagery
salvamento [salßa'mento] *nm* rescue
salvar [sal'ßar] *vt* (*rescatar*) to save,
rescue; (*resolver*) to overcome, resolve;
(*cubrir distancias*) to cover, travel;
(*hacer excepción*) to except, exclude;
(*barco*) to salvage
salvavidas [salßa'ßiðas] *adj inv*:
bote/chaleco/cinturón ~ lifeboat/life
jacket/life belt
salvo, a ['salßo, a] *adj* safe ♦ *adv*
except (for), save; **a ~** out of danger;
~ que unless; **~conducto** *nm* safe-
conduct
san [san] *adj* saint; **S~ Juan** St John
sanar [sa'nar] *vt* (*herida*) to heal;
(*persona*) to cure ♦ *vi* (*persona*) to get
well, recover; (*herida*) to heal
sanatorio [sana'torjo] *nm* sanatorium
sanción [san'θjon] *nf* sanction;
sancionar *vt* to sanction
sandalia [san'dalja] *nf* sandal
sandez [san'deθ] *nf* foolishness
sandía [san'dia] *nf* watermelon
sandwich ['sandwitʃ] (*pl* **~s, ~es**) *nm*
sandwich
saneamiento [sanea'mjento] *nm*
sanitation
sanear [sane'ar] *vt* to clean up;
(*terreno*) to drain

The **Sanfermines** *is a week-long
festival in Pamplona made famous by
Ernest Hemingway. From the 7th
July, the feast of "San Fermín",
crowds of mainly young people take to
the streets drinking, singing and*

*dancing. Early in the morning bulls
are released along the narrow streets
leading to the bullring, and young
men risk serious injury to show their
bravery by running out in front of
them, a custom which is also typical
of many Spanish villages.*

sangrar [san'grar] *vt, vi* to bleed;
sangre *nf* blood
sangría [san'gria] *nf* sangria, sweetened
drink of red wine with fruit
sangriento, a [san'grjento, a] *adj*
bloody
sanguijuela [sangi'xwela] *nf* (ZOOL,
fig) leech
sanguinario, a [sangi'narjo, a] *adj*
bloodthirsty
sanguíneo, a [san'gineo, a] *adj* blood
cpd
sanidad [sani'ðað] *nf*: **~ (pública)**
public health

San Isidro *is the patron saint of
Madrid, and gives his name to the
week-long festivities which take place
around the 15th May. Originally an
18th-century trade fair, the San
Isidro celebrations now include
music, dance, a famous romería,
theatre and bullfighting.*

sanitario, a [sani'tarjo, a] *adj* health
cpd; **~s** *nmpl* toilets (*BRIT*), washroom
(*US*)
sano, a ['sano, a] *adj* healthy; (*sin
daños*) sound; (*comida*) wholesome;
(*entero*) whole, intact; **~ y salvo** safe
and sound
Santiago [san'tjavo] *nm*: **~ (de Chile)**
Santiago
santiamén [santja'men] *nm*: **en un ~**
in no time at all
santidad [santi'ðað] *nf* holiness,
sanctity
santiguarse [santi'xwarse] *vr* to make

the sign of the cross

santo, a ['santo, a] *adj* holy; *(fig)* wonderful, miraculous ♦ *nm/f* saint ♦ *nm* saint's day; **~ y seña** password

santuario [san'twarjo] *nm* sanctuary, shrine

saña ['saɲa] *nf* rage, fury

sapo ['sapo] *nm* toad

saque ['sake] *nm* (*TENIS*) service, serve; (*FÚTBOL*) throw-in; **~ de esquina** corner (kick)

saquear [sake'ar] *vt* (*MIL*) to sack; (*robar*) to loot, plunder; *(fig)* to ransack; **saqueo** *nm* sacking; looting, plundering; ransacking

sarampión [saram'pjon] *nm* measles *sg*

sarcasmo [sar'kasmo] *nm* sarcasm; **sarcástico, a** *adj* sarcastic

sardina [sar'ðina] *nf* sardine

sargento [sar'xento] *nm* sergeant

sarmiento [sar'mjento] *nm* (*BOT*) vine shoot

sarna ['sarna] *nf* itch; (*MED*) scabies

sarpullido [sarpu'ʎiðo] *nm* (*MED*) rash

sarro ['sarro] *nm* (*en dientes*) tartar, plaque

sartén [sar'ten] *nf* frying pan

sastre ['sastre] *nm* tailor; **~ría** *nf* (*arte*) tailoring; (*tienda*) tailor's (shop)

Satanás [sata'nas] *nm* Satan

satélite [sa'telite] *nm* satellite

sátira ['satira] *nf* satire

satisfacción [satisfak'θjon] *nf* satisfaction

satisfacer [satisfa'θer] *vt* to satisfy; (*gastos*) to meet; (*pérdida*) to make good; **~se** *vr* to satisfy o.s, be satisfied; (*vengarse*) to take revenge; **satisfecho, a** *adj* satisfied; (*contento*) content(ed), happy; (*tb*: **satisfecho de sí mismo**) self-satisfied, smug

saturar [satu'rar] *vt* to saturate; **~se** *vr* (*mercado, aeropuerto*) to reach saturation point

sauce ['sauθe] *nm* willow; **~ llorón** weeping willow

sauna ['sauna] *nf* sauna

savia ['saβja] *nf* sap

saxofón [sakso'fon] *nm* saxophone

sazonar [saθo'nar] *vt* to ripen; (*CULIN*) to flavour, season

SE *abr* (= *sudeste*) SE

se [se] *pron* 1 (*reflexivo*: *sg*: *m*) himself; (: *f*) herself; (: *pl*) themselves; (: *cosa*) itself; (: *de Vd*) yourself; (: *de Vds*) yourselves; **~ está preparando** she's preparing herself; *para usos léxicos del pron ver el vb en cuestión, p.ej.* **arrepentirse**

2 (*con complemento indirecto*) to him; to her; to them; to it; to you; **a usted ~ lo dije ayer** I told you yesterday; **~ compró un sombrero** he bought himself a hat; **~ rompió la pierna** he broke his leg

3 (*uso recíproco*) each other, one another; **~ miraron (el uno al otro)** they looked at each other o one another

4 (*en oraciones pasivas*): **se han vendido muchos libros** a lot of books have been sold

5 (*impers*): **~ dice que** people say that, it is said that; **allí ~ come muy bien** the food there is very good, you can eat very well there

sé *vb ver* **saber; ser**

sea *etc vb ver* **ser**

sebo ['seβo] *nm* fat, grease

secador [seka'ðor] *nm*: **~ de pelo** hair-dryer

secadora [seka'ðora] *nf* tumble dryer

secar [se'kar] *vt* to dry; **~se** *vr* to dry (off); (*río, planta*) to dry up

sección [sek'θjon] *nf* section

seco, a ['seko, a] *adj* dry; (*carácter*) cold; (*respuesta*) sharp, curt; **habrá pan a secas** there will be just bread; **decir algo a secas** to say sth curtly; **parar en ~** to stop dead

secretaría [sekreta'ria] nf secretariat
secretario, a [sekre'tarjo, a] nm/f
secretary

secreto, a [se'kreto, a] adj secret;
(persona) secretive ♦ nm secret;
(calidad) secrecy

secta ['sekta] nf sect; **~rio, a** adj
sectarian

sector [sek'tor] nm sector

secuela [se'kwela] nf consequence

secuencia [se'kwenθja] nf sequence

secuestrar [sekwes'trar] vt to kidnap;
(bienes) to seize, confiscate; **secuestro**
nm kidnapping; seizure, confiscation

secular [seku'lar] adj secular

secundar [sekun'dar] vt to second,
support

secundario, a [sekun'darjo, a] adj
secondary

sed [seð] nf thirst; **tener ~** to be thirsty

seda ['seða] nf silk

sedal [se'ðal] nm fishing line

sedante [se'ðante] nm sedative

sede ['seðe] nf (de gobierno) seat; (de
compañía) headquarters pl; **Santa S~**
Holy See

sedentario, a [seðen'tarjo, a] adj
sedentary

sediento, a [se'ðjento, a] adj thirsty

sedimento [seði'mento] nm sediment

sedoso, a [se'ðoso, a] adj silky, silken

seducción [seðuk'θjon] nf seduction

seducir [seðu'θir] vt to seduce;
(cautivar) to charm, fascinate; (atraer)
to attract; **seductor, a** adj seductive;
charming, fascinating; attractive ♦ nm/f
seducer

segar [se'ɣar] vt (mies) to reap, cut;
(hierba) to mow, cut

seglar [se'ɣlar] adj secular, lay

segregación [seɣreɣa'θjon] nf
segregation. **~ racial** racial segregation

segregar [seɣre'ɣar] vt to segregate,
separate

seguida [se'ɣiða] nf: **en ~** at once,
right away

seguido, a [se'ɣiðo, a] adj (continuo)

continuous, unbroken; (recto) straight
♦ adv (directo) straight (on); (después)
after; (AM: a menudo) often; **~s**
consecutive, successive; **5 días ~s** 5
days running, 5 days in a row

seguimiento [seɣi'mjento] nm chase,
pursuit; (continuación) continuation

seguir [se'ɣir] vt to follow; (venir
después) to follow on, come after;
(proseguir) to continue; (perseguir) to
chase, pursue ♦ vi (gen) to follow;
(continuar) to continue, carry o go on;
~se vr to follow; **sigo sin
comprender** I still don't understand;
sigue lloviendo it's still raining

según [se'ɣun] prep according to
♦ adv: **¿irás? — ~** are you going? — it
all depends ♦ conj as; **~ caminamos**
while we walk

segundo, a [se'ɣundo, a] adj second
♦ nm second ♦ nf second meaning; **de
segunda mano** second-hand;
segunda (clase) second class;
segunda enseñanza secondary
education; **segunda (marcha)** (AUT)
second (gear)

seguramente [seɣura'mente] adv
surely; (con certeza) for sure, with
certainty

seguridad [seɣuri'ðað] nf safety; (del
estado, de casa etc) security;
(certidumbre) certainty; (confianza)
confidence; (estabilidad) stability;
~ social social security

seguro, a [se'ɣuro, a] adj (cierto) sure,
certain; (fiel) trustworthy; (libre de
peligro) safe; (bien defendido, firme)
secure ♦ adv for sure, certainly ♦ nm
(COM) insurance; **~ contra terceros/a
todo riesgo** third party/
comprehensive insurance; **~s sociales**
social security sg

seis [seis] num six

seísmo [se'ismo] nm tremor,
earthquake

selección [selek'θjon] nf selection;
seleccionar vt to pick, choose, select

selectividad |selektiβi'ðað| (*ESP*) nf university entrance examination

selecto, a |se'lekto, a| adj select, choice; (*escogido*) selected

sellar |se'ʎar| vt (*documento oficial*) to seal; (*pasaporte, visado*) to stamp

sello |'seʎo| nm stamp; (*precinto*) seal

selva |'selβa| nf (*bosque*) forest, woods pl; (*jungla*) jungle

semáforo |se'maforo| nm (*AUTO*) traffic lights pl; (*FERRO*) signal

semana |se'mana| nf week; **entre ~** during the week; **S~ Santa** Holy Week; **semanal** adj weekly; **~rio** nm weekly magazine

---

Semana Santa

In Spain celebrations for **Semana Santa** *(Holy Week) are often spectacular. "Viernes Santo", "Sábado Santo" and "Domingo de Resurrección" (Good Friday, Holy Saturday, Easter Sunday) are all national public holidays, with additional days being given as local holidays. There are fabulous* **procesiones** *all over the country, with members of "cofradías" (brotherhoods) dressing in hooded robes and parading their "pasos" (religious floats and sculptures) through the streets. Seville has the most famous Holy Week processions.*

---

semblante |sem'blante| nm face; (*fig*) look

sembrar |sem'brar| vt to sow; (*objetos*) to sprinkle, scatter about; (*noticias etc*) to spread

semejante |seme'xante| adj (*parecido*) similar ♦ nm fellow man, fellow creature; **~s** alike, similar; **nunca hizo cosa ~** he never did any such thing; **semejanza** nf similarity

semejar |seme'xar| vi to seem like, resemble; **~se** vr to look alike, be similar

semen |'semen| nm semen

semestral |semes'tral| adj half-yearly, bi-annual

semicírculo |semi'θirkulo| nm semicircle

semidesnatado, a |semiðesna'taðo, a| adj semi-skimmed

semifinal |semifi'nal| nf semifinal

semilla |se'miʎa| nf seed

seminario |semi'narjo| nm (*REL*) seminary; (*ESCOL*) seminar

sémola |'semola| nf semolina

Sena |'sena| nm: **el ~** the (river) Seine

senado |se'naðo| nm senate; **senador, a** nm/f senator

sencillez |senθi'ʎeθ| nf simplicity; (*de persona*) naturalness; **sencillo, a** adj simple; natural, unaffected

senda |'senda| nf path, track

senderismo |sende'rismo| nm hiking

sendero |sen'dero| nm path, track

sendos, as |'sendos, as| adj pl: **les dio ~ golpes** he hit both of them

senil |se'nil| adj senile

seno |'seno| nm (*ANAT*) bosom, bust; (*fig*) bosom; **~s** breasts

sensación |sensa'θjon| nf sensation; (*sentido*) sense; (*sentimiento*) feeling; **sensacional** adj sensational

sensato, a |sen'sato, a| adj sensible

sensible |sen'sible| adj sensitive; (*apreciable*) perceptible, appreciable; (*pérdida*) considerable; **~ro, a** adj sentimental

sensitivo, a |sensi'tiβo, a| adj sense cpd

sensorial |senso'rjal| adj sensory

sensual |sen'swal| adj sensual

sentada |sen'taða| nf sitting; (*protesta*) sit-in

sentado, a |sen'taðo, a| adj: **estar ~** to sit, be sitting (down); **dar por ~** to take for granted, assume

sentar |sen'tar| vt to sit, seat; (*fig*) to establish ♦ vi (*vestido*) to suit; (*alimento*): **~ bien/mal a** to agree/ disagree with; **~se** vr (*persona*) to sit, sit down; (*los depósitos*) to settle

sentencia [sen'tenθja] nf (máxima)
maxim, saying; (JUR) sentence;
sentenciar vt to sentence

sentido, a [sen'tiðo, a] adj (pérdida)
regrettable; (carácter) sensitive ♦ nm
sense; (sentimiento) feeling; (significado)
sense, meaning; (dirección) direction;
mi más ~ pésame my deepest
sympathy; **~ del humor** sense of
humour; **~ único** one-way (street);
tener ~ to make sense

sentimental [sentimen'tal] adj
sentimental; **vida ~** love life

sentimiento [senti'mjento] nm
feeling

sentir [sen'tir] vt to feel; (percibir) to
perceive, sense; (lamentar) to regret,
be sorry for ♦ vi (tener la sensación) to
feel; (lamentarse) to feel sorry ♦ nm
opinion, judgement; **~se bien/mal** to
feel well/ill; **lo siento** I'm sorry

seña ['seɲa] nf sign; (MIL) password; **~s**
nfpl (dirección) address sg; **~s
personales** personal description sg

señal [se'ɲal] nf sign; (síntoma)
symptom; (FERRO, TELEC) signal;
(marca) mark; (COM) deposit; **en ~ de**
as a token of, as a sign of; **~ar** vt to
mark; (indicar) to point out, indicate

señor [se'ɲor] nm (hombre) man;
(caballero) gentleman; (dueño) owner,
master; (trato: antes de nombre propio)
Mr; (: hablando directamente) sir; **muy
~ mío** Dear Sir; **el ~ alcalde/
presidente** the mayor/president

señora [se'ɲora] nf (dama) lady; (trato:
antes de nombre propio) Mrs;
(: hablando directamente) madam;
(esposa) wife; **Nuestra S~** Our Lady

señorita [seɲo'rita] nf (con nombre y/o
apellido) Miss; (mujer joven) young lady

señorito [seɲo'rito] nm young
gentleman; (pey) rich kid

señuelo [se'ɲwelo] nm decoy

sepa etc vb ver **saber**

separación [separa'θjon] nf
separation; (división) division; (hueco)
gap

separar [sepa'rar] vt to separate;
(dividir) to divide; **~se** vr (parte) to
come away; (partes) to come apart;
(persona) to leave, go away;
(matrimonio) to separate;

separatismo nm separatism

sepia ['sepja] nf cuttlefish

septentrional [septentrjo'nal] adj
northern

septiembre [sep'tjembre] nm
September

séptimo, a ['septimo, a] adj, nm
seventh

sepulcral [sepul'kral] adj (fig: silencio,
atmósfera) deadly; **sepulcro** nm tomb,
grave

sepultar [sepul'tar] vt to bury;
sepultura nf (acto) burial; (tumba)
grave, tomb

sequedad [seke'ðað] nf dryness; (fig)
brusqueness, curtness

sequía [se'kia] nf drought

séquito ['sekito] nm (de rey etc)
retinue; (seguidores) followers pl

PALABRA CLAVE

---

ser [ser] vi **1** (descripción) to be; **es
médica/muy alta** she's a doctor/very
tall; **la familia es de Cuzco** his (o her
etc) family is from Cuzco; **soy Ana**
(TELEC) Ana speaking o here

2 (propiedad): **es de Joaquín** it's
Joaquín's, it belongs to Joaquín

3 (horas, fechas, números): **es la una**
it's one o'clock; **son las seis y media**
it's half-past six; **es el 1 de junio** it's
the first of June; **somos/son seis**
there are six of us/them

4 (en oraciones pasivas): **ha sido
descubierto ya** it's already been
discovered

5: es de esperar que ... it is to be
hoped o I etc hope that ...

6 (locuciones con sub): **o sea** that is to
say; **sea él sea su hermana** either
him o his sister

7: a no ~ por él ... but for him ...

8: a no ~ que: a no ~ que tenga uno ya unless he's got one already
♦ *nm* being; **~ humano** human being

---

serenarse [sere'narse] *vr* to calm down

sereno, a [se'reno, a] *adj* (*persona*) calm, unruffled; (*el tiempo*) fine, settled; (*ambiente*) calm, peaceful ♦ *nm* night watchman

serial [ser'jal] *nm* serial

serie ['serje] *nf* series; (*cadena*) sequence, succession; **fuera de ~** out of order; (*fig*) special, out of the ordinary; **fabricación en ~** mass production

seriedad [serje'ðað] *nf* seriousness; (*formalidad*) reliability; **serio, a** *adj* serious; reliable, dependable; grave, serious; **en serio** *adv* seriously

serigrafía [seriɣra'fia] *nf* silk-screen printing

sermón [ser'mon] *nm* (*REL*) sermon

seropositivo, a [seroposi'tiβo] *adj* HIV positive

serpentear [serpente'ar] *vi* to wriggle; (*camino, río*) to wind, snake

serpentina [serpen'tina] *nf* streamer

serpiente [ser'pjente] *nf* snake; **~ de cascabel** rattlesnake

serranía [serra'nia] *nf* mountainous area

serrar [se'rrar] *vt* = **aserrar**

serrín [se'rrin] *nm* = **aserrín**

serrucho [se'rrutʃo] *nm* saw

servicio [ser'βiθjo] *nm* service; **~s** *nmpl* toilet(s); **~ incluido** service charge included; **~ militar** military service

servidumbre [serβi'ðumbre] *nf* (*sujeción*) servitude; (*criados*) servants *pl*, staff

servil [ser'βil] *adj* servile

servilleta [serβi'ʎeta] *nf* serviette, napkin

servir [ser'βir] *vt* to serve ♦ *vi* to serve;

(*tener utilidad*) to be of use, be useful; **~se** *vr* to serve o help o.s.; **~se de algo** to make use of sth, use sth; **sírvase pasar** please come in

sesenta [se'senta] *num* sixty

sesgo ['sesɣo] *nm* slant; (*fig*) slant, twist

sesión [se'sjon] *nf* (*POL*) session, sitting; (*CINE*) showing

seso ['seso] *nm* brain; **sesudo, a** *adj* sensible, wise

seta ['seta] *nf* mushroom; **~ venenosa** toadstool

setecientos [sete'θjentos, as] *adj*, *num* seven hundred

setenta [se'tenta] *num* seventy

seto ['seto] *nm* hedge

seudónimo [seu'ðonimo] *nm* pseudonym

severidad [seβeri'ðað] *nf* severity; **severo, a** *adj* severe

Sevilla [se'βiʎa] *n* Seville; **sevillano, a** *adj* of o from Seville ♦ *nm/f* native o inhabitant of Seville

sexo ['sekso] *nm* sex

sexto, a ['seksto, a] *adj*, *nm* sixth

sexual [sek'swal] *adj* sexual; **vida ~** sex life

si [si] *conj* if; **me pregunto ~** ... I wonder if o whether ...

sí [si] *adv* yes ♦ *nm* consent ♦ *pron* (*uso impersonal*) oneself; (*sg: m*) himself; (: *f*) herself; (: *de cosa*) itself; (*de usted*) yourself; (*pl*) themselves; (*de ustedes*) yourselves; (*recíproco*) each other; **él no quiere pero yo ~** he doesn't want to but I do; **ella ~ vendrá** she will certainly come, she is sure to come; **claro que ~** of course; **creo que ~** I think so

siamés, esa [sja'mes, esa] *adj*, *nm/f* Siamese

SIDA ['siða] *nm abr* (= *Síndrome de Inmunodeficiencia Adquirida*) AIDS

siderúrgico, a [siðe'rurxico, a] *adj* iron and steel *cpd*

sidra ['siðra] *nf* cider

siembra ['sjembra] nf sowing

siempre ['sjempre] adv always; (todo el tiempo) all the time; **~ que** (cada vez) whenever; (dado que) provided that; **como ~** as usual; **para ~** for ever

sien [sjen] nf temple

siento etc vb ver **sentar**; **sentir**

sierra ['sjerra] nf (TEC) saw; (cadena de montañas) mountain range

siervo, a ['sjerßo, a] nm/f slave

siesta ['sjesta] nf siesta, nap; **echar la ~** to have an afternoon nap o a siesta

siete ['sjete] num seven

sífilis ['sifilis] nf syphilis

sifón [si'fon] nm syphon; **whisky con ~** whisky and soda

sigla ['sixla] nf abbreviation; acronym

siglo ['sixlo] nm century; (fig) age

significación [sixnifika'θjon] nf significance

significado [sixnifi'kaðo] nm (de palabra etc) meaning

significar [sixnifi'kar] vt to mean, signify; (notificar) to make known, express; **significativo, a** adj significant

signo ['sixno] nm sign; **~ de admiración o exclamación** exclamation mark; **~ de interrogación** question mark

sigo etc vb ver **seguir**

siguiente [si'xjente] adj next, following

siguió etc vb ver **seguir**

sílaba ['silaßa] nf syllable

silbar [sil'ßar] vt, vi to whistle; **silbato** nm whistle; **silbido** nm whistle, whistling

silenciador [silenθja'ðor] nm silencer

silenciar [silen'θjar] vt (persona) to silence; (escándalo) to hush up; **silencio** nm silence, quiet; **silencioso, a** adj silent, quiet

silla ['siʎa] nf (asiento) chair; (tb: **~ de montar**) saddle; **~ de ruedas** wheelchair

sillón [si'ʎon] nm armchair, easy chair

silueta [si'lweta] nf silhouette; (de edificio) outline; (figura) figure

silvestre [sil'ßestre] adj wild

simbólico, a [sim'boliko, a] adj symbolic(al)

simbolizar [simboli'θar] vt to symbolize

símbolo ['simbolo] nm symbol

simetría [sime'tria] nf symmetry

simiente [si'mjente] nf seed

similar [simi'lar] adj similar

simio ['simjo] nm ape

simpatía [simpa'tia] nf liking; (afecto) affection; (amabilidad) kindness; **simpático, a** adj nice, pleasant; kind

simpatizante [simpati'θante] nm/f sympathizer

simpatizar [simpati'θar] vi: **~ con** to get on well with

simple ['simple] adj simple; (elemental) simple, easy; (mero) mere; (puro) pure, sheer ♦ nm/f simpleton; **~za** nf simpleness; (necedad) silly thing; **simplificar** vt to simplify

simposio [sim'posjo] nm symposium

simular [simu'lar] vt to simulate

simultáneo, a [simul'taneo, a] adj simultaneous

sin [sin] prep without; **la ropa está ~ lavar** the clothes are unwashed; **~ que** without; **~ embargo** however, still

sinagoga [sina'xoxa] nf synagogue

sinceridad [sinθeri'ðað] nf sincerity; **sincero, a** adj sincere

sincronizar [sinkroni'θar] vt to synchronize

sindical [sindi'kal] adj union cpd, trade-union cpd; **~ista** adj, nm/f trade unionist

sindicato [sindi'kato] nm (de trabajadores) trade(s) union; (de negociantes) syndicate

síndrome ['sindrome] nm (MED) syndrome; **~ de abstinencia** (MED) withdrawal symptoms

sinfín [sin'fin] nm: **un ~ de** a great

many, no end of

sinfonía [sinfo'nia] nf symphony

singular [singu'lar] adj singular; (fig) outstanding, exceptional; (raro) peculiar, odd; **~idad** nf singularity, peculiarity; **~izarse** vr to distinguish o.s., stand out

siniestro, a [si'njestro, a] adj sinister ♦ nm (accidente) accident

sinnúmero [sin'numero] nm = **sinfin**

sino ['sino] nm fate, destiny ♦ conj (pero) but; (salvo) except, save

sinónimo, a [si'nonimo, a] adj synonymous ♦ nm synonym

síntesis ['sintesis] nf synthesis; **sintético, a** adj synthetic

sintetizar [sinteti'θar] vt to synthesize

sintió vb ver **sentir**

síntoma ['sintoma] nm symptom

sintonía [sinto'nia] nf (RADIO, MUS: de programa) tuning; **sintonizar** vt (RADIO: emisora) to tune (in)

sinvergüenza [simber'ɣwenθa] nm/f rogue, scoundrel; **¡es un ~!** he's got a nerve!

siquiera [si'kjera] conj even if, even though ♦ adv at least; **ni ~** not even

sirena [si'rena] nf siren

Siria ['sirja] nf Syria

sirviente, a [sir'βjente, a] nm/f servant

sirvo etc vb ver **servir**

sisear [sise'ar] vt, vi to hiss

sistema [sis'tema] nm system; (método) method; **sistemático, a** adj systematic

---
Sistema educativo

The reform of the Spanish **sistema educativo** (education system) begun in the early 90s has replaced the courses EGB, BUP and COU with the following: "Primaria" a compulsory 6 years; "Secundaria" a compulsory 4 years and "Bachillerato" an optional 2-year secondary school course, essential for those wishing to go on to higher education.

---

sitiar [si'tjar] vt to besiege, lay siege to

sitio ['sitjo] nm (lugar) place; (espacio) room, space; (MIL) siege

situación [sitwa'θjon] nf situation, position; (estatus) position, standing

situado, a [situ'aðo] adj situated, placed

situar [si'twar] vt to place, put; (edificio) to locate, situate

slip [slip] nm pants pl, briefs pl

smoking ['smokin, es'mokin] (pl **~s**) nm dinner jacket (BRIT), tuxedo (US)

snob [es'nob] = **esnob**

SO abr (= suroeste) SW

sobaco [so'βako] nm armpit

sobar [so'βar] vt (ropa) to rumple; (comida) to play around with

soberanía [soβera'nia] nf sovereignty; **soberano, a** adj sovereign; (fig) supreme ♦ nm/f sovereign

soberbia [so'βerβja] nf pride; haughtiness, arrogance; magnificence

soberbio, a [so'βerβjo, a] adj (orgulloso) proud; (altivo) haughty, arrogant; (estupendo) magnificent, superb

sobornar [soβor'nar] vt to bribe; **soborno** nm bribe

sobra ['soβra] nf excess, surplus; **~s** nfpl left-overs, scraps; **de ~** surplus, extra; **tengo de ~** I've more than enough; **~do, a** adj (más que suficiente) more than enough; (superfluo) excessive; **sobrante** remaining, extra ♦ nm surplus, remainder

sobrar [so'βrar] vt to exceed, surpass ♦ vi (tener de más) to be more than enough; (quedar) to remain, be left (over)

sobrasada [soβra'saða] nf pork sausage spread

sobre ['soβre] prep (gen) on; (encima) on (top of); (por encima de, arriba de) over, above; (*más que*) more than; (*además*) in addition to, besides; (*alrededor de*) about ♦ *nm* envelope; **~ todo** above all

sobrecama [soβre'kama] *nf* bedspread

sobrecargar [soβrekar'ɣar] *vt* (*camión*) to overload; (*COM*) to surcharge

sobredosis [soβre'ðosis] *nf inv* overdose

sobreentender [soβre(e)nten'der] *vt* to deduce, infer; **~se** *vr*: **se sobreentiende que ...** it is implied that ...

sobrehumano, a [soβreu'mano, a] *adj* superhuman

sobrellevar [soβreʎe'βar] *vt* to bear, endure

sobremesa [soβre'mesa] *nf*: **durante la ~** after dinner; **ordenador de ~** desktop computer

sobrenatural [soβrenatu'ral] *adj* supernatural

sobrenombre [soβre'nombre] *nm* nickname

sobrepasar [soβrepa'sar] *vt* to exceed, surpass

sobreponerse [soβrepo'nerse] *vr*: **~ a** to overcome

sobresaliente [soβresa'ljente] *adj* outstanding, excellent

sobresalir [soβresa'lir] *vi* to project, jut out; (*fig*) to stand out, excel

sobresaltar [soβresal'tar] *vt* (*asustar*) to scare, frighten; (*sobrecoger*) to startle; **sobresalto** *nm* (*movimiento*) start; (*susto*) scare; (*turbación*) sudden shock

sobretodo [soβre'toðo] *nm* overcoat

sobrevenir [soβreβe'nir] *vi* (*ocurrir*) to happen (unexpectedly); (*resultar*) to follow, ensue

sobreviviente [soβreβi'βjente] *adj* surviving ♦ *nm/f* survivor

sobrevivir [soβreβi'βir] *vi* to survive

sobrevolar [soβreβo'lar] *vt* to fly over

sobriedad [soβrje'ðað] *nf* sobriety, soberness; (*moderación*) moderation, restraint

sobrino, a [so'βrino, a] *nm/f* nephew/niece

sobrio, a [so'βrjo, a] *adj* sober; (*moderado*) moderate, restrained

socarrón, ona [soka'rron, ona] *adj* (*sarcástico*) sarcastic, ironic(al)

socavar [soka'βar] *vt* (*tb fig*) to undermine

socavón [soka'βon] *nm* (*hoyo*) hole

sociable [so'θjaβle] *adj* (*persona*) sociable, friendly; (*animal*) social

social [so'θjal] *adj* social; (*COM*) company *cpd*

socialdemócrata [soθjalde'mokrata] *nm/f* social democrat

socialista [soθja'lista] *adj, nm/f* socialist

socializar [soθjali'θar] *vt* to socialize

sociedad [soθje'ðað] *nf* society; (*COM*) company; **~ anónima** limited company; **~ de consumo** consumer society

socio, a ['soθjo, a] *nm/f* (*miembro*) member; (*COM*) partner

sociología [soθjolo'xia] *nf* sociology; **sociólogo, a** *nm/f* sociologist

socorrer [soko'rrer] *vt* to help; **socorrista** *nm/f* first aider; (*en piscina, playa*) lifeguard; **socorro** *nm* (*ayuda*) help, aid; (*MIL*) relief; **¡socorro!** help!

soda ['soða] *nf* (*sosa*) soda; (*bebida*) soda (water)

sofá [so'fa] (*pl ~s*) *nm* sofa, settee; **~-cama** *nm* studio couch; sofa bed

sofisticación [sofistika'θjon] *nf* sophistication

sofocar [sofo'kar] *vt* to suffocate; (*apagar*) to smother, put out; **~se** *vr* to suffocate; (*fig*) to blush, feel embarrassed; **sofoco** *nm* suffocation; embarrassment

sofreír [sofre'ir] *vt* (*CULIN*) to fry lightly

soga ['soɣa] *nf* rope

sois *vb ver* **ser**

soja ['soxa] nf soya

sol [sol] nm sun; (luz) sunshine, sunlight; **hace ~** it is sunny

solamente [sola'mente] adv only, just

solapa [so'lapa] nf (de chaqueta) lapel; (de libro) jacket

solapado, a [sola'paðo, a] adj (intenciones) underhand; (gestos, movimiento) sly

solar [so'lar] adj solar, sun cpd

solaz [so'laθ] nm recreation, relaxation; **~ar** vt (divertir) to amuse

soldado [sol'daðo] nm soldier; **~ raso** private

soldador [solda'ðor] nm soldering iron; (persona) welder

soldar [sol'dar] vt to solder, weld

soleado, a [sole'aðo, a] adj sunny

soledad [sole'ðað] nf solitude; (estado infeliz) loneliness

solemne [so'lemne] adj solemn; **solemnidad** nf solemnity

soler [so'ler] vi to be in the habit of, be accustomed to; **suele salir a las ocho** she usually goes out at 8 o'clock

solfeo [sol'feo] nm solfa

solicitar [soliθi'tar] vt (permiso) to ask for, seek; (puesto) to apply for; (votos) to canvass for; (atención) to attract

solícito, a [so'liθito, a] adj (diligente) diligent; (cuidadoso) careful; **solicitud** nf (calidad) great care; (petición) request; (a un puesto) application

solidaridad [soliðari'ðað] nf solidarity; **solidario, a** adj (participación) joint, common; (compromiso) mutually binding

solidez [soli'ðeθ] nf solidity; **sólido, a** adj solid

soliloquio [soli'lokjo] nm soliloquy

solista [so'lista] nm/f soloist

solitario, a [soli'tarjo, a] adj (persona) lonely, solitary; (lugar) lonely, desolate ♦ nm/f (recluso) recluse; (en la sociedad) loner ♦ nm solitaire

solo, a ['solo, a] adj (único) single, sole; (sin compañía) alone; (solitario) lonely; **hay una sola dificultad** there is just one difficulty; **a solas** alone, by oneself

sólo ['solo] adv only, just

solomillo [solo'miʎo] nm sirloin

soltar [sol'tar] vt (dejar ir) to let go of; (desprender) to unfasten, loosen; (librar) to release, set free; (risa etc) to let out

soltero, a [sol'tero, a] adj single, unmarried ♦ nm/f bachelor/single woman; **solterón, ona** nm/f old bachelor/spinster

soltura [sol'tura] nf looseness, slackness; (de los miembros) agility, ease of movement; (en el hablar) fluency, ease

soluble [so'luβle] adj (QUÍM) soluble; (problema) solvable; **~ en agua** soluble in water

solución [solu'θjon] nf solution; **solucionar** vt (problema) to solve; (asunto) to settle, resolve

solventar [solβen'tar] vt (pagar) to settle, pay; (resolver) to resolve;

solvente adj (ECON: empresa, persona) solvent

sombra ['sombra] nf shadow; (como protección) shade; **~s** nfpl (oscuridad) darkness sg, shadows; **tener buena/mala ~** to be lucky/unlucky

sombrero [som'brero] nm hat

sombrilla [som'briʎa] nf parasol, sunshade

sombrío, a [som'brio, a] adj (oscuro) dark; (triste) sombre, sad; (persona) gloomy

somero, a [so'mero, a] adj superficial

someter [some'ter] vt (país) to conquer; (persona) to subject to one's will; (informe) to present, submit; **~se** vr to give in, yield, submit; **~ a** to subject to

somier [so'mjer] (pl somiers) n spring mattress

somnífero [som'nifero] nm sleeping

pill
somnolencia [somno'lenθja] nf sleepiness, drowsiness
somos vb ver **ser**
son [son] vb ver **ser** ♦ nm sound; **en ~ de broma** as a joke
sonajero [sona'xero] nm (baby's) rattle
sonambulismo [sonambu'lismo] nm sleepwalking; **sonámbulo, a** nm/f sleepwalker
sonar [so'nar] vt to ring ♦ vi to sound; (hacer ruido) to make a noise; (pronunciarse) to be sounded, be pronounced; (ser conocido) to sound familiar; (campana) to ring; (reloj) to strike, chime; **~se** vr: **~se (las narices)** to blow one's nose; **me suena ese nombre** that name rings a bell
sonda ['sonda] nf (NAUT) sounding; (TEC) bore, drill; (MED) probe
sondear [sonde'ar] vt to sound; to bore (into), drill; to probe, sound; (fig) to sound out; **sondeo** nm sounding, boring, drilling; (fig) poll, enquiry
sonido [so'niðo] nm sound
sonoro, a [so'noro, a] adj sonorous; (resonante) loud, resonant
sonreír [sonre'ir] vi to smile; **~se** vr to smile; **sonriente** adj smiling; **sonrisa** nf smile
sonrojarse [sonro'xarse] vr to blush, go red; **sonrojo** nm blush
soñador, a [sona'ðor, a] nm/f dreamer
soñar [so'nar] vt, vi to dream; **~ con** to dream about o of
soñoliento, a [sono'ljento, a] adj sleepy, drowsy
sopa ['sopa] nf soup
sopesar [sope'sar] vt to consider, weigh up
soplar [so'plar] vt (polvo) to blow away, blow off; (inflar) to blow up; (vela) to blow out ♦ vi to blow; **soplo** nm blow, puff; (de viento) puff, gust
soplón, ona [so'plon, ona] (fam),

nm/f (niño) telltale; (de policía) grass (fam)
sopor [so'por] nm drowsiness
soporífero [sopo'rifero] nm sleeping pill
soportable [sopor'taβle] adj bearable
soportar [sopor'tar] vt to bear, carry; (fig) to bear, put up with; **soporte** nm support; (fig) pillar, support
soprano [so'prano] nf soprano
sorber [sor'βer] vt (chupar) to sip; (absorber) to soak up, absorb
sorbete [sor'βete] nm iced fruit drink
sorbo ['sorβo] nm (trago: grande) gulp, swallow; (: pequeño) sip
sordera [sor'ðera] nf deafness
sórdido, a [sor'ðiðo, a] adj dirty, squalid
sordo, a ['sorðo, a] adj (persona) deaf ♦ nm/f deaf person; **~mudo, a** adj deaf and dumb
sorna ['sorna] nf sarcastic tone
soroche [so'rotʃe] (AM) nm mountain sickness
sorprendente [sorpren'dente] adj surprising
sorprender [sorpren'der] vt to surprise; **sorpresa** nf surprise
sortear [sorte'ar] vt to draw lots for; (rifar) to raffle; (dificultad) to avoid; **sorteo** nm (en lotería) draw; (rifa) raffle
sortija [sor'tixa] nf ring; (rizo) ringlet, curl
sosegado, a [sose'vaðo, a] adj quiet, calm
sosegar [sose'var] vt to quieten, calm; (el ánimo) to reassure ♦ vi to rest; **sosiego** nm quiet(ness), calm(ness)
soslayo [sos'lajo]: **de ~** adv obliquely, sideways
soso, a ['soso, a] adj (CULIN) tasteless; (aburrido) dull, uninteresting
sospecha [sos'petʃa] nf suspicion
sospechar vt to suspect
sospechoso, a adj suspicious; (testimonio, opinión) suspect ♦ nm/f

suspect

sostén [sos'ten] nm (apoyo) support; (sujetador) bra; (alimentación) sustenance, food

sostener [soste'ner] vt to support; (mantener) to keep up, maintain; (alimentar) to sustain, keep going; **~se** vr to support o.s.; (seguir) to continue, remain; **sostenido, a** adj continuous, sustained; (prolongado) prolonged

sotana [so'tana] nf (REL) cassock

sótano ['sotano] nm basement

soviético, a [so'βjetiko, a] adj Soviet; **los ~s** the Soviets

soy vb ver **ser**

Sr. abr (= Señor) Mr

Sra. abr (= Señora) Mrs

S.R.C. abr (= se ruega contestación) R.S.V.P.

Sres. abr (= Señores) Messrs

Srta. abr (= Señorita) Miss

Sta. abr (= Santa) St

status ['status, e'status] nm inv status

Sto. abr (= Santo) St

su [su] pron (de él) his; (de ella) her; (de una cosa) its; (de ellos, ellas) their; (de usted, ustedes) your

suave ['swaβe] adj gentle; (superficie) smooth; (trabajo) easy; (música, voz) soft, gentle; **suavidad** nf gentleness; smoothness; softness, sweetness; **suavizante** nm (de ropa) softener; (del pelo) conditioner; **suavizar** vt to soften; (quitar la aspereza) to smooth (out)

subalimentado, a [suβalimen'taðo, a] adj undernourished

subasta [su'βasta] nf auction; **subastar** vt to auction (off)

subcampeón, ona [suβkampe'on, ona] nm/f runner-up

subconsciente [suβkons'θjente] adj, nm subconscious

subdesarrollado, a [suβðesarro-'ʎaðo, a] adj underdeveloped

subdesarrollo [suβðesa'rroʎo] nm underdevelopment

subdirector, a [suβðirek'tor, a] nm/f assistant director

súbdito, a ['suβðito, a] nm/f subject

subestimar [suβesti'mar] vt to underestimate, underrate

subida [su'βiða] nf (de montaña etc) ascent, climb; (de precio) rise, increase; (pendiente) slope, hill

subir [su'βir] vt (objeto) to raise, lift up; (cuesta, calle) to go up; (colina, montaña) to climb; (precio) to raise, put up ♦ vi to go up, come up; (a un coche) to get in; (a un autobús, tren o avión) to get on, board; (precio) to rise, go up; (río, marea) to rise; **~se** vr to get up, climb

súbito, a ['suβito, a] adj (repentino) sudden; (imprevisto) unexpected

subjetivo, a [suβxe'tiβo, a] adj subjective

sublevación [suβleβa'θjon] nf revolt, rising

sublevar [suβle'βar] vt to rouse to revolt; **~se** vr to revolt, rise

sublime [su'βlime] adj sublime

submarinismo [suβmari'nismo] nm scuba diving

submarino, a [suβma'rino, a] adj underwater ♦ nm submarine

subnormal [suβnor'mal] adj subnormal ♦ nm/f subnormal person

subordinado, a [suβorði'naðo, a] adj, nm/f subordinate

subrayar [suβra'jar] vt to underline

subsanar [suβsa'nar] vt to rectify

subscribir [suβskri'βir] vt = **suscribir**

subsidio [suβ'siðjo] nm (ayuda) aid, financial help; (subvención) subsidy, grant; (de enfermedad, paro etc) benefit, allowance

subsistencia [suβsis'tenθja] nf subsistence

subsistir [suβsis'tir] vi to subsist; (sobrevivir) to survive, endure

subterráneo, a [suβte'rraneo, a] adj underground, subterranean ♦ nm underpass, underground passage

subtítulo [suβ'titulo] nm (CINE) subtitle

suburbano, a [suβur'βano, a] adj suburban

suburbio [su'βurβjo] nm (barrio) slum quarter

subvención [subβen'θjon] nf (ECON) subsidy, grant; **subvencionar** vt to subsidize

subversión [subβer'sjon] nf subversion; **subversivo, a** adj subversive

subyugar [subʝu'var] vt (país) to subjugate, subdue; (enemigo) to overpower; (voluntad) to dominate

sucedáneo, a [suθe'ðaneo, a] adj substitute ♦ nm substitute (food)

suceder [suθe'ðer] vt, vi to happen; (seguir) to succeed, follow; **lo que sucede es que ...** the fact is that ...; **sucesión** nf succession; (serie) sequence, series

sucesivamente [suθesiβa'mente] adv: **y así ~** and so on

sucesivo, a [suθe'siβo, a] adj successive, following; **en lo ~** in future, from now on

suceso [su'θeso] nm (hecho) event, happening; (incidente) incident

suciedad [suθje'ðað] nf (estado) dirtiness; (mugre) dirt, filth

sucinto, a [su'θinto, a] adj (conciso) succinct, concise

sucio, a [su'θjo, a] adj dirty

suculento, a [suku'lento, a] adj succulent

sucumbir [sukum'bir] vi to succumb

sucursal [sukur'sal] nf branch (office)

sudadera [suða'ðera] nf sweatshirt

Sudáfrica [su'ðafrika] nf South Africa

Sudamérica [suða'merika] nf South America; **sudamericano, a** adj, nm/f South American

sudar [su'ðar] vt, vi to sweat

sudeste [su'ðeste] nm south-east

sudoeste [suðo'este] nm south-west

sudor [su'ðor] nm sweat; **~oso, a** adj sweaty, sweating

Suecia ['sweθja] nf Sweden; **sueco, a** adj Swedish ♦ nm/f Swede

suegro, a ['swexro, a] nm/f father-/ mother-in-law

suela ['swela] nf sole

sueldo ['sweldo] nm pay, wage(s) (pl)

suele etc vb ver **soler**

suelo ['swelo] nm (tierra) ground; (de casa) floor

suelto, a ['swelto, a] adj loose; (libre) free; (separado) detached; (ágil) quick, agile ♦ nm (loose) change, small change

sueño etc ['sweɲo] vb ver **soñar** ♦ nm sleep; (somnolencia) sleepiness, drowsiness; (lo soñado, fig) dream; **tener ~** to be sleepy

suero ['swero] nm (MED) serum; (de leche) whey

suerte ['swerte] nf (fortuna) luck; (azar) chance; (destino) fate, destiny; (especie) sort, kind; **tener ~** to be lucky; **de otra ~** otherwise, if not; **de ~ que** so that, in such a way that

suéter ['sweter] nm sweater

suficiente [sufi'θjente] adj enough, sufficient ♦ nm (ESCOL) pass

sufragio [su'fraxjo] nm (voto) vote; (derecho de voto) suffrage

sufrido, a [su'friðo, a] adj (persona) tough; (paciente) long-suffering, patient

sufrimiento [sufri'mjento] nm (dolor) suffering

sufrir [su'frir] vt (padecer) to suffer; (soportar) to bear, put up with; (apoyar) to hold up, support ♦ vi to suffer

sugerencia [suxe'renθja] nf suggestion

sugerir [suxe'rir] vt to suggest; (sutilmente) to hint

sugestión [suxes'tjon] nf suggestion; (sutil) hint; **sugestionar** vt to influence

sugestivo, a [suxes'tiβo, a] adj stimulating; (fascinante) fascinating

suicida [sui'θiδa] adj suicidal ♦ nm/f suicidal person; (muerto) suicide, person who has committed suicide; **suicidarse** vr to commit suicide, kill o.s.; **suicidio** nm suicide

Suiza ['swiθa] nf Switzerland; **suizo, a** adj, nm/f Swiss

sujeción [suxe'θjon] nf subjection

sujetador [suxeta'δor] nm (sostén) bra

sujetar [suxe'tar] vt (fijar) to fasten; (detener) to hold down; **~se** vr to subject o.s.; **sujeto, a** adj fastened, secure ♦ nm subject; (individuo) individual; **sujeto a** subject to

suma ['suma] nf (cantidad) total, sum; (de dinero) sum; (acto) adding (up), addition; **en ~** in short

sumamente [suma'mente] adv extremely, exceedingly

sumar [su'mar] vt to add (up) ♦ vi to add up

sumario, a [su'marjo, a] adj brief, concise ♦ nm summary

sumergir [sumer'xir] vt to submerge; (hundir) to sink

suministrar [sumini'strar] vt to supply, provide; **suministro** nm supply; (acto) supplying, providing

sumir [su'mir] vt to sink, submerge; (fig) to plunge

sumisión [sumi'sjon] nf (acto) submission; (calidad) submissiveness, docility; **sumiso, a** adj submissive, docile

sumo, a ['sumo, a] adj great, extreme; (autoridad) highest, supreme

suntuoso, a [sun'twoso, a] adj sumptuous, magnificent

supe etc vb ver **saber**

supeditar [supeδi'tar] vt: **~ algo a algo** to subordinate sth to sth

super... [super] prefijo super..., over...; **~bueno** adj great, fantastic

súper ['super] nf (gasolina) three-star (petrol)

superar [supe'rar] vt (sobreponerse a) to overcome; (rebasar) to surpass, do better than; (pasar) to go beyond; **~se** vr to excel o.s.

superávit [supe'raβit] nm inv surplus

superficial [superfi'θjal] adj superficial; (medida) surface cpd, of the surface

superficie [superfi'θje] nf surface; (área) area

superfluo, a [su'perflwo, a] adj superfluous

superior [supe'rjor] adj (piso, clase) upper; (temperatura, número, nivel) higher; (mejor: calidad, producto) superior, better ♦ nm/f superior; **~idad** nf superiority

supermercado [supermer'kaδo] nm supermarket

superponer [superpo'ner] vt to superimpose

supersónico, a [super'soniko, a] adj supersonic

superstición [supersti'θjon] nf superstition; **supersticioso, a** adj superstitious

supervisar [superßi'sar] vt to supervise

supervivencia [superßi'ßenθja] nf survival

superviviente [superßi'ßjente] adj surviving

supiera etc vb ver **saber**

suplantar [suplan'tar] vt to supplant

suplemento [suple'mento] nm supplement

suplente [su'plente] adj, nm/f substitute

supletorio, a [suple'torjo, a] adj supplementary ♦ nm supplement; **teléfono ~** extension

súplica ['suplika] nf request; (JUR) petition

suplicar [supli'kar] vt (cosa) to beg (for), plead for; (persona) to beg, plead with

suplicio [su'pliθjo] nm torture

suplir [su'plir] vt (compensar) to make good, make up for; (reemplazar) to replace, substitute ♦ vi: ~ **a** to take the place of, substitute for

supo etc vb ver **saber**

suponer [supo'ner] vt to suppose; **suposición** nf supposition

supremacía [suprema'θia] nf supremacy

supremo, a [su'premo, a] adj supreme

supresión [supre'sjon] nf suppression; (de derecho) abolition; (de palabra etc) deletion; (de restricción) cancellation; lifting

suprimir [supri'mir] vt to suppress; (derecho, costumbre) to abolish; (palabra etc) to delete; (restricción) to cancel, lift

supuesto, a [su'pwesto, a] pp de **suponer** ♦ adj (hipotético) supposed ♦ nm assumption, hypothesis; **~ que** since; **por ~** of course

sur [sur] nm south

surcar [sur'kar] vt to plough; **surco** nm (en metal, disco) groove; (AGR) furrow

surgir [sur'xir] vi to arise, emerge; (dificultad) to come up, crop up

suroeste [suro'este] nm south-west

surtido, a [sur'tiðo, a] adj mixed, assorted ♦ nm (selección) selection, assortment; (abastecimiento) supply, stock; **~r** nm (also: **~r de gasolina**) petrol pump (BRIT), gas pump (US)

surtir [sur'tir] vt to supply, provide ♦ vi to spout, spurt

susceptible [susθep'tiβle] adj susceptible; (sensible) sensitive; **~ de** capable of

suscitar [susθi'tar] vt to cause, provoke; (interés, sospechas) to arouse

suscribir [suskri'βir] vt (firmar) to sign; (respaldar) to subscribe to, endorse; **~se** vr to subscribe; **suscripción** nf subscription

susodicho, a [suso'ðitʃo, a] adj above-mentioned

suspender [suspen'der] vt (objeto) to hang (up), suspend; (trabajo) to stop, suspend; (ESCOL) to fail; (interrumpir) to adjourn; (atrasar) to postpone

suspensión nf suspension; (fig) stoppage, suspension

suspenso, a [sus'penso, a] adj hanging, suspended; (ESCOL) failed ♦ nm (ESCOL) fail; **quedar** o **estar en ~** to be pending

suspicacia [suspi'kaθja] nf suspicion, mistrust; **suspicaz** adj suspicious, distrustful

suspirar [suspi'rar] vi to sigh; **suspiro** nm sigh

sustancia [sus'tanθja] nf substance

sustentar [susten'tar] vt (alimentar) to sustain, nourish; (objeto) to hold up, support; (idea, teoría) to maintain, uphold; (fig) to sustain, keep going; **sustento** nm support; (alimento) sustenance, food

sustituir [sustitu'ir] vt to substitute, replace; **sustituto, a** nm/f substitute, replacement

susto [susto] nm fright, scare

sustraer [sustra'er] vt to remove, take away; (MAT) to subtract

susurrar [susu'rrar] vi to whisper; **susurro** nm whisper

sutil [su'til] adj (aroma, diferencia) subtle; (tenue) thin; (inteligencia, persona) sharp; **~eza** nf subtlety; thinness

suyo, a ['sujo, a] (con artículo o después del verbo **ser**) adj (de él) his; (de ella) hers; (de ellos, ellas) theirs; (de Ud, Uds) yours; **un amigo ~** a friend of his (o hers o theirs o yours)

T, t

tabacalera [taβaka'lera] nf: **T~** Spanish state tobacco monopoly

tabaco [ta'βako] nm tobacco; (fam)

cigarettes *pl*

taberna [ta'βerna] *nf* bar, pub (BRIT)

tabique [ta'βike] *nm* partition (wall)

tabla ['taβla] *nf* (de madera) plank; (estante) shelf; (de vestido) pleat; (ARTE) panel; ~s *nfpl*: estar o quedar en ~s to draw; ~do *nm* (plataforma) platform; (TEATRO) stage

tablao [ta'βlao] *nm* (tb: ~ flamenco) flamenco show

tablero [ta'βlero] *nm* (de madera) plank, board; (de ajedrez, damas) board; ~ de anuncios notice (BRIT) o bulletin (US) board

tableta [ta'βleta] *nf* (MED) tablet; (de chocolate) bar

tablón [ta'βlon] *nm* (de suelo) plank; (de techo) beam; ~ de anuncios notice board (BRIT), bulletin board (US)

tabú [ta'βu] *nm* taboo

tabular [taβu'lar] *vt* to tabulate

taburete [taβu'rete] *nm* stool

tacaño, a [ta'kaɲo, a] *adj* mean

tacha ['tatʃa] *nf* flaw; (TEC) stud;

tachar *vt* (borrar) to cross out; **tachar de** to accuse of

tácito, a ['taθito, a] *adj* tacit

taciturno, a [taθi'turno, a] *adj* silent

taco ['tako] *nm* (BILLAR) cue; (libro de billetes) book; (AM: de zapato) heel; (tarugo) peg; (palabrota) swear word

tacón [ta'kon] *nm* heel; **de ~ alto** high-heeled; **taconeo** *nm* (heel) stamping

táctica ['taktika] *nf* tactics *pl*

táctico, a ['taktiko, a] *adj* tactical

tacto ['takto] *nm* touch; (fig) tact

taimado, a [tai'maðo, a] *adj* (astuto) sly

tajada [ta'xaða] *nf* slice

tajante [ta'xante] *adj* sharp

tajo ['taxo] *nm* (corte) cut; (GEO) cleft

tal [tal] *adj* such; ~ **vez** perhaps ♦ *pron* (persona) someone, such a one; (cosa) something, such a thing; ~ **como** such as; ~ **para cual** (dos iguales) two of a kind ♦ *adv*: ~ **como** (igual) just as;

~ **cual** (como es) just as it is; ¿qué ~? how are things?; ¿qué ~ te gusta? how do you like it? ♦ *conj*: **con ~ de que** provided that

taladrar [tala'ðrar] *vt* to drill; **taladro** *nm* drill

talante [ta'lante] *nm* (humor) mood; (voluntad) will, willingness

talar [ta'lar] *vt* to fell, cut down; (devastar) to devastate

talco ['talko] *nm* (polvos) talcum powder

talego [ta'leɣo] *nm* sack

talento [ta'lento] *nm* talent; (capacidad) ability

TALGO ['talɣo] (ESP) *nm abr* (= tren articulado ligero Goicoechea-Oriol) ≈ HST (BRIT)

talismán [talis'man] *nm* talisman

talla ['taʎa] *nf* (estatura, fig, MED) height, stature; (palo) measuring rod; (ARTE) carving; (medida) size

tallado, a [ta'ʎaðo, a] *adj* carved ♦ *nm* carving

tallar [ta'ʎar] *vt* (madera) to carve; (metal etc) to engrave; (medir) to measure

tallarines [taʎa'rines] *nmpl* noodles

talle ['taʎe] *nm* (ANAT) waist; (fig) appearance

taller [ta'ʎer] *nm* (TEC) workshop; (de artista) studio

tallo ['taʎo] *nm* (de planta) stem; (de hierba) blade; (brote) shoot

talón [ta'lon] *nm* (ANAT) heel; (COM) counterfoil; (cheque) cheque (BRIT), check (US)

talonario [talo'narjo] *nm* (de cheques) chequebook (BRIT), checkbook (US); (de recibos) receipt book

tamaño, a [ta'maɲo, a] *adj* (tan grande) such a big; (tan pequeño) such a small ♦ *nm* size; **de ~ natural** full-size

tamarindo [tama'rindo] *nm* tamarind

tambalearse [tambale'arse] *vr* (persona) to stagger; (vehículo) to sway

también |tam'bjen| adv (igualmente) also, too, as well; (además) besides

tambor |tam'bor| nm drum; (ANAT) eardrum; **~ del freno** brake drum

tamiz |ta'miθ| nm sieve; **~ar** vt to sieve

tampoco |tam'poko| adv nor, neither; **yo ~ lo compré** I didn't buy it either

tampón |tam'pon| nm tampon

tan |tan| adv so; **~ es así que ...** so much so that ....

tanda |'tanda| nf (gen) series; (turno) shift

tangente |tan'xente| nf tangent

Tánger |'tanxer| n Tangier(s)

tangible |tan'xiβle| adj tangible

tanque |'tanke| nm (cisterna, MIL) tank; (AUTO) tanker

tantear |tante'ar| vt (calcular) to reckon (up); (medir) to take the measure of; (probar) to test, try out; (tomar la medida: persona) to take the measurements of; (situación) to weigh up; (persona: opinión) to sound out ♦ vi (DEPORTE) to score; **tanteo** nm (cálculo) (rough) calculation; (prueba) test, trial; (DEPORTE) scoring

tanto, a |'tanto, a| adj (cantidad) so much, as much; **~s** so many, as many; **20 y ~s** 20-odd ♦ adv (cantidad) so much, as much; (tiempo) so long, as long ♦ conj: **en ~ que** while; **hasta ~ (que)** until such time as ♦ nm (suma) certain amount; (proporción) so much; (punto) point; (gol) goal; **un ~ perezoso** somewhat lazy ♦ pron: **cado uno paga ~** each one pays so much; **~ tú como yo** both you and I; **~ como eso** as much as that; **~ más ... cuanto que** all the more ... because; **~ mejor/peor** so much the better/the worse; **si viene como si va** whether he comes or whether he goes; **~ es así que** so much so that; **por o por lo ~** therefore; **me he vuelto ronco de o con ~ hablar** I have become hoarse with so much

talking; **a ~s de agosto** on such and such a day in August

tapa |'tapa| nf (de caja, olla) lid; (de botella) top; (de libro) cover; (comida) snack

tapadera |tapa'ðera| nf lid, cover

tapar |ta'par| vt (cubrir) to cover; (envolver) to wrap o cover up; (la vista) to obstruct; (persona, falta) to conceal; (AM) to fill; **~se** vr to wrap o.s. up

taparrabo |tapa'rraβo| nm loincloth

tapete |ta'pete| nm table cover

tapia |'tapja| nf (garden) wall; **tapiar** vt to wall in

tapicería |tapiθe'ria| nf tapestry; (para muebles) upholstery; (tienda) upholsterer's (shop)

tapiz |ta'piθ| nm (alfombra) carpet; (tela tejida) tapestry; **~ar** vt (muebles) to upholster

tapón |ta'pon| nm (de botella) top; (de lavabo) plug; **~ de rosca** screw-top

taquigrafía |takiɣra'fia| nf shorthand; **taquígrafo, a** nm/f shorthand writer, stenographer

taquilla |ta'kiʎa| nf (donde se compra) booking office; (suma recogida) takings pl; **taquillero, a** adj: **función taquillera** box office success ♦ nm/f ticket clerk

tara |'tara| nf (defecto) defect; (COM) tare

tarántula |ta'rantula| nf tarantula

tararear |tarare'ar| vi to hum

tardar |tar'ðar| vi (tomar tiempo) to take a long time; (llegar tarde) to be late; (demorar) to delay; **¿tarda mucho el tren?** does the train take (very) long?; **a más tardar** at the latest; **no tardes en venir** come soon

tarde |'tarðe| adv late ♦ nf (de día) afternoon; (al anochecer) evening; **de ~ en ~** from time to time; **¡buenas ~s!** good afternoon!; **a o por la ~** in the afternoon, in the evening

tardío, a |tar'ðio, a| adj (retrasado) late; (lento) slow (to arrive)

tarea [ta'rea] nf task; (faena) chore; (ESCOL) homework

tarifa [ta'rifa] nf (lista de precios) price list; (precio) tariff

tarima [ta'rima] nf (plataforma) platform

tarjeta [tar'xeta] nf card; ~ postal/de crédito/de Navidad postcard/credit card/Christmas card

tarro ['tarro] nm jar, pot

tarta ['tarta] nf (pastel) cake; (de base dura) tart

tartamudear [tartamuðe'ar] vi to stammer; **tartamudo, a** adj stammering ♦ nm/f stammerer

tártaro, a ['tartaro, a] adj: **salsa tártara** tartar(e) sauce

tasa ['tasa] nf (precio) (fixed) price, rate; (valoración) valuation; (medida, norma) measure, standard; ~ de cambio/interés exchange/interest rate; ~s universitarias university fees; ~s de aeropuerto airport tax; ~ción nf valuation; ~dor, a nm/f valuer

tasar [ta'sar] vt (arreglar el precio) to fix a price for; (valorar) to value, assess

tasca ['taska] (fam) nf pub

tatarabuelo, a [tatara'ßwelo, a] nm/f great-great-grandfather/mother

tatuaje [ta'twaxe] nm (dibujo) tattoo; (acto) tattooing

tatuar [ta'twar] vt to tattoo

taurino, a [tau'rino, a] adj bullfighting cpd

Tauro ['tauro] nm Taurus

tauromaquia [tauro'makja] nf tauromachy, (art of) bullfighting

taxi ['taksi] nm taxi

taxista [tak'sista] nm/f taxi driver

taza ['taθa] nf cup; (de retrete) bowl; ~ para café coffee cup; **tazón** nm (taza grande) mug, large cup; (de fuente) basin

te [te] pron (complemento de objeto) you; (complemento indirecto) (to) you; (reflexivo) (to) yourself; ¿~ duele mucho el brazo? does your arm hurt

a lot?; ~ equivocas you're wrong; ¡~ cálma~! calm down!

té [te] nm tea

tea ['tea] nf torch

teatral [tea'tral] adj theatre cpd; (fig) theatrical

teatro [te'atro] nm theatre; (LITERATURA) plays pl, drama

tebeo [te'ßeo] nm comic

techo ['tetʃo] nm (externo) roof; (interno) ceiling; ~ corredizo sunroof

tecla ['tekla] nf key; ~do nm keyboard; **teclear** vi (MUS) to strum; (con los dedos) to tap ♦ vt (INFORM) to key in

técnica ['teknika] nf technique; (tecnología) technology; ver tb **técnico**

técnico, a ['tekniko, a] adj technical ♦ nm/f technician; (experto) expert

tecnología [teknolo'xia] nf technology; **tecnológico, a** adj technological

tedio ['teðjo] nm boredom, tedium; ~**so, a** adj boring, tedious

teja ['texa] nf tile; (BOT) lime (tree); ~**do** nm (tiled) roof

tejemaneje [texema'nexe] nm (lío) fuss; (intriga) intrigue

tejer [te'xer] vt to weave; (hacer punto) to knit; (fig) to fabricate; **tejido** nm (tela) material, fabric; (telaraña) web; (ANAT) tissue

tel [tel] abr (= teléfono) tel

tela ['tela] nf (tejido) material; (telaraña) web; (en líquido) skin; **telar** nm (máquina) loom

telaraña [tela'raɲa] nf cobweb

tele ['tele] (fam) nf telly (BRIT), tube (US)

tele... ['tele] pref tele...; ~**comunicación** nf telecommunication; ~**control** nm remote control; ~**diario** nm television news; ~**difusión** nf (television) broadcast; ~**dirigido, a** adj remote-controlled

teléf abr (= teléfono) tel

teleférico [tele'feriko] nm (de esquí)

ski-lift

telefonear [telefone'ar] vi to
telephone

telefónico, a [tele'foniko, a] adj
telephone cpd

telefonillo [telefo'niʎo] nm (de puerta)
intercom

telefonista [telefo'nista] nm/f
telephonist

teléfono [te'lefono] nm (tele)phone;
estar hablando al ~ to be on the
phone; **llamar a uno por ~** to ring sb
(up) o phone sb (up); **~ móvil** car
phone; **~ portátil** mobile phone

telegrafía [teleɣra'fia] nf telegraphy

telégrafo [te'leɣrafo] nm telegraph

telegrama [tele'ɣrama] nm telegram

tele-: **~impresor** nm teleprinter (BRIT),
teletype (US); **~novela** nf soap (opera);
~objetivo nm telephoto lens; **~patía**
nf telepathy; **~pático, a** adj telepathic;
~scópico, a adj telescopic; **~scopio**
nm telescope; **~silla** nm chairlift;
~spectador, a nm/f viewer; **~squí**
nm ski-lift; **~tarjeta** nf phonecard;
~tipo nm teletype

televidente [teleßi'ðente] nm/f viewer

televisar [teleßi'sar] vt to televise

televisión [teleßi'sjon] nf television;
~ en colores colour television

televisor [teleßi'sor] nm television set

télex ['teleks] nm inv telex

telón [te'lon] nm curtain; **~ de acero**
(POL) iron curtain; **~ de fondo**
backcloth, background

tema ['tema] nm (asunto) subject,
topic; (MUS) theme; **temática** nf
(social, histórica, artística) range of
topics; **temático, a** adj thematic

temblar [tem'blar] vi to shake,
tremble; (de frío) to shiver; **temblón,
ona** adj shaking; **temblor** nm
trembling; (de tierra) earthquake;
tembloroso, a adj trembling

temer [te'mer] vt to fear ♦ vi to be
afraid; **temo que llegue tarde** I am
afraid he may be late

temerario, a [teme'rarjo, a] adj
(descuidado) reckless; (irreflexivo) hasty;
temeridad nf (imprudencia) rashness;
(audacia) boldness

temeroso, a [teme'roso, a] adj
(miedoso) fearful; (que inspira temor)
frightful

temible [te'mißle] adj fearsome

temor [te'mor] nm (miedo) fear; (duda)
suspicion

témpano ['tempano] nm: **~ de hielo**
ice-floe

temperamento [tempera'mento] nm
temperament

temperatura [tempera'tura] nf
temperature

tempestad [tempes'taθ] nf storm;
tempestuoso, a adj stormy

templado, a [tem'plaðo, a] adj
(moderado) moderate; (frugal) frugal;
(agua) lukewarm; (clima) mild; (MUS)
well-tuned; **templanza** nf moderation;
mildness

templar [tem'plar] vt (moderar) to
moderate; (furia) to restrain; (calor) to
reduce; (afinar) to tune (up); (acero) to
temper; (tuerca) to tighten up; **temple**
nm (ajuste) tempering; (afinación)
tuning; (pintura) tempera

templo ['templo] nm (iglesia) church;
(pagano etc) temple

temporada [tempo'raða] nf time,
period; (estación) season

temporal [tempo'ral] adj (no
permanente) temporary; (REL) temporal
♦ nm storm

temprano, a [tempra'nero, a] adj
(BOT) early; (persona) early-rising

temprano, a [tem'prano, a] adj early;
(demasiado pronto) too soon, too early

ten vb ver **tener**

tenaces [te'naθes] adj pl ver **tenaz**

tenacidad [tenaθi'ðaθ] nf tenacity;
(dureza) toughness; (terquedad)
stubbornness

tenacillas [tena'θiʎas] nfpl tongs;
(para el pelo) curling tongs (BRIT) o iron

sg (*US*); (*MED*) forceps

tenaz [te'naθ] *adj* (*material*) tough; (*persona*) tenacious; (*creencia, resistencia*) stubborn

tenaza(s) [te'naθa(s)] *nf(pl)* (*MED*) forceps; (*TEC*) pliers; (*ZOOL*) pincers

tendedero [tende'ðero] *nm* (*para ropa*) drying place; (*cuerda*) clothes line

tendencia [ten'denθja] *nf* tendency; **tener ~ a** to have a tendency to; **tendencioso, a** *adj* tendentious

tender [ten'der] *vt* (*extender*) to spread out; (*colgar*) to hang out; (*vía férrea, cable*) to lay; (*estirar*) to stretch ♦ *vi*: **~ a** to tend to, have a tendency towards; **~se** *vr* to lie down; **~ la cama/la mesa** (*AM*) to make the bed/lay (*BRIT*) o set (*US*) the table

tenderete [tende'rete] *nm* (*puesto*) stall; (*exposición*) display of goods

tendero, a [ten'dero, a] *nm/f* shopkeeper

tendido, a [ten'diðo, a] *adj* (*acostado*) lying down, flat; (*colgado*) hanging ♦ *nm* (*TAUR*) front rows of seats; **a galope ~** flat out

tendón [ten'don] *nm* tendon

tendré *etc vb ver* **tener**

tenebroso, a [tene'βroso, a] *adj* (*oscuro*) dark; (*fig*) gloomy

tenedor [tene'ðor] *nm* (*CULIN*) fork; **~ de libros** book-keeper

tenencia [te'nenθja] *nf* (*de casa*) tenancy; (*de oficio*) tenure; (*de propiedad*) ownership

---

PALABRA CLAVE

---

tener [te'ner] *vt* **1** (*poseer, gen*) to have; (*en la mano*) to hold; **¿tienes un boli?** have you got a pen?; **va a ~ un niño** she's going to have a baby; **ven (o tenga)!, ¡aquí tienes (o tiene)!** here you are!

2 (*edad, medidas*) to be; **tiene 7 años** she's 7 (years old); **tiene 15 cm de largo** it's 15 cm long; *ver* **calor; hambre** *etc*

3 (*considerar*): **lo tengo por brillante** I consider him to be brilliant; **~ en mucho a uno** to think very highly of sb

4 (+ *pp*: = *pretérito*): **tengo terminada ya la mitad del trabajo** I've done half the work already

5: **~ que hacer algo** to have to do sth; **tengo que acabar este trabajo hoy** I have to finish this job today

6: **¿qué tienes, estás enfermo?** what's the matter with you, are you ill?

♦ **~se** *vr* **1**: **~se en pie** to stand up

2: **~se por** to think o.s.; **se tiene por muy listo** he thinks himself very clever

---

tengo *etc vb ver* **tener**

tenia ['tenja] *nf* tapeworm

teniente [te'njente] *nm* (*rango*) lieutenant; (*ayudante*) deputy

tenis ['tenis] *nm* tennis; **~ de mesa** table tennis; **~ta** *nm/f* tennis player

tenor [te'nor] *nm* (*sentido*) meaning; (*MUS*) tenor; **a ~ de** on the lines of

tensar [ten'sar] *vt* to tighten; (*arco*) to draw

tensión [ten'sjon] *nf* tension; (*TEC*) stress; (*MED*): **~ arterial** blood pressure; **tener la ~ alta** to have high blood pressure

tenso, a ['tenso, a] *adj* tense

tentación [tenta'θjon] *nf* temptation

tentáculo [ten'takulo] *nm* tentacle

tentador, a [tenta'ðor, a] *adj* tempting

tentar [ten'tar] *vt* (*seducir*) to tempt; (*atraer*) to attract; **tentativa** *nf* attempt; **tentativa de asesinato** attempted murder

tentempié [tentem'pje] *nm* snack

tenue ['tenwe] *adj* (*delgado*) thin, slender; (*neblina*) light; (*lazo, vínculo*) slight

teñir [te'nir] *vt* to dye; (*fig*) to tinge; **~se** *vr* to dye; **~se el pelo** to dye one's hair

teología [teolo'xia] *nf* theology

teoría |teoˈria| nf theory; **en ~** in theory; **teóricamente** adv theoretically; **teórico, a** adj theoretic(al) ♦ nm/f theoretician, theorist; **teorizar** vi to theorize

terapéutico, a |teraˈpeutiko, a| adj therapeutic

terapia |teˈrapja| nf therapy

tercer |terˈθer| adj ver **tercero**

tercermundista |terθermunˈdista| adj Third World cpd

tercero, a |terˈθero, a| adj (delante de nmsg: **tercer**) third ♦ nm (JUR) third party

terceto |terˈθeto| nm trio

terciar |terˈθjar| vi (participar) to take part; (hacer de árbitro) to mediate; **~se** vr to come up; **~io, a** adj tertiary

tercio |ˈterθjo| nm third

terciopelo |terθjoˈpelo| nm velvet

terco, a |ˈterko, a| adj obstinate

tergal ® |terˈval| nm type of polyester

tergiversar |terxiβerˈsar| vt to distort

termal |terˈmal| adj thermal

termas |ˈtermas| nfpl hot springs

térmico, a |ˈtermiko, a| adj thermal

terminación |terminaˈθjon| nf (final) end; (conclusión) conclusion, ending

terminal |termiˈnal| adj, nm, nf terminal

terminante |termiˈnante| adj (final) final, definitive; (tajante) categorical; **~mente** adv: **~mente prohibido** strictly forbidden

terminar |termiˈnar| vt (completar) to complete, finish; (concluir) to end ♦ vi (llegar a su fin) to end; (parar) to stop; (acabar) to finish; **~se** vr to come to an end; **~ por hacer algo** to end up (by) doing sth

término |ˈtermino| nm end, conclusion; (parada) terminus; (límite) boundary; **~ medio** average; (fig) middle way; **en último ~** (a fin de cuentas) in the last analysis; (como último recurso) as a last resort

terminología |terminoloˈxia| nf terminology

termodinámico, a |termoðiˈnamiko, a| adj thermodynamic

termómetro |terˈmometro| nm thermometer

termonuclear |termonukleˈar| adj thermonuclear

termo(s) ® |ˈtermo(s)| nm Thermos ® (flask)

termostato |termosˈtato| nm thermostat

ternero, a |terˈnero, a| nm/f (animal) calf ♦ nf (carne) veal

ternura |terˈnura| nf (trato) tenderness; (palabra) endearment; (cariño) fondness

terquedad |terkeˈðað| nf obstinacy

terrado |teˈrraðo| nm terrace

terraplén |terraˈplen| nm embankment

terrateniente |terrateˈnjente| nm/f landowner

terraza |teˈrraθa| nf (balcón) balcony; (tejado) (flat) roof; (AGR) terrace

terremoto |terreˈmoto| nm earthquake

terrenal |terreˈnal| adj earthly

terreno |teˈrreno| nm (tierra) land; (parcela) plot; (suelo) soil; (fig) field; **un ~** a piece of land

terrestre |teˈrrestre| adj terrestrial; (ruta) land cpd

terrible |teˈrriβle| adj terrible, awful

territorio |terriˈtorjo| nm territory

terrón |teˈrron| nm (de azúcar) lump; (de tierra) clod, lump

terror |teˈrror| nm terror; **~ífico, a** adj terrifying; **~ista** adj, nm/f terrorist

terso, a |ˈterso, a| adj (liso) smooth; (pulido) polished; **tersura** nf smoothness

tertulia |terˈtulja| nf (reunión informal) social gathering; (grupo) group, circle

tesis |ˈtesis| nf inv thesis

tesón |teˈson| nm (firmeza) firmness; (tenacidad) tenacity

tesorero, a |tesoˈrero, a| nm/f

treasurer

tesoro |te'soro| nm treasure; (COM, POL) treasury

testaferro |testa'ferro| nm figurehead

testamentario, a |testamen'tarjo, a| adj testamentary ♦ nm/f executor/executrix

testamento |testa'mento| nm will

testar |tes'tar| vi to make a will

testarudo, a |testa'ruðo, a| adj stubborn

testículo |tes'tikulo| nm testicle

testificar |testifi'kar| vt to testify; (fig) to attest ♦ vi to give evidence

testigo |tes'tiɣo| nm/f witness; ~ de cargo/descargo witness for the prosecution/defence; ~ ocular eye witness

testimoniar |testimo'njar| vt to testify to; (fig) to show; **testimonio** nm testimony

teta |'teta| nf (de biberón) teat; (ANAT: fam) breast

tétanos |'tetanos| nm tetanus

tetera |te'tera| nf teapot

tétrico, a |'tetriko, a| adj gloomy, dismal

textil |teks'til| adj textile

texto |'teksto| nm text; **textual** adj textual

textura |teks'tura| nf (de tejido) texture

tez |teθ| nf (cutis) complexion

ti |ti| pron you; (reflexivo) yourself

tía |'tia| nf (pariente) aunt; (fam) chick, bird

tibieza |ti'ßjeθa| nf (temperatura) tepidness; (actitud) coolness; **tibio, a** adj lukewarm

tiburón |tiβu'ron| nm shark

tic |tik| nm (ruido) click; (de reloj) tick; (MED): ~ **nervioso** nervous tic

tictac |tik'tak| nm (de reloj) tick tock

tiempo |'tjempo| nm time; (época, período) age, period; (METEOROLOGÍA) weather; (LING) tense; (DEPORTE) half; a ~ in time; a un o al mismo ~ at the same time; al poco ~ very soon

(after); **se quedó poco** ~ he didn't stay very long; **hace poco** ~ not long ago; **mucho** ~ a long time; **de** ~ **en** ~ from time to time; **the weather is fine/bad; estar a** ~ to be in time; **hace** ~ some time ago; **hacer** ~ to while away the time; **motor de 2** ~s two-stroke engine; **primer** ~ first half

tienda |'tjenda| nf shop, store; ~ (de campaña) tent; ~ de alimentación o comestibles grocer's (BRIT), grocery store (US)

tienes etc vb ver **tener**

tienta etc |'tjenta| vb ver **tentar** ♦ nf: **andar a** ~s to grope one's way along

tiento |'tjento| vb ver **tentar** ♦ nm (tacto) touch; (precaución) wariness

tierno, a |'tjerno, a| adj (blando) tender; (fresco) fresh; (amable) sweet

tierra |'tjerra| nf earth; (suelo) soil; (mundo) earth, world; (país) country, land; ~ **adentro** inland

tieso, a |'tjeso, a| adj (rígido) rigid; (duro) stiff; (fam: orgulloso) conceited

tiesto |'tjesto| nm flowerpot

tifoidea |tifoi'ðea| nf typhoid

tifón |ti'fon| nm typhoon

tifus |'tifus| nm typhus

tigre |'tiɣre| nm tiger

tijera |ti'xera| nf scissors pl; (ZOOL) claw; ~s nfpl scissors; (para plantas) shears

tijeretear |tixerete'ar| vt to snip

tila |'tila| nf lime blossom tea

tildar |til'dar| vt: ~ **de** to brand as

tilde |'tilde| nf (TIP) tilde

tilín |ti'lin| nm tinkle

tilo |'tilo| nm lime tree

timar |ti'mar| vt (estafar) to swindle

timbal |tim'bal| nm small drum

timbrar |tim'brar| vt to stamp

timbre |'timbre| nm (sello) stamp; (campanilla) bell; (tono) timbre; (COM) stamp duty

timidez |timi'ðeθ| nf shyness; **tímido, a** adj shy

timo ['timo] *nm* swindle

timón [ti'mon] *nm* helm, rudder; **timonel** *nm* helmsman

tímpano ['timpano] *nm* (ANAT) eardrum; (MUS) small drum

tina ['tina] *nf* tub; (*baño*) bath(tub); **tinaja** *nf* large jar

tinglado [tiŋ'glaðo] *nm* (*cobertizo*) shed; (*fig: truco*) trick; (*intriga*) intrigue

tinieblas [ti'nieβlas] *nfpl* darkness *sg*; (*sombras*) shadows

tino ['tino] *nm* (*habilidad*) skill; (*juicio*) insight

tinta ['tinta] *nf* ink; (TEC) dye; (ARTE) colour

tinte ['tinte] *nm* dye

tintero [tin'tero] *nm* inkwell

tintinear [tintine'ar] *vt* to tinkle

tinto ['tinto] *nm* red wine

tintorería [tintore'ria] *nf* dry cleaner's

tintura [tin'tura] *nf* (QUÍM) dye; (*farmacéutico*) tincture

tío ['tio] *nm* (*pariente*) uncle; (*fam: individuo*) bloke (BRIT), guy

tiovivo [tio'βiβo] *nm* merry-go-round

típico, a ['tipiko, a] *adj* typical

tipo ['tipo] *nm* (*clase*) type, kind; (*hombre*) fellow; (ANAT: *de hombre*) build; (: *de mujer*) figure; (IMPRENTA) type; **~ bancario/de descuento/de interés/de cambio** bank/discount/ interest/exchange rate

tipografía [tipoxra'fia] *nf* printing *cpd*; **tipográfico, a** *adj* printing *cpd*

tiquet [ti'ket] (*pl* **~s**) *nm* ticket; (*en tienda*) cash slip

tiquismiquis [tikis'mikis] *nm inv* fussy person ♦ *nmpl* (*querellas*) squabbling *sg*; (*escrúpulos*) silly scruples

tira ['tira] *nf* strip; (*fig*) abundance; **~ y afloja** give and take

tirabuzón [tiraβu'θon] *nm* (*rizo*) curl

tirachinas [tira'tʃinas] *nm inv* catapult

tirada [ti'raða] *nf* (*acto*) cast, throw; (*serie*) series; (TIP) printing, edition; **de una ~** at one go

tirado, a [ti'raðo, a] *adj* (*barato*) dirt-

cheap; (*fam: fácil*) very easy

tirador [tira'ðor] *nm* (*mango*) handle

tiranía [tira'nia] *nf* tyranny; **tirano, a** *adj* tyrannical ♦ *nm/f* tyrant

tirante [ti'rante] *adj* (*cuerda etc*) tight, taut; (*relaciones*) strained ♦ *nm* (ARQ) brace; (TEC) stay; **~s** *nmpl* (*de pantalón*) braces (BRIT), suspenders (US); **tirantez** *nf* tightness; (*fig*) tension

tirar [ti'rar] *vt* to throw; (*dejar caer*) to drop; (*volcar*) to upset; (*derribar*) to knock down o over; (*desechar*) to throw out o away; (*dinero*) to squander; (*imprimir*) to print ♦ *vi* (*disparar*) to shoot; (*de la puerta etc*) to pull; (*fam: andar*) to go; (*tender a, buscar realizar*) to tend to; (DEPORTE) to shoot; **~se** *vr* to throw o.s.; (*abalanzarse*) to rush, to dash; **va tirando** to manage; **a todo ~** at the most

tirita [ti'rita] *nf* (sticking) plaster (BRIT), bandaid (US)

tiritar [tiri'tar] *vi* to shiver

tiro ['tiro] *nm* (*lanzamiento*) throw; (*disparo*) shot; (DEPORTE) shot; (GOLF, TENIS) drive; (*alcance*) range; **~ al blanco** target practice; **caballo de ~** cart-horse; **andar de ~s largos** to be all dressed up; **al ~** (AM) at once

tirón [ti'ron] *nm* (*sacudida*) pull, tug; **de un ~** in one go, all at once

tiroteo [tiro'teo] *nm* exchange of shots, shooting

tísico, a ['tisiko, a] *adj* consumptive

tisis ['tisis] *nf inv* consumption, tuberculosis

títere ['titere] *nm* puppet

titiritero, a [titiri'tero, a] *nm/f* puppeteer

titubeante [tituβe'ante] *adj* (*al andar*) shaky, tottering; (*al hablar*) stammering; (*dudoso*) hesitant

titubear [tituβe'ar] *vi* to stagger; to stammer; (*fig*) to hesitate; **titubeo** *nm* staggering; stammering; hesitation

titulado, a [titu'laðo, a] *adj* (*libro*) entitled; (*persona*) titled

titular [titu'lar] *adj* titular ♦ *nm/f* holder ♦ *nm* headline ♦ *vt* to title; to head; **título** *nm* title; (*de diario*) headline; (*certificado*) professional qualification; (*universitario*) (university) degree; **a título de** in the capacity of

tiza ['tiθa] *nf* chalk

tiznar [tiθ'nar] *vt* to blacken

tizón [ti'θon] *nm* brand

toalla [to'aʎa] *nf* towel

tobillo [to'βiʎo] *nm* ankle

tobogán [toβo'van] *nm* (*montaña rusa*) roller-coaster; (*de niños*) chute, slide

tocadiscos [toka'ðiskos] *nm inv* record player

tocado, a [to'kaðo, a] *adj* (*fam*) touched ♦ *nm* headdress

tocador [toka'ðor] *nm* (*mueble*) dressing table; (*cuarto*) boudoir; (*fam*) ladies' toilet (BRIT) o room (US)

tocante [to'kante]: **~ a** *prep* with regard to

tocar [to'kar] *vt* to touch; (MUS) to play; (*referirse a*) to allude to; (*timbre*) to ring ♦ *vi* (*a la puerta*) to knock (on o at the door); (*ser de turno*) to fall to, be the turn of; (*ser hora*) to be due; **~se** *vr* (*cubrirse la cabeza*) to cover one's head; (*tener contacto*) to touch (each other); **por lo que a mí me toca** as far as I am concerned; **te toca a ti** it's your turn

tocayo, a [to'kajo, a] *nm/f* namesake

tocino [to'θino] *nm* bacon

todavía [toða'βia] *adv* (*aun*) even; (*aún*) still, yet; **~ más** yet more; **~ no** not yet

PALABRA CLAVE

todo, a ['toðo, a] *adj* **1** (*con artículo sg*) all; **toda la carne** all the meat; **toda la noche** all night, the whole night; **~ el libro** the whole book; **toda una botella** a whole bottle; **~ lo contrario** quite the opposite; **está toda sucia** she's all dirty; **por ~ el país** throughout the whole country

2 (*con artículo pl*) all; every; **~s los libros** all the books; **todas las noches** every night; **~s los que quieran salir** all those who want to leave

♦ *pron* **1** everything, all; **~s** everyone, everybody; **lo sabemos ~** we know everything; **~s querían más tiempo** everybody o everyone wanted more time; **nos marchamos ~s** all of us left

2: con ~: con ~ él me sigue gustando even so I still like him

♦ *adv* all; **vaya ~ seguido** keep straight on o ahead

♦ *nm*: **como un ~** as a whole; **del ~: no me agrada del ~** I don't entirely like it

todopoderoso, a [toðopoðe'roso, a] *adj* all powerful; (REL) almighty

toga ['toya] *nf* toga; (ESCOL) gown

Tokio ['tokjo] *n* Tokyo

toldo ['toldo] *nm* (*para el sol*) sunshade (BRIT), parasol; (*tienda*) marquee

tolerancia [tole'ranθja] *nf* tolerance;

tolerante [tole'rante] *adj* (*sociedad*) liberal; (*persona*) open-minded

tolerar [tole'rar] *vt* to tolerate; (*resistir*) to endure

toma ['toma] *nf* (*acto*) taking; (MED) dose; **~ (de corriente)** socket

tomar [to'mar] *vt* to take; (*aspecto*) to take on; (*beber*) to drink ♦ *vi* to take; (AM) to drink; **~se** *vr* to take; **~se por** to consider o.s. to be; **~ a bien/a mal** to take well/badly; **~ en serio** to take seriously; **~ el pelo a alguien** to pull sb's leg; **~la con uno** to pick a quarrel with sb; **¡tome!** here you are!; **~ el sol** to sunbathe

tomate [to'mate] *nm* tomato

tomillo [to'miʎo] *nm* thyme

tomo ['tomo] nm (libro) volume

ton [ton] abr = **tonelada ♦** nm: **sin ~ ni son** without rhyme or reason

tonada [to'naða] nf tune

tonalidad [tonali'ðað] nf tone

tonel [to'nel] nm barrel

tonelada [tone'laða] nf ton; **tonelaje** nm tonnage

tónica ['tonika] nf (estupidez) tonic; (fig) keynote

tónico, a [to'niko, a] adj tonic ♦ nm (MED) tonic

tonificar [tonifi'kar] vt to tone up

tono ['tono] nm tone; **fuera de ~** inappropriate; **darse ~** to put on airs

tontería [tonte'ria] nf (estupidez) foolishness; (cosa) stupid thing; (acto) foolish act; **~s** nfpl (disparates) rubbish sg, nonsense sg

tonto, a ['tonto, a] adj stupid, silly ♦ nm/f fool

topar [to'par] vi: **~ contra** o **en** to run into; **~ con** to run up against

tope ['tope] adj maximum ♦ nm (fin) end; (límite) limit; (FERRO) buffer; (AUTO) bumper; **al ~** end to end

tópico, a ['topiko, a] adj topical ♦ nm platitude

topo ['topo] nm (ZOOL) mole; (fig) blunderer

topografía [topoɣra'fia] nf topography; **topógrafo, a** nm/f topographer

toque etc ['toke] vb ver **tocar** ♦ nm touch; (MUS) beat; (de campana) peal; **dar un ~ a** to warn; **~ de queda** curfew

toqué vb ver **tocar**

toquetear [tokete'ar] vt to finger

toquilla [to'kiʎa] nf (pañuelo) headscarf; (chal) shawl

tórax ['toraks] nm thorax

torbellino [torbe'ʎino] nm whirlwind; (fig) whirl

torcedura [torθe'ðura] nf twist; (MED) sprain

torcer [tor'θer] vt to twist; (la esquina) to turn; (MED) to sprain ♦ vi (desviar) to turn off; **~se** vr (ladearse) to bend; (desviarse) to go astray; (fracasar) to go wrong; **torcido, a** adj twisted; (fig) crooked ♦ nm curl

tordo, a ['torðo, a] adj dappled ♦ nm thrush

torear [tore'ar] vt (fig: evadir) to avoid; (jugar con) to tease ♦ vi to fight bulls; **toreo** nm bullfighting; **torero, a** nm/f bullfighter

tormenta [tor'menta] nf storm; (fig: confusión) turmoil

tormento [tor'mento] nm torture; (fig) anguish

tornar [tor'nar] vt (devolver) to return, give back; (transformar) to transform ♦ vi to go back; **~se** vr (ponerse) to become

tornasolado, a [tornaso'laðo, a] adj (brillante) iridescent; (reluciente) shimmering

torneo [tor'neo] nm tournament

tornillo [tor'niʎo] nm screw

torniquete [torni'kete] nm (MED) tourniquet

torno ['torno] nm (TEC) winch; (tambor) drum; **en ~ (a)** round, about

toro ['toro] nm bull; (fam) he-man; **los ~s** bullfighting

toronja [to'ronxa] nf grapefruit

torpe ['torpe] adj (poco hábil) clumsy, awkward; (necio) dim; (lento) slow

torpedo [tor'peðo] nm torpedo

torpeza [tor'peθa] nf (falta de agilidad) clumsiness; (lentitud) slowness; (error) mistake

torre ['torre] nf tower; (de petróleo) derrick

torrefacto, a [torre'fakto, a] adj roasted

torrente [to'rrente] nm torrent

tórrido, a ['torriðo, a] adj torrid

torrija [to'rrixa] nf French toast

torsión [tor'sjon] nf twisting

torso ['torso] nm torso

torta ['torta] nf cake; (fam) slap

torticolis [tor'tikolis] nm inv stiff neck

tortilla [tor'tiʎa] nf omelette; (AM) maize pancake; ~ **francesa/española** plain/potato omelette

tórtola ['tortola] nf turtledove

tortuga [tor'tuɣa] nf tortoise

tortuoso, a [tor'twoso, a] adj winding

tortura [tor'tura] nf torture; **torturar** vt to torture

tos [tos] nf cough; ~ **ferina** whooping cough

tosco, a ['tosko, a] adj coarse

toser [to'ser] vi to cough

tostada, a [tos'taða] nf piece of toast; **tostado, a** adj toasted; (por el sol) dark brown; (piel) tanned

tostador [tosta'ðor] nm toaster

tostar [tos'tar] vt to toast; (café) to roast; (persona) to tan; ~**se** vr to get brown

total [to'tal] adj total ♦ adv in short; (al fin y al cabo) when all is said and done ♦ nm total; ~ **que** to cut (BRIT) o make (US) a long story short

totalidad [totali'ðað] nf whole

totalitario, a [totali'tarjo, a] adj totalitarian

tóxico, a ['toksiko, a] adj toxic ♦ nm poison; **toxicómano, a** nm/f drug addict

toxina [to'ksina] nf toxin

tozudo, a [to'θuðo, a] adj obstinate

traba ['traβa] nf bond, tie; (cadena) shackle

trabajador, a [traβaxa'ðor, a] adj hard-working ♦ nm/f worker

trabajar [traβa'xar] vt to till; (AGR) to till; (empeñarse en) to work at; (convencer) to persuade ♦ vi to work; (esforzarse) to strive; **trabajo** nm work; (tarea) task; (POL) labour; (fig) effort; **tomarse el trabajo de** to take the trouble to; **trabajo por turno/a destajo** shift work/piecework; **trabajoso, a** adj hard

trabalenguas [traβa'lengwas] nm inv tongue twister

trabar [tra'βar] vt (juntar) to join, unite; (atar) to tie down, fetter; (agarrar) to seize; (amistad) to strike up; ~**se** vr to become entangled; **trabársele a uno la lengua** to be tongue-tied

tracción [trak'θjon] nf traction; ~ **delantera/trasera** front-wheel/rear-wheel drive

tractor [trak'tor] nm tractor

tradición [traði'θjon] nf tradition; **tradicional** adj traditional

traducción [traðuk'θjon] nf translation

traducir [traðu'θir] vt to translate; **traductor, a** nm/f translator

traer [tra'er] vt to bring; (llevar) to carry; (llevar puesto) to wear; (incluir) to carry; (causar) to cause; ~**se** vr: ~**se algo** to be up to sth

traficar [trafi'kar] vi to trade

tráfico ['trafiko] nm (COM) trade; (AUTO) traffic

tragaluz [traɣa'luθ] nm skylight

tragaperras [traɣa'perras] nm o f inv slot machine

tragar [tra'ɣar] vt to swallow; (devorar) to devour, bolt down; ~**se** vr to swallow

tragedia [tra'xeðja] nf tragedy; **trágico, a** adj tragic

trago ['traɣo] nm (líquido) drink; (bocado) gulp; (fam: de bebida) swig; (desgracia) blow

traición [trai'θjon] nf treachery; (JUR) treason; (una ~) act of treachery; **traicionar** vt to betray

traicionero, a [traiθjo'nero, a] adj treacherous

traidor, a [trai'ðor, a] adj treacherous ♦ nm/f traitor

traigo etc vb ver **traer**

traje ['traxe] vb ver **traer** ♦ nm (de hombre) suit; (de mujer) dress; (vestido típico) costume; ~ **de baño** swimsuit; ~ **de luces** bullfighter's costume

trajera etc vb ver **traer**

trajín |tra'xin| nm (fam: movimiento) bustle; **trajinar** vi (moverse) to bustle about

trama |'trama| nf (intriga) plot; (de tejido) weft (BRIT), woof (US); **tramar** vt to plot; (TEC) to weave

tramitar |trami'tar| vt (asunto) to transact; (negociar) to negotiate

trámite |'tramite| nm (paso) step; (JUR) transaction; **~s** nmpl (burocracia) procedure sg; (JUR) proceedings

tramo |'tramo| nm (de tierra) plot; (de escalera) flight; (de vía) section

tramoya |tra'moja| nf (TEATRO) piece of stage machinery; **tramoyista** nm/f scene shifter; (fig) trickster

trampa |'trampa| nf trap; (en el suelo) trapdoor; (truco) trick; (engaño) fiddle; **trampear** vt, vi to cheat

trampolín |trampo'lin| nm (de piscina etc) diving board

tramposo, a |tram'poso, a| adj crooked, cheating ♦ nm/f crook, cheat

tranca |'tranka| nf (palo) stick; (de puerta, ventana) bar; **trancar** vt to bar

trance |'tranθe| nm (momento difícil) difficult moment o juncture; (estado hipnotizado) trance

tranquilidad |trankili'ðað| nf (calma) calmness, stillness; (paz) peacefulness

tranquilizar |trankili'θar| vt (calmar) to calm (down); (asegurar) to reassure; **~se** vr to calm down; **tranquilo, a** adj (calmado) calm; (apacible) peaceful; (mar) calm; (mente) untroubled

transacción |transak'θjon| nf transaction

transbordador |transβorða'ðor| nm ferry

transbordar |transβor'ðar| vt to transfer; **transbordo** nm transfer; **hacer transbordo** to change (trains etc)

transcurrir |transku'rrir| vi (tiempo) to pass; (hecho) to take place

transcurso |trans'kurso| nm: **~ del tiempo** lapse (of time)

transeúnte |transe'unte| nm/f passer-by

transferencia |transfe'renθja| nf transference; (COM) transfer

transferir |transfe'rir| vt to transfer

transformador |transforma'ðor| nm (ELEC) transformer

transformar |transfor'mar| vt to transform; (convertir) to convert

tránsfuga |'transfuva| nm/f (MIL) deserter; (POL) turncoat

transfusión |transfu'sjon| nf transfusion

transición |transi'θjon| nf transition

transigir |transi'xir| vi to compromise, make concessions

transistor |transis'tor| nm transistor

transitar |transi'tar| vi to go (from place to place); **tránsito** nm transit; (AUTO) traffic; **transitorio, a** adj transitory

transmisión |transmi'sjon| nf (TEC) transmission; (transferencia) transfer; **~ en directo/exterior** live/outside broadcast

transmitir |transmi'tir| vt to transmit; (RADIO, TV) to broadcast

transparencia |transpa'renθja| nf transparency; (claridad) clearness, clarity; (foto) slide

transparentar |transparen'tar| vt to reveal ♦ vi to be transparent; **transparente** adj transparent; (claro) clear

transpirar |transpi'rar| vi to perspire

transportar |transpor'tar| vt to transport; (llevar) to carry; **transporte** nm transport; (COM) haulage

transversal |transβer'sal| adj transverse, cross

tranvía |tram'bia| nm tram

trapecio |tra'peθjo| nm trapeze; **trapecista** nm/f trapeze artist

trapero, a |tra'pero, a| nm/f ragman

trapichео |trapi'tʃeo| (fam) nm scheme, fiddle

trapo |'trapo| nm (tela) rag; (de cocina)

cloth

tráquea [ˈtrakea] nf windpipe

traqueteo [trakeˈteo] nm rattling

tras [tras] prep (detrás) behind; (después) after

trasatlántico [trasatˈlantiko] nm (barco) (cabin) cruiser

trascendencia [trasθenˈdenθja] nf (importancia) importance; (FILOSOFÍA) transcendence

trascendental [trasθendenˈtal] adj important; (FILOSOFÍA) transcendental

trascender [trasθenˈder] vi (noticias) to come out; (suceso) to have a wide effect

trasero, a [traˈsero, a] adj back, rear ♦ nm (ANAT) bottom

trasfondo [trasˈfondo] nm background

trasgredir [trasɣreˈðir] vt to contravene

trashumante [trasuˈmante] adj (animales) migrating

trasladar [traslaˈðar] vt to move; (persona) to transfer; (postergar) to postpone; (copiar) to copy; ~se vr (mudarse) to move; **traslado** nm move; (mudanza) move, removal

traslucir [trasluˈθir] vt to show; ~se vr to be translucent; (fig) to be revealed

trasluz [trasˈluθ] nm reflected light; **al ~** against o up to the light

trasnochador, a [trasnotʃaˈðor, a] nm/f night owl

trasnochar [trasnoˈtʃar] vi (acostarse tarde) to stay up late

traspapelar [traspapeˈlar] vt (document, carta) to mislay, misplace

traspasar [traspaˈsar] vt (suj: bala etc) to pierce, go through; (propiedad) to sell, transfer; (calle) to cross over; (límites) to go beyond; (ley) to break; **traspaso** nm (venta) transfer, sale

traspié [trasˈpje] nm (tropezón) trip; (error) blunder

trasplantar [trasplanˈtar] vt to transplant

traste [ˈtraste] nm (MÚS) fret; **dar al ~ con algo** to ruin sth

trastero [trasˈtero] nm storage room

trastienda [trasˈtjenda] nf back of shop

trasto [ˈtrasto] nm (pey) nm (cosa) piece of junk; (persona) dead loss

trastornado, a [trastorˈnaðo, a] adj (loco) mad, crazy

trastornar [trastorˈnar] vt (fig: planes) to disrupt; (: nervios) to shatter; (: persona) to drive crazy; ~se vr (volverse loco) to go mad o crazy; **trastorno** nm (acto) overturning; (confusión) confusion

tratable [traˈtaßle] adj friendly

tratado [traˈtaðo] nm (POL) treaty; (COM) agreement

tratamiento [trataˈmjento] nm treatment; ~ **de textos** (INFORM) word processing cpd

tratar [traˈtar] vt (ocuparse de) to treat; (manejar, TEC) to handle; (MED) to treat; (dirigirse a: persona) to address ♦ vi: ~ **de** (hablar sobre) to deal with, be about; (intentar) to try to; ~se vr to treat each other; ~ **con** (COM) to trade in; (negociar) to negotiate with; (tener contactos) to have dealings with; **¿de qué se trata?** what's it about?; **trato** nm dealings pl; (relaciones) relationship; (comportamiento) manner; (COM) agreement

trauma [ˈtrauma] nm trauma

través [traˈßes] nm (fig) reverse; **al ~** across, crossways; **a ~ de** across; (sobre) over; (por) through

travesaño [traßeˈsaɲo] nm (ARQ) crossbeam; (DEPORTE) crossbar

travesía [traßeˈsia] nf (calle) cross-street; (NAUT) crossing

travesura [traßeˈsura] nf (broma) prank; (ingenio) wit

traviesa [traˈßjesa] nf (ARQ) crossbeam

travieso, a [traˈßjeso, a] adj (niño) naughty

trayecto [traˈjekto] nm (ruta) road,

way; (*viaje*) journey; (*tramo*) stretch;
~ría *nf* trajectory; (*fig*) path

traza ['traθa] *nf* (*aspecto*) look;
(*señal*) sign; **~do, a** *adj*: **bien ~do**
shapely, well-formed ♦ *nm* (*ARQ*) plan,
design; (*fig*) outline

trazar [tra'θar] *vt* (*ARQ*) to plan; (*ARTE*)
to sketch; (*fig*) to trace; (*plan*) to draw
up; **trazo** *nm* (*línea*) line; (*bosquejo*)
sketch

trébol ['treβol] *nm* (*BOT*) clover

trece ['treθe] *num* thirteen

trecho ['tretʃo] *nm* (*distancia*) distance;
(*de tiempo*) while; **de ~ en ~** at
intervals

tregua ['treɣwa] *nf* (*MIL*) truce; (*fig*)
respite

treinta ['treinta] *num* thirty

tremendo, a [tre'mendo, a] *adj*
(*terrible*) terrible; (*imponente: cosa*)
imposing; (*fam: fabuloso*) tremendous

trémulo, a ['tremulo, a] *adj* quiver-
ing

tren [tren] *nm* train; **~ de aterrizaje**
undercarriage

trenca ['trenka] *nf* duffel coat

trenza ['trenθa] *nf* (*de pelo*) plait
(*BRIT*), braid (*US*); **trenzar** *vt* (*pelo*) to
plait, braid; **trenzarse** *vr* (*AM*) to
become involved

trepadora [trepa'ðora] *nf* (*BOT*)
climber

trepar [tre'par] *vt, vi* to climb

trepidante [trepi'ðante] *adj* (*acción*)
fast; (*ritmo*) hectic

tres [tres] *num* three

tresillo [tre'siʎo] *nm* three-piece suite;
(*MUS*) triplet

treta ['treta] *nf* trick

triángulo ['trjangulo] *nm* triangle

tribu ['triβu] *nf* tribe

tribuna [tri'βuna] *nf* (*plataforma*)
platform; (*DEPORTE*) (grand)stand

tribunal [triβu'nal] *nm* (*JUR*) court;
(*comisión, fig*) tribunal

tributar [triβu'tar] *vt* (*gen*) to pay;
tributo *nm* (*COM*) tax

tricotar [triko'tar] *vi* to knit

trigal [tri'ɣal] *nm* wheat field

trigo ['triɣo] *nm* wheat

trigueño, a [tri'ɣeɲo, a] *adj* (*pelo*)
corn-coloured

trillado, a [tri'ʎaðo, a] *adj* threshed;
(*asunto*) trite, hackneyed; **trilladora** *nf*
threshing machine

trillar [tri'ʎar] *vt* (*AGR*) to thresh

trimestral [trimes'tral] *adj* quarterly;
(*ESCOL*) termly

trimestre [tri'mestre] *nm* (*ESCOL*) term

trinar [tri'nar] *vi* (*pájaros*) to sing;
(*rabiar*) to fume, be angry

trinchar [trin'tʃar] *vt* to carve

trinchera [trin'tʃera] *nf* (*fosa*) trench

trineo [tri'neo] *nm* sledge

trinidad [trini'ðað] *nf* trio; (*REL*): **la T~**
the Trinity

trino ['trino] *nm* trill

tripa ['tripa] *nf* (*ANAT*) intestine; (*fam:
tb: ~s*) insides *pl*

triple ['triple] *adj* triple

triplicado, a [tripli'kaðo, a] *adj*: **por ~**
in triplicate

tripulación [tripula'θjon] *nf* crew

tripulante [tripu'lante] *nm/f*
crewman/woman

tripular [tripu'lar] *vt* (*barco*) to man;
(*AUTO*) to drive

triquiñuela [triki'ŋwela] *nf* trick

tris [tris] *nm inv* crack; **en un ~ in an**
instant

triste ['triste] *adj* sad; (*lamentable*)
sorry, miserable; **~za** *nf* (*aflicción*)
sadness; (*melancolía*) melancholy

triturar [tritu'rar] *vt* (*moler*) to grind;
(*mascar*) to chew

triunfar [trjun'far] *vi* (*tener éxito*) to
triumph; (*ganar*) to win; **triunfo** *nm*
triumph

trivial [tri'βjal] *adj* trivial; **~izar** *vt* to
minimize, play down

triza ['triθa] *nf*: **hacer ~s** to smash to
bits; (*papel*) to tear to shreds

trocar [tro'kar] *vt* to exchange

trocear [troθe'ar] *vt* (*carne, manzana*)

to cut up, cut into pieces

trocha ['trotʃa] nf short cut

troche ['trotʃe]: **a ~ y moche** adv helter-skelter, pell-mell

trofeo [tro'feo] nm (premio) trophy; (éxito) success

tromba ['tromba] nf downpour

trombón [trom'bon] nm trombone

trombosis [trom'bosis] nf inv thrombosis

trompa ['trompa] nf horn; (trompo) humming top; (hocico) snout; (fam): **cogerse una ~** to get tight

trompazo [trom'paθo] nm bump, bang

trompeta [trom'peta] nf trumpet; (clarín) bugle

trompicón [trompi'kon]: **a ~es** adv in fits and starts

trompo ['trompo] nm spinning top

trompón [trom'pon] nm bump

tronar [tro'nar] vt (AM) to shoot ♦ vi to thunder; (fig) to rage

tronchar [tron'tʃar] vt (árbol) to chop down; (fig: vida) to cut short; (: esperanza) to shatter; (persona) to tire out; **~se** vr to fall down

tronco ['tronko] nm (de árbol, ANAT) trunk

trono ['trono] nm throne

tropa ['tropa] nf (MIL) troop; (soldados) soldiers pl

tropel [tro'pel] nm (muchedumbre) crowd

tropezar [trope'θar] vi to trip, stumble; (error) to slip up; **~ con** to run into; (topar con) to bump into; **tropezón** nm trip; (fig) blunder

tropical [tropi'kal] adj tropical

trópico ['tropiko] nm tropic

tropiezo [tro'pjeθo] etc vb ver **tropezar** ♦ nm (error) slip, blunder; (desgracia) misfortune; (obstáculo) snag

trotamundos [trota'mundos] nm inv globetrotter

trotar [tro'tar] vi to trot; **trote** nm trot; (fam) travelling; **de mucho trote**

hard-wearing

trozo ['troθo] nm bit, piece

trucha ['trutʃa] nf trout

truco ['truko] nm (habilidad) knack; (engaño) trick

trueno ['trweno] nm thunder; (estampido) bang

trueque etc ['trweke] vb ver **trocar** ♦ nm exchange; (COM) barter

trufa ['trufa] nf (BOT) truffle

truhán, ana [tru'an, ana] nm/f rogue

truncar [trun'kar] vt (cortar) to truncate; (fig: la vida etc) to cut short; (: el desarrollo) to stunt

tu [tu] adj your

tú [tu] pron you

tubérculo [tu'ßerkulo] nm (BOT) tuber

tuberculosis [tußerku'losis] nf inv tuberculosis

tubería [tuße'ria] nf pipes pl; (conducto) pipeline

tubo ['tußo] nm tube, pipe; **~ de ensayo** test tube; **~ de escape** exhaust (pipe)

tuerca ['twerka] nf nut

tuerto, a ['twerto, a] adj blind in one eye ♦ nm/f one-eyed person

tuerza etc vb ver **torcer**

tuétano ['twetano] nm marrow; (BOT) pith

tufo ['tufo] nm (hedor) stench

tul [tul] nm tulle

tulipán [tuli'pan] nm tulip

tullido, a [tu'ʎiðo, a] adj crippled

tumba ['tumba] nf (sepultura) tomb

tumbar [tum'bar] vt to knock down; **~se** vr (echarse) to lie down; (extenderse) to stretch out

tumbo ['tumbo] nm: **dar ~s** to stagger

tumbona [tum'bona] nf (butaca) easy chair; (de playa) deckchair (BRIT), beach chair (US)

tumor [tu'mor] nm tumour

tumulto [tu'multo] nm turmoil

tuna ['tuna] nf (MUS) student music group; ver tb **tuno**

Tuna

A tuna is a musical group made up of university students or former students who dress up in costumes from the "Edad de Oro", the Spanish Golden Age. These groups go through the town playing their guitars, lutes and tambourines and serenade the young ladies in the halls of residence or make impromptu appearances at weddings or parties singing traditional Spanish songs for a few pesetas.

---

tunante [tu'nante] *nm/f* rascal
tunda ['tunda] *nf (golpeo)* beating
túnel ['tunel] *nm* tunnel
Túnez ['tuneθ] *nm* Tunisia; *(ciudad)* Tunis
tuno, a ['tuno, a] *nm/f (fam)* rogue ♦ *nm* member of student music group
tupido, a [tu'piðo, a] *adj (denso)* dense; *(tela)* close-woven
turba ['turβa] *nf* crowd
turbante [tur'βante] *nm* turban
turbar [tur'βar] *vt (molestar)* to disturb; *(incomodar)* to upset; **~se** *vr* to be disturbed
turbina [tur'βina] *nf* turbine
turbio, a ['turβjo, a] *adj* cloudy; *(tema etc)* confused
turbulencia [turβu'lenθja] *nf* turbulence; *(fig)* restlessness;
turbulento, a *adj* turbulent; *(fig: intranquilo)* restless; *(: ruidoso)* noisy
turco, a ['turko, a] *adj* Turkish ♦ *nm/f* Turk
turismo [tu'rismo] *nm* tourism; *(coche)* car; **turista** *nm/f* tourist; **turístico, a** *adj* tourist *cpd*
turnar [tur'nar] *vi* to take (it in) turns; **~se** *vr* to take (it in) turns; **turno** *nm (de trabajo)* shift; *(juegos etc)* turn
turquesa [tur'kesa] *nf* turquoise
Turquía [tur'kia] *nf* Turkey
turrón [tu'rron] *nm (dulce)* nougat
tutear [tute'ar] *vt* to address as familiar

"tú"; **~se** *vr* to be on familiar terms
tutela [tu'tela] *nf (legal)* guardianship;
tutelar *adj* tutelary ♦ *vt* to protect
tutor, a [tu'tor, a] *nm/f (legal)* guardian; *(ESCOL)* tutor
tuve *etc vb ver* **tener**
tuviera *etc vb ver* **tener**
tuyo, a ['tujo, a] *adj* yours, of yours
♦ *pron* yours; **un amigo ~** a friend of yours; **los ~s** *(fam)* your relations, your family
TV ['te'βe] *nf abr (= televisión)* TV
TVE *nf abr =* **Televisión Española**

U, u

u [u] *conj* or
ubicar [uβi'kar] *vt* to place, situate; *(AM: encontrar)* to find; **~se** *vr* to lie, be located
ubre ['uβre] *nf* udder
UCI *nf abr (= Unidad de Cuidados Intensivos)* ICU
Ud(s) *abr =* **usted(es)**
UE *nf abr (= Unión Europea)* EU
ufanarse [ufa'narse] *vr* to boast; **~ de** to pride o.s. on; **ufano, a** *adj (arrogante)* arrogant; *(presumido)* conceited
UGT *nf abr =* **Unión General de Trabajadores**
ujier [u'xjer] *nm* usher; *(portero)* doorkeeper
úlcera ['ulθera] *nf* ulcer
ulcerar [ulθe'rar] *vt* to make sore; **~se** *vr* to ulcerate
ulterior [ulte'rjor] *adj (más allá)* farther, further; *(subsecuente, siguiente)* subsequent
últimamente ['ultimamente] *adv (recientemente)* lately, recently
ultimar [ulti'mar] *vt* to finish; *(finalizar)* to finalize; *(AM: rematar)* to finish off
ultimátum [ulti'matum] *(pl ~s)* *nm* ultimatum

último, a ['ultimo, a] *adj* last; (*más reciente*) latest, most recent; (*más bajo*) bottom; (*más alto*) top; **en las últimas** on one's last legs; **por ~** finally

ultra ['ultra] *adj* ultra ♦ *nm/f* extreme right-winger

ultrajar [ultra'xar] *vt* (*ofender*) to outrage; (*insultar*) to insult, abuse; **ultraje** *nm* outrage; insult

ultramar [ultra'mar] *nm*: **de o en ~** abroad, overseas

ultramarinos [ultrama'rinos] *nmpl* groceries; **tienda de ~** grocer's (shop)

ultranza [ul'tranθa] **a ~** *adv* (*a todo trance*) at all costs; (*completo*) outright

ultratumba [ultra'tumba] *nf*: **la vida de ~** the next life

umbral [um'bral] *nm* (*gen*) threshold

umbrío, a [um'brio, a] *adj* shady

PALABRA CLAVE

un, una [un, 'una] *art indef* a; (*antes de vocal*) an; **una mujer/naranja** a woman/an orange
♦ *adj*: **unos** (o **unas**): **hay unos regalos para ti** there are some presents for you; **hay unas cervezas en la nevera** there are some beers in the fridge

unánime [u'nanime] *adj* unanimous; **unanimidad** *nf* unanimity

undécimo, a [un'deθimo, a] *adj* eleventh

ungir [un'xir] *vt* to anoint

ungüento [un'gwento] *nm* ointment

únicamente ['unikamente] *adv* solely, only

único, a ['uniko, a] *adj* only, sole; (*sin par*) unique

unidad [uni'ðað] *nf* unity; (*COM, TEC etc*) unit

unido, a [u'niðo, a] *adj* joined, linked; (*fig*) united

unificar [unifi'kar] *vt* to unite, unify

uniformar [unifor'mar] *vt* to make

uniform, level up; (*persona*) to put into uniform

uniforme [uni'forme] *adj* uniform, equal; (*superficie*) even ♦ *nm* uniform; **uniformidad** *nf* uniformity; (*de terreno*) levelness, evenness

unilateral [unilate'ral] *adj* unilateral

unión [u'njon] *nf* union; (*acto*) uniting, joining; (*unidad*) unity; (*TEC*) joint; **la U~ Europea** the European Union; **la U~ Soviética** the Soviet Union

unir [u'nir] *vt* (*juntar*) to join, unite; (*atar*) to tie, fasten; (*combinar*) to combine; **~se** *vr* to join together, unite; (*empresas*) to merge

unísono [u'nisono] *nm*: **al ~** in unison

universal [uniβer'sal] *adj* universal; (*mundial*) world *cpd*

universidad [uniβersi'ðað] *nf* university

universitario, a [uniβersi'tarjo, a] *adj* university *cpd* ♦ *nm/f* (*profesor*) lecturer; (*estudiante*) (university) student; (*graduado*) graduate

universo [uni'βerso] *nm* universe

PALABRA CLAVE

uno, a ['uno, a] *adj* one; **es todo ~** it's all one and the same; **~s pocos** a few; **~s cien** about a hundred
♦ *pron* **1** one; **quiero sólo ~** I only want one; **~ de ellos** one of them
2 (*alguien*) somebody, someone; **conozco a ~ que se te parece** I know somebody o someone who looks like you; **~ mismo** oneself; **~s querían quedarse** some (people) wanted to stay
3: (**los**) **~s ... (los) otros** ... some ... others; **una y otra son muy agradables** they're both very nice ♦ *nf* one; **es la una** it's one o'clock ♦ *nm* (number) one

untar [un'tar] *vt* (*mantequilla*) to spread; (*engrasar*) to grease, oil

uña ['uɲa] *nf* (*ANAT*) nail; (*garra*) claw;

(casco) hoof; (arrancaclavos) claw

uranio [u'ranjo] *nm* uranium

urbanidad [urβani'ðað] *nf* courtesy, politeness

urbanismo [urβa'nismo] *nm* town planning

urbanización [urβaniθa'θjon] *nf* (barrio, colonia) housing estate

urbanizar [urβani'θar] *vt* (zona) to develop, urbanize

urbano, a [ur'βano, a] *adj* (de ciudad) urban; (cortés) courteous, polite

urbe ['urβe] *nf* large city

urdimbre [ur'ðimbre] *nf* (de tejido) warp; (intriga) intrigue

urdir [ur'ðir] *vt* to warp; (complot) to plot, contrive

urgencia [ur'xenθja] *nf* urgency; (prisa) haste, rush; (emergencia) emergency; **servicios de ~** emergency services; **"Urgencias"** "Casualty"; **urgente** *adj* urgent

urgir [ur'xir] *vi* to be urgent; **me urge** I'm in a hurry for it

urinario, a [uri'narjo, a] *adj* urinary ♦ *nm* urinal

urna ['urna] *nf* urn; (POL) ballot box

urraca [u'rraka] *nf* magpie

URSS *nf*: **la ~** the USSR

Uruguay [uru'ɣwai] *nm*: **el ~** Uruguay; **uruguayo, a** *adj, nm/f* Uruguayan

usado, a [u'saðo, a] *adj* used; (de segunda mano) secondhand

usar [u'sar] *vt* to use; (ropa) to wear; (tener costumbre) to be in the habit of; **~se** *vr* to be used; **uso** *nm* use; wear; (costumbre) usage, custom; (moda) fashion; **al uso** in keeping with custom; **al uso de** in the style of

usted [us'teð] *pron* (sg) you sg; (pl): **~es** you pl

usual [u'swal] *adj* usual

usuario, a [u'swarjo, a] *nm/f* user

usura [u'sura] *nf* usury; **usurero, a** *nm/f* usurer

usurpar [usur'par] *vt* to usurp

utensilio [uten'siljo] *nm* tool; (CULIN) utensil

útero ['utero] *nm* uterus, womb

útil ['util] *adj* useful ♦ *nm* tool; **utilidad** *nf* usefulness; (COM) profit; **utilizar** *vt* to use, utilize

utopía [uto'pia] *nf* Utopia; **utópico, a** *adj* Utopian

uva ['uβa] *nf* grape

Las Uvas

In Spain **Las uvas** play a big part on New Year's Eve (**Nochevieja**), when on the stroke of midnight people gather at home, in restaurants or in the **plaza mayor** and eat a grape for each stroke of the clock of the **Puerta del Sol** in Madrid. It is said to bring luck for the following year.

V, v

v *abr* (= *voltio*) v

va *vb ver* **ir**

vaca ['baka] *nf* (animal) cow; **carne de ~** beef

vacaciones [baka'θjones] *nfpl* holidays

vacante [ba'kante] *adj* vacant, empty ♦ *nf* vacancy

vaciar [ba'θjar] *vt* to empty out; (ahuecar) to hollow out; (moldear) to cast; **~se** *vr* to empty

vacilante [baθi'lante] *adj* unsteady; (habla) faltering; (dudoso) hesitant

vacilar [baθi'lar] *vi* to be unsteady; (al hablar) to falter; (dudar) to hesitate, waver; (memoria) to fail

vacío, a [ba'θio, a] *adj* empty; (puesto) vacant; (desocupado) idle; (vano) vain ♦ *nm* emptiness; (FÍSICA) vacuum; (un ~) (empty) space

vacuna [ba'kuna] *nf* vaccine; **vacunar** *vt* to vaccinate

vacuno, a [ba'kuno, a] *adj* cow *cpd*; **ganado ~** cattle

vacuo, a ['bakwo, a] *adj* empty

adear [baðe'ar] vt (río) to ford; **vado** nm ford

agabundo, a [baɣa'ßundo, a] adj wandering ♦ nm tramp

agamente [baɣa'mente] adv vaguely

agancia [baɣa'ɣanθja] nf (pereza) idleness, laziness

ago, a ['baɣo, a] adj vague; (perezoso) lazy ♦ nm/f (vagabundo) tramp; (flojo)

agina [ba'xina] nf vagina

agón [ba'ɣon] nm (FERRO: de pasajeros) carriage; (: de mercancías) wagon

aguedad [baɣe'ðað] nf vagueness

aho ['bao] nm (vapor) vapour, steam; (respiración) breath

aina ['baina] nf sheath

ainilla [bai'niʎa] nf vanilla

ainita [bai'nita] nf (AM) green o French bean

ais vb ver **ver**

aivén [bai'ßen] nm to-and-fro movement; (de tránsito) coming and going; **vaivenes** nmpl (fig) ups and downs

ajilla [ba'xiʎa] nf crockery, dishes pl; **lavar la ~** to do the washing-up (BRIT), wash the dishes (US)

aldré etc vb ver **valer**

ale ['bale] nm voucher; (recibo) receipt; (pagaré) IOU

aledero, a [bale'ðero, a] adj valid

alenciano, a [balen'θjano, a] adj Valencian

alentía [balen'tia] nf courage, bravery

aler [ba'ler] vt to be worth; (MAT) to equal; (costar) to cost ♦ vi (ser útil) to be useful; (ser válido) to be valid; **~se** vr to take care of oneself; **~se de** to make use of, take advantage of; **~ la pena** to be worthwhile; **¿vale?** (ESP) OK?

aleroso, a [bale'roso, a] adj brave, valiant

valgo etc vb ver **valer**

valía [ba'lia] nf worth, value

validar [bali'ðar] vt to validate; **validez** nf validity; **válido, a** adj valid ♦ nm hero

valioso, a [ba'ljoso, a] adj valuable

valla ['baʎa] nf fence; (DEPORTE) hurdle; **~ publicitaria** hoarding; **vallar** vt to fence in

valle ['baʎe] nm valley

valor [ba'lor] nm value, worth; (precio) price; (valentía) valour, courage; (importancia) importance; **~es** nmpl (COM) securities; **~ar** vt to value

vals [bals] nm inv waltz

válvula ['balßula] nf valve

vamos vb ver **ir**

vampiro, resa [bam'piro, 'resa] nm/f vampire

van vb ver **ir**

vanagloriarse [banaɣlo'rjarse] vr to boast

vandalismo [banda'lismo] nm vandalism; **vándalo, a** nm/f vandal

vanguardia [ban'gwarðja] nf vanguard; (ARTE etc) avant-garde

vanidad [bani'ðað] nf vanity; **vanidoso, a** adj vain, conceited

vano, a ['bano, a] adj vain

vapor [ba'por] nm vapour; (vaho) steam; **al ~** (CULIN) steamed; **~izador** nm atomizer; **~izar** vt to vaporize; **~oso, a** adj vaporous

vapulear [bapule'ar] vt to beat, thrash

vaquero, a [ba'kero, a] adj cattle cpd ♦ nm cowboy; **~s** nmpl (pantalones) jeans

vaquilla [ba'kiʎa] nf (ZOOL) heifer

vara ['bara] nf stick; (TEC) rod; **~ mágica** magic wand

variable [ba'rjaßle] adj, nf variable

variación [barja'θjon] nf variation

variar [bar'jar] vt to vary; (modificar) to modify; (cambiar de posición) to switch around ♦ vi to change

varicela [bari'θela] nf chickenpox

varices |ba'riθes| *nfpl* varicose veins

variedad |barje'ðað| *nf* variety

varilla |ba'riʎa| *nf* stick; (*BOT*) twig; (*TEC*) rod; (*de rueda*) spoke

vario, a |'barjo, a| *adj* varied; **~s** various, several

varita |ba'rita| *nf*: **~ mágica** magic wand

varón |ba'ron| *nm* male, man; **varonil** *adj* manly, virile

Varsovia |bar'soβja| *n* Warsaw

vas *vb ver* **ir**

vasco, a |'basko, a| *adj, nm/f* Basque

vascongado, a |baskon'gaðo, a| *adj* Basque; **las Vascongadas** the Basque Country

vascuence |bas'kwenθe| *adj* = **vascongado**

vaselina |base'lina| *nf* Vaseline ®

vasija |ba'sixa| *nf* container, vessel

vaso |'baso| *nm* glass, tumbler; (*ANAT*) vessel

vástago |'bastaγo| *nm* (*BOT*) shoot; (*TEC*) rod; (*fig*) offspring

vasto, a |'basto, a| *adj* vast, huge

Vaticano |bati'kano| *nm*: **el ~** the Vatican

vatio |'batjo| *nm* (*ELEC*) watt

vaya *etc vb ver* **ir**

Vd(s) *abr* = **usted(es)**

ve *vb ver* **ir; ver**

veces |'beθes| *nfpl de* **vez**

vecindad |beθin'dað| *nf* neighbourhood; (*habitantes*) residents *pl*

vecindario |beθin'darjo| *nm* neighbourhood; residents *pl*

vecino, a |be'θino, a| *adj* neighbouring ♦ *nm/f* neighbour; (*residente*) resident

veda |'beða| *nf* prohibition

vedar |be'ðar| *vt* (*prohibir*) to ban, prohibit; (*impedir*) to stop, prevent

vegetación |bexeta'θjon| *nf* vegetation

vegetal |bexe'tal| *adj, nm* vegetable

vegetariano, a |bexeta'rjano, a| *adj, nm/f* vegetarian

vehemencia |be(e)'menθja| *nf* vehemence; **vehemente** *adj* vehement

vehículo |be'ikulo| *nm* vehicle; (*MED*) carrier

veia *etc vb ver* **ver**

veinte |'beinte| *num* twenty

vejación |bexa'θjon| *nf* vexation; (*humillación*) humiliation

vejar |be'xar| *vt* (*irritar*) to annoy, vex; (*humillar*) to humiliate

vejez |be'xeθ| *nf* old age

vejiga |be'xiγa| *nf* (*ANAT*) bladder

vela |'bela| *nf* (*de cera*) candle; (*NAUT*) sail; (*insomnio*) sleeplessness; (*vigilia*) vigil; (*MIL*) sentry duty; **estar a dos ~s** (*fam: sin dinero*) to be skint

velado, a |be'laðo, a| *adj* veiled; (*sonido*) muffled; (*FOTO*) blurred ♦ *nf* soirée

velar |be'lar| *vt* (*vigilar*) to keep watch over ♦ *vi* to stay awake; **~ por** to watch over, look after

velatorio |bela'torjo| *nm* (*funeral*) wake

veleidad |belei'ðað| *nf* (*ligereza*) fickleness; (*capricho*) whim

velero |be'lero| *nm* (*NAUT*) sailing ship (*AVIAT*) glider

veleta |be'leta| *nf* weather vane

veliz |be'lis| (*AM*) *nm* suitcase

vello |'beʎo| *nm* down, fuzz

velo |'belo| *nm* veil

velocidad |beloθi'ðað| *nf* speed; (*TEC, AUTO*) gear

velocímetro |belo'θimetro| *nm* speedometer

veloz |be'loθ| *adj* fast

ven *vb ver* **venir**

vena |'bena| *nf* vein

venado |be'naðo| *nm* deer

vencedor, a |benθe'ðor, a| *adj* victorious ♦ *nm/f* victor, winner

vencer |ben'θer| *vt* (*dominar*) to defeat, beat; (*derrotar*) to vanquish; (*superar, controlar*) to overcome, master ♦ *vi* (*triunfar*) to win (through), triumph; (*plazo*) to expire; **vencido, a** *adj* (*derrotado*) defeated, beaten; (COM)

due ♦ *adv*: **pagar vencido** to pay in arrears; **vencimiento** *nm* (COM) maturity

enda ['benda] *nf* bandage; **vendaje** *nm* bandage, dressing; **vendar** *vt* to bandage; **vendar los ojos** to blindfold

endaval [benda'βal] *nm* (*viento*) gale

endedor, a [bende'ðor, a] *nm/f* seller

ender [ben'der] *vt* to sell; **~ al contado/al por mayor/al por menor** to sell for cash/wholesale/retail

endimia [ben'dimja] *nf* grape harvest

endré *etc vb ver* **venir**

eneno [be'neno] *nm* poison; (*de serpiente*) venom; **~so, a** *adj* poisonous; venomous

enerable [bene'raβle] *adj* venerable; **venerar** *vt* (*respetar*) to revere; (*adorar*) to worship

enéreo, a [be'nereo, a] *adj*:
enfermedad venérea venereal disease

enezolano, a [beneθo'lano, a] *adj* Venezuelan

enezuela [bene'θwela] *nf* Venezuela

enganza [ben'ganθa] *nf* vengeance, revenge; **vengar** *vt* to avenge; **vengarse** *vr* to take revenge; **vengativo, a** *adj* (*persona*) vindictive

engo *etc vb ver* **venir**

enia [benja] *nf* (*perdón*) pardon; (*permiso*) consent

enial [be'njal] *adj* venial

enida [be'niða] *nf* (*llegada*) arrival; (*regreso*) return

enidero, a [beni'ðero, a] *adj* coming, future

enir [be'nir] *vi* to come; (*llegar*) to arrive; (*ocurrir*) to happen; (*fig*): **~ de** to stem from; **~ bien/mal** to be suitable/unsuitable; **el año que viene** next year; **~se abajo** to collapse

enta [benta] *nf* (COM) sale; **~ a plazos** hire purchase; **~ al contado/**

al por mayor/al por menor *o* al detalle cash sale/wholesale/retail; **~ con derecho a retorno** sale or return; **"en ~"** "for sale"

ventaja [ben'taxa] *nf* advantage; **ventajoso, a** *adj* advantageous

ventana [ben'tana] *nf* window; **ventanilla** *nf* (*de taquilla*) window (*of booking office etc*)

ventilación [bentila'θjon] *nf* ventilation; (*corriente*) draught; **ventilador** [bentila'ðor] *nm* fan

ventilar [benti'lar] *vt* to ventilate; (*para secar*) to put out to dry; (*asunto*) to air, discuss

ventisca [ben'tiska] *nf* blizzard

ventrílocuo, a [ben'trilokwo, a] *nm/f* ventriloquist

ventura [ben'tura] *nf* (*felicidad*) happiness; (*buena suerte*) luck; (*destino*) fortune; **a la (buena) ~** at random; **venturoso, a** *adj* happy; (*afortunado*) lucky, fortunate

veo *etc vb ver* **ver**

ver [ber] *vt* to see; (*mirar*) to look at, watch; (*entender*) to understand; (*investigar*) to look into; ♦ *vi* to see; to understand; **~se** *vr* (*encontrarse*) to meet; (*dejarse ~*) to be seen; (*hallarse: en un apuro*) to find o.s., be; **a ~** let's see; **no tener nada que ~ con** to have nothing to do with; **a mi modo de ~** as I see it

vera ['bera] *nf* edge, verge; (*de río*) bank

veracidad [beraθi'ðað] *nf* truthfulness

veranear [berane'ar] *vi* to spend the summer; **veraneo** *nm* summer holiday; **veraniego, a** *adj* summer *cpd*

verano [be'rano] *nm* summer

veras ['beras] *nfpl* truth *sg*; **de ~** really, truly

veraz [be'raθ] *adj* truthful

verbal [ber'βal] *adj* verbal

verbena [ber'βena] *nf* (*baile*) open-air dance

verbo ['berβo] *nm* verb; **~so, a** *adj* verbose

verdad [ber'ðað] nf truth; (fiabilidad) reliability; **de ~** real, proper; **a decir ~** to tell the truth; **~ero, a** adj (veraz) true, truthful; (fiable) reliable; (fig) real

verde ['berðe] adj green; (chiste) blue, dirty ♦ nm green; **viejo ~** dirty old man; **~ar** vi to turn green; **verdor** nm greenness

verdugo [ber'ðuɣo] nm executioner

verdulero, a [berðu'lero, a] nm/f greengrocer

verduras [ber'ðuras] nfpl (CULIN) greens

vereda [be'reða] nf path; (AM) pavement (BRIT), sidewalk (US)

veredicto [bere'ðikto] nm verdict

vergonzoso, a [berɣon'θoso, a] adj shameful; (tímido) timid, bashful

vergüenza [ber'ɣwenθa] nf shame, sense of shame; (timidez) bashfulness; (pudor) modesty; **me da ~** I'm ashamed

verídico, a [be'riðiko, a] adj true, truthful

verificar [berifi'kar] vt to check; (corroborar) to verify; (llevar a cabo) to carry out; **~se** vr (predicción) to prove to be true

verja ['berxa] nf (cancela) iron gate; (valla) iron railings pl; (de ventana) grille

vermut [ber'mut] (pl ~s) nm vermouth

verosímil [bero'simil] adj likely, probable; (relato) credible

verruga [be'rruxa] nf wart

versado, a [ber'saðo, a] adj: **~ en** versed in

versátil [ber'satil] adj versatile

versión [ber'sjon] nf version

verso ['berso] nm verse; **un ~** a line of poetry

vértebra ['berteßra] nf vertebra

verter [ber'ter] vt (líquido: adrede) to empty, pour (out); (: sin querer) to spill; (basura) to dump ♦ vi to flow

vertical [berti'kal] adj vertical

vértice ['bertiθe] nm vertex, apex

vertidos [ber'tiðos] nmpl waste sg

vertiente [ber'tjente] nf slope; (fig) aspect

vertiginoso, a [bertixi'noso, a] adj giddy, dizzy

vértigo ['bertiɣo] nm vertigo; (mareo) dizziness

vesícula [be'sikula] nf blister

vespino ® [bes'pino] nm o nf moped

vestíbulo [bes'tißulo] nm hall; (de teatro) foyer

vestido [bes'tiðo] pp de vestir; **~ de azul/marinero** dressed in blue/as a sailor ♦ nm (ropa) clothes pl, clothing; (de mujer) dress, frock

vestigio [bes'tixjo] nm (huella) trace; **~s** nmpl (restos) remains

vestimenta [besti'menta] nf clothing

vestir [bes'tir] vt (poner: ropa) to put on; (llevar: ropa) to wear; (proveer de ropa a) to clothe; (suj: sastre) to make clothes for ♦ vi to dress; (verse bien) to look good; **~se** vr to get dressed, dress o.s.

vestuario [bes'twarjo] nm clothes pl, wardrobe; (TEATRO: cuarto) dressing room; (DEPORTE) changing room

veta ['beta] nf (vena) vein, seam; (en carne) streak; (de madera) grain

vetar [be'tar] vt to veto

veterano, a [bete'rano, a] adj, nm veteran

veterinaria [beteri'narja] nf veterinary science; ver tb **veterinario**

veterinario, a [beteri'narjo, a] nm/f vet(erinary surgeon)

veto ['beto] nm veto

vez [beθ] nf time; (turno) turn; **a la ~ que** at the same time as; **a su ~** in its turn; **otra ~** again; **una ~** once; **de una ~** in one go; **de una ~ para siempre** once and for all; **en ~ de** instead of; **a o algunas veces** sometimes; **una y otra ~** repeatedly; **de ~ en cuando** from time to time; **veces** 9 7 times 9; **hacer las veces de** to stand in for; **tal ~** perhaps

vía 297 **VIH**

vía ['bia] nf track, route; (FERRO) line; (fig) way; (ANAT) passage, tube ♦ prep via, by way of; **por ~ judicial** by legal means; **por ~ oficial** through official channels; **en ~s de** in the process of; **~ aérea** airway; **V~ Láctea** Milky Way; **~ pública** public road o thoroughfare

viable ['bjaβle] adj (solución, plan, alternativa) feasible

viaducto [bja'ðukto] nm viaduct

viajante [bja'xante] nm commercial traveller

viajar [bja'xar] vi to travel; **viaje** nm journey; (gira) tour; (NAUT) voyage; **estar de viaje** to be on a trip; **viaje de ida y vuelta** round trip; **viaje de novios** honeymoon; **viajero, a** adj travelling; (ZOOL) migratory ♦ nm/f (quien viaja) traveller; (pasajero) passenger

vial [bjal] adj road cpd, traffic cpd

víbora ['biβora] nf viper; (AM) poisonous snake

vibración [biβra'θjon] nf vibration

vibrar [bi'βrar] vt, vi to vibrate

vicario [bi'karjo] nm curate

vicepresidente [biθepresi'ðente] nm/f vice-president

viceversa [biθe'βersa] adv vice versa

viciado, a [bi'θjaðo, a] adj (corrompido) corrupt; (contaminado) foul, contaminated; **viciar** vt (pervertir) to pervert; (JUR) to nullify; (estropear) to spoil; **viciarse** vr to become corrupted

vicio ['biθjo] nm vice; (mala costumbre) bad habit; **~so, a** adj (muy malo) vicious; (corrompido) depraved ♦ nm/f depraved person

vicisitud [biθisi'tuð] nf vicissitude

víctima ['biktima] nf victim

victoria [bik'torja] nf victory; **victorioso, a** adj victorious

vid [bið] nf vine

never; **estar con ~** to be still alive; **ganarse la ~** to earn one's living

vídeo ['biðeo] nm video ♦ adj inv: **película ~** video film; **~cámara** nf camcorder; **~casete** nm video cassette, videotape; **~club** nm video club; **~juego** nm video game

vidriero, a [bi'ðrjero, a] nm/f glazier ♦ nf (ventana) stained-glass window; (AM: de tienda) shop window; (puerta) glass door

vidrio ['biðrjo] nm glass

vieira ['bjeira] nf scallop

viejo, a ['bjexo, a] adj old ♦ nm/f old man/woman; **hacerse ~** to get old

Viena ['bjena] n Vienna

vienes etc vb ver **venir**

vienés, esa [bje'nes, esa] adj Viennese

viento ['bjento] nm wind; **hacer ~** to be windy

vientre ['bjentre] nm belly; (matriz) womb

viernes ['bjernes] nm inv Friday; **V~ Santo** Good Friday

Vietnam [bjet'nam] nm: **el ~** Vietnam; **vietnamita** adj Vietnamese

viga ['biɣa] nf beam, rafter; (de metal) girder

vigencia [bi'xenθja] nf validity; **estar en ~** to be in force; **vigente** adj valid, in force; (imperante) prevailing

vigésimo, a [bi'xesimo, a] adj twentieth

vigía [bi'xia] nm look-out

vigilancia [bixi'lanθja] nf: **tener a uno bajo ~** to keep watch on sb

vigilar [bixi'lar] vt to watch over ♦ vi (gen) to be vigilant; (hacer guardia) to keep watch; **~ por** to take care of

vigilia [vi'xilja] nf wakefulness, being awake; (REL) fast

vigor [bi'ɣor] nm vigour, vitality; **en ~** in force; **entrar/poner en ~** to come/put into effect; **~oso, a** adj vigorous

VIH nm abr (= virus de la inmunodeficiencia humana) HIV;

~ **positivo/negativo** HIV-positive/-negative

vil [bil] *adj* vile, low; **~eza** *nf* vileness; (*acto*) base deed

vilipendiar [bilipen'djar] *vt* to vilify, revile

villa ['biʎa] *nf* (*casa*) villa; (*pueblo*) small town; (*municipalidad*) municipality; **~ miseria** (*AM*) shantytown

villancico [biʎan'θiko] *nm* (Christmas) carol

villorrio [bi'ʎorrjo] *nm* shantytown

vilo ['bilo]: **en ~** *adv* in the air, suspended; (*fig*) on tenterhooks, in suspense

vinagre [bi'navre] *nm* vinegar

vinagreta [bina'xreta] *nf* vinaigrette, French dressing

vinculación [binkula'θjon] *nf* (*lazo*) link, bond; (*acción*) linking

vincular [binku'lar] *vt* to link, bind; **vínculo** *nm* link, bond

vine *etc vb ver* **venir**

vinicultura [binikul'tura] *nf* wine growing

viniera *etc vb ver* **venir**

vino ['bino] *vb ver* **venir** ♦ *nm* wine; **~ blanco/tinto** white/red wine

viña ['biɲa] *nf* vineyard; **viñedo** *nm* vineyard

viola ['bjola] *nf* viola

violación [bjola'θjon] *nf* violation; **~** (**sexual**) rape

violar [bjo'lar] *vt* to violate; (*sexualmente*) to rape

violencia [bjo'lenθja] *nf* violence, force; (*incomodidad*) embarrassment; (*acto injusto*) unjust act; **violentar** *vt* to force; (*casa*) to break into; (*agredir*) to assault; (*violar*) to violate; **violento, a** *adj* violent; (*furioso*) furious; (*situación*) embarrassing; (*acto*) forced, unnatural

violeta [bjo'leta] *nf* violet

violín [bjo'lin] *nm* violin

violón [bjo'lon] *nm* double bass

viraje [bi'raxe] *nm* turn; (*de vehículo*) swerve; (*fig*) change of direction; **virar** *vi* to change direction

virgen ['birxen] *adj, nf* virgin

Virgo ['birxo] *nm* Virgo

viril [bi'ril] *adj* virile; **~idad** *nf* virility

virtud [bir'tuð] *nf* virtue; **en ~ de** by virtue of; **virtuoso, a** *adj* virtuous ♦ *nm/f* virtuoso

viruela [bi'rwela] *nf* smallpox

virulento, a [biru'lento, a] *adj* virulent

virus ['birus] *nm inv* virus

visa ['bisa] (*AM*) *nf* = **visado**

visado [bi'saðo] *nm* visa

víscera ['bisθera] *nf* (*ANAT, ZOOL*) gut, bowel; **~s** *nfpl* entrails

visceral [bisθe'ral] *adj* (*odio*) intense; **reacción ~** gut reaction

viscoso, a [bis'koso, a] *adj* viscous

visera [bi'sera] *nf* visor

visibilidad [bisiβili'ðað] *nf* visibility; **visible** *adj* visible; (*fig*) obvious

visillos [bi'siʎos] *nmpl* lace curtains

visión [bi'sjon] *nf* (*ANAT*) vision, (*eye*)sight; (*fantasía*) vision, fantasy

visita [bi'sita] *nf* call, visit; (*persona*) visitor; **hacer una ~** to pay a visit

visitar [bisi'tar] *vt* to visit, call on

vislumbrar [bislum'brar] *vt* to glimpse, catch a glimpse of

viso ['biso] *nm* (*del metal*) glint, gleam; (*de tela*) sheen; (*aspecto*) appearance

visón [bi'son] *nm* mink

visor [bi'sor] *nm* (*FOTO*) viewfinder

víspera ['bispera] *nf*: **la ~ de ...** the day before ...

vista ['bista] *nf* sight, vision; (*capacidad de ver*) (eye)sight; (*mirada*) look(s) (*pl*); **a primera ~** at first glance; **hacer la ~ gorda** to turn a blind eye; **volver la ~** to look back; **está a la ~ que** it's obvious that; **en ~ de** in view of; **en ~ de que** in view of the fact that; **¡hasta la ~!** so long!, see you!; **con ~s a** with a view to; **~zo** *nm* glance; **dar** o **echar un ~zo a** to glance at

visto, a ['bisto, a] *pp de ver* ♦ *adj*

tb vestir ♦ *adj* seen; (*considerado*) considered ♦ *nm*: **~ bueno** approval; **"~ bueno"** "approved"; **por lo ~** apparently; **está ~ que** it's clear that; **está bien/mal ~** it's acceptable/unacceptable; **~ que** since, considering that

visual [bi'swal] *adj* visual

vital [bi'tal] *adj* life *cpd*, living *cpd*; (*fig*) vital; (*persona*) lively, vivacious; **~icio, a** *adj* for life; **~idad** (*de persona, negocio*) energy; (*de ciudad*) liveliness

vitamina [bita'mina] *nf* vitamin

viticultor, a [bitikul'tor, a] *nm/f* wine grower; **viticultura** *nf* wine growing

vitorear [bitore'ar] *vt* to cheer, acclaim

vitrina [bi'trina] *nf* show case; (*AM*) shop window

viudez *nf* widowhood

viudo, a [ˈbjuðo, a] *nm/f* widower/widow

viva [ˈbiβa] *excl* hurrah!: **¡~ el rey!** long live the king!

vivacidad [biβaθiˈðað] *nf* (*vigor*) vigour; (*vida*) liveliness

vivaracho, a [biβaˈratʃo, a] *adj* jaunty, lively; (*ojos*) bright, twinkling

vivaz [biˈβaθ] *adj* lively

víveres [ˈbiβeres] *nmpl* provisions

vivero [biˈβero] *nm* (*para plantas*) nursery; (*para peces*) fish farm; (*fig*) hotbed

viveza [biˈβeθa] *nf* liveliness; (*agudeza mental*) sharpness

vivienda [biˈβjenda] *nf* housing; (*una ~*) house; (*piso*) flat (*BRIT*), apartment (*US*)

viviente [biˈβjente] *adj* living

vivir [biˈβir] *vt, vi* to live ♦ *nm* life, living

vivo, a [ˈbiβo, a] *adj* living, alive; (*fig: descripción*) vivid; (*persona: astuto*) smart, clever; **en ~** (*transmisión etc*) live

vocablo [boˈkaβlo] *nm* (*palabra*) word; (*término*) term

vocabulario [bokaβuˈlarjo] *nm* vocabulary

vocación [bokaˈθjon] *nf* vocation; **vocacional** (*AM*) *nf* ≈ technical college

vocal [boˈkal] *adj* vocal ♦ *nf* vowel; **~izar** *vt* to vocalize

vocear [boθeˈar] *vt* (*para vender*) to cry; (*aclamar*) to acclaim; (*fig*) to proclaim ♦ *vi* to yell; **vocerío** *nm* shouting

vocero [boˈθero] *nm/f* spokesman/woman

voces [ˈboθes] *pl de* **voz**

vociferar [boθifeˈrar] *vt* to shout ♦ *vi* to yell

vodka [ˈboðka] *nm o f* vodka

vol *abr* = **volumen**

volador, a [bolaˈðor, a] *adj* flying

volandas [boˈlandas]: **en ~** *adv* in the air

volante [boˈlante] *adj* flying ♦ *nm* (*de coche*) steering wheel; (*de reloj*) balance

volar [boˈlar] *vt* (*edificio*) to blow up ♦ *vi* to fly

volátil [boˈlatil] *adj* volatile

volcán [bolˈkan] *nm* volcano; **~ico, a** *adj* volcanic

volcar [bolˈkar] *vt* to upset, overturn; (*tumbar, derribar*) to knock over; (*vaciar*) to empty out ♦ *vi* to overturn; **~se** *vr* to tip over

voleibol [boleiˈβol] *nm* volleyball

volqué *etc vb ver* **volcar**

voltaje [bolˈtaxe] *nm* voltage

voltear [bolteˈar] *vt* to turn over; (*volcar*) to turn upside down

voltereta [bolteˈreta] *nf* somersault

voltio [ˈboltjo] *nm* volt

voluble [boˈluβle] *adj* fickle

volumen [boˈlumen] (*pl* **volúmenes**) *nm* volume; **voluminoso, a** *adj* voluminous; (*enorme*) massive

voluntad [bolunˈtað] *nf* will; (*resolución*) willpower; (*deseo*) desire, wish

voluntario, a [bolunˈtarjo, a] *adj*

voluntary ♦ nm/f volunteer

voluntarioso, a [bolunta'rjoso, a] adj headstrong

voluptuoso, a [bolup'twoso, a] adj voluptuous

volver [bol'βer] vt (gen) to turn; (dar vuelta a) to turn (over); (voltear) to turn round, turn upside down; (poner al revés) to turn inside out; (devolver) to return ♦ vi to return, go back, come back; **~se** vr to turn round; **~ la espalda** to turn one's back; **~ triste** etc **a uno** to make sb sad etc; **~ a hacer** to do again; **~ en sí** to come to; **~se insoportable/muy caro** to get o become unbearable/very expensive; **~se loco** to go mad

vomitar [bomi'tar] vt, vi to vomit; **vómito** nm vomit

voraz [bo'raθ] adj voracious

vos [bos] (AM) pron you

vosotros, as [bo'sotros, as] pron you; (reflexivo): **entre/para ~** among/for yourselves

votación [bota'θjon] nf (acto) voting; (voto) vote

votar [bo'tar] vi to vote; **voto** nm vote; (promesa) vow; **votos** (good) wishes

voy vb ver **ir**

voz [boθ] nf voice; (grito) shout; (rumor) rumour; (LING) word; **dar voces** to shout, yell; **a media ~** in a low voice; **a ~ en cuello o en grito** at the top of one's voice; **de viva ~** verbally; **en ~ alta** aloud; **~ de mando** command

vuelco ['bwelko] vb ver **volcar** ♦ nm spill, overturning

vuelo ['bwelo] vb ver **volar** ♦ nm flight; (encaje) lace, frill; **coger al ~** to catch in flight; **~ charter/regular** charter/scheduled flight; **~ libre** (DEPORTE) hang-gliding

vuelque etc vb ver **volcar**

vuelta ['bwelta] nf (gen) turn; (curva) bend, curve; (regreso) return;

(revolución) revolution; (de circuito) lap; (de papel, tela) reverse; (cambio) change; **a la ~** on one's return; **a ~ de correo** by return of post; **dar ~s** (suj: cabeza) to spin; **dar ~s a una idea** to turn over an idea (in one's head); **estar de ~** to be back; **dar una ~** to go for a walk; (en coche) to go for a drive; **~ ciclista** (DEPORTE) (cycle) tour

vuelto pp de **volver**

vuelvo etc vb ver **volver**

vuestro, a ['bwestro, a] adj your; **un amigo ~** a friend of yours ♦ pron: **el ~/la vuestra, los ~s/las vuestras** yours

vulgar [bul'var] adj (ordinario) vulgar; (común) common; **~idad** nf commonness; (acto) vulgarity; (expresión) coarse expression; **~izar** vt to popularize

vulgo ['bulɣo] nm common people

vulnerable [bulne'raßle] adj vulnerable

vulnerar [bulne'rar] vt (ley, acuerdo) to violate, breach; (derechos, intimidad) to violate; (reputación) to damage

W, w

Walkman ® [wak'man] nm Walkman ®

wáter ['bater] nm toilet

whisky ['wiski] nm whisky, whiskey

X, x

xenofobia [kseno'foßja] nf xenophobia

xilófono [ksi'lofono] nm xylophone

Y, y

y [i] conj and

ya [ja] adv (gen) already; (ahora) now;

(en seguida) at once; (pronto) soon
♦ excl all right! ♦ conj (ahora que) now
that; ~ **lo sé** I know; ~ **que** since

▼acer [ja'θer] vi to lie

▼acimiento [jaθi'mjento] nm (de
mineral) deposit; (arqueológico) site

▼anqui ['janki] adj, nm/f Yankee

▼ate ['jate] nm yacht

▼azco etc vb ver **yacer**

▼edra ['jeðra] nf ivy

▼egua ['jeɣwa] nf mare

▼ema ['jema] nf (del huevo) yoke; (BOT)
leaf bud; (fig) best part; ~ **del dedo**
fingertip

▼ergo etc vb ver **erguir**

▼ermo, a ['jermo, a] adj (estéril, fig)
barren ♦ nm wasteland

▼erno ['jerno] nm son-in-law

▼erro etc vb ver **errar**

▼eso ['jeso] nm plaster

▼o [jo] pron I; **soy ~** it's me, it is I

▼odo ['joðo] nm iodine

▼oga ['joɣa] nm yoga

▼ogur(t) [jo'ɣur(t)] nm yoghurt

▼ugo ['juɣo] nm yoke

▼ugoslavia [juɣos'laßja] nf Yugoslavia

▼ugular [juɣu'lar] adj jugular

▼unque ['junke] nm anvil

▼unta ['junta] nf yoke

▼uxtaponer [jukstapo'ner] vt to
juxtapose; **yuxtaposición** nf
juxtaposition

Z, z

▼afar [θa'far] vt (soltar) to untie;
(superficie) to clear; **~se** vr (escaparse)
to escape; (TEC) to slip off

▼afio, a ['θafjo, a] adj coarse

▼afiro [θa'firo] nm sapphire

▼aga ['θaɣa] nf: **a la ~** behind, in the
rear

▼aguán [θa'ɣwan] nm hallway

▼aherir [θae'rir] vt (criticar) to criticize

▼aino, a ['θaino, a] adj (caballo)
chestnut

zalamería [θalame'ria] nf flattery;
zalamero, a adj flattering; (cobista)
suave

zamarra [θa'marra] nf (chaqueta)
sheepskin jacket

zambullirse [θambu'ʎirse] vr to dive

zampar [θam'par] vt to gobble down

zanahoria [θana'orja] nf carrot

zancada [θan'kaða] nf stride

zancadilla [θanka'ðiʎa] nf trip

zanco ['θanko] nm stilt

zancudo, a [θan'kuðo, a] adj long-
legged ♦ nm (AM) mosquito

zángano ['θangano] nm drone

zanja ['θanxa] nf ditch; **zanjar** vt
(resolver) to resolve

zapata [θa'pata] nf (MECÁNICA) shoe

zapatear [θapate'ar] vi to tap with
one's feet

zapatería [θapate'ria] nf (oficio)
shoemaking; (tienda) shoe shop;
(fábrica) shoe factory; **zapatero, a**
nm/f shoemaker

zapatilla [θapa'tiʎa] nf slipper; ~ **de
deporte** training shoe

zapato [θa'pato] nm shoe

zapping ['θapin] nm channel-hopping;
hacer ~ to flick through the channels

zar [θar] nm tsar, czar

zarandear [θarande'ar] vt (fam) to
shake vigorously

zarpa ['θarpa] nf (garra) claw

zarpar [θar'par] vi to weigh anchor

zarza ['θarθa] nf (BOT) bramble; **zarzal**
nm (matorral) bramble patch

zarzamora [θarθa'mora] nf blackberry

zarzuela [θar'θwela] nf Spanish light
opera

zigzag [θiɣ'θaɣ] nm zigzag;
zigzaguear vi to zigzag

zinc [θink] nm zinc

zócalo ['θokalo] nm (ARQ) plinth, base

zodíaco [θo'ðiako] nm (ASTRO) zodiac

zona ['θona] nf zone; ~ **fronteriza**
border area

zoo ['θoo] nm zoo

zoología [θoolo'xia] nf zoology;

zoológico, a adj zoological ♦ nm (tb: parque ~) zoo; **zoólogo, a** nm/f zoologist

zoom ['θum] nm zoom lens

zopilote [θopi'lote] (AM) nm buzzard

zoquete [θo'kete] nm (fam) blockhead

zorro, a ['θorro, a] adj crafty ♦ nm/f fox/vixen

zozobra [θo'θoβra] nf (fig) anxiety; **zozobrar** vi (hundirse) to capsize; (fig) to fail

zueco ['θweko] nm clog

zumbar [θum'bar] vt (golpear) to hit ♦ vi to buzz; **zumbido** nm buzzing

zumo ['θumo] nm juice

zurcir [θur'θir] vt (coser) to darn

zurdo, a ['θurðo, a] adj (persona) left-handed

zurrar [θu'rrar] (fam) vt to wallop

ENGLISH · SPANISH
INGLÉS · ESPAÑOL

ENGLISH-SPANISH
INGLÉS-ESPAÑOL

A, a

A [eɪ] n (MUS) la m

a [ə] indef art (before vowel or silent h: an) **1** un(a); **~ book** un libro; **an apple** una manzana; **she's ~ doctor** (ella) es médica
2 (instead of the number "one") un(a); **~ year ago** hace un año; **~ hundred/thousand etc pounds** cien/mil etc libras
3 (in expressing ratios, prices etc): **3 ~ day/week** 3 al día/a la semana; **10 km an hour** 10 km por hora; **£5 ~ person** £5 por persona; **30p ~ kilo** 30p el kilo

A.A. n abbr (= Automobile Association: BRIT) ≈ RACE m (SP); (= Alcoholics Anonymous) Alcohólicos Anónimos
A.A.A. (US) n abbr (= American Automobile Association) ≈ RACE m (SP)
aback [ə'bæk] adv: **to be taken ~** quedar desconcertado
abandon [ə'bændən] vt abandonar; (give up) renunciar a
abate [ə'beɪt] vi (storm) amainar; (anger) aplacarse; (terror) disminuir
abattoir ['æbətwɑː*] (BRIT) n matadero
abbey ['æbɪ] n abadía
abbot ['æbət] n abad m
abbreviation [əbriːvɪ'eɪʃən] n (short form) abreviatura
abdicate ['æbdɪkeɪt] vt renunciar a ♦ vi abdicar
abdomen ['æbdəmən] n abdomen m
abduct [æb'dʌkt] vt raptar, secuestrar
abeyance [ə'beɪəns] n: **in ~** (law) en

desuso; (matter) en suspenso
abide [ə'baɪd] vt: **I can't ~ it/him** no lo/le puedo ver; **~ by** vt fus atenerse a
ability [ə'bɪlɪtɪ] n habilidad f, capacidad f; (talent) talento
abject ['æbdʒekt] adj (poverty) miserable; (apology) rastrero
ablaze [ə'bleɪz] adj en llamas, ardiendo
able ['eɪbl] adj capaz; (skilled) hábil; **to be ~ to do sth** poder hacer algo; **~-bodied** adj sano; **ably** adv hábilmente
abnormal [æb'nɔːməl] adj anormal
aboard [ə'bɔːd] adv a bordo ♦ prep a bordo de
abode [ə'bəud] n: **of no fixed ~** sin domicilio fijo
abolish [ə'bɔlɪʃ] vt suprimir, abolir
aborigine [æbə'rɪdʒɪnɪ] n aborigen m/f
abort [ə'bɔːt] vt, vi abortar; **~ion** [ə'bɔːʃən] n aborto; **to have an ~ion** abortar, hacerse abortar; **~ive** adj malogrado

about [ə'baut] adv **1** (approximately) más o menos, aproximadamente; **~ a hundred/thousand etc** unos(unas) cien/mil etc; **it takes ~ 10 hours** se tarda unas o más o menos 10 horas; **at ~ 2 o'clock** sobre las dos; **I've just ~ finished** casi he terminado
2 (referring to place) por todas partes; **to leave things lying ~** dejar las cosas (tiradas) por todas partes; **to run ~** correr por todas partes; **to walk ~** pasearse, ir y venir
3: to be ~ to do sth estar a punto de hacer algo

above ♦ prep **1** (relating to) de, sobre, acerca de; **a book ~ London** un libro sobre or acerca de Londres; **what is it ~?** ¿de qué se trata?, ¿qué pasa?; **we talked ~ it** hablamos de eso or ello; **what or how ~ doing this?** ¿qué tal si hacemos esto? **2** (referring to place) por; **to walk ~ the town** caminar por la ciudad

above [ə'bʌv] adv encima, por encima, arriba ♦ prep encima de; (greater than: in number) más de; (: in rank) superior a; **mentioned ~** susodicho; **~ all** sobre todo; **~ board** adj legítimo

abrasive [ə'breɪzɪv] adj abrasivo; (manner) brusco

abreast [ə'brɛst] adv de frente; **to keep ~ of** (fig) mantenerse al corriente de

abroad [ə'brɔːd] adv (to be) en el extranjero; (to go) al extranjero

abrupt [ə'brʌpt] adj (sudden) brusco; (curt) áspero

abruptly [ə'brʌptlɪ] adv (leave) repentinamente; (speak) bruscamente

abscess ['æbsɪs] n absceso

abscond [əb'skɒnd] vi (thief): **to ~ with** fugarse con; (prisoner): **to ~ (from)** escaparse (de)

absence ['æbsəns] n ausencia

absent ['æbsənt] adj ausente; **~ee** [-'tiː] n ausente m/f; **~-minded** adj distraído

absolute ['æbsəluːt] adj absoluto; **~ly** [-'luːtlɪ] adv (totally) totalmente; (certainly!) ¡por supuesto (que sí)!

absolve [əb'zɒlv] vt: **to ~ sb (from)** absolver a alguien de

absorb [əb'zɔːb] vt absorber; **to be ~ed in a book** estar absorto en un libro; **~ent cotton** (US) n algodón m hidrófilo; **~ing** adj absorbente

absorption [əb'zɔːpʃən] n absorción f

abstain [əb'steɪn] vi: **to ~ (from)** abstenerse (de)

abstinence ['æbstɪnəns] n abstinencia

abstract ['æbstrækt] adj abstracto

absurd [əb'səːd] adj absurdo

abundance [ə'bʌndəns] n abundancia

abuse [n ə'bjuːs, vb ə'bjuːz] n (insults) insultos mpl, injurias fpl; (ill-treatment) malos tratos mpl; (misuse) abuso ♦ vt insultar; maltratar; abusar de; **abusive** adj ofensivo

abysmal [ə'bɪzməl] adj pésimo; (failure) garrafal; (ignorance) supino

abyss [ə'bɪs] n abismo

AC abbr (= alternating current) corriente f alterna

academic [ækə'dɛmɪk] adj académico, universitario; (pej: issue) puramente teórico ♦ n estudioso/a; profesor(a) m/f universitario/a

academy [ə'kædəmɪ] n (learned body) academia; (school) instituto, colegio; **~ of music** conservatorio

accelerate [æk'sɛləreɪt] vt, vi acelerar; **accelerator** (BRIT) n acelerador m

accent ['æksɛnt] n acento; (fig) énfasis m

accept [ək'sɛpt] vt aceptar; (responsibility, blame) admitir; **~able** adj aceptable; **~ance** n aceptación f

access ['æksɛs] n acceso; **to have ~ to** tener libre acceso a; **~ible** [-'sɛsəbl] adj (place, person) accesible; (knowledge etc) asequible

accessory [æk'sɛsərɪ] n accesorio; (LAW): **~ to** cómplice de

accident ['æksɪdənt] n accidente m; (chance event) casualidad f; **by ~** (unintentionally) sin querer; (by chance) por casualidad; **~al** [-'dɛntl] adj accidental, fortuito; **~ally** [-'dɛntəlɪ] adv sin querer; por casualidad; **~ insurance** n seguro contra accidentes; **~-prone** adj propenso a los accidentes

acclaim [ə'kleɪm] vt aclamar, aplaudir ♦ n aclamación f, aplausos mpl

acclimatize [ə'klaɪmətaɪz] (US: **acclimate**) vt: **to become ~d** aclimatarse

accommodate [əˈkɔmədeɪt] vt (subj: person) alojar, hospedar; (: car, hotel etc) tener cabida para; (oblige, please) complacer; **accommodating** adj servicial, complaciente

accommodation [əkɔməˈdeɪʃən] n (us accommodations npl) alojamiento

accompany [əˈkʌmpəni] vt acompañar

accomplice [əˈkʌmplis] n cómplice m/f

accomplish [əˈkʌmpliʃ] vt (finish) concluir; (achieve) lograr; **~ed** adj experto, hábil; **~ment** n (skill: gen pl) talento; (completion) realización f

accord [əˈkɔːd] n acuerdo ♦ vt conceder; **of his own ~** espontáneamente; **~ance** n: **in ~ance with** de acuerdo con, conforme a; **~ing: ~ing to** prep según; (in accordance with) conforme a; (this) adv (appropriately) de acuerdo con esto; (as a result) en consecuencia

accordion [əˈkɔːdiən] n acordeón m

accost [əˈkɔst] vt abordar, dirigirse a

account [əˈkaunt] n (COMM) cuenta; (report) informe m; **~s** npl (COMM) cuentas fpl; **of no ~** de ninguna importancia; **on ~** a cuenta; **on no ~** bajo ningún concepto; **on ~ of** a causa de, por motivo de; **to take into ~**, **take ~ of** tener en cuenta; **~ for** vt fus (explain) explicar; (represent) representar; **~able** adj: **~able (to)** responsable (ante); **~ancy** n contabilidad f; **~ant** n contable m/f, contador(a) m/f; **~ number** (at bank etc) número de cuenta

accrued interest [əˈkruːd-] n interés m acumulado

accumulate [əˈkjuːmjuleɪt] vt acumular ♦ vi acumularse

accuracy [ˈækjurəsi] n (of total) exactitud f; (of description etc) precisión f

accurate [ˈækjurit] adj (total) exacto;

(description) preciso; (person) cuidadoso; (device) de precisión; **~ly** adv con precisión

accusation [ækjuˈzeɪʃən] n acusación f

accuse [əˈkjuːz] vt: **to ~ sb (of sth)** acusar a uno (de algo); **~d** n (LAW) acusado/a

accustom [əˈkʌstəm] vt acostumbrar; **~ed** adj: **~ed to** acostumbrado a

ace [eɪs] n as m

ache [eɪk] n dolor m ♦ vi doler; **my head ~s** me duele la cabeza

achieve [əˈtʃiːv] vt (aim, result) alcanzar; (success) lograr, conseguir; **~ment** n (completion) realización f; (success) éxito

acid [ˈæsɪd] adj ácido; (taste) agrio ♦ n (CHEM, inf: LSD) ácido; **~ rain** n lluvia ácida

acknowledge [əkˈnɔlɪdʒ] vt (letter: also: ~ receipt of) acusar recibo de; (fact, situation, person) reconocer; **~ment** n acuse m de recibo

acne [ˈækni] n acné m

acorn [ˈeɪkɔːn] n bellota

acoustic [əˈkuːstɪk] adj acústico; **~s** n, npl acústica sg

acquaint [əˈkweɪnt] vt: **to ~ sb with sth** (inform) poner a uno al corriente de algo; **to be ~ed with** conocer; **~ance** n (person) conocido/a; (with person, subject) conocimiento

acquire [əˈkwaɪəʳ] vt adquirir; **acquisition** [ækwiˈzɪʃən] n adquisición f

acquit [əˈkwɪt] vt absolver, exculpar; **to ~ o.s. well** salir con éxito

acre [ˈeɪkəʳ] n acre m

acrid [ˈækrɪd] adj acre

acrobat [ˈækrəbæt] n acróbata m/f

across [əˈkrɔs] prep (on the other side of) al otro lado de, del otro lado de; (crosswise) a través de ♦ adv de un lado a otro, de una parte a otra; a través, al través; (measurement): **the road is 10m ~** la carretera tiene 10m de ancho; **to run/swim ~** atravesar corriendo/nadando; **~ from** enfrente de

acrylic [ə'krɪlɪk] *adj* acrílico ♦ *n* acrílica

act [ækt] *n* acto, acción *f*; (*of play*) acto; (*in music hall etc*) número; (*LAW*) decreto, ley *f* ♦ *vi* (*behave*) comportarse; (*have effect: drug, chemical*) hacer efecto; (*THEATRE*) actuar; (*pretend*) fingir; (*take action*) obrar ♦ *vt* (*part*) hacer el papel de; **in the ~ of**: **to catch sb in the ~ of ...** pillar a uno en el momento en que ...; **to ~ as** actuar or hacer de; **~ing** *adj* suplente ♦ *n* (*activity*) actuación *f*; (*profession*) profesión *f* de actor

action ['ækʃən] *n* acción *f*, acto; (*MIL*) acción *f*, batalla; (*LAW*) proceso, demanda; **out of ~** (*person*) fuera de combate; (*thing*) estropeado; **to take ~** tomar medidas; **~ replay** *n* (*TV*) repetición *f*

activate ['æktɪveɪt] *vt* activar

active ['æktɪv] *adj* activo, enérgico; (*volcano*) en actividad; **~ly** *adv* (*participate*) activamente; (*discourage, dislike*) enérgicamente; **activity** [-'tɪvɪtɪ] *n* actividad *f*; **activity holiday** *n* vacaciones *fpl* con actividades organizadas

actor ['æktə*] *n* actor *m*

actress ['æktrɪs] *n* actriz *f*

actual ['æktjuəl] *adj* verdadero, real; (*emphatic use*) propiamente dicho; **~ly** *adv* realmente, en realidad; (*even*) incluso

acumen ['ækjumən] *n* perspicacia

acute [ə'kjuːt] *adj* agudo

ad [æd] *n abbr* = **advertisement**

A.D. *adv abbr* (= *anno Domini*) A.C.

adamant ['ædəmənt] *adj* firme, inflexible

adapt [ə'dæpt] *vt* adaptar ♦ *vi*: **to ~ (to)** adaptarse (a), ajustarse (a); **~able** *adj* adaptable; **~er, ~or** *n* (*ELEC*) adaptador *m*

add [æd] *vt* añadir, agregar; (*figures: also: ~ up*) sumar ♦ *vi*: **to ~ to**

(*increase*) aumentar, acrecentar; **it doesn't ~ up** (*fig*) no tiene sentido

adder ['ædə*] *n* víbora

addict ['ædɪkt] *n* adicto/a; (*enthusiast*) entusiasta *m/f*; **~ed** [ə'dɪktɪd] *adj*: **to be ~ed to** ser adicto a; (*football etc*) ser fanático de; **~ion** [ə'dɪkʃən] *n* (*to drugs etc*) adicción *f*; **~ive** [ə'dɪktɪv] *adj* que causa adicción

addition [ə'dɪʃən] *n* (*adding up*) adición *f*; (*thing added*) añadidura, añadido; **in ~** además, por añadidura; **in ~ to** además de; **~al** *adj* adicional

additive ['ædɪtɪv] *n* aditivo

address [ə'drɛs] *n* dirección *f*, señas *fpl*; (*speech*) discurso ♦ *vt* (*letter*) dirigir; (*speak to*) dirigirse a, dirigir la palabra a; (*problem*) tratar

adept ['ædɛpt] *adj*: **~ at** experto or hábil en

adequate ['ædɪkwɪt] *adj* (*satisfactory*) adecuado; (*enough*) suficiente

adhere [əd'hɪə*] *vi*: **to ~ to** (*stick to*) pegarse a; (*fig: abide by*) observar; (*: belief etc*) ser partidario de

adhesive [əd'hiːzɪv] *adj* adhesivo, ~ **tape** *n* (*BRIT*) cinta adhesiva; (*US: MED*) esparadrapo

ad hoc [æd'hɔk] *adj* ad hoc

adjacent [ə'dʒeɪsənt] *adj*: **~ to** contiguo a, inmediato a

adjective ['ædʒɛktɪv] *n* adjetivo

adjoining [ə'dʒɔɪnɪŋ] *adj* contiguo, vecino

adjourn [ə'dʒəːn] *vt* aplazar ♦ *vi* suspenderse

adjudicate [ə'dʒuːdɪkeɪt] *vi* sentenciar

adjust [ə'dʒʌst] *vt* (*change*) modificar; (*clothing*) ajustar; (*machine*) ajustar ♦ *vi*: **to ~ (to)** adaptarse (a); **~able** *adj* ajustable; **~ment** *n* adaptación *f*; (*to machine, prices*) ajuste *m*

ad-lib [æd'lɪb] *vt, vi* improvisar; **ad lib** *adv* de forma improvisada

administer [əd'mɪnɪstə*] *vt* administrar; **administration** [-'treɪʃən] *n* (*management*)

administración f; (government)
gobierno; **administrative** [-trətɪv] adj
administrativo

admiral ['ædmərəl] n almirante m;
A~ty (BRIT) n Ministerio de Marina,
Almirantazgo

admiration [ædmə'reɪʃən] n
admiración f

admire [əd'maɪə*] vt admirar; **~r** n
(fan) admirador/a m/f

admission [əd'mɪʃən] n (to university,
club) ingreso; (entry fee) entrada;
(confession) confesión f

admit [əd'mɪt] vt (confess) confesar;
(permit to enter) dejar entrar, dar
entrada a; (to club, organization)
admitir; (accept: defeat) reconocer; **to
be ~ted to** hospital ingresar en el
hospital; **~ to** vt fus confesarse
culpable de; **~tance** n entrada; **~tedly**
adv es cierto or verdad que

admonish [əd'mɒnɪʃ] vt amonestar

ad nauseam [æd'nɔ:siæm] adv hasta
el cansancio

ado [ə'du:] n: **without (any) more ~**
sin más (ni más)

adolescent [ædəu'lesnt] adj, n
adolescente m/f

adopt [ə'dɒpt] vt adoptar; **~ed** adj
adoptivo; **~ion** [ə'dɒpʃən] n adopción f

adore [ə'dɔ:*] vt adorar

Adriatic [eɪdrɪ'ætɪk] n: **the ~ (Sea)** el
(Mar) Adriático

adrift [ə'drɪft] adv a la deriva

adult ['ædʌlt] n adulto/a ♦ adj (grown-
up) adulto; (for adults) para adultos

adultery [ə'dʌltərɪ] n adulterio

advance [əd'vɑ:ns] n (progress)
adelanto, progreso; (money) anticipo,
préstamo; (MIL) avance m ♦ adj:
~ booking venta anticipada;
~ notice, ~ warning previo aviso ♦ vt
(money) anticipar; (theory, idea)
proponer (para la discusión) ♦ vi
avanzar, adelantarse; **to make ~s (to
sb)** hacer proposiciones (a alguien); **in**

~ por adelantado; ~d adj avanzado;
(SCOL: studies) adelantado

advantage [əd'vɑ:ntɪdʒ] n (also
TENNIS) ventaja; **to take ~ of** (person)
aprovecharse de; (opportunity)
aprovechar

Advent ['ædvənt] n (REL) Adviento

adventure [əd'ventʃə*] n aventura;
adventurous [-tʃərəs] adj atrevido;
aventurero

adverb ['ædvə:b] n adverbio

adverse ['ædvə:s] adj adverso,
contrario

adversity [əd'və:sɪtɪ] n infortunio

advert ['ædvə:t] n abbr =
advertisement

advertise ['ædvətaɪz] vi (in newspaper
etc) anunciar, hacer publicidad; **to
~ for** (staff, accommodation etc) buscar
por medio de anuncios ♦ vt anunciar;
~ment [əd'və:tɪsmənt] n (COMM)
anuncio; **~r** n anunciante m/f;
advertising n publicidad f, anuncios
mpl; (industry) industria publicitaria

advice [əd'vaɪs] n consejo, consejos
mpl; (notification) aviso; **a piece of ~**
un consejo; **to take legal ~** consultar
con un abogado

advisable [əd'vaɪzəbl] adj aconsejable,
conveniente

advise [əd'vaɪz] vt aconsejar; (inform):
to ~ sb of sth informar a uno de
algo; **to ~ sb against sth/doing sth**
desaconsejar algo a uno/aconsejar a
uno que no haga algo; **~dly**
[əd'vaɪzɪdlɪ] adv (deliberately)
deliberadamente; **~r** n = **advisor**;
advisor n consejero/a, (consultant)
asesor/a m/f; **advisory** adj consultivo

advocate [vb 'ædvəkeɪt] vt abogar por
♦ n [-kɪt] (lawyer) abogado/a,
(supporter): **~ of** defensor(a) m/f de

Aegean [i:'dʒi:ən] n: **the ~ (Sea)** el
(Mar) Egeo

aerial ['eərɪəl] n antena ♦ adj aéreo

aerobics [eə'rəubɪks] n aerobic m

aeroplane ['eərəpleɪn] (BRIT) n

avión m

aerosol ['eərəsɒl] n aerosol m

aesthetic [iːs'θetɪk] adj estético

afar [ə'fɑː*] adv: **from ~** desde lejos

affair [ə'fɛə*] n asunto; (also: love ~) aventura (amorosa)

affect [ə'fɛkt] vt (influence) afectar, influir en; (afflict, concern) afectar; (move) conmover; **~ed** adj afectado

affection [ə'fɛkʃən] n afecto, cariño; **~ate** adj afectuoso, cariñoso

affinity [ə'fɪnɪtɪ] n (bond, rapport): **to feel an ~ with** sentirse identificado con; (resemblance) afinidad f

afflict [ə'flɪkt] vt afligir

affluence ['æfluəns] n opulencia, riqueza

affluent ['æfluənt] adj (wealthy) acomodado; **the ~ society** la sociedad opulenta

afford [ə'fɔːd] vt (provide) proporcionar; **can we ~ (to buy) it?** ¿tenemos bastante dinero para comprarlo?

Afghanistan [æf'gænɪstæn] n Afganistán m

afield [ə'fiːld] adv: **far ~** muy lejos

afloat [ə'fləut] adv (floating) a flote

afoot [ə'fut] adv: **there is something ~** algo se está tramando

afraid [ə'freɪd] adj: **to be ~ of** (person) tener miedo a; (thing) tener miedo de; **to be ~ to** tener miedo a, temer; **I am ~ that** me temo que; **I am ~ not/so** lo siento, pero no/es así

afresh [ə'frɛʃ] adv de nuevo, otra vez

Africa ['æfrɪkə] n África; **~n** adj, n africano/a m

after ['ɑːftə*] prep (time) después de; (place, order) detrás de, tras ♦ adv después ♦ conj después (de) que; **what/who are you ~?** ¿qué/a quién busca usted?; **~ having done/he left** después de haber hecho/después de que se marchó; **to name sb ~ sb** llamar a uno por uno; **it's twenty ~ eight** (US) son las ocho y veinte; **to**

ask ~ sb preguntar por alguien; **~ all** después de todo, al fin y al cabo; **~ you!** ¡pase usted!; **~-effects** npl consecuencias fpl, efectos mpl; **~math** n consecuencias fpl, resultados mpl; **~noon** n tarde f; **~s** (inf) n (dessert) postre m; **~-sales service** (BRIT) n servicio de asistencia pos-venta; **~-shave (lotion)** n loción (lotion); **~sun (lotion/cream)** n loción f/crema para después del sol, aftersun m; **~thought** n ocurrencia (tardía); **~wards** (US **~ward**) adv después, más tarde

again [ə'gɛn] adv otra vez, de nuevo; **to do sth ~** volver a hacer algo; **~ and ~** una y otra vez

against [ə'gɛnst] prep (in opposition to) en contra de; (leaning on, touching) contra, junto a

age [eɪdʒ] n edad f; (period) época ♦ vi envejecer(se) ♦ vt envejecer; **she is 20 years of ~** tiene 20 años; **to come of ~** llegar a la mayoría de edad; **it's been ~s since I saw you** hace siglos que no te veo; **~d 10** de 10 años de edad; **the ~d** ['eɪdʒɪd] npl los ancianos; **~ group** n: **to be in the same ~ group** tener la misma edad; **~ limit** n edad f mínima (or máxima)

agency ['eɪdʒənsɪ] n agencia

agenda [ə'dʒɛndə] n orden m del día

agent ['eɪdʒənt] n agente m/f; (COMM: holding concession) representante m/f, delegado/a; (CHEM, fig) agente m

aggravate ['ægrəveɪt] vt (situation) agravar; (person) irritar

aggregate ['ægrɪgət] n conjunto

aggressive [ə'grɛsɪv] adj (belligerent) agresivo; (assertive) enérgico

aggrieved [ə'griːvd] adj ofendido, agraviado

aghast [ə'gɑːst] adj horrorizado

agile ['ædʒaɪl] adj ágil

agitate ['ædʒɪteɪt] vt (trouble) inquietar ♦ vi: **to ~ for/against** hacer campaña pro or en favor de/en contra de

AGM n abbr (= annual general meeting)

asamblea anual

ago [əˈgəu] adv: **2 days ~** hace 2 días; **not long ~** hace poco; **how long ~?** ¿hace cuánto tiempo?

agog [əˈgɔg] adj (eager) ansioso; (excited) emocionado

agonizing [ˈægənaızıŋ] adj (pain) atroz; (decision, wait) angustioso

agony [ˈægənı] n (pain) dolor m agudo; (distress) angustia; **to be in ~** retorcerse de dolor

agree [əˈgriː] vt (price, date) acordar, quedar en ♦ vi (have same opinion): **to ~ (with/that)** estar de acuerdo (con/que); (correspond) coincidir, concordar; (consent) acceder; **to ~ with** (subj: person) estar de acuerdo con, ponerse de acuerdo con; (: food) sentar bien a; (LING) concordar con; **to ~ to sth/to do sth** consentir en algo/aceptar hacer algo; **to ~ that** (admit) estar de acuerdo en que; **~able** adj (sensation) agradable; (person) simpático; (willing) de acuerdo, conforme; **~d** adj (time, place) convenido; **~ment** n acuerdo; (contract) contrato; **in ~ment** de acuerdo, conforme

agricultural [ægrıˈkʌltʃərəl] adj agrícola

agriculture [ˈægrıkʌltʃəˈ] n agricultura

aground [əˈgraund] adv: **to run ~** (NAUT) encallar, embarrancar

ahead [əˈhɛd] adv (in front) delante; (into the future): **she had no time to think ~** no tenía tiempo de hacer planes para el futuro; **~ of** delante de; (in advance of) antes de; **~ of time** antes de la hora; **go right** or **straight ~** (direction) siga adelante; (permission) hazlo (or hágalo)

aid [eıd] n ayuda, auxilio; (device) aparato ♦ vt ayudar, auxiliar; **in ~ of** a beneficio de

aide [eıd] n (person, also: MIL) ayudante m/f

AIDS [eıdz] n abbr (= acquired immune deficiency syndrome) SIDA m

ailment [ˈeılmənt] n enfermedad f, achaque m

aim [eım] vt (gun, camera) apuntar; (missile, remark) dirigir; (blow) asestar ♦ vi (also: take ~) apuntar ♦ n (in shooting: skill) puntería; (objective) propósito, meta; **to ~ at** (with weapon) apuntar a; (objective) aspirar a, pretender; **to ~ to do** tener la intención de hacer; **~less** adj sin propósito, sin objeto

ain't [eınt] (inf) = **am not; aren't; isn't**

air [ɛəˈ] n aire m; (appearance) aspecto ♦ vt (room) ventilar; (clothes, ideas) airear ♦ cpd aéreo; **to throw sth into the ~** (ball etc) lanzar algo al aire; **by ~** (travel) en avión; **to be on the ~** (RADIO, TV) estar en antena; **~bed** (BRIT) n colchón m neumático; **~-conditioned** adj climatizado; **~ conditioning** n aire acondicionado; **~craft** n inv avión m; **~craft carrier** n porta(a)viones m inv; **~field** n campo de aviación; **A~ Force** n fuerzas fpl aéreas, aviación f; **~ freshener** n ambientador m; **~gun** n escopeta de aire comprimido; **~ hostess** (BRIT) n azafata; **~ letter** (BRIT) n carta aérea; **~lift** n puente m aéreo; **~line** n línea aérea; **~liner** n avión m de pasajeros; **~mail** n: **by ~mail** por avión; **~plane** (US) n avión m; **~port** n aeropuerto; **~ raid** n ataque m aéreo; **~sick** adj: **to be ~sick** marearse (en avión); **~space** n espacio aéreo; **~tight** adj hermético; **~-traffic controller** n controlador(a) m/f aéreo/a; **~y** adj (room) bien ventilado; (fig: manner) desenfadado

aisle [aıl] n (of church) nave f; (of theatre, supermarket) pasillo; **~ seat** n (on plane) asiento de pasillo

ajar [əˈdʒɑː²] adj entreabierto

alarm [əˈlɑːm] n (in shop, bank) alarma; (anxiety) inquietud f ♦ vt asustar, inquietar; **~ call** n (in hotel etc) alarma; **~ clock** n despertador m

alas [ə'læs] *adv* desgraciadamente

albeit [ɔːl'biːit] *conj* aunque

album ['ælbəm] n álbum m; (L.P.) elepé m

alcohol ['ælkəhɔl] n alcohol m; **~ic** [-'hɔlik] *adj*, n alcohólico/a m/f

ale [eil] n cerveza

alert [ə'ləːt] *adj* (attentive) atento; (to danger, opportunity) alerta ♦ n alerta m, alarma ♦ vt poner sobre aviso; **to be on the ~** (also MIL) estar alerta o sobre aviso

algebra ['ældʒibrə] n álgebra

Algeria [æl'dʒiəriə] n Argelia

alias ['eiliəs] *adv* alias, conocido por ♦ n (of criminal) apodo; (of writer) seudónimo

alibi ['ælibai] n coartada

alien ['eiliən] n (foreigner) extranjero/a; (extraterrestrial) extraterrestre m/f ♦ *adj*: **~ to** ajeno a; **~ate** vt enajenar, alejar

alight [ə'lait] *adj* ardiendo; (eyes) brillante ♦ vi (person) apearse, bajar; (bird) posarse

align [ə'lain] vt alinear

alike [ə'laik] *adj* semejantes, iguales ♦ *adv* igualmente, del mismo modo; **to look ~** parecerse

alimony ['æliməni] n manutención f

alive [ə'laiv] *adj* vivo; (lively) alegre

KEYWORD

all [ɔːl] *adj* (sg) todo/a; (pl) todos/as; **~ day** todo el día; **~ night** toda la noche; **~ men** todos los hombres; **~ five came** vinieron los cinco; **~ the books** todos los libros; **~ his life** toda su vida

♦ *pron* 1 todo; **I ate it ~, I ate ~ of it** me lo comí todo; **~ of us went** fuimos todos; **~ the boys went** fueron todos los chicos; **is that ~?** ¿eso es todo?, ¿algo más?; (in shop) ¿algo más?, ¿alguna cosa más?

2 (in phrases): **above ~** sobre todo; por encima de todo; **after ~** después

de todo; **at ~: not at ~** (in answer to question) en absoluto; (in answer to thanks) ¡de nada!, ¡no hay de qué!; **I'm not at ~ tired** no estoy nada cansado/a; **anything at ~ will do** cualquier cosa viene bien; **~ in ~** a fin de cuentas

♦ *adv*: **~ alone** completamente solo/a; **it's not as hard as ~ that** no es tan difícil como lo pintas; **~ the more/the better** tanto más/mejor; **~ but** casi; **the score is ~** = están empatados a 2

all clear n (after attack etc) fin m de la alerta; (fig) luz f verde

allege [ə'ledʒ] vt pretender; **~dly** [ə'ledʒidli] *adv* supuestamente, según se afirma

allegiance [ə'liːdʒəns] n lealtad f

allergy ['ælədʒi] n alergia

alleviate [ə'liːvieit] vt aliviar

alley ['æli] n callejuela

alliance [ə'laiəns] n alianza

allied ['ælaid] *adj* aliado

alligator ['æligeitə*] n (ZOOL) caimán m

all-in (BRIT) *adj*, *adv* (charge) todo incluido

all-night *adj* (café, shop) abierto toda la noche; (party) que dura toda la noche

allocate ['æləkeit] vt (money etc) asignar

allot [ə'lɔt] vt asignar; **~ment** n ración f; (garden) parcela

all-out *adj* (effort etc) supremo; **all out** *adv* con todas las fuerzas

allow [ə'lau] vt permitir, dejar; (a claim) admitir; (sum, time etc) dar, conceder; (concede): **to ~ that** reconocer que; **to ~ sb to do** permitir a alguien hacer; **he is ~ed to ...** se le permite ...; **~ for** vt fus tener en cuenta; **~ance** n subvención f; (welfare payment) subsidio, pensión f; (pocket money) dinero de bolsillo; (tax ~ance) desgravación f; **to make ~ances for** (person) disculpar a; (thing) tener en cuenta

alloy ['ælɔɪ] n mezcla

all: ~ **right** adv bien; (as answer) ¡conforme!, ¡está bien!; ~**rounder** n: **he's a good** ~**rounder** es todo a la vez todo; ~**time** adj (record) de todos los tiempos

alluring [ə'ljuərɪŋ] adj atractivo, tentador(a)

ally ['ælaɪ] n aliado/a ♦ vt: **to** ~ **o.s. with** aliarse con

almighty [ɔːl'maɪtɪ] adj todopoderoso; (row etc) imponente

almond ['ɑːmənd] n almendra

almost ['ɔːlməust] adv casi

alone [ə'ləun] adj, adv solo; **to leave sb** ~ dejar a uno en paz; **to leave sth** ~ no tocar algo, dejar algo sin tocar; **let** ~ ... y mucho menos ...

along [ə'lɒŋ] prep a lo largo de, por ♦ adv: **is he coming** ~ **with us?** ¿viene con nosotros?; **he was limping** ~ iba cojeando; ~ **with** junto con; **all** ~ (all the time) desde el principio; ~**side** prep al lado de ♦ adv al lado

aloof [ə'luːf] adj reservado ♦ adv: **to stand** ~ mantenerse apartado

aloud [ə'laud] adv en voz alta

alphabet ['ælfəbet] n alfabeto

Alps [ælps] npl: **the** ~ los Alpes

already [ɔːl'redɪ] adv ya

alright ['ɔːl'raɪt] (BRIT) adv = **all right**

Alsatian [æl'seɪʃən] n (dog) pastor m alemán

also ['ɔːlsəu] adv también, además

altar ['ɔːltə*] n altar m

alter ['ɔːltə*] vt cambiar, modificar ♦ vi cambiar; ~**ation** [ɔːltə'reɪʃən] n cambio; (to clothes) arreglo; (to building) arreglo mpl

alternate [adj ɔl'tɜːnɪt, vb 'ɔːltəneɪt] adj (actions etc) alternativos; (events) alterno; (US) = **alternative** ♦ vi: **to** ~ **(with)** alternar (con); **on** ~ **days** un día sí y otro no; **alternating current** [-neɪtɪŋ-] n corriente f alterna

alternative [ɔl'tɜːnətɪv] adj alternativo ♦ n alternativa; ~ **medicine** medicina alternativa; ~**ly** adv: ~**ly one could ...** por otra parte se podría ...

although [ɔːl'ðəu] conj aunque

altitude ['æltɪtjuːd] n altura

alto ['æltəu] n (female) contralto f; (male) alto

altogether [ɔːltə'geðə*] adv completamente, del todo; (on the whole) en total, en conjunto

always ['ɔːlweɪz] adv siempre

Alzheimer's (disease) ['æltshaɪməz-] n enfermedad f de Alzheimer

am [æm] vb see **be**

a.m. adv abbr (= ante meridiem) de la mañana

amalgamate [ə'mælgəmeɪt] vi amalgamarse ♦ vt amalgamar, unir

amateur ['æmətə*] n aficionado/a, amateur m/f; ~**ish** adj inexperto, superficial

amaze [ə'meɪz] vt asombrar, pasmar; **to be** ~**d (at)** quedar pasmado (de); ~**ment** n asombro, sorpresa; **amazing** adj extraordinario; (fantastic) increíble

Amazon ['æməzən] n (GEO) Amazonas m

ambassador [æm'bæsədə*] n embajador(a) m/f

amber ['æmbə*] n ámbar m; **at** ~ (BRIT: AUT) en el amarillo

ambiguous [æm'bɪgjuəs] adj ambiguo

ambition [æm'bɪʃən] n ambición f; **ambitious** [-ʃəs] adj ambicioso

ambulance ['æmbjuləns] n ambulancia

ambush ['æmbuʃ] n emboscada ♦ vt tender una emboscada a

amenable [ə'miːnəbl] adj: **to be** ~ **to** dejarse influir por

amend [ə'mend] vt enmendar; **to make** ~**s** dar cumplida satisfacción

amenities [ə'miːnɪtɪz] npl

comodidades *fpl*

America [əˈmerɪkə] *n* (*USA*) Estados *mpl* Unidos; **~n** *adj, n* norteamericano/a *m/f*; estadounidense *m/f*

amiable [ˈeɪmɪəbl] *adj* amable, simpático

amicable [ˈæmɪkəbl] *adj* amistoso, amigable

amid(st) [əˈmɪd(st)] *prep* entre, en medio de

amiss [əˈmɪs] *adv:* **to take sth ~** tomar algo a mal; **there's something ~** pasa algo

ammonia [əˈməunɪə] *n* amoníaco

ammunition [æmjuˈnɪʃən] *n* municiones *fpl*

amnesty [ˈæmnɪstɪ] *n* amnistía

amok [əˈmɔk] *adv:* **to run ~** enloquecerse, desbocarse

among(st) [əˈmʌŋ(st)] *prep* entre, en medio de

amorous [ˈæmərəs] *adj* amoroso

amount [əˈmaunt] *n* (*gen*) cantidad *f*; (*of bill etc*) suma, importe *m* ♦ *vi:* **to ~ to** sumar; (*be same as*) equivaler a, significar

amp(ère) [ˈæmp(ɛə*)] *n* amperio

ample [ˈæmpl] *adj* (*large*) grande; (*abundant*) abundante; (*enough*) bastante, suficiente

amplifier [ˈæmplɪfaɪə*] *n* amplificador *m*

amuse [əˈmjuːz] *vt* divertir; (*distract*) distraer, entretener; **~ment** *n* diversión *f*; (*pastime*) pasatiempo; (*laughter*) risa; **~ment arcade** *n* salón *m* de juegos; **~ment park** *n* parque *m* de atracciones

an [æn] *indef art see* a

anaemic [əˈniːmɪk] (*US* **anemic**) *adj* anémico; (*fig*) soso, insípido

anaesthetic [ænɪsˈθetɪk] *n* (*US* **anesthetic**) anestesia

analog(ue) [ˈænəlɔg] *adj* (*computer, watch*) analógico

analyse [ˈænəlaɪz] (*US* **analyze**) *vt*

analizar; **analysis** [əˈnæləsɪs] (*pl* **analyses**) *n* análisis *m inv*; **analyst** [-lɪst] *n* (*political analyst, psychoanalyst*) analista *m/f*

analyze [ˈænəlaɪz] (*US*) *vt* = **analyse**

anarchist [ˈænəkɪst] *n* anarquista *m/f*

anatomy [əˈnætəmɪ] *n* anatomía

ancestor [ˈænsɪstə*] *n* antepasado

anchor [ˈæŋkə*] *n* ancla, áncora *vi* (*also:* to drop ~) anclar ♦ *vt* anclar; **to weigh ~** levar anclas

anchovy [ˈæntʃəvɪ] *n* anchoa

ancient [ˈeɪnʃənt] *adj* antiguo

ancillary [ænˈsɪlərɪ] *adj* auxiliar

and [ænd] *conj* y; (*before i-, hi- + consonant*) e; **men ~ women** hombres y mujeres; **father ~ son** padre e hijo; **trees ~ grass** árboles y hierba; **so on** etcétera, y así sucesivamente; **try ~ come** procura venir; **he talked ~ talked** habló sin parar; **better ~ better** cada vez mejor

Andes [ˈændiːz] *npl:* **the ~** los Andes

anemic *etc* [əˈniːmɪk] (*US*) = **anaemic** *etc*

anesthetic *etc* [ænɪsˈθetɪk] (*US*) = **anaesthetic** *etc*

anew [əˈnjuː] *adv* de nuevo, otra vez

angel [ˈeɪndʒəl] *n* ángel *m*

anger [ˈæŋgə*] *n* cólera

angina [ænˈdʒaɪnə] *n* angina (del pecho)

angle [ˈæŋgl] *n* ángulo; **from their ~** desde su punto de vista

angler [ˈæŋglə*] *n* pescador(a) *m/f* (de caña)

Anglican [ˈæŋglɪkən] *adj, n* anglicano/a *m/f*

angling [ˈæŋglɪŋ] *n* pesca con caña

Anglo... [ˈæŋgləu] *prefix* anglo...

angrily [ˈæŋgrɪlɪ] *adv* coléricamente, airadamente

angry [ˈæŋgrɪ] *adj* enfadado, airado; (*wound*) inflamado; **to be ~ with sb/ at sth** estar enfadado con alguien/por algo; **to get ~** enfadarse, enojarse

anguish [ˈæŋgwɪʃ] *n* (*physical*)

tormentos *mpl*; (*mental*) angustia

animal ['ænɪməl] *n* animal *m*; (*pej: person*) bestia ♦ *adj* animal

animate ['ænɪmɪt] *adj* vivo; **~d** [-meɪtɪd] *adj* animado

aniseed ['ænɪsiːd] *n* anís *m*

ankle ['æŋkl] *n* tobillo *m*; **~ sock** *n* calcetín *m* corto

annex [*n* 'æneks, *vb* æ'neks] *n* (*also: BRIT: annexe*) (*building*) edificio anexo ♦ *vt* (*territory*) anexionar

annihilate [ə'naɪəleɪt] *vt* aniquilar

anniversary [ænɪ'vɜːsərɪ] *n* aniversario *m*

announce [ə'nauns] *vt* anunciar; **~ment** *n* anuncio; (*official*) declaración *f*; **~r** *n* (*RADIO*) locutor(a) *m/f*; (*TV*) presentador(a) *m/f*

annoy [ə'nɔɪ] *vt* molestar, fastidiar; **don't get ~ed!** ¡no se enfade!; **~ance** *n* enojo; **~ing** *adj* molesto, fastidioso; (*person*) pesado

annual ['ænjuəl] *adj* anual ♦ *n* (*BOT*) anual *m*; (*book*) anuario; **~ly** *adv* anualmente, cada año

annul [ə'nʌl] *vt* anular

annum ['ænəm] *n see* **per**

anonymous [ə'nɔnɪməs] *adj* anónimo

anorak ['ænəræk] *n* anorak *m*

anorexia [ænə'reksɪə] *n* (*MED: also: ~ nervosa*) anorexia

another [ə'nʌðə*] *adj* (*one more, a different one*) otro ♦ *pron* otro; *see* **one**

answer ['ɑːnsə*] *n* contestación *f*, respuesta; (*to problem*) solución *f* ♦ *vi* contestar, responder ♦ *vt* (*reply to*) contestar a, responder a; (*problem*) resolver; (*prayer*) escuchar; **in ~ to your letter** contestando *or* en contestación a su carta; **to ~ the phone** contestar *or* coger el teléfono; **to ~ the bell** *or* **the door** acudir a la puerta; **~ back** *vi* replicar, ser respondón/ona; **~ for** *vt fus* responder de *or* por; **~ to** *vt fus* (*description*) corresponder a; **~able** *adj*: **~able to sb for sth** responsable ante uno de algo; **~ing machine** *n* contestador *m*

automático

ant [ænt] *n* hormiga

antagonism [æn'tægənɪzm] *n* antagonismo, hostilidad *f*

antagonize [æn'tægənaɪz] *vt* provocar la enemistad de

Antarctic [ænt'ɑːktɪk] *n*: **the ~** el Antártico

antelope ['æntɪləup] *n* antílope *m*

antenatal [æntɪ'neɪtl] *adj* antenatal, prenatal; **~ clinic** *n* clínica prenatal

anthem ['ænθəm] *n*: **national ~** himno nacional

anthropology [ænθrə'pɔlədʒɪ] *n* antropología

anti... [æntɪ] *prefix* anti...; **~-aircraft** [-'eəkrɑːft] *adj* antiaéreo; **~biotic** [-baɪ'ɔtɪk] *n* antibiótico; **~body** ['æntɪbɔdɪ] *n* anticuerpo

anticipate [æn'tɪsɪpeɪt] *vt* prever; (*expect*) esperar, contar con; (*look forward to*) esperar con ilusión; (*do first*) anticiparse a, adelantarse a; **anticipation** [-'peɪʃən] *n* (*expectation*) previsión *f*; (*eagerness*) ilusión *f*, expectación *f*

anticlimax [æntɪ'klaɪmæks] *n* decepción *f*

anticlockwise [æntɪ'klɔkwaɪz] (*BRIT*) *adv* en dirección contraria a la de las agujas del reloj

antics ['æntɪks] *npl* gracias *fpl*

anticyclone [æntɪ'saɪkləun] *n* anticiclón *m*

antidote ['æntɪdəut] *n* antídoto

antifreeze ['æntɪfriːz] *n* anticongelante *m*

antihistamine [æntɪ'hɪstəmiːn] *n* antihistamínico

antiquated ['æntɪkweɪtɪd] *adj* anticuado

antique [æn'tiːk] *n* antigüedad *f* ♦ *adj* antiguo; **~ dealer** *n* anticuario/a; **~ shop** *n* tienda de antigüedades

antiquity [æn'tɪkwɪtɪ] *n* antigüedad *f*

anti-Semitism [æntɪ'semɪtɪzm] *n* antisemitismo

antiseptic [ænti'sɛptik] *adj, n*
antiséptico

antlers ['æntləz] *npl* cuernas *fpl*,
cornamenta *sg*

anus ['eɪnəs] *n* ano

anvil ['ænvɪl] *n* yunque *m*

anxiety [æŋ'zaɪətɪ] *n* inquietud *f*; (MED)
ansiedad *f*; **~ to do** deseo de hacer

anxious ['æŋkʃəs] *adj* inquieto,
preocupado; (*worrying*) preocupante;
(*keen*): **to be ~ to do** tener muchas
ganas de hacer

KEYWORD

any ['ɛnɪ] *adj* **1** (*in questions etc*)
algún/alguna; **have you ~ butter/**
children? ¿tienes mantequilla/hijos?; **if**
there are ~ tickets left si quedan
billetes, si queda algún billete

2 (*with negative*): **I haven't ~**
money/books no tengo dinero/
libros

3 (*no matter which*) cualquier;
~ excuse will do valdrá *or* servirá
cualquier excusa; **choose ~ book you**
like escoge el libro que quieras;
~ teacher you ask will tell you
cualquier profesor al que preguntes te
lo dirá

4 (*in phrases*): **in ~ case** de todas
formas, en cualquier caso; **~ day now**
cualquier día de estos; **at ~ moment**
en cualquier momento, de un
momento a otro; **at ~ rate** en todo
caso; **~ time: come (at) ~ time** ven
cuando quieras; **he might come (at)**
~ time podría llegar de un momento a
otro

♦ *pron* **1** (*in questions etc*): **have you**
got ~? ¿tienes alguno(s)/a(s)?; **can**
~ of you sing? ¿sabe cantar alguno
de vosotros/ustedes?

2 (*with negative*): **I haven't ~ (of**
them) no tengo ninguno

3 (*no matter which one(s)*): **take ~ of**
those books (you like) toma el libro
que quieras de ésos

♦ *adv* **1** (*in questions etc*): **do you**
want ~ more soup/sandwiches?
¿quieres más sopa/bocadillos?; **are**
you feeling ~ better? ¿te sientes
algo mejor?

2 (*with negative*): **I can't hear him**
~ more ya no le oigo; **don't wait**
~ longer no esperes más

anybody ['ɛnɪbɒdɪ] *pron* cualquiera; (*in
interrogative sentences*) alguien; (*in
negative sentences*) **I don't see ~** no
veo a nadie; **if ~ should phone ...** si
llama alguien ...

anyhow ['ɛnɪhaʊ] *adv* (*at any rate*) de
todos modos, de todas formas;
(*haphazard*): **do it ~ you like** hazlo
como quieras; **she leaves things just**
~ deja las cosas como quiera *or* de
cualquier modo; **I shall go ~** de todos
modos iré

anyone ['ɛnɪwʌn] *pron* = **anybody**

anything ['ɛnɪθɪŋ] *pron* (*in questions
etc*) algo, alguna cosa; (*with negative*)
nada; **can you see ~?** ¿ves algo?; **if**
~ happens to me ... si algo me
ocurre ...; (*no matter what*): **you can**
say ~ you like puedes decir lo que
quieras; **~ will do** vale todo *or*
cualquier cosa; **he'll eat ~** come de
todo *or* lo que sea

anyway ['ɛnɪweɪ] *adv* (*at any rate*) de
todos modos, de todas formas; **I shall**
go ~ iré de todos modos; (*besides*): **~,**
I couldn't come even if I wanted
to además, no podría venir aunque
quisiera; **why are you phoning, ~?**
¿entonces, por qué llamas? ¿por qué
llamas, pues?

anywhere ['ɛnɪweə*] *adv* (*in questions
etc*): **can you see him ~?** ¿le ves por
algún lado?; **are you going ~?** ¿vas a
algún sitio?; **I can't**
see him ~ no le veo por ninguna
parte; **~ in the world** (*no matter
where*) en cualquier parte (del mundo);
put the books down ~ deja los

libros donde quieras

apart [ə'pɑːt] adv (aside) aparte;
(situation): ~ (from) separado (de);
(movement): to pull ~ separar; **10
miles** ~ separados por 10 millas; to
take ~ desmontar; ~ from prep aparte
de

apartheid [ə'pɑːteɪt] n apartheid m

apartment [ə'pɑːtmənt] n (US) piso
(SP), departamento (AM), apartamento;
(room) cuarto; ~ building (US) n
edificio de apartamentos

apathetic [æpə'θetɪk] adj apático,
indiferente

ape [eɪp] n mono ♦ vt imitar, remedar

aperitif [ə'perɪtɪf] n aperitivo

aperture ['æpətjuə*] n rendija,
resquicio; (PHOT) abertura

APEX ['eɪpeks] n abbr (= Advanced
Purchase Excursion Fare) tarifa APEX f

apex n ápice m; (fig) cumbre f

apiece [ə'piːs] adv cada uno

aplomb [ə'plɔm] n aplomo

apologetic [əpɔlə'dʒetɪk] adj de
disculpa; (person) arrepentido

apologize [ə'pɔlədʒaɪz] vi: to ~ (for
sth to sb) disculparse (con alguien de
algo)

apology [ə'pɔlədʒɪ] n disculpa, excusa

apostrophe [ə'pɔstrəfɪ] n apóstrofo m

appal [ə'pɔːl] vt horrorizar, espantar;
~ling adj espantoso; (awful) pésimo

apparatus [æpə'reɪtəs] n (equipment)
equipo; (organization) aparato; (in
gymnasium) aparatos mpl

apparel [ə'pærl] (US) n ropa

apparent [ə'pærənt] adj aparente;
(obvious) evidente; ~ly adv por lo visto,
al parecer

appeal [ə'piːl] vi (LAW) apelar ♦ n
(LAW) apelación f; (request)
llamamiento; (plea) petición f; (charm)
atractivo; to ~ for reclamar; to ~ to
(be attractive to) atraer; it doesn't
~ to me no me atrae, no me llama la
atención; ~ing adj (attractive) atractivo

appear [ə'pɪə*] vi aparecer;

presentarse; (LAW) comparecer;
(publication) salir (a la luz), publicarse;
(seem) parecer; to ~ on TV/in
"Hamlet" salir por la tele/hacer un
papel en "Hamlet"; it would ~ that
parecería que; ~ance n aparición f;
(look) apariencia, aspecto

appease [ə'piːz] vt (pacify) apaciguar;
(satisfy) satisfacer

appendices [ə'pendɪsiːz] npl of
appendix

appendicitis [əpendɪ'saɪtɪs] n
apendicitis f

appendix [ə'pendɪks] (pl appendices)
n apéndice m

appetite ['æpɪtaɪt] n apetito; (fig)
deseo, anhelo

appetizer ['æpɪtaɪzə*] n (drink)
aperitivo; (food) tapas fpl (SP)

applaud [ə'plɔːd] vt, vi aplaudir

applause [ə'plɔːz] n aplausos mpl

apple ['æpl] n manzana; ~ tree n
manzano

appliance [ə'plaɪəns] n aparato

applicable [ə'plɪkəbl] adj (relevant): to
be ~ (to) referirse (a)

applicant ['æplɪkənt] n candidato/a;
solicitante m/f

application [æplɪ'keɪʃən] n aplicación
f; (for a job etc) solicitud f, petición f;
~ form n solicitud f

applied [ə'plaɪd] adj aplicado

apply [ə'plaɪ] vt (paint etc) poner; (law
etc: put into practice) poner en vigor
♦ vi: to ~ to (ask) dirigirse a; (be
applicable) ser aplicable a; to ~ for
(permit, grant, job) solicitar; to ~ o.s.
to aplicarse a, dedicarse a

appoint [ə'pɔɪnt] vt (to post) nombrar;
~ed adj: at the ~ed time a la hora
señalada; ~ment n (with client) cita;
(act) nombramiento; (post) puesto; (at
hairdresser etc) hora; to have an ~ment
tener hora; to make an ~ment (with
sb) citarse (con uno)

appraisal [ə'preɪzl] n valoración f

appreciate [ə'priːʃɪeɪt] vt apreciar,

tener en mucho; (be grateful for)
agradecer; (be aware of) comprender
♦ vi (COMM) aumentar(se) en valor;
appreciation [-'eɪʃən] n apreciación f;
(gratitude) reconocimiento,
agradecimiento; (COMM) aumento en
valor
appreciative [ə'priːʃɪətɪv] adj
apreciativo; (comment) agradecido
apprehensive [æprɪ'hensɪv] adj
aprensivo
apprentice [ə'prentɪs] n aprendiz/a
m/f; **~ship** n aprendizaje m
approach [ə'prəʊtʃ] vi acercarse ♦ vt
acercarse a; (ask, apply to) dirigirse a;
(situation, problem) abordar ♦ n
acercamiento; (access) acceso; (to
problem, situation): ~ actitud f
(ante); **~able** adj (person) abordable;
(place) accesible
appropriate [adj ə'prəʊprɪɪt, vb
ə'prəʊprɪeɪt] adj apropiado,
conveniente ♦ vt (take) apropiarse de
approval [ə'pruːvəl] n aprobación f,
visto bueno; (permission)
consentimiento; **on** ~ (COMM) a prueba
approve [ə'pruːv] vt aprobar; ~ **of** vt
fus (thing) aprobar; (person): **they
don't** ~ **of her** (ella) no les parece
bien
approximate [ə'prɒksɪmɪt] adj
aproximado; **~ly** adv
aproximadamente, más o menos
apricot ['eɪprɪkɒt] n albaricoque m (SP),
damasco (AM)
April ['eɪprəl] n abril m; ~ **Fools' Day**
n el primero de abril; ≈ día m de los
Inocentes (28 December)
apron ['eɪprən] n delantal m
apt [æpt] adj acertado, apropiado;
(likely): ~ **to do** propenso a hacer
aquarium [ə'kwɛərɪəm] n acuario
Aquarius [ə'kwɛərɪəs] n Acuario
Arab ['ærəb] adj, n árabe m/f
Arabian [ə'reɪbɪən] adj árabe
Arabic ['ærəbɪk] adj árabe; (numerals)
arábigo ♦ n árabe m

arable ['ærəbl] adj cultivable
Aragon ['ærəgən] n Aragón m
arbitrary ['ɑːbɪtrərɪ] adj arbitrario
arbitration [ɑːbɪ'treɪʃən] n arbitraje m
arcade [ɑː'keɪd] n (round a square)
soportales mpl; (shopping mall) galería
comercial
arch [ɑːtʃ] n arco; (of foot) arco del pie
♦ vt arquear
archaeologist [ɑːkɪ'ɒlədʒɪst] n (US
archeologist) n arqueólogo/a
archaeology [ɑːkɪ'ɒlədʒɪ] n (US
archeology) n arqueología
archbishop [ɑːtʃ'bɪʃəp] n arzobispo
archeology etc [ɑːkɪ'ɒlədʒɪ] (US) =
archaeology etc
archery ['ɑːtʃərɪ] n tiro al arco
architect ['ɑːkɪtekt] n arquitecto/a;
~ure n arquitectura
archives ['ɑːkaɪvz] npl archivo
Arctic ['ɑːktɪk] adj ártico ♦ n: **the** ~ el
Ártico
ardent ['ɑːdənt] adj ardiente,
apasionado
arduous ['ɑːdjuəs] adj (task) arduo;
(journey) agotador(a)
are [ɑː*] vb see **be**
area ['ɛərɪə] n área, región f; (part of
place) zona; (MATH etc) área, superficie
f; (in room: e.g. dining ~) parte f; (of
knowledge, experience) campo
arena [ə'riːnə] n estadio; (of circus)
pista
Argentina [ɑːdʒən'tiːnə] n Argentina;
Argentinian [-'tɪnɪən] adj, n
argentino/a m/f
arguably ['ɑːgjuəblɪ] adv posiblemente
argue ['ɑːgjuː] vi (quarrel) discutir,
pelearse; (reason) razonar, argumentar;
to ~ **that** sostener que
argument ['ɑːgjumənt] n discusión f,
pelea; (reasons) argumento; **~ative**
[-'mentətɪv] adj discutidor(a)
Aries ['ɛərɪz] n Aries m
arise [ə'raɪz] (pt **arose**, pp **arisen**) vi
surgir, presentarse

arisen [ə'rɪzn] pp of **arise**

aristocrat ['ærɪstəkræt] n aristócrata m/f

arithmetic [ə'rɪθmətɪk] n aritmética f

ark [ɑːk] n: **Noah's A~** el Arca f de Noé

arm [ɑːm] n brazo ♦ vt armar; **~s** npl armas fpl; **~ in ~** cogidos del brazo

armaments ['ɑːməmənts] npl armamento

armchair ['ɑːmtʃeə*] n sillón m, butaca

armed [ɑːmd] adj armado; **~ robbery** n robo a mano armada

armour ['ɑːmə*] (US **armor**) n armadura, (MIL: tanks) blindaje m; **~ed car** n coche m (SP) or carro (AM) blindado

armpit ['ɑːmpɪt] n sobaco, axila

armrest ['ɑːmrest] n apoyabrazos m inv

army ['ɑːmɪ] n ejército m, (fig) multitud f

aroma [ə'rəumə] n aroma m, fragancia; **~therapy** n aromaterapia

arose [ə'rəuz] pt of **arise**

around [ə'raund] adv alrededor; (in the area): **there is no one else ~** no hay nadie más por aquí ♦ prep alrededor de

arouse [ə'rauz] vt despertar; (anger) provocar

arrange [ə'reɪndʒ] vt arreglar, ordenar; (organize) organizar; **to ~ to do sth** quedar en hacer algo; **~ment** n arreglo; (agreement) acuerdo; **~ments** npl (preparations) preparativos mpl

array [ə'reɪ] n: **~ of** (things) serie f de; (people) conjunto de

arrears [ə'rɪəz] npl atrasos mpl; **to be in ~ with one's rent** estar retrasado en el pago del alquiler

arrest [ə'rest] vt detener; (sb's attention) llamar ♦ n detención f; **under ~** detenido

arrival [ə'raɪvl] n llegada; **new ~** recién llegado/a; (baby) recién nacido

arrive [ə'raɪv] vi llegar; (baby) nacer

arrogant ['ærəgənt] adj arrogante

arrow ['ærəu] n flecha

arse [ɑːs] (BRIT: inf!) n culo, trasero

arson ['ɑːsn] n incendio premeditado

art [ɑːt] n arte m; (skill) destreza; **A~s** npl (SCOL) Letras fpl

artery ['ɑːtərɪ] n arteria

art gallery n pinacoteca; (saleroom) galería de arte

arthritis [ɑː'θraɪtɪs] n artritis f

artichoke ['ɑːtɪtʃəuk] n alcachofa; **Jerusalem ~** aguaturma

article ['ɑːtɪkl] n artículo; (BRIT: LAW: training) **~s** npl contrato de aprendizaje; **~ of clothing** prenda de vestir

articulate [adj ɑː'tɪkjulɪt, vb ɑː'tɪkjuleɪt] adj claro, bien expresado ♦ vt expresar; **~d lorry** (BRIT) n trailer m

artificial [ɑːtɪ'fɪʃəl] adj artificial; (affected) afectado

artillery [ɑː'tɪlərɪ] n artillería

artisan [ɑːtɪzæn] n artesano

artist ['ɑːtɪst] n artista m/f; (MUS) intérprete m/f; **~ic** [ɑː'tɪstɪk] adj artístico; **~ry** n arte m, habilidad f (artística)

art school n escuela de bellas artes

KEYWORD

as [æz] conj **1** (referring to time) cuando, mientras; a medida que; **~ the years went by** con el paso de los años; **he came in ~ I was leaving** entró cuando me marchaba; **~ from tomorrow** desde or a partir de mañana

2 (in comparisons): **~ big ~** tan grande como; **twice ~ big ~** el doble de grande que; **~ much money/many books ~** tanto dinero/tantos libros como; **~ soon ~** en cuanto

3 (since, because) como, ya que; **he left early ~ he had to be home by 10** se fue temprano ya que tenía que estar en casa a las 10

4 (referring to manner, way): **do ~ you**

wish haz lo que quieras; **~ she said** como dijo; **he gave it to me ~ a present** me lo dio de regalo
5 (*in the capacity of*): **he works ~ a barman** trabaja de barman; **~ chairman of the company, he ...** como presidente de la compañía, ...
6 (*concerning*): **~ for** o **to that** por o en lo que respecta a eso
7: **~ if** o **though** como si; **he looked ~ if he was ill** parecía como si estuviera enfermo, tenía aspecto de enfermo; *see also* **long; such; well**

a.s.a.p. *abbr* (= *as soon as possible*) cuanto antes
asbestos [æz'bɛstəs] *n* asbesto, amianto
ascend [ə'sɛnd] *vt* subir; (*throne*) ascender *or* subir a
ascent [ə'sɛnt] *n* subida; (*slope*) cuesta, pendiente *f*
ascertain [æsə'teɪn] *vt* averiguar
ash [æʃ] *n* ceniza; (*tree*) fresno
ashamed [ə'feɪmd] *adj* avergonzado, apenado (*AM*); **to be ~ of** avergonzarse de
ashore [ə'ʃɔːr] *adv* en tierra; (*swim etc*) a tierra
ashtray ['æʃtreɪ] *n* cenicero
Ash Wednesday *n* miércoles *m* de Ceniza
Asia ['eɪʃə] *n* Asia; **~n** *adj*, *n* asiático/a *m/f*
aside [ə'saɪd] *adv* a un lado ♦ *n* aparte *m*
ask [ɑːsk] *vt* (*question*) preguntar; (*invite*) invitar; **to ~ sb sth/to do sth** preguntar algo a alguien/pedir a alguien que haga algo; **to ~ sb about sth** preguntar algo a alguien; **to ~ (sb) a question** hacer una pregunta (a alguien); **to ~ sb out to dinner** invitar a cenar a uno; **~ after** *vt fus* preguntar por; **~ for** *vt fus* pedir; (*trouble*) buscar
asking price *n* precio inicial

asleep [ə'sliːp] *adj* dormido; **to fall ~** dormirse, quedarse dormido
asparagus [əs'pærəgəs] *n* (*plant*) espárrago; (*food*) espárragos *mpl*
aspect ['æspɛkt] *n* aspecto, apariencia; (*direction in which a building etc faces*) orientación *f*
aspersions [əs'pəːʃənz] *npl*: **to cast ~ on** difamar a, calumniar a
asphyxiation [æsfiksi'eɪʃən] *n* asfixia
aspire [əs'paɪər] *vi*: **to ~ to** aspirar a, ambicionar
aspirin ['æsprɪn] *n* aspirina
ass [æs] *n* asno, burro; (*inf: idiot*) imbécil *m/f*; (*US: inf!*) culo, trasero
assailant [ə'seɪlənt] *n* asaltador(a) *m/f*, agresor(a) *m/f*
assassinate [ə'sæsɪneɪt] *vt* asesinar
assassination [əsæsɪ'neɪʃən] *n* asesinato
assault [ə'sɔːlt] *n* asalto, (*LAW*) agresión *f* ♦ *vt* asaltar, atacar; (*sexually*) violar
assemble [ə'sɛmbl] *vt* reunir, juntar; (*TECH*) montar ♦ *vi* reunirse, juntarse
assembly [ə'sɛmblɪ] *n* reunión *f*, asamblea; (*parliament*) parlamento; (*construction*) montaje *m*; **~ line** *n* cadena de montaje
assent [ə'sɛnt] *n* asentimiento, aprobación *f*
assert [ə'səːt] *vt* afirmar; (*authority*) hacer valer; **~ion** [-ʃən] *n* afirmación *f*
assess [ə'sɛs] *vt* valorar, calcular; (*tax, damages*) fijar; (*for tax*) gravar; **~ment** *n* valoración *f*; (*for tax*) gravamen *m*; **~or** *n* asesor(a) *m/f*
asset ['æsɛt] *n* ventaja; **~s** *npl* (*COMM*) activo; (*property, funds*) fondos *mpl*
assign [ə'saɪn] *vt*: **~ (to)** (*date*) fijar (para); (*task*) asignar (a); (*resources*) destinar (a); **~ment** *n* tarea
assist [ə'sɪst] *vt* ayudar; **~ance** *n* ayuda, auxilio; **~ant** *n* ayudante *m/f*; (*BRIT: also: shop ~ant*) dependiente/a *m/f*
associate [*adj*, *n* ə'səuʃɪɪt, *vb*

association [əˈsəʊʃɪeɪt] *adj* asociado ♦ *n* (*at work*) colega *m/f* ♦ *vt* asociar; (*ideas*) relacionar ♦ *vi*: **to ~ with sb** tratar con alguien

association [əsəʊsɪˈeɪʃən] *n* asociación f

assorted [əˈsɔːtɪd] *adj* surtido, variado

assortment [əˈsɔːtmənt] *n* (*of shapes, colours*) surtido; (*of books*) colección f; (*of people*) mezcla

assume [əˈsjuːm] *vt* suponer; (*responsibilities*) asumir; (*attitude*) adoptar, tomar

assumption [əˈsʌmpʃən] *n* suposición f, presunción f; (*of power etc*) toma f

assurance [əˈʃʊərəns] *n* garantía, promesa; (*confidence*) confianza, aplomo; (*insurance*) seguro

assure [əˈʃʊə*] *vt* asegurar

asthma [ˈæsmə] *n* asma

astonish [əˈstɒnɪʃ] *vt* asombrar, pasmar; **~ment** *n* asombro, sorpresa

astound [əˈstaʊnd] *vt* asombrar, pasmar

astray [əˈstreɪ] *adv*: **to go ~** extraviarse; **to lead ~** (*morally*) llevar por mal camino

astride [əˈstraɪd] *prep* a caballo *or* horcajadas sobre

astrology [əsˈtrɒlədʒɪ] *n* astrología

astronaut [ˈæstrənɔːt] *n* astronauta *m/f*

astronomy [əsˈtrɒnəmɪ] *n* astronomía

asylum [əˈsaɪləm] *n* (*refuge*) asilo; (*mental hospital*) manicomio

---

KEYWORD

---

at [æt] *prep* **1** (*referring to position*) en; (*direction*) a; **~ the top** en lo alto; **~ home/school** en casa/la escuela; **to look ~ sth/sb** mirar algo/a uno

2 (*referring to time*): **~ 4 o'clock** a las 4; **~ night** por la noche; **~ Christmas** en Navidad; **~ times** a veces

3 (*referring to rates, speed etc*): **~ £1 a kilo** a una libra el kilo; **two ~ a time** de dos en dos; **~ 50 km/h** a 50 km/h

4 (*referring to manner*): **~ a stroke** de un golpe; **~ peace** en paz

5 (*referring to activity*): **to be ~ work** estar trabajando; (*in the office etc*) estar en el trabajo; **to play ~ cowboys** jugar a los vaqueros; **to be good ~ sth** ser bueno en algo

6 (*referring to cause*): **shocked/surprised/annoyed ~ sth** asombrado/sorprendido/fastidiado por algo; **I went ~ his suggestion** fui a instancias suyas

ate [eɪt] *pt of* **eat**

atheist [ˈeɪθɪɪst] *n* ateo/a

Athens [ˈæθɪnz] *n* Atenas

athlete [ˈæθliːt] *n* atleta *m/f*

athletic [æθˈletɪk] *adj* atlético; **~s** *n* atletismo

Atlantic [ətˈlæntɪk] *adj* atlántico ♦ *n*: **the ~ (Ocean)** el (Océano) Atlántico

atlas [ˈætləs] *n* atlas *m*

A.T.M. *n abbr* (= *automated telling machine*) cajero automático

atmosphere [ˈætməsfɪə*] *n* atmósfera; (*of place*) ambiente *m*

atom [ˈætəm] *n* átomo; **~ic** [əˈtɒmɪk] *adj* atómico; **~(ic) bomb** *n* bomba atómica; **~izer** [ˈætəmaɪzə*] *n* atomizador *m*

atone [əˈtəʊn] *vi*: **to ~ for** expiar

atrocious [əˈtrəʊʃəs] *adj* atroz

attach [əˈtætʃ] *vt* (*fasten*) atar; (*join*) unir, sujetar; (*document, letter*) adjuntar; (*importance etc*) dar, conceder; **to be ~ed to sb/sth** (*to like*) tener cariño a alguien/algo

attaché case [əˈtæʃeɪ–] *n* maletín *m*

attachment [əˈtætʃmənt] *n* (*tool*) accesorio; (*love*): **~ (to)** apego *m*

attack [əˈtæk] *vt* (*MIL*) atacar; (*subj: criminal*) agredir, asaltar; (*criticize*) criticar; (*task*) emprender ♦ *n* ataque *m*, asalto; (*on sb's life*) atentado; (*fig: criticism*) crítica; (*of illness*) ataque *m*; **heart ~** infarto (de miocardio); **~er** *n* agresor/a *m/f*, asaltante *m/f*

attain [ə'teɪn] vt (also: ~ to) alcanzar; (achieve) lograr, conseguir

attempt [ə'tempt] n tentativa, intento; (attack) atentado ♦ vt intentar; **~ed** adj: **~ed** burglary/murder/suicide tentativa o intento de robo/asesinato/suicidio

attend [ə'tend] vt asistir a; (patient) atender; **~ to** vt fus ocuparse de; (customer, patient) atender a; **~ance** n asistencia, presencia; (people present) concurrencia; **~ant** n ayudante m/f; (in garage etc) encargado/a ♦ adj (dangers) concomitante

attention [ə'tenʃən] n atención f; (care) atenciones fpl; **~!** (MIL) ¡firme(s)!; **for the ~ of ...** (ADMIN) atención ...

attentive [ə'tentɪv] adj atento

attic ['ætɪk] n desván m

attitude ['ætɪtjuːd] n actitud f; (disposition) disposición f

attorney [ə'tɜːnɪ] n (lawyer) abogado/a; **A~ General** n (BRIT) ≈ Presidente m del Consejo del Poder Judicial (SP); (US) ≈ ministro de justicia

attract [ə'trækt] vt atraer; (sb's attention) llamar; **~ion** [ə'trækʃən] n encanto; (gen pl: amusements) diversiones fpl; (PHYSICS) atracción f; (fig: towards sb, sth) atractivo m; **~ive** adj guapo; (interesting) atrayente

attribute ['ætrɪbjuːt, vb ə'trɪbjuːt] n atributo ♦ vt: **to ~ sth to** atribuir algo a

attrition [ə'trɪʃən] n: **war of ~** guerra de agotamiento

aubergine ['əʊbəʒiːn] (BRIT) n berenjena; (colour) morado

auburn ['ɔːbən] adj color castaño rojizo

auction ['ɔːkʃən] n (also: sale by ~) subasta ♦ vt subastar; **~eer** [-'nɪə*] n subastador/a m/f

audible ['ɔːdɪbl] adj audible, que se puede oír

audience ['ɔːdɪəns] n público m; (RADIO)

radioescuchas mpl; (TV) telespectadores mpl; (interview) audiencia

audio-visual [ɔːdɪəʊ'vɪzjuəl] adj audiovisual; **~ aid** n ayuda audiovisual

audit ['ɔːdɪt] vt revisar, intervenir

audition [ɔː'dɪʃən] n audición f

auditor ['ɔːdɪtə*] n interventor/a m/f, censor(a) m/f de cuentas

augment [ɔːg'ment] vt aumentar

augur ['ɔːgə*] vi: **it ~s well** es un buen augurio

August ['ɔːgəst] n agosto

aunt [ɑːnt] n tía; **~ie** n diminutive of aunt; **~y** n diminutive of aunt

au pair ['əʊ'peə*] n (also: ~ girl) (chica) au pair f

auspicious [ɔːs'pɪʃəs] adj propicio, de buen augurio

Australia [ɔs'treɪlɪə] n Australia; **~n** adj, n australiano/a m/f

Austria ['ɒstrɪə] n Austria; **~n** adj, n austríaco/a m/f

authentic [ɔː'θentɪk] adj auténtico

author ['ɔːθə] n autor(a) m/f

authoritarian [ɔːθɔrɪ'teərɪən] adj autoritario

authoritative [ɔː'θɔrɪtətɪv] adj autorizado; (manner) autoritario

authority [ɔː'θɔrɪtɪ] n autoridad f; (official permission) autorización f; **the authorities** npl las autoridades

authorize ['ɔːθəraɪz] vt autorizar

auto ['ɔːtəu] (US) n coche m (SP), carro (AM), automóvil m

auto-: **~biography** [ɔːtəbaɪ'ɒgrəfɪ] n autobiografía; **~graph** ['ɔːtəgrɑːf] n autógrafo ♦ vt (photo etc) dedicar; (programme) firmar; **~mated** ['ɔːtəmeɪtɪd] adj automatizado; **~matic** [ɔːtə'mætɪk] adj automático ♦ n (gun) pistola automática; (car) coche m automático; **~matically** adv automáticamente; **~mation** [ɔːtə'meɪʃən] n reconversión f; **~mobile** ['ɔːtəməbiːl] (US) n coche m (SP), carro (AM), automóvil m; **~nomy** [ɔː'tɒnəmɪ] n autonomía

autumn ['ɔːtəm] n otoño
auxiliary [ɔːɡ'zɪlɪərɪ] adj, n auxiliar m/f
avail [ə'veɪl] vt: to ~ o.s. of aprovechar(se) de ♦ n: to no ~ en vano, sin resultado
available [ə'veɪləbl] adj disponible; (unoccupied) libre; (person: unattached) soltero y sin compromiso
avalanche ['ævəlɑːnʃ] n alud m, avalancha
avant-garde ['æṽːŋ'ɡɑːd] adj de vanguardia
Ave. abbr = **avenue**
avenge [ə'vendʒ] vt vengar
avenue ['ævɪnjuː] n avenida; (fig) camino
average ['ævərɪdʒ] n promedio, término medio ♦ adj medio, de término medio; (ordinary) regular, corriente ♦ vt sacar un promedio de; **on ~** por regla general; **~ out** vi: **to ~ out at** salir en un promedio de
averse [ə'vɜːs] adj: **to be ~ to sth/doing** sentir aversión o antipatía por algo/por hacer
avert [ə'vɜːt] vt prevenir; (blow) desviar; (one's eyes) apartar
aviary ['eɪvɪərɪ] n pajarera, avería
avocado [ævə'kɑːdəʊ] n (also: BRIT: ~ pear) aguacate m (SP), palta (AM)
avoid [ə'vɔɪd] vt evitar, eludir
await [ə'weɪt] vt esperar, aguardar
awake [ə'weɪk] (pt awoke, pp awoken or awaked) adj despierto ♦ vt despertar ♦ vi despertarse; **to be ~** estar despierto; **~ning** n el despertar
award [ə'wɔːd] n premio; (LAW: damages) indemnización f ♦ vt otorgar, conceder; (LAW: damages) adjudicar
aware [ə'weə] adj: ~ (of) consciente (de); **to become ~ of/that** darse cuenta de/de que; (learn) enterarse de/de que; **~ness** n conciencia; (knowledge) conocimiento
away [ə'weɪ] adv fuera; (movement): **she went ~** se marchó; (far ~) lejos; **two kilometres ~** a dos kilómetros

de distancia; **two hours ~ by car** a dos horas en coche; **the holiday was two weeks ~** faltaban dos semanas para las vacaciones; **he's ~ for a week** estará ausente una semana; **to take ~ (from)** quitar (a); (subtract) substraer de; **to work/pedal ~** seguir trabajando/pedaleando; **to fade ~** (colour) desvanecerse; (sound) apagarse; **~ game** n (SPORT) partido de fuera
awe [ɔː] n admiración f respetuosa; **~-inspiring** adj imponente
awful ['ɔːfəl] adj horroroso; (quantity): **an ~ lot (of)** cantidad de (de); **~ly** adv (very) terriblemente
awkward ['ɔːkwəd] adj desmañado, torpe; (shape) incómodo; (embarrassing) delicado, difícil
awning ['ɔːnɪŋ] n (of tent, caravan, shop) toldo
awoke [ə'wəʊk] pt of awake
awoken [ə'wəʊkən] pp of awake
awry [ə'raɪ] adv: **to be ~** estar descolocado o mal puesto
axe [æks] (US **ax**) n hacha ♦ vt (project) cortar; (jobs) reducir
axes ['æksiːz] npl of axis
axis ['æksɪs] (pl axes) n eje m
axle ['æksl] n eje m, árbol m
ay(e) [aɪ] excl sí

B, b

B [biː] n (MUS) si m
B.A. abbr = **Bachelor of Arts**
baby ['beɪbɪ] n bebé m/f; (US: inf: darling) mi amor; **~ carriage** (US) n cochecito; **~-sit** vi hacer de canguro; **~-sitter** n canguro/a; **~ wipe** n toallita húmeda (para bebés)
bachelor ['bætʃələ] n soltero; **B~ of Arts/Science** licenciado/a en Filosofía y Letras/Ciencias
back [bæk] n (of person) espalda; (of animal) lomo; (of hand) dorso; (as

opposed to front) parte *f* de atrás; (*of chair*) respaldo; (*of page*) reverso; (*of book*) final *m*; (FOOTBALL) defensa *m*; (*of crowd*): **the ones at the ~** los del fondo ♦ vt (*candidate: also: ~ up*) respaldar, apoyar; (*horse: at races*) apostar a; (*car*) dar marcha atrás a or con ♦ vi (*car etc*) ir (or salir or entrar) marcha atrás ♦ adj (*payment, rent*) atrasado; (*seats, wheels*) de atrás ♦ adv (*not forward*) (hacia) atrás; (*returned*): **he's ~** está de vuelta, ha vuelto; **he ran ~** volvió corriendo; (*restitution*): **throw the ball ~** devuelve la pelota; **can I have it ~?** ¿me lo devuelve?; (*again*): **he called ~** llamó de nuevo; **~ down** vi echarse atrás; **~ out** vi (*of promise*) volverse atrás; **~ up** vt (*person*) apoyar, respaldar; (*theory*) defender; (COMPUT) hacer una copia preventiva or de reserva; **~bencher** (BRIT) *n* miembro del parlamento sin cargo relevante; **~bone** *n* columna vertebral; **~date** vt (*pay rise*) dar efecto retroactivo a; (*letter*) poner fecha atrasada a; **~drop** *n* telón de fondo; **~fire** vi (AUT) petardear; (*plans*) fallar, salir mal; **~ground** *n* fondo; (*of events*) antecedentes *mpl*; (*basic knowledge*) bases *fpl*; (*experience*) conocimientos *mpl*, educación *f*; **family ~ground** origen *m*, antecedentes *mpl*; (TENNIS: also: **~hand stroke**) revés *m*; **~hander** (BRIT) *n* (*bribe*) soborno; **~ing** *n* (*fig*) apoyo, respaldo; **~lash** *n* reacción *f*; **~log** *n*: **~log of work** trabajo atrasado; **~ number** *n* (*of magazine etc*) número atrasado; **~pack** *n* mochila; **~packer** *n* mochilero(a); **~ pay** *n* pago atrasado; **~side** (*inf*) *n* trasero, culo; **~slash** *n* barra entre bastidores; **~stroke** *n* espalda; **~up** adj suplementario; (COMPUT) de reserva ♦ *n* (*support*) apoyo; (*also: ~up file*) copia preventiva or de reserva; **~ward** adj (*person, country*) atrasado; **~wards** adv hacia atrás; (*read a list*) al revés;

(*fall*) de espaldas; **~yard** *n* traspatio
bacon ['beɪkən] *n* tocino, beicon *m*
bad [bæd] adj malo; (*mistake, accident*) grave; (*food*) podrido, pasado; **his ~ leg** su pierna lisiada; **to go ~** (*food*) pasarse
badge [bædʒ] *n* insignia; (*policeman's*) chapa, placa
badger ['bædʒə*] *n* tejón *m*
badly ['bædlɪ] adv mal; **to reflect ~ on sb** influir negativamente en la reputación de uno; **~ wounded** gravemente herido; **he needs it ~** le hace gran falta; **to be ~ off** (*for money*) andar mal de dinero
badminton ['bædmɪntən] *n* bádminton *m*
bad-tempered adj de mal genio or carácter; (*temporarily*) de mal humor
bag [bæg] *n* bolsa; (*handbag*) bolso; (*satchel*) mochila; (*case*) maleta; **~s of** (*inf*) un montón de; **~gage** *n* equipaje *m*; **~gage allowance** *n* límite *m* de equipaje; **~gage reclaim** *n* recogida de equipajes; **~gy** adj amplio; **~pipes** *npl* gaita
Bahamas [bə'hɑːməz] *npl*: **the ~** las Islas Bahamas
bail [beɪl] *n* fianza ♦ vt (*prisoner: gen: grant ~ to*) poner en libertad bajo fianza; (*boat: also: ~ out*) achicar; **on ~** (*prisoner*) bajo fianza; **to ~ sb out** obtener la libertad de uno bajo fianza; *see also* **bale**
bailiff ['beɪlɪf] *n* alguacil *m*
bait [beɪt] *n* cebo ♦ vt poner cebo en; (*tease*) tomar el pelo a
bake [beɪk] vt cocer (al horno) ♦ vi cocerse; **~d beans** *npl* judías *fpl* en salsa de tomate; **~d potato** *n* patata al horno; **~r** *n* panadero; **~ry** *n* panadería; (*for cakes*) pastelería; **baking** *n* (*act*) amasar *m*; (*batch*) hornada; **baking powder** *n* levadura (en polvo)
balance ['bæləns] *n* equilibrio; (COMM: *sum*) balance *m*; (*remainder*) resto;

(scales) balanza ♦ vt equilibrar; (budget) nivelar; (account) saldar; (make equal) equilibrar; ~ **of trade/payments** balanza de comercio/pagos; **~d** adj (personality, diet) equilibrado; (report) objetivo; **~ sheet** n balance m

balcony ['bælkənɪ] n (open) balcón m; (closed) galería; (in theatre) anfiteatro

bald [bɔːld] adj calvo; (tyre) liso

bale [beɪl] n (AGR) paca, fardo; (of papers etc) fajo; **~ out** vi lanzarse en paracaídas

Balearics [bælɪˈærɪks] npl: **the ~** las Baleares

ball [bɔːl] n pelota; (football) balón m; (of wool, string) ovillo; (dance) baile m; **to play ~** (fig) cooperar

ballast ['bæləst] n lastre m

ball bearings npl cojinetes mpl de bolas

ballerina [bælə'riːnə] n bailarina

ballet ['bæleɪ] n ballet m; **~ dancer** n bailarín/ina m/f

balloon [bə'luːn] n globo

ballot ['bælət] n votación f; **~ paper** n papeleta (para votar)

ballpoint (pen) ['bɔːlpɔɪnt-] n bolígrafo

ballroom ['bɔːlrʊm] n salón m de baile

Baltic ['bɔːltɪk] n: **the ~ (Sea)** el (Mar) Báltico

ban [bæn] n prohibición f, proscripción f ♦ vt prohibir, proscribir

banal [bə'nɑːl] adj banal, vulgar

banana [bə'nɑːnə] n plátano (SP), banana (AM)

band [bænd] n grupo; (strip) faja, tira; (stripe) lista; (MUS: jazz) orquesta; (: rock) grupo; (: MIL) banda; **~ together** vi juntarse, asociarse

bandage ['bændɪdʒ] n venda, vendaje m ♦ vt vendar

Bandaid ® ['bændeɪd] (US) n tirita

bandit ['bændɪt] n bandido

bandy-legged ['bændɪ'legd] adj estevado

bang [bæŋ] n (of gun, exhaust)

estallido, detonación f; (of door) portazo; (blow) golpe m ♦ vt (door) cerrar de golpe; (one's head) golpear ♦ vi estallar; (door) cerrar de golpe

Bangladesh [bɑːŋglə'deʃ] n Bangladesh m

bangs [bæŋz] (US) npl flequillo

banish ['bænɪʃ] vt desterrar

banister(s) ['bænɪstə(z)] n(pl) barandilla, pasamanos m inv

bank [bæŋk] n (COMM) banco; (of river, lake) ribera, orilla; (of earth) terraplén m ♦ vi (AVIAT) ladearse; **~ on** vt fus contar con; **~ account** n cuenta de banco; **~ card** n tarjeta bancaria; **~er** n banquero; **~er's card** (BRIT) n = **~ card**; **B~ holiday** (BRIT) n día m festivo; **~ing** n banca; **~note** n billete m de banco; **~ rate** n tipo de interés bancario

---

bank holiday

El término **bank holiday** *se aplica en el Reino Unido a todo día festivo oficial en el que cierran bancos y comercios. Los más importantes son en Navidad, Semana Santa, finales de mayo y finales de agosto y, al contrario que en los países de tradición católica, no coinciden necesariamente con una celebración religiosa.*

---

bankrupt ['bæŋkrʌpt] adj quebrado, insolvente; **to go ~** hacer bancarrota; **to be ~** estar en quiebra; **~cy** n quiebra

bank statement n balance m or detalle m de cuenta

banner ['bænə*] n pancarta

bannister(s) ['bænɪstə(z)] n(pl) = **banister(s)**

baptism ['bæptɪzəm] n bautismo; (act) bautizo

bar [bɑː*] n (in pub) bar m; (counter) mostrador m; (rod) barra; (of window, cage) reja; (of soap) pastilla; (of *chocolate*) tableta; (*fig: hindrance*) obstáculo; (*prohibition*) proscripción f; (*MUS*) barra ♦ vt (*road*) obstruir; (*person*) excluir; (*activity*) prohibir; **the B~** (*LAW*) la abogacía; **behind ~s** entre rejas; **~ none** sin excepción

barbaric [baːˈbærɪk] *adj* bárbaro

barbecue [ˈbaːbɪkjuː] *n* barbacoa

barbed wire [ˈbaːbd-] *n* alambre *m* de púas

barber [ˈbaːbə*] *n* peluquero, barbero

bar code *n* código de barras

bare [bɛə*] *adj* desnudo; (*trees*) sin hojas; (*necessities etc*) básico ♦ *vt* desnudar; (*teeth*) enseñar; **~back** *adv* a pelo, sin silla; **~faced** *adj* descarado; **~foot** *adj, adv* descalzo; **~ly** *adv* apenas

bargain [ˈbaːgɪn] *n* pacto, negocio; (*good buy*) ganga ♦ *vi* negociar; (*haggle*) regatear; **into the ~** además, por añadidura; **~ for** *vt fus*: **he got more than he ~ed for** le resultó peor de lo que esperaba

barge [baːdʒ] *n* barcaza; **~ in** *vi* irrumpir; (*interrupt: conversation*) interrumpir

bark [baːk] *n* (*of tree*) corteza; (*of dog*) ladrido ♦ *vi* ladrar

barley [ˈbaːlɪ] *n* cebada

barmaid [ˈbaːmeɪd] *n* camarera

barman [ˈbaːmən] *n* camarero, barman *m*

barn [baːn] *n* granero

barometer [bəˈrɒmɪtə*] *n* barómetro

baron [ˈbærən] *n* barón *m*; (*press ~ etc*) magnate *m*; **~ess** *n* baronesa

barracks [ˈbærəks] *npl* cuartel *m*

barrage [ˈbæraːʒ] *n* (*MIL*) descarga, bombardeo; (*dam*) presa; (*of criticism*) lluvia, aluvión *m*

barrel [ˈbærəl] *n* barril *m*; (*of gun*) cañón *m*

barren [ˈbærən] *adj* estéril

barricade [bærɪˈkeɪd] *n* barricada

barrier [ˈbærɪə*] *n* barrera

barring [ˈbaːrɪŋ] *prep* excepto, salvo

barrister [ˈbærɪstə*] (*BRIT*) *n* abogado/a

barrow [ˈbærəu] *n* (*cart*) carretilla (de mano)

bartender [ˈbaːtɛndə*] (*US*) *n* camarero, barman *m*

barter [ˈbaːtə*] *vt*: **to ~ sth for sth** trocar algo por algo

base [beɪs] *n* base f ♦ *vt*: **to ~ sth on** basar o fundar algo en ♦ *adj* bajo, infame

baseball [ˈbeɪsbɔːl] *n* béisbol *m*

basement [ˈbeɪsmənt] *n* sótano

bases¹ [ˈbeɪsɪz] *npl of* **basis**

bases² [ˈbeɪsɪz] *npl of* **base**

bash [bæʃ] (*inf*) *vt* golpear

bashful [ˈbæʃful] *adj* tímido, vergonzoso

basic [ˈbeɪsɪk] *adj* básico; **~ally** *adv* fundamentalmente, en el fondo; (*simply*) sencillamente; **~s** *npl*: **the ~s** los fundamentos

basil [ˈbæzl] *n* albahaca

basin [ˈbeɪsn] *n* cuenco, tazón *m*; (*GEO*) cuenca; (*also: wash~*) lavabo

basis [ˈbeɪsɪs] *n* (*pl* **bases**) *n* base f; **on a part-time/trial ~** a tiempo parcial/a prueba

bask [baːsk] *vi*: **to ~ in the sun** tomar el sol

basket [ˈbaːskɪt] *n* cesta, cesto; canasta; **~ball** *n* baloncesto

Basque [bæsk] *adj, n* vasco/a *m/f*; **~ Country** *n* Euskadi *m*, País *m* Vasco

bass [beɪs] *n* (*MUS: instrument*) bajo; (*double ~*) contrabajo; (*singer*) bajo

bassoon [bəˈsuːn] *n* fagot *m*

bastard [ˈbaːstəd] *n* bastardo; (*inf!*) hijo de puta (!)

bat [bæt] *n* (*ZOOL*) murciélago; (*for ball games*) bate; (*BRIT: for table tennis*) pala ♦ *vt*: **he didn't ~ an eyelid** ni pestañeó

batch [bætʃ] *n* (*of bread*) hornada; (*of letters etc*) lote *m*

bated [ˈbeɪtɪd] *adj*: **with ~ breath** sin respirar

bath [bɑːθ, pl baːðz] n (action) baño; (~tub) baño (SP), bañera (SP), tina (AM) ♦ vt bañar; **to have a ~** bañarse, tomar un baño; see also **baths**

bathe [beɪð] vi bañarse ♦ vt (wound) lavar; **~r** n bañista m/f

bathing ['beɪðɪŋ] n el bañarse; **~ costume** (US = **suit**) n traje m de baño

bath: **~robe** n (man's) batín m; (woman's) bata; **~room** n (cuarto de) baño; **~s** [bɑːðz] npl (also: swimming ~s) piscina; **~ towel** n toalla de baño

baton ['bætən] n (MUS) batuta; (ATHLETICS) testigo; (weapon) porra

batter ['bætə*] vt maltratar; (subj: rain etc) azotar ♦ n masa (para rebozar); **~ed** adj (hat, pan) estropeado

battery ['bætəri] n (AUT) batería; (of torch) pila

battle ['bætl] n batalla; (fig) lucha ♦ vi luchar; **~ship** n acorazado

bawl [bɔːl] vi chillar, gritar; (child) berrear

bay [beɪ] n (GEO) bahía; **B~ of Biscay** ≈ mar Cantábrico; **to hold sb at ~** mantener a alguien a raya; **~ leaf** n hoja de laurel

bay window n ventana salediza

bazaar [bə'zɑː*] n bazar m; (fete) venta con fines benéficos

B. & B. n abbr (= bed and breakfast) cama y desayuno

BBC n abbr (= British Broadcasting Corporation) cadena de radio y televisión estatal británica

B.C. adv abbr (= before Christ) a. de C.

KEYWORD

be [biː] n (pt **was**, **were**, pp **been**) aux vb 1 (with present participle: forming continuous tenses): **what are you doing?** ¿qué estás haciendo?, ¿qué haces?; **they're coming tomorrow** vienen mañana; **I've been waiting for you for hours** llevo horas esperándote

2 (with pp: forming passives) ser (but often replaced by active or reflective constructions); **to ~ murdered** ser asesinado; **the box had been opened** habían abierto la caja; **the thief was nowhere to ~ seen** no se veía al ladrón por ninguna parte

3 (in tag questions): **it was fun, wasn't it?** fue divertido, ¿no? or ¿verdad?; **he's good-looking, isn't he?** es guapo, ¿no te parece?; **she's back again, is she?** entonces, ¿ha vuelto?

4 (+ to + infin): **the house is to ~ sold** (necessity) hay que vender la casa; (future) van a vender la casa; **he's not to open it** no tiene que abrirlo

♦ vb + complement 1 (with n or num complement, but see also 3, 4, 5 and impers vb below) ser; **he's a doctor** es médico; **2 and 2 are 4** 2 y 2 son 4

2 (with adj complement: expressing permanent or inherent quality) ser; (: expressing state seen as temporary or reversible) estar; **I'm English** soy inglés/esa; **he's tall/pretty** es alta/bonita; **he's young** es joven; **~ careful/good/quiet** ten cuidado/ pórtate bien/cállate; **I'm tired** estoy cansado/a; **it's dirty** está sucio/a

3 (of health) estar; **how are you?** ¿cómo estás?; **he's very ill** está muy enfermo; **I'm better now** ya estoy mejor

4 (of age) tener; **how old are you?** ¿cuántos años tienes?; **I'm sixteen (years old)** tengo dieciséis años

5 (cost) costar; ser; **how much was the meal?** ¿cuánto fue or costó la comida?; **that'll ~ £5.75, please** son £5.75, por favor; **this shirt is £17** esta camisa cuesta £17

♦ vi 1 (exist, occur etc) existir, haber; **the best singer that ever was** el mejor cantante que existió jamás; **is there a God?** ¿hay un Dios?; ¿existe

Dios?; ~ **that as it may** sea como sea; **so ~ it** así sea
2 (*referring to place*) estar; **I won't ~ here tomorrow** no estaré aquí mañana
3 (*referring to movement*): **where have you been?** ¿dónde has estado?
♦ *impers vb* **1** (*referring to time*): **it's 3 o'clock** son las 5; **it's the 28th of April** estamos a 28 de abril
2 (*referring to distance*): **it's 10 km to the village** el pueblo está a 10 km
3 (*referring to the weather*): **it's too hot/cold** hace demasiado calor/frío; **it's windy today** hace viento hoy
4 (*emphatic*): **it's me** soy yo; **it was Maria who paid the bill** fue María la que pagó la cuenta

beach [biːtʃ] *n* playa ♦ *vt* varar
beacon ['biːkən] *n* (*lighthouse*) faro; (*marker*) guía
bead [biːd] *n* cuenta; (*of sweat etc*) gota
beak [biːk] *n* pico
beaker ['biːkə*] *n* vaso de plástico
beam [biːm] *n* (*ARCH*) viga, travesaño; (*of light*) rayo, haz *m* de luz ♦ *vi* brillar; (*smile*) sonreír
bean [biːn] *n* judía; **runner/broad ~** habichuela/haba; **coffee ~** grano de café; **~sprouts** *npl* brotes *mpl* de soja
bear [bɛə*] (*pt* **bore**, *pp* **borne**) *n* oso ♦ *vt* (*weight etc*) llevar; (*cost*) pagar; (*responsibility*) tener; (*endure*) soportar, aguantar; (*children*) parir, tener; (*fruit*) dar ♦ *vi*: **to ~ right/left** torcer a la derecha/izquierda; **~ out** *vt* (*suspicions*) corroborar, confirmar; (*person*) dar la razón a; **~ up** *vi* (*remain cheerful*) mantenerse animado
beard [biəd] *n* barba; **~ed** *adj* con barba, barbudo
bearer ['bɛərə*] *n* portador(a) *m/f*
bearing ['bɛərɪŋ] *n* porte *m*, comportamiento; (*connection*) relación

f; **~s** *npl* (*also*: **ball ~s**) cojinetes *mpl* a bolas; **to take a ~** tomar marcaciones; **to find one's ~s** orientarse
beast [biːst] *n* bestia; (*inf*) bruto, salvaje *m*; **~ly** (*inf*) *adj* horrible
beat [biːt] (*pt* **beat**, *pp* **beaten**) *n* (*of heart*) latido; (*MUS*) ritmo, compás *m*; (*of policeman*) ronda ♦ *vt* pegar, golpear; (*eggs*) batir; (*defeat*) opponent) vencer, derrotar; (: *record*) sobrepasar ♦ *vi* (*heart*) latir; (*drum*) redoblar; (*rain, wind*) azotar; **off the ~en track** aislado; **to ~ it** (*inf*) largarse; **~ off** *vt* rechazar; **~ up** *vt* (*attack*) dar una paliza a; **~ing** *n* paliza
beautiful ['bjuːtɪful] *adj* precioso, hermoso, bello; **~ly** *adv* maravillosamente
beauty ['bjuːtɪ] *n* belleza; **~ salon** *n* salón *m* de belleza; **~ spot** *n* (*TOURISM*) lugar *m* pintoresco
beaver ['biːvə*] *n* castor *m*
became [bɪ'keɪm] *pt of* **become**
because [bɪ'kɒz] *conj* porque; **~ of** debido a, a causa de
beckon ['bɛkən] *vt* (*also*: **~ to**) llamar con señas
become [bɪ'kʌm] (*irreg*: *like* **come**) *vt* (*suit*) favorecer, sentar bien a ♦ *vi* (+ *n*) hacerse, llegar a ser; (+ *adj*) ponerse, volverse; **to ~ fat** engordar
becoming [bɪ'kʌmɪŋ] *adj* (*behaviour*) decoroso; (*clothes*) favorecedor(a)
bed [bɛd] *n* cama; (*of flowers*) macizo; (*of coal, clay*) capa; (*of river*) lecho; (*of sea*) fondo; **to go to ~** acostarse; **~ and breakfast** *n* (*place*) pensión *f*; (*terms*) cama y desayuno; **~clothes** *npl* ropa de cama; **~ding** *n* ropa de cama

---

Bed and Breakfast

Se llama Bed and Breakfast *a una forma de alojamiento, en el campo o la ciudad, que ofrece cama y desayuno a precios inferiores a los de un hotel. El servicio se suele anunciar* con carteles en los que a menudo se usa únicamente la abreviatura B. & B.

bedraggled [bɪ'dræɡld] *adj* (*untidy: person*) desastrado; (*clothes, hair*) desordenado

bed: ~**ridden** *adj* postrado (en cama); ~**room** *n* dormitorio; ~**side** *n*: **at the** ~**side of a** la cabecera de; ~**sit(ter)** (*BRIT*) *n* estudio (*SP*), suite *m* (*AM*); ~**spread** *n* cubrecama *m*, colcha; ~**time** *n* hora de acostarse

bee [bi:] *n* abeja

beech [bi:tʃ] *n* haya

beef [bi:f] *n* carne *f* de vaca; **roast** ~ rosbif *m*; ~**burger** *n* hamburguesa; **B~eater** *n* alabardero de la Torre de Londres

beehive ['bi:haɪv] *n* colmena

beeline ['bi:laɪn] *n*: **to make a** ~ **for** ir derecho a

been [bi:n] *pp of* **be**

beer [bɪə*] *n* cerveza

beet [bi:t] (*US*) *n* (*also:* **red** ~) remolacha

beetle ['bi:tl] *n* escarabajo

beetroot ['bi:tru:t] (*BRIT*) *n* remolacha

before [bɪ'fɔ:*] *prep* (*of time*) antes de; (*of space*) delante de ♦ *conj* antes de que ♦ *adv* antes, anteriormente; delante, adelante; ~ **going** antes de marcharse; ~ **she goes** antes de que se vaya; **the week** ~ la semana anterior; **I've never seen it** ~ no lo he visto nunca; ~**hand** *adv* de antemano, con anticipación

beg [beɡ] *vi* pedir limosna ♦ *vt* pedir, rogar; (*entreat*) suplicar; **to** ~ **sb to do sth** rogar a uno que haga algo; *see also* **pardon**

began [bɪ'ɡæn] *pt of* **begin**

beggar ['beɡə*] *n* mendigo/a

begin [bɪ'ɡɪn] (*pt* **began**, *pp* **begun**) *vt, vi* empezar, comenzar; **to** ~ **doing** *or* **to do sth** empezar a hacer algo; ~**ner** *n* principiante *m/f*; ~**ning** *n* principio, comienzo

begun [bɪ'ɡʌn] *pp of* **begin**

behalf [bɪ'hɑ:f] *n*: **on** ~ **of** en nombre de, por; (*for benefit of*) en beneficio de; **on my/his** ~ por mí/él

behave [bɪ'heɪv] *vi* (*person*) portarse, comportarse; (*well: also:* ~ **o.s.**) portarse bien; **behaviour** (*US* **behavior**) *n* comportamiento, conducta

behind [bɪ'haɪnd] *prep* detrás de; (*supporting*): **to be** ~ **sb** apoyar a alguien ♦ *adv* detrás, por detrás, atrás ♦ *n* trasero; **to be** ~ (*schedule*) ir retrasado; ~ **the scenes** (*fig*) entre bastidores

behold [bɪ'həʊld] (*irreg: like* **hold**) *vt* contemplar

beige [beɪʒ] *adj* color beige

Beijing ['beɪ'dʒɪŋ] *n* Pekín *m*

being ['bi:ɪŋ] *n* ser *m*; (*existence*): **in** ~ existente; **to come into** ~ aparecer

Beirut [beɪ'ru:t] *n* Beirut *m*

Belarus [belə'rus] *n* Bielorrusia

belated [bɪ'leɪtɪd] *adj* atrasado, tardío

belch [beltʃ] *vi* eructar ♦ *vt* (*gen:* ~ **out:** *smoke etc*) arrojar

Belgian ['beldʒən] *adj*, *n* belga *m/f*

Belgium ['beldʒəm] *n* Bélgica

belief [bɪ'li:f] *n* opinión *f*; (*faith*) fe *f*

believe [bɪ'li:v] *vt, vi* creer; **to** ~ **in** creer en; ~**r** *n* partidario/a; (*REL*) creyente *m/f*, fiel *m/f*

belittle [bɪ'lɪtl] *vt* quitar importancia a

bell [bel] *n* campana; (*small*) campanilla; (*on door*) timbre *m*

belligerent [bɪ'lɪdʒərənt] *adj* agresivo

bellow ['beləʊ] *vi* bramar; (*person*) rugir

belly ['belɪ] *n* barriga, panza

belong [bɪ'lɒŋ] *vi*: **to** ~ **to** pertenecer a; (*club etc*) ser socio de; **this book** ~**s here** este libro va aquí; ~**ings** *npl* pertenencias *fpl*

beloved [bɪ'lʌvɪd] *adj* querido/a

below [bɪ'ləʊ] *prep* bajo, debajo de; (*less than*) inferior a ♦ *adv* abajo, (por) debajo; **see** ~ véase más abajo

belt [belt] *n* cinturón *m*; (*TECH*) correa, cinta ♦ *vt* (*thrash*) pegar con correa; **~way** (*US*) *n* (*AUT*) carretera de circunvalación

bench [bentʃ] *n* banco; (*BRIT: POL*): **the Government/Opposition ~es** (los asientos de) los miembros del Gobierno/de la Oposición; **the B~** (*LAW: judges*) magistratura

bend [bend] (*pt*, *pp* **bent**) *vt* doblar ♦ *vi* inclinarse ♦ *n* (*BRIT: in road*, *river*) curva; (*in pipe*) codo; **~ down** *vi* inclinarse, doblarse; **~ over** *vi* inclinarse

beneath [bɪˈniːθ] *prep* bajo, debajo de; (*unworthy of*) indigno de ♦ *adv* abajo, (por) debajo

benefactor [ˈbenɪfæktə*] *n* bienhechor *m*

beneficial [benɪˈfɪʃəl] *adj* beneficioso

benefit [ˈbenɪfɪt] *n* beneficio; (*allowance of money*) subsidio ♦ *vt* beneficiar ♦ *vi*: **he'll ~ from it** sacará provecho

benevolent [bɪˈnevələnt] *adj* (*person*) benévolo

benign [bɪˈnaɪn] *adj* benigno; (*smile*) afable

bent [bent] *pt*, *pp* of **bend** ♦ *n* inclinación *f* ♦ *adj*: **to be ~ on** estar empeñado en

bequest [bɪˈkwest] *n* legado

bereaved [bɪˈriːvd] *npl*: **the ~** los íntimos de una persona afligidos por su muerte

beret [ˈbereɪ] *n* boina

Berlin [bɜːˈlɪn] *n* Berlín

berm [bɜːm] (*US*) *n* (*AUT*) arcén *m*

Bermuda [bɜːˈmjuːdə] *n* las Bermudas

berry [ˈberɪ] *n* baya

berserk [bəˈsɜːk] *adj*: **to go ~** perder los estribos

berth [bɜːθ] *n* (*bed*) litera; (*cabin*) camarote *m*; (*for ship*) amarradero ♦ *vi* atracar, amarrar

beseech [bɪˈsiːtʃ] (*pt*, *pp* **besought**) *vt* suplicar

beset [bɪˈset] (*pt*, *pp* **beset**) *vt* (*person*) acosar

beside [bɪˈsaɪd] *prep* junto a, al lado de; **to be ~ o.s. with anger** estar fuera de sí; **that's ~ the point** eso no tiene nada que ver; **~s** *adv* además ♦ *prep* además de

besiege [bɪˈsiːdʒ] *vt* sitiar; (*fig*) asediar

best [best] *adj* (*el/la*) mejor ♦ *adv* (lo) mejor; **the ~ part of** (*quantity*) la mayor parte de; **at ~** en el mejor de los casos; **to make the ~ of sth** sacar el mejor partido de algo; **to do one's ~** hacer todo lo posible; **to the ~ of my knowledge** que yo sepa; **to the ~ of my ability** como mejor puedo; **~-before date** *n* fecha de consumo preferente; **~ man** *n* padrino de boda

bestow [bɪˈstəʊ] *vt* (*title*) otorgar

bestseller [ˈbestˈselə*] *n* éxito de librería, bestseller *m*

bet [bet] (*pt*, *pp* **bet** or **betted**) *n* apuesta ♦ *vt*: **to ~ money on** apostar dinero por; **to ~ sb sth** apostar algo a uno ♦ *vi* apostar

betray [bɪˈtreɪ] *vt* traicionar; (*trust*) faltar a; **~al** *n* traición *f*

better [ˈbetə*] *adj*, *adv* mejor ♦ *vt* superar ♦ *n*: **to get the ~ of sb** quedar por encima de alguien; **you had ~ do it** más vale que lo hagas; **he thought ~ of it** cambió de parecer; **to get ~** (*MED*) mejorar(se); **~ off** *adj* mejor; (*wealthier*) más acomodado

betting [ˈbetɪŋ] *n* juego, el apostar; **~ shop** (*BRIT*) *n* agencia de apuestas

between [bɪˈtwiːn] *prep* entre ♦ *adv* (*time*) mientras tanto; (*place*) en medio

beverage [ˈbevərɪdʒ] *n* bebida

beware [bɪˈweə*] *vi*: **to ~ (of)** tener cuidado (con); **"~ of the dog"** "perro peligroso"

bewildered [bɪˈwɪldəd] *adj* aturdido, perplejo

beyond [bɪˈjɒnd] *prep* más allá de; (*past: understanding*) fuera de; (*after:*

date) después de, más allá de; (*above*) superior a ♦ *adv* (*in space*) más allá; (*in time*) posteriormente; **~ doubt** fuera de toda duda; **~ repair** irreparable

bias ['baɪəs] *n* (*prejudice*) prejuicio, pasión *f*; (*preference*) predisposición *f*; **~(s)ed** *adj* parcial

bib [bɪb] *n* babero

Bible ['baɪbl] *n* Biblia

bicarbonate of soda [baɪ'kɑ:bənɪt-] *n* bicarbonato sódico

bicker ['bɪkə*] *vi* pelearse

bicycle ['baɪsɪkl] *n* bicicleta

bid [bɪd] (*pt* **bade** or **bid**, *pp* **bidden** or **bid**) *n* oferta, postura; (*in tender*) licitación *f*; (*attempt*) tentativa, conato ♦ *vi* hacer una oferta ♦ *vt* (*offer*) ofrecer; **to ~ sb good day** dar a uno los buenos días; **~der** *n*: **the highest ~der** el mejor postor; **~ding** *n* (*at auction*) ofertas *fpl*

bide [baɪd] *vt*: **to ~ one's time** esperar el momento adecuado

bifocals [baɪ'fəʊklz] *npl* gafas *fpl* (*SP*) or anteojos *mpl* (*AM*) bifocales

big [bɪg] *adj* grande; (*brother, sister*) mayor

bigheaded ['bɪg'hedɪd] *adj* engreído

bigot ['bɪgət] *n* fanático/a, intolerante *m/f*; **~ed** *adj* fanático, intolerante; **~ry** *n* fanatismo, intolerancia

big top *n* (*at circus*) carpa

bike [baɪk] *n* bici *f*

bikini [bɪ'ki:nɪ] *n* bikini *m*

bilingual [baɪ'lɪŋgwəl] *adj* bilingüe

bill [bɪl] *n* cuenta; (*invoice*) factura; (*POL*) proyecto de ley; (*US*: *banknote*) billete *m*; (*of bird*) pico; (*of show*) programa *m*; **"post no ~s"** "prohibido fijar carteles"; **to fit** or **fill the ~** (*fig*) cumplir con los requisitos; **~board** (*US*) *n* cartelera

billet ['bɪlɪt] *n* alojamiento

billfold ['bɪlfəʊld] (*US*) *n* cartera

billiards ['bɪljədz] *n* billar *m*

billion ['bɪljən] *n* (*BRIT*) billón *m* (*millón de millones*); (*US*) mil millones *mpl*

bimbo ['bɪmbəʊ] (*inf*) *n* tía buena sin seso

bin [bɪn] *n* (*for rubbish*) cubo (*SP*) or bote *m* (*AM*) de la basura; (*container*) recipiente *m*

bind [baɪnd] (*pt*, *pp* **bound**) *vt* atar; (*book*) encuadernar; (*oblige*) obligar ♦ *n* (*inf*: *nuisance*) lata; **~ing** *adj* (*contract*) obligatorio

binge [bɪndʒ] (*inf*) *n*: **to go on a ~** ir de juerga

bingo ['bɪŋgəʊ] *n* bingo *m*

binoculars [bɪ'nɒkjʊləz] *npl* prismáticos *mpl*

bio... [baɪə] *prefix*: **~chemistry** *n* bioquímica; **~degradable** [baɪəʊdɪ'greɪdəbl] *adj* biodegradable; **~graphy** [baɪ'ɒgrəfɪ] *n* biografía; **~logical** [baɪə'lɒdʒɪkl] *adj* biológico; **~logy** [baɪ'ɒlədʒɪ] *n* biología

birch [bɜːtʃ] *n* (*tree*) abedul *m*

bird [bɜːd] *n* ave *f*, pájaro; (*BRIT*: *inf*: *girl*) chica; **~'s eye view** *n* (*aerial view*) vista de pájaro; (*overview*) visión *f* de conjunto; **~ watcher** *n* ornitólogo/a

Biro ® ['baɪərəʊ] *n* bolígrafo

birth [bɜːθ] *n* nacimiento; **to give ~ to** parir, dar a luz; **~ certificate** *n* partida de nacimiento; **~ control** *n* (*policy*) control *m* de natalidad; (*methods*) métodos *mpl* anticonceptivos; **~day** *n* cumpleaños *m inv* ♦ *cpd* (*cake, card etc*) de cumpleaños; **~place** *n* lugar *m* de nacimiento; **~ rate** *n* (tasa de) natalidad *f*

biscuit ['bɪskɪt] (*BRIT*) *n* galleta, bizcocho (*AM*)

bisect [baɪ'sekt] *vt* bisecar

bishop ['bɪʃəp] *n* obispo; (*CHESS*) alfil *m*

bit [bɪt] *pt* of **bite** *n* trozo, pedazo, pedacito; (*COMPUT*) bit *m*, bitio; (*for horse*) freno, bocado; **a ~ of** un poco de; **a ~ mad** un poco loco; **~ by ~** poco a poco

bitch [bɪtʃ] *n* perra; (*inf!*: *woman*) zorra (!)

bite [baɪt] (*pt* **bit**, *pp* **bitten**) *vt*, *vi* morder; (*insect etc*) picar ♦ *n* (*insect ~*) picadura; (*mouthful*) bocado; **to ~ one's nails** comerse las uñas; **let's have a ~ (to eat)** (*inf*) vamos a comer algo

bitter ['bɪtə*] *adj* amargo; (*wind*) cortante, penetrante; (*battle*) encarnizado ♦ *n* (*BRIT*: *beer*) cerveza típica británica a base de lúpulos; **~ness** *n* lo amargo, amargura; (*anger*) rencor *m*

bizarre [bɪ'zɑ:*] *adj* raro, extraño

black [blæk] *adj* negro; (*tea, coffee*) solo ♦ *n* color *m* negro; (*person*): **B~** negro/a ♦ *vt* (*BRIT*: *INDUSTRY*) boicotear; **to give sb a ~ eye** ponerle a uno el ojo morado; **~ and blue** (*bruised*) amoratado; **to be in the ~** (*bank account*) estar en números negros; **~berry** *n* zarzamora; **~bird** *n* mirlo; **~board** *n* pizarra; **~ coffee** *n* café *m* solo; **~currant** *n* grosella negra; **~en** *vt* (*fig*) desacreditar; **~ ice** *n* hielo invisible en la carretera; **~leg** (*BRIT*) *n* esquirol *m*, rompehuelgas *m inv*; **~list** *n* lista negra; **~mail** *n* chantaje *m* ♦ *vt* chantajear; **~ market** *n* mercado negro; **~out** *n* (*MIL*) oscurecimiento; (*power cut*) apagón *m*; (*TV*, *RADIO*) interrupción *f* de programas; (*fainting*) desvanecimiento; **B~ Sea** *n*: **the B~ Sea** el Mar Negro; **~ sheep** *n* (*fig*) oveja negra; **~smith** *n* herrero; **~ spot** *n* (*AUT*) lugar *m* peligroso; (*for unemployment etc*) punto negro

bladder ['blædə*] *n* vejiga

blade [bleɪd] *n* hoja; (*of propeller*) paleta; **a ~ of grass** una brizna de hierba

blame [bleɪm] *n* culpa ♦ *vt*: **to ~ sb for sth** echar a uno la culpa de algo; **to be to ~** tener la culpa de

bland [blænd] *adj* (*music, taste*) soso

blank [blæŋk] *adj* en blanco; (*look*) sin expresión ♦ *n* (*of memory*): **my mind is a ~** no puedo recordar nada; (*on form*) blanco, espacio en blanco;

(*cartridge*) cartucho sin bala *or* de fogueo; **~ cheque** *n* cheque *m* en blanco

blanket ['blæŋkɪt] *n* manta (*SP*), cobija (*AM*); (*of snow*) capa; (*of fog*) manto

blare [blɛə*] *vi* sonar estrepitosamente

blasé ['blɑ:zeɪ] *adj* hastiado

blast [blɑ:st] *n* (*of wind*) ráfaga, soplo; (*of explosive*) explosión *f* ♦ *vt* (*blow up*) volar; **~-off** *n* (*SPACE*) lanzamiento

blatant ['bleɪtənt] *adj* descarado

blaze [bleɪz] *n* (*fire*) fuego; (*fig*: *of colour*) despliegue *m*; (: *of glory*) esplendor *m* ♦ *vi* arder en llamas; (*fig*) brillar ♦ *vt*: **to ~ a trail** (*fig*) abrir (un) camino; **in a ~ of publicity** con gran publicidad

blazer ['bleɪzə*] *n* chaqueta de uniforme de colegial *o* de socio de club

bleach [bli:tʃ] *n* (*also*: *household ~*) lejía ♦ *vt* blanquear; **~ed** *adj* (*hair*) teñido (de rubio); **~ers** (*US*) *npl* (*SPORT*) gradas *fpl* al sol

bleak [bli:k] *adj* (*countryside*) desierto; (*prospect*) poco prometedor(a); (*weather*) crudo; (*smile*) triste

bleat [bli:t] *vi* balar

bleed [bli:d] (*pt*, *pp* **bled**) *vt*, *vi* sangrar; **my nose is ~ing** me está sangrando la nariz

bleeper ['bli:pə*] *n* busca *m*

blemish ['blemɪʃ] *n* marca, mancha; (*on reputation*) tacha

blend [blend] *n* mezcla ♦ *vt* mezclar; (*colours etc*) combinar, mezclar ♦ *vi* (*colours etc*: *also*: ~ *in*) combinarse, mezclarse

bless [bles] (*pt*, *pp* **blessed** *or* **blest**) *vt* bendecir; **~ you!** (*after sneeze*) ¡Jesús!; **~ing** *n* (*approval*) aprobación *f*; (*godsend*) don *m* del cielo, bendición *f*; (*advantage*) beneficio, ventaja

blew [blu:] *pt of* **blow**

blind [blaɪnd] *adj* ciego; (*fig*): **~ (to)** ciego (a) ♦ *n* (*for window*) persiana ♦ *vt* cegar; (*dazzle*) deslumbrar; (*deceive*): **to ~ sb to ...** cegar a uno a ...; **the ~**

npl los ciegos; **~ alley** *n* callejón *m* sin salida; **~ corner** (*BRIT*) *n* esquina escondida; **~fold** *n* venda ♦ *adv* con los ojos vendados ♦ *vt* vendar los ojos a; **~ly** *adv* a ciegas, ciegamente; **~ness** *n* ceguera; **~ spot** *n* (*AUT*) ángulo ciego

blink [blɪŋk] *vi* parpadear, pestañear; (*light*) oscilar; **~ers** *npl* anteojeras *fpl*

bliss [blɪs] *n* felicidad *f*

blister ['blɪstə*] *n* ampolla ♦ *vi* (*paint*) ampollarse

blizzard ['blɪzəd] *n* ventisca

bloated ['bləʊtɪd] *adj* hinchado; (*person: full*) ahíto

blob [blɒb] *n* (*drop*) gota; (*indistinct object*) bulto

bloc [blɒk] *n* (*POL*) bloque *m*

block [blɒk] *n* bloque *m*; (*in pipes*) obstáculo; (*of buildings*) manzana (*SP*), cuadra (*AM*) ♦ *vt* obstruir, cerrar; (*progress*) estorbar; **~ of flats** (*BRIT*) bloque *m* de pisos; **mental ~ade** [-'keɪd] *n* bloqueo ♦ *vt* bloquear; **~age** *n* estorbo, obstrucción *f*; **~buster** *n* (*book*) bestséller *m*; (*film*) éxito de público; **~ letters** *npl* letras *fpl* de molde

bloke [bləʊk] (*BRIT: inf*) *n* tipo, tío

blond(e) [blɒnd] *adj, n* rubio/a *m/f*

blood [blʌd] *n* sangre *f*; **~ donor** *n* donante *m/f* de sangre; **~ group** *n* grupo sanguíneo; **~hound** *n* sabueso; **~ poisoning** *n* envenenamiento de la sangre; **~ pressure** *n* presión *f* sanguínea; **~shed** *n* derramamiento de sangre; **~shot** *adj* inyectado en sangre; **~stream** *n* corriente *f* sanguínea; **~ test** *n* análisis *m inv* de sangre; **~thirsty** *adj* sanguinario; **~ vessel** *n* vaso sanguíneo; **~y** *adj* sangriento; (*nose etc*) lleno de sangre; (*BRIT: inf!*): **this ~y ...** este condenado o puñetero ... (*!*) ♦ *adv*: **~y strong/good** (*BRIT: inf!*) terriblemente fuerte/bueno; **~y-minded** (*BRIT: inf*) *adj* puñetero (*!*)

bloom [bluːm] *n* flor *f* ♦ *vi* florecer

blossom ['blɒsəm] *n* flor *f* ♦ *vi* (*also fig*) florecer

blot [blɒt] *n* borrón *m*; (*fig*) mancha ♦ *vt* (*stain*) manchar; **~ out** *vt* (*view*) tapar

blotchy ['blɒtʃɪ] *adj* (*complexion*) lleno de manchas

blotting paper ['blɒtɪŋ-] *n* papel *m* secante

blouse [blauz] *n* blusa

blow [bləʊ] (*pt* **blew**, *pp* **blown**) *n* golpe *m*; (*with sword*) espadazo ♦ *vi* soplar; (*dust, sand etc*) volar; (*fuse*) fundirse ♦ *vt* (*subj: wind*) llevarse; (*fuse*) quemar; (*instrument*) tocar; **to ~ one's nose** sonarse; **~ away** *vt* llevarse, arrancar; **~ down** *vt* derribar; **~ off** *vt* arrebatar; **~ out** *vi* apagarse; **~ over** *vi* amainar; **~ up** *vi* estallar ♦ *vt* volar; (*tyre*) inflar; (*PHOT*) ampliar; **~-dry** *n* moldeado (con secador); **~lamp** (*BRIT*) *n* soplete *m*, lámpara de soldar; **~-out** *n* (*of tyre*) pinchazo; **~torch** *n* = **~lamp**

blue [bluː] *adj* azul; (*depressed*) deprimido; **~ film/joke** película/chiste *m* verde; **out of the ~** (*fig*) de repente; **~bell** *n* campanilla, campánula azul; **~bottle** *n* moscarda, mosca azul; **~print** *n* (*fig*) anteproyecto

bluff [blʌf] *vi* tirarse un farol, farolear ♦ *n* farol *m*; **to call sb's ~** coger a uno la palabra

blunder ['blʌndə*] *n* patinazo, metedura de pata ♦ *vi* cometer un error, meter la pata

blunt [blʌnt] *adj* (*pencil*) despuntado; (*knife*) desafilado, romo; (*person*) franco, directo

blur [bləː*] *n* (*shape*): **to become a ~** hacerse borroso ♦ *vt* (*vision*) enturbiar; (*distinction*) borrar

blush [blʌʃ] *vi* ruborizarse, ponerse colorado ♦ *n* rubor *m*

blustery ['blʌstərɪ] *adj* (*weather*)

tempestuoso, tormentoso

boar [bɔːʳ] n verraco, cerdo

board [bɔːd] n (card~) cartón m; (wooden) tabla, tablero; (on wall) tablón m; (for chess etc) tablero; (committee) junta, consejo; (in firm) mesa or junta directiva; (NAUT, AVIAT): **on ~ a bordo ♦ vt (ship) embarcar en; (train) subir a; full ~ (BRIT) pensión completa; half ~ (BRIT) media pensión; to go by the ~ (fig) ser abandonado or olvidado; ~ up vt (door) tapiar; ~ and lodging n casa y comida; ~er n (SCOL) interno/a; ~ing card n (BRIT) n tarjeta de embarque; ~ing house n casa de huéspedes; ~ing pass n (US) n = ~ing card; ~ing school n internado; ~ room n sala de juntas**

boast [bəʊst] vi: **to ~ (about or of) alardear (de)**

boat [bəʊt] n barco, buque m; (small) barca, bote m

bob [bɔb] vi (also: ~ up and down) menearse, balancearse; ~ up vi (re)aparecer de repente

bobby [ˈbɔbi] (BRIT: inf) n poli m

bobsleigh [ˈbɔbsleɪ] n bob m

bode [bəʊd] vi: **to ~ well/ill (for) ser prometedor/poco prometedor (para)**

bodily [ˈbɔdɪlɪ] adj corporal ♦ adv (move: person) en peso

body [ˈbɔdɪ] n cuerpo; (corpse) cadáver m; (of car) caja, carrocería; (fig: group) grupo; (: organization) organismo; **~-building** n culturismo; **~guard** n guardaespaldas m inv; **~work** n carrocería

bog [bɔg] n pantano, ciénaga ♦ vt: **to get ~ged down (fig) empantanarse, atascarse**

bogus [ˈbəʊgəs] adj falso, fraudulento

boil [bɔɪl] vt (water) hervir; (eggs) pasar por agua, cocer ♦ vi hervir; (fig: with anger) estar furioso; (: with heat) asfixiarse ♦ n (MED) furúnculo, divieso; **to come to the ~, to come to a ~ (US) comenzar a hervir; to ~ down to**

(fig) reducirse a; **~ over vi salirse, rebosar; (anger etc) llegar al colmo; ~ed egg** n huevo cocido (SP) or pasado (AM); **~ed potatoes** npl patatas fpl (SP) or papas fpl (AM) hervidas; **~er** n caldera; **~er suit** (BRIT) n mono; **~ing point** n punto de ebullición

boisterous [ˈbɔɪstərəs] adj (noisy) bullicioso; (excitable) exuberante; (crowd) tumultuoso

bold [bəʊld] adj valiente, audaz; (pej) descarado; (colour) llamativo

Bolivia [bəˈlɪvɪə] n Bolivia; **~n** adj, n boliviano/a m/f

bollard [ˈbɔləd] (BRIT) n (AUT) poste m

bolt [bəʊlt] n (lock) cerrojo; (with nut) perno, tornillo ♦ adv: **~ upright** rígido, erguido ♦ vt (door) echar el cerrojo a; (also: ~ together) sujetar con tornillos; (food) engullir ♦ vi fugarse; (horse) desbocarse

bomb [bɔm] n bomba ♦ vt bombardear; **~ disposal** n desmontaje m de explosivos; **~er** n (AVIAT) bombardero; **~shell** n (fig) bomba

bond [bɔnd] n (promise) fianza; (FINANCE) bono; (link) vínculo, lazo; (COMM): **in ~** en depósito bajo fianza

bondage [ˈbɔndɪdʒ] n esclavitud f

bone [bəʊn] n hueso; (of fish) espina ♦ vt deshuesar; quitar las espinas a; **~ idle** adj gandul; **~ marrow** n médula

bonfire [ˈbɔnfaɪəʳ] n hoguera, fogata

bonnet [ˈbɔnɪt] n gorra; (BRIT: of car) capó m

bonus [ˈbəʊnəs] n (payment) paga extraordinaria, plus m; (fig) bendición f

bony [ˈbəʊnɪ] adj (arm, face) huesudo; (MED: tissue) óseo; (meat) lleno de huesos; (fish) lleno de espinas

boo [buː] excl ¡uh! ♦ vt abuchear, rechiflar

booby trap [ˈbuːbɪ-] n trampa explosiva

book [buk] n libro; (of tickets) taco; (of

stamps etc) librito ♦ *vt (ticket)* sacar; *(seat, room)* reservar; **~s** *npl (COMM)* cuentas *fpl*, contabilidad *f*; **~case** *n* librería, estante *m* para libros; **~ing office** *n (BRIT: RAIL)* despacho de billetes *(SP)* or boletos *(AM)*; *(THEATRE)* taquilla *(SP)*, boletería *(AM)*; **~keeping** *n* contabilidad *f*; **~let** *n* folleto; **~maker** *n* corredor *m* de apuestas; **~seller** *n* librero; **~shop**, **~ store** *n* librería

boom [buːm] *n (noise)* trueno, estampido; *(in prices etc)* alza rápida; *(ECON, in population)* boom *m* ♦ *vi (cannon)* hacer gran estruendo, retumbar; *(ECON)* estar en alza

boon [buːn] *n* favor *m*, beneficio

boost [buːst] *n* estímulo, empuje *m* ♦ *vt* estimular, empujar; **~er** *n (MED)* reinyección *f*

boot [buːt] *n* bota; *(BRIT: of car)* maleta, maletero *m* ♦ *vt (COMPUT)* arrancar; **to ~** *(in addition)* además, por añadidura

booth [buːð] *n (telephone ~, voting ~)* cabina

booze [buːz] *(inf) n* bebida

border ['bɔːdə*] *n* borde *m*, margen *m*; *(of a country)* frontera; *(for flowers)* arriate *m* ♦ *vt (road)* bordear; *(another country: also: ~ on)* lindar con; **B~s** *n*: **the B~s** región fronteriza entre Escocia e Inglaterra; **~ on** *vt fus (insanity etc)* rayar en; **~line** *n*: **on the ~line** en el límite; **~line case** *n* caso dudoso

bore [bɔː*] *pt of* **bear** ♦ *vt (hole)* hacer un agujero en; *(well)* perforar; *(person)* aburrir ♦ *n (person)* pelmazo, pesado; *(of gun)* calibre *m*; **to be ~d** estar aburrido; **~dom** *n* aburrimiento

boring ['bɔːrɪŋ] *adj* aburrido

born [bɔːn] *adj*: **to be ~** nacer; **I was ~ in 1960** nací en 1960

borne [bɔːn] *pp of* **bear**

borough ['bʌrə] *n* municipio

borrow ['bɔrəu] *vt*: **to ~ sth (from sb)** tomar algo prestado (a alguien)

Bosnia(-Herzegovina) ['bɔznɪə-(heːtzə'gəuviːnə)] *n* Bosnia (-Herzegovina)

bosom ['buzəm] *n* pecho

boss [bɔs] *n* jefe *m* ♦ *vt (also: ~ about or around)* mangonear; **~y** *adj* mandón/ona

bosun ['bəusn] *n* contramaestre *m*

botany ['bɔtənɪ] *n* botánica

botch [bɔtʃ] *vt (also: ~ up)* arruinar, estropear

both [bəuθ] *adj, pron* ambos/as, los/las dos; **~ of us went, we ~ went** fuimos los dos, ambos fuimos ♦ *adv*: **~ A and B** tanto A como B

bother ['bɔðə*] *vt (worry)* preocupar; *(disturb)* molestar, fastidiar ♦ *vi (also: ~ o.s.)* molestarse ♦ *n (trouble)* dificultad *f*; *(nuisance)* molestia, lata; **to ~ doing** tomarse la molestia de hacer

bottle ['bɔtl] *n* botella; *(small)* frasco; *(baby's)* biberón *m* ♦ *vt* embotellar; **~ up** *vt* suprimir; **~ bank** *n* contenedor *m* de vidrio; **~neck** *n (AUT)* embotellamiento; *(in supply)* obstáculo; **~-opener** *n* abrebotellas *m inv*

bottom ['bɔtəm] *n (of box, sea)* fondo; *(buttocks)* trasero, culo; *(of page)* pie *m*; *(of list)* final *m*; *(of class)* último/a ♦ *adj (lowest)* más bajo; *(last)* último

bough [bau] *n* rama

bought [bɔːt] *pt, pp of* **buy**

boulder ['bəuldə*] *n* canto rodado

bounce [bauns] *vi (ball)* (re)botar; *(cheque)* ser rechazado ♦ *vt* hacer (re)botar ♦ *n (rebound)* (re)bote *m*; **~r** *(inf) n* gorila *m (que echa a los alborotadores de un bar, club etc)*

bound [baund] *pt, pp of* **bind** ♦ *n (leap)* salto; *(gen pl: limit)* límite *m* ♦ *vi (leap)* saltar ♦ *vt (border)* rodear ♦ *adj*: **~ by** rodeado de; **to be ~ to do** sth *(obliged)* tener el deber de hacer algo; **he's ~ to come** es seguro que vendrá; **out of ~s** prohibido el paso; **~ for** con destino a

boundary ['baundri] n límite m

bouquet ['bukeɪ] n (of flowers) ramo

bourgeois ['buəʒwa:] adj burgués/esa m/f

bout [baut] n (of malaria etc) ataque m; (of activity) período; (BOXING etc) combate m, encuentro

bow¹ [bau] n (knot) lazo; (weapon, MUS) arco

bow² [bau] n (of the head) reverencia; (NAUT: also: ~s) proa ♦ vi inclinarse, hacer una reverencia; (yield): **to ~ to** or **before** ceder ante, someterse a

bowels [bauəlz] npl intestinos mpl, vientre m; (fig) entrañas fpl

bowl [baul] n tazón m, cuenco; (ball) bola ♦ vi (CRICKET) arrojar la pelota; see also **bowls**

bow-legged ['bəu'legɪd] adj estevado

bowler ['baulə*] n (CRICKET) lanzador m (de la pelota); (BRIT: also: ~ hat) hongo, bombín m

bowling ['bəulɪŋ] n (game) bochas fpl, bolos mpl; **~ alley** n bolera; **~ green** n pista para bochas

bowls [baulz] n juego de las bochas, bolos mpl

bow tie ['bəu-] n corbata de lazo, pajarita

box [bɔks] n (also: cardboard ~) caja, cajón m; (THEATRE) palco ♦ vt encajonar ♦ vi (SPORT) boxear; **~er** ['bɔksə*] n (person) boxeador m; **~ing** ['bɔksɪŋ] n (SPORT) boxeo; **B~ing Day** (BRIT) n día en que se dan los aguinaldos, 26 de diciembre; **~ing gloves** npl guantes mpl de boxeo; **~ing ring** n ring m, cuadrilátero; **~ office** n taquilla (SP), boletería (AM); **~room** n trastero

carteros y otros proveedores en este día, y de ahí el nombre.

boy [bɔɪ] n (young) niño m; (older) muchacho, chico; (son) hijo

boycott ['bɔɪkɔt] n boicot m ♦ vt boicotear

boyfriend ['bɔɪfrend] n novio

boyish ['bɔɪɪʃ] adj juvenil; (girl) con aspecto de muchacho

B.R. n abbr (formerly = British Rail) ≈ RENFE f (SP)

bra [bra:] n sostén m, sujetador m

brace [breɪs] n (BRIT: also: ~s: on teeth) corrector m, aparato; (tool) berbiquí m ♦ vt (knees, shoulders) tensionar; **~s** npl (BRIT) tirantes mpl; **to ~ o.s.** (fig) prepararse

bracelet ['breɪslɪt] n pulsera, brazalete m

bracing ['breɪsɪŋ] adj vigorizante, tónico

bracket ['brækɪt] n (TECH) soporte m, puntal m; (group) clase f, categoría; (also: brace ~) paréntesis m inv; (also: round ~) paréntesis m inv; (also: square ~) corchete m ♦ vt (word etc) poner entre paréntesis

brag [bræg] vi jactarse

braid [breɪd] n (trimming) galón m; (of hair) trenza

brain [breɪn] n cerebro; **~s** npl sesos mpl; **she's got ~s** es muy lista; **~wash** vt lavar el cerebro; **~wave** n idea luminosa; **~y** adj muy inteligente

braise [breɪz] vt cocer a fuego lento

brake [breɪk] n (on vehicle) freno ♦ vi frenar; **~ light** n luz f de frenado

bran [bræn] n salvado

branch [bra:ntʃ] n rama; (COMM) sucursal f; **~ out** vi (fig) extenderse

brand [brænd] n marca; (fig: type) tipo ♦ vt (cattle) marcar con hierro candente; **~-new** adj flamante, completamente nuevo

brandy ['brændɪ] n coñac m

brash [bræʃ] adj (forward) descarado

brass [brɑːs] n latón m; **the ~** (MUS) los cobres; **~ band** n banda de metal

brat [bræt] (pej) n mocoso/a

brave [breɪv] adj valiente, valeroso ♦ vt (face up to) desafiar; **~ry** n valor m, valentía

brawl [brɔːl] n pelea, reyerta

brazen ['breɪzn] adj descarado, cínico ♦ vt: **to ~ it out** echarle cara

Brazil [brə'zɪl] n (el) Brasil; **~ian** adj, n brasileño/a m/f

breach [briːtʃ] vt abrir brecha en ♦ n (gap) brecha; (breaking): **~ of contract** infracción f de contrato; **~ of the peace** perturbación f del órden público

bread [bred] n pan m; **~ and butter** n pan con mantequilla f; (fig) pan (de cada día); **~bin** n panera; **~crumbs** npl migajas fpl; (CULIN) pan rallado; **~line** n: **on the ~line** en la miseria

breadth [bretθ] n anchura; (fig) amplitud f

breadwinner ['bredwɪnə*] n sustento m de la familia

break [breɪk] (pt broke, pp broken) vt romper; (promise) faltar a; (law) violar, infringir; (record) batir ♦ vi romperse, quebrarse; (storm) estallar; (weather) cambiar; (dawn) despuntar; (news etc) darse a conocer ♦ n (gap) abertura; (fracture) fractura; (time) intervalo; (: at school) (período de) recreo; (chance) oportunidad f; **to ~ the news to sb** comunicar la noticia a uno; **~ down** vt (figures, data) analizar, descomponer ♦ vi (machine) estropearse; (AUT) averiarse; (person) romper a llorar; (talks) fracasar; **~ even** vi cubrir los gastos; **~ free** or **loose** vi escaparse; **~ in** vt (horse etc) domar ♦ vi (burglar) forzar una entrada; (interrupt) interrumpir; **~ into** vt fus (house) forzar; **~ off** vi (speaker) pararse, detenerse; (branch) partir; **~ open** vt (door etc) abrir por la fuerza, forzar; **~ out** vi estallar; (prisoner) escaparse;

to ~ out in spots salirle a uno granos; **~ up** vi (ship) hacerse pedazos; (crowd, meeting) disolverse; (marriage) deshacerse; (SCOL) terminar (el curso) ♦ vt (rocks etc) partir; (journey) partir; (fight etc) acabar con; **~age** n rotura; **~down** n (AUT) avería; (in communications) interrupción f; (MED: also: nervous ~down) colapso, crisis f nerviosa; (of marriage, talks) fracaso; (of statistics) análisis m; **~er** n (ola) rompiente f

breakfast ['brekfəst] n desayuno

break-: **~-in** n robo con allanamiento de morada; **~ing and entering** n (LAW) violación f de domicilio, allanamiento de morada; **~through** n (also fig) avance m; **~water** n rompeolas m inv

breast [brest] n (of woman) pecho, seno; (chest) pecho; (of bird) pechuga; **~-feed** (irreg: like feed) vt, vi amamantar, criar a los pechos; **~-stroke** n braza (de pecho)

breath [breθ] n aliento, respiración f; **to take a deep ~** respirar hondo; **out of ~** sin aliento, sofocado

Breathalyser ® ['breθəlaɪzə*] (BRIT) n alcoholímetro m

breathe [briːð] vt, vi respirar; **~ in** vt, vi aspirar; **~ out** vt, vi espirar; **~r** n respiro; **breathing** n respiración f

breath-: **~less** adj sin aliento, jadeante; **~taking** adj imponente, pasmoso

breed [briːd] (pt, pp bred) vt criar ♦ vi reproducirse, procrear ♦ n (ZOOL) raza, casta; (type) tipo; **~ing** n (of person) educación f

breeze [briːz] n brisa

breezy ['briːzɪ] adj de mucho viento, ventoso; (person) despreocupado

brevity ['brevɪtɪ] n brevedad f

brew [bruː] vt (tea) hacer; (beer) elaborar ♦ vi (fig: trouble) prepararse; (storm) amenazar; **~ery** n fábrica de cerveza, cervecería

bribe [braɪb] n soborno ♦ vt sobornar, cohechar; **~ry** n soborno, cohecho

bric-a-brac ['brɪkəbræk] n inv baratijas fpl

brick [brɪk] n ladrillo; **~layer** n albañil m

bridal ['braɪdl] adj nupcial

bride [braɪd] n novia; **~groom** n novio; **~smaid** n dama de honor

bridge [brɪdʒ] n puente m; (NAUT) puente m de mando; (of nose) caballete m; (CARDS) bridge m ♦ vt (fig): **to ~ a gap** llenar un vacío

bridle ['braɪdl] n brida, freno; **~ path** n camino de herradura

brief [briːf] adj breve, corto ♦ n (LAW) escrito; (task) cometido, encargo ♦ vt informar; **~s** npl (for men) calzoncillos mpl; (for women) bragas fpl; **~case** n cartera (SP), portafolio (AM); **~ing** n (PRESS) informe m; **~ly** adv (glance) fugazmente; (say) en pocas palabras

brigadier [brɪgə'dɪə*] n general m de brigada

bright [braɪt] adj brillante; (room) luminoso; (day) de sol; (person: clever) listo, inteligente; (: lively) alegre; (colour) vivo; (future) prometedor(a); **~en** (also: **~en up**) vt (room) hacer más alegre; (event) alegrar ♦ vi (weather) despejarse; (person) animarse, alegrarse; (prospects) mejorar

brilliance ['brɪljəns] n brillo, brillantez f; (of talent etc) brillantez

brilliant ['brɪljənt] adj brillante; (inf) fenomenal

brim [brɪm] n borde m; (of hat) ala

brine [braɪn] n (CULIN) salmuera

bring [brɪŋ] (pt, pp **brought**) vt (thing, person: with you) traer; (: to sb) llevar, conducir; (trouble, satisfaction) causar; **~ about** vt ocasionar, producir; **~ back** vt volver a traer; (return) devolver; **~ down** vt (government, plane) derribar; (price) rebajar; **~ forward** vt adelantar; **~ off** vt (task, plan) lograr, conseguir; **~ out** vt sacar;

(book etc) publicar; (meaning) subrayar; **~ round** vt (unconscious person) hacer volver en sí; **~ up** vt subir; (person) educar, criar; (question) sacar a colación; (food: vomit) devolver, vomitar

brink [brɪŋk] n borde m

brisk [brɪsk] adj (abrupt: tone) brusco; (person) enérgico, vigoroso; (pace) rápido; (trade) activo

bristle ['brɪsl] n cerda ♦ vi: **to ~ in anger** temblar de rabia

Britain ['brɪtən] n (also: **Great ~**) Gran Bretaña

British ['brɪtɪʃ] adj británico ♦ npl: **the ~ los británicos; ~ Isles** npl: **the ~ Isles** las Islas Británicas; **~ Rail** ≈ RENFE f (SP)

Briton ['brɪtən] n británico/a

brittle ['brɪtl] adj quebradizo, frágil

broach [brəʊtʃ] vt (subject) abordar

broad [brɔːd] adj ancho; (range) amplio; (smile) abierto; (general: outlines etc) general; (accent) cerrado; **in ~ daylight** en pleno día; **~cast** (irreg: like cast) n emisión f ♦ vt (RADIO) emitir; (TV) transmitir ♦ vi emitir; transmitir; **~en** vt ampliar ♦ vi ensancharse; **to ~en one's mind** hacer más tolerante a uno; **~ly** adv en general; **~-minded** adj tolerante, liberal

broccoli ['brɔkəlɪ] n brécol m

brochure ['brəʊʃjuə*] n folleto

broil [brɔɪl] vt (CULIN) asar a la parrilla

broke [brəʊk] pt of **break** ♦ adj (inf) pelado, sin blanca

broken ['brəʊkən] pp of **break** ♦ adj roto; (machine: also: ~ down) averiado; **~ leg** pierna rota; **in ~ English** en un inglés imperfecto; **~-hearted** adj con el corazón partido

broker ['brəʊkə*] n agente m/f, bolsista m/f; (insurance) ~ agente de seguros

brolly ['brɔlɪ] (BRIT: inf) n paraguas m inv

bronchitis [brɔŋ'kaɪtɪs] n bronquitis f

bronze [brɔnz] n bronce m

brooch [brəʊtʃ] n prendedor m, broche m

brood [bruːd] n camada, cría ♦ vi (person) dejarse obsesionar

broom [brum] n escoba; (BOT) retama

Bros. abbr (= Brothers) Hnos

broth [brɔθ] n caldo

brothel ['brɔθl] n burdel m

brother ['brʌðəʳ] n hermano; **~-in-law** n cuñado

brought [brɔːt] pt, pp of **bring**

brow [braʊ] n (forehead) frente m; (eye~) ceja; (of hill) cumbre f

brown [braʊn] adj (colour) marrón; (hair) castaño; (tanned) bronceado, moreno ♦ n (colour) color m marrón or pardo ♦ vt (CULIN) dorar; **~ bread** n pan integral

Brownie ['braʊnɪ] n niña exploradora; **b~** (US: cake) pastel de chocolate con nueces

brown paper n papel m de estraza

brown sugar n azúcar m terciado

browse [braʊz] vi (through book) hojear; (in shop) mirar

bruise [bruːz] n cardenal m (SP), moretón m (AM) ♦ vt magullar

brunch [brʌntʃ] n desayuno-almuerzo

brunette [bruː'net] n morena

brunt [brʌnt] n: **to bear the ~ of** llevar el peso de

brush [brʌʃ] n cepillo; (for painting, shaving etc) brocha; (artist's) pincel m; (with police etc) roce m ♦ vt (sweep) barrer; (groom) cepillar; (also: **~ against**) rozar al pasar; **~ aside** vt rechazar, no hacer caso a; **~ up** vt (knowledge) repasar, refrescar; **~wood** n (sticks) leña

Brussels ['brʌslz] n Bruselas; **~ sprout** n col f de Bruselas

brute [bruːt] n bruto; (person) bestia ♦ adj: **by ~ force** a fuerza bruta

B.Sc. abbr (= Bachelor of Science) licenciado en Ciencias

BSE n abbr (= bovine spongiform encephalopathy) encefalopatía espongiforme bovina

bubble ['bʌbl] n burbuja ♦ vi burbujear, borbotar; **~ bath** n espuma para el baño; **~ gum** n chicle m de globo

buck [bʌk] n (rabbit) conejo macho; (deer) gamo; (US: inf) dólar m ♦ vi corcovear; **to pass the ~ (to sb)** echar a (uno) el muerto; **~ up** vi (cheer up) animarse, cobrar ánimo

---

Buckingham Palace

Buckingham Palace es la residencia oficial del monarca británico en Londres. El palacio se concluyó en 1703 y fue residencia del Duque de Buckingham hasta que, en 1762, pasó a manos de Jorge III. Fue reconstruido en el siglo XIX y posteriormente reformado a principios de este siglo. Una parte del palacio está actualmente abierta al público.

---

bucket ['bʌkɪt] n cubo, balde m

buckle ['bʌkl] n hebilla ♦ vt abrochar con hebilla ♦ vi combarse

bud [bʌd] n (of plant) brote m, yema; (of flower) capullo ♦ vi brotar, echar brotes

Buddhism ['budɪzm] n Budismo

budding ['bʌdɪŋ] adj en ciernes, en embrión

buddy ['bʌdɪ] (US) n compañero, compinche m

budge [bʌdʒ] vt mover; (fig) hacer ceder ♦ vi moverse, ceder

budgerigar ['bʌdʒərɪgɑː*] n periquito

budget ['bʌdʒɪt] n presupuesto ♦ vi: **to ~ for sth** presupuestar algo

budgie ['bʌdʒɪ] n = **budgerigar**

buff [bʌf] adj (colour) color de ante ♦ n (inf: enthusiast) entusiasta m/f

buffalo ['bʌfələʊ] (pl ~ or ~es) n (BRIT) búfalo; (US: bison) bisonte m

buffer ['bʌfə*] n (COMPUT) memoria

intermedia; (RAIL) tope m

buffet¹ ['bufei] n (BRIT: in station) bar m, cafetería; (food) buffet m; ~ **car** (BRIT) n (RAIL) coche-comedor m

buffet² ['bʌfit] vt golpear

bug [bʌg] n (esp US: insect) bicho, sabandija; (COMPUT) error m; (germ) microbio, bacilo; (spy device) micrófono oculto ♦ vt (inf: annoy) fastidiar; (room) poner micrófono oculto en

buggy ['bʌgi] n cochecito de niño

bugle ['bjuːgl] n corneta, clarín m

build [bild] (pt, pp **built**) n (of person) tipo ♦ vt construir, edificar; ~ **up** vt (morale, forces, production) acrecentar; (stocks) acumular; ~**er** n (contractor) contratista m/f; (structure) edificio; ~**ing** n construcción f; ~**ing society** (BRIT) n sociedad f inmobiliaria, cooperativa de construcciones

built [bilt] pt, pp of **build** ♦ adj: ~**-in** (wardrobe etc) empotrado; ~**-up area** n zona urbanizada

bulb [bʌlb] n (BOT) bulbo; (ELEC) bombilla (SP), foco (AM)

Bulgaria [bʌl'gɛəriə] n Bulgaria; ~**n** adj, n búlgaro/a m/f

bulge [bʌldʒ] n bulto, protuberancia ♦ vi bombearse, pandearse; (pocket etc): **to ~ (with)** rebosar (de)

bulk [bʌlk] n masa, mole f; **in ~** (COMM) a granel; **the ~ of** la mayor parte de; ~**y** adj voluminoso, abultado

bull [bul] n toro; (male elephant, whale) macho; ~**dog** n dogo

bulldozer ['buldəuzə*] n bulldozer m

bullet ['bulit] n bala

bulletin ['bulitin] n anuncio, parte m; (journal) boletín m

bulletproof ['bulitpruːf] adj a prueba de balas

bullfight ['bulfait] n corrida de toros; ~**er** n torero; ~**ing** n los toros, el toreo

bullion ['buljən] n oro (or plata) en barras

bullock ['bulək] n novillo

bullring ['bulrin] n plaza de toros

bull's-eye n centro del blanco

bully ['buli] n valentón m, matón m ♦ vt intimidar, tiranizar

bum [bʌm] n (BRIT: backside) culo; (esp US: tramp) vagabundo

bumblebee ['bʌmblbiː] n abejorro

bump [bʌmp] n (blow) tope m, choque m; (jolt) sacudida; (on road etc) bache m; (on head etc) chichón m ♦ vt (strike) chocar contra; ~ **into** vt fus chocar contra, tropezar con; (person) topar con; ~**er** n (AUT) parachoques m inv ♦ adj: ~**er crop/harvest** cosecha abundante; ~**er cars** npl coches mpl de choque; ~**y** adj (road) lleno de baches

bun [bʌn] n (BRIT: cake) pastel m; (US: bread) bollo; (of hair) moño

bunch [bʌntʃ] n (of flowers) ramo; (of keys) manojo; (of bananas) piña; (of people) grupo; (pej) pandilla; ~**es** npl (in hair) coletas fpl

bundle ['bʌndl] n bulto, fardo; (of sticks) haz m; (of papers) legajo ♦ vt (also: ~ up) atar, envolver; **to ~ sth/sb into** meter algo/a alguien precipitadamente

bungalow ['bʌngələu] n bungalow m, chalé m

bungle ['bʌngl] vt hacer mal

bunion ['bʌnjən] n juanete m

bunk [bʌnk] n litera; ~ **beds** npl literas fpl

bunker ['bʌnkə*] n (coal store) carbonera; (MIL) refugio; (GOLF) bunker m

bunny ['bʌni] n (also: ~ **rabbit**) conejito

buoy [bɔi] n boya; ~**ant** adj (ship) capaz de flotar; (economy) boyante; (person) optimista

burden ['bəːdn] n carga ♦ vt cargar

bureau [bjuə'rəu] (pl **bureaux**) n (BRIT: writing desk) escritorio, buró m; (US: chest of drawers) cómoda; (office) oficina, agencia

bureaucracy [bjuə'rɔkrəsi] n

burocracia

burglar ['bɜːglə*] n ladrón/ona m/f;
~ **alarm** n alarma f antirrobo;
~**y** n robo con allanamiento, robo de una casa

burial ['bɛrɪəl] n entierro

burly ['bɜːlɪ] adj fornido, membrudo

Burma ['bɜːmə] n Birmania

burn [bɜːn] (pt, pp **burned** or **burnt**)
vt quemar; (house) incendiar ♦ vi quemarse, arder; incendiarse; (sting) escocer ♦ n quemadura; ~ **down** vt incendiar; ~**er** n (on cooker etc) quemador m; ~**ing** adj (building etc) en llamas; (hot: sand etc) abrasador(a); (ambition) ardiente

burrow ['bʌrəu] n madriguera ♦ vi hacer una madriguera; (rummage) hurgar

bursary ['bɜːsərɪ] (BRIT) n beca

burst [bɜːst] (pt, pp **burst**) vt reventar;
(subj: river: banks etc) romper ♦ vi reventarse; (tyre) pincharse ♦ n (of gunfire) ráfaga; (also: ~ pipe) reventón m; a ~ **of energy/speed/enthusiasm** una explosión de energía/un ímpetu de velocidad/un arranque de entusiasmo; to ~ **into flames** estallar en llamas; to ~ **into tears** deshacerse en lágrimas; to ~ **out laughing** soltar la carcajada; to ~ **open** abrirse de golpe; to be ~**ing with** (subj: container) estar lleno a rebosar de; (person) reventar por de; ~ **into** vt fus (room etc) irrumpir en

bury ['bɛrɪ] vt enterrar; (body) enterrar, sepultar

bus [bʌs] (pl ~es) n autobús m

bush [buʃ] n arbusto; (scrub land) monte m; to beat about the ~ andar(se) con rodeos

bushy [buʃɪ] adj (thick) espeso, poblado

busily ['bɪzɪlɪ] adv afanosamente

business ['bɪznɪs] n (matter) asunto;
(trading) comercio, negocios mpl; (firm) empresa, casa; (occupation) oficio; to **be away on** ~ estar en viaje de negocios; **it's my** ~ **to ...** me toca or corresponde ...; **it's none of my** ~ yo no tengo nada que ver; **he means** ~ habla en serio; ~**like** adj eficiente; ~**man** n hombre m de negocios;
~ **trip** n viaje m de negocios;
~**woman** n mujer f de negocios

busker ['bʌskə*] (BRIT) n músico/a ambulante

bus: ~ **shelter** n parada cubierta;
~ **station** n estación f de autobuses;
~**stop** n parada de autobús

bust [bʌst] n (ANAT) pecho; (sculpture) busto ♦ adj (inf: broken) roto, estropeado; to **go** ~ quebrar

bustle ['bʌsl] n bullicio, movimiento ♦ vi menearse, apresurarse; **bustling** adj (town) animado, bullicioso

busy ['bɪzɪ] adj ocupado, atareado;
(shop, street) concurrido, animado; (TEL: line) comunicando ♦ vt: to ~ **o.s. with** ocuparse en; ~**body** n entrometido/a; ~ **signal** (US) n (TEL) señal f de comunicando

but [bʌt] conj **1** pero; **he's not very bright, but he's hard-working** no es muy inteligente, pero es trabajador
2 (in direct contradiction) sino; **he's not English ~ French** no es inglés sino francés; **he didn't sing ~ he shouted** no cantó sino que gritó
3 (showing disagreement, surprise etc):
~ **that's far too expensive!** ¡pero eso es carísimo!; ~ **it does work!** ¡(pero) sí que funciona!
♦ prep (apart from, except) menos, salvo; **we've had nothing ~ trouble** no hemos tenido más que problemas;
no-one ~ him can do it nadie más que él puede hacerlo; **who ~ a lunatic would do such a thing?** ¿sólo un loco haría una cosa así!; ~ **for you/your help** si no fuera por ti/tu ayuda; **anything ~ that** cualquier

cosa menos eso
♦ *adv* (*just, only*): **she's a child** no es más que una niña; **had I known** si lo hubiera sabido; **I can try at least** al menos lo puedo intentar; **it's all finished** está casi acabado

butcher ['butʃə*] *n* carnicero ♦ *vt* hacer una carnicería con; (*cattle etc*) matar; **~'s (shop)** *n* carnicería
butler ['bʌtlə*] *n* mayordomo
butt [bʌt] *n* (*barrel*) tonel *m*; (*of gun*) culata *f*; (*of cigarette*) colilla; (BRIT: *fig: target*) blanco ♦ *vt* dar cabezadas contra, top(et)ar; **~ in** *vi* (*interrupt*) interrumpir
butter ['bʌtə*] *n* mantequilla ♦ *vt* untar con mantequilla; **~cup** *n* botón *m* de oro
butterfly ['bʌtəflaɪ] *n* mariposa; (SWIMMING: *also*: **~ stroke**) braza de mariposa
buttocks ['bʌtəks] *npl* nalgas *fpl*
button ['bʌtn] *n* botón *m*; (US) placa, chapa *f* ♦ *vt* (*also*: **~ up**) abotonar, abrochar ♦ *vi* abrocharse
buttress ['bʌtrɪs] *n* contrafuerte *m*
buy [baɪ] (*pt, pp* **bought**) *vt* comprar ♦ *n* compra; **to sth/sth from sb** comprarle algo a alguien; **to sb a drink** invitar a alguien a tomar algo; **~er** *n* comprador(a) *m/f*
buzz [bʌz] *n* zumbido; (*inf: phone call*) llamada (por teléfono) ♦ *vi* zumbar; **~er** *n* timbre *m*; **~ word** *n* palabra que está de moda

---KEYWORD---

by [baɪ] *prep* **1** (*referring to cause, agent*) por; de; **killed ~ lightning** muerto por un relámpago; **a painting ~ Picasso** un cuadro de Picasso
2 (*referring to method, manner, means*): **~ bus/car/train** en autobús/coche/tren; **to pay ~ cheque** pagar con un cheque; **~ moonlight/candlelight** a la luz de la luna/una vela; **~ saving**

hard, he ... ahorrando, ...
3 (*via, through*) por; **we came ~ Dover** vinimos por Dover
4 (*close to, past*): **the house ~ the river** la casa junto al río; **she rushed ~ me** pasó a mi lado como una exhalación; **I go ~ the post office every day** paso por delante de Correos todos los días
5 (*time: not later than*) para; (*: during*): **~ daylight** de día; **~ 4 o'clock** para las cuatro; **~ this time tomorrow** mañana a estas horas; **~ the time I got here it was too late** cuando llegué ya era demasiado tarde
6 (*amount*): **~ the metre/kilo** por metro/kilo; **paid ~ the hour** pagado por hora
7 (MATH, *measure*): **to divide/multiply ~ 3** dividir/multiplicar por 3; **a room 3 metres ~ 4** una habitación de 3 metros por 4; **it's broader ~ a metre** es un metro más ancho
8 (*according to*) según, de acuerdo con; **it's 3 o'clock ~ my watch** según mi reloj, son las tres; **it's all right ~ me** por mí, está bien
9: (**all**) **~ oneself** *etc* todo solo; **he did it (all) ~ himself** lo hizo él solo; **he was standing (all) ~ himself in a corner** estaba de pie solo en un rincón
10: **~ the way** a propósito, por cierto; **this wasn't my idea, ~ the way** pues, no fue idea mía
♦ *adv* **1** *see* **go**; **pass** *etc*
2: **~ and ~** finalmente; **they'll come back ~ and ~** acabarán volviendo; **~ and large** en líneas generales, en general

bye(-bye) ['baɪ('baɪ)] *excl* adiós, hasta luego
bye(e)-law *n* ordenanza municipal
by-: **~election** (BRIT) *n* elección *f* parcial; **~gone** ['baɪgɔn] *adj* pasado, del pasado ♦ *n*: **let ~gones be**

~gones lo pasado, pasado está; **~pass** ['baɪpɑːs] n carretera de circunvalación; (MED) (operación f de) by-pass m ♦ vt evitar; **~product** n subproducto, derivado; (of situation) consecuencia; **~stander** ['baɪstændə*] n espectador(a) m/f

byte [baɪt] n (COMPUT) byte m, octeto

byword ['baɪwɜːd] n: **to be a ~ for** ser conocidísimo por

C, c

C [siː] n (MUS) do m

C. abbr (= centigrade) C.

C.A. abbr = **chartered accountant**

cab [kæb] n taxi m; (of truck) cabina

cabbage ['kæbɪdʒ] n col f, berza

cabin ['kæbɪn] n cabaña; (on ship) camarote m; (on plane) cabina; **~ crew** n tripulación f de cabina; **~ cruiser** n yate m de motor

cabinet ['kæbɪnɪt] n (POL) consejo de ministros; (furniture) armario; (also: display ~) vitrina

cable ['keɪbl] n cable m ♦ vt cablegrafiar; **~car** n teleférico; **~ television** n televisión f por cable

cache [kæʃ] n (of arms, drugs etc) alijo

cackle ['kækl] vi lanzar risotadas; (hen) cacarear

cactus ['kæktəs] (pl cacti) cacto

cadge [kædʒ] (inf) vt gorronear

Caesarean [siː'zɛərɪən] adj: **~ (section)** cesárea

café ['kæfeɪ] n café m

cafeteria [kæfɪ'tɪərɪə] n cafetería

cage [keɪdʒ] n jaula

cagey ['keɪdʒɪ] (inf) adj cauteloso, reservado

cagoule [kə'guːl] n chubasquero

cajole [kə'dʒəul] vt engatusar

cake [keɪk] n (CULIN: large) tarta; (: small) pastel m; (of soap) pastilla; **~d** adj: **~d with** cubierto de

calculate ['kælkjuleɪt] vt calcular;

calculation [-'leɪʃən] n cálculo, cómputo; **calculator** n calculadora

calendar ['kæləndə*] n calendario; **~ month/year** n mes m/año civil

calf [kɑːf] (pl calves) n (of cow) ternero, becerro; (of other animals) cría; (also: ~skin) piel f de becerro; (ANAT) pantorrilla

calibre ['kælɪbə*] (US caliber) n calibre m

call [kɔːl] vt llamar; (meeting) convocar ♦ vi (shout) llamar; (TEL) llamar (por teléfono), telefonear (esp AM); (visit: also: ~ in, ~ round) hacer una visita ♦ n llamada; (of bird) canto; **to be ~ed** llamarse; **on ~** (nurse, doctor etc) de guardia; **~ back** vi (return) volver; (TEL) volver a llamar; **~ for** vt fus (demand) pedir, exigir; (fetch) venir por (SP), pasar por (AM); **~ off** vt (cancel: meeting, race) cancelar; (: deal) anular; (: strike) desconvocar; **~ on** vt fus (visit) visitar; (turn to) acudir a; **~ out** vi gritar, dar voces; **~ up** vt (MIL) llamar al servicio militar; (TEL) llamar; **~box** (BRIT) n cabina telefónica; **~er** n visita; (TEL) usuario/a; **~ girl** n prostituta; **~in** (US) n (programa m) coloquio (por teléfono); **~ing** n vocación f; (occupation) profesión f; **~ing card** (US) n tarjeta comercial or de visita

callous ['kæləs] adj insensible, cruel

calm [kɑːm] adj tranquilo; (sea) liso, en calma ♦ n calma, tranquilidad f ♦ vt calmar, tranquilizar; **~ down** vi calmarse, tranquilizarse ♦ vt calmar, tranquilizar

Calor gas ® ['kælə*-] n butano

calorie ['kælərɪ] n caloría

calves [kɑːvz] npl of **calf**

Cambodia [kæm'bəudjə] n Camboya

camcorder ['kæmkɔːdə*] n videocámara

came [keɪm] pt of **come**

camel ['kæməl] n camello

camera ['kæmərə] n máquina fotográfica; (CINEMA, TV) cámara; **in ~** (LAW) a puerta cerrada; **~man** n cámara m

camouflage ['kæməflɑːʒ] n camuflaje m ♦ vt camuflar

camp [kæmp] n campamento, camping m; (MIL) campamento; (for prisoners) campo; (fig: faction) bando ♦ vi acampar ♦ adj afectado, afeminado

campaign [kæm'peɪn] n (MIL, also POL) campaña ♦ vi hacer campaña

camp: ~**bed** (BRIT) n cama de campaña; ~**er** n campista m/f; (vehicle) caravana; ~**ing** n camping m; **to go** ~**ing** hacer camping; ~**site** n camping m

campus ['kæmpəs] n ciudad f universitaria

can¹ [kæn] n (of oil, water) bidón m; (tin) lata, bote m ♦ vt enlatar

---
KEYWORD
---

can² [kæn] (negative **cannot, can't**; conditional and pt could) aux vb **1** (be able to) poder; **you ~ do it if you try** puedes hacerlo si lo intentas; **I ~'t see you** no te veo

2 (know how to) saber; **I ~ swim/play tennis/drive** sé nadar/jugar al tenis/conducir; **~ you speak French?** ¿hablas or sabes hablar francés?

3 (may) poder; **~ I use your phone?** ¿me dejas or puedo usar tu teléfono?

4 (expressing disbelief, puzzlement etc): **it ~'t be true!** ¡no puede ser (verdad)!; **what CAN he want?** ¿qué querrá?

5 (expressing possibility, suggestion etc): **he could be in the library** podría estar en la biblioteca; **she could have been delayed** pudo haberse retrasado

Canada ['kænədə] n (el) Canadá; **Canadian** [kə'neɪdɪən] adj, n canadiense m/f

canal [kə'næl] n canal m

canary [kə'nɛərɪ] n canario m; **the C~ Islands** npl las (Islas) Canarias

cancel ['kænsəl] vt cancelar; (train) suprimir; (cross out) tachar, borrar; ~**lation** [-'leɪʃən] n cancelación f; supresión f

cancer ['kænsə*] n cáncer m; **C~** (ASTROLOGY) Cáncer m

candid ['kændɪd] adj franco, abierto

candidate ['kændɪdeɪt] n candidato/a

candle ['kændl] n vela; (in church) cirio; ~**light** n: **by ~light** a la luz de una vela; ~**stick** n (single) candelero; (low) palmatoria; (bigger, ornate) candelabro

candour ['kændə*] (US **candor**) n franqueza

candy ['kændɪ] n azúcar m cande; (US) caramelo; ~**floss** (BRIT) n algodón m (azucarado)

cane [keɪn] n (BOT) caña; (stick) vara, palmeta; (for furniture) mimbre f ♦ (BRIT) vt (SCOL) castigar (con vara)

canister ['kænɪstə*] n bote m, lata; (of gas) bombona

cannabis ['kænəbɪs] n marijuana

canned [kænd] adj en lata, de lata

cannon ['kænən] (pl ~ or ~**s**) n cañón m

cannot ['kænɔt] = **can not**

canoe [kə'nuː] n canoa; (SPORT) piragua; ~**ing** n piragüismo

canon ['kænən] n (clergyman) canónigo; (standard) canon m

can-opener n abrelatas m inv

canopy ['kænəpɪ] n dosel m; toldo

can't [kænt] = **can not**

canteen [kæn'tiːn] n (eating place) cantina; (BRIT: of cutlery) juego

canter ['kæntə*] vi ir a medio galope

canvas ['kænvəs] n (material) lona; (painting) lienzo; (NAUT) velas fpl

canvass ['kænvəs] vi (POL): **to ~ for** solicitar votos por ♦ vt (COMM) sondear

canyon ['kænjən] n cañón m

cap [kæp] n (hat) gorra; (of pen) capuchón m; (of bottle) tapa, tapón m; (contraceptive) diafragma m; (for toy gun) cápsula ♦ vt (outdo) superar;

(*limit*) recortar

capability [keɪpə'bɪlɪtɪ] *n* capacidad *f*

capable ['keɪpəbl] *adj* capaz

capacity [kə'pæsɪtɪ] *n* capacidad *f*; (*position*) calidad *f*

cape [keɪp] *n* capa; (GEO) cabo

caper ['keɪpə*] *n* (*also: ~s*) (CULIN: *gen: ~s*) alcaparra; (*prank*) broma

capital ['kæpɪtl] *n* (*also: ~ city*) capital *f*; (*money*) capital *m*; (*also: ~ letter*) mayúscula; **~ gains tax** *n* impuesto sobre las ganancias de capital; **~ism** *n* capitalismo; **~ist** *adj*, *n* capitalista *m/f*; **~ize on** *vt fus* aprovechar; **~ punishment** *n* pena de muerte

Capitol

El Capitolio (**Capitol**) es el edificio del Congreso (**Congress**) de los Estados Unidos, situado en la ciudad de Washington. Por extensión, también se suele llamar así al edificio en el que tienen lugar las sesiones parlamentarias de la cámara de representantes de muchos de los estados.

Capricorn ['kæprɪkɔːn] *n* (ASTROLOGY) Capricornio

capsize [kæp'saɪz] *vt* volcar, hacer zozobrar ♦ *vi* volcarse, zozobrar

capsule ['kæpsjuːl] *n* cápsula

captain ['kæptɪn] *n* capitán *m*

caption ['kæpʃən] *n* (*heading*) título; (*to picture*) leyenda

captive ['kæptɪv] *adj*, *n* cautivo/a *m/f*

capture ['kæptʃə*] *vt* prender, apresar; (*animal*, COMPUT) capturar; (*place*) tomar; (*attention*) captar, llamar ♦ *n* apresamiento; captura; toma; (*data ~*) formulación *f* de datos

car [kɑː*] *n* coche *m*, carro (AM), automóvil *m*; (US: RAIL) vagón *m*

carafe [kə'ræf] *n* jarra

carat ['kærət] *n* quilate *m*

caravan ['kærəvæn] *n* (BRIT) caravana, ruló *f*; (*in desert*) caravana; **~ning** *n*: to

go ~ning ir de vacaciones en caravana, viajar en caravana; **~ site** (BRIT) *n* camping *m* para caravanas

carbohydrate [kɑːbəu'haɪdreɪt] *n* hidrato de carbono; (*food*) fécula

carbon ['kɑːbən] *n* carbono; **~ paper** *n* papel *m* carbón

car boot sale *n* mercadillo organizado en un aparcamiento, en el que se exponen las mercancías en el maletero del coche

carburettor [kɑːbju'retə*] (US **carburetor**) *n* carburador *m*

card [kɑːd] *n* (*material*) cartulina; (*index ~ etc*) ficha; (*playing ~*) carta, naipe *m*; (*visiting ~, greetings ~ etc*) tarjeta; **~board** *n* cartón *m*

cardiac ['kɑːdɪæk] *adj* cardíaco

cardigan ['kɑːdɪgən] *n* rebeca

cardinal ['kɑːdɪnl] *adj* cardinal; (*importance*, *principal*) esencial ♦ *n* cardenal *m*

card index *n* fichero

care [keə*] *n* cuidado; (*worry*) inquietud *f*; (*charge*) cargo, custodia ♦ *vi*: to **~ about** (*person*, *animal*) tener cariño a; (*thing*, *idea*) preocuparse por; **~ of** en casa de, al cuidado de; **in sb's ~** a cargo de uno; to **take ~** to cuidarse de, tener cuidado de; to **take ~ of** cuidar; (*problem etc*) ocuparse de; **I don't ~** no me importa; **I couldn't ~ less** eso me trae sin cuidado; **~ for** *vt fus* cuidar a; (*like*) querer

career [kə'rɪə*] *n* profesión *f*; (*in work*, *school*) carrera ♦ *vi* (*also: ~ along*) correr a toda velocidad; **~ woman** *n* mujer *f* dedicada a su profesión

care: **~free** *adj* despreocupado; **~ful** *adj* cuidadoso; (*cautious*) cauteloso; **(be) ~ful!** ¡tenga cuidado!; **~fully** *adv* con cuidado, cuidadosamente; con cautela; **~less** *adj* descuidado; (*heedless*) poco atento; **~lessness** *n* descuido; falta de atención; **~r** ['keərə*] *n* enfermero/a *m/f* (*official*); (*unpaid*) persona que cuida a un pariente o vecino

caress [kəˈres] n caricia ♦ vt acariciar

caretaker [ˈkeəteɪkə*] n portero/a, conserje m/f

car-ferry n transbordador m para coches

cargo [ˈkɑːgəu] (pl ~es) n cargamento, carga

car hire n alquiler m de automóviles

Caribbean [kærɪˈbiːən] n: **the ~ (Sea)** el (Mar) Caribe

caring [ˈkeərɪŋ] adj humanitario; (behaviour) afectuoso

carnation [kɑːˈneɪʃən] n clavel m

carnival [ˈkɑːnɪvəl] n carnaval m; (US: funfair) parque m de atracciones

carol [ˈkærəl] n: **(Christmas) ~** villancico

carp [kɑːp] n (fish) carpa

car park (BRIT) n aparcamiento, parking m

carpenter [ˈkɑːpɪntə*] n carpintero/a

carpet [ˈkɑːpɪt] n alfombra; (fitted) moqueta ♦ vt alfombrar

car phone n teléfono movil

car rental (US) n alquiler m de coches

carriage [ˈkærɪdʒ] n (BRIT: RAIL) vagón m; (horse-drawn) coche m; (of goods) transporte m; (: cost) porte m, flete m; **~way** (BRIT) n (part of road) calzada

carrier [ˈkærɪə*] n (transport company) transportista, empresa de transportes; (MED) portador m/a; **~ bag** (BRIT) n bolsa de papel or plástico

carrot [ˈkærət] n zanahoria

carry [ˈkærɪ] vt (subj: person) llevar; (transport) transportar; (involve: responsibilities etc) entrañar, implicar; (MED) ser portador de ♦ vi (sound) oírse; **to get carried away** (fig) entusiasmarse; **~ on** vi (continue) seguir (adelante), continuar ♦ vt proseguir, continuar; **~ out** vt (orders) cumplir; (investigation) llevar a cabo, realizar; **~ cot** (BRIT) n cuna portátil; **~-on** (inf) n (fuss) lío

cart [kɑːt] n carro, carreta ♦ vt (inf: transport) acarrear

carton [ˈkɑːtən] n (box) caja (de cartón); (of milk etc) bote m; (of yogurt) tarrina

cartoon [kɑːˈtuːn] n (PRESS) caricatura; (comic strip) tira cómica; (film) dibujos mpl animados

cartridge [ˈkɑːtrɪdʒ] n cartucho; (of pen) recambio; (of record player) cápsula

carve [kɑːv] vt (meat) trinchar; (wood, stone) cincelar, esculpir; (initials etc) grabar; **~ up** vt dividir, repartir; **carving** n (object) escultura; (design) talla; (art) tallado; **carving knife** n trinchante m

car wash n lavado de coches

case [keɪs] n (container) caja; (MED) caso; (for jewels etc) estuche m; (LAW) causa, proceso; (BRIT: also: suit~) maleta; **in ~ of** en caso de; **in any ~** en todo caso; **just in ~** por si acaso

cash [kæʃ] n dinero en efectivo, dinero contante ♦ vt cobrar, hacer efectivo; **to pay (in) ~** pagar al contado; **~ on delivery** cóbrese al entregar; **~book** n libro de caja; **~ card** n tarjeta f dinero; **~ desk** (BRIT) n caja; **~ dispenser** n cajero automático

cashew [kæˈʃuː] n (also: ~ nut) anacardo

cash flow n flujo de fondos, cash-flow m

cashier [kæˈʃɪə*] n cajero/a

cashmere [kæʃˈmɪə*] n cachemira

cash register n caja

casing [ˈkeɪsɪŋ] n revestimiento

casino [kəˈsiːnəu] n casino

casket [ˈkɑːskɪt] n cofre m, estuche m; (US: coffin) ataúd m

casserole [ˈkæsərəul] n (food, pot) cazuela

cassette [kæˈset] n cassette f; **~ player/recorder** n tocacassettes m inv, cassette m

cast [kɑːst] (pt, pp cast) vt (throw) echar, arrojar, lanzar; (glance, eyes) dirigir; (THEATRE): **to ~ sb as Othello**

dar a uno el papel de Otelo ♦ vi (FISHING) lanzar ♦ n (THEATRE) reparto; (also: plaster ~) vaciado; **to ~ one's vote** votar; **to ~ doubt on** suscitar dudas acerca de; **~ off** vt (NAUT) desamarrar; (KNITTING) cerrar (los puntos); **~ on** vi (KNITTING) poner los puntos

castanets [kæstə'nɛts] npl castañuelas fpl

castaway ['kɑ:stəweɪ] n náufrago/a

caster sugar ['kɑ:stə*-] n (BRIT) n azúcar m extrafino

Castile [kæs'ti:l] n Castilla; **Castilian** adj, n castellano/a m/f

casting vote ['kɑ:stɪŋ-] (BRIT) n voto decisivo

cast iron n hierro fundido

castle ['kɑ:sl] n castillo; (CHESS) torre f

castor oil ['kɑ:stə*-] n aceite m de ricino

casual ['kæʒjul] adj fortuito; (irregular: work etc) eventual, temporero; (unconcerned) despreocupado; (clothes) de sport; **~ly** adv de manera despreocupada; (dress) de sport

casualty ['kæʒjultɪ] n víctima, herido; (dead) muerto; (MED: department) urgencias fpl

cat [kæt] n gato; (big ~) felino

Catalan ['kætəlæn] adj, n catalán/ana m/f

catalogue ['kætəlɒg] (US **catalog**) n catálogo ♦ vt catalogar

Catalonia [kætə'ləunɪə] n Cataluña

catalyst ['kætəlɪst] n catalizador m

catalytic convertor [kætə'lɪtɪk kən'vɜ:tə*] n catalizador m

catapult ['kætəpʌlt] n tirachinas m inv

catarrh [kə'tɑ:*] n catarro

catastrophe [kə'tæstrəfɪ] n catástrofe f

catch [kætʃ] (pt, pp **caught**) vt coger (SP), agarrar (AM); (arrest) detener; (grasp) asir; (breath) contener; (surprise: person) sorprender; (attract: attention) captar; (hear) oír; (MED) contagiarse de; coger; (also: ~ up) alcanzar ♦ vi (fire)

encenderse; (in branches etc) enredarse ♦ n (fish etc) pesca; (act of catching) cogida; (hidden problem) dificultad f; (game) pilla-pilla; (of lock) pestillo, cerradura; **to ~ fire** encenderse; **to ~ sight of** divisar; **~ on** vi (understand) caer en la cuenta; (grow popular) hacerse popular; **~ up** vi (fig) ponerse al día; **~ing** ['kætʃɪŋ] adj (MED) contagioso; **~ment area** ['kætʃmənt-] (BRIT) n zona de captación; **~phrase** ['kætʃfreɪz] n lema m, eslogan m; **~y** ['kætʃɪ] adj (tune) pegadizo

category ['kætɪgərɪ] n categoría, clase f

cater ['keɪtə*] vi: **to ~ for** (BRIT) abastecer a; (needs) atender a; (COMM: parties etc) proveer comida a; **~er** n abastecedor(a) m/f, proveedor(a) m/f; **~ing** n (trade) hostelería

caterpillar ['kætəpɪlə*] n oruga, gusano

cathedral [kə'θi:drəl] n catedral f

catholic ['kæθəlɪk] adj (tastes etc) amplio; **C~** adj, n (REL) católico/a m/f

CAT scan [kæt-] n TAC f, tomografía

Cat'seye ® ['kæts'aɪ] (BRIT) n (AUT) catafoto

cattle ['kætl] npl ganado

catty ['kætɪ] adj malicioso, rencoroso

caucus ['kɔ:kəs] n (POL) camarilla política; (: US: to elect candidates) comité m electoral

caught [kɔ:t] pt, pp of **catch**

cauliflower ['kɒlɪflauə*] n coliflor f

cause [kɔ:z] n causa, motivo, razón f; (principle: also: POL) causa ♦ vt causar

caution ['kɔ:ʃən] n cautela, prudencia; (warning) advertencia, amonestación f ♦ vt amonestar; **cautious** adj cauteloso, prudente, precavido

cavalry ['kævəlrɪ] n caballería

cave [keɪv] n cueva, caverna; **~ in** vi (roof etc) derrumbarse, hundirse

caviar(e) ['kævɪɑ:*] n caviar m

CB n abbr (= Citizens' Band (Radio))

banda ciudadana

CBI n abbr (= Confederation of British Industry) ≈ C.E.O.E. f (SP)

cc abbr = cubic centimetres; = **carbon copy**

CD n abbr (= compact disc) DC m; (player) (reproductor m de) disco compacto; ~ **player** n lector m de compact disc, reproductor m de compact disc; ~**-ROM** [si:di:'rɔm] n abbr CD-ROM m

cease [si:s] vt, vi cesar; ~**fire** n alto m el fuego; ~**less** adj incesante

cedar ['si:də*] n cedro

ceiling ['si:lɪŋ] n techo; (fig) límite m

celebrate ['selɪbreɪt] vt celebrar ♦ vi divertirse; ~**d** adj célebre; **celebration** [-'breɪʃən] n fiesta, celebración f

celery ['selərɪ] n apio

cell [sel] n celda; (BIOL) célula; (ELEC) elemento

cellar ['selə*] n sótano; (for wine) bodega

cello ['tʃeləu] n violoncelo

Cellophane ® ['seləfeɪn] n celofán m

cellphone ['selfəun] n teléfono celular

Celt [kelt, selt] adj, n celta m/f; ~**ic** adj celta

cement [sə'ment] n cemento; ~ **mixer** n hormigonera

cemetery ['semɪtrɪ] n cementerio

censor ['sensə*] n censor m ♦ vt (cut) censurar; ~**ship** n censura

censure ['senʃə*] vt censurar

census ['sensəs] n censo

cent [sent] n (US) (coin) centavo, céntimo; see also **per**

centenary [sen'ti:nərɪ] n centenario

center ['sentə*] (US) = **centre**

centi... [sentɪ] prefix: ~**grade** adj centígrado; ~**litre** (US ~**liter**) n centilitro; ~**metre** (US ~**meter**) n centímetro

centipede ['sentɪpi:d] n ciempiés n inv

central ['sentrəl] adj central; (of house etc) céntrico; **C~ America** n

Centroamérica; ~ **heating** n calefacción f central; ~**ize** vt centralizar

centre ['sentə*] (US **center**) n centro; (fig) núcleo ♦ vt centrar; ~**-forward** n (SPORT) delantero centro; ~**-half** n (SPORT) medio centro

century ['sentjurɪ] n siglo; **20th** ~ siglo veinte

ceramic [sɪ'ræmɪk] adj cerámico; ~**s** n cerámica

cereal ['si:rɪəl] n cereal m

ceremony ['serɪmənɪ] n ceremonia; **to stand on** ~ hacer ceremonias, estar de cumplido

certain ['sə:tən] adj seguro; (person): **a ~ Mr Smith** un tal Sr Smith; (particular, some) cierto; **for** ~ a ciencia cierta; ~**ly** adv (undoubtedly) ciertamente; (of course) desde luego, por supuesto; ~**ty** n certeza, certidumbre f, seguridad f; (inevitability) certeza

certificate [sə'tɪfɪkɪt] n certificado

certified ['sə:tɪfaɪd]: ~ **mail** n (US) n correo certificado; ~ **public accountant** (US) n contable m/f diplomado/a

certify ['sə:tɪfaɪ] vt certificar; (award diploma to) conceder un diploma a; (declare insane) declarar loco

cervical ['sə:vɪkl] adj cervical

cervix ['sə:vɪks] n cuello del útero

cf. abbr (= compare) cfr

CFC n abbr (= chlorofluorocarbon) CFC m

ch. abbr (= chapter) cap

chain [tʃeɪn] n cadena; (of mountains) cordillera; (of events) sucesión f ♦ vt (also: ~ up) encadenar; ~ **reaction** n reacción f en cadena; ~**-smoke** vi fumar un cigarrillo tras otro; ~ **store** n tienda de una cadena, ≈ gran almacén

chair [tʃeə*] n silla; (armchair) sillón m, butaca; (of university) cátedra; (of meeting etc) presidencia ♦ vt (meeting) presidir; ~**lift** n telesilla; ~**man** n presidente m

chalk [tʃɔːk] n (GEO) creta; (for writing) tiza (SP), gis m (AM)

challenge ['tʃælɪndʒ] n desafío, reto ♦ vt desafiar, retar; (statement, right) poner en duda; **to ~ sb to do sth** retar a uno a que haga algo; **challenging** adj exigente; (tone) de desafío

chamber ['tʃeɪmbə*] n cámara, sala; (POL) cámara; (BRIT: LAW: gen pl) despacho; **~ of commerce** cámara de comercio; **~maid** n camarera; **~ music** n música de cámara

chamois ['ʃæmwɑː] n gamuza

champagne [ʃæm'peɪn] n champaña m, champán m

champion ['tʃæmpɪən] n campeón/ona m/f; (of cause) defensor(a) m/f; **~ship** n campeonato

chance [tʃɑːns] n (opportunity) ocasión f, oportunidad f; (likelihood) posibilidad f; (risk) riesgo ♦ vt arriesgar, probar ♦ adj fortuito, casual; **to ~ it** arriesgarse, intentarlo; **to take a ~** arriesgarse; **by ~** por casualidad

chancellor ['tʃɑːnsələ*] n canciller m; **C~ of the Exchequer** (BRIT) n Ministro de Hacienda

chandelier [ʃændə'lɪə*] n araña (de luces)

change [tʃeɪndʒ] vt cambiar; (replace) cambiar, reemplazar; (gear, clothes, job) cambiar de; (transform) transformar ♦ vi cambiar(se); (trains) hacer transbordo; (traffic lights) cambiar de color; (be transformed): **to ~ into** transformarse en ♦ n cambio; (alteration) modificación f, transformación f; (of clothes) muda; (coins) suelto, sencillo; (money returned) vuelta; **to ~ gear** (AUT) cambiar de marcha; **to ~ one's mind** cambiar de opinión o idea; **for a ~** para variar; **~able** adj (weather) cambiable; **~ machine** n máquina de cambio; **~over** n (to new system) cambio; **changing** adj cambiante; **changing**

room (BRIT) n vestuario

channel ['tʃænl] n (TV) canal m; (of river) cauce m; (groove) conducto m; (fig: medium) medio ♦ vt (river etc) encauzar; **the (English) C~** el Canal de la Mancha; **the C~ Islands** las Islas Normandas; **the C~ Tunnel** el túnel del Canal de la Mancha, el Eurotúnel; **~-hopping** n (TV) zapping m

chant [tʃɑːnt] n (of crowd) gritos mpl; (REL) canto ♦ vt (slogan, word) repetir a gritos

chaos ['keɪɔs] n caos m

chap [tʃæp] (BRIT: inf) n (man) tío, tipo

chapel ['tʃæpl] n capilla

chaperone ['ʃæpərəʊn] n carabina

chaplain ['tʃæplɪn] n capellán m

chapped [tʃæpt] adj agrietado

chapter ['tʃæptə*] n capítulo

char [tʃɑː*] vt (burn) carbonizar, chamuscar

character ['kærɪktə*] n carácter m, naturaleza, índole f; (moral strength, personality) carácter; (in novel, film) personaje m; **~istic** adj característico ♦ n característica

charcoal ['tʃɑːkəʊl] n carbón m vegetal; (ART) carboncillo

charge [tʃɑːdʒ] n (LAW) cargo, acusación f; (cost) precio, coste m; (responsibility) cargo ♦ vt (LAW): **to ~ (with)** acusar (de); (battery) cargar; (price) pedir; (customer) cobrar ♦ vi precipitarse; (MIL) cargar, atacar; **~s** npl: **to reverse the ~s** (BRIT: TEL) revertir el cobro; **to take ~ of** hacerse cargo de, encargarse de; **to be in ~ of** estar encargado de; (business) mandar; **how much do you ~?** ¿cuánto cobra usted?; **to ~ an expense (up) to sb's account** cargar algo a cuenta de alguien; **~ card** n tarjeta de cuenta

charity ['tʃærɪtɪ] n caridad f; (organization) sociedad f benéfica; (money, gifts) limosnas fpl

charm [tʃɑːm] n encanto, atractivo; (talisman) hechizo; (on bracelet) dije m

chart 348 **chestnut**

♦ vt encantar; **~ing** adj encantador(a)

chart [tʃɑːt] n (diagram) cuadro; (graph) gráfica; (map) carta de navegación ♦ vt (course) trazar; (progress) seguir; **~s** npl (Top 40): **the ~s** ≈ los 40 principales (SP)

charter [ˈtʃɑːtə*] vt (plane) alquilar; (ship) fletar ♦ n (document) carta; (of university, company) estatutos mpl; **~ed accountant** (BRIT) n contable m/f diplomado/a; **~ flight** n vuelo chárter

chase [tʃeɪs] vt (pursue) perseguir; (also: ~ away) ahuyentar ♦ n persecución f

chasm [ˈkæzəm] n sima

chassis [ˈʃæsɪ] n chasis m

chat [tʃæt] vi (also: have a ~) charlar ♦ n charla; **~ show** (BRIT) n programa m de entrevistas

chatter [ˈtʃætə*] vi (person) charlar; (teeth) castañetear ♦ n (of birds) parloteo; (of people) charla, cháchara; **~box** (inf) n parlanchín/ina m/f

chatty [ˈtʃætɪ] adj (style) informal; (person) hablador(a)

chauffeur [ˈʃəʊfə*] n chófer m

chauvinist [ˈʃəʊvɪnɪst] n (male ~) machista m; (nationalist) chovinista m/f

cheap [tʃiːp] adj barato; (joke) de mal gusto; (poor quality) de mala calidad ♦ adv barato; **~ day return** n billete m de ida y vuelta al mismo día; **~er** adj más barato; **~ly** adv barato, a bajo precio

cheat [tʃiːt] vi hacer trampa ♦ vt: to ~ sb (out of sth) estafar (algo) a uno ♦ n (person) tramposo/a

check [tʃek] vt (examine) controlar; (facts) comprobar; (halt) parar, detener; (restrain) refrenar, restringir ♦ n (inspection) control m, inspección f; (curb) freno; (US: bill) nota, cuenta; (US) = **cheque**; (pattern: gen pl) cuadro ♦ adj (also: ~ed: pattern, cloth) a cuadros; **~ in** vi (at hotel) firmar el registro; (at airport) facturar el equipaje ♦ vt (luggage) facturar; **~ out** vi (of hotel) marcharse; **~ up** vi: to ~ up on

sth comprobar algo; to ~ up on sb investigar a alguien; **~ered** (US) adj = **check**; **chequered**; **~ers** (US) n juego de damas; **~-in (desk)** n mostrador m de facturación; **~ing account** (US) n cuenta corriente; **~mate** n jaque m mate; **~out** n caja; **~point** n (punto de) control m; **~room** (US) n consigna; **~up** n (MED) reconocimiento general

cheek [tʃiːk] n mejilla; (impudence) descaro; **what a ~!** ¡qué cara!; **~bone** n pómulo; **~y** adj fresco, descarado

cheep [tʃiːp] vi piar

cheer [tʃɪə*] vt vitorear, aplaudir; (gladden) alegrar, animar ♦ vi dar vivas ♦ n viva m; **~s** npl aplausos mpl; **~s!** ¡salud!; **~ up** vi animarse ♦ vt alegrar, animar; **~ful** adj alegre

cheerio [tʃɪərɪˈəʊ] excl (BRIT) ¡hasta luego!

cheese [tʃiːz] n queso; **~board** n tabla de quesos

cheetah [ˈtʃiːtə] n leopardo cazador

chef [ʃef] n jefe/a m/f de cocina

chemical [ˈkemɪkəl] adj químico ♦ n producto químico

chemist [ˈkemɪst] n (BRIT: pharmacist) farmacéutico/a; (scientist) químico/a; **~ry** n química; **~'s (shop)** (BRIT) n farmacia

cheque [tʃek] (US **check**) n cheque m; **~book** n talonario de cheques (SP), chequera (AM); **~ card** n tarjeta de cheque

chequered [ˈtʃekəd] (US **checkered**) adj (fig) accidentado

cherish [ˈtʃerɪʃ] vt (love) querer, apreciar; (protect) cuidar; (hope etc) abrigar

cherry [ˈtʃerɪ] n cereza; (also: ~ tree) cerezo

chess [tʃes] n ajedrez m; **~board** n tablero de ajedrez

chest [tʃest] n (ANAT) pecho; (box) cofre m, cajón m; **~ of drawers** n cómoda

chestnut [ˈtʃesnʌt] n castaña; **~ (tree)**

n castaño

chew [tʃuː] vt mascar, masticar; **~ing gum** n chicle m

chic [ʃiːk] adj elegante

chick [tʃik] n pollito, polluelo; (inf: girl) chica

chicken ['tʃikin] n gallina, pollo; (food) pollo; (inf: coward) gallina m/f; **~ out** (inf) vi rajarse; **~pox** n varicela

chicory ['tʃikəri] n (for coffee) achicoria; (salad) escarola

chief [tʃiːf] n jefe.a m/f ♦ adj principal; **~ executive** n director(a) m/f general; **~ly** adv principalmente

chilblain ['tʃilblein] n sabañón m

child [tʃaild] n (pl **children**) niño/a; (offspring) hijo/a; **~birth** n parto; **~hood** n niñez f, infancia; **~ish** adj pueril, aniñado; **~like** adj de niño; **~ minder** (BRIT) n madre f de día; **~ren** ['tʃildrən] npl of **child**

Chile ['tʃili] n Chile m; **~an** adj, n chileno.a m/f

chill [tʃil] n frío; (MED) resfriado ♦ vt enfriar; (CULIN) congelar

chil(l)i ['tʃili] (BRIT) n chile m (SP), ají m (AM)

chilly ['tʃili] adj frío

chime [tʃaim] n repique m; (of clock) campanada ♦ vi repicar; sonar

chimney ['tʃimni] n chimenea; **~ sweep** n deshollinador m

chimpanzee [tʃimpæn'ziː] n chimpancé m

chin [tʃin] n mentón m, barbilla

china ['tʃainə] n porcelana; (crockery) loza

China ['tʃainə] n China; **Chinese** [tʃai'niːz] adj chino ♦ n inv chino/a; (LING) chino

chink [tʃiŋk] n (opening) grieta, hendedura; (noise) tintineo

chip [tʃip] n (gen pl CULIN: BRIT) patata (SP) or papa (AM) frita; (: US: also: potato ~) patata or papa frita; (of wood) astilla; (of glass, stone) lasca; (at poker) ficha; (COMPUT) chip m ♦ vt (cup, plate)

desconchar

chiropodist [kɪ'rɔpədist] (BRIT) n pedicuro/a, callista m/f

chirp [tʃəːp] vi (bird) gorjear, piar

chisel ['tʃizl] n (for wood) escoplo; (for stone) cincel m

chit [tʃit] n nota

chitchat ['tʃittʃæt] n chismes mpl, habladurías fpl

chivalry ['ʃivəlri] n caballerosidad f

chives [tʃaivz] npl cebollinos mpl

chlorine ['klɔːriːn] n cloro

chock-a-block ['tʃɔkə'blɔk] adj atestado

chock-full ['tʃɔk'ful] adj atestado

chocolate ['tʃɔklit] n chocolate m; (sweet) bombón m

choice [tʃɔis] n elección f, selección f; (option) opción f; (preference) preferencia ♦ adj escogido

choir ['kwaiə*] n coro; **~boy** n niño de coro

choke [tʃəuk] vi ahogarse; (on food) atragantarse ♦ vt estrangular, ahogar; (block): **to be ~d with** estar atascado de ♦ n (AUT) estárter m

cholesterol [kə'lestərɔl] n colesterol m

choose [tʃuːz] (pt **chose**, pp **chosen**) vt escoger, elegir; (team) seleccionar; **to ~ to do sth** optar por hacer algo

choosy ['tʃuːzi] adj delicado

chop [tʃɔp] vt (wood) cortar, tajar; (CULIN: also: ~ up) picar ♦ n (CULIN) chuleta; **~s** npl (jaws) boca, labios mpl

chopper ['tʃɔpə*] n (helicopter) helicóptero

choppy ['tʃɔpi] adj (sea) picado, agitado

chopsticks ['tʃɒpstɪks] npl palillos mpl

chord [kɔːd] n (MUS) acorde m

chore [tʃɔː*] n faena, tarea; (routine task) trabajo rutinario

chorus ['kɔːrəs] n coro; (repeated part of song) estribillo

chose [tʃəuz] pt of **choose**

chosen ['tʃəuzn] pp of **choose**

chowder ['tʃaudə*] n (esp US) sopa de pescado

Christ [kraɪst] n Cristo

christen ['krɪsn] vt bautizar

Christian ['krɪstɪən] adj, n cristiano/a m/f; **~ity** [-'ænɪtɪ] n cristianismo; **~ name** n nombre m de pila

Christmas ['krɪsməs] n Navidad f; **Merry ~!** ¡Felices Pascuas!; **~ card** n crismas m inv, tarjeta de Navidad; **~ Day** n día m de Navidad; **~ Eve** n Nochebuena; **~ tree** n árbol m de Navidad

chrome [krəum] n cromo

chronic ['krɒnɪk] adj crónico

chronological [krɒnə'lɔdʒɪkəl] adj cronológico

chubby ['tʃʌbɪ] adj regordete

chuck [tʃʌk] (inf) vt lanzar, arrojar; (BRIT: also: ~ up) abandonar; **~ out** vt (person) echar (fuera); (rubbish etc) tirar

chuckle ['tʃʌkl] vi reírse entre dientes

chug [tʃʌg] vi resoplar; (car, boat: also: ~ along) avanzar traqueteando

chum [tʃʌm] n compañero/a

chunk [tʃʌŋk] n pedazo, trozo

church [tʃəːtʃ] n iglesia; **~yard** n cementerio

churn [tʃəːn] n (for butter) mantequera; (for milk) lechera; **~ out** vt producir en serie

chute [ʃuːt] n (also: rubbish ~) vertedero; (for coal etc) rampa de caída

chutney ['tʃʌtnɪ] n condimento a base de frutas de la India

CIA (US) n abbr (= Central Intelligence Agency) CIA f

CID (BRIT) n abbr (= Criminal Investigation Department) ≈ B.I.C. f (SP)

cider ['saɪdə*] n sidra

cigar [sɪ'gaː*] n puro

cigarette [sɪgə'ret] n cigarrillo (SP), cigarro (AM); pitillo; **~ case** n pitillera; **~ end** n colilla

Cinderella [sɪndə'relə] n Cenicienta

cinders ['sɪndəz] npl cenizas fpl

cine camera ['sɪnɪ-] (BRIT) n cámara cinematográfica

cinema ['sɪnəmə] n cine m

cinnamon ['sɪnəmən] n canela

circle ['səːkl] n círculo; (in theatre) anfiteatro ♦ vi dar vueltas ♦ vt (surround) rodear, cercar; (move round) dar la vuelta a

circuit ['səːkɪt] n circuito; (tour) gira; (track) pista; (lap) vuelta; **~ous** [səː'kjuːtəs] adj indirecto

circular ['səːkjulə*] adj circular ♦ n circular f

circulate ['səːkjuleɪt] vi circular; (person: at party etc) hablar con los invitados ♦ vt poner en circulación; **circulation** [-'leɪʃən] n circulación f; (of newspaper) tirada

circumstances ['səːkəmstənsɪz] npl circunstancias fpl; (financial condition) situación f económica

circus ['səːkəs] n circo

CIS n abbr (= Commonwealth of Independent States) CEI f

cistern ['sɪstən] n tanque m, depósito; (in toilet) cisterna

citizen ['sɪtɪzn] n (POL) ciudadano/a; (of city) vecino/a, habitante m/f; **~ship** n ciudadanía

citrus fruits ['sɪtrəs-] npl agrios mpl

city ['sɪtɪ] n ciudad f; **the C~** centro financiero de Londres

civic ['sɪvɪk] adj cívico; (authorities) municipal; **~ centre** (BRIT) n centro público

civil ['sɪvɪl] adj civil; (polite) atento, cortés; **~ engineer** n ingeniero de caminos, canales y puertos); **~ian** [sɪ'vɪlɪən] adj civil (no militar) ♦ n civil m/f, paisano/a

civilization [sɪvɪlaɪˈzeɪʃən] *n* civilización *f*

civilized [ˈsɪvɪlaɪzd] *adj* civilizado

civil [ˈsɪvəl]: ~ **law** *n* derecho civil; ~ **servant** *n* funcionario *m* del Estado; **C~ Service** *n* administración *f* pública; ~ **war** *n* guerra civil

claim [kleɪm] *vt* exigir, reclamar; *(rights etc)* reivindicar; *(assert)* pretender ♦ *vi (for insurance)* reclamar ♦ *n* reclamación *f*; pretensión *f*; ~**ant** *n* demandante *m/f*

clairvoyant [klɛəˈvɔɪənt] *n* clarividente *m/f*

clam [klæm] *n* almeja

clamber [ˈklæmbə*] *vi* trepar

clammy [ˈklæmɪ] *adj* frío y húmedo

clamour [ˈklæmə*] *(US* **clamor**) *vi:* **to ~ for** clamar por, pedir a voces

clamp [klæmp] *n* abrazadera, grapa ♦ *vt (2 things together)* cerrar fuertemente; *(one thing on another)* afianzar (con abrazadera); *(AUT: wheel)* poner el cepo a; ~ **down on** *vt fus (subj: government, police)* reforzar la lucha contra

clang [klæŋ] *vi* sonar, hacer estruendo

clap [klæp] *vi* aplaudir; ~**ping** *n* aplausos *mpl*

claret [ˈklærət] *n* burdeos *m inv*

clarify [ˈklærɪfaɪ] *vt* aclarar

clarinet [klærɪˈnet] *n* clarinete *m*

clash [klæʃ] *n* enfrentamiento; choque *m*; desacuerdo; estruendo ♦ *vi (fight)* enfrentarse; *(beliefs)* chocar; *(disagree)* estar en desacuerdo; *(colours)* desentonar; *(two events)* coincidir

clasp [klɑːsp] *n (hold)* apretón *m*; *(of necklace, bag)* cierre *m* ♦ *vt* apretar; abrazar

class [klɑːs] *n* clase *f* ♦ *vt* clasificar

classic [ˈklæsɪk] *adj, n* clásico; ~**al** *adj* clásico

classified [ˈklæsɪfaɪd] *adj (information)* reservado; ~ **advertisement** *n* anuncio por palabras

classmate [ˈklɑːsmeɪt] *n* compañero/a

de clase

classroom [ˈklɑːsrum] *n* aula

clatter [ˈklætə*] *n* estrépito ♦ *vi* hacer ruido *or* estrépito

clause [klɔːz] *n* cláusula; *(LING)* oración *f*

claw [klɔː] *n (of cat)* uña; *(of bird of prey)* garra; *(of lobster)* pinza

clay [kleɪ] *n* arcilla

clean [kliːn] *adj* limpio; *(record, reputation)* bueno, intachable; *(joke)* decente ♦ *vt* limpiar; *(hands etc)* lavar; ~ **out** *vt* limpiar; ~ **up** *vt* limpiar, asear; ~**-cut** *adj (person)* bien parecido; ~**er** *n (person)* asistenta; *(substance)* producto para la limpieza; ~**er's** *n* tintorería; ~**ing** *n* limpieza; ~**liness** [ˈklɛnlɪnɪs] *n* limpieza

cleanse [klɛnz] *vt* limpiar; ~**r** *n (for face)* crema limpiadora

clean-shaven *adj* sin barba, afeitado

cleansing department *(BRIT) n* departamento de limpieza

clear [klɪə*] *adj* claro; *(road, way)* libre; *(conscience)* limpio, tranquilo; *(skin)* terso; *(sky)* despejado ♦ *vt (space)* despejar, limpiar; *(LAW: suspect)* absolver; *(obstacle)* salvar, saltar por encima de; *(cheque)* aceptar ♦ *vi (fog etc)* despejarse ♦ *adv:* ~ **of** a distancia de; **to ~ the table** recoger *or* levantar la mesa; ~ **up** *vt* limpiar; *(mystery)* aclarar, resolver; ~**ance** *n (removal)* despeje *m*; *(permission)* acreditación *f*; ~**-cut** *adj* bien definido, nítido; ~**ing** *n (in wood)* claro; ~**ing bank** *(BRIT) n* cámara de compensación; ~**ly** *adv* claramente; *(evidently)* sin duda; ~**way** *(BRIT) n* carretera donde no se puede parar

clef [klef] *n (MUS)* clave *f*

cleft [kleft] *n (in rock)* grieta, hendedura

clench [klentʃ] *vt* apretar, cerrar

clergy [ˈklɜːdʒɪ] *n* clero; ~**man** *n* clérigo

clerical [ˈklerɪkəl] *adj* de oficina; *(REL)*

clerical

clerk [klɑːk, (US) klɜːrk] n (BRIT) oficinista m/f; (US) dependiente/a m/f, vendedor(a) m/f

clever ['klɛvə*] adj (intelligent) inteligente, listo; (skilful) hábil; (device, arrangement) ingenioso

click [klɪk] vt (tongue) chasquear; (heels) taconear

client ['klaɪənt] n cliente m/f

cliff [klɪf] n acantilado

climate ['klaɪmɪt] n clima m

climax ['klaɪmæks] n (of battle, career) apogeo; (of film, book) punto culminante; (sexual) orgasmo

climb [klaɪm] vi subir; (plant) trepar; (move with effort): **to ~ over a wall/into a car** trepar a una tapia/subir a un coche ♦ vt (stairs) subir; (tree) trepar a; (mountain) escalar ♦ n subida; **~-down** n vuelta atrás; **~er** n alpinista m/f (SP), andinista m/f (AM); **~ing** n alpinismo (SP), andinismo (AM)

clinch [klɪntʃ] vt (deal) cerrar; (argument) remachar

cling [klɪŋ] (pt, pp **clung**) vi: **to ~ to** agarrarse a; (clothes) pegarse a

clinic ['klɪnɪk] n clínica; **~al** adj clínico; (fig) frío

clink [klɪŋk] vi tintinar

clip [klɪp] n (for hair) horquilla; (also: **paper ~**) sujetapapeles m inv, clip m; (TV, CINEMA) fragmento ♦ vt (cut) cortar; (also: **~ together**) unir; **~pers** npl (for gardening) tijeras fpl; **~ping** n (newspaper) recorte m

clique [kliːk] n camarilla

cloak [kləuk] n capa, manto ♦ vt (fig) encubrir, disimular; **~room** n guardarropa; (BRIT: WC) lavabo (SP), aseos mpl (SP), baño (AM)

clock [klɒk] n reloj m; **~ in** or **on** vi fichar, picar; **~ off** or **out** vi fichar or picar la salida; **~wise** adv en el sentido de las agujas del reloj; **~work** n aparato de relojería ♦ adj (toy) de cuerda

clog [klɒg] n zueco, chanclo ♦ vt atascar ♦ vi (also: **~ up**) atascarse

cloister ['klɔɪstə*] n claustro

close¹ [kləus] adj (near): **~ (to)** cerca (de); (friend) íntimo; (connection) estrecho; (examination) detallado, minucioso; (weather) bochornoso; **to have a ~ shave** (fig) escaparse por un pelo ♦ adv cerca; **~ by**, **~ at hand** muy cerca; **~ to** prep cerca de

close² [kləuz] vt (shut) cerrar; (end) concluir, terminar ♦ vi (shop etc) cerrarse; (end) concluirse, terminarse ♦ n (end) fin m, final m, conclusión f; **~ down** vi cerrarse definitivamente; **~d** adj (shop etc) cerrado; **~d shop** n taller m gremial

close-knit [kləus'nɪt] adj (fig) muy unido

closely ['kləuslɪ] adv (study) con detalle; (watch) de cerca; (resemble) estrechamente

closet ['klɒzɪt] n armario

close-up ['kləusʌp] n primer plano

closure ['kləuʒə*] n cierre m

clot [klɒt] n (gen: blood ~) coágulo; (inf: idiot) imbécil m/f ♦ vi (blood) coagularse

cloth [klɒθ] n (material) tela, paño; (rag) trapo

clothe [kləuð] vt vestir; **~s** npl ropa; **~s brush** n cepillo (para la ropa); **~s line** n cuerda (para tender la ropa); **~s peg** (US **~s pin**) n pinza

clothing ['kləuðɪŋ] n = **clothes**

cloud [klaud] n nube f; **~burst** n aguacero; **~y** adj nublado, nubloso; (liquid) turbio

clout [klaut] vt dar un tortazo a

clove [kləuv] n clavo; **~ of garlic** diente m de ajo

clover ['kləuvə*] n trébol m

clown [klaun] n payaso ♦ vi (also: **~ about**, **~ around**) hacer el payaso

cloying ['klɔɪɪŋ] adj empalagoso

club [klʌb] n (society) club m; (weapon) porra, cachiporra; (also: golf ~) palo

♦ vt aporrear ♦ vi: **to ~ together** (for gift) comprar entre todos; **~s nut** (CARDS) tréboles mpl; **~ class** n (AVIAT) clase f preferente; **~house** n local social, sobre todo en clubs deportivos

cluck [klʌk] vi cloquear

clue [kluː] n pista; (in crosswords) indicación f; **I haven't a ~** no tengo ni idea

clump [klʌmp] n (of trees) grupo

clumsy ['klʌmzɪ] adj (person) torpe, desmañado; (tool) difícil de manejar; (movement) desgarbado

clung [klʌŋ] pt, pp of **cling**

cluster ['klʌstə*] n grupo ♦ vi agruparse, apiñarse

clutch [klʌtʃ] n (AUT) embrague m; (grasp): **~es garras** fpl ♦ vt asir; agarrar

clutter ['klʌtə*] vt atestar

cm abbr (= centimetre) cm

CND n abbr (= Campaign for Nuclear Disarmament) plataforma pro desarme nuclear

Co. abbr = **county; company**

c/o abbr (= care of) c/a, a/c

coach [kəutʃ] n autocar m (SP), coche m de línea; (horse-drawn) coche m; (of train) vagón m, coche m; (SPORT) entrenador(a) m/f, instructor(a) m/f; (tutor) profesor(a) m/f particular ♦ vt (SPORT) entrenar; (student) preparar, enseñar; **~ trip** n excursión f en autocar

coal [kəul] n carbón m; **~ face** n frente m de carbón; **~field** n yacimiento de carbón

coalition [kəuə'lɪʃən] n coalición f

coalman ['kəulmən] (irreg) n carbonero

coalmine ['kəulmaɪn] n mina de carbón

coarse [kɔːs] adj basto, burdo; (vulgar) grosero, ordinario

coast [kəust] n costa, litoral m ♦ vi (AUT) ir en punto muerto; **~al** adj costero, costanero; **~guard** n guardacostas m inv; **~line** n litoral m

coat [kəut] n abrigo; (of animal) pelaje m, lana; (of paint) mano f, capa ♦ vt cubrir, revestir; **~ of arms** n escudo de armas; **~ hanger** n percha (SP), gancho (AM); **~ing** n capa, baño

coax [kəuks] vt engatusar

cobbler ['kɔblə*] n zapatero (remendón)

cobbles ['kɔblz] npl, **cobblestones** ['kɔblstəunz] npl adoquines mpl

cobweb ['kɔbwɛb] n telaraña

cocaine [kə'keɪn] n cocaína

cock [kɔk] n (rooster) gallo; (male bird) macho ♦ vt (gun) amartillar; **~erel** n gallito

cockle ['kɔkl] n berberecho

cockney ['kɔknɪ] n habitante de ciertos barrios de Londres

cockpit ['kɔkpɪt] n cabina

cockroach ['kɔkrəutʃ] n cucaracha

cocktail ['kɔkteɪl] n coctel m, cóctel m; **~ cabinet** n mueble-bar m; **~ party** n coctel m, cóctel m

cocoa ['kəukəu] n cacao; (drink) chocolate m

coconut ['kəukənʌt] n coco

cod [kɔd] n bacalao

C.O.D. abbr (= cash on delivery) C.A.E.

code [kəud] n código; (cipher) clave f; (dialling ~) prefijo; (post ~) código postal

cod-liver oil ['kɔdlɪvər-] n aceite m de hígado de bacalao

coercion [kəu'əːʃən] n coacción f

coffee ['kɔfɪ] n café m; **~ bar** (BRIT) n cafetería; **~ bean** n grano de café; **~ break** n descanso (para tomar café); **~pot** n cafetera; **~ table** n mesita (para servir el café)

coffin ['kɔfɪn] n ataúd m

cog [kɔg] n (wheel) rueda dentada; (tooth) diente m

cogent ['kəudʒənt] adj convincente

cognac ['kɔnjæk] n coñac m

coil [kɔɪl] n rollo; (ELEC) bobina, carrete m; (contraceptive) espiral f ♦ vt enrollar

coin [kɔɪn] n moneda ♦ vt (word)

inventar, idear; **~age** n moneda; **~-box** (BRIT) n cabina telefónica

coincide [kəʊɪnˈsaɪd] vi coincidir; (agree) estar de acuerdo; **coincidence** [kəʊˈɪnsɪdəns] n casualidad f

Coke ® [kəʊk] n Coca-Cola ®

coke [kəʊk] n (coal) coque m

colander [ˈkɔləndə*] n colador m, escurridor m

cold [kəʊld] adj frío ♦ n frío; (MED) resfriado; **it's ~** hace frío; **to be ~** (person) tener frío; **to catch ~** enfriarse; **to catch a ~** resfriarse, acatarrarse; **in ~ blood** a sangre fría; **~-shoulder** vt dar o volver la espalda a; **~ sore** n herpes mpl o fpl

coleslaw [ˈkəʊlslɔː] n especie de ensalada de col

colic [ˈkɔlɪk] n cólico

collapse [kəˈlæps] vi hundirse, derrumbarse; (MED) sufrir un colapso ♦ n hundimiento, derrumbamiento; (MED) colapso; **collapsible** adj plegable

collar [ˈkɔlə*] n (of coat, shirt) cuello; (of dog etc) collar; **~bone** n clavícula

collateral [kɔˈlætərəl] n garantía colateral

colleague [ˈkɔliːg] n colega m/f; (at work) compañero, a

collect [kəˈlekt] vt (litter, mail etc) recoger; (as a hobby) coleccionar; (BRIT: call and pick up) recoger; (debts, subscriptions etc) recaudar ♦ vi reunirse; (dust) acumularse; **to call ~** (US: TEL) llamar a cobro revertido; **~ion** [kəˈlekʃən] n colección f, (of mail, for charity) recogida; **~or** n coleccionista m/f

college [ˈkɔlɪdʒ] n colegio mayor; (of agriculture, technology) escuela universitaria

collide [kəˈlaɪd] vi chocar

colliery [ˈkɔlɪərɪ] (BRIT) n mina de carbón

collision [kəˈlɪʒən] n choque m

colloquial [kəˈləʊkwɪəl] adj familiar, coloquial

Colombia [kəˈlɔmbɪə] n Colombia; **~n** adj, n colombiano/a

colon [ˈkəʊlən] n (sign) dos puntos; (MED) colon m

colonel [ˈkɜːnl] n coronel m

colonial [kəˈləʊnɪəl] adj colonial

colony [ˈkɔlənɪ] n colonia

colour [ˈkʌlə*] (US **color**) n color m ♦ vt color(e)ar; (dye) teñir; (fig: account) adornar; (: judgement) distorsionar ♦ vi (blush) sonrojarse; **~s** npl (of party, club) colores mpl; **in ~** en color; **~ in** vt colorear; **~ bar** n segregación f racial; **~-blind** adj daltónico; **~ed** adj de color; (photo) en color; **~ film** n película en color; **~ful** adj lleno de color; (story) fantástico; (person) excéntrico; **~ing** n (complexion) tez f; (in food) colorante m; **~ scheme** n combinación f de colores; **~ television** n televisión f en color

colt [kəʊlt] n potro

column [ˈkɔləm] n columna; **~ist** [ˈkɔləmnɪst] n columnista m/f

coma [ˈkəʊmə] n coma m

comb [kəʊm] n peine m; (ornamental) peineta ♦ vt (hair) peinar; (area) registrar a fondo

combat [ˈkɔmbæt] n combate m ♦ vt combatir

combination [kɔmbɪˈneɪʃən] n combinación f

combine [vb kəmˈbaɪn, n ˈkɔmbaɪn] vt combinar; (qualities) reunir ♦ vi combinarse ♦ n (ECON) cartel m; **~ (harvester)** n cosechadora

┌─────────────────┐
│ **KEYWORD** │
└─────────────────┘

come [kʌm] (pt **came**, pp **come**) vi **1** (movement towards) venir; **to ~ running** venir corriendo

2 (arrive) llegar; **he's ~ here to work** ha venido aquí para trabajar; **to ~ home** volver a casa

3 (reach): **to ~ to** llegar a; **the bill**

came to £40 la cuenta ascendía a cuarenta libras

4 (*occur*): **an idea came to me** se me ocurrió una idea

5 (*be, become*): **to ~ loose/undone** *etc* aflojarse/desabrocharse, desatarse *etc*; **I've ~ to like him** por fin ha llegado a gustarme

come about *vi* suceder, ocurrir

come across *vt fus* (*person*) topar con; (*thing*) dar con

come away *vi* (*leave*) marcharse; (*become detached*) desprenderse

come back *vi* (*return*) volver

come by *vt fus* (*acquire*) conseguir

come down *vi* (*price*) bajar; (*tree, building*) ser derribado

come forward *vi* presentarse

come from *vt fus* (*place, source*) ser de

come in *vi* (*visitor*) entrar; (*train, report*) llegar; (*fashion*) ponerse de moda; (*on deal etc*) entrar

come in for *vt fus* (*criticism etc*) recibir

come into *vt fus* (*money*) heredar; (*be involved*) tener que ver con; **to ~ into fashion** ponerse de moda

come off *vi* (*button*) soltarse, desprenderse; (*attempt*) salir bien

come on *vi* (*pupil*) progresar; (*work, project*) desarrollarse; (*lights*) encenderse; (*electricity*) volver; **~ on!** ¡vamos!

come out *vi* (*fact*) salir a la luz; (*book, sun*) salir; (*stain*) quitarse

come round *vi* (*after faint, operation*) volver en sí

come to *vi* (*wake*) volver en sí

come up *vi* (*sun*) salir; (*problem*) surgir; (*event*) aproximarse; (*in conversation*) mencionarse

come up against *vt fus* (*resistance etc*) tropezar con

come up with *vt fus* (*idea*) sugerir; (*money*) conseguir

come upon *vt fus* (*find*) dar con

comeback ['kʌmbæk] *n:* **to make a ~** (THEATRE) volver a las tablas

comedian [kə'miːdɪən] *n* cómico; **comedienne** [-'ɛn] *n* cómica

comedy ['kɒmɪdɪ] *n* comedia; (*humour*) comicidad *f*

comet ['kɒmɪt] *n* cometa *m*

comeuppance [kʌm'ʌpəns] *n:* **to get one's ~** llevar su merecido

comfort ['kʌmfət] *n* bienestar *m*; (*relief*) alivio ♦ *vt* consolar; **~s** *npl* (*of home etc*) comodidades *fpl*; **~able** *adj* cómodo; (*financially*) acomodado; (*easy*) fácil; **~ably** *adv* (*sit*) cómodamente; (*live*) holgadamente; **~ station** (US) *n* servicios *mpl*

comic ['kɒmɪk] *adj* (*also:* **~al**) cómico ♦ *n* (*comedian*) cómico; (BRIT: for children) tebeo; (BRIT: for adults) comic *m*; **~ strip** *n* tira cómica

coming ['kʌmɪŋ] *n* venida, llegada ♦ *adj* que viene; **~(s) and going(s)** *n(pl)* ir y venir *m*, ajetreo

comma ['kɒmə] *n* coma

command [kə'mɑːnd] *n* orden *f*, mandato; (MIL: *authority*) mando; (*mastery*) dominio ♦ *vt* (*troops*) mandar; (*give orders to*): **to ~ sb to do** mandar or ordenar a uno hacer; **~eer** [kɒmən'dɪə*] *vt* requisar; **~er** *n* (MIL) comandante *m/f*, jefe/a *m/f*

commemorate [kə'mɛməreɪt] *vt* conmemorar

commence [kə'mɛns] *vt*, *vi* comenzar, empezar

commend [kə'mɛnd] *vt* elogiar, alabar; (*recommend*) recomendar

commensurate [kə'mɛnsjərɪt] *adj:* **~ with** en proporción a, que corresponde a

comment ['kɒmɛnt] *n* comentario ♦ *vi:* **to ~ on** hacer comentarios sobre; **"no ~"** (*written*) "sin comentarios"; (*spoken*) "no tengo nada que decir"; **~ary** ['kɒmɛntərɪ] *n* comentario; **~ator** ['kɒmɛnteɪtə*] *n* comentarista *m/f* commerce ['kɒmə:s] n comercio

commercial [kə'mə:ʃəl] adj comercial
♦ n (TV, RADIO) anuncio

commiserate [kə'mɪzəreɪt] vi: to
~ with compadecerse de, condolerse
de

commission [kə'mɪʃən] n (committee,
fee) comisión f ♦ vt (work of art)
encargar; out of ~ fuera de servicio;
~aire [kəmɪʃə'neə*] (BRIT) n portero;
~er n (POLICE) comisario de policía

commit [kə'mɪt] vt (act) cometer;
(resources) dedicar; (to sb's care)
entregar; to ~ o.s. (to do)
comprometerse (a hacer); to
~ suicide suicidarse; ~ment n
compromiso; (to ideology etc) entrega
f

committee [kə'mɪtɪ] n comité m

commodity [kə'mɒdɪtɪ] n mercancía

common ['kɒmən] adj común; (pej)
ordinario ♦ n campo común; the C~s
npl (BRIT) (la Cámara de) los Comunes
mpl; in ~ en común; ~er n plebeyo;
~ law n ley f consuetudinaria; ~ly adv
comúnmente; C~ Market n Mercado
Común; ~place adj de lo más común;
~room n sala común; ~ sense n
sentido común; the C~wealth n la
Commonwealth

commotion [kə'məuʃən] n tumulto,
confusión f

commune [n 'kɒmju:n, vb kə'mju:n]
n (group) comuna ♦ vi: to ~ with
comulgar o conversar con

communicate [kə'mju:nɪkeɪt] vt
comunicar ♦ vi: to ~ (with)
comunicarse (con); (in writing) estar en
contacto (con)

communication [kəmju:nɪ'keɪʃən] n
comunicación f; ~ cord (BRIT) n timbre
m de alarma

communion [kə'mju:nɪən] n (also:
Holy C~) comunión f

communiqué [kə'mju:nɪkeɪ] n
comunicado, parte f

communism ['kɒmjunɪzəm] n
comunismo; communist adj,

comunista m/f

community [kə'mju:nɪtɪ] n
comunidad f; (large group) colectividad
f; ~ centre n centro social; ~ chest
(US) n arca comunitaria, fondo común

commutation ticket [kɒmju'teɪʃən-]
(US) n billete m de abono

commute [kə'mju:t] vi viajar a diario
de la casa al trabajo ♦ vt conmutar; ~r
n persona (que viaja ... see vi)

compact [adj kəm'pækt, n 'kɒmpækt]
adj compacto ♦ n (also: powder ~)
polvera; ~ disc n compact disc m;
~ disc player n reproductor m de
disco compacto, compact disc m

companion [kəm'pænɪən] n
compañero/a; ~ship n compañerismo

company ['kʌmpənɪ] n compañía;
(COMM) sociedad f, compañía; to keep
sb ~ acompañar a uno; ~ secretary
(BRIT) n secretario/a de compañía

comparative [kəm'pærətɪv] adj
relativo; (study) comparativo; ~ly adv
(relatively) relativamente

compare [kəm'peə*] vt: to ~ sth/sb
with/to comparar algo/a uno con
♦ vi: to ~ (with) compararse (con);
comparison [-'pærɪsn] n
comparación f

compartment [kəm'pɑ:tmənt] n
(also: RAIL) compartim(i)ento

compass ['kʌmpəs] n brújula; ~es npl
(MATH) compás m

compassion [kəm'pæʃən] n
compasión f; ~ate adj compasivo

compatible [kəm'pætɪbl] adj
compatible

compel [kəm'pel] vt obligar

compensate ['kɒmpənseɪt] vt
compensar ♦ vi: to ~ for compensar;
compensation [-'seɪʃən] n (for loss)
indemnización f

compère ['kɒmpeə*] n presentador m

compete [kəm'pi:t] vi (take part)
tomar parte, concurrir; (vie with): to
~ with competir con, hacer
competencia a

competent ['kɒmpɪtənt] *adj* competente, capaz

competition [kɒmpɪ'tɪʃən] *n* (*contest*) concurso; (*rivalry*) competencia

competitive [kəm'petɪtɪv] *adj* (*ECON*, *SPORT*) competitivo

competitor [kəm'petɪtə*] *n* (*rival*) competidor(a) *m/f*; (*participant*) concursante *m/f*

complacency [kəm'pleɪsnsɪ] *n* autosatisfacción *f*

complacent [kəm'pleɪsənt] *adj* autocomplaciente

complain [kəm'pleɪn] *vi* quejarse; (*COMM*) reclamar; **~t** *n* queja; reclamación *f*; (*MED*) enfermedad *f*

complement [*n* 'kɒmplɪmənt, *vb* 'kɒmplɪment] *n* complemento; (*esp* of ship's crew) dotación *f* ♦ *vt* (*enhance*) complementar; **~ary** [kɒmplɪ'mentərɪ] *adj* complementario

complete [kəm'pli:t] *adj* (*full*) completo; (*finished*) acabado ♦ *vt* (*fulfil*) completar; (*finish*) acabar; (*a form*) llenar; **~ly** *adv* completamente; **completion** [-'pli:ʃən] *n* terminación *f*; (*of contract*) realización *f*

complex ['kɒmpleks] *adj*, *n* complejo

complexion [kəm'plekʃən] *n* (*of face*) tez *f*, cutis *m*

compliance [kəm'plaɪəns] *n* (*submission*) sumisión *f*; (*agreement*) conformidad *f*; **in ~ with** de acuerdo con

complicate ['kɒmplɪkeɪt] *vt* complicar; **~d** *adj* complicado; **complication** [-'keɪʃən] *n* complicación *f*

compliment [*n* 'kɒmplɪmənt, *vb* 'kɒmplɪment] *n* (*formal*) cumplido ♦ *vt* felicitar; **~s** *npl* (*regards*) saludos *mpl*; **to pay sb a ~** hacer cumplidos a uno; **~ary** [-'mentərɪ] *adj* lisonjero; (*free*) de favor

comply [kəm'plaɪ] *vi*: **to ~ with** cumplir con

component [kəm'pəunənt] *adj* componente ♦ *n* (*TECH*) pieza

compose [kəm'pəuz] *vt*: **to be ~d of**

componerse de; (*music etc*) componer; **to ~ o.s.** tranquilizarse; **~d** *adj* sosegado; **~r** *n* (*MUS*) compositor(a) *m/f*; **composition** [kɒmpə'zɪʃən] *n* composición *f*

compost ['kɒmpɒst] *n* abono (vegetal)

composure [kəm'pəuʒə*] *n* serenidad *f*, calma

compound ['kɒmpaund] *n* (*CHEM*) compuesto; (*LING*) palabra compuesta; (*enclosure*) recinto ♦ *adj* compuesto; (*fracture*) complicado

comprehend [kɒmprɪ'hend] *vt* comprender; **comprehension** [-'henʃən] *n* comprensión *f*

comprehensive [kɒmprɪ'hensɪv] *adj* exhaustivo; (*INSURANCE*) contra todo riesgo; **~ (school)** *n* centro estatal de enseñanza secundaria, ≈ Instituto Nacional de Bachillerato (*SP*)

compress [*vb* kəm'pres, *n* 'kɒmpres] *vt* comprimir; (*information*) condensar ♦ *n* (*MED*) compresa

comprise [kəm'praɪz] *vt* (*also*: **be ~d of**) comprender, constar de; (*constitute*) constituir

compromise ['kɒmprəmaɪz] *n* (*agreement*) arreglo ♦ *vt* comprometer ♦ *vi* transigir

compulsion [kəm'pʌlʃən] *n* compulsión *f*; (*force*) obligación *f*

compulsive [kəm'pʌlsɪv] *adj* compulsivo; (*viewing*, *reading*) obligado

compulsory [kəm'pʌlsərɪ] *adj* obligatorio

computer [kəm'pju:tə*] *n* ordenador *m*, computador *m*, computadora; **~ game** *n* juego para ordenador; **~-generated** *adj* realizado por ordenador, creado por ordenador; **~ize** *vt* (*data*) computarizar; (*system*) informatizar; **~ programmer** *n* programador(a) *m/f*; **~ programming** *n* programación *f*; **~ science** *n* informática; **computing** [kəm'pju:tɪŋ] *n* (*activity*, *science*) informática

comrade ['kɒmrɪd] *n* (*POL*, *MIL*)

camarada; (*friend*) compañero/a;
~ship n camaradería, compañerismo
con [kɔn] vt (*deceive*) engañar; (*cheat*)
estafar ♦ n estafa
conceal [kən'si:l] vt ocultar
conceit [kən'si:t] n presunción f; **~ed**
adj presumido
conceive [kən'si:v] vt, vi concebir
concentrate ['kɔnsəntreit] vi
concentrarse ♦ vt concentrar
concentration [kɔnsən'treiʃən] n
concentración f
concept ['kɔnsept] n concepto
concern [kən'sə:n] n (*matter*) asunto;
(COMM) empresa; (*anxiety*)
preocupación f ♦ vt (*worry*) preocupar;
(*involve*) afectar; (*relate to*) tener que
ver con; **to be ~ed** (**about**)
interesarse (por), preocuparse (por);
~ing prep sobre, acerca de
concert ['kɔnsət] n concierto; **~ed**
[kən'sə:tid] adj (*efforts etc*)
concertado; **~ hall** n sala de conciertos
concerto [kən'tʃə:təu] n concierto
concession [kən'seʃən] n concesión f;
tax ~ privilegio fiscal
conclude [kən'klu:d] vt concluir;
(*treaty etc*) firmar; (*agreement*) llegar a;
(*decide*) llegar a la conclusión de;
conclusion [-'klu:ʒən] n conclusión f;
firma; **conclusive** [-'klu:siv] adj
decisivo, concluyente
concoct [kən'kɔkt] vt confeccionar;
(*plot*) tramar; **~ion** [-'kɔkʃən] n mezcla
concourse ['kɔŋkɔ:s] n vestíbulo
concrete ['kɔnkri:t] n hormigón m
♦ adj de hormigón; (*fig*) concreto
concur [kən'kə:*] vi estar de acuerdo,
asentir
concurrently [kən'kʌrntlı] adv al
mismo tiempo
concussion [kən'kʌʃən] n conmoción
f cerebral
condemn [kən'dɛm] vt condenar;
(*building*) declarar en ruina
condense [kən'dɛns] vi condensarse
♦ vt condensar, abreviar; **~d milk** n

leche f condensada
condition [kən'dıʃən] n condición f,
estado; (*requirement*) condición f ♦ vt
condicionar; **on ~ that** a condición
(de) que; **~er** n suavizante
condolences [kən'dəulənsız] npl
pésame m
condom ['kɔndəm] n condón m
condone [kən'dəun] vt condonar
conducive [kən'dju:sıv] adj: **~ to**
conducente a
conduct [n 'kɔndʌkt, vb kən'dʌkt] n
conducta, comportamiento ♦ vt (*lead*)
conducir; (*manage*) llevar a cabo,
dirigir; (MUS) dirigir; **to ~ o.s.**
comportarse; **~ed tour** (BRIT) n visita
acompañada; **~or** n (of orchestra)
director m; (US: on train) revisor(a) m/f;
(on bus) cobrador m; (ELEC) conductor
m; **~ress** n (on bus) cobradora
cone [kəun] n cono; (*pine ~*) piña; (on
road) pivote m; (for ice-cream)
cucurucho
confectioner [kən'fɛkʃənə*] n
repostero/a; **~'s (shop)** n confitería;
~y n dulces mpl
confer [kən'fə:*] vt: **to ~ sth on**
otorgar algo a ♦ vi conferenciar
conference ['kɔnfərns] n (*meeting*)
reunión f; (*convention*) congreso
confess [kən'fɛs] vt confesar ♦ vi
admitir; **~ion** [-'fɛʃən] n confesión f
confetti [kən'fɛti] n confeti m
confide [kən'faid] vi: **to ~ in** confiar
en
confidence ['kɔnfıdns] n (also: self-~)
confianza; (*secret*) confidencia; in **~**
(*speak, write*) en confianza; **~ trick** n
timo; **confident** adj seguro de sí
mismo; (*certain*) seguro; **confidential**
[kɔnfı'dɛnʃəl] adj confidencial
confine [kən'faın] vt (*limit*) limitar;
(*shut up*) encerrar; **~d** adj (*space*)
reducido; **~ment** n (in prison) prisión f;
~s ['kɔnfaınz] npl confines mpl
confirm [kən'fə:m] vt confirmar;
~ation [kɔnfə'meıʃən] n confirmación

f; **~ed** adj empedernido
confiscate ['kɒnfɪskeɪt] vt confiscar
conflict [n 'kɒnflɪkt, vb kən'flɪkt] n
conflicto ♦ vi (opinions) chocar; **~ing**
adj contradictorio
conform [kən'fɔ:m] vi conformarse; **to
~ to** ajustarse a
confound [kən'faund] vt confundir
confront [kən'frʌnt] vt (problems)
hacer frente a; (enemy, danger)
enfrentarse con; **~ation**
[kɒnfrən'teɪʃən] n enfrentamiento
confuse [kən'fju:z] vt (perplex) aturdir,
desconcertar; (mix up) confundir;
(complicate) complicar; **~d** adj confuso;
(person) perplejo; **confusing** adj
confuso; **confusion** [-'fju:ʒən] n
confusión f
congeal [kən'dʒi:l] vi (blood)
coagularse; (sauce etc) cuajarse
congested [kən'dʒestɪd] adj
congestionado; **congestion** [-'dʒestʃən] n
congestión f
congratulate [kən'grætjuleɪt] vt: **to
~ sb (on)** felicitar a uno (por);
congratulations [-'leɪʃənz] npl
felicitaciones fpl; **congratulations!**
¡enhorabuena!
congregate ['kɒŋgrɪgeɪt] vi
congregarse; **congregation** [-'geɪʃən]
n (of a church) feligreses mpl
congress ['kɒŋgres] n congreso; (US):
C~ Congreso; **C~man** (irreg) (US) n
miembro del Congreso
conifer ['kɒnɪfə*] n conífera
conjunctivitis [kəndʒʌŋktɪ'vaɪtɪs] n
conjuntivitis f
conjure ['kʌndʒə*] vi hacer juegos de
manos; **~ up** vt (ghost, spirit) hacer
aparecer; (memories) evocar; **~r** n
ilusionista m/f
con man ['kɒn-] n estafador m
connect [kə'nekt] vt juntar, unir;
(ELEC) conectar; (TEL: subscriber) poner;
(: caller) poner al habla; (fig) relacionar,
asociar ♦ vi: **to ~ with** (train) enlazar
con; **to be ~ed with** (associated) estar

relacionado con; **~ion** [-ʃən] n juntura,
unión f; (ELEC) conexión f; (RAIL) enlace
m; (TEL) comunicación f; (fig) relación f
connive [kə'naɪv] vi: **to ~ at** hacer la
vista gorda a
connoisseur [kɒnɪ'sə*] n experto/a,
entendido/a
conquer ['kɒŋkə*] vt (territory)
conquistar; (enemy, feelings) vencer;
~or n conquistador m
conquest ['kɒŋkwest] n conquista
cons [kɒnz] npl see **convenience**; **pro**
conscience ['kɒnʃəns] n conciencia
conscientious [kɒnʃɪ'enʃəs] adj
concienzudo; (objection) de conciencia
conscious ['kɒnʃəs] adj (deliberate)
deliberado; (awake, aware) consciente;
~ness n conciencia f; (MED)
conocimiento
conscript ['kɒnskrɪpt] n recluta m;
~ion [kən'skrɪpʃən] n servicio militar
(obligatorio)
consensus [kən'sensəs] n consenso
consent [kən'sent] n consentimiento
♦ vi: **to ~ (to)** consentir (en)
consequence ['kɒnsɪkwəns] n
consecuencia f; (significance) importancia
consequently ['kɒnsɪkwəntlɪ] adv por
consiguiente
conservation [kɒnsə'veɪʃən] n
conservación f
conservative [kən'sə:vətɪv] adj
conservador(a); (estimate etc)
cauteloso; **C~** (BRIT) adj, n (POL)
conservador(a) m/f
conservatory [kən'sə:vətrɪ] n
invernadero; (MUS) conservatorio
conserve [kən'sə:v] vt conservar ♦ n
conserva
consider [kən'sɪdə*] vt considerar;
(take into account) tener en cuenta;
(study) estudiar, examinar; **to ~ doing**
sth pensar en (la posibilidad de) hacer
algo; **~able** adj considerable; **~ably**
adv notablemente; **~ate** adj
considerado; **consideration** [-'reɪʃən]
n consideración f; (factor) factor m; **to**

give sth further consideration
estudiar algo más a fondo; **~ing** prep
teniendo en cuenta

consign [kən'saɪn] vt: **to ~ to** (sth
unwanted) relegar a; (person) destinar
a; **~ment** n envío

consist [kən'sɪst] vi: **to ~ of** consistir
en

consistency [kən'sɪstənsɪ] n (of
argument etc) coherencia;
consecuencia; (thickness) consistencia

consistent [kən'sɪstənt] adj (person)
consecuente; (argument etc) coherente

consolation [kɒnsə'leɪʃən] n consuelo

console[1] [kən'səʊl] vt consolar

console[2] ['kɒnsəʊl] n consola

consonant ['kɒnsənənt] n consonante
f

consortium [kən'sɔːtɪəm] n consorcio

conspicuous [kən'spɪkjʊəs] adj
(visible) visible

conspiracy [kən'spɪrəsɪ] n conjura,
complot m

constable ['kʌnstəbl] (BRIT) n policía
m/f; **chief ~** ≈ jefe m de policía

constabulary [kən'stæbjʊlərɪ] n ≈
policía

constant ['kɒnstənt] adj constante;
~ly adv constantemente

constipated ['kɒnstɪpeɪtɪd] adj
estreñido; **constipation**
[kɒnstɪ'peɪʃən] n estreñimiento

constituency [kən'stɪtjʊənsɪ] n (POL:
area) distrito electoral; (: electors)
electorado; **constituent** [-ənt] n (POL)
elector/a m/f; (part) componente m

constitution [kɒnstɪ'tjuːʃən] n
constitución f; **~al** adj constitucional

constraint [kən'streɪnt] n obligación f;
(limit) restricción f

construct [kən'strʌkt] vt construir;
~ion [-ʃən] n construcción f; **~ive** adj
constructivo

consul ['kɒnsl] n cónsul m/f; **~ate**
['kɒnsjʊlɪt] n consulado

consult [kən'sʌlt] vt consultar; **~ant** n
(BRIT: MED) especialista m/f; (other

specialist) asesor(a) m/f; **~ation**
[kɒnsl'teɪʃən] n consulta; **~ing room**
(BRIT) n consultorio

consume [kən'sjuːm] vt (eat) comerse;
(drink) beberse; (fire etc, COMM)
consumir; **~r** n consumidor(a) m/f; **~r
goods** npl bienes mpl de consumo

consummate ['kɒnsʌmeɪt] vt
consumar

consumption [kən'sʌmpʃən] n
consumo

cont. abbr (= continued) sigue

contact ['kɒntækt] n contacto; (person)
contacto; (: pej) enchufe m ♦ vt
ponerse en contacto con; **~ lenses** npl
lentes fpl de contacto

contagious [kən'teɪdʒəs] adj
contagioso

contain [kən'teɪn] vt contener; **to
~ o.s.** contenerse; **~er** n recipiente m;
(for shipping etc) contenedor m

contaminate [kən'tæmɪneɪt] vt
contaminar

cont'd abbr (= continued) sigue

contemplate ['kɒntəmpleɪt] vt
contemplar; (reflect upon) considerar

contemporary [kən'tempərərɪ] adj, n
contemporáneo/a m/f

contempt [kən'tempt] n desprecio;
~ of court (LAW) desacato (a los
tribunales); **~ible** adj despreciable;
~uous adj desdeñoso

contend [kən'tend] vt (argue) afirmar
♦ vi: **to ~ with/for** luchar contra/por;
~er n (SPORT) contendiente m/f

content [adj, vb kən'tent, n 'kɒntent]
adj (happy) contento; (satisfied)
satisfecho ♦ vt contentar; satisfacer ♦ n
contenido; **~s** npl contenido; (table
of) **~s** índice m de materias; **~ed** adj
contento; satisfecho

contention [kən'tenʃən] n (assertion)
aseveración f; (disagreement) discusión f

contest [n 'kɒntest, vb kən'test] n
lucha; (competition) concurso ♦ vt
(dispute) impugnar; (POL) presentarse
como candidato/a en; **~ant**

[kən'testənt] n concursante m/f; (in fight) contendiente m/f

context ['kɔntekst] n contexto

continent ['kɔntinənt] n continente m; **the C~** (BRIT) el continente europeo; **~al** [-'nentl] adj continental; **~al breakfast** n desayuno estilo europeo; **~al quilt** (BRIT) n edredón m

contingency [kən'tindʒənsi] n contingencia

continual [kən'tinjual] adj continuo; **~ly** adv constantemente

continuation [kəntinju'eiʃən] n prolongación f; (after interruption) reanudación f

continue [kən'tinju:] vi, vt seguir, continuar

continuous [kən'tinjuəs] adj continuo

contort [kən'tɔ:t] vt retorcer

contour ['kɔntuə*] n contorno; (also: ~ line) curva de nivel

contraband ['kɔntrəbænd] n contrabando

contraceptive [kɔntrə'septiv] adj, n anticonceptivo

contract [n 'kɔntrækt, vb kən'trækt] n contrato ♦ vi (COMM): **to ~ to do sth** comprometerse por contrato a hacer algo; (become smaller) contraerse, encogerse ♦ vt contraer; **~ion** [kən'trækʃən] n contracción f; **~or** n contratista m/f

contradict [kɔntrə'dikt] vt contradecir; **~ion** [-ʃən] n contradicción f

contraption [kən'træpʃən] n (pej) artilugio m

contrary[1] ['kɔntrəri] adj contrario ♦ n lo contrario; **on the ~** al contrario; **unless you hear to the ~** a no ser que le digan lo contrario

contrary[2] [kən'trɛəri] adj (perverse) terco

contrast [n 'kɔntrɑ:st, vt kən'trɑ:st] n contraste m ♦ vt comparar; **in ~ to** en contraste con

contravene [kɔntrə'vi:n] vt infringir

contribute [kən'tribju:t] vi contribuir

♦ vt: **to ~ £10/an article to** contribuir con 10 libras/un artículo a; **to ~ to** (charity) donar a; (newspaper) escribir para; (discussion) intervenir en; **contribution** [kɔntri'bju:ʃən] n (donation) donativo; (BRIT: for social security) cotización f; (to debate) intervención f; (to journal) colaboración f; **contributor** n contribuyente m/f; (to newspaper) colaborador(a) m/f

contrive [kən'traiv] vt (invent) idear ♦ vi: **to ~ to do** lograr hacer

control [kən'trəul] vt controlar; (process etc) dirigir; (machinery) manejar; (temper) dominar; (disease) contener ♦ n control m; **~s** npl (of vehicle) instrumentos mpl de mando; (of radio) controles mpl; (governmental) medidas fpl de control; **under ~** bajo control; **to be in ~ of** tener el mando de; **the car went out of ~** se perdió el control del coche; **~led substance** n sustancia controlada; **~ panel** n tablero de instrumentos; **~ room** n sala de mando; **~ tower** n (AVIAT) torre f de control

controversial [kɔntrə'və:ʃl] adj polémico

controversy ['kɔntrəvə:si] n polémica

convalesce [kɔnvə'les] vi convalecer

convector [kən'vektə*] n calentador m de aire

convene [kən'vi:n] vt convocar ♦ vi reunirse

convenience [kən'vi:niəns] n (easiness) comodidad f; (suitability) idoneidad f; (advantage) ventaja; **at your ~** cuando le sea conveniente; **all modern ~s, all mod cons** (BRIT) todo confort

convenient [kən'vi:niənt] adj (useful) útil; (place, time) conveniente

convent ['kɔnvənt] n convento

convention [kən'venʃən] n convención f; (meeting) asamblea; (agreement) convenio; **~al** adj convencional

converge [kən'vɜːdʒ] *vi* convergir; *(people)*: **to ~ on** dirigirse todos a

conversant [kən'vɜːsnt] *adj*: **to be ~ with** estar al tanto de

conversation [kɔnvə'seɪʃən] *n* conversación *f*; **~al** *adj* familiar; **~al skill** facilidad *f* de palabra

converse [*n* 'kɔnvɜːs, *vb* kən'vɜːs] *n* inversa ♦ *vi* conversar; **~ly** [-'vɜːslɪ] *adv* a la inversa

conversion [kən'vɜːʃən] *n* conversión *f*

convert [*vb* kən'vɜːt, *n* 'kɔnvɜːt] *vt* *(REL, COMM)* convertir; *(alter)*: **~ sth into/to** transformar algo en/convertir algo a ♦ *n* converso/a; **~ible** *adj* convertible ♦ *n* descapotable *m*

convey [kən'veɪ] *vt* llevar; *(thanks)* comunicar; *(idea)* expresar; **~or belt** *n* cinta transportadora

convict [*vb* kən'vɪkt, *n* 'kɔnvɪkt] *vt* *(find guilty)* declarar culpable a ♦ *n* presidiario/a; **~ion** [-ʃən] *n* condena; *(belief, certainty)* convicción *f*

convince [kən'vɪns] *vt* convencer; **~d** *adj*: **~d of/that** convencido de/de que; **convincing** *adj* convincente

convoluted ['kɔnvəluːtɪd] *adj* *(argument etc)* enrevesado

convoy ['kɔnvɔɪ] *n* convoy *m*

convulse [kən'vʌls] *vt*: **to be ~d with laughter** desternillarse de risa; **convulsion** [-'vʌlʃən] *n* convulsión *f*

cook [kuk] *vt* *(stew etc)* guisar; *(meal)* preparar ♦ *vi* cocer; *(person)* cocinar ♦ *n* cocinero/a; **~ book** *n* libro de cocina; **~er** *n* cocina; **~ery** *n* cocina; **~ery book** *(BRIT)* *n* = **~ book**; **~ie** *(US)* *n* galleta; **~ing** *n* cocina

cool [kuːl] *adj* fresco; *(not afraid)* tranquilo; *(unfriendly)* frío ♦ *vt* enfriar ♦ *vi* enfriarse; **~ness** *n* frescura; tranquilidad *f*; *(indifference)* falta de entusiasmo

coop [kuːp] *n* gallinero ♦ *vt*: **to ~ up** *(fig)* encerrar

cooperate [kəu'ɔpəreɪt] *vi* cooperar,

colaborar; **cooperation** [-'reɪʃən] *n* cooperación *f*, colaboración *f*;

cooperative [-rətɪv] *adj* cooperativo; *(person)* servicial ♦ *n* cooperativa

coordinate [*vb* kəu'ɔːdɪneɪt, *n* kəu'ɔːdɪnət] *vt* coordinar ♦ *n* *(MATH)* coordenada; **~s** *npl* *(clothes)* coordinados *mpl*; **coordination** [-'neɪʃən] *n* coordinación *f*

co-ownership [kəu'əunəʃɪp] *n* co-propiedad *f*

cop [kɔp] *(inf)* *n* poli *m* *(SP)*, tira *m* *(AM)*

cope [kəup] *vi*: **to ~ with** *(problem)* hacer frente a

copper ['kɔpə*] *n* *(metal)* cobre *m*; *(BRIT: inf)* poli *m*; **~s** *npl* *(money)* calderilla *(SP)*, centavos *mpl* *(AM)*

copulate ['kɔpjuleɪt] *vi* copularse

copy ['kɔpɪ] *n* copia; *(of book etc)* ejemplar *m* ♦ *vt* copiar; **~right** *n* derechos *mpl* de autor

coral ['kɔrəl] *n* coral *m*

cord [kɔːd] *n* cuerda; *(ELEC)* cable *m*; *(fabric)* pana

cordial ['kɔːdɪəl] *adj* cordial ♦ *n* cordial *m*

cordon ['kɔːdn] *n* cordón *m*; **~ off** *vt* acordonar

corduroy ['kɔːdərɔɪ] *n* pana

core [kɔː*] *n* centro, núcleo; *(of fruit)* corazón *m*; *(of problem)* meollo ♦ *vt* quitar el corazón de

coriander [kɔrɪ'ændə*] *n* culantro

cork [kɔːk] *n* corcho; *(tree)* alcornoque *m*; **~screw** *n* sacacorchos *m inv*

corn [kɔːn] *n* *(BRIT: cereal crop)* trigo; *(US: maize)* maíz *m*; *(on foot)* callo; **~ on the cob** *(CULIN)* maíz en la mazorca *(SP)*, choclo *(AM)*

corned beef [kɔːnd-] *n* carne *f* acecinada (en lata)

corner ['kɔːnə*] *n* *(outside)* esquina; *(inside)* rincón *m*; *(in road)* curva; *(FOOTBALL)* córner *m*; *(BOXING)* esquina ♦ *vt* *(trap)* arrinconar; *(COMM)* acaparar ♦ *vi* *(in car)* tomar las curvas; **~stone** *n* *(also fig)* piedra angular

cornet ['kɔːnɪt] *n* (MUS) corneta; (BRIT: *of ice-cream*) cucurucho

cornflakes ['kɔːnfleɪks] *npl* copos *mpl* de maíz, cornflakes *mpl*

cornflour ['kɔːnflauə*] (BRIT), **cornstarch** ['kɔːnstɑːtʃ] (US) *n* harina de maíz

Cornwall ['kɔːnwəl] *n* Cornualles *f*

corny ['kɔːnɪ] *(inf)* adj gastado

coronary ['kɔrənərɪ] *n* (*also*: ~ *thrombosis*) infarto

coronation [kɔrə'neɪʃən] *n* coronación *f*

coroner ['kɔrənə*] *n* juez *m* (de instrucción)

corporal ['kɔːpərl] *n* cabo ♦ *adj*: ~ **punishment** castigo corporal

corporate ['kɔːpərɪt] *adj* (action, ownership) colectivo; (finance, image) corporativo

corporation [kɔːpə'reɪʃən] *n* (of town) ayuntamiento; (COMM) corporación *f*

corps [kɔː*, *pl* kɔːz] *n inv* cuerpo; **diplomatic** ~ cuerpo diplomático; **press** ~ gabinete *m* de prensa

corpse [kɔːps] *n* cadáver *m*

correct [kə'rekt] *adj* justo, exacto; (proper) correcto ♦ *vt* corregir; (exam) corregir, calificar; **~ion** [-ʃən] *n* (act) corrección *f*; (instance) rectificación *f*

correspond [kɔrɪs'pɔnd] *vi* (write): **to** ~ **(with)** escribirse (con); (be equivalent to): **to** ~ **(to)** corresponder (a); (be in accordance): **to** ~ **(with)** corresponder (con); **~ence** *n* correspondencia *f*; **~ence course** *n* curso por correspondencia; **~ent** *n* corresponsal *m/f*

corridor ['kɔrɪdɔː*] *n* pasillo

corrode [kə'rəud] *vt* corroer ♦ *vi* corroerse

corrugated ['kɔrəgeɪtɪd] *adj* ondulado; ~ **iron** *n* chapa ondulada

corrupt [kə'rʌpt] *adj* (person) corrupto; (COMPUT) corrompido ♦ *vt* corromper; (COMPUT) degradar

Corsica ['kɔːsɪkə] *n* Córcega

cosmetic [kɔz'metɪk] *adj*, *n* cosmético

cosmopolitan [kɔzmə'pɔlɪtn] *adj* cosmopolita

cost [kɔst] (*pt*, *pp* cost) *n* (price) precio; **~s** *npl* (COMM) costes *mpl*; (LAW) costas *fpl* ♦ *vi* costar, valer ♦ *vt* preparar el presupuesto de; **how much does it** ~? ¿cuánto cuesta?; **to** ~ **sb time/effort** costarle a uno tiempo/esfuerzo; **it** ~ **him his life** le costó la vida; **at all** ~s cueste lo que cueste

co-star ['kəustɑː*] *n* coprotagonista *m/f*

Costa Rica ['kɔstə'riːkə] *n* Costa Rica; **~n** *adj*, *n* costarriqueño/a *m/f*

cost-effective [kɔstɪ'fektɪv] *adj* rentable

costly ['kɔstlɪ] *adj* costoso

cost-of-living [kɔstəv'lɪvɪŋ] *adj*: ~ **allowance** plus *m* de carestía de vida; ~ **index** índice *m* del costo de vida

cost price (BRIT) *n* precio de coste

costume ['kɔstjuːm] *n* traje *m*; (BRIT: *also*: *swimming* ~) traje de baño; ~ **jewellery** *n* bisutería

cosy ['kəuzɪ] (US **cozy**) *adj* (person) cómodo; (room) acogedor(a)

cot [kɔt] *n* (BRIT: child's) cuna; (US: *campbed*) cama de campaña

cottage ['kɔtɪdʒ] *n* casita de campo; (rustic) barraca; ~ **cheese** *n* requesón *m*

cotton ['kɔtn] *n* algodón *m*; (thread) hilo; ~ **on to** (inf) *vt fus* caer en la cuenta de; ~ **candy** (US) *n* algodón *m* (azucarado); ~ **wool** (BRIT) *n* algodón *m* (hidrófilo)

couch [kautʃ] *n* sofá *m*; (doctor's etc) diván *m*

couchette [kuː'ʃet] *n* litera

cough [kɔf] *vi* toser ♦ *n* tos *f*; ~ **drop** *n* pastilla para la tos

could [kud] *pt of* **can²**; **~n't** = could not

council ['kaunsl] n consejo; **city** or **town** ~ consejo municipal; ~ **estate** (BRIT) n urbanización f de viviendas municipales de alquiler; ~ **house** (BRIT) n vivienda municipal de alquiler; ~**lor** n concejal(a) m/f

counsel ['kaunsl] n (advice) consejo; (lawyer) abogado/a ♦ vt aconsejar; ~**lor** n consejero/a; ~**or** (US) n abogado/a

count [kaunt] vt contar; (include) incluir ♦ vi contar ♦ n cuenta; (of votes) escrutinio; (level) nivel m; (nobleman) conde m; ~ **on** vt fus contar con; ~**down** n cuenta atrás

countenance ['kauntinəns] n semblante m, rostro ♦ vt (tolerate) aprobar, tolerar

counter ['kauntə*] n (in shop) mostrador m; (in game) ficha ♦ vt contrarrestar ♦ adv: **to run** ~ **to** ser contrario a, ir en contra de; ~**act** vt contrarrestar

counterfeit ['kauntəfit] n falsificación f, simulación f ♦ vt falsificar ♦ adj falso, falsificado

counterfoil ['kauntəfɔil] n talón m

counterpart ['kauntəpɑːt] n homólogo/a

counter-productive [kauntəprə'-dʌktiv] adj contraproducente

countersign ['kauntəsain] vt refrendar

countess ['kauntis] n condesa

countless ['kauntlis] adj innumerable

country ['kʌntri] n país m; (native land) patria; (as opposed to town) campo; (region) región f, tierra; ~ **dancing** (BRIT) n baile m regional; ~ **house** n casa de campo; ~**man** (irreg) (compatriot) compatriota m; (rural) campesino, paisano; ~**side** n campo

county ['kaunti] n condado

coup [kuː] (pl ~**s**) n (also: ~ **d'état**) golpe m (de estado); (achievement) éxito

couple ['kʌpl] n (of things) par m; (of people) pareja; (married ~) matrimonio; **a** ~ **of** un par de

coupon ['kuːpɔn] n cupón m; (voucher) valé m

courage ['kʌrɪdʒ] n valor m, valentía; ~**ous** [kə'reɪdʒəs] adj valiente

courgette [kuə'ʒet] (BRIT) n calabacín m (SP), calabacita (AM)

courier ['kuriə*] n mensajero/a; (for tourists) guía m/f (de turismo)

course [kɔːs] n (direction) dirección f; (of river, SCOL) curso; (process) transcurso; (MED): ~ **of treatment** tratamiento; (of ship) rumbo; (part of meal) plato; (GOLF) campo; **of** ~ desde luego, naturalmente; **of** ~! ¡claro!

court [kɔːt] n (royal) corte f; (LAW) tribunal m, juzgado; (TENNIS etc) pista, cancha ♦ vt (woman) cortejar a; **to take to** ~ demandar

courteous ['kɜːtiəs] adj cortés

courtesy ['kɜːtəsi] n cortesía; **(by)** ~ **of** por cortesía de; ~ **bus**, ~ **coach** n autobús m gratuito

court-house ['kɔːthaus] (US) n palacio de justicia

courtier ['kɔːtiə*] n cortesano

court-martial (pl **courts-martial**) n consejo de guerra

courtroom ['kɔːtrum] n sala de justicia

courtyard ['kɔːtjɑːd] n patio

cousin ['kʌzn] n primo/a; **first** ~ primo/a carnal, primo/a hermano/a

cove [kəuv] n cala, ensenada

covenant ['kʌvənənt] n pacto

cover ['kʌvə*] vt (cover, mistake) ocultar; (with lid) tapar; (book etc) forrar; (distance) recorrer; (include) abarcar; (protect: also: INSURANCE) cubrir; (PRESS) investigar; (discuss) tratar ♦ n cubierta; (lid) tapa; (for chair etc) funda; (envelope) sobre m; (for book) forro; (of magazine) portada; (shelter) abrigo; (INSURANCE) cobertura; (of spy) cobertura; ~**s** npl (on bed) sábanas; mantas; **to take** ~ (shelter) protegerse, resguardarse; **under** ~ (indoors) bajo techo; **under ~ of darkness** al amparo de la oscuridad; **under separate ~** (COMM) por separado; **~ up** vi: **to ~ up for sb** encubrir a uno; **~age** n (TV, PRESS) cobertura; **~alls** (US) npl mono; **~ charge** n precio del cubierto; **~ing** n capa; **~ing letter** (US ~ letter) n carta de explicación; **~ note** n (INSURANCE) póliza provisional

covert ['kʌvət] adj secreto, encubierto

cover-up n encubrimiento

cow [kau] n vaca; (inf: woman) bruja ♦ vt intimidar

coward ['kauəd] n cobarde m/f; **~ice** [-ıs] n cobardía; **~ly** adj cobarde

cowboy ['kaubɔɪ] n vaquero

cower ['kauə*] vi encogerse (de miedo)

coy [kɔɪ] adj tímido

cozy ['kəuzı] (US) adj = **cosy**

CPA (US) n abbr = **certified public accountant**

crab [kræb] n cangrejo; **~ apple** n manzana silvestre

crack [kræk] n grieta; (noise) crujido; (drug) crack m ♦ vt agrietar, romper; (nut) cascar; (solve: problem) resolver; (: code) descifrar; (whip etc) chasquear; (knuckles) crujir; (joke) contar ♦ adj (expert) de primera; **~ down on** vt fus adoptar fuertes medidas contra; **~ up** vi (MED) sufrir una crisis nerviosa; **~er** n (biscuit) cráquer m; (Christmas ~er) petardo sorpresa

crackle ['krækl] vi crepitar

cradle ['kreɪdl] n cuna

craft [krɑːft] n (skill) arte m; (trade) oficio; (cunning) astucia; (boat: pl inv) barco; (plane: pl inv) avión m

craftsman ['krɑːftsmən] n artesano; **~ship** n (quality) destreza

crafty ['krɑːftı] adj astuto

crag [kræg] n peñasco

cram [kræm] vt (fill): **to ~ sth with** llenar algo (a reventar) de; (put): **to ~ sth into** meter algo a la fuerza en

♦ vi (for exams) empollar

cramp [kræmp] n (MED) calambre m; **~ed** adj apretado, estrecho

cranberry ['krænbərı] n arándano agrio

crane [kreɪn] n (TECH) grúa; (bird) grulla

crank [kræŋk] n manivela; (person) chiflado

cranny ['krænı] n see **nook**

crash [kræʃ] n (noise) estrépito; (of cars etc) choque m; (of plane) accidente m de aviación; (COMM) quiebra ♦ vt (car, plane) estrellar ♦ vi (car, plane) estrellarse; (two cars) chocar; (COMM) quebrar; **~ course** n curso acelerado; **~ helmet** n casco (protector); **~ landing** n aterrizaje m forzado

crass [kræs] adj grosero, maleducado

crate [kreɪt] n cajón m de embalaje; (for bottles) caja

cravat(e) [krə'væt] n pañuelo

crave [kreɪv] vt, vi: **to ~ (for)** ansiar, anhelar

crawl [krɔːl] vi (drag o.s.) arrastrarse; (child) andar a gatas, gatear; (vehicle) avanzar (lentamente) ♦ n (SWIMMING) crol m

crayfish ['kreɪfıʃ] n inv (freshwater) cangrejo de río; (saltwater) cigala

crayon ['kreɪən] n lápiz m de color

craze [kreɪz] n (fashion) moda

crazy ['kreɪzı] adj (person) loco; (idea) disparatado; (inf: keen): **~ about sb/ sth** loco por uno/algo

creak [kriːk] vi (floorboard) crujir; (hinge etc) chirriar, rechinar

cream [kriːm] n (of milk) nata, crema; (lotion) crema; (fig) flor f y nata ♦ adj (colour) color crema; **~ cake** n pastel m de nata; **~ cheese** n queso blanco; **~y** adj cremoso; (colour) color crema

crease [kriːs] n (fold) pliegue m; (in trousers) raya; (wrinkle) arruga ♦ vt (wrinkle) arrugar ♦ vi (wrinkle up) arrugarse

create [kriː'eɪt] vt crear; **creation**

[-fən] n creación f; **creative** adj
creativo; **creator** n creador/a m/f
creature ['kriːtʃə*] n (animal) animal
m, bicho; (person) criatura
crèche [krɛʃ] n guardería (infantil)
credence ['kriːdəns] n: **to lend** or
give ~ to creer en, dar crédito a
credentials [krɪ'denʃlz] npl (references)
referencias fpl; (identity papers)
documentos mpl de identidad
credible ['krɛdɪbl] adj creíble;
(trustworthy) digno de confianza
credit ['krɛdɪt] n crédito; (merit) honor
m, mérito ♦ vt (COMM) abonar; (believe:
also: **give ~ to**) creer, prestar fe a ♦ adj
crediticio; **~s** npl (CINEMA) fichas fpl
técnicas; **to be in ~** (person) tener
saldo a favor; **to ~ sb with** (fig)
reconocer a uno el mérito de; **~ card**
n tarjeta de crédito; **~or** n acreedor/a
m/f
creed [kriːd] n credo
creek [kriːk] n cala, ensenada; (US)
riachuelo
creep [kriːp] (pt, pp crept) vi
arrastrarse; **~er** n enredadera; **~y**
(frightening) horripilante
cremate [krɪ'meɪt] vt incinerar
crematorium [krɛmə'tɔːrɪəm] (pl
crematoria) n crematorio
crêpe [kreɪp] n (fabric) crespón m;
(also: ~ rubber) crepé m; **~ bandage**
(BRIT) n venda de crepé
crept [krɛpt] pt, pp of **creep**
crescent ['krɛsnt] n media luna;
(street) calle f (en forma de semicírculo)
cress [krɛs] n berro
crest [krɛst] n (of bird) cresta; (of hill)
cima, cumbre f; (of coat of arms)
blasón m; **~fallen** adj alicaído
crevice ['krɛvɪs] n grieta, hendidura
crew [kruː] n (of ship etc) tripulación f;
(TV, CINEMA) equipo; **~-cut** n corte m
al rape; **~-neck** n cuello a la caja
crib [krɪb] n cuna ♦ vt (inf) plagiar
crick [krɪk] n (in neck) tortícolis f
cricket ['krɪkɪt] n (insect) grillo; (game)

cricket m
crime [kraɪm] n (no pl: illegal activities)
crimen m; (illegal action) delito;
criminal ['krɪmɪnl] n criminal m/f,
delincuente m/f ♦ adj criminal; (illegal)
delictivo; (law) penal
crimson ['krɪmzn] adj carmesí
cringe [krɪndʒ] vi agacharse, encogerse
crinkle ['krɪŋkl] vt arrugar
cripple ['krɪpl] n lisiado/a, cojo/a ♦ vt
lisiar, mutilar
crisis ['kraɪsɪs] (pl **crises**) n crisis f inv
crisp [krɪsp] adj fresco; (vegetables etc)
crujiente; (manner) seco; **~s** (BRIT) npl
patatas fpl (SP) or papas fpl (AM) fritas
crisscross ['krɪskrɔs] adj entrelazado
criterion [kraɪ'tɪərɪən] (pl **criteria**) n
criterio
critic ['krɪtɪk] n crítico/a; **~al** adj
crítico; (illness) grave; **~ally** adv (speak
etc) en tono crítico; (ill) gravemente;
~ism ['krɪtɪsɪzm] n crítica; **~ize**
['krɪtɪsaɪz] vt criticar
croak [krəuk] vi (frog) croar; (raven)
graznar; (person) gruñir
Croatia [krəu'eɪʃə] n Croacia
crochet ['krəuʃeɪ] n ganchillo
crockery ['krɔkərɪ] n loza, vajilla
crocodile ['krɔkədaɪl] n cocodrilo
crocus ['krəukəs] n croco, crocus m
croft [krɔft] n granja pequeña
crony ['krəunɪ] (inf: pej) n compinche
m/f
crook [kruk] n ladrón/ona m/f; (of
shepherd) cayado; **~ed** ['krukɪd] adj
torcido; (dishonest) nada honrado
crop [krɔp] n (produce) cultivo; (amount
produced) cosecha; (riding ~) látigo de
montar ♦ vt cortar, recortar; **~ up** vi
surgir, presentarse
cross [krɔs] n cruz f; (hybrid) cruce m
♦ vt (street etc) cruzar, atravesar ♦ adj
de mal humor, enojado; **~ out** vt
tachar; **~ over** vi cruzar; **~bar** n
travesaño; **~country (race)** n carrera
a campo traviesa, cross m; **~-examine**
vt interrogar; **~-eyed** adj bizco; **~fire**

n fuego cruzado; **~ing** *n* (*sea passage*) travesía; (*also: pedestrian ~ing*) paso para peatones; **~ing guard** (*US*) *n* persona encargada de ayudar a los niños a cruzar la calle; **~ purposes** *npl*: **to be at ~ purposes** no comprenderse uno a otro; **~reference** *n* referencia, llamada; **~roads** *n* cruce *m*, encrucijada; **~ section** *n* corte *m* transversal; (*of population*) muestra (*representativa*); **~walk** (*US*) *n* paso de peatones; **~wind** *n* viento de costado; **~word** *n* crucigrama *m*

crotch [krɔtʃ] *n* (*ANAT, of garment*) entrepierna

crotchet [ˈkrɔtʃɪt] *n* (*MUS*) negra

crouch [krautʃ] *vi* agacharse, acurrucarse

crow [krəu] *n* (*bird*) cuervo; (*of cock*) canto, cacareo ♦ *vi* (*cock*) cantar

crowbar [ˈkrəubɑ:*] *n* palanca

crowd [kraud] *n* muchedumbre *f*, multitud *f* ♦ *vt* (*fill*) llenar ♦ *vi* (*gather*): **to ~ round** reunirse en torno a; (*cram*): **to ~ in** entrar en tropel; **~ed** *adj* (*full*) atestado; (*densely populated*) superpoblado

crown [kraun] *n* corona; (*of head*) coronilla; (*for tooth*) funda; (*of hill*) cumbre *f* ♦ *vt* coronar; (*fig*) completar, rematar; **~ jewels** *npl* joyas *fpl* reales; **~ prince** *n* heredero

crow's feet *npl* patas *fpl* de gallo

crucial [ˈkru:ʃl] *adj* decisivo

crucifix [ˈkru:sɪfɪks] *n* crucifijo; **~ion** [-ˈfɪkʃən] *n* crucifixión *f*

crude [kru:d] *adj* (*materials*) bruto; (*fig: basic*) tosco; (: *vulgar*) ordinario; **~ (oil)** *n* (*petróleo*) crudo

cruel [ˈkruəl] *adj* cruel; **~ty** *n* crueldad *f*

cruise [kru:z] *n* crucero ♦ *vi* (*ship*) hacer un crucero; (*car*) ir a velocidad de crucero; **~r** *n* (*motorboat*) yate *m* de motor; (*warship*) crucero

crumb [krʌm] *n* miga, migaja

crumble [ˈkrʌmbl] *vt* desmenuzar ♦ *vi*

(*building, also fig*) desmoronarse; **crumbly** *adj* que se desmigaja fácilmente

crumpet [ˈkrʌmpɪt] *n* ≈ bollo para tostar

crumple [ˈkrʌmpl] *vt* (*paper*) estrujar; (*material*) arrugar

crunch [krʌntʃ] *vt* (*with teeth*) mascar; (*underfoot*) hacer crujir ♦ *n* (*fig*) hora o momento de la verdad; **~y** *adj* crujiente

crusade [kru:ˈseɪd] *n* cruzada

crush [krʌʃ] *n* (*crowd*) aglomeración *f*; (*infatuation*): **to have a ~ on sb** estar loco por uno; (*drink*): **lemon ~** limonada ♦ *vt* aplastar; (*paper*) estrujar; (*cloth*) arrugar; (*fruit*) exprimir; (*opposition*) aplastar; (*hopes*) destruir

crust [krʌst] *n* corteza; (*of snow, ice*) costra

crutch [krʌtʃ] *n* muleta

crux [krʌks] *n*: **the ~ of** lo esencial de, el quid de

cry [kraɪ] *vi* llorar; (*shout: also: ~ out*) gritar ♦ *n* (*shriek*) chillido; (*shout*) grito; **~ off** *vi* echarse atrás

cryptic [ˈkrɪptɪk] *adj* enigmático, secreto

crystal [ˈkrɪstl] *n* cristal *m*; **~-clear** *adj* claro como el agua

cub [kʌb] *n* cachorro; (*also: ~ scout*) niño explorador

Cuba [ˈkju:bə] *n* Cuba; **~n** *adj*, *n* cubano/a *m/f*

cube [kju:b] *n* cubo ♦ *vt* (*MATH*) cubicar; **cubic** *adj* cúbico

cubicle [ˈkju:bɪkl] *n* (*at pool*) caseta; (*for bed*) cubículo

cuckoo [ˈkuku:] *n* cuco; **~ clock** *n* reloj *m* de cucú

cucumber [ˈkju:kʌmbə*] *n* pepino

cuddle [ˈkʌdl] *vt* ♦ *vi* abrazarse

cue [kju:] *n* (*snooker*) taco; (*THEATRE etc*) señal *f*

cuff [kʌf] *n* (*of sleeve*) puño; (*US: of trousers*) vuelta; (*blow*) bofetada; **off the ~** *adv* de improviso; **~links** *npl* gemelos *mpl*

cuisine [kwi'zi:n] *n* cocina

cul-de-sac ['kʌldəsæk] *n* callejón *m* sin salida

cull [kʌl] *vt* (*idea*) sacar ♦ *n* (*of animals*) matanza selectiva

culminate ['kʌlmɪneɪt] *vi*: **to ~ in** terminar en; **culmination** [-'neɪʃən] *n* culminación *f*, colmo

culottes [ku:'lɒts] *npl* falda pantalón *f*

culprit ['kʌlprɪt] *n* culpable *m/f*

cult [kʌlt] *n* culto

cultivate ['kʌltɪveɪt] *vt* (*also fig*) cultivar; **~d** *adj* culto; **cultivation** [-'veɪʃən] *n* cultivo

cultural ['kʌltʃərəl] *adj* cultural

culture ['kʌltʃə*] *n* (*also fig*) cultura; (*BIO*) cultivo; **~d** *adj* culto

cumbersome ['kʌmbəsəm] *adj* de mucho bulto, voluminoso; (*process*) enrevesado

cunning ['kʌnɪŋ] *n* astucia ♦ *adj* astuto

cup [kʌp] *n* taza; (*as prize*) copa

cupboard ['kʌbəd] *n* armario; (*kitchen*) alacena

cup tie (*BRIT*) *n* partido de copa

curate ['kjuərɪt] *n* cura *m*

curator [kjuə'reɪtə*] *n* director(a) *m/f*

curb [kə:b] *vt* refrenar; (*person*) reprimir ♦ *n* freno; (*US*) bordillo

curdle ['kə:dl] *vi* cuajarse

cure [kjuə*] *vt* curar ♦ *n* cura, curación *f*; (*fig: solution*) remedio

curfew ['kə:fju:] *n* toque *m* de queda

curiosity [kjuərɪ'ɔsɪtɪ] *n* curiosidad *f*

curious ['kjuərɪəs] *adj* curioso; (*person: interested*): **to be ~** sentir curiosidad

curl [kə:l] *n* rizo ♦ *vt* (*hair*) rizar ♦ *vi* rizarse; **~ up** *vi* (*person*) hacerse un ovillo; **~er** *n* rulo; **~y** *adj* rizado

currant ['kʌrnt] *n* pasa (de Corinto); (*black~, red~*) grosella

currency ['kʌrnsɪ] *n* moneda; **to gain ~** (*fig*) difundirse

current ['kʌrnt] *n* corriente *f* ♦ *adj* (*accepted*) corriente; (*present*) actual; **~ account** (*BRIT*) *n* cuenta corriente;

~ affairs *npl* noticias *fpl* de actualidad; **~ly** *adv* actualmente

curriculum [kə'rɪkjuləm] (*pl* **~s** or **curricula**) *n* plan *m* de estudios; **~ vitae** *n* currículum *m*

curry ['kʌrɪ] *n* curry *m* ♦ *vt*: **to ~ favour with** buscar favores con; **~ powder** *n* curry *m* en polvo

curse [kə:s] *vi* soltar tacos ♦ *vt* maldecir ♦ *n* maldición *f*; (*swearword*) palabrota, taco

cursor ['kə:sə*] *n* (*COMPUT*) cursor *m*

cursory ['kə:sərɪ] *adj* rápido, superficial

curt [kə:t] *adj* corto, seco

curtail [kə:'teɪl] *vt* (*visit etc*) acortar; (*freedom*) restringir; (*expenses etc*) reducir

curtain ['kə:tn] *n* cortina; (*THEATRE*) telón *m*

curts(e)y ['kə:tsɪ] *vi* hacer una reverencia

curve [kə:v] *n* curva ♦ *vi* (*road*) hacer una curva; (*line etc*) curvarse

cushion ['kuʃən] *n* cojín *m*; (*of air*) colchón *m* ♦ *vt* (*shock*) amortiguar

custard ['kʌstəd] *n* natillas *fpl*

custody ['kʌstədɪ] *n* custodia; **to take into ~** detener

custom ['kʌstəm] *n* costumbre *f*; (*COMM*) clientela; **~ary** *adj* acostumbrado

customer ['kʌstəmə*] *n* cliente *m/f*

customized ['kʌstəmaɪzd] *adj* (*car etc*) hecho a encargo

custom-made *adj* hecho a la medida

customs ['kʌstəmz] *npl* aduana; **~ officer** *n* aduanero/a

cut [kʌt] (*pt, pp* **cut**) *vt* cortar; (*price*) rebajar; (*text, programme*) acortar; (*reduce*) reducir ♦ *vi* cortar ♦ *n* (*of garment*) corte *m*; (*in skin*) cortadura, tajada; (*in salary etc*) rebaja; (*in spending*) reducción *f*, recorte *m*; (*slice of meat*) tajada; **to ~ a tooth** echar un diente; **~ down** *vt* (*tree*) derribar; (*reduce*) reducir; **~ off** *vt* cortar; (*person, place*) aislar; (*TEL*) desconectar; **~ out** *vt* (*shape*) recortar; (*stop: activity etc*) dejar; (*remove*) quitar; **~ up** *vt* cortar (en pedazos); **~back** *n* reducción *f*

cute [kju:t] *adj* mono

cuticle ['kju:tɪkl] *n* cutícula

cutlery ['kʌtlərɪ] *n* cubiertos *mpl*

cutlet ['kʌtlɪt] *n* chuleta; (*nut etc ~*) plato vegetariano hecho con nueces y verdura en forma de chuleta

cut: **~out** *n* (*switch*) dispositivo de seguridad, disyuntor *m*; (*cardboard ~out*) recortable *m*; **~-price** (*US* **~-rate**) *adj* a precio reducido; **~throat** *n* asesino/a ♦ *adj* feroz

cutting ['kʌtɪŋ] *adj* (*remark*) mordaz ♦ *n* (*BRIT: from newspaper*) recorte *m*; (*from plant*) esqueje *m*

CV *n abbr* = **curriculum vitae**

cwt *abbr* = **hundredweight(s)**

cyanide ['saɪənaɪd] *n* cianuro

cycle ['saɪkl] *n* ciclo; (*bicycle*) bicicleta ♦ *vi* ir en bicicleta; **~ lane** *n* carril-bici *m*; **~ path** *n* carril-bici *m*; **cycling** *n* ciclismo; **cyclist** *n* ciclista *m/f*

cyclone ['saɪkləun] *n* ciclón *m*

cygnet ['sɪgnɪt] *n* pollo de cisne

cylinder ['sɪlɪndə*] *n* cilindro; (*of gas*) bombona; **~-head gasket** *n* junta de culata

cymbals ['sɪmblz] *npl* platillos *mpl*

cynic ['sɪnɪk] *n* cínico/a; **~al** *adj* cínico; **~ism** ['sɪnɪsɪzəm] *n* cinismo

Cyprus ['saɪprəs] *n* Chipre *f*

cyst [sɪst] *n* quiste *m*; **~itis** [-'taɪtɪs] *n* cistitis *f*

czar [zɑ:*] *n* zar *m*

Czech [tʃek] *adj, n* checo/a *m/f*; **~ Republic** *n* la República Checa

D, d

D [di:] *n* (*MUS*) re *m*

dab [dæb] *vt* (*eyes, wound*) tocar (ligeramente); (*paint, cream*) poner un poco de

dabble ['dæbl] *vi*: **to ~ in** ser algo

aficionado a

dad [dæd] *n* = **daddy**

daddy ['dædɪ] *n* papá *m*

daffodil ['dæfədɪl] *n* narciso

daft [dɑ:ft] *adj* tonto

dagger ['dægə*] *n* puñal *m*, daga

daily ['deɪlɪ] *adj* diario, cotidiano ♦ *adv* todos los días, cada día

dainty ['deɪntɪ] *adj* delicado

dairy ['dɛərɪ] *n* (*shop*) lechería; (*on farm*) vaquería; **~ farm** *n* granja; **~ products** *npl* productos *mpl* lácteos; **~ store** (*US*) *n* lechería

daisy ['deɪzɪ] *n* margarita

dale [deɪl] *n* valle *m*

dam [dæm] *n* presa ♦ *vt* construir una presa sobre, represar

damage ['dæmɪdʒ] *n* lesión *f*; daño; (*dents etc*) desperfectos *mpl*; (*fig*) perjuicio ♦ *vt* dañar, perjudicar; (*spoil, break*) estropear; **~s** *npl* (*LAW*) daños *mpl* y perjuicios

damn [dæm] *vt* condenar; (*curse*) maldecir ♦ *n* (*inf*): **I don't give a ~** me importa un pito ♦ *adj* (*inf: also:* **~ed**) maldito; **~ (it)!** ¡maldito sea!; **~ing** *adj* (*evidence*) irrecusable

damp [dæmp] *adj* húmedo, mojado ♦ *n* humedad *f* ♦ *vt* (*also:* **~en:** *cloth, rag*) mojar; (*: enthusiasm*) enfriar

damson ['dæmzən] *n* ciruela damascena

dance [dɑ:ns] *n* baile *m* ♦ *vi* bailar; **~ hall** *n* salón *m* de baile; **~r** *n* bailador/a *m/f*, (*professional*) bailarín/ina *m/f*; **dancing** *n* baile *m*

dandelion ['dændɪlaɪən] *n* diente de león

dandruff ['dændrəf] *n* caspa

Dane [deɪn] *n* danés/esa *m/f*

danger ['deɪndʒə*] *n* peligro; (*risk*) riesgo; **~!** (*on sign*) ¡peligro de muerte!; **to be in ~** correr riesgo de; **~ous** *adj* peligroso; **~ously** *adv* peligrosamente

dangle ['dæŋgl] *vt* colgar ♦ *vi* pender, colgar

Danish ['deɪnɪʃ] adj danés/esa ♦ n
(LING) danés m

dare [dɛə*] vt: **to ~ sb to do** desafiar
a uno a hacer ♦ vi: **to ~ (to) do sth**
atreverse a hacer algo; **I ~ say** (I
suppose) puede ser (que); **daring** adj
atrevido, osado ♦ n atrevimiento,
osadía

dark [dɑːk] adj oscuro; (hair,
complexion) moreno ♦ n: **in the ~** a
oscuras; **to be in the ~ about** (fig) no
saber nada de; **after ~** después del
anochecer; **~en** vt (colour) hacer más
oscuro ♦ vi oscurecerse; **~ glasses** npl
gafas fpl negras (SP), anteojos mpl
negros (AM); **~ness** n oscuridad f;
~room n cuarto oscuro

darling ['dɑːlɪŋ] adj, n querido/a m/f

darn [dɑːn] vt zurcir

dart [dɑːt] n dardo; (in sewing) sisa ♦ vi
precipitarse; **~ away/along** vi salir/
marchar disparado; **~board** n diana;
~s n dardos mpl

dash [dæʃ] n (small quantity: of liquid)
gota, chorrito; (: of solid) pizca; (sign)
raya ♦ vt (throw) lanzar; (hopes)
defraudar ♦ vi precipitarse, ir de prisa;
~ away or **off** vi marcharse
apresuradamente

dashboard ['dæʃbɔːd] n (AUT)
salpicadero

dashing ['dæʃɪŋ] adj gallardo

data ['deɪtə] npl datos mpl; **~base** n
base f de datos; **~ processing** n
proceso de datos

date [deɪt] n (day) fecha; (with friend)
cita; (fruit) dátil m ♦ vt fechar; (person)
salir con; **~ of birth** fecha de
nacimiento; **to ~** adv hasta la fecha;
~d adj anticuado; **~ rape** n violación
ocurrida durante una cita con un
conocido

daub [dɔːb] vt embadurnar

daughter ['dɔːtə*] n hija; **~-in-law** n
nuera, hija política

daunting ['dɔːntɪŋ] adj
desalentador(a)

dawdle ['dɔːdl] vi (go slowly) andar
muy despacio

dawn [dɔːn] n alba, amanecer m; (fig)
nacimiento ♦ vi (day) amanecer; (fig):
it ~ed on him that ... cayó en la
cuenta de que ...

day [deɪ] n día m; (working ~) jornada;
(hey~) tiempos mpl, días mpl; **the
~ before/after** el día anterior/
siguiente; **the ~ after tomorrow**
pasado mañana; **the ~ before
yesterday** anteayer; **the following ~**
el día siguiente; **by ~** de día; **~break** n
amanecer m; **~dream** vi soñar
despierto; **~light** n luz f (del día);
~ return (BRIT) n billete m de ida y
vuelta (en un día); **~time** n día m; **~-
to-~** adj cotidiano

daze [deɪz] vt (stun) aturdir ♦ n: **in a ~**
aturdido

dazzle ['dæzl] vt deslumbrar

DC abbr (= direct current) corriente f
continua

dead [dɛd] adj muerto; (limb) dormido;
(telephone) cortado; (battery) agotado
♦ adv (completely) totalmente; (exactly)
exactamente; **to shoot sb ~** matar a
uno a tiros; **~ tired** muerto de
cansancio); **to stop ~** parar en seco;
the ~ npl los muertos; **to be a ~ loss**
(inf: person) ser un inútil; **~en** vt (blow,
sound) amortiguar; (pain etc) aliviar;
~ end n callejón m sin salida; **~ heat**
n (SPORT) empate m; **~line** n fecha (or
hora) tope; **~lock** n: **to reach ~lock**
llegar a un punto muerto; **~ly** adj
mortal, fatal; **~pan** adj sin expresión;
the D~ Sea n el Mar Muerto

deaf [dɛf] adj sordo; **~en** vt
ensordecer; **~ness** n sordera

deal [diːl] n (pt, pp **dealt**) n (agreement)
pacto, convenio; (business ~) trato ♦ vt
dar; (card) repartir; **a great ~ (of)**
bastante, mucho; **~ in** vt fus tratar en,
comerciar en; **~ with** vt fus (people)
tratar con; (problem) ocuparse de;
(subject) tratar de; **~ings** npl (COMM)

transacciones *fpl*; (*relations*) relaciones *fpl*

dealt [delt] *pt, pp of* **deal**

dean [di:n] *n* (*REL*) deán *m*; (*SCOL: BRIT*) decano; (: *US*) decano; rector *m*

dear [dɪə*] *adj* querido; (*expensive*) caro ♦ *n*: **my ~** mi querido/a ♦ *excl* **~ me!** ¡Dios mío!; **D~ Sir/Madam** (*in letter*) Muy Señor Mío, Estimado Señor/ Estimada Señora; **D~ Mr/Mrs X** Estimado/a Señor(a) X; **~ly** *adv* (*love*) mucho; (*pay*) caro

death [deθ] *n* muerte *f*; **~ certificate** *n* partida de defunción; **~ly** *adj* (*white*) como un muerto; (*silence*) sepulcral; **~ penalty** *n* pena de muerte; **~ rate** *n* mortalidad *f*; **~ toll** *n* número de víctimas

debacle [deɪˈbɑːkl] *n* desastre *m*

debase [dɪˈbeɪs] *vt* degradar

debatable [dɪˈbeɪtəbl] *adj* discutible

debate [dɪˈbeɪt] *n* debate *m* ♦ *vt* discutir

debit [ˈdebɪt] *n* debe *m* ♦ *vt*: **to ~ a sum to sb** *or* **to sb's account** cargar una suma en cuenta a alguien

debris [ˈdebriː] *n* escombros *mpl*

debt [det] *n* deuda; **to be in ~** tener deudas; **~or** *n* deudor(a) *m/f*

début [ˈdeɪbjuː] *n* presentación *f*

decade [ˈdekeɪd] *n* decenio, década

decadence [ˈdekədəns] *n* decadencia

decaff [ˈdiːkæf] (*inf*) *n* descafeinado

decaffeinated [dɪˈkæfɪneɪtɪd] *adj* descafeinado

decanter [dɪˈkæntə*] *n* garrafa

decay [dɪˈkeɪ] *n* (*of building*) desmoronamiento; (*of tooth*) caries *f inv* ♦ *vi* (*rot*) pudrirse

deceased [dɪˈsiːst] *n*: **the ~** el/la difunto/a

deceit [dɪˈsiːt] *n* engaño; **~ful** *adj* engañoso; **deceive** [dɪˈsiːv] *vt* engañar

December [dɪˈsembə*] *n* diciembre *m*

decent [ˈdiːsənt] *adj* (*proper*) decente; (*person: kind*) amable, bueno

deception [dɪˈsepʃən] *n* engaño

deceptive [dɪˈseptɪv] *adj* engañoso

decibel [ˈdesɪbel] *n* decibel(io) *m*

decide [dɪˈsaɪd] *vt* (*person*) decidir; (*question, argument*) resolver ♦ *vi* decidir; **to ~ to do/that** decidir hacer/que; **to ~ on sth** decidirse por algo; **~d** *adj* (*resolute*) decidido; (*clear, definite*) indudable; **~dly** [-dɪdlɪ] *adv* decididamente; (*emphatically*) con resolución

deciduous [dɪˈsɪdjuəs] *adj* de hoja caduca

decimal [ˈdesɪml] *adj* decimal ♦ *n* decimal *m*; **~ point** *n* coma decimal

decipher [dɪˈsaɪfə*] *vt* descifrar

decision [dɪˈsɪʒən] *n* decisión *f*

decisive [dɪˈsaɪsɪv] *adj* decisivo; (*person*) decidido

deck [dek] *n* (*NAUT*) cubierta; (*of bus*) piso; (*record ~*) platina; (*of cards*) baraja; **~chair** *n* tumbona

declaration [dekləˈreɪʃən] *n* declaración *f*

declare [dɪˈkleə*] *vt* declarar

decline [dɪˈklaɪn] *n* disminución *f*, descenso ♦ *vt* rehusar ♦ *vi* (*person, business*) decaer; (*strength*) disminuir

decoder [diːˈkəʊdə*] *n* (*TV*) decodificador *m*

décor [ˈdeɪkɔː*] *n* decoración *f*; (*THEATRE*) decorado

decorate [ˈdekəreɪt] *vt* (*adorn*): **to ~ (with)** adornar (de), decorar (de); (*paint*) pintar; (*paper*) empapelar; **decoration** [-ˈreɪʃən] *n* adorno; (*act*) decoración *f*; (*medal*) condecoración *f*; **decorator** (*workman*) pintor *m* (decorador)

decorum [dɪˈkɔːrəm] *n* decoro

decoy [ˈdiːkɔɪ] *n* señuelo

decrease [*n* ˈdiːkriːs, *vb* diˈkriːs] *n*: **~ (in)** disminución *f* (de) ♦ *vt* disminuir, reducir ♦ *vi* reducirse

decree [dɪˈkriː] *n* decreto; **~ nisi** *n* sentencia provisional de divorcio

dedicate [ˈdedɪkeɪt] *vt* dedicar; **dedication** [-ˈkeɪʃən] *n* (*devotion*)

dedicación f; (*in book*) dedicatoria
deduce [dɪ'djuːs] *vt* deducir
deduct [dɪ'dʌkt] *vt* restar; descontar; **~ion** [dɪ'dʌkʃən] *n* (*amount deducted*) descuento; (*conclusion*) deducción f, conclusión f
deed [diːd] *n* hecho, acto; (*feat*) hazaña; (LAW) escritura
deep [diːp] *adj* profundo; (*expressing measurements*) de profundidad; (*voice*) bajo; (*breath*) profundo; (*colour*) intenso ♦ *adv*: **the spectators stood 20 ~** los espectadores se formaron de 20 en fondo; **to be 4 metres ~** tener 4 metros de profundidad; **~en** *vt* ahondar, profundizar ♦ *vi* aumentar, crecer; **~-freeze** *n* congelador *m*; **~-fry** *vt* freír en aceite abundante; **~ly** *adv* (*breathe*) a pleno pulmón; (*interested, moved, grateful*) profundamente, hondamente; **~-sea diving** *n* buceo de altura; **~-seated** *adj* (*beliefs*) (profundamente) arraigado
deer [dɪə*] *n inv* ciervo
deface [dɪ'feɪs] *vt* (*wall, surface*) estropear, pintarrajear
default [dɪ'fɔːlt] *n*: **by ~** (*win*) por incomparecencia ♦ *adj* (COMPUT) por defecto
defeat [dɪ'fiːt] *n* derrota ♦ *vt* derrotar, vencer; **~ist** *adj, n* derrotista *m/f*
defect [*n* 'diːfekt, *vb* dɪ'fekt] *n* defecto ♦ *vi*: **to ~ to the enemy** pasarse al enemigo; **~ive** [dɪ'fektɪv] *adj* defectuoso
defence [dɪ'fens] (US **defense**) *n* defensa; **~less** *adj* indefenso
defend [dɪ'fend] *vt* defender; **~ant** *n* acusado/a; (*in civil case*) demandado/a; **~er** *n* defensor(a) *m/f*; (SPORT) defensa *m/f*
defense [dɪ'fens] (US) *n* = **defence**
defensive [dɪ'fensɪv] *adj* defensivo ♦ *n*: **on the ~** a la defensiva
defer [dɪ'fəː*] *vt* aplazar
defiance [dɪ'faɪəns] *n* desafío; **in ~ of** en contra de; **defiant** [dɪ'faɪənt] *adj*

(*challenging*) desafiante, retador(a)
deficiency [dɪ'fɪʃənsɪ] *n* (*lack*) falta; (*defect*) defecto; **deficient** [dɪ'fɪʃənt] *adj* deficiente
deficit ['defɪsɪt] *n* déficit *m*
define [dɪ'faɪn] *vt* (*word etc*) definir; (*limits etc*) determinar
definite ['defɪnɪt] *adj* (*fixed*) determinado; (*obvious*) claro; (*certain*) indudable; **he was ~ about it** no dejó lugar a dudas (sobre ello); **~ly** *adv* desde luego, por supuesto
definition [defɪ'nɪʃən] *n* definición f; (*clearness*) nitidez f
deflate [diː'fleɪt] *vt* desinflar
deflect [dɪ'flekt] *vt* desviar
defraud [dɪ'frɔːd] *vt*: **to ~ sb of sth** estafar algo a uno
defrost [diː'frɔst] *vt* descongelar; **~er** (US) *n* (*demister*) eliminador *m* de vaho
deft [deft] *adj* diestro, hábil
defunct [dɪ'fʌŋkt] *adj* difunto; (*organization etc*) ya que no existe
defuse [diː'fjuːz] *vt* desactivar; (*situation*) calmar
defy [dɪ'faɪ] *vt* (*resist*) oponerse a; (*challenge*) desafiar; (*fig*): **it defies description** resulta imposible describirlo
degenerate [*vb* dɪ'dʒenəreɪt, *adj* dɪ'dʒenərət] *vi* degenerar ♦ *adj* degenerado
degree [dɪ'griː] *n* grado; (SCOL) título; **to have a ~ in maths** tener una licenciatura en matemáticas; **by ~s** (*gradually*) poco a poco, por etapas; **to some ~** hasta cierto punto
dehydrated [diːhaɪ'dreɪtɪd] *adj* deshidratado; (*milk*) en polvo
de-ice [diː'aɪs] *vt* deshelar
deign [deɪn] *vi*: **to ~ to do** dignarse hacer
dejected [dɪ'dʒektɪd] *adj* abatido, desanimado
delay [dɪ'leɪ] *vt* demorar, aplazar; (*person*) entretener; (*train*) retrasar ♦ *vi* tardar ♦ *n* demora, retraso; **to be ~ed**

retrasarse; **without ~** en seguida, sin tardar

delectable [dɪ'lektəbl] *adj* (*person*) encantador(a); (*food*) delicioso

delegate [*n* 'delɪgɪt, *vb* 'delɪgeɪt] *n* delegado/a ♦ *vt* (*person*) delegar en; (*task*) delegar

delete [dɪ'liːt] *vt* suprimir, tachar

deliberate [*adj* dɪ'lɪbərɪt, *vb* dɪ'lɪbəreɪt] *adj* (*intentional*) intencionado; (*slow*) pausado, lento ♦ *vi* deliberar; **~ly** *adv* (*on purpose*) a propósito

delicacy ['delɪkəsɪ] *n* delicadeza; (*choice food*) manjar *m*

delicate ['delɪkɪt] *adj* delicado; (*fragile*) frágil

delicatessen [delɪkə'tesn] *n* ultramarinos *mpl* finos

delicious [dɪ'lɪʃəs] *adj* delicioso

delight [dɪ'laɪt] *n* (*feeling*) placer *m*, deleite *m*; (*person, experience etc*) encanto, delicia ♦ *vt* encantar, deleitar; **to take ~ in** deleitarse en; **~ed** *adj*: **~ed** (**at** *or* **with/to do**) encantado (con/de hacer); **~ful** *adj* encantador(a), delicioso

delinquent [dɪ'lɪŋkwənt] *adj, n* delincuente *m/f*

delirious [dɪ'lɪrɪəs] *adj*: **to be ~** delirar, desvariar; **to be ~ with** estar loco de

deliver [dɪ'lɪvə*] *vt* (*distribute*) repartir; (*hand over*) entregar; (*message*) comunicar; (*speech*) pronunciar; (*MED*) asistir al parto de; **~y** *n* reparto; entrega; (*of speaker*) modo de expresarse; (*MED*) parto, alumbramiento; **to take ~y of** recibir

delude [dɪ'luːd] *vt* engañar

deluge ['deljuːdʒ] *n* diluvio

delusion [dɪ'luːʒən] *n* ilusión *f*, engaño

de luxe [də'lʌks] *adj* de lujo

demand [dɪ'mɑːnd] *vt* (*gen*) exigir; (*rights*) reclamar ♦ *n* exigencia; (*claim*) reclamación *f*; (*ECON*) demanda; **to be in ~** ser muy solicitado; **on ~** a

solicitud; **~ing** *adj* (*boss*) exigente; (*work*) absorbente

demean [dɪ'miːn] *vt*: **to ~ o.s.** rebajarse

demeanour [dɪ'miːnə*] (*US* **demeanor**) *n* porte *m*, conducta

demented [dɪ'mentɪd] *adj* demente

demise [dɪ'maɪz] *n* (*death*) fallecimiento

demister [diː'mɪstə*] *n* (*AUT*) eliminador *m* de vaho

demo ['deməu] (*inf*) *n abbr* (= *demonstration*) manifestación *f*

democracy [dɪ'mɔkrəsɪ] *n* democracia; **democrat** ['deməkræt] *n* demócrata *m/f*; **democratic** [demə'krætɪk] *adj* democrático; (*US*) demócrata

demolish [dɪ'mɔlɪʃ] *vt* derribar, demoler; (*fig: argument*) destruir

demon ['diːmən] *n* (*evil spirit*) demonio

demonstrate ['demənstreɪt] *vt* demostrar; (*skill, appliance*) mostrar ♦ *vi* manifestarse; **demonstration** [-'streɪʃən] *n* (*POL*) manifestación *f*; (*proof, exhibition*) demostración *f*; **demonstrator** *n* (*POL*) manifestante *m/f*; (*COMM*) demostrador/a *m/f*, vendedor(a) *m/f*

demote [dɪ'məut] *vt* degradar

demure [dɪ'mjuə*] *adj* recatado

den [den] *n* (*of animal*) guarida; (*room*) habitación *f*

denial [dɪ'naɪəl] *n* (*refusal*) negativa; (*of report etc*) negación *f*

denim ['denɪm] *n* tela vaquera; **~s** *npl* vaqueros *mpl*

Denmark ['denmɑːk] *n* Dinamarca

denomination [dɪnɔmɪ'neɪʃən] *n* valor *m*; (*REL*) confesión *f*

denounce [dɪ'nauns] *vt* denunciar

dense [dens] *adj* (*crowd*) denso; (*thick*) espeso; (: *foliage etc*) tupido; (*inf: stupid*) torpe; **~ly** *adv*: **~ly populated** con una alta densidad de población

density ['densɪtɪ] *n* densidad *f*; **single/double-~ disk** *n* (*COMPUT*) disco de densidad sencilla/doble densidad

dent [dɛnt] n abolladura ♦ vt (also: make a ~ in) abollar

dental ['dɛntl] adj dental; ~ **surgeon** n odontólogo/a

dentist ['dɛntɪst] n dentista m/f

dentures ['dɛntʃəz] npl dentadura (postiza)

deny [dɪ'naɪ] vt negar; (charge) rechazar

deodorant [diː'əudərənt] n desodorante m

depart [dɪ'pɑːt] vi irse, marcharse; (train) salir; **to ~ from** (fig: differ from) apartarse de

department [dɪ'pɑːtmənt] n (COMM) sección f; (SCOL) departamento; (POL) ministerio; ~ **store** n gran almacén m

departure [dɪ'pɑːtʃə*] n partida, ida; (of train) salida; (of employee) marcha; **a new ~** un nuevo rumbo; ~ **lounge** n (at airport) sala de embarque

depend [dɪ'pɛnd] vi: **to ~ on** depender de; (rely on) contar con; **it ~s** depende, según; **~ing on the result** según el resultado; **~able** adj (person) formal, serio; (watch) exacto; (car) seguro; **~ant** n dependiente m/f; **~ent** adj: **to be ~ent on** depender de ♦ n = **dependant**

depict [dɪ'pɪkt] vt (in picture) pintar; (describe) representar

depleted [dɪ'pliːtɪd] adj reducido

deploy [dɪ'plɔɪ] vt desplegar

deport [dɪ'pɔːt] vt deportar

deposit [dɪ'pɔzɪt] n depósito; (CHEM) sedimento; (of ore, oil) yacimiento ♦ vt (gen) depositar; **~ account** (BRIT) n cuenta de ahorros

depot ['dɛpəu] n (storehouse) depósito; (for vehicles) parque m; (US) estación f

depreciate [dɪ'priːʃɪeɪt] vi depreciarse, perder valor

depress [dɪ'prɛs] vt deprimir; (wages etc) hacer bajar; (press down) apretar; **~ed** adj deprimido; **~ing** adj

depriment; **~ion** [dɪ'prɛʃən] n depresión f

deprivation [dɛprɪ'veɪʃən] n privación f

deprive [dɪ'praɪv] vt: **to ~ sb of** privar a uno de; **~d** adj necesitado

depth [dɛpθ] n profundidad f; (of cupboard) fondo; **to be in the ~s of despair** sentir la mayor desesperación; **to be out of one's ~** (in water) no hacer pie; (fig) sentirse totalmente perdido

deputize ['dɛpjutaɪz] vi: **to ~ for sb** suplir a uno

deputy ['dɛpjutɪ] adj: **~ head** subdirector(a) m/f ♦ n sustituto/a, suplente m/f; (US: POL) diputado/a; (US: also: **~ sheriff**) agente m (del sheriff)

derail [dɪ'reɪl] vt: **to be ~ed** descarrilarse

deranged [dɪ'reɪndʒd] adj trastornado

derby ['dɑːbɪ] (US) n (hat) hongo

derelict ['dɛrɪlɪkt] adj abandonado

derisory [dɪ'raɪzərɪ] adj (sum) irrisorio

derive [dɪ'raɪv] vt (benefit etc) obtener ♦ vi: **to ~ from** derivarse de

derogatory [dɪ'rɔgətərɪ] adj despectivo

descend [dɪ'sɛnd] vt, vi descender, bajar; **to ~ from** descender de; **to ~ to** rebajarse a; **~ant** n descendiente m/f

descent [dɪ'sɛnt] n descenso; (origin) descendencia

describe [dɪs'kraɪb] vt describir; **description** [-'krɪpʃən] n descripción f; (sort) clase f, género

desecrate ['dɛsɪkreɪt] vt profanar

desert [n 'dɛzət, vb dɪ'zəːt] n desierto ♦ vt abandonar ♦ vi (MIL) desertar; **~er** [dɪ'zəːtə*] n desertor(a) m/f; **~ion** [dɪ'zəːʃən] n deserción f; (LAW) abandono; **~ island** n isla desierta; **~s** [dɪ'zəːts] npl: **to get one's just ~s** llevar su merecido

deserve [dɪ'zəːv] vt merecer, ser digno de; **deserving** adj (person) digno;

(*action, cause*) meritorio

design [dɪ'zaɪn] n (*sketch*) bosquejo; (*layout, shape*) diseño; (*pattern*) dibujo; (*intention*) intención f ♦ vt diseñar

designate [vb 'dezɪgneɪt, adj 'dezɪgnɪt] vt (*appoint*) nombrar; (*destine*) designar ♦ adj designado

designer [dɪ'zaɪnə*] n diseñador(a) m/f; (*fashion*) → modisto/a, diseñador(a) m/f de moda

desirable [dɪ'zaɪərəbl] adj (*proper*) deseable; (*attractive*) atractivo

desire [dɪ'zaɪə*] n deseo ♦ vt desear

desk [desk] n (*in office*) escritorio; (*for pupil*) pupitre m; (*in hotel, at airport*) recepción f; (*BRIT: in shop, restaurant*) caja

desk-top publishing ['desktɔp-] n autoedición f

desolate ['desəlɪt] adj (*place*) desierto; (*person*) afligido

despair [dɪs'peə*] n desesperación f ♦ vi: **to ~ of** perder la esperanza de

despatch [dɪs'pætʃ] n, vt = **dispatch**

desperate ['despərɪt] adj desesperado; (*fugitive*) peligroso; **to be ~ for sth/to do** necesitar urgentemente algo/hacer; **~ly** adv desesperadamente; (*very*) terriblemente, gravemente

desperation [despə'reɪʃən] n desesperación f; **in (sheer) ~** (absolutamente) desesperado

despicable [dɪs'pɪkəbl] adj vil, despreciable

despise [dɪs'paɪz] vt despreciar

despite [dɪs'paɪt] prep a pesar de, pese a

despondent [dɪs'pɔndənt] adj deprimido, abatido

dessert [dɪ'zə:t] n postre m; **~spoon** n cuchara (de postre)

destination [destɪ'neɪʃən] n destino

destiny ['destɪnɪ] n destino

destitute ['destɪtjuːt] adj desamparado, indigente

destroy [dɪs'trɔɪ] vt destruir; (*animal*) sacrificar; **~er** n (*NAUT*) destructor m

destruction [dɪs'trʌkʃən] n destrucción f

detach [dɪ'tætʃ] vt separar; (*unstick*) despegar; **~ed** adj (*attitude*) objetivo, imparcial; **~ed house** n → chalé m, ≈ chalet m; **~ment** n (*aloofness*) frialdad f; (*MIL*) destacamento

detail ['diːteɪl] n detalle m; (*no pl: in picture etc*) detalles mpl; (*trifle*) pequeñez f ♦ vt detallar; (*MIL*) destacar; **in ~** detalladamente; **~ed** adj detallado

detain [dɪ'teɪn] vt retener; (*in captivity*) detener

detect [dɪ'tekt] vt descubrir; (*MED, POLICE*) identificar; (*MIL, RADAR, TECH*) detectar; **~ion** [dɪ'tekʃən] n descubrimiento, identificación f; **~ive** n detective m/f; **~ive story** n novela policíaca; **~or** n detector m

detention [dɪ'tenʃən] n detención f, arresto; (*SCOL*) castigo

deter [dɪ'tə:*] vt (*dissuade*) disuadir

detergent [dɪ'tə:dʒənt] n detergente m

deteriorate [dɪ'tɪərɪəreɪt] vi deteriorarse; **deterioration** [-'reɪʃən] n deterioro

determination [dɪtə:mɪ'neɪʃən] n resolución f

determine [dɪ'tə:mɪn] vt determinar; **~d** adj (*person*) resuelto, decidido; **~d to do** resuelto a hacer

deterrent [dɪ'terənt] n (*MIL*) fuerza de disuasión

detest [dɪ'test] vt aborrecer

detonate ['detəneɪt] vi estallar ♦ vt hacer detonar

detour ['diːtuə*] n (*gen, US: AUT*) desviación f

detract [dɪ'trækt] vt: **to ~ from** quitar mérito a, desvirtuar

detriment ['detrɪmənt] n: **to the ~ of** en perjuicio de; **~al** [detrɪ'mentl] adj: **~al (to)** perjudicial (a)

devaluation [dɪvælju'eɪʃən] n devaluación f

devalue [diː'væljuː] vt (currency) devaluar; (fig) quitar mérito a

devastate ['dɛvəsteɪt] vt devastar; (fig): **to be ~d by** quedar destrozado por; **devastating** adj devastador(a); (fig) arrollador(a)

develop [dɪ'vɛləp] vt desarrollar; (PHOT) revelar; (disease) coger; (habit) adquirir; (fault) empezar a tener ♦ vi desarrollarse; (advance) progresar; (facts, symptoms) aparecer; **~er** n promotor m; **~ing country** n país m en (vías de) desarrollo; **~ment** n desarrollo; (advance) progreso; (of affair, case) desenvolvimiento; (of land) urbanización f

deviation [diːvɪ'eɪʃən] n desviación f

device [dɪ'vaɪs] n (apparatus) aparato, mecanismo

devil ['dɛvl] n diablo, demonio

devious ['diːvɪəs] adj taimado

devise [dɪ'vaɪz] vt idear, inventar

devoid [dɪ'vɔɪd] adj: **~ of** desprovisto de

devolution [diːvə'luːʃən] n (POL) descentralización f

devote [dɪ'vəʊt] vt: **to ~ sth to** dedicar algo a; **~d** adj (loyal) leal, fiel; **to be ~d to sb** querer con devoción a alguien; **the book is ~d to politics** el libro trata de la política; **~e** [dɛvəʊ'tiː] n entusiasta m/f; (REL) devoto/a; **devotion** n dedicación f; (REL) devoción f

devour [dɪ'vaʊə*] vt devorar

devout [dɪ'vaʊt] adj devoto

dew [djuː] n rocío

diabetes [daɪə'biːtiːz] n diabetes f; **diabetic** [-'bɛtɪk] adj, n diabético/a m/f

diabolical [daɪə'bɔlɪkəl] (inf) adj (weather, behaviour) pésimo

diagnosis [daɪəg'nəʊsɪs] (pl **-ses**) n diagnóstico

diagonal [daɪ'ægənl] adj, n diagonal f

diagram ['daɪəgræm] n diagrama m, esquema m

dial ['daɪəl] n esfera, cuadrante m, cara (AM); (on radio etc) selector m; (of phone) disco ♦ vt (number) marcar

dialling ['daɪəlɪŋ]: **~ code** n prefijo; **~ tone** (US **dial tone**) n (BRIT) señal f or tono de marcar

dialogue ['daɪəlɔg] (US **dialog**) n diálogo

diameter [daɪ'æmɪtə*] n diámetro

diamond ['daɪəmənd] n diamante m; (shape) rombo; **~s** npl (CARDS) diamantes mpl

diaper ['daɪəpə*] (US) n pañal m

diaphragm ['daɪəfræm] n diafragma m

diarrhoea [daɪə'riːə] (US **diarrhea**) n diarrea

diary ['daɪərɪ] n (daily account) diario; (book) agenda

dice [daɪs] n inv dados mpl ♦ vt (CULIN) cortar en cuadritos

Dictaphone ® ['dɪktəfəʊn] n dictáfono ®

dictate [dɪk'teɪt] vt dictar; (conditions) imponer; **dictation** [-'teɪʃən] n dictado; (giving of orders) órdenes fpl

dictator [dɪk'teɪtə*] n dictador m; **~ship** n dictadura

dictionary ['dɪkʃənrɪ] n diccionario

did [dɪd] pt of **do**

didn't ['dɪdənt] = **did not**

die [daɪ] vi morir; (fig: fade) desvanecerse, desaparecer; **to be dying for sth/to do sth** morirse por algo/de ganas de hacer algo; **~ away** vi (sound, light) perderse; **~ down** vi apagarse; (wind) amainar; **~ out** vi desaparecer

diesel ['diːzəl] n vehículo con motor Diesel; **~ engine** n motor m Diesel; **~ (oil)** n gasoil m

diet ['daɪət] n dieta; (restricted food) régimen m ♦ vi (also: **be on a ~**) estar a dieta, hacer régimen

differ ['dɪfə*] vi: **to ~ (from)** (be different) ser distinto (a), diferenciarse (de); (disagree) discrepar (de); **~ence** n diferencia; (disagreement) desacuerdo;

~ent adj diferente, distinto; ~entiate
[-'renʃieɪt] vi: to ~entiate (between)
distinguir (entre); ~ently adv de otro
modo, en forma distinta

difficult ['dɪfɪkəlt] adj difícil; ~y n
dificultad f

diffident ['dɪfɪdənt] adj tímido

dig [dɪg] (pt, pp dug) vt (hole, ground)
cavar ♦ n (prod) empujón m;
(archaeological) excavación f; (remark)
indirecta; to ~ one's nails into clavar
las uñas en; ~ into vt fus (savings)
consumir; ~ up vt (information)
desenterrar; (plant) desarraigar

digest [vb daɪ'dʒest, n 'daɪdʒest] vt
(food) digerir; (facts) asimilar ♦ n
resumen m; ~ion [dɪ'dʒestʃən] n
digestión f

digit ['dɪdʒɪt] n (number) dígito; (finger)
dedo; ~al adj digital

dignified ['dɪgnɪfaɪd] adj grave,
solemne

dignity ['dɪgnɪtɪ] n dignidad f

digress [daɪ'gres] vi: to ~ from
apartarse de

digs [dɪgz] (BRIT: inf) npl pensión f,
alojamiento

dilapidated [dɪ'læpɪdeɪtɪd] adj
desmoronado, ruinoso

dilemma [daɪ'lemə] n dilema m

diligent ['dɪlɪdʒənt] adj diligente

dilute [daɪ'luːt] vt diluir

dim [dɪm] adj (light) débil; (outline)
indistinto; (room) oscuro; (inf: stupid)
lerdo ♦ vt (light) bajar

dime [daɪm] (US) n moneda de diez
centavos

dimension [dɪ'menʃən] n dimensión f

diminish [dɪ'mɪnɪʃ] vt, vi disminuir

diminutive [dɪ'mɪnjutɪv] adj diminuto
♦ n (LING) diminutivo

dimmers ['dɪməz] (US) npl (AUT: dipped
headlights) luces fpl cortas; (: parking
lights) luces fpl de posición

dimple ['dɪmpl] n hoyuelo

din [dɪn] n estruendo, estrépito

dine [daɪn] vi cenar; ~r n (person)

comensal m/f; (US) restaurante m
económico

dinghy ['dɪŋgɪ] n bote m; (also: rubber
~) lancha (neumática)

dingy ['dɪndʒɪ] adj (room) sombrío;
(colour) sucio

dining car ['daɪnɪŋ-] (BRIT) n (RAIL)
coche-comedor m

dining room n comedor m

dinner ['dɪnə*] n (evening meal) cena;
(lunch) comida; (public) cena, banquete
m; ~ jacket n smoking m; ~ party n
cena; ~ time n (evening) hora de
cenar; (midday) hora de comer

dinosaur ['daɪnəsɔː*] n dinosaurio m

diocese ['daɪəsɪs] n diócesis f inv

dip [dɪp] n (slope) pendiente f; (in sea)
baño; (CULIN) salsa ♦ vt (in water)
mojar; (ladle etc) meter; (BRIT: AUT): to
~ one's lights poner luces de cruce
♦ vi (road etc) descender, bajar

diploma [dɪ'pləumə] n diploma m

diplomacy [dɪ'pləuməsɪ] n diplomacia f

diplomat ['dɪpləmæt] n diplomático/a;
~ic [dɪplə'mætɪk] adj diplomático

diprod ['dɪprod] (US) n = dipstick

dipstick ['dɪpstɪk] (BRIT) n (AUT) varilla
de nivel (del aceite)

dipswitch ['dɪpswɪtʃ] (BRIT) n (AUT)
interruptor m

dire [daɪə*] adj calamitoso

direct [daɪ'rekt] adj directo; (in straight line)
claro; (person) franco ♦ vt dirigir;
(order): to ~ sb to do sth mandar a
uno hacer algo ♦ adv derecho; can
you ~ me to...? ¿puede indicarme
dónde está...?; ~ debit (BRIT) n
domiciliación f bancaria de recibos

direction [dɪ'rekʃən] n dirección f;
sense of ~ sentido de la dirección; ~s
npl (instructions) instrucciones fpl; ~s
for use modo de empleo

directly [dɪ'rektlɪ] adv (in straight line)
directamente; (at once) en seguida

director [dɪ'rektə*] n director(a) m/f

directory [dɪ'rektərɪ] n (TEL) guía
(telefónica); (COMPUT) directorio;

~ **enquiries**, ~ **assistance** (*us*) *n*
(servicio de) información *f*

dirt [də:t] *n* suciedad *f*; (*earth*) tierra;
~**-cheap** *adj* baratísimo; ~**y** *adj* sucio;
(*joke*) verde (*SP*), colorado (*AM*) ♦ *vt*
ensuciar; (*stain*) manchar; ~**y trick** *n*
juego sucio

disability [dɪsə'bɪlɪtɪ] *n* incapacidad *f*

disabled [dɪs'eɪbld] *adj*: **to be**
physically ~ ser minusválido/a; **to be**
mentally ~ ser deficiente mental

disadvantage [dɪsəd'vɑːntɪdʒ] *n*
desventaja, inconveniente *m*

disagree [dɪsə'griː] *vi* (*differ*) discrepar;
to ~ (**with**) no estar de acuerdo (con);
~**able** *adj* desagradable; (*person*)
antipático; ~**ment** *n* desacuerdo

disallow [dɪsə'lau] *vt* (*goal*) anular;
(*claim*) rechazar

disappear [dɪsə'pɪə*] *vi* desaparecer;
~**ance** *n* desaparición *f*

disappoint [dɪsə'pɔɪnt] *vt*
decepcionar, defraudar; ~**ed** *adj*
decepcionado; ~**ing** *adj*
decepcionante; ~**ment** *n* decepción *f*

disapproval [dɪsə'pruːvəl] *n*
desaprobación *f*

disapprove [dɪsə'pruːv] *vi*: **to** ~ **of** ver
mal

disarmament [dɪs'ɑːməmənt] *n*
desarme *m*

disarray [dɪsə'reɪ] *n*: **in** ~ (*army*,
organization) desorganizado; (*hair*,
clothes) desarreglado

disaster [dɪ'zɑːstə*] *n* desastre *m*

disband [dɪs'bænd] *vt* disolver ♦ *vi*
desbandarse

disbelief [dɪsbə'liːf] *n* incredulidad *f*

disc [dɪsk] *n* disco; (*COMPUT*) = **disk**

discard [dɪs'kɑːd] *vt* (*old things*) tirar;
(*fig*) descartar

discern [dɪ'sɜːn] *vt* percibir, discernir;
(*understand*) comprender; ~**ing** *adj*
perspicaz

discharge [*vb* dɪs'tʃɑːdʒ, *n* 'dɪstʃɑːdʒ]
vt (*task, duty*) cumplir; (*waste*) verter;
(*patient*) dar de alta; (*employee*)

despedir; (*soldier*) licenciar; (*defendant*)
poner en libertad ♦ *n* (*ELEC*) descarga;
(*MED*) supuración *f*; (*dismissal*)
despedida; (*of duty*) desempeño *f*; (*of
debt*) pago, descargo

discipline ['dɪsɪplɪn] *n* disciplina ♦ *vt*
disciplinar; (*punish*) castigar

disc jockey *n* pinchadiscos *m/f inv*

disclaim [dɪs'kleɪm] *vt* negar

disclose [dɪs'kləuz] *vt* revelar;
disclosure [-'kləuʒə*] *n* revelación *f*

disco ['dɪskəu] *n abbr* = **discothèque**

discomfort [dɪs'kʌmfət] *n*
incomodidad *f*; (*unease*) inquietud *f*;
(*physical*) malestar *m*

disconcert [dɪskən'sɜːt] *vt*
desconcertar

disconnect [dɪskə'nekt] *vt* separar;
(*ELEC etc*) desconectar

discontent [dɪskən'tent] *n*
descontento; ~**ed** *adj* descontento

discontinue [dɪskən'tɪnjuː] *vt*
interrumpir; (*payments*) suspender;
"~**d**" (*COMM*) "ya no se fabrica"

discord ['dɪskɔːd] *n* discordia; (*MUS*)
disonancia

discothèque ['dɪskəutek] *n* discoteca

discount [*n* 'dɪskaunt, *vb* dɪs'kaunt] *n*
descuento ♦ *vt* descontar

discourage [dɪs'kʌrɪdʒ] *vt* desalentar;
(*advise against*): **to** ~ **sb from doing**
disuadir a uno de hacer

discover [dɪs'kʌvə*] *vt* descubrir;
(*error*) darse cuenta de; ~**y** *n*
descubrimiento

discredit [dɪs'kredɪt] *vt* desacreditar

discreet [dɪs'kriːt] *adj* (*tactful*) discreto;
(*careful*) circunspecto, prudente

discrepancy [dɪs'krepənsɪ] *n*
diferencia

discretion [dɪs'kreʃən] *n* (*tact*)
discreción *f*; **at the** ~ **of** a criterio de

discriminate [dɪs'krɪmɪneɪt] *vi*: **to**
~ **between** distinguir entre; **to**
~ **against** discriminar contra;
discriminating *adj* entendido;
discrimination [-'neɪʃən] *n*

(discernment) perspicacia; *(bias)* discriminación f

discuss [dɪs'kʌs] vt discutir; *(a theme)* tratar; ~**ion** [dɪs'kʌʃən] n discusión f

disdain [dɪs'deɪn] n desdén m

disease [dɪ'ziːz] n enfermedad f

disembark [dɪsɪm'bɑːk] vt, vi desembarcar

disentangle [dɪsɪn'tæŋgl] vt soltar; *(wire, thread)* desenredar

disfigure [dɪs'fɪgə*] vt *(person)* desfigurar; *(object)* afear

disgrace [dɪs'greɪs] n ignominia; *(shame)* vergüenza, ignominia f ♦ vt deshonrar; ~**ful** adj vergonzoso

disgruntled [dɪs'grʌntld] adj disgustado, descontento

disguise [dɪs'gaɪz] n disfraz m ♦ vt disfrazar; **in ~** disfrazado

disgust [dɪs'gʌst] n repugnancia ♦ vt repugnar, dar asco a; ~**ing** adj repugnante, asqueroso; *(behaviour etc)* vergonzoso

dish [dɪʃ] n *(gen)* plato; **to do** or **wash the ~es** fregar los platos; ~ **out** vt repartir; ~ **up** vt servir; ~**cloth** n estropajo

dishearten [dɪs'hɑːtn] vt desalentar

dishevelled [dɪ'ʃevəld] *(US* **disheveled)** adj *(hair)* despeinado; *(appearance)* desarreglado

dishonest [dɪs'ɒnɪst] adj *(person)* poco honrado, tramposo; *(means)* fraudulento; ~**y** n falta de honradez

dishonour [dɪs'ɒnə*] *(US* **dishonor)** n deshonra; ~**able** adj deshonroso

dishtowel ['dɪʃtauəl] *(US)* n estropajo

dishwasher ['dɪʃwɒʃə*] n lavaplatos m inv

disillusion [dɪsɪ'luːʒən] vt desilusionar

disinfect [dɪsɪn'fekt] vt desinfectar; ~**ant** n desinfectante m

disintegrate [dɪs'ɪntɪgreɪt] vi disgregarse, desintegrarse

disinterested [dɪs'ɪntrɪstɪd] adj desinteresado

disjointed [dɪs'dʒɔɪntɪd] adj inconexo

disk [dɪsk] n *(esp US)* = **disc**; *(COMPUT)* disco, disquete m; **single-/double-sided** ~ disco de una cara/dos caras; ~ **drive** n disc drive m; ~**ette** n = **disk**

dislike [dɪs'laɪk] n antipatía, aversión f ♦ vt tener antipatía a

dislocate ['dɪsləkeɪt] vt dislocar

dislodge [dɪs'lɒdʒ] vt sacar

disloyal [dɪs'lɔɪəl] adj desleal

dismal ['dɪzml] adj *(gloomy)* deprimente, triste; *(very bad)* malísimo, fatal

dismantle [dɪs'mæntl] vt desmontar, desarmar

dismay [dɪs'meɪ] n consternación f ♦ vt consternar

dismiss [dɪs'mɪs] vt *(worker)* despedir; *(pupils)* dejar marchar; *(soldiers)* dar permiso para irse; *(idea, LAW)* rechazar; *(possibility)* descartar; ~**al** n despido

dismount [dɪs'maunt] vi apearse

disobedient [dɪsə'biːdɪənt] adj desobediente

disobey [dɪsə'beɪ] vt desobedecer

disorder [dɪs'ɔːdə*] n desorden m; *(rioting)* disturbios mpl; *(MED)* trastorno; ~**ly** adj desordenado; *(meeting)* alborotado; *(conduct)* escandaloso

disorientated [dɪs'ɔːrɪenteɪtəd] adj desorientado

disown [dɪs'aun] vt *(action)* renegar de; *(person)* negar cualquier tipo de relación con

disparaging [dɪs'pærɪdʒɪŋ] adj despreciativo

dispassionate [dɪs'pæʃənɪt] adj *(unbiased)* imparcial

dispatch [dɪs'pætʃ] vt enviar ♦ n *(sending)* envío; *(PRESS)* informe m; *(MIL)* parte m

dispel [dɪs'pel] vt disipar

dispense [dɪs'pens] vt *(medicines)* preparar; ~ **with** vt fus prescindir de; ~**r** n *(container)* distribuidor m automático; **dispensing chemist** *(BRIT)* n farmacia

disperse [dɪs'pɜːs] vt dispersar ♦ vi
dispersarse

dispirited [dɪ'spɪrɪtɪd] adj desanimado,
desalentado

displace [dɪs'pleɪs] vt desplazar,
reemplazar; **~d person** n (POL)
desplazado/a f

display [dɪs'pleɪ] n (in shop window)
escaparate m; (exhibition) exposición f;
(COMPUT) visualización f; (of feeling)
manifestación f ♦ vt exponer;
manifestar; (ostentatiously) lucir

displease [dɪs'pliːz] vt (offend)
ofender; (annoy) fastidiar; **~d** adj: **~d
with** disgustado con; **displeasure**
[-'pleʒə*] n disgusto

disposable [dɪs'pəuzəbl] adj
desechable; (income) disponible;
~ nappy n pañal m desechable

disposal [dɪs'pəuzl] n (of rubbish)
destrucción f; at one's **~** a su
disposición

dispose [dɪs'pəuz] vi: **to ~ of**
(unwanted goods) deshacerse de;
(problem etc) resolver; **~d to do** dispuesto a hacer; **to be well-~d
towards sb** estar bien dispuesto hacia
uno; **disposition** [dɪspə'zɪʃən] n
(nature) temperamento m; (inclination)
propensión f

disprove [dɪs'pruːv] vt refutar

dispute [dɪs'pjuːt] n disputa; (also:
industrial ~) conflicto (laboral) ♦ vt
(argue) disputar, discutir; (question)
cuestionar

disqualify [dɪs'kwɔlɪfaɪ] vt (SPORT)
desclasificar; **to ~ sb for sth/from
doing sth** incapacitar a alguien para
algo/hacer algo

disquiet [dɪs'kwaɪət] n preocupación f,
inquietud f

disregard [dɪsrɪ'gɑːd] vt (ignore) no
hacer caso de

disrepair [dɪsrɪ'peə*] n: **to fall into ~**
(building) desmoronarse

disreputable [dɪs'repjutəbl] adj
(person) de mala fama; (behaviour)

vergonzoso

disrespectful [dɪsrɪ'spektful] adj
irrespetuoso

disrupt [dɪs'rʌpt] vt (plans) desbaratar,
trastornar; (conversation) interrumpir

dissatisfaction [dɪssætɪs'fækʃən] n
disgusto, descontento

dissect [dɪ'sekt] vt disecar

dissent [dɪ'sent] n disensión f

dissertation [dɪsə'teɪʃən] n tesina

disservice [dɪs'sɜːvɪs] n: **to do sb a ~**
perjudicar a alguien

dissimilar [dɪ'sɪmɪlə*] adj distinto

dissipate ['dɪsɪpeɪt] vt disipar; (waste)
desperdiciar

dissolve [dɪ'zɔlv] vt disolver ♦ vi
disolverse; **to ~ in(to) tears**
deshacerse en lágrimas

dissuade [dɪ'sweɪd] vt: **to ~ sb
(from)** disuadir a uno (de)

distance ['dɪstəns] n distancia; **in the
~ a lo lejos**

distant ['dɪstənt] adj lejano; (manner)
reservado, frío

distaste [dɪs'teɪst] n repugnancia; **~ful**
adj repugnante, desagradable

distended [dɪs'tendɪd] adj (stomach)
hinchado

distil [dɪs'tɪl] (US **distill**) vt destilar;
~lery n destilería

distinct [dɪs'tɪŋkt] adj (different)
distinto; (clear) claro; (unmistakeable)
inequívoco; **as ~ from** a diferencia de;
~ion [dɪs'tɪŋkʃən] n distinción f;
(honour) honor m; (in exam)
sobresaliente m; **~ive** adj distintivo

distinguish [dɪs'tɪŋgwɪʃ] vt distinguir;
to ~ o.s. destacarse; **~ed** adj (eminent)
distinguido; **~ing** adj (feature)
distintivo

distort [dɪs'tɔːt] vt distorsionar; (shape,
image) deformar; **~ion** [dɪs'tɔːʃən] n
distorsión f; deformación f

distract [dɪs'trækt] vt distraer; **~ed** adj
distraído; **~ion** [dɪs'trækʃən] n
distracción f; (confusion) aturdimiento

distraught [dɪs'trɔːt] adj loco de

inquietud

distress [dɪs'tres] n (anguish) angustia, aflicción f ♦ vt afligir; **~ing** adj angustioso; doloroso; **~ signal** n señal f de socorro

distribute [dɪs'trɪbjuːt] vt distribuir; (share out) repartir; **distribution** [-'bjuːʃən] n distribución f, reparto; **distributor** n (AUT) distribuidor m; (COMM) distribuidora

district ['dɪstrɪkt] n (of country) zona, región f; (of town) barrio; (ADMIN) distrito; **~ attorney** (US) n fiscal m/f; **~ nurse** (BRIT) n enfermera que atiende a pacientes a domicilio

distrust [dɪs'trʌst] n desconfianza ♦ vt desconfiar de

disturb [dɪs'təːb] vt (person: bother, interrupt) molestar; (: upset) perturbar, inquietar; (disorganize) alterar; **~ance** n (upheaval) perturbación f; (political etc: gen pl) disturbio; (of mind) trastorno; **~ed** adj (worried, upset) preocupado, angustiado; **emotionally ~ed** trastornado; (childhood) inseguro; **~ing** adj inquietante, perturbador(a)

disuse [dɪs'juːs] n: **to fall into ~** caer en desuso

disused [dɪs'juːzd] adj abandonado

ditch [dɪtʃ] n zanja; (irrigation ~) acequia ♦ vt (inf: partner) deshacerse de; (: plan, car etc) abandonar

dither ['dɪðə*] (pej) vi vacilar

ditto ['dɪtəu] adv ídem, lo mismo

divan [dɪ'væn] n (also: ~ bed) cama turca

dive [daɪv] n (from board) salto; (underwater) buceo; (of submarine) sumersión f ♦ vi (swimmer: into water) saltar; (: under water) zambullirse, bucear; (fish, submarine) sumergirse; (bird) lanzarse en picado; **to ~ into** (bag etc) meter la mano en; (place) meterse de prisa en; **~r** n (underwater) buzo

diverse [daɪ'vəːs] adj diversos/as, varios/as

diversion [daɪ'vəːʃən] n (BRIT: AUT) desviación f; (distraction, MIL) diversión f; (of funds) distracción f

divert [daɪ'vəːt] vt (turn aside) desviar

divide [dɪ'vaɪd] vt (also: separate) separar ♦ vi dividirse; (road) bifurcarse; **~d highway** (US) n carretera de doble calzada

dividend ['dɪvɪdend] n dividendo; (fig): **to pay ~s** proporcionar beneficios

divine [dɪ'vaɪn] adj (also fig) divino

diving ['daɪvɪŋ] n (SPORT) salto; (underwater) buceo; **~ board** n trampolín m

divinity [dɪ'vɪnɪtɪ] n divinidad f; (SCOL) teología

division [dɪ'vɪʒən] n división f; (sharing out) reparto; (disagreement) diferencias fpl; (COMM) sección f

divorce [dɪ'vɔːs] n divorcio ♦ vt divorciarse de; **~d** adj divorciado; **~e** [-'siː] n divorciado/a

divulge [daɪ'vʌldʒ] vt divulgar, revelar

D.I.Y. (BRIT) adj, n abbr = **do-it-yourself**

dizzy ['dɪzɪ] adj (spell) de mareo; **to feel ~** marearse

DJ n abbr = **disc jockey**

KEYWORD

do [duː] (pt **did**, pp **done**) n (inf: party etc): **we're having a little ~ on Saturday** damos una fiestecita el sábado; **it was rather a grand ~** fue un acontecimiento a lo grande
♦ aux vb **1** (in negative constructions: not translated) **I don't understand** no entiendo
2 (to form questions: not translated) **didn't you know?** ¿no lo sabías?; **what ~ you think?** ¿qué opinas?
3 (for emphasis, in polite expressions): **people ~ make mistakes sometimes** sí que se cometen errores a veces; **she does seem rather late** a mí también me parece que se ha

retrasado; **~ sit down/help yourself** siéntate/sírvete por favor; **~ take care!** ¡ten cuidado!, ¡te pido)!

4 (used to avoid repeating vb): **she sings better than I ~** canta mejor que yo; **~ you agree? — yes, I ~/no, I don't** ¿estás de acuerdo? — sí (lo estoy)/no (lo estoy); **she lives in Glasgow — so ~ I** vive en Glasgow — yo también; **he didn't like it and neither did we** no le gustó y a nosotros tampoco; **who made this mess? — I did** ¿quién hizo esta chapuza? — yo; **he asked me to help him and I did** me pidió que le ayudara y lo hice

5 (in question tags): **you like him, don't you?** te gusta, ¿verdad? or ¿no?; **I don't know him, ~ I?** creo que no le conozco

♦ vt **1** (gen, carry out, perform etc): **what are you ~ing tonight?** ¿qué haces esta noche?; **what can I ~ for you?** ¿en qué puedo servirle?; **to ~ the washing-up/cooking** fregar los platos/cocinar; **to ~ one's teeth/ hair/nails** lavarse los dientes/ arreglarse el pelo/arreglarse las uñas
2 (AUT etc): **the car was ~ing 100** el coche iba a 100; **we've done 200 km already** ya hemos hecho 200 km; **he can ~ 100 in that car** puede ir a 100 en ese coche

♦ vi **1** (act, behave) hacer; **~ as I ~** haz como yo
2 (get on, fare): **he's ~ing well/badly at school** va bien/mal en la escuela; **the firm is ~ing well** la empresa anda or va bien; **how ~ you ~?** mucho gusto; (less formal) ¿qué tal?
3 (suit): **will it ~?** ¿sirve?, ¿está or va bien?
4 (be sufficient) bastar; **will £10 ~?** ¿será bastante con £10?; **that'll ~** así está bien; **that'll ~!** (in annoyance) ¡ya está bien!, ¡basta ya!; **to make ~ (with)** arreglárselas (con)

do away with vt fus (kill, disease) eliminar; (abolish: law etc) abolir; (withdraw) retirar
do up vt (laces) atar; (zip, dress, shirt) abrochar; (renovate: room, house) renovar
do with vt fus (need): **I could ~ with a drink/some help** no me vendría mal un trago/un poco de ayuda; (be connected) tener que ver con; **what has it got to ~ with you?** ¿qué tiene que ver contigo?
do without vi pasar sin; **if you're late for tea then you'll ~ without** si llegas tarde tendrás que quedarte sin cenar ♦ vt fus pasar sin; **I can ~ without a car** puedo pasar sin coche

dock [dɔk] n (NAUT) muelle m; (LAW) banquillo (de los acusados); **~s** npl (NAUT) muelles mpl, puerto sg ♦ vi (enter ~) atracar (a) la muelle; (SPACE) acoplarse; **~er** n trabajador m portuario, estibador m; **~yard** n astillero

doctor ['dɔktə*] n médico/a; (Ph.D. etc) doctor(a) m/f ♦ vt (drink) adulterar; **D~ of Philosophy** n Doctor en Filosofía y Letras

document ['dɔkjumənt] n documento; **~ary** [-'mɛntəri] adj documental ♦ n documental m

dodge [dɔdʒ] n (fig) truco ♦ vt evadir; (blow) esquivar

dodgems ['dɔdʒəmz] (BRIT) npl coches mpl de choque

doe [dəu] n (deer) cierva, gama; (rabbit) coneja

does [dʌz] vb see do; **~n't** = does not

dog [dɔg] n perro ♦ vt seguir los pasos de; (subj: bad luck) perseguir; **~ collar** n collar m de perro; (of clergyman) alzacuellos m inv; **~-eared** adj sobado

dogged ['dɔgid] adj tenaz, obstinado

dogsbody ['dɔgzbɔdi] (BRIT: inf) n

burro de carga

doings ['duɪŋz] npl (activities)
actividades fpl

do-it-yourself n bricolaje m

doldrums ['dɔldrəmz] npl: **to be in
the ~** (person) estar abatido; (business)
estar estancado

dole [dəul] (BRIT) n (payment) subsidio
de paro; **on the ~** parado; **~ out** vt
repartir

doll [dɔl] n muñeca; (US: inf: woman)
muñeca, gachí f

dollar ['dɔlə*] n dólar m

dolled up (inf) adj arreglado

dolphin ['dɔlfin] n delfín m

domain [də'meɪn] n (fig) campo,
competencia; (land) dominios mpl

dome [dəum] n (ARCH) cúpula

domestic [də'mestɪk] adj (animal,
duty) doméstico; (flight, policy)
nacional; **~ated** adj domesticado;
(home-loving) casero, hogareño

dominate ['dɔmɪneɪt] vt dominar

domineering [dɔmɪ'nɪərɪŋ] adj
dominante

dominion [də'mɪnɪən] n dominio

domino ['dɔmɪnəu] (pl **~es**) n ficha de
dominó; **~es** n (game) dominó

don [dɔn] (BRIT) n profesor(a) m/f
universitario/a

donate [də'neɪt] vt donar; **donation**
[də'neɪʃən] n donativo

done [dʌn] pp of **do**

donkey ['dɔŋkɪ] n burro

donor ['dəunə*] n donante m/f;
~ card n carnet m de donante de
órganos

don't [dəunt] = **do not**

donut ['dəunʌt] (US) n = **doughnut**

doodle ['du:dl] vi hacer dibujitos or
garabatos

doom [du:m] n (fate) suerte f ♦ vt: **to
be ~ed to failure** estar condenado al
fracaso

door [dɔ:*] n puerta; **~bell** n timbre m;
~ handle n tirador m; (of car) manija;
~man (irreg) n (in hotel) portero;

~mat n felpudo, estera; **~step** n
peldaño; **~-to-~** adj de puerta en
puerta; **~way** n entrada, puerta

dope [dəup] n (inf: illegal drug) droga;
(: person) imbécil m/f ♦ vt (horse etc)
drogar

dormant ['dɔ:mənt] adj inactivo

dormitory ['dɔ:mɪtrɪ] n (BRIT)
dormitorio; (US) colegio mayor

dormouse ['dɔ:maus] n (pl **-mice**) n
lirón m

DOS n abbr (= disk operating system)
DOS m

dosage ['dəusɪdʒ] n dosis f inv

dose [dəus] n dósis f inv

doss house [dɔss-] (BRIT) n pensión f
de mala muerte

dossier ['dɔsɪeɪ] n expediente m,
dosier m

dot [dɔt] n punto ♦ vt: **~ted with**
salpicado de; **on the ~** en punto

double ['dʌbl] adj doble ♦ adv (twice):
to cost ~ costar el doble ♦ n doble m
♦ vt doblar ♦ vi doblarse; **on the ~, at
the ~** (BRIT) corriendo; **~ bass** n
contrabajo; **~ bed** n cama de
matrimonio; **~ bend** (BRIT) n doble
curva; **~-breasted** adj cruzado;
~cross vt (trick) engañar; (betray)
traicionar; **~-decker** n autobús m de
dos pisos; **~ glazing** (BRIT) n doble
acristalamiento; **~ room** n habitación f
doble; **~s** n (TENNIS) juego de dobles;
doubly adv doblemente

doubt [daut] n duda ♦ vt dudar;
(suspect) dudar de; **to ~ that** dudar
que; **~ful** adj dudoso; (person): **to be
~ful about sth** tener dudas sobre
algo; **~less** adv sin duda

dough [dəu] n masa, pasta; **~nut** (US
donut) n ≈ rosquilla

dove [dʌv] n paloma

dovetail ['dʌvteɪl] vi (fig) encajar

dowdy ['daudɪ] adj (person) mal
vestido; (clothes) pasado de moda

down [daun] n (feathers) plumón m,
flojel m ♦ adv (~wards) abajo, hacia

abajo; (*on the ground*) por o en tierra ♦ *prep* abajo ♦ *vt* (*inf: drink*) beberse; ~ **with X!** ¡abajo X!; **~-and-out** *n* vagabundo/a; **~-at-heel** *adj* venido a menos; (*appearance*) desaliñado; **~cast** *adj* abatido; **~fall** *n* caída, ruina; **~hearted** *adj* abatido; **~hill** *adv*: **to go ~hill** (*also fig*) ir cuesta abajo; ~ **payment** *n* entrada, pago al contado; **~pour** *n* aguacero; **~right** *adj* (*nonsense, lie*) manifiesto; (*refusal*) terminante; **~size** *vi* (*ECON: company*) reducir la plantilla de

Downing Street

Downing Street *es la calle de Londres en la que están las residencias oficiales del Presidente del Gobierno (Prime Minister), tradicionalmente en el No. 10, y del Ministro de Economía (Chancellor of the Exchequer). La calle está situada en el céntrico barrio londinense de Westminster y está cerrada al tráfico de peatones y vehículos. En lenguaje periodístico, se usa también* Downing Street *para referirse al primer ministro o al Gobierno.*

Down's syndrome ['daʊnz-] *n* síndrome *m* de Down

down: **~stairs** *adv* (*below*) (en la casa de) abajo; (*~wards*) escaleras abajo; **~stream** *adv* aguas o río abajo; **~to-earth** *adj* práctico; **~town** *adv* en el centro de la ciudad; ~ **under** *adv* en Australia (or Nueva Zelanda); **~ward** [-wəd] *adj, adv* hacia abajo; **~wards** [-wədz] *adv* hacia abajo

dowry ['daʊrɪ] *n* dote *f*

doz. *abbr* = **dozen**

doze [dəʊz] *vi* dormitar; ~ **off** *vi* quedarse medio dormido

dozen ['dʌzn] *n* docena; **a** ~ **books** una docena de libros; **~s of** cantidad de

Dr. *abbr* = **doctor; drive**

drab [dræb] *adj* gris, monótono

draft [drɑːft] *n* (*first copy*) borrador *m*; (*POL: of bill*) anteproyecto; (*US: call-up*) quinta ♦ *vt* (*plan*) preparar; (*write roughly*) hacer un borrador de; *see also* **draught**

draftsman ['drɑːftsmən] (*US*) *n* = **draughtsman**

drag [dræg] *vt* arrastrar; (*river*) dragar, rastrear ♦ *vi* (*time*) pasar despacio; (*play, film etc*) hacerse pesado ♦ *n* (*inf*) lata; (*women's clothing*): **in ~** vestido de travesti; ~ **on** *vi* ser interminable; ~ **and drop** *vt* (*COMPUT*) arrastrar y soltar

dragon ['drægən] *n* dragón *m*

dragonfly ['drægənflaɪ] *n* libélula

drain [dreɪn] *n* desaguadero; (*in street*) sumidero; (*source of loss*): **to be a ~ on** consumir, agotar ♦ *vt* (*land, marshes*) desaguar; (*reservoir*) desecar; (*vegetables*) escurrir ♦ *vi* escurrirse; **~age** *n* (*act*) desagüe *m*; (*MED, AGR*) drenaje *m*; (*sewage*) alcantarillado; **~ing board** (*US* **~board**) *n* escurridera, escurridor *m*; **~pipe** *n* tubo de desagüe

drama ['drɑːmə] *n* (*art*) teatro; (*play*) drama *m*; (*excitement*) emoción f; **~tic** [drəˈmætɪk] *adj* dramático; (*sudden, marked*) espectacular; **~tist** ['dræmətɪst] *n* dramaturgo/a; **~tize** ['dræmətaɪz] *vt* (*events*) dramatizar

drank [dræŋk] *pt of* **drink**

drape [dreɪp] *vt* (*cloth*) colocar; (*flag*) colgar; **~s** (*US*) *npl* cortinas fpl

drastic ['dræstɪk] *adj* (*measure*) severo; (*change*) radical, drástico

draught [drɑːft] (*US* **draft**) *n* (*of air*) corriente f de aire; (*NAUT*) calado; **on ~** (*beer*) de barril; ~ **beer** *n* cerveza de barril; **~board** (*BRIT*) *n* tablero de damas; **~s** (*BRIT*) *n* (*game*) juego de damas

draughtsman ['drɑːftsmən] (*US* **draftsman**) (*irreg*) *n* delineante *m*

draw [drɔː] (*pt* **drew**, *pp* **drawn**) *vt*

(picture) dibujar; (cart) tirar de; (curtain) correr; (take out) sacar; (attract) atraer; (money) retirar; (wages) cobrar ♦ vi (SPORT) empatar ♦ n empate m; (lottery) sorteo; ~ **near** vi acercarse; ~ **out** vi (lengthen) alargarse ♦ vt sacar; ~ **up** vi (stop) pararse ♦ vt (document) redactar; **~back** n inconveniente m, desventaja; **~bridge** n puente m levadizo

drawer [drɔː*] n

drawing ['drɔːɪŋ] n dibujo; ~ **board** n tablero (de dibujante); ~ **pin** (BRIT) n chincheta; ~ **room** n salón m

drawl [drɔːl] n habla lenta y cansina

drawn [drɔːn] pp of **draw**

dread [drɛd] n pavor m, terror m ♦ vt temer, tener miedo or pavor a; **~ful** adj horroroso

dream [driːm] (pt, pp **dreamed** or **dreamt**) n sueño ♦ vt, vi soñar; **~y** adj (distracted) soñador(a), distraído; (music) suave

dreary ['drɪərɪ] adj monótono

dredge [drɛdʒ] vt dragar

dregs [drɛgz] npl posos mpl; (of humanity) hez f

drench [drɛntʃ] vt empapar

dress [drɛs] n vestido; (clothing) ropa ♦ vt vestir; (wound) vendar ♦ vi vestirse; **to get ~ed** vestirse; ~ **up** vi vestirse de etiqueta; (in fancy dress) disfrazarse; ~ **circle** (BRIT) n principal m; **~er** n (furniture) aparador m; (: US) cómoda (con espejo); **~ing** n (MED) vendaje m; (CULIN) aliño; **~ing gown** (BRIT) n bata; **~ing room** n (THEATRE) camarín m; (SPORT) vestuario; **~ing table** n tocador m; **~maker** n modista, costurera; ~ **rehearsal** n ensayo general

drew [druː] pt of **draw**

dribble ['drɪbl] vi (baby) babear ♦ vt (ball) regatear

dried [draɪd] adj (fruit) seco; (milk) en polvo

drier ['draɪə*] n = **dryer**

drift [drɪft] n (of current etc) flujo; (of snow) ventisquero; (meaning) significado ♦ vi (boat) ir a la deriva; (sand, snow) amontonarse; **~wood** n madera de deriva

drill [drɪl] n (~ bit) broca; (tool for DIY etc) taladro; (of dentist) fresa; (for mining etc) perforadora, barrena; (MIL) instrucción f ♦ vt perforar, taladrar; (troops) enseñar la instrucción a ♦ vi (for oil) perforar

drink [drɪŋk] (pt **drank**, pp **drunk**) n bebida; (sip) trago ♦ vt, vi beber; **to have a ~** tomar algo; tomar una copa or un trago; **a ~ of water** un trago de agua; **~er** n bebedor(a) m/f; **~ing water** n agua potable

drip [drɪp] n (act) goteo; (one ~) gota; (MED) gota a gota m ♦ vi gotear; **~-dry** adj (shirt) inarrugable; **~ping** n (animal fat) pringue m

drive [draɪv] (pt **drove**, pp **driven**) n (journey) viaje m (en coche); (also: **~way**) entrada; (energy) energía, vigor m; (COMPUT: also: disk ~) drive m ♦ vt (car) conducir, manejar (AM); (nail) clavar; (push) empujar; (TECH: motor) impulsar ♦ vi (AUT: at controls) conducir; (: travel) pasearse en coche; **left-/right-hand ~** conducción f a la izquierda/derecha; **to ~ sb mad** volverle loco a uno

drivel ['drɪvl] (inf) n tonterías fpl

driven ['drɪvn] pp of **drive**

driver ['draɪvə*] n conductor(a) m/f (SP), chofer m (AM); (of train) maquinista m/f; (of taxi, bus) chofer; **~'s license** (US) n carnet m de conducir

driveway ['draɪvweɪ] n entrada

driving ['draɪvɪŋ] n el conducir (SP), el manejar (AM); ~ **instructor** n instructor/a m/f de conducción or manejo; ~ **lesson** n clase f de conducción or manejo; ~ **licence** (BRIT) n permiso de conducir; ~ **school** n autoescuela; ~ **test** n examen m de conducción or manejo

drizzle ['drɪzl] n llovizna

drool [druːl] vi babear

droop [druːp] vi (flower) marchitarse; (shoulders) encorvarse; (head) inclinarse

drop [drɒp] n (of water) gota; (lessening) baja; (fall) caída ♦ vt dejar caer; (voice, eyes, price) bajar; (passenger) dejar; (omit) omitir ♦ vi (object) caer; (wind) amainar; **~s off** (MED) gotas fpl; **~ off** vi (sleep) dormirse ♦ vt (passenger) dejar; **~ out** vi (withdraw) retirarse; **~out** n marginado/a; (SCOL) estudiante que abandona los estudios; **~per** n cuentagotas m inv; **~pings** npl excremento

drought [draut] n sequía

drove [drəuv] pt of **drive**

drown [draun] vt ahogar ♦ vi ahogarse

drowsy ['drauzɪ] adj soñoliento; **to be ~** tener sueño

drug [drʌg] n medicamento; (narcotic) droga ♦ vt drogar; **to be on ~s** drogarse; **~ addict** n drogadicto/a; **~gist** (US) n farmacéutico; **~store** (US) n farmacia

drum [drʌm] n tambor m; (for oil, petrol) bidón m; **~s** npl batería; **~mer** n tambor m

drunk [drʌŋk] pp of **drink** ♦ adj borracho ♦ n (also: ~ard) borracho/a; **~en** adj borracho; (laughter, party) de borrachos

dry [draɪ] adj seco; (day) sin lluvia; (climate) árido, seco ♦ vt secar; (tears) enjugarse ♦ vi secarse; **~ up** vi (river) secarse; **~-cleaner's** n tintorería; **~-cleaning** n lavado en seco; **~er** n (for hair) secador m; (US: for clothes) secadora; **~ rot** n putrefacción f fungoide

DSS n abbr = **Department of Social Security**

DTP n abbr (= desk-top publishing) autoedición f

dual ['djuəl] adj doble; **~ carriageway** (BRIT) n carretera de

doble calzada; **~-purpose** adj de doble uso

dubbed [dʌbd] adj (CINEMA) doblado

dubious ['djuːbɪəs] adj indeciso; (reputation, company) sospechoso

duchess ['dʌtʃɪs] n duquesa

duck [dʌk] n pato ♦ vi agacharse; **~ling** n patito

duct [dʌkt] n conducto, canal m

dud [dʌd] n (object, tool) engaño, engañifa ♦ adj: **~ cheque** (BRIT) cheque m sin fondos

due [djuː] adj (owed): **he is ~ £10** se le deben 10 libras; (expected: event): **the meeting is ~ on Wednesday** la reunión tendrá lugar el miércoles; (: arrival) **the train is ~ at 8am** el tren tiene su llegada para las 8; (proper) debido ♦ n: **to give sb his** (or her) **~** ser justo con alguien ♦ adv: **~ north** derecho al norte; **~s** npl (for club, union) cuota; (in harbour) derechos mpl; **in ~ course** a su debido tiempo; **~ to** debido a; **to be ~ to** deberse a

duet [djuːˈet] n dúo

duffel bag ['dʌfəl] n bolsa de lona

duffel coat n trenca, abrigo de tres cuartos

dug [dʌg] pt, pp of **dig**

duke [djuːk] n duque m

dull [dʌl] adj (light) débil; (stupid) torpe; (boring) pesado; (sound, pain) sordo; (weather, day) gris ♦ vt (pain, grief) aliviar; (mind, senses) entorpecer

duly ['djuːlɪ] adv debidamente; (on time) a su debido tiempo

dumb [dʌm] adj mudo; (pej: stupid) estúpido; **~founded** [dʌmˈfaundɪd] adj pasmado

dummy ['dʌmɪ] n (tailor's ~) maniquí m; (mock-up) maqueta; (BRIT: for baby) chupete m ♦ adj falso, postizo

dump [dʌmp] n (also: rubbish ~) basurero, vertedero; (inf: place) cuchitril m ♦ vt (put down) dejar; (get rid of) deshacerse de; (COMPUT: data) transferir

dumpling ['dʌmplɪŋ] *n* bola de masa hervida

dumpy ['dʌmpɪ] *adj* regordete/a

dunce [dʌns] *n* zopenco

dung [dʌŋ] *n* estiércol *m*

dungarees [dʌŋgə'riːz] *npl* mono

dungeon ['dʌndʒən] *n* calabozo

duplex ['djuːpleks] *n* dúplex *m*

duplicate [*n* 'djuːplɪkət, *vb* 'djuːplɪkeɪt] *n* duplicado ♦ *vt* duplicar; (*photocopy*) fotocopiar; (*repeat*) repetir; **in ~** por duplicado

durable ['djuərəbl] *adj* duradero

duration [djuə'reɪʃən] *n* duración *f*

during ['djuərɪŋ] *prep* durante

dusk [dʌsk] *n* crepúsculo, anochecer *m*

dust [dʌst] *n* polvo ♦ *vt* quitar el polvo a, desempolvar; (*cake etc*): **to ~ with** espolvorear de; **~bin** (BRIT) *n* cubo de la basura (SP), balde *m* (AM); **~er** *n* paño, trapo; (*feather*) (BRIT irreg) *n* basurero; **~y** *adj* polvoriento

Dutch [dʌtʃ] *adj* holandés/esa ♦ *n* (LING) holandés *m*; **the ~** *npl* los holandeses; **to go ~** (*inf*) pagar cada uno lo suyo; **~man/woman** (irreg) *n* holandés/esa *m/f*

duty ['djuːtɪ] *n* deber *m*; (*tax*) derechos *mpl* de aduana; **on ~** de servicio; (*at night etc*) de guardia; **off ~** libre (de servicio); **~-free** *adj* libre de impuestos

duvet ['duːveɪ] (BRIT) *n* edredón *m*

dwarf [dwɔːf] (*pl* **dwarves**) *n* enano/a ♦ *vt* empequeñecer

dwell [dwel] (*pt, pp* **dwelt**) *vi* morar; **~ on** *vt fus* explayarse en

dwindle ['dwɪndl] *vi* menguar, disminuir

dye [daɪ] *n* tinte *m* ♦ *vt* teñir

dying ['daɪɪŋ] *adj* moribundo, agonizante

dyke [daɪk] (BRIT) *n* dique *m*

dynamic [daɪ'næmɪk] *adj* dinámico

dynamite ['daɪnəmaɪt] *n* dinamita

dynamo ['daɪnəməu] *n* dinamo *f*

dynasty ['dɪnəstɪ] *n* dinastía *f*

E, e

E [iː] *n* (MUS) mi *m*

each [iːtʃ] *adj* cada *inv* ♦ *pron* cada uno; **~ other** el uno al otro; **they hate ~ other** se odian (entre ellos or mutuamente); **they have 2 books ~** tienen 2 libros por persona

eager ['iːgə*] *adj* (*keen*) entusiasmado; **to be ~ to do sth** tener muchas ganas de hacer algo, impacientarse por hacer algo; **to be ~ for** tener muchas ganas de

eagle ['iːgl] *n* águila

ear [ɪə*] *n* oreja; oído; (*of corn*) espiga; **~ache** *n* dolor *m* de oídos; **~drum** *n* tímpano

earl [əːl] *n* conde *m*

earlier ['əːlɪə*] *adj* anterior ♦ *adv* antes

early ['əːlɪ] *adv* temprano; (*before time*) con tiempo, con anticipación ♦ *adj* temprano; (*settlers etc*) primitivo; (*death, departure*) prematuro; (*reply*) pronto; **to have an ~ night** acostarse temprano; **in the ~ or ~ in the spring/19th century** a principios de primavera/del siglo diecinueve; **~ retirement** *n* jubilación *f* anticipada

earmark ['ɪəmɑːk] *vt*: **to ~ (for)** reservar (para), destinar (a)

earn [əːn] *vt* (*salary*) percibir; (*interest*) devengar; (*praise*) merecerse

earnest ['əːnɪst] *adj* (*wish*) fervoroso; (*person*) serio, formal; **in ~** en serio

earnings ['əːnɪŋz] *npl* (*personal*) sueldo, ingresos *mpl*; (*company*) ganancias *fpl*

ear: ~phones *npl* auriculares *mpl*; **~ring** *n* pendiente *m*, arete *m*; **~shot** *n*: **within ~shot** al alcance del oído

earth [əːθ] *n* tierra; (BRIT: ELEC) cable *m* de toma de tierra ♦ *vt* (BRIT: ELEC) conectar a tierra; **~enware** *n* loza (de barro); **~quake** *n* terremoto; **~y** *adj* (*fig: vulgar*) grosero

ease [iːz] n facilidad f; (comfort) comodidad f ♦ vt (lessen: problem) mitigar; (: pain) aliviar; (: tension) reducir; **to ~ sth in/out** meter/sacar algo con cuidado; **at ~!** (MIL) ¡descansen!; **~ off** or **up** vi (wind, rain) amainar; (slow down) aflojar la marcha

easel [ˈiːzl] n caballete m

easily [ˈiːzɪlɪ] adv fácilmente

east [iːst] n este m ♦ adj del este, oriental; (wind) este ♦ adv al este, hacia el este; **the E~** el Oriente; (POL) los países del Este

Easter [ˈiːstəʳ] n Pascua (de Resurrección); **~ egg** n huevo de Pascua

east: ~erly [ˈiːstəlɪ] adj (to the east) al este; (from the east) del este; **~ern** [ˈiːstən] adj del este, oriental; (oriental) oriental; (communist) del este; **~ward(s)** [ˈiːstwəd(z)] adv hacia el este

easy [ˈiːzɪ] adj fácil; (simple) sencillo; (comfortable) holgado, cómodo; (relaxed) tranquilo ♦ adv: **to take it** or **things ~** (not worry) tomarlo con calma; (rest) descansar; **~ chair** n sillón m; **~-going** adj acomodadizo

eat [iːt] (pt **ate**, pp **eaten**) vt comer; **~ away** at vt fus corroer; mermar; **~ into** vt fus corroer; (savings) mermar

eaves [iːvz] npl alero

eavesdrop [ˈiːvzdrɒp] vi: **to ~ (on)** escuchar a escondidas

ebb [eb] n reflujo ♦ vi bajar; (fig: also: **~ away**) decaer

ebony [ˈebənɪ] n ébano

EC n abbr (= European Community) CE f

eccentric [ɪkˈsentrɪk] adj, n excéntrico/a m/f

echo [ˈekəu] (pl **~es**) n eco m ♦ vt (sound) repetir ♦ vi resonar, hacer eco

éclair [ɪˈklɛəʳ] n pastelillo relleno de crema y con chocolate por encima

eclipse [ɪˈklɪps] n eclipse m

ecology [ɪˈkɒlədʒɪ] n ecología

economic [iːkəˈnɒmɪk] adj económico;

(business etc) rentable; **~al** adj económico; **~s** n (SCOL) economía ♦ npl (of project etc) rentabilidad f

economize [ɪˈkɒnəmaɪz] vi economizar, ahorrar

economy [ɪˈkɒnəmɪ] n economía; **~ class** n (AVIAT) clase f económica; **~ size** n tamaño económico

ecstasy [ˈekstəsɪ] n éxtasis m inv; (drug) éxtasis m inv; **ecstatic** [eksˈtætɪk] adj extático

ECU [ˈeɪkjuː] n (= European Currency Unit) ECU m

Ecuador [ˈekwədɔːʳ] n Ecuador m; **~ian** adj, n ecuatoriano/a m/f

eczema [ˈeksɪmə] n eczema m

edge [edʒ] n (of knife etc) filo; (of object) borde m; (of lake etc) orilla ♦ vt (SEWING) ribetear; **on** (fig) = **edgy**; **to ~ away from** alejarse poco a poco de; **~ways** adv: **he couldn't get a word in ~ways** no pudo meter ni baza

edgy [ˈedʒɪ] adj nervioso, inquieto

edible [ˈedɪbl] adj comestible

Edinburgh [ˈedɪnbərə] n Edimburgo

edit [ˈedɪt] vt (be editor of) dirigir; (text, report) corregir, preparar; **~ion** [ɪˈdɪʃən] n edición f; **~or** n (of newspaper) director(a) m/f; (of column): **foreign/political ~or** encargado de la sección de extranjero/político; (of book) redactor(a) m/f; **~orial** [-ˈtɔːrɪəl] adj editorial ♦ n editorial m

educate [ˈedjukeɪt] vt (gen) educar; (instruct) instruir

education [edjuˈkeɪʃən] n educación f; (schooling) enseñanza; (SCOL) pedagogía; **~al** adj (policy etc) educacional; (experience) docente; (toy) educativo

EEC n abbr (= European Economic Community) CEE f

eel [iːl] n anguila

eerie [ˈɪərɪ] adj misterioso

effect [ɪˈfekt] n efecto ♦ vt efectuar, llevar a cabo; **to take ~** (law) entrar en vigor or vigencia; (*drug*) surtir efecto; **in ~** en realidad; **~ive** *adj* eficaz; (*actual*) verdadero; **~ively** *adv* eficazmente; (*in reality*) efectivamente; **~iveness** *n* eficacia

effeminate [ɪˈfɛmɪnɪt] *adj* afeminado
efficiency [ɪˈfɪʃənsɪ] *n* eficiencia; rendimiento
efficient [ɪˈfɪʃənt] *adj* eficiente; (*machine*) de buen rendimiento
effort [ˈɛfət] *n* esfuerzo; **~less** *adj* sin ningún esfuerzo; (*style*) natural
effusive [ɪˈfjuːsɪv] *adj* efusivo
e.g. *adv abbr* (= *exempli gratia*) p. ej.
egg [ɛg] *n* huevo; **hard-boiled/soft-boiled ~** huevo duro/pasado por agua; **~ on** vt incitar; **~cup** *n* huevera; **~ plant** (*esp US*) *n* berenjena; **~shell** *n* cáscara de huevo
ego [ˈiːgəu] *n* ego; **~tism** *n* egoísmo; **~tist** *n* egoísta *m/f*
Egypt [ˈiːdʒɪpt] *n* Egipto; **~ian** [ɪˈdʒɪpʃən] *adj*, *n* egipcio/a *m/f*
eiderdown [ˈaɪdədaun] *n* edredón *m*
eight [eɪt] *num* ocho; **~een** *num* diez y ocho; dieciocho; **eighth** [eɪtθ] *num* octavo; **~y** *num* ochenta
Eire [ˈɛərə] *n* Eire *m*
either [ˈaɪðə*] *adj* cualquiera de los dos; (*both, each*) cada ♦ *pron:* **~ (of them)** cualquiera (de los dos) ♦ *adv* tampoco; **on ~ side** en ambos lados; **I don't like ~** no me gusta ninguno/a de los/las dos; **no, I don't ~** no, yo tampoco ♦ *conj:* **~ yes or no** o sí o no
eject [ɪˈdʒɛkt] vt echar, expulsar; (*tenant*) desahuciar; **~or seat** *n* asiento proyectable
elaborate [*adj* ɪˈlæbərɪt, *vb* ɪˈlæbəreɪt] *adj* (*complex*) complejo ♦ vt (*expand*) ampliar; (*refine*) refinar ♦ vi explicar con más detalles
elastic [ɪˈlæstɪk] *n* elástico ♦ *adj* elástico; (*fig*) flexible; **~ band** (*BRIT*) *n* gomita
elated [ɪˈleɪtɪd] *adj:* **to be ~** regocijarse
elbow [ˈɛlbəu] *n* codo

elder [ˈɛldə*] *adj* mayor ♦ *n* (*tree*) saúco; (*person*) mayor; **~ly** *adj* de edad, mayor ♦ *npl:* **the ~ly** los mayores
eldest [ˈɛldɪst] *adj, n* el/la mayor
elect [ɪˈlɛkt] vt elegir ♦ *adj:* **the president ~** el presidente electo; **to ~ to do** optar por hacer; **~ion** *n* elección *f*; **~ioneering** [ɪlɛkʃəˈnɪərɪŋ] *n* campaña electoral; **~or** *n* elector/a *m/f*; **~oral** *adj* electoral; **~orate** *n* electorado
electric [ɪˈlɛktrɪk] *adj* eléctrico; **~al** *adj* eléctrico; **~ blanket** *n* manta eléctrica; **~ fire** *n* estufa eléctrica; **~ian** [ɪlɛkˈtrɪʃən] *n* electricista *m/f*; **~ity** [ɪlɛkˈtrɪsɪtɪ] *n* electricidad *f*; **electrify** [ɪˈlɛktrɪfaɪ] vt (*RAIL*) electrificar; (*fig: audience*) electrizar
electronic [ɪlɛkˈtrɒnɪk] *adj* electrónico; **~ mail** *n* correo electrónico; **~s** *n* electrónica
elegant [ˈɛlɪgənt] *adj* elegante
element [ˈɛlɪmənt] *n* elemento; (*of kettle etc*) resistencia; **~ary** [-ˈmɛntərɪ] *adj* elemental; (*primitive*) rudimentario; (*school*) primario
elephant [ˈɛlɪfənt] *n* elefante *m*
elevation [ɛlɪˈveɪʃən] *n* elevación *f*; (*height*) altura
elevator [ˈɛlɪveɪtə*] *n* (*US*) ascensor *m*; (*in warehouse etc*) montacargas *m inv*
eleven [ɪˈlɛvn] *num* once; **~ses** (*BRIT*) *npl* café *m* de las once; **~th** *num* undécimo
elicit [ɪˈlɪsɪt] vt: **to ~ (from)** sacar (de)
eligible [ˈɛlɪdʒəbl] *adj:* **an ~ young man/woman** un buen partido; **to be ~ for sth** llenar los requisitos para algo
elm [ɛlm] *n* olmo
elongated [ˈiːlɒŋgeɪtɪd] *adj* alargado
elope [ɪˈləup] vi fugarse (para casarse)
eloquent [ˈɛləkwənt] *adj* elocuente
else [ɛls] *adv:* **something ~** otra cosa; **somewhere ~** en otra parte; **everywhere ~** en todas partes menos aquí; **where ~?** ¿dónde más?, ¿en qué

otra parte?; **there was little ~ to do** apenas quedaba otra cosa que hacer; **nobody ~ spoke** no habló nadie más; **~where** adv (be) en otra parte; (go) a otra parte

elude [ɪ'luːd] vt (subj: idea etc) escaparse a; (capture) esquivar

elusive [ɪ'luːsɪv] adj esquivo; (quality) difícil de encontrar

emaciated [ɪ'meɪsɪeɪtɪd] adj demacrado

E-mail, e-mail ['iːmeɪl] n abbr (= electronic mail) correo electrónico, e-mail m

emancipate [ɪ'mænsɪpeɪt] vt emancipar

embankment [ɪm'bæŋkmənt] n terraplén m

embark [ɪm'bɑːk] vi embarcarse ♦ vt embarcar; **to ~ on** (journey) emprender; (course of action) lanzarse a; **~ation** [embɑː'keɪʃən] n (people) embarco; (goods) embarque m

embarrass [ɪm'bærəs] vt avergonzar; (government etc) dejar en mal lugar; **~ed** adj (laugh, silence) embarazoso; **~ing** adj (situation) violento; (question) embarazoso; **~ment** n (shame) vergüenza; (problem): **to be an ~ment for sb** poner en un aprieto a uno

embassy ['embəsɪ] n embajada

embedded [ɪm'bedɪd] adj (object) empotrado; (thorn etc) clavado

embellish [ɪm'belɪʃ] vt embellecer; (story) adornar

embers ['embəz] npl rescoldo, ascua

embezzle [ɪm'bezl] vt desfalcar, malversar

embitter [ɪm'bɪtə*] vt (fig: sour) amargar

embody [ɪm'bɔdɪ] vt (spirit) encarnar; (include) incorporar

embossed [ɪm'bɔst] adj realzado

embrace [ɪm'breɪs] vt abrazar, dar un abrazo a; (include) abarcar ♦ vi abrazarse ♦ n abrazo

embroider [ɪm'brɔɪdə*] vt bordar; **~y** n bordado

embryo ['embrɪəu] n embrión m

emerald ['emərəld] n esmeralda

emerge [ɪ'mɜːdʒ] vi salir; (arise) surgir

emergency [ɪ'mɜːdʒənsɪ] n crisis f inv; **in an ~** en caso de urgencia; **state of ~** estado de emergencia; **~ cord** (US) n timbre m de alarma; **~ exit** n salida de emergencia; **~ landing** n aterrizaje m forzoso; **~ services** npl (fire, police, ambulance) servicios mpl de urgencia or emergencia

emery board ['emərɪ-] n lima de uñas

emigrate ['emɪgreɪt] vi emigrar

emissions [ɪ'mɪʃənz] npl emisión f

emit [ɪ'mɪt] vt emitir; (smoke) arrojar; (smell) despedir; (sound) producir

emotion [ɪ'məuʃən] n emoción f; **~al** adj (needs) emocional; (person) sentimental; (scene) conmovedor(a), emocionante; (speech) emocionado

emperor ['empərə*] n emperador m

emphasis ['emfəsɪs] (pl **-ses**) n énfasis m inv

emphasize ['emfəsaɪz] vt (word, point) subrayar, recalcar; (feature) hacer resaltar

emphatic [ɛm'fætɪk] adj (reply) categórico; (person) insistente

empire ['empaɪə*] n (also fig) imperio

employ [ɪm'plɔɪ] vt emplear; **~ee** [-'iː] n empleado/a; **~er** n patrón/ona m/f; empresario; **~ment** n (work) trabajo; **~ment agency** n agencia de colocaciones

empower [ɪm'pauə*] vt: **to ~ sb to do sth** autorizar a uno para hacer algo

empress ['emprɪs] n emperatriz f

emptiness ['emptɪnɪs] n vacío; (of life etc) vaciedad f

empty ['emptɪ] adj vacío; (place) desierto; (house) desocupado; (threat) vano ♦ vt vaciar; (place) dejar vacío ♦ vi vaciarse; (house etc) quedar desocupado; **~-handed** adj con las manos vacías

EMU n abbr (= European Monetary Union) UME f

emulate ['emjuleɪt] vt emular

emulsion [ɪ'mʌlʃən] n emulsión f; (also: ~ paint) pintura emulsión

enable [ɪ'neɪbl] vt: to ~ sb to do sth permitir a uno hacer algo

enamel [ɪ'næməl] n esmalte m; (also: ~ paint) pintura esmaltada

enchant [ɪn'tʃɑːnt] vt encantar; **~ing** adj encantador(a)

encl. abbr (= enclosed) adj

enclose [ɪn'kləuz] vt (land) cercar; (letter etc) adjuntar; **please find ~d** le mandamos adjunto

enclosure [ɪn'kləuʒə*] n cercado, recinto

encompass [ɪn'kʌmpəs] vt abarcar

encore [ɔŋ'kɔː*] excl ¡otra!, ¡bis! ♦ n bis m

encounter [ɪn'kauntə*] n encuentro ♦ vt encontrar, encontrarse con; (difficulty) tropezar con

encourage [ɪn'kʌrɪdʒ] vt alentar, animar; (activity) fomentar; (growth) estimular; **~ment** n estímulo; (of industry) fomento

encroach [ɪn'krəutʃ] vi: to ~ (up)on invadir; (rights) usurpar; (time) adueñarse de

encyclo(p)aedia [ensaɪkləu'piːdɪə] n enciclopedia

end [end] n (gen, also aim) fin m; (of table) extremo; (of street) final m; (SPORT) lado ♦ vt terminar, acabar; (also: bring to an ~, put an ~ to) acabar con ♦ vi terminar, acabar; **in the ~** al fin; **on ~** (object) de punta, de cabeza; **to stand on ~** (hair) erizarse; **for hours on ~** hora tras hora; **~ up** vi: **to ~ up in** terminar en; (place) ir a parar en

endanger [ɪn'deɪndʒə*] vt poner en peligro; **an ~ed species** una especie en peligro de extinción

endearing [ɪn'dɪərɪŋ] adj simpático, atractivo

endeavour [ɪn'devə*] (US **endeavor**) n esfuerzo; (attempt) tentativa ♦ vi: **to ~ to do** esforzarse por hacer; (try) procurar hacer

ending ['endɪŋ] n (of book) desenlace m; (LING) terminación f

endive ['endaɪv] n (chicory) endibia; (curly) escarola

endless ['endlɪs] adj interminable, inacabable

endorse [ɪn'dɔːs] vt (cheque) endosar; (approve) aprobar; **~ment** n (on driving licence) nota de inhabilitación

endure [ɪn'djuə*] vt (bear) aguantar, soportar ♦ vi (last) durar

enemy ['enəmɪ] adj, n enemigo/a m/f

energetic [enə'dʒetɪk] adj enérgico

energy ['enədʒɪ] n energía

enforce [ɪn'fɔːs] vt (LAW) hacer cumplir

engage [ɪn'geɪdʒ] vt (attention) llamar; (interest) ocupar; (in conversation) abordar; (worker) contratar; (AUT): **to ~ the clutch** embragar ♦ vi (TECH) engranar; **to ~ in** dedicarse a, ocuparse en; **~d** adj (BRIT: busy, in use) ocupado; (betrothed) prometido; **to get ~d** prometerse; **~d tone** (BRIT) n (TEL) señal f de comunicando; **~ment** n (appointment) compromiso, cita; (booking) contratación f; (to marry) compromiso; (period) noviazgo; **~ment ring** n anillo de prometida

engaging [ɪn'geɪdʒɪŋ] adj atractivo

engine ['endʒɪn] n (AUT) motor m; (RAIL) locomotora; **~ driver** n (RAIL) maquinista m/f

engineer [endʒɪ'nɪə*] n ingeniero; (BRIT: for repairs) mecánico; (on ship, US: RAIL) maquinista m; **~ing** n ingeniería

England ['ɪŋlənd] n Inglaterra

English ['ɪŋlɪʃ] adj inglés/esa ♦ n (LING) inglés m; **the ~** npl los ingleses mpl; **the ~ Channel** n (el Canal de) la Mancha; **~man/woman** (irreg) n inglés/esa m/f

engraving [ɪn'greɪvɪŋ] n grabado

engrossed [ɪnˈgrəʊst] adj: ~ **in** absorto en

engulf [ɪnˈgʌlf] vt (subj: water) sumergir, hundir; (: fire) prender; (: fear) apoderarse de

enhance [ɪnˈhɑːns] vt (gen) aumentar; (beauty) realzar

enjoy [ɪnˈdʒɔɪ] vt (health, fortune) disfrutar de, gozar de; (like) gustarle a uno; **to ~ o.s.** divertirse; **~able** adj agradable; (amusing) divertido; **~ment** n (joy) placer m; (activity) diversión f

enlarge [ɪnˈlɑːdʒ] vt aumentar; (broaden) extender; (PHOT) ampliar ♦ vi: **to ~ on** (subject) tratar con más detalles; **~ment** n (PHOT) ampliación f

enlighten [ɪnˈlaɪtn] vt (inform) informar; **~ed** adj comprensivo; **the E~ment** n (HISTORY) ≈ la Ilustración, ≈ el Siglo de las Luces

enlist [ɪnˈlɪst] vt alistar; (support) conseguir ♦ vi alistarse

enmity [ˈenmɪtɪ] n enemistad f

enormous [ɪˈnɔːməs] adj enorme

enough [ɪˈnʌf] adj: ~ **time/books** bastante tiempo/bastantes libros ♦ pron bastante(s) ♦ adv: **big ~** bastante grande; **he has not worked ~** no ha trabajado bastante; **have you got ~?** ¿tiene usted bastante(s)?; **~ to eat** lo suficiente or (lo) bastante para comer; **~!** ¡basta ya!; **that's ~, thanks** con eso basta, gracias; **I've had ~ of him** estoy harto de él; ... **which, funnily** or **oddly ~** ... lo que, por extraño que parezca ...

enquire [ɪnˈkwaɪə*] vt, vi = **inquire**

enrage [ɪnˈreɪdʒ] vt enfurecer

enrol [ɪnˈrəʊl] (US **enroll**) vt (members) inscribir; (SCOL) matricular ♦ vi inscribirse; matricularse; **~ment** (US **enrollment**) n inscripción f; matriculación f

en route [ɒnˈruːt] adv durante el viaje

en suite [ɒnˈswiːt] adj: **with ~ bathroom** con baño

ensure [ɪnˈʃʊə*] vt asegurar

entail [ɪnˈteɪl] vt suponer

entangled [ɪnˈtæŋgld] adj: **to become ~ (in)** quedarse enredado (en) or enmarañado (en)

enter [ˈentə*] vt (room) entrar en; (club) hacerse socio de; (army) alistarse en; (sb for a competition) inscribir; (write down) anotar, apuntar; (COMPUT) meter ♦ vi entrar; **~ for** vt fus presentarse para; **~ into** vt fus (discussion etc) entablar; (agreement) llegar a, firmar

enterprise [ˈentəpraɪz] n empresa; (spirit) iniciativa; **free ~** la libre empresa; **private ~** la iniciativa privada; **enterprising** adj emprendedor(a)

entertain [entəˈteɪn] vt (amuse) divertir; (invite: guest) invitar a (casa); (idea) abrigar; **~er** n artista m/f; **~ing** adj divertido, entretenido; **~ment** n (amusement) diversión f; (show) espectáculo

enthralled [ɪnˈθrɔːld] adj encantado

enthusiasm [ɪnˈθuːzɪæzəm] n entusiasmo

enthusiast [ɪnˈθuːzɪæst] n entusiasta m/f; **~ic** [-ˈæstɪk] adj entusiasta; **to be ~ic about** entusiasmarse por

entire [ɪnˈtaɪə*] adj entero; **~ly** adv totalmente; **~ty** [ɪnˈtaɪərətɪ] n: **in its ~ty** en su totalidad

entitle [ɪnˈtaɪtl] vt: **to ~ sb to sth** dar a uno derecho a algo; **~d** adj (book) titulado; **to be ~d to do** tener derecho a hacer

entrance [n ˈentrəns, vb ɪnˈtrɑːns] n entrada ♦ vt encantar, hechizar; **to gain ~ to** (university etc) ingresar en; **~ examination** n examen m de ingreso; **~ fee** n cuota; **~ ramp** (US) n (AUT) rampa de acceso

entrant [ˈentrənt] n (in race, competition) participante m/f; (in examination) candidato/a

entrenched [enˈtrentʃd] adj inamovible

entrepreneur [ɔntrəprə'nə:] n empresario

entrust [ɪn'trʌst] vt: **to ~ sth to** sb confiar algo a uno

entry ['entrɪ] n entrada; (in competition) participación f; (in register) apunte m; (in account) partida; (in reference book) artículo; **"no ~"** "prohibido el paso"; (AUT) "dirección prohibida"; **~ form** n hoja de inscripción; **~ phone** n portero automático

envelop [ɪn'veləp] vt envolver

envelope ['envələup] n sobre m

envious ['envɪəs] adj envidioso; (look) de envidia

environment [ɪn'vaɪərnmənt] n (surroundings) entorno; (natural world): **the ~** el medio ambiente; **~al** [-'mentl] adj ambiental; medioambiental; **~-friendly** adj no perjudicial para el medio ambiente

envisage [ɪn'vɪzɪdʒ] vt prever

envoy ['envɔɪ] n enviado

envy ['envɪ] n envidia ♦ vt tener envidia a; **to ~ sb sth** envidiar algo a uno

epic ['epɪk] n épica ♦ adj épico

epidemic [epɪ'demɪk] n epidemia

epilepsy ['epɪlepsɪ] n epilepsia

episode ['epɪsəud] n episodio

epitomize [ɪ'pɪtəmaɪz] vt epitomar, resumir

equal ['i:kwl] adj igual; (treatment) equitativo ♦ n igual m/f ♦ vt ser igual a; (fig) igualar; **to be ~ to** (task) estar a la altura de; **~ity** [i:'kwɔlɪtɪ] n igualdad f; **~ize** vi (SPORT) empatar; **~ly** adv igualmente; (share etc) a partes iguales

equate [ɪ'kweɪt] vt: **to ~ sth with** equiparar algo con; **equation** [ɪ'kweɪʒən] n (MATH) ecuación f

equator [ɪ'kweɪtə*] n ecuador m

equilibrium [i:kwɪ'lɪbrɪəm] n equilibrio

equip [ɪ'kwɪp] vt equipar; (person) proveer; **to be well ~ped** estar bien

equipado; **~ment** n equipo; (tools) avíos mpl

equities ['ekwɪtɪz] (BRIT) npl (COMM) derechos mpl sobre or en el activo

equivalent [ɪ'kwɪvələnt] adj: **~ (to)** equivalente (a) ♦ n equivalente m

era ['ɪərə] n era, época

eradicate [ɪ'rædɪkeɪt] vt erradicar

erase [ɪ'reɪz] vt borrar; **~r** n goma de borrar

erect [ɪ'rekt] adj erguido ♦ vt erigir, levantar; (assemble) montar; **~ion** [-ʃən] n construcción f; (assembly) montaje m; (PHYSIOL) erección f

ERM n abbr (= Exchange Rate Mechanism) tipo de cambio europeo

erode [ɪ'rəud] vt (GEO) erosionar; (metal) corroer, desgastar; (fig) desgastar

erotic [ɪ'rɔtɪk] adj erótico

errand [ɪ'rænd] n recado (SP), mandado (AM)

erratic [ɪ'rætɪk] adj desigual, poco uniforme

error ['erə*] n error m, equivocación f

erupt [ɪ'rʌpt] vi entrar en erupción; (fig) estallar; **~ion** [ɪ'rʌpʃən] n erupción f; (of war) estallido

escalate ['eskəleɪt] vi extenderse, intensificarse

escalator ['eskəleɪtə*] n escalera móvil

escapade [eskə'peɪd] n travesura

escape [ɪ'skeɪp] n fuga ♦ vi escaparse; (flee) huir, evadirse; (leak) fugarse ♦ vt (responsibility) evitar, eludir; (consequences) escapar a; (elude): **his name ~s me** no me sale su nombre; **to ~ from** (place) escaparse de; (person) escapar a

escort [n 'eskɔ:t, vb ɪ'skɔ:t] n acompañante m/f; (MIL) escolta ♦ vt acompañar

Eskimo ['eskɪməu] n esquimal m/f

especially [ɪ'speʃlɪ] adv (above all) sobre todo; (particularly) en particular, especialmente

espionage ['espɪənɑ:ʒ] n espionaje m

esplanade [esplə'neɪd] *n* (*by sea*) paseo marítimo

Esquire [ɪ'skwaɪə] (*abbr* Esq.) *n*: J. Brown, ~ Sr. D. J. Brown

essay ['eseɪ] *n* (*LITERATURE*) ensayo; (*SCOL*: *short*) redacción *f*; (: *long*) trabajo

essence ['esns] *n* esencia

essential [ɪ'senʃl] *adj* (*necessary*) imprescindible; (*basic*) esencial; ~s *npl* lo imprescindible, lo esencial; **~ly** *adv* esencialmente

establish [ɪ'stæblɪʃ] *vt* establecer; (*prove*) demostrar; (*relations*) entablar; (*reputation*) ganarse; **~ed** *adj* (*business*) conocido; (*practice*) arraigado; **~ment** *n* establecimiento; **the E~ment** *n* la clase dirigente

estate [ɪ'steɪt] *n* (*land*) finca, hacienda; (*inheritance*) herencia; (*BRIT*: *also*: *housing* ~) urbanización *f*; ~ **agent** (*BRIT*) *n* agente *m/f* inmobiliario/a; ~ **car** (*BRIT*) *n* furgoneta

esteem [ɪ'stiːm] *n*: **to hold sb in high** ~ estimar en mucho a uno

esthetic [ɪs'θetɪk] (*US*) *adj* = **aesthetic**

estimate [*n* 'estɪmət, *vb* 'estɪmeɪt] *n* estimación *f*, apreciación *f*; (*assessment*) tasa, cálculo; (*COMM*) presupuesto ♦ *vt* estimar, tasar; calcular; **estimation** [-'meɪʃən] *n* opinión *f*, juicio; cálculo

estranged [ɪs'streɪndʒd] *adj* separado

estuary ['estjuərɪ] *n* estuario, ría

etc *abbr* (= *et cetera*) etc

eternal [ɪ'tɜːnl] *adj* eterno

eternity [ɪ'tɜːnɪtɪ] *n* eternidad *f*

ethical ['eθɪkl] *adj* ético; **ethics** ['eθɪks] *n* ética ♦ *npl* moralidad *f*

Ethiopia [iːθɪ'əupɪə] *n* Etiopía

ethnic ['eθnɪk] *adj* étnico; ~ **minority** *n* minoría étnica

ethos ['iːθɒs] *n* genio, carácter *m*

etiquette ['etɪket] *n* etiqueta

EU *n abbr* (= *European Union*) UE *f*

euro *n* euro

Eurocheque ['juərəutʃek] *n* Eurocheque *m*

Europe ['juərəp] *n* Europa; **~an** [-'piːən] *adj*, *n* europeo/a *m/f*; **~an Community** *n* Comunidad *f* Europea; **~an Union** *n* Unión *f* Europea

evacuate [ɪ'vækjueɪt] *vt* (*people*) evacuar; (*place*) desocupar

evade [ɪ'veɪd] *vt* evadir, eludir

evaporate [ɪ'væpəreɪt] *vi* evaporarse; (*fig*) desvanecerse; **~d milk** *n* leche *f* evaporada

evasion [ɪ'veɪʒən] *n* evasión *f*

eve [iːv] *n*: **on the ~** en vísperas de

even ['iːvn] *adj* (*level*) llano; (*smooth*) liso; (*speed, temperature*) uniforme; (*number*) par ♦ *adv* hasta, incluso; (*introducing a comparison*) aún, todavía; ~ **if**, ~ **though** aunque + *sub*; ~ **more** aun más; ~ **so** aun así; **not** ~ ni siquiera; **he was there** ~ hasta él estuvo allí; ~ **on Sundays** incluso los domingos; **to get** ~ **with sb** ajustar cuentas con uno

evening ['iːvnɪŋ] *n* tarde *f*; (*late*) noche *f*; **in the** ~ por la tarde; ~ **class** *n* clase *f* nocturna; ~ **dress** *n* (*no pl*: *formal clothes*) traje *m* de etiqueta; (*woman's*) traje *m* de noche

event [ɪ'vent] *n* suceso, acontecimiento; (*SPORT*) prueba; **in the** ~ **of** en caso de; **~ful** *adj* (*life*) activo; (*day*) ajetreado

eventual [ɪ'ventʃuəl] *adj* final; **~ity** [-'ælɪt] *n* eventualidad *f*; **~ly** *adv* (*finally*) finalmente; (*in time*) con el tiempo

ever ['evə*] *adv* (*at any time*) nunca, jamás; (*at all times*) siempre; (*in question*) **why** ~ **not?** ¿y por qué no?; **the best** ~ lo nunca visto; **have you** ~ **seen it?** ¿lo ha visto usted alguna vez?; **better than** ~ mejor que nunca; ~ **since** *adv* desde entonces ♦ *conj* después de que; **~green** *n* árbol *m* de hoja perenne; **~lasting** *adj* eterno, perpetuo

KEYWORD

every ['evrɪ] adj **1** (each) cada; **~ one of them** (persons) todos ellos/as; (objects) cada uno de ellos/as; **~ shop in the town was closed** todas las tiendas de la ciudad estaban cerradas **2** (all possible) todo/a; **I gave you ~ assistance** te di toda la ayuda posible; **I have ~ confidence in him** tiene toda mi confianza; **we wish you ~ success** te deseamos toda suerte de éxitos **3** (showing recurrence) todo/a; **~ day/ week** todos los días/todas las semanas; **~ other car had been broken into** habían forzado uno de cada dos coches; **she visits me ~ other/third day** me visita cada dos/tres días; **~ now and then** de vez en cuando

every: ~body pron = **everyone**; **~day** adj (daily) cotidiano, de todos los días; (usual) acostumbrado; **~one** pron todos/as, todo el mundo; **~thing** pron todo; **this shop sells ~thing** esta tienda vende de todo; **~where** adv: **I've been looking for you ~where** te he estado buscando por todas partes; **~where you go you meet ...** en todas partes encuentras ...

evict [ɪ'vɪkt] vt desahuciar; **~ion** [ɪ'vɪkʃən] n desahucio

evidence ['evɪdəns] n (proof) prueba; (of witness) testimonio; (sign) indicios mpl; **to give ~** prestar declaración, dar testimonio

evident ['evɪdənt] adj evidente, manifiesto; **~ly** adv por lo visto

evil ['iːvl] adj malo; (influence) funesto ♦ n mal m

evoke [ɪ'vəuk] vt evocar

evolution [iːvə'luːʃən] n evolución f

evolve [ɪ'vɒlv] vt desarrollar ♦ vi evolucionar, desarrollarse

ewe [juː] n oveja

ex- [eks] prefix ex

exact [ɪg'zækt] adj exacto; (person) meticuloso ♦ vt: **to ~ sth (from)** exigir algo (de); **~ing** adj exigente; (conditions) arduo; **~ly** adv exactamente; (indicating agreement) exacto

exaggerate [ɪg'zædʒəreɪt] vt, vi exagerar; **exaggeration** [-'reɪʃən] n exageración f

exalted [ɪg'zɔːltɪd] adj eminente

exam [ɪg'zæm] n abbr (SCOL) = **examination**

examination [ɪgzæmɪ'neɪʃən] n examen m; (MED) reconocimiento

examine [ɪg'zæmɪn] vt examinar; (inspect) inspeccionar, escudriñar; (MED) reconocer; **~r** n examinador(a) m/f

example [ɪg'zɑːmpl] n ejemplo; **for ~** por ejemplo

exasperate [ɪg'zɑːspəreɪt] vt exasperar, irritar; **exasperation** [-'ʃən] n exasperación f, irritación f

excavate ['ekskəveɪt] vt excavar

exceed [ɪk'siːd] vt (amount) exceder; (number) pasar de; (speed limit) sobrepasar; (powers) excederse en; (hopes) superar; **~ingly** adv sumamente, sobremanera

excellent ['eksələnt] adj excelente

except [ɪk'sept] prep (also: **~ for, ~ing**) excepto, salvo ♦ vt exceptuar, excluir; **~ if/when** excepto si/cuando; **~ that** salvo que; **~ion** [ɪk'sepʃən] n excepción f; **to take ~ion to** ofenderse por; **~ional** [ɪk'sepʃənl] adj excepcional

excerpt ['eksɜːpt] n extracto

excess [ɪk'ses] n exceso; **~es** npl (of cruelty etc) atrocidades fpl; **~ baggage** n exceso de equipaje; **~ fare** n suplemento; **~ive** adj excesivo

exchange [ɪks'tʃeɪndʒ] n intercambio; (conversation) diálogo; (also: **telephone ~**) central f (telefónica) ♦ vt: **to ~ (for)** cambiar (por); **~ rate** n tipo de cambio

exchequer [ɪks'tʃekə*] (BRIT) n: **the E~** la Hacienda del Fisco

excise ['eksaɪz] n impuestos mpl sobre el alcohol y el tabaco

excite [ɪk'saɪt] vt (stimulate) estimular; (arouse) excitar; **~d** adj: **to get ~d** emocionarse; **~ment** n (agitation) excitación f; (exhilaration) emoción f; **exciting** adj emocionante

exclaim [ɪk'skleɪm] vi exclamar; **exclamation** [eksklə'meɪʃən] n exclamación f; **exclamation mark** n punto de admiración

exclude [ɪk'skluːd] vt excluir; exceptuar

exclusive [ɪk'skluːsɪv] adj exclusivo; (club, district) selecto; **~ of tax** excluyendo impuestos; **~ly** adv únicamente

excruciating [ɪk'skruːʃieɪtɪŋ] adj (pain) agudísimo, atroz; (noise, embarrassment) horrible

excursion [ɪk'skɜːʃən] n (tourist ~) excursión f

excuse [n ɪk'skjuːs, vb ɪk'skjuːz] n disculpa, excusa; (pretext) pretexto ♦ vt (justify) justificar; (forgive) disculpar, perdonar; **to ~ sb from doing sth** dispensar a uno de hacer algo; **~ me!** (attracting attention) ¡por favor!; (apologizing) ¡perdón!; **if you will ~ me** con su permiso

ex-directory ['eksdɪ'rektərɪ] (BRIT) adj que no consta en la guía

execute ['eksɪkjuːt] vt (plan) realizar; (order) cumplir; (person) ajusticiar, ejecutar; **execution** [-'kjuːʃən] n realización f; cumplimiento; ejecución f

executive [ɪg'zekjutɪv] n (person, committee) ejecutivo; (POL: committee) poder m ejecutivo ♦ adj ejecutivo

exemplify [ɪg'zemplɪfaɪ] vt ejemplificar; (illustrate) ilustrar

exempt [ɪg'zempt] adj: **~ from** exento de ♦ vt: **to ~ sb from** eximir a uno de; **~ion** [-ʃən] n exención f

exercise ['eksəsaɪz] n ejercicio ♦ vt (patience) usar de; (right) valerse de; (dog) llevar de paseo; (mind) preocupar ♦ vi (also: **to take ~**) hacer ejercicio(s); **~ bike** n ciclostático ®, bicicleta estática; **~ book** n cuaderno

exert [ɪg'zɜːt] vt ejercer; **to ~ o.s.** esforzarse; **~ion** [-ʃən] n esfuerzo

exhale [eks'heɪl] vt despedir ♦ vi exhalar

exhaust [ɪg'zɔːst] n (AUT: also: **~ pipe**) escape m; (: fumes) gases mpl de escape ♦ vt agotar; **~ed** adj agotado; **~ion** [ɪg'zɔːstʃən] n agotamiento; **nervous ~ion** postración f nerviosa; **~ive** adj exhaustivo

exhibit [ɪg'zɪbɪt] n (ART) obra expuesta; (LAW) objeto expuesto ♦ vt (show: emotions) manifestar; (: courage, skill) demostrar; (paintings) exponer; **~ion** [eksɪ'bɪʃən] n exposición f; (of talent etc) demostración f

exhilarating [ɪg'zɪləreɪtɪŋ] adj estimulante, tónico

exile ['eksaɪl] n exilio; (person) exiliado/a ♦ vt desterrar, exiliar

exist [ɪg'zɪst] vi existir; (live) vivir; **~ence** n existencia; **~ing** adj existente, actual

exit ['eksɪt] n salida ♦ vi (THEATRE) hacer mutis; (COMPUT) salir (al sistema); **~ poll** n encuesta a la salida de los colegios electorales; **~ ramp** (US) n (AUT) vía de acceso

exodus ['eksədəs] n éxodo

exonerate [ɪg'zɒnəreɪt] vt: **to ~ from** exculpar de

exotic [ɪg'zɒtɪk] adj exótico

expand [ɪk'spænd] vt ampliar; (number) aumentar ♦ vi (population) aumentar; (trade etc) expandirse; (gas, metal) dilatarse

expanse [ɪk'spæns] n extensión f

expansion [ɪk'spænʃən] n (of population) aumento; (of trade) expansión f

expect [ɪk'spekt] vt esperar; (require)

contar con; (*suppose*) suponer ♦ *vi*: **to be ~ing** (*pregnant woman*) estar embarazada; **~ancy** *n* (*anticipation*) esperanza; **life ~ancy** esperanza de vida; **~ant mother** *n* futura madre *f*; **~ation** [ɛkspɛk'teɪʃən] *n* (*hope*) esperanza; (*belief*) expectativa

expedient [ɪk'spiːdɪənt] *adj* conveniente, oportuno ♦ *n* recurso, expediente *m*

expedition [ɛkspə'dɪʃən] *n* expedición *f*

expel [ɪk'spɛl] *vt* arrojar; (*from place*) expulsar

expend [ɪk'spɛnd] *vt* (*money*) gastar; (*time, energy*) consumir; **~iture** *n* gastos *mpl*, desembolso; consumo

expense [ɪk'spɛns] *n* gasto, gastos *mpl*; (*high cost*) costas *npl* (COMM) gastos *mpl*; **at the ~ of** a costa de; **~ account** *n* cuenta de gastos

expensive [ɪk'spɛnsɪv] *adj* caro, costoso

experience [ɪk'spɪərɪəns] *n* experiencia ♦ *vt* experimentar; (*suffer*) sufrir; **~d** *adj* experimentado

experiment [ɪk'spɛrɪmənt] *n* experimento ♦ *vi* hacer experimentos

expert ['ɛkspɜːt] *adj* experto, perito ♦ *n* experto/a, perito/a; (*specialist*) especialista *m/f*; **~ise** [-'tiːz] *n* pericia

expire [ɪk'spaɪə*] *vi* caducar, vencer; **expiry** *n* vencimiento

explain [ɪk'spleɪn] *vt* explicar; **explanation** [ɛksplə'neɪʃən] *n* explicación *f*; **explanatory** [ɪk'splænətrɪ] *adj* explicativo; aclaratorio

explicit [ɪk'splɪsɪt] *adj* explícito

explode [ɪk'spləʊd] *vi* estallar, explotar; (*population*) crecer rápidamente; (*with anger*) reventar

exploit [*n* 'ɛksplɔɪt, *vb* ɪk'splɔɪt] *n* hazaña ♦ *vt* explotar; **~ation** [-'teɪʃən] *n* explotación *f*

exploratory [ɪk'splɔrətrɪ] *adj* de exploración; (*fig: talks*) exploratorio,

preliminar

explore [ɪk'splɔː*] *vt* explorar; (*fig*) examinar; investigar; **~r** *n* explorador(a) *m/f*

explosion [ɪk'spləʊʒən] *n* (*also fig*) explosión *f*; **explosive** [ɪks'pləʊsɪv] *adj*, *n* explosivo

exponent [ɪk'spəʊnənt] *n* (*of theory etc*) partidario/a; (*of skill etc*) exponente *m/f*

export [*vb* ɛk'spɔːt, *n* 'ɛkspɔːt] *vt* exportar ♦ *n* (*process*) exportación *f*; (*product*) producto de exportación ♦ *cpd* de exportación; **~er** *n* exportador *m*

expose [ɪk'spəʊz] *vt* exponer; (*unmask*) desenmascarar; **~d** *adj* expuesto

exposure [ɪk'spəʊʒə*] *n* exposición *f*; (*publicity*) publicidad *f*; (PHOT: *speed*) velocidad *f* de obturación; (: *shot*) fotografía; **to die from ~** (MED) morir de frío; **~ meter** *n* fotómetro

express [ɪk'sprɛs] *adj* (*definite*) expreso, explícito; (BRIT: *letter etc*) urgente ♦ *n* (*train*) rápido ♦ *vt* expresar; **~ion** [ɪk'sprɛʃən] *n* expresión *f*; (*of actor etc*) sentimiento; **~ly** *adv* expresamente; **~way** *n* (US) (*urban motorway*) autopista

exquisite [ɛk'skwɪzɪt] *adj* exquisito

extend [ɪk'stɛnd] *vt* (*visit, street*) prolongar; (*building*) ampliar; (*invitation*) ofrecer ♦ *vi* (*land*) extenderse; (*period of time*) prolongarse

extension [ɪk'stɛnʃən] *n* extensión *f*; (*building*) ampliación *f*; (*of time*) prolongación *f*; (TEL: *in private house*) línea derivada; (: *in office*) extensión *f*

extensive [ɪk'stɛnsɪv] *adj* extenso; (*damage*) importante; (*knowledge*) amplio; **~ly** *adv*: **he's travelled ~ly** ha viajado por muchos países

extent [ɪk'stɛnt] *n* (*breadth*) extensión *f*; (*scope*) alcance *m*; **to some ~** hasta cierto punto; **to the ~ of...** hasta el punto de...; **to such an ~ that...** hasta tal punto que...; **to what ~?**

¿hasta qué punto?

extenuating [ɪk'stɛnjueɪtɪŋ] adj: ~ **circumstances** circunstancias fpl atenuantes

exterior [ɛk'stɪərɪə*] adj exterior, externo ♦ n exterior m

external [ɛk'stɔːnl] adj externo

extinct [ɪk'stɪŋkt] adj (volcano) extinguido; (race) extinto

extinguish [ɪk'stɪŋgwɪʃ] vt extinguir, apagar; ~**er** n extintor m

extort [ɪk'stɔːt] vt obtener por fuerza; ~**ionate** adj excesivo, exorbitante

extra ['ɛkstrə] adj adicional ♦ adv (in addition) de más ♦ n (luxury, addition) extra m; (CINEMA, THEATRE) extra m/f, comparsa m/f

extra... ['ɛkstrə] prefix extra...

extract [vb ɪk'strækt, n 'ɛkstrækt] vt sacar; (tooth) extraer; (money, promise) obtener ♦ n extracto

extracurricular [ɛkstrəkə'rɪkjulə*] adj extraescolar, extra-académico

extradite ['ɛkstrədaɪt] vt extraditar

extra: ~marital [ɛkstrə'mærɪtl] adj extramatrimonial; ~**mural** [ɛkstrə'mjuərl] adj extraescolar; ~**ordinary** [ɪk'strɔːdnrɪ] adj extraordinario; (odd) raro

extravagance [ɪk'strævəgəns] n derroche m, despilfarro; (thing bought) extravagancia

extravagant [ɪk'strævəgənt] adj (lavish: person) pródigo, (: gift) (demasiado) caro; (wasteful) despilfarrador/a

extreme [ɪk'striːm] adj extremo, extremado ♦ n extremo; ~**ly** adv sumamente, extremadamente

extricate ['ɛkstrɪkeɪt] vt: to ~ **sth/sb from** librar algo/a uno de

extrovert ['ɛkstrəvɜːt] n extrovertido/a

eye [aɪ] n ojo ♦ vt mirar de soslayo, ojear; **to keep an ~ on** vigilar; ~**bath** n ojera; ~**brow** n ceja; ~**drops** npl gotas fpl para los ojos, colino; ~**lash** n pestaña; ~**lid** n párpado; ~**liner** n lápiz m de ojos; ~-**opener** n revelación f,

gran sorpresa; ~**shadow** n sombreador m de ojos; ~**sight** n vista; ~**sore** n monstruosidad f; ~ **witness** n testigo m/f presencial

F, f

F [ɛf] n (MUS) fa m

F. abbr = **Fahrenheit**

fable ['feɪbl] n fábula

fabric ['fæbrɪk] n tejido, tela

fabulous ['fæbjuləs] adj fabuloso

façade [fə'sɑːd] n fachada

face [feɪs] n (ANAT) cara, rostro; (of clock) esfera (SP), cara (AM); (of mountain) cara, ladera; (of building) fachada ♦ vt (direction) estar de cara a; (situation) hacer frente a; (facts) aceptar; ~ **down** (person, card) boca abajo; **to lose** ~ desprestigiarse; **to make** or **pull a** ~ hacer muecas; **in the ~ of** (difficulties etc) ante; **on the ~ of it** a primera vista; ~ **to** ~ cara a cara; ~ **up to** vt fus hacer frente a, arrostrar; ~ **cloth** (BRIT) n manopla; ~ **cream** n crema (de belleza); ~ **lift** n estirado facial; (of building) renovación f; ~ **powder** n polvos mpl; ~**saving** adj para salvar las apariencias; ~ **value** n (of stamp) valor m nominal; **to take sth at** ~ **value** (fig) tomar algo en sentido literal

facilities [fə'sɪlɪtɪz] npl (buildings) instalaciones fpl; (equipment) servicios mpl; **credit** ~ facilidades fpl de crédito

facing ['feɪsɪŋ] prep frente a

facsimile [fæk'sɪmɪlɪ] n (replica) facsímil(e) m; (machine) telefax m; (fax) fax m

fact [fækt] n hecho; **in** ~ en realidad

factor ['fæktə*] n factor m

factory ['fæktərɪ] n fábrica

factual ['fæktjuəl] adj basado en los hechos

faculty ['fækəltɪ] n facultad f; (US: teaching staff) personal m docente

fad [fæd] n novedad f, moda

fade [feɪd] vi desteñirse; (sound, smile) desvanecerse; (light) apagarse; (flower) marchitarse; (hope, memory) perderse

fag [fæg] (BRIT: inf) n (cigarette) pitillo (SP), cigarro

fail [feɪl] vt (candidate) suspender; (exam) no aprobar (SP), reprobar (AM); (subj: memory etc) fallar a ♦ vi suspender; (be unsuccessful) fracasar; (strength, brakes) fallar; (light) acabarse; **to ~ to do sth** (neglect) dejar de hacer algo; (be unable) no poder hacer algo; **without ~** sin falta; **~ing** n falta, defecto ♦ prep a falta de; **~ure** ['feɪljə*] n fracaso; (person) fracasado/a; (mechanical etc) fallo

faint [feɪnt] adj débil; (recollection) vago; (mark) apenas visible ♦ n desmayo ♦ vi desmayarse; **to feel ~** estar mareado, marearse

fair [fɛə*] adj justo; (hair, person) rubio; (weather) bueno; (good enough) regular; (considerable) considerable ♦ adv (play) limpio ♦ n feria; (funfair) parque m de atracciones; **~ly** adv (justly) con justicia, (quite) bastante; **~ness** n justicia, imparcialidad f; **~ play** n juego limpio

fairy ['fɛərɪ] n hada; **~ tale** n cuento de hadas

faith [feɪθ] n fe f; (trust) confianza; (sect) religión f; **~ful** adj (loyal: troops etc) leal; (spouse) fiel; (account) exacto; **~fully** adv fielmente; **yours ~fully** (BRIT: in letters) le saluda atentamente

fake [feɪk] n (painting etc) falsificación f; (person) impostor(a) m/f ♦ adj falso ♦ vt fingir; (painting etc) falsificar

falcon ['fɔːlkən] n halcón m

fall [fɔːl] (pt fell, pp fallen) n caída; (in price etc) descenso; (US) otoño ♦ vi caer(se); (price) bajar, descender; **~s** npl (water~) cascada, salto de agua; **to ~ flat** (on one's face) caerse (boca abajo); (plan) fracasar; (joke, story) no hacer gracia; **~ back** vi retroceder;

~ back on vt fus (remedy etc) recurrir a; **~ behind** vi quedarse atrás; **~ down** vi (person) caerse; (building, hopes) derrumbarse; **~ for** vt fus (trick) dejarse engañar por; (person) enamorarse de; **~ in** vi (roof) hundirse; (MIL) alinearse; **~ off** vi caerse; (diminish) disminuir; **~ out** vi (friends etc) reñir; (hair, teeth) caerse; **~ through** vi (plan, project) fracasar

fallacy ['fæləsɪ] n error m

fallen ['fɔːlən] pp of **fall**

fallout ['fɔːlaut] n lluvia radioactiva

fallow ['fæləu] adj en barbecho

false [fɔːls] adj falso; **under ~ pretences** con engaños; **~ alarm** n falsa alarma; **~ teeth** (BRIT) npl dentadura postiza

falter ['fɔːltə*] vi vacilar; (engine) fallar

fame [feɪm] n fama

familiar [fə'mɪlɪə*] adj conocido, familiar; (tone) de confianza; **to be ~ with** (subject) conocer (bien)

family ['fæmɪlɪ] n familia; **~ business** n negocio familiar; **~ doctor** n médico/a de cabecera

famine ['fæmɪn] n hambre f, hambruna

famished ['fæmɪʃt] adj hambriento

famous ['feɪməs] adj famoso, célebre; **~ly** adv (get on) estupendamente

fan [fæn] n abanico; (ELEC) ventilador m; (of pop star) fan m/f; (SPORT) hincha m/f ♦ vt abanicar; (fire, quarrel) atizar

fanatic [fə'nætɪk] n fanático/a

fan belt n correa del ventilador

fanciful ['fænsɪful] adj (design, name) fantástico

fancy ['fænsɪ] n (whim) capricho, antojo; (imagination) imaginación f ♦ adj (luxury) lujoso, de lujo ♦ vt (feel like, want) tener ganas de; (imagine) imaginarse; (think) creer; **to take a ~ to sb** tomar cariño a uno; **he fancies her** (inf) le gusta mucho; **~ dress** n disfraz m; **~-dress ball** n baile m de disfraces

fanfare ['fænfeəʳ] n fanfarria (de trompeta)

fang [fæŋ] n colmillo

fantastic [fæn'tæstɪk] adj (enormous) enorme; (strange, wonderful) fantástico

fantasy ['fæntəzɪ] n (dream) sueño; (unreality) fantasía

far [fɑ:ʳ] adj (distant) lejano ♦ adv lejos; (much, greatly) mucho; ~ **away**, ~ **off** (a lo lejos); ~ **better** mucho mejor; ~ **from** lejos de; **by** ~ con mucho; **go as** ~ **as the farm** vaya hasta la granja; **as** ~ **as I know** que yo sepa; **how** ~? ¿hasta dónde?; (fig) ¿hasta qué punto?; **~away** adj remoto; (look) distraído

farce [fɑ:s] n farsa

fare [feəʳ] n (on trains, buses) precio (del billete); (in taxi: cost) tarifa; (food) comida; **half** ~ medio pasaje m; **full** ~ pasaje completo

Far East n: **the** ~ el Extremo Oriente

farewell [feə'wel] excl, n adiós m

farm [fɑ:m] n granja (sp), finca (sp), estancia (AM) ♦ vt cultivar; **~er** n granjero (sp), estanciero (AM); **~hand** n peón m; **~house** n granja, casa de hacienda (AM); **~ing** n agricultura; (of crops) cultivo; (of animals) cría; **~land** n tierra de cultivo; ~ **worker** n = **~hand**; **~yard** n corral m

far-reaching [fɑ:'ri:tʃɪŋ] adj (reform, effect) de gran alcance

fart [fɑ:t] (inf!) vi tirarse un pedo (!)

farther ['fɑ:ðəʳ] adv más lejos, más allá ♦ adj más lejano

farthest ['fɑ:ðɪst] superlative of **far**

fascinate ['fæsɪneɪt] vt fascinar

fascination [-'neɪʃən] n fascinación f

fascism ['fæʃɪzəm] n fascismo

fashion ['fæʃən] n (fashion) moda; (~ industry) industria de la moda; (manner) manera ♦ vt formar; **in** ~ a la moda; **out of** ~ pasado de moda; **~able** adj de moda; ~ **show** n desfile m de modelos

fast [fɑ:st] adj rápido; (dye, colour) resistente; (clock): **to be** ~ estar adelantado ♦ adv rápidamente, de

prisa; (stuck, held) firmemente ♦ n ayuno ♦ vi ayunar; ~ **asleep** profundamente dormido

fasten ['fɑ:sn] vt atar, sujetar; (coat, belt) abrochar ♦ vi atarse; abrocharse; **~er**, **~ing** n cierre m; (of door etc) cerrojo

fast food n comida rápida, platos mpl preparados

fastidious [fæs'tɪdɪəs] adj (fussy) quisquilloso

fat [fæt] adj gordo; (book) grueso; (profit) grande, pingüe ♦ n grasa; (on person) carnes fpl; (lard) manteca

fatal ['feɪtl] adj (mistake) fatal; (injury) mortal; **~ity** [fə'tælɪtɪ] n (road death etc) víctima; **~ly** adv fatalmente; mortalmente

fate [feɪt] n destino; (of person) suerte f; **~ful** adj fatídico

father ['fɑ:ðəʳ] n padre m; **~-in-law** n suegro; **~ly** adj paternal

fathom ['fæðəm] n braza ♦ vt (mystery) desentrañar; (understand) lograr comprender

fatigue [fə'ti:g] n fatiga, cansancio

fatten ['fætn] vt, vi engordar

fatty ['fætɪ] adj (food) graso ♦ n (inf) gordito/a, gordinflón/ona mf

fatuous ['fætjuəs] adj fatuo, necio

faucet ['fɔ:sɪt] (US) n grifo (sp), llave f

fault [fɔ:lt] n (blame) culpa; (defect: in person, machine) defecto; (GEO) falla ♦ vt criticar; **it's my** ~ es culpa mía; **to find** ~ **with** criticar, poner peros a; **at** ~ culpable; **~y** adj defectuoso

fauna ['fɔ:nə] n fauna

favour ['feɪvəʳ] (US **favor**) n favor m; (approval) aprobación f ♦ vt (proposition) estar a favor de, aprobar; (assist) ser propicio a; **to do sb a** ~ hacer un favor a uno; **to find** ~ **with sb** caer en gracia a uno; **in** ~ **of** a favor de; **~able** adj favorable; **~ite** ['feɪvrɪt] adj, n favorito, preferido

fawn [fɔ:n] n cervato ♦ adj (also: ~-

coloured) color de cervato, leonado
♦ *vi*: **to ~ (up)on** adular

fax [fæks] *n* (*document*) fax *m*;
(*machine*) telefax *m* ♦ *vt* mandar por
telefax

FBI (*US*) *n abbr* (= *Federal Bureau of
Investigation*) ≈ BIC *f* (*SP*)

fear [fɪə*] *n* miedo, temor *m* ♦ *vt* tener
miedo de, temer; **for ~ of** por si; **~ful**
adj temeroso, miedoso; (*awful*) terrible;
~less *adj* audaz

feasible ['fi:zəbl] *adj* factible

feast [fi:st] *n* banquete *m*, (*REL*: *also*:
~ *day*) fiesta ♦ *vi* festejar

feat [fi:t] *n* hazaña

feather ['feðə*] *n* pluma

feature ['fi:tʃə*] *n* característica,
(*article*) artículo de fondo ♦ *vt* (*subj*:
film) presentar ♦ *vi*: **to ~ in** tener un
papel destacado en; **~s** *npl* (*of face*)
facciones *fpl*; **~ film** *n* largometraje *m*

February ['februərɪ] *n* febrero

fed [fed] *pt*, *pp of* **feed**

federal ['fedərəl] *adj* federal

fed up [fed'ʌp] *adj*: **to be ~ (with)**
estar harto (de)

fee [fi:] *n* pago; (*professional*) derechos
mpl, honorarios *mpl*; (*of club*) cuota;
school ~s matrícula

feeble ['fi:bl] *adj* débil; (*joke*) flojo

feed [fi:d] (*pt*, *pp* **fed**) *n* comida; (*of
animal*) pienso; (*on printer*) dispositivo
de alimentación ♦ *vt* alimentar; (*BRIT*:
baby: *breast~*) dar el pecho a; (*animal*)
dar de comer a; (*data, information*): **to
~ into** meter en; (*on*) **on** *vt fus*
alimentarse de, comer; **~back** *n* reacción *f*,
feedback *m*

feel [fi:l] (*pt*, *pp* **felt**) *n* (*sensation*)
sensación *f*; (*sense of touch*) tacto;
(*impression*): **to have the ~ of**
parecerse a ♦ *vt* tocar; (*pain etc*) sentir;
(*think, believe*) creer; **to ~ hungry/
cold** tener hambre/frío; **to ~ lonely/
better** sentirse solo/mejor; **I don't
~ well** no me siento bien; **it ~s soft**
es suave al tacto; **to ~ like** (*want*)

tener ganas de; **~ about** or **around** *vi*
tantear; **~er** *n* (*of insect*) antena; **~ing**
n (*physical*) sensación *f*; (*foreboding*)
presentimiento; (*emotion*) sentimiento

feet [fi:t] *npl of* **foot**

feign [feɪn] *vt* fingir

fell [fel] *pt of* **fall** ♦ *vt* (*tree*) talar

fellow ['feləu] *n* tipo, tío (*SP*);
(*comrade*) compañero; (*of learned
society*) socio/a ♦ *cpd*: **~ citizen** *n*
conciudadano/a; **~ countryman**
(*irreg*) *n* compatriota *m*; **~ men** *npl*
semejantes *mpl*; **~ship** *n*
compañerismo; (*grant*) beca

felony ['feləni] *n* crimen *m*

felt [felt] *pt*, *pp of* **feel** ♦ *n* fieltro; **~-tip
pen** *n* rotulador *m*

female ['fi:meɪl] *n* (*pej*: *woman*) mujer
f, tía; (*ZOOL*) hembra ♦ *adj* femenino;
hembra

feminine ['femɪnɪn] *adj* femenino

feminist ['femɪnɪst] *n* feminista

fence [fens] *n* valla, cerca ♦ *vt* (*also*:
~ *in*) cercar ♦ *vi* (*SPORT*) hacer esgrima;
fencing *n* esgrima

fend [fend] *vi*: **to ~ for o.s.** valerse por
sí mismo; **~ off** *vt* (*attack*) rechazar;
(*questions*) evadir

fender ['fendə*] *n* guardafuego; (*US*:
AUT) parachoques *m inv*

ferment [*vb* fə'ment, *n* 'fɜ:ment] *vi*
fermentar ♦ *n* (*fig*) agitación *f*

fern [fɜ:n] *n* helecho

ferocious [fə'rəuʃəs] *adj* feroz

ferret ['ferɪt] *n* hurón

ferry ['ferɪ] *n* (*small*) barca (de pasaje),
balsa; (*large*: *also*: ~*boat*) transbordador
m (*SP*), embarcadero (*AM*) ♦ *vt*
transportar

fertile ['fɜ:taɪl] *adj* fértil; (*BIOL*)
fecundo; **fertilize** ['fɜ:tɪlaɪz] *vt* (*BIOL*)
fecundar; (*AGR*) abonar; **fertilizer** *n*
abono

fester ['festə*] *vi* ulcerarse

festival ['festɪvl] *n* (*REL*) fiesta; (*ART,
MUS*) festival *m*

festive ['festɪv] *adj* festivo; **the**

~ **season** (BRIT: Christmas) las
Navidades
festivities [fes'tɪvɪtɪz] npl fiestas fpl
festoon [fes'tu:n] vt: **to ~ with**
engalanar de
fetch [fetʃ] vt ir a buscar; (sell for)
venderse por
fête [feɪt] n fiesta
fetus [fi:təs] (US) n = **foetus**
feud [fju:d] n (hostility) enemistad f;
(quarrel) disputa
fever [fi:və*] n fiebre f; **~ish** adj febril
few [fju:] adj (not many) pocos ♦ pron
pocos; algunos; **a ~** adj unos pocos,
algunos; **~er** adj menos; **~est** adj los/
las menos
fiancé [fɪ'ã:nseɪ] n novio, prometido;
~e n novia, prometida
fib [fɪb] n mentirilla
fibre [faɪbə*] (US **fiber**) n fibra; **~glass**
(**Fiberglass** ℝ (US)) n fibra de vidrio
fickle [fɪkl] adj inconstante
fiction [fɪkʃən] n ficción f; **~al** adj
novelesco; **fictitious** [fɪk'tɪʃəs] adj
ficticio
fiddle [fɪdl] n (MUS) violín m; (cheating)
trampa ♦ vt (BRIT: accounts) falsificar;
~ with fus juguetear con
fidget [fɪdʒɪt] vi enredar; **stop ~ing!**
¡estáte quieto!
field [fi:ld] n campo; (fig) campo,
esfera; (SPORT) campo, cancha (AM);
~ marshal n mariscal m; **~work** n
trabajo de campo
fiend [fi:nd] n demonio
fierce [fɪəs] adj feroz; (wind, heat)
fuerte; (fighting, enemy) encarnizado
fiery [faɪərɪ] adj (burning) ardiente;
(temperament) apasionado
fifteen [fɪf'ti:n] num quince
fifth [fɪfθ] num quinto
fifty [fɪftɪ] num cincuenta; **~-~** adj
(deal, split) a medias ♦ adv a medias,
mitad por mitad
fig [fɪg] n higo
fight [faɪt] (pt, pp **fought**) n (gen)
pelea; (MIL) combate m; (struggle)

lucha ♦ vt luchar contra; (cancer,
alcoholism) combatir; (election) intentar
ganar; (emotion) resistir ♦ vi pelear,
luchar; **~er** n combatiente m/f; (plane)
caza m; **~ing** n combate m, pelea
figment [fɪgmənt] n: **a ~ of the
imagination** una quimera
figurative [fɪgjurətɪv] adj (meaning)
figurado; (style) figurativo
figure [fɪgə*] n (DRAWING, GEOM)
figura, dibujo; (number, cipher) cifra;
(body, outline) tipo; (personality) figura
♦ vt (esp US) imaginar ♦ vi (appear)
figurar; **~ out** vt (work out) resolver;
~head n (NAUT) mascarón m de proa;
(pej: leader) figura decorativa; **~ of
speech** n figura retórica
file [faɪl] n (tool) lima; (dossier)
expediente m; (folder) carpeta;
(COMPUT) fichero; (row) fila ♦ vt limar;
(LAW: claim) presentar; (store) archivar;
~ in/out vi entrar/salir en fila; **filing
cabinet** n fichero, archivador m
fill [fɪl] vt (space): **to ~ (with)** llenar
(de); (vacancy, need) cubrir ♦ n: **to eat
one's ~** llenarse; **~ in** vt rellenar; **~ up**
vt llenar (hasta el borde) ♦ vi (AUT)
poner gasolina
fillet [fɪlɪt] n filete m; **~ steak** n filete
m de ternera
filling [fɪlɪŋ] n (CULIN) relleno; (for
tooth) empaste m; **~ station** n
estación f de servicio
film [fɪlm] n película ♦ vt (scene) filmar
♦ vi rodar (una película); **~ star** n
astro, estrella de cine
filter [fɪltə*] n filtro ♦ vt filtrar; **~ lane**
(BRIT) n carril m de selección; **~-tipped**
adj con filtro
filth [fɪlθ] n suciedad f; **~y** adj sucio;
(language) obsceno
fin [fɪn] n (gen) aleta
final [faɪnl] adj (last) final, último;
(definitive) definitivo, terminante ♦ n
(BRIT: SPORT) final f; **~s** npl (SCOL)
examen m final; (US: SPORT) final f
finale [fɪ'nɑ:lɪ] n final m

final: ~ist n (SPORT) finalista m/f; **~ize**
vt concluir, completar; **~ly** adv (lastly)
por último, finalmente; (eventually) por
fin

finance [faɪˈnæns] n (money) fondos
mpl; **~s** npl finanzas fpl; (personal ~s)
situación f económica ♦ vt financiar;
financial [-ˈnænʃəl] adj financiero

find [faɪnd] (pt, pp **found**) vt
encontrar, hallar; (come upon)
descubrir ♦ n hallazgo; descubrimiento;
to ~ sb guilty (LAW) declarar culpable
a uno; **to ~** vt averiguar; (truth,
secret) descubrir; **to ~ out about**
(subject) informarse sobre; (by chance)
enterarse de; **~ings** npl (LAW)
veredicto, fallo; (of report)
recomendaciones fpl

fine [faɪn] adj excelente; (thin) fino
♦ adv (well) bien ♦ n (LAW) multa ♦ vt
(LAW) multar; **to be ~** (person) estar
bien; (weather) hacer buen tiempo;
~ arts npl bellas artes fpl

finery [ˈfaɪnərɪ] n adornos mpl

finger [ˈfɪŋɡə*] n dedo ♦ vt (touch)
manosear; **little/index ~** (dedo)
meñique m/índice m; **~nail** n uña;
~print n huella dactilar; **~tip** n yema
del dedo

finish [ˈfɪnɪʃ] n (end) fin m; (SPORT)
meta; (polish etc) acabado ♦ vt, vi
terminar; **to ~ doing sth** acabar de
hacer algo; **to ~ third** llegar el tercero;
~ off vt acabar, terminar; (kill) acabar
con; **~ up** vt acabar, terminar ♦ vi ir a
parar, terminar; **~ing line** n línea de
llegada o meta

finite [ˈfaɪnaɪt] adj finito; (verb)
conjugado

Finland [ˈfɪnlənd] n Finlandia

Finn [fɪn] n finlandés/esa m/f; **~ish** adj
finlandés/esa ♦ n (LING) finlandés m

fir [fə:*] n abeto

fire [ˈfaɪə*] n fuego; (in hearth) lumbre
f; (accidental) incendio; (heater) estufa
♦ vt (gun) disparar; (interest) despertar;
(inf: dismiss) despedir ♦ vi (shoot)

disparar; **on ~** ardiendo, en llamas;
~ alarm n alarma de incendios; **~
arm** n arma de fuego; **~ brigade** (US
~ department) n (cuerpo de)
bomberos mpl; **~ engine** n coche m
de bomberos; **~ escape** n escalera de
incendios; **~ extinguisher** n extintor
m (de incendios); **~guard** n rejilla de
protección; **~man** (irreg) n bombero;
~place n chimenea; **~side** n: **by the
~side** al lado de la chimenea; **~
station** n parque m de bomberos;
~wood n leña; **~works** npl fuegos
mpl artificiales

firing squad [ˈfaɪrɪŋ-] n pelotón m de
ejecución

firm [fə:m] adj firme; (look, voice)
resuelto ♦ n firma, empresa; **~ly** adv
firmemente; resueltamente

first [fə:st] adj primero ♦ adv (before
others) primero; (when listing reasons
etc) en primer lugar, primeramente ♦ n
(person: in race) primero/a; (AUT)
primera; (BRIT: SCOL) título de licenciado
con calificación de sobresaliente; **at ~** al
principio; **~ of all** ante todo; **~ aid** n
primera ayuda, primeros auxilios mpl;
~-aid kit n botiquín m; **~-class** adj
(excellent) de primera categoría;
(ticket etc) de primera clase; **~-hand**
adj de primera mano; **F~ Lady** n (esp
US) n primera dama; **~ly** adv en primer
lugar; **~ name** n nombre m (de pila);
~-rate adj estupendo

fish [fɪʃ] n inv pez m; (food) pescado
♦ vt, vi pescar; **to go ~ing** ir de pesca;
~erman (irreg) n pescador m; **~ farm**
n criadero de peces; **~ fingers** (BRIT)
npl croquetas fpl de pescado; **~ing
boat** n barca de pesca; **~ing line** n
sedal m; **~ing rod** n caña (de pescar);
~monger's (shop) (BRIT) n
pescadería; **~ sticks** (US) npl =
~ fingers; **~y** (inf) adj sospechoso

fist [fɪst] n puño

fit [fɪt] adj (healthy) en (buena) forma;
(proper) adecuado, apropiado ♦ vt

(subj: clothes) estar or sentar bien a; (instal: equip) proveer, dotar; (facts) cuadrar or corresponder con ♦ vi (clothes) sentar bien; (in space, gap) caber; (facts) coincidir ♦ n (MED) ataque m; ~ **to** (ready) a punto de; ~ **for** apropiado para; **a ~ of anger/ pride** un arranque de cólera/orgullo; **this dress is a ~** este vestido me sienta bien; **by ~s and starts a** rachas; ~ **in** vi (fig: person) llevarse bien (con todos); ~**ful** adj espasmódico, intermitente; ~**ment** n módulo adosable; ~**ness** n (MED) salud f; ~**ted carpet** n moqueta; ~**ted kitchen** n cocina amueblada; ~**ter** n ajustador m; ~**ting** adj apropiado ♦ n (of dress) prueba; (of piece of equipment) instalación f; ~**ting room** n probador m; ~**tings** npl instalaciones fpl

five [faɪv] num cinco; ~**r** n (inf) (BRIT) billete m de cinco libras; (US) billete m de cinco dólares

fix [fɪks] vt (secure) fijar, asegurar; (mend) arreglar; (prepare) preparar ♦ n **to be in a ~** estar en un aprieto; ~ **up** vt (meeting) arreglar; **to ~ sb up with sth** proveer a uno de algo; ~**ation** [fɪkˈseɪʃən] n obsesión f; ~**ed** adj (prices etc) fijo; ~**ture** n (SPORT) encuentro; ~**tures** npl (cupboards etc) instalaciones fpl fijas

fizzy [ˈfɪzɪ] adj (drink) gaseoso

fjord [fjɔːd] n fiordo

flabbergasted [ˈflæbəɡɑːstɪd] adj pasmado, alucinado

flabby [ˈflæbɪ] adj gordo

flag [flæɡ] n bandera; (stone) losa ♦ vi decaer; **to ~ sb down** hacer señas a uno para que se pare; ~**pole** n asta de bandera; ~**ship** n buque m insignia; (fig) bandera

flair [flɛə*] n aptitud f especial

flak [flæk] n (MIL) fuego antiaéreo; (inf: criticism) lluvia de críticas

flake [fleɪk] n (of rust, paint) escama; (of snow, soap powder) copo ♦ vi (also:

~ off) desconcharse

flamboyant [flæmˈbɔɪənt] adj (dress) vistoso; (person) extravagante

flame [fleɪm] n llama

flamingo [fləˈmɪŋɡəʊ] n flamenco

flammable [ˈflæməbl] adj inflamable

flan [flæn] (BRIT) n tarta

flank [flæŋk] n (of animal) ijar m; (of army) flanco ♦ vt flanquear

flannel [ˈflænl] n (BRIT: also: face ~) manopla; (fabric) franela

flap [flæp] n (of pocket, envelope) solapa ♦ vt (wings, arms) agitar ♦ vi (sail, flag) ondear

flare [flɛə*] n llamarada; (MIL) bengala; (in skirt etc) vuelo; ~ **up** vi encenderse; (fig: person) encolerizarse; (: revolt) estallar

flash [flæʃ] n relámpago; (also: news ~) noticias fpl de última hora; (PHOT) flash m ♦ vt (light, headlights) lanzar un destello con; (news, message) transmitir; (smile) lanzar ♦ vi brillar; (hazard light etc) lanzar destellos; **in a ~** en un instante; **he ~ed by** or **past** pasó como un rayo; ~**back** n (CINEMA) flashback m; ~**bulb** n bombilla fusible; ~ **cube** n cubo de flash; ~**light** n linterna

flashy [ˈflæʃɪ] (pej) adj ostentoso

flask [flɑːsk] n frasco; (also: vacuum ~) termo

flat [flæt] adj llano; (smooth) liso; (tyre) desinflado; (battery) descargado; (beer) muerto; (refusal etc) rotundo; (MUS) desafinado; (rate) fijo ♦ n (BRIT: apartment) piso (SP), departamento (AM), apartamento, (AUT) pinchazo; (MUS) bemol m; **to work ~ out** trabajar a toda mecha; ~**ly** adv terminantemente, de plano; ~**ten** vt (also: ~ten out) allanar; (smooth out) alisar; (building, plants) arrasar

flatter [ˈflætə*] vt adular, halagar; ~**ing** adj halagüeño; (dress) que favorece; ~**y** n adulación f

flaunt [flɔːnt] vt ostentar, lucir

flavour ['fleɪvə*] (US **flavor**) n sabor m,
gusto ♦ vt sazonar, condimentar;
strawberry-~ed con sabor a fresa;
~ing n (in product) aromatizante m

flaw [flɔː] n defecto; **~less** adj
impecable

flax [flæks] n lino

flea [fliː] n pulga

fleck [flek] n (mark) mota

flee [fliː] (pt, pp **fled**) vt huir de ♦ vi
huir, fugarse

fleece [fliːs] n vellón m; (wool) lana
♦ vt (inf) desplumar

fleet [fliːt] n flota; (of lorries etc)
escuadra

fleeting ['fliːtɪŋ] adj fugaz

Flemish ['flemɪʃ] adj flamenco

flesh [fleʃ] n carne f; (skin) piel f; (of
fruit) pulpa; **~ wound** n herida
superficial

flew [fluː] pt of **fly**

flex [fleks] n cordón m ♦ vt (muscles)
tensar; **~ible** adj flexible

flick [flɪk] n capirotazo; chasquido ♦ vt
(with hand) dar un capirotazo a; (whip
etc) chasquear; (switch) accionar;
~ through vt fus hojear

flicker ['flɪkə*] vi (light) parpadear;
(flame) vacilar

flier ['flaɪə*] n aviador(a) m/f

flight [flaɪt] n vuelo; (escape) huida,
fuga; (also: **~ of steps**) tramo (de
escaleras); **~ attendant** (US) n
camarero/azafata; **~ deck** n (AVIAT)
cabina de mandos; (NAUT) cubierta de
aterrizaje

flimsy ['flɪmzɪ] adj (thin) muy ligero;
(building) endeble; (excuse) flojo

flinch [flɪntʃ] vi encogerse; **to ~ from**
retroceder ante

fling [flɪŋ] (pt, pp **flung**) vt arrojar

flint [flɪnt] n pedernal m; (in lighter)
piedra

flip [flɪp] vt dar la vuelta a; (switch: turn
on) encender; (: turn off) apagar; (coin)
echar a cara o cruz

flippant ['flɪpənt] adj poco serio

flipper ['flɪpə*] n aleta

flirt [flɜːt] vi coquetear, flirtear ♦ n
coqueta

float [fləʊt] n flotador m; (in procession)
carroza; (money) reserva ♦ vi flotar;
(swimmer) hacer la plancha

flock [flɒk] n (of sheep) rebaño; (of
birds) bandada ♦ vi: **to ~ to** acudir en
tropel a

flog [flɒg] vt azotar

flood [flʌd] n inundación f; (of letters,
imports etc) avalancha ♦ vt inundar ♦ vi
(place) inundarse; (people): **to ~ into**
inundar; **~ing** n inundaciones fpl;
~light n foco

floor [flɔː*] n suelo; (storey) piso; (of
sea) fondo ♦ vt (subj: question) dejar
sin respuesta; (: blow) derribar;
ground ~, **first ~** (US) planta baja;
first ~, **second ~** (US) primer piso;
~board n tabla; **~ show** n cabaret m

flop [flɒp] n fracaso ♦ vi (fail) fracasar;
(fall) derrumbarse; **~py** adj flojo ♦ n
(COMPUT: also: **~py disk**) floppy m

flora ['flɔːrə] n flora

floral ['flɔːrl] adj (pattern) floreado

florid ['flɒrɪd] adj florido; (complexion)
rubicundo

florist ['flɒrɪst] n florista m/f; **~'s
(shop)** n florería

flounder ['flaʊndə*] vi (swimmer)
patalear; (fig: economy) estar en
dificultades ♦ n (ZOOL) platija

flour ['flaʊə*] n harina

flourish ['flʌrɪʃ] vi florecer ♦ n ademán
m, movimiento (ostentoso)

flout [flaʊt] vt burlarse de

flow [fləʊ] n (movement) flujo; (of
traffic) circulación f; (tide) corriente f
♦ vi (river, blood) fluir; (traffic) circular;
~ chart n organigrama m

flower ['flaʊə*] n flor f ♦ vi florecer;
~ bed n macizo; **~pot** n tiesto; **~y** adj
(fragrance) floral; (pattern) floreado;
(speech) florido

flown [fləʊn] pp of **fly**

flu [fluː] n: **to have ~** tener la gripe

fluctuate ['flʌktjʊeɪt] *vi* fluctuar

fluent ['flu:ənt] *adj* (*linguist*) que habla perfectamente; (*speech*) elocuente; **he speaks ~ French, he's ~ in French** domina el francés; **~ly** *adv* con fluidez

fluff [flʌf] *n* pelusa; **~y** *adj* de pelo suave

fluid ['flu:ɪd] *adj* (*movement*) fluido, líquido; (*situation*) inestable ♦ *n* fluido, líquido

fluke [flu:k] (*inf*) *n* chiripa

flung [flʌŋ] *pt, pp of* **fling**

fluoride ['flʊəraɪd] *n* fluoruro

flurry ['flʌrɪ] *n* (*of snow*) temporal *m*; **~ of activity** frenesí *m* de actividad

flush [flʌʃ] *n* rubor *m*; (*fig: of youth etc*) resplandor *m* ♦ *vt* limpiar con agua ♦ *vi* ruborizarse ♦ *adj*: **~ with** a ras de; **to ~ the toilet** hacer funcionar la cisterna; **~ed** *adj* ruborizado

flustered ['flʌstəd] *adj* aturdido

flute [flu:t] *n* flauta

flutter ['flʌtə*] *n* (*of wings*) revoloteo, aleteo; **a ~ of panic/excitement** una oleada de pánico/excitación ♦ *vi* revolotear

flux [flʌks] *n*: **to be in a state of ~** estar continuamente cambiando

fly [flaɪ] (*pt* **flew,** *pp* **flown**) *n* mosca; (*on trousers: also:* **flies**) bragueta ♦ *vt* (*plane*) pilot(e)ar; (*cargo*) transportar (en avión) ♦ *vi* volar; (*passengers*) ir en avión; (*escape*) evadirse; (*flag*) ondear; **~ away** *or* **off** *vi* emprender el vuelo; **~-drive** *n*: **~-drive holiday** vacaciones que incluyen vuelo y alquiler de coche; **~ing** *n* (*activity*) (el) volar; (*action*) vuelo ♦ *adj*: **~ing visit** visita relámpago; **with ~ing colours** con lucimiento; **~ing saucer** *n* platillo volante; **~ing start** *n*: **to get off to a ~ing start** empezar con buen pie; **~over** (*BRIT*) *n* paso a desnivel *or* superior; **~sheet** *n* (*for tent*) doble techo

foal [fəul] *n* potro

foam [fəum] *n* espuma ♦ *vi* hacer espuma; **~ rubber** *n* goma espuma

fob [fɔb] *vt*: **to ~ sb off with sth** despachar a uno con algo

focal point ['fəukl-] *n* (*fig*) centro de atención

focus ['fəukəs] (*pl* **~es**) *n* foco; (*centre*) centro ♦ *vt* (*field glasses etc*) enfocar ♦ *vi*: **to ~ (on)** enfocar (a); (*issue etc*) centrarse en; **in/out of ~** enfocado/ desenfocado

fodder ['fɔdə*] *n* pienso

foetus ['fi:təs] (*US* **fetus**) *n* feto

fog [fɔg] *n* niebla; **~gy** *adj*: **it's ~gy** hay niebla, está brumoso; **~ lamp** (*US* **~ light**) *n* (*AUT*) faro de niebla

foil [fɔɪl] *vt* frustrar ♦ *n* hoja; (*kitchen ~*) papel *m* (de) aluminio; (*complement*) complemento; (*FENCING*) florete *m*

fold [fəuld] *n* (*bend, crease*) pliegue *m*; (*AGR*) redil *m* ♦ *vt* doblar; (*arms*) cruzar; **~ up** *vi* plegarse, doblarse; (*business*) quebrar ♦ *vt* (*map etc*) plegar; **~er** *n* (*for papers*) carpeta; **~ing** *adj* (*chair, bed*) plegable

foliage ['fəulɪdʒ] *n* follaje *m*

folk [fəuk] *npl* gente *f* ♦ *adj* popular, folklórico; **~s** *npl* (*family*) familia *sg*, parientes *mpl*; **~lore** ['fəuklɔ:*] *n* folklore *m*; **~ song** *n* canción *f* popular *or* folklórica

follow ['fɔləu] *vt* seguir ♦ *vi* seguir; (*result*) resultar; **to ~ suit** hacer lo mismo; **~ up** *vt* (*letter, offer*) responder a; (*case*) investigar; **~er** *n* (*of person, belief*) partidario/a, **~ing** *adj* siguiente ♦ *n* afición *f*, partidarios *mpl*

folly ['fɔlɪ] *n* locura

fond [fɔnd] *adj* (*memory, smile etc*) cariñoso; (*hopes*) ilusorio; **to be ~ of** tener cariño a; (*pastime, food*) ser aficionado a

fondle ['fɔndl] *vt* acariciar

font [fɔnt] *n* pila bautismal; (*TYP*) fundición *f*

food [fu:d] *n* comida; **~ mixer** *n* batidora; **~ poisoning** *n* intoxicación *f* alimenticia; **~ processor** n robot m de cocina; **~stuffs** npl comestibles mpl

fool [fu:l] n tonto/a f, (CULIN) puré m de frutas con nata ♦ vt engañar ♦ vi (gen: ~ around) bromear; **~hardy** adj temerario; **~ish** adj tonto; (careless) imprudente; **~proof** adj (plan etc) infalible

foot [fut] (pl feet) n pie m; (measure) pie m (= 304 mm); (of animal) pata ♦ vt (bill) pagar; **on ~** a pie; **~age** n (CINEMA) imágenes fpl; **~ball** n balón m; (game: BRIT) fútbol m; (: US) fútbol m americano; **~ball player** n (BRIT: also: ~baller) futbolista m; (US) jugador m de fútbol americano; **~brake** n freno de pie; **~bridge** n puente m para peatones; **~hills** npl estribaciones fpl; **~hold** n pie m firme; **~ing** n (fig) posición f; **to lose one's ~ing** perder el pie; **~lights** npl candilejas fpl; **~note** n nota (al pie de la página); **~path** n sendero; **~print** n huella, pisada; **~step** n paso; **~wear** n calzado

---

KEYWORD

for [fɔ:] prep **1** (indicating destination, intention) para; **the train ~ London** el tren con destino a or de Londres; **he left ~ Rome** marchó para Roma; **he went ~ the paper** fue por el periódico; **is this ~ me?** ¿es esto para mí?; **it's time ~ lunch** es la hora de comer

2 (indicating purpose) para; **what's it ~?** ¿para qué (es)?; **to pray ~ peace** rezar por la paz

3 (on behalf of, representing): **the MP ~ Hove** el diputado por Hove; **he works ~ the government/a local firm** trabaja para el gobierno/en una empresa local; **I'll ask him ~ you** se lo pediré por ti; **G ~ George** G de Gerona

4 (because of) por esta razón; **~ fear of being criticized** por temor a ser criticado

5 (with regard to) para; **it's cold ~ July** hace frío para julio; **he has a gift ~ languages** tiene don de lenguas

6 (in exchange for) por; **I sold it ~ £5** lo vendí por £5; **to pay 50 pence ~ a ticket** pagar 50 peniques por un billete

7 (in favour of): **are you ~ or against us?** ¿estás con nosotros o contra nosotros?; **I'm all ~ it** estoy totalmente a favor; **vote ~ X** vote (a) X

8 (referring to distance): **there are roadworks ~ 5 km** hay obras en 5 km; **we walked ~ miles** caminamos kilómetros y kilómetros

9 (referring to time): **he was away ~ 2 years** estuvo fuera (durante) dos años; **it hasn't rained ~ 3 weeks** no ha llovido durante en 3 semanas; **I have known her ~ years** la conozco desde hace años; **can you do it ~ tomorrow?** ¿lo podrás hacer para mañana?

10 (with infinitive clauses): **it is not ~ me to decide** la decisión no es cosa mía; **it would be best ~ you to leave** sería mejor que te fueras; **there is still time ~ you to do it** todavía te queda tiempo para hacerlo; **~ this to be possible ...** para que esto sea posible ...

11 (in spite of) a pesar de; **~ all his complaints** a pesar de sus quejas ♦ conj (since, as: rather formal) puesto que

forage ['fɔrɪdʒ] vi (animal) forrajear; (person): **to ~ for** hurgar en busca de

foray ['fɔreɪ] n incursión f

forbid [fə'bɪd] (pt **forbad(e)**, pp **forbidden**) vt prohibir; **to ~ sb to do sth** prohibir a uno hacer algo; **~ding** adj amenazador/a

force [fɔ:s] n fuerza ♦ vt forzar; (push)

meter a la fuerza; **to ~ o.s. to do** hacer un esfuerzo por hacer; **the F~s** *npl* (*BRIT*) las Fuerzas Armadas; **in ~** en vigor; **~d** [fɔːst] *adj* forzado; **~feed** *vt* alimentar a la fuerza; **~ful** *adj* enérgico

forcibly ['fɔːsəbli] *adv* a la fuerza; (*speak*) enérgicamente

ford [fɔːd] *n* vado

fore [fɔː*] *n*: **to come to the ~** empezar a destacar

fore: **~arm** *n* antebrazo; **~boding** *n* presentimiento; **~cast** *n* pronóstico ♦ *vt* (*irreg*: *like* cast) pronosticar; **~court** *n* patio; **~finger** (dedo) índice *m*; **~front** *n*: **in the ~front of** en la vanguardia de

forego *vt* = **forgo**

foregone ['fɔːgɔn] *pp of* **forego** ♦ *adj*: **it's a ~ conclusion** es una conclusión evidente

foreground ['fɔːgraund] *n* primer plano

forehead ['fɔrɪd] *n* frente *f*

foreign ['fɔrɪn] *adj* extranjero; (*trade*) exterior; (*object*) extraño; **~er** *n* extranjero/a; **~ exchange** *n* divisas *fpl*; **F~ Office** (*BRIT*) *n* Ministerio de Asuntos Exteriores; **F~ Secretary** (*BRIT*) *n* Ministro de Asuntos Exteriores

fore: **~leg** *n* pata delantera; **~man** (*irreg*) *n* capataz *m*; (*in construction*) maestro de obras; **~most** *adj* principal ♦ *adv*: **first and ~most** ante todo

forensic [fə'rɛnsɪk] *adj* forense

fore: **~runner** *n* precursor(a) *m/f*; **~see** (*pt* **foresaw**, *pp* **foreseen**) *vt* prever; **~seeable** *adj* previsible; **~shadow** *vt* prefigurar, anunciar; **~sight** *n* previsión *f*

forest ['fɔrɪst] *n* bosque *m*

forestry ['fɔrɪstri] *n* silvicultura

foretaste ['fɔːteɪst] *n* muestra

foretell [fɔː'tɛl] (*pt*, *pp* **foretold**) *vt* predecir, pronosticar

forever [fə'rɛvə*] *adv* para siempre; (*endlessly*) constantemente

foreword ['fɔːwəːd] *n* prefacio

forfeit ['fɔːfɪt] *vt* perder

forgave [fə'geɪv] *pt of* **forgive**

forge [fɔːdʒ] *n* herrería ♦ *vt* (*signature*, *money*) falsificar; (*metal*) forjar; **~ ahead** *vi* avanzar mucho; **~ry** *n* falsificación *f*

forget [fə'gɛt] (*pt* **forgot**, *pp* **forgotten**) *vt* olvidar ♦ *vi* olvidarse; **~ful** *adj* despistado; **~-me-not** *n* nomeolvides *f inv*

forgive [fə'gɪv] (*pt* **forgave**, *pp* **forgiven**) *vt* perdonar; **to ~ sb for sth** perdonar algo a uno; **~ness** *n* perdón *m*

forgo [fɔː'gəu] (*pt* **forwent**, *pp* **forgone**) *vt* (*give up*) renunciar a; (*go without*) privarse de

forgot [fə'gɔt] *pt of* **forget**

forgotten [fə'gɔtn] *pp of* **forget**

fork [fɔːk] *n* (*for eating*) tenedor *m*; (*for gardening*) horca; (*of roads*) bifurcación *f* ♦ *vi* (*road*) bifurcarse; **~ out** (*inf*) *vt* (*pay*) desembolsar; **~-lift truck** *n* máquina elevadora

forlorn [fə'lɔːn] *adj* (*person*) triste, melancólico; (*place*) abandonado; (*attempt*, *hope*) desesperado

form [fɔːm] *n* forma; (*BRIT*: *SCOL*) clase *f*; (*document*) formulario ♦ *vt* formar; (*idea*) concebir; (*habit*) adquirir; **in top ~** en plena forma; **to ~ a queue** hacer cola

formal ['fɔːməl] *adj* (*offer*, *receipt*) por escrito; (*person etc*) correcto; (*occasion*, *dinner*) de etiqueta; (*dress*) correcto; (*garden*) de (estilo) clásico; **~ity** [-'mælɪti] *n* (*procedure*) trámite *m*; corrección *f*; etiqueta; **~ly** *adv* oficialmente

format ['fɔːmæt] *n* formato ♦ *vt* (*COMPUT*) formatear

formative ['fɔːmətɪv] *adj* (*years*) de formación; (*influence*) formativo

former ['fɔːmə*] *adj* anterior; (*earlier*) antiguo; (*ex*) ex; **the ~ ... the latter ...** aquél ... éste ...; **~ly** *adv* antes

formula ['fɔːmjulə] *n* fórmula

forsake [fə'seɪk] (pt **forsook**, pp **forsaken**) vt (gen) abandonar; (plan) renunciar a

fort [fɔːt] n fuerte m

forte ['fɔːtɪ] n fuerte m

forth [fɔːθ] adv: **back and ~** de acá para allá; **and so ~** y así sucesivamente; **~coming** adj próximo, venidero; (help, information) disponible; (character) comunicativo; **~right** adj franco; **~with** adv en el acto

fortify ['fɔːtɪfaɪ] vt (city) fortificar; (person) fortalecer

fortitude ['fɔːtɪtjuːd] n fortaleza

fortnight ['fɔːtnaɪt] (BRIT) n quince días mpl; quincena f; **~ly** adj de cada quince días, quincenal ♦ adv cada quince días, quincenalmente

fortress ['fɔːtrɪs] n fortaleza

fortunate ['fɔːtʃənɪt] adj afortunado; **it is ~ that ...** (es una) suerte que ...; **~ly** adv afortunadamente

fortune ['fɔːtʃən] n suerte f; (wealth) fortuna; **~-teller** n adivino/a

forty ['fɔːtɪ] num cuarenta

forum ['fɔːrəm] n foro

forward ['fɔːwəd] adj (movement, position) avanzado; (front) delantero; (in time) adelantado; (not shy) atrevido ♦ n (SPORT) delantero m ♦ vt (letter) remitir; (career) promocionar; **to move ~** avanzar; **~(s)** adv (hacia) adelante

fossil ['fɔsl] n fósil m

foster ['fɔstə*] vt (child) acoger en una familia; fomentar; **~ child** n hijo/a adoptivo/a

fought [fɔːt] pt, pp of **fight**

foul [faul] adj sucio, puerco; (weather, smell etc) asqueroso; (language) grosero; (temper) malísimo ♦ n (SPORT) falta ♦ vt (dirty) ensuciar; **~ play** n (LAW) muerte f violenta

found [faund] pt, pp of **find** ♦ vt fundar; **~ation** [-'deɪʃən] n (act) fundación f; (basis) base f; (also: **~ation cream**) crema base; **~ations** npl (of building) cimientos mpl

founder ['faundə*] n fundador(a) m/f ♦ vi hundirse

foundry ['faundrɪ] n fundición f

fountain ['fauntɪn] n fuente f; **~ pen** n pluma (estilográfica) (SP), pluma-fuente f (AM)

four [fɔː*] num cuatro; **on all ~s** a gatas; **~-poster** n cama de dosel; **~teen** num catorce; **~th** num cuarto

fowl [faul] n ave f (de corral)

fox [fɔks] n zorro ♦ vt confundir

foyer ['fɔɪeɪ] n vestíbulo

fraction ['frækʃən] n fracción f

fracture ['fræktʃə*] n fractura

fragile ['frædʒaɪl] adj frágil

fragment ['frægmənt] n fragmento

fragrant ['freɪgrənt] adj fragante, oloroso

frail [freɪl] adj frágil; (person) débil

frame [freɪm] n (TECH) armazón m; (of person) cuerpo; (of picture, door etc) marco; (of spectacles: also: **~s**) montura ♦ vt enmarcar; **~ of mind** n estado de ánimo; **~work** n marco

France [frɑːns] n Francia

franchise ['fræntʃaɪz] n (POL) derecho de voto, sufragio; (COMM) licencia, concesión f

frank [fræŋk] adj franco ♦ vt (letter) franquear; **~ly** adv francamente

frantic ['fræntɪk] adj (distraught) desesperado; (hectic) frenético

fraternity [frə'təːnɪtɪ] n (feeling) fraternidad f; (group of people) círculos mpl

fraud [frɔːd] n fraude m; (person) impostor(a) m/f

fraught [frɔːt] adj: **~ with** lleno de

fray [freɪ] vi deshilacharse

freak [friːk] n (person) fenómeno; (event) suceso anormal

freckle ['frekl] n peca

free [friː] adj libre; (gratis) gratuito ♦ vt (prisoner etc) poner en libertad; (jammed object) soltar; **~ (of charge)**, **for ~** gratis; **~dom** ['friːdəm] n

libertad f; **F~fone** ® ['fri:fəun] n número gratuito; **~for-all** n riña general; **~ gift** n prima; **~hold** n propiedad f vitalicia; **~ kick** n tiro libre; **~lance** adj independiente ♦ adv por cuenta propia; **~ly** adv libremente; (liberally) generosamente; **F~mason** n francmasón m; **F~post** ® n porte m pagado; **~range** adj (hen, eggs) de granja; **~ trade** n libre comercio; **~way** (US) n autopista; **~ will** n libre albedrío; **of one's own ~ will** por su propia voluntad

freeze [fri:z] (pt **froze**, pp **frozen**) vi (weather) helar; (liquid, pipe, person) helarse, congelarse ♦ vt helar; (food, prices, salaries) congelar ♦ n helada; (on arms, wages) congelación f; **~-dried** adj liofilizado; **~r** n congelador m (SP), congeladora (AM)

freezing ['fri:zɪŋ] adj helado; **3 degrees below ~** tres grados bajo cero; **~ point** n punto de congelación

freight [freɪt] n (goods) carga; (money charged) flete m; **~ train** (US) n tren m de mercancías

French [frentʃ] adj francés/esa ♦ n (LING) francés m; **the ~** npl los franceses; **~ bean** n judía verde; **~ fried potatoes** npl patatas fpl (SP) or papas fpl (AM) fritas; **~ fries** (US) npl = **~ fried potatoes**; **~man/woman** (irreg) n francés/esa m/f; **~ window** n puerta de cristal

frenzy ['frenzɪ] n frenesí m

frequent [adj 'fri:kwənt, vb frɪ'kwent] adj frecuente ♦ vt frecuentar; **~ly** [-əntlɪ] adv frecuentemente, a menudo

fresh [freʃ] adj fresco; (bread) tierno; (new) nuevo; **~en** vi (wind, air) soplar más recio; **~en up** vi (person) arreglarse, lavarse; **~er** (BRIT: inf) n (UNIV) estudiante m/f de primer año; **~ly** adv (made, painted etc) recién; **~man** (US irreg) n = **~er**; **~ness** n frescura; **~water** adj (fish) de agua dulce

fret [fret] vi inquietarse

friar ['fraɪə*] n fraile m; (before name) fray m

friction ['frɪkʃən] n fricción f

Friday ['fraɪdɪ] n viernes m inv

fridge [frɪdʒ] (BRIT) n nevera (SP), refrigeradora (AM)

fried [fraɪd] adj frito

friend [frend] n amigo/a; **~ly** adj simpático; (government) amigo; (place) acogedor(a); (match) amistoso; **~ fire** fuego amigo, disparos mpl del propio bando; **~ship** n amistad f

frieze [fri:z] n friso

fright [fraɪt] n (terror) terror m; (scare) susto; **to take ~** asustarse; **~en** vt asustar; **~ened** adj asustado; **~ening** adj espantoso; **~ful** adj espantoso, horrible

frill [frɪl] n volante m

fringe [frɪndʒ] n (BRIT: of hair) flequillo; (on lampshade etc) flecos mpl; (of forest etc) borde m, margen m; **~ benefits** npl beneficios mpl marginales

frisk [frɪsk] vt cachear, registrar

frisky ['frɪskɪ] adj juguetón/ona

fritter ['frɪtə*] n buñuelo; **~ away** vt desperdiciar

frivolous ['frɪvələs] adj frívolo

frizzy ['frɪzɪ] adj rizado

fro [frəu] see **to**

frock [frɒk] n vestido

frog [frɒg] n rana; **~man** n hombre-rana m

frolic ['frɒlɪk] vi juguetear

KEYWORD

from [frɒm] prep 1 (indicating starting place) de, desde; **where do you come ~?** ¿de dónde eres?; **~ London to Glasgow** de Londres a Glasgow; **to escape ~ sth/sb** escaparse de algo/alguien
2 (indicating origin etc) de; **a letter/telephone call ~ my sister** una carta/llamada de mi hermana; **tell him ~ me that ...** dígale de mi

parte que ...
3 (*indicating time*): ~ **one o'clock** to
or **until** o **till two** de(sde) la una a or
hasta las dos; ~ **January (on)** a partir
de enero
4 (*indicating distance*) de; **the hotel is
1 km ~ the beach** el hotel está a 1
km de la playa
5 (*indicating price, number etc*) de;
prices range ~ £10 to £50 los
precios van desde £10 a or hasta £50;
**the interest rate was increased
~ 9% to 10%** el tipo de interés fue
incrementado en un 9% a un 10%
6 (*indicating difference*) de; **he can't
tell red ~ green** no sabe distinguir el
rojo del verde; **to be different ~** sb/
sth ser diferente o algo/alguien
7 (*because of, on the basis of*): ~ **what
he says** por lo que dice; **weak
~ hunger** debilitado por el hambre

front [frʌnt] *n* (*foremost part*) parte *f*
delantera; (*of house*) fachada; (*of dress*)
delantero; (*promenade: also: sea ~*)
paseo marítimo; (MIL, POL,
METEOROLOGY) frente *m* ♦ *adj*
(*wheel, leg*) delantero; (*row, line*)
primero; **in ~ (of)** delante (de);
~ **door** *n* puerta principal; **~ier**
['frʌntɪə*] *n* frontera; ~ **page** *n*
primera plana; ~ **room** (BRIT) *n* salón
m, sala; **~-wheel drive** *n* tracción *f*
delantera

frost [frɔst] *n* helada; (*also: hoar~*)
escarcha; **~bite** *n* congelación *f*; **~ed**
adj (*glass*) deslustrado; **~y** *adj*
(*weather*) de helada; (*welcome etc*)
glacial

froth [frɔθ] *n* espuma

frown [fraun] *vi* fruncir el ceño

froze [frəuz] *pt* of freeze

frozen ['frəuzn] *pp* of freeze

fruit [fruːt] *n inv* fruta; (*fig*) fruto;
resultados *mpl*; **~erer** *n* frutero/a;
~erer's (shop) *n* frutería; **~ful** *adj*

provechoso; **~ion** [fruː'ɪʃən] *n*: **to
come to ~ion** realizarse; ~ **juice** *n*
zumo (SP) or jugo (AM) de fruta;
~ **machine** (BRIT) *n* máquina *f*
tragaperras; ~ **salad** *n* macedonia (SP)
or ensalada (AM) de frutas

frustrate [frʌs'treɪt] *vt* frustrar

fry [fraɪ] (*pt, pp* fried) *vt* freír; **small ~**
npl gente *f* menuda; **~ing pan** *n* sartén *f*

ft. *abbr* = **foot**; **feet**

fudge [fʌdʒ] *n* (CULIN) caramelo blando

fuel [fjuəl] *n* (*for heating*) combustible
m; (*coal*) carbón *m*; (*wood*) leña; (*for
engine*) carburante *m*; ~ **oil** *n* fuel oil
m; ~ **tank** *n* depósito (de combustible)

fugitive ['fjuːdʒɪtɪv] *n* fugitivo/a

fulfil [ful'fɪl] *vt* (*function*) cumplir con;
(*condition*) satisfacer; (*wish, desire*)
realizar; **~ment** (US fulfillment) *n*
satisfacción *f*; (*of promise, desire*)
realización *f*

full [ful] *adj* pleno; (*fig*) lleno;
(*complete*) completo; (*maximum*)
máximo; (*information*) detallado; (*price*)
íntegro; (*skirt*) amplio ♦ *adv*: **to know
~ well that** saber perfectamente que;
I'm ~ (up) no puedo más; **~
employment** pleno empleo; **a ~ two
hours** dos horas completas; **at
~ speed** a máxima velocidad; **in ~**
(*reproduce, quote*) íntegramente; **~-
length** *adj* (*novel etc*) entero; (*coat*)
largo; (*portrait*) de cuerpo entero; **~
moon** *n* luna llena; **~-scale** *adj*
(*attack, war*) en gran escala; (*model*) de
tamaño natural; **~ stop** *n* punto; **~-
time** *adj* (*work*) de tiempo completo
♦ *adv*: **to work ~-time** trabajar a
tiempo completo; **~y** *adv*
completamente; (*at least*) por lo
menos; **~y-fledged** *adj* (*teacher,
barrister*) diplomado

fumble ['fʌmbl] *vi*: **to ~ with** manejar
torpemente

fume [fjuːm] *vi* (*rage*) estar furioso; **~s**
npl humo, gases *mpl*

fun [fʌn] *n* (*amusement*) diversión *f*; **to**

have ~ divertirse; **for** ~ en broma; **to make** ~ **of** burlarse de

function ['fʌŋkʃən] n función f ♦ vi funcionar; **~al** adj (operational) en buen estado; (practical) funcional

fund [fʌnd] n fondo; (reserve) reserva; **~s** npl (money) fondos mpl

fundamental [fʌndə'mentl] adj fundamental

funeral ['fjuːnərəl] n (burial) entierro; (ceremony) funerales mpl; ~ **parlour** (BRIT) n funeraria; ~ **service** n misa de difuntos, funeral m

funfair ['fʌnfɛə*] (BRIT) n parque m de atracciones

fungus ['fʌŋgəs] (pl fungi) n hongo; (mould) moho

funnel ['fʌnl] n embudo; (of ship) chimenea

funny ['fʌni] adj gracioso, divertido; (strange) curioso, raro

fur [fəː*] n piel f; (BRIT: in kettle etc) sarro; ~ **coat** n abrigo de pieles

furious ['fjuərɪəs] adj furioso; (effort) violento

furlong ['fəːlɔŋ] n octava parte de una milla, = 201.17 m

furnace ['fəːnɪs] n horno

furnish ['fəːnɪʃ] vt amueblar; (supply) suministrar; (information) facilitar; **~ings** npl muebles mpl

furniture ['fəːnɪtʃə*] n muebles mpl; **piece of** ~ mueble m

furrow ['fʌrəu] n surco

furry ['fəːrɪ] adj peludo

further ['fəːðə*] adj (new) nuevo, adicional ♦ adv más lejos; (more) más; (moreover) además ♦ vt promover, adelantar; ~ **education** n educación f superior; **~more** [fəːðə'mɔː*] adv además

furthest ['fəːðɪst] superlative of **far**

fury ['fjuərɪ] n furia

fuse [fjuːz] (US fuze) n fusible m; (for bomb etc) mecha ♦ vt (metal) fundir; (fig) fusionar ♦ vi fundirse; fusionarse; (BRIT: ELEC): **to ~ the lights** fundir los plomos; ~ **box** n caja de fusibles

fuss [fʌs] n (excitement) conmoción f; (trouble) alboroto; **to make a** ~ armar un lío or jaleo; **to make a ~ of sb** mimar a uno; **~y** adj (person) exigente; (too ornate) recargado

futile ['fjuːtaɪl] adj vano

future ['fjuːtʃə*] adj futuro; (coming) venidero ♦ n futuro; (prospects) porvenir; **in** ~ de ahora en adelante

fuze [fjuːz] (US) = **fuse**

fuzzy ['fʌzɪ] adj (PHOT) borroso; (hair) muy rizado

G, g

G [dʒiː] n (MUS) sol m

g. abbr (= gram(s)) gr.

G7 abbr (= Group of Seven) el grupo de los 7

gabble ['gæbl] vi hablar atropelladamente

gable ['geɪbl] n aguilón m

gadget ['gædʒɪt] n aparato

Gaelic ['geɪlɪk] adj, n (LING) gaélico

gag [gæg] n (on mouth) mordaza; (joke) chiste m ♦ vt amordazar

gaiety ['geɪɪtɪ] n alegría

gaily ['geɪlɪ] adv alegremente

gain [geɪn] n: ~ **(in)** aumento (de); (profit) ganancia ♦ vt ganar ♦ vi (watch) adelantarse; **to ~ from/by sth** sacar provecho de algo; **to ~ on sb** ganar terreno a uno; **to ~ 3 lbs (in weight)** engordar 3 libras

gal. abbr = **gallon**

gala ['gaːlə] n fiesta

gale [geɪl] n (wind) vendaval m

gallant ['gælənt] adj valiente; (towards ladies) atento

gall bladder ['gɔːl-] n vesícula biliar

gallery ['gælərɪ] n (also: **art** ~: public) pinacoteca; (: private) galería de arte; (for spectators) tribuna

gallon ['gælən] n galón m (BRIT = 4,546 litros, US = 3,785 litros)

gallop ['gæləp] n galope m ♦ vi galopar

gallows ['gæləuz] n horca

gallstone ['gɔ:lstəun] n cálculo biliario

galore [gə'lɔ:*] adv en cantidad, en abundancia

gambit ['gæmbit] n (fig): (opening) ~ estrategia (inicial)

gamble ['gæmbl] n (risk) riesgo ♦ vt jugar, apostar ♦ vi (take a risk) jugárselas; (bet) apostar; to ~ on apostar a; (success etc) contar con; ~r n jugador(a) m/f; **gambling** n juego

game [geɪm] n juego; (match) partido; (of cards) partida; (HUNTING) caza ♦ adj (willing): to be ~ for anything atreverse a todo; big ~ caza mayor; ~keeper n guardabosques m inv

gammon ['gæmən] n (bacon) tocino ahumado; (ham) jamón m ahumado

gamut ['gæmət] n gama

gang [gæŋ] n (of criminals) pandilla; (of friends etc) grupo; (of workmen) brigada; **~ up** vi: to ~ up on sb aliarse contra uno

gangster ['gæŋstə*] n gángster m

gangway ['gæŋweɪ] n (on ship) pasarela; (BRIT: in theatre, bus etc) pasillo

gaol [dʒeɪl] (BRIT) n, vt = **jail**

gap [gæp] n vacío, hueco (AM); (in trees, traffic) claro; (in time) intervalo; (difference): ~ (between) diferencia (entre)

gape [geɪp] vi mirar boquiabierto; (shirt etc) abrirse (completamente); **gaping** adj (completamente) abierto

garage ['gærɑ:ʒ] n garaje m; (for repairs) taller m

garbage ['gɑ:bɪdʒ] (US) n basura; (inf: nonsense) tonterías fpl; **~ can** n cubo (SP) or bote m (AM) de la basura

garbled ['gɑ:bld] adj (distorted) falsificado, amañado

garden ['gɑ:dn] n jardín m; **~s** npl (park) parque m; **~er** n jardinero,a; **~ing** n jardinería

gargle ['gɑ:gl] vi hacer gárgaras, gargarear (AM)

garish ['gɛərɪʃ] adj chillón/ona

garland ['gɑ:lənd] n guirnalda

garlic ['gɑ:lɪk] n ajo

garment ['gɑ:mənt] n prenda (de vestir)

garnish ['gɑ:nɪʃ] vt (CULIN) aderezar

garrison ['gærɪsn] n guarnición f

garter ['gɑ:tə*] n (for sock) liga; (US) liguero

gas [gæs] n gas m; (fuel) combustible m; (US: gasoline) gasolina ♦ vt asfixiar con gas; **~ cooker** (BRIT) n cocina de gas; **~ cylinder** n bombona de gas; **~ fire** n estufa de gas

gash [gæʃ] n raja; (wound) cuchillada ♦ vt rajar; acuchillar

gasket ['gæskɪt] n (AUT) junta de culata

gas mask n careta antigás

gas meter n contador m de gas

gasoline ['gæsəli:n] (US) n gasolina

gasp [gɑ:sp] n boqueada; (of shock etc) grito sofocado ♦ vi (pant) jadear

gas station (US) n gasolinera

gastric ['gæstrɪk] adj gástrico

gate [geɪt] n puerta; (iron ~) verja; **~crash** (BRIT) vt colarse en; **~way** n (also fig) puerta

gather ['gæðə*] vt (flowers, fruit) coger (SP), recoger; (assemble) reunir; (pick up) recoger; (SEWING) fruncir; (understand) entender ♦ vi (assemble) reunirse; to ~ speed ganar velocidad; **~ing** n reunión f, asamblea

gaudy ['gɔ:dɪ] adj chillón/ona

gauge [geɪdʒ] n (instrument) indicador m ♦ vt medir; (fig) juzgar

gaunt [gɔ:nt] adj (haggard) demacrado; (stark) desolado

gauntlet ['gɔ:ntlɪt] n (fig): to run the ~ of exponerse a; to throw down the ~ arrojar el guante

gauze [gɔ:z] n gasa

gave [geɪv] pt of **give**

gay [geɪ] adj (homosexual) gay; (joyful)

alegre; (*colour*) vivo
gaze [geɪz] *n* mirada fija ♦ *vi*: to ~ at sth mirar algo fijamente
gazelle [gəˈzɛl] *n* gacela
gazumping [gəˈzʌmpɪŋ] (*BRIT*) *n* la subida del precio de una casa una vez que ya ha sido apalabrado
GB *abbr* = **Great Britain**
GCE *n abbr* (*BRIT*) = *General Certificate of Education*
GCSE (*BRIT*) *n abbr* (= *General Certificate of Secondary Education*) examen de reválida que se hace a los 16 años
gear [gɪə*] *n* equipo, herramientas *fpl*, (*TECH*) engranaje *m*; (*AUT*) velocidad *f*, marcha ♦ *vt* (*fig: adapt*): to ~ sth to adaptar or ajustar algo a; **top** *or* **high** (*US*)/**low** ~ cuarta/primera velocidad; **in** ~ en marcha; ~ **box** *n* caja de cambios; ~ **lever** *n* palanca de cambio; ~ **shift** (*US*) *n* = ~ **lever**
geese [giːs] *npl of* **goose**
gel [dʒɛl] *n* gel *m*
gem [dʒɛm] *n* piedra preciosa
Gemini [ˈdʒɛmɪnaɪ] *n* Géminis *m*, Gemelos *mpl*
gender [ˈdʒɛndə*] *n* género
gene [dʒiːn] *n* gen(e) *m*
general [ˈdʒɛnərl] *n* general *m* ♦ *adj* general; **in** ~ en general; ~ **delivery** (*US*) *n* lista de correos; ~ **election** *n* elecciones *fpl* generales; ~**ly** *adv* generalmente, en general; ~ **practitioner** *n* médico general
generate [ˈdʒɛnəreɪt] *vt* (*ELEC*) generar; (*jobs, profits*) producir
generation [dʒɛnəˈreɪʃən] *n* generación *f*
generator [ˈdʒɛnəreɪtə*] *n* generador *m*
generosity [dʒɛnəˈrɔsɪtɪ] *n* generosidad *f*
generous [ˈdʒɛnərəs] *adj* generoso
genetic [dʒɪˈnɛtɪk] *adj*: ~ **engineering** ingeniería genética; ~ **fingerprinting** identificación *f* genética

Geneva [dʒɪˈniːvə] *n* Ginebra
genial [ˈdʒiːnɪəl] *adj* afable, simpático
genitals [ˈdʒɛnɪtlz] *npl* (órganos *mpl*) genitales *mpl*
genius [ˈdʒiːnɪəs] *n* genio
genteel [dʒɛnˈtiːl] *adj* fino, elegante
gentle [ˈdʒɛntl] *adj* apacible, dulce; (*animal*) manso; (*breeze, curve etc*) suave
gentleman [ˈdʒɛntlmən] (*irreg*) *n* señor *m*; (*well-bred man*) caballero
gently [ˈdʒɛntlɪ] *adv* dulcemente, suavemente
gentry [ˈdʒɛntrɪ] *n* alta burguesía
gents [dʒɛnts] *n* aseos *mpl* (de caballeros)
genuine [ˈdʒɛnjuɪn] *adj* auténtico; (*person*) sincero
geography [dʒɪˈɔɡrəfɪ] *n* geografía
geology [dʒɪˈɔlədʒɪ] *n* geología
geometric(al) [dʒɪəˈmɛtrɪk(l)] *adj* geométrico
geranium [dʒɪˈreɪnjəm] *n* geranio
geriatric [dʒɛrɪˈætrɪk] *adj*, *n* geriátrico a m/f
germ [dʒəːm] *n* (*microbe*) microbio, bacteria; (*seed, fig*) germen *m*
German [ˈdʒəːmən] *adj* alemán/ana ♦ *n* alemán/ana *m/f*; (*LING*) alemán *m*; ~ **measles** *n* rubéola
Germany [ˈdʒəːmənɪ] *n* Alemania
gesture [ˈdʒɛstjə*] *n* gesto; (*symbol*) muestra

┌─────────────────┐
│ KEYWORD │
└─────────────────┘

get [gɛt] (*pt*, *pp* **got**, *pp* **gotten** (*US*)) *vi*
1 (*become, be*) ponerse, volverse; **to ~ old/tired** envejecer/cansarse; **to ~ drunk** emborracharse; **to ~ dirty** ensuciarse; **to ~ married** casarse; **when do I ~ paid?** ¿cuándo me pagan or se me paga?; **it's ~ting late** se está haciendo tarde
2 (*go*): **to ~ to/from** llegar a/de; **to ~ home** llegar a casa
3 (*begin*) empezar a; **to ~ to know sb** (llegar a) conocer a uno; **I'm ~ting to**

like him me está empezando a gustar;
let's ~ going or **started** ¡vamos (a
empezar)!

4 (modal aux vb): **you've got to do it**
tienes que hacerlo

♦ vt **1: to ~ sth done** (finish) terminar
algo; (have done) mandar hacer algo;
to ~ one's hair cut cortarse el pelo;
to ~ the car going or **to go** arrancar
el coche; **to ~ sb to do sth** conseguir
or hacer que alguien haga algo; **to ~
sth/sb ready** preparar algo/a
alguien

2 (obtain: money, permission, results)
conseguir; (find: job, flat) encontrar;
(fetch: person, doctor) buscar; (object) ir
a buscar, traer; **to ~ sth for sb**
conseguir algo para alguien; **~ me Mr
Jones, please** (TEL) póngame or
comuníqueme (AM) con el Sr. Jones,
por favor; **can I ~ you a drink?**
¿quieres algo de beber?

3 (receive: present, letter) recibir;
(acquire: reputation) alcanzar; (: prize)
ganar; **what did you ~ for your
birthday?** ¿qué te regalaron por tu
cumpleaños?; **how much did you
~ for the painting?** ¿cuánto sacaste
por el cuadro?

4 (catch) coger (SP), agarrar (AM); (hit:
target etc) dar en; **to ~ sb by the
arm/throat** coger or agarrar a uno
por el brazo/cuello; **~ him!** ¡cógelo!
(SP), ¡atrápalo! (AM); **the bullet got
him in the leg** la bala le dio en la
pierna

5 (take, move) llevar; **to ~ sth to sb**
hacer llegar algo a alguien; **do you
think we'll ~ it through the door?**
¿crees que lo podremos meter por la
puerta?

6 (catch, take: plane, bus etc) coger
(SP), tomar (AM); **where do I ~ the
train for Birmingham?** ¿dónde se
coge or se toma el tren para
Birmingham?

7 (understand) entender; (hear) oír;

I've got it! ¡ya lo tengo!, ¡eureka!; **I
don't ~ your meaning** no te
entiendo; **I'm sorry, I didn't ~ your
name** lo siento, no cogí tu nombre

8 (have, possess): **to have got** tener

get about vi salir mucho; (news)
divulgarse

get along vi (agree) llevarse bien;
(depart) marcharse; (manage) = **get
by**

get at vt fus (attack) atacar; (reach)
alcanzar

get away vi marcharse; (escape)
escaparse

get away with vt fus hacer
impunemente

get back vi (return) volver ♦ vt
recobrar

get by vi (pass) lograr pasar;
(manage) arreglárselas

get down vi bajarse ♦ vt fus bajar ♦ vt
bajar; (depress) deprimir

get down to vt fus (work) ponerse a

get in vi entrar; (train) llegar; (arrive
home) volver a casa, regresar

get into vt fus entrar en; (vehicle)
subir a; **to ~ into a rage** enfadarse

get off vi (from train etc) bajar;
(depart: person, car) marcharse ♦ vt
(remove) quitar ♦ vt fus (train, bus)
bajar de

get on vi (at exam etc): **how are you
~ting on?** ¿cómo te va?; (agree): **to
~ on (with)** llevarse bien (con) ♦ vt fus
subir a

get out vi salir; (of vehicle) bajar ♦ vt
sacar

get out of vt fus salir de; (duty etc)
escaparse de

get over vt fus (illness) recobrarse de

get round vt fus rodear; (fig: person)
engatusar

get through vi (TEL) lograr
comunicarse

get through to vt fus (TEL)
comunicar con

get together vi reunirse ♦ vt reunir,

juntar
get up vi (rise) levantarse ♦ vt fus subir
get up to vt fus (reach) llegar a; (prank) hacer

geyser ['giːzə*] n (water heater) calentador m de agua; (GEO) géiser m
ghastly ['gɑːstlɪ] adj horrible
gherkin ['gəːkɪn] n pepinillo
ghetto blaster ['getəʊblɑːstə*] n cassette m portátil de gran tamaño
ghost [gəʊst] n fantasma m
giant ['dʒaɪənt] n gigante m/f ♦ adj gigantesco, gigante
gibberish ['dʒɪbərɪʃ] n galimatías m
giblets ['dʒɪblɪts] npl menudillos mpl
Gibraltar [dʒɪ'brɔːltə*] n Gibraltar m
giddy ['gɪdɪ] adj mareado
gift [gɪft] n regalo; (ability) talento; **~ed** adj dotado; **~ token** or **voucher** n vale m canjeable por un regalo
gigantic [dʒaɪ'gæntɪk] adj gigantesco
giggle ['gɪgl] vi reírse tontamente
gill [dʒɪl] n (measure) = 0.25 pints (BRIT = 0.148l, US = 0.118l)
gills [gɪlz] npl (of fish) branquias fpl, agallas fpl
gilt [gɪlt] adj, n dorado; **~-edged** adj (COMM) de máxima garantía
gimmick ['gɪmɪk] n truco
gin [dʒɪn] n ginebra
ginger ['dʒɪndʒə*] n jengibre m; **~ ale** = **~ beer**; **~ beer** (BRIT) n gaseosa de jengibre; **~bread** n pan m (or galleta) de jengibre
gingerly ['dʒɪndʒəlɪ] adv con cautela
gipsy ['dʒɪpsɪ] n = **gypsy**
giraffe [dʒɪ'rɑːf] n jirafa
girder ['gəːdə*] n viga
girl [gəːl] n (small) niña; (young woman) chica, joven f, muchacha; (daughter) hija; **an English ~** una (chica) inglesa; **~friend** n (of girl) amiga; (of boy) novia; **~ish** adj de niña
giro ['dʒaɪrəʊ] n (BRIT: bank ~) giro bancario; (post office ~) giro postal; (state benefit) cheque quincenal del

subsidio de desempleo
gist [dʒɪst] n lo esencial
give [gɪv] (pt gave, pp given) vt dar; (deliver) entregar; (as gift) regalar ♦ vi (break) romperse; (stretch: fabric) dar de sí; **to ~ sb sth**, **~ sth to sb** dar algo a uno; **~ away** vt (give free) regalar; (betray) traicionar; (disclose) revelar; **~ back** vt devolver; **~ in** vi ceder ♦ vt entregar; **~ off** vt despedir; **~ out** vt distribuir; **~ up** vi rendirse, darse por vencido ♦ vt renunciar a; **to ~ up smoking** dejar de fumar; **to ~ o.s. up** entregarse; **~ way** vi ceder; (BRIT: AUT) ceder el paso
glacier ['glæsɪə*] n glaciar m
glad [glæd] adj contento
gladly ['glædlɪ] adv con mucho gusto
glamorous ['glæmərəs] adj encantador(a), atractivo; **glamour** ['glæmə*] n encanto, atractivo
glance [glɑːns] n ojeada, mirada ♦ vi: **to ~** echar una ojeada a; **glancing** adj (blow) oblicuo
gland [glænd] n glándula
glare [glɛə*] n (of anger) mirada feroz; (of light) deslumbramiento, brillo; **to be in the ~ of publicity** ser el foco de la atención pública ♦ vi deslumbrar; **to ~** mirar con odio a; **glaring** adj (mistake) manifiesto
glass [glɑːs] n vidrio, cristal m; (for drinking) vaso; (: with stem) copa; **~es** npl (spectacles) gafas fpl; **~house** n invernadero; **~ware** n cristalería
glaze [gleɪz] vt (window) poner cristales a; (pottery) vidriar ♦ n vidriado; **glazier** ['gleɪzɪə*] n vidriero/a
gleam [gliːm] vi brillar
glean [gliːn] vt (information) recoger
glee [gliː] n alegría, regocijo
glen [glɛn] n cañada
glib [glɪb] adj de mucha labia; (promise, response) poco sincero
glide [glaɪd] vi deslizarse; (AVIAT, birds) planear; **~r** n (AVIAT) planeador m; **gliding** n (AVIAT) vuelo sin motor

glimmer ['glɪmə*] n luz f tenue; (of interest) muestra; **~y** adj (dark) oscuro; (sad) triste, (pessimistic) pesimista

glimpse [glɪmps] n vislumbre m ♦ vt vislumbrar, entrever

glint [glɪnt] vi centellear

glisten ['glɪsn] vi relucir, brillar

glitter ['glɪtə*] vi relucir, brillar

gloat [gləʊt] vi: **to ~ over** recrearse en

global ['gləʊbl] adj mundial; **~ warming** (re)calentamiento global or de la tierra

globe [gləʊb] n globo; (model) globo terráqueo

gloom [gluːm] n tinieblas fpl, oscuridad f; (sadness) tristeza, melancolía; **~y** adj (dark) oscuro; (sad) triste, (pessimistic) pesimista

glorious ['glɔːrɪəs] adj glorioso; (weather etc) magnífico

glory ['glɔːrɪ] n gloria

gloss [glɒs] n (shine) brillo; (paint) pintura de aceite; **~ over** vt fus disimular

glossary ['glɒsərɪ] n glosario

glossy ['glɒsɪ] adj lustroso; (magazine) de lujo

glove [glʌv] n guante m; **~ compartment** n (AUT) guantera

glow [gləʊ] vi brillar

glower ['glaʊə*] vi: **to ~ at** mirar con ceño

glue [gluː] n goma (de pegar), cemento ♦ vt pegar

glum [glʌm] adj (person, tone) melancólico

glut [glʌt] n superabundancia

glutton ['glʌtn] n glotón/ona m/f; **a ~ for work** un(a) trabajador(a) incansable

gnat [næt] n mosquito

gnaw [nɔː] vt roer

gnome [nəʊm] n gnomo

go [gəʊ] (pt **went**, pp **gone**, pl **~es**) vi ir; (travel) viajar; (depart) irse, marcharse; (work) funcionar, marchar; (be sold) venderse; (time) pasar; (fit, suit): **to ~ with** hacer juego con;

(become) ponerse; (break etc) estropearse, romperse ♦ n: **to have a ~ (at)** probar suerte (con); **to be on the ~** no parar; **whose ~ is it?** ¿a quién le toca?; **he's going to do it** va a hacerlo; **to ~ for a walk** ir de paseo; **to ~ dancing** ir a bailar; **how did it ~?** ¿qué tal salió or resultó?, ¿cómo ha ido?; **to ~ round the back** pasar por detrás; **~ about** vi (rumour) propagarse ♦ vt fus: **how do I ~ about this?** ¿cómo me las arreglo para hacer esto?; **~ ahead** vi seguir adelante; **~ along** vi ir ♦ vt fus bordear; **to ~ along with** (agree) estar de acuerdo con; **~ away** vi irse, marcharse; **~ back** vi volver; **~ back on** vt fus (promise) faltar a; **~ by** vi (time) pasar ♦ vt fus guiarse por; **~ down** vi bajar; (ship) hundirse; (sun) ponerse ♦ vt fus bajar; **~ for** vt fus (fetch) ir por; (like) gustar; (attack) atacar; **~ in** vi entrar; **~ in for** vt fus (competition) presentarse a; **~ into** vt fus entrar en; (investigate) investigar; (embark on) dedicarse a; **~ off** vi irse, marcharse; (food) pasarse; (explode) estallar; (event) realizarse ♦ vt fus dejar de gustar; **I'm going off him/the idea** ya no me gusta tanto él/la idea; **~ on** vi (continue) seguir, continuar; (happen) pasar, ocurrir; **to ~ on doing sth** seguir haciendo algo; **~ out** vi salir; (fire, light) apagarse; **~ over** vi (ship) zozobrar ♦ vt fus (check) revisar; **~ through** vt fus (town etc) atravesar; **~ up** vi, vt fus subir; **~ without** vt fus pasarse sin

goad [gəʊd] vt aguijonear

go-ahead adj (person) dinámico; (firm) innovador(a) ♦ n luz f verde

goal [gəʊl] n meta; (score) gol m; **~keeper** n portero; **~-post** n poste m (de la portería)

goat [gəʊt] n cabra

gobble ['gɒbl] vt (also: **~ down**, **~ up**) tragarse, engullir

go-between n intermediario/a
god [gɔd] n dios m; **G~** n Dios m;
~child n ahijado/a; **~daughter** n
ahijada; **~dess** n diosa; **~father** n
padrino; **~-forsaken** adj dejado de la
mano de Dios; **~mother** n madrina;
~send n don m del cielo; **~son** n
ahijado

goggles ['gɔglz] npl gafas fpl

going ['gəʊɪŋ] n (conditions) estado del
terreno ♦ adj: the **~ rate** la tarifa
corriente or en vigor

gold [gəʊld] n oro ♦ adj de oro; **~en**
adj (made of ~) de oro; (~ in colour)
dorado; **~fish** n pez m de colores;
~mine n (also fig) mina de oro; **~-
plated** adj chapado en oro; **~smith** n
orfebre m/f

golf [gɔlf] n golf m; **~ ball** n (for game)
pelota de golf; (on typewriter) esfera;
~ club n club m de golf; (stick) palo
(de golf); **~ course** n campo de golf;
~er n golfista m/f

gone [gɔn] pp of **go**

good [gʊd] adj bueno; (pleasant)
agradable; (kind) bueno, amable;
(well-behaved) educado ♦ n bien m,
provecho; **~s** npl (COMM) mercancías
fpl; **~!** ¡qué bien!; **to be ~ at** tener
aptitud para; **to be ~ for** servir para;
it's ~ for you te hace bien; **would
you be ~ enough to ...?** ¿podría
hacerme el favor de ...?, ¿sería tan
amable de ...?; **a ~ deal (of)** mucho; **a
~ many** muchos; **to make ~** reparar;
it's no ~ complaining no vale la
pena (de) quejarse; **for ~** para siempre,
definitivamente; **~ morning/
afternoon!** ¡buenos días/buenas
tardes!; **~ evening!** ¡buenas noches!;
~ night! ¡buenas noches!; **~bye!**
¡adiós!; **to say ~bye** despedirse;
G~ Friday n Viernes m Santo; **~-
looking** adj guapo; **~-natured** adj
amable, simpático; **~ness** n (of person)
bondad f; for **~ness sake!** ¡por Dios!;
~ness gracious! ¡Dios mío!; **~s train**

(BRIT) n tren m de mercancías; **~will** n
buena voluntad f

goose [guːs] n (pl **geese**) n ganso, oca

gooseberry ['guzbəri] n grosella
espinosa; **to play** ~ hacer de carabina

gooseflesh ['guːsfleʃ] n = **goose
pimples**

goose pimples npl carne f de gallina

gore [gɔː*] vt cornear ♦ n sangre f

gorge [gɔːdʒ] n barranco ♦ vr: **to
~ o.s. (on)** atracarse (de)

gorgeous ['gɔːdʒəs] adj (thing)
precioso; (weather) espléndido; (person)
guapísimo

gorilla [gə'rɪlə] n gorila m

gorse [gɔːs] n tojo

gory ['gɔːrɪ] adj sangriento

go-slow (BRIT) n huelga de manos
caídas

gospel ['gɔspl] n evangelio

gossip ['gɔsɪp] n (scandal) cotilleo,
chismes mpl; (chat) charla;
(scandalmonger) cotilla m/f, chismoso/a
♦ vi cotillear

got [gɔt] pt, pp of **get**; **~ten** (US) pp of
get

gout [gaʊt] n gota

govern ['gʌvən] vt gobernar;
(influence) dominar; **~ess** n institutriz f;
~ment n gobierno; **~or** n
gobernador(a) m/f; (of school etc)
miembro del consejo; (of jail)
director(a) m/f

gown [gaʊn] n traje m; (of teacher,
BRIT: of judge) toga

G.P. n abbr = **general practitioner**

grab [græb] vt coger (SP) or agarrar
(AM), arrebatar ♦ vi: **to ~ at** intentar
agarrar

grace [greɪs] n gracia ♦ vt honrar;
(adorn) adornar; **5 days'** ~ un plazo
de 5 días; **~ful** adj grácil, ágil; (style,
shape) elegante, gracioso; **gracious**
['greɪʃəs] adj amable

grade [greɪd] n (quality) clase f, calidad
f; (in hierarchy) grado; (SCOL: mark)
nota; (US: school class) curso ♦ vt

clasificar; **~ crossing** (US) n paso a nivel; **~ school** (US) n escuela primaria

gradient ['greidiənt] n pendiente f

gradual ['grædjuəl] adj paulatino; **~ly** adv paulatinamente

graduate [n 'grædjut, vb 'grædjueit] n (US: of high school) graduado/a; (of university) licenciado/a ♦ vi graduarse; licenciarse; **graduation** ['eiʃən] n (ceremony) entrega del título

graffiti [grə'fi:ti] n pintadas fpl

graft [grɑ:ft] n (AGR, MED) injerto; (BRIT: inf) trabajo duro; (bribery) corrupción f ♦ vt injertar

grain [grein] n (single particle) grano; (corn) granos mpl, cereales mpl; (of wood) fibra

gram [græm] n gramo

grammar ['græmə*] n gramática; **~ school** (BRIT) n ≈ instituto de segunda enseñanza, liceo (SP)

grammatical [grə'mætikl] adj gramatical

gramme [græm] n = gram

gramophone ['græməfəun] (BRIT) n tocadiscos m inv

grand [grænd] adj magnífico, imponente; (wonderful) estupendo; (gesture etc) grandioso; **~children** npl nietos mpl; **~dad** (inf) n yayo, abuelito; **~daughter** n nieta; **~eur** ['grændjə*] n magnificencia f, lo grandioso; **~father** n abuelo; **~ma** (inf) n yaya, abuelita; **~mother** n abuela; **~pa** (inf) n = **~dad**; **~parents** npl abuelos mpl; **~ piano** n piano de cola; **~son** n nieto; **~stand** n (SPORT) tribuna

granite ['grænit] n granito

granny ['grænɪ] (inf) n abuelita, yaya

grant [grɑ:nt] vt (concede) conceder; (admit) reconocer ♦ n (SCOL) beca; (ADMIN) subvención f; **to take sth/sb for ~ed** dar algo por sentado/no hacer ningún caso a uno

granulated sugar ['grænjuleitid-] (BRIT) n azúcar m blanquilla

grape [greip] n uva

grapefruit ['greipfru:t] n pomelo (SP), toronja (AM)

graph [grɑ:f] n gráfica; **~ic** ['græfik] adj gráfico; **~ics** n artes fpl gráficas ♦ npl (drawings) dibujos mpl

grapple ['græpl] vi: **to ~ with sth/sb** agarrar a algo/uno

grasp [grɑ:sp] vt agarrar, asir; (understand) comprender ♦ n (grip) asimiento; (understanding) comprensión f; **~ing** adj (mean) avaro

grass [grɑ:s] n hierba; (lawn) césped m; **~hopper** n saltamontes m inv; **~roots** adj (fig) popular

grate [greit] n parrilla de chimenea ♦ vi: **to ~ (on)** chirriar (sobre) ♦ vt (CULIN) rallar

grateful ['greitful] adj agradecido

grater ['greitə*] n rallador m

gratifying ['grætifaiiŋ] adj grato

grating ['greitiŋ] n (iron bars) reja ♦ adj (noise) áspero

gratitude ['grætitju:d] n agradecimiento

gratuity [grə'tju:iti] n gratificación f

grave [greiv] n tumba ♦ adj serio, grave

gravel ['grævl] n grava

gravestone ['greivstəun] n lápida

graveyard ['greivjɑ:d] n cementerio

gravity ['græviti] n gravedad f

gravy ['greivi] n salsa de carne

gray [grei] adj = **grey**

graze [greiz] vi pacer ♦ vt (touch lightly) rozar; (scrape) raspar ♦ n (MED) abrasión f

grease [gri:s] n (fat) grasa; (lubricant) lubricante m ♦ vt engrasar; lubrificar; **~proof paper** (BRIT) n papel m apergaminado; **greasy** adj grasiento

great [greit] adj grande; (inf) magnífico, estupendo; **G~ Britain** n Gran Bretaña; **~-grandfather** n bisabuelo; **~-grandmother** n bisabuela; **~ly** adv muy; (with verb) mucho; **~ness** n grandeza

Greece [gri:s] n Grecia

greed [gri:d] n (also: ~iness) codicia, avaricia; (for food) gula; (for power etc) avidez f; **~y** adj avaro; (for food) glotón/ona

Greek [gri:k] adj griego ♦ n griego/a; (LING) griego

green [gri:n] adj (also POL) verde; (inexperienced) novato ♦ n verde m; (stretch of grass) césped m; (GOLF) green m; **~s** npl (vegetables) verduras fpl; **~ belt** n zona verde; **~ card** n (AUT) carta verde; (US: work permit) permiso de trabajo para los extranjeros en EE. UU.; **~ery** n verdura; **~grocer** (BRIT) n verdulero/a; **~house** n invernadero; **~house effect** n efecto invernadero; **~house gas** n gases mpl de invernadero; **~ish** adj verdoso

Greenland ['gri:nlənd] n Groenlandia

greet [gri:t] vt (welcome) dar la bienvenida a; (receive: news) recibir; **~ing** n (welcome) bienvenida; **~ing(s) card** n tarjeta de felicitación

grenade [grə'neɪd] n granada

grew [gru:] pt of **grow**

grey [greɪ] adj gris; (weather) sombrío; **~-haired** adj canoso; **~hound** n galgo

grid [grɪd] n reja; (ELEC) red f; **~lock** n (traffic jam) retención f

grief [gri:f] n dolor m, pena

grievance ['gri:vəns] n motivo de queja, agravio

grieve [gri:v] vi afligirse, acongojarse ♦ vt dar pena a; **to ~ for** llorar por

grievous ['gri:vəs] adj: **~ bodily harm** (LAW) daños mpl corporales graves

grill [grɪl] n (on cooker) parrilla; (also: mixed ~) parrillada ♦ vt (BRIT) asar a la parrilla; (inf: question) interrogar

grille [grɪl] n reja; (AUT) rejilla

grim [grɪm] adj (place) sombrío; (situation) triste; (person) ceñudo

grimace ['grɪmeɪs] n mueca ♦ vi hacer muecas

grime [graɪm] n mugre f, suciedad f

grin [grɪn] n sonrisa abierta ♦ vi sonreír abiertamente

grind [graɪnd] (pt, pp **ground**) vt (coffee, pepper etc) moler; (US: meat) picar; (make sharp) afilar ♦ n (work) rutina

grip [grɪp] n (hold) asimiento; (control) control m, dominio; (of tyre etc) adherencia; (handle) asidero; (holdall) maletín m ♦ vt agarrar; (viewer, reader) fascinar; **to get to ~s with** enfrentarse con; **~ping** adj absorbente

grisly ['grɪzlɪ] adj horripilante, horrible

gristle ['grɪsl] n ternilla

grit [grɪt] n gravilla; (courage) valor m ♦ vt (road) poner gravilla en; **to ~ one's teeth** apretar los dientes

groan [grəun] n gemido; quejido ♦ vi gemir; quejarse

grocer ['grəusə*] n tendero de ultramarinos (SP); **~ies** npl comestibles mpl; **~'s (shop)** n tienda de ultramarinos or de abarrotes (AM)

groin [grɔɪn] n ingle f

groom [gru:m] n mozo/a de cuadra; (also: bride~) novio ♦ vt (horse) almohazar; (fig): **to ~ sb for** prepararse a uno para; **well-~ed** de buena presencia

groove [gru:v] n ranura, surco

grope [grəup] n: **to ~ for** vt fus buscar a tientas

gross [grəus] adj (neglect, injustice) grave; (vulgar: behaviour) grosero; (: appearance) de mal gusto; (COMM) bruto; **~ly** adv (greatly) enormemente

grotto ['grɔtəu] n gruta

grotty ['grɔtɪ] (inf) adj horrible

ground [graund] pt, pp of **grind** ♦ n suelo, tierra; (SPORT) campo, terreno; (reason: gen pl) causa, razón f; (US: also: ~ wire) tierra ♦ vt (plane) mantener en tierra; (US: also) conectar con tierra; **~s** npl (of coffee etc) poso; (gardens etc) jardines mpl, parque m; **on the ~** en el suelo; **to the ~** al suelo; **to gain/lose ~** ganar/perder terreno; **~ cloth** (US) n

= **~sheet**; **~ing** *n* (*in education*) conocimientos *mpl* básicos; **~less** *adj* infundado; **~sheet** (*BRIT*) *n* tela impermeable; suelo; **~ staff** *n* personal *m* de tierra; **~work** *n* preparación *f*

group [gruːp] *n* grupo; (*musical*) conjunto ♦ *vt* (*also*: **~ together**) agrupar ♦ *vi* (*also*: **~ together**) agruparse

grouse [graʊs] *n inv* (*bird*) urogallo ♦ *vi* (*complain*) quejarse

grove [grəʊv] *n* arboleda

grovel ['grɒvl] *vi* (*fig*): **to ~ before** humillarse ante

grow [grəʊ] (*pt* **grew**, *pp* **grown**) *vi* crecer; (*increase*) aumentar; (*expand*) desarrollarse; (*become*) volverse; **to ~ rich/weak** enriquecerse/debilitarse ♦ *vt* cultivar; (*hair, beard*) dejar crecer; **~ up** *vi* crecer, hacerse hombre/mujer; **~er** *n* cultivador(a) *m/f*, productor(a) *m/f*; **~ing** *adj* creciente

growl [graʊl] *vi* gruñir

grown [grəʊn] *pp* of **grow**; **~-up** *n* adulto, mayor *m/f*

growth [grəʊθ] *n* crecimiento, desarrollo; (*what has grown*) brote *m*; (*MED*) tumor *m*

grub [grʌb] *n* larva, gusano; (*inf*: *food*) comida

grubby ['grʌbi] *adj* sucio, mugriento

grudge [grʌdʒ] *n* (motivo de) rencor *m* ♦ *vt*: **to ~ sb sth** dar algo a uno de mala gana; **to bear sb a ~** guardar rencor a uno

gruelling ['grʊəlɪŋ] (*US* **grueling**) *adj* penoso, duro

gruesome ['gruːsəm] *adj* horrible

gruff [grʌf] *adj* (*voice*) ronco; (*manner*) brusco

grumble ['grʌmbl] *vi* refunfuñar, quejarse

grumpy ['grʌmpi] *adj* gruñón/ona

grunt [grʌnt] *vi* gruñir

G-string ['dʒiːstrɪŋ] *n* taparrabo

guarantee [gærən'tiː] *n* garantía ♦ *vt* garantizar

guard [gɑːd] *n* (*squad*) guardia; (*one man*) guardia *m*; (*BRIT*: *RAIL*) jefe *m* de tren; (*on machine*) dispositivo de seguridad; (*also*: **fire~**) rejilla de protección ♦ *vt* guardar; (*prisoner*) vigilar; **to be on one's ~** estar alerta; **~ against** *vt fus* (*prevent*) protegerse de; **~ed** *adj* (*fig*) cauteloso; **~ian** *n* guardián/ana *m/f*; (*of minor*) tutor(a) *m/f*; **~'s van** *n* (*BRIT*: *RAIL*) furgón *m*

Guatemala [gwætɪ'mɑːlə] *n* Guatemala; **~n** *adj*, *n* guatemalteco/a *m/f*

guerrilla [gə'rɪlə] *n* guerrillero/a

guess [ges] *vt, vi* (*estimate*); (*US*) suponer ♦ *vt* adivinar; suponer ♦ *n* suposición *f*, conjetura; **to take** *or* **have a ~** tratar de adivinar; **~work** *n* conjeturas *fpl*

guest [gest] *n* invitado/a, (*in hotel*) huésped/a *m/f*; **~ house** *n* casa de huéspedes, pensión *f*; **~ room** *n* cuarto de huéspedes

guffaw [gʌ'fɔː] *vi* reírse a carcajadas

guidance ['gaɪdəns] *n* (*advice*) consejos *mpl*

guide [gaɪd] *n* (*person*) guía *m/f*; (*book*, *fig*) guía ♦ *vt* (*round museum etc*) guiar; (*lead*) conducir; (*direct*) orientar; (**girl**) **~** *n* exploradora; **~book** *n* guía; **~ dog** *n* perro *m* guía; **~lines** *npl* (*advice*) directrices *fpl*

guild [gɪld] *n* gremio

guilt [gɪlt] *n* culpabilidad *f*; **~y** *adj* culpable

guinea pig ['gɪnɪ-] *n* cobaya, (*fig*) conejillo de Indias

guise [gaɪz] *n*: **in** *or* **under the ~ of** bajo apariencia de

guitar [gɪ'tɑː*] *n* guitarra

gulf [gʌlf] *n* golfo; (*abyss*) abismo

gull [gʌl] *n* gaviota

gullible ['gʌlɪbl] *adj* crédulo

gully ['gʌlɪ] *n* barranco

gulp [gʌlp] *vi* tragar saliva ♦ *vt* (*also*: **~ down**) tragarse

gum [gʌm] *n* (*ANAT*) encía; (*glue*) goma, cemento; (*sweet*) caramelo de goma; (*also*: **chewing-~**) chicle *m* ♦ *vt* pegar con goma; **~boots** (BRIT) npl botas fpl de goma

gun [gʌn] n (small) pistola, revólver m; (shotgun) escopeta; (rifle) fusil m; (cannon) cañón m; **~boat** n cañonero; **~fire** n disparos mpl; **~man** n pistolero; **~ at ~point** n: at a mano armada; **~powder** n pólvora; **~shot** n escopetazo

gurgle ['gə:gl] vi (baby) gorgotear; (water) borbotear

gush [gʌʃ] vi salir a raudales; (person) deshacerse en efusiones

gust [gʌst] n (of wind) ráfaga

gusto ['gʌstəu] n entusiasmo

gut [gʌt] n intestino; **~s** npl (ANAT) tripas fpl; (courage) valor m

gutter ['gʌtə*] n (of roof) canalón m; (in street) cuneta

guy [gaɪ] n (also: **~rope**) cuerda; (inf: man) tío (SP), tipo; (figure) monigote m

---

Guy Fawkes' Night

La noche del cinco de noviembre, **Guy Fawkes' Night**, se celebra en el Reino Unido el fracaso de la conspiración de la pólvora ("Gunpowder Plot"), un intento fallido de volar el parlamento de Jaime I en 1605. Esa noche se lanzan fuegos artificiales y se hacen hogueras en las que se queman unos muñecos de trapo que representan a **Guy Fawkes**, uno de los cabecillas de la revuelta. Días antes, los niños tienen por costumbre pedir a los transeúntes "a penny for the guy", dinero que emplean en comprar cohetes y petardos.

---

guzzle ['gʌzl] vi tragar ♦ vt engullir

gym [dʒɪm] n (also: gymnasium) gimnasio; (also: gymnastics) gimnasia; **~nast** n gimnasta m/f; **~ shoes** npl zapatillas fpl (de deporte); **~ slip** (BRIT) n túnica de colegiala

gynaecologist [gaɪnɪ'kɔlədʒɪst] (US

gynecologist) n ginecólogo/a

gypsy ['dʒɪpsɪ] n gitano/a

H, h

haberdashery [hæbə'dæʃərɪ] (BRIT) n mercería

habit ['hæbɪt] n hábito, costumbre f; (drug ~) adicción f; (costume) hábito

habitual [hə'bɪtjuəl] adj acostumbrado, habitual; (drinker, liar) empedernido

hack [hæk] vt (cut) cortar; (slice) tajar ♦ n (pej: writer) escritor(a) m/f a sueldo; **~er** n (COMPUT) pirata m/f informático/a

hackneyed ['hæknɪd] adj trillado

had [hæd] pt, pp of **have**

haddock ['hædək] (pl ~ or ~s) n especie de merluza

hadn't ['hædnt] = **had not**

haemorrhage ['hemərɪdʒ] (US **hemorrhage**) n hemorragia

haemorrhoids ['heməroɪdz] (US **hemorrhoids**) npl hemorroides fpl

haggle ['hægl] vi regatear

Hague [heɪg] n: **The ~** La Haya

hail [heɪl] n granizo; (fig) lluvia ♦ vt saludar; (taxi) llamar a; (acclaim) aclamar ♦ vi granizar; **~stone** n (piedra de) granizo

hair [heə*] n pelo, cabellos mpl; (one ~) pelo, cabello; (on legs etc) vello; **to do one's ~** arreglarse el pelo; **to have grey ~** tener canas fpl; **~brush** n cepillo (para el pelo); **~cut** n corte m (de pelo); **~do** n peinado; **~dresser** n peluquero/a; **~dresser's** n peluquería; **~ dryer** n secador m de pelo; **~grip** n horquilla; **~ net** n redecilla; **~piece** n postizo; **~pin** n horquilla; **~pin bend** (US **~pin curve**) n curva de horquilla; **~raising** adj espeluznante; **~ removing cream** n crema depilatoria; **~ spray** n laca; **~style** n peinado; **~y** adj peludo; velludo; (inf:

frightening) espeluznante

hake [heɪk] *(pl inv or ~s) n* merluza

half [hɑːf] *(pl* **halves**) *n* mitad *f; (of beer)* ≈ caña (SP), media pinta; (RAIL, BUS) billete *m* de niño ♦ *adj* medio ♦ *adv* medio, a medias; **two and a ~** dos y media; **~ a dozen** media docena; **~ a pound** media libra; **to cut sth in ~** cortar algo por la mitad; **~-caste** ['hɑːfkɑːst] *n* mestizo/a; **~-hearted** *adj* indiferente, poco entusiasta; **~-hour** *n* media hora; **~-mast** *n:* **at ~-mast** *(flag)* a media asta; **~-price** *adj, adv* a mitad de precio; **~ term** *(BRIT) n (SCOL)* vacaciones de mediados del trimestre; **~-time** *n* descanso; **~way** *adv* a medio camino; *(in period of time)* a mitad de camino

hall [hɔːl] *n (for concerts)* sala; *(entrance way)* hall *m;* vestíbulo; **~ of residence** *(BRIT) n* residencia

hallmark ['hɔːlmɑːk] *n* sello

hallo [hə'ləu] *excl =* **hello**

Hallowe'en [hæləu'iːn] *n* víspera de Todos los Santos

Hallowe'en

La tradición anglosajona dice que en la noche del 31 de octubre, **Hallowe'en***, víspera de Todos los Santos, es posible ver a brujas y fantasmas. En este día los niños se disfrazan y van de puerta en puerta llevando un farol hecho con una calabaza en forma de cabeza humana. Cuando se les abre la puerta gritan "trick or treat", amenazando con gastar una broma a quien no les dé golosinas o algo de calderilla.*

---

hallucination [həluːsɪ'neɪʃən] *n* alucinación *f*

hallway ['hɔːlweɪ] *n* vestíbulo

halo ['heɪləu] *n (of saint)* halo, aureola

halt [hɔːlt] *n (stop)* alto, parada ♦ *vt* parar; interrumpir ♦ *vi* pararse

halve [hɑːv] *vt* partir por la mitad

halves [hɑːvz] *npl of* **half**

ham [hæm] *n* jamón *m* (cocido)

hamburger ['hæmbɜːgə*] *n* hamburguesa

hamlet ['hæmlɪt] *n* aldea

hammer ['hæmə*] *n* martillo ♦ *vt (nail)* clavar; *(force):* **to ~ an idea into sb/a message across** meter una idea en la cabeza a uno/machacar una idea ♦ *vi* dar golpes

hammock ['hæmək] *n* hamaca

hamper ['hæmpə*] *vt* estorbar ♦ *n* cesto

hand [hænd] *n* mano *f; (of clock)* aguja; *(writing)* letra; *(worker)* obrero ♦ *vt* pasar; **to give** or **lend sb a ~** echar una mano a uno, ayudar a uno; **at ~** a mano; **in ~** *(time)* libre; *(job etc)* entre manos; **on ~** *(person, services)* a mano, al alcance; **to ~** *(information etc)* a mano; **on the one ~ ...**, **on the other ~ ...** por una parte ... por otra (parte) ...; ♦ *in* **~** entregar; ♦ *out vt* distribuir; ♦ *over vt (deliver)* entregar; **~bag** *n* bolso (SP), cartera (AM); **~book** *n* manual *m;* **~brake** *n* freno de mano; **~cuffs** *npl* esposas *fpl;* **~ful** *n* puñado

handicap ['hændɪkæp] *n* minusvalía; *(disadvantage)* desventaja; *(SPORT)* handicap *m* ♦ *vt* estorbar; **mentally/physically ~ped** deficiente *m/f* (mental)/minusválido/a (físico/a)

handicraft ['hændɪkrɑːft] *n* artesanía; *(object)* objeto de artesanía

handiwork ['hændɪwɜːk] *n* obra

handkerchief ['hæŋkətʃɪf] *n* pañuelo

handle ['hændl] *n (of door etc)* tirador *m; (of cup etc)* asa; *(of knife etc)* mango; *(for winding)* manivela ♦ *vt (touch)* tocar; *(deal with)* encargarse de; *(treat: people)* manejar; **"~ with care"** "(manéjese) con cuidado"; **to fly off the ~** perder los estribos; **~bar(s)** *n(pl)* manillar *m*

hand: ~ luggage *n* equipaje *m* de

mano; **~made** adj hecho a mano; **~out** n (money etc) limosna; (leaflet) folleto; **~rail** n pasamanos m inv; **~shake** n apretón m de manos

handsome ['hænsəm] adj guapo; (building) bello; (fig: profit) considerable

handwriting ['hændraɪtɪŋ] n letra

handy ['hændɪ] adj (close at hand) a la mano; (tool etc) práctico; (skilful) hábil, diestro

hang [hæŋ] (pt, pp hung) vt colgar; (criminal: pt, pp hanged) ahorcar ♦ vi (painting, coat etc) colgar; (hair, drapery) caer; **to get the ~ of sth** (inf) lograr dominar algo; **~ about** or **around** vi haraganear; **~ on** vi esperar; **~ up** vi (TEL) colgar ♦ vt colgar

hanger ['hæŋə*] n percha; **~-on** n parásito

hang-: ~gliding ['-glaɪdɪŋ] n vuelo libre; **~over** n (after drinking) resaca; **~-up** n complejo

hanker ['hæŋkə*] vi: **to ~ after** añorar

hankie, hanky ['hæŋkɪ] n abbr = **handkerchief**

haphazard [hæp'hæzəd] adj fortuito

happen ['hæpən] vi suceder, ocurrir; (chance): **he ~ed to hear/see** dió la casualidad de que oyó/vió; **as it ~s** da la casualidad de que; **~ing** n suceso, acontecimiento

happily ['hæpɪlɪ] adv (luckily) afortunadamente; (cheerfully) alegremente

happiness ['hæpɪnɪs] n felicidad f; (cheerfulness) alegría

happy ['hæpɪ] adj feliz; (cheerful) alegre; **to be ~ (with)** estar contento (con); **to be ~ to do** estar encantado de hacer; **~ birthday!** ¡feliz cumpleaños!; **~-go-lucky** adj despreocupado; **~ hour** n horas en las que la bebida es más barata, happy hour f

harass ['hærəs] vt acosar, hostigar; **~ment** n persecución f

harbour ['hɑːbə*] (US **harbor**) n puerto ♦ vt (fugitive) dar abrigo a; (hope etc) abrigar

hard [hɑːd] adj duro; (difficult) difícil; (work) arduo; (person) severo; (fact) innegable ♦ adv (work) mucho, duro; (think) profundamente; **to look ~ at** clavar los ojos en; **to try ~** esforzarse; **no ~ feelings!** ¡sin rencor(es)!; **to be ~ of hearing** ser duro de oído; **to be ~ done by** ser tratado injustamente; **~back** n libro en cartoné; **~ cash** n dinero contante; **~ disk** n (COMPUT) disco duro or rígido; **~en** vt endurecer; (fig) curtir ♦ vi endurecerse; curtirse; **~-headed** adj realista; **~ labour** n trabajos mpl forzados

hardly ['hɑːdlɪ] adv apenas; **~ ever** casi nunca

hard-: ~ship n privación f; **~ shoulder** (BRIT) n (AUT) arcén m; **~-up** (inf) adj sin un duro (SP), sin plata (AM); **~ware** n ferretería; (COMPUT) hardware m; (MIL) armamento; **~ware shop** n ferretería; **~-wearing** adj resistente, duradero; **~-working** adj trabajador(a)

hardy ['hɑːdɪ] adj fuerte; (plant) resistente

hare [hɛə*] n liebre f; **~-brained** adj descabellado

harm [hɑːm] n daño, mal m ♦ vt (person) hacer daño a; (health, interests) perjudicar; (thing) dañar; **out of ~'s way** a salvo; **~ful** adj dañino; **~less** adj (person) inofensivo; (joke etc) inocente

harmony ['hɑːmənɪ] n armonía

harness ['hɑːnɪs] n arreos mpl; (for child) arnés m; (safety ~) arneses mpl ♦ vt (horse) enjaezar; (resources) aprovechar

harp [hɑːp] n arpa ♦ vi: **to ~ on (about)** machacar (con)

harrowing ['hærəʊɪŋ] adj angustioso

harsh [hɑːʃ] adj (cruel) duro, cruel; (severe) severo; (sound) áspero; (light) deslumbrador(a)

harvest ['hɑːvɪst] n (~ time) siega; (of cereals etc) cosecha; (of grapes) vendimia ♦ vt cosechar

has [hæz] vb see **have**

hash [hæʃ] n (CULIN) picadillo; (fig: mess) lío

hashish ['hæʃɪʃ] n hachís m

hasn't ['hæznt] = **has not**

hassle ['hæsl] (inf) n lata

haste [heɪst] n prisa; ~n ['heɪsn] vt acelerar ♦ vi darse prisa; **hastily** adv de prisa; precipitadamente; **hasty** adj apresurado; (rash) precipitado

hat [hæt] n sombrero

hatch [hætʃ] n (NAUT: also: ~way) escotilla; (also: service ~) ventanilla ♦ vi (bird) salir del cascarón ♦ vt incubar; (plot) tramar; **5 eggs have ~ed** han salido 5 pollos

hatchback ['hætʃbæk] n (AUT) tres or cinco puertas m

hatchet ['hætʃɪt] n hacha

hate [heɪt] vt odiar, aborrecer ♦ n odio; **~ful** adj odioso; **hatred** ['heɪtrɪd] n odio

haughty ['hɔːtɪ] adj altanero

haul [hɔːl] vt tirar ♦ n (of fish) redada; (of stolen goods etc) botín m; **~age** (BRIT) n transporte m; (costs) gastos mpl de transporte; **~ier** (US ~er) n transportista m/f

haunch [hɔːntʃ] n anca; (of meat) pierna

haunt [hɔːnt] vt (subj: ghost) aparecerse en; (obsess) obsesionar ♦ n guarida

---

KEYWORD

have [hæv] (pt, pp **had**) aux vb **1** (gen) haber; **to ~ arrived/eaten** haber llegado/comido; **having finished** or **when he had finished, he left** cuando hubo acabado, se fue **2** (in tag questions): **you've done it, ~n't you?** lo has hecho, ¿verdad? or ¿no?

3 (in short answers and questions): **I**

~**n't** no; **so I ~** pues, es verdad; **we ~n't paid — yes we ~!** no hemos pagado — ¡sí que hemos pagado!; **I've been there before, ~ you?** he estado allí antes, ¿y tú?

♦ modal aux vb (be obliged): **to ~ (got) to do sth** tener que hacer algo; **you ~n't to tell her** no hay que or no debes decírselo

♦ vt **1** (possess): **he has (got) blue eyes/dark hair** tiene los ojos azules/el pelo negro

2 (referring to meals etc): **to ~ breakfast/lunch/dinner** desayunar/comer/cenar; **to ~ a drink/a cigarette** tomar algo/fumar un cigarrillo

3 (receive) recibir; (obtain) obtener; **may I ~ your address?** ¿puedes darme tu dirección?; **you can ~ it for £5** te lo puedes quedar por £5; **I must ~ it by tomorrow** lo necesito para mañana; **to ~ a baby** tener un niño or bebé

4 (maintain, allow): **I won't ~ it/this nonsense!** ¡no lo permitiré!/¡no permitiré estas tonterías!; **we can't ~ that** no podemos permitir eso

5: **to ~ sth done** hacer or mandar hacer algo; **to ~ one's hair cut** cortarse el pelo; **to ~ sb do sth** hacer que alguien haga algo

6 (experience, suffer): **to ~ a cold/flu** tener un resfriado/la gripe; **she had her bag stolen/her arm broken** le robaron el bolso/se rompió un brazo; **to ~ an operation** operarse

7 (+ noun): **to ~ a swim/walk/bath/rest** nadar/dar un paseo/darse un baño/descansar; **let's ~ a look** vamos a ver; **to ~ a meeting/party** celebrar una reunión/una fiesta; **let me ~ a try** déjame intentarlo

have out vt: **to ~ it out with sb** (settle a problem etc) dejar las cosas en claro con alguien

haven ['heɪvn] n puerto; (fig) refugio

haven't ['hævnt] = **have not**

havoc ['hævək] n estragos mpl

hawk [hɔːk] n halcón m

hay [heɪ] n heno; ~ **fever** n fiebre f del heno; **~stack** n almiar m

haywire ['heɪwaɪə*] (inf) adj: **to go** ~ (plan) embrollarse

hazard ['hæzəd] n peligro ♦ vt aventurar; **~ous** adj peligroso; ~ **warning lights** npl (AUT) señales fpl de emergencia

haze [heɪz] n neblina

hazelnut ['heɪzlnʌt] n avellana

hazy ['heɪzɪ] adj brumoso; (idea) vago

he [hiː] pron él; ~ **who** ... el que ..., quien ...

head [hed] n cabeza; (leader) jefe/a m/f; (of school) director(a) m/f ♦ vt (list) encabezar; (group) capitanear; (company) dirigir; ~**s (or tails)** cara (o cruz); ~ **first** de cabeza; ~ **over heels** (in love) perdidamente; **to** ~ **the ball** cabecear (la pelota); ~ **for** vt fus dirigirse a; (disaster) ir camino de; **~ache** n dolor m de cabeza; **~dress** n tocado; **~ing** n título; **~lamp** (BRIT) n = **~light**; **~land** n promontorio; **~light** n faro; **~line** n titular m; **~long** adv (fall) de cabeza; (rush) precipitadamente; **~master/mistress** n director(a) m/f (de escuela); ~ **office** n oficina central, central f; **~-on** adj (collision) de frente; **~phones** npl auriculares mpl; **~quarters** npl sede f central; (MIL) cuartel m general; ~ **rest** n reposa-cabezas m inv; **~room** n (in car) altura interior; (under bridge) (límite m de) altura; **~scarf** n pañuelo; **~strong** adj testarudo; ~ **waiter** n maître m; ~ **way** n: **to make ~way** (fig) hacer progresos; **~wind** n viento contrario; **~y** adj (experience, period) apasionante; (wine) cabezón; (atmosphere) embriagador(a)

heal [hiːl] vt curar ♦ vi cicatrizarse

health [helθ] n salud f; ~ **food** n

alimentos mpl orgánicos; **the H~ Service** (BRIT) n el servicio de salud pública; ≈ el Insalud (SP); **~y** adj sano, saludable

heap [hiːp] n montón m ♦ vt: **to** ~ **(up)** amontonar; **to** ~ **sth with** llenar algo hasta arriba de; **~s of** un montón de

hear [hɪə*] (pt, pp **heard**) vt (also LAW) oír; (news) saber ♦ vi oír; **to** ~ **about** oír hablar de; **to** ~ **from sb** tener noticias de uno; **~ing** n (sense) oído; (LAW) vista; **~ing aid** n audífono; **~say** n rumores mpl, hablillas fpl

hearse [həːs] n coche m fúnebre

heart [hɑːt] n corazón m; (fig) valor m; (of lettuce) cogollo; **~s** npl (CARDS) corazones mpl; **to lose/take** ~ descorazonarse/cobrar ánimo; **at** ~ en el fondo; **by** ~ (learn, know) de memoria; **~ attack** n infarto (de miocardio); **~beat** n latido (del corazón); **~breaking** adj desgarrador(a); **~broken** adj: **she was ~broken about it** esto le partió el corazón; **~burn** n acedía; ~ **failure** n fallo cardíaco; **~felt** adj (deeply felt) más sentido

hearth [hɑːθ] n (fireplace) chimenea

hearty ['hɑːtɪ] adj (person) campechano; (laugh) sano; (dislike, support) absoluto

heat [hiːt] n calor m; (SPORT: also: qualifying ~) prueba eliminatoria ♦ vt calentar; ~ **up** vi calentarse ♦ vt calentar; **~ed** adj caliente; (fig) acalorado; **~er** n estufa; (in car) calefacción f

heath [hiːθ] (BRIT) n brezal m

heather ['heðə*] n brezo

heating ['hiːtɪŋ] n calefacción f

heatstroke ['hiːtstrəuk] n insolación f

heatwave ['hiːtweɪv] n ola de calor

heave [hiːv] vt (pull) tirar; (push) empujar con esfuerzo; (lift) levantar (con esfuerzo) ♦ vi (chest) palpitar; (retch) tener náuseas ♦ n tirón m;

empujón m; **to ~ a sigh** suspirar

heaven ['hɛvn] n cielo; (fig) una maravilla; **~ly** adj celestial; (fig) maravilloso

heavily ['hɛvɪlɪ] adv pesadamente; (drink, smoke) con exceso; (sleep, sigh) profundamente; (depend) mucho

heavy ['hɛvɪ] adj pesado; (work, blow) duro; (sea, rain, meal) fuerte; (drinker, smoker) grande; (responsibility) grave; (schedule) ocupado; (weather) bochornoso; **~ goods vehicle** n vehículo pesado; **~weight** n (SPORT) peso pesado

Hebrew ['hi:bru:] adj, n (LING) hebreo

heckle ['hɛkl] vt interrumpir

hectic ['hɛktɪk] adj agitado

he'd [hi:d] = he would; he had

hedge [hɛdʒ] n seto ♦ vi contestar con evasivas; **to ~ one's bets** (fig) cubrirse

hedgehog ['hɛdʒhɒg] n erizo

heed [hi:d] vt (also: take ~ of) (pay attention to) hacer caso de; **~less** adj: **to be ~less (of)** no hacer caso (de)

heel [hi:l] n talón m; (of shoe) tacón m ♦ vt (shoe) poner tacón a

hefty ['hɛftɪ] adj (person) fornido; (parcel, profit) gordo

heifer ['hɛfə*] n novilla, ternera

height [haɪt] n (of person) estatura; (of building) altura; (high ground) cerro; (altitude) altitud f; (fig: of season): **at the ~ of summer** en los días más calurosos del verano; (: of power etc) cúspide f; (: of stupidity etc) colmo; **~en** vt elevar; (fig) aumentar

heir [ɛə*] n heredero; **~ess** n heredera; **~loom** n reliquia de familia

held [hɛld] pt, pp of **hold**

helicopter ['hɛlɪkɒptə*] n helicóptero

hell [hɛl] n infierno; **~!** (inf) ¡demonios!

he'll [hi:l] = he will; he shall

hello [hə'ləu] excl ¡hola!; (to attract attention) ¡oiga!; (surprise) ¡caramba!

helm [hɛlm] n (NAUT) timón m

helmet ['hɛlmɪt] n casco

help [hɛlp] n ayuda; (cleaner etc)

criada, asistenta ♦ vt ayudar; **~!** ¡socorro!; **~ yourself** sírvete; **he can't ~ it** no es culpa suya; **~er** n ayudante m/f; **~ful** adj útil; (person) servicial; **~ing** n ración f; **~less** adj (incapable) incapaz; (defenceless) indefenso

hem [hɛm] n dobladillo ♦ vt poner o coser el dobladillo; **~ in** vt cercar

hemorrhage ['hɛmərɪdʒ] (US) n = **haemorrhage**

hemorrhoids ['hɛmərɔɪdz] (US) npl = **haemorrhoids**

hen [hɛn] n gallina; (female bird) hembra

hence [hɛns] adv (therefore) por lo tanto; **2 years ~** de aquí a 2 años; **~forth** adv de hoy en adelante

hepatitis [hɛpə'taɪtɪs] n hepatitis f

her [hə:*] pron (direct) la; (indirect) le; (stressed, after prep) ella ♦ adj su; see also **me**; **my**

herald ['hɛrəld] n heraldo ♦ vt anunciar; **~ry** n heráldica

herb [hə:b] n hierba

herd [hə:d] n rebaño

here [hɪə*] adv aquí; (at this point) en este punto; **~!** (present) ¡presente!; **~ is/are** aquí está/están; **~ she is** aquí está; **~after** adv en el futuro; **~by** adv (in letter) por la presente

heritage ['hɛrɪtɪdʒ] n patrimonio

hermit ['hə:mɪt] n ermitaño/a

hernia ['hə:nɪə] n hernia

hero ['hɪərəu] (pl **~es**) n héroe m; (in book, film) protagonista m

heroin ['hɛrəuɪn] n heroína

heroine ['hɛrəuɪn] n heroína; (in book, film) protagonista

heron ['hɛrən] n garza

herring ['hɛrɪŋ] n arenque m

hers [hə:z] pron (el) suyo/(la) suya etc; see also **mine[1]**

herself [hə:'sɛlf] pron (reflexive) se; (emphatic) ella misma; (after prep) sí (misma); see also **oneself**

he's [hi:z] = he is; he has

hesitant ['hezɪtənt] *adj* vacilante

hesitate ['hezɪteɪt] *vi* vacilar; (*in speech*) titubear; (*be unwilling*) resistirse a; **hesitation** [-'teɪʃən] *n* indecisión f; titubeo; dudas *fpl*

heterosexual [hetərəʊ'seksjuəl] *adj* heterosexual

heyday ['heɪdeɪ] *n*: **the ~ of** el apogeo de

HGV *n abbr* = **heavy goods vehicle**

hi [haɪ] *excl* ¡hola!; (*to attract attention*) ¡oiga!

hiatus [haɪ'eɪtəs] *n* vacío

hibernate ['haɪbəneɪt] *vi* invernar

hiccough ['hɪkʌp] = **hiccup**

hiccup ['hɪkʌp] *vi* hipar; **~s** *npl* hipo

hide [haɪd] (*pt* **hid**, *pp* **hidden**) *n* (*skin*) piel f ♦ *vt* esconder, ocultar ♦ *vi*: **to ~ (from sb)** esconderse or ocultarse (de uno); **~-and-seek** *n* escondite m

hideous ['hɪdɪəs] *adj* horrible

hiding ['haɪdɪŋ] *n* (*beating*) paliza; **to be in ~** (*concealed*) estar escondido

hierarchy ['haɪərɑːkɪ] *n* jerarquía

hi-fi ['haɪfaɪ] *n* estéreo, hifi *m* ♦ *adj* de alta fidelidad

high [haɪ] *adj* alto; (*speed, number*) grande; (*price*) elevado; (*wind*) fuerte; (*voice*) agudo ♦ *adv* alto, a gran altura; **it is 20 m ~** tiene 20 m de altura; **~ in the air** en las alturas; **~brow** *adj* intelectual; **~chair** *n* silla alta; **~er education** *n* educación f or enseñanza superior; **~-handed** *adj* despótico; **~-heeled** *adj* de tacón alto; **~ jump** *n* (*SPORT*) salto de altura; **the H~lands** *npl* las tierras altas de Escocia; **~light** *n* (*fig: of event*) punto culminante; (*in hair*) reflejo ♦ *vt* subrayar; **~ly** *adv* (*paid*) muy bien; (*critical, confidential*) sumamente; (*a lot*): **to speak/think ~ly of** hablar muy bien de/tener en mucho a; **~ly strung** *adj* hipertenso; **~ness** *n* altura; **Her** or **His H~ness** Su Alteza; **~-pitched** *adj* agudo; **~-rise block** *n* torre f de pisos; **~ school** *n* ≈ Instituto Nacional de Bachillerato (*SP*);

~ season (*BRIT*) *n* temporada alta; **~ street** (*BRIT*) *n* calle f mayor; **~way** *n* carretera; (*US*) carretera nacional; autopista; **H~way Code** (*BRIT*) *n* código de la circulación

hijack ['haɪdʒæk] *vt* secuestrar; **~er** *n* secuestrador(a) *m/f*

hike [haɪk] *vi* (*go walking*) ir de excursión (a pie) ♦ *n* caminata; **~r** *n* excursionista *m/f*; **hiking** *n* senderismo

hilarious [hɪ'lɛərɪəs] *adj* divertidísimo

hill [hɪl] *n* colina; (*high*) montaña; (*slope*) cuesta; **~side** *n* ladera; **~ walking** *n* senderismo de (montaña); **~y** *adj* montañoso

hilt [hɪlt] *n* (*of sword*) empuñadura; **to the ~** (*fig: support*) incondicionalmente

him [hɪm] *pron* (*direct*) le, lo; (*indirect*) le; (*stressed, after prep*) él; *see also* **me**; **~self** *pron* (*reflexive*) se; (*emphatic*) él mismo; (*after prep*) sí (mismo); *see also* **oneself**

hinder ['hɪndə*] *vt* estorbar, impedir; **hindrance** ['hɪndrəns] *n* estorbo

hindsight ['haɪndsaɪt] *n*: **with ~** en retrospectiva

Hindu ['hɪnduː] *n* hindú *m/f*

hinge [hɪndʒ] *n* bisagra, gozne *m* ♦ *vi* (*fig*): **to ~ on** depender de

hint [hɪnt] *n* indirecta; (*advice*) consejo; (*sign*) dejo ♦ *vt*: **to ~ that** insinuar que ♦ *vi*: **to ~ at** hacer alusión a

hip [hɪp] *n* cadera

hippopotamus [hɪpə'pɔtəməs] (*pl* **~es** or **hippopotami**) *n* hipopótamo

hire ['haɪə*] *vt* (*BRIT: car, equipment*) alquilar; (*worker*) contratar ♦ *n* alquiler *m*; **for ~** se alquila; (*taxi*) libre; **~(d) car** (*BRIT*) *n* coche m de alquiler; **~ purchase** (*BRIT*) *n* compra a plazos

his [hɪz] *pron* (el) suyo/(la) suya *etc* ♦ *adj* su; *see also* **mine**[1]; **my**

Hispanic [hɪs'pænɪk] *adj* hispánico

hiss [hɪs] *vi* silbar

historian [hɪ'stɔːrɪən] *n* historiador(a) *m/f*

historic(al) [hɪ'stɔrɪk(l)] *adj* histórico

history ['hɪstərɪ] n historia

hit [hɪt] (pt, pp **hit**) vt (strike) golpear, pegar; (reach: target) alcanzar; (collide with: car) chocar contra; (fig: affect) afectar ♦ n golpe m; (success) éxito; **to ~ it off with sb** llevarse bien con uno; **~-and-run driver** n conductor(a) que atropella y huye

hitch [hɪtʃ] vt (fasten) atar, amarrar; (also: ~ up) remangar ♦ n (difficulty) dificultad f; **to ~ a lift** hacer autostop

hitch-hike vi hacer autostop; **~hiking** n autostop m

hi-tech [haɪ'tek] adj de alta tecnología

hitherto ['hɪðə'tuː] adv hasta ahora

HIV n abbr (= human immunodeficiency virus) VIH m; **~-negative/positive** adj VIH negativo/positivo

hive [haɪv] n colmena

HMS abbr = **His (Her) Majesty's Ship**

hoard [hɔːd] n (treasure) tesoro; (stockpile) provisión f ♦ vt acumular; (goods in short supply) acaparar; **~ing** n (for posters) cartelera

hoarse [hɔːs] adj ronco

hoax [həʊks] n trampa

hob [hɔb] n quemador m

hobble ['hɔbl] vi cojear

hobby ['hɔbɪ] n pasatiempo, afición f

hobo ['həʊbəʊ] (US) n vagabundo

hockey ['hɔkɪ] n hockey m

hog [hɔg] n cerdo, puerco ♦ vt (fig) acaparar; **to go the whole ~** poner toda la carne en el asador

hoist [hɔɪst] n (crane) grúa ♦ vt levantar, alzar; (flag, sail) izar

hold [həʊld] (pt, pp **held**) vt sostener; (contain) contener; (have: power, qualification) tener; (keep back) retener; (believe) sostener; (consider) considerar; (keep in position): **to ~ one's head up** mantener la cabeza alta; (meeting) celebrar ♦ vi (withstand pressure) resistir; (be valid) valer ♦ n (grasp) asimiento; (fig) dominio; (on ship): **the ~ la bodega** ♦ vt (fig) defenderse; **to catch** or **get (a) ~ of** agarrarse or asirse de; **~ back** vt retener; (secret) ocultar; **~ down** vt (person) sujetar; (job) mantener; **~ off** vt (enemy) rechazar; **~ on** vi agarrarse bien; (wait) esperar; **~ on!** (TEL) ¡(espere) un momento!; **~ on to** vt fus agarrarse a; (keep) guardar; **~ out** vt ofrecer ♦ vi (resist) resistir; **~ up** vt (raise) levantar; (support) apoyar; (delay) retrasar; (rob) asaltar; **~all** (BRIT) n bolsa; **~er** n (container) receptáculo; (of ticket, record) poseedor(a) m/f; (of office, title etc) titular m/f; **~ing** n (share) interés m; (farmland) parcela; **~up** n (robbery) atraco; (delay) retraso; (BRIT: in traffic) embotellamiento

hole [həʊl] n agujero

holiday ['hɔlədɪ] n vacaciones fpl; (public ~) día m de fiesta, día m feriado; **on ~** de vacaciones; **~ camp** n (BRIT: also: **~ centre**) centro de vacaciones; **~-maker** (BRIT) n turista m/f; **~ resort** n centro turístico

holiness ['həʊlɪnɪs] n santidad f

Holland ['hɔlənd] n Holanda

hollow ['hɔləʊ] adj hueco; (claim) vacío; (eyes) hundido; (sound) sordo ♦ n hueco; (in ground) hoyo ♦ vt: **to ~ out** excavar

holly ['hɔlɪ] n acebo

holocaust ['hɔləkɔːst] n holocausto

holy ['həʊlɪ] adj santo, sagrado; (water) bendito

homage ['hɔmɪdʒ] n homenaje m

home [həʊm] n casa; (country) patria; (institution) asilo ♦ cpd (domestic) casero, de casa; (ECON, POL) nacional ♦ adv (direction) a casa; (right in: nail etc) a fondo; **at ~** en casa; (in country) en el país; (fig) como pez en el agua; **to go/come ~** ir/volver a casa; **make yourself at ~** ¡estás en tu casa!; **~ address** n domicilio; **~land** n tierra natal; **~less** adj sin hogar, sin casa; **~ly** adj (simple) sencillo; **~-made** adj casero; **H~ Office** (BRIT) n Ministerio

del Interior; **~ rule** n autonomía;
H~ Secretary (BRIT) n Ministro del
Interior; **~sick** adj: **to be ~sick** tener
morriña, sentir nostalgia; **~ town** n
ciudad f natal; **~ward** ['həumwəd] adj
(journey) hacia casa; **~work** n deberes
mpl

homoeopathic [həumɪə'pæθɪk] (US
homeopathic) adj homeopático

homosexual [hɔməu'seksjuəl] adj, n
homosexual m/f

Honduran [hɔn'djuərən] adj, n
hondureño/a m/f

Honduras [hɔn'djuərəs] n Honduras f

honest ['ɔnɪst] adj honrado; (sincere)
franco, sincero; **~ly** adv honradamente;
francamente; **~y** n honradez f

honey ['hʌnɪ] n miel f; **~comb** n
panal m; **~moon** n luna de miel;
~suckle n madreselva

honk [hɔŋk] vi (AUT) tocar el pito, pitar

honorary ['ɔnərərɪ] adj (member,
president) de honor; (title) honorífico;
~ degree n doctorado honoris causa

honour ['ɔnə*] (US **honor**) vt honrar;
(commitment, promise) cumplir con ♦ n
honor m, honra f; **~able** adj honorable;
~s degree n (SCOL) título de licenciado
con calificación alta

hood [hud] n capucha; (BRIT: AUT)
capota; (US: AUT) capó m; (of cooker)
campana de humos

hoof [hu:f] (pl **hooves**) n pezuña

hook [huk] n gancho; (on dress)
corchete m, broche m; (for fishing)
anzuelo ♦ vt enganchar; (fish) pescar

hooligan ['hu:lɪɡən] n gamberro

hoop [hu:p] n aro

hooray [hu:'reɪ] excl = **hurray**

hoot [hu:t] (BRIT) vi (AUT) tocar el pito,
pitar; (siren) sonar la sirena; (owl)
ulular; **~er** (BRIT) n (AUT) pito, claxon
m; (NAUT) sirena

Hoover ® ['hu:və*] (BRIT) n aspiradora
♦ vt: **h~** pasar la aspiradora por

hooves [hu:vz] npl of **hoof**

hop [hɔp] vi saltar, brincar; (on one

foot) saltar con un pie

hope [həup] vt, vi esperar ♦ n
esperanza; **I ~ so/not** espero que sí/
no; **~ful** adj (person) optimista;
(situation) prometedor(a); **~fully** adv
con esperanza; (one hopes): **~fully he
will recover** esperamos que se
recupere; **~less** adj desesperado;
(person): **to be ~less** ser un desastre

hops [hɔps] npl lúpulo

horizon [hə'raɪzn] n horizonte m; **~tal**
[hɔrɪ'zɔntl] adj horizontal

hormone ['hɔ:məun] n hormona

horn [hɔ:n] n cuerno; (MUS: also: French
~) trompa; (AUT) pito, claxon m

hornet ['hɔ:nɪt] n avispón m

horoscope ['hɔrəskəup] n horóscopo

horrible ['hɔrɪbl] adj horrible

horrid ['hɔrɪd] adj horrible, horroroso

horrify ['hɔrɪfaɪ] vt horrorizar

horror ['hɔrə*] n horror m; **~ film** n
película de horror

hors d'œuvre [ɔ:'də:vrə] n entremeses
mpl

horse [hɔ:s] n caballo; **~back** n: **on
~back** a caballo; **~ chestnut** n (tree)
castaño de Indias; (nut) castaña de
Indias; **~man/woman** (irreg) n
jinete/a m/f; **~power** n caballo (de
fuerza); **~-racing** n carreras fpl de
caballos; **~radish** n rábano picante;
~shoe n herradura

hose [həuz] n (also: ~**pipe**) manguera

hospitable ['hɔspɪtəbl] adj hospitalario

hospital ['hɔspɪtl] n hospital m

hospitality [hɔspɪ'tælɪtɪ] n
hospitalidad f

host [həust] n anfitrión m; (TV, RADIO)
presentador m; (REL) hostia; (large
number): **a ~ of** multitud de

hostage ['hɔstɪdʒ] n rehén m

hostel ['hɔstl] n hostal m; (youth) ~
albergue m juvenil

hostess ['həustɪs] n anfitriona; (BRIT:
air ~) azafata; (TV, RADIO) presentadora

hostile ['hɔstaɪl] adj hostil

hot [hɔt] adj caliente; (weather)

caluroso, de calor; (as opposed to warm) muy caliente; (spicy) picante; to be ~ (person) tener calor; (object) estar caliente; (weather) hacer calor; **~bed** n (fig) semillero; **~ dog** n perro caliente

hotel [hau'tɛl] n hotel m

hot: **~house** n invernadero; **~ line** n (POL) teléfono rojo; **~ly** adv con pasión, apasionadamente; **~water bottle** n bolsa de agua caliente

hound [haund] vt acosar ♦ n perro de (caza)

hour ['auə*] n hora; **~ly** adj (de) cada hora

house [n haus, pl 'hauziz, vb hauz] n (gen, firm) casa; (POL) cámara; (THEATRE) sala ♦ vt (person) alojar; (collection) albergar; **on the ~** (fig) la casa invita; **~ arrest** n arresto domiciliario; **~boat** n casa flotante; **~bound** adj confinado en casa; **~breaking** n allanamiento de morada; **~hold** n familia; (home) casa; **~keeper** n ama de llaves; **~keeping** n (work) trabajos mpl domésticos; **~keeping (money)** n dinero para gastos domésticos; **~warming party** n fiesta de estreno de una casa; **~wife** (irreg) n ama de casa; **~work** n faenas fpl (de la casa)

housing ['hauziŋ] n (act) alojamiento; (houses) viviendas fpl; **~ development** n urbanización f; **~ estate** (BRIT) n = **~ development**

hovel ['hɒvl] n casucha

hover ['hɒvə*] vi flotar (en el aire); **~craft** n aerodeslizador m

how [hau] adv (in what way) cómo; **~ are you?** ¿cómo estás?; **~ much milk/many people?** ¿cuánta leche/ gente?; **~ much does it cost?** ¿cuánto cuesta?; **~ long have you been here?** ¿cuánto tiempo hace que estás aquí?; **~ old are you?** ¿cuántos años tienes?; **~ tall is he?** ¿cómo es de alto?; **~ is school?** ¿cómo (te) va en la escuela?; **~ was the film?** ¿qué tal

la película?; **~ lovely/awful!** ¡qué bonito/horror!

however [hau'ɛvə*] adv: **~ I do it** lo haga como lo haga; **~ cold it is** por mucho frío que haga; **~ fast he runs** por muy rápido que corra; **~ did you do it?** ¿cómo lo hiciste? ♦ conj sin embargo, no obstante

howl [haul] n aullido ♦ vi aullar; (person) dar alaridos; (wind) ulular

H.P. n abbr = **hire purchase**

h.p. abbr = **horse power**

HQ n abbr = **headquarters**

hub [hʌb] n (of wheel) cubo; (fig) centro

hubcap ['hʌbkæp] n tapacubos m inv

huddle ['hʌdl] vi: **to ~ together** acurrucarse

hue [hju:] n color m, matiz m

huff [hʌf] n: **in a ~** enojado

hug [hʌg] vt abrazar; (thing) apretar con los brazos

huge [hju:dʒ] adj enorme

hull [hʌl] n (of ship) casco

hullo [hə'lau] excl = **hello**

hum [hʌm] vt tararear, canturrear ♦ vi tararear, canturrear; (insect) zumbar

human ['hju:mən] adj humano; **~e** [hju:'mein] adj humano, humanitario; **~itarian** [hju:mænɪ'tɛərɪən] adj humanitario; **~ity** [hju:'mænɪtɪ] n humanidad f

humble ['hʌmbl] adj humilde

humdrum ['hʌmdrʌm] adj (boring) monótono, aburrido

humid ['hju:mɪd] adj húmedo

humiliate [hju:'mɪlɪeɪt] vt humillar

humorous ['hju:mərəs] adj gracioso, divertido

humour ['hju:mə*] (US humor) n humorismo, sentido del humor; (mood) humor m ♦ vt (person) complacer

hump [hʌmp] n (in ground) montículo; (camel's) giba

hunch [hʌntʃ] n (premonition) presentimiento; **~back** n joroba m/f; **~ed** adj jorobado

hundred ['hʌndrəd] num ciento; (before n) cien; **~s of** centenares de; **~weight** n (BRIT) = 50.8 kg; 112 lb; (US) = 45.3 kg; 100 lb

hung [hʌŋ] pt, pp of **hang**

Hungarian [hʌŋ'geərɪən] adj, n húngaro/a m/f

Hungary ['hʌŋgərɪ] n Hungría

hunger ['hʌŋgə*] n hambre f ♦ vi: to ~ for (fig) tener hambre de, anhelar; ~ strike n huelga de hambre

hungry ['hʌŋgrɪ] adj: ~ (for) hambriento (de); **to be** ~ tener hambre

hunk [hʌŋk] n (of bread etc) trozo, pedazo

hunt [hʌnt] vt (seek) buscar; (SPORT) cazar ♦ vi (search): to ~ (for) buscar; (SPORT) cazar ♦ n búsqueda; caza, cacería; **~er** n cazador(a) m/f; **~ing** n caza

hurdle ['hə:dl] n (in SPORT) valla; (fig) obstáculo

hurl [hə:l] vt lanzar, arrojar

hurrah [hu'rɑ:] excl = **hurray**

hurray [hu'reɪ] excl ¡viva!

hurricane ['hʌrɪkən] n huracán m

hurried ['hʌrɪd] adj (rushed) hecho de prisa; **~ly** adv con prisa, apresuradamente

hurry ['hʌrɪ] n prisa ♦ vi (also: ~ up) apresurarse, darse prisa ♦ vt (also: ~ up: person) dar prisa a; (: work) apresurar, hacer de prisa; **to be in a** ~ tener prisa

hurt [hə:t] (pt, pp **hurt**) vt hacer daño a ♦ vi doler ♦ adj lastimado; **~ful** adj (remark etc) hiriente

hurtle ['hə:tl] vi: to ~ past pasar como un rayo; **to ~ down** ir a toda velocidad

husband ['hʌzbənd] n marido

hush [hʌʃ] n silencio ♦ vt hacer callar; **~!** ¡chitón!, ¡cállate!; **~ up** vt encubrir

husk [hʌsk] n (of wheat) cáscara

husky ['hʌskɪ] adj ronco ♦ n perro esquimal

hustle ['hʌsl] vt (hurry) dar prisa a ♦ n: ~ **and bustle** ajetreo

hut [hʌt] n cabaña; (shed) cobertizo

hutch [hʌtʃ] n conejera

hyacinth ['haɪəsɪnθ] n jacinto

hydrant ['haɪdrənt] n (also: fire ~) boca de incendios

hydraulic [haɪ'drɔ:lɪk] adj hidráulico

hydroelectric [haɪdrəu'lektrɪk] adj hidroeléctrico

hydrofoil ['haɪdrəfɔɪl] n aerodeslizador m

hydrogen ['haɪdrədʒən] n hidrógeno

hygiene ['haɪdʒi:n] n higiene f; **hygienic** [-'dʒi:nɪk] adj higiénico

hymn [hɪm] n himno

hype [haɪp] (inf) n bombardeo publicitario

hypermarket ['haɪpəmɑ:kɪt] n hipermercado

hyphen ['haɪfn] n guión m

hypnotize ['hɪpnətaɪz] vt hipnotizar

hypocrisy [hɪ'pɔkrɪsɪ] n hipocresía; **hypocrite** ['hɪpəkrɪt] n hipócrita m/f; **hypocritical** [hɪpə'krɪtɪkl] adj hipócrita

hypothesis [haɪ'pɔθɪsɪs] (pl **hypotheses**) n hipótesis f inv

hysteria [hɪ'stɪərɪə] n histeria; **hysterical** [-'sterɪkl] adj histérico; (funny) para morirse de risa; **hysterics** [-'sterɪks] npl histeria; **to be in hysterics** (fig) morirse de risa

I, i

I [aɪ] pron yo

ice [aɪs] n hielo; (~ cream) helado ♦ vt (cake) alcorzar ♦ vi (also: ~ over, ~ up) helarse; **~berg** n iceberg m; **~box** n (BRIT) congelador m; (US) nevera (SP), refrigeradora (AM); **~ cream** n helado; ~ **cube** n cubito de hielo; **~d** adj (cake) escarchado; (drink) helado; ~ **hockey** n hockey m sobre hielo

Iceland ['aɪslənd] n Islandia

ice: ~ **lolly** (BRIT) n polo; ~ **rink** n pista de hielo; ~ **skating** n patinaje m sobre hielo

icicle ['aɪsɪkl] n carámbano

icing ['aɪsɪŋ] n (CULIN) alcorza; ~ **sugar** (BRIT) n azúcar m glas(eado)

icy ['aɪsɪ] adj helado

I'd [aɪd] = **I would; I had**

idea [aɪ'dɪə] n idea

ideal [aɪ'dɪəl] n ideal m ♦ adj ideal

identical [aɪ'dentɪkl] adj idéntico

identification [aɪdentɪfɪ'keɪʃən] n identificación f; (means of) ~ documentos mpl personales

identify [aɪ'dentɪfaɪ] vt identificar

Identikit ® [aɪ'dentɪkɪt] n: ~ (picture) retrato-robot m

identity [aɪ'dentɪtɪ] n identidad f; ~ **card** n carnet m de identidad

ideology [aɪdɪ'ɔlədʒɪ] n ideología

idiom ['ɪdɪəm] n modismo; (style of speaking) lenguaje m

idiosyncrasy [ɪdɪəʊ'sɪŋkrəsɪ] n idiosincrasia

idiot ['ɪdɪət] n idiota m/f; ~**ic** [-'ɔtɪk] adj tonto

idle ['aɪdl] adj (inactive) ocioso; (lazy) holgazán/ana; (unemployed) parado, desocupado; (machinery etc) parado; (talk etc) frívolo ♦ vi (machine) marchar en vacío

idol ['aɪdl] n ídolo; ~**ize** vt idolatrar

i.e. abbr (= that is) esto es

if [ɪf] conj si; ~ **necessary** si fuera necesario, si hiciese falta; ~ **I were you** yo en tu lugar; ~ **so/not** de ser así/si no; ~ **only I could!** ¡ojalá pudiera!; see also **as; even**

igloo ['ɪgluː] n iglú m

ignite [ɪg'naɪt] vt (set fire to) encender ♦ vi encenderse

ignition [ɪg'nɪʃən] n (AUT: process) ignición f; (: mechanism) encendido; **to switch on/off the** ~ arrancar/apagar el motor; ~ **key** n (AUT) llave f de contacto

ignorant ['ɪgnərənt] adj ignorante; **to**

be ~ **of** ignorar

ignore [ɪg'nɔː*] vt (person, advice) no hacer caso de; (fact) pasar por alto

I'll [aɪl] = **I will; I shall**

ill [ɪl] adj enfermo, malo ♦ n mal m ♦ adv mal; **to be taken** ~ ponerse enfermo; ~**-advised** adj (decision) imprudente; ~**-at-ease** adj incómodo

illegal [ɪ'liːgl] adj ilegal

illegible [ɪ'ledʒɪbl] adj ilegible

illegitimate [ɪlɪ'dʒɪtɪmət] adj ilegítimo

ill-fated adj malogrado

ill feeling n rencor m

illicit [ɪ'lɪsɪt] adj ilícito

illiterate [ɪ'lɪtərət] adj analfabeto

ill: ~**-mannered** adj mal educado; ~**ness** n enfermedad f; ~**-treat** vt maltratar

illuminate [ɪ'luːmɪneɪt] vt (room, street) iluminar, alumbrar; **illumination** [-'neɪʃən] n alumbrado; **illuminations** npl (decorative lights) iluminaciones fpl, luces fpl

illusion [ɪ'luːʒən] n ilusión f; (trick) truco

illustrate ['ɪləstreɪt] vt ilustrar

illustration [ɪlə'streɪʃən] n (act of illustrating) ilustración f; (example) ejemplo, ilustración f; (in book) lámina

illustrious [ɪ'lʌstrɪəs] adj ilustre

I'm [aɪm] = **I am**

image ['ɪmɪdʒ] n imagen f; ~**ry** [-ərɪ] n imágenes fpl

imaginary [ɪ'mædʒɪnərɪ] adj imaginario

imagination [ɪmædʒɪ'neɪʃən] n imaginación f; (inventiveness) inventiva

imaginative [ɪ'mædʒɪnətɪv] adj imaginativo

imagine [ɪ'mædʒɪn] vt imaginarse

imbalance [ɪm'bæləns] n desequilibrio

imitate ['ɪmɪteɪt] vt imitar; **imitation** [ɪmɪ'teɪʃən] n imitación f; (copy) copia

immaculate [ɪ'mækjulət] adj inmaculado

immaterial [ɪmə'tɪərɪəl] adj (unimportant) sin importancia

immature [ɪmə'tjuə*] adj (person) inmaduro

immediate [ɪ'miːdɪət] adj inmediato; (pressing) urgente, apremiante; (nearest: family) próximo; (: neighbourhood) inmediato; **~ly** adv (at once) en seguida; (directly) inmediatamente; **~ly next to** muy junto a

immense [ɪ'mɛns] adj inmenso, enorme; (importance) enorme

immerse [ɪ'məːs] vt (submerge) sumergir; **to be ~d in** (fig) estar absorto en

immersion heater [ɪ'məːʃən-] (BRIT) n calentador m de inmersión

immigrant ['ɪmɪgrənt] n inmigrante m/f; **immigration** [ɪmɪ'greɪʃən] n inmigración f

imminent ['ɪmɪnənt] adj inminente

immobile [ɪ'məʊbaɪl] adj inmóvil

immoral [ɪ'mɔrl] adj inmoral

immortal [ɪ'mɔːtl] adj inmortal

immune [ɪ'mjuːn] adj: **~ (to)** inmune (a); **immunity** n (MED, of diplomat) inmunidad f

immunize ['ɪmjʊnaɪz] vt inmunizar

impact ['ɪmpækt] n impacto

impair [ɪm'pɛə*] vt perjudicar

impart [ɪm'pɑːt] vt comunicar; (flavour) proporcionar

impartial [ɪm'pɑːʃl] adj imparcial

impassable [ɪm'pɑːsəbl] adj (barrier) infranqueable; (river, road) intransitable

impassive [ɪm'pæsɪv] adj impasible

impatience [ɪm'peɪʃəns] n impaciencia

impatient [ɪm'peɪʃənt] adj impaciente; **to get** or **grow ~** impacientarse

impeccable [ɪm'pekəbl] adj impecable

impede [ɪm'piːd] vt estorbar

impediment [ɪm'pedɪmənt] n obstáculo, estorbo; (also: speech ~) defecto (del habla)

impending [ɪm'pendɪŋ] adj inminente

imperative [ɪm'perətɪv] adj (tone) imperioso; (need) imprescindible

imperfect [ɪm'pəːfɪkt] adj (goods etc) defectuoso ♦ n (LING: also: ~ tense) imperfecto

imperial [ɪm'pɪərɪəl] adj imperial

impersonal [ɪm'pəːsənl] adj impersonal

impersonate [ɪm'pəːsəneɪt] vt hacerse pasar por; (THEATRE) imitar

impertinent [ɪm'pəːtɪnənt] adj impertinente, insolente

impervious [ɪm'pəːvɪəs] adj impermeable; (fig): **~ to** insensible a

impetuous [ɪm'petjuəs] adj impetuoso

impetus ['ɪmpətəs] n ímpetu m; (fig) impulso

impinge [ɪm'pɪndʒ]: **to ~ on** vt fus (affect) afectar a

implement [n 'ɪmplɪmənt, vb 'ɪmplɪment] n herramienta; (for cooking) utensilio ♦ vt (regulation) hacer efectivo; (plan) realizar

implicit [ɪm'plɪsɪt] adj implícito; (belief, trust) absoluto

imply [ɪm'plaɪ] vt (involve) suponer; (hint) dar a entender que

impolite [ɪmpə'laɪt] adj mal educado

import [vb ɪm'pɔːt, n 'ɪmpɔːt] vt importar ♦ n (COMM) importación f; (: article) producto importado; (meaning) significado, sentido

importance [ɪm'pɔːtəns] n importancia

important [ɪm'pɔːtənt] adj importante; **it's not ~** no importa, no tiene importancia

importer [ɪm'pɔːtə*] n importador(a) m/f

impose [ɪm'pəʊz] vt imponer ♦ vi: **to ~ on sb** abusar de uno; **imposing** adj imponente, impresionante

imposition [ɪmpə'zɪʃn] n (of tax etc) imposición f; **to be an ~ on** (person) molestar a

impossible [ɪm'pɔsɪbl] adj imposible; (person) insoportable

impotent ['ɪmpətənt] adj impotente

impound [ɪm'paund] vt embargar

impoverished [ɪm'pɔvərɪʃt] adj

necesitado

impractical [ɪm'præktɪkl] adj (person, plan) poco práctico

imprecise [ɪmprɪ'saɪs] adj impreciso

impregnable [ɪm'prɛgnəbl] adj (castle) inexpugnable

impress [ɪm'prɛs] vt impresionar; (mark) estampar; **to ~ sth on sb** hacer entender algo a uno

impression [ɪm'prɛʃən] n impresión f; (imitation) imitación f; **to be under the ~ that** tener la impresión de que; **~ist** n impresionista m/f

impressive [ɪm'prɛsɪv] adj impresionante

imprint ['ɪmprɪnt] n (outline) huella; (PUBLISHING) pie m de imprenta

imprison [ɪm'prɪzn] vt encarcelar; **~ment** n encarcelamiento; (term of ~ment) cárcel f

improbable [ɪm'prɔbəbl] adj improbable, inverosímil

improper [ɪm'prɔpə*] adj (unsuitable: conduct etc) incorrecto; (: activities) deshonesto

improve [ɪm'pru:v] vt mejorar; (foreign language) perfeccionar ♦ vi mejorarse; **~ment** n mejoramiento; perfección f; progreso

improvise ['ɪmprəvaɪz] vt, vi improvisar

impulse ['ɪmpʌls] n impulso; **to act on ~** obrar sin reflexión; **impulsive** [-'pʌlsɪv] adj irreflexivo

impure [ɪm'pjuə*] adj (adulterated) adulterado; (morally) impuro; **impurity** n impureza

---

KEYWORD

in [ɪn] prep **1** (indicating place, position, with place names) en; **the house/garden** en (la) casa/el jardín; **~ here/there** aquí/ahí or allí dentro; **~ London/England** en Londres/Inglaterra

2 (indicating time) en; **~ spring** en (la) primavera; **~ the afternoon** por la tarde; **at 4 o'clock ~ the afternoon** a las 4 de la tarde; **I did it ~ 3 hours/days** lo hice en 3 horas/días; **I'll see you ~ 2 weeks** or **2 weeks' time** te veré dentro de 2 semanas

3 (indicating manner etc) en; **~ a loud/soft voice** en voz alta/baja; **~ pencil/ink** a lápiz/bolígrafo; **the boy ~ the blue shirt** el chico de la camisa azul

4 (indicating circumstances): **~ the sun/shade/rain** al sol/a la sombra/bajo la lluvia; **a change ~ policy** un cambio de política

5 (indicating mood, state): **~ tears** en lágrimas, llorando; **~ anger/despair** enfadado/desesperado; **to live ~ luxury** vivir lujosamente

6 (with ratios, numbers): **1 ~ 10 households, 1 household ~ 10** una de cada 10 familias; **20 pence ~ the pound** 20 peniques por libra; **they lined up ~ twos** se alinearon de dos en dos

7 (referring to people, works) en; entre; **the disease is common ~ children** la enfermedad es común entre los niños; **~ (the works of) Dickens** en (las obras de) Dickens

8 (indicating profession etc): **to be ~ teaching** estar en la enseñanza

9 (after superlative) de; **the best pupil ~ the class** el/la mejor alumno/a de la clase

10 (with present participle): **~ saying this** al decir esto

♦ adv: **to be ~** (person: at home) estar en casa; (work) estar; (train, ship, plane) haber llegado; (in fashion) estar de moda; **she'll be ~ later** today llegará más tarde hoy; **to ask sb ~** hacer pasar a uno; **to run/limp etc ~** entrar corriendo/cojeando etc

♦ n: **the ~s and outs** (of proposal, situation etc) los detalles

in. abbr = **inch**

inability [ɪnə'bɪlɪtɪ] n: ~ **(to do)** incapacidad f (de hacer)

inaccurate [ɪn'ækjʊrət] adj inexacto, incorrecto

inadequate [ɪn'ædɪkwət] adj (income, reply etc) insuficiente; (person) incapaz

inadvertently [ɪnəd'vɜːtntlɪ] adv por descuido

inadvisable [ɪnəd'vaɪzəbl] adj poco aconsejable

inane [ɪ'neɪn] adj necio, fatuo

inanimate [ɪn'ænɪmət] adj inanimado

inappropriate [ɪnə'prəʊprɪət] adj inadecuado; (improper) poco oportuno

inarticulate [ɪnɑː'tɪkjʊlət] adj (person) incapaz de expresarse; (speech) mal pronunciado

inasmuch as [ɪnəz'mʌtʃ-] conj puesto que, ya que

inauguration [ɪnɔːgjʊ'reɪʃən] n ceremonia de apertura

inborn [ɪn'bɔːn] adj (quality) innato

inbred [ɪn'bred] adj innato; (family) engendrado por endogamia

Inc. abbr (US: = incorporated) S.A.

incapable [ɪn'keɪpəbl] adj incapaz

incapacitate [ɪnkə'pæsɪtət] vt: **to ~ sb** incapacitar a uno

incense [n 'ɪnsens, vb ɪn'sens] n incienso ♦ vt (anger) indignar, encolerizar

incentive [ɪn'sentɪv] n incentivo, estímulo

incessant [ɪn'sesnt] adj incesante, continuo; **~ly** adv constantemente

incest ['ɪnsest] n incesto

inch [ɪntʃ] n pulgada; **to be within an ~ of** estar a dos dedos de; **he didn't give an ~** no dio concesión alguna

incident ['ɪnsɪdnt] n incidente m

incidental [ɪnsɪ'dentl] adj accesorio; **~ to** relacionado con; **~ly** [-'dentlɪ] adv (by the way) a propósito

incite [ɪn'saɪt] vt provocar

inclination [ɪnklɪ'neɪʃən] n (tendency)

tendencia, inclinación f; (desire) deseo; (disposition) propensión f

incline [n 'ɪnklaɪn, vb ɪn'klaɪn] n pendiente m, cuesta ♦ vt (head) poner de lado ♦ vi inclinarse; **to be ~d to** (tend) ser propenso a

include [ɪn'kluːd] vt (incorporate) incluir; (in letter) adjuntar; **including** prep incluso, inclusive

inclusion [ɪn'kluːʒən] n inclusión f

inclusive [ɪn'kluːsɪv] adj inclusivo; **~ of tax** incluidos los impuestos

income ['ɪŋkʌm] n (earned) ingresos mpl; (from property etc) renta; (from investment etc) rédito; **~ tax** n impuesto sobre la renta

incoming ['ɪnkʌmɪŋ] adj (flight, government etc) entrante

incomparable [ɪn'kɒmpərəbl] adj incomparable, sin par

incompatible [ɪnkəm'pætɪbl] adj incompatible

incompetent [ɪn'kɒmpɪtənt] adj incompetente

incomplete [ɪnkəm'pliːt] adj (partial: achievement etc) incompleto; (unfinished: painting etc) inacabado

incongruous [ɪn'kɒŋgruəs] adj (strange) discordante; (inappropriate) incongruente

inconsiderate [ɪnkən'sɪdərət] adj desconsiderado

inconsistent [ɪnkən'sɪstənt] adj inconsecuente; (contradictory) incongruente; **~ with** (que) no concuerda con

inconspicuous [ɪnkən'spɪkjuəs] adj (colour, building etc) discreto; (person) que llama poco la atención

inconvenience [ɪnkən'viːnjəns] n inconvenientes mpl; (trouble) molestia, incomodidad f ♦ vt incomodar

inconvenient [ɪnkən'viːnjənt] adj incómodo, poco práctico; (time, place, visitor) inoportuno

incorporate [ɪn'kɔːpəreɪt] vt incorporar; (contain) comprender;

(add) agregar; **~d** adj: **~d company** (US) ≈ sociedad f anónima

incorrect [ɪnkəˈrɛkt] adj incorrecto

increase [n ˈɪnkriːs, vb ɪnˈkriːs] n aumento ♦ vi aumentar; (grow) crecer; (price) subir ♦ vt aumentar; (price) subir; **increasing** adj creciente; **increasingly** adv cada vez más, más y más

incredible [ɪnˈkrɛdɪbl] adj increíble

incubator [ˈɪnkjubeɪtə*] n incubadora

incumbent [ɪnˈkʌmbənt] adj: **it is ~ on him to ...** le incumbe ...

incur [ɪnˈkəː*] vt (expenditure) incurrir; (loss) sufrir; (anger, disapproval) provocar

indebted [ɪnˈdɛtɪd] adj: **to be ~ to sb** estar agradecido a uno

indecent [ɪnˈdiːsnt] adj indecente; **~ assault** (BRIT) n atentado contra el pudor; **~ exposure** n exhibicionismo

indecisive [ɪndɪˈsaɪsɪv] adj indeciso

indeed [ɪnˈdiːd] adv efectivamente, en realidad; (in fact) en efecto; (furthermore) es más; **yes ~!** ¡claro que sí!

indefinitely [ɪnˈdɛfɪnɪtlɪ] adv (wait) indefinidamente

indemnity [ɪnˈdɛmnɪtɪ] n (insurance) indemnidad f; (compensation) indemnización f

independence [ɪndɪˈpɛndns] n independencia

Independence Day

El cuatro de julio es **Independence Day**, *la fiesta nacional de Estados Unidos, que se celebra en conmemoración de la Declaración de Independencia, escrita por Thomas Jefferson y aprobada en 1776. En ella se proclamaba la independencia total de Gran Bretaña de las trece colonias americanas que serían el origen de los Estados Unidos de América.*

independent [ɪndɪˈpɛndənt] adj independiente

index [ˈɪndɛks] (pl **~es**) n (in book) índice m; (: in library etc) catálogo; (pl **indices**: ratio, sign) exponente m; **~ card** n ficha; **~ed** (US) adj = **~-linked**; **~ finger** n índice m; **~-linked** (BRIT) adj vinculado al índice del coste de la vida

India [ˈɪndɪə] n la India; **~n** adj, n indio/a m/f; **Red ~n** piel roja m/f; **~n Ocean** n: **the ~n Ocean** el Océano Índico

indicate [ˈɪndɪkeɪt] vt indicar; **indication** [-ˈkeɪʃən] n indicio, señal f; **indicative** [ɪnˈdɪkətɪv] adj: **to be indicative of** indicar; **indicator** n indicador m; (AUT) intermitente m

indices [ˈɪndɪsiːz] npl of **index**

indictment [ɪnˈdaɪtmənt] n acusación f

indifferent [ɪnˈdɪfrənt] adj indiferente; (mediocre) regular

indigenous [ɪnˈdɪdʒɪnəs] adj indígena

indigestion [ɪndɪˈdʒɛstʃən] n indigestión f

indignant [ɪnˈdɪgnənt] adj: **to be ~ at sth/with sb** indignarse por algo/con uno

indigo [ˈɪndɪgəu] adj de color añil ♦ n añil m

indirect [ɪndɪˈrɛkt] adj indirecto

indiscreet [ɪndɪˈskriːt] adj indiscreto, imprudente

indiscriminate [ɪndɪˈskrɪmɪnət] adj indiscriminado

indisputable [ɪndɪˈspjuːtəbl] adj incontestable

indistinct [ɪndɪˈstɪŋkt] adj (noise, memory etc) confuso

individual [ɪndɪˈvɪdjuəl] n individuo ♦ adj individual; (personal) personal; (particular) particular; **~ly** adv (singly) individualmente

indoctrinate [ɪnˈdɔktrɪneɪt] vt adoctrinar

indoor [ˈɪndɔː*] adj (swimming pool) cubierto; (plant) de interior; (sport)

bajo cubierta; **~s** [ɪn'dɔːz] adv dentro
induce [ɪn'djuːs] vt inducir, persuadir;
(bring about) producir; (birth) provocar;
~ment n (incentive) incentivo; (pej:
bribe) soborno
indulge [ɪn'dʌldʒ] vt (whim) satisfacer;
(person) complacer; (child) mimar ♦ vi:
to ~ in darse el gusto de; **~nce** n
vicio; (leniency) indulgencia; **~nt** adj
indulgente
industrial [ɪn'dʌstrɪəl] adj industrial;
~ action n huelga; **~ estate** (BRIT) n
polígono (SP) or zona (AM) industrial;
~ist n industrial m/f; **~ize** vt
industrializar; **~ park** (US) n =
~ estate
industrious [ɪn'dʌstrɪəs] adj
trabajador(a); (student) aplicado
industry ['ɪndəstrɪ] n industria;
(diligence) aplicación f
inebriated [ɪ'niːbrɪeɪtɪd] adj borracho
inedible [ɪn'edɪbl] adj incomible;
(poisonous) no comestible
ineffective [ɪnɪ'fektɪv] adj ineficaz,
inútil
ineffectual [ɪnɪ'fektjʊəl] adj =
ineffective
inefficient [ɪnɪ'fɪʃənt] adj ineficaz,
ineficiente
inept [ɪ'nept] adj incompetente
inequality [ɪnɪ'kwɔlɪtɪ] n desigualdad f
inert [ɪ'nɜːt] adj inerte, inactivo;
(immobile) inmóvil
inescapable [ɪnɪ'skeɪpəbl] adj
ineludible
inevitable [ɪn'evɪtəbl] adj inevitable;
inevitably adv inevitablemente
inexcusable [ɪnɪks'kjuːzəbl] adj
imperdonable
inexpensive [ɪnɪk'spensɪv] adj
económico
inexperienced [ɪnɪk'spɪərɪənst] adj
inexperto
infallible [ɪn'fælɪbl] adj infalible
infamous ['ɪnfəməs] adj infame
infancy ['ɪnfənsɪ] n infancia
infant ['ɪnfənt] n niño/a; (baby) niño

pequeño, bebé m; (pej) aniñado
infantry ['ɪnfəntrɪ] n infantería
infant school (BRIT) n parvulario
infatuated [ɪn'fætjʊeɪtɪd] adj: **~ with**
(in love) loco por
infatuation [ɪnfætjʊ'eɪʃən] n
enamoramiento, pasión f
infect [ɪn'fekt] vt (wound) infectar;
(food) contaminar; (person, animal)
contagiar; **~ion** [ɪn'fekʃən] n infección
f; (fig) contagio; **~ious** [ɪn'fekʃəs] adj
(also fig) contagioso
infer [ɪn'fɜː*] vt deducir, inferir
inferior [ɪn'fɪərɪə*] adj, n inferior m/f;
~ity [-rɪ'ɔrɪtɪ] n inferioridad f
infertile [ɪn'fɜːtaɪl] adj estéril; (person)
infecundo
infested [ɪn'festɪd] adj: **~ with**
plagado de
in-fighting n (fig) lucha(s) f(pl)
interna(s)
infinite ['ɪnfɪnɪt] adj infinito
infinitive [ɪn'fɪnɪtɪv] n infinitivo
infinity [ɪn'fɪnɪtɪ] n infinito; (an ~)
infinidad f
infirmary [ɪn'fɜːmərɪ] n hospital m
inflamed [ɪn'fleɪmd] adj: **to become**
~ inflamarse
inflammable [ɪn'flæməbl] adj
inflamable
inflammation [ɪnflə'meɪʃən] n
inflamación f
inflatable [ɪn'fleɪtəbl] adj (ball, boat)
inflable
inflate [ɪn'fleɪt] vt (tyre, price etc) inflar;
(fig) hinchar; **inflation** [ɪn'fleɪʃən] n
(ECON) inflación f
inflexible [ɪn'fleksəbl] adj (rule) rígido;
(person) inflexible
inflict [ɪn'flɪkt] vt: **to ~ sth on sb**
infligir algo en uno
influence ['ɪnfluəns] n influencia ♦ vt
influir en, influenciar; **under the ~ of**
alcohol en estado de embriaguez;
influential [-'enʃl] adj influyente
influenza [ɪnflu'enzə] n gripe f
influx ['ɪnflʌks] n afluencia

inform [ɪnˈfɔːm] vt: **to ~ sb of sth** informar a uno sobre or de algo ♦ vi: **to ~ on sb** delatar a uno

informal [ɪnˈfɔːməl] adj (manner, tone) familiar; (dress, interview, occasion) informal; (visit, meeting) extraoficial; **~ity** [-ˈmælɪtɪ] n informalidad f; sencillez f

informant [ɪnˈfɔːmənt] n informante m/f

information [ɪnfəˈmeɪʃən] n información f; (knowledge) conocimientos mpl; **a piece of ~** un dato; **~ desk** n (mostrador m de) información f; **~ office** n información f

informative [ɪnˈfɔːmətɪv] adj informativo

informer [ɪnˈfɔːmə*] n (also: police ~) soplón/ona m/f

infra-red [ɪnfrəˈred] adj infrarrojo

infrastructure [ˈɪnfrəstrʌktʃə*] n (of system etc) infraestructura

infringe [ɪnˈfrɪndʒ] vt infringir, violar ♦ vi: **to ~ on** abusar de; **~ment** n infracción f; (of rights) usurpación f

infuriating [ɪnˈfjuərɪeɪtɪŋ] adj (habit, noise) enloquecedor(a)

ingenious [ɪnˈdʒiːnjəs] adj ingenioso; **ingenuity** [-dʒɪˈnjuːɪtɪ] n ingeniosidad f

ingenuous [ɪnˈdʒenjuəs] adj ingenuo

ingot [ˈɪŋɡət] n lingote m, barra

ingrained [ɪnˈɡreɪnd] adj arraigado

ingratiate [ɪnˈɡreɪʃɪeɪt] vt: **to ~ o.s. with** congraciarse con

ingredient [ɪnˈɡriːdɪənt] n ingrediente m

inhabit [ɪnˈhæbɪt] vt vivir en; **~ant** n habitante m/f

inhale [ɪnˈheɪl] vt inhalar ♦ vi (breathe in) aspirar; (in smoking) tragar

inherent [ɪnˈhɪərənt] adj: **~ in** or **to** inherente a

inherit [ɪnˈherɪt] vt heredar; **~ance** n herencia; (fig) patrimonio

inhibit [ɪnˈhɪbɪt] vt inhibir, impedir; **~ed** adj (PSYCH) cohibido; **~ion**

[-ˈbɪʃən] n cohibición f

inhospitable [ɪnhɒsˈpɪtəbl] adj (person) inhospitalario; (place) inhóspito

inhuman [ɪnˈhjuːmən] adj inhumano

initial [ɪˈnɪʃl] adj primero ♦ n inicial f ♦ vt firmar con las iniciales; **~s** npl (as signature) iniciales fpl; (abbreviation) siglas fpl; **~ly** adv al principio

initiate [ɪˈnɪʃɪeɪt] vt iniciar; **to ~ proceedings against sb** (LAW) entablar proceso contra uno

initiative [ɪˈnɪʃətɪv] n iniciativa

inject [ɪnˈdʒekt] vt inyectar; **to ~ sb with sth** inyectar algo a uno; **~ion** [ɪnˈdʒekʃən] n inyección f

injunction [ɪnˈdʒʌŋkʃən] n interdicto

injure [ˈɪndʒə*] vt (hurt) herir, lastimar; (fig: reputation etc) perjudicar; **~d** adj (person, arm) herido, lastimado; **injury** n herida, lesión f; (wrong) perjuicio, daño; **injury time** n (SPORT) (tiempo de) descuento

injustice [ɪnˈdʒʌstɪs] n injusticia

ink [ɪŋk] n tinta

inkling [ˈɪŋklɪŋ] n sospecha; (idea) idea

inlaid [ˈɪnleɪd] adj (with wood, gems etc) incrustado

inland [adj ˈɪnlənd, adv ɪnˈlænd] adj (waterway, port etc) interior ♦ adv tierra adentro; **I~ Revenue** (BRIT) n departamento de impuestos; ≈ Hacienda (SP)

in-laws npl suegros mpl

inlet [ˈɪnlet] n (GEO) ensenada, cala; (TECH) admisión f, entrada

inmate [ˈɪnmeɪt] n (in prison) preso/a; presidiario/a; (in asylum) internado/a

inn [ɪn] n posada, mesón m

innate [ɪˈneɪt] adj innato

inner [ˈɪnə*] adj (courtyard, calm) interior; (feelings) íntimo; **~ city** n barrios deprimidos del centro de una ciudad; **~ tube** n (of tyre) cámara (SP), llanta (AM)

innings [ˈɪnɪŋz] n (CRICKET) entrada, turno

innocent ['ɪnəsnt] adj inocente
innocuous [ɪ'nɔkjuəs] adj inocuo
innovation [ɪnəu'veɪʃən] n novedad f
innuendo [ɪnju'endəu] (pl **-es**) n indirecta
inoculation [ɪnɔkju'leɪʃən] n inoculación f
in-patient n paciente m/f interno/a
input ['ɪnput] n entrada; (of resources) inversión f; (COMPUT) entrada de datos
inquest ['ɪnkwest] n (coroner's) encuesta judicial
inquire [ɪn'kwaɪə*] vi preguntar ♦ vt: **to ~ whether** preguntar si; **to ~ about** (person) preguntar por; (fact) informarse de; **~ into** vt fus investigar, indagar; **inquiry** n pregunta; (investigation) investigación f, pesquisa; **"Inquiries"** "Información"; **inquiry office** (BRIT) n oficina de información
inquisitive [ɪn'kwɪzɪtɪv] adj (curious) curioso
ins. abbr = **inches**
insane [ɪn'seɪn] adj loco; (MED) demente
insanity [ɪn'sænɪtɪ] n demencia, locura
inscription [ɪn'skrɪpʃən] n inscripción f; (in book) dedicatoria
inscrutable [ɪn'skruːtəbl] adj inescrutable, insondable
insect ['ɪnsekt] n insecto; **~icide** [ɪn'sektɪsaɪd] n insecticida m; **~ repellent** n loción f contra insectos
insecure [ɪnsɪ'kjuə*] adj inseguro
insemination [ɪnsemɪ'neɪʃn] n: **artificial ~** inseminación f artificial
insensitive [ɪn'sensɪtɪv] adj insensible
insert [vb ɪn'sɜːt, n 'ɪnsɜːt] vt (into sth) introducir ♦ n encarte m; **~ion** [ɪn'sɜːʃən] n inserción f
in-service [ɪnsə:'viːs] adj (training, course) a cargo de la empresa
inshore [ɪn'ʃɔː*] adj de bajura ♦ adv (be) cerca de la orilla; (move) hacia la orilla
inside ['ɪn'saɪd] n interior m ♦ adj interior, interno ♦ adv (be) (por)

dentro; (go) hacia dentro ♦ prep dentro de; (of time): **~ 10 minutes** en menos de 10 minutos; **~s** npl (inf: stomach) tripas fpl; **~ information** n información f confidencial; **~ lane** n (AUT: in Britain) carril m izquierdo; (: in US, Europe etc) carril m derecho; **~ out** adv (turn) al revés; (know) a fondo
insider dealing, insider trading n (STOCK EXCHANGE) abuso de información privilegiada
insight ['ɪnsaɪt] n perspicacia
insignificant [ɪnsɪg'nɪfɪknt] adj insignificante
insincere [ɪnsɪn'sɪə*] adj poco sincero
insinuate [ɪn'sɪnjueɪt] vt insinuar
insipid [ɪn'sɪpɪd] adj soso, insulso
insist [ɪn'sɪst] vi insistir; **to ~ on** insistir en; **to ~ that** insistir en que; (claim) exigir que; **~ent** adj insistente; (noise, action) persistente
insole ['ɪnsəul] n plantilla
insolent ['ɪnsələnt] adj insolente, descarado
insomnia [ɪn'sɔmnɪə] n insomnio
inspect [ɪn'spekt] vt inspeccionar, examinar; (troops) pasar revista a; **~ion** [ɪn'spekʃən] n inspección f, examen m; (of troops) revista; **~or** n inspector(a) m/f; (BRIT: on buses, trains) revisor(a) m/f
inspiration [ɪnspə'reɪʃən] n inspiración f; **inspire** [ɪn'spaɪə*] vt inspirar
instability [ɪnstə'bɪlɪtɪ] n inestabilidad f
install [ɪn'stɔːl] vt instalar; (official) nombrar; **~ation** [ɪnstə'leɪʃən] n instalación f
instalment [ɪn'stɔːlmənt] (US **installment**) n plazo; (of story) entrega; (of TV serial etc) capítulo; **in ~s** (pay, receive) a plazos
instance ['ɪnstəns] n ejemplo, caso; **for ~** por ejemplo; **in the first ~** en primer lugar
instant ['ɪnstənt] n instante m, momento ♦ adj inmediato; (coffee etc)

instantáneo; **~ly** adv en seguida

instead [ɪnˈsted] adv en cambio; **~ of** en lugar de, en vez de

instep [ˈɪnstep] n empeine m

instil [ɪnˈstɪl] vt: **to ~ sth into** inculcar algo a

instinct [ˈɪnstɪŋkt] n instinto

institute [ˈɪnstɪtjuːt] n instituto; (professional body) colegio ♦ vt (begin) iniciar, empezar; (proceedings) entablar; (system, rule) establecer

institution [ɪnstɪˈtjuːʃən] n institución f; (MED: home) asilo; (: asylum) manicomio; (of system etc) establecimiento; (of custom) iniciación f

instruct [ɪnˈstrʌkt] vt: **to ~ sb in** instruir a uno en or sobre algo; **to ~ sb to do sth** dar instrucciones a uno de hacer algo; **~ion** [ɪnˈstrʌkʃən] n (teaching) instrucción f; **~ions** npl (orders) órdenes fpl; **~ions (for use)** modo de empleo; **~or** n instructor(a) m/f

instrument [ˈɪnstrəmənt] n instrumento; **~al** [-ˈmentl] adj (MUS) instrumental; **to be ~al in** ser (el) artífice de; **~ panel** n tablero (de instrumentos)

insufficient [ɪnsəˈfɪʃənt] adj insuficiente

insular [ˈɪnsjulə] adj insular; (person) estrecho de miras

insulate [ˈɪnsjuleɪt] vt aislar; **insulation** [-ˈleɪʃən] n aislamiento

insulin [ˈɪnsjulɪn] n insulina

insult [n ˈɪnsʌlt, vb ɪnˈsʌlt] n insulto ♦ vt insultar; **~ing** adj insultante

insurance [ɪnˈʃuərəns] n seguro; **fire/ life ~** seguro contra incendios/sobre la vida; **~ agent** n agente m/f de seguros; **~ policy** n póliza (de seguros)

insure [ɪnˈʃuə] vt asegurar

intact [ɪnˈtækt] adj íntegro, intacto; (unharmed) ileso

intake [ˈɪnteɪk] n (of food) ingestión f; (of air) consumo; (BRIT: SCOL): **an ~ of 200 a year** 200 matriculados al año

integral [ˈɪntɪgrəl] adj (whole) íntegro; (part) integrante

integrate [ˈɪntɪgreɪt] vt integrar ♦ vi integrarse

integrity [ɪnˈtegrɪtɪ] n honradez f, rectitud f

intellect [ˈɪntəlekt] n intelecto; **~ual** [-ˈlektjuəl] adj, n intelectual m/f

intelligence [ɪnˈtelɪdʒəns] n inteligencia

intelligent [ɪnˈtelɪdʒənt] adj inteligente

intelligible [ɪnˈtelɪdʒɪbl] adj inteligible, comprensible

intend [ɪnˈtend] vt (gift etc): **to ~ sth for** destinar algo a; **to ~ to do sth** tener intención de or pensar hacer algo

intense [ɪnˈtens] adj intenso; **~ly** adv (extremely) sumamente

intensify [ɪnˈtensɪfaɪ] vt intensificar; (increase) aumentar

intensive [ɪnˈtensɪv] adj intensivo; **~ care unit** n unidad f de vigilancia intensiva

intent [ɪnˈtent] n propósito; (LAW) premeditación f ♦ adj (absorbed) absorto; (attentive) atento; **to all ~s and purposes** prácticamente; **to be ~ on doing sth** estar resuelto a hacer algo

intention [ɪnˈtenʃən] n intención f, propósito; **~al** adj deliberado; **~ally** adv a propósito

intently [ɪnˈtentlɪ] adv atentamente, fijamente

interact [ɪntərˈækt] vi influirse mutuamente; **~ive** adj (COMPUT) interactivo

interchange [ˈɪntətʃeɪndʒ] n intercambio; (on motorway) intersección f; **~able** adj intercambiable

intercom [ˈɪntəkɔm] n interfono

intercourse [ˈɪntəkɔːs] n (sexual) relaciones fpl sexuales

interest [ˈɪntrɪst] n (also COMM) interés m ♦ vt interesar; **to be ~ed in**

interesarse por; **~ing** adj interesante; **~ rate** n tipo o tasa de interés

interface ['ɪntəfeɪs] n (COMPUT) junción f

interfere [ɪntə'fɪə*] vi: **to ~ in** (quarrel, other people's business) entrometerse en; **to ~ with** (hinder) estorbar; (damage) estropear

interference [ɪntə'fɪərəns] n intromisión f; (RADIO, TV) interferencia

interim ['ɪntərɪm] n: **in the ~** en el ínterin ♦ adj provisional

interior [ɪn'tɪərɪə*] n interior m ♦ adj interior; **~ designer** n interiorista m/f

interjection [ɪntə'dʒɛkʃən] n interposición f; (LING) interjección f

interlock [ɪntə'lɔk] vi entrelazarse

interlude ['ɪntəluːd] n intervalo; (THEATRE) intermedio

intermediate [ɪntə'miːdɪət] adj intermedio

intermission [ɪntə'mɪʃən] n intermisión f; (CINEMA) descanso

intern [vb ɪn'tə:n, n 'ɪntə:n] vt internar ♦ n (US) interno/a

internal [ɪn'tə:nl] adj (layout, pipes, security) interior; (injury, structure, memo) internal; **~ly** adv: **"not to be taken ~ly"** "uso externo"; **I~ Revenue Service** (US) n departamento de impuestos; ≈ Hacienda (SP)

international [ɪntə'næʃənl] adj internacional ♦ n (BRIT: match) partido internacional

Internet ['ɪntənɛt] n: **the ~** Internet m or f

interplay ['ɪntəpleɪ] n interacción f

interpret [ɪn'tə:prɪt] vt interpretar; (translate) traducir; (understand) entender ♦ vi hacer de intérprete; **~er** n intérprete m/f

interrelated [ɪntərɪ'leɪtɪd] adj interrelacionados

interrogate [ɪn'tɛrəʊgeɪt] vt interrogar; **interrogation** [-'geɪʃən] n interrogatorio

interrupt [ɪntə'rʌpt] vt, vi interrumpir; **~ion** [-'rʌpʃən] n interrupción f

intersect [ɪntə'sɛkt] vi (roads) cruzarse; **~ion** [-'sɛkʃən] n (of roads) cruce m

intersperse [ɪntə'spə:s] vt: **to ~ with** salpicar de

intertwine [ɪntə'twaɪn] vt entrelazarse

interval ['ɪntəvl] n intervalo; (BRIT: THEATRE, SPORT) descanso; (: SCOL) recreo; **at ~s** a ratos, de vez en cuando

intervene [ɪntə'viːn] vi intervenir; (event) interponerse; (time) transcurrir; **intervention** n intervención f

interview ['ɪntəvjuː] n entrevista ♦ vt entrevistar con; **~er** n entrevistador(a) m/f

intestine [ɪn'tɛstɪn] n intestino

intimacy ['ɪntɪməsɪ] n intimidad f

intimate [adj 'ɪntɪmət, vb 'ɪntɪmeɪt] adj íntimo; (friendship) estrecho; (knowledge) profundo ♦ vt dar a entender

into ['ɪntu:] prep en; (towards) a; (inside) hacia el interior de; **~ 3 pieces/French** en 3 pedazos/al francés

intolerable [ɪn'tɔlərəbl] adj intolerable, insoportable

intolerant [ɪn'tɔlərnt] adj: **~ (of)** intolerante (con o para)

intoxicated [ɪn'tɔksɪkeɪtɪd] adj embriagado

intractable [ɪn'træktəbl] adj (person) intratable; (problem) espinoso

intransitive [ɪn'trænsɪtɪv] adj intransitivo

intravenous [ɪntrə'viːnəs] adj intravenoso

in-tray n bandeja de entrada

intricate ['ɪntrɪkət] adj (design, pattern) intrincado

intrigue [ɪn'triːg] n intriga ♦ vt fascinar; **intriguing** adj fascinante

intrinsic [ɪn'trɪnsɪk] adj intrínseco

introduce [ɪntrə'djuːs] vt introducir, meter; (speaker, TV show etc) presentar;

to ~ **sb** (**to sb**) presentar uno (a otro); to ~ **sb to** (*pastime, technique*) introducir a uno a; **introduction** [-'dʌkʃən] n introducción f; (*of person*) presentación f; **introductory** [-'dʌktərɪ] adj introductorio; (*lesson, offer*) de introducción

introvert ['ɪntrəvə:t] n introvertido/a ♦ adj (also: ~ed) introvertido

intrude [ɪn'tru:d] vi (*person*) entrometerse; to ~ **on** estorbar; ~r n intruso/a; **intrusion** [-ʒən] n invasión f

intuition [ɪntju:'ɪʃən] n intuición f

inundate ['ɪnʌndeɪt] vt: to ~ **with** inundar de

invade [ɪn'veɪd] vt invadir

invalid [n 'ɪnvəlɪd, adj ɪn'vælɪd] n (*MED*) minusválido/a ♦ adj (*not valid*) inválido, nulo

invaluable [ɪn'væljuəbl] adj inestimable

invariable [ɪn'vɛərɪəbl] adj invariable

invent [ɪn'vent] vt inventar; ~**ion** [ɪn'venʃən] n invento; (*lie*) ficción f, mentira; ~**ive** adj inventivo; ~**or** n inventor(a) m/f

inventory ['ɪnvəntrɪ] n inventario

invert [ɪn'və:t] vt invertir

inverted commas (*BRIT*) npl comillas fpl

invest [ɪn'vest] vt invertir ♦ vi: to ~ **in** (*company etc*) invertir dinero en; (*fig: sth useful*) comprar

investigate [ɪn'vestɪgeɪt] vt investigar; **investigation** [-'geɪʃən] n investigación f, pesquisa

investment [ɪn'vestmənt] n inversión f

investor [ɪn'vestə*] n inversionista m/f

invigilator [ɪn'vɪdʒɪleɪtə*] n persona que vigila en un examen

invigorating [ɪn'vɪgəreɪtɪŋ] adj vigorizante

invisible [ɪn'vɪzɪbl] adj invisible

invitation [ɪnvɪ'teɪʃən] n invitación f

invite [ɪn'vaɪt] vt invitar; (*opinions etc*) solicitar, pedir; **inviting** adj atractivo;

(*food*) apetitoso

invoice ['ɪnvɔɪs] n factura ♦ vt facturar

involuntary [ɪn'vɔləntrɪ] adj involuntario

involve [ɪn'vɔlv] vt suponer, implicar; tener que ver con; (*concern, affect*) corresponder; to ~ **sb** (**in sth**) comprometer a uno (con algo); ~**d** adj complicado; to be ~**d in** (*take part*) tomar parte en; (*be engrossed*) estar muy metido en; ~**ment** n participación f; dedicación f

inward ['ɪnwəd] adj (*movement*) interior, interno; (*thought, feeling*) íntimo; ~(**s**) adv hacia dentro

I/O abbr (*COMPUT* = input/output) entrada/salida

iodine ['aɪəudi:n] n yodo

ion ['aɪən] n ion m; **ioniser** ['aɪənaɪzə*] n ionizador m

iota [aɪ'əutə] n jota, ápice m

IOU n abbr (= I owe you) pagaré m

IQ n abbr (= intelligence quotient) cociente m intelectual

IRA n abbr (= Irish Republican Army) IRA m

Iran [ɪ'rɑ:n] n Irán m; ~**ian** ['reɪnɪən] adj, n iraní m/f

Iraq [ɪ'rɑ:k] n Iraq; ~**i** adj, n iraquí m/f

irate [aɪ'reɪt] adj enojado, airado

Ireland ['aɪələnd] n Irlanda

iris ['aɪrɪs] (pl ~**es**) n (*ANAT*) iris m; (*BOT*) lirio

Irish ['aɪrɪʃ] adj irlandés/esa ♦ npl: **the** ~ los irlandeses; ~**man/woman** (*irreg*) n irlandés/esa m/f; ~ **Sea** n: **the** ~ **Sea** el mar de Irlanda

iron ['aɪən] n hierro; (*for clothes*) plancha ♦ cpd de hierro ♦ vt (*clothes*) planchar; ~ **out** vt (*fig*) allanar

ironic(al) [aɪ'rɒnɪk(l)] adj irónico

ironing ['aɪənɪŋ] n (*activity*) planchado; (*clothes: ironed*) ropa planchada; (: *to be ironed*) ropa por planchar; ~ **board** n tabla de planchar

ironmonger's (shop) ['aɪənmʌŋgəz] (*BRIT*) n ferretería, quincallería

irony ['aɪərənɪ] n ironía

irrational [ɪ'ræʃənl] adj irracional

irreconcilable [ɪrekən'saɪləbl] adj (ideas) incompatible; (enemies) irreconciliable

irregular [ɪ'regjulə*] adj irregular; (surface) desigual; (action, event) anómalo; (behaviour) poco ortodoxo

irrelevant [ɪ'reləvənt] adj fuera de lugar, inoportuno

irresolute [ɪ'rezəluːt] adj indeciso

irrespective [ɪrɪ'spektɪv]: ~ of prep sin tener en cuenta, no importa

irresponsible [ɪrɪ'spɒnsɪbl] adj (act) irresponsable; (person) poco serio

irrigate ['ɪrɪgeɪt] vt regar; **irrigation** [-'geɪʃən] n riego

irritable ['ɪrɪtəbl] adj (person) de mal humor

irritate ['ɪrɪteɪt] vt fastidiar; (MED) picar; **irritating** adj fastidioso; **irritation** [-'teɪʃən] n fastidio; irritación; picazón f, picor m

IRS (US) n abbr = **Internal Revenue Service**

is [ɪz] vb see **be**

Islam ['ɪzlɑːm] n Islam m; **~ic** [ɪz'læmɪk] adj islámico

island ['aɪlənd] n isla; **~er** n isleño/a

isle [aɪl] n isla

isn't ['ɪznt] = **is not**

isolate ['aɪsəleɪt] vt aislar; **~d** adj aislado; **isolation** [-'leɪʃən] n aislamiento

Israel ['ɪzreɪl] n Israel m; **~i** [ɪz'reɪlɪ] adj, n israelí m/f

issue ['ɪsjuː] n (problem, subject, most important part) cuestión f; (outcome) resultado; (of banknotes etc) emisión f; (of newspaper etc) edición f ♦ vt (rations, equipment) distribuir, repartir; (orders) dar; (certificate, passport) expedir; (decree) promulgar; (magazine) publicar; (cheques) extender; (banknotes, stamps) emitir; **at ~** en cuestión; **to take ~ with sb (over)** estar en desacuerdo con uno

(sobre); **to make an ~ of sth** hacer una cuestión de algo

Istanbul [ɪstæn'buːl] n Estambul m

─┤ KEYWORD ├─

it [ɪt] pron **1** (specific: subject: not generally translated) él/ella; (: direct object) lo, la; (: indirect object) le; (after prep) él/ella; (abstract concept) ello; **~'s on the table** está en la mesa; **I can't find ~** no lo (or la) encuentro; **give ~ to me** dámelo (or dámela); **I spoke to him about ~** le hablé del asunto; **what did you learn from ~?** ¿qué aprendiste de él (or ella)?; **did you go to ~?** (party, concert etc) ¿fuiste?

2 (impersonal): **~'s raining** llueve, está lloviendo; **~'s 6 o'clock/the 10th of August** son las 6/es el 10 de agosto; **how far is ~?** — **~'s 10 miles/2 hours on the train** ¿a qué distancia está? — a 10 millas/2 horas en tren; **who is ~?** — **~'s me** ¿quién es? — soy yo

Italian [ɪ'tæljən] adj italiano ♦ n italiano/a; (LING) italiano

italics [ɪ'tælɪks] npl cursiva

Italy ['ɪtəlɪ] n Italia

itch [ɪtʃ] n picazón f ♦ vi (part of body) picar; **to ~ to do sth** rabiar por hacer algo; **~y** adj: **my hand is ~y** me pica la mano

it'd ['ɪtd] = **it would**; **it had**

item ['aɪtəm] n artículo; (on agenda) asunto (a tratar); (also: news ~) noticia; **~ize** vt detallar

itinerary [aɪ'tɪnərərɪ] n itinerario

it'll ['ɪtl] = **it will**; **it shall**

its [ɪts] adj su; sus pl

it's [ɪts] = **it is**; **it has**

itself [ɪt'self] pron (reflexive) sí mismo/a; (emphatic) mismo/a, él/ella misma

ITV n abbr (BRIT: = Independent Television) cadena de televisión comercial independiente del Estado

I.U.D. n abbr (= intra-uterine device)

I've [aɪv] = **I have**

ivory ['aɪvərɪ] n marfil m

ivy ['aɪvɪ] n (BOT) hiedra

J, j

jab [dʒæb] vt: **to ~ sth into sth** clavar algo en algo ♦ n (inf) (MED) pinchazo

jack [dʒæk] n (AUT) gato; (CARDS) sota; **~ up** vt (AUT) levantar con gato

jackal ['dʒækɔːl] n (ZOOL) chacal m

jacket ['dʒækɪt] n chaqueta, americana, saco (AM); (of book) sobrecubierta

jack: **~-knife** vi colear; **~ plug** n (ELEC) enchufe m de clavija; **~pot** n premio gordo

jaded ['dʒeɪdɪd] adj (tired) cansado; (fed-up) hastiado

jagged ['dʒægɪd] adj dentado

jail [dʒeɪl] n cárcel f ♦ vt encarcelar

jam [dʒæm] n mermelada; (also: traffic ~) embotellamiento; (inf: difficulty) apuro ♦ vt (passage etc) obstruir; (mechanism, drawer etc) atascar; (RADIO) interferir ♦ vi atascarse, trabarse; **to ~ sth into sth** meter algo a la fuerza en algo

Jamaica [dʒə'meɪkə] n Jamaica

jangle ['dʒæŋgl] vi entrechocar (ruidosamente)

janitor ['dʒænɪtə*] n (caretaker) portero, conserje m

January ['dʒænjuərɪ] n enero

Japan [dʒə'pæn] n (el) Japón; **~ese** [dʒæpə'niːz] adj japonés/esa ♦ n inv japonés/esa m/f; (LING) japonés m

jar [dʒɑː*] n tarro, bote m ♦ vi (sound) chirriar; (colours) desentonar

jargon ['dʒɑːgən] n jerga

jasmine ['dʒæzmɪn] n jazmín m

jaundice ['dʒɔːndɪs] n icteria

jaunt [dʒɔːnt] n excursión f

javelin ['dʒævlɪn] n jabalina

jaw [dʒɔː] n mandíbula

jay [dʒeɪ] n (ZOOL) arrendajo

jaywalker ['dʒeɪwɔːkə*] n peatón/ona m/f imprudente

jazz [dʒæz] n jazz m; **~ up** vt (liven up) animar, avivar

jealous ['dʒeləs] adj celoso; (envious) envidioso; **~y** n celos mpl; envidia

jeans [dʒiːnz] npl vaqueros mpl, tejanos mpl

Jeep ® [dʒiːp] n jeep m

jeer [dʒɪə*] vi: **to ~ (at)** (mock) mofarse (de)

jelly ['dʒelɪ] n (jam) jalea; (dessert etc) gelatina; **~fish** n inv medusa (SP), aguaviva (AM)

jeopardy ['dʒepədɪ] n: **to be in ~** estar en peligro

jerk [dʒɜːk] n (jolt) sacudida; (wrench) tirón m; (inf) imbécil m/f ♦ vt tirar bruscamente de ♦ vi (vehicle) traquetear

jersey ['dʒɜːzɪ] n jersey m; (fabric) (tejido de) punto

Jesus ['dʒiːzəs] n Jesús m

jet [dʒet] n (of gas, liquid) chorro; (AVIAT) avión m a reacción; **~-black** adj negro como el azabache; **~ engine** n motor m a reacción; **~ lag** n desorientación f después de un largo vuelo

jettison ['dʒetɪsn] vt desechar

jetty ['dʒetɪ] n muelle m, embarcadero

Jew [dʒuː] n judío

jewel ['dʒuːəl] n joya; (in watch) rubí m; **~ler** (US **~er**) n joyero/a; **~ler's (shop)** (US **~ry store**) n joyería; **~lery** (US **~ry**) n joyas fpl, alhajas fpl

Jewess ['dʒuːɪs] n judía

Jewish ['dʒuːɪʃ] adj judío

jibe [dʒaɪb] n mofa

jiffy ['dʒɪfɪ] (inf) n: **in a ~** en un santiamén

jigsaw ['dʒɪgsɔː] n (also: ~ puzzle) rompecabezas m inv, puzle m

jilt [dʒɪlt] vt dejar plantado a

jingle ['dʒɪŋgl] n musiquilla ♦ vi tintinear

jinx [dʒɪŋks] n: **there's a ~ on it** está

gafado

jitters ['dʒɪtəz] (inf) npl: **to get the ~** ponerse nervioso

job [dʒɔb] n (task) tarea; (post) empleo; **it's not my ~** no me incumbe a mí; **it's a good ~ that ...** menos mal que ...; **just the ~!** ¡estupendo!; **~ centre** (BRIT) n oficina estatal de colocaciones; **~less** adj sin trabajo

jockey ['dʒɔkɪ] n jockey m/f ♦ vi: to **~ for position** maniobrar para conseguir una posición

jog [dʒɔg] vt empujar (ligeramente) ♦ vi (run) hacer footing; **to ~ sb's memory** refrescar la memoria a uno; **~ along** vi (fig) ir tirando; **~ging** n footing m

join [dʒɔɪn] vt (things) juntar, unir; (club) hacerse socio de; (POL: party) afiliarse a; (queue) ponerse en; (meet: people) reunirse con ♦ vi (roads) juntarse; (rivers) confluir ♦ n juntura; **~ in** vi tomar parte, participar ♦ vt fus tomar parte or participar en; **~ up** vi reunirse; (MIL) alistarse

joiner ['dʒɔɪnə*] (BRIT) n carpintero/a; **~y** n carpintería

joint [dʒɔɪnt] n (TECH) junta, unión f; (ANAT) articulación f; (BRIT: CULIN) pieza de carne (para asar); (inf: place) tugurio; (: of cannabis) porro ♦ adj (common) común; (combined) combinado; **~ account** (with bank etc) cuenta común

joke [dʒəuk] n chiste m; (also: practical **~**) broma ♦ vi bromear; **to play a ~ on** gastar una broma a; **~r** n (CARDS) comodín m

jolly ['dʒɔlɪ] adj (merry) alegre; (enjoyable) divertido ♦ adv (BRIT: inf) muy, terriblemente

jolt [dʒəult] n (jerk) sacudida; (shock) susto ♦ vt (physically) sacudir; (emotionally) asustar

jostle ['dʒɔsl] vt dar empellones a, codear

jot [dʒɔt] n: **not one ~** ni jota, ni

pizca; **~ down** vt apuntar; **~ter** (BRIT) n bloc m

journal ['dʒəːnl] n (magazine) revista; (diary) periódico, diario; **~ism** n periodismo; **~ist** n periodista m/f, reportero/a

journey ['dʒəːnɪ] n viaje m; (distance covered) trayecto

jovial ['dʒəuvɪəl] adj risueño, jovial

joy [dʒɔɪ] n alegría; **~ful** adj alegre; **~ous** adj alegre; **~ ride** n (illegal) paseo en coche robado; **~rider** n gamberro que roba un coche para dar una vuelta y luego abandonarlo; **~ stick** n (AVIAT) palanca de mando; (COMPUT) palanca de control

JP n abbr = **Justice of the Peace**

Jr abbr = **junior**

jubilant ['dʒuːbɪlnt] adj jubiloso

judge [dʒʌdʒ] n juez m/f; (fig: expert) perito ♦ vt juzgar; (consider) considerar; **judg(e)ment** n juicio

judiciary [dʒuːˈdɪʃɪərɪ] n poder m judicial

judicious [dʒuːˈdɪʃəs] adj juicioso

judo ['dʒuːdəu] n judo

jug [dʒʌg] n jarra

juggernaut ['dʒʌgənɔːt] (BRIT) n (huge truck) trailer m

juggle ['dʒʌgl] vi hacer juegos malabares; **~r** n malabarista m/f

juice [dʒuːs] n zumo, jugo (esp AM); **juicy** adj jugoso

jukebox ['dʒuːkbɔks] n máquina de discos

July [dʒuːˈlaɪ] n julio

jumble ['dʒʌmbl] n revoltijo ♦ vt (also: **~ up**) revolver; **~ sale** (BRIT) n venta de objetos usados con fines benéficos

jumble sale

*Los **jumble sales** son unos mercadillos que se organizan con fines benéficos en los locales de un colegio, iglesia u otro centro público. En ellos puede comprarse todo tipo de artículos baratos de segunda mano, sobre todo*

ropa, juguetes, libros, vajillas o muebles.

jumbo (jet) ['dʒʌmbəʊ-] *n* jumbo
jump [dʒʌmp] *vi* saltar, dar saltos; *(with fear etc)* pegar un bote; *(increase)* aumentar ♦ *vt* saltar ♦ *n* salto; aumento; **to ~ the queue** *(BRIT)* colarse
jumper ['dʒʌmpə*] *n* *(BRIT: pullover)* suéter *m*, jersey *m*; *(US: dress)* mandil *m*; **~ cables** *(US)* *npl* = **jump leads**
jump leads *(BRIT)* *npl* cables *mpl* puente de batería
jumpy ['dʒʌmpɪ] *(inf)* *adj* nervioso
Jun. *abbr* = **junior**
junction ['dʒʌŋkʃn] *n* *(BRIT: of roads)* cruce *m*; *(RAIL)* empalme *m*
juncture ['dʒʌŋktʃə*] *n*: **at this ~** en este momento, en esta coyuntura
June [dʒuːn] *n* junio
jungle ['dʒʌŋgl] *n* selva, jungla
junior ['dʒuːnɪə*] *adj* *(in age)* menor, más joven; *(brother/sister etc)*: **3 years her ~** siete años menor que ella; *(position)* subalterno ♦ *n* menor *m/f*, joven *m/f*; **~ school** *(BRIT)* *n* escuela primaria
junk [dʒʌŋk] *n* *(cheap goods)* baratijas *fpl*; *(rubbish)* basura; **~ food** *n* alimentos preparados y envasados de escaso valor nutritivo
junkie ['dʒʌŋkɪ] *(inf)* *n* drogadicto/a, yonqui *m/f*
junk mail *n* propaganda de buzón
junk shop *n* tienda de objetos usados
Junr *abbr* = **junior**
juror ['dʒʊərə*] *n* jurado
jury ['dʒʊərɪ] *n* jurado
just [dʒʌst] *adj* justo ♦ *adv* *(exactly)* exactamente; *(only)* sólo, solamente; **he's ~ done it/left** acaba de hacerlo/irse; **~ right** perfecto; **~ two o'clock** las dos en punto; **she's ~ as clever as you** (ella) es tan lista como tú; **~ as well that ...** menos mal que ...; **~ as he was leaving** en el momento en que se marchaba;

~ before/enough justo antes/lo suficiente; **~ here** aquí mismo; **he ~ missed** ha fallado por poco; **~ listen to this** escucha esto un momento
justice ['dʒʌstɪs] *n* justicia; *(US: judge)* juez *m*; **to do ~ to** *(fig)* hacer justicia a; **J~ of the Peace** *n* juez *m* de paz
justify ['dʒʌstɪfaɪ] *vt* justificar; *(text)* alinear
jut [dʒʌt] *vi* *(also: ~ out)* sobresalir
juvenile ['dʒuːvənaɪl] *adj* *(court)* de menores; *(humour, mentality)* infantil ♦ *n* menor *m* de edad

K, k

K *abbr* (= *one thousand*) mil; (= *kilobyte*) kilobyte m, kilooocteto
kangaroo [kæŋgə'ruː] *n* canguro
karate [kə'rɑːtɪ] *n* karate *m*
kebab [kə'bæb] *n* pincho moruno
keel [kiːl] *n* quilla; **on an even ~** *(fig)* en equilibrio
keen [kiːn] *adj* *(interest, desire)* grande, vivo; *(eye, intelligence)* agudo; *(competition)* reñido; *(edge)* afilado; *(eager)* entusiasta; **to be ~ to do** or **on doing sth** tener muchas ganas de hacer algo; **to be ~ on sth/sb** interesarse por algo/uno
keep [kiːp] *(pt, pp kept)* *vt* *(preserve, store)* guardar; *(hold back)* quedarse con; *(maintain)* mantener; *(detain)* detener; *(shop)* ser propietario de; *(feed: family etc)* mantener; *(promise)* cumplir; *(chickens, bees etc)* criar; *(accounts)* llevar; *(diary)* escribir; *(prevent)*: **to ~ sb from doing sth** impedir a uno hacer algo ♦ *vi* *(food)* conservarse; *(remain)* seguir, continuar ♦ *n* *(of castle)* torreón *m*; *(food)* comida, subsistencia; *(inf)*: **for ~s** para siempre; **to ~ doing sth** seguir haciendo algo; **to ~ sb happy** tener a uno contento; **to ~ a place tidy**

mantener un lugar limpio; **to ~ sth to o.s.** guardar algo para sí mismo; **to ~ sth (back) from sb** ocultar algo a uno; **to ~ time** (clock) mantener la hora exacta; **~ on** vi: **to ~ on doing** seguir o continuar haciendo; **to ~ on (about sth)** no parar de hablar (de algo); **~ out** vi (stay out) permanecer fuera; **"~ out"** "prohibida la entrada"; **~ up** vt mantener, conservar ♦ vi no retrasarse; **to ~ up with** (pace) ir al paso de; (level) mantenerse a la altura de; **~er** n guardián/ana m/f; **~-fit** n gimnasia (para mantenerse en forma); **~ing** n (care) cuidado; **in ~ing with** de acuerdo con; **~sake** n recuerdo

kennel ['kɛnl] n perrera; **~s** npl residencia canina

Kenya ['kɛnjə] n Kenia

kept [kɛpt] pt, pp of **keep**

kerb [kəːb] (BRIT) n bordillo

kernel ['kəːnl] n (nut) almendra; (fig) meollo

ketchup ['kɛtʃəp] n salsa de tomate, catsup m

kettle ['kɛtl] n hervidor m de agua; **~ drum** n (MUS) timbal m

key [kiː] n llave f; (MUS) tono; (of piano, typewriter) tecla ♦ adj (issue etc) clave inv ♦ vt (also: **~ in**) teclear; **~board** n teclado; **~ed up** adj (person) nervioso; **~hole** n ojo (de la cerradura); **~hole surgery** n cirugía cerrada, cirugía no invasiva; **~note** n (MUS) tónica; (of speech) punto principal or clave; **~ring** n llavero

khaki ['kɑːki] n caqui

kick [kɪk] vt dar una patada or un puntapié a; (inf: habit) quitarse de ♦ vi (horse) dar coces ♦ n patada; puntapié m; (of animal) coz f; (thrill): **he does it for ~s** lo hace por pura diversión; **~ off** vi (SPORT) hacer el saque inicial

kid [kɪd] n (inf: child) chiquillo m; (animal) cabrito; (leather) cabritilla ♦ vi (inf) bromear

kidnap ['kɪdnæp] vt secuestrar; **~per** n

secuestrador(a) m/f; **~ping** n secuestro

kidney ['kɪdnɪ] n riñón m

kill [kɪl] vt matar; (murder) asesinar ♦ n matanza; **to ~ time** matar el tiempo; **~er** n asesino/a; **~ing** n (one) asesinato; (several) matanza; **to make a ~ing** (fig) hacer su agosto; **~joy** (BRIT) n aguafiestas m/f inv

kiln [kɪln] n horno

kilo ['kiːləʊ] n kilo; **~byte** n (COMPUT) kilobyte m, kilocteto; **~gram(me)** ['kɪləɡræm] n kilo, kilogramo; **~metre** ['kɪləmiːtə*] (US **~meter**) n kilómetro; **~watt** ['kɪləʊwɔt] n kilovatio

kilt [kɪlt] n falda escocesa

kin [kɪn] n see **next**

kind [kaɪnd] adj amable, atento ♦ n clase f, especie f; (species) género; **in ~** (COMM) en especie; **a ~ of** una especie de; **to be two of a ~** tener algo que ver la cual

kindergarten ['kɪndəɡɑːtn] n jardín m de la infancia

kind-hearted adj bondadoso, de buen corazón

kindle ['kɪndl] vt encender; (arouse) despertar

kindly ['kaɪndlɪ] adj bondadoso, cariñoso ♦ adv bondadosamente, amablemente; **will you ~** ... sea usted tan amable de ...

kindness ['kaɪndnɪs] n (quality) bondad f, amabilidad f; (act) favor m

king [kɪŋ] n rey m; **~dom** n reino; **~fisher** n martín m pescador; **~-size** adj de tamaño extra

kiosk ['kiːɔsk] n quiosco; (BRIT: TEL) cabina

kipper ['kɪpə*] n arenque m ahumado

kiss [kɪs] n beso ♦ vt besar; **to ~ (each other)** besarse; **~ of life** n respiración f boca a boca

kit [kɪt] n (equipment) equipo; (tools etc) caja de herramientas fpl; (assembly) ~) juego de armar

kitchen ['kɪtʃɪn] n cocina; **~ sink** n fregadero

kite [kaɪt] n (toy) cometa

kitten ['kɪtn] n gatito/a

kitty ['kɪtɪ] n (pool of money) fondo común

km abbr (= kilometre) km

knack [næk] n: **to have the ~ of doing sth** tener el don de hacer algo

knapsack ['næpsæk] n mochila

knead [ni:d] vt amasar

knee [ni:] n rodilla; **~cap** n rótula

kneel [ni:l] (pt, pp **knelt**) vi (also: **~ down**) arrodillarse

knew [nju:] pt of **know**

knickers ['nɪkəz] (BRIT) npl bragas fpl

knife [naɪf] (pl **knives**) n cuchillo ♦ vt acuchillar

knight [naɪt] n caballero; (CHESS) caballo; **~hood** (BRIT) n (title): **to receive a ~hood** recibir el título de Sir

knit [nɪt] vt tejer, tricotar ♦ vi hacer punto, tricotar; (bones) soldarse; **to ~ one's brows** fruncir el ceño; **~ting** n labor f de punto; **~ting machine** n máquina de tricotar; **~ting needle** n aguja de hacer punto; **~wear** n prendas fpl de punto

knives [naɪvz] npl of **knife**

knob [nɔb] n (of door) tirador m; (of stick) puño; (on radio, TV) botón m

knock [nɔk] vt (strike) golpear; (bump into) chocar contra; (inf) criticar ♦ vi (at door etc): **to ~ at/on** llamar a ♦ n golpe m; (on door) llamada; **~ down** vt atropellar; **~ off** (inf) vi (finish) salir del trabajo ♦ vt (from price) descontar; (inf: steal) birlar; **~ out** vt dejar sin sentido; (BOXING) poner fuera de combate, dejar K.O.; (in competition) eliminar; **~ over** vt (object) tirar; (person) atropellar; **~er** n (on door) aldabón m; **~out** n (BOXING) K.O. m, knockout m ♦ cpd (competition etc) eliminatorio

knot [nɔt] n nudo ♦ vt anudar

know [nəu] (pt **knew**, pp **known**) vt (facts) saber; (be acquainted with) conocer; (recognize) reconocer, conocer; **to ~ how to swim** saber nadar; **to ~ about** or **of sb/sth** saber de uno/algo; **~-all** n sabelotodo m/f; **~-how** n conocimientos mpl; **~ing** adj (look) de complicidad; **~ingly** adv (purposely) adrede; (smile, look) con complicidad

knowledge ['nɔlɪdʒ] n conocimiento; (learning) saber m, conocimientos mpl; **~able** adj entendido

knuckle ['nʌkl] n nudillo

Koran [kɔ'rɑ:n] n Corán m

Korea [kə'rɪə] n Corea

kosher ['kəuʃə*] adj autorizado por la ley judía

L, l

L (BRIT) abbr = **learner driver**

l. abbr (= litre) l

lab [læb] n abbr = **laboratory**

label ['leɪbl] n etiqueta ♦ vt poner etiqueta a

labor etc ['leɪbə*] (US) = **labour**

laboratory [lə'bɔrətəri] n laboratorio

laborious [lə'bɔ:rɪəs] adj penoso

labour ['leɪbə*] (US **labor**) n (hard work) trabajo; (~ force) mano f de obra; (MED): **to be in ~** estar de parto ♦ vi: **to ~ (at sth)** trabajar (en algo) ♦ vt: **to ~ a point** insistir en un punto; **L~, the L~ party** (BRIT) el partido laborista, los laboristas mpl; **~ed** (breathing) fatigoso; **~er** n peón m; **farm ~er** peón m; (day ~er) jornalero

lace [leɪs] n encaje m; (of shoe etc) cordón m; (shoes: also: **~ up**) atarse (los zapatos)

lack [læk] n (absence) falta ♦ vt faltarle a uno, carecer de; **through** or **for ~ of** por falta de, por la falta de; **to be ~ing** faltar, no haber; **to be ~ing in sth** faltarle a uno algo

lacquer ['lækə*] n laca

lad [læd] n muchacho, chico

ladder ['lædə*] n escalera (de mano); (BRIT: in tights) carrera

laden ['leɪdn] adj: ~ (with) cargado (de)

ladle ['leɪdl] n cucharón m

lady ['leɪdɪ] n señora; (dignified, graceful) dama; "**ladies and gentlemen ...**" "señoras y caballeros ..."; **young ~** señorita; **the ladies' (room)** los servicios de señoras; **~bird** (US **~bug**) n mariquita; **~like** adj fino; **L~ship** n: **your L~ship** su Señoría

lag [læg] n retraso ♦ vi (also: ~ behind) retrasarse, quedarse atrás ♦ vt (pipes) revestir

lager ['lɑːgə*] n cerveza (rubia)

lagoon [lə'guːn] n laguna

laid [leɪd] pt, pp of **lay**; **~ back** (inf) adj relajado; **~ up** adj: **to be ~ up (with)** tener que guardar cama (a causa de)

lain [leɪn] pp of **lie**

lake [leɪk] n lago

lamb [læm] n cordero; (meat) (carne f de) cordero; **~ chop** n chuleta de cordero; **lambswool** n lana de cordero

lame [leɪm] adj cojo; (excuse) poco convincente

lament [lə'ment] n quejo ♦ vt lamentarse de

laminated ['læmɪneɪtd] adj (metal) laminado; (wood) contrachapado; (surface) plastificado

lamp [læmp] n lámpara; **~post** (BRIT) n (poste m de) farol m; **~shade** n pantalla

lance [lɑːns] vt (MED) abrir con lanceta

land [lænd] n tierra; (country) país m; (piece of ~) terreno; (estate) tierras fpl, finca ♦ vi (from ship) desembarcar; (AVIAT) aterrizar; (fig: fall) caer, terminar ♦ vt (passengers, goods) desembarcar; **to ~ sb with sth** (inf) hacer cargar a uno con algo; **~ up** vi: **to ~ up in/at** ir a parar a/en; **~fill site** ['lændfɪl-] n vertedero; **~ing** n aterrizaje m; (of staircase) rellano; **~ing**

gear n (AVIAT) tren m de aterrizaje; **~lady** n (of rented house, pub etc) dueña; **~lord** n propietario; (of pub etc) patrón m; **~mark** n lugar m conocido; **to be a ~mark** (fig) marcar un hito histórico; **~owner** n terrateniente m/f; **~scape** n paisaje m; **~scape gardener** n arquitecto de jardines; **~slide** n (GEO) corrimiento de tierras; (fig: POL) victoria arrolladora

lane [leɪn] n (in country) camino; (AUT) carril m; (in race) calle f

language ['læŋgwɪdʒ] n lenguaje m; (national tongue) idioma m, lengua; **bad ~** palabrotas fpl; **~ laboratory** n laboratorio de idiomas

lank [læŋk] adj (hair) lacio

lanky ['læŋkɪ] adj larguirucho

lantern ['læntn] n linterna, farol m

lap [læp] n (of track) vuelta; (of body) regazo; **to sit on sb's ~** sentarse en las rodillas de uno ♦ vt (also: ~ up) beber a lengüetadas ♦ vi (waves) chapotear; **~ up** vt (fig) tragarse

lapel [lə'pel] n solapa

Lapland ['læplænd] n Laponia

lapse [læps] n fallo; (moral) desliz m; (of time) intervalo ♦ vi (expire) caducar; (time) pasar, transcurrir; **to ~ into bad habits** caer en malos hábitos

laptop (computer) ['læptɒp-] n (ordenador m) portátil m

larch [lɑːtʃ] n alerce m

lard [lɑːd] n manteca (de cerdo)

larder ['lɑːdə*] n despensa

large [lɑːdʒ] adj grande; **at ~** (free) en libertad; (generally) en general; **~ly** adv (mostly) en su mayor parte; (introducing reason) en gran parte; **~-scale** adj (map) en gran escala; (fig) importante

lark [lɑːk] n (bird) alondra; (joke) broma

laryngitis [lærɪn'dʒaɪtɪs] n laringitis f

laser ['leɪzə*] n láser m; **~ printer** n impresora (por) láser

lash [læʃ] n latigazo; (also: eye~) pestaña; (of whip) azotar; (tie): **to ~ to/together** atar a/atar; **~ out** vi: **to**

~ out (at sb) (hit) arremeter (contra uno); **to ~ out against sb** lanzar invectivas contra uno

lass [læs] (BRIT) n chica

lasso [læˈsuː] n lazo

last [lɑːst] adj último; (end: of series etc) final ♦ adv (most recently) la última vez; (finally) por último ♦ vi durar; (continue) continuar, seguir; **~ night** anoche; **~ week** la semana pasada; **at ~** por fin; **~ but one** penúltimo; **~ ditch** adj (attempt) último, desesperado; **~ing** adj duradero; **~ly** adv por último, finalmente; **~-minute** adj de última hora

latch [lætʃ] n pestillo

late [leɪt] adj (far on: in time, process etc) al final de; (not on time) tarde, atrasado; (dead) fallecido ♦ adv tarde; (behind time, schedule) con retraso; **of ~** últimamente; **~ at night** a última hora de la noche; **in ~ May** hacia fines de mayo; **the ~ Mr X** el difunto Sr X; **~comer** n recién llegado/a; **~ly** adv últimamente; **~r** adj (date etc) posterior; (version etc) más reciente ♦ adv más tarde, después; **~st** ['leɪtɪst] adj último; **at the ~st** a más tardar

lathe [leɪð] n torno

lather ['lɑːðə*] n espuma (de jabón) ♦ vt enjabonar

Latin ['lætɪn] n latín m ♦ adj latino; **~ America** n América latina; **~-American** adj, n latinoamericano/a

latitude ['lætɪtjuːd] n latitud f; (fig) libertad f

latter ['lætə*] adj último; (of two) segundo ♦ n: **the ~** el último, éste; **~ly** adv últimamente

laudable ['lɔːdəbl] adj loable

laugh [lɑːf] n risa ♦ vi reír(se); **(to do sth) for a ~** (hacer algo) en broma; **~ at** vt fus reírse de; **~ off** vt tomar algo a risa; **~able** adj ridículo; **~ing stock** n: **the ~ing stock of** el hazmerreír de; **~ter** n risa

launch [lɔːntʃ] n lanzamiento; (boat)

lancha ♦ vt (ship) botar; (rocket etc) lanzar; (fig) comenzar; **~ into** vt fus lanzarse a; **~(ing) pad** n plataforma de lanzamiento

launder ['lɔːndə*] vt lavar

Launderette ® [lɔːnˈdrɛt] (BRIT) n lavandería (automática)

Laundromat ® ['lɔːndrəmæt] (US) n = **Launderette**

laundry ['lɔːndrɪ] n (dirty) ropa sucia; (clean) colada; (room) lavadero

lavatory ['lævətərɪ] n wáter m

lavender ['lævəndə*] n lavanda

lavish ['lævɪʃ] adj (amount) abundante; (person): **~ with** pródigo en ♦ vt: **to ~ sth on sb** colmar a uno de algo

law [lɔː] n ley f; (SCOL) derecho; (a rule) regla; (professions connected with ~) jurisprudencia; **~-abiding** adj respetuoso de la ley; **~ and order** n orden m público; **~ court** n tribunal m (de justicia); **~ful** adj legítimo, lícito; **~less** adj (action) criminal

lawn [lɔːn] n césped m; **~ mower** n cortacésped m; **~ tennis** n tenis m sobre hierba

law school n (US) (SCOL) facultad f de derecho

lawsuit ['lɔːsuːt] n pleito

lawyer ['lɔːjə*] n abogado/a; (for sales, wills etc) notario/a

lax [læks] adj (joose) laxo

laxative ['læksətɪv] n laxante m

lay [leɪ] (pt, pp **laid**) pt of **lie** ♦ adj laico; (not expert) lego ♦ vt (place) colocar; (eggs, table) poner; (cable) tender; (carpet) extender; **~ aside** or **by** vt dejar a un lado; **~ down** vt (pen etc) dejar; (rules etc) establecer; **to ~ down the law** (pej) imponer las normas; **~ off** vt (workers) despedir; **~ on** vt (meal, facilities) proveer; **~ out** vt (spread out) disponer, exponer; **~about** (inf) n vago/a; **~-by** (BRIT: AUT) n área de aparcamiento

layer ['leɪə*] n capa

layman ['leɪmən] (irreg) n lego

layout ['leɪaut] n (design) plan m, trazado; (PRESS) composición f

laze [leɪz] vi (also: ~ about) holgazanear

lazy ['leɪzɪ] adj perezoso, vago; (movement) lento

lb. abbr = **pound** (weight)

lead¹ [liːd] (pt, pp **led**) n (front position) delantera; (clue) pista; (ELEC) cable m; (for dog) correa; (THEATRE) papel m principal ♦ vt (walk etc in front of) ir a la cabeza de; (guide): **to ~ sb somewhere** conducir a uno a algún sitio; (be leader of) dirigir; (start, guide: activity) protagonizar ♦ vi (road, pipe etc) conducir a; (SPORT) ir primero; **to be in the ~** (SPORT) llevar la delantera; (fig) ir a la cabeza; **to ~ the way** (also fig) llevar la delantera; **~ away** vi llevar; **~ back** vi (person, route) llevar de vuelta; **~ on** vt (tease) engañar; **~ to** vt fus producir, provocar; **~ up to** vt fus (events) conducir a; (in conversation) preparar el terreno para

lead² [lɛd] n (metal) plomo; (in pencil) mina; **~ed petrol** n gasolina con plomo

leader ['liːdə*] n jefe/a m/f, líder m; (SPORT) líder m; **~ship** n dirección f; (position) mando; (quality) iniciativa f

leading ['liːdɪŋ] adj (main) principal; (first) primero; (front) delantero; **~ lady** n (THEATRE) primera actriz f; **~ light** n (person) figura principal; **~ man** (irreg) n (THEATRE) primer galán m

lead singer [liːd-] n cantante m/f

leaf [liːf] (pl **leaves**) n hoja f ♦ vi: **to ~ through** hojear; **to turn over a new ~** reformarse

leaflet ['liːflɪt] n folleto

league [liːg] n (competition: FOOTBALL) liga; **to be in ~ with** haberse confabulado con

leak [liːk] n (of liquid, gas) escape m, fuga; (in pipe) agujero; (in roof) gotera; (in security) filtración f ♦ vi (shoes, ship) hacer agua; (pipe) tener (un) escape;

(roof) gotear; (liquid, gas) escaparse, fugarse; (fig) divulgarse ♦ vt (fig) filtrar

lean [liːn] (pt, pp **leaned** or **leant**) adj (thin) flaco; (meat) magro ♦ vt: **to ~ sth on sth** apoyar algo en algo ♦ vi (slope) inclinarse; **to ~ against** apoyarse contra; **to ~ on** apoyarse en; **~ back/forward** vi inclinarse hacia atrás/adelante; **~ out** vi asomarse; **~ over** vi inclinarse; **~ing** n: **~ing (towards)** inclinación f (hacia); **leant** [lɛnt] pt, pp of **lean**

leap [liːp] (pt, pp **leaped** or **leapt**) n salto ♦ vi saltar; **~frog** n pídola; **~ year** n año bisiesto

learn [lɜːn] (pt, pp **learned** or **learnt**) vt aprender ♦ vi aprender; **to ~ about sth** enterarse de algo; **to ~ to do sth** aprender a hacer algo; **~ed** ['lɜːnɪd] adj erudito; **~er** n (BRIT: also: **~er driver**) principiante m/f; **~ing** n el saber m, conocimientos mpl

lease [liːs] n arriendo ♦ vt arrendar

leash [liːʃ] n correa

least [liːst] adj: **the ~** (slightest) el menor, el más pequeño; (smallest amount of) mínimo ♦ adv (+ vb) menos; (+ adj): **the ~ expensive** el/la menos costoso/a; **the ~ possible effort** el menor esfuerzo posible; **at ~** por lo menos, al menos; **you could at ~ have written** por lo menos podías haber escrito; **not in the ~** en absoluto

leather ['lɛðə*] n cuero

leave [liːv] (pt, pp **left**) vt dejar; (go away from) abandonar; (place etc: permanently) salir de ♦ vi irse; (train etc) salir ♦ n permiso; **to ~ sth to sb** (money etc) legar algo a uno; (responsibility etc) encargar a uno de algo; **to be left** quedar, sobrar; **there's some milk left over** sobra or queda algo de leche; **on ~** de permiso; **~ behind** vt (on purpose) dejar; (accidentally) dejarse; **~ out** vt omitir; **~ of absence** n permiso de ausentarse

leaves [li:vz] npl of **leaf**

Lebanon ['lebənən] n: **the ~** el Líbano

lecherous ['letʃərəs] (pej) adj lascivo

lecture ['lektʃə*] n conferencia; (SCOL) clase f ♦ vi dar una clase ♦ vt (scold): **to ~ sb on** or **about sth** echar una reprimenda a uno por algo; **to give a ~ on** dar una conferencia sobre; **~r** n conferenciante m/f; (BRIT: at university) profesor(a) m/f

led [led] pt, pp of **lead**

ledge [ledʒ] n repisa; (of window) alféizar m; (of mountain) saliente m

ledger ['ledʒə*] n libro mayor

leech [li:tʃ] n sanguijuela

leek [li:k] n puerro

leer [lɪə*] vi: **to ~ at sb** mirar de manera lasciva a uno

leeway ['li:weɪ] n (fig): **to have some ~** tener cierta libertad de acción

left [left] pt, pp of **leave** ♦ adj izquierdo; (remaining): **there are 2 ~** quedan dos ♦ n izquierda ♦ adv a la izquierda; **on** or **to the ~** a la izquierda; **the L~** (POL) la izquierda; **~-handed** adj zurdo; **the ~-hand side** n la izquierda; **~-luggage (office)** (BRIT) n consigna; **~-overs** npl sobras fpl; **~-wing** adj (POL) de izquierdas, izquierdista

leg [leg] n pierna; (of animal, chair) pata; (trouser ~) pernera; (CULIN: of lamb) pierna; (of chicken) pata; (of journey) etapa

legacy ['legəsɪ] n herencia

legal ['li:gl] adj (permitted by law) lícito; (of law) legal; **~ holiday** (US) n fiesta oficial; **~ize** vt legalizar; **~ly** adv legalmente; **~ tender** n moneda de curso legal

legend ['ledʒənd] n (also fig: person) leyenda

legislation [ledʒɪs'leɪʃən] n legislación f

legislature ['ledʒɪslətʃə*] n cuerpo legislativo

legitimate [lɪ'dʒɪtɪmət] adj legítimo

leg-room n espacio para las piernas

leisure ['leʒə*] n ocio, tiempo libre; **at ~** con tranquilidad; **~ centre** n centro de recreo; **~ly** adj sin prisa; lento

lemon ['lemən] n limón m; **~ade** n (fizzy) gaseosa; **~ tea** n té m con limón

lend [lend] (pt, pp **lent**) vt: **to ~ sth to sb** prestar algo a alguien; **~ing library** n biblioteca de préstamo

length [leŋθ] n (size) largo, longitud f; (distance): **the ~ of** todo lo largo de; (of swimming pool, cloth) largo; (of wood, string) trozo; (amount of time) duración f; **at ~** (at last) por fin, finalmente; (lengthily) largamente; **~en** vt alargar ♦ vi alargarse; **~ways** adv a lo largo; **~y** adj largo, extenso

lenient ['li:nɪənt] adj indulgente

lens [lenz] n (of spectacles) lente f; (of camera) objetivo

Lent [lent] n Cuaresma

lent [lent] pt, pp of **lend**

lentil ['lentl] n lenteja

Leo ['li:əu] n Leo

leotard ['li:ətɑ:d] n mallas fpl

leprosy ['leprəsɪ] n lepra

lesbian ['lezbɪən] n lesbiana

less [les] adj (in size, degree etc) menor; (in quality) menos ♦ pron, adv menos ♦ prep: **~ tax/10% discount** menos impuestos/el 10 por ciento de descuento; **~ than half** menos de la mitad; **~ than ever** menos que nunca; **~ and ~** cada vez menos; **the ~ he works ...** cuanto menos trabaja ...; **~en** vi disminuir, reducirse ♦ vt disminuir, reducir; **~er** ['lesə*] adj menor; **to a ~er extent** en menor grado

lesson ['lesn] n clase f; (warning) lección f

let [let] (pt, pp **let**) vt (allow) dejar, permitir; (BRIT: lease) alquilar; **to ~ sb do sth** dejar que uno haga algo; **to ~ sb know sth** comunicar algo a uno; **~'s go** ¡vamos!; **~ him come** que venga; **"to ~"** "se alquila"; **~ down** vt *(tyre)* desinflar; *(disappoint)* defraudar; **~ go** *vi*, *vt* soltar; **~ in** *vt* dejar entrar; *(visitor etc)* hacer pasar; **~ off** *vt* *(culprit)* dejar escapar; *(gun)* disparar; *(bomb)* accionar; *(firework)* hacer estallar; **~ on** *(inf)* *vi* divulgar; **~ out** *vt* dejar salir; *(sound)* soltar; **~ up** *vi* amainar, disminuir

lethal ['li:θl] *adj* *(weapon)* mortífero; *(poison, wound)* mortal

letter ['letə*] *n* *(of alphabet)* letra; *(correspondence)* carta; **~ bomb** *n* carta-bomba; **~box** *(BRIT)* *n* buzón *m*; **~ing** *n* letras *fpl*

lettuce ['letis] *n* lechuga

let-up *n* disminución *f*

leukaemia [lu:'ki:mɪə] *(US* **leukemia**) *n* leucemia

level ['levl] *adj* *(flat)* llano ♦ *adv:* **to draw ~ with** llegar a la altura de ♦ *n* nivel *m*; *(height)* altura ♦ *vt* nivelar; allanar; *(destroy: building)* derribar; (: *forest)* arrasar; **to be ~ with** estar a nivel de; **"A" ~s** *(BRIT)* *npl* ≈ exámenes *mpl* de bachillerato superior, B.U.P.; **"O" ~s** *(BRIT)* *npl* ≈ exámenes *mpl* de octavo de básica; **on the ~** *(fig: honest)* serio; **~ off** *or* **out** *vi* *(prices etc)* estabilizarse; **~ crossing** *(BRIT)* *n* paso a nivel; **~-headed** *adj* sensato

lever ['li:və*] *n* *(also fig)* palanca ♦ *vt:* **to ~ up** levantar con palanca; **~age** *n* *(using bar etc)* apalancamiento; *(fig: influence)* influencia

levy ['levi] *n* impuesto ♦ *vt* exigir, recaudar

lewd [lu:d] *adj* lascivo; *(joke)* obsceno, colorado *(AM)*

liability [laɪə'bɪlətɪ] *n* *(pej: person, thing)* estorbo, lastre *m*; *(JUR: responsibility)* responsabilidad *f*; **liabilities** *npl* *(COMM)* pasivo

liable ['laɪəbl] *adj* *(subject):* **~** sujeto a; *(responsible):* **~** for responsable de; *(likely):* **~ to do** propenso a hacer

liaise [lɪ'eɪz] *vi:* **to ~ with** enlazar con; **liaison** [lɪ:'eɪzɔn] *n* *(coordination)*

enlace *m*; *(affair)* relaciones *fpl* amorosas

liar ['laɪə*] *n* mentiroso/a

libel ['laɪbl] *n* calumnia ♦ *vt* calumniar

liberal ['lɪbərəl] *adj* liberal; *(offer, amount etc)* generoso

liberate ['lɪbəreɪt] *vt* *(people: from poverty etc)* librar; *(prisoner)* libertar; *(country)* liberar

liberty ['lɪbətɪ] *n* libertad *f*; *(criminal):* **to be at ~** estar en libertad; **to be at ~ to do** estar libre para hacer; **to take the ~ of doing sth** tomarse la libertad de hacer algo

Libra ['li:brə] *n* Libra

librarian [laɪ'breərɪən] *n* bibliotecario/a

library ['laɪbrərɪ] *n* biblioteca

libretto [lɪ'bretəʊ] *n* libreto

Libya ['lɪbɪə] *n* Libia; **~n** *adj*, *n* libio/a *m/f*

lice [laɪs] *npl of* **louse**

licence ['laɪsəns] *(US* **license**) *n* licencia; *(permit)* permiso; *(also: driving ~, (US)* driver's *~)* carnet *m* de conducir *(SP)*, permiso *(AM)*

license ['laɪsəns] *n* *(US)* = **licence** ♦ *vt* autorizar, dar permiso a; **~d** *adj* *(for alcohol)* autorizado para vender bebidas alcohólicas; *(car)* matriculado; **~ plate** *(US)* *n* placa *(de* matrícula*)*

lick [lɪk] *vt* lamer; *(inf: defeat)* dar una paliza a; **to ~ one's lips** relamerse

licorice ['lɪkərɪs] *(US)* *n* = **liquorice**

lid [lɪd] *n* *(of box, case)* tapa; *(of pan)* tapadera

lido ['laɪdəʊ] *n* *(BRIT)* piscina

lie [laɪ] *(pt* **lay**, *pp* **lain**) *vi* *(rest)* estar echado, estar acostado; *(of object: be situated)* estar, encontrarse; *(tell lies: pt, pp* **lied**) mentir ♦ *n* mentira; **to ~ low** *(fig)* mantenerse a escondidas; **~ about** *or* **around** *vi* *(things)* estar tirado; *(BRIT: people)* estar tumbado; **~-down** *(BRIT)* *n:* **to have a ~-down** echarse *(una siesta)*; **~-in** *(BRIT)* *n:* **to have a ~-in** quedarse en la cama

lieu [lu:]: **in ~ of** *prep* en lugar de

lieutenant [lɛfˈtɛnənt, (US) luːˈtɛnənt] n (MIL) teniente m

life [laɪf] (pl **lives**) n vida; **to come to ~** animarse; **~ assurance** (BRIT) n seguro de vida; **~belt** (BRIT) n salvavidas m inv; **~boat** n lancha de socorro; **~guard** n vigilante m, socorrista m/f; **~ insurance** n = **~ assurance**; **~ jacket** n chaleco salvavidas; **~less** adj sin vida; (dull) soso; **~like** adj (model etc) que parece vivo; (realistic) realista; **~long** adj de toda la vida; **~ preserver** (US) n cinturón m/chaleco salvavidas; **~ sentence** n cadena perpetua; **~size** adj de tamaño natural; **~ span** n vida; **~style** n estilo de vida; **~ support system** n (MED) sistema m de respiración asistida; **~time** n (of person) vida; (of thing) período de vida

lift [lɪft] vt levantar; (end: ban, rule) levantar, suprimir ♦ vi (fog) disiparse ♦ n (BRIT: machine) ascensor m; **to give sb a ~** (BRIT) llevar a uno en el coche; **~off** n despegue m

light [laɪt] (pt, pp **lighted** or **lit**) n luz f; (lamp) luz f, lámpara; (AUT) luz f; (for cigarette etc): **have you got a ~?** ¿tienes fuego? ♦ vt (candle, cigarette, fire) encender ♦ (SP), prender (AM); (room) alumbrar ♦ adj (colour) claro; (not heavy, also fig) ligero; (room) con mucha luz; (gentle, graceful) ágil; **~s** npl (traffic ~s) semáforos mpl; **to come to ~** salir a luz; **in the ~ of** (of new evidence etc) a la luz de; **~ up** vi (smoke) encender un cigarrillo; (face) iluminarse ♦ vt (illuminate) iluminar, alumbrar; (set fire to) encender; **~ bulb** n bombilla (SP), foco (AM); **~en** vt (also: make less heavy) aligerar; **~er** n (also: cigarette ~er) encendedor m, mechero; **~-headed** adj (dizzy) mareado; (excited) exaltado; **~-hearted** adj (person) alegre; (remark etc) divertido; **~house** n faro; **~ing** n (system) alumbrado; **~ly** adv ligeramente; (not

seriously) con poca seriedad; **to get off ~ly** ser castigado con poca severidad; **~ness** n (in weight) ligereza

lightning [ˈlaɪtnɪŋ] n relámpago, rayo; **~ conductor** (US **~ rod**) n pararrayos m inv

light: **~ pen** n lápiz m óptico; **~weight** adj (suit) ligero ♦ n (BOXING) peso ligero; **~ year** n año luz

like [laɪk] vt gustarle a uno ♦ prep como ♦ adj parecido, semejante ♦ n: **and the ~** y otros por el estilo; **his ~s and dislikes** sus gustos y aversiones; **I would ~, I'd ~** me gustaría; (for purchase) quisiera; **would you ~ a coffee?** ¿te apetece un café?; **I ~ swimming** me gusta nadar; **she ~s apples** le gustan las manzanas; **to be or look ~ sb/sth** parecerse a alguien/algo; **what does it look/taste/sound ~?** ¿cómo es/a qué sabe/cómo suena?; **that's just ~ him** es muy de él, es característico de él; **do it ~ this** hazlo así; **it is nothing ~ ...** no tiene parecido alguno con ...; **~able** adj simpático, agradable

likelihood [ˈlaɪklɪhʊd] n probabilidad f

likely [ˈlaɪklɪ] adj probable; **he's ~ to leave** es probable que se vaya; **not ~!** ¡ni hablar!

likeness [ˈlaɪknɪs] n semejanza, parecido; **that's a good ~** se parece mucho

likewise [ˈlaɪkwaɪz] adv igualmente; **to do ~** hacer lo mismo

liking [ˈlaɪkɪŋ] n: **~ (for)** (person) cariño (a); (thing) afición (a); **to be to sb's ~** ser del gusto de uno

lilac [ˈlaɪlək] n (tree) lilo; (flower) lila

lily [ˈlɪlɪ] n lirio, azucena; **~ of the valley** n lirio de los valles

limb [lɪm] n miembro

limber [ˈlɪmbəˈ]: **to ~ up** vi (SPORT) hacer ejercicios de calentamiento

limbo [ˈlɪmbəʊ] n: **to be in ~** (fig) quedar a la expectativa

lime [laɪm] n (tree) limero; (fruit) lima;

(GEO) cal f

limelight ['laɪmlaɪt] n: **to be in the ~** (fig) ser el centro de atención

limerick ['lɪmərɪk] n especie de poema humorístico

limestone ['laɪmstəʊn] n piedra caliza

limit ['lɪmɪt] n límite m ♦ vt limitar; **~ed** adj limitado; **to be ~ed to** limitarse a; **~ed (liability) company** (BRIT) n sociedad f anónima

limousine ['lɪməzi:n] n limusina

limp [lɪmp] n: **to have a ~** tener cojera ♦ vi cojear ♦ adj flojo; (material) fláccido

limpet ['lɪmpɪt] n lapa

line [laɪn] n línea; (rope) cuerda; (for fishing) sedal m; (wire) hilo; (row, series) fila, hilera; (of writing) renglón m, línea; (of song) verso; (on face) arruga; (RAIL) vía ♦ vt (road etc) llenar; (SEWING) forrar; **to ~ the streets** llenar las aceras; **in ~ with** alineado con; (according to) de acuerdo con; **~ up** vi hacer cola ♦ vt alinear; (prepare) preparar; organizar

lined [laɪnd] adj (face) arrugado; (paper) rayado

linen ['lɪnɪn] n ropa blanca; (cloth) lino

liner ['laɪnə*] n vapor m de línea, transatlántico; (for bin) bolsa (de basura)

linesman ['laɪnzmən] n (SPORT) juez m de línea

line-up n (US: queue) cola; (SPORT) alineación f

linger ['lɪŋgə*] vi retrasarse, tardar en marcharse; (smell, tradition) persistir

lingerie ['lænʒəri:] n lencería

linguist ['lɪŋgwɪst] n lingüista m/f; **~ics** n lingüística

lining ['laɪnɪŋ] n forro; (ANAT) (membrana) mucosa

link [lɪŋk] n (of a chain) eslabón m; (relationship) relación f, vínculo ♦ vt vincular, unir; (associate): **to ~ with** or **to** relacionar con; **~s** npl (GOLF) campo de golf; **~ up** vt acoplar ♦ vi unirse

lino ['laɪnəʊ] n = **linoleum**

linoleum [lɪ'nəʊlɪəm] n linóleo

lion ['laɪən] n león m; **~ess** n leona

lip [lɪp] n labio

liposuction ['lɪpəʊsʌkʃən] n liposucción f

lip: ~read vi leer los labios; **~ salve** n crema protectora para labios; **~ service** n: **to pay ~ service to sth** (pej) prometer algo de boquilla; **~stick** n lápiz m de labios, carmín m

liqueur [lɪ'kjuə*] n licor m

liquid ['lɪkwɪd] adj, n líquido; **~ize** [-aɪz] vt (CULIN) licuar; **~izer** [-aɪzə*] n licuadora

liquor ['lɪkə*] n licor m, bebidas fpl alcohólicas

liquorice ['lɪkərɪs] (BRIT) n regaliz m

liquor store (US) n bodega, tienda de vinos y bebidas alcohólicas

Lisbon ['lɪzbən] n Lisboa

lisp [lɪsp] n ceceo ♦ vi cecear

list [lɪst] n lista ♦ vt (mention) enumerar; (put on a list) poner en una lista; **~ed building** (BRIT) n monumento declarado de interés histórico-artístico

listen ['lɪsn] vi escuchar, oír; **to ~ to sb/sth** escuchar a uno/algo; **~er** n oyente m/f; (RADIO) radioyente m/f

listless ['lɪstlɪs] adj apático, indiferente

lit [lɪt] pt, pp of **light**

liter ['li:tə*] (US) n = **litre**

literacy ['lɪtərəsɪ] n capacidad f de leer y escribir

literal ['lɪtərəl] adj literal

literary ['lɪtərərɪ] adj literario

literate ['lɪtərət] adj que sabe leer y escribir; (educated) culto

literature ['lɪtərɪtʃə*] n literatura; (brochures etc) folletos mpl

lithe [laɪð] adj ágil

litigation [lɪtɪ'geɪʃən] n litigio

litre ['li:tə*] (US **liter**) n litro

litter ['lɪtə*] n (rubbish) basura; (young animals) camada, cría; **~ bin** (BRIT) n papelera; **~ed** adj: **~ed with**

(scattered) lleno de

little ['lɪtl] adj (small) pequeño ♦ (not much) poco ♦ adv poco; **a ~** un poco (de); **~ house/bird** casita/pajarito; **a ~ bit** un poquito; **by ~ and ~** poco a poco; **~ finger** n dedo meñique

live¹ [laɪv] adj (animal) vivo; (wire) conectado; (broadcast) en directo; (shell) cargado

live² [lɪv] vi vivir; **~ down** vt hacer olvidar; **~ on** vt fus (food, salary) vivir de; **~ together** vi vivir juntos; **~ up to** vt fus (fulfil) cumplir con

livelihood ['laɪvlɪhud] n sustento

lively ['laɪvlɪ] adj vivo; (interesting: place, book etc) animado

liven up ['laɪvn-] vt animar ♦ vi animarse

liver ['lɪvə*] n hígado

lives [laɪvz] npl of **life**

livestock ['laɪvstɔk] n ganado

livid ['lɪvɪd] adj lívido; (furious) furioso

living ['lɪvɪŋ] adj (alive) vivo ♦ n: to **earn** or **make a ~** ganarse la vida; **~ conditions** npl condiciones fpl de vida; **~ room** n sala (de estar); **~ standards** npl nivel m de vida; **~ wage** n jornal m suficiente para vivir

lizard ['lɪzəd] n lagarto; (small) lagartija

load [ləud] n carga; (weight) peso ♦ vt (COMPUT) cargar; (also: **~ up**): to **~ (with)** cargar (con or de); **a ~ of rubbish** (inf) tonterías fpl; **a ~ of, ~s of** (fig) cantidad de, montones de; **~ed** adj (vehicle): to **be ~ed** with estar cargado de; (question) intencionado; (inf: rich) forrado (de dinero)

loaf [ləuf] (pl loaves) n (barra de pan m

loan [ləun] n préstamo ♦ vt prestar; **on ~** prestado

loath [ləuθ] adj: to **be ~ to do sth** estar poco dispuesto a hacer algo

loathe [ləuð] vt aborrecer; (person) odiar; **loathing** n aversión f; odio

loaves [ləuvz] npl of **loaf**

lobby ['lɔbɪ] n vestíbulo, sala de espera; (POL: pressure group) grupo de presión ♦ vt presionar

lobster ['lɔbstə*] n langosta

local ['ləukl] adj local ♦ n (pub) bar m; **the ~s** los vecinos, los del lugar; **~ anaesthetic** n (MED) anestesia local; **~ authority** n municipio, ayuntamiento (SP); **~ call** n (TEL) llamada local; **~ government** n gobierno municipal; **~ity** [-'kælɪtɪ] n localidad f; **~ly** [-kəlɪ] adv en la vecindad; por aquí

locate [ləu'keɪt] vt (find) localizar; (situate): to **be ~d in** estar situado en

location [ləu'keɪʃən] n situación f; **on ~** (CINEMA) en exteriores

loch [lɔx] n lago

lock [lɔk] n (of door, box) cerradura; (of canal) esclusa; (of hair) mechón m ♦ vt (with key) cerrar (con llave) ♦ vi (door etc) cerrarse (con llave); (wheels) trabarse; **~ in** vt encerrar; **~ out** vt (person) cerrar la puerta a; **~ up** vt (criminal) meter en la cárcel; (mental patient) encerrar; (house) cerrar (con llave) ♦ vi echar la llave

locker ['lɔkə*] n casillero

locket ['lɔkɪt] n medallón m

locksmith ['lɔksmɪθ] n cerrajero/a

lockup ['lɔkʌp] n (jail, cell) cárcel f

locum ['ləukəm] n (MED) (médico/a) interino/a

locust ['ləukəst] n langosta

lodge [lɔdʒ] n casita (del guarda) ♦ vi (person): to **~ (with)** alojarse (en casa de); (bullet, bone) incrustarse ♦ vt (complaint) presentar; **~r** n huésped(a) m/f

lodgings ['lɔdʒɪŋz] npl alojamiento

loft [lɔft] n desván m

lofty ['lɔftɪ] adj (noble) sublime; (haughty) altanero

log [lɔg] n (of wood) leño, tronco; (written account) diario ♦ vt anotar

logbook ['lɔgbuk] n (NAUT) diario de a bordo; (AVIAT) libro de vuelo; (of car)

loggerheads 458 **look**

documentación f (del coche (SP) or carro (AM))

loggerheads ['lɔgəhedz] npl: **to be at ~ (with)** estar en desacuerdo (con)

logic ['lɔdʒɪk] n lógica; **~al** adj lógico

logo ['ləʊgəʊ] n logotipo

loin [lɔɪn] n (CULIN) lomo, solomillo

loiter ['lɔɪtə*] vi (linger) entretenerse

loll [lɔl] vi (also: **~ about**) repantigarse

lollipop ['lɔlɪpɔp] n chupa-chups ® inv, piruli m; **~ man/lady** (BRIT irreg) n persona encargada de ayudar a los niños a cruzar la calle

---
lollipop man/lollipop lady

En el Reino Unido, se llama **lollipop man** o **lollipop lady** a la persona que se ocupa de parar el tráfico en los alrededores de los colegios para que los niños crucen sin peligro. Suelen ser personas ya jubiladas, vestidas con una gabardina de color llamativo y llevan una señal de stop portátil, la cual recuerda por su forma a una piruleta, y de ahí su nombre.

London ['lʌndən] n Londres; **~er** n londinense m/f

lone [ləʊn] adj solitario

loneliness ['ləʊnlɪnɪs] n soledad f; aislamiento

lonely ['ləʊnlɪ] adj (situation) solitario; (person) solo; (place) aislado

long [lɔŋ] adj largo ♦ adv mucho tiempo, largamente ♦ vi: **to ~ for sth** anhelar algo; **so** or **as ~ as** mientras, con tal que; **don't be ~!** ¡no tardes!, ¡vuelve pronto!; **how ~ is the street?** ¿cuánto tiene la calle de largo?; **how ~ is the lesson?** ¿cuánto dura la clase?; **6 metres ~** que mide 6 metros, de 6 metros de largo; **6 months ~** que dura 6 meses, de 6 meses de duración; **all night ~** toda la noche; **he no ~er comes** ya no viene; **~ before** mucho antes; **before ~** (+ future) dentro de poco; (+ past)

poco tiempo después; **at ~ last** al fin, por fin; **~-distance** adj (race) de larga distancia; (call) interurbano; **~-haired** adj de pelo largo; **~hand** n escritura sin abreviaturas; **~ing** n anhelo, ansia; (nostalgia) nostalgia ♦ adj anhelante

longitude ['lɔŋgɪtjuːd] n longitud f

long: **~ jump** n salto de longitud; **~-life** adj (batteries) de larga duración; (milk) uperizado; **~-lost** adj desaparecido hace mucho tiempo; **~-range** adj (plan) de gran alcance; (missile) de largo alcance; **~-sighted** (BRIT) adj présbita; **~-standing** adj de mucho tiempo; **~-suffering** adj sufrido; **~-term** adj a largo plazo; **~ wave** n onda larga; **~-winded** adj prolijo

loo [luː] (BRIT: inf) n wáter m

look [lʊk] vi mirar; (seem) parecer; (building etc): **to ~ south/on to the sea** dar al sur/al mar ♦ n (gen): **to have a ~** mirar; (glance) mirada; (appearance) aire m, aspecto; **~s** npl (good ~s) belleza; **~ (here)!** (expressing annoyance etc) ¡oye!; **~!** (expressing surprise) ¡mira!; **~ after** vt fus (care for) cuidar a; (deal with) encargarse de; **~ at** vt fus mirar; (read quickly) echar un vistazo a; **~ back** vi mirar hacia atrás; **~ down on** vt fus (fig) despreciar, mirar con desprecio; **~ for** vt fus buscar; **~ forward to** vt fus esperar con ilusión; (in letters): **we ~ forward to hearing from you** quedamos a la espera de sus gratas noticias; **~ into** vt investigar; **~ on** vi mirar (como espectador); **~ out** vi (beware): **~ out (for)** tener cuidado (de); **~ out for** vt fus (seek) buscar; (await) esperar; **~ round** vi volver la cabeza; **~ through** vt fus (examine) examinar; **~ to** vt fus (rely on) contar con; **~ up** vi mirar hacia arriba; (improve) mejorar ♦ vt (word) buscar; **~ up to** vt fus admirar; **~out** n (tower etc) puesto de observación; (person) vigía m/f; **to be on the ~-out** for sth estar al acecho de algo

loom [lu:m] vi: **~ (up)** (threaten) surgir, amenazar; (event: approach) aproximarse

loony ['lu:nɪ] (inf) adj, n loco/a m/f

loop [lu:p] n lazo ♦ vt: **to ~ sth round sth** pasar algo alrededor de algo; **~hole** n escapatoria

loose [lu:s] adj suelto; (clothes) ancho; (morals, discipline) relajado; **to be on the ~** estar en libertad; **to be at a ~ end** or **at ~ ends** (US) no saber qué hacer; **~ change** n cambio; **~ chippings** npl (on road) gravilla suelta; **~ly** adv libremente, aproximadamente; **~n** vt aflojar

loot [lu:t] n botín m ♦ vt saquear

lop off [lɔp-] vt (branches) podar

lop-sided adj torcido

lord [lɔ:d] n señor m; **L~ Smith** Lord Smith; **the L~** el Señor; **my ~** (to bishop) Ilustrísima; (to noble etc) Señor; **good L~!** ¡Dios mío!; **the (House of) L~s** (BRIT) la Cámara de los Lores; **~ship** n: **your L~ship** su Señoría

lore [lɔ:*] n tradiciones fpl

lorry ['lɔrɪ] (BRIT) n camión m; **~ driver** n camionero/a

lose [lu:z] (pt, pp lost) vt perder ♦ vi perder, ser vencido; **to ~ (time)** (clock) atrasarse; **~r** n perdedor(a) m/f

loss [lɔs] n pérdida; **heavy ~es** (MIL.) grandes pérdidas; **to be at a ~** no saber qué hacer; **to make a ~** sufrir pérdidas

lost [lɔst] pt, pp of lose ♦ adj perdido; **~ property** (US **~ and found**) n objetos mpl perdidos

lot [lɔt] n (group: of things) grupo; (at auctions) lote m; **the ~** el todo, todos; **a ~** (large number: of books etc) muchos; (a great deal) mucho, bastante; **a ~ of, ~s of** mucho(s) (pl); **I read a ~** leo bastante; **to draw ~s (for sth)** echar suertes (para decidir algo)

lotion ['ləuʃən] n loción f

lottery ['lɔtərɪ] n lotería

loud [laud] adj (voice, sound) fuerte; (laugh, shout) estrepitoso; (condemnation etc) enérgico; (gaudy) chillón/ona ♦ adv (speak etc) fuerte; **out ~** en voz alta; **~hailer** (BRIT) n megáfono; **~ly** adv (noisily) fuerte; (aloud) en voz alta; **~speaker** n altavoz m

lounge [laundʒ] n salón m, sala (de estar); (at airport etc) sala; (BRIT: also: **~-bar**) salón-bar m ♦ vi (also: **~ about** or **around**) reposar, holgazanear

louse [laus] (pl lice) n piojo

lousy ['lauzɪ] (inf) adj (bad quality) malísimo, asqueroso; (ill) fatal

lout [laut] n gamberro/a

lovable ['lʌvəbl] adj amable, simpático

love [lʌv] n (romantic, sexual) amor m; (kind, caring) cariño ♦ vt amar, querer; (thing, activity) encantarle a uno; **"~ from Anne"** (on letter) "un abrazo (de) Anne"; **to ~ to do** encantarle a uno hacer; **to be/fall in ~ with** estar enamorado/enamorarse de; **to make ~** hacer el amor; **for the ~ of** por amor de; **"15 ~"** (TENNIS) "15 a cero"; **I ~ paella** me encanta la paella; **~ affair** n aventura sentimental; **~ letter** n carta de amor; **~ life** n vida sentimental

lovely ['lʌvlɪ] adj (delightful) encantador(a); (beautiful) precioso

lover ['lʌvə*] n amante m/f; (person in love) enamorado; (amateur): **a ~ of** un(a) aficionado/a or un(a) amante de

loving ['lʌvɪŋ] adj amoroso, cariñoso; (action) tierno

low [ləu] adj, ad bajo ♦ n (METEOROLOGY) área de baja presión; **to be ~ on** (supplies etc) andar mal de; **to feel ~** sentirse deprimido; **to turn (down)** ~ bajar; **~-alcohol** adj de bajo contenido en alcohol; **~-calorie** adj bajo en calorías; **~-cut** adj (dress) escotado

lower ['ləʊə*] adj más bajo; (less important) menos importante ♦ vt bajar; (reduce) reducir ♦ vr: **to ~ o.s. to** (fig) rebajarse a

low: **~-fat** adj (milk, yoghurt) desnatado; (diet) bajo en calorías; **~lands** npl (GEO) tierras fpl bajas; **~ly** adj humilde, inferior; **~ season** n la temporada baja

loyal ['lɔɪəl] adj leal; **~ty** n lealtad f

lozenge ['lɒzɪndʒ] n (MED) pastilla

L.P. n abbr (= long-playing record) elepé m

L-plates ['ɛl-] npl (BRIT) placas fpl de aprendiz de conductor

---
L-Plates

En el Reino Unido las personas que están aprendiendo a conducir deben llevar en la parte delantera y trasera de su vehículo unas placas blancas con una L en rojo conocidas como **L-Plates** (de **learner**). No es necesario que asistan a clases teóricas sino que, desde el principio, se les entrega un carnet de conducir provisional ("provisional driving licence") para que realicen sus prácticas, aunque no pueden circular por las autopistas y deben ir siempre acompañadas por un conductor con carnet definitivo ("full driving licence").

Ltd abbr (= limited company) S.A.

lubricate ['lu:brɪkeɪt] vt lubricar, engrasar

luck [lʌk] n suerte f; **bad ~** mala suerte; **good ~!** ¡que tengas suerte!, ¡suerte!; **bad** or **hard** or **tough ~!** ¡qué pena!; **~ily** adv afortunadamente; **~y** adj afortunado; (at cards etc) con suerte; (object) que trae suerte

ludicrous ['lu:dɪkrəs] adj absurdo

lug [lʌg] vt (drag) arrastrar

luggage ['lʌgɪdʒ] n equipaje m; **~ rack** n (on car) baca, portaequipajes m inv

lukewarm ['lu:kwɔ:m] adj tibio

lull [lʌl] n tregua ♦ vt: **to ~ sb to sleep** arrullar a uno; **to ~ sb into a false sense of security** dar a alguien una falsa sensación de seguridad

lullaby ['lʌləbaɪ] n nana

lumbago [lʌm'beɪgəu] n lumbago

lumber ['lʌmbə*] n (junk) trastos mpl viejos; (wood) maderos mpl; **~ with** vt: **to be ~ed with** tener que cargar con algo; **~jack** n maderero

luminous ['lu:mɪnəs] adj luminoso

lump [lʌmp] n terrón m; (fragment) trozo; (swelling) bulto ♦ vt (also: ~ **together**) juntar; **~ sum** n suma global; **~y** adj (sauce) lleno de grumos; (mattress) lleno de bultos

lunatic ['lu:nətɪk] adj loco

lunch [lʌntʃ] n almuerzo, comida ♦ vi almorzar

luncheon ['lʌntʃən] n almuerzo; **~ voucher** (BRIT) n vale m de comida

lunch time n hora de comer

lung [lʌŋ] n pulmón m

lunge [lʌndʒ] vi (also: ~ **forward**) abalanzarse; **to ~ at** arremeter contra

lurch [lə:tʃ] vi dar sacudidas ♦ n sacudida; **to leave sb in the ~** dejar a uno plantado

lure [luə*] n (attraction) atracción f ♦ vt tentar

lurid ['luərɪd] adj (colour) chillón/ona; (account) espeluznante

lurk [lə:k] vi (person, animal) estar al acecho; (fig) acechar

luscious ['lʌʃəs] adj (attractive: person, thing) precioso; (food) delicioso

lush [lʌʃ] adj exuberante

lust [lʌst] n lujuria; (greed) codicia

lustre ['lʌstə*] (US **luster**) n lustre m, brillo

lusty ['lʌstɪ] adj robusto, fuerte

Luxembourg ['lʌksəmbə:g] n Luxemburgo

luxuriant [lʌg'zjuərɪənt] adj exuberante

luxurious [lʌg'zjuərɪəs] adj lujoso

luxury ['lʌkʃəri] n lujo ♦ cpd de lujo
lying ['laiiŋ] n mentiras fpl ♦ adj mentiroso
lyrical ['lirikl] adj lírico
lyrics ['liriks] npl (of song) letra

M, m

m. abbr = metre; mile; million
M.A. abbr = Master of Arts
mac [mæk] n (BRIT) impermeable m
macaroni [mækə'rəuni] n macarrones mpl
machine [mə'ʃiːn] n máquina ♦ vt (dress etc) coser a máquina; (TECH) hacer a máquina; ~ **gun** n ametralladora; ~ **language** n (COMPUT) lenguaje m máquina; ~**ry** n maquinaria; (fig) mecanismo
macho ['mætʃəu] adj machista
mackerel ['mækrl] n inv caballa
mackintosh ['mækintɔʃ] (BRIT) n impermeable m
mad [mæd] adj loco; (idea) disparatado; (angry) furioso; (keen): **to be ~ about sth** volverle loco a uno algo
madam ['mædəm] n señora
madden ['mædn] vt volver loco
made [meid] pt, pp of **make**
Madeira [mə'diərə] n (GEO) Madera; (wine) vino de Madera
made-to-measure [BRIT] adj hecho a la medida
madly ['mædli] adv locamente
madman ['mædmən] (irreg) n loco
madness ['mædnis] n locura
Madrid [mə'drid] n Madrid
magazine [mægə'ziːn] n revista; (RADIO, TV) programa m magazina
maggot ['mægət] n gusano
magic ['mædʒik] n magia ♦ adj mágico; ~**ian** [mə'dʒiʃən] n mago/a; (conjurer) prestidigitador(a) m/f
magistrate ['mædʒistreit] n juez m/f (municipal)

magnet ['mægnit] n imán m; ~**ic** [-'netik] adj magnético; (personality) atrayente
magnificent [mæg'nifisənt] adj magnífico
magnify ['mægnifai] vt (object) ampliar; (sound) aumentar; ~**ing glass** n lupa
magpie ['mægpai] n urraca
mahogany [mə'hɔgəni] n caoba
maid [meid] n criada; **old ~** (pej) solterona
maiden ['meidn] n doncella ♦ adj (aunt etc) solterona; (speech, voyage) inaugural; ~ **name** n nombre m de soltera
mail [meil] n correo; (letters) cartas fpl ♦ vt echar al correo; ~**box** (US) n buzón m; ~**ing list** n lista de direcciones; ~-**order** n pedido postal
maim [meim] vt mutilar, lisiar
main [mein] adj principal, mayor ♦ n (pipe) cañería maestra; (US) red f eléctrica; **the ~s** npl (BRIT: ELEC) la red eléctrica; **in the ~** en general; ~**frame** n (COMPUT) ordenador m central; ~**land** n tierra firme; ~**ly** adv principalmente; ~ **road** n carretera; ~**stay** n (fig) pilar m; ~**stream** n corriente f principal
maintain [mein'tein] vt mantener; **maintenance** ['meintənəns] n mantenimiento; (LAW) manutención f
maize [meiz] (BRIT) n maíz m (SP), choclo (AM)
majestic [mə'dʒestik] adj majestuoso
majesty ['mædʒisti] n majestad f; (title): **Your M~** Su Majestad
major ['meidʒə*] n (MIL) comandante m ♦ adj principal; (MUS) mayor
Majorca [mə'jɔːkə] n Mallorca
majority [mə'dʒɔriti] n mayoría
make [meik] (pt, pp **made**) vt hacer; (manufacture) fabricar; (mistake) cometer; (speech) pronunciar; (cause to be): **to ~ sb sad** poner triste a alguien; (force): **to ~ sb do sth**

obligar a alguien a hacer algo; (*earn*) ganar; (*equal*): **2 and 2 ~ 4** 2 y 2 son 4 ♦ *n* marca; **to ~ the bed** hacer la cama; **to ~ a fool of sb** poner a alguien en ridículo; **to ~ a profit/loss** obtener ganancias/sufrir pérdidas; **to ~ it** (*arrive*) llegar; (*achieve sth*) tener éxito; **what time do you ~ it?** ¿qué hora tienes?; **to ~ do with** contentarse con; **~ for** *vt fus* (*place*) dirigirse a; **~ out** *vt* (*decipher*) descifrar; (*understand*) entender; (*see*) distinguir; (*cheque*) extender; **~ up** *vt* (*invent*) inventar; (*prepare*) hacer; (*constitute*) constituir ♦ *vi* reconciliarse; (*with cosmetics*) maquillarse; **~ up for** *vt fus* compensar; **~-believe** *n* ficción *f*, invención *f*; **~r** *n* fabricante *m/f*; (*of film, programme*) autor(a) *m/f*; **~-shift** *adj* improvisado; **~up** *n* maquillaje *m*; **~-up remover** *n* desmaquillador *m*

making ['meiking] *n* (*fig*): **in the ~** en vías de formación; **to have the ~s of** (*person*) tener madera de

Malaysia [mə'leiziə] *n* Malasia, Malaysia

male [meil] *n* (BIOL) macho ♦ *adj* (*sex, attitude*) masculino; (*child etc*) varón

malfunction [mæl'fʌŋkʃən] *n* mal funcionamiento

malice ['mælis] *n* malicia; **malicious** [mə'lɪʃəs] *adj* malicioso; rencoroso

malignant [mə'lignənt] *adj* (MED) maligno

mall [mɔ:l] (US) *n* (*also*: **shopping ~**) centro comercial

mallet ['mælit] *n* mazo

malnutrition [mælnju:'trɪʃən] *n* desnutrición *f*

malpractice [mæl'præktis] *n* negligencia profesional

malt [mɔ:lt] *n* malta; (*whisky*) whisky *m* de malta

Malta ['mɔ:ltə] *n* Malta; **Maltese** [-'ti:z] *adj*, *n inv* maltés/esa *m/f*

mammal ['mæml] *n* mamífero

mammoth ['mæməθ] *n* mamut *m*

♦ *adj* gigantesco

man [mæn] (*pl* **men**) *n* hombre *m*; (**~kind**) el hombre ♦ *vt* (NAUT) tripular; (MIL) guarnecer; (*operate*: *machine*) manejar; **an old ~** un viejo; **~ and wife** marido y mujer

manage ['mænidʒ] *vi* arreglárselas, ir tirando ♦ *vt* (*be in charge of*) dirigir; (*control*: *person*) manejar; (: *ship*) gobernar; **~able** *adj* manejable; **~ment** *n* dirección *f*; **~r** *n* director(a) *m/f*; (*of pop star*) mánayer *m/f*; (SPORT) entrenador *m/f*; **~ress** *n* directora; entrenadora; **~rial** [-ə'dʒɪərɪəl] *adj* directivo; **managing director** *n* director(a) *m/f* general

mandarin ['mændərɪn] *n* (*also*: **~ orange**) mandarina; (*person*) mandarín *m*

mandatory ['mændətərɪ] *adj* obligatorio

mane [mein] *n* (*of horse*) crin *f*; (*of lion*) melena

maneuver [mə'nu:və*] (US) = **manoeuvre**

manfully ['mænfəlɪ] *adv* valientemente

mangle ['mæŋgl] *vt* mutilar, destrozar

man: **~handle** *vt* maltratar; **~hole** *n* agujero de acceso; **~hood** *n* edad *f* viril; (*state*) virilidad *f*; **~hour** *n* hora-hombre *f*; **~hunt** *n* (POLICE) búsqueda y captura

mania ['meɪnɪə] *n* manía; **~c** ['meɪnɪæk] *n* maníaco/a; (*fig*) maníático

manic ['mænɪk] *adj* frenético; **~-depressive** *n* maníaco/a depresivo/a

manicure ['mænɪkjuə*] *n* manicura

manifest ['mænɪfest] *vt* manifestar, mostrar ♦ *adj* manifiesto

manifesto [mænɪ'festəu] *n* manifiesto

manipulate [mə'nɪpjuleit] *vt* manipular

man: **~kind** [mæn'kaind] *n* humanidad *f*, género humano; **~ly** *adv* varonil; **~-made** *adj* artificial

manner ['mænə*] *n* manera, modo;

(*behaviour*) conducta, manera de ser;
(*type*): **all ~ of things** toda clase de
cosas; **~s** npl (*behaviour*) modales mpl;
bad ~s mala educación; **~ism** n
peculiaridad f de lenguaje (*or de
comportamiento*)

manoeuvre [məˈnuːvə*] (*US
maneuver*) vt, vi maniobrar ♦ n
maniobra

manor [ˈmænə*] n (*also: ~ house*) casa
solariega

manpower [ˈmænpauə*] n mano f de
obra

mansion [ˈmænʃən] n palacio, casa
grande

manslaughter [ˈmænslɔːtə*] n
homicidio no premeditado

mantelpiece [ˈmæntlpiːs] n repisa,
chimenea

manual [ˈmænjuəl] adj manual ♦ n
manual m

manufacture [mænjuˈfæktʃə*] vt
fabricar ♦ n fabricación f; **~r** n
fabricante m/f

manure [məˈnjuə*] n estiércol m

manuscript [ˈmænjuskrɪpt] n
manuscrito

many [ˈmenɪ] adj, pron muchos/as; **a
great ~** muchísimos, un buen número
de; **~ a time** muchas veces

map [mæp] n mapa m; **to ~ out** vt
proyectar

maple [ˈmeɪpl] n arce m (SP), maple m
(AM)

mar [mɑː*] vt estropear

marathon [ˈmærəθən] n maratón m

marble [ˈmɑːbl] n mármol m; (*toy*)
canica

March [mɑːtʃ] n marzo

march [mɑːtʃ] vi (MIL) marchar;
(*demonstrators*) manifestarse ♦ n
marcha; (*demonstration*) manifestación
f

mare [meə*] n yegua

margarine [mɑːdʒəˈriːn] n margarina

margin [ˈmɑːdʒɪn] n margen m;
(COMM: *profit* ~) margen m de

beneficios; **~al** adj marginal; **~al seat**
n (POL) escaño electoral difícil de
asegurar

marigold [ˈmærɪɡəʊld] n caléndula

marijuana [mærɪˈwɑːnə] n marijuana

marina [məˈriːnə] n puerto deportivo

marinate [ˈmærɪneɪt] vt marinar

marine [məˈriːn] adj marino ♦ n
soldado de marina

marital [ˈmærɪtl] adj matrimonial;
~ status estado civil

marjoram [ˈmɑːdʒərəm] n mejorana

mark [mɑːk] n marca, señal f; (*in snow,
mud etc*) huella; (*stain*) mancha; (BRIT:
SCOL) nota; (*currency*) marco ♦ vt
marcar; manchar; (*damage: furniture*)
rayar; (*indicate: place etc*) señalar; (BRIT:
SCOL) calificar, corregir; **to ~ time**
marcar el paso; (*fig*) marcar(se) un
ritmo; **~ed** adj (*obvious*) marcado,
acusado; **~er** n (*sign*) marcador m;
(*bookmark*) señal f (de libro)

market [ˈmɑːkɪt] n mercado ♦ vt
(COMM) comercializar; **~ garden** (BRIT)
n huerto; **~ing** n márketing m; **~place**
n mercado; **~ research** n análisis m
inv de mercados

marksman [ˈmɑːksmən] n tirador m

marmalade [ˈmɑːməleɪd] n
mermelada de naranja

maroon [məˈruːn] vt: **to be ~ed**
quedar aislado; (*fig*) quedar
abandonado

marquee [mɑːˈkiː] n entoldado

marriage [ˈmærɪdʒ] n (*relationship,
institution*) matrimonio; (*wedding*)
boda; (*act*) casamiento; **~ certificate**
n partida de casamiento

married [ˈmærɪd] adj casado; (*life, love*)
conyugal

marrow [ˈmærəʊ] n médula;
(*vegetable*) calabacín m

marry [ˈmærɪ] vt casarse con; (*subj:
father, priest etc*) casar ♦ vi (*also: get
married*) casarse

Mars [mɑːz] n Marte m

marsh [mɑːʃ] n pantano; (*salt ~*)

marisma

marshal ['mɑːʃl] n (MIL) mariscal m; (at sports meeting etc) oficial m; (US: of police, fire department) jefe/a m/f ♦ vt (thoughts etc) ordenar; (soldiers) formar

marshy ['mɑːʃɪ] adj pantanoso

martial law ['mɑːʃl-] n ley f marcial

martyr ['mɑːtə*] n mártir m/f; **~dom** n martirio

marvel ['mɑːvl] n maravilla, prodigio ♦ vi: **to ~ (at)** maravillarse (de); **~lous** (US **~ous**) adj maravilloso

Marxist ['mɑːksɪst] adj, n marxista m/f

marzipan ['mɑːzɪpæn] n mazapán m

mascara [mæs'kɑːrə] n rímel m

masculine ['mæskjulɪn] adj masculino

mash [mæʃ] vt machacar; **~ed potatoes** npl puré m de patatas (SP) or papas (AM)

mask [mɑːsk] n máscara ♦ vt (cover): **to ~ one's face** ocultarse la cara; (hide: feelings) esconder

mason ['meɪsn] n (also: stone~) albañil m; (also: free~) masón m; **~ry** n (in building) mampostería

masquerade [mæskə'reɪd] vi: **to ~ as** disfrazarse de, hacerse pasar por

mass [mæs] n (people) muchedumbre f; (of air, liquid etc) masa; (of detail, hair etc) gran cantidad f; (REL) misa ♦ cpd masivo ♦ vi reunirse; concentrarse; the **~es** npl las masas; **~es of** (inf) montones de

massacre ['mæsəkə*] n masacre f

massage ['mæsɑːʒ] n masaje m ♦ vt dar masaje a

masseur [mæ'sə:*] n masajista m

masseuse [mæ'sə:z] n masajista f

massive ['mæsɪv] adj enorme; (support, changes) masivo

mass media npl medios mpl de comunicación

mass production n fabricación f en serie

mast [mɑːst] n (NAUT) mástil m; (RADIO etc) torre f

master ['mɑːstə*] n (of servant) amo;

(of situation) dueño, maestro; (in primary school) maestro; (in secondary school) profesor m; (title for boys): **M~ X** Señorito X ♦ vt dominar; **M~ of Arts/Science** n licenciatura superior en Letras/Ciencias; **~ly** adj magistral; **~mind** n inteligencia superior ♦ vt dirigir, planear; **~piece** n obra maestra; **~y** n maestría

mat [mæt] n estera; (also: door~) felpudo; (also: table ~) salvamanteles m inv, posavasos m inv ♦ adj = **matt**

match [mætʃ] n cerilla, fósforo; (game) partido; (equal) igual m/f ♦ vt (go well with) hacer juego con; (equal) igualar; (correspond to) corresponderse con; (pair: also: ~ up) casar con ♦ vi hacer juego; **to be a good ~** hacer juego; **~box** n caja de cerillas; **~ing** adj que hace juego

mate [meɪt] n (work~) colega m/f; (inf: friend) amigo/a; (animal) macho m/ hembra f; (in merchant navy) segundo de a bordo ♦ vi acoplarse, aparearse ♦ vt aparear

material [mə'tɪərɪəl] n (substance) materia; (information) material m; (cloth) tela, tejido ♦ adj material; (important) esencial; **~s** npl materiales mpl

maternal [mə'tɜːnl] adj maternal

maternity [mə'tɜːnɪtɪ] n maternidad f; **~ dress** n vestido premamá

math [mæθ] (US) n = **mathematics**

mathematical [mæθə'mætɪkl] adj matemático

mathematician [mæθəmə'tɪʃən] n matemático/a

mathematics [mæθə'mætɪks] n matemáticas fpl

maths [mæθs] (BRIT) n = **mathematics**

matinée ['mætɪneɪ] n sesión f de tarde

matrices ['meɪtrɪsiːz] npl of **matrix**

matriculation [mətrɪkju'leɪʃən] n (formalización f de) matrícula

matrimony ['mætrɪmənɪ] n

matrimonio
matrix ['meɪtrɪks] (pl **matrices**) n
matriz f
matron ['meɪtrən] n enfermera f jefe;
(in school) ama de llaves
matt(t) [mæt] adj mate
matted ['mætɪd] adj enmarañado
matter ['mætə*] n cuestión f, asunto;
(PHYSICS) sustancia, materia; (reading ~)
material m; (MED: pus) pus m ♦ vi
importar; **~s** npl (affairs) asuntos mpl,
temas mpl; **it doesn't ~** no importa;
what's the ~? ¿qué pasa?; **no**
~ what pase lo que pase; **as a ~ of**
course por rutina; **as a ~ of fact** de
hecho; **~-of-fact** adj prosaico, práctico
mattress ['mætrɪs] n colchón m
mature [mə'tjʊə*] adj maduro ♦ vi
madurar; **maturity** n madurez f
maul [mɔ:l] vt magullar
mauve [məʊv] adj de color malva (SP)
or guinda (AM)
maximum ['mæksɪməm] (pl **maxima**)
adj máximo ♦ n máximo
May [meɪ] n mayo
may [meɪ] (conditional: **might**) vi
(indicating possibility): **he ~ come**
puede que venga; (be allowed to): **~ I**
smoke? ¿puedo fumar?; (wishes):
~ God bless you! ¡que Dios le
bendiga!; **you ~ as well go** bien
puedes irte
maybe ['meɪbi] adv quizá(s)
May Day n el primero de Mayo
mayhem ['meɪhem] n caos m total
mayonnaise [meɪə'neɪz] n mayonesa
mayor [meə*] n alcalde m; **~ess** n
alcaldesa
maze [meɪz] n laberinto
M.D. abbr = Doctor of Medicine
me [mi:] pron (direct) me; (stressed,
after pron) mí; **can you hear ~?** ¿me
oyes?; **he heard me** me oyó a mí; **it's**
~ soy yo; **give them to ~** dámelos;
las; **with/without ~** conmigo/sin mí
meadow ['medəʊ] n prado, pradera
meagre ['mi:gə*] (US **meager**) adj

escaso, pobre
meal [mi:l] n comida; (flour) harina;
~time n hora de comer
mean [mi:n] (pt, pp **meant**) adj (with
money) tacaño; (unkind) mezquino,
malo; (shabby) humilde; (average)
medio ♦ vt (signify) querer decir,
significar; (refer to) referirse a; (intend):
to ~ to do sth pensar or pretender
hacer algo ♦ n medio, término medio;
~s npl (way) medio, manera; (money)
recursos mpl, medios mpl; **by ~s of**
mediante, por medio de; **by all ~s!**
¡naturalmente!, ¡claro que sí!; **do you**
~ it? ¿lo dices en serio?; **what do**
you ~? ¿qué quiere decir?; **to be**
meant for sb/sth ser para uno/algo
meander [mɪ'ændə*] vi (river)
serpentear
meaning ['mi:nɪŋ] n significado,
sentido; (purpose) sentido, propósito;
~ful adj significativo; **~less** adj sin
sentido
meanness ['mi:nnɪs] n (with money)
tacañería; (unkindness) maldad f,
mezquindad f; (shabbiness) humildad f
meant [ment] pt, pp of **mean**
meantime ['mi:ntaɪm] adv (also: in
the ~) mientras tanto
meanwhile ['mi:nwaɪl] adv =
meantime
measles ['mi:zlz] n sarampión m
measure ['meʒə*] vt, vi medir ♦ n
medida; (ruler) regla; **~ments** npl
medidas fpl
meat [mi:t] n carne f; **cold ~** fiambre
m; **~ball** n albóndiga; **~ pie** n pastel
m de carne
Mecca ['mekə] n La Meca
mechanic [mɪ'kænɪk] n mecánico/a;
~s n mecánica ♦ npl mecanismo; **~al**
adj mecánico
mechanism ['mekənɪzəm] n
mecanismo
medal ['medl] n medalla; **~lion**
[mɪ'dælɪən] n medallón m; **~list** (US
~ist) n (SPORT) medallista m/f

meddle ['mɛdl] vi: **to ~ in** entrometerse en; **to ~ with sth** manosear algo

media ['miːdɪə] npl medios mpl de comunicación ♦ npl of **medium**

mediaeval [mɛdɪ'iːvl] adj = **medieval**

mediate ['miːdɪeɪt] vi mediar; **mediator** n intermediario/a, mediador(a) m/f

Medicaid ® ['mɛdɪkeɪd] (US) n programa m de ayuda médica para los pobres

medical ['mɛdɪkl] adj médico ♦ n reconocimiento médico

Medicare ® ['mɛdɪkeə*] (US) n programa m de ayuda médica para los ancianos

medication [mɛdɪ'keɪʃən] n medicación f

medicine ['mɛdsɪn] n medicina; (drug) medicamento

medieval [mɛdɪ'iːvl] adj medieval

mediocre [miːdɪ'əʊkə*] adj mediocre

meditate ['mɛdɪteɪt] vi meditar

Mediterranean [mɛdɪtə'reɪnɪən] adj mediterráneo; **the ~ (Sea)** el (Mar) Mediterráneo

medium ['miːdɪəm] (pl **media**) adj mediano, regular ♦ n (means) medio; (pl **mediums**: person) médium m/f; **~ wave** n onda media

meek [miːk] adj manso, sumiso

meet [miːt] (pt, pp **met**) vt encontrar; (accidentally) encontrarse con, tropezar con; (by arrangement) reunirse con; (for the first time) conocer; (go and fetch) ir a buscar; (opponent) enfrentarse con; (obligations) cumplir; (encounter: problem) hacer frente a; (need) satisfacer ♦ vi encontrarse; (in session) reunirse; (join: objects) unirse; (for the first time) conocerse; ~ **with** vt fus (difficulty) tropezar con; **to ~ with success** tener éxito; **~ing** n encuentro; (arranged) cita, compromiso; (business ~ing) reunión f;

(POL) mitin m

megabyte ['mɛgəbaɪt] n (COMPUT) megabyte m, megaocteto

megaphone ['mɛgəfəʊn] n megáfono

melancholy ['mɛlənkəlɪ] n melancolía ♦ adj melancólico

mellow ['mɛləʊ] adj (wine) añejo; (sound, colour) suave ♦ vi (person) ablandar

melody ['mɛlədɪ] n melodía

melon ['mɛlən] n melón m

melt [mɛlt] vi (metal) fundirse; (snow) derretirse ♦ vt fundir; **~down** n (in nuclear reactor) fusión f de un reactor (nuclear); **~ing pot** n (fig) crisol m

member ['mɛmbə*] n (gen, ANAT) miembro; (of club) socio/a; **M~ of Parliament** (BRIT) diputado/a; **M~ of the European Parliament** (BRIT) eurodiputado/a; **~ship** n (members) número de miembros; (state) filiación f; **~ship card** n carnet m de socio

memento [mə'mɛntəʊ] n recuerdo

memo ['mɛməʊ] n apunte m, nota

memoirs ['mɛmwɑːz] npl memorias fpl

memorandum [mɛmə'rændəm] n (pl **memoranda**) n apunte m, nota; (official note) acta

memorial [mɪ'mɔːrɪəl] n monumento conmemorativo ♦ adj conmemorativo

memorize ['mɛməraɪz] vt aprender de memoria

memory ['mɛmərɪ] n (also: COMPUT) memoria; (instance) recuerdo; (of dead person): **in ~ of** a la memoria de

men [mɛn] npl of **man**

menace ['mɛnəs] n amenaza ♦ vt amenazar; **menacing** adj amenazador(a)

mend [mɛnd] vt reparar, arreglar; (darn) zurcir ♦ vi reponerse ♦ n arreglo, reparación f; zurcido n: **to be on the ~** ir mejorando; **to ~ one's ways** enmendarse; **~ing** n reparación f; (clothes) ropa por remendar

meningitis [mɛnɪn'dʒaɪtɪs] n meningitis f

menopause ['mɛnəʊpɔːz] n menopausia f

menstruation [mɛnstru'eɪʃən] n menstruación f

mental ['mɛntl] adj mental; **~ity** [-'tælɪtɪ] n mentalidad f

mention ['mɛnʃən] n mención f ♦ vt mencionar; (speak of) hablar de; **don't ~ it!** ¡de nada!

menu ['mɛnjuː] n (set ~) menú m; (printed) carta; (COMPUT) menú m

MEP n abbr = **Member of the European Parliament**

merchandise ['mɜːtʃəndaɪz] n mercancías fpl

merchant ['mɜːtʃənt] n comerciante m/f; **~ bank** (BRIT) n banco comercial; **~ navy** (US = **marine**) n marina mercante

merciful ['mɜːsɪful] adj compasivo; (fortunate) afortunado

merciless ['mɜːsɪlɪs] adj despiadado

mercury ['mɜːkjurɪ] n mercurio

mercy ['mɜːsɪ] n compasión f; (REL) misericordia f; **at the ~ of** a la merced de

merely ['mɪəlɪ] adv simplemente, sólo

merge [mɜːdʒ] vt (join) unir ♦ vi unirse; (COMM) fusionarse; (colours etc) fundirse; **~r** n (COMM) fusión f

meringue [mə'ræŋ] n merengue m

merit ['mɛrɪt] n mérito ♦ vt merecer

mermaid ['mɜːmeɪd] n sirena

merry ['mɛrɪ] adj alegre; **M~ Christmas!** ¡Felices Pascuas!; **~-go-round** n tiovivo

mesh [mɛʃ] n malla

mesmerize ['mɛzməraɪz] vt hipnotizar

mess [mɛs] n (muddle: of situation) confusión f; (: of room) revoltijo; (dirt) porquería; (MIL) comedor m; **~ about** or **around** (inf) vi perder el tiempo; (pass the time) entretenerse; **~ about** or **around with** (inf) vt fus divertirse con; **~ up** vt (spoil) estropear; (dirty) ensuciar

message ['mɛsɪdʒ] n recado, mensaje

m

messenger ['mɛsɪndʒə*] n mensajero/a

Messrs abbr (on letters: = Messieurs) Sres

messy ['mɛsɪ] adj (dirty) sucio; (untidy) desordenado

met [mɛt] pt, pp of **meet**

metal ['mɛtl] n metal m; **~lic** [-'tælɪk] adj metálico

metaphor ['mɛtəfə*] n metáfora

meteor ['miːtɪə*] n meteoro; **~ite** [-aɪt] n meteorito

meteorology [miːtɪə'rɔlədʒɪ] n meteorología

meter ['miːtə*] n (instrument) contador m; (US: unit) = **metre** ♦ vt (US: POST) franquear

method ['mɛθəd] n método

meths [mɛθs] (BRIT) n, **methylated spirit** ['mɛθɪleɪtɪd-] (BRIT) n alcohol m metilado or desnaturalizado

metre ['miːtə*] (US **meter**) n metro

metric ['mɛtrɪk] adj métrico

metropolitan [mɛtrə'pɔlɪtən] adj metropolitano; **the M~ Police** (BRIT) la policía londinense

mettle ['mɛtl] n: **to be on one's ~** estar dispuesto a mostrar todo lo que uno vale

mew [mjuː] vi (cat) maullar

mews [mjuːz] n: **~ flat** (BRIT) piso acondicionado en antiguos establos o cocheras

Mexican ['mɛksɪkən] adj, n mejicano/a m/f, mexicano/a m/f

Mexico ['mɛksɪkəu] n Méjico (SP), México (AM); **~ City** n Ciudad f de Méjico or México

miaow [miːˈau] vi maullar

mice [maɪs] npl of **mouse**

micro... ['maɪkrəu] prefix micro...; **~chip** n microplaqueta; **~(computer)** n microordenador m; **~phone** n micrófono; **~processor** n microprocesador m; **~scope** n microscopio; **~wave** n (also: ~wave oven) horno microondas

mid [mɪd] adj: **in ~ May** a mediados de mayo; **in ~ afternoon** a media tarde; **in ~ air** en el aire; **~day** n mediodía m

middle ['mɪdl] n centro; (half-way point) medio; (waist) cintura ♦ adj de en medio; (course, way) intermedio; **in the ~ of the night** en plena noche; **~-aged** adj de mediana edad; **the M~ Ages** npl la Edad Media; **~-class** adj de clase media; **the ~ class(es)** n(pl) la clase media; **M~ East** n Oriente m Medio; **~man** n intermediario; **~ name** n segundo nombre; **~-of-the-road** adj moderado; **~weight** n (BOXING) peso medio

middling ['mɪdlɪŋ] adj mediano

midge [mɪdʒ] n mosquito

midget ['mɪdʒɪt] n enano/a

Midlands ['mɪdləndz] npl: **the ~** la región central de Inglaterra

midnight ['mɪdnaɪt] n medianoche f

midst [mɪdst] n: **in the ~ of** (crowd) en medio de; (situation, action) en mitad de

midsummer [mɪd'sʌmə*] n: **in ~** en pleno verano

midway ['mɪdweɪ] adj, adv: **~ (between)** a medio camino (entre); **~ through** a la mitad (de)

midweek [mɪd'wiːk] adv entre semana

midwife ['mɪdwaɪf] (pl midwives) n comadrona, partera

might [maɪt] vb see **may** ♦ n fuerza, poder m; **~y** adj fuerte, poderoso

migraine ['miːgreɪn] n jaqueca

migrant ['maɪgrənt] adj (bird) migratorio; (worker) emigrante

migrate [maɪ'greɪt] vi emigrar

mike [maɪk] n abbr (= microphone) micro

mild [maɪld] adj (person) apacible; (climate) templado; (slight) ligero; (taste) suave; (illness) leve; **~ly** adv ligeramente; suavemente; **to put it**

~ly para no decir más

mile [maɪl] n milla; **~age** n número de millas, ≈ kilometraje m; **~ometer** [maɪ'lɒmɪtə*] n ≈ cuentakilómetros m inv; **~stone** n mojón m

militant ['mɪlɪtənt] adj, n militante m/f

military ['mɪlɪtərɪ] adj militar

militia [mɪ'lɪʃə] n milicia

milk [mɪlk] n leche f ♦ vt (cow) ordeñar; (fig) chupar; **~ chocolate** n chocolate m con leche; **~man** (irreg) n lechero; **~ shake** n batido, malteada (AM); **~y** adj lechoso; **M~y Way** n Vía Láctea

mill [mɪl] n (windmill etc) molino; (coffee ~) molinillo; (factory) fábrica ♦ vt moler ♦ vi (also: **~ about**) arremolinarse

millennium [mɪ'lenɪəm] (pl **~s** or **millennia**) n milenio, milenario

miller ['mɪlə*] n molinero

milli... ['mɪlɪ] prefix: **~gram(me)** n miligramo; **~metre** (US **~meter**) n milímetro

million ['mɪljən] n millón m; **a ~ times** un millón de veces; **~aire** [-jə'neə*] n millonario/a

milometer [maɪ'lɒmɪtə*] (BRIT) n = **mileometer**

mime [maɪm] n mímica; (actor) mimo/a ♦ vt remedar ♦ vi actuar de mimo

mimic ['mɪmɪk] n imitador(a) m/f ♦ adj mímico ♦ vt remedar, imitar

min. abbr = **minimum**; **minute(s)**

mince [mɪns] vt picar ♦ n (BRIT: CULIN) carne f picada; **~meat** n conserva de fruta picada; (US: meat) carne f picada; **~ pie** n empanadilla rellena de fruta picada; **~r** n picadora de carne

mind [maɪnd] n mente f; (intellect) intelecto; (contrasted with matter) espíritu m ♦ vt (attend to, look after) ocuparse de, cuidar; (be careful of) tener cuidado con; (object to): **I don't ~ the noise** no me molesta el ruido; **it is on my ~** me preocupa; **to bear**

sth in ~ tomar or tener algo en cuenta; **to make up one's** ~ decidirse; **I don't** ~ me es igual; **~ you, ...** te advierto que ...; **never ~!** ¡es igual!, ¡no importa!; *(don't worry)* ¡no te preocupes!; **"~ the step"** "cuidado con el escalón!"; **~er** n guardaespaldas m inv; *(child ~er)* ≈ niñera; **~ful** adj ~ful of consciente de; **~less** adj *(crime)* sin motivo; *(work)* de autómata

mine¹ [maɪn] pron el mío/la mía etc; **a friend of ~** n un(a) amigo/a mío/mía ♦ adj: **this book is ~** este libro es mío

mine² [maɪn] n mina ♦ vt *(coal)* extraer; *(bomb: beach etc)* minar; **~field** n campo de minas; **miner** n minero/a

mineral ['mɪnərəl] adj mineral ♦ n mineral m; **~s** npl *(BRIT: soft drinks)* refrescos mpl; **~ water** n agua mineral

mingle ['mɪŋɡl] vi: **to ~ with** mezclarse con

miniature ['mɪnətʃə*] adj (en) miniatura ♦ n miniatura f

minibus ['mɪnɪbʌs] n microbús m

minimal ['mɪnɪml] adj mínimo

minimize ['mɪnɪmaɪz] vt minimizar; *(play down)* empequeñecer

minimum ['mɪnɪməm] n *(pl minima* n), adj mínimo

mining ['maɪnɪŋ] n explotación f minera

miniskirt ['mɪnɪskə:t] n minifalda

minister ['mɪnɪstə*] n *(BRIT: POL)* ministro/a *(SP)*, secretario/a *(AM)*; *(REL)* pastor m ♦ vi: **to ~ to** atender a

ministry ['mɪnɪstrɪ] n *(BRIT: POL)* ministerio *(SP)*, secretaría *(AM)*; *(REL)* sacerdocio

mink [mɪŋk] n visón m

minnow ['mɪnəu] n pececillo *(de agua dulce)*

minor ['maɪnə*] adj *(repairs, injuries)* leve; *(poet, planet)* menor; *(MUS)* menor ♦ n *(LAW)* menor m de edad

Minorca [mɪ'nɔ:kə] n Menorca

minority [maɪ'nɔrɪtɪ] n minoría

mint [mɪnt] n *(plant)* menta, hierbabuena; *(sweet)* caramelo de menta ♦ vt *(coins)* acuñar; **(the Royal) M~, the (US) M~** la Casa de la Moneda; **in ~ condition** en perfecto estado

minus ['maɪnəs] n *(also: ~ sign)* signo de menos ♦ prep menos; **12 ~ 6 equals 6** 12 menos 6 son 6; **~ 24°C** menos 24 grados

minute¹ ['mɪnɪt] n minuto; *(fig)* momento; **~s** npl *(of meeting)* actas fpl; **at the last ~** a última hora

minute² [maɪ'nju:t] adj diminuto; *(search)* minucioso

miracle ['mɪrəkl] n milagro

mirage ['mɪra:ʒ] n espejismo

mirror ['mɪrə*] n espejo; *(in car)* retrovisor m

mirth [mə:θ] n alegría

misadventure [mɪsəd'ventʃə*] n desgracia

misapprehension [mɪsæprɪ'henʃən] n equivocación f

misappropriate [mɪsə'prəuprɪeɪt] vt malversar

misbehave [mɪsbɪ'heɪv] vi portarse mal

miscalculate [mɪs'kælkjuleɪt] vt calcular mal

miscarriage [mɪs'kærɪdʒ] n *(MED)* aborto; **~ of justice** error m judicial

miscellaneous [mɪsɪ'leɪnɪəs] adj varios/as, diversos/as

mischief ['mɪstʃɪf] n travesuras fpl, diabluras fpl; *(maliciousness)* malicia; **mischievous** [-ʃɪvəs] adj travieso

misconception [mɪskən'sepʃən] n idea equivocada; equivocación f

misconduct [mɪs'kɔndʌkt] n mala conducta; **professional ~** falta profesional

misdemeanour [mɪsdɪ'mi:nə*] *(US* **misdemeanor)** n delito, ofensa

miser ['maɪzə*] n avaro/a

miserable ['mɪzərəbl] adj *(unhappy)*

triste, desgraciado; (*unpleasant, contemptible*) miserable

miserly ['maɪzəlɪ] *adj* avariento, tacaño

misery ['mɪzərɪ] *n* tristeza; (*wretchedness*) miseria, desdicha

misfire [mɪs'faɪə*] *vi* fallar

misfit ['mɪsfɪt] *n* inadaptado/a

misfortune [mɪs'fɔːtʃən] *n* desgracia

misgiving [mɪs'gɪvɪŋ] *n* (*apprehension*) presentimiento; **to have ~s about sth** tener dudas acerca de algo

misguided [mɪs'gaɪdɪd] *adj* equivocado

mishandle [mɪs'hændl] *vt* (*mismanage*) manejar mal

mishap [mɪs'hæp] *n* desgracia, contratiempo

misinform [mɪsɪn'fɔːm] *vt* informar mal

misinterpret [mɪsɪn'tɜːprɪt] *vt* interpretar mal

misjudge [mɪs'dʒʌdʒ] *vt* juzgar mal

mislay [mɪs'leɪ] (*irreg*) *vt* extraviar, perder

mislead [mɪs'liːd] (*irreg*) *vt* llevar a conclusiones erróneas; **~ing** *adj* engañoso

mismanage [mɪs'mænɪdʒ] *vt* administrar mal

misplace [mɪs'pleɪs] *vt* extraviar

misprint ['mɪsprɪnt] *n* errata, error *m* de imprenta

Miss [mɪs] *n* Señorita

miss [mɪs] *vt* (*train etc*) perder; (*fail to hit: target*) errar; (*regret the absence of*): **I ~ him** (yo) le echo de menos *o* a faltar; (*fail to see*): **you can't ~ it** no tiene pérdida ♦ *vi* fallar ♦ *n* (*shot*) tiro fallido *o* perdido; **~ out** (*BRIT*) *vt* omitir

misshapen [mɪs'ʃeɪpən] *adj* deforme

missile ['mɪsaɪl] *n* (*AVIAT*) misil *m*; (*object thrown*) proyectil *m*

missing ['mɪsɪŋ] *adj* (*pupil*) ausente; (*thing*) perdido; (*MIL*): **~ in action** desaparecido en combate

mission ['mɪʃən] *n* misión *f*; (*official*

representation) delegación *f*; **~ary** *n* misionero/a

mist [mɪst] *n* (*light*) neblina; (*heavy*) niebla; (*at sea*) bruma ♦ *vi* (*eyes: also:* ~ *over*, ~ *up*) llenarse de lágrimas; (*BRIT: windows: also:* ~ *over*, ~ *up*) empañarse

mistake [mɪs'teɪk] (*vt: irreg*) *n* error *m* ♦ *vt* entender mal; **by ~** por equivocación; **to make a ~** equivocarse; **to ~ A for B** confundir A con B; **mistaken** *pp* of **mistake** ♦ *adj* equivocado; **to be mistaken** equivocarse, engañarse

mister ['mɪstə*] (*inf*) *n* señor *m*; *see* **Mr**

mistletoe ['mɪsltəʊ] *n* muérdago

mistook [mɪs'tʊk] *pt* of **mistake**

mistress ['mɪstrɪs] *n* (*lover*) amante *f*; (*of house*) señora (de la casa); (*BRIT: in primary school*) maestra; (*in secondary school*) profesora; (*of situation*) dueña

mistrust [mɪs'trʌst] *vt* desconfiar de

misty ['mɪstɪ] *adj* (*day*) de niebla; (*glasses etc*) empañado

misunderstand [mɪsʌndə'stænd] (*irreg*) *vt, vi* entender mal; **~ing** *n* malentendido

misuse [*n* mɪs'juːs, *vb* mɪs'juːz] *n* mal uso; (*of power*) abuso; (*of funds*) malversación *f* ♦ *vt* abusar de; malversar

mitt(en) ['mɪt(n)] *n* manopla

mix [mɪks] *vt* mezclar; (*combine*) unir ♦ *vi* mezclarse; (*people*) llevarse bien ♦ *n* mezcla; **~ up** *vt* mezclar; (*confuse*) confundir; **~ed** *adj* mixto; (*feelings etc*) encontrado; **~ed-up** *adj* (*confused*) confuso, revuelto; **~er** *n* (*for food*) licuadora; (*for drinks*) coctelera; (*person*): **he's a good ~er** tiene don de gentes; **~ture** *n* mezcla; (*also: cough ~ture*) jarabe *m*; **~-up** *n* confusión *f*

mm *abbr* (= *millimetre*) mm

moan [məʊn] *n* gemido ♦ *vi* gemir; (*inf: complain*): **to ~ (about)** quejarse (de)

moat [məʊt] n foso

mob [mɒb] n multitud f ♦ vt acosar

mobile ['məʊbaɪl] adj móvil ♦ n móvil m; **~ home** n caravana; **~ phone** n teléfono portátil

mock [mɒk] vt (ridicule) ridiculizar; (laugh at) burlarse de ♦ adj fingido; **~ exam** examen preparatorio antes de los exámenes oficiales; **~ery** n burla; **~-up** n maqueta

mod [mɒd] adj see **convenience**

mode [məʊd] n modo

model ['mɒdl] n modelo; (fashion ~, artist's ~) modelo m/f ♦ adj fingido ♦ vt (with clay etc) modelar (copy): **to ~ o.s. on** tomar como modelo a ♦ vi ser modelo; **to ~ clothes** pasar modelos, ser modelo; **~ railway** n ferrocarril m de juguete

modem ['məʊdəm] n modem m

moderate [adj 'mɒdərət, vb 'mɒdəreɪt] adj moderado/a ♦ vi moderarse, calmarse ♦ vt moderar

modern ['mɒdən] adj moderno; **~ize** vt modernizar

modest ['mɒdɪst] adj modesto; (small) módico; **~y** n modestia

modify ['mɒdɪfaɪ] vt modificar

mogul ['məʊgəl] n (fig) magnate m

mohair ['məʊhɛə*] n mohair m

moist [mɔɪst] adj húmedo; **~en** ['mɔɪsn] vt humedecer; **~ure** ['mɔɪstʃə*] n humedad f; **~urizer** ['mɔɪstʃəraɪzə*] n crema hidratante

molar ['məʊlə*] n muela

mold [məʊld] (US) n, vt = **mould**

mole [məʊl] n (animal, spy) topo; (spot) lunar m

molest [məʊ'lest] vt importunar; (assault sexually) abusar sexualmente de

mollycoddle ['mɒlɪkɒdl] vt mimar

molt [məʊlt] (US) vi = **moult**

molten ['məʊltən] adj fundido; (lava) líquido

mom [mɒm] (US) n = **mum**

moment ['məʊmənt] n momento; at **the ~** de momento, por ahora; **~ary** adj momentáneo; **~ous** [-'mentəs] adj trascendental, importante

momentum [məʊ'mentəm] n momento; (fig) ímpetu m; **to gather ~** cobrar velocidad; (fig) ganar fuerza

mommy ['mɒmɪ] (US) n = **mummy**

Monaco ['mɒnəkəʊ] n Mónaco

monarch ['mɒnək] n monarca m/f; **~y** n monarquía

monastery ['mɒnəstərɪ] n monasterio

Monday ['mʌndɪ] n lunes m inv

monetary ['mʌnɪtərɪ] adj monetario

money ['mʌnɪ] n dinero; (currency) moneda; **to make ~** ganar dinero; **~ order** n giro; **~-spinner** (inf) n: **to be a ~-spinner** dar mucho dinero

mongrel ['mʌŋgrəl] n (dog) perro mestizo

monitor ['mɒnɪtə*] n (SCOL) monitor m; (also: television ~) receptor m de control; (of computer) monitor m ♦ vt controlar

monk [mʌŋk] n monje m

monkey ['mʌŋkɪ] n mono; **~ nut** (BRIT) n cacahuete m (SP), maní m (AM); **~ wrench** n llave f inglesa

monopoly [mə'nɒpəlɪ] n monopolio

monotone ['mɒnətəʊn] n voz f (or tono) monocorde

monotonous [mə'nɒtənəs] adj monótono

monsoon [mɒn'su:n] n monzón m

monster ['mɒnstə*] n monstruo

monstrous ['mɒnstrəs] adj (huge) enorme; (atrocious, ugly) monstruoso

month [mʌnθ] n mes m; **~ly** adj mensual ♦ adv mensualmente

monument ['mɒnjumənt] n monumento

moo [mu:] vi mugir

mood [mu:d] n humor m; (of crowd, group) clima m; **to be in a good/bad ~** estar de buen/mal humor; **~y** adj (changeable) de humor variable; (sullen) malhumorado

moon [mu:n] n luna; **~light** n luz f de

la luna; **~lighting** n pluriempleo; **~lit** adj: **a ~lit night** una noche de luna

Moor [muə*] n moro/a

moor [muə*] n páramo ♦ vt (ship) amarrar ♦ vi echar las amarras

Moorish ['muərɪʃ] adj moro; (architecture) árabe, morisco

moorland ['muələnd] n páramo, brezal m

moose [mu:s] n inv alce m

mop [mɔp] n fregona; (of hair) greña, melena ♦ vt fregar; **~ up** vt limpiar

mope [məup] vi estar o andar deprimido

moped ['məuped] n ciclomotor m

moral ['mɔrl] adj moral o n moraleja; **~s** npl moralidad f, moral f

morale [mɔ'rɑːl] n moral f

morality [mə'rælɪt] n moralidad f

morass [mə'ræs] n pantano

KEYWORD

more [mɔː*] adj **1** (greater in number etc) más; **~ people/work than before** más gente/trabajo que antes **2** (additional) más; **do you want (some) ~ tea?** ¿quieres más té?; **is there any ~ wine?** ¿queda vino?; **it'll take a few ~ weeks** tardará unas semanas más; **it's 2 kms ~ to the house** faltan 2 kms para la casa; **~ time/letters than we expected** más tiempo del que/más cartas de las que esperábamos

♦ pron (greater amount, additional amount) más; **~ than 10** más de 10; **it cost ~ than the other one/than we expected** costó más que el otro/más de lo que esperábamos; **is there any ~?** ¿hay más?; **many/much ~** muchos(as)/mucho(a) más

♦ adv más; **~ dangerous/easily (than)** más peligroso/fácilmente (que); **~ and ~ expensive** cada vez más caro; **~ or less** más o menos; **~ than ever** más que nunca

moreover [mɔː'rəuvə*] adv además, por otra parte

morning ['mɔːnɪŋ] n mañana; (early ~) madrugada ♦ cpd matutino, de la mañana; **in the ~** por la mañana; **7 o'clock in the ~** las 7 de la mañana; **~ sickness** n náuseas fpl matutinas

Morocco [mə'rɔkəu] n Marruecos m

moron ['mɔːrɔn] (inf) n imbécil m/f

morphine ['mɔːfiːn] n morfina

Morse [mɔːs] n (also: **~ code**) (código) Morse

morsel ['mɔːsl] n (of food) bocado

mortar ['mɔːtə*] n argamasa

mortgage ['mɔːgɪdʒ] n hipoteca ♦ vt hipotecar; **~ company** (US) n ≈ banco hipotecario

mortuary ['mɔːtjuəri] n depósito de cadáveres

Moscow ['mɔskəu] n Moscú

Moslem ['mɔzləm] adj, n = **Muslim**

mosque [mɔsk] n mezquita

mosquito [mɔs'kiːtəu] (pl **~es**) n mosquito (SP), zancudo (AM)

moss [mɔs] n musgo

most [məust] adj la mayor parte de, la mayoría de ♦ pron la mayor parte, la mayoría ♦ adv el más; (very) muy; **the ~** (also: **+ adj**) el más; **~ of them** la mayor parte de ellos; **I saw the ~** yo vi el que más; **at the (very) ~** a lo sumo, todo lo más; **to make the ~ of** aprovechar (al máximo); **a ~ interesting book** un libro interesantísimo; **~ly** adv en su mayor parte, principalmente

MOT (BRIT) n abbr (= Ministry of Transport): **the ~ (test)** inspección (anual) obligatoria de coches y camiones

motel [məu'tel] n motel m

moth [mɔθ] n mariposa nocturna; (clothes ~) polilla

mother ['mʌðə*] n madre f ♦ adj materno ♦ vt (care for) cuidar (como una madre); **~hood** n maternidad f; **~-in-law** n suegra; **~ly** adj maternal

~-of-pearl n nácar m; **~-to-be** n futura madre f; **~ tongue** n lengua materna

motion ['məuʃən] n movimiento; (gesture) ademán m, señal f; (at meeting) moción f ♦ vt, vi: **to ~ (to) sb to do sth** hacer señas a uno para que haga algo; **~less** adj inmóvil; **~ picture** n película

motivated ['məutɪveɪtɪd] adj motivado

motive ['məutɪv] n motivo

motley ['mɔtlɪ] adj variado

motor ['məutə*] n motor m; (BRIT: inf: vehicle) coche m (SP), carro (AM), automóvil m ♦ adj motor (f: motora or motriz); **~bike** n moto f; **~boat** n lancha motora; **~car** (BRIT) n coche m, carro, automóvil m; **~cycle** n motocicleta; **~cycle racing** n motociclismo; **~cyclist** n motociclista m/f; **~ing** (BRIT) n automovilismo; **~ist** n conductor(a) m/f, automovilista m/f; **~ racing** (BRIT) n carreras fpl de coches, automovilismo; **~ vehicle** n automóvil m; **~way** (BRIT) n autopista

mottled ['mɔtld] adj abigarrado, multicolor

motto ['mɔtəu] (pl **~es**) n lema m, (watchword) consigna

mould [məuld] (US **mold**) n molde m; (mildew) moho ♦ vt moldear; (fig) formar; **~y** adj enmohecido

moult [məult] (US **molt**) vi mudar la piel (or las plumas)

mound [maund] n montón m, montículo

mount [maunt] n monte m ♦ vt montar, subir a; (jewel) engarzar; (picture) enmarcar; (exhibition etc) organizar ♦ vi (increase) aumentar; **~ up** vi aumentar

mountain ['mauntɪn] n montaña ♦ cpd de montaña; **~ bike** n bicicleta de montaña; **~eer** [-'nɪə*] n montañero/a (SP), andinista m/f (AM); **~eering** [-'nɪərɪŋ] n montañismo,

andinismo; **~ous** adj montañoso; **~ rescue team** n equipo de rescate de montaña; **~side** n ladera de la montaña

mourn [mɔːn] vt llorar, lamentar ♦ vi: **to ~ for** llorar la muerte de; **~er** n doliente m/f; dolorido/a; **~ing** n luto; **in ~ing** de luto

mouse [maus] (pl **mice**) n (ZOOL, COMPUT) ratón m; **~trap** n ratonera

mousse [muːs] n (CULIN) crema batida; (for hair) espuma (moldeadora)

moustache [məs'tɑːʃ] (US **mustache**) n bigote m

mousy ['mausɪ] adj (hair) pardusco

mouth [mauθ] (pl **mouths** [-ðz]) n boca; (of river) desembocadura; **~ful** n bocado; **~ organ** n armónica; **~piece** n (of musical instrument) boquilla; (spokesman) portavoz m/f; **~wash** n enjuague m; **~-watering** adj apetitoso

movable ['muːvəbl] adj mobible

move [muːv] n (movement) movimiento; (in game) jugada; (: turn to play) turno; (change: of house) mudanza; (: of job) cambio de trabajo ♦ vt mover; (emotionally) conmover; (POL: resolution etc) proponer ♦ vi moverse; (traffic) circular; (also: ~ house) trasladarse, mudarse; **to ~ sb to do sth** mover a uno a hacer algo; **to get a ~ on** darse prisa; **~ about** or **around** vi moverse; (travel) viajar; **~ along** vi avanzar, adelantarse; **~ away** vi alejarse; **~ back** vi retroceder; **~ forward** vi avanzar; **~ in** vi (to a house) instalarse; (police, soldiers) intervenir; **~ 'on** vi ponerse en camino; **~ out** vi (of house) mudarse; **~ over** vi apartarse, hacer sitio; **~ up** vi (employee) ser ascendido

moveable ['muːvəbl] adj = **movable**

movement ['muːvmənt] n movimiento

movie ['muːvɪ] n película; **to go to the ~s** al ir al cine

moving ['muːvɪŋ] adj (emotional)

conmovedor(a); *(that moves)* móvil

mow [mǝʊ] *(pt mowed, pp mowed or mown) vt (grass, corn)* cortar, segar; **~ down** *vt (shoot)* acribillar; **~er** *n (also: lawn~er)* cortacéspedes *m inv*, segadora

MP *n abbr* = **Member of Parliament**

m.p.h. *abbr* = **miles per hour** (60 *m.p.h.* = 96 *k.p.h.*)

Mr ['mɪstǝ*]* (*US* **Mr.**) *n*: **~ Smith** (el) Sr. Smith

Mrs ['mɪsɪz] (*US* **Mrs.**) *n*: **~ Smith** (la) Sra. Smith

Ms [mɪz] (*US* **Ms.**) *n* (= *Miss or Mrs*): **~ Smith** (la) Sr(t)a. Smith

M.Sc. *abbr* = **Master of Science**

much [mʌtʃ] *adj* mucho ♦ *adv* mucho; *(before pp)* muy ♦ *n or pron* mucho; **how ~ is it?** ¿cuánto es?, ¿cuánto cuesta?; **too ~** demasiado; **it's not ~** no es mucho; **as ~ as** tanto como; **however ~ he tries** por mucho que se esfuerce

muck [mʌk] *n* suciedad *f*; **~ about or around** *(inf) vi* perder el tiempo; *(enjoy o.s.)* entretenerse; **~ up** *(inf) vt* arruinar, estropear

mud [mʌd] *n* barro, lodo

muddle ['mʌdl] *n* desorden *m*, confusión *f*; *(mix-up)* embrollo, lío ♦ *vt* (*also: ~ up)* embrollar, confundir; **~ through** *vi* salir del paso

muddy ['mʌdɪ] *adj* fangoso, cubierto de lodo

mudguard ['mʌdɡɑːd] *n* guardabarros *m inv*

muffin ['mʌfɪn] *n* panecillo dulce

muffle ['mʌfl] *vt (sound)* amortiguar; *(against cold)* embozar; **~d** *adj (noise etc)* amortiguado, apagado; **~r** (*US*) *n (AUT)* silenciador *m*

mug [mʌɡ] *n* taza grande *(sin platillo)*; *(for beer)* jarra; *(inf: face)* jeta; (: *fool)* bobo ♦ *vt (assault)* asaltar; **~ging** *n* asalto

muggy ['mʌɡɪ] *adj* bochornoso

mule [mjuːl] *n* mula

multi... [mʌltɪ] *prefix* multi...

multi-level [mʌltɪ'levl] (*US*) *adj* = **multistorey**

multiple ['mʌltɪpl] *adj* múltiple ♦ *n* múltiplo; **~ sclerosis** *n* esclerosis *f* múltiple

multiplex cinema ['mʌltɪpleks-] *n* multicines *mpl*

multiplication [mʌltɪplɪ'keɪʃǝn] *n* multiplicación *f*

multiply ['mʌltɪplaɪ] *vt* multiplicar ♦ *vi* multiplicarse

multistorey [mʌltɪ'stɔːrɪ] (*BRIT*) *adj* de muchos pisos

multitude ['mʌltɪtjuːd] *n* multitud *f*

mum [mʌm] (*BRIT: inf)* *n* mamá ♦ *adj*: **to keep ~** mantener la boca cerrada

mumble ['mʌmbl] *vt*, *vi* hablar entre dientes, refunfuñar

mummy ['mʌmɪ] *n* (*BRIT: mother)* mamá; *(embalmed)* momia

mumps [mʌmps] *n* paperas *fpl*

munch [mʌntʃ] *vt*, *vi* mascar

mundane [mʌn'deɪn] *adj* trivial

municipal [mjuː'nɪsɪpl] *adj* municipal

murder ['mɜːdǝ*]* *n* asesinato; *(in law)* homicidio ♦ *vt* asesinar, matar; **~er/ess** *n* asesino/a; **~ous** *adj* homicida

murky ['mɜːkɪ] *adj (water)* turbio; *(street, night)* lóbrego

murmur ['mɜːmǝ*]* *n* murmullo ♦ *vt*, *vi* murmurar

muscle ['mʌsl] *n* músculo; *(fig: strength)* garra, fuerza; **~ in** *vi* entrometerse; **muscular** ['mʌskjʊlǝ*]* *adj* muscular; *(person)* musculoso

muse [mjuːz] *vi* meditar ♦ *n* musa

museum [mjuː'zɪǝm] *n* museo

mushroom ['mʌʃrʊm] *n* seta, hongo; *(CULIN)* champiñón *m* ♦ *vi* crecer de la noche a la mañana

music ['mjuːzɪk] *n* música; **~al** *adj* musical; *(sound)* melodioso; *(person)* con talento musical ♦ *n (show)* comedia musical; **~al instrument** *n* instrumento musical; **~ hall** *n* teatro de variedades; **~ian** [-'zɪʃǝn] *n*

músico/a
Muslim [ˈmʌzlɪm] adj, n musulmán/
ana m/f
muslin [ˈmʌzlɪn] n muselina
mussel [ˈmʌsl] n mejillón m
must [mʌst] aux vb (obligation): **I ~ do
it** debo hacerlo, tengo que hacerlo;
(probability): **he ~ be there by now**
ya debe (de) estar allí ♦ n: **it's a ~** es
imprescindible
mustache [ˈmʌstæʃ] (US) n =
moustache
mustard [ˈmʌstəd] n mostaza
muster [ˈmʌstə*] vt juntar, reunir
mustn't [ˈmʌsnt] = **must not**
mute [mjuːt] adj, n mudo/a m/f
muted [ˈmjuːtɪd] adj callado; (colour)
apagado
mutiny [ˈmjuːtɪnɪ] n motín m ♦ vi
amotinarse
mutter [ˈmʌtə*] vt, vi murmurar
mutton [ˈmʌtn] n carne f de cordero
mutual [ˈmjuːtʃuəl] adj mutuo;
(interest) común; **~ly** adv mutuamente
muzzle [ˈmʌzl] n hocico; (for dog)
bozal m; (of gun) boca ♦ vt (dog) poner
un bozal a
my [maɪ] adj mi(s); **~ house/
brother/sisters** mi casa/mi
hermano/mis hermanas; **I've washed
~ hair/cut ~ finger** me he lavado el
pelo/cortado un dedo; **is this ~ pen
or yours?** ¿es este bolígrafo mío o
tuyo?
myself [maɪˈself] pron (reflexive) me;
(emphatic) yo mismo; (after prep) mí
(mismo); see also **oneself**
mysterious [mɪsˈtɪərɪəs] adj misterioso
mystery [ˈmɪstərɪ] n misterio
mystify [ˈmɪstɪfaɪ] vt (perplex) dejar
perplejo
myth [mɪθ] n mito

N, n

n/a abbr (= not applicable) no interesa
nag [næg] vt (scold) regañar; **~ging** adj
(doubt) persistente; (pain) continuo
nail [neɪl] n (human) uña; (metal) clavo
♦ vt (fasten) to **~ sth to sth** clavar algo
en algo; **to ~ sb down to doing sth**
comprometer a uno a que haga algo;
~brush n cepillo para las uñas; **~file** n
lima para las uñas; **~ polish** n esmalte
m or laca para las uñas; **~ polish
remover** n quitaesmalte m;
~ scissors npl tijeras fpl para las uñas;
~ varnish (BRIT) n = **~ polish**
naïve [naɪˈiːv] adj ingenuo
naked [ˈneɪkɪd] adj (nude) desnudo;
(flame) expuesto al aire
name [neɪm] n nombre m; (surname)
apellido; (reputation) fama, renombre
m ♦ vt (child) poner nombre a;
(criminal) identificar; (price, date etc)
fijar; **what's your ~?** ¿cómo se
llama?; **by ~** de nombre; **in the ~ of**
en nombre de; **to give one's ~ and
address** dar sus señas; **~ly** adv a
saber; **~sake** n tocayo/a
nanny [ˈnænɪ] n niñera
nap [næp] n (sleep) sueñecito, siesta
nape [neɪp] n: **~ of the neck** nuca,
cogote m
napkin [ˈnæpkɪn] n (also: table ~)
servilleta
nappy [ˈnæpɪ] (BRIT) n pañal m;
~ rash n prurito
narcotic [naːˈkɔtɪk] adj, n narcótico
narrow [ˈnærəʊ] adj (road) estrecho,
angosto (fig: majority etc) corto; (: ideas etc)
estrecho ♦ vi (road) estrecharse;
(diminish) reducirse; **to have a
~ escape** escaparse por los pelos; **to
~ sth down** reducir algo; **~ly** adv
(miss) por poco; **~-minded** adj de
miras estrechas
nasty [ˈnɑːstɪ] adj (remark) feo;

(person) antipático; (revolting: taste, smell) asqueroso; (wound, disease etc) peligroso, grave

nation ['neɪʃən] n nación f

national ['næʃənl] adj, n nacional m/f;
~ **dress** n vestido nacional;
N~ Health Service (BRIT) n servicio nacional de salud pública; ≈ Insalud m (SP); **N~ Insurance** (BRIT) n seguro social nacional; ~**ism** n nacionalismo; ~**ist** adj, n nacionalista m/f; ~**ity** [-'nælɪtɪ] n nacionalidad f; ~**ize** vt nacionalizar; ~**ly** adv (nationwide) en escala nacional; (as a nation) nacionalmente, como nación; ~ **park** (BRIT) n parque m nacional

nationwide ['neɪʃənwaɪd] adj en escala or a nivel nacional

native ['neɪtɪv] n (local inhabitant) natural m/f, nacional m/f ♦ adj (indigenous) indígena; (country) natal; (innate) natural, innato; **a ~ of Russia** un(a) natural m/f de Rusia; **a ~ speaker of French** un hablante nativo de francés; **N~ American** adj, n americano/a indígena, amerindio/a;
~ **language** n lengua materna

Nativity [nə'tɪvɪtɪ] n: **the ~** Navidad f

NATO ['neɪtəʊ] n abbr (= North Atlantic Treaty Organization) OTAN f

natural ['nætʃrəl] adj natural; ~**ly** adv (speak etc) naturalmente; (of course) desde luego, por supuesto

nature ['neɪtʃə*] n (also: N~) naturaleza f; (group, sort) género, clase f; (character) carácter m, genio; **by ~** por or de naturaleza

naught [nɔ:t] n = **nought**

naughty ['nɔ:tɪ] adj (child) travieso

nausea ['nɔ:sɪə] n náuseas fpl

nautical ['nɔ:tɪkl] adj náutico, marítimo; (mile) marino

naval ['neɪvl] adj naval, de marina;
~ **officer** n oficial m/f de marina

nave [neɪv] n nave f

navel ['neɪvl] n ombligo

navigate ['nævɪgeɪt] vt gobernar ♦ vi

navegar; (AUT) ir de copiloto;

navigation [-'geɪʃən] n (action) navegación f; (science) náutica

navigator n navegador(a) m/f, navegante m/f (AUT) copiloto m/f

navvy ['nævɪ] (BRIT) n peón m caminero

navy ['neɪvɪ] n marina de guerra; (ships) armada, flota; ~**(-blue)** adj azul marino

Nazi ['nɑ:tsɪ] n nazi m/f

NB abbr (= nota bene) nótese

near [nɪə*] adj (place, relation) cercano; (time) próximo ♦ adv cerca ♦ prep (also: ~ to: space) cerca de, junto a; (: time) cerca de ♦ vt acercarse a, aproximarse a; ~**by** [nɪə'baɪ] adj cercano, próximo ♦ adv cerca; ~**ly** adv casi, por poco; **I ~ly fell** por poco me caigo; ~ **miss** n tiro cercano; ~**side** n (AUT: in Britain) lado izquierdo; (: in US, Europe etc) lado derecho; ~**-sighted** adj miope, corto de vista

neat [ni:t] adj (place) ordenado, bien cuidado; (person) pulcro; (plan) ingenioso; (spirits) solo; ~**ly** adv (tidily) con esmero; (skilfully) ingeniosamente

necessarily ['nesɪsrɪlɪ] adv necesariamente

necessary ['nesɪsrɪ] adj necesario, preciso

necessitate [nɪ'sesɪteɪt] vt hacer necesario

necessity [nɪ'sesɪtɪ] n necesidad f; **necessities** npl artículos mpl de primera necesidad

neck [nek] n (of person, garment, bottle) cuello; (of animal) pescuezo ♦ vi (inf) besuquearse; ~ **and ~** parejos; ~**lace** ['neklɪs] n collar m; ~**line** n escote m; ~**tie** ['nektaɪ] n corbata

née [neɪ] adj: ~ **Scott** de soltera Scott

need [ni:d] n (lack) escasez f, falta; (necessity) necesidad f ♦ vt (require) necesitar; **I ~ to do it** tengo que or debo hacerlo; **you don't ~ to go** no hace falta que (te) vayas

needle ['niːdl] n aguja ♦ vt (fig: inf) picar, fastidiar

needless ['niːdlɪs] adj innecesario; ~ **to say** huelga decir que

needlework ['niːdlwɜːk] n (activity) costura, labor f de aguja

needn't ['niːdnt] = **need not**

needy ['niːdɪ] adj necesitado

negative ['negətɪv] n (PHOT) negativo; (LING) negación f ♦ adj negativo; ~ **equity** n situación que se da cuando el valor de la vivienda es menor que el de la hipoteca que pesa sobre ella

neglect [nɪ'glekt] vt (one's duty) faltar a, no cumplir con; (child) descuidar, desatender ♦ n (of house, garden etc) abandono; (of child) desatención f; (of duty) incumplimiento

negligee ['neglɪʒeɪ] n (nightgown) salto de cama

negotiate [nɪ'gəʊʃɪeɪt] vt (treaty, loan) negociar; (obstacle) franquear; (bend in road) tomar ♦ vi: **to ~ (with)** negociar (con); **negotiation** [-'eɪʃən] n negociación f, gestión f

neigh [neɪ] vi relinchar

neighbour ['neɪbə*] (US **neighbor**) n vecino/a; ~**hood** n (place) vecindad f, barrio; (people) vecindario; ~**ing** adj vecino; ~**ly** adj (person) amable; (attitude) de buen vecino

neither ['naɪðə*] adj ni ♦ conj: **I didn't move and ~ did John** no me he movido, ni Juan tampoco ♦ pron ninguno ♦ adv: ~ **good nor bad** ni bueno ni malo; ~ **is true** ninguno/a de los/las dos es cierto/a

neon ['niːɒn] n neón m; ~ **light** n lámpara de neón

nephew ['nevjuː] n sobrino

nerve [nɜːv] n (ANAT) nervio; (courage) valor m; (impudence) descaro, frescura; **a fit of ~s** un ataque de nervios; ~**racking** adj desquiciante

nervous ['nɜːvəs] adj (anxious, ANAT) nervioso; (timid) tímido, miedoso; ~ **breakdown** n crisis f nerviosa

nest [nest] n (of bird) nido; (wasps' ~) avispero ♦ vi anidar; ~ **egg** n (fig) ahorros mpl

nestle ['nesl] vi: **to ~ down** acurrucarse

net [net] n (gen) red f; (fabric) tul m ♦ adj (COMM) neto, líquido ♦ vt coger (SP) or agarrar (AM) con red; (SPORT) marcar; ~**ball** n básquet m

Netherlands ['neðələndz] npl: **the ~** los Países Bajos

nett [net] adj = **net**

netting ['netɪŋ] n red f, redes fpl

nettle ['netl] n ortiga

network ['netwɜːk] n red f

neurotic [njuə'rɒtɪk] adj, n neurótico/a m/f

neuter ['njuːtə*] adj (LING) neutro ♦ vt castrar, capar

neutral ['njuːtrəl] adj (person) neutral; (colour etc, ELEC) neutro ♦ n (AUT) punto muerto; ~**ize** vt neutralizar

never ['nevə*] adv nunca, jamás; **I ~ went** no fui nunca, ~ **in my life** jamás en la vida; see also **mind**; ~-**ending** adj interminable, sin fin; ~**theless** [nevəðə'les] adv sin embargo, no obstante

new [njuː] adj nuevo; (brand new) a estrenar; (recent) reciente; **N~ Age** n Nueva Era; ~**born** adj recién nacido; ~**comer** ['njuːkʌmə*] n recién venido/a or llegado/a; ~**fangled** (pej) adj modernísimo; ~**found** adj (friend) nuevo; (enthusiasm) recién adquirido; ~**ly** adv nuevamente, recién; ~**lyweds** npl recién casados mpl

news [njuːz] n noticias fpl; **a piece of ~** una noticia; **the ~** (RADIO, TV) las noticias fpl; ~ **agency** n agencia de noticias; ~ **agent** (BRIT) n vendedor/a m/f de periódicos; ~**caster** n presentador/a m/f, locutor/a m/f; ~ **flash** n noticia de última hora; ~**letter** n hoja informativa, boletín m; ~**paper** n periódico, diario; ~**print** n papel m de periódico; ~**reader** n =

~caster; ~reel n noticiario; **~ stand** n quiosco or puesto de periódicos

newt [njuːt] n tritón m

New Year n Año Nuevo; **~'s Day** n Día m de Año Nuevo; **~'s Eve** n Nochevieja

New York [njuːˈjɔːk] n Nueva York

New Zealand [njuːˈziːlənd] n Nueva Zelanda; **~er** n neozelandés/esa m/f

next [nekst] adj (house, room) vecino; (bus stop, meeting) próximo; (following: page etc) siguiente ♦ adv después; **the ~ day** el día siguiente; **~ time** la próxima vez; **~ year** el año próximo or que viene; **~ to** junto a, al lado de; **~ to nothing** casi nada; **~ please!** ¡el siguiente! **~ door** adv en la casa de al lado ♦ adj vecino, de al lado; **~-of-kin** n pariente m más cercano

NHS n abbr = **National Health Service**

nib [nɪb] n plumilla

nibble [ˈnɪbl] vt mordisquear, mordiscar

Nicaragua [nɪkəˈrægjuə] n Nicaragua; **~n** adj, n nicaragüense m/f

nice [naɪs] adj (likeable) simpático; (kind) amable; (pleasant) agradable; (attractive) bonito, mono, lindo (AM); **~ly** adv amablemente; bien

nick [nɪk] n (wound) rasguño; (cut, indentation) mella, muesca ♦ vt (inf) birlar, robar; **in the ~ of time** justo a tiempo

nickel [ˈnɪkl] n níquel m; (US) moneda de 5 centavos

nickname [ˈnɪkneɪm] n apodo, mote m ♦ vt apodar

nicotine [ˈnɪkətiːn] n nicotina

niece [niːs] n sobrina

Nigeria [naɪˈdʒɪərɪə] n Nigeria; **~n** adj, n nigeriano/a m/f

niggling [ˈnɪɡlɪŋ] adj (trifling) nimio, insignificante; (annoying) molesto

night [naɪt] n noche f; (evening) tarde f; **the ~ before last** anteanoche; **at ~, by ~** de noche, por la noche; **~cap** n

(drink) bebida que se toma antes de acostarse; **~ club** n cabaret m; **~dress** (BRIT) n camisón m; **~fall** n anochecer m; **~gown** n = **~dress**; **~ie** [ˈnaɪtɪ] n = **~dress**

nightingale [ˈnaɪtɪŋɡeɪl] n ruiseñor m

night: ~life n vida nocturna; **~ly** adj de todas las noches ♦ adv todas las noches, cada noche; **~mare** n pesadilla; **~ porter** n portero de noche; **~ school** n clase(s) f(pl) nocturna(s); **~ shift** n turno nocturno or de noche; **~time** n noche f; **~ watchman** n vigilante m nocturno

nil [nɪl] (BRIT) n (SPORT) cero, nada

Nile [naɪl] n: **the ~** el Nilo

nimble [ˈnɪmbl] adj (agile) ágil, ligero; (skilful) diestro

nine [naɪn] num nueve; **~teen** num diecinueve, diez y nueve; **~ty** num noventa

ninth [naɪnθ] adj noveno

nip [nɪp] vt (pinch) pellizcar; (bite) morder

nipple [ˈnɪpl] n (ANAT) pezón m

nitrogen [ˈnaɪtrədʒən] n nitrógeno

KEYWORD

---

no [nəʊ] (pl **~es**) adv (opposite of "yes") no; **are you coming?** — ~ **(I'm not)** ¿vienes? — no; **would you like some more?** — ~ **thank you** ¿quieres más? — no gracias ♦ adj (not any): **I have ~ money/ time/books** no tengo dinero/tiempo/ libros; **~ other man would have done it** ningún otro lo hubiera hecho; **"~ entry"** "prohibido el paso"; **"~ smoking"** "prohibido fumar" ♦ n no m

---

nobility [nəʊˈbɪlɪtɪ] n nobleza

noble [ˈnəʊbl] adj noble

nobody [ˈnəʊbədɪ] pron nadie

nod [nɒd] vi saludar con la cabeza; (in agreement) decir que sí con la cabeza; (doze) dar cabezadas ♦ vt: **to ~ one's**

head inclinar la cabeza ♦ n inclinación f de cabeza; **~ off** vi dar cabezadas
noise [nɔɪz] n ruido; (din) escándalo, estrépito; **noisy** adj ruidoso; (child) escandaloso
nominate ['nɒmɪneɪt] vt (propose) proponer; (appoint) nombrar; **nominee** [-'niː] n candidato/a
non... [nɒn] prefix no, des..., in...; **~-alcoholic** adj no alcohólico; **~chalant** adj indiferente; **~-committal** adj evasivo; **~descript** adj soso
none [nʌn] pron ninguno/a ♦ adv de ninguna manera; **~ of you** ninguno de vosotros; **I've ~ left** no me queda ninguno/a; **he's ~ the worse for it** no le ha hecho ningún mal
nonentity [nɒ'nɛntɪtɪ] n cero a la izquierda, nulidad f
nonetheless [nʌnðə'lɛs] adv sin embargo, no obstante
non-existent adj inexistente
non-fiction n literatura no novelesca
nonplussed [nɒn'plʌst] adj perplejo
nonsense ['nɒnsəns] n tonterías fpl, disparates fpl; **~!** ¡qué tonterías!
non: ~-smoker n no fumador(a) m/f; **~-smoking** adj (de) no fumador; **~-stick** adj (pan, surface) antiadherente; **~-stop** adj continuo; (RAIL) directo ♦ adv sin parar
noodles ['nuːdlz] npl tallarines mpl
nook [nuk] n: **~s and crannies** escondrijos mpl
noon [nuːn] n mediodía m
no-one pron = **nobody**
noose [nuːs] n (hangman's) dogal m
nor [nɔː*] conj = **neither** ♦ adv see **neither**
norm [nɔːm] n norma
normal ['nɔːml] adj normal; **~ly** adv normalmente
north [nɔːθ] n norte m ♦ adj del norte, norteño ♦ adv al or hacia el norte; **N~ Africa** n África del Norte; **N~ America** n América del Norte; **~east** n nor(d)este m; **~erly** ['nɔːðəlɪ]

adj (point, direction) norteño; **~ern** ['nɔːðən] adj norteño, del norte; **N~ern Ireland** n Irlanda del Norte; **N~ Pole** n Polo Norte; **N~ Sea** n Mar m del Norte; **~ward(s)** ['nɔːθwəd(z)] adv hacia el norte; **~-west** n nor(d)oeste m
Norway ['nɔːweɪ] n Noruega; **Norwegian** [-'wiːdʒən] adj noruego/a ♦ n noruego/a; (LING) noruego
nose [nəuz] n (ANAT) nariz f; (ZOOL) hocico; (sense of smell) olfato ♦ vi: **to ~ about** curiosear; **~bleed** n hemorragia nasal; **~-dive** n (of plane: deliberate) picado vertical; (: involuntary) caída en picado; **~y** (inf) adj curioso, fisgón/ona
nostalgia [nɒs'tældʒɪə] n nostalgia
nostril ['nɒstrɪl] n ventana de la nariz
nosy ['nəuzɪ] (inf) adj = **nosey**
not [nɒt] adv no; **~ that** ... no es que ...; **it's too late, isn't it?** es demasiado tarde, ¿verdad or no?; **~ yet/now** todavía/ahora no; **why ~?** ¿por qué no?; (see also) **only**
notably ['nəutəblɪ] adv especialmente
notary ['nəutərɪ] n notario m
notch [nɒtʃ] n muesca, corte m
note [nəut] n (MUS, record, letter) nota; (banknote) billete m; (tone) tono ♦ vt (observe) notar, observar; (write down) apuntar, anotar; **~book** n libreta, cuaderno; **~d** ['nəutɪd] adj célebre, conocido; **~pad** n bloc m; **~paper** n papel m para cartas
nothing ['nʌθɪŋ] n nada; (zero) cero; **he does ~** no hace nada; **~ new** nada nuevo; **~ much** no mucho; **for ~** (free) gratis, sin pago; (in vain) en balde
notice ['nəutɪs] n (announcement) anuncio; (warning) aviso; (dismissal) despido; (resignation) dimisión f; (period of time) plazo ♦ vt (observe) notar, observar; **to bring sth to sb's ~** (attention) llamar la atención de uno sobre algo; **to take ~ of** tomar nota de, prestar atención a; **at short ~** con

poca anticipación; **until further ~** hasta nuevo aviso; **to hand in one's ~** dimitir; **~able** adj evidente, obvio; **~ board** (BRIT) n tablón m de anuncios

notify ['nəutɪfaɪ] vt: **to ~ sb (of sth)** comunicar (algo) a

notion ['nəuʃən] n idea; (opinion) opinión f

notorious [nəu'tɔ:rɪəs] adj notorio

nougat ['nu:ga:] n turrón m

nought [nɔ:t] n cero

noun [naun] n nombre m, sustantivo

nourish ['nʌrɪʃ] vt nutrir; (fig) alimentar; **~ing** adj nutritivo; **~ment** n alimento, sustento

novel ['nɔvl] n novela ♦ adj (new) nuevo, original; (unexpected) insólito; **~ist** n novelista m/f; **~ty** n novedad f

November [nəu'vɛmbə*] n noviembre m

novice ['nɔvɪs] n (REL) novicio/a

now [nau] adv (at the present time) ahora; (these days) actualmente, hoy día ♦ conj: **~ (that)** ya que, ahora que; **right ~** ahora mismo; **by ~** ya; **just ~** ahora mismo; **~ and then, ~ and again** de vez en cuando; **from ~ on** de ahora en adelante; **~adays** ['nauədeɪz] adv hoy (en) día, actualmente

nowhere ['nəuwɛə*] adv (direction) a ninguna parte; (location) en ninguna parte

nozzle ['nɔzl] n boquilla

nuance ['nju:ɑ:ns] n matiz m

nuclear ['nju:klɪə*] adj nuclear

nucleus ['nju:klɪəs] n (pl nuclei) n núcleo

nude [nju:d] adj, n desnudo m/f; **in the ~** desnudo

nudge [nʌdʒ] vt dar un codazo a

nudist ['nju:dɪst] n nudista m/f

nuisance ['nju:sns] n molestia, fastidio; (person) pesado, latoso; **what a ~!** ¡qué lata!

null [nʌl] adj: **~ and void** nulo y sin efecto

numb [nʌm] adj: **~ with cold/fear** entumecido por el frío/paralizado de miedo

number ['nʌmbə*] n número; (quantity) cantidad f ♦ vt (pages etc) numerar, poner número a; (amount to) sumar, ascender a; **to be ~ed among** figurar entre; **a ~ of** varios, algunos; **they were ten in ~** eran diez; **~ plate** (BRIT) n matrícula, placa

numeral ['nju:mərəl] n número, cifra

numerate ['nju:mərɪt] adj competente en la aritmética

numerous ['nju:mərəs] adj numeroso

nun [nʌn] n monja, religiosa

nurse [nə:s] n enfermero/a (♦ vt (patient) cuidar, atender

nursery ['nə:sərɪ] n (institution) guardería infantil; (room) cuarto de los niños; (for plants) criadero, semillero; **~ rhyme** n canción f infantil; **~ school** n parvulario, escuela de párvulos; **~ slope** (BRIT) n (SKI) cuesta para principiantes

nursing ['nə:sɪŋ] n (profession) profesión f de enfermera; (care) asistencia, cuidado; **~ home** n clínica de reposo

nut [nʌt] n (TECH) tuerca; (BOT) nuez f; **~crackers** npl cascanueces m inv

nutmeg ['nʌtmeg] n nuez f moscada

nutritious [nju:'trɪʃəs] adj nutritivo, alimenticio

nuts [nʌts] (inf) adj loco

nutshell ['nʌtʃɛl] n: **in a ~** en resumidas cuentas

nylon ['naɪlɔn] n nilón m ♦ adj de nilón

O, o

oak [əuk] n roble m ♦ adj de roble

O.A.P. (BRIT) n abbr = **old-age pensioner**

oar [ɔ:*] n remo

oasis [əu'eɪsɪs] (pl **oases**) n oasis m inv
oath [əuθ] n juramento; (swear word) palabrota; **on** (BRIT) or **under ~** bajo juramento
oatmeal ['əutmiːl] n harina de avena
oats [əuts] n avena
obedience [ə'biːdɪəns] n obediencia
obedient [ə'biːdɪənt] adj obediente
obey [ə'beɪ] vt obedecer; (instructions, regulations) cumplir
obituary [ə'bɪtjuərɪ] n necrología
object [n 'ɔbdʒɪkt, vb əb'dʒɛkt] n objeto; (purpose) objeto, propósito; (LING) complemento ♦ vi: **to ~ to** estar en contra de; (proposal) oponerse a; **to ~ that** objetar que; **expense is no ~** no importa cuánto cuesta; **I ~!** ¡yo protesto!; **~ion** [əb'dʒɛkʃən] n protesta; **I have no ~ion to ...** no tengo inconveniente en que ...; **~ionable** [əb'dʒɛkʃənəbl] adj desagradable; (conduct) censurable; **~ive** adj, n objetivo
obligation [ɔblɪ'geɪʃən] n obligación f; (debt) deber m; **without ~** sin compromiso
oblige [ə'blaɪdʒ] vt (do a favour for) complacer, hacer un favor a; **to ~ sb to do sth** forzar or obligar a uno a hacer algo; **to be ~d to sb for sth** estarle agradecido a uno por algo; **obliging** adj servicial, atento
oblique [ə'bliːk] adj oblicuo; (allusion) indirecto
obliterate [ə'blɪtəreɪt] vt borrar
oblivion [ə'blɪvɪən] n olvido; **oblivious** [-ɪəs] adj: **oblivious of** inconsciente de
oblong ['ɔblɔŋ] adj rectangular ♦ n rectángulo
obnoxious [əb'nɔkʃəs] adj odioso, detestable; (smell) nauseabundo
oboe ['əubəu] n oboe m
obscene [əb'siːn] adj obsceno
obscure [əb'skjuə*] adj oscuro ♦ vt oscurecer; (hide: sun) esconder
observant [əb'zəːvnt] adj

observador(a)
observation [ɔbzə'veɪʃən] n observación f; (MED) examen m
observe [əb'zəːv] vt observar; (rule) cumplir; **~r** n observador(a) m/f
obsess [əb'sɛs] vt obsesionar; **~ive** adj obsesivo; obsesionante
obsolete ['ɔbsəliːt] adj: **to be ~** estar en desuso
obstacle ['ɔbstəkl] n obstáculo; (nuisance) estorbo; **~ race** n carrera de obstáculos
obstinate ['ɔbstɪnɪt] adj terco, porfiado; (determined) obstinado
obstruct [əb'strʌkt] vt obstruir; (hinder) estorbar, obstaculizar; **~ion** [əb'strʌkʃən] n (action) obstrucción f; (object) estorbo, obstáculo
obtain [əb'teɪn] vt obtener; (achieve) conseguir
obvious ['ɔbvɪəs] adj obvio, evidente; **~ly** adv evidentemente, naturalmente; **~ly not** por supuesto que no
occasion [ə'keɪʒən] n oportunidad f, ocasión f; (event) acontecimiento m; **~al** adj poco frecuente, ocasional; **~ally** adv de vez en cuando
occupant ['ɔkjupənt] n (of house) inquilino/a; (of car) ocupante m/f
occupation [ɔkju'peɪʃən] n ocupación f; (job) trabajo; (pastime) ocupaciones fpl; **~al hazard** n riesgo profesional
occupier ['ɔkjupaɪə*] n inquilino/a
occupy ['ɔkjupaɪ] vt (seat, post, time) ocupar; (house) habitar; **to ~ o.s. in doing** pasar el tiempo haciendo
occur [ə'kəː*] vi pasar, suceder; **to ~ to sb** ocurrírsele a uno; **~rence** [ə'kʌrəns] n acontecimiento m; (existence) existencia
ocean ['əuʃən] n océano
o'clock [ə'klɔk] adv: **it is 5 ~** son las 5
OCR n abbr = **optical character recognition/reader**
October [ɔk'təubə*] n octubre m
octopus ['ɔktəpəs] n pulpo
odd [ɔd] adj extraño, raro; (number)

impar; (sock, shoe etc) suelto; **60-~** 60 y pico; **at ~ times** de vez en cuando; **to be the ~ one out** estar de más; **~ity** n rareza; (person) excentricidad f; **~job man** n chico para todo; **~ jobs** npl bricolaje m; **~ly** adv curiosamente, extrañamente; see also **enough**; **~ments** npl (COMM) retales mpl; **~s** npl (in betting) puntos mpl de ventaja; **it makes no ~s** da lo mismo; **at ~s** reñidos/as; **~s and ends** minucias fpl

odometer [ɔ'dɔmɪtə*] (US) n cuentakilómetros m inv

odour ['əudə*] (US **odor**) n olor m; (unpleasant) hedor m

KEYWORD

of [ɔv, əv] prep 1 (gen) de; **a friend ~ ours** un amigo nuestro; **a boy ~ 10** un chico de 10 años; **that was kind ~ you** eso fue muy amable por or de tu parte

2 (expressing quantity, amount, dates etc) de; **a kilo ~ flour** un kilo de harina; **there were 3 ~ them** había tres; **3 ~ us went** tres de nosotros fuimos; **the 5th ~ July** el 5 de julio

3 (from, out of) de; **made ~ wood** (hecho) de madera

off [ɔf] adj, adv (engine) desconectado; (light) apagado; (tap) cerrado; (BRIT: food: bad) pasado, malo; (: milk) cortado; (cancelled) cancelado ♦ prep de; **to be ~** (to leave) irse, marcharse; **to be ~ sick** estar enfermo or de baja; **a day ~** un día libre or sin trabajar; **to have an ~ day** tener un día malo; **he had his coat ~** se había quitado el abrigo; **10% ~** (COMM) (con el) 10% de descuento; **5 km ~** (the road) a 5 km (de la carretera); **~ the coast** frente a la costa; **I'm ~ meat** (no longer eat/like it) paso de la carne; **on the ~ chance** por si acaso; **~ and on** de vez en cuando

offal ['ɔfl] (BRIT) n (CULIN) menudencias fpl

off-colour [ɔf'kʌlə*] (BRIT) adj (ill) indispuesto

offence [ə'fɛns] (US **offense**) n (crime) delito; **to take ~ at** ofenderse por

offend [ə'fɛnd] vt (person) ofender; **~er** n delincuente m/f

offensive [ə'fɛnsɪv] adj ofensivo; (smell etc) repugnante ♦ n (MIL) ofensiva

offer ['ɔfə*] n oferta, ofrecimiento; (proposal) propuesta ♦ vt ofrecer; (opportunity) facilitar; **"on ~"** (COMM) "en oferta"; **~ing** n ofrenda

offhand [ɔf'hænd] adj informal ♦ adv de improviso

office ['ɔfɪs] n (place) oficina; (room) despacho; (position) carga, oficio; **doctor's ~** (US) consultorio; **to take ~** entrar en funciones; **~ automation** n ofimática, buromática; **~ block** (US **~ building**) n bloque m de oficinas; **~ hours** npl horas fpl de oficina; (US: MED) horas fpl de consulta

officer ['ɔfɪsə*] n (MIL etc) oficial m/f; (also: police ~) agente m/f de policía; (of organization) director(a) m/f

office worker n oficinista m/f

official [ə'fɪʃl] adj oficial, autorizado ♦ n funcionario, oficial m

offing ['ɔfɪŋ] n: **in the ~** (fig) en perspectiva

off-: **~licence** (BRIT) n (shop) bodega, tienda de vinos y bebidas alcohólicas ♦ **~line** adj, adv (COMPUT) fuera de línea; **~peak** adj (electricity) de banda económica; (ticket) billete de precio reducido por viajar fuera de las horas punta; **~putting** (BRIT) adj (person) asqueroso; (remark) desalentador(a); **~season** adj, adv fuera de temporada

Off-licence

En el Reino Unido la venta de bebidas alcohólicas está estrictamente regulada y se necesita una licencia especial, con la que cuentan los bares, restaurantes y los establecimientos de

off-licence, *los únicos lugares en donde se pueden adquirir bebidas alcohólicas para su consumo fuera del local, de donde viene su nombre. También venden bebidas no alcohólicas, tabaco, chocolatinas, patatas fritas, etc. y a menudo forman parte de una cadena nacional.*

offset ['ɔfset] (*irreg*) *vt* contrarrestar, compensar

offshoot ['ɔfʃuːt] *n* (*fig*) ramificación *f*

offshore [ɔf'ʃɔː*] *adj* (*breeze, island*) costera; (*fishing*) de bajura

offside ['ɔf'saɪd] *adj* (*SPORT*) fuera de juego; (*AUT: in UK*) del lado derecho; (: *in US, Europe etc*) del lado izquierdo

offspring ['ɔfsprɪŋ] *n inv* descendencia

off: **~stage** *adv* entre bastidores; **~-the-peg** (*US* **~-the-rack**) *adj* confeccionado/a; **~-white** *adj* color crudo

often ['ɔfn] *adv* a menudo, con frecuencia; **how ~ do you go?** ¿cada cuánto vas?

oh [əu] *excl* ¡ah!

oil [ɔɪl] *n* aceite *m*; (*petroleum*) petróleo; (*for heating*) aceite *m* combustible ♦ *vt* engrasar; **~can** *n* lata de aceite; **~field** *n* campo petrolífero; **~ filter** *n* (*AUT*) filtro de aceite; **~ painting** *n* pintura al óleo; **~ rig** *n* torre *f* de perforación; **~ tanker** *n* petrolero; (*truck*) camión *m* cisterna; **~ well** *n* pozo *m* (de petróleo); **~y** *adj* aceitoso; (*food*) grasiento

ointment ['ɔɪntmənt] *n* ungüento

O.K., okay ['əu'keɪ] *excl* O.K., ¡está bien!, ¡vale! (*SP*) ♦ *adj* bien ♦ *vt* dar el visto bueno a

old [əuld] *adj* viejo; (*former*) antiguo; **how ~ are you?** ¿cuántos años tienes?; ¿qué edad tienes?; **he's 10 years ~** tiene 10 años; **~er brother** hermano mayor; **~ age** *n* vejez *f*; **~-age pensioner** (*BRIT*) *n* jubilado/a; **~-fashioned** *adj* anticuado, pasado de moda

olive ['ɔlɪv] *n* (*fruit*) aceituna; (*tree*) olivo ♦ *adj* (*also*: **~-green**) verde oliva; **~ oil** *n* aceite *m* de oliva

Olympic [əu'lɪmpɪk] *adj* olímpico; **the ~ Games, the ~s** las Olimpiadas

omelet(te) ['ɔmlɪt] *n* tortilla (*SP*), tortilla de huevo (*AM*)

omen ['əumən] *n* presagio

ominous ['ɔmɪnəs] *adj* de mal agüero, amenazador(a)

omit [əu'mɪt] *vt* omitir

on [ɔn] *prep* **1** (*indicating position*) en; sobre; **~ the wall** en la pared; **it's ~ the table** está sobre *or* en la mesa; **~ the left** a la izquierda

2 (*indicating means, method, condition etc*): **~ foot** a pie; **~ the train/plane** (*go*) en tren/avión; (*be*) en el tren/avión; **~ the radio/television/telephone** por *or* en la radio/televisión/al teléfono; **to be ~ drugs** drogarse; (*MED*) estar a tratamiento; **to be ~ holiday/business** estar de vacaciones/en viaje de negocios

3 (*referring to time*): **~ Friday** el viernes; **~ Fridays** los viernes; **~ June 20th** el 20 de junio; **a week ~ Friday** del viernes en una semana; **~ arrival** al llegar; **~ seeing this** al ver esto

4 (*about, concerning*) sobre, acerca de; **a book ~ physics** un libro de *or* sobre física

♦ *adv* **1** (*referring to dress*): **to have one's coat ~** tener *or* llevar el abrigo puesto; **she put her gloves ~** se puso los guantes

2 (*referring to covering*): **"screw the lid ~ tightly"** "cerrar bien la tapa"

3 (*further, continuously*): **to walk** *etc* **~** seguir caminando *etc*

♦ *adj* **1** (*functioning, in operation: machine, radio, TV, light*) encendido/a (*SP*), prendido/a (*AM*); (: *tap*) abierto/a; (: *brakes*) echado/a, puesto/a; **is the**

meeting still ~? (*in progress*) ¿todavía continúa la reunión?; (*not cancelled*) ¿va a haber reunión al fin? **there's a good film ~ at the cinema** ponen una buena película en el cine 2: **that's not ~!** (*inf: not possible*) ¡eso ni hablar!; (: *not acceptable*) ¡eso no se hace!

once [wʌns] *adv* una vez; (*formerly*) antiguamente ♦ *conj* una vez que; **~ he had left/it was done** una vez que se había marchado/se hizo; **at ~** en seguida, inmediatamente; (*simultaneously*) a la vez; **~ a week** una vez por semana; **~ more** otra vez; **~ and for all** de una vez por todas; **~ upon a time** érase una vez

oncoming ['ɒnkʌmɪŋ] *adj* (*traffic*) que viene de frente

─────────────────
KEYWORD
─────────────────

one [wʌn] *num* un(o)/una; **~ hundred and fifty** ciento cincuenta; **~ by ~** uno a uno
♦ *adj* 1 (*sole*) único; **the ~ book which** el único libro que; **the ~ man who** el único que
2 (*same*) mismo/a; **they came in the ~ car** vinieron en un solo coche
♦ *pron* 1: **this ~** éste/ésta; **that ~** ése/ésa; (*more remote*) aquél/aquélla; **I've already got (a red) ~** ya tengo uno/a (rojo/a); **~ by ~** uno/a por uno/a
2: **~ another** os (*SP*), se (+ *el uno al otro, unos a otros etc*); **do they ever see ~ another?** ¿vosotros dos os veis alguna vez? (*SP*), ¿se ven ustedes dos alguna vez?; **the boys didn't dare look at ~ another** los chicos no se atrevieron a mirarse (el uno al otro); **they all kissed ~ another** se besaron unos a unos
3 (*impers*): **~ never knows** nunca se sabe; **to cut ~'s finger** cortarse el dedo; **~ needs to eat** hay que comer

one: ~-day excursion (*US*) *n* billete *m* de ida y vuelta en un día; **~-man** *adj* (*business*) individual; **~-man band** *n* hombre-orquesta *m*; **~-off** (*BRIT: inf*) *n* (*event*) acontecimiento único

oneself [wʌn'self] *pron* (*reflexive*) se; (*after prep*) sí; (*emphatic*) mismo/a uno/a mismo/a; **to hurt ~** hacerse daño; **to keep sth for ~** guardarse algo; **to talk to ~** hablar solo

one: ~-sided *adj* (*argument*) parcial; **~-to-~** *adj* (*relationship*) de dos; **~-way** *adj* (*street*) de sentido único

ongoing ['ɒngəʊɪŋ] *adj* continuo

onion ['ʌnjən] *n* cebolla

on-line *adj, adv* (*COMPUT*) en línea

onlooker ['ɒnlʊkə*] *n* espectador(a) *m/f*

only ['əʊnlɪ] *adv* solamente, sólo ♦ *adj* único, solo ♦ *conj* solamente que, pero; **an ~ child** un hijo único; **not ~ ... but also ...** no sólo ... sino también ...

onset ['ɒnset] *n* comienzo

onshore ['ɒnʃɔ:*] *adj* (*wind*) que sopla del mar hacia la tierra

onslaught ['ɒnslɔ:t] *n* ataque *m*, embestida

onto ['ɒntu] *prep* = **on to**

onward(s) ['ɒnwəd(z)] *adv* (*move*) (hacia) adelante; **from that time ~** desde entonces en adelante

onyx ['ɒnɪks] *n* ónice *m*

ooze [u:z] *vi* rezumar

opaque [əʊ'peɪk] *adj* opaco

OPEC ['əʊpek] *n abbr* (= *Organization of Petroleum-Exporting Countries*) OPEP *f*

open ['əʊpn] *adj* abierto; (*car*) descubierto; (*road, view*) despejado; (*meeting*) público; (*admiration*) manifiesto ♦ *vt* abrir ♦ *vi* abrirse; (*book etc: commence*) comenzar; **in the ~ (-air)** al aire libre; **~ on to** *vt fus* (*subj: room, door*) dar a; **~ up** *vt* abrir; (*blocked road*) despejar ♦ *vi* abrirse, empezar; **~ing** *n* abertura; (*start*) comienzo; (*opportunity*) oportunidad *f*;

~ing hours npl horario de apertura;
~ learning educación flexible a
tiempo parcial; ~ly adv abiertamente;
~-minded adj imparcial; ~-necked
adj (shirt) desabrochado; sin corbata;
~-plan adj: ~-plan office gran oficina
sin particiones

Open University

La **Open University**, fundada en
1969, está especializada en impartir
cursos a distancia que no exigen una
dedicación exclusiva. Cuenta con sus
propios materiales de apoyo, entre
ellos programas de radio y televisión
emitidos por la BBC y para conseguir
los créditos de la licenciatura es
necesaria la presentación de unos
trabajos y la asistencia a los cursos de
verano.

opera ['ɔpərə] n ópera; ~ **house** n
teatro de la ópera
operate ['ɔpəreit] vt (machine) hacer
funcionar; (company) dirigir ♦ vi
funcionar; **to ~ on sb** (MED) operar a
uno
operatic [ɔpə'rætik] adj de ópera
operating table ['ɔpəreitiŋ-] n mesa
de operaciones
operating theatre n sala de
operaciones
operation [ɔpə'reɪʃən] n operación f;
(of machine) funcionamiento; **to be in
~** estar funcionando o en
funcionamiento; **to have an ~** (MED)
ser operado; ~**al** adj operacional, en
buen estado
operative ['ɔpərətiv] adj en vigor
operator ['ɔpəreitə*] n (of machine)
maquinista m/f, operario/a; (TEL)
operador/a m/f, telefonista m/f
opinion [ə'pinjən] n opinión f; **in my
~** en mi opinión, a mi juicio; ~**ated**
adj testarudo; ~ **poll** n encuesta, sondeo
opponent [ə'pəunənt] n adversario/a,
contrincante m/f

opportunity [ɔpə'tjuːniti] n
oportunidad f; **to take the ~ of
doing** aprovechar la ocasión para
hacer
oppose [ə'pəuz] vt oponerse a; **to be
~d to sth** oponerse a algo; **as ~d to**
a diferencia de; **opposing** adj
opuesto, contrario
opposite ['ɔpəzit] adj opuesto,
contrario a; (house etc) de enfrente
♦ adv en frente ♦ prep en frente de,
frente a ♦ n lo contrario
opposition [ɔpə'zɪʃən] n oposición f
oppressive [ə'presiv] adj opresivo;
(weather) agobiante
opt [ɔpt] vi: **to ~ for** optar por; **to
~ to do** optar por hacer; **~ out** vi: **to
~ out of** optar por no hacer
optical ['ɔptikl] adj óptico
optician [ɔp'tɪʃən] n óptico m/f
optimist ['ɔptimist] n optimista m/f;
~**ic** [-'mistik] adj optimista
option ['ɔpʃən] n opción f; ~**al** adj
facultativo, discrecional
or [ɔː*] conj o; (before o, ho) u; (with
negative): **he hasn't seen ~ heard
anything** no ha visto ni oído nada; **~
else** si no
oral ['ɔːrəl] adj oral ♦ n examen m oral
orange ['ɔrɪndʒ] n (fruit) naranja ♦ adj
color naranja
orbit ['ɔːbit] n órbita ♦ vt, vi orbitar
orchard ['ɔːtʃəd] n huerto
orchestra ['ɔːkɪstrə] n orquesta; (US:
seating) platea
orchid ['ɔːkɪd] n orquídea
ordain [ɔː'deɪn] vt (REL) ordenar,
decretar
ordeal [ɔː'diːl] n experiencia horrorosa
order ['ɔːdə*] n orden m; (command)
orden f; (good ~) buen estado; (COMM)
pedido ♦ vt (also: put in ~) arreglar,
poner en orden; (COMM) mandar,
pedir; (command) mandar, ordenar; **in ~** en
orden; (of document) en regla; **in
(working) ~** en funcionamiento; **in
~ to do/that** para hacer/que; **on ~**

(COMM) pedido; **to be out of ~** estar desordenado; (not working) no funcionar; **to ~ sb to do sth** mandar a uno hacer algo; **~ form** n hoja de pedido; **~ly** n (MIL) ordenanza m; (MED) enfermero/a (auxiliar) ♦ adj ordenado

ordinary ['ɔːdnrɪ] adj corriente, normal; (pej) común y corriente; **out of the ~** fuera de lo común

Ordnance Survey ['ɔːdnəns-] (BRIT) n servicio oficial de topografía

ore [ɔː*] n mineral m

organ ['ɔːgən] n órgano; **~ic** [ɔː'gænɪk] adj orgánico; **~ism** n organismo

organization [ɔːgənaɪ'zeɪʃən] n organización f

organize ['ɔːgənaɪz] vt organizar; **~r** n organizador(a) m/f

orgasm ['ɔːgæzəm] n orgasmo

orgy ['ɔːdʒɪ] n orgía

Orient ['ɔːrɪənt] n Oriente m; **oriental** [-'entl] adj oriental

orientate ['ɔːrɪənteɪt] vt: **to ~ o.s.** orientarse

origin ['ɒrɪdʒɪn] n origen m

original [ə'rɪdʒɪnl] adj original; (first) primero; (earlier) primitivo ♦ n original m; **~ly** adv al principio

originate [ə'rɪdʒɪneɪt] vi: **to ~ from, to ~ in** surgir de, tener su origen en

Orkneys ['ɔːknɪz] npl: **the ~** (also: the Orkney Islands) las Orcadas

ornament ['ɔːnəmənt] n adorno; (trinket) chuchería; **~al** [-'mentl] adj decorativo, de adorno

ornate [ɔː'neɪt] adj muy ornado, vistoso

orphan ['ɔːfn] n huérfano/a

orthopaedic [ɔːθə'piːdɪk] (US **orthopedic**) adj ortopédico

ostensibly [ɔs'tensɪblɪ] adv aparentemente

ostentatious [ɔsten'teɪʃəs] adj ostentoso

osteopath ['ɔstɪəpæθ] n osteópata m/f

ostracize ['ɔstrəsaɪz] vt hacer el vacío a

ostrich ['ɔstrɪtʃ] n avestruz m

other ['ʌðə*] adj otro ♦ pron: **than the ~** (one) otro que; **~ than** aparte de; **~s** (~ people) otros; **the ~ day** adv el otro día; **~wise** adv de otra manera ♦ conj (if not) si no

otter ['ɔtə*] n nutria

ouch [autʃ] excl ¡ay!

ought [ɔːt] (pt ought) aux vb: **I ~ to do it** debería hacerlo; **this ~ to have been corrected** esto debiera haberse corregido; **he ~ to win** (probability) debe or debiera ganar

ounce [auns] n onza (28.35g)

our ['auə*] adj nuestro; see also **my**; **~s** pron (el) nuestro/(la) nuestra etc; see also **mine¹**; **~selves** pron pl (reflexive, after prep) nosotros; (emphatic) nosotros mismos; see also **oneself**

oust [aust] vt desalojar

out [aut] adv fuera, afuera; (not at home) fuera de casa; (light, fire) apagado; **~ there** allí (fuera); **he's ~** (absent) no está, ha salido; **to be ~ in one's calculations** equivocarse (en sus cálculos); **to run ~** salir corriendo; **~ loud** en alta voz; **~ of** (outside) fuera de; (because of: anger etc) por; **~ of petrol** sin gasolina; **"~ of order"** "no funciona"; **~-and-~** adj (liar, thief etc) redomado, empedernido; **~back** n interior m; **~board** adj: **~board motor** (motor m) fuera borda m; **~break** n (of war) comienzo; (of disease) epidemia; (of violence etc) ola; **~burst** n explosión f, arranque m; **~cast** n paria m/f; **~come** n resultado; **~crop** n (of rock) afloramiento m; **~cry** n protestas fpl; **~dated** adj anticuado, fuera de moda; **~do** (irreg) vt superar; **~door** adj exterior, de aire libre; (clothes) de calle; **~doors** adv al aire libre

outer ['autə*] adj exterior, externo; **~ space** n espacio exterior

outfit [ˈautfɪt] n (clothes) conjunto

out: **~going** adj (character)
extrovertido; (retiring: president etc)
saliente; **~goings** (BRIT) npl gastos
mpl; **~grow** (irreg) vt **he has
~grown his clothes** su ropa le queda
pequeña ya; **~house** n dependencia;
~ing [ˈautɪŋ] n excursión f, paseo

out: **~law** n proscrito ♦ vt proscribir;
~lay n inversión f; **~let** n salida; (of
pipe) desagüe m; (US: ELEC) toma de
corriente; (also: retail ~let) punto de
venta; **~line** n (shape) contorno, perfil
m; (sketch, plan) esbozo ♦ vt (plan etc)
esbozar; **in ~line** (fig) a grandes
rasgos; **~live** vt sobrevivir a; **~look**
n (fig: prospects) perspectivas fpl; (: for
weather) pronóstico; **~lying** adj
remoto, aislado; **~moded** adj
anticuado, pasado de moda;
~number vt superar en número; **~-
of-date** adj (passport) caducado;
(clothes) pasado de moda; **~-of-the-
way** adj apartado; **~patient** n
paciente m/f externo/a; **~post** n
puesto avanzado; **~put** n (volumen m
de) producción f, rendimiento;
(COMPUT) salida

outrage [ˈautreɪdʒ] n escándalo;
(atrocity) atrocidad f ♦ vt ultrajar; **~ous**
[-ˈreɪdʒəs] adj monstruoso

outright [adv autˈraɪt, adj ˈautraɪt] adv
(ask, deny) francamente; (refuse)
rotundamente; (win) de manera
absoluta; (be killed) en el acto ♦ adj
franco; rotundo

outset [ˈautset] n principio

outside [autˈsaɪd] n exterior m ♦ adj
exterior, externo ♦ adv fuera ♦ prep
fuera de; (beyond) más allá de; **at the
~** (fig) a lo sumo; **~ lane** n (AUT: in
Britain) carril m de la derecha; (: in US,
Europe etc) carril m de la izquierda;
~ line n (TEL) línea (exterior); **~r** n
(stranger) extraño, forastero

out: **~size** adj (clothes) de talla grande;
~skirts npl alrededores mpl, afueras

fpl; **~spoken** adj muy franco;
~standing adj excepcional,
destacado; (remaining) pendiente;
~stay vt: **to ~stay one's welcome**
quedarse más de la cuenta;
~stretched adj (hand) extendido;
~strip vt (competitors, demand) dejar
atrás, aventajar; **~tray** n bandeja de
salida

outward [ˈautwəd] adj externo;
(journey) de ida

outweigh [autˈweɪ] vt pesar más que

outwit [autˈwɪt] vt ser más listo que

oval [ˈəuvl] adj ovalado ♦ n óvalo

ovary [ˈəuvərɪ] n ovario

oven [ˈʌvn] n horno; **~proof** adj
resistente al horno

over [ˈəuvə*] adv encima, por encima
♦ adj (or adv) (finished) terminado;
(surplus) de sobra ♦ prep (por) encima
de; (above) sobre; (on the other side of)
al otro lado de; (more than) más de;
(during) durante; **~ here** (por) aquí;
~ there (por) allí or allá; **all ~**
(everywhere) por todas partes; **~ and
~ (again)** una y otra vez; **~ and
above** además de; **to ask sb ~** invitar
a uno a casa; **to bend ~** inclinarse

overall [adj, n ˈəuvərɔːl, adv əuvərˈɔːl]
adj (length etc) total; (study) de
conjunto ♦ adv en conjunto ♦ n (BRIT)
guardapolvo; **~s** npl mono (SP), overol
m (AM)

over: **~awe** vt: **to be ~awed (by)**
quedar impresionado (con); **~balance**
vi perder el equilibrio; **~board** adv
(NAUT) por la borda; **~book**
[əuvəˈbuk] vt sobrereservar

overcast [ˈəuvəkɑːst] adj encapotado

overcharge [əuvəˈtʃɑːdʒ] vt: **to ~ sb**
cobrar un precio excesivo a uno

overcoat [ˈəuvəkəut] n abrigo,
sobretodo

overcome [əuvəˈkʌm] (irreg) vt
vencer; (difficulty) superar

over: **~crowded** adj atestado de
gente; (city, country) superpoblado;

~do (*irreg*) *vt* exagerar; (*overcook*) cocer demasiado; **to ~do it** (*work etc*) pasarse; **~dose** *n* sobredosis *f inv*; **~draft** *n* saldo deudor; **~drawn** *adj* (*account*) en descubierto; **~due** *adj* retrasado; **~estimate** [auvər'estimeit] *vt* sobreestimar

overflow [*vb* auvə'fləu, *n* 'auvəfləu] *vi* desbordarse *n* (*also*: **~ pipe**) (cañería de) desagüe *m*

overgrown [auvə'grəun] *adj* (*garden*) invadido por la vegetación

overhaul [*vb* auvə'hɔːl, *n* 'auvəhɔːl] *vt* revisar, repasar ♦ *n* revisión *f*

overhead [*adv* auvə'hed, *adj*, *n* 'auvəhed] *adv* por arriba or encima ♦ *adj* (*cable*) aéreo ♦ *n* (*US*) = **~s**; **~s** *npl* (*expenses*) gastos *mpl* generales

over: ~hear (*irreg*) *vt* oír por casualidad; **~heat** *vi* (*engine*) recalentarse; **~joyed** *adj* encantado, lleno de alegría

overland ['auvəlænd] *adj*, *adv* por tierra

overlap [auvə'læp] *vi* traslaparse

over: ~leaf *adv* al dorso; **~load** *vt* sobrecargar; **~look** *vt* (*have view of*) dar a, tener vistas a; (*miss: by mistake*) pasar por alto; (*excuse*) perdonar

overnight [auvə'naɪt] *adv* durante la noche; (*fig*) de la noche a la mañana ♦ *adj* de noche; **to stay ~** pasar la noche

overpass ['auvəpɑːs] (*US*) *n* paso superior

overpower [auvə'pauə*] *vt* dominar; (*fig*) embargar; **~ing** *adj* (*heat*) agobiante; (*smell*) penetrante

over: ~rate *vt* sobreestimar; **~ride** (*irreg*) *vt* no hacer caso de; **~riding** *adj* predominante; **~rule** *vt* (*decision*) anular; (*claim*) denegar; **~run** (*irreg*) *vt* (*country*) invadir; (*time limit*) rebasar, exceder

overseas [auvə'siːz] *adv* (*abroad: live*) en el extranjero; (*: travel*) al extranjero ♦ *adj* (*trade*) exterior; (*visitor*)

extranjero

overshadow [auvə'ʃædəu] *vt*: **to be ~ed by** estar a la sombra de

overshoot [auvə'ʃuːt] (*irreg*) *vt* excederse

oversight ['auvəsaɪt] *n* descuido

oversleep [auvə'sliːp] (*irreg*) *vi* quedarse dormido

overstep [auvə'step] *vt*: **to ~ the mark** pasarse de la raya

overt [au'vɜːt] *adj* abierto

overtake [auvə'teɪk] (*irreg*) *vt* sobrepasar; (*BRIT: AUT*) adelantar

over: ~throw (*irreg*) *vt* (*government*) derrocar; **~time** *n* horas *fpl* extraordinarias; **~tone** *n* (*fig*) tono

overture ['auvətʃuə*] *n* (*MUS*) obertura, (*fig*) preludio

over: ~turn *vt* volcar; (*fig: plan*) desbaratar; (*: government*) derrocar ♦ *vi* volcar; **~weight** *adj* demasiado gordo or pesado; **~whelm** *vt* aplastar; (*subj: emotion*) sobrecoger; **~whelming** *adj* (*victory, defeat*) arrollador(a); (*feeling*) irresistible; **~work** *vt* trabajar demasiado; **~wrought** [auvə'rɔːt] *adj* sobreexcitado

owe [əu] *vt*: **to ~ sb sth**, **to ~ sth to sb** deber algo a uno; **owing to** *prep* debido a, por causa de

owl [aul] *n* búho, lechuza

own [aun] *vt* tener, poseer ♦ *adj* propio; **a room of my ~** una habitación propia; **to get one's ~ back** tomar revancha; **on one's ~** solo, a solas; **~ up** *vi* confesar; **~er** *n* dueño/a; **~ership** *n* posesión *f*

ox [ɔks] (*pl* **~en**) *n* buey *m*; **~tail** *n*: **~tail soup** sopa de rabo de buey

oxygen ['ɔksɪdʒən] *n* oxígeno

oyster ['ɔistə*] *n* ostra

oz. *abbr* = **ounce(s)**

ozone ['auzəun]: **~ friendly** *adj* que no daña la capa de ozono; **~ hole** *n* agujero *m* de/en la capa de ozono; **~ layer** *n* capa *f* de ozono

P, p

p [pi:] *abbr* = **penny; pence**
P.A. *n abbr* = **personal assistant; public address system**
p.a. *abbr* = **per annum**
pa [pɑ:] *(inf) n* papá *m*
pace [peɪs] *n* paso *m* ♦ *vi*: **to ~ up and down** pasearse de un lado a otro; **to keep ~ with** llevar el mismo paso que; **~maker** *n* (MED) regulador *m* cardíaco, marcapasos *m inv*; (SPORT: *also*: ~setter) liebre *f*
Pacific [pə'sɪfɪk] *n*: **the ~ (Ocean)** el (Océano) Pacífico
pack [pæk] *n* (*packet*) paquete *m*; (*of hounds*) jauría; (*of people*) manada, bando; (*of cards*) baraja; (*bundle*) fardo; (*US: of cigarettes*) paquete *m*; (*back ~*) mochila ♦ *vt* (*fill*) llenar; (*in suitcase etc*) meter, poner; (*cram*) llenar, atestar; **to ~ (one's bags)** hacerse la maleta; **to ~ sb off** despachar a uno; **~ it in!** (*inf*) ¡déjalo!
package [ˈpækɪdʒ] *n* paquete *m*; (*bulky*) bulto; (*also*: ~ deal) acuerdo global; **~ holiday** *n* vacaciones *fpl* organizadas; **~ tour** *n* viaje *m* organizado
packed lunch *n* almuerzo frío
packet [ˈpækɪt] *n* paquete *m*
packing [ˈpækɪŋ] *n* embalaje *m*; **~ case** *n* cajón *m* de embalaje
pact [pækt] *n* pacto *m*
pad [pæd] *n* (*of paper*) bloc *m*; (*cushion*) cojinete *m*; (*inf: home*) casa ♦ *vt* rellenar; **~ding** *n* (*material*) relleno
paddle [ˈpædl] *n* (*oar*) canalete *m*; (*US: for table tennis*) paleta ♦ *vt* impulsar con canalete ♦ *vi* (*with feet*) chapotear;
paddling pool (BRIT) *n* estanque *m* de juegos
paddock [ˈpædək] *n* corral *m*
padlock [ˈpædlɒk] *n* candado
paediatrics [pi:dɪˈætrɪks] (*US*

pediatrics) *n* pediatría
pagan [ˈpeɪɡən] *adj, n* pagano/a *m/f*
page [peɪdʒ] *n* (*of book*) página; (*of newspaper*) plana; (*also*: ~ boy) paje *m* ♦ *vt* (*in hotel etc*) llamar por altavoz a
pageant [ˈpædʒənt] *n* (*procession*) desfile *m*; (*show*) espectáculo; **~ry** *n* pompa
pager [ˈpeɪdʒə*] *n* (TEL) busca *m*
paging device [ˈpeɪdʒɪŋ-] *n* = **pager**
paid [peɪd] *pt, pp of* **pay** ♦ *adj* (*work*) remunerado; (*holiday*) pagado; (*official etc*) a sueldo; **to put ~ to** (BRIT) acabar con
pail [peɪl] *n* cubo, balde *m*
pain [peɪn] *n* dolor *m*; **to be in ~** sufrir; **to take ~s to do sth** tomarse grandes molestias en hacer algo; **~ed** *adj* (*expression*) afligido; **~ful** *adj* doloroso; (*difficult*) penoso; (*disagreeable*) desagradable; **~fully** *adv* (*fig: very*) terriblemente; **~killer** *n* analgésico; **~less** *adj* que no causa dolor; **~staking** [ˈpeɪnzteɪkɪŋ] *adj* (*person*) concienzudo, esmerado
paint [peɪnt] *n* pintura ♦ *vt* pintar; **to ~ the door blue** pintar la puerta de azul; **~brush** *n* (*artist's*) pincel *m*; (*decorator's*) brocha; **~er** *n* pintor(a) *m/f*; **~ing** *n* pintura; **~work** *n* pintura
pair [peə*] *n* (*of shoes, gloves etc*) par *m*; (*of people*) pareja; **a ~ of scissors** unas tijeras; **a ~ of trousers** unos pantalones, un pantalón
pajamas [pəˈdʒɑːməz] (*US*) *npl* pijama *m*
Pakistan [pɑːkɪˈstɑːn] *n* Paquistán *m*; **~i** *adj, n* paquistaní *m/f*
pal [pæl] *(inf) n* compinche *m/f*, compañero/a
palace [ˈpæləs] *n* palacio
palatable [ˈpælɪtəbl] *adj* sabroso
palate [ˈpælɪt] *n* paladar *m*
pale [peɪl] *adj* (*gen*) pálido; (*colour*) claro ♦ *n*: **to be beyond the ~** pasarse de la raya
Palestine [ˈpæləstaɪn] *n* Palestina;

Palestinian [-'tɪnɪən] *adj, n* palestino/a *m/f*

palette ['pælɪt] *n* paleta

pall [pɔːl] *vi* perder el sabor

pallet ['pælɪt] *n (for goods)* pallet *m*

pallid ['pælɪd] *adj* pálido

palm [pɑːm] *n (ANAT)* palma; *(also: ~ tree)* palmera, palma ♦ *vt:* **to ~ sth off on sb** *(inf)* encajar algo a uno; **P~ Sunday** *n* Domingo de Ramos

paltry ['pɔːltrɪ] *adj* irrisorio

pamper ['pæmpə*] *vt* mimar

pamphlet ['pæmflət] *n* folleto

pan [pæn] *n (also: sauce~)* cacerola, cazuela, olla; *(also: frying ~)* sartén *f*

Panama ['pænəmɑː] *n* Panamá *m;* **the ~ Canal** el Canal de Panamá

pancake ['pænkeɪk] *n* crepe *f*

panda ['pændə] *n* panda *m;* **~ car** *(BRIT)* *n* coche *m* Z *(SP)*

pandemonium [pændɪ'məunɪəm] *n* jaleo

pander ['pændə*] *vi:* **to ~ to** complacer a

pane [peɪn] *n* cristal *m*

panel ['pænl] *n (of wood etc)* panel *m; (RADIO, TV)* panel *m* de invitados; **~ling** *(US* **~ing)** *n* paneles *mpl*

pang [pæŋ] *n:* **a ~ of regret** (una punzada de) remordimiento; **hunger ~s** dolores *mpl* del hambre

panic ['pænɪk] *n* (terror *m*) pánico ♦ *vi* dejarse llevar por el pánico; **~ky** *adj (person)* asustadizo; **~-stricken** *adj* preso de pánico

pansy ['pænzɪ] *n (BOT)* pensamiento; *(inf: pej)* maricón *m*

pant [pænt] *vi* jadear

panther ['pænθə*] *n* pantera

panties ['pæntɪz] *npl* bragas *fpl*, pantis *mpl*

pantihose ['pæntɪhəuz] *(US) n* pantimedias *fpl*

pantomime ['pæntəmaɪm] *(BRIT) n* revista musical representada en Navidad, basada en cuentos de hadas

---

Pantomime

En época navideña se ponen en escena en los teatros británicos las llamadas **pantomimes**, *que son versiones libres de cuentos tradicionales como* Aladino *o* El gato con botas. *En ella nunca faltan personajes como la dama ("dame"), papel que siempre interpreta un actor, el protagonista joven ("principal boy"), normalmente interpretado por una actriz, y el malvado ("villain"). Es un espectáculo familiar en el que se anima al público a participar y aunque va dirigido principalmente a los niños, cuenta con grandes dosis de humor para adultos.*

---

pantry ['pæntrɪ] *n* despensa

pants [pænts] *n (BRIT: underwear: woman's)* bragas *fpl; (: man's)* calzoncillos *mpl; (US: trousers)* pantalones *mpl*

paper ['peɪpə*] *n (also: news~)* periódico, diario; *(academic essay)* ensayo; *(exam)* examen *m* ♦ de papel ♦ *vt* empapelar *(SP)*, tapizar *(AM);* **~s** *npl (also: identity ~s)* papeles *mpl*, documentos *mpl;* **~back** *n* libro en rústica; **~ bag** *n* bolsa de papel; **~ clip** *n* clip *m;* **~ hankie** *n* pañuelo de papel; **~weight** *n* pisapapeles *m inv;* **~work** *n* trabajo administrativo

paprika ['pæprɪkə] *n* pimentón *m*

par [pɑː*] *n (GOLF)* par *m;* **to be on a ~ with** estar a la par con

parachute ['pærəʃuːt] *n* paracaídas *m inv*

parade [pə'reɪd] *n* desfile *m* ♦ *vt (show off)* hacer alarde de ♦ *vi* desfilar; *(MIL)* pasar revista

paradise ['pærədaɪs] *n* paraíso

paradox ['pærədɔks] *n* paradoja; **~ically** [-'dɔksɪklɪ] *adv* paradójicamente

paraffin ['pærəfɪn] *(BRIT) n (also: ~ oil)*

parafina

paragon ['pærəgən] n modelo

paragraph ['pærəgrɑːf] n párrafo

parallel ['pærəlɛl] adj en paralelo; (fig) semejante ♦ n (line) paralela; (fig, GEO) paralelo

paralyse ['pærəlaiz] vt paralizar

paralysis [pə'rælisis] n parálisis f inv

paralyze ['pærəlaiz] (US) vt = **paralyse**

paramount ['pærəmaunt] adj: **of ~ importance** de suma importancia

paranoid ['pærənɔid] adj (person, feeling) paranoico

paraphernalia [pærəfə'neɪliə] n (gear) avíos mpl

parasite ['pærəsait] n parásito/a

parasol ['pærəsɔl] n sombrilla, quitasol m

paratrooper ['pærətruːpə*] n paracaidista m/f

parcel ['pɑːsl] n paquete m ♦ vt (also: ~ up) empaquetar, embalar

parched [pɑːtʃt] adj (person) muerto de sed

parchment ['pɑːtʃmənt] n pergamino

pardon ['pɑːdn] n (LAW) indulto ♦ vt perdonar; ~ **me!, I beg your ~!** (I'm sorry!) ¡perdone usted!; **(I beg your) ~?, ~ me?** (US) (what did you say) ¿cómo?

parent ['pɛərənt] n (mother) madre f; (father) padre m; ~s npl padres mpl; ~al [pə'rɛntl] adj paternal/maternal

parenthesis [pə'rɛnθisis] n (pl **parentheses**) n paréntesis m inv

Paris ['pæris] n París

parish ['pæriʃ] n parroquia

Parisian [pə'riziən] adj, n parisiense m/f

park [pɑːk] n parque m ♦ vt aparcar, estacionar ♦ vi aparcar, estacionarse

parking ['pɑːkiŋ] n aparcamiento, estacionamiento; **"no ~"** "prohibido estacionarse"; ~ **lot** (US) n parking m; ~ **meter** n parquímetro; ~ **ticket** n multa de aparcamiento

parliament ['pɑːləmənt] n parlamento; (Spanish) Cortes fpl; ~**ary** [-'mɛntəri] adj parlamentario

parlour ['pɑːlə*] (US **parlor**) n sala de recibo, salón m, living m (AM)

parochial [pə'rəukiəl] (pej) adj de miras estrechas

parole [pə'rəul] n: **on ~** libre bajo palabra

parquet ['pɑːkei] n: ~ **floor(ing)** parquet m

parrot ['pærət] n loro, papagayo

parry ['pæri] vt parar

parsley ['pɑːsli] n perejil m

parsnip ['pɑːsnip] n chirivía

parson ['pɑːsn] n cura m

part [pɑːt] n (gen, MUS) parte f; (bit) trozo; (of machine) pieza; (THEATRE etc) papel m; (of serial) entrega; (US: in hair) raya ♦ adv = **partly** ♦ vt separar ♦ vi (people) separarse; (crowd) apartarse; **to take ~ in** tomar parte or participar en; **to take sth in good ~** tomar algo en buena parte; **to take sb's ~** defender a uno; **for my ~** por mi parte; **for the most ~** en su mayor parte; **to ~ one's hair** hacerse la raya; **~ with** vt fus ceder, entregar; (money) pagar; **~ exchange** (BRIT) n: **in ~ exchange** como parte del pago

partial ['pɑ:ʃl] adj parcial; **to be ~ to** ser aficionado a

participant [pɑ:'tɪsɪpənt] n (in competition) concursante m/f; (in campaign etc) participante m/f

participate [pɑ:'tɪsɪpeɪt] vi: **to ~ in** participar en; **participation** [-'peɪʃən] n participación f

participle ['pɑ:tɪsɪpl] n participio

particle ['pɑ:tɪkl] n partícula; (of dust) grano

particular [pə'tɪkjulə*] adj (special) particular; (concrete) concreto; (given) determinado; (fussy) quisquilloso; (demanding) exigente; **~s** npl (information) datos mpl; (details) pormenores mpl; **in ~** en particular; **~ly** adv (in particular) sobre todo; (difficult, good etc) especialmente

parting ['pɑ:tɪŋ] n (act of separation) separación f; (farewell) despedida; (BRIT: in hair) raya ♦ adj de despedida

partisan [pɑ:tɪ'zæn] adj partidista ♦ n partidario/a

partition [pɑ:'tɪʃən] n (POL) división f; (wall) tabique m

partly ['pɑ:tlɪ] adv en parte

partner ['pɑ:tnə*] n (COMM) socio/a; (SPORT, at dance) pareja f; (spouse) cónyuge m/f; (lover) compañero/a; **~ship** n asociación f; (COMM) sociedad f

partridge ['pɑ:trɪdʒ] n perdiz f

part-time adj, adv a tiempo parcial

party ['pɑ:tɪ] n (POL) partido; (celebration) fiesta; (group) grupo; (LAW) parte f interesada ♦ cpd (POL) de partido; **~ dress** n vestido de fiesta

pass [pɑ:s] vt (time, object) pasar; (place) pasar por; (overtake) rebasar;

(exam) aprobar; (approve) aprobar ♦ vi pasar; (SCOL) aprobar, ser aprobado ♦ n (permit) permiso; (membership card) carnet m; (in mountains) puerto, desfiladero; (SPORT) pase m; (SCOL: also: **~ mark**): **to get a ~** in aprobar en; **to ~ sth through sth** pasar algo por algo; **to make a ~ at sb** (inf) hacer proposiciones a uno; **~ away** vi fallecer; **~ by** vi pasar ♦ vt (ignore) pasar por alto; **~ for** vt fus pasar por; **~ on** vt transmitir; **~ out** vi desmayarse; **~ up** vt (opportunity) renunciar a; **~able** adj (road) transitable; (tolerable) pasable

passage ['pæsɪdʒ] n (also: **~way**) pasillo; (act of passing) tránsito; (fare, in book) pasaje m; (by boat) travesía f; (ANAT) tubo

passbook ['pɑ:sbuk] n libreta de banco

passenger ['pæsɪndʒə*] n pasajero/a, viajero/a

passer-by [pɑ:sə'baɪ] n transeúnte m/f

passing ['pɑ:sɪŋ] adj pasajero; **in ~** de paso; **~ place** n (AUT) apartadero

passion ['pæʃən] n pasión f; **~ate** adj apasionado

passive ['pæsɪv] adj (gen, also LING) pasivo; **~ smoking** n efectos del tabaco en fumadores pasivos

Passover ['pɑ:səuvə*] n Pascua (de los judíos)

passport ['pɑ:spɔ:t] n pasaporte m; **~ control** n control m de pasaporte; **~ office** n oficina de pasaportes

password ['pɑ:swɜ:d] n contraseña

past [pɑ:st] prep (in front of) por delante de; (further than) más allá de; (later than) después de ♦ adj pasado; (president etc) antiguo ♦ n (time) pasado; (of person) antecedentes mpl; **he's ~ forty** tiene más de cuarenta años; **ten/quarter ~ eight** las ocho y diez/cuarto; **for the ~ few/3 days** durante los últimos días/últimos 3 días; **to run ~ sb** pasar a uno corriendo

pasta ['pæstə] n pasta

paste [peɪst] n pasta; (glue) engrudo ♦ vt pegar

pasteurized ['pæstəraɪzd] adj pasteurizado

pastille ['pæstl] n pastilla

pastime ['pɑːstaɪm] n pasatiempo

pastry ['peɪstrɪ] n (dough) pasta; (cake) pastel m

pasture ['pɑːstʃə*] n pasto

pasty¹ ['pæstɪ] n empanada

pasty² ['peɪstɪ] adj (complexion) pálido

pat [pæt] vt dar una palmadita a; (dog etc) acariciar

patch [pætʃ] n (of material, eye ~) parche m; (mended tear) remiendo; (of land) terreno ♦ vt remendar; (to go through) a bad ~ (pasar por) una mala racha; ~ up vt reparar; (quarrel) hacer las paces en; ~work n labor m de retazos; ~y adj desigual

pâté ['pæteɪ] n paté m

patent ['peɪtnt] n patente f ♦ vt patentar ♦ adj patente, evidente; ~ leather n charol m

paternal [pə'tɜːnl] adj paternal; (relation) paterno

path [pɑːθ] n camino, sendero; (trail, track) pista; (of missile) trayectoria

pathetic [pə'θetɪk] adj patético, lastimoso; (very bad) malísimo

pathological [pæθə'lɔdʒɪkəl] adj patológico

pathway ['pɑːθweɪ] n sendero, vereda

patience ['peɪʃns] n paciencia; (BRIT: CARDS) solitario

patient ['peɪʃnt] n paciente m/f ♦ adj paciente, sufrido

patio ['pætɪəu] n patio

patriot ['peɪtrɪət] n patriota m/f; ~ic [pætrɪ'ɔtɪk] adj patriótico

patrol [pə'trəul] n patrulla ♦ vt patrullar por; ~ car n coche m patrulla; ~man (US irreg) n policía m

patron ['peɪtrən] n (in shop) cliente m/f; (of charity) patrocinador(a) m/f; ~ of the arts mecenas m; ~ize

['pætrənaɪz] vt (shop) ser cliente de; (artist etc) proteger; (look down on) condescender con; ~ saint n santo/a patrón/ona m/f

patter ['pætə*] n golpeteo; (sales talk) labia ♦ vi (rain) tamborilear

pattern ['pætən] n (SEWING) patrón m; (design) dibujo

pauper ['pɔːpə*] n pobre m/f

pause [pɔːz] n pausa ♦ vi hacer una pausa

pave [peɪv] vt pavimentar; to ~ the way for preparar el terreno para

pavement ['peɪvmənt] n (BRIT) acera (SP), vereda (AM)

pavilion [pə'vɪlɪən] n (SPORT) caseta

paving ['peɪvɪŋ] n pavimento, enlosado; ~ stone n losa

paw [pɔː] n pata

pawn [pɔːn] n (CHESS) peón m; (fig) instrumento ♦ vt empeñar; ~ broker n prestamista m/f; ~shop n monte m de piedad

pay [peɪ] (pt, pp paid) n (wage etc) sueldo, salario ♦ vt pagar ♦ vi (be profitable) rendir; to ~ attention (to) prestar atención (a); to ~ sb a visit hacer una visita a uno; to ~ one's respects to sb presentar sus respetos a uno; ~ back vt (money) reembolsar; (person) pagar; ~ for vt fus pagar; ~ in vt ingresar; ~ off vt saldar ♦ vi (scheme, decision) dar resultado; ~ up vt pagar (de mala gana); ~able adj: ~able to pagadero a; ~ day n día m de paga; ~ee n portador(a) m/f; ~ envelope (US) n = ~ packet; ~ment n pago; monthly ~ment mensualidad f; ~ packet (BRIT) n sobre m de (paga); ~ phone n teléfono público; ~roll n nómina; ~ slip n recibo de sueldo; ~ television n televisión f de pago

PC n abbr = personal computer; (BRIT) = police constable ♦ adv abbr = politically correct

p.c. abbr = per cent

pea [piː] n guisante m (SP), chícharo

(AM), arveja (AM)

peace |pi:s| n paz f; (calm) paz f, tranquilidad f; **~ful** adj (gentle) pacífico; (calm) tranquilo, sosegado

peach |pi:tʃ| n melocotón m (SP), durazno (AM)

peacock |'pi:kɔk| n pavo real

peak |pi:k| n (of mountain) cumbre f, cima; (of cap) visera f, (fig) cumbre f; **~ hours** npl, **~ period** n horas fpl punta

peal |pi:l| n (of bells) repique m; **~ of laughter** carcajada

peanut |'pi:nʌt| n cacahuete m (SP), maní m (AM); **~ butter** manteca de cacahuete or maní

pear |peə*| n pera f

pearl |pə:l| n perla

peasant |'peznt| n campesino/a

peat |pi:t| n turba

pebble |'pebl| n guijarro

peck |pek| vt (also: **~ at**) picotear ♦ n picotazo; (kiss) besito; **~ing order** n orden m de jerarquía; **~ish** (BRIT: inf) adj: **I feel ~ish** tengo ganas de picar algo

peculiar |pɪ'kju:lɪə*| adj (odd) extraño, raro; (typical) propio, característico; **~ to** propio de

pedal |'pedl| n pedal m ♦ vi pedalear

pedantic |pɪ'dæntɪk| adj pedante

peddler |'pedlə*| n: **drug ~** traficante m/f; camello

pedestrian |pɪ'destrɪən| n peatón/ona m/f ♦ adj pedestre; **~ crossing** (BRIT) n paso de peatones; **~ precinct** (BRIT), **~ zone** (US) n zona peatonal

pediatrics |pi:dɪ'ætrɪks| (US) n = **paediatrics**

pedigree |'pedɪgri:| n genealogía; (of animal) raza, pedigrí m ♦ cpd (animal) de raza, de casta

pee |pi:| (inf) vi mear

peek |pi:k| vi mirar a hurtadillas

peel |pi:l| n piel f; (of orange, lemon) cáscara; (: removed) peladuras fpl ♦ vt pelar ♦ vi (paint etc) desconcharse;

(wallpaper) despegarse, desprenderse; (skin) pelar

peep |pi:p| n (BRIT: look) mirada furtiva; (sound) pío ♦ vi (BRIT: look) mirar furtivamente; **~ out** vi salir (un poco); **~hole** n mirilla

peer |pɪə*| vi: **to ~ at** esdruññar ♦ n (noble) par m; (equal) igual m; (contemporary) contemporáneo/a; **~age** n nobleza

peeved |pi:vd| adj enojado

peg |peg| n (for coat etc) gancho, colgadero; (BRIT: also: **clothes ~**) pinza

Pekingese |pi:kɪ'ni:z| n (dog) pequinés/esa m/f

pelican |'pelɪkən| n pelícano; **~ crossing** (BRIT) n (AUT) paso de peatones señalizado

pellet |'pelɪt| n bolita; (bullet) perdigón m

pelt |pelt| vt: **to ~ sb with sth** arrojarle algo a uno ♦ vi (rain) llover a cántaros; (: run) correr ♦ n pellejo

pen |pen| n (fountain ~) pluma; (ballpoint ~) bolígrafo; (for sheep) redil m

penal |'pi:nl| adj penal; **~ize** vt castigar

penalty |'penltɪ| n (gen) pena; (fine) multa; **~ (kick)** n (FOOTBALL) penalty m; (RUGBY) golpe m de castigo

penance |'penəns| n penitencia

pence |pens| npl of **penny**

pencil |'pensl| n lápiz m, lapicero (AM); **~ case** n estuche (1); **~ sharpener** n sacapuntas m inv

pendant |'pendnt| n pendiente m

pending |'pendɪŋ| prep antes de ♦ adj pendiente

pendulum |'pendjuləm| n péndulo

penetrate |'penɪtreɪt| vt penetrar

penfriend |'penfrend| (BRIT) n amigo/ a por carta

penguin |'pengwɪn| n pingüino

penicillin |penɪ'sɪlɪn| n penicilina

peninsula |pə'nɪnsjulə| n península

penis |'pi:nɪs| n pene m

penitentiary [peni'tenʃərɪ] (US) n cárcel f, presidio

penknife ['pennaɪf] n navaja

pen name n seudónimo

penniless ['penɪlɪs] adj sin dinero

penny ['penɪ] (pl **pennies** or (BRIT) **pence**) n penique m; (US) centavo

penpal ['penpæl] n amigo/a por carta

pension ['penʃən] n (state benefit) jubilación f; **~er** (BRIT) n jubilado/a; **~ fund** n caja or fondo de pensiones

pentagon ['pentəgən] n: **the P~** (US: POL) el Pentágono

Pentagon

Se conoce como **Pentagon** al edificio de planta pentagonal que acoge las dependencias del Ministerio de Defensa estadounidense ("Department of Defense") en Arlington, Virginia. En lenguaje periodístico se aplica también a la dirección militar del país.

Pentecost ['pentɪkɔst] n Pentecostés m

penthouse ['penthaus] n ático de lujo

pent-up ['pentʌp] adj reprimido

people ['pi:pl] npl gente f; (citizens) pueblo, ciudadanos mpl; (POL): **the ~** el pueblo ♦ n (nation, race) pueblo, nación f; **several ~ came** vinieron varias personas; **~ say that ...** dice la gente que ...

pep [pep] (inf): **~ up** vt animar

pepper ['pepə*] n (spice) pimienta; (vegetable) pimiento ♦ vt: **to ~ with** (fig) salpicar de; **~mint** n (sweet) pastilla de menta

peptalk ['peptɔːk] n: **to give sb a ~** darle a uno una inyección de ánimo

per [pə:*] prep por; **~ day/person** por día/persona; **~ annum** al año; **~ capita** adj, adv per cápita

perceive [pə'si:v] vt percibir; (realize) darse cuenta de

per cent n por ciento

percentage [pə'sentɪdʒ] n porcentaje m

perception [pə'sepʃən] n percepción f; (insight) perspicacia; (opinion etc) opinión f; **perceptive** [-'septɪv] adj perspicaz

perch [pə:tʃ] n (fish) perca; (for bird) percha ♦ vi: **to ~ (on)** (bird) posarse (en); (person) encaramarse (en)

percolator ['pə:kəleɪtə*] n (also: coffee ~) cafetera de filtro

perennial [pə'reniəl] adj perenne

perfect [adj, n 'pə:fɪkt, vb pə'fekt] adj perfecto ♦ n (also: ~ tense) perfecto ♦ vt perfeccionar; **~ly** ['pə:fɪktlɪ] adv perfectamente

perforate ['pə:fəreɪt] vt perforar

perform [pə'fɔ:m] vt (carry out) realizar, llevar a cabo; (THEATRE) representar; (piece of music) interpretar ♦ vi (well, badly) funcionar; **~ance** n (of a play) representación f; (of actor, athlete etc) actuación f; (of car, engine, company) rendimiento; (of economy) resultados mpl; **~er** n (actor) actor m, actriz f

perfume ['pə:fju:m] n perfume m

perhaps [pə'hæps] adv quizá(s), tal vez

peril ['perɪl] n peligro, riesgo

perimeter [pə'rɪmɪtə*] n perímetro

period ['pɪərɪəd] n período; (SCOL) clase f; (full stop) punto; (MED) regla ♦ adj (costume, furniture) de época; **~ic(al)** [-'ɔdɪk(l)] adj periódico; **~ical** [-'ɔdɪkl] n periódico; **~ically** [-'ɔdɪklɪ] adv de vez en cuando, cada cierto tiempo

peripheral [pə'rɪfərəl] adj periférico ♦ n (COMPUT) periférico, unidad f periférica

perish ['perɪʃ] vi perecer; (decay) echarse a perder; **~able** adj perecedero

perjury ['pə:dʒərɪ] n (LAW) perjurio

perk [pə:k] n extra m; **~ up** vi (cheer up) animarse

perm [pə:m] n permanente f

permanent ['pə:mənənt] adj permanente

permeate ['pə:mieit] vi penetrar, trascender ♦ vt penetrar, trascender a

permissible [pə'misibl] adj permisible, lícito

permission [pə'miʃən] n permiso

permissive [pə'misiv] adj permisivo

permit [n 'pə:mit, vt pə'mit] n permiso, licencia ♦ vt permitir

perplex [pə'pleks] vt dejar perplejo

persecute ['pə:sikju:t] vt perseguir

persevere [pə:si'viə*] vi persistir

Persian ['pə:ʃən] adj, n persa m/f; **the ~ Gulf** el Golfo Pérsico

persist [pə'sist] vi: **to ~ (in doing sth)** persistir (en hacer algo); **~ence** n empeño; **~ent** adj persistente; (determined) porfiado

person ['pə:sn] n persona; **in ~** en persona; **~al** adj personal; individual; (visit) en persona; **~al assistant** n ayudante m/f personal; **~al column** n anuncios mpl personales; **~al computer** n ordenador m personal; **~ality** [-'næliti] n personalidad f; **~ally** adv personalmente; (in person) en persona; **to take sth ~ally** tomarse algo a mal; **~al organizer** n agenda; **~al stereo** n Walkman ® m; **~ify** [-'sonifai] vt encarnar

personnel [pə:sə'nel] n personal m

perspective [pə'spektiv] n perspectiva

Perspex ® ['pə:speks] n plexiglás ® m

perspiration [pə:spi'reiʃən] n transpiración f

persuade [pə'sweid] vt: **to ~ sb to do sth** persuadir a uno para que haga algo

Peru [pə'ru:] n el Perú; **Peruvian** adj, n peruano/a m/f

perverse [pə'və:s] adj perverso; (wayward) travieso

pervert [n 'pə:və:t, vb pə'və:t] n pervertido/a ♦ vt pervertir; (truth, sb's words) tergiversar

pessimist ['pesimist] n pesimista m/f;

~ic [-'mistik] adj pesimista

pest [pest] n (insect) insecto nocivo; (fig) lata, molestia

pester ['pestə*] vt molestar, acosar

pesticide ['pestisaid] n pesticida m

pet [pet] n animal m doméstico ♦ cpd favorito ♦ vt acariciar; **teacher's ~** favorito/a (del profesor); **~ hate** manía

petal ['petl] n pétalo

peter ['pi:tə*]: **to ~ out** vi agotarse, acabarse

petite [pə'ti:t] adj chiquita

petition [pə'tiʃən] n petición f

petrified ['petrifaid] adj horrorizado

petrol ['petrəl] (BRIT) n gasolina; **two/four-star ~** gasolina normal/súper; **~ can** n bidón m de gasolina

petroleum [pə'trəuliəm] n petróleo

petrol: ~ pump (BRIT) n (in garage) surtidor m de gasolina; **~ station** (BRIT) n gasolinera; **~ tank** (BRIT) n depósito (de gasolina)

petticoat ['petikaut] n enaguas fpl

petty ['peti] adj (mean) mezquino; (unimportant) insignificante; **~ cash** n dinero para gastos menores; **~ officer** n contramaestre m

petulant ['petjulant] adj malhumorado

pew [pju:] n banco

pewter ['pju:tə*] n peltre m

phantom ['fæntəm] n fantasma m

pharmacist ['fɑ:məsist] n farmacéutico/a

pharmacy ['fɑ:məsi] n farmacia

phase [feiz] n fase f ♦ vt: **to ~ sth in/out** introducir/retirar algo por etapas

Ph.D. abbr = **Doctor of Philosophy**

pheasant ['feznt] n faisán m

phenomenon [fə'nɔminən] (pl **phenomena**) n fenómeno

philanthropist [fi'lænθrəpist] n filántropo/a

Philippines ['filipi:nz] npl: **the ~** las Filipinas

philosopher [fi'lɔsəfə*] n filósofo/a

philosophy [fi'lɔsəfi] n filosofía

phobia ['fəubjə] n fobia

phone [fəun] n teléfono ♦ vt telefonear, llamar por teléfono; **to be on the ~** tener teléfono; (be calling) estar hablando por teléfono; **~ back** vt, vi volver a llamar; **~ up** vt, vi llamar por teléfono; **~ book** n guía telefónica; **~ booth** n cabina telefónica; **~ box** (BRIT) n = **~ booth**; **~ call** n llamada (telefónica); **~card** n teletarjeta; **~-in** (BRIT) n (RADIO, TV) programa m de participación (telefónica)

phonetics [fə'nɛtɪks] n fonética

phoney ['fəunɪ] adj falso

photo ['fəutəu] n foto f; **~copier** n fotocopiadora; **~copy** n fotocopia ♦ vt fotocopiar

photograph ['fəutəgrɑːf] n fotografía ♦ vt fotografiar; **~er** [fə'tɔgrəfə*] n fotógrafo; **~y** [fə'tɔgrəfɪ] n fotografía

phrase [freɪz] n frase f ♦ vt expresar; **~ book** n libro de frases

physical ['fɪzɪkl] adj físico; **~ education** n educación f física; **~ly** adv físicamente

physician [fɪ'zɪʃən] n médico/a

physicist ['fɪzɪsɪst] n físico/a

physics ['fɪzɪks] n física

physiotherapy [fɪzɪəu'θerəpɪ] n fisioterapia

physique [fɪ'ziːk] n físico

pianist ['piːənɪst] n pianista m/f

piano [pɪ'ænəu] n piano

pick [pɪk] n (tool: also: ~axe) pico, piqueta ♦ vt (select) escoger, elegir; (gather) coger (SP), recoger; (remove, take out) sacar, quitar; (lock) abrir con ganzúa; **take your ~** escoja lo que quiera; **the ~ of** lo mejor de; **to ~ one's nose/teeth** hurgarse las narices/limpiarse los dientes; **to ~ a quarrel with sb** meterse con alguien; **~ at** vt fus: **to ~ at one's food** comer con poco apetito; **~ on** vt fus (person) meterse con; **~ out** vt escoger; (distinguish) identificar; **~ up** vi (improve: sales) ir a mejor; (: patient) reponerse; (: FINANCE) recobrarse ♦ vt

recoger; (learn) aprender; (POLICE: arrest) detener; (person: for sex) ligar; (RADIO) captar; **to ~ up speed** acelerarse; **to ~ o.s. up** levantarse

picket ['pɪkɪt] n piquete m ♦ vt piquetear

pickle ['pɪkl] n (also: ~s: as condiment) escabeche m; (fig: mess) apuro ♦ vt encurtir

pickpocket ['pɪkpɔkɪt] n carterista m/f

pickup ['pɪkʌp] n (small truck) furgoneta

picnic ['pɪknɪk] n merienda ♦ vi ir de merienda; **~ area** n zona de picnic; (AUT) área de descanso

picture ['pɪktʃə*] n cuadro; (painting) pintura; (photograph) fotografía; (TV) imagen f; (film) película; (fig: description) descripción f; (: situation) situación f ♦ vt (imagine) imaginar; **~s** npl: **the ~s** (BRIT) el cine; **~ book** n libro de dibujos

picturesque [pɪktʃə'resk] adj pintoresco

pie [paɪ] n pastel m; (open) tarta; (small: of meat) empanada

piece [piːs] n pedazo, trozo; (of cake) trozo; (item): **a ~ of clothing/ furniture/advice** una prenda (de vestir)/un mueble/un consejo ♦ vt: **to ~ together** juntar; (TECH) unir; **to take to ~s** desmontar; **~meal** adv poco a poco; **~work** n trabajo a destajo

pie chart n gráfico de sectores or tarta

pier [pɪə*] n muelle m, embarcadero

pierce [pɪəs] vt perforar

piercing ['pɪəsɪŋ] adj penetrante

pig [pɪg] n cerdo (SP), puerco (SP), chancho (AM); (pej: unkind person) asqueroso; (: greedy person) glotón/ona m/f

pigeon ['pɪdʒən] n paloma; (as food) pichón m; **~hole** n casilla

piggy bank ['pɪgɪ-] n hucha (en forma de cerdito)

pig: ~headed ['pɪg'hedɪd] adj terco,

testarudo; **~skin** ['paɪglt] n cochinillo;
~skin n piel f de cerdo; **~sty** ['pɪgstaɪ]
n pocilga; **~tail** n (girl's) trenza;
(Chinese, TAUR) coleta

pike [paɪk] n (fish) lucio

pilchard ['pɪltʃəd] n sardina

pile [paɪl] n montón m; (of carpet,
cloth) pelo ♦ vt (also: ~ up) amontonar;
(fig) acumular ♦ vi (also: ~ up)
amontonarse; acumularse; **~ into** vt
fus (car) meterse en; **~s** [paɪlz] npl
(MED) almorranas fpl, hemorroides mpl;
~-up n (AUT) accidente m múltiple

pilfering ['pɪlfərɪŋ] n ratería

pilgrim ['pɪlgrɪm] n peregrino/a; **~age**
n peregrinación f, romería

pill [pɪl] n píldora; **the ~** la píldora

pillage ['pɪlɪdʒ] vt pillar, saquear

pillar ['pɪlə*] n pilar m; **~ box** (BRIT) n
buzón m

pillion ['pɪljən] n (of motorcycle)
asiento trasero

pillow ['pɪləu] n almohada; **~case** n
funda

pilot ['paɪlət] n piloto ♦ cpd (scheme
etc) piloto ♦ vt pilotar; **~ light** n piloto

pimp [pɪmp] n chulo (SP), cafiche m
(AM)

pimple ['pɪmpl] n grano

PIN n abbr (= personal identification
number) número personal

pin [pɪn] n alfiler m ♦ vt prender (con
alfiler); **~s and needles** hormigueo;
to ~ sb down (fig) hacer que uno
concrete; **to ~ sth on sb** (fig) colgarle
a uno el sambenito de algo

pinafore ['pɪnəfɔ:*] n delantal m;
~ dress (BRIT) n mandil m

pinball ['pɪnbɔ:l] n mesa americana

pincers ['pɪnsəz] npl pinzas fpl, tenazas
fpl

pinch [pɪntʃ] n (of salt etc) pizca ♦ vt
pellizcar; (inf: steal) birlar; **at a ~** en
caso de apuro

pincushion ['pɪnkuʃən] n acerico

pine [paɪn] n (also: ~ tree, wood) pino
♦ vi: **to ~ for** suspirar por; **~ away** vi
morirse de pena

pineapple ['paɪnæpl] n piña, ananás m

ping [pɪŋ] n (noise) sonido agudo; **~-
pong** ® n pingpong ®

pink [pɪŋk] adj rosado, (color de) rosa
♦ n (colour) rosa; (BOT) clavel m,
clavellina

pinpoint ['pɪnpɔɪnt] vt precisar

pint [paɪnt] n pinta (BRIT = 568cc; US
= 473cc); (BRIT: inf: of beer) pinta de
cerveza, ≈ jarra (SP)

pin-up n fotografía erótica

pioneer [paɪə'nɪə*] n pionero/a

pious ['paɪəs] adj piadoso, devoto

pip [pɪp] n (seed) pepita; **the ~s** (BRIT)
la señal

pipe [paɪp] n tubo, caño; (for smoking)
pipa ♦ vt conducir en cañerías; **~s** npl
(gen) cañería; (also: bag-s) gaita;
~ cleaner n limpiapipas m inv;
~ dream n sueño imposible; **~line** n
(for oil) oleoducto; (for gas) gasoducto;
~r n gaitero/a

piping ['paɪpɪŋ] adv: **to be ~ hot** estar
que quema

piquant ['pi:kənt] adj picante; (fig)
agudo

pique [pi:k] n pique m, resentimiento

pirate ['paɪərət] n pirata m/f ♦ vt
(cassette, book) piratear; **~ radio** (BRIT)
n emisora pirata

Pisces ['paɪsi:z] n Piscis m

piss [pɪs] (inf!) vi mear; **~ed** (inf!) adj
(drunk) borracho

pistol ['pɪstl] n pistola

piston ['pɪstən] n pistón m, émbolo

pit [pɪt] n hoyo; (also: coal ~) mina; (in
garage) foso de inspección; (also:
orchestra ~) platea ♦ vt: **to ~ one's
wits against sb** medir fuerzas con
uno; **~s** npl (AUT) box m

pitch [pɪtʃ] n (MUS) tono; (BRIT: SPORT)
campo, terreno; (fig) punto; (tar) brea
♦ vt (throw) arrojar, lanzar ♦ vi (fall)
caer(se); **to ~ a tent** montar una
tienda (de campaña); **~-black** adj
negro como boca de lobo; **~ed battle**

n batalla campal

pitfall ['pɪtfɔ:l] *n* riesgo

pith [pɪθ] *n (of orange)* médula

pithy ['pɪθɪ] *adj (fig)* jugoso

pitiful ['pɪtɪful] *adj (touching)* lastimoso, conmovedor(a)

pitiless ['pɪtɪlɪs] *adj* despiadado

pittance ['pɪtns] *n* miseria

pity ['pɪtɪ] *n* compasión *f*, piedad *f* ♦ *vt* compadecer(se de); **what a ~!** ¡qué pena!

pizza ['pi:tsə] *n* pizza

placard ['plækɑ:d] *n* letrero; *(in march etc)* pancarta

placate [plə'keɪt] *vt* apaciguar

place [pleɪs] *n* lugar *m*, sitio; *(post)* puesto; *(home)*: **at/to his ~** en/a su casa; *(role: in society etc)* papel *m* ♦ *vt (object)* poner, colocar; *(identify)* reconocer; **to take ~** tener lugar; **to be ~d** *(in race, exam)* colocarse; **out of ~** *(not suitable)* fuera de lugar; **in the first ~** en primer lugar; **to change ~s with sb** cambiarse de sitio con uno; **~ of birth** lugar *m* de nacimiento

placid ['plæsɪd] *adj* apacible

plague [pleɪg] *n* plaga; *(MED)* peste *f* ♦ *vt (fig)* acosar, atormentar

plaice [pleɪs] *n inv* platija

plaid [plæd] *n (material)* tartán *m*

plain [pleɪn] *adj (unpatterned)* liso; *(clear)* claro, evidente; *(simple)* sencillo; *(not handsome)* poco atractivo ♦ *adv* claramente ♦ *n* llano, llanura; **~ chocolate** *n* chocolate *m* amargo; **~-clothes** *adj (police)* vestido de paisano; **~ly** *adv* claramente

plaintiff ['pleɪntɪf] *n* demandante *m/f*

plait [plæt] *n* trenza

plan [plæn] *n (drawing)* plano; *(scheme)* plan *m*, proyecto ♦ *vt* proyectar, planificar ♦ *vi* hacer proyectos; **to ~ to do** pensar hacer

plane [pleɪn] *n (AVIAT)* avión *m*; *(MATH, fig)* plano; *(also: ~ tree)* plátano; *(tool)* cepillo

planet ['plænɪt] *n* planeta *m*

plank [plæŋk] *n* tabla

planner ['plænə*] *n* planificador(a) *m/f*

planning ['plænɪŋ] *n* planificación *f*; **family ~** planificación familiar; **~ permission** *n* permiso para realizar obras

plant [plɑ:nt] *n* planta; *(machinery)* maquinaria; *(factory)* fábrica ♦ *vt* plantar; *(field)* sembrar; *(bomb)* colocar

plaster ['plɑ:stə*] *n (for walls)* yeso; *(also: ~ of Paris)* yeso mate; *(BRIT: also: sticking ~)* tirita *(SP)*, esparadrapo, curita *(AM)* ♦ *vt* enyesar; *(cover)*: **to ~ with** llenar or cubrir de; **~ed** *(inf) adj* borracho; **~er** *n* yesero

plastic ['plæstɪk] *n* plástico ♦ *adj* de plástico; **~ bag** *n* bolsa de plástico

Plasticine ® ['plæstɪsi:n] *(BRIT) n* plastilina ®

plastic surgery *n* cirujía plástica

plate [pleɪt] *n (dish)* plato; *(metal, in book)* lámina; *(dental ~)* placa de dentadura postiza

plateau ['plætəʊ] *(pl ~s or ~x) n* meseta, altiplanicie *f*

plateaux ['plætəʊz] *npl of* plateau

plate glass *n* vidrio cilindrado

platform ['plætfɔ:m] *n (RAIL)* andén *m*; *(stage, BRIT: on bus)* plataforma; *(at meeting)* tribuna; *(POL)* programa *m* (electoral)

platinum ['plætɪnəm] *adj, n* platino

platoon [plə'tu:n] *n* pelotón *m*

platter ['plætə*] *n* fuente *f*

plausible ['plɔ:zɪbl] *adj* verosímil; *(person)* convincente

play [pleɪ] *n (THEATRE)* obra, comedia ♦ *vt (game)* jugar; *(compete against)* jugar contra; *(instrument)* tocar; *(part: in play etc)* hacer el papel de; *(tape, record)* poner ♦ *vi* jugar; *(band)* tocar; *(tape, record)* sonar; **to ~ safe** ir a lo seguro; **~ down** *vt* quitar importancia a; **~ up** *vi (cause trouble)* dar guerra; **~boy** *n* playboy *m*; **~er** *n* jugador(a) *m/f*; *(THEATRE)* actor/actriz *m/f*; *(MUS)* músico/a; **~ful** adj juguetón/ona; **~ground** n (in school) patio de recreo; (in park) parque m infantil; **~group** n jardín m de niños; **~ing card** n naipe m, carta; **~ing field** n campo de deportes; **~mate** n compañero/a de juego; **~off** n (SPORT) partido de desempate m; **~pen** n corral m; **~ing** n juguete m; **~time** n (SCOL) recreo; **~wright** n dramaturgo n

plc abbr (= public limited company) ≈ S.A.

plea [pliː] n súplica, petición f; (LAW) alegato, defensa; **~ bargaining** n (LAW) acuerdo entre fiscal y defensor para agilizar los trámites judiciales

plead [pliːd] vt (LAW): **to ~ sb's case** defender a uno; (give as excuse) poner como pretexto ♦ vi (LAW) declararse; (beg): **to ~ with sb** suplicar o rogar a uno

pleasant ['plɛznt] adj agradable; **~ries** npl cortesías fpl

please [pliːz] excl ¡por favor! ♦ vt (give pleasure to) dar gusto a, agradar ♦ vi (think fit): **do as you ~** haz lo que quieras; **~ yourself!** (inf) ¡haz lo que quieras!, ¡como quieras!; **~d** adj (happy) alegre, contento; **~d (with)** satisfecho (de); **~d to meet you** ¡encantado!, ¡tanto gusto!; **pleasing** adj agradable, grato

pleasure ['plɛʒə*] n placer m, gusto; **"it's a ~"** "el gusto es mío"

pleat [pliːt] n pliegue m

pledge [plɛdʒ] n (promise) promesa, voto ♦ vt prometer

plentiful ['plɛntɪful] adj copioso, abundante

plenty ['plɛntɪ] n: **~ of** mucho(s)/a(s)

pliable ['plaɪəbl] adj flexible

pliers ['plaɪəz] npl alicates mpl, tenazas fpl

plight [plaɪt] n situación f difícil

plimsolls ['plɪmsəlz] (BRIT) npl zapatos mpl de tenis

plinth [plɪnθ] n plinto

plod [plɒd] vi caminar con paso pesado; (fig) trabajar laboriosamente

plonk [plɒŋk] (inf) n (BRIT: wine) vino peleón ♦ vt: **to ~ sth down** dejar caer algo

plot [plɒt] n (scheme) complot m, conjura; (of story, play) argumento; (of land) terreno, lote m (AM) ♦ vt (mark out) trazar; (conspire) tramar, urdir ♦ vi conspirar

plough [plau] (US plow) n arado ♦ vt (earth) arar; **to ~ money into** invertir dinero en; **~ through** vt fus (crowd) abrirse paso por la fuerza por; **~man's lunch** (BRIT) n almuerzo de pub a base de pan, queso y encurtidos

pluck [plʌk] vt (fruit) coger (SP), recoger (AM); (musical instrument) puntear; (bird) desplumar; (eyebrows) depilar; **to ~ up courage** hacer de tripas corazón

plug [plʌg] n tapón m; (ELEC) enchufe m, clavija; (AUT: also: spark(ing) ~) bujía ♦ vt (hole) tapar; (inf: advertise) dar publicidad a; **~ in** vt (ELEC) enchufar

plum [plʌm] n (fruit) ciruela

plumb [plʌm] vt: **to ~ the depths** alcanzar los mayores extremos de

plumber ['plʌmə*] n fontanero/a (SP), plomero/a (AM)

plumbing ['plʌmɪŋ] n (trade) fontanería, plomería; (piping) cañería

plummet ['plʌmɪt] vi: **to ~ (down)** caer a plomo

plump [plʌmp] adj rechoncho, rollizo ♦ vi: **to ~ for** (inf: choose) optar por; **~ up** vt mullir

plunder ['plʌndə*] vt pillar, saquear

plunge [plʌndʒ] n zambullida ♦ vt sumergir, hundir ♦ vi (fall) caer; (dive) saltar; (person) arrojarse; **to take the ~** lanzarse; **plunging** adj: **plunging neckline** escote m pronunciado

pluperfect [pluːˈpəːfɪkt] n pluscuamperfecto

plural ['pluərl] adj plural ♦ n plural m

plus [plʌs] n (also: ~ sign) signo más

♦ *prep* más, y, además de; **ten/ twenty ~** más de diez/veinte

plush [plʌʃ] *adj* lujoso

plutonium [plu:'təʊnɪəm] *n* plutonio

ply [plaɪ] *vt (a trade)* ejercer ♦ *vi (ship)* ir y venir ♦ *n (of wool, rope)* cabo; **to ~ sb with drink** insistir en ofrecer a uno muchas copas; **~wood** *n* madera contrachapada

P.M. *n abbr* = **Prime Minister**

p.m. *adv abbr* (= *post meridiem*) de la tarde o noche

pneumatic [nju:'mætɪk] *adj* neumático; **~ drill** *n* martillo neumático

pneumonia [nju:'məʊnɪə] *n* pulmonía

poach [pəʊtʃ] *vt (cook)* escalfar; *(steal)* cazar (*or* pescar) en vedado ♦ *vi* cazar (*or* pescar) en vedado; **~ed** *adj* escalfado; **~er** *n* cazador(a) *m/f* furtivo/a

P.O. Box *n abbr* = **Post Office Box**

pocket [ˈpɔkɪt] *n* bolsillo; *(fig: small area)* bolsa ♦ *vt* meter en el bolsillo; *(steal)* embolsar; **to be out of ~** *(BRIT)* salir perdiendo; **~book** *(US)* *n* cartera; **~ calculator** *n* calculadora de bolsillo; **~ knife** *n* navaja; **~ money** *n* asignación *f*

pod [pɔd] *n* vaina

podgy [ˈpɔdʒɪ] *adj* gordinflón/ona

podiatrist [pɔˈdiːətrɪst] *(US)* *n* pedicuro/a

poem [ˈpəʊɪm] *n* poema *m*

poet [ˈpəʊɪt] *n* poeta *m/f*; **~ic** [-ˈetɪk] *adj* poético; **~ry** *n* poesía

poignant [ˈpɔɪnjənt] *adj* conmovedor(a)

point [pɔɪnt] *n* punto; *(tip)* punta; *(purpose)* fin *m*, propósito; *(use)* utilidad *f*; *(significant part)* lo significativo; *(moment)* momento; *(ELEC)* toma (de corriente); *(also: decimal ~)*: **2 ~ 3 (2.3)** dos coma tres (2,3) ♦ *vt* señalar; *(gun etc)*: **to ~ sth at sb** apuntar algo a uno ♦ *vi*: **to ~ at** señalar; **~s** *npl* *(AUT)* contactos *mpl*;

(RAIL) agujas *fpl*; **to be on the ~ of doing sth** estar a punto de hacer algo; **to make a ~ of** poner empeño en; **to get/miss the ~** comprender/ no comprender; **to come to the ~** ir al meollo; **there's no ~ (in doing)** no tiene sentido (hacer); **~ out** *vt* señalar; **~ to** *vt fus (fig)* indicar, señalar; **~-blank** *adv* (*say*, *refuse*) sin más hablar; *(also: at ~-blank range)* a quemarropa; **~ed** *adj (shape)* puntiagudo, afilado; *(remark)* intencionado; **~edly** *adv* intencionadamente; **~er** *n (needle)* aguja, indicador *m*; **~less** *adj* sin sentido; **~ of view** *n* punto de vista

poise [pɔɪz] *n* aplomo, elegancia

poison [ˈpɔɪzn] *n* veneno ♦ *vt* envenenar; **~ing** *n* envenenamiento; **~ous** *adj* venenoso; *(fumes etc)* tóxico

poke [pəʊk] *vt (jab with finger, stick etc)* empujar; *(put)*: **to ~ sth in(to)** introducir algo en; **~ about** *vi* fisgonear

poker [ˈpəʊkə*] *n* atizador *m*; *(CARDS)* póker *m*

Poland [ˈpəʊlənd] *n* Polonia

polar [ˈpəʊlə*] *adj* polar; **~ bear** *n* oso polar

Pole [pəʊl] *n* polaco/a

pole [pəʊl] *n* palo; *(fixed)* poste *m*; *(GEO)* polo; **~ bean** *(US)* *n* = judía verde; **~ vault** *n* salto con pértiga

police [pəˈliːs] *n* policía ♦ *vt* vigilar; **~ car** *n* coche-patrulla *m*; **~man** *(irreg)* *n* policía *m*, guardia *m*; **~ state** *n* estado policial; **~ station** *n* comisaría; **~woman** *(irreg)* *n* mujer *f* policía

policy [ˈpɔlɪsɪ] *n* política; *(also: insurance ~)* póliza

polio [ˈpəʊlɪəʊ] *n* polio *f*

Polish [ˈpəʊlɪʃ] *adj* polaco ♦ *n* *(LING)* polaco

polish [ˈpɔlɪʃ] *n* *(for shoes)* betún *m*; *(for floor)* cera (de lustrar); *(shine)* brillo, lustre *m*; *(fig: refinement)* educación *f* ♦ *vt* *(shoes)* limpiar; *(make*

shiny) pulir, sacar brillo a; ~ **off** vt
(*food*) despachar; **~ed** adj (*fig: person*)
elegante

polite [pə'laɪt] adj cortés, atento;
~ness n cortesía

political [pə'lɪtɪkl] adj político; **~ly** adv
políticamente; **~ly correct**
políticamente correcto

politician [pɒlɪ'tɪʃən] n político/a

politics ['pɒlɪtɪks] n política

poll [pəʊl] n (*election*) votación f; (*also:
opinion* ~) sondeo, encuesta ♦ vt
(*votes*) obtener

pollen ['pɒlən] n polen m

polling day ['pəʊlɪŋ-] n día m de
elecciones

polling station n centro electoral

pollute [pə'luːt] vt contaminar

pollution [pə'luːʃən] n polución f,
contaminación f del medio ambiente

polo ['pəʊləʊ] n (*sport*) polo; **~-
necked** adj de cuello vuelto; **~ shirt** n
polo, niqui m

polyester [pɒlɪ'estə*] n poliéster m

polystyrene [pɒlɪ'staɪriːn] n
poliestireno

polythene ['pɒlɪθiːn] (*BRIT*) n politeno

pomegranate ['pɒmɪɡrænɪt] n
granada

pomp [pɒmp] n pompa

pompous ['pɒmpəs] adj pomposo

pond [pɒnd] n (*natural*) charca;
(*artificial*) estanque m

ponder ['pɒndə*] vt meditar

ponderous ['pɒndərəs] adj pesado

pong [pɒŋ] (*BRIT: inf*) n hedor m

pony ['pəʊnɪ] n poney m, jaca, potro
(*AM*); **~tail** n cola de caballo;
~ trekking (*BRIT*) n excursión f a
caballo

poodle ['puːdl] n caniche m

pool [puːl] n (*natural*) charca; (*also:
swimming* ~) piscina (*SP*), alberca (*AM*);
(*fig: of light etc*) charco; (*SPORT*)
chapolín m ♦ vt juntar; **~s** npl (*football
~s*) quinielas fpl; **typing ~** servicio de
mecanografía

poor [puə*] adj pobre; (*bad*) de mala
calidad ♦ npl: **the ~** los pobres; **~ly** adj
mal, enfermo ♦ adv mal

pop [pɒp] n (*sound*) ruido seco; (*MUS*)
(música) pop m; (*inf: father*) papá m;
(*drink*) gaseosa ♦ vt (*put quickly*) meter
(de prisa) ♦ vi reventar; (*cork*) saltar;
~ **in/out** vi entrar/salir un momento;
~ **up** vi aparecer inesperadamente;
~corn n palomitas fpl

pope [pəʊp] n papa m

poplar ['pɒplə*] n álamo

popper ['pɒpə*] (*BRIT*) n automático

poppy ['pɒpɪ] n amapola

Popsicle ® ['pɒpsɪkl] (*US*) n polo

pop star n estrella del pop

populace ['pɒpjʊləs] n pueblo, plebe f

popular ['pɒpjʊlə*] adj popular

population [pɒpjʊ'leɪʃən] n población
f

porcelain ['pɔːslɪn] n porcelana

porch [pɔːtʃ] n pórtico, entrada; (*US*)
veranda

porcupine ['pɔːkjʊpaɪn] n puerco m
espín

pore [pɔː*] n poro ♦ vi: **to ~ over**
engolfarse en

pork [pɔːk] n carne f de cerdo (*SP*) or
chancho (*AM*)

pornography [pɔː'nɒɡrəfɪ] n
pornografía

porpoise ['pɔːpəs] n marsopa

porridge ['pɒrɪdʒ] n gachas fpl de
avena

port [pɔːt] n puerto; (*NAUT: left side*)
babor m; (*wine*) vino de Oporto; **~ of
call** puerto de escala

portable ['pɔːtəbl] adj portátil

porter ['pɔːtə*] n (*for luggage*)
maletero; (*doorkeeper*) portero/a,
conserje m/f

portfolio [pɔːt'fəʊlɪəʊ] n cartera

porthole ['pɔːthəʊl] n portilla

portion ['pɔːʃən] n porción f; (*of food*)
ración f

portrait ['pɔːtreɪt] n retrato

portray [pɔː'treɪ] vt retratar; (*subj:*

actor) representar

Portugal ['pɔːtjʊɡl] n Portugal m

Portuguese [pɔːtjuˈgiːz] adj
portugués/esa ♦ n inv portugués/esa
m/f; (LING) portugués m

pose [pəuz] n postura, actitud f ♦ vi
(*pretend*): **to ~ as** hacerse pasar por
♦ vt (*question*) plantear; **to ~ for** posar
para

posh [pɔʃ] (*inf*) adj elegante, de lujo

position [pəˈzɪʃən] n posición f; (*job*)
puesto; (*situation*) situación f ♦ vt
colocar

positive ['pɔzɪtɪv] adj positivo; (*certain*)
seguro; (*definite*) definitivo

possess [pəˈzes] vt poseer; **~ion**
[pəˈzeʃən] n posesión f; **~ions** npl
(*belongings*) pertenencias fpl

possibility [pɔsɪˈbɪlɪtɪ] n posibilidad f

possible ['pɔsɪbl] adj posible; **as big
as ~** lo más grande posible; **possibly**
adv posiblemente; **I cannot possibly
come** me es imposible venir

post [pəust] n (BRIT: *system*) correos
mpl; (BRIT: *letters, delivery*) correo; (*job,
situation*) puesto; (*pole*) poste m ♦ vt
(BRIT: *send by post*) echar al correo;
(BRIT: *appoint*): **to ~ to** enviar a; **~age**
n porte m, franqueo; **~age stamp** n
sello de correos; **~al order** n giro postal;
~box (BRIT) n buzón m; **~card** n tarjeta
postal; **~code** (BRIT) n código postal

postdate [pəust'deɪt] vt (*cheque*)
poner fecha adelantada a

poster ['pəustə*] n cartel m

poste restante [pəust'restɒnt] (BRIT)
n lista de correos

postgraduate ['pəust'grædjuət] n
posgraduado/a

posthumous ['pɔstjuməs] adj
póstumo

postman ['pəustmən] (*irreg*) n cartero

postmark ['pəustmɑːk] n matasellos m
inv

post-mortem [-'mɔːtəm] n autopsia

post office n (*building*) (oficina de)

correos m; (*organization*): **the Post
Office** Administración f General de
Correos; **Post Office Box** n apartado
postal (SP), casilla de correos (AM)

postpone [pəs'pəun] vt aplazar

postscript ['pəustskrɪpt] n posdata

posture ['pɔstʃə*] n postura, actitud f

postwar [pəust'wɔː*] adj de la
posguerra

posy ['pəuzɪ] n ramillete m (de flores)

pot [pɔt] n (*for cooking*) olla; (*tea~*)
tetera; (*coffee~*) cafetera; (*for flowers*)
maceta; (*for jam*) tarro, pote m; (*inf:
marijuana*) chocolate m ♦ vt (*plant*)
poner en tiesto; **to go to ~** (*inf*) irse al
traste

potato [pəˈteɪtəu] (*pl* **~es**) n patata
(SP), papa (AM); **~ peeler** n pelapatatas
m inv

potent ['pəutnt] adj potente,
poderoso; (*drink*) fuerte

potential [pəˈtenʃl] adj potencial,
posible ♦ n potencial m; **~ly** adv en
potencia

pothole ['pɔthəul] n (*in road*) bache
m; (BRIT: *underground*) gruta; **~**
potholing (BRIT) n: **to go potholing**
dedicarse a la espeleología

potluck [pɔt'lʌk] n: **to take ~** tomar
lo que haya

potted ['pɔtɪd] adj (*food*) en conserva;
(*plant*) en tiesto o maceta; (*shortened*)
resumido

potter ['pɔtə*] n alfarero/a ♦ vi: **to
~ around, ~ about** (BRIT) hacer
trabajitos; **~y** n cerámica; (*factory*)
alfarería

potty ['pɔtɪ] n orinal m de niño

pouch [pautʃ] n (ZOOL) bolsa; (*for
tobacco*) petaca

poultry ['pəultrɪ] n aves fpl de corral;
(*meat*) pollo

pounce [pauns] vi: **to ~ on**
precipitarse sobre

pound [paund] n libra (*weight* = 453g
or 16oz; *money* = 100 pence) ♦ vt
(*beat*) golpear; (*crush*) machacar ♦ vi

(*heart*) latir; ~ **sterling** *n* libra esterlina

pour [pɔː*] *vt* echar; (*tea etc*) servir ♦ *vi* correr, fluir; to ~ **sb a drink** servirle a uno una copa; ~ **away** *or* **off** *vt* vaciar, verter; ~ **in** *vi* (*people*) entrar en tropel; ~ **out** *vi* salir en tropel ♦ *vt* (*drink*) echar, servir; (*fig*): to ~ **out one's feelings** desahogarse; ~**ing** *adj*: ~**ing rain** lluvia torrencial

pout [paut] *vi* hacer pucheros

poverty ['pɔvəti] *n* pobreza, miseria; ~**-stricken** *adj* necesitado

powder ['paudə*] *n* polvo; (*face* ~) polvos *mpl* ♦ *vt* polvorear; to ~ **one's face** empolvarse la cara; ~ **compact** *n* polvera; ~**ed milk** *n* leche *f* en polvo; ~ **room** *n* aseos *mpl*

power ['pauə*] *n* poder *m*; (*strength*) fuerza; (*nation, TECH*) potencia; (*drive*) empuje *m*; (*ELEC*) fuerza, energía ♦ *vt* impulsar; to **be in** ~ (*POL*) estar en el poder; ~ **cut** (*BRIT*) *n* apagón *m*; ~**ed** *adj*: ~**ed by** impulsado por; ~ **failure** *n* = ~ **cut**; ~**ful** *adj* poderoso; (*engine*) potente; (*speech etc*) convincente; ~**less** *adj*: ~**less (to do)** incapaz (de hacer); ~ **point** (*BRIT*) *n* enchufe *m*; ~ **station** *n* central *f* eléctrica

p.p. *abbr* (= *per procurationem*): ~ **J. Smith** p.p. (por poder de) J. Smith; (= *pages*) págs

PR *n abbr* = **public relations**

practical ['præktɪkl] *adj* práctico; ~**ity** [-'kælɪtɪ] *n* factibilidad *f*; ~ **joke** *n* broma pesada; ~**ly** *adv* (*almost*) casi

practice ['præktɪs] *n* (*habit*) costumbre *f*; (*exercise*) práctica, ejercicio; (*training*) adiestramiento; (*MED: of profession*) práctica, ejercicio; (*MED, LAW: business*) consulta ♦ *vt*, *vi* (*US*) = **practise**; **in** ~ (*in reality*) en la práctica; **out of** ~ desentrenado

practise ['præktɪs] (*US* **practice**) *vt* (*carry out*) practicar; (*profession*) ejercer; (*train at*) practicar ♦ *vi* ejercer; (*train*) practicar; **practising** *adj* (*Christian etc*) practicante; (*lawyer*) en

ejercicio

practitioner [præk'tɪʃənə*] *n* (*MED*) médico/a

prairie ['preəri] *n* pampa

praise [preɪz] *n* alabanza(s) *f(pl)*, elogio(s) *m(pl)* ♦ *vt* alabar, elogiar; ~**worthy** *adj* loable

pram [præm] (*BRIT*) *n* cochecito de niño

prank [præŋk] *n* travesura

prawn [prɔːn] *n* gamba; ~ **cocktail** *n* cóctel *m* de gambas

pray [preɪ] *vi* rezar

prayer [preə*] *n* oración *f*, rezo; (*entreaty*) ruego, súplica

preach [priːtʃ] *vi* (*also fig*) predicar; ~**er** *n* predicador/a *m/f*

precaution [prɪ'kɔːʃən] *n* precaución *f*

precede [prɪ'siːd] *vt, vi* preceder

precedent ['presɪdənt] *n* precedente *m*

preceding [prɪ'siːdɪŋ] *adj* anterior

precinct ['priːsɪŋkt] *n* recinto; ~**s** *npl* contornos *mpl*; **pedestrian** ~ (*BRIT*) zona peatonal; **shopping** ~ (*BRIT*) centro comercial

precious ['preʃəs] *adj* precioso

precipitate [prɪ'sɪpɪteɪt] *vt* precipitar

precise [prɪ'saɪs] *adj* preciso, exacto; ~**ly** *adv* precisamente, exactamente

precocious [prɪ'kəuʃəs] *adj* precoz

precondition [priːkən'dɪʃən] *n* condición *f* previa

predecessor [priːdɪsesə*] *n* antecesor(a) *m/f*

predicament [prɪ'dɪkəmənt] *n* apuro

predict [prɪ'dɪkt] *vt* pronosticar; ~**able** *adj* previsible; ~**ion** [-'dɪkʃən] *n* predicción *f*

predominantly [prɪ'dɔmɪnəntlɪ] *adv* en su mayoría

pre-empt [priː'emt] *vt* adelantarse a

preen [priːn] *vt*: to ~ **itself** (*bird*) limpiarse (las plumas); to ~ **o.s.** pavonearse

preface ['prefəs] *n* prefacio

prefect ['priːfekt] (*BRIT*) *n* (*in school*)

monitor(a) m/f

prefer [prɪˈfəː*] vt preferir; **to ~ doing**
or **to do** preferir hacer; **~able**
[ˈprefrəbl] adj preferible; **~ably**
[ˈprefrəblɪ] adv de preferencia; **~ence**
[ˈprefrəns] n preferencia; (*priority*)
prioridad f; **~ential** [prefəˈrenʃəl] adj
preferente

prefix [ˈpriːfɪks] n prefijo

pregnancy [ˈpregnənsɪ] n (*of woman*)
embarazo; (*of animal*) preñez f

pregnant [ˈpregnənt] adj (*woman*)
embarazada; (*animal*) preñada

prehistoric [ˈpriːhɪsˈtɔrɪk] adj
prehistórico

prejudice [ˈpredʒudɪs] n prejuicio; **~d**
adj (*person*) predispuesto

premarital [ˈpriːˈmærɪtl] adj premarital

premature [ˈprematʃuə*] adj
prematuro

premier [ˈpremɪə*] adj primero,
principal ♦ n (POL) primer(a) ministro/a

première [ˈpremɪeə*] n estreno

premise [ˈpremɪs] n premisa; **~s** npl
(*of business etc*) local m; **on the ~s** en
el lugar mismo

premium [ˈpriːmɪəm] n premio;
(*insurance*) prima; **to be at a ~** ser
muy solicitado; **~ bond** n (BRIT) n bono
del estado que participa en una lotería
nacional

premonition [preməˈnɪʃən] n
presentimiento

preoccupied [priːˈɒkjupaɪd] adj
ensimismado

prep [prep] n (SCOL: *study*) deberes mpl

prepaid [priːˈpeɪd] adj porte pagado

preparation [prepəˈreɪʃən] n
preparación f; **~s** npl preparativos mpl

preparatory [prɪˈpærətərɪ] adj
preparatorio, preliminar; **~ school** n
escuela preparatoria

prepare [prɪˈpeə*] vt preparar,
disponer; (CULIN) preparar ♦ vi: **to
~ for** (*action*) prepararse or disponerse
para; (*event*) hacer preparativos para;
~d to dispuesto a; **~d for** listo para

preposition [prepəˈzɪʃən] n
preposición f

preposterous [prɪˈpɒstərəs] adj
absurdo, ridículo

prep school n = **preparatory school**

prerequisite [priːˈrekwɪzɪt] n requisito

Presbyterian [prezbɪˈtɪərɪən] adj, n
presbiteriano/a m/f

preschool [ˈpriːˈskuːl] adj preescolar

prescribe [prɪˈskraɪb] vt (MED) recetar

prescription [prɪˈskrɪpʃən] n (MED)
receta

presence [ˈprezns] n presencia; **in
sb's ~** en presencia de uno; **~ of
mind** aplomo

present [adj, n ˈpreznt, vb prɪˈzent]
adj (*in attendance*) presente; (*current*)
actual ♦ n (*gift*) regalo; (*actuality*): **the
~** la actualidad, el presente ♦ vt
(*introduce, describe*) presentar;
(*expound*) exponer; (*give*) presentar,
dar, ofrecer; (THEATRE) representar; **to
give sb a ~** regalar algo a uno; **at ~**
actualmente; **~able** [prɪˈzentəbl] adj:
to make o.s. ~able arreglarse;
~ation [-ˈteɪʃən] n presentación f; (*of
report etc*) exposición f; (*formal
ceremony*) entrega de un regalo; **~-day**
adj actual; **~er** [prɪˈzentə*] n (RADIO,
TV) locutor(a) m/f; **~ly** adv (*soon*)
dentro de poco; (*now*) ahora

preservative [prɪˈzəːvətɪv] n
conservante m

preserve [prɪˈzəːv] vt (*keep safe*)
preservar, proteger; (*maintain*)
mantener; (*food*) conservar ♦ n (*for
game*) coto, vedado; (*often pl: jam*)
conserva, confitura

president [ˈprezɪdənt] n presidente
m/f; **~ial** [-ˈdenʃl] adj presidencial

press [pres] n (*newspapers*) la
prensa; (*printer's*) imprenta; (*of button*)
pulsación f ♦ vt (*push*) empujar; (*button etc*)
apretar; (*clothes: iron*) planchar; (*put
pressure on: person*) presionar; (*insist*):
to ~ sth on sb insistir en que uno
acepte algo ♦ vi (*squeeze*) apretar;

(*pressurize*): **to ~ for** presionar por; **we are ~ed for time/money** estamos apurados de tiempo/dinero; **~ on** vi avanzar; (*hurry*) apretar el paso; **~ agency** n agencia de prensa; **~ conference** n rueda de prensa; **~ing** adj apremiante; **~ stud** (BRIT) n botón m de presión; **~-up** (BRIT) n plancha

pressure ['prɛʃə*] n presión f; **to put ~ on sb** presionar a uno; **~ cooker** n olla a presión; **~ gauge** n manómetro; **~ group** n grupo de presión; **pressurized** adj (*container*) a presión

prestige [prɛs'ti:ʒ] n prestigio

presumably [prɪ'zju:məblɪ] adv es de suponer que, cabe presumir que

presume [prɪ'zju:m] vt: **to ~ (that)** presumir (que), suponer (que)

pretence [prɪ'tɛns] (US **pretense**) n fingimiento; **under false ~s** con engaños

pretend [prɪ'tɛnd] vt, vi (*feign*) fingir

pretentious [prɪ'tɛnʃəs] adj presumido; (*ostentatious*) ostentoso, aparatoso

pretext ['pri:tɛkst] n pretexto

pretty ['prɪtɪ] adj bonito (SP), lindo (AM) ♦ adv bastante

prevail [prɪ'veɪl] vi (*gain mastery*) prevalecer; (*be current*) predominar; **~ing** adj (*dominant*) predominante

prevalent ['prɛvələnt] adj (*widespread*) extendido

prevent [prɪ'vɛnt] vt: **to ~ sb from doing sth** impedir a uno hacer algo; **to ~ sth from happening** evitar que ocurra algo; **~ative** adj = **preventive**; **~ive** adj preventivo

preview ['pri:vju:] n (*of film*) preestreno

previous ['pri:vɪəs] adj previo, anterior; **~ly** adv antes

prewar [pri:'wɔ:*] adj de antes de la guerra

prey [preɪ] n presa ♦ vi: **to ~ on** (*feed on*) alimentarse de; **it was ~ing on**

his mind le preocupaba, le obsesionaba

price [praɪs] n precio ♦ vt (*goods*) fijar el precio de; **~less** adj que no tiene precio; **~ list** n tarifa

prick [prɪk] n (*sting*) picadura ♦ vt pinchar; (*hurt*) picar; **to ~ up one's ears** aguzar el oído

prickle ['prɪkl] n (*sensation*) picor m; (BOT) espina; **prickly** adj espinoso; (*fig: person*) enojadizo; **prickly heat** n sarpullido causado por exceso de calor

pride [praɪd] n orgullo; (*pej*) soberbia ♦ vt: **to ~ o.s. on** enorgullecerse de

priest [pri:st] n sacerdote m; **~hood** n sacerdocio

prim [prɪm] adj (*demure*) remilgado; (*prudish*) gazmoño

primarily ['praɪmərɪlɪ] adv ante todo

primary ['praɪmərɪ] adj (*first in importance*) principal ♦ n (US: POL) (*elección f*) primaria; **~ school** (BRIT) n escuela primaria

prime [praɪm] adj primero, principal; (*excellent*) selecto, de primera clase ♦ n: **in the ~ of life** en la flor de la vida ♦ vt (*wood, fig*) preparar; **~ example** ejemplo típico; **P~ Minister** n primer(a) ministro/a

primeval [praɪ'mi:vəl] adj primitivo

primitive ['prɪmɪtɪv] adj primitivo; (*crude*) rudimentario

primrose ['prɪmrəʊz] n primavera, prímula

Primus (stove) ® ['praɪməs-] (BRIT) n hornillo de camping

prince [prɪns] n príncipe m

princess [prɪn'sɛs] n princesa

principal ['prɪnsɪpl] adj principal, mayor ♦ n director(a) m/f; **~ity** [-'pælɪtɪ] n principado

principle ['prɪnsɪpl] n principio; **in ~** en principio; **on ~** por principio

print [prɪnt] n (*foot~*) huella; (*finger~*) huella dactilar; (*letters*) letra de molde; (*fabric*) estampado; (ART) grabado; (PHOT) impresión f ♦ vt imprimir; (*cloth*)

estampar; (*write in capitals*) escribir en
letras de molde; **out of ~** agotado;
~ed matter n impresos mpl; **~er** n
(*person*) impresor(a) m/f; (*machine*)
impresora; **~ing** n (*art*) imprenta; (*act*)
impresión f; **~out** n (COMPUT)
impresión f

prior ['praɪə*] adj anterior, previo;
(*more important*) más importante; **~ to**
antes de

priority [praɪ'ɔrɪtɪ] n prioridad f; **to
have ~ (over)** tener prioridad (sobre)

prison ['prɪzn] n cárcel f, prisión f
♦ cpd carcelario; **~er** n (*in prison*)
preso/a; (*captured person*) prisionero/a;
~-of-war n prisionero de guerra

privacy ['prɪvəsɪ] n intimidad f

private ['praɪvɪt] adj (*personal*)
particular; (*property, industry, discussion
etc*) privado; (*person*) reservado; (*place*)
tranquilo ♦ n soldado raso; **"~"** (*on
envelope*) "confidencial"; (*on door*)
"prohibido el paso"; **in ~** en privado;
~ enterprise n empresa privada;
~ eye n detective m/f privado/a;
~ property n propiedad f privada;
~ school n colegio particular

privet ['prɪvɪt] n alheña

privilege ['prɪvɪlɪdʒ] n privilegio;
(*prerogative*) prerrogativa

privy ['prɪvɪ] adj: **to be ~ to** estar
enterado de

prize [praɪz] n premio ♦ adj de primera
clase ♦ vt apreciar, estimar; **~-giving** n
distribución f de premios; **~-winner** n
premiado/a

pro [prəʊ] n (SPORT) profesional m/f
♦ prep a favor de; **the ~s and cons**
los pros y los contras

probability [prɔbə'bɪlɪtɪ] n
probabilidad f; **in all ~** con toda
probabilidad

probable ['prɔbəbl] adj probable

probably ['prɔbəblɪ] adv
probablemente

probation [prə'beɪʃən] n: **on ~**
(*employee*) a prueba; (LAW) en libertad

condicional

probe [prəʊb] n (MED, SPACE) sonda;
(*enquiry*) encuesta, investigación f ♦ vt
sondar; (*investigate*) investigar

problem ['prɔbləm] n problema m

procedure [prə'siːdʒə*] n
procedimiento; (*bureaucratic*) trámites
mpl

proceed [prə'siːd] vi (*do afterwards*):
to ~ to do sth proceder a hacer algo;
(*continue*): **to ~ (with)** continuar or
seguir (con); **~ings** npl acto(s) (pl);
(LAW) proceso; **~s** ['prəʊsiːdz] npl
(*money*) ganancias fpl, ingresos mpl

process ['prəʊses] n proceso ♦ vt
tratar, elaborar; **~ing** n tratamiento,
elaboración f; (PHOT) revelado

procession [prə'seʃən] n desfile m;
funeral ~ cortejo fúnebre

pro-choice [prəʊ'tʃɔɪs] adj en favor del
derecho a elegir de la madre

proclaim [prə'kleɪm] vt (*announce*)
anunciar

procrastinate [prəʊ'kræstɪneɪt] vi
demorarse

procure [prə'kjuə*] vt conseguir

prod [prɔd] vt empujar ♦ n empujón m

prodigy ['prɔdɪdʒɪ] n prodigio

produce [n 'prɔdjuːs, vt prə'djuːs] n
(AGR) productos mpl agrícolas ♦ vt
producir; (*play, film, programme*)
presentar; **~r** n productor(a) m/f; (*of
film, programme*) director(a) m/f; (*of
record*) productor(a) m/f

product ['prɔdʌkt] n producto

production [prə'dʌkʃən] n producción
f; (THEATRE) presentación f; **~ line** n
línea de producción

productivity [prɔdʌk'tɪvɪtɪ] n
productividad f

profession [prə'feʃən] n profesión f;
~al adj profesional ♦ n profesional m/f;
(*skilled person*) perito

professor [prə'fesə*] n (BRIT)
catedrático/a; (US, Canada) profesor(a)
m/f

proficient [prə'fɪʃənt] adj experto,

profile 508 propaganda

hábil

profile ['prəufaıl] n perfil m

profit ['prɒfɪt] n (COMM) ganancia ♦ vi:
to ~ by or **from** aprovechar or sacar
provecho de; **~ability** [-ə'bɪlɪtɪ] n
rentabilidad f; **~able** adj (ECON)
rentable

profound [prə'faund] adj profundo

profusely [prə'fjuːslɪ] adv
profusamente

programme ['prəugræm] (US
program) n programa m ♦ vt
programar; **~r** (US **programer**) n
programador(a) m/f; **programming**
(US **programing**) n programación f

progress [n 'prəugres, vi prə'gres] n
progreso, (development) desarrollo ♦ vi
progresar, avanzar; **in ~** en curso; **~ive**
[-'gresɪv] adj progresivo; (person)
progresista

prohibit [prə'hɪbɪt] vt prohibir; **to
~ sb from doing sth** prohibir a uno
hacer algo; **~ion** [-'bɪʃn] n prohibición
f; (US): **P~ion** Ley f Seca

project [n 'prɒdʒekt, vb prə'dʒekt] n
proyecto ♦ vt proyectar ♦ vi (stick out)
salir, sobresalir; **~ion** [prə'dʒekʃən] n
proyección f; (overhang) saliente m;
~or [prə'dʒektə*] n proyector m

pro-life [prəu'laɪf] adj pro-vida

prolong [prə'lɒŋ] vt prolongar,
extender

prom [prɒm] n abbr = **promenade**;
(US: ball) baile m de gala

Prom

*El ciclo de conciertos de música
clásica más conocido de Londres es el
llamado* the Proms (promenade
concerts), *que se celebra anualmente
en el Royal Albert Hall. Su nombre se
debe a que originalmente el público
paseaba durante las actuaciones,
costumbre que en la actualidad se
mantiene de forma simbólica,
permitiendo que parte de los
asistentes permanezcan de pie. En*

Estados Unidos se llama prom *a un
baile de gala en un centro de
educación secundaria o universitaria.*

---

promenade [prɒmə'nɑːd] n (by sea)
paseo marítimo; **~ concert** (BRIT) n
concierto (en que parte del público
permanece de pie)

prominence ['prɒmɪnəns] n
importancia

prominent ['prɒmɪnənt] adj (standing
out) saliente; (important) eminente,
importante

promiscuous [prə'mɪskjuəs] adj
(sexually) promiscuo

promise ['prɒmɪs] n promesa ♦ vt, vi
prometer; **promising** adj
prometedor(a)

promote [prə'məut] vt (employee)
ascender; (product, pop star) hacer
propaganda por; (ideas) fomentar; **~r** n
(of event) promotor(a) m/f; (of cause
etc) impulsor(a) m/f; **promotion**
[-'məuʃən] n (advertising campaign)
campaña de promoción f; (in rank)
ascenso

prompt [prɒmpt] adj rápido ♦ adv: **at
6 o'clock ~** a las seis en punto ♦ n
(COMPUT) aviso ♦ vt (urge) mover,
incitar; (when talking) instar; (THEATRE)
apuntar; **to ~ sb to do sth** instar a
uno a hacer algo; **~ly** adv
rápidamente; (exactly) puntualmente

prone [prəun] adj (lying) postrado;
~ to propenso a

prong [prɒŋ] n diente m, punta

pronoun ['prəunaun] n pronombre m

pronounce [prə'nauns] vt pronunciar;
~d adj (marked) marcado

pronunciation [prənʌnsɪ'eɪʃən] n
pronunciación f

proof [pruːf] n prueba ♦ adj:
~ against a prueba de

prop [prɒp] n apoyo, (fig) sostén m ♦ vt
(also: ~ up) apoyar, (lean): **to ~ sth
against** apoyar algo contra

propaganda [prɒpə'gændə] n

propaganda

propel [prə'pɛl] vt impulsar, propulsar; **~ler** n hélice f

propensity [prə'pɛnsɪtɪ] n propensión f

proper ['prɒpə*] adj (suited, right) propio; (exact) justo; (seemly) correcto, decente; (authentic) verdadero; (referring to place): **the village ~** el pueblo mismo; **~ly** adv (adequately) correctamente; (decently) decentemente; **~ noun** n nombre m propio

property ['prɒpətɪ] n propiedad f; (personal) bienes mpl muebles; **~ owner** n dueño/a de propiedades

prophecy ['prɒfɪsɪ] n profecía f

prophesy ['prɒfɪsaɪ] vt (fig) predecir

prophet ['prɒfɪt] n profeta m

proportion [prə'pɔːʃən] n proporción f; (share) parte f; **~al** adj: **~al (to)** en proporción (con); **~al representation** n representación f proporcional; **~ate** adj: **~ate (to)** en proporción (con)

proposal [prə'pəuzl] n (offer of marriage) oferta de matrimonio; (plan) proyecto

propose [prə'pəuz] vt proponer ♦ vi declararse; **to ~ to do** tener intención de hacer

proposition [prɒpə'zɪʃən] n propuesta

proprietor [prə'praɪətə*] n propietario/a, dueño/a

propriety [prə'praɪətɪ] n decoro

pro rata [-'rɑːtə] adv a prorrateo

prose [prəuz] n prosa

prosecute ['prɒsɪkjuːt] vt (LAW) procesar; **prosecution** [-'kjuːʃən] n proceso, causa; (accusing side) acusación f; **prosecutor** n acusador(a) m/f; (also: **public prosecutor**) fiscal m

prospect [n 'prɒspɛkt, vb prə'spɛkt] n (possibility) posibilidad f; (outlook) perspectiva ♦ vi: **to ~ for** buscar; **~s** npl (for work etc) perspectivas fpl; **~ing** n prospección f; **~ive** [prə'spɛktɪv] adj futuro

prospectus [prə'spɛktəs] n prospecto

prosper ['prɒspə*] vi prosperar; **~ity** [-'spɛrɪtɪ] n prosperidad f; **~ous** adj próspero

prostitute ['prɒstɪtjuːt] n prostituta; (male) hombre que se dedica a la prostitución

protect [prə'tɛkt] vt proteger; **~ion** [-'tɛkʃən] n protección f; **~ive** adj protector(a)

protein ['prəutiːn] n proteína

protest [n 'prəutɛst, vb prə'tɛst] n protesta ♦ vi: **to ~ about** or **at/against** protestar de/contra ♦ vt (insist): **to ~ (that)** insistir en (que)

Protestant ['prɒtɪstənt] adj, n protestante m/f

protester [prə'tɛstə*] n manifestante m/f

protracted [prə'træktɪd] adj prolongado

protrude [prə'truːd] vi salir, sobresalir

proud [praud] adj orgulloso; (pej) soberbio, altanero

prove [pruːv] vt probar; (show) demostrar ♦ vi: **to ~ (to be) correct** resultar correcto; **to ~ o.s.** probar su valía

proverb ['prɒvəːb] n refrán m

provide [prə'vaɪd] vt proporcionar, dar; **to ~ sb with sth** proveer a uno de algo; **~d that** conj con tal de que, a condición de que; **~ for** vt fus (person) mantener a; (problem etc) tener en cuenta; **providing** [prə'vaɪdɪŋ] conj: **providing (that)** a condición de que, con tal de que

province ['prɒvɪns] n provincia; (fig) esfera; **provincial** [prə'vɪnʃəl] adj provincial; (pej) provinciano

provision [prə'vɪʒən] n (supplying) suministro, abastecimiento; (of contract etc) disposición f; **~s** npl (food) comestibles mpl; **~al** adj provisional

proviso [prə'vaɪzəu] n condición f, estipulación f

provocative [prə'vɒkətɪv] adj

provoke   510   pull

provocativo

provoke [prəˈvəʊk] vt (cause)
provocar, incitar; (anger) enojar
prowess [ˈpraʊɪs] n destreza
prowl [praʊl] vi (also: ~ about,
~ around) merodear ♦ n: **on the ~** de
merodeo; **~er** n merodeador(a) m/f
proxy [ˈprɒksɪ] n: **by ~** por poderes
prudent [ˈpruːdənt] adj prudente
prune [pruːn] n ciruela pasa ♦ vt podar
pry [praɪ] vi: **to ~ (into)** entrometerse
(en)
PS n abbr (= postscript) P.D.
psalm [sɑːm] n salmo
pseudonym [ˈsjuːdənɪm] n
seudónimo
psyche [ˈsaɪkɪ] n psique f
psychiatric [saɪkɪˈætrɪk] adj
psiquiátrico
psychiatrist [saɪˈkaɪətrɪst] n psiquiatra
m/f
psychic [ˈsaɪkɪk] adj (also: ~al) psíquico
psychoanalyse [saɪkəʊˈænəlaɪz] vt
psicoanalizar; **psychoanalysis**
[-əˈnælɪsɪs] n psicoanálisis m inv
psychological [saɪkəˈlɒdʒɪkl] adj
psicológico
psychologist [saɪˈkɒlədʒɪst] n
psicólogo/a
psychology [saɪˈkɒlədʒɪ] n psicología
PTO abbr (= please turn over) sigue
pub [pʌb] n abbr (= public house) pub
m, bar m

┌─── pub ───┐

*Un pub es un local público donde se
pueden consumir bebidas alcohólicas.
La estricta regulación sobre la venta
de alcohol prohíbe que se sirva a
menores de 18 años y controla las
horas de apertura, aunque éstas son
más flexibles desde hace unos años.
El pub es, además, un lugar de
encuentro donde se sirven comidas
ligeras o se juega a los dardos o al
billar, entre otras actividades.*

└─────────────┘

puberty [ˈpjuːbətɪ] n pubertad f
public [ˈpʌblɪk] adj público ♦ n: **the ~**
el público; **in ~** en público; **to make
~** hacer público; **~ address system** n
megafonía
publican [ˈpʌblɪkən] n tabernero/a
publication [pʌblɪˈkeɪʃən] n
publicación f
public: ~ company n sociedad f
anónima; **~ convenience** (BRIT) n
aseos mpl públicos (SP), sanitarios mpl
(AM); **~ holiday** n día de fiesta (SP),
(día) feriado (AM); **~ house** (BRIT) n
bar m, pub m
publicity [pʌbˈlɪsɪtɪ] n publicidad f
publicize [ˈpʌblɪsaɪz] vt publicitar
publicly [ˈpʌblɪklɪ] adv públicamente,
en público
public: ~ opinion n opinión f pública;
~ relations n relaciones fpl públicas;
~ school n (BRIT) escuela privada; (US)
instituto; **~-spirited** adj que tiene
sentido del deber ciudadano;
~ transport n transporte m público
publish [ˈpʌblɪʃ] vt publicar; **~er** n
(person) editor(a) m/f; (firm) editorial f;
~ing n (industry) industria del libro
pub lunch n almuerzo que se sirve en
un pub; **to go for a ~** almorzar o
comer en un pub
pucker [ˈpʌkə*] vt (pleat) arrugar;
(brow etc) fruncir
pudding [ˈpʊdɪŋ] n pudín m;
(BRIT: dessert) postre m; **black ~**
morcilla
puddle [ˈpʌdl] n charco
puff [pʌf] n soplo; (of smoke, air)
bocanada; (of breathing) resoplido ♦ vt:
to ~ one's pipe chupar la pipa ♦ vi
(pant) jadear; **~ out** vi hinchar;
~ pastry n hojaldre m; **~y** adj
hinchado
pull [pʊl] n (tug): **to give sth a ~** dar
un tirón a algo ♦ vt tirar de; (press:
trigger) apretar; (haul) tirar, arrastrar;
(close: curtain) echar ♦ vi tirar; **to ~ to
pieces** hacer pedazos; **to not ~ one's**

punches no andarse con bromas; **to ~ one's weight** hacer su parte; **to ~ o.s. together** sobreponerse; **to ~ sb's leg** tomar el pelo a uno; **~ apart** vt (break) romper; **~ down** vt (building) derribar; **~ in** vi (car etc) parar (junto a la acera); (train) llegar a la estación; **~ off** vt (deal etc) cerrar; **~ out** vi (car, train etc) salir ♦ vt sacar, arrancar; **~ over** vi (AUT) hacerse a un lado; **~ through** vi (MED) reponerse; **~ up** vi (stop) parar ♦ vt (raise) levantar; (uproot) arrancar, desarraigar

pulley ['pulı] n polea

pullover ['puləuvə*] n jersey m, suéter m

pulp [pʌlp] n (of fruit) pulpa

pulpit ['pulpıt] n púlpito

pulsate [pʌl'seıt] vi pulsar, latir

pulse [pʌls] n (ANAT) pulso; (rhythm) pulsación f; (BOT) legumbre f

pump [pʌmp] n bomba; (shoe) zapatilla ♦ vt sacar con una bomba; **~ up** vt inflar

pumpkin ['pʌmpkın] n calabaza

pun [pʌn] n juego de palabras

punch [pʌntʃ] n (blow) golpe m, puñetazo; (tool) punzón m; (drink) ponche m ♦ vt (hit): **to ~ sb/sth** dar un puñetazo or golpear a uno/algo; **~line** n palabras que rematan un chiste; **~-up** n (BRIT: inf) riña

punctual ['pʌŋktjuəl] adj puntual

punctuation [pʌŋktju'eıʃən] n puntuación f

puncture ['pʌŋktʃə*] (BRIT) n pinchazo ♦ vt pinchar

pungent ['pʌndʒənt] adj acre

punish ['pʌnıʃ] vt castigar; **~ment** n castigo

punk [pʌŋk] n (also: ~ rocker) música punk m/f; (also: ~ rock) música punk; (US: inf: hoodlum) rufián m

punt [pʌnt] n (boat) batea

punter ['pʌntə*] (BRIT) n (gambler) jugador(a) m/f; (inf) cliente m/f

puny ['pju:nı] adj débil

pup [pʌp] n cachorro

pupil ['pju:pl] n alumno/a; (of eye) pupila

puppet ['pʌpıt] n títere m

puppy ['pʌpı] n cachorro, perrito

purchase ['pə:tʃıs] n compra ♦ vt comprar; **~r** n comprador(a) m/f

pure [pjuə*] adj puro

purée ['pjuəreı] n puré m

purely ['pjuəlı] adv puramente

purge [pə:dʒ] n (MED, POL) purga ♦ vt purgar

purify ['pjuərıfaı] vt purificar, depurar

purple ['pə:pl] adj purpúreo; morado

purpose ['pə:pəs] n propósito; **on ~** a propósito, adrede; **~ful** adj resuelto, determinado

purr [pə:*] vi ronronear

purse [pə:s] n monedero; (US) bolsa (SP), cartera (AM) ♦ vt fruncir

pursue [pə'sju:] vt seguir; **~r** n perseguidor(a) m/f

pursuit [pə'sju:t] n (chase) caza; (occupation) actividad f

push [puʃ] n empuje m, empujón m; (of button) presión f; (drive) empuje m ♦ vt empujar; (button) apretar; (promote) promover ♦ vi empujar; (demand): **to ~ for** luchar por; **~ aside** vt apartar con la mano; **~ off** vi (inf) largarse; **~ on** vi seguir adelante; **~ through** vi (crowd) abrirse paso a empujones ♦ vt (measure) despachar; **~ up** vt (total, prices) hacer subir; **~chair** (BRIT) n sillita de ruedas; **~er** n (drug ~er) traficante m/f de drogas; **~over** (inf) n: **it's a ~over** está tirado; **~-up** (US) n plancha; **~y** (pej) adj agresivo

puss [pus] (inf) n minino

pussy(-cat) ['pusı-] (inf) n = **puss**

put [put] (pt, pp **put**) vt (place) poner, colocar; (~ into) meter; (say) expresar; (a question) hacer; (estimate) estimar; **~ about** or **around** vt (rumour) diseminar; **~ across** vt (ideas etc) comunicar; **~ away** vt (store) guardar;

~ **back** vt (replace) devolver a su lugar; (postpone) aplazar; ~ **by** vt (money) guardar; ~ **down** vt (on ground) poner en el suelo; (animal) sacrificar; (in writing) apuntar; (revolt etc) sofocar; (attribute): **to** ~ **sth down to** atribuir algo a; ~ **forward** vt (ideas) presentar, proponer; (time) adelantar; ~ **in** vt (complaint) presentar; (time) dedicar; ~ **off** vt (postpone) aplazar; (discourage) desanimar; ~ **on** vt ponerse; (light etc) encender; (play etc) presentar; (gain): **to** ~ **on weight** engordar; (brake) echar; (record, kettle etc) poner; (assume) adoptar; ~ **out** vt (fire, light) apagar; (rubbish etc) sacar; (cat etc) echar; (one's hand) alargar; (inf: person): **to be** ~ **out** alterarse; ~ **through** vt (TEL) poner; (plan etc) hacer aprobar; ~ **up** vt (raise) levantar, alzar; (hang) colgar; (build) construir; (increase) aumentar; (accommodate) alojar; ~ **up with** vt fus aguantar

putt [pʌt] n putt m, golpe m corto; ~**ing green** n green m; minigolf m
putty ['pʌtɪ] n masilla
put-up ['putʌp] adj: ~ **job** (BRIT) amaño
puzzle ['pʌzl] n rompecabezas m inv; (also: crossword ~) crucigrama m, (mystery) misterio ♦ vt dejar perplejo, confundir ♦ vi: **to** ~ **over sth** devanarse los sesos con algo; **puzzling** adj misterioso, extraño
pyjamas [pɪ'dʒɑːməz] (BRIT) npl pijama m
pylon ['paɪlən] n torre f de conducción eléctrica
pyramid ['pɪrəmɪd] n pirámide f
Pyrenees [pɪrə'niːz] npl: **the** ~ los Pirineos
python ['paɪθən] n pitón m

Q, q

quack [kwæk] n graznido; (pej: doctor) curandero/a
quad [kwɒd] n abbr = **quadrangle**; **quadruplet**
quadrangle ['kwɒdræŋgl] n patio
quadruple [kwɒ'druːpl] vt, vi cuadruplicar
quadruplets [kwɔː'druːplɪts] npl cuatrillizos/as
quail [kweɪl] n codorniz f ♦ vi: **to** ~ **at** or **before** amedrentarse ante
quaint [kweɪnt] adj extraño; (picturesque) pintoresco
quake [kweɪk] vi temblar ♦ n abbr = **earthquake**
Quaker ['kweɪkə*] n cuáquero/a
qualification [kwɒlɪfɪ'keɪʃən] n (ability) capacidad f; (often pl: diploma etc) título; (reservation) salvedad f
qualified ['kwɒlɪfaɪd] adj capacitado; (professionally) titulado; (limited) limitado
qualify ['kwɒlɪfaɪ] vt (make competent) capacitar; (modify) modificar ♦ vi (in competition): **to** ~ (**for**) calificarse (para); (pass examination(s)): **to** ~ (**as**) calificarse (de), graduarse (en); (be eligible): **to** ~ (**for**) reunir los requisitos (para)
quality ['kwɒlɪtɪ] n calidad f; (of person) cualidad f; ~ **time** n tiempo dedicado a la familia y a los amigos

---

quality press

La expresión **quality press** se refiere a los periódicos que dan un tratamiento serio de las noticias, ofreciendo información detallada sobre un amplio espectro de temas y un análisis en profundidad de la actualidad. Por su tamaño, considerablemente mayor que el de los *periódicos sensacionalistas, se les conoce también como "broadsheets".*

qualm [kwɑːm] n escrúpulo

quandary ['kwɔndrɪ] n: **to be in a ~** tener dudas

quantity ['kwɔntɪtɪ] n cantidad f; **in ~** en grandes cantidades; **~ surveyor** n aparejador(a) m/f

quarantine ['kwɔrntiːn] n cuarentena

quarrel ['kwɔrl] n riña, pelea ♦ vi reñir, pelearse

quarry ['kwɔrɪ] n cantera

quart [kwɔːt] n ≈ litro

quarter ['kwɔːtə*] n cuarto, cuarta parte f; (US: coin) moneda de 25 centavos; (of year) trimestre m; (district) barrio ♦ vt dividir en cuartos; (MIL: lodge) alojar; **~s** npl (barracks) cuartel m; (living ~s) alojamiento; **a ~ of an hour** un cuarto de hora; **~ final** n cuarto de final; **~ly** adj trimestral ♦ adv cada 3 meses, trimestralmente

quartet(te) [kwɔː'tet] n cuarteto

quartz [kwɔːts] n cuarzo

quash [kwɔʃ] vt (verdict) anular

quaver ['kweɪvə*] (BRIT) n (MUS) corchea ♦ vi temblar

quay [kiː] n (also: ~side) muelle m

queasy ['kwiːzɪ] adj: **to feel ~** tener náuseas

queen [kwiːn] n reina; (CARDS etc) dama; **~ mother** n reina madre

queer [kwɪə*] adj raro, extraño ♦ n (inf: highly offensive) maricón m

quell [kwel] vt (feeling) calmar; (rebellion etc) sofocar

quench [kwentʃ] vt: **to ~ one's thirst** apagar la sed

query ['kwɪərɪ] n (question) pregunta ♦ vt dudar de

quest [kwest] n busca, búsqueda

question ['kwestʃən] n pregunta; (doubt) duda; (matter) asunto, cuestión f ♦ vt (doubt) dudar de; (interrogate) interrogar, hacer preguntas a; **beyond ~** fuera de toda duda; **out of the ~**

imposible; ni hablar; **~able** adj dudoso; **~ mark** n punto de interrogación; **~naire** [-'nɛə*] n cuestionario

queue [kjuː] (BRIT) n cola ♦ vi (also: ~ up) hacer cola

quibble ['kwɪbl] vi sutilizar

quick [kwɪk] adj rápido; (agile) ágil; (mind) listo ♦ n: **cut to the ~** (fig) herido en lo vivo; **be ~!** ¡date prisa!; **~en** vt apresurar ♦ vi apresurarse, darse prisa; **~ly** adv rápidamente, de prisa; **~sand** n arenas fpl movedizas; **~-witted** adj perspicaz

quid [kwɪd] (BRIT: inf) n inv libra

quiet ['kwaɪət] adj (voice, music etc) bajo; (person, place) tranquilo; (ceremony) íntimo ♦ n silencio; (calm) tranquilidad f ♦ vt, vi (US) = **~en**; **~en** (also: ~en down) vi calmarse; (grow silent) callarse ♦ vt calmar; hacer callar; **~ly** adv tranquilamente; (silently) silenciosamente; **~ness** n silencio; tranquilidad f

quilt [kwɪlt] n edredón m

quin [kwɪn] n abbr = **quintuplet**

quintet(te) [kwɪn'tet] n quinteto

quintuplets [kwɪn'tjuːplɪts] npl quintillizos/as

quip [kwɪp] n pulla

quirk [kwəːk] n peculiaridad f; (accident) capricho

quit [kwɪt] (pt, pp quit or quitted) vt dejar, abandonar; (premises) desocupar ♦ vi (give up) renunciar; (resign) dimitir

quite [kwaɪt] adv (rather) bastante; (entirely) completamente; **that's not ~ big enough** no acaba de ser lo bastante grande; **~ a few of them** un buen número de ellos; **~ (so)!** ¡así es!, ¡exactamente!

quits [kwɪts] adj: **~ (with)** en paz (con); **let's call it ~** dejémoslo en tablas

quiver ['kwɪvə*] vi estremecerse

quiz [kwɪz] n concurso ♦ vt interrogar; **~zical** adj burlón(ona)

quota ['kwəutə] n cuota

quotation [kwəu'teiʃən] n cita; (estimate) presupuesto; ~ **marks** npl comillas fpl

quote [kwəut] n cita; (estimate) presupuesto ♦ vt citar; (price) cotizar ♦ vi: **to ~ from** citar de; **~s** npl (inverted commas) comillas fpl

R, r

rabbi ['ræbai] n rabino

rabbit ['ræbit] n conejo; ~ **hutch** n conejera

rabble ['ræbl] (pej) n chusma, populacho

rabies ['reibi:z] n rabia

RAC (BRIT) n abbr = **Royal Automobile Club**

rac(c)oon [rə'ku:n] n mapache m

race [reis] n carrera; (species) raza ♦ vt (horse) hacer correr; (engine) acelerar ♦ vi (compete) competir; (run) correr; (pulse) latir a ritmo acelerado; ~ **car** (US) n = **racing car**; ~ **car driver** (US) n = **racing driver**; **~course** n hipódromo; **~horse** n caballo de carreras; **~track** n pista; (for cars) autódromo

racial ['reiʃl] adj racial

racing ['reisiŋ] n carreras fpl; ~ **car** (BRIT) n coche m de carreras; ~ **driver** (BRIT) n corredor(a) m/f de coches

racism ['reisizəm] n racismo; **racist** [-sist] adj, n racista m/f

rack [ræk] n (also: luggage ~) rejilla; (shelf) estante m; (also: roof ~) baca, portaequipajes m inv; (dish ~) escurreplatos m inv; (clothes ~) percha ♦ vt atormentar; **to ~ one's brains** devanarse los sesos

racket ['rækit] n (for tennis) raqueta; (noise) ruido, estrépito; (swindle) estafa, timo

racquet ['rækit] n raqueta

racy ['reisi] adj picante, salado

radar ['reidɑ:*] n radar m

radiant ['reidiənt] adj radiante (de felicidad)

radiate ['reidieit] vt (heat) radiar; (emotion) irradiar ♦ vi (lines) extenderse

radiation [reidi'eiʃən] n radiación f

radiator ['reidieitə*] n radiador m

radical ['rædikl] adj radical

radii ['reidiai] npl of **radius**

radio ['reidiəu] n radio f; **on the ~** por radio

radio... [reidiəu] prefix: **~active** adj radioactivo; **~graphy** [reidi'ɔgrəfi] n radiografía; **~logy** [reidi'ɔlədʒi] n radiología

radio station n emisora

radiotherapy [-'θerəpi] n radioterapia

radish ['rædiʃ] n rábano

radius ['reidiəs] (pl **radii**) n radio

RAF n abbr = **Royal Air Force**

raffle ['ræfl] n rifa, sorteo

raft [rɑ:ft] n balsa; (also: life ~) balsa salvavidas

rafter ['rɑ:ftə*] n viga

rag [ræg] n (piece of cloth) trapo; (torn cloth) harapo; (pej: newspaper) periodicucho; (for charity) actividades estudiantiles benéficas; **~s** npl (torn clothes) harapos mpl; ~ **doll** n muñeca de trapo

rage [reidʒ] n rabia, furor m ♦ vi (person) rabiar, estar furioso; (storm) bramar; **it's all the ~** (very fashionable) está muy de moda

ragged ['rægid] adj (edge) desigual, mellado; (appearance) andrajoso, harapiento

raid [reid] n (MIL) incursión f; (criminal) asalto; (by police) redada ♦ vt invadir, atacar; asaltar

rail [reil] n (on stair) barandilla, pasamanos m inv; (on bridge, balcony) pretil m; (of ship) barandilla; (also: towel ~) toallero; **~s** npl (RAIL) vía; **by ~** por ferrocarril; **~ing(s)** n(pl) vallado; **~road** (US) n = **~way**; **~way** (BRIT) n ferrocarril m, vía férrea; **~way line**

(BRIT) n línea (de ferrocarril);
~wayman (BRIT irreg) n ferroviario;
~way station (BRIT) n estación f de
ferrocarril

rain [reɪn] n lluvia ♦ vi llover; **in the ~**
bajo la lluvia; **it's ~ing** llueve, está
lloviendo; **~bow** n arco iris; **~coat** n
impermeable m; **~drop** n gota de
lluvia; **~fall** n lluvia; **~forest** n selvas
fpl tropicales; **~y** adj lluvioso

raise [reɪz] n aumento ♦ vt levantar;
(increase) aumentar; (improve: morale)
subir; (: standards) mejorar; (doubts)
suscitar; (a question) plantear; (cattle,
family) criar; (crop) cultivar; (army)
reclutar; (loan) obtener; **to ~ one's
voice** alzar la voz

raisin ['reɪzn] n pasa de Corinto

rake [reɪk] n (tool) rastrillo; (person)
libertino ♦ vt (garden) rastrillar

rally ['rælɪ] n (POL etc) reunión f, mitin
m; (AUT) rallye m; (TENNIS) peloteo ♦ vt
reunir ♦ vi recuperarse; **~ round** vt fus
(fig) dar apoyo a

RAM [ræm] n abbr (= random access
memory) RAM f

ram [ræm] n carnero; (also: battering ~)
ariete m ♦ vt (crash into) dar contra,
chocar con; (push: fist etc) empujar con
fuerza

ramble ['ræmbl] n caminata, excursión
f en el campo ♦ vi (pej: also: ~ on)
divagar; **~r** n excursionista m/f; (BOT)
trepadera; **rambling** adj (speech)
inconexo; (house) laberíntico; (BOT)
trepador(a)

ramp [ræmp] n rampa; **on/off ~** (US:
AUT) vía de acceso/salida

rampage [ræm'peɪdʒ] n: **to be on
the ~** desmandarse ♦ vi: **they went
rampaging through the town**
recorrieron la ciudad armando alboroto

rampant ['ræmpənt] adj (disease etc):
to be ~ estar extendiéndose mucho

ram raid vt atracar (rompiendo el
escaparate con un coche)

ramshackle ['ræmʃækl] adj

destartalado

ran [ræn] pt of **run**

ranch [rɑːntʃ] n hacienda, estancia;
~er n ganadero

rancid ['rænsɪd] adj rancio

rancour ['ræŋkə*] (US **rancor**) n rencor
m

random ['rændəm] adj fortuito, sin
orden; (COMPUT, MATH) aleatorio ♦ n:
at ~ al azar

randy ['rændɪ] (BRIT: inf) adj cachondo

rang [ræŋ] pt of **ring**

range [reɪndʒ] n (of mountains) cadena
de montañas, cordillera; (BRIT: also: missile)
alcance f; (of voice) registro; (series)
serie f; (of products) surtido; (MIL: also:
shooting ~) campo de tiro; (also:
kitchen ~) fogón m ♦ vt (place) colocar;
(arrange) arreglar ♦ vi: **to ~ over**
(extend) extenderse por; **to ~ from ...
to ...** oscilar entre ... y ...

ranger [reɪndʒə*] n guardabosques m
inv

rank [ræŋk] n (row) fila; (MIL) rango;
(status) categoría; (BRIT: also: taxi ~)
parada de taxis ♦ vi: **to ~ among**
figurar entre ♦ adj rancio, rancio; **the
~ and file** (fig) la base

ransack ['rænsæk] vt (search) registrar;
(plunder) saquear

ransom ['rænsəm] n rescate m; **to
hold to ~** (fig) hacer chantaje a

rant [rænt] vi divagar, desvariar

rap [ræp] vt golpear, dar un golpecito
en ♦ n (music) rap m

rape [reɪp] n violación f; (BOT) colza
♦ vt violar; **~ (seed) oil** n aceite m de
colza

rapid ['ræpɪd] adj rápido; **~ity**
[rə'pɪdɪtɪ] n rapidez f; **~s** npl (GEO)
rápidos mpl

rapist ['reɪpɪst] n violador m

rapport [ræ'pɔː*] n simpatía

rapturous ['ræptʃərəs] adj extático

rare [reə*] adj raro, poco común;
(CULIN: steak) poco hecho

rarely ['reəlɪ] adv pocas veces

raring ['reərɪŋ] adj: **to be ~ to go** (inf) tener muchas ganas de empezar

rascal ['rɑːskl] n pillo, pícaro

rash [ræʃ] adj imprudente, precipitado ♦ n (MED) sarpullido, erupción f (cutánea); (of events) serie f

rasher ['ræʃə*] n lonja

raspberry ['rɑːzbərɪ] n frambuesa

rasping ['rɑːspɪŋ] adj: **a ~ noise** un ruido áspero

rat [ræt] n rata

rate [reɪt] n (ratio) razón f; (price) precio; (: of hotel etc) tarifa; (of interest) tipo; (speed) velocidad f ♦ vt (value) tasar; (estimate) estimar; **~s** npl (BRIT: property tax) impuesto municipal; (fees) tarifa; **to ~ sth/sb as** considerar algo/a uno como; **~able value** (BRIT) n valor m impuesto; **~payer** (BRIT) n contribuyente m/f

rather ['rɑːðə*] adv: **it's ~ expensive** es algo caro; (too much) es demasiado caro; (to some extent) más bien; **there's ~ a lot** hay bastante; **I would** or **I'd ~ go** preferiría ir; **or ~** mejor dicho

rating ['reɪtɪŋ] n tasación f; (score) índice m; (of ship) clase f; **~s** npl (RADIO, TV) niveles mpl de audiencia

ratio ['reɪʃɪəu] n razón f; **in the ~ of 100 to 1** a razón de 100 a 1

ration ['ræʃən] n ración f ♦ vt racionar; **~s** npl víveres mpl

rational ['ræʃənl] adj (solution, reasoning) lógico, razonable; (person) cuerdo, sensato; **~e** [-'nɑːl] n razón f fundamental; **~ize** vt justificar

rat race n lucha incesante por la supervivencia

rattle ['rætl] n golpeteo; (of train etc) traqueteo; (for baby) sonaja, sonajero ♦ vi castañetear; (car, bus): **to ~ along** traquetear ♦ vt hacer sonar agitando; **~snake** n serpiente f de cascabel

raucous ['rɔːkəs] adj estridente, ronco

ravage ['rævɪdʒ] vt hacer estragos en, destrozar; **~s** npl estragos mpl

rave [reɪv] vi (in anger) encolerizarse; (with enthusiasm) entusiasmarse; (MED) delirar, desvariar ♦ n (inf: party) rave m

raven ['reɪvən] n cuervo

ravenous ['rævənəs] adj hambriento

ravine [rə'viːn] n barranco

raving ['reɪvɪŋ] adj: **~ lunatic** loco/a de atar

ravishing ['rævɪʃɪŋ] adj encantador(a)

raw [rɔː] adj crudo; (not processed) bruto; (sore) vivo; (inexperienced) novato, inexperto; **~ deal** (inf) n injusticia; **~ material** n materia prima

ray [reɪ] n rayo; **~ of hope** (rayo de) esperanza

raze [reɪz] vt arrasar

razor ['reɪzə*] n (open) navaja; (safety ~) máquina de afeitar; (electric ~) máquina (eléctrica) de afeitar; **~ blade** n hoja de afeitar

Rd abbr = **road**

re [riː] prep con referencia a

reach [riːtʃ] n alcance m; (of river etc) extensión f entre dos recodos ♦ vt alcanzar, llegar a; (achieve) lograr ♦ vi extenderse; **within ~** al alcance (de la mano); **out of ~** fuera del alcance; **~ out** vt (hand) tender ♦ vi: **to ~ out for sth** alargar or tender la mano para tomar algo

react [riː'ækt] vi reaccionar; **~ion** n reacción f

reactor [riː'æktə*] n (also: nuclear ~) reactor m (nuclear)

read [riːd, pt, pp red] (pt, pp **read**) vi leer ♦ vt leer; (understand) entender; (study) estudiar; **~ out** vt leer en alta voz; **~able** adj (writing) legible; (book) leíble; **~er** n lector(a) m/f; (BRIT: at university) profesor(a) m/f adjunto/a; **~ership** n (of paper etc) (número de) lectores mpl

readily ['redɪlɪ] adv (willingly) de buena gana; (easily) fácilmente; (quickly) en seguida

readiness ['redɪnɪs] n buena voluntad f; (preparedness) preparación f; **in ~**

(*prepared*) listo, preparado
reading ['ri:dɪŋ] *n* lectura; (*on instrument*) indicación *f*
ready ['rɛdɪ] *adj* listo, preparado; (*willing*) dispuesto; (*available*) disponible ♦ *adv:* **~-cooked** listo para comer ♦ *n:* **at the ~** (MIL) listo para tirar; **to get ~** *vi* prepararse ♦ *vt* preparar; **~-made** *adj* confeccionado; **~-to-wear** *adj* confeccionado
real [rɪəl] *adj* verdadero, auténtico; **in ~ terms** en términos reales; **~ estate** *n* bienes *mpl* raíces; **~istic** [-'lɪstɪk] *adj* realista
reality [rɪ:'ælɪtɪ] *n* realidad *f*
realization [rɪəlaɪ'zeɪʃən] *n* comprensión *f*; (*fulfilment*, COMM) realización *f*
realize ['rɪəlaɪz] *vt* (*understand*) darse cuenta de
really ['rɪəlɪ] *adv* realmente; (*for emphasis*) verdaderamente; (*actually*): **what ~ happened** lo que pasó en realidad; **~?** ¿de veras?; **~!** (*annoyance*) ¡vamos!, ¡por favor!
realm [rɛlm] *n* reino, (*fig*) esfera
realtor ® ['rɪəltɔ:*] (US) *n* corredor(a) *m/f* de bienes raíces
reap [ri:p] *vt* segar; (*fig*) cosechar, recoger
reappear [ri:ə'pɪə*] *vi* reaparecer
rear [rɪə*] *adj* trasero ♦ *n* parte *f* trasera ♦ *vt* (*cattle, family*) criar ♦ *vi* (*also:* **~ up**) (*animal*) encabritarse; **~guard** *n* retaguardia
rearmament [ri:'ɑ:məmənt] *n* rearme *m*
rearrange [ri:ə'reɪndʒ] *vt* ordenar or arreglar de nuevo
rear-view mirror *n* (AUT) (*espejo*) retrovisor *m*
reason ['ri:zn] *n* razón *f* ♦ *vi:* **to ~ with sb** tratar de que uno entre en razón; **it stands to ~ that** es lógico que; **~able** *adj* razonable; (*sensible*) sensato; **~ably** *adv* razonablemente; **~ing** *n* razonamiento, argumentos *mpl*

reassurance [ri:ə'ʃuərəns] *n* consuelo
reassure [ri:ə'ʃuə*] *vt* tranquilizar, alentar; **to ~ sb that** tranquilizar a uno asegurando que
rebate ['ri:beɪt] *n* (*on tax etc*) desgravación *f*
rebel [*n* 'rɛbl, *vi* rɪ'bɛl] *n* rebelde *m/f* ♦ *vi* rebelarse, sublevarse; **~lious** [rɪ'bɛljəs] *adj* rebelde; (*child*) revoltoso
rebirth [ri:'bə:θ] *n* renacimiento
rebound [*vi* rɪ'baund, *n* 'ri:baund] *vi* (*ball*) rebotar ♦ *n* rebote *m*; **on the ~** (*also fig*) de rebote
rebuff [rɪ'bʌf] *n* desaire *m*, rechazo
rebuild [ri:'bɪld] (*irreg*) *vt* reconstruir
rebuke [rɪ'bju:k] *n* reprimenda ♦ *vt* reprender
rebut [rɪ'bʌt] *vt* rebatir
recall [*vb* rɪ'kɔ:l, *n* 'ri:kɔl] *vt* (*remember*) recordar; (*ambassador etc*) retirar ♦ *n* recuerdo; retirada
recap ['ri:kæp], **recapitulate** [ri:kə'pɪtjuleɪt] *vt, vi* recapitular
rec'd *abbr* (= *received*) rbdo
recede [rɪ:si:d] *vi* (*tide*) bajar; retirarse or borrándose; (*hair*) retroceder; **receding** *adj* (*forehead, chin*) huidizo; **to have a receding hairline** tener entradas
receipt [rɪ'si:t] *n* (*document*) recibo, (*for parcel etc*) acuse *m* de recibo; (*act of receiving*) recepción *f*; **~s** *npl* (COMM) ingresos *mpl*
receive [rɪ'si:v] *vt* recibir; (*guest*) acoger; (*wound*) sufrir; **~r** *n* (TEL) auricular *m*, (RADIO) receptor *m*; (*of stolen goods*) perista *m/f*; (COMM) administrador *m* jurídico
recent ['ri:snt] *adj* reciente; **~ly** *adv* recientemente; **~ly arrived** recién llegado
receptacle [rɪ'sɛptɪkl] *n* receptáculo
reception [rɪ'sɛpʃən] *n* recepción *f*; (*welcome*) acogida; **~ desk** *n* recepción *f*; **~ist** *n* recepcionista *m/f*
recess [rɪ'sɛs] *n* (*in room*) hueco; (*for bed*) nicho; (*secret place*) escondrijo;

(POL etc: holiday) clausura
recession [rɪ'seʃən] n recesión f
recipe ['resɪpɪ] n receta; (for disaster, success) fórmula
recipient [rɪ'sɪpɪənt] n recibidor(a) m/f; (of letter) destinatario/a
recital [rɪ'saɪtl] n recital m
recite [rɪ'saɪt] vt (poem) recitar
reckless ['rekləs] adj temerario, imprudente; (driving, driver) peligroso; **~ly** adv imprudentemente; de modo peligroso
reckon ['rekən] vt calcular; (consider) considerar; (think:) **I ~ that ...** me parece que ...; **~ on** vt fus contar con; **~ing** n cálculo
reclaim [rɪ'kleɪm] vt (land, waste) recuperar; (land: from sea) rescatar; (demand back) reclamar
reclamation [reklə'meɪʃən] n (of land) acondicionamiento de tierras
recline [rɪ'klaɪn] vi reclinarse; **reclining** adj (seat) reclinable
recluse [rɪ'kluːs] n recluso/a
recognition [rekəg'nɪʃən] n reconocimiento; **transformed beyond ~** irreconocible
recognizable ['rekəgnaɪzəbl] adj: **~ (by)** reconocible (por)
recognize ['rekəgnaɪz] vt: **to ~ (by/ as)** reconocer (por/como)
recoil [vi rɪ'kɔɪl, n 'riːkɔɪl] vi (person): **to ~ from doing sth** retraerse de hacer algo ♦ n (of gun) retroceso
recollect [rekə'lekt] vt recordar, acordarse de; **~ion** [-'lekʃən] n recuerdo
recommend [rekə'mend] vt recomendar
reconcile ['rekənsaɪl] vt (two people) reconciliar; (two facts) compaginar; **to ~ o.s. to sth** conformarse a algo
recondition [riːkən'dɪʃən] vt (machine) reacondicionar
reconnoitre [rekə'nɔɪtə*] (US **reconnoiter**) vt, vi (MIL) reconocer
reconsider [riːkən'sɪdə*] vt repensar

reconstruct [riːkən'strʌkt] vt reconstruir
record [n 'rekɔːd, vt rɪ'kɔːd] n (MUS) disco; (of meeting etc) acta; (register) registro, partida; (file) archivo; (also: **criminal ~**) antecedentes mpl; (written) expediente m; (SPORT, COMPUT) récord m ♦ vt registrar; (MUS: song etc) grabar; **in ~ time** en un tiempo récord; **off the ~** adj no oficial ♦ adv confidencialmente; **~ card** n (in file) ficha; **~ed delivery** (BRIT) n (POST) entrega con acuse de recibo; **~er** n (MUS) flauta de pico; (file) archivo; **~ holder** n (SPORT) actual poseedor(a) m/f del récord; **~ing** n (MUS) grabación f; **~ player** n tocadiscos m inv
recount [rɪ'kaunt] vt contar
re-count ['riːkaunt] n (POL: of votes) segundo escrutinio
recoup [rɪ'kuːp] vt: **to ~ one's losses** recuperar las pérdidas
recourse [rɪ'kɔːs] n: **to have ~ to** recurrir a
recover [rɪ'kʌvə*] vt recuperar ♦ vi (from illness, shock) recuperarse; **~y** n recuperación f
recreation [rekrɪ'eɪʃən] n recreo; **~al** adj de recreo; **~al drug** droga recreativa
recruit [rɪ'kruːt] n recluta m/f ♦ vt reclutar; (staff) contratar
rectangle ['rektæŋgl] n rectángulo; **rectangular** [-'tæŋgjulə*] adj rectangular
rectify ['rektɪfaɪ] vt rectificar
rector ['rektə*] n (REL) párroco; **~y** n casa del párroco
recuperate [rɪ'kuːpəreɪt] vi reponerse, restablecerse
recur [rɪ'kɜː*] vi repetirse; (pain, illness) producirse de nuevo; **~rence** [rɪ'kʌrəns] n repetición f; **~rent** [rɪ'kʌrənt] adj repetido
recycle [riː'saɪkl] vt reciclar
red [red] n rojo ♦ adj rojo; (hair) pelirrojo; (wine) tinto; **to be in the ~**

(*account*) estar en números rojos; (*business*) tener un saldo negativo; **to give sb the ~ carpet treatment** recibir a uno con todos los honores; **R~ Cross** n Cruz f Roja; **~currant** n grosella roja; **~den** vt enrojecer ♦ vi enrojecerse

redeem [rɪ'di:m] vt redimir; (*promises*) cumplir; (*sth in pawn*) desempeñar; (*fig, also* REL) rescatar; **~ing** adj: **~ing feature** rasgo bueno or favorable

redeploy [ri:dɪ'plɔɪ] vt (*resources*) reorganizar

red: **~-haired** adj pelirrojo; **~-handed** adj: **to be caught ~-handed** cogerse (SP) or pillarse (AM) con las manos en la masa; **~head** n pelirrojo/a; **~ herring** n (*fig*) pista falsa; **~-hot** adj candente

redirect [ri:daɪ'rekt] vt (*mail*) reexpedir

red light n: **to go through a ~** (AUT) pasar la luz roja; **red-light district** n barrio chino

redo [ri:'du:] (*irreg*) vt rehacer

redress [rɪ'dres] n reparar

Red Sea n: **the ~** el mar Rojo

redskin ['redskɪn] n piel roja m/f

red tape n (*fig*) trámites mpl

reduce [rɪ'dju:s] vt reducir; **to ~ sb to tears** hacer llorar a uno; **to be ~d to begging** no quedarle a uno otro remedio que pedir limosna; *"~ speed now"* (AUT) "reduzca la velocidad"; **at a ~d price** (*of goods*) (a precio) rebajado; **reduction** [rɪ'dʌkʃən] n reducción f; (*of price*) rebaja; (*discount*) descuento; (*smaller-scale copy*) copia reducida

redundancy [rɪ'dʌndənsɪ] n (*dismissal*) despido; (*unemployment*) desempleo

redundant [rɪ'dʌndnt] adj (BRIT: *worker*) parado, sin trabajo; (*detail, object*) superfluo; **to be made ~** quedar(se) sin trabajo

reed [ri:d] n (BOT) junco, caña; (MUS) lengüeta

reef [ri:f] n (*at sea*) arrecife m

reek [ri:k] vi: **to ~ (of)** apestar (a)

reel [ri:l] n carrete m, bobina; (*of film*) rollo; (*dance*) baile m escocés ♦ vt (also: **~ up**) devanar; (also: **~ in**) sacar ♦ vi (*sway*) tambalear(se)

ref [vt ref] (*inf*) n abbr = **referee**

refectory [rɪ'fektərɪ] n comedor m

refer [rɪ'fə:*] vt (*send: patient*) referir; (: *matter*) remitir ♦ vi: **to ~ to** (*allude to*) referirse a, aludir a; (*apply to*) relacionarse con; (*consult*) consultar

referee [refə'ri:] n árbitro; (BRIT: *for job application*): **to be a ~ for sb** proporcionar referencias a uno ♦ vt (*match*) arbitrar en

reference ['refrəns] n referencia; (*for job application: letter*) carta de recomendación; **with ~ to** (COMM: *in letter*) me remito a; **~ book** n libro de consulta; **~ number** n número de referencia

refill [vt ri:'fɪl, n 'ri:fɪl] vt rellenar ♦ n repuesto, recambio

refine [rɪ'faɪn] vt refinar; **~d** adj (*person*) fino; **~ment** n cultura, educación f; (*of system*) refinamiento

reflect [rɪ'flekt] vt reflejar ♦ vi (*think*) reflexionar, pensar; **it ~s badly/well on him** le perjudica/le hace honor; **~ion** [-'flekʃən] n (*act*) reflexión f; (*image*) reflejo; (*criticism*) crítica; **on ~ion** pensándolo bien; **~or** n (AUT) captafaros m inv; (*of light, heat*) reflector m

reflex ['ri:fleks] adj, n reflejo; **~ive** [rɪ'fleksɪv] adj (LING) reflexivo

reform [rɪ'fɔ:m] n reforma ♦ vt reformar; **~atory** (US) n reformatorio

refrain [rɪ'freɪn] vi: **to ~ from doing** abstenerse de hacer ♦ n estribillo

refresh [rɪ'freʃ] vt refrescar; **~er course** (BRIT) n curso de repaso; **~ing** adj refrescante; **~ments** npl refrescos mpl

refrigerator [rɪ'frɪdʒəreɪtə*] n nevera (SP), refrigeradora (AM)

refuel [ri:'fjuəl] vi repostar (combustible)

refuge ['rɛfjuːdʒ] n refugio, asilo; **to take ~ in** refugiarse en

refugee [rɛfjuˈdʒiː] n refugiado/a

refund [n 'riːfʌnd, vb rɪ'fʌnd] n reembolso ♦ vt devolver, reembolsar

refurbish [riː'fəːbɪʃ] vt restaurar, renovar

refusal [rɪ'fjuːzəl] n negativa; **to have first ~** on tener la primera opción a

refuse¹ ['rɛfjuːs] n basura; **~ collection** n recolección f de basuras

refuse² [rɪ'fjuːz] vt rechazar; (invitation) declinar; (permission) denegar ♦ vi: **to ~ to do sth** negarse a hacer algo; (horse) rehusar

regain [rɪ'geɪn] vt recobrar, recuperar

regal ['riːɡl] adj regio, real

regard [rɪ'ɡɑːd] n mirada; (esteem) respeto; (attention) consideración f ♦ vt (consider) considerar; **to give one's ~s to** saludar de su parte a; **''with kindest ~s''** ''con muchos recuerdos''; **~ing, as ~s, with ~ to** con respecto a, en cuanto a; **~less** adv a pesar de todo; **~less of** sin reparar en

régime [reɪ'ʒiːm] n régimen m

regiment ['rɛdʒɪmənt] n regimiento; **~al** [-'mɛntl] adj militar

region ['riːdʒən] n región f; **in the ~ of** (fig) alrededor de; **~al** adj regional

register ['rɛdʒɪstə*] n registro ♦ vt (birth) declarar; (car) matricular; (letter) certificar; (subj: instrument) marcar, indicar ♦ vi (at hotel) registrarse; (as student) matricularse; (make impression) producir impresión; **~ed** adj (letter, parcel) certificado; **~ed trademark** n marca registrada

registrar ['rɛdʒɪstrɑː*] n secretario/a (del registro civil)

registration [rɛdʒɪs'treɪʃən] n (act) declaración f; (AUT: also: **~ number**) matrícula

registry ['rɛdʒɪstrɪ] n registro; **~ office** (BRIT) n registro civil; **to get married**

in a ~ office casarse por lo civil

regret [rɪ'ɡrɛt] n sentimiento, pesar m ♦ vt sentir, lamentar; **~fully** adv con pesar; **~table** adj lamentable

regular ['rɛɡjulə*] adj regular; (soldier) profesional; (usual) habitual; (: doctor) de cabecera ♦ n (client etc) cliente/a m/f habitual; **~ly** adv con regularidad; (often) repetidas veces

regulate ['rɛɡjuleɪt] vt controlar; regular

regulation [-'leɪʃən] n (rule) regla, reglamento

rehearsal [rɪ'həːsəl] n ensayo

rehearse [rɪ'həːs] vt ensayar

reign [reɪn] n reinado; (fig) predominio ♦ vi reinar; (fig) imperar

reimburse [riːɪm'bəːs] vt reembolsar

rein [reɪn] n (for horse) rienda

reindeer ['reɪndɪə*] n inv reno

reinforce [riːɪn'fɔːs] vt reforzar; **~d concrete** n hormigón m armado; **~ments** npl (MIL) refuerzos mpl

reinstate [riːɪn'steɪt] vt reintegrar; (tax, law) reinstaurar

reiterate [riː'ɪtəreɪt] vt reiterar, repetir

reject [n 'riːdʒɛkt, vb rɪ'dʒɛkt] n (thing) desecho ♦ vt rechazar; (suggestion) descartar; (coin) expulsar; **~ion** [rɪ'dʒɛkʃən] n rechazo

rejoice [rɪ'dʒɔɪs] vi: **to ~ at** or **over** regocijarse or alegrarse de

rejuvenate [rɪ'dʒuːvəneɪt] vt rejuvenecer

relapse [rɪ'læps] n recaída

relate [rɪ'leɪt] vt (tell) contar, relatar; (connect) relacionar ♦ vi relacionarse; **~d** adj afín; (person) emparentado; **~d to** (subject) relacionado con; **relating to** prep referente a

relation [rɪ'leɪʃən] n (person) familiar m/f, pariente/a m/f; (link) relación f; **~s** npl (relatives) familiares mpl; (relationship) relación f; (personal) relaciones fpl; **~ship** n relación f; (personal) relaciones fpl; (also: family ~ship) parentesco

relative ['rɛlətɪv] n pariente/a m/f, familiar m/f ♦ adj relativo; **~ly** adv (comparatively) relativamente

relax [rɪˈlæks] vi descansar; (unwind) relajarse ♦ vt (one's grip) soltar, aflojar; (control) relajar; (mind, person) descansar; **~ation** [riːlækˈseɪʃən] n descanso; (of rule, control) relajamiento; (entertainment) diversión f; **~ed** adj relajado; (tranquil) tranquilo; **~ing** adj relajante

relay [ˈriːleɪ] n (race) carrera de relevos ♦ vt (RADIO, TV) retransmitir

release [rɪˈliːs] n (liberation) liberación f; (from prison) puesta en libertad; (of gas etc) escape m; (of film etc) estreno; (of record) lanzamiento ♦ vt (prisoner) poner en libertad; (gas) despedir, arrojar; (from wreckage) soltar; (catch, spring etc) desenganchar; (film) estrenar; (book) publicar; (news) difundir

relegate [ˈrelɪgeɪt] vt relegar; (BRIT: SPORT): **to be ~d** bajar a

relent [rɪˈlent] vi ablandarse; **~less** adj implacable

relevant [ˈrelɪvənt] adj (fact) pertinente; **~ to** relacionado con

reliable [rɪˈlaɪəbl] adj (person, firm) de confianza, de fiar; (method, machine) seguro; (source) fidedigno; **reliably** adv: **to be reliably informed that ...** saber de fuente fidedigna que ...

reliance [rɪˈlaɪəns] n: **~ (on)** dependencia de

relic [ˈrelɪk] n (REL) reliquia; (of the past) vestigio

relief [rɪˈliːf] n (from pain, anxiety) alivio; (help, supplies) socorro, ayuda; (ART, GEO) relieve m

relieve [rɪˈliːv] vt (pain) aliviar; (bring help to) ayudar, socorrer; (take over from) sustituir; (: guard) relevar; **to ~ sb of sth** quitar algo a uno; **to ~ o.s.** hacer sus necesidades

religion [rɪˈlɪdʒən] n religión f; **religious** adj religioso

relinquish [rɪˈlɪŋkwɪʃ] vt abandonar; (plan, habit) renunciar a

relish [ˈrelɪʃ] n (CULIN) salsa;

(enjoyment) entusiasmo ♦ vt (food etc) saborear; (enjoy): **to ~ sth** hacerle mucha ilusión a uno algo

relocate [riːləuˈkeɪt] vt cambiar de lugar, mudar ♦ vi mudarse

reluctance [rɪˈlʌktəns] n renuencia

reluctant [rɪˈlʌktənt] adj renuente; **~ly** adv de mala gana

rely on [rɪˈlaɪ] vi depender de; (trust) contar con

remain [rɪˈmeɪn] vi (survive) quedar; (be left) sobrar; (continue) quedar(se), permanecer; **~der** n resto; **~ing** adj que queda(n); (surviving) restante(s); **~s** npl restos mpl

remand [rɪˈmɑːnd] n: **on ~** detenido (bajo custodia) ♦ vt: **to be ~ed in custody** quedar detenido bajo custodia; **~ home** (BRIT) n reformatorio

remark [rɪˈmɑːk] n comentario ♦ vt comentar; **~able** adj (outstanding) extraordinario

remarry [riːˈmærɪ] vi volver a casarse

remedial [rɪˈmiːdɪəl] adj de recuperación

remedy [ˈremədɪ] n remedio ♦ vt remediar, curar

remember [rɪˈmembə*] vt recordar, acordarse de; (bear in mind) tener presente; (send greetings to): **~ me to him** dale recuerdos de mi parte; **remembrance** n recuerdo; **R~ Day** n ≈ día en el que se recuerda a los caídos en las dos guerras mundiales

---

Remembrance Day

En el Reino Unido el domingo más próximo al 11 de noviembre se conoce como **Remembrance Sunday** o **Remembrance Day**, aniversario de la firma del armisticio de 1918 que puso fin a la Primera Guerra Mundial. Ese día, a las once de la mañana (hora en que se firmó el armisticio), se recuerda a los que murieron en las dos guerras

*mundiales con dos minutos de
silencio ante los monumentos a los
caídos. Allí se colocan coronas de
amapolas, flor que también se suele
llevar prendida en el pecho tras pagar
un donativo destinado a los inválidos
de guerra.*

remind [rɪ'maɪnd] *vt*: **to ~ sb to do
sth** recordar a uno que haga algo; **to
~ sb of sth** (*of fact*) recordar algo a
uno; **she ~s me of her mother** me
recuerda a su madre; **~er** *n*
notificación *f*; (*memento*) recuerdo

reminisce [remɪ'nɪs] *vi* recordar (viejas
historias); **reminiscent** *adj*: **to be
reminiscent of sth** recordar algo

remiss [rɪ'mɪs] *adj* descuidado; **it was
~ of him** fue un descuido de su parte

remission [rɪ'mɪʃən] *n* remisión *f*; (*of
prison sentence*) disminución *f* de pena;
(*REL*) perdón *m*

remit [rɪ'mɪt] *vt* (*send: money*) remitir,
enviar; **~tance** *n* remesa, envío

remnant [ˈremnənt] *n* resto; (*of cloth*)
retal *m*; **~s** *npl* (*COMM*) restos *mpl* de
serie

remorse [rɪ'mɔːs] *n* remordimientos
mpl; **~ful** *adj* arrepentido; **~less** *adj*
(*fig*) implacable, inexorable

remote [rɪ'məʊt] *adj* (*distant*) lejano;
(*person*) distante; **~ control** *n*
telecontrol *m*; **~ly** *adv* remotamente;
(*slightly*) levemente

remould [ˈriːməʊld] (*BRIT*) *n* (*tyre*)
neumático *m*/llanta (*AM*)
recauchutado/a

removable [rɪ'muːvəbl] *adj*
(*detachable*) separable

removal [rɪ'muːvəl] *n* (*taking away*) el
quitar; (*BRIT: from house*) mudanza;
(*from office: dismissal*) destitución *f*;
(*MED*) extirpación *f*; **~ van** (*BRIT*) *n*
camión *m* de mudanzas

remove [rɪ'muːv] *vt* quitar; (*employee*)
destituir; (*name: from list*) tachar,
borrar; (*doubt*) disipar; (*abuse*)

suprimir, acabar con; (*MED*) extirpar

Renaissance [rɪ'neɪsɑ̃s] *n*: **the ~** el
Renacimiento

render [ˈrendə*] *vt* (*thanks*) dar; (*aid*)
proporcionar, prestar; (*make*): **to ~ sth
useless** hacer algo inútil; **~ing** *n* (*MUS
etc*) interpretación *f*

rendezvous [ˈrɒndɪvuː] *n* cita

renew [rɪ'njuː] *vt* renovar; (*resume*)
reanudar; (*loan etc*) prorrogar; **~able**
adj renovable; **~al** *n* reanudación *f*;
prórroga

renounce [rɪ'naʊns] *vt* renunciar a;
(*right, inheritance*) renunciar

renovate [ˈrenəveɪt] *vt* renovar

renown [rɪ'naʊn] *n* renombre *m*; **~ed**
adj renombrado

rent [rent] *n* (*for house*) arriendo, renta
♦ *vt* alquilar; **~al** *n* (*for television, car*)
alquiler *m*

rep [rep] *n abbr* = **representative**;
repertory

repair [rɪ'pɛə*] *n* reparación *f*,
compostura ♦ *vt* reparar, componer;
(*shoes*) remendar; **in good/bad ~** en
buen/mal estado; **~ kit** *n* caja de
herramientas

repatriate [riː'pætrɪeɪt] *vt* repatriar

repay [riː'peɪ] (*irreg*) *vt* (*money*)
devolver, reembolsar; (*person*) pagar;
(*debt*) liquidar; (*sb's efforts*) devolver,
corresponder a; **~ment** *n* reembolso,
devolución *f*; (*sum of money*)
recompensa

repeal [rɪ'piːl] *n* revocación *f* ♦ *vt*
revocar

repeat [rɪ'piːt] *n* (*RADIO, TV*) reposición
f ♦ *vt* repetir ♦ *vi* repetirse; **~edly** *adv*
repetidas veces

repel [rɪ'pel] *vt* (*drive away*) rechazar;
(*disgust*) repugnar; **~lent** *adj*
repugnante ♦ *n*: **insect ~lent** crema
(*or loción f*) anti-insectos

repent [rɪ'pent] *vi*: **to ~ (of)**
arrepentirse (de); **~ance** *n*
arrepentimiento

repercussions [riːpə'kʌʃənz] *npl*

consecuencias *fpl*

repertory ['repətəri] *n* (*also:* ~ theatre) teatro de repertorio

repetition [repɪ'tɪʃən] *n* repetición *f*

repetitive [rɪ'petɪtɪv] *adj* repetitivo

replace [rɪ'pleɪs] *vt* (*put back*) devolver a su sitio; (*take the place of*) reemplazar, sustituir; **~ment** *n* (*act*) reposición *f*; (*thing*) recambio; (*person*) suplente *m/f*

replay ['riːpleɪ] *n* (SPORT) desempate *m*; (*of tape, film*) repetición *f*

replenish [rɪ'plenɪʃ] *vt* rellenar; (*stock etc*) reponer

replica ['replɪkə] *n* copia, reproducción *f* (exacta)

reply [rɪ'plaɪ] *n* respuesta, contestación *f* ♦ *vi* contestar, responder

report [rɪ'pɔːt] *n* informe *m*; (PRESS etc) reportaje *m*; (BRIT: *also:* school ~) boletín *m* escolar; (*of gun*) estallido ♦ *vt* informar de; (PRESS etc) hacer un reportaje sobre; (*notify: accident, culprit*) denunciar ♦ *vi* (*make a report*) presentar un informe; (*present o.s.*): **to ~ (to sb)** presentarse (ante uno); **~ card** *n* (US, Scottish) cartilla escolar; **~edly** *adv* según se dice; **~er** *n* periodista *m/f*

repose [rɪ'pəuz] *n*: **in ~** (*face, mouth*) en reposo

reprehensible [reprɪ'hensɪbl] *adj* reprensible, censurable

represent [reprɪ'zent] *vt* representar; (COMM) ser agente de; (*describe*): **to ~ sth as** describir algo como; **~ation** [-'teɪʃən] *n* representación *f*; **~ations** *npl* (*protest*) quejas *fpl*; **~ative** *n* representante *m/f*; (US: POL) diputado/a *m/f* ♦ *adj* representativo

repress [rɪ'pres] *vt* reprimir; **~ion** [-'preʃən] *n* represión *f*

reprieve [rɪ'priːv] *n* (LAW) indulto *m*; (*fig*) alivio

reprisals [rɪ'praɪzlz] *npl* represalias *fpl*

reproach [rɪ'prəutʃ] *n* reproche *m* ♦ *vt*: **to ~ sb for sth** reprochar algo a uno;

~ful *adj* de reproche, de acusación

reproduce [riːprə'djuːs] *vt* reproducir ♦ *vi* reproducirse; **reproduction** [-'dʌkʃən] *n* reproducción *f*

reprove [rɪ'pruːv] *vt*: **to ~ sb for sth** reprochar algo a uno

reptile ['reptaɪl] *n* reptil *m*

republic [rɪ'pʌblɪk] *n* república *f*; **~an** *adj, n* republicano/a *m/f*

repudiate [rɪ'pjuːdɪeɪt] *vt* rechazar; (*violence etc*) repudiar

repulsive [rɪ'pʌlsɪv] *adj* repulsivo

reputable ['repjutəbl] *adj* (*make etc*) de renombre

reputation [repju'teɪʃən] *n* reputación *f*

reputed [rɪ'pjuːtɪd] *adj* supuesto; **~ly** *adv* según dicen o se dice

request [rɪ'kwest] *n* petición *f*; (*formal*) solicitud *f* ♦ *vt*: **to ~ sth of** or **from sb** solicitar algo a uno; **~ stop** *n* (BRIT) parada discrecional

require [rɪ'kwaɪə*] *vt* (*need: subj: person*) necesitar, tener necesidad de; (: *thing, situation*) exigir; (*want*) pedir; **to ~ sb to do sth** pedir a uno que haga algo; **~ment** *n* requisito; (*need*) necesidad *f*

requisition [rekwɪ'zɪʃən] *n*: **~ (for)** solicitud *f* (de) ♦ *vt* (MIL) requisar

rescue ['reskjuː] *n* rescate *m* ♦ *vt* rescatar; **~ party** *n* expedición *f* de salvamento; **~r** *n* salvador(a) *m/f*

research [rɪ'sɜːtʃ] *n* investigaciones *fpl* ♦ *vt* investigar; **~er** *n* investigador(a) *m/f*

resemblance [rɪ'zembləns] *n* parecido *m*

resemble [rɪ'zembl] *vt* parecerse a

resent [rɪ'zent] *vt* tomar a mal; **~ful** *adj* resentido; **~ment** *n* resentimiento *m*

reservation [rezə'veɪʃən] *n* reserva

reserve [rɪ'zɜːv] *n* reserva; (SPORT) suplente *m/f* ♦ *vt* (*seats etc*) reservar; **~s** *npl* (MIL) reserva; **in ~** de reserva; **~d** *adj* reservado

reshuffle [riː'ʃʌfl] *n*: **Cabinet ~** (POL) remodelación *f* del gabinete

residence ['rezɪdəns] n (formal: home) domicilio; (length of stay) permanencia; **~ permit** (BRIT) n permiso de permanencia

resident ['rezɪdənt] n (of area) vecino/a; (in hotel) huésped(a) m/f ♦ adj (population) permanente; (doctor) residente; **~ial** [-'denʃəl] adj residencial

residue ['rezɪdjuː] n resto

resign [rɪ'zaɪn] vt renunciar a ♦ vi dimitir; **to ~ o.s. to** (situation) resignarse a; **~ation** [rezɪg'neɪʃən] n dimisión f; (state of mind) resignación f; **~ed** adj resignado

resilient [rɪ'zɪlɪənt] adj (material) elástico; (person) resistente

resist [rɪ'zɪst] vt resistir, oponerse a; **~ance** n resistencia

resolute ['rezəluːt] adj resuelto; (refusal) tajante

resolution [rezə'luːʃən] n (gen) resolución f

resolve [rɪ'zɔlv] n resolución f ♦ vt resolver ♦ vi: **to ~ to do** resolver hacer; **~d** adj resuelto

resort [rɪ'zɔːt] n (town) centro turístico; (recourse) recurso ♦ vi: **to ~ to** recurrir a; **in the last ~** como último recurso

resounding [rɪ'zaundɪŋ] adj sonoro, (fig) clamoroso

resource [rɪ'sɔːs] n recurso; **~s** npl recursos mpl; **~ful** adj despabilado, ingenioso

respect [rɪs'pekt] n respeto ♦ vt respetar; **~s** npl recuerdos mpl, saludos mpl; **with ~ to** con respecto a; **in this ~** en cuanto a eso; **~able** adj respetable; (large: amount) apreciable; (passable) tolerable; **~ful** adj respetuoso

respective [rɪs'pektɪv] adj respectivo; **~ly** adv respectivamente

respite ['respaɪt] n respiro

respond [rɪs'pɔnd] vi responder; (react) reaccionar; **response** [-'pɔns] n respuesta; reacción f

responsibility [rɪspɔnsɪ'bɪlɪtɪ] n

responsabilidad f

responsible [rɪs'pɔnsɪbl] adj (character) serio, formal; (job) de confianza; (liable): **~ (for)** responsable (de)

responsive [rɪs'pɔnsɪv] adj sensible

rest [rest] n descanso, reposo; (MUS, pause) pausa, silencio; (support) apoyo; (remainder) resto ♦ vi descansar; (be supported): **to ~ on** descansar sobre ♦ vt (lean): **to ~ sth on/against** apoyar algo en o sobre/contra; **the ~ of them** (people, objects) los demás; **it ~s with him to ...** depende de él lo que ...

restaurant ['restərɔŋ] n restaurante m; **~ car** (BRIT) n (RAIL) coche-comedor m

restful ['restful] adj descansado, tranquilo

rest home n residencia para jubilados

restive ['restɪv] adj inquieto; (horse) rebelón(ona)

restless ['restlɪs] adj inquieto

restoration [restə'reɪʃən] n restauración f; devolución f

restore [rɪ'stɔː*] vt (building) restaurar; (sth stolen) devolver; (health) restablecer; (to power) volver a poner a

restrain [rɪs'treɪn] vt (feeling) contener, refrenar; (person): **to ~ (from doing)** disuadir (de hacer); **~ed** adj reservado; **~t** n (restriction) restricción f; (moderation) moderación f; (of manner) reserva

restrict [rɪs'trɪkt] vt restringir, limitar; **~ion** [-kʃən] n restricción f, limitación f; **~ive** adj restrictivo

rest room (US) n aseos mpl

result [rɪ'zʌlt] n resultado ♦ vi: **to ~ in** terminar en, tener por resultado; **as a ~ of** a consecuencia de

resume [rɪ'zjuːm] vt reanudar ♦ vi comenzar de nuevo

résumé ['reɪzjuːmeɪ] n resumen m; (US) currículum m

resumption [rɪ'zʌmpʃən] n reanudación f

resurgence [rɪ'sɜːdʒəns] n resurgimiento

resurrection [rezə'rekʃən] n resurrección f

resuscitate [rɪ'sʌsɪteɪt] vt (MED) resucitar

retail ['riːteɪl] adj, adv por menor; **~er** n detallista m/f; **~ price** n precio de venta al público

retain [rɪ'teɪn] vt (keep) retener, conservar; **~er** n (fee) anticipo

retaliate [rɪ'tælɪeɪt] vi: **to ~ (against)** tomar represalias (contra); **retaliation** [-'eɪʃən] n represalias fpl

retarded [rɪ'tɑːdɪd] adj retrasado

retch [retʃ] vi dársele a uno arcadas

retentive [rɪ'tentɪv] adj (memory) retentivo

retire [rɪ'taɪə*] vi (give up work) jubilarse; (withdraw) retirarse; (go to bed) acostarse; **~d** adj (person) jubilado; **~ment** n (giving up work: state) retiro; (: act) jubilación f; **retiring** adj (leaving) saliente; (shy) retraído

retort [rɪ'tɔːt] vi contestar

retrace [riː'treɪs] vt: **to ~ one's steps** volver sobre sus pasos, desandar lo andado

retract [rɪ'trækt] vt (statement) retirar; (claws) retraer; (undercarriage, aerial) replegar

retrain [riː'treɪn] vt reciclar; **~ing** n readaptación f profesional

retread ['riːtred] n neumático (SP) or llanta (AM) recauchutado/a

retreat [rɪ'triːt] n (place) retiro; (MIL) retirada ♦ vi retirarse

retribution [retrɪ'bjuːʃən] n desquite m

retrieval [rɪ'triːvəl] n recuperación f

retrieve [rɪ'triːv] vt recobrar; (situation, honour) salvar; (COMPUT) recuperar; (error) reparar; **~r** n perro cobrador

retrospect ['retrəspekt] n: **in ~** retrospectivamente; **~ive** [-'spektɪv] adj retrospectivo; (law) retroactivo

return [rɪ'tɜːn] n (going or coming back) vuelta, regreso; (of sth stolen etc) devolución f; (FINANCE: from land, shares) ganancia, ingresos mpl ♦ cpd (journey) de regreso; (BRIT: ticket) de ida y vuelta; (match) de vuelta ♦ vi (person etc: come or go back) volver, regresar; (symptoms etc) reaparecer; (regain): **to ~ to** volver a ♦ vt devolver; (favour, love etc) corresponder a; (verdict) pronunciar; (POL: candidate) elegir; **~s** npl (COMM) ingresos mpl; **in ~ (for)** a cambio (de); **by ~ of post** a vuelta de correo; **many happy ~s (of the day)!** ¡feliz cumpleaños!

reunion [riː'juːnɪən] n (of family) reunión f; (of two people, school) reencuentro

reunite [riːjuː'naɪt] vt reunir; (reconcile) reconciliar

rev [rev] n abbr (AUT) (= revolution) revolución f ♦ vt (also: ~ up) acelerar

reveal [rɪ'viːl] vt revelar; **~ing** adj revelador/a

revel ['revl] vi: **to ~ in sth/in doing sth** gozar de algo/con hacer algo

revenge [rɪ'vendʒ] n venganza; **to take ~ on** vengarse de

revenue ['revənjuː] n ingresos mpl, rentas fpl

reverberate [rɪ'vɜːbəreɪt] vi (sound) resonar, retumbar; (fig: shock) repercutir

reverence ['revərəns] n reverencia

Reverend ['revərənd] adj (in titles): **the ~ John Smith** (Anglican) el Reverendo John Smith; (Catholic) el Padre John Smith; (Protestant) el Pastor John Smith

reversal [rɪ'vɜːsl] n (of order) inversión f; (of direction, policy) cambio; (of decision) revocación f

reverse [rɪ'vɜːs] n (opposite) contrario; (back: of cloth) revés m; (: of coin) reverso; (: of paper) dorso; (AUT: also: ~ gear) marcha atrás; (setback) revés m

♦ adj (order) inverso; (direction) contrario; (process) opuesto ♦ vt (decision, AUT) dar marcha atrás a; (position, function) invertir ♦ vi (BRIT: AUT) dar marcha atrás; **~-charge call** (BRIT) n llamada a cobro revertido; **reversing lights** (BRIT) npl (AUT) luces fpl de retroceso

revert [rɪ'vəːt] vi: to ~ to volver a

review [rɪ'vjuː] n (magazine, MIL) revista; (of deal, film) reseña; (US: examination) repaso, examen m ♦ vt repasar, examinar; (MIL) pasar revista a; (book, film) reseñar; **~er** n crítico/a

revise [rɪ'vaɪz] vt (manuscript) corregir; (opinion) modificar; (price, procedure) revisar ♦ vi (study) repasar; **revision** [rɪ'vɪʒən] n corrección f; modificación f; (for exam) repaso

revival [rɪ'vaɪvəl] n (recovery) reanimación f; (of interest) renacimiento m; (THEATRE) reestreno m; (of faith) despertar m

revive [rɪ'vaɪv] vt resucitar; (custom) restablecer; (hope) despertar; (play) reestrenar ♦ vi (person) volver en sí; (business) reactivarse

revolt [rɪ'vəult] n rebelión f ♦ vi rebelarse, sublevarse ♦ vt dar asco a, repugnar; **~ing** adj asqueroso, repugnante

revolution [rɛvə'luːʃən] n revolución f; **~ary** adj, n revolucionario/a m/f; **~ize** vt revolucionar

revolve [rɪ'vɔlv] vi dar vueltas, girar; (life, discussion): to ~ (a)round girar en torno a

revolver [rɪ'vɔlvə*] n revólver m

revolving [rɪ'vɔlvɪŋ] adj (chair, door etc) giratorio

revue [rɪ'vjuː] n (THEATRE) revista

revulsion [rɪ'vʌlʃən] n asco, repugnancia

reward [rɪ'wɔːd] n premio, recompensa f ♦ vt: to ~ (for) recompensar o premiar (por); **~ing** adj (fig) valioso

rewind [riː'waɪnd] (irreg) vt rebobinar

rewire [riː'waɪə*] vt (house) renovar la instalación eléctrica de

rheumatism [ˈruːmətɪzəm] n reumatismo, reúma m

Rhine [raɪn] n: the ~ el (río) Rin

rhinoceros [raɪ'nɔsərəs] n rinoceronte m

rhododendron [rəudə'dɛndrn] n rododendro

Rhone [rəun] n: the ~ el (río) Ródano

rhubarb [ˈruːbɑːb] n ruibarbo

rhyme [raɪm] n rima; (verse) poesía

rhythm [ˈrɪðm] n ritmo

rib [rɪb] n (ANAT) costilla ♦ vt (mock) tomar el pelo a

ribbon [ˈrɪbən] n cinta; **in ~s** (torn) hecho trizas

rice [raɪs] n arroz m; **~ pudding** n arroz m con leche

rich [rɪtʃ] adj rico; (soil) fértil; (food) pesado; (: sweet) empalagoso; (abundant): **~ in** (minerals etc) rico en; **the ~** npl los ricos; **~es** npl riqueza; **~ly** adv ricamente; (deserved, earned) bien

rickets [ˈrɪkɪts] n raquitismo

rid [rɪd] (pt, pp **rid**) vt: to ~ **sb of sth** librar a uno de algo; to **get ~ of** deshacerse o desembarazarse de

ridden [ˈrɪdn] pp of **ride**

riddle [ˈrɪdl] n (puzzle) acertijo; (mystery) enigma m, misterio ♦ vt: to **be ~d with** (with holes) lleno o plagado de

ride [raɪd] (pt **rode**, pp **ridden**) n paseo; (distance covered) viaje m, recorrido ♦ vi (as sport) montar; (go somewhere: on horse, bicycle) dar un paseo, pasearse; (travel: on bicycle, motorcycle, bus) viajar ♦ vt (a horse) montar a; (a bicycle, motorcycle) andar en; (distance) recorrer; to **take sb for a ~** (fig) engañar a uno; **~r** n (on horse) jinete/a m/f; (on bicycle) ciclista m/f; (on motorcycle) motociclista m/f

ridge [rɪdʒ] n (of hill) cresta; (of roof) caballete m; (wrinkle) arruga

ridicule ['rɪdɪkjuːl] n irrisión f, burla
♦ vt poner en ridículo, burlarse de;
ridiculous [-'dɪkjʊləs] adj ridículo

riding ['raɪdɪŋ] n equitación f; **I like ~
me gusta montar a caballo; ~ school**
n escuela de equitación

rife [raɪf] adj: **to be ~** ser muy común;
to be ~ with abundar en

riffraff ['rɪfræf] n gentuza

rifle ['raɪfl] n rifle m, fusil m ♦ vt
saquear; **~ through** vt (papers)
registrar; **~ range** n campo de tiro; (at
fair) tiro al blanco

rift [rɪft] n (in clouds) claro; (fig:
disagreement) desavenencia

rig [rɪg] n (also: **oil ~: at sea**) plataforma
petrolera ♦ vt (election etc) amañar;
~ out (BRIT) vt disfrazar; **~ up** vt
improvisar; **~ging** n (NAUT) aparejo

right [raɪt] adj (correct) correcto,
exacto; (suitable) indicado, debido; (proper) apropiado; (just) justo; (morally good) bueno; (not left) derecho ♦ n
bueno; (title, claim) derecho; (not left)
derecha ♦ adv bien, correctamente;
(not left) a la derecha; (exactly): **~ now**
ahora mismo ♦ vt enderezar; (correct)
corregir ♦ excl ¡bueno!, ¡está bien!; **to
be ~** (person) tener razón; (answer) ser
correcto; **is that the ~ time?** (of
clock) ¿es esa la hora buena?; **by ~s** en
justicia; **on the ~** a la derecha; **to be
in the ~** tener razón; **~ away** en
seguida; **~ in the middle**
exactamente en el centro; **~ angle** n
ángulo recto; **~eous** ['raɪtʃəs] adj
justado, honrado; (anger) justificado;
~ful adj legítimo; **~-handed** adj
diestro; **~-hand man** n brazo
derecho; **~-hand side** n derecha; **~ly**
adv correctamente, debidamente; (with
reason) con razón; **~ of way** n (on
path etc) derecho de paso; (AUT)
prioridad f; **~-wing** adj (POL)
derechista

rigid ['rɪdʒɪd] adj rígido; (person, ideas)
inflexible

rigmarole ['rɪgmərəʊl] n galimatías m
inv

rigorous ['rɪgərəs] adj riguroso

rile [raɪl] vt irritar

rim [rɪm] n borde m; (of spectacles) aro;
(of wheel) llanta

rind [raɪnd] n (of bacon) corteza; (of
lemon etc) cáscara; (of cheese) costra

ring [rɪŋ] (pt **rang**, pp **rung**) n (of
metal) aro; (on finger) anillo; (of people)
corro; (of objects) círculo; (of gang)
banda; (for boxing) cuadrilátero; (of
circus) pista; (bull ~) ruedo, plaza;
(sound of bell) toque m ♦ vi (on
telephone) llamar por teléfono; (bell)
repicar; (doorbell, phone) sonar; (also:
~ out) sonar; (ears) zumbar ♦ vt (BRIT:
TEL) llamar, telefonear; (bell etc) hacer
sonar; (doorbell) tocar; **to give sb a ~**
(BRIT: TEL) llamar o telefonear a
alguien; **~ back** (BRIT) vt, vi (TEL)
devolver la llamada; **~ off** (BRIT) vi
(TEL) colgar, cortar la comunicación;
~ up (BRIT) vt (TEL) llamar, telefonear;
~ing n (of bell) repique m; (of phone)
el sonar; (in ears) zumbido; **~ing tone**
n (TEL) tono de llamada; **~leader** n (of
gang) cabecilla m; **~lets** ['rɪŋlɪts] npl
rizos mpl, bucles mpl; **~ road** (BRIT) n
carretera periférica o de circunvalación

rink [rɪŋk] n (also: **ice ~**) pista de hielo

rinse [rɪns] n aclarado; (dye) tinte m
♦ vt aclarar; (mouth) enjuagar

riot ['raɪət] n motín m, disturbio ♦ vi
amotinarse; **to run ~** desmandarse;
~ous adj alborotado; (party) bullicioso

rip [rɪp] n rasgón m, rasgadura ♦ vt
rasgar, desgarrar ♦ vi rasgarse,
desgarrarse; **~cord** n cabo de desgarre

ripe [raɪp] adj maduro; **~n** vt madurar;
(cheese) curar ♦ vi madurar

ripple ['rɪpl] n onda, rizo; (sound)
murmullo ♦ vi rizarse

rise [raɪz] (pt **rose**, pp **risen**) n (slope)
cuesta, pendiente f; (hill) altura; (BRIT:
in wages) aumento; (in prices,
temperature) subida; (fig: to power etc)

ascenso ♦ vi subir; (waters) crecer; (sun, moon) salir; (person: from bed etc) levantarse; (also: ~ up: rebel) sublevarse; (in rank) ascender; **to give ~ to** dar lugar o origen a; **to ~ to the occasion** ponerse a la altura de las circunstancias; **risen** [rɪzn] pp of **rise; rising** adj (increasing: number) creciente; (: prices) en aumento or alza; (tide) creciente; (sun, moon) naciente

risk [rɪsk] n riesgo, peligro ♦ vt arriesgar; (run the ~ of) exponerse a; **to take** or **run the ~ of doing** correr el riesgo de hacer; **at ~** en peligro; **at one's own ~** bajo su propia responsabilidad; **~y** adj arriesgado, peligroso

rissole ['rɪsəʊl] n croqueta

rite [raɪt] n rito; **last ~s** exequias fpl

ritual ['rɪtjʊəl] adj ritual ♦ n ritual m, rito

rival ['raɪvl] n rival m/f; (in business) competidor(a) m/f ♦ adj rival, opuesto ♦ vt competir con; **~ry** n competencia

river ['rɪvə*] n río ♦ cpd (port) de río; (traffic) fluvial; **up/down ~** río arriba/abajo; **~bank** n orilla (del río); **~bed** n lecho, cauce m

rivet ['rɪvɪt] n roblón m, remache m ♦ vt (fig) captar

Riviera [rɪvɪ'eərə] n: **the (French) ~** la Costa Azul (francesa)

road [rəʊd] n camino; (motorway etc) carretera; (in town) calle f ♦ cpd (accident) de tráfico; **major/minor ~** carretera principal/secundaria; **~ accident** n accidente m de tráfico; **~block** n barricada; **~hog** n loco/a del volante; **~ map** n mapa m de carreteras; **~ rage** n agresividad en la carretera; **~ safety** n seguridad f vial; **~side** n borde m (del camino); **~sign** n señal f de tráfico; **~ user** n usuario/a de la vía pública; **~way** n calzada; **~works** npl obras fpl; **~worthy** adj (car) en buen estado para circular

roam [rəʊm] vi vagar

roar [rɔ:*] n rugido, (of vehicle, storm) estruendo; (of laughter) carcajada ♦ vi rugir; hacer estruendo; **to ~ with laughter** reírse a carcajadas; **to do a ~ing trade** hacer buen negocio

roast [rəʊst] n carne f asada, asado ♦ vt asar; (coffee) tostar; **~ beef** n rosbif m

rob [rɒb] vt robar; **to ~ sb of sth** robar algo a uno; (fig: deprive) quitar algo a uno; **~ber** n ladrón/ona m/f; **~bery** n robo

robe [rəʊb] n (for ceremony etc) toga; (also: bath~, us) albornoz m

robin ['rɒbɪn] n petirrojo

robot ['rəʊbɒt] n robot m

robust [rəʊ'bʌst] adj robusto, fuerte

rock [rɒk] n roca; (boulder) peña, peñasco; (us: small stone) piedrecita; (BRIT: sweet) ≈ pirulí ♦ vt (swing gently: cradle) balancear, mecer; (: child) arrullar; (shake) sacudir ♦ vi mecerse, balancearse; sacudirse; **on the ~s** (drink) con hielo; (marriage etc) en ruinas; **~ and roll** n rocanrol m; **~-bottom** adj (fig) punto más bajo; **~ery** n cuadro alpino

rocket ['rɒkɪt] n cohete m

rocking ['rɒkɪŋ]: **~ chair** n mecedora; **~ horse** n caballo de balancín

rocky ['rɒkɪ] adj rocoso

rod [rɒd] n vara, varilla; (also: fishing ~) caña

rode [rəʊd] pt of **ride**

rodent ['rəʊdnt] n roedor m

roe [rəʊ] n (species: also: ~ deer) corzo; (of fish): **hard/soft ~** hueva/lecha

rogue [rəʊg] n pícaro, pillo

role [rəʊl] n papel m

roll [rəʊl] n rollo; (of bank notes) fajo; (also: bread ~) panecillo; (register, list) lista, nómina; (sound: of drums etc) redoble m ♦ vt hacer rodar; (also: ~ up: string) enrollar; (: sleeves) arremangar; (cigarette) liar; (also: ~ out: pastry) aplanar; (flatten: road, lawn) apisonar ♦ vi rodar; (drum) redoblar; (ship) balancearse; **~ about** or **around** vi (person) revolcarse; (object) rodar (por); **~ by** vi (time) pasar; **~ over** vi dar una vuelta; **~ up** vi (inf: arrive) aparecer ♦ vt (carpet) arrollar; **~ call** n: **to take a ~ call** pasar lista; **~er** n (road) apisonadora; (wheel) rueda; (for hair) rulo; **~erblade** n patín m (en línea); **~er coaster** n montaña rusa; **~er skates** npl patines mpl de rueda

rolling ['rəʊlɪŋ] adj (landscape) ondulado; **~ pin** n rodillo (de cocina); **~ stock** n (RAIL) material m rodante

ROM [rɔm] n abbr (COMPUT: = read only memory) ROM f

Roman ['rəʊmən] adj romano/a; **~ Catholic** adj, n católico/a m/f (romano/a)

romance [rə'mæns] n (love affair) amor m; (charm) lo romántico; (novel) novela de amor

Romania [ruː'meɪnɪə] n = **Rumania**

Roman numeral n número romano

romantic [rə'mæntɪk] adj romántico

Rome [rəʊm] n Roma

romp [rɔmp] n retozo, juego ♦ vi (also: **~ about**) jugar, brincar

rompers ['rɔmpəz] npl pelele m

roof [ruːf] (pl **~s**) n (gen) techo; (of house) techo, tejado ♦ vt techar, poner techo a; **the ~ of the mouth** el paladar; **~ing** n techumbre f; **~ rack** n (AUT) baca, portaequipajes m inv

rook [rʊk] n (bird) graja; (CHESS) torre f

room [ruːm] n cuarto, habitación f, pieza (esp AM); (also: **bed~**) dormitorio; (in school etc) sala; (space, scope) sitio, cabida; **~s** npl (lodging) alojamiento; **"~s to let"**, **"~s for rent"** (US) "se alquilan cuartos"; **single/double ~** habitación individual/doble o para dos personas; **~ing house** (US) n pensión f; **~mate** n compañero/a de cuarto; **~ service** n servicio de habitaciones; **~y** adj espacioso; (garment) amplio

roost [ruːst] vi pasar la noche

rooster ['ruːstə*] n gallo

root [ruːt] n raíz f ♦ vi arraigarse; **~ about** vi (fig) buscar y rebuscar; **~ for** vt fus (support) apoyar a; **~ out** vt desarraigar

rope [rəʊp] n cuerda; (NAUT) cable m ♦ vt (tie) atar o amarrar con (una) cuerda; (climbers: also: **~ together**) encordarse; (an area: also: **~ off**) acordonar; **to know the ~s** (fig) conocer los trucos (del oficio); **~ in** vt (fig): **to ~ sb in** persuadir a uno a tomar parte

rosary ['rəʊzərɪ] n rosario

rose [rəʊz] pt of **rise** ♦ n rosa; (shrub) rosal m; (on watering can) roseta

rosé ['rəʊzeɪ] n vino rosado

rosebud ['rəʊzbʌd] n capullo de rosa

rosebush ['rəʊzbʊʃ] n rosal m

rosemary ['rəʊzmərɪ] n romero

roster ['rɔstə*] n: **duty ~** lista de deberes

rostrum ['rɔstrəm] n tribuna

rosy ['rəʊzɪ] adj rosado, sonrosado; **a ~ future** un futuro prometedor

rot [rɔt] n podredumbre f; (fig: pej) tonterías fpl ♦ vt pudrir ♦ vi pudrirse

rota ['rəʊtə] n (sistema m de) turnos mpl

rotary ['rəʊtərɪ] adj rotativo

rotate [rəʊ'teɪt] vt (revolve) hacer girar, dar vueltas a; (jobs) alternar ♦ vi girar, dar vueltas; **rotating** adj rotativo; **rotation** [-'teɪʃən] n rotación f

rotten ['rɔtn] adj podrido; (dishonest) corrompido; (inf: bad) pocho; **to feel ~** (ill) sentirse fatal

rotund [rəʊ'tʌnd] adj regordete

rouble ['ruːbl] (US **ruble**) n rublo

rough [rʌf] adj (skin, surface) áspero; (terrain) quebrado; (road) desigual, (voice) bronco; (person, manner) tosco, grosero; (weather) borrascoso; (treatment) brutal; (sea) picado; (town, area) peligroso; (cloth) basto; (plan) preliminar; (guess) aproximado ♦ n (GOLF): **in the ~** en las hierbas altas; **to ~ it** vivir sin comodidades; **to sleep ~**

(BRIT) pasar la noche al raso; **~age** n fibra(s) f(pl); **~-and-ready** adj improvisado; **~ copy** n borrador m; **~ draft** n = **~ copy**; **~ly** adv (handle) torpemente; (make) toscamente; (speak) groseramente; (approximately) aproximadamente; **~ness** n (of surface) aspereza; (of person) rudeza

roulette [ru:'let] n ruleta

Rumania [ru:'meɪnɪə] n = **Rumania**

round [raund] adj redondo ♦ n círculo; (BRIT: of toast) rebanada; (of policeman) ronda; (of milkman) recorrido; (of doctor) visitas fpl; (game: of cards, in competition) partida; (of ammunition) cartucho; (BOXING) asalto; (of talks) ronda ♦ vt (corner) doblar ♦ prep alrededor de; (surrounding): **~ his neck/the table** su cuello/alrededor de la mesa; (in a circular movement): **to move ~ the room/sail ~ the world** dar una vuelta a la habitación/ circumnavigar el mundo; (in various directions): **to move ~ a room/house** moverse por toda la habitación/casa; (approximately) alrededor de ♦ adv: **all ~** por todos lados; **the long way ~** por el camino menos directo; **all the year ~** durante todo el año; **it's just ~ the corner** (fig) está a la vuelta de la esquina; **the clock** adv las 24 horas; **to go ~ to sb's (house)** ir a casa de uno; **to go ~ the back** pasar por atrás; **enough to go ~** bastante (para todos); **a ~ of applause** una salva de aplausos; **a ~ of drinks/ sandwiches** una ronda de bebidas/ bocadillos; **~ off** vt (speech etc) acabar, poner término a; **~ up** vt (cattle) acorralar; (people) reunir; (price) redondear; **~about** (BRIT) n (AUT) isleta; (at fair) tiovivo ♦ adj (route, means) indirecto; **~ers** n (game) juego similar al béisbol; **~ly** adv (fig) rotundamente; **~ trip** n viaje m de ida y vuelta; **~up** n rodeo; (of criminals) redada; (of news) resumen m

rouse [rauz] vt (wake up) despertar; (stir up) suscitar; **rousing** adj (cheer, welcome) caluroso

route [ru:t] n ruta, camino; (of bus) recorrido; (of shipping) derrota

routine [ru:'ti:n] adj rutinario ♦ n rutina; (THEATRE) número

rove [rəuv] vt vagar o errar por

row¹ [rəu] n (line) fila, hilera; (KNITTING) pasada ♦ vi (in boat) remar ♦ vt conducir remando; **4 days in a ~** 4 días seguidos

row² [rau] n (racket) escándalo; (dispute) bronca, pelea; (scolding) regaño ♦ vi pelear(se)

rowboat ['rəubəut] (US) n bote m de remos

rowdy ['raudɪ] adj (person: noisy) ruidoso; (occasion) alborotado

rowing ['rəuɪŋ] n remo; **~ boat** (BRIT) n bote m de remos

royal ['rɔɪəl] adj real; **R~ Air Force** n Fuerzas fpl Aéreas Británicas; **~ty** n (~ persons) familia real; (payment to author) derechos mpl de autor

rpm abbr (= revs per minute) r.p.m.

R.S.V.P. abbr (= répondez s'il vous plaît) SRC

Rt. Hon. abbr (BRIT: = Right Honourable) título honorífico de diputado

rub [rʌb] vt frotar; (scrub) restregar ♦ n: **to give sth a ~** frotar algo; **to ~ sb up or ~ sb** (US) **the wrong way** entrarle uno por mal ojo; **~ off** vi borrarse; **~ off on** vt fus influir en; **~ out** vt borrar

rubber ['rʌbə*] n caucho, goma; (BRIT: eraser) goma de borrar; **~ band** n goma, gomita; **~ plant** n ficus m

rubbish ['rʌbɪʃ] n basura; (waste) desperdicios mpl; (fig: pej) tonterías fpl; (junk) pacotilla; **~ bin** (BRIT) n cubo (SP) or bote m (AM) de la basura; **~ dump** n vertedero, basurero

rubble ['rʌbl] n escombros mpl

ruble ['ru:bl] (US) n = **rouble**

ruby ['ru:bɪ] n rubí m

rucksack [ˈrʌksæk] n mochila

rudder [ˈrʌdə*] n timón m

ruddy [ˈrʌdɪ] adj (face) rubicundo; (inf: damned) condenado

rude [ruːd] adj (impolite: person) mal educado; (: word, manners) grosero; (crude) crudo; (indecent) indecente; **~ness** n descortesía

ruffle [ˈrʌfl] vt (hair) despeinar; (clothes) arrugar; **to get ~d** (fig: person) alterarse

rug [rʌg] n alfombra; (BRIT: blanket) manta

rugby [ˈrʌgbɪ] n (also: ~ football) rugby m

rugged [ˈrʌgɪd] adj (landscape) accidentado; (features) robusto

ruin [ˈruːɪn] n ruina ♦ vt arruinar; (spoil) estropear; **~s** npl ruinas fpl, restos mpl

rule [ruːl] n (norm) norma, costumbre f; (regulation, ruler) regla; (government) dominio ♦ vt (country, person) gobernar ♦ vi gobernar; (LAW) fallar; **as a ~** por regla general; **~ out** vt excluir; **~d** adj (paper) rayado; **~r** n (sovereign) soberano; (for measuring) regla; **ruling** adj (party) gobernante, (class) dirigente ♦ n (LAW) fallo, decisión f

rum [rʌm] n ron m

Rumania [ruːˈmeɪnɪə] n Rumanía; **~n** adj rumano/a ♦ n rumano/a m/f; (LING) rumano

rumble [ˈrʌmbl] n (noise) ruido sordo ♦ vi retumbar, hacer un ruido sordo; (stomach, pipe) sonar

rummage [ˈrʌmɪdʒ] vi (search) hurgar

rumour [ˈruːmə*] (US **rumor**) n rumor m ♦ vt: **it is ~ed that ...** se rumorea que ...

rump [rʌmp] n (of animal) ancas fpl, grupa; **~ steak** n filete m de lomo

rumpus [ˈrʌmpəs] n lío, gresca

run [rʌn] (pt **ran**, pp **run**) n (fast pace): **at a ~** corriendo; (SPORT, in tights) carrera; (outing) paseo, excursión f; (distance travelled) trayecto; (series)

serie f; (THEATRE) temporada; (SKI) pista ♦ vt (operate: business) dirigir; (: competition, course) organizar; (: hotel, house) administrar, llevar; (COMPUT) ejecutar; (pass: hand) pasar; (PRESS: feature) publicar ♦ vi correr; (work: machine) funcionar, marchar; (bus, train: operate) circular, ir; (: travel) ir; (continue: play) seguir; (: contract) ser válido; (flow: river) fluir; (colours, washing) desteñirse; (in election) ser candidato; **there was a ~ on** (meat, tickets) hubo mucha demanda de; **in the long ~** a la larga; **on the ~** en fuga; **I'll ~ you to the station** te llevaré a la estación (en coche); **to ~ a risk** correr un riesgo; **to ~ a bath** llenar la bañera; **~ about** or **around** vi (children) correr por todos lados; **~ across** vt fus (find) dar or topar con; **~ away** vi huir; **~ down** vt (production) ir reduciendo; (factory) ir restringiendo la producción en; (subj: car) atropellar; (criticize) criticar; **to be ~ down** (person: tired) estar debilitado; **~ in** (BRIT) vt (car) rodar; **~ into** vt fus (meet: person, trouble) tropezar con; (collide with) chocar con; **~ off** vt (water) dejar correr; (copies) sacar ♦ vi huir corriendo; **~ out** vi (person) salir corriendo; (liquid) irse; (lease) caducar, vencer; (money etc) acabarse; **~ out of** vt fus quedar sin; **~ over** vt (AUT) atropellar ♦ vt fus (revise) repasar; **~ through** vt fus (instructions) repasar; **~ up** vt (debt) contraer; **to ~ up against** (difficulties) tropezar con; **~away** adj (horse) desbocado; (truck) sin frenos; (child) escapado de casa

rung [rʌŋ] pp of **ring** ♦ n (of ladder) escalón m, peldaño

runner [ˈrʌnə*] n (in race: person) corredor(a) m/f; (: horse) caballo; (on sledge) patín m; **~ bean** (BRIT) n ≈ judía verde; **~-up** n subcampeón/ona m/f

running [ˈrʌnɪŋ] n (sport) atletismo;

(business) administración f ♦ adj (water, costs) corriente; (commentary) continuo; **to be in/out of the ~ for sth** tener/no tener posibilidades de ganar algo; **6 days** ~ 6 días seguidos; **~ commentary** n (TV, RADIO) comentario en directo; (on guided tour etc) comentario detallado; **~ costs** npl gastos mpl corrientes

runny ['rʌnɪ] adj fluido; (nose, eyes) gastante

run-of-the-mill adj común y corriente

runt [rʌnt] n (also pej) redrojo, enano

run-up n: ~ **to** (election etc) período previo a

runway ['rʌnweɪ] n (AVIAT) pista de aterrizaje

rural ['ruərl] adj rural

rush [rʌʃ] n ímpetu m; (hurry) prisa; (COMM) demanda repentina; (current) corriente f fuerte; (of feeling) torrente; (BOT) junco ♦ vt apresurar; (work) hacer de prisa ♦ vi correr, precipitarse; **~ hour** n horas fpl punta

rusk [rʌsk] n bizcocho tostado

Russia ['rʌʃə] n Rusia; **~n** adj ruso/a ♦ n ruso/a m/f; (LING) ruso

rust [rʌst] n herrumbre f, moho ♦ vi oxidarse

rustic ['rʌstɪk] adj rústico

rustle ['rʌsl] vi susurrar ♦ vt (paper) hacer crujir

rustproof ['rʌstpru:f] adj inoxidable

rusty ['rʌstɪ] adj oxidado

rut [rʌt] n surco; (ZOOL) celo; **to be in a ~** ser esclavo de la rutina

ruthless ['ru:θlɪs] adj despiadado

rye [raɪ] n centeno

S, s

Sabbath ['sæbəθ] n domingo; (Jewish) sábado

sabotage ['sæbətɑ:ʒ] n sabotaje m ♦ vt sabotear

saccharin(e) ['sækərɪn] n sacarina

sachet ['sæʃeɪ] n sobrecito

sack [sæk] n (bag) saco, costal m ♦ vt (dismiss) despedir; (plunder) saquear; **to get the ~** ser despedido; **~ing** n despido; (material) arpillera

sacred ['seɪkrɪd] adj sagrado, santo

sacrifice ['sækrɪfaɪs] n sacrificio ♦ vt sacrificar

sad [sæd] adj (unhappy) triste; (deplorable) lamentable

saddle ['sædl] n silla (de montar); (of cycle) sillín m ♦ vt (horse) ensillar; **to be ~d with sth** (inf) quedar cargado con algo; **~bag** n alforja

sadistic [sə'dɪstɪk] adj sádico

sadly ['sædlɪ] adv lamentablemente; **to be ~ lacking** in estar por desgracia carente de

sadness ['sædnɪs] n tristeza

s.a.e. abbr (= stamped addressed envelope) sobre con las propias señas de uno y con sello

safari [sə'fɑ:rɪ] n safari m

safe [seɪf] adj (out of danger) fuera de peligro; (not dangerous, sure) seguro; (unharmed) ileso ♦ n caja de caudales, caja fuerte; **~ and sound** sano y salvo; **(just) to be on the ~ side** para mayor seguridad; **~-conduct** n salvoconducto; **~-deposit** n (vault) cámara acorazada; (box) caja de seguridad; **~guard** n protección f, garantía ♦ vt proteger, defender; **~keeping** n custodia; **~ly** adv seguramente, con seguridad; **to arrive ~ly** llegar bien; **~ sex** n sexo seguro or sin riesgo

safety ['seɪftɪ] n seguridad f; **~ belt** n cinturón m (de seguridad); **~ pin** n imperdible m (SP), seguro (AM); **~ valve** n válvula de seguridad

saffron ['sæfrən] n azafrán m

sag [sæg] vi aflojarse

sage [seɪdʒ] n (herb) salvia; (man) sabio

Sagittarius [sædʒɪ'tɛərɪəs] n Sagitario

Sahara [sə'hɑ:rə] n: **the ~ (Desert)** el (desierto del) Sáhara

said [sed] pt, pp of **say**

sail [seɪl] n (on boat) vela; (trip): **to go for a ~** dar un paseo en barco ♦ vt (boat) gobernar ♦ vi (travel: ship) navegar; (SPORT) hacer vela; (begin voyage) salir; **they ~ed into Copenhagen** arribaron a Copenhague; **~ through** vt fus (exam) aprobar sin ningún problema; **~boat** (US) n velero, barco de vela; **~ing** n (SPORT) vela; **to go ~ing** hacer vela; **~ing boat** n barco de vela; **~ing ship** n velero; **~or** n marinero, marino

saint [seɪnt] n santo; **~ly** adj santo

sake [seɪk] n: **for the ~ of** por

salad ['sæləd] n ensalada; **~ bowl** n ensaladera; **~ cream** (BRIT) n (especie f de) mayonesa; **~ dressing** n aliño

salary ['sælərɪ] n sueldo

sale [seɪl] n venta; (at reduced prices) liquidación f, saldo; (auction) subasta; **~s** npl (total amount sold) ventas fpl, facturación f; **"for ~"** "se vende"; **~ en venta; on ~ or return** (goods) venta por reposición; **~room** n sala de subastas; **~s assistant** (US **~s clerk**) n dependiente/a m/f; **salesman/woman** (irreg) n (in shop) dependiente/a m/f; (representative) viajante m/f

salmon ['sæmən] n inv salmón m

salon ['sælɔn] n (hairdressing ~) peluquería; (beauty ~) salón m de belleza

saloon [sə'lu:n] n (US) bar m, taberna; (BRIT: AUT) (coche m de) turismo; (ship's lounge) cámara, salón m

salt [sɔlt] n sal f ♦ vt salar; (put ~ on) poner sal en; **~ cellar** n salero; **~water** adj de agua salada; **~y** adj salado

salute [sə'lu:t] n saludo; (of guns) salva ♦ vt saludar

salvage ['sælvɪdʒ] n (saving) salvamento, recuperación f; (things saved) objetos mpl salvados ♦ vt salvar

salvation [sæl'veɪʃən] n salvación f;

S~ Army n Ejército de Salvación

same [seɪm] adj mismo ♦ pron: **the ~** el/la mismo/a, los/las mismos/as; **the ~ book as** el mismo libro que; **at the ~ time** (at the ~ moment) al mismo tiempo; (yet) sin embargo; **all ~ or just the ~** sin embargo, aun así; **to do the ~ (as sb)** hacer lo mismo (que uno); **the ~ to you!** ¡igualmente!

sample ['sɑ:mpl] n muestra ♦ vt (food) probar; (wine) catar

sanction ['sæŋkʃən] n aprobación f ♦ vt sancionar; aprobar; **~s** npl (POL) sanciones fpl

sanctity ['sæŋktɪtɪ] n santidad f; (inviolability) inviolabilidad f

sanctuary ['sæŋktjuərɪ] n santuario; (refuge) asilo, refugio; (for wildlife) reserva

sand [sænd] n arena; (beach) playa ♦ vt (also: ~ down) lijar

sandal ['sændl] n sandalia

sand: ~box (US) n = **~pit; ~castle** n castillo de arena; **~ dune** n duna; **~paper** n papel m de lija; **~pit** n (for children) cajón m de arena; **~stone** n piedra arenisca

sandwich ['sændwɪtʃ] n bocadillo (SP), sandwich m, emparedado (AM) ♦ vt intercalar; **~ed between** apretujado entre; **cheese/ham ~** sandwich de queso/jamón; **~ course** (BRIT) n curso de medio tiempo

sandy ['sændɪ] adj arenoso; (colour) rojizo

sane [seɪn] adj cuerdo; (sensible) sensato

sang [sæŋ] pt of **sing**

sanitary ['sænɪtərɪ] adj sanitario; (clean) higiénico; **~ towel** (US **~ napkin**) n paño higiénico, compresa

sanitation [sænɪ'teɪʃən] n (in house) servicios mpl higiénicos; (in town) servicio de desinfección; **~ department** (US) n departamento de limpieza y recogida de basuras

sanity ['sænɪtɪ] n cordura; (of

judgment) sensatez f

sank [sæŋk] pt of **sink**

Santa Claus [sænta'klɔːz] n San Nicolás, Papá Noel

sap [sæp] n (of plants) savia ♦ vt (strength) minar, agotar

sapling ['sæplɪŋ] n árbol nuevo or joven

sapphire ['sæfaɪə*] n zafiro

sarcasm ['sɑːkæzm] n sarcasmo

sardine [sɑː'diːn] n sardina

Sardinia [sɑː'dɪnɪə] n Cerdeña

sash [sæʃ] n faja

sat [sæt] pt, pp of **sit**

Satan ['seɪtn] n Satanás m

satchel ['sætʃl] n (child's) cartera (SP), mochila (AM)

satellite ['sætəlaɪt] n satélite m; ~ **dish** n antena de televisión por satélite; ~ **television** n televisión f vía satélite

satin ['sætɪn] n raso ♦ adj de raso

satire ['sætaɪə*] n sátira

satisfaction [sætɪs'fækʃən] n satisfacción f

satisfactory [sætɪs'fæktərɪ] adj satisfactorio

satisfy ['sætɪsfaɪ] vt satisfacer; (convince) convencer; ~**ing** adj satisfactorio

Saturday ['sætədɪ] n sábado

sauce [sɔːs] n salsa; (sweet) crema; jarabe m; ~**pan** n cacerola, olla

saucer ['sɔːsə*] n platillo

Saudi ['saʊdɪ]: ~ **Arabia** n Arabia Saudí or Saudita; ~ **(Arabian)** adj, n saudí m/f, saudita m/f

sauna ['sɔːnə] n sauna

saunter ['sɔːntə*] vi: **to** ~ **in/out** entrar/salir sin prisa

sausage ['sɔsɪdʒ] n salchicha; ~ **roll** n empanadita de salchicha

sauté ['səʊteɪ] adj salteado

savage ['sævɪdʒ] adj (cruel, fierce) feroz, furioso; (primitive) salvaje ♦ n salvaje m/f ♦ vt (attack) embestir

save [seɪv] vt (rescue) salvar, rescatar; (money, time) ahorrar; (put by, keep;

seat) guardar; (COMPUT) salvar (y guardar); (avoid: trouble) evitar; (SPORT) parar ♦ vi (also: ~ up) ahorrar ♦ n (SPORT) parada ♦ prep salvo, excepto

saving ['seɪvɪŋ] n (on price etc) economía ♦ adj: **the** ~ **grace** of el único mérito de; ~**s** npl ahorros mpl; ~**s account** n cuenta de ahorros; ~**s bank** n caja de ahorros

saviour ['seɪvjə*] (US **savior**) n salvador(a) m/f

savour ['seɪvə*] (US **savor**) vt saborear; ~**y** adj sabroso; (dish: not sweet) salado

saw [sɔː] (pt **sawed**, pp **sawed** or **sawn**) pt of **see** ♦ n (tool) sierra ♦ vt serrar; ~**dust** n (a)serrín m; ~**mill** n aserradero; ~**n-off shotgun** n escopeta de cañones recortados

saxophone ['sæksəfəʊn] n saxófono

say [seɪ] (pt, pp **said**) n: **to have one's** ~ expresar su opinión ♦ vt decir; **to have a** or **some** ~ **in sth** tener voz or tener que ver en algo; **to** ~ **yes/no** decir que sí/no; **could you** ~ **that again?** ¿podría repetir eso?; **that is to** ~ es decir; **that goes without** ~**ing** ni que decir tiene; ~**ing** n dicho, refrán m

scab [skæb] n costra; (pej) esquirol m

scaffold ['skæfəʊld] n cadalso; ~**ing** n andamio, andamiaje m

scald [skɔːld] n escaldadura ♦ vt escaldar

scale [skeɪl] n (gen, MUS) escala; (of fish) escama; (of salaries, fees etc) escalafón m ♦ vt (mountain) escalar; (tree) trepar; ~**s** npl (for weighing: small) balanza; (: large) báscula; **on a large** ~ en gran escala; ~ **of charges** tarifa, lista de precios; ~ **down** vt reducir a escala

scallop ['skɒləp] n (ZOOL) venera; (SEWING) festón m

scalp [skælp] n cabellera ♦ vt escalpar

scampi ['skæmpɪ] npl gambas fpl

scan [skæn] vt (examine) escudriñar; (glance at quickly) dar un vistazo a; (TV,

RADAR) explorar, registrar ♦ *n* (*MED*): **to have a ~** pasar por el escáner

scandal ['skændl] *n* escándalo; (*gossip*) chismes *mpl*

Scandinavia [skændɪ'neɪvɪə] *n* Escandinavia; **~n** *adj*, *n* escandinavo/a *m/f*

scant [skænt] *adj* escaso; **~y** *adj* (*meal*) insuficiente; (*clothes*) ligero

scapegoat ['skeɪpgəut] *n* cabeza de turco, chivo expiatorio

scar [skɑ:] *n* cicatriz *f*; (*fig*) señal *f* ♦ *vt* dejar señales en

scarce [skɛəs] *adj* escaso; **to make o.s. ~** (*inf*) esfumarse; **~ly** *adv* apenas; **scarcity** *n* escasez *f*

scare [skɛə*] *n* susto, sobresalto; (*panic*) pánico ♦ *vt* asustar, espantar; **to ~ sb stiff** dar a uno un susto de muerte; **bomb ~** amenaza de bomba; **~ off** *or* **away** *vt* ahuyentar; **~crow** *n* espantapájaros *m inv*; **~d** *adj*: **to be ~d** estar asustado

scarf [skɑ:f] (*pl* **~s** *or* **scarves**) *n* (*long*) bufanda; (*square*) pañuelo

scarlet ['skɑ:lɪt] *adj* escarlata; **~ fever** *n* escarlatina

scarves [skɑ:vz] *npl of* **scarf**

scary ['skɛərɪ] (*inf*) *adj* espeluznante

scathing ['skeɪðɪŋ] *adj* mordaz

scatter ['skætə*] *vt* (*spread*) esparcir, desparramar; (*put to flight*) dispersar ♦ *vi* desparramarse; dispersarse; **~brained** *adj* ligero de cascos

scavenger ['skævəndʒə*] *n* (*person*) basurero/a

scenario [sɪ'nɑːrɪəu] *n* (*THEATRE*) argumento; (*CINEMA*) guión *m*; (*fig*) escenario

scene [si:n] *n* (*THEATRE, fig etc*) escena; (*of crime etc*) escenario; (*view*) panorama *m*; (*fuss*) escándalo; **~ry** *n* (*THEATRE*) decorado; (*landscape*) paisaje *m*; **scenic** *adj* pintoresco

scent [sɛnt] *n* perfume *m*, olor *m*; (*fig: track*) rastro, pista

sceptic ['skɛptɪk] (*US* **skeptic**) *n*

escéptico/a; **~al** *adj* escéptico

sceptre ['sɛptə*] (*US* **scepter**) *n* cetro

schedule ['ʃɛdjuːl, (*US*) 'skɛdjuːl] *n* (*timetable*) horario; (*of events*) programa *m*; (*list*) lista ♦ *vt* (*visit*) fijar la hora de; **to arrive on ~** llegar a la hora debida; **to be ahead of/behind ~** estar adelantado/en retraso; **~d flight** *n* vuelo regular

scheme [ski:m] *n* (*plan*) plan *m*, proyecto; (*plot*) intriga; (*arrangement*) disposición *f*; (*pension ~*) sistema *m* ♦ *vi* (*intrigue*) intrigar; **scheming** *adj* intrigante ♦ *n* intrigas *fpl*

schizophrenic [skɪtsə'frɛnɪk] *adj* esquizofrénico

scholar ['skɒlə*] *n* (*pupil*) alumno/a; (*learned person*) sabio/a, erudito/a; **~ship** *n* erudición *f*; (*grant*) beca

school [skuːl] *n* escuela, colegio; (*in university*) facultad *f* ♦ *cpd* escolar; **~ age** *n* edad *f* escolar; **~book** *n* libro de texto; **~boy** *n* alumno; **~ children** *npl* alumnos *mpl*; **~girl** *n* alumna; **~ing** *n* enseñanza; **~master/mistress** *n* (*primary*) maestro/a; (*secondary*) profesor(a) *m/f*; **~teacher** *n* (*primary*) maestro/a; (*secondary*) profesor/a *m/f*

schooner ['skuːnə*] *n* (*ship*) goleta

sciatica [saɪ'ætɪkə] *n* ciática

science ['saɪəns] *n* ciencia; **~ fiction** *n* ciencia-ficción *f*; **scientific** [-'tɪfɪk] *adj* científico; **scientist** *n* científico/a

scissors ['sɪzəz] *npl* tijeras *fpl*; **a pair of ~** unas tijeras

scoff [skɒf] *vt* (*BRIT: inf: eat*) engullir ♦ *vi*: **to ~ (at)** (*mock*) mofarse (de)

scold [skəuld] *vt* regañar

scone [skɒn] *n* pastel de pan

scoop [sku:p] *n* (*for flour etc*) pala; (*PRESS*) exclusiva; **~ out** *vt* excavar; **~ up** *vt* recoger

scooter ['skuːtə*] *n* moto *f*; (*toy*) patinete *m*

scope [skəup] *n* (*of plan*) ámbito; (*of person*) competencia; (*opportunity*) libertad *f* (de acción)

scorch [skɔ:tʃ] vt (clothes) chamuscar; (earth, grass) quemar, secar

score [skɔ:*] n (points etc) puntuación f; (MUS) partitura; (twenty) veintena ♦ vt (goal, point) ganar; (mark) rayar; (achieve: success) conseguir ♦ vi marcar un tanto; (FOOTBALL) marcar (un) gol; (keep score) llevar el tanteo; **~s of** (very many) decenas de; **on that** ~ en lo que se refiere a eso; **to ~ 6 out of 10** obtener una puntuación de 6 sobre 10; **~ out** vt tachar; **~ over** vt fus obtener una victoria sobre; **~board** n marcador m

scorn [skɔ:n] n desprecio; **~ful** adj desdeñoso, despreciativo

Scorpio ['skɔ:pɪəu] n Escorpión m

scorpion ['skɔ:pɪən] n alacrán m

Scot [skɔt] n escocés/esa m/f

Scotch [skɔtʃ] n whisky m escocés

Scotland ['skɔtlənd] n Escocia

Scots [skɔts] adj escocés/esa; **~man/ woman** (irreg) n escocés/esa m/f

Scottish ['skɔtɪʃ] adj escocés/esa

scoundrel ['skaundrl] n canalla m/f, sinvergüenza m/f

scout [skaut] n (MIL, also: boy ~) explorador m; **girl ~** (US) niña exploradora; **~ around** vi reconocer el terreno

scowl [skaul] vi fruncir el ceño; **to ~ at sb** mirar con ceño a uno

scrabble ['skræbl] vi (claw): **to ~ (at)** arañar; (also: **~ around:** search) revolver todo buscando ♦ n: **S~** ® Scrabble ® m

scraggy ['skrægɪ] adj descarnado

scram [skræm] (inf) vi largarse

scramble ['skræmbl] n (climb) subida (difícil); (struggle) pelea ♦ vi: **to ~ through/out** abrirse paso/salir con dificultad; **to ~ for** pelear por; **~d eggs** npl huevos mpl revueltos

scrap [skræp] n (bit) pedacito, (fig) pizca; (fight) riña, bronca; (also: **~ iron**) chatarra, hierro viejo ♦ vt (discard) desechar, descartar ♦ vi reñir, armar

(una) bronca; **~s** npl (waste) sobras fpl, desperdicios mpl; **~book** n álbum m de recortes; **~ dealer** n chatarrero/a

scrape [skreɪp] n: **to get into a ~** meterse en un lío ♦ vt raspar; (skin etc) rasguñar; (~ against) rozar ♦ vi: to **~ through** (exam) aprobar por los pelos; (~ together) (money) arañar, juntar

scrap: **~ heap** n (fig): **to be on the ~ heap** estar acabado; **~ merchant** (BRIT) n chatarrero/a; **~ paper** n pedazos mpl de papel

scratch [skrætʃ] n rasguño; (from claw) arañazo ♦ cpd: **~ team** equipo improvisado ♦ vt (paint, car) rayar; (with claw, nail) rasguñar, arañar; (rub: nose etc) rascarse ♦ vi rascarse; **to start from ~** partir de cero; **to be up to ~** cumplir con los requisitos

scrawl [skrɔ:l] n garabatos mpl ♦ vi hacer garabatos

scrawny ['skrɔ:nɪ] adj flaco

scream [skri:m] n chillido ♦ vi chillar

screech [skri:tʃ] vi chirriar

screen [skri:n] n (CINEMA, TV) pantalla; (movable barrier) biombo ♦ vt (conceal) tapar; (from the wind etc) proteger; (film) proyectar; (candidates etc) investigar a; **~ing** n (MED) investigación f médica; **~play** n guión m

screw [skru:] n tornillo ♦ vt (also: **~ in**) atornillar; **~ up** vt (paper etc) arrugar; **to ~ up one's eyes** arrugar el entrecejo; **~driver** n destornillador m

scribble ['skrɪbl] n garabatos mpl ♦ vt, vi garabatear

script [skrɪpt] n (CINEMA etc) guión m; (writing) escritura, letra

Scripture(s) ['skrɪptʃə*(z)] n(pl) Sagrada Escritura

scroll [skrəul] n rollo

scrounge [skraundʒ] (inf) vt: **to ~ sth off or from sb** obtener algo de uno de gorra ♦ n: **on the ~** de gorra; **~r** n gorrón/ona m/f

scrub [skrʌb] n (land) maleza ♦ vt fregar, restregar; (inf: reject) cancelar, anular

scruff [skrʌf] n: **by the ~ of the neck** por el pescuezo

scruffy ['skrʌfɪ] adj desaliñado, piojoso

scrum(mage) ['skrʌm(mɪdʒ)] n (RUGBY) melée f

scruple ['skru:pl] n (gen pl) escrúpulo

scrutinize ['skru:tɪnaɪz] vt escudriñar; (votes) escrutar; **scrutiny** ['skru:tɪnɪ] n escrutinio, examen m

scuff [skʌf] vt (shoes, floor) rayar

scuffle ['skʌfl] n refriega

sculptor ['skʌlptə*] n escultor(a) m/f

sculpture ['skʌlptʃə*] n escultura

scum [skʌm] n (on liquid) espuma; (pej: people) escoria

scurry ['skʌrɪ] vi correr; **to ~ off** escabullirse

scuttle ['skʌtl] n (also: coal ~) cubo, carbonera ♦ vt (ship) barrenar ♦ vi (scamper): **to ~ away, ~ off** escabullirse

scythe [saɪð] n guadaña

SDP (BRIT) n abbr = **Social Democratic Party**

sea [si:] n mar m ♦ cpd de mar, marítimo; **by ~** (travel) en barco; **on the ~** (boat) en el mar; (town) junto al mar; **to be all at ~** (fig) estar despistado; **out to ~, at ~** en alta mar; **~board** n litoral m; **~food** n mariscos mpl; **~ front** n paseo marítimo; **~-going** adj de altura; **~gull** n gaviota

seal [si:l] n (animal) foca; (stamp) sello ♦ vt (close) cerrar; **~ off** vt (area) acordonar

sea level n nivel m del mar

sea lion n león m marino

seam [si:m] n costura; (of metal) juntura; (of coal) veta, filón m

seaman ['si:mən] (irreg) n marinero

seance ['seɪɒns] n sesión f de espiritismo

seaplane ['si:pleɪn] n hidroavión m

seaport ['si:pɔ:t] n puerto de mar

search [sə:tʃ] n (for person, thing) busca, búsqueda; (COMPUT) búsqueda; (inspection: of sb's home) registro ♦ vt (look in) buscar en; (examine) examinar; (person, place) registrar ♦ vi: **to ~ for** buscar; **in ~ of** en busca de; **~ through** vt fus registrar; **~ing** adj penetrante; **~light** n reflector m; **~ party** n pelotón m de salvamento; **~ warrant** n mandamiento (judicial)

sea: ~shore n playa, orilla del mar; **~sick** adj mareado; **~side** n playa, orilla del mar; **~side resort** n centro turístico costero

season ['si:zn] n (of year) estación f; (sporting etc) temporada; (of films etc) ciclo ♦ vt (food) sazonar; **in/out of ~** en sazón/fuera de temporada; **~al** adj estacional; **~ed** adj (fig) experimentado; **~ing** n condimento, aderezo; **~ ticket** n abono

seat [si:t] n (in bus, train) asiento; (chair) silla; (PARLIAMENT) escaño; (buttocks) culo, trasero; (of trousers) culera ♦ vt sentar; (have room for) tener cabida para; **to be ~ed** sentarse; **~ belt** n cinturón m de seguridad

sea: ~ water n agua del mar; **~weed** n alga marina; **~worthy** adj en condiciones de navegar

sec. abbr = **second(s)**

secluded [sɪ'klu:dɪd] adj retirado

seclusion [sɪ'klu:ʒən] n reclusión f

second ['sekənd] adj segundo ♦ adv en segundo lugar ♦ n segundo; (AUT: also: ~ gear) segunda; (COMM) artículo con algún desperfecto; (BRIT: SCOL: degree) título de licenciado con calificación de notable ♦ vt (motion) apoyar; **~ary** adj secundario; **~ary school** n escuela secundaria; **~-class** adj de segunda clase ♦ adv (RAIL) en segunda; **~hand** adj de segunda mano, usado; **~ hand** n (on clock) segundero; **~ly** adv en segundo lugar; **~ment** [sɪ'kɔndmənt] n (BRIT) traslado temporal; **~rate** adj de segunda categoría; **~ thoughts** npl: **to have ~ thoughts** cambiar de opinión; **on ~ thoughts** or **thought** (US) pensándolo bien

secrecy ['si:krəsi] n secreto

secret ['si:krit] adj, n secreto; **in ~** en secreto

secretarial [sekrə'teəriəl] adj de secretario; (course, staff) de secretariado

secretary ['sekrətəri] n secretario/a; **S~ of State (for)** (BRIT: POL) Ministro (de)

secretive ['si:krətiv] adj reservado, sigiloso

secretly ['si:kritli] adv en secreto

sect [sekt] n secta; **~arian** [-'teəriən] adj sectario

section ['sekʃən] n sección f; (part) parte f; (of document) artículo; (of opinion) sector m; (cross-~) corte m transversal

sector ['sektə*] n sector m

secular ['sekjulə*] adj secular, seglar

secure [si'kjuə*] adj seguro; (firmly fixed) firme, fijo ♦ vt (fix) asegurar, afianzar; (get) conseguir

security [si'kjuəriti] n seguridad f; (for loan) fianza f; (: object) prenda

sedate [si'deit] adj tranquilo ♦ vt tratar con sedantes

sedation [si'deiʃən] n (MED) sedación f

sedative ['seditiv] n sedante m, sedativo

seduce [si'dju:s] vt seducir; **seduction** [-'dʌkʃən] n seducción f; **seductive** [-'dʌktiv] adj seductor(a)

see [si:] (pt **saw**, pp **seen**) vt ver; (accompany): **to ~ sb to the door** acompañar a uno a la puerta; (understand) ver, comprender ♦ vi ver ♦ n (arz)obispado; **to ~ that** (ensure) asegurar que; **~ you soon!** ¡hasta pronto!; **~ about** vt fus atender a, encargarse de; **~ off** vt despedir; **~ through** vt fus (fig) calar ♦ vt (plan)

llevar a cabo; **~ to** vt fus atender a, encargarse de

seed [si:d] n semilla; (in fruit) pepita; (fig: gen pl) germen m; (TENNIS etc) preseleccionado/a; **to go to ~** (plant) granar, (fig) descuidarse; **~ling** n planta de semillero; **~y** adj (shabby) desaseado, raído

seeing ['si:iŋ] conj: **~ (that)** visto que, en vista de que

seek [si:k] (pt, pp **sought**) vt buscar; (post) solicitar

seem [si:m] vi parecer; **there ~s to be ... parece que hay ...; ~ingly** adv aparentemente, según parece

seen [si:n] pp of **see**

seep [si:p] vi filtrarse

seesaw ['si:sɔ:] n subibaja

seethe [si:ð] vi hervir; **to ~ with anger** estar furioso

see-through adj transparente

segment ['segmənt] n (part) sección f; (of orange) gajo

segregate ['segrigeit] vt segregar

seize [si:z] vt (grasp) agarrar, asir; (take possession of) secuestrar; (: territory) apoderarse de; (opportunity) aprovecharse de; **~ (up)on** vt fus aprovechar; **~ up** vi (TECH) agarrotarse

seizure ['si:ʒə*] n (MED) ataque m; (LAW, of power) incautación f

seldom ['seldəm] adv rara vez

select [si'lekt] adj selecto, escogido ♦ vt escoger, elegir; (SPORT) seleccionar; **~ion** [-'lekʃən] n selección f; (COMM) surtido

self [self] (pl **selves**) n uno mismo; **the ~** el yo ♦ prefix auto...; **~-assured** adj seguro de sí mismo; **~-catering** (BRIT) adj (flat etc) con cocina; **~-centred** (US **~-centered**) adj egocéntrico; **~-confidence** n confianza en sí mismo; **~-conscious** adj cohibido; **~-contained** (BRIT) adj (flat) con entrada particular; **~-control** n autodominio; **~-defence** (US **~-defense**) n defensa propia; **~-discipline** n autodisciplina;

~-**employed** *adj* que trabaja por cuenta propia; ~-**evident** *adj* patente; ~-**governing** *adj* autónomo; ~-**indulgent** *adj* autocomplaciente; ~-**interest** *n* egoísmo; ~-**ish** *adj* egoísta; ~-**ishness** *n* egoísmo; ~-**less** *adj* desinteresado; ~-**made** *adj*: ~-**made man** hombre *m* que se ha hecho a sí mismo; ~-**pity** *n* lástima de sí mismo; ~-**portrait** *n* autorretrato; ~-**possessed** *adj* sereno, dueño de sí mismo; ~-**preservation** *n* propia conservación *f*; ~-**respect** *n* amor *m* propio; ~-**righteous** *adj* santurrón/ona; ~-**sacrifice** *n* abnegación *f*; ~-**satisfied** *adj* satisfecho de sí mismo; ~-**service** *adj* de autoservicio; ~-**sufficient** *adj* autosuficiente; ~-**taught** *adj* autodidacta

sell [sel] (*pt, pp* **sold**) *vt* vender ♦ *vi* venderse; **to ~ at** *o* **for £10** venderse a 10 libras; ~ **off** *vt* liquidar; ~ **out** *vi*: **to ~ out of tickets/milk** vender todas las entradas/toda la leche; ~-**by date** *n* fecha de caducidad; ~**er** *n* vendedor(a) *m/f*; ~-**ing price** *n* precio de venta

Sellotape ® ['seləʊteɪp] (*BRIT*) *n* cinta adhesiva, celo (*SP*), scotch *m* (*AM*)

selves [selvz] *npl of* **self**

semblance ['sembləns] *n* apariencia

semen ['siːmən] *n* semen *m*

semester [sɪ'mestə*] (*US*) *n* semestre *m*

semi... [semɪ] *prefix* semi-, medio...; ~**circle** *n* semicírculo; ~**colon** *n* punto y coma; ~**conductor** *n* semiconductor *m*; ~**detached (house)** *n* (casa) semiseparada; ~**final** *n* semi-final *m*

seminar ['semɪnɑː*] *n* seminario

seminary ['semɪnərɪ] (*REL*) *n* seminario

semiskilled ['semɪskɪld] *adj* (*work, worker*) semi-cualificado

semi-skimmed (milk) *n* leche semidesnatada

senate ['senɪt] *n* senado; **senator** *n* senador(a) *m/f*

send [send] (*pt, pp* **sent**) *vt* mandar,

enviar; (*signal*) transmitir; ~ **away** *vt* despachar; ~ **away for** *vt fus* pedir; ~ **back** *vt* devolver; ~ **for** *vt fus* mandar traer; ~ **off** *vt* (*goods*) despachar; (*BRIT: SPORT: player*) expulsar; ~ **out** *vt* (*invitation*) mandar; (*signal*) emitir; ~ **up** *vt* (*person, price*) hacer subir; (*BRIT: parody*) parodiar; ~**er** *n* remitente *m/f*; ~-**off** *n*: **a good ~off** una buena despedida

senior ['siːnɪə*] *adj* (*older*) mayor, más viejo; (: *on staff*) de más antigüedad; (*of higher rank*) superior; ~ **citizen** *n* persona de la tercera edad; ~**ity** [-'ɒrɪtɪ] *n* antigüedad *f*

sensation [sen'seɪʃən] *n* sensación *f*; ~**al** *adj* sensacional

sense [sens] *n* (*faculty, meaning*) sentido; (*feeling*) sensación *f*; (*good ~*) sentido común, juicio ♦ *vt* sentir, percibir; **it makes ~** tiene sentido; ~**less** *adj* estúpido, insensato; (*unconscious*) sin conocimiento; ~ **of humour** *n* sentido del humor

sensible ['sensɪbl] *adj* sensato; (*reasonable*) razonable, lógico

sensitive ['sensɪtɪv] *adj* sensible; (*touchy*) susceptible

sensual ['sensjuəl] *adj* sensual

sensuous ['sensjuəs] *adj* sensual

sent [sent] *pt, pp of* **send**

sentence ['sentns] *n* (*LING*) oración *f*; (*LAW*) sentencia, fallo ♦ *vt*: **to ~ sb to death/to 5 years (in prison)** condenar a uno a muerte/a 5 años de cárcel

sentiment ['sentɪmənt] *n* sentimiento; (*opinion*) opinión *f*; ~**al** [-'mentl] *adj* sentimental

sentry ['sentrɪ] *n* centinela *m*

separate [*adj* 'seprɪt, *vb* 'sepəreɪt] *adj* separado; (*distinct*) distinto ♦ *vt* separar; (*part*) dividir ♦ *vi* separarse; ~**s** *npl* (*clothes*) coordinados *mpl*; ~**ly** *adv* por separado; **separation** [-'reɪʃən] *n* separación *f*

September [sep'tembə*] *n*

se(p)tiembre m

septic ['septik] adj séptico; ~ **tank** n fosa séptica

sequel ['siːkwl] n consecuencia, resultado; (of story) continuación f

sequence ['siːkwəns] n sucesión f, serie f; (CINEMA) secuencia

sequin ['siːkwɪn] n lentejuela

serene [sɪ'riːn] adj sereno, tranquilo

sergeant ['saːdʒənt] n sargento

serial ['sɪərɪəl] n (TV) telenovela, serie f televisiva; (BOOK) serie f; **~ize** vt emitir como serial; **~ killer** n asesino/a múltiple; **~ number** n número de serie

series ['sɪəriːz] n inv serie f

serious ['sɪərɪəs] adj serio; (grave) grave; **~ly** adv en serio; (ill, wounded etc) gravemente

sermon ['səːmən] n sermón m

serrated [sɪ'reɪtɪd] adj serrado, dentellado

serum ['sɪərəm] n suero

servant ['səːvənt] n servidor(a) m/f; (house ~) criado/a

serve [səːv] vt servir; (customer) atender; (subj: train) pasar por; (apprenticeship) cumplir ♦ vi (at table) servir; (TENNIS) sacar; to ~ **as/for/to do** servir de/para/para hacer ♦ n (TENNIS) saque m; **it ~s him right** se lo tiene merecido; ~ **out** vt (food) servir; ~ **up** vt = ~ **out**

service ['səːvɪs] n servicio; (REL) misa; (AUT) mantenimiento; (dishes etc) juego ♦ vt (car etc) revisar; (: repair) reparar; **the S~s** npl las fuerzas armadas; **to be of ~ to sb** ser útil a uno; ~ **included/not included** servicio incluído/no incluído; **~able** adj servible, utilizable; ~ **area** n (on motorway) área de servicio; ~ **charge** (BRIT) n servicio; **~man** n militar m; ~ **station** n estación f de servicio

serviette [səːvɪ'et] (BRIT) n servilleta

session ['seʃən] n sesión f; **to be in ~** estar en sesión

set [set] (pt, pp set) n juego m; (RADIO)

aparato; (TV) televisor m; (of utensils) batería; (of cutlery) cubierto; (of books) colección f; (TENNIS) set m; (group of people) grupo; (CINEMA) plató m; (THEATRE) decorado; (HAIRDRESSING) marcado ♦ adj (fixed) fijo; (ready) listo ♦ vt (place) poner, colocar; (fix) fijar; (adjust) ajustar, arreglar; (decide: rules etc) establecer, decidir ♦ vi (sun) ponerse; (jam, jelly) cuajarse; (concrete) fraguar; (bone) componerse; **to be ~ on doing sth** estar empeñado en hacer algo; **to ~ to music** poner música a; **to ~ on fire** incendiar, poner fuego a; **to ~ free** poner en libertad; **to ~ sth going** poner algo en marcha; **to ~ sail** zarpar, hacerse a la vela; ~ **about** vt fus ponerse a; ~ **aside** vt poner aparte, dejar de lado; (money, time) reservar; ~ **back** vt (cost): **to ~ sb back £5** costar a uno cinco libras; (: in time): **to ~ back (by)** retrasar (por); ~ **off** vi partir ♦ vt (bomb) hacer estallar; (events) poner en marcha; (show up well) hacer resaltar; ~ **out** vi partir ♦ vt (arrange) disponer; (state) exponer; **to ~ out to do sth** proponerse hacer algo; ~ **up** vt establecer; **~back** n revés m, contratiempo; ~ **menu** n menú m

settee [se'tiː] n sofá m

setting ['setɪŋ] n (scenery) marco; (position) disposición f; (of sun) puesta; (of jewel) engaste m, montadura

settle ['setl] vt (argument) resolver; (accounts) ajustar, liquidar; (MED: calm) calmar, sosegar ♦ vi (dust etc) depositarse; (also: ~ **down**) instalarse; tranquilizarse; (weather) serenarse; ~ **for sth** convenir en aceptar algo; ~ **on sth** decidirse por algo; **to ~ in** vi instalarse; ~ **up** vi: **to ~ up with sb** ajustar cuentas con uno; **~ment** n (payment) liquidación f; (agreement) acuerdo, convenio; (village etc) pueblo; **~r** n colono/a, colonizador(a) m/f

setup ['setʌp] n sistema m; (situation)

situación f

seven ['sɛvn] num siete; **~teen** num diez y siete, diecisiete; **~th** num séptimo; **~ty** num setenta

sever ['sɛvə*] vt cortar; (relations) romper

several ['sɛvərl] adj, pron varios/as m/fpl, algunos/as m/fpl; **~ of us** varios de nosotros

severance ['sɛvərəns] n (of relations) ruptura; **~ pay** n indemnización f por despido

severe [sɪ'vɪə*] adj severo; (serious) grave; (hard) duro; (pain) intenso;

severity [sɪ'vɛrɪtɪ] n severidad f; gravedad f; intensidad f

sew [səu] (pt sewed, pp sewn) vt, vi coser; **~ up** vt coser, zurcir

sewage ['su:ɪdʒ] n aguas fpl residuales

sewer ['su:ə*] n alcantarilla, cloaca

sewing ['səuɪŋ] n costura; **~ machine** n máquina de coser

sewn [səun] pp of **sew**

sex [sɛks] n sexo; (lovemaking): **to have ~** hacer el amor; **~ist** adj, n sexista m/f; **~ual** ['sɛksjuəl] adj sexual; **~y** adj sexy

shabby ['ʃæbɪ] adj (person) desharrapado; (clothes) raído, gastado; (behaviour) ruin xxx

shack [ʃæk] n choza, chabola

shackles ['ʃæklz] npl grillos mpl, grilletes mpl

shade [ʃeɪd] n sombra; (for lamp) pantalla; (for eyes) visera; (of colour) matiz m, tonalidad f; (small quantity): **a ~ (too big/more)** un poquitín (grande/más) ♦ vt dar sombra a; (eyes) proteger del sol; **in the ~** en la sombra

shadow ['ʃædəu] n sombra ♦ vt (follow) seguir y vigilar; **~ cabinet** (BRIT) n (POL) gabinete paralelo formado por el partido de oposición; **~y** adj oscuro; (dim) indistinto

shady ['ʃeɪdɪ] adj sombreado; (fig: dishonest) sospechoso; (: deal) turbio

shaft [ʃɑ:ft] n (of arrow, spear) astil m;

(AUT, TECH) eje m, árbol m; (of mine) pozo; (of lift) hueco, caja; (of light) rayo

shaggy ['ʃægɪ] adj peludo

shake [ʃeɪk] (pt shook, pp shaken) vt sacudir; (building) hacer temblar; (bottle, cocktail) agitar ♦ vi (tremble) temblar; **to ~ one's head** (in refusal) negar con la cabeza; (in dismay) mover or menear la cabeza, incrédulo; **to ~ hands with sb** estrechar la mano a uno; **~ off** vt sacudirse; (fig) deshacerse de; **~ up** vt agitar; (fig) reorganizar; **shaky** adj (hand, voice) trémulo; (building) inestable

shall [ʃæl] aux vb: **~ I help you?** ¿quieres que te ayude?; **I'll buy three, ~ I?** compro tres, ¿no te parece?

shallow ['ʃæləu] adj poco profundo; (fig) superficial

sham [ʃæm] n fraude m, engaño ♦ vt fingir, simular

shambles ['ʃæmblz] n confusión f

shame [ʃeɪm] n vergüenza ♦ vt avergonzar; **it is a ~ that/to do** es una lástima que/hacer; **what a ~!** ¡qué lástima!; **~ful** adj vergonzoso; **~less** adj desvergonzado

shampoo [ʃæm'pu:] n champú m ♦ vt lavar con champú; **~ and set** n lavado y marcado

shamrock ['ʃæmrɔk] n trébol m (emblema nacional irlandés)

shandy ['ʃændɪ] n mezcla de cerveza con gaseosa

shan't [ʃɑ:nt] = **shall not**

shantytown ['ʃæntɪtaun] n barrio de chabolas

shape [ʃeɪp] n forma ♦ vt formar, dar forma a; (sb's ideas) formar; (sb's life) determinar; **to take ~** tomar forma; **~ up** vi (events) desarrollarse; (person) formarse; **~d** suffix: **heart-~d** en forma de corazón; **~less** adj informe, sin forma definida; **~ly** adj (body etc) esbelto

share [ʃɛə*] n (part) parte f, porción f; (contribution) cuota; (COMM) acción f

♦ vt dividir; (have in common) compartir; **to ~ out** (among or between) repartir (entre); **~holder** (BRIT) n accionista m/f

shark [ʃɑːk] n tiburón m

sharp [ʃɑːp] adj (blade, nose) afilado; (point) puntiagudo; (outline) definido; (pain) intenso; (MUS) desafinado; (contrast) marcado; (voice) agudo; (person: quick-witted) astuto; (: dishonest) poco escrupuloso ♦ n (MUS) sostenido ♦ adv: **at 2 o'clock ~** a las 2 en punto; **~en** vt afilar; (pencil) sacar punta a; (fig) aguzar; **~ener** n (also: pencil ~ener) sacapuntas m inv; **~-eyed** adj de vista aguda; **~ly** adv (turn, stop) bruscamente; (stand out, contrast) claramente; (criticize, retort) severamente

shatter ['ʃætə*] vt hacer añicos or pedazos; (fig: ruin) destruir, acabar con ♦ vi hacerse añicos

shave [ʃeɪv] vt afeitar, rasurar ♦ vi afeitarse, rasurarse ♦ n: **to have a ~** afeitarse; **~r** n (also: electric ~r) máquina de afeitar (eléctrica)

shaving ['ʃeɪvɪŋ] n (action) el afeitarse, rasurado; **~s** npl (of wood etc) virutas fpl; **~ brush** n brocha (de afeitar); **~ cream** n crema de afeitar; **~ foam** n espuma de afeitar

shawl [ʃɔːl] n chal m

she [ʃiː] pron ella; **~-cat** n gata

sheaf [ʃiːf] (pl **sheaves**) n (of corn) gavilla; (of papers) fajo

shear [ʃɪə*] (pt **sheared**, pp **sheared** or **shorn**) vt esquilar, trasquilar; **~s** npl (for hedge) tijeras fpl de jardín

sheath [ʃiːθ] n vaina; (contraceptive) preservativo

sheaves [ʃiːvz] npl of **sheaf**

shed [ʃed] (pt, pp **shed**) n cobertizo ♦ vt (skin) mudar; (tears, blood) derramar; (load) derramar; (workers) despedir

she'd [ʃiːd] = **she had; she would**

sheen [ʃiːn] n brillo, lustre m

sheep [ʃiːp] n inv oveja; **~dog** n perro pastor; **~skin** n piel f de carnero

sheer [ʃɪə*] adj (utter) puro, completo; (steep) escarpado; (material) diáfano ♦ adv verticalmente

sheet [ʃiːt] n (on bed) sábana; (of paper) hoja; (of glass, metal) lámina; (of ice) capa

sheik(h) [ʃeɪk] n jeque m

shelf [ʃelf] (pl **shelves**) n estante m

shell [ʃel] n (on beach) concha; (of egg, nut etc) cáscara; (explosive) proyectil m, obús m; (of building) armazón f ♦ vt (peas) desenvainar; (MIL) bombardear

she'll [ʃiːl] = **she will; she shall**

shellfish ['ʃelfɪʃ] n inv crustáceo; (as food) mariscos mpl

shell suit n chándal m de calle

shelter ['ʃeltə*] n abrigo, refugio ♦ vt (aid) amparar, proteger; (give lodging to) abrigar ♦ vi abrigarse, refugiarse; **~ed** adj (life) protegido; (spot) abrigado; **~ed housing** n viviendas vigiladas para ancianos y minusválidos

shelve [ʃelv] vt (fig) aplazar; **~s** npl of **shelf**

shepherd ['ʃepəd] n pastor m ♦ vt (guide) guiar, conducir; **~'s pie** (BRIT) n pastel de carne y patatas

sherry ['ʃerɪ] n jerez m

she's [ʃiːz] = **she is; she has**

Shetland ['ʃetlənd] n (also: **the ~s, the ~ Isles**) las Islas de Zetlandia

shield [ʃiːld] n escudo; (protection) blindaje m ♦ vt: **to ~ (from)** proteger (de)

shift [ʃɪft] n (change) cambio; (at work) turno ♦ vt trasladar; (remove) quitar ♦ vi moverse; **~ work** n trabajo a turnos; **~y** adj tramposo; (eyes) furtivo

shimmer ['ʃɪmə*] n reflejo trémulo

shin [ʃɪn] n espinilla

shine [ʃaɪn] (pt, pp **shone**) n brillo, lustre m ♦ vi brillar, relucir ♦ vt (shoes) lustrar, sacar brillo a; **to ~ a torch on sth** dirigir una linterna hacia algo

shingle ['ʃɪŋgl] n (on beach) guijarros

mpl; **~s** *n* (MED) herpes *mpl* or *fpl*

shiny ['ʃaɪnɪ] *adj* brillante, lustroso

ship [ʃɪp] *n* buque *m*, barco ♦ *vt* (goods) embarcar; (send) transportar o enviar por vía marítima; **~building** *n* construcción *f* de buques; **~ment** *n* (goods) envío; **~ping** *n* (act) embarque *m*; (traffic) buques *mpl*; **~wreck** *n* naufragio ♦ *vt*: **to be ~wrecked** naufragar; **~yard** *n* astillero

shire ['ʃaɪə*] (BRIT) *n* condado

shirt [ʃɜːt] *n* camisa; **in (one's) ~ sleeves** en mangas de camisa

shit [ʃɪt] (inf!) excl ¡mierda! (!)

shiver ['ʃɪvə*] *n* escalofrío ♦ *vi* temblar, estremecerse; (with cold) tiritar

shoal [ʃəʊl] *n* (of fish) banco *m*; (fig: also: ~s) tropel *m*

shock [ʃɒk] *n* (impact) choque *m*; (ELEC) descarga (eléctrica); (emotional) conmoción *f*; (start) sobresalto, susto; (MED) postración *f* nerviosa ♦ *vt* dar un susto a; (offend) escandalizar; **~ absorber** *n* amortiguador *m*; **~ing** *adj* espantoso; (outrageous) escandaloso

shoddy ['ʃɒdɪ] *adj* de pacotilla

shoe [ʃuː] *n* (pt, pp **shod**) zapato; (for horse) herradura ♦ *vt* (horse) herrar; **~brush** *n* cepillo para zapatos; **~lace** *n* cordón *m*; **~ polish** *n* betún *m*; **~shop** *n* zapatería; **~string** *n* (fig): **on a ~string** con muy poco dinero

shone [ʃɒn] *pt, pp* of **shine**

shook [ʃʊk] *pt* of **shake**

shoot [ʃuːt] *n* (pt, pp **shot**) *n* (on branch, seedling) retoño, vástago ♦ *vt* disparar; (kill) matar a tiros; (wound) pegar un tiro; (execute) fusilar; (film) rodar, filmar ♦ *vi* (FOOTBALL) chutar; **~ down** *vt* (plane) derribar; **~ in/out** *vi* entrar corriendo/salir disparado; **~ up** *vi* (prices) dispararse; **~ing** *n* (shots) tiros *mpl*; (HUNTING) caza con escopeta; **~ing star** *n* estrella fugaz

shop [ʃɒp] *n* tienda; (workshop) taller *m* ♦ *vi* (also: go **~ping**) ir de compras;

~ assistant (BRIT) *n* dependiente/a *m/f*; **~ floor** (BRIT) *n* (fig) taller *m*, fábrica; **~keeper** *n* tendero/a; **~lifting** *n* mechería; **~per** *n* comprador(a) *m/f*; **~ping** *n* (goods) compras *fpl*; **~ping bag** *n* bolsa (de compras); **~ping centre** (US **~ping center**) *n* centro comercial; **~-soiled** *adj* deteriorado; **~ steward** (BRIT) *n* (INDUSTRY) enlace *m* sindical; **~ window** *n* escaparate *m* (SP), vidriera (AM)

shore [ʃɔː*] *n* orilla ♦ *vt*: **to ~ (up)** reforzar; **on ~** en tierra

shorn [ʃɔːn] *pp* of **shear**

short [ʃɔːt] *adj* corto; (in time) breve, de corta duración; (person) bajo; (curt) brusco, seco; (insufficient) insuficiente; **(a pair of) ~s** (unos) pantalones *mpl* cortos; **to be ~ of sth** estar falto de algo; **in ~** en pocas palabras; **~ of doing ...** fuera de hacer ...; **it is ~ for** es la forma abreviada de; **to cut ~** (speech, visit) interrumpir, terminar inesperadamente; **everything ~ of ...** todo menos ...; **to fall ~ of** no alcanzar; **to run ~ of** quedarle a uno poco; **to stop ~** parar en seco; **to stop ~ of** detenerse antes de; **~age** *n*: **a ~age of** una falta de; **~bread** *n* especie de mantecado; **~change** *vt* no dar bien el cambio completo a; **~ circuit** *n* cortocircuito; **~coming** *n* defecto, deficiencia; **~(crust) pastry** (BRIT) *n* pasta quebradiza; **~cut** *n* atajo; **~en** *vt* acortar; (visit) interrumpir; **~fall** *n* déficit *m*; **~hand** (BRIT) *n* taquigrafía; **~hand typist** *n* taquimecanógrafo/a; **~ list** (BRIT) *n* (for job) lista de candidatos escogidos; **~-lived** *adj* efímero; **~ly** *adv* en breve, dentro de poco; **~-sighted** *adj* miope; (fig) imprudente; **~-staffed** *adj*: **to be ~-staffed** estar falto de personal; **~ story** *n* cuento; **~-tempered** *adj* enojadizo; **~-term** *adj* (effect) a corto plazo; **~-wave** *n* (RADIO) onda corta

shot [ʃɒt] *pt, pp* of **shoot** *n* (sound)

tiro, disparo; (try) tentativa; (injection) inyección f; (PHOT) toma, fotografía; **to be a good/poor ~** (person) tener buena/mala puntería; **like a ~** (without any delay) como un rayo; **~gun** n escopeta

should [ʃud] aux vb: **I ~ go now** debo irme ahora; **he ~ be there now** debe de haber llegado (ya); **I ~ go if I were you** yo en tu lugar me iría; **I ~ like to** me gustaría

shoulder ['ʃəuldə*] n hombro ♦ vt (fig) cargar con; **~ bag** n cartera de bandolera; **~ blade** n omóplato

shouldn't ['ʃudnt] = **should not**

shout [ʃaut] n grito ♦ vt gritar ♦ vi gritar, dar voces; **~ down** vt acallar a gritos; **~ing** n griterío

shove [ʃʌv] n empujón m ♦ vt empujar; (inf: put): **to ~ sth in** meter algo a empellones; **~ off** (inf) vi largarse

shovel ['ʃʌvl] n pala; (mechanical) excavadora ♦ vt mover con pala

show [ʃəu] (pt showed, pp shown) n (of emotion) demostración f; (semblance) apariencia; (exhibition) exposición f; (THEATRE) función f, espectáculo; (TV) show m ♦ vt mostrar, enseñar; (courage etc) mostrar, manifestar; (exhibit) exponer; (film) proyectar ♦ vi mostrarse; (appear) aparecer; **for ~** para impresionar; **on ~** (exhibits etc) expuesto; **~ in** vt (person) hacer pasar; **~ off** (pej) vi presumir ♦ vt (display) lucir; **~ out** vt: **to ~ sb out** acompañar a uno a la puerta; **~ up** vi (stand out) destacar; (inf: turn up) aparecer ♦ vt (unmask) desenmascarar; **~ business** n mundo del espectáculo; **~down** n enfrentamiento (final)

shower ['ʃauə*] n (rain) chaparrón m, chubasco; (of stones etc) lluvia; (for bathing) ducha (SP), regadera (AM) ♦ vi llover ♦ vt (fig): **to ~ sb with sth** colmar a uno de algo; **to have a ~** ducharse; **~proof** adj impermeable

showing ['ʃəuiŋ] n (of film) proyección f

show jumping n hípica

shown [ʃəun] pp of **show**

show: **~-off** (inf) n presumido/a; **~piece** n (of exhibition etc) objeto cumbre; **~room** n sala de muestras

shrank [ʃræŋk] pt of **shrink**

shrapnel ['ʃræpnl] n metralla

shred [ʃred] n (gen pl) triza, jirón m ♦ vt hacer trizas; (CULIN) desmenuzar; **~der** n (vegetable ~der) picadora; (document ~der) trituradora (de papel)

shrewd [ʃruːd] adj astuto

shriek [ʃriːk] n chillido ♦ vi chillar

shrill [ʃril] adj agudo, estridente

shrimp [ʃrimp] n camarón m

shrine [ʃrain] n santuario, sepulcro

shrink [ʃriŋk] (pt shrank, pp shrunk) vi encogerse; (be reduced) reducirse; (also: ~ away) retroceder ♦ vt encoger ♦ n (inf: pej) loquero/a; **to ~ from (doing) sth** no atreverse a hacer algo; **~wrap** vt embalar con película de plástico

shrivel ['ʃrivl] (also: ~ up) vt (dry) secar ♦ vi secarse

shroud [ʃraud] n sudario ♦ vt: **~ed in mystery** envuelto en el misterio

Shrove Tuesday ['ʃrəuv-] n martes m de carnaval

shrub [ʃrʌb] n arbusto; **~bery** n arbustos mpl

shrug [ʃrʌg] n encogimiento de hombros ♦ vt, vi: **to ~ (one's shoulders)** encogerse de hombros; **~ off** vt negar importancia a

shrunk [ʃrʌŋk] pp of **shrink**

shudder ['ʃʌdə*] n estremecimiento, escalofrío ♦ vi estremecerse

shuffle ['ʃʌfl] vt (cards) barajar ♦ vi: **to ~ (one's feet)** arrastrar los pies

shun [ʃʌn] vt rehuir, esquivar

shunt [ʃʌnt] vt (train) maniobrar; (object) empujar

shut [ʃʌt] (pt, pp shut) vt cerrar ♦ vi

cerrarse; **~ down** vt, vi cerrar; **~ off** vt (supply etc) cortar; **~ up** vi (inf: keep quiet) callarse ♦ vt (close) cerrar; (silence) hacer callar; **~ter** n contraventana; (PHOT) obturador m

shuttle ['ʃʌtl] n lanzadera; (also: ~ service) servicio rápido y continuo entre dos puntos: (: AVIAT) puente m aéreo; **~cock** n volante m; **~ diplomacy** n viajes mpl diplomáticos

shy [ʃaɪ] adj tímido; **~ness** n timidez f

Sicily ['sɪsɪlɪ] n Sicilia

sick [sɪk] adj (ill) enfermo; (nauseated) mareado; (humour) negro; (vomiting): **to be ~** (BRIT) vomitar; **to feel ~** tener náuseas; **to be ~ of** (fig) estar harto de; **~ bay** n enfermería; **~en** vt dar asco a; **~ening** adj asqueroso

sickle ['sɪkl] n hoz f

sick: ~ leave n baja por enfermedad; **~ly** adj enfermizo; (smell) nauseabundo; **~ness** n enfermedad f, mal m; (vomiting) náuseas fpl; **~ pay** n subsidio de enfermedad

side [saɪd] n (gen) lado, (of body) costado; (of lake) orilla; (of hill) ladera; (team) equipo ♦ adj (door, entrance) lateral ♦ vi: **to side with sb** tomar el partido de uno; **by the ~ of** al lado de; **~ by ~** juntos/as; **from ~ to ~** de un lado para otro; **from all ~s** de todos lados; **to take ~s (with)** tomar partido (con); **~board** n aparador m; **~boards** (BRIT) npl = **~burns**; **~burns** npl patillas fpl; **~ drum** n tambor m; **~ effect** n efecto secundario; **~light** n (AUT) luz f lateral; **~line** n (SPORT) línea de banda; (fig) empleo suplementario; **~long** adj de soslayo; **~ order** n plato de acompañamiento; **~ show** n (stall) caseta; **~step** vt (fig) esquivar; **~ street** n calle f lateral; **~track** vt (fig) desviar de su propósito); **~walk** (US) n acera; **~ways** adv de lado

siding ['saɪdɪŋ] n (RAIL) apartadero, vía

muerta

siege [si:dʒ] n cerco, sitio

sieve [sɪv] n colador m ♦ vt cribar

sift [sɪft] vt cribar; (fig: information) escudriñar

sigh [saɪ] n suspiro ♦ vi suspirar

sight [saɪt] n (faculty) vista; (spectacle) espectáculo; (on gun) mira, alza ♦ vt divisar; **in ~** a la vista; **out of ~** fuera de (la) vista; **on ~** (shoot) sin previo aviso; **~seeing** n excursionismo, turismo; **to go ~seeing** hacer turismo

sign [saɪn] n (with hand) señal f, seña; (trace) huella, rastro; (notice) letrero; (written) signo ♦ vt firmar; (SPORT) fichar; **to ~ sth over to sb** firmar el traspaso de algo a uno; **~ on** vi (BRIT: as unemployed) registrarse como desempleado; (for course) inscribirse ♦ vt (MIL) alistar; (employee) contratar; **~ up** vi (MIL) alistarse; (for course) inscribirse ♦ vt (player) fichar

signal ['sɪgnl] n señal f ♦ vi señalizar ♦ vt (person) hacer señas a; (message) comunicar por señales; **~man** (irreg) n (RAIL) guardavía n

signature ['sɪgnətʃə*] n firma; **~ tune** n sintonía de apertura de un programa

signet ring ['sɪgnət-] n anillo de sello

significance [sɪg'nɪfɪkəns] n (importance) trascendencia

significant [sɪg'nɪfɪkənt] adj significativo; (important) trascendente

signify ['sɪgnɪfaɪ] vt significar

sign language n lenguaje m para sordomudos

signpost ['saɪnpəust] n indicador m

silence ['saɪləns] n silencio ♦ vt acallar; (guns) reducir al silencio; **~r** n (on gun), BRIT: AUT) silenciador m

silent ['saɪlənt] adj silencioso; (not speaking) callado; (film) mudo; **to remain ~** guardar silencio; **~ partner** n (COMM) socio/a comanditario/a

silhouette [sɪlu:'et] n silueta

silicon chip ['sɪlɪkən-] n plaqueta de silicio

silk [sɪlk] *n* seda ♦ *adj* de seda; **~y** *adj* sedoso

silly ['sɪlɪ] *adj* (*person*) tonto; (*idea*) absurdo

silt [sɪlt] *n* sedimento

silver ['sɪlvə*] *n* plata; (*money*) moneda suelta ♦ *adj* de plata; (*colour*) plateado; **~ paper** (*BRIT*) *n* papel *m* de plata; **~-plated** *adj* plateado; **~smith** *n* platero/a; **~ware** *n* plata; **~y** *adj* argentino

similar ['sɪmɪlə*] *adj*: **~ (to)** parecido *or* semejante (a); **~ity** [-'lærɪtɪ] *n* semejanza; **~ly** *adv* del mismo modo

simmer ['sɪmə*] *vi* hervir a fuego lento

simple ['sɪmpl] *adj* (*easy*) sencillo; (*foolish*, *COMM*: *interest*) simple; **simplicity** [-'plɪsɪtɪ] *n* sencillez *f*; **simplify** ['sɪmplɪfaɪ] *vt* simplificar

simply ['sɪmplɪ] *adv* (*live*, *talk*) sencillamente; (*just*, *merely*) sólo

simulate ['sɪmjuleɪt] *vt* fingir, simular; **~d** *adj* simulado; (*fur*) de imitación

simultaneous [sɪməl'teɪnɪəs] *adj* simultáneo; **~ly** *adv* simultáneamente

sin [sɪn] *n* pecado ♦ *vi* pecar

since [sɪns] *adv* desde entonces, después ♦ *prep* desde ♦ *conj* (*time*) desde que; (*because*) ya que, puesto que; **~ then, ever ~** desde entonces

sincere [sɪn'sɪə*] *adj* sincero; **~ly** *adv*: **yours ~ly** (*in letters*) le saluda atentamente; **sincerity** [-'serɪtɪ] *n* sinceridad *f*

sinew ['sɪnjuː] *n* tendón *m*

sing [sɪŋ] (*pt* **sang**, *pp* **sung**) *vt*, *vi* cantar

Singapore [sɪŋə'pɔː*] *n* Singapur *m*

singe [sɪndʒ] *vt* chamuscar

singer ['sɪŋə*] *n* cantante *m/f*

singing ['sɪŋɪŋ] *n* canto

single ['sɪŋgl] *adj* único, solo; (*unmarried*) soltero; (*not double*) simple, sencillo ♦ *n* (*BRIT*: *also*: **~ ticket**) billete *m* sencillo; (*record*) sencillo, single *m*; **~s** *npl* (*TENNIS*) individual *m*; **~ out** *vt* (*choose*) escoger; **~ bed** cama

individual; **~-breasted** *adj* recto; **~ file** *n*: **in ~ file** en fila de uno; **~-handed** *adv* sin ayuda; **~-minded** *adj* resuelto, firme; **~ parent** *n* padre *m* soltero, madre *f* soltera (*o divorciado etc*); **~ parent family** familia monoparental; **~ room** *n* cuarto individual

singly ['sɪŋglɪ] *adv* uno por uno

singular ['sɪŋgjulə*] *adj* (*odd*) raro, extraño; (*outstanding*) excepcional ♦ *n* (*LING*) singular *m*

sinister ['sɪnɪstə*] *adj* siniestro

sink [sɪŋk] (*pt* **sank**, *pp* **sunk**) *n* fregadero ♦ *vt* (*ship*) hundir, echar a pique; (*foundations*) excavar ♦ *vi* (*gen*) hundirse; **to ~ sth into** hundir algo en; **~ in** *vi* (*fig*) penetrar, calar

sinner ['sɪnə*] *n* pecador/a *m/f*

sinus ['saɪnəs] *n* (*ANAT*) seno

sip [sɪp] *n* sorbo ♦ *vt* sorber, beber a sorbitos

siphon ['saɪfən] *n* sifón *m*; **~ off** *vt* desviar

sir [sə*] *n* señor *m*; **S~ John Smith** Sir John Smith; **yes ~** sí, señor

siren ['saɪərn] *n* sirena

sirloin ['sɜːlɔɪn] *n* (*also*: **~ steak**) solomillo

sister ['sɪstə*] *n* hermana; (*BRIT*: *nurse*) enfermera jefe; **~-in-law** *n* cuñada

sit [sɪt] (*pt*, *pp* **sat**) *vi* sentarse; (*be sitting*) estar sentado; (*assembly*) reunirse; (*for painter*) posar ♦ *vt* (*exam*) presentarse a; **~ down** *vi* sentarse; **~ in on** *vt fus* asistir a; **~ up** *vi* incorporarse; (*not go to bed*) velar

sitcom ['sɪtkɔm] *n abbr* (= situation comedy) comedia de situación

site [saɪt] *n* sitio; (*also*: **building ~**) solar *m* ♦ *vt* situar

sit-in (*demonstration*) sentada

sitting ['sɪtɪŋ] *n* (*of assembly etc*) sesión *f*; (*in canteen*) turno; **~ room** *n* sala de estar

situated ['sɪtjueɪtɪd] *adj* situado

situation [sɪtju'eɪʃən] *n* situación *f*;

"~s vacant" (*BRIT*) "ofrecen trabajo"

six [sɪks] *num* seis; **~teen** *num* dieciséis; **~th** *num* sexto; **~ty** *num* sesenta

size [saɪz] *n* tamaño; (*extent*) extensión f; (*of clothing*) talla; (*of shoes*) número; **~ up** *vt* formarse una idea de; **~able** *adj* importante, considerable

sizzle ['sɪzl] *vi* crepitar

skate [skeɪt] *n* patín *m*; (*fish: pl inv*) raya ♦ *vi* patinar; **~board** *n* monopatín *m*; **~boarding** *n* monopatín *m*; **~r** *n* patinador(a) *m/f*; **skating** *n* patinaje *m*; **skating rink** *n* pista de patinaje

skeleton ['skelɪtn] *n* esqueleto *m*; (*TECH*) armazón f; (*outline*) esquema *m*; **~ staff** *n* personal *m* reducido

skeptic *etc* ['skeptɪk] (*US*) = **sceptic**

sketch [sketʃ] *n* (*drawing*) dibujo; (*outline*) esbozo, bosquejo; (*THEATRE*) sketch *m* ♦ *vt* dibujar; (*plan etc: also: ~ out*) esbozar; **~ book** *n* libro de dibujos; **~y** *adj* incompleto

skewer ['skju:ə*] *n* broqueta

ski [ski:] *n* esquí *m* ♦ *vi* esquiar; **~ boot** *n* bota de esquí

skid [skɪd] *n* patinazo ♦ *vi* patinar

ski: ~er *n* esquiador(a) *m/f*; **~ing** *n* esquí *m*; **~ jump** *n* salto con esquís

skilful ['skɪlful] (*BRIT*) *adj* diestro, experto

ski lift *n* telesilla *m*, telesquí *m*

skill [skɪl] *n* destreza, pericia, técnica; **~ed** *adj* hábil, diestro; (*worker*) cualificado; **~full** (*US*) *adj* = **skilful**

skim [skɪm] *vt* (*milk*) desnatar; (*glide over*) rozar, rasar ♦ *vi*: **to ~ through** (*book*) hojear; **~med milk** *n* leche f desnatada

skimp [skɪmp] *vt* (*also: ~ on: work*) chapucear; (*cloth etc*) escatimar; **~y** *adj* escaso; (*skirt*) muy corto

skin [skɪn] *n* piel f; (*complexion*) cutis *m* ♦ *vt* (*fruit etc*) pelar; (*animal*) despellejar; **~ cancer** *n* cáncer *m* de piel; **~-deep** *adj* superficial; **~ diving** *n* buceo; **~ny** *adj* flaco; **~tight** *adj*

(*dress etc*) muy ajustado

skip [skɪp] *n* brinco, salto; (*BRIT: container*) contenedor *m* ♦ *vi* brincar; (*with rope*) saltar a la comba ♦ *vt* saltarse

ski: ~ pass *n* forfait *m* (de esquí); **~ pole** *n* bastón *m* de esquiar

skipper ['skɪpə*] *n* (*NAUT, SPORT*) capitán *m*

skipping rope ['skɪpɪŋ-] (*BRIT*) *n* comba

skirmish ['skə:mɪʃ] *n* escaramuza

skirt [skə:t] *n* falda (*SP*), pollera (*AM*) ♦ *vt* (*go round*) ladear; **~ing board** (*BRIT*) *n* rodapié *m*

ski slope *n* pista de esquí

ski suit *n* traje *m* de esquiar

ski tow *n* remonte *m*

skittle ['skɪtl] *n* bolo; **~s** *n* (*game*) boliche *m*

skive [skaɪv] (*BRIT: inf*) *vi* gandulear

skull [skʌl] *n* calavera; (*ANAT*) cráneo

skunk [skʌŋk] *n* mofeta

sky [skaɪ] *n* cielo; **~light** *n* tragaluz *m*, claraboya; **~scraper** *n* rascacielos *m inv*

slab [slæb] *n* (*stone*) bloque *m*; (*flat*) losa; (*of cake*) trozo

slack [slæk] *adj* (*loose*) flojo; (*slow*) de poca actividad; (*careless*) descuidado; **~s** *npl* pantalones *mpl*; **~en** (*also: ~en off*) *vi* aflojarse ♦ *vt* aflojar; (*speed*) disminuir

slag heap ['slæg-] *n* escorial *m*, escombrera

slag off (*BRIT: inf*) *vt* poner como un trapo

slam [slæm] *vt* (*throw*) arrojar (*violentamente*); (*criticize*) criticar duramente ♦ *vi* (*door*) cerrarse de golpe; **to ~ the door** dar un portazo

slander ['slɑ:ndə*] *n* calumnia, difamación f

slang [slæŋ] *n* argot *m*; (*jargon*) jerga

slant [slɑ:nt] *n* sesgo, inclinación f; (*fig*) interpretación f; **~ed** *adj* (*fig*) parcial; **~ing** *adj* inclinado; (*eyes*) rasgado

slap |slæp| n palmada; (in face) bofetada ♦ vt dar una palmada or bofetada a; (paint etc): **to ~ sth on sth** embadurnar algo con algo ♦ adv (directly) exactamente, directamente; **~dash** adj descuidado; **~stick** n comedia de golpe y porrazo; **~up** adj: **a ~up meal** (BRIT) un banquetazo, una comilona

slash |slæʃ| vt acuchillar; (fig: prices) fulminar

slat |slæt| n tablilla, listón m

slate |sleɪt| n pizarra ♦ vt (fig: criticize) criticar duramente

slaughter |'slɔːtə*| n (of animals) matanza; (of people) carnicería ♦ vt matar; **~house** n matadero

Slav |slɑːv| adj eslavo

slave |sleɪv| n esclavo/a ♦ vi (also: ~ away) sudar tinta; **~ry** n esclavitud f

slay |sleɪ| (pt slew, pp slain) vt matar

sleazy |'sliːzɪ| adj de mala fama

sledge |slɛdʒ| n trineo; **~hammer** n mazo

sleek |sliːk| adj (shiny) lustroso; (car etc) elegante

sleep |sliːp| (pt, pp slept) n sueño ♦ vi dormir; **to go to ~** quedarse dormido; **~ around** vi acostarse con cualquiera; **~ in** vi (oversleep) quedarse dormido; **~er** n (person) durmiente m/f; (BRIT, RAIL: on track) traviesa; (: train) coche-cama m; **~ing bag** n saco de dormir; **~ing car** n coche-cama m; **~ing partner** (BRIT) n (COMM) socio comanditario; **~ing pill** n somnífero; **~less** adj: **a ~less night** una noche en blanco; **~walker** n sonámbulo/a; **~y** adj soñoliento; (place) soporífero

sleet |sliːt| n aguanieve f

sleeve |sliːv| n manga; (TECH) manguito; (of record) portada; **~less** adj sin mangas

sleigh |sleɪ| n trineo

sleight |slaɪt| n: **~ of hand** escamoteo

slender |'slɛndə*| adj delgado; (means)

escaso

slept |slɛpt| pt, pp of **sleep**

slew |sluː| pt of **slay** ♦ vi (BRIT: veer) torcerse

slice |slaɪs| n (of meat) tajada; (of bread) rebanada; (of lemon) rodaja; (utensil) pala ♦ vt cortar (en tajos), rebanar

slick |slɪk| adj (skilful) hábil, diestro; (clever) astuto ♦ n (also: oil ~) marea negra

slide |slaɪd| (pt, pp slid) n (movement) descenso, desprendimiento; (in playground) tobogán m; (PHOT) diapositiva; (BRIT: also: hair ~) pasador m ♦ vt correr, deslizar ♦ vi (slip) resbalarse; (glide) deslizarse; **sliding** adj (door) corredizo; **sliding scale** n escala móvil

slight |slaɪt| adj (slim) delgado; (frail) delicado; (pain etc) leve; (trivial) insignificante; (small) pequeño ♦ n desaire m ♦ vt (insult) ofender, desairar; **not in the ~est** en absoluto; **~ly** adv ligeramente, un poco

slim |slɪm| adj delgado, esbelto; (fig: chance) remoto ♦ vi adelgazar

slime |slaɪm| n limo, cieno

slimming |'slɪmɪŋ| n adelgazamiento

slimy |'slaɪmɪ| adj cenagoso

sling |slɪŋ| (pt, pp slung) n (MED) cabestrillo; (weapon) honda ♦ vt tirar, arrojar

slip |slɪp| n (slide) resbalón m; (mistake) descuido; (underskirt) combinación f; (of paper) papelito ♦ vt (slide) deslizar ♦ vi deslizarse; (stumble) resbalar(se); (decline) decaer; (move smoothly): **to ~ into/out of** (room etc) introducirse en/salirse de; **to give sb the ~** eludir a uno; **a ~ of the tongue** un lapsus; **to ~ sth on/off** ponerse/quitarse algo; **~ away** vi escabullirse; **~ in** vt meter ♦ vi meterse; **~ out** vi (go out) salir (un momento); **~ up** vi (make mistake) equivocarse; meter la pata; **~ped disc** n vértebra dislocada

slipper ['slɪpə*] n zapatilla, pantufla
slippery ['slɪpərɪ] adj resbaladizo
slip: ~ **road** (BRIT) n carretera de acceso; **~-up** n (error) desliz m; **~way** n grada, gradas fpl
slit [slɪt] (pt, pp **slit**) n raja; (cut) corte m ♦ vt rajar; cortar
slither ['slɪðə*] vi deslizarse
sliver ['slɪvə*] n (of glass, wood) astilla; (of cheese etc) raja
slob [slɔb] (inf) n abandonado/a
slog [slɔg] (BRIT) vi sudar tinta; **it was a ~** costó trabajo (hacerlo)
slogan ['sləugən] n eslogan m, lema m
slope [sləup] n (up) cuesta, pendiente f; (down) declive m; (side of mountain) falda, vertiente m ♦ vi: **to ~ down** estar en declive; **to ~ up** inclinarse; **sloping** adj en pendiente; en declive; (writing) inclinado
sloppy ['slɔpɪ] adj (work) descuidado; (appearance) desaliñado
slot [slɔt] n ranura ♦ vt: **to ~ into** encajar en
slot machine n (BRIT: vending machine) distribuidor m automático; (for gambling) tragaperras m inv
slouch [slautʃ] vi andar etc con los hombros caídos
Slovenia [sləu'vi:nɪə] n Eslovenia
slovenly ['slʌvənlɪ] adj desaliñado, desaseado; (careless) descuidado
slow [sləu] adj lento; (not clever) lerdo; (watch): **to be ~** atrasar ♦ adv lentamente, despacio ♦ vt, vi (also: **~ down, ~ up**) retardar; **"~"** (road sign) "disminuir velocidad"; **~down** (US) n huelga de manos caídas; **~ly** adv lentamente, despacio; **~ motion** n: **in ~ motion** a cámara lenta
sludge [slʌdʒ] n lodo, fango
slug [slʌg] n babosa; (bullet) posta; **~gish** adj lento; (person) perezoso
sluice [slu:s] n (gate) esclusa; (channel) canal m
slum [slʌm] n casucha
slump [slʌmp] n (economic) depresión

f ♦ vi hundirse; (prices) caer en picado
slung [slʌŋ] pt, pp of **sling**
slur [slə:*] n: **to cast a ~ on** insultar ♦ vt (speech) pronunciar mal
slush [slʌʃ] n nieve f a medio derretir
slut [slʌt] n putona
sly [slaɪ] adj astuto; (smile) taimado
smack [smæk] n bofetada ♦ vt dar con la mano a; (child, on face) abofetear ♦ vi: **to ~ of** saber a, oler a
small [smɔ:l] adj pequeño; **~ ads** (BRIT) npl anuncios mpl por palabras; **~ change** n suelto, cambio; **~holder** (BRIT) n granjero/a, parcelero/a; **~ hours** npl: **in the ~ hours** a las altas horas (de la noche); **~pox** n viruela; **~ talk** n cháchara
smart [sma:t] adj elegante; (clever) listo, inteligente; (quick) rápido, vivo ♦ vi escocer, picar; **~en up** vi arreglarse ♦ vt arreglar
smash [smæʃ] n (also: **~-up**) choque m; (MUS) exitazo ♦ vt (break) hacer pedazos; (car etc) estrellar; (SPORT: record) batir ♦ vi hacerse pedazos; (against wall etc) estrellarse; **~ing** (inf) adj estupendo
smattering ['smætərɪŋ] n: **a ~ of** algo de
smear [smɪə*] n mancha; (MED) frotis m inv ♦ vt untar; **~ campaign** n campaña de desprestigio
smell [smel] (pt, pp **smelt** or **smelled**) n olor m; (sense) olfato ♦ vt, vi oler; **~y** adj maloliente
smile [smaɪl] n sonrisa ♦ vi sonreír
smirk [smə:k] n sonrisa falsa o afectada
smith [smɪθ] n herrero; **~y** ['smɪðɪ] n herrería
smog [smɔg] n esmog m
smoke [sməuk] n humo ♦ vi fumar; (chimney) echar humo ♦ vt (cigarettes) fumar; **~d** adj (bacon, glass) ahumado; **~r** n fumador(a) m/f; (RAIL) coche m fumador; **~ screen** n cortina de humo; **~ shop** (US) n estanco (SP),

tabaquería (*AM*); **smoking** *n*: "no smoking" "prohibido fumar";
smoky *adj* (*room*) lleno de humo; (*taste*) ahumado

smolder ['sməʊldə*] (*US*) *vi* = **smoulder**

smooth [smu:ð] *adj* liso; (*sea*) tranquilo; (*flavour, movement*) suave; (*sauce*) fino; (*person: pej*) meloso ♦ *vt* (*also: ~ out*) alisar; (*creases, difficulties*) allanar

smother ['smʌðə*] *vt* sofocar; (*repress*) contener

smoulder ['sməʊldə*] (*US* **smolder**) *vi* arder sin llama

smudge [smʌdʒ] *n* mancha ♦ *vt* manchar

smug [smʌg] *adj* presumido; orondo

smuggle ['smʌgl] *vt* pasar de contrabando; **~r** *n* contrabandista *m/f*; **smuggling** *n* contrabando

smutty ['smʌtɪ] *adj* (*fig*) verde, obsceno

snack [snæk] *n* bocado; **~ bar** *n* cafetería

snag [snæg] *n* problema *m*

snail [sneɪl] *n* caracol *m*

snake [sneɪk] *n* serpiente *f*

snap [snæp] *n* (*sound*) chasquido; (*photograph*) foto *f* ♦ *adj* (*decision*) instantáneo ♦ *vt* (*break*) quebrar; (*fingers*) castañetear ♦ *vi* quebrarse; (*fig: speak sharply*) contestar bruscamente; **to ~ shut** cerrarse de golpe; **~ at** *vt fus* (*subj: dog*) intentar morder; **~ off** *vi* partirse; **~ up** *vt* agarrar; **~ fastener** (*US*) *n* botón *m* de presión; **~py** (*inf*) *adj* (*answer*) instantáneo; (*slogan*) conciso; **make it ~py!** (*hurry up*) ¡date prisa!; **~shot** *n* foto *f* (instantánea)

snare [snɛə*] *n* trampa

snarl [snɑːl] *vi* gruñir

snatch [snætʃ] *n* (*small piece*) fragmento ♦ *vt* (*~ away*) arrebatar; (*fig*) agarrar; **to ~ some sleep** encontrar tiempo para dormir

sneak [sni:k] (*pt* (*US*) **snuck**) *vi*: **to ~ in/out** entrar/salir a hurtadillas ♦ *n* (*inf*) soplón/ona *m/f*; **to ~ up on sb** aparecérsele de improviso a uno; **~ers** *npl* zapatos *mpl* de lona; **~y** *adj* furtivo

sneer [snɪə*] *vi* reír con sarcasmo; (*mock*): **to ~ at** burlarse de

sneeze [sni:z] *vi* estornudar

sniff [snɪf] *vi* sollozar ♦ *vt* husmear, oler; (*drugs*) esnifar

snigger ['snɪgə*] *vi* reírse con disimulo

snip [snɪp] *n* tijeretazo; (*BRIT: inf: bargain*) ganga ♦ *vt* tijeretear

sniper ['snaɪpə*] *n* francotirador(a) *m/f*

snippet ['snɪpɪt] *n* retazo

snob [snɔb] *n/f*; **~bery** *n* (e)snobismo; **~bish** *adj* (e)snob

snooker ['snu:kə*] *n* especie de billar

snoop [snu:p] *vi*: **to ~ about** fisgonear

snooze [snu:z] *n* siesta ♦ *vi* echar una siesta

snore [snɔː*] *n* ronquido ♦ *vi* roncar

snorkel ['snɔːkl] *n* (tubo) respirador *m*

snort [snɔːt] *n* bufido ♦ *vi* bufar

snout [snaʊt] *n* hocico, morro

snow [snəʊ] *n* nieve *f* ♦ *vi* nevar; **~ball** *n* bola de nieve ♦ *vi* (*fig*) agrandirse, ampliarse; **~bound** *adj* bloqueado por la nieve; **~drift** *n* ventisquero; **~drop** *n* campanilla; **~fall** *n* nevada; **~flake** *n* copo de nieve; **~man** (*irreg*) *n* figura de nieve; **~plough** (*US* **~plow**) *n* quitanieves *m inv*; **~shoe** *n* raqueta (de nieve); **~storm** *n* nevada, nevasca

snub [snʌb] *vt* (*person*) desairar ♦ *n* desaire *m*, repulsa; **~-nosed** *adj* chato

snuff [snʌf] *n* rapé *m*

snug [snʌg] *adj* (*cosy*) cómodo; (*fitted*) ajustado

snuggle ['snʌgl] *vi*: **to ~ up to sb** arrimarse a uno

KEYWORD

so [səʊ] *adv* **1** (*thus, likewise*) así, de este modo; **if ~** de ser así; **I like swimming — ~ do I** a mí me gusta nadar — a mí también; **I've got work**

to do — ~ has Paul tengo trabajo que hacer — Paul también; **it's 5 o'clock — ~ it is!** son las cinco — ¡pues es verdad!; **I hope/think ~** espero/creo que sí; **(in past)** hasta este momento

2 (in comparisons etc: to such a degree) tan; **~ quickly (that)** tan rápido (que); **~ big (that)** tan grande (que); **she's not ~ clever as her brother** no es tan lista como su hermano; **we were ~ worried** estábamos preocupadísimos

3: ~ much adj, adv tanto; **~ many** tantos/as

4 (phrases): **10 or ~** unos 10, 10 o así; **~ long!** (inf: goodbye) ¡hasta luego! ♦ conj **1** (expressing purpose): **~ as to do** para hacer; **~ (that)** para que + sub **2** (expressing result) así que; **~ you see, I could have gone** así que ya ves, (yo) podría haber ido

soak [səuk] vt (drench) empapar; (steep in water) remojar ♦ vi remojarse, estar a remojo; **~ in** vi penetrar; **~ up** vt absorber

soap [səup] n jabón m; **~flakes** npl escamas fpl de jabón; **~ opera** n telenovela; **~ powder** n jabón m en polvo; **~y** adj jabonoso

soar [sɔː*] vi (on wings) remontarse; (rocket, prices) dispararse; (building etc) elevarse

sob [sɔb] n sollozo ♦ vi sollozar

sober ['səubə*] adj (serious) serio; (not drunk) sobrio; (colour, style) discreto; **~ up** vt quitar la borrachera

so-called adj así llamado

soccer ['sɔkə*] n fútbol m

social ['səuʃl] adj social ♦ n velada, fiesta; **~ club** n club m; **~ism** n socialismo; **~ist** n, adj socialista m/f; **~ize** vi: **to ~ize (with)** alternar (con); **~ly** adv socialmente; **~ security** n seguridad f social; **~ work** n asistencia social; **~ worker** n asistente/a m/f

social

society [sə'saɪətɪ] n sociedad f; (club) asociación f; (also: high ~) alta sociedad

sociology [səusɪ'ɒlədʒɪ] n sociología

sock [sɔk] n calcetín m (SP), media (AM)

socket ['sɔkɪt] n cavidad f; (BRIT: ELEC) enchufe m

sod [sɔd] n (of earth) césped m; (BRIT: inf!) cabrón/ona m/f (!)

soda ['səudə] n (CHEM) sosa; (also: ~ water) soda; (US: also: ~ pop) gaseosa

sofa ['səufə] n sofá m

soft [sɔft] adj (lenient, not hard) blando; (gentle, not bright) suave; **~ drink** n bebida no alcohólica; **~en** ['sɔfn] vt ablandar; suavizar; (effect) amortiguar ♦ vi ablandarse; suavizarse; **~ly** adv suavemente; (gently) delicadamente, con delicadeza; **~ness** n blandura; suavidad f; **~ware** n (COMPUT) software m

soggy ['sɔgɪ] adj empapado

soil [sɔɪl] n (earth) tierra, suelo ♦ vt ensuciar; **~ed** adj sucio

solar ['səulə*] adj: **~ energy** n energía solar; **~ panel** n panel m solar

sold [səuld] pt, pp of **sell**; **~ out** adj (COMM) agotado

solder ['səuldə*] vt soldar ♦ n soldadura

soldier ['səuldʒə*] n soldado; (army man) militar m

sole [səul] n (of foot) planta; (of shoe) suela; (fish: pl inv) lenguado ♦ adj único

solemn ['sɔləm] adj solemne

sole trader n (COMM) comerciante m exclusivo

solicit [sə'lɪsɪt] vt (request) solicitar ♦ vi (prostitute) importunar

solicitor [sə'lɪsɪtə*] n (BRIT) n (for wills etc) ≈ notario/a; (in court) ≈ abogado/a

solid ['sɔlɪd] adj sólido; (gold etc) macizo ♦ n sólido; **~s** npl (food) alimentos mpl sólidos

solidarity [sɔli'dærɪti] n solidaridad f

solitary ['sɔlɪtərɪ] adj solitario, solo; **~ confinement** n incomunicación f

solo ['səuləu] n solo ♦ adv (fly) en solitario; **~ist** n solista m/f

soluble ['sɔljubl] adj soluble

solution [sə'lu:ʃən] n solución f

solve [sɔlv] vt resolver, solucionar

solvent ['sɔlvənt] adj (COMM) solvente ♦ n (CHEM) solvente m

KEYWORD

some [sʌm] adj 1 (a certain amount or number of): **~ tea/water/biscuits** té/agua/(unas) galletas; **there's ~ milk in the fridge** hay leche en el frigo; **there were ~ people outside** había algunas personas fuera; **I've got ~ money, but not much** tengo algo de dinero, pero no mucho

2 (certain: in contrasts) algunos/as; **~ people say that ...** hay quien dice que ...; **~ films were excellent, but most were mediocre** hubo películas excelentes, pero la mayoría fueron mediocres

3 (unspecified): **~ woman was asking for you** una mujer estuvo preguntando por ti; **he was asking for ~ book (or other)** pedía un libro; **~ day** algún día; **~ day next week** un día de la semana que viene

♦ pron 1 (a certain number): **I've got ~** (books etc) tengo algunos/as

2 (a certain amount): **I've got ~** (money, milk) tengo algo; **could I have ~ of that cheese?** ¿me puede dar un poco de ese queso?; **I've read ~ of the book** he leído parte del libro

♦ adv: **~ 10 people** unas 10 personas, una decena de personas

some: **~body** ['sʌmbədi] pron = **someone**; **~how** adv de alguna manera; (for some reason) por una u otra razón; **~one** pron alguien; **~place** (US) adv = **somewhere**

somersault ['sʌməsɔ:lt] n (deliberate) salto mortal; (accidental) vuelco ♦ vi dar un salto mortal; dar vueltos

some: **~thing** pron algo; **would you like ~thing to eat/drink?** ¿te gustaría cenar/tomar algo?; **~time** adv (in future) algún día, en algún momento; (in past): **~time last month** durante el mes pasado; **~times** adv a veces; **~what** adv algo; **~where** adv (be) en alguna parte; (go) a alguna parte; **~where else** (be) en otra parte; (go) a otra parte

son [sʌn] n hijo

song [sɔŋ] n canción f

son-in-law n yerno

soon [su:n] adv pronto, dentro de poco; **~ afterwards** poco después; see also **as**; **~er** adv (time) antes, más temprano; (preference): **I would ~er do that** preferiría hacer eso; **~er or later** tarde o temprano

soot [sut] n hollín m

soothe [su:ð] vt tranquilizar; (pain) aliviar

sophisticated [sə'fɪstɪkeɪtɪd] adj sofisticado

sophomore ['sɔfəmɔ:*] (US) n estudiante m/f de segundo año

sopping ['sɔpɪŋ] adj: **~ (wet)** empapado

soppy ['sɔpɪ] (pej) adj tonto

soprano [sə'prɑ:nəu] n soprano f

sorcerer ['sɔ:sərə*] n hechicero

sore [sɔ:*] adj (painful) doloroso, que duele ♦ n llaga; **~ly** adv: **I am ~ly tempted to** estoy muy tentado a

sorrow ['sɔrəu] n pena, dolor m; **~s** npl pesares mpl; **~ful** adj triste

sorry ['sɔrɪ] adj (regretful) arrepentido; (condition, excuse) lastimoso; **~!** ¡perdón!, ¡perdone!; **~?** ¿cómo?; **to feel ~ for sb** tener lástima a uno; **I feel ~ for him** me da lástima

sort [sɔ:t] n clase f, género, tipo ♦ vt (also: **~ out**: papers) clasificar; (: problems) arreglar, solucionar; **~ing**

office n sala de batalla

SOS n SOS m

so-so adv regular, así así

soufflé ['su:fleɪ] n suflé m

sought [sɔːt] pt, pp of **seek**

soul [səul] n alma; **~ful** adj lleno de sentimiento

sound [saund] n (noise) sonido, ruido; (volume: on TV etc) volumen m; (GEO) estrecho ♦ adj (healthy) sano; (safe, not damaged) en buen estado; (reliable: person) digno de confianza; (sensible) sensato, razonable; (secure: investment) seguro ♦ adv: **~ asleep** profundamente dormido ♦ vt (alarm) sonar ♦ vi sonar, resonar; (fig: seem) parecer; **to ~ like** sonar a; **~ out** vt sondear; **~ barrier** n barrera del sonido; **~bite** n cita jugosa; **~ effects** npl efectos mpl sonoros; **~ly** adv (sleep) profundamente; (defeated) completamente; **~proof** adj insonorizado; **~track** n (of film) banda sonora

soup [suːp] n (thick) sopa; (thin) caldo; **~ plate** n plato sopero; **~spoon** n cuchara sopera

sour ['sauə*] adj agrio; (milk) cortado; **it's ~ grapes** (fig) están verdes

source [sɔːs] n fuente f

south [sauθ] n sur m ♦ adj del sur, sureño ♦ adv al sur, hacia el sur; **S~ Africa** n África del Sur; **S~ African** adj, n sudafricano/a m/f; **S~ America** n América del Sur, Sudamérica; **S~ American** adj, n sudamericano/a m/f; **~-east** n sudeste m; **~erly** ['sʌðəlɪ] adj sur; (from the ~) del sur; **~ern** ['sʌðən] adj del sur, meridional; **S~ Pole** n Polo Sur; **~ward(s)** adv hacia el sur; **~-west** n suroeste m

souvenir [suːvə'nɪə*] n recuerdo

sovereign ['sɔvrɪn] adj, n soberano/a m/f; **~ty** n soberanía

soviet ['səuvɪət] adj soviético; **the S~ Union** la Unión Soviética

sow[1] [səu] (pt **sowed**, pp **sown**) vt sembrar

sow[2] [sau] n cerda (SP), puerca (SP), chancha (AM)

soy [sɔɪ] (US) n = **soya**

soya ['sɔɪə] (BRIT) n soja; **~ bean** n haba de soja; **~ sauce** n salsa de soja

spa [spaː] n balneario

space [speɪs] n espacio; (room) sitio ♦ cpd espacial ♦ vt (also: **~ out**) espaciar; **~craft** n nave f espacial; **~man/woman** (irreg) n astronauta m/f, cosmonauta m/f; **~ship** n = **~craft**; **spacing** n espaciado

spacious ['speɪʃəs] adj amplio

spade [speɪd] n (tool) pala, laya; **~s** npl (CARDS: British) picas fpl; (: Spanish) espadas fpl

spaghetti [spə'gɛtɪ] n espaguetis mpl, fideos mpl

Spain [speɪn] n España

span [spæn] n (of bird, plane) envergadura; (of arch) luz f; (in time) lapso ♦ vt extenderse sobre, cruzar; (fig) abarcar

Spaniard ['spænjəd] n español(a) m/f

spaniel ['spænjəl] n perro de aguas

Spanish ['spænɪʃ] adj español(a) ♦ n (LING) español m, castellano; **the ~** npl los españoles

spank [spæŋk] vt zurrar

spanner ['spænə*] (BRIT) n llave f (inglesa)

spare [spɛə*] adj de reserva; (surplus) sobrante, de más ♦ n = **~ part** ♦ vt (do without) pasarse sin; (refrain from hurting) perdonar; **to ~** (surplus) sobrante, de sobra; **~ part** n pieza de repuesto; **~ time** n tiempo libre; **~ wheel** n (AUT) rueda de recambio

sparingly ['spɛərɪŋlɪ] adv con moderación

spark [spaːk] n chispa; (fig) chispazo; **~(ing) plug** n bujía

sparkle ['spaːkl] n centelleo, destello ♦ vi (shine) relucir, brillar; **sparkling** adj (eyes, conversation) brillante; (wine) espumoso; (*mineral water*) con gas

sparrow ['spærəu] *n* gorrión *m*

sparse [spɑːs] *adj* esparcido, escaso

spartan ['spɑːtən] *adj* (*fig*) espartano

spasm ['spæzəm] *n* (*MED*) espasmo

spastic ['spæstik] *n* espástico/a

spat [spæt] *pt, pp of* **spit**

spate [speit] *n* (*fig*): **a ~ of** un torrente
de

spawn [spɔːn] *vi* desovar, frezar ♦ *n*
huevas *fpl*

speak [spiːk] (*pt* **spoke**, *pp* **spoken**)
vt (*language*) hablar; (*truth*) decir ♦ *vi*
hablar; (*make a speech*) intervenir; **to
~ to sb/of** *or* **about sth** hablar con
uno/de *or* sobre algo; **~ up!** ¡habla
fuerte!; **~er** *n* (*in public*) orador(a) *m/f*;
(*also: loud~er*) altavoz *m*; (*for stereo etc*)
bafle *m*; (*POL*) **the S~er** (*BRIT*) el
Presidente de la Cámara de los
Comunes, (*US*) el Presidente del Congreso

spear [spiə*] *n* lanza ♦ *vt* alancear;
~head *vt* (*attack etc*) encabezar

spec [spek] (*inf*) *n*: **on ~** como
especulación

special ['spɛʃl] *adj* especial; (*edition etc*)
extraordinario; (*delivery*) urgente; **~ist**
n especialista *m/f*; **~ity** [spɛʃiˈælɪtɪ]
(*BRIT*) *n* especialidad *f*; **~ize** *vi*: **to ~ize
(in)** especializarse (en); **~ly** *adv* sobre
todo, en particular; **~ty** (*US*) *n* = **~ity**

species ['spiːʃiːz] *n inv* especie *f*

specific [spəˈsɪfɪk] *adj* específico; **~ally**
adv específicamente

specify ['spesɪfaɪ] *vt, vi* especificar,
precisar

specimen ['spesɪmən] *n* ejemplar *m*;
(*MED: of urine*) espécimen *m* (: *of blood*)
muestra

speck [spek] *n* grano, mota

speckled ['spekld] *adj* moteado

specs [speks] (*inf*) *npl* gafas *fpl* (*SP*),
anteojos *mpl*

spectacle ['spektəkl] *n* espectáculo; **~s**
npl (*BRIT: glasses*) gafas *fpl* (*SP*),
anteojos *mpl*; **spectacular** [-'tækjulə*]
adj espectacular; (*success*)

impresionante

spectator [spek'teɪtə*] *n* espectador(a)
m/f

spectrum ['spektrəm] (*pl* **spectra**) *n*
espectro

speculate ['spekjuleɪt] *vi*: **to ~ (on)**
especular (en); **speculation**
[spekjuˈleɪʃən] *n* especulación *f*

speech [spiːtʃ] *n* (*faculty*) habla; (*formal
talk*) discurso; (*spoken language*)
lenguaje *m*; **~less** *adj* mudo,
estupefacto; **~ therapist** *n* especialista
que corrige defectos de pronunciación en
los niños

speed [spiːd] *n* velocidad *f*; (*haste*)
prisa; (*promptness*) rapidez *f*; **at full** *or*
top ~ a máxima velocidad; **~ up** *vi*
acelerarse ♦ *vt* acelerar; **~boat** *n*
lancha motora; **~ily** *adv* rápido,
rápidamente; **~ing** *n* (*AUT*) exceso de
velocidad; **~ limit** *n* límite *m* de
velocidad, velocidad *f* máxima;
~ometer [spɪˈdɒmɪtə*] *n* velocímetro;
~way *n* (*sport*) pista de carrera; **~y** *adj*
(*fast*) veloz, rápido; (*prompt*) pronto

spell [spel] (*pt, pp* **spelt** (*BRIT*) *or*
spelled) *n* (*also: magic ~*) encanto,
hechizo; (*period of time*) rato, período
♦ *vt* deletrear; (*fig*) anunciar, presagiar;
to cast a ~ on sb hechizar a uno; **he
can't ~** pone faltas de ortografía;
~bound *adj* embelesado, hechizado;
~ing *n* ortografía

spend [spend] (*pt, pp* **spent**) *vt*
(*money*) gastar; (*time*) pasar; (*life*)
dedicar; **~thrift** *n* derrochador(a) *m/f*,
pródigo/a

sperm [spɜːm] *n* esperma

sphere [sfɪə*] *n* esfera

sphinx [sfɪŋks] *n* esfinge *f*

spice [spaɪs] *n* especia ♦ *vt*
condimentar

spicy ['spaɪsɪ] *adj* picante

spider ['spaɪdə*] *n* araña

spike [spaɪk] *n* (*point*) punta; (*BOT*)
espiga

spill [spɪl] (*pt, pp* **spilt** *or* **spilled**) *vt*

derramar, verter ♦ vi derramarse; **to ~ over** desbordarse

spin [spɪn] (pt, pp **spun**) n (AVIAT) barrena; (trip in car) paseo (en coche); (on ball) efecto m ♦ vt (wool etc) hilar; (ball etc) hacer girar ♦ vi girar, dar vueltas

spinach ['spɪnɪtʃ] n espinaca; (as food) espinacas fpl

spinal ['spaɪnl] adj espinal; **~ cord** n columna vertebral

spin doctor n informador(a) parcial al servicio de un partido político etc

spin-dryer (BRIT) n secador m centrífugo

spine [spaɪn] n espinazo, columna vertebral; (thorn) espina; **~less** adj (fig) débil, pusilánime

spinning ['spɪnɪŋ] n hilandería; **~ top** n peonza

spin-off n derivado, producto secundario

spinster ['spɪnstə*] n soltera

spiral ['spaɪərl] n espiral f ♦ vi (fig: prices) subir desorbitadamente; **~ staircase** n escalera de caracol

spire ['spaɪə*] n aguja, chapitel m

spirit ['spɪrɪt] n (soul) alma f; (ghost) fantasma m; (attitude, sense) espíritu m; (courage) valor m, ánimo; **~s** npl (drink) licor(es) m(pl); **in good ~s** alegre, de buen ánimo; **~ed** adj enérgico, vigoroso

spiritual ['spɪrɪtjuəl] adj espiritual ♦ n espiritual m

spit [spɪt] (pt, pp **spat**) n (for roasting) asador m, espetón m; (saliva) saliva ♦ vi escupir; (sound) chisporrotear; (rain) lloviznar

spite [spaɪt] n rencor m, ojeriza ♦ vt causar pena a, mortificar; **in ~ of** a pesar de, pese a; **~ful** adj rencoroso, malévolo

spittle ['spɪtl] n saliva, baba

splash [splæʃ] n (sound) chapoteo; (of colour) mancha ♦ vi salpicar ♦ vi (also: **~ about**) chapotear

spleen [spli:n] n (ANAT) bazo

splendid ['splendɪd] adj espléndido

splint [splɪnt] n tablilla

splinter ['splɪntə*] n (of wood etc) astilla; (in finger) espigón m ♦ vi astillarse, hacer astillas

split [splɪt] (pt, pp **split**) n hendedura, raja; (fig) división f; (POL) escisión f ♦ vt partir, rajar; (party) dividir; (share) repartir ♦ vi dividirse, escindirse; **~ up** vi (couple) separarse; (meeting) acabarse

spoil [spɔɪl] (pt, pp **spoilt** or **spoiled**) vt (damage) dañar; (mar) estropear; (child) mimar, consentir; **~s** npl despojo, botín m; **~sport** n aguafiestas m inv

spoke [spəuk] pt of **speak** ♦ n rayo, radio

spoken ['spəukn] pp of **speak**

spokesman ['spəuksmən] (irreg) n portavoz m; **spokeswoman** ['spəukswumən] (irreg) n portavoz f

sponge [spʌndʒ] n esponja; (also: **~ cake**) bizcocho ♦ vt (wash) lavar con esponja ♦ vi: **to ~ off** or **on sb** vivir a costa de uno; **~ bag** (BRIT) n esponjera

sponsor ['spɒnsə*] n patrocinador(a) m/f ♦ vt (applicant, proposal etc) proponer; **~ship** n patrocinio

spontaneous [spɒn'teɪnɪəs] adj espontáneo

spooky ['spu:kɪ] (inf) adj espeluznante, horripilante

spool [spu:l] n carrete m

spoon [spu:n] n cuchara; **~-feed** vt dar de comer con cuchara a; (fig) tratar como un niño a; **~ful** n cucharada

sport [spɔ:t] n deporte m; (person): **to be a good ~** ser muy majo ♦ vt (wear) lucir, ostentar; **~ing** adj deportivo; (generous) caballeroso; **to give sb a ~ing chance** darle a uno la (buena) oportunidad; **~ jacket** (US) n = **~s jacket**; **~s car** n coche m deportivo; **~s jacket** (BRIT) n chaqueta deportiva; **~sman** (irreg) n deportista m;

~**smanship** n deportividad f; ~**swear** n trajes mpl de deporte or sport; ~**swoman** (irreg) n deportista; ~**y** adj deportista

spot [spɔt] n sitio, lugar m; (dot: on pattern) punto, mancha; (pimple) grano; (RADIO) cuña publicitaria; (TV) espacio publicitario; (small amount): **a** ~ **of** un poquito de ♦ vt (notice) notar, observar; **on the** ~ allí mismo; ~ **check** n reconocimiento rápido; ~**less** adj perfectamente limpio; ~**light** n foco, reflector m; (AUT) faro auxiliar; ~**ted** adj (pattern) de puntos; ~**ty** adj (face) con granos

spouse [spauz] n cónyuge m/f

spout [spaut] n (of jug) pico; (of pipe) caño ♦ vi salir en chorro

sprain [spreɪn] n torcedura ♦ vt: **to** ~ **one's ankle/wrist** torcerse el tobillo/la muñeca

sprang [spræŋ] pt of **spring**

sprawl [sprɔːl] vi tumbarse

spray [spreɪ] n rociada; (of sea) espuma; (container) atomizador m; (for paint etc) pistola rociadora; (of flowers) ramita ♦ vt rociar; (crops) regar

spread [spred] (pt, pp **spread**) n extensión f; (of idea etc) difusión f; (PRESS, TYP: two pages) plana; (CULIN: for bread etc) pasta para untar; (inf: food) comilona ♦ vt extender; (butter) untar; (wings, sails) desplegar; (work, wealth) repartir; (scatter) esparcir ♦ vi (also: ~ **out**: stain) extenderse; (news) diseminarse; ~ **out** vi (move apart) separarse; ~**-eagled** adj a pata tendida; ~**sheet** n hoja electrónica or de cálculo

spree [spriː] n: **to go on a** ~ ir de juerga

sprightly [ˈspraɪtlɪ] adj vivo, enérgico

spring [sprɪŋ] (pt **sprang**, pp **sprung**) n (season) primavera; (leap) salto, brinco; (coiled metal) resorte m; (of water) fuente f, manantial m ♦ vi saltar, brincar; ~ **up** vi (thing: appear) aparecer; (problem) surgir; ~**board** n trampolín m; ~**-clean(ing)** n limpieza general; ~**time** n primavera

sprinkle [ˈsprɪŋkl] vt (pour: liquid) rociar; (: salt, sugar) espolvorear; **to** ~ **water etc on,** ~ **with water etc** rociar o salpicar de agua etc; ~**r** n (for lawn) rociadera; (: to put out fire) aparato de rociadura automática

sprint [sprɪnt] n esprint m ♦ vi esprintar

sprout [spraut] vi brotar, retoñar; **(Brussels)** ~**s** npl coles fpl de Bruselas

spruce [spruːs] n inv (BOT) pícea ♦ adj aseado, pulcro

sprung [sprʌŋ] pp of **spring**

spun [spʌn] pt, pp of **spin**

spur [spəː*] n espuela; (fig) estímulo, aguijón m ♦ vt (also: ~ **on**) estimular, incitar; **on the** ~ **of the moment** de improviso

spurious [ˈspjuərɪəs] adj falso

spurn [spəːn] vt desdeñar, rechazar

spurt [spəːt] n chorro; (of energy) arrebato ♦ vi chorrear

spy [spaɪ] n espía m/f ♦ vi: **to** ~ **on** espiar a ♦ vt (see) divisar, lograr ver; ~**ing** n espionaje m

sq. abbr = **square**

squabble [ˈskwɔbl] vi reñir, pelear

squad [skwɔd] n (MIL) pelotón m; (POLICE) brigada; (SPORT) equipo

squadron [ˈskwɔdrn] n (MIL) escuadrón m; (AVIAT, NAUT) escuadra

squalid [ˈskwɔlɪd] adj vil; (fig: sordid) sórdido

squall [skwɔːl] n (storm) chubasco; (wind) ráfaga

squalor [ˈskwɔlə*] n miseria

squander [ˈskwɔndə*] vt (money) derrochar, despilfarrar; (chances) desperdiciar

square [skweə*] n cuadro; (in town) plaza; (inf: person) carca m/f ♦ adj cuadrado; (inf: ideas, tastes) trasnochado ♦ vt (arrange) arreglar; (MATH) cuadrar; (reconcile) compaginar; **all** ~ igual(es); **to have a** ~ **meal** comer caliente; **2 metres** ~ 2 metros en cuadro; **2 ~ metres** 2 metros cuadrados; **~ly** adv de lleno

squash [skwɒʃ] n (BRIT: drink): **lemon/orange ~** zumo (SP) or jugo (AM) de limón/naranja; (US: BOT) calabacín m; (SPORT) squash m, frontenis m ♦ vt aplastar

squat [skwɒt] adj achaparrado ♦ vi (also: ~ down) agacharse, sentarse en cuclillas; **~ter** n persona que ocupa ilegalmente una casa

squeak [skwi:k] vi (hinge) chirriar, rechinar; (mouse) chillar

squeal [skwi:l] vi chillar, dar gritos agudos

squeamish ['skwi:mɪʃ] adj delicado, remilgado

squeeze [skwi:z] n presión f; (of hand) apretón m; (COMM) restricción f ♦ vt (hand, arm) apretar; **~ out** vt exprimir

squelch [skwɛltʃ] vi chapotear

squid [skwɪd] n inv calamar m; (CULIN) calamares mpl

squiggle ['skwɪgl] n garabato

squint [skwɪnt] vi bizquear, ser bizco ♦ n (MED) estrabismo

squirm [skwə:m] vi retorcerse, revolverse

squirrel ['skwɪrəl] n ardilla

squirt [skwə:t] vi salir a chorros ♦ vt chiscar

Sr abbr = **senior**

St abbr = **saint**; **street**

stab [stæb] n (with knife) puñalada, (of pain) pinchazo; (inf: try): **to have a ~ at (doing) sth** intentar (hacer) algo ♦ vt apuñalar

stable ['steɪbl] adj estable ♦ n cuadra, caballeriza

stack [stæk] n montón m, pila ♦ vt amontonar, apilar

stadium ['steɪdɪəm] n estadio

staff [stɑ:f] n (work force) personal m, plantilla; (BRIT: SCOL) cuerpo docente ♦ vt proveer de personal

stag [stæg] n ciervo, venado

stage [steɪdʒ] n escena; (point) etapa;

(platform) plataforma; (profession): **the ~** el teatro ♦ vt (play) poner en escena, representar; (organize) montar, organizar; **in ~s** por etapas; **~coach** n diligencia; **~ manager** n director(a) m/f de escena

stagger ['stægə*] vi tambalearse ♦ vt (amaze) asombrar; (hours, holidays) escalonar; **~ing** adj asombroso

stagnant ['stægnənt] adj estancado

stag party n despedida de soltero

staid [steɪd] adj serio, formal

stain [steɪn] n mancha; (colouring) tintura ♦ vt manchar; (wood) teñir; **~ed glass window** n vidriera de colores; **~less steel** n acero inoxidable; **~ remover** n quitamanchas m inv

stair [stɛə*] n (step) peldaño, escalón m; **~s** npl escaleras fpl; **~case** n = **~way**; **~way** n escalera

stake [steɪk] n estaca, poste m; (COMM) interés m; (BETTING) apuesta ♦ vt (money) apostar; (life) arriesgar; (reputation) poner en juego; (claim) presentar una reclamación; **to be at ~** estar en juego

stale [steɪl] adj (bread) duro; (food) pasado; (smell) rancio; (beer) agrio

stalemate ['steɪlmeɪt] n tablas fpl (por ahogado); (fig) estancamiento

stalk [stɔ:k] n tallo, caña ♦ vt acechar, cazar al acecho; **~ off** vi irse airado

stall [stɔ:l] n (in market) puesto; (in stable) casilla de (establo) ♦ vt (AUT) calar; (fig) dar largas a ♦ vi (AUT) calarse; (fig) andarse con rodeos; **~s** npl (BRIT: in cinema, theatre) butacas fpl

stallion ['stæljən] n semental m

stamina ['stæmɪnə] n resistencia

stammer ['stæmə*] n tartamudeo ♦ vi tartamudear

stamp [stæmp] n sello (SP), estampilla (AM); (mark, also fig) marca, huella; (on document) timbre m ♦ vi (also: **~ one's foot**) patear ♦ vt (mark) marcar; (letter) poner sellos or estampillas en; (with rubber ~) sellar; **~ album** n álbum m para sellos or estampillas; **~ collecting** n filatelia

stampede [stæm'pi:d] n estampida

stance [stæns] n postura

stand [stænd] (pt, pp **stood**) n (position) posición f, postura; (for taxis) parada; (hall ~) perchero; (music ~) atril m; (SPORT) tribuna; (at exhibition) stand m ♦ vi (be) estar, encontrarse; (be on foot) estar de pie; (rise) levantarse; (remain) quedar en pie; (in election) presentar candidatura ♦ vt (place) poner, colocar; (withstand) aguantar, soportar; (invite to) invitar; **to make a ~** (fig) mantener una postura firme; **to ~ for parliament** (BRIT) presentarse (como candidato) a las elecciones; **~ by vi** (be ready) estar listo ♦ vt fus (opinion) aferrarse a; (person) apoyar; **~ down** vi (withdraw) ceder el puesto; **~ for** vt fus (signify) significar; (tolerate) aguantar, permitir; **~ in for** vt fus suplir a; **~ out** vi destacarse; **~ up** vi levantarse, ponerse de pie; **~ up for** vt fus defender; **~ up to** vt fus hacer frente a

standard ['stændəd] n patrón m, norma; (level) nivel m; (flag) estandarte m ♦ adj (size etc) normal, corriente; (text) básico; **~s** npl (morals) valores mpl morales; **~ lamp** (BRIT) n lámpara de pie; **~ of living** n nivel m de vida

stand-by ['stændbaɪ] n (reserve) recurso seguro; **to be on ~** estar sobre aviso; **~ ticket** n (AVIAT) (billete m) standby m

stand-in ['stændɪn] n suplente m/f

standing ['stændɪŋ] adj (on foot) de pie, en pie; (permanent) permanente ♦ n reputación f; **of many years' ~** que lleva muchos años; **~ joke** n broma permanente; **~ order** (BRIT) n (at bank) orden f de pago permanente; **~ room** n sitio para estar de pie

stand: **~point** n punto de vista; **~still** n: **at a ~still** (industry, traffic) paralizado; (car) parado; **to come to**

a ~still quedar paralizado; pararse

stank [stæŋk] pt of **stink**

staple ['steɪpl] n (for papers) grapa ♦ adj (food etc) básico ♦ vt grapar; **~r** n grapadora

star [stɑ:*] n estrella; (celebrity) estrella, astro ♦ vt (THEATRE, CINEMA) ser el/la protagonista de; **the ~s** npl (ASTROLOGY) el horóscopo

starboard ['stɑ:bəd] n estribor m

starch [stɑ:tʃ] n almidón m

stardom ['stɑ:dəm] n estrellato

stare [steə*] n mirada fija ♦ vi: **to ~ at** mirar fijo

starfish ['stɑ:fɪʃ] n estrella de mar

stark [stɑ:k] adj (bleak) severo, escueto ♦ adv: **~ naked** en cueros

starling ['stɑ:lɪŋ] n estornino

starry ['stɑ:rɪ] adj estrellado; **~-eyed** adj (innocent) inocentón/ona, ingenuo

start [stɑ:t] n principio, comienzo; (departure) salida; (sudden movement) salto, sobresalto; (advantage) ventaja ♦ vt empezar, comenzar; (cause) causar; (found) fundar; (engine) poner en marcha ♦ vi comenzar, empezar; (with fright) asustarse, sobresaltarse; (train etc) salir; **to ~ doing** or **to do sth** empezar a hacer algo; **~ off** vi empezar, comenzar; (leave) salir, ponerse en camino; **~ up** vi comenzar; (car) ponerse en marcha ♦ vt comenzar; poner en marcha; **~er** n (AUT) botón m de arranque; (SPORT: official) juez m/f de salida; (BRIT: CULIN) entrada; **~ing point** n punto de partida

startle ['stɑ:tl] vt asustar, sobrecoger; **startling** adj alarmante

starvation [stɑ:'veɪʃən] n hambre f

starve [stɑ:v] vi tener mucha hambre; (to death) morir de hambre ♦ vt hacer pasar hambre

state [steɪt] n estado ♦ vt (say, declare) afirmar; **the S~s** los Estados Unidos; **to be in a ~** estar agitado; **~ly** adj majestuoso, imponente; **~ly home** n casa señorial, casa solariega; **~ment** n afirmación f; **~sman** (irreg) n estadista m

static ['stætɪk] n (RADIO) parásitos mpl ♦ adj estático; **~ electricity** n estática f; **~** (RADIO) emisora f

station ['steɪʃən] n (gen) estación f, (RADIO) emisora f, (rank) posición f social ♦ vt colocar, situar; (MIL) apostar

stationary ['steɪʃnərɪ] adj estacionario, fijo

stationer ['steɪʃənə*] n papelero/a; **~'s (shop)** (BRIT) n papelería f; **~y** [-nərɪ] n papel m de escribir, articulos mpl de escritorio

station master n (RAIL) jefe m de estación

station wagon (US) n ranchera

statistic [stə'tɪstɪk] n estadística f; **~s** n (science) estadística f

statue ['stætjuː] n estatua f

status ['steɪtəs] n estado; (reputation) estatus m; **~ symbol** n símbolo m de prestigio

statute ['stætjuːt] n estatuto, ley f; **statutory** adj estatutario

staunch [stɔːntʃ] adj leal, incondicional

stay [steɪ] n estancia ♦ vi quedar(se); (as guest) hospedarse; **to ~ put** seguir en el mismo sitio; **to ~ the night/5 days** pasar la noche/estar 5 días; **~ behind** vi quedar atrás; **~ in** vi quedarse en casa; **~ on** vi quedarse; **~ out** vi (of house) no volver a casa; (on strike) permanecer en huelga; **~ up** vi (at night) velar, no acostarse; **~ing power** n aguante m

stead [sted] n: **in sb's ~** en lugar de uno; **to stand sb in good ~** ser muy útil a uno

steadfast ['stedfɑːst] adj firme, resuelto

steadily ['stedɪlɪ] adv constantemente; (firmly) firmemente; (work, walk) sin parar; (gaze) fijamente

steady ['stedɪ] adj (firm) firme; (regular) regular; (person, character) sensato, juicioso; (boyfriend) formal; (look, voice)

tranquilo ♦ vt (stabilize) estabilizar; (nerves) calmar

steak [steɪk] n (gen) filete m; (beef) bistec m

steal [stiːl] (pt **stole**, pp **stolen**) vt robar ♦ vi robar; (move secretly) andar a hurtadillas

stealth [stelθ] n: **by ~** a escondidas, sigilosamente; **~y** adj cauteloso, sigiloso

steam [stiːm] n vapor m; (mist) vaho, humo ♦ vt (CULIN) cocer al vapor ♦ vi echar vapor; **~ engine** n máquina de vapor; **~er** n (buque m de) vapor m; **~roller** n apisonadora; **~ship** n = **~er**; **~y** adj (room) lleno de vapor; (window) empañado; (heat, atmosphere) bochornoso

steel [stiːl] n acero ♦ adj de acero; **~works** n acería

steep [stiːp] adj escarpado, abrupto; (stair) empinado; (price) exhorbitante, excesivo ♦ vt empapar, remojar

steeple ['stiːpl] n aguja, torre; **~chase** n carrera de obstáculos

steer [stɪə*] vt (car) conducir (SP), manejar (AM); (person) dirigir ♦ vi conducir, manejar; **~ing** n (AUT) dirección f; **~ing wheel** n volante m

stem [stem] n (of plant) tallo; (of glass) pie m ♦ vt detener; (blood) restañar; **~ from** vt fus ser consecuencia de

stench [stentʃ] n hedor m

stencil ['stensl] n (pattern) plantilla ♦ vt hacer un cliché de

stenographer [ste'nɔgrəfə*] (US) n taquígrafo/a

step [step] n paso; (on stair) peldaño, escalón m ♦ vi: **to ~ forward/back** dar un paso adelante/hacia atrás; **~s** npl (BRIT) = **~ladder**; **in/out of** **~ (with)** acorde/en disonancia (con); **~ down** vi (fig) retirarse; **~ on** vt fus pisar; **~ up** vt (increase) aumentar; **~brother** n hermanastro; **~daughter** n hijastra; **~father** n padrastro; **~ladder** n escalera doble or de tijera;

~mother n madrastra; **~ping stone** n pasadera; **~sister** n hermanastra; **~son** n hijastro

stereo ['stɛrɪəu] n estéreo ♦ adj (also: **~phonic**) estéreo, estereofónico

sterile ['stɛraɪl] adj estéril; **sterilize** ['stɛrɪlaɪz] vt esterilizar

sterling ['stə:lɪŋ] adj (silver) de ley ♦ n (ECON) (libras fpl) esterlinas fpl; **one pound ~** una libra esterlina

stern [stə:n] adj severo, austero ♦ n (NAUT) popa

stew [stju:] n cocido (SP), estofado (SP), guisado (AM) ♦ vt estofar, guisar; (fruit) cocer

steward ['stju:əd] n camarero; **~ess** n (esp on plane) azafata

stick [stɪk] (pt, pp stuck) n palo; (of dynamite) barreno; (as weapon) porra; (walking ~) bastón m ♦ vt (of glue) pegar; (inf: put) meter; (: tolerate) aguantar, soportar; (thrust): **to ~ sth into** clavar o hincar algo en ♦ vi pegarse; (be unmoveable) quedarse parado; (in mind) quedarse grabado; **~ out** vi sobresalir; **~ up** vi sobresalir; **~ up for** vt fus defender; **~er** n (label) etiqueta engomada; (with slogan) pegatina; **~ing plaster** n esparadrapo

stick-up ['stɪkʌp] (inf) n asalto, atraco

sticky ['stɪkɪ] adj pegajoso; (label) engomado; (fig) difícil

stiff [stɪf] adj rígido, tieso; (hard) duro; (manner) estirado; (difficult) difícil; (person) inflexible; (price) exorbitante ♦ adv: **scared/bored ~** muerto de miedo/aburrimiento; **~en** vi (muscles etc) agarrotarse; **~ neck** n tortícolis m inv; **~ness** n rigidez f, tiesura

stifle ['staɪfl] vt ahogar, sofocar; **stifling** adj (heat) sofocante, bochornoso

stigma ['stɪgmə] n (fig) estigma m

stile [staɪl] n portillo, portilla

stiletto [stɪ'lɛtəu] (BRIT) n (also: ~ heel) tacón m de aguja

still [stɪl] adj inmóvil, quieto ♦ adv todavía; (even) aun; (nonetheless) sin embargo, aun así; **~born** adj nacido muerto; **~ life** n naturaleza muerta

stilt [stɪlt] n zanco; (pile) pilar m, soporte m

stilted ['stɪltɪd] adj afectado

stimulate ['stɪmjuleɪt] vt estimular

stimulus ['stɪmjuləs] (pl stimuli) n estímulo, incentivo

sting [stɪŋ] (pt, pp stung) n picadura; (pain) escozor m, picazón f; (organ) aguijón m ♦ vt, vi picar

stingy ['stɪndʒɪ] adj tacaño

stink [stɪŋk] n tufo, hedor m; (pt stank, pp stunk) vi heder, apestar; **~ing** adj hediondo, fétido; (fig: inf) horrible

stint [stɪnt] n tarea, trabajo ♦ vi: **to ~ on** escatimar

stir [stə:*] n (fig: agitation) conmoción f ♦ vt (tea etc) remover; (fig: emotions) provocar ♦ vi moverse; **~ up** vt (trouble) fomentar

stirrup ['stɪrəp] n estribo

stitch [stɪtʃ] n (SEWING) puntada; (KNITTING) punto; (MED) punto de sutura; (pain) punzada ♦ vt coser; (MED) suturar

stoat [stəut] n armiño

stock [stɔk] n (COMM: reserves) existencias fpl, stock m; (: selection) surtido; (AGR) ganado, ganadería; (CULIN) caldo; (descent) raza, estirpe f; (FINANCE) capital m ♦ adj (fig: reply etc) clásico ♦ vt (have in ~) tener existencias de; **~s and shares** acciones y valores; **in ~** en existencia o almacén; **out of ~** agotado; **to take ~ of** (fig) asesorar, examinar; **~ up with** vt fus abastecerse de; **~broker** ['stɔkbrəukə*] n agente m/f o corredor(a) m/f de bolsa; **~ cube** (BRIT) n pastilla de caldo; **~ exchange** n bolsa

stocking ['stɔkɪŋ] n media

stock: **~ market** n bolsa (de valores); **~pile** n reserva ♦ vt acumular, almacenar; **~taking** (BRIT) n (COMM) inventario

stocky ['stɔkɪ] adj (strong) robusto; (short) achaparrado

stodgy ['stɔdʒɪ] adj indigesto, pesado

stoke [stəuk] vt atizar

stole [stəul] pt of **steal** ♦ n estola

stolen ['stəuln] pp of **steal**

stomach ['stʌmək] n (ANAT) estómago; (belly) vientre m ♦ vt tragar, aguantar; **~ache** n dolor m de estómago

stone [stəun] n piedra; (in fruit) hueso; = 6.348 kg; 14 libras ♦ adj de piedra ♦ vt apedrear; (fruit) deshuesar; **~-cold** adj helado; **~-deaf** adj sordo como una tapia; **~work** n (art) cantería; **stony** adj pedregoso; (fig) frío

stood [stud] pt, pp of **stand**

stool [stu:l] n taburete m

stoop [stu:p] vi (also: ~ down) doblarse, agacharse; (also: have a ~) ser cargado de espaldas

stop [stɔp] n parada; (in punctuation) punto ♦ vt parar, detener; (break off) suspender; (block: pay) suspender; (: cheque) invalidar; (also: put a ~ to) poner término a ♦ vi pararse, detenerse; (end) acabarse; **to ~ doing sth** dejar de hacer algo; **~ dead** vi pararse en seco; **~ off** vi interrumpir el viaje; **~ up** vt (hole) tapar; **~gap** n (person) interino/a; (thing) recurso provisional; **~over** n parada; (AVIAT) escala

stoppage ['stɔpɪdʒ] n (strike) paro; (blockage) obstrucción f

stopper ['stɔpə*] n tapón m

stop press n noticias fpl de última hora

stopwatch ['stɔpwɔtʃ] n cronómetro m

storage ['stɔːrɪdʒ] n almacenaje m; **~ heater** n acumulador m

store [stɔː*] n (stock) provisión f; (depot: BRIT: large shop) almacén m; (US) tienda; (reserve) reserva, repuesto ♦ vt almacenar; **~s** npl víveres mpl; **in ~** (fig): **to be in ~ for sb** esperarle a

uno; **~ up** vt acumular; **~room** n despensa

storey ['stɔːrɪ] (US **story**) n piso

stork [stɔːk] n cigüeña

storm [stɔːm] n tormenta; (fig: of applause) salva; (: of criticism) nube f ♦ vi (fig) rabiar ♦ vt tomar por asalto; **~y** adj tempestuoso

story ['stɔːrɪ] n historia; (lie) mentira; (US) = **storey**; **~book** n libro de cuentos

stout [staut] adj (strong) sólido; (fat) gordo, corpulento; (resolute) resuelto ♦ n cerveza negra

stove [stəuv] n (for cooking) cocina; (for heating) estufa

stow [stəu] vt (also: ~ away) meter, poner; (NAUT) estibar; **~away** n polizón/ona m/f

straggle ['strægl] vi (houses etc) extenderse; (lag behind) rezagarse

straight [streɪt] adj recto, derecho; (frank) franco, directo; (simple) sencillo ♦ adv derecho, directamente; (drink) sin mezcla; **to put o get sth ~** dejar algo en claro; **~ away, ~ off** en seguida; **~en** vt (also: ~en out) enderezar, poner derecho; **~-faced** adj serio; **~forward** adj (simple) sencillo; (honest) honrado, franco

strain [streɪn] n tensión f; (TECH) presión f; (MED) torcedura; (breed) tipo, variedad f ♦ vt (back etc) torcerse; (resources) agotar; (stretch) estirar; (food, tea) colar; **~s** npl (MUS) son m; **~ed** adj (muscle) torcido; (laugh) forzado; (relations) tenso; **~er** n colador m

strait [streɪt] n (GEO) estrecho; **to be in dire ~s** pasar grandes apuros; **~-jacket** n camisa de fuerza; **~-laced** adj mojigato, gazmoño

strand [strænd] n (of thread) hebra; (of hair) trenza; (of rope) ramal m

stranded ['strændɪd] adj (person: without money) desamparado; (: without transport) colgado

strange [streɪndʒ] adj (not known) desconocido; (odd) extraño, raro; **~ly** adv de un modo raro; see also **enough**; **~r** n desconocido/a; (from another area) forastero/a

strangle ['stræŋgl] vt estrangular; **~hold** n (fig) dominio completo

strap [stræp] n correa; (of slip, dress) tirante m

strategic [strə'tiːdʒɪk] adj estratégico

strategy ['strætɪdʒɪ] n estrategia

straw [strɔː] n paja; (drinking ~) caña, pajita; **that's the last ~!** ¡eso es el colmo!

strawberry ['strɔːbərɪ] n fresa (SP), frutilla (AM)

stray [streɪ] adj (animal) extraviado; (bullet) perdido; (scattered) disperso ♦ vi extraviarse, perderse

streak [striːk] n raya; (in hair) raya ♦ vt rayar ♦ vi: **to ~ past** pasar como un rayo

stream [striːm] n riachuelo, arroyo; (of people, vehicles) riada, caravana; (of smoke, insults etc) chorro ♦ vt (SCOL) dividir en grupos por habilidad ♦ vi correr, fluir; **to ~ in/out** (people) entrar/salir en tropel

streamer ['striːmə*] n serpentina

streamlined ['striːmlaɪnd] adj aerodinámico

street [striːt] n calle f; **~car** (US) n tranvía m; **~ lamp** n farol m; **~ plan** n plano; **~wise** (inf) adj que tiene mucha calle

strength [streŋθ] n fuerza; (of girder, knot etc) resistencia; (fig: power) poder m; **~en** vt fortalecer, reforzar

strenuous ['strenjuəs] adj (energetic, determined) enérgico

stress [stres] n presión f; (mental strain) estrés m; (accent) acento ♦ vt subrayar, recalcar; (syllable) acentuar

stretch [stretʃ] n (of sand etc) trecho ♦ vi estirarse; (extend): **to ~ to** or **as far as** extenderse hasta ♦ vt extender, estirar; (make demands of) exigir el máximo esfuerzo a; **~ out** vi tenderse ♦ vt (arm etc) extender; (spread) estirar

stretcher ['stretʃə*] n camilla

strewn [struːn] adj: **~ with** cubierto or sembrado de

stricken ['strɪkən] adj (person) herido; (city, industry etc) condenado; **~ with** (disease) afectado por

strict [strɪkt] adj severo; (exact) estricto; **~ly** adv severamente; estrictamente

stride [straɪd] (pt **strode**, pp **stridden**) n zancada, tranco ♦ vi dar zancadas, andar a trancos

strife [straɪf] n lucha

strike [straɪk] (pt, pp **struck**) n huelga; (of oil etc) descubrimiento; (attack) ataque m ♦ vt golpear, pegar; (oil etc) descubrir; (bargain, deal) cerrar ♦ vi declarar la huelga; (attack) atacar; (clock) dar la hora; **on ~** (workers) en huelga; **to ~ a match** encender un fósforo; **~ down** vt derribar; **~ up** vt (MUS) empezar a tocar; (conversation) entablar; (friendship) trabar; **~r** n huelguista m/f; (SPORT) delantero; **striking** adj llamativo

string [strɪŋ] (pt, pp **strung**) n (gen) cuerda; (row) hilera ♦ vt: **to ~ together** ensartar; **to ~ out** extenderse; **the ~s** npl (MUS) los instrumentos de cuerda; **to pull ~s** (fig) mover palancas; **~ bean** n judía verde, habichuela; **~(ed) instrument** n (MUS) instrumento de cuerda

stringent ['strɪndʒənt] adj riguroso, severo

strip [strɪp] n tira; (of land) franja; (of metal) cinta, lámina ♦ vt desnudar; (paint) quitar; (also: **~ down**: machine) desmontar ♦ vi desnudarse; **~ cartoon** n tira cómica (SP), historieta (AM)

stripe [straɪp] n raya; (MIL) galón m; **~d** adj a rayas, rayado

strip lighting n alumbrado fluorescente

stripper ['strɪpə*] n artista m/f de

striptease

strive [straɪv] (pt **strove**, pp **striven**) vi: **to ~ for sth/to do sth** luchar por conseguir/hacer algo

strode [strəʊd] pt of **stride**

stroke [strəʊk] n (blow) golpe m; (SWIMMING) brazada; (MED) apoplejía; (of paintbrush) toque m ♦ vt acariciar; **at a ~** de un solo golpe

stroll [strəʊl] n paseo, vuelta ♦ vi dar un paseo or una vuelta; **~er** (US) n (for child) sillita de ruedas

strong [strɒŋ] adj fuerte; **they are 50 ~** son 50; **~hold** n fortaleza; (fig) baluarte m; **~ly** adv fuertemente, con fuerza; (believe) firmemente; **~room** n cámara acorazada

strove [strəʊv] pt of **strive**

struck [strʌk] pt, pp of **strike**

structure ['strʌktʃə*] n estructura; (building) construcción f

struggle ['strʌgl] n lucha ♦ vi luchar

strum [strʌm] vt (guitar) rasguear

strung [strʌŋ] pt, pp of **string**

strut [strʌt] n puntal m ♦ vi pavonearse

stub [stʌb] n (of ticket etc) talón m; (of cigarette) colilla; **to ~ one's toe on sth** dar con el dedo (del pie) contra algo; **~ out** vt apagar

stubble ['stʌbl] n rastrojo; (on chin) barba (incipiente)

stubborn ['stʌbən] adj terco, testarudo

stuck [stʌk] pt, pp of **stick** ♦ adj (jammed) atascado; **~-up** adj engreído, presumido

stud [stʌd] n (shirt ~) corchete m; (of boot) taco; (earring) pendiente m (de bolita); (also: ~ farm) caballeriza; (also: ~ horse) caballo semental ♦ vt (fig): **~ded with** salpicado de

student ['stju:dənt] n estudiante m/f ♦ adj estudiantil; **~ driver** (US) n aprendiz/a m/f

studio ['stju:dɪəʊ] n estudio; (artist's) taller m; **~ flat** (US **~ apartment**) n estudio

studious ['stju:dɪəs] adj estudioso;

(studied) calculado; **~ly** adv (carefully) con esmero

study ['stʌdɪ] n estudio ♦ vt estudiar; (examine) examinar, investigar ♦ vi estudiar

stuff [stʌf] n materia; (substance) material m, sustancia; (things) cosas fpl ♦ vt llenar; (CULIN) rellenar; (animals) disecar; (inf. push) meter; **~ing** n relleno; **~y** adj (room) mal ventilado; (person) de miras estrechas

stumble ['stʌmbl] vi tropezar, dar un traspié; **to ~ across, ~ on** (fig) tropezar con; **stumbling block** n tropiezo, obstáculo

stump [stʌmp] n (of tree) tocón m; (of limb) muñón m ♦ vt: **to be ~ed for an answer** no saber qué contestar

stun [stʌn] vt dejar sin sentido

stung [stʌŋ] pt, pp of **sting**

stunk [stʌŋk] pp of **stink**

stunning ['stʌnɪŋ] adj (fig: news) pasmoso; (: outfit etc) sensacional

stunt [stʌnt] n (in film) escena peligrosa; (publicity ~) truco publicitario; **~man** (irreg) n doble m

stupid ['stju:pɪd] adj estúpido, tonto; **~ity** [-'pɪdɪtɪ] n estupidez f

sturdy ['stɜ:dɪ] adj robusto, fuerte

stutter ['stʌtə*] n tartamudeo ♦ vi tartamudear

sty [staɪ] n (for pigs) pocilga

stye [staɪ] n (MED) orzuelo

style [staɪl] n estilo; **stylish** adj elegante, a la moda

stylus ['staɪləs] n aguja

suave [swɑːv] adj cortés

sub... [sʌb] prefix sub...; **~conscious** adj subconsciente; **~contract** vt subcontratar; **~divide** vt subdividir

subdue [səb'dju:] vt sojuzgar; (passions) dominar; **~d** adj (light) tenue; (person) sumiso, manso

subject [n 'sʌbdʒɪkt, vb səb'dʒɛkt] n súbdito; (SCOL) asignatura; (matter) tema m; (GRAMMAR) sujeto ♦ vt (fig): **to ~ sb to sth** someter a uno a algo; **to**

be ~ to (*law*) estar sujeto a; (*subj: person*) ser propenso a; **~ive** [-'dʒektɪv] *adj* subjetivo; **~ matter** *n* (*content*) contenido

sublet [sʌb'let] *vt* subarrendar

submarine [sʌbmə'ri:n] *n* submarino ♦ *vi* sumergirse

submerge [sǝb'mǝ:dʒ] *vt* sumergir ♦ *vi* sumergirse

submissive [sǝb'mɪsɪv] *adj* sumiso

submit [sǝb'mɪt] *vt* someter ♦ *vi:* **to ~ to sth** someterse a algo

subnormal [sʌb'nɔ:məl] *adj* anormal

subordinate [sǝ'bɔ:dɪnət] *adj, n* subordinado/a *m/f*

subpoena [sǝb'pi:nǝ] *n* (*LAW*) citación *f*

subscribe [sǝb'skraɪb] *vi* suscribir; **to ~ to** (*opinion, fund*) suscribir, aprobar; (*newspaper*) suscribirse a; **~r** *n* (*to periodical*) suscriptor(a) *m/f*; (*to telephone*) abonado/a

subscription [sǝb'skrɪpʃǝn] *n* abono; (*to magazine*) subscripción *f*

subsequent ['sʌbsɪkwǝnt] *adj* subsiguiente, posterior; **~ly** *adv* posteriormente, más tarde

subside [sǝb'saɪd] *vi* hundirse o; (*flood*) bajar; (*wind*) amainar; **subsidence** [-'saɪdns] *n* hundimiento; (*in road*) socavón *m*

subsidiary [sǝb'sɪdɪǝrɪ] *adj* secundario ♦ *n* sucursal *f*, filial *f*

subsidize ['sʌbsɪdaɪz] *vt* subvencionar

subsidy ['sʌbsɪdɪ] *n* subvención *f*

subsistence [sǝb'sɪstǝns] *n* subsistencia; **~ allowance** *n* salario mínimo

substance ['sʌbstǝns] *n* sustancia

substantial [sǝb'stænʃl] *adj* sustancial, sustancioso; (*fig*) importante

substantiate [sǝb'stænʃɪeɪt] *vt* comprobar

substitute ['sʌbstɪtju:t] *n* (*person*) suplente *m/f*; (*thing*) sustituto ♦ *vt:* **to ~ A for B** sustituir A por B, reemplazar B por A

subtitle ['sʌbtaɪtl] *n* subtítulo

subtle ['sʌtl] *adj* sutil; **~ty** *n* sutileza

subtotal [sʌb'tǝutl] *n* total *m* parcial

subtract [sǝb'trækt] *vt* restar, sustraer; **~ion** [-'trækʃǝn] *n* resta, sustracción *f*

suburb ['sʌbǝ:b] *n* barrio residencial; **the ~s** las afueras (de la ciudad); **~an** [sǝ'bǝ:bǝn] *adj* suburbano; (*train etc*) de cercanías; **~ia** [sǝ'bǝ:bɪǝ] *n* barrios *mpl* residenciales

subway ['sʌbweɪ] *n* (*BRIT*) paso subterráneo or inferior; (*US*) metro

succeed [sǝk'si:d] *vi* (*person*) tener éxito; (*plan*) salir bien ♦ *vt* suceder a; **to ~ in doing** lograr hacer; **~ing** *adj* (*following*) sucesivo

success [sǝk'ses] *n* éxito; **~ful** *adj* exitoso; (*business*) próspero; **to be ~ful (in doing)** lograr (hacer); **~fully** *adv* con éxito

succession [sǝk'seʃǝn] *n* sucesión *f*, serie *f*

successive [sǝk'sesɪv] *adj* sucesivo, consecutivo

succinct [sǝk'sɪŋkt] *adj* sucinto

such [sʌtʃ] *adj* tal, semejante; (*of that kind*): **~ a book** tal libro; (*so much*): **~ courage** tanto valor ♦ *adv* tan; **~ a long trip** un viaje tan largo; **~ a lot of** tanto(s)/a(s); **~ as** (*like*) tal como; **as ~** como tal; **~-and-~** *adj* tal o cual

suck [sʌk] *vt* chupar; (*bottle*) sorber; (*breast*) mamar; **~er** *n* (*ZOOL*) ventosa; (*inf*) bobo, primo

suction ['sʌkʃǝn] *n* succión *f*

Sudan [su'dæn] *n* Sudán *m*

sudden ['sʌdn] *adj* (*rapid*) repentino, súbito; (*unexpected*) imprevisto; **all of a ~** de repente, **~ly** *adv* de repente

suds [sʌdz] *npl* espuma de jabón

sue [su:] *vt* demandar

suede [sweɪd] *n* ante *m* (*SP*), gamuza (*AM*)

suet ['suɪt] *n* sebo

Suez ['su:ɪz] *n:* **the ~ Canal** el Canal de Suez

suffer ['sʌfǝ*] *vt* sufrir, padecer; (*tolerate*) aguantar, soportar ♦ *vi* sufrir;

to ~ from (*illness etc*) padecer; **~er** n víctima; (*MED*) enfermo/a; **~ing** n sufrimiento

sufficient [sə'fɪʃənt] *adj* suficiente, bastante; **~ly** *ad* suficientemente, bastante

suffocate ['sʌfəkeɪt] *vi* ahogarse, asfixiarse; **suffocation** [-'keɪʃən] n asfixia

sugar ['ʃugə*] n azúcar m ♦ *vt* echar azúcar a, azucarar; **~ beet** n remolacha; **~ cane** n caña de azúcar

suggest [sə'dʒest] *vt* sugerir; **~ion** [-'dʒestʃən] n sugerencia; **~ive** (*pej*) *adj* indecente

suicide ['suɪsaɪd] n suicidio; (*person*) suicida m/f; *see also* **commit**

suit [suːt] n (*man's*) traje m; (*woman's*) conjunto; (*LAW*) pleito; (*CARDS*) palo ♦ *vt* convenir; (*clothes*) sentar a, ir bien a; (*adapt*): **to ~ sth to** adaptar or ajustar algo a; **well ~ed** (*well matched: couple*) hecho el uno para el otro; **~able** *adj* conveniente; (*apt*) indicado; **~ably** *adv* convenientemente; (*impressed*) apropiadamente

suitcase ['suːtkeɪs] n maleta (*SP*), valija (*AM*)

suite [swiːt] n (*of rooms, MUS*) suite f; (*furniture*): **bedroom/dining room ~** (juego de) dormitorio/comedor

suitor ['suːtə*] n pretendiente m

sulfur ['sʌlfə*] (*US*) n = **sulphur**

sulk [sʌlk] *vi* estar de mal humor; **~y** *adj* malhumorado

sullen ['sʌlən] *adj* hosco, malhumorado

sulphur ['sʌlfə*] (*US* **sulfur**) n azufre m

sultana [sʌl'tɑːnə] n (*fruit*) pasa de Esmirna

sultry ['sʌltrɪ] *adj* (*weather*) bochornoso

sum [sʌm] n suma; (*total*) total m; **~ up** *vt* resumir ♦ *vi* hacer un resumen

summarize ['sʌmə raɪz] *vt* resumir

summary ['sʌmərɪ] n resumen m ♦ *adj* (*justice*) sumario

summer ['sʌmə*] n verano ♦ *cpd* de verano; **in ~** en verano; **~ holidays** *npl* vacaciones *fpl* de verano; **~house** n (*in garden*) cenador m, glorieta; **~time** n (*season*) verano; **~ time** n (*by clock*) hora de verano

summit ['sʌmɪt] n cima, cumbre f; (*also*: **~ conference, ~ meeting**) (conferencia) cumbre f

summon ['sʌmən] *vt* (*person*) llamar; (*meeting*) convocar; (*LAW*) citar; **~ up** *vt* (*courage*) armarse de; **~s** n llamamiento, llamada ♦ *vt* (*LAW*) citar

sump [sʌmp] (*BRIT*) n (*AUT*) cárter m

sumptuous ['sʌmptjuəs] *adj* suntuoso

sun [sʌn] n sol m; **~bathe** *vi* tomar el sol; **~block** n filtro solar; **~burn** n (*painful*) quemadura; (*tan*) bronceado; **~burnt** *adj* quemado por el sol

Sunday ['sʌndɪ] n domingo; **~ school** n catequesis f dominical

sundial ['sʌndaɪəl] n reloj m de sol

sundown ['sʌndaun] n anochecer m

sundry ['sʌndrɪ] *adj* varios/as, diversos/as; **all and ~** todos sin excepción; **sundries** *npl* géneros *mpl* diversos

sunflower ['sʌnflauə*] n girasol m

sung [sʌŋ] *pp* of **sing**

sunglasses ['sʌnglɑːsɪz] *npl* gafas *fpl* (*SP*) or anteojos *mpl* de sol

sunk [sʌŋk] *pp* of **sink**

sun: ~light n luz f del sol; **~lit** *adj* iluminado por el sol; **~ny** *adj* soleado; (*day*) de sol; (*fig*) alegre; **~rise** n salida del sol; **~ roof** n (*AUT*) techo corredizo; **~screen** n protector m solar; **~set** n puesta del sol; **~shade** n (*over table*) sombrilla; **~shine** n sol m; **~stroke** n insolación f; **~tan** n bronceado; **~tan oil** n aceite m bronceador

super ['suːpə*] (*inf*) *adj* genial

superannuation [suːpərænju'eɪʃən] n cuota de jubilación

superb [suː'pəːb] *adj* magnífico, espléndido

supercilious [suːpə'sɪlɪəs] *adj* altanero

superfluous [su'pə:fluəs] *adj*
superfluo, de sobra
superhuman [su:pə'hju:mən] *adj*
sobrehumano
superimpose ['su:pərim'pəuz] *vt*
sobreponer
superintendent [su:pərin'tendənt] *n*
director(a) *m/f*; (POLICE) subjefe/a *m/f*
superior [su'pɪərɪə*] *adj* superior;
(smug) desdeñoso ♦ *n* superior *m*; **~ity**
[-'ɔrɪtɪ] *n* superioridad *f*
superlative [su'pə:lətɪv] *n* superlativo
superman ['su:pəmæn] (irreg) *n*
superhombre *m*
supermarket ['su:pəma:kɪt] *n*
supermercado
supernatural [su:pə'nætʃərəl] *adj*
sobrenatural ♦ *n*: **the ~** lo sobrenatural
superpower ['su:pəpauə*] *n* (POL)
superpotencia
supersede [su:pə'si:d] *vt* suplantar
superstar ['su:pəsta:*] *n* gran estrella
superstitious [su:pə'stɪʃəs] *adj*
supersticioso
supertanker ['su:pətæŋkə*] *n*
superpetrolero
supervise ['su:pəvaɪz] *vt* supervisar;
supervision [-'vɪʒən] *n* supervisión *f*;
supervisor *n* supervisor(a) *m/f*
supper ['sʌpə*] *n* cena
supple ['sʌpl] *adj* flexible
supplement [*n* 'sʌplɪmənt, *vb*
sʌplɪ'mɛnt] *n* suplemento ♦ *vt* suplir;
~ary [-'mɛntərɪ] *adj* suplementario;
~ary benefit (BRIT) *n* subsidio
suplementario de la seguridad social
supplier [sə'plaɪə*] *n* (COMM)
distribuidor(a) *m/f*
supply [sə'plaɪ] *vt* (provide) suministrar;
(equip): **to ~ (with)** proveer (de) ♦ *n*
provisión *f*; (gas, water etc) suministro;
supplies *npl* (food) víveres *mpl*; (MIL)
pertrechos *mpl*; **~ teacher** *n*
profesor(a) *m/f* suplente
support [sə'pɔ:t] *n* apoyo; (TECH)
soporte *m* ♦ *vt* apoyar; (financially)
mantener; (uphold, TECH) sostener; **~er**

n (POL etc) partidario/a; (SPORT)
aficionado/a
suppose [sə'pəuz] *vt* suponer;
(imagine) imaginarse; **to be ~d**
to do sth deber hacer algo; **~dly**
[sə'pəuzɪdlɪ] *adv* según cabe suponer;
supposing *conj* en caso de que
suppress [sə'prɛs] *vt* suprimir; (yawn)
ahogar
supreme [su'pri:m] *adj* supremo
surcharge ['sə:tʃa:dʒ] *n* sobretasa,
recargo
sure [ʃuə*] *adj* seguro; (definite,
convinced) cierto; **to make ~ of sth/**
that asegurarse de algo/asegurar que;
~! (of course) ¡claro!, ¡por supuesto!;
~ enough efectivamente; **~ly** *adv*
(certainly) seguramente
surf [sə:f] *n* olas *fpl*
surface ['sə:fɪs] *n* superficie *f* ♦ *vt*
(road) revestir ♦ *vi* (also fig) salir a la
superficie; **by ~ mail** por vía terrestre
surfboard ['sə:fbɔ:d] *n* tabla (de surf)
surfeit ['sə:fɪt] *n*: **a ~ of** un exceso de
surfing ['sə:fɪŋ] *n* surf *m*
surge [sə:dʒ] *n* oleada, oleaje *m* ♦ *vi*
(wave) romper; (people) avanzar en
tropel
surgeon ['sə:dʒən] *n* cirujano/a
surgery ['sə:dʒərɪ] *n* cirugía; (BRIT:
room) consultorio; **~ hours** (BRIT) *npl*
horas *fpl* de consulta
surgical ['sə:dʒɪkl] *adj* quirúrgico;
~ spirit (BRIT) *n* alcohol *m* de 90°
surname ['sə:neim] *n* apellido
surpass [sə:'pa:s] *vt* superar, exceder
surplus ['sə:pləs] *n* excedente *m*;
(COMM) superávit *m* ♦ *adj* excedente,
sobrante
surprise [sə'praɪz] *n* sorpresa ♦ *vt*
sorprender; **surprising** *adj*
sorprendente; **surprisingly** *adv*: **it**
was surprisingly easy me *etc*
sorprendió lo fácil que fue
surrender [sə'rɛndə*] *n* rendición *f*,
entrega ♦ *vi* rendirse, entregarse
surreptitious [sʌrəp'tɪʃəs] *adj*

subrepticio

surrogate ['sʌrəgɪt] n sucedáneo; **~ mother** n madre f portadora

surround [sə'raund] vt rodear, circundar; (MIL etc) cercar; **~ing** adj circundante; **~ings** npl alrededores mpl, cercanías fpl

surveillance [sə:'veɪləns] n vigilancia

survey [n 'sə:veɪ, vb sə:'veɪ] n inspección f, reconocimiento f; (inquiry) encuesta ♦ vt examinar, inspeccionar; (look at) mirar, contemplar; **~or** n agrimensor(a) m/f

survival [sə'vaɪvl] n supervivencia

survive [sə'vaɪv] vi sobrevivir; (custom etc) perdurar ♦ vt sobrevivir a; **survivor** n superviviente m/f

susceptible [sə'septəbl] adj: **~ (to)** (disease) susceptible (a); (flattery) sensible (a)

suspect [adj, n 'sʌspekt, vb sə'spekt] adj, n sospechoso/a m/f ♦ vt (person) sospechar de; (think) sospechar

suspend [səs'pend] vt suspender; **~ed sentence** n (LAW) libertad f condicional; **~er belt** n portaligas m inv; **~ers** npl (BRIT) ligas fpl; (US) tirantes mpl

suspense [səs'pens] n incertidumbre f, duda; (in film etc) suspense m; **to keep sb in ~** mantener a uno en suspense

suspension [səs'penʃən] n (gen, AUT) suspensión f; (of driving licence) privación f; **~ bridge** n puente m colgante

suspicion [səs'pɪʃən] n sospecha; (distrust) recelo; **suspicious** [-ʃəs] adj receloso; (causing suspicion) sospechoso

sustain [səs'teɪn] vt sostener, apoyar; (suffer) sufrir, padecer; **~able** adj sostenible; **~ed effort** (old) (effort) sostenido

sustenance ['sʌstɪnəns] n sustento

swab [swɔb] n (MED) algodón m

swagger ['swægə*] vi pavonearse

swallow ['swɔləu] n (bird) golondrina ♦ vt tragar; (fig, pride) tragarse; **~ up** vt (savings etc) consumir

swam [swæm] pt of **swim**

swamp [swɔmp] n pantano, ciénaga ♦ vt (with water etc) inundar; (fig) abrumar, agobiar; **~y** adj pantanoso

swan [swɔn] n cisne m

swap [swɔp] n canje m, intercambio ♦ vt: **to ~ (for)** cambiar (por)

swarm [swɔ:m] n (of bees) enjambre m; (fig) multitud f ♦ vi (bees) formar un enjambre; (people) pulular; **to be ~ing with** ser un hervidero de

swastika ['swɔstɪkə] n esvástika

swat [swɔt] vt aplastar

sway [sweɪ] vi mecerse, balancearse ♦ vt (influence) mover, influir en

swear [swɛə*] (pt **swore**, pp **sworn**) vi (curse) maldecir; (promise) jurar ♦ vt jurar; **~word** n taco, palabrota

sweat [swet] n sudor m ♦ vi sudar

sweater ['swetə*] n suéter m

sweatshirt ['swetʃə:t] n suéter m

sweaty ['swetɪ] adj sudoroso

Swede [swi:d] n sueco/a

swede [swi:d] (BRIT) n nabo

Sweden ['swi:dn] n Suecia; **Swedish** ['swi:dɪʃ] adj sueco ♦ n (LING) sueco

sweep [swi:p] (pt, pp **swept**) n (act) barrido; (also: chimney ~) deshollinador(a) m/f ♦ vt barrer; (with arm) empujar; (subj: current) arrastrar ♦ vi barrer; (arm etc) moverse rápidamente; (wind) soplar con violencia; **~ away** vt barrer; **~ past** vi pasar majestuosamente; **~ up** vi barrer; **~ing** adj (gesture) dramático; (generalized) statement generalizado

sweet [swi:t] n (candy) dulce m, caramelo; (BRIT: pudding) postre m ♦ adj dulce; (fig: kind) dulce, amable; (: attractive) mono; **~corn** n maíz m; **~en** vt (add sugar to) poner azúcar a; (person) endulzar; **~heart** n novio/a; **~ness** n dulzura; **~ pea** n guisante m de olor

swell [swel] (pt **swelled**, pp **swollen** or **swelled**) n (of sea) marejada, oleaje m ♦ adj (US: inf: excellent) estupendo,

fenomenal ♦ vt hinchar, inflar ♦ vi
(also: ~ up) hincharse; (numbers)
aumentar; (sound, feeling) ir
aumentando; **~ing** n (MED) hinchazón
f

sweltering ['sweltərɪŋ] adj sofocante,
de mucho calor

swept [swept] pt, pp de **sweep**

swerve [swə:v] vi desviarse
bruscamente

swift [swɪft] n (bird) vencejo ♦ adj
rápido, veloz; **~ly** adv rápidamente

swig [swɪg] (inf) n (drink) trago

swill [swɪl] vt (also: ~ out, ~ down)
lavar, limpiar con agua

swim [swɪm] (pt **swam**, pp **swum**) n:
to go for a ~ ir a nadar o a bañarse
♦ vi nadar; (head, room) dar vueltas
♦ vt nadar; (the Channel etc) cruzar a
nado; **~mer** n nadador(a) m/f; **~ming**
n natación f; **~ming cap** n gorro de
baño; **~ming costume** (BRIT) n
bañador m, traje m de baño; **~ming
pool** n piscina (SP), alberca (AM);
~ming trunks n bañador m (de
hombre); **~suit** n = **~ming costume**

swindle ['swɪndl] n estafa ♦ vt estafar

swine [swaɪn] (inf!) n canalla (!)

swing [swɪŋ] (pt, pp **swung**) n (in
playground) columpio; (movement)
balanceo, vaivén m; (change of
direction) viraje m; (rhythm) ritmo ♦ vt
balancear; (also: ~ round) voltear, girar
♦ vi balancearse, columpiarse; (also:
~ round) dar media vuelta; **to be in
full ~** estar en plena marcha; **~ bridge**
n puente m giratorio; **~ door** (US **~ing
door**) n puerta giratoria

swingeing ['swɪndʒɪŋ] (BRIT) adj (cuts)
atroz

swipe [swaɪp] vt (hit) golpear fuerte;
(inf: steal) guindar

swirl [swə:l] vi arremolinarse

Swiss [swɪs] adj, n inv suizo/a m/f

switch [swɪtʃ] n (for light etc)
interruptor m; (change) cambio ♦ vt
(change) cambiar de; **~ off** vt apagar;

(engine) parar; **~ on** vt encender (SP),
prender (AM); (engine, machine)
arrancar; **~board** n (TEL) centralita (de
teléfonos) (SP), conmutador m (AM)

Switzerland ['swɪtsələnd] n Suiza

swivel ['swɪvl] vi (also: ~ round) girar

swollen ['swəʊlən] pp of **swell**

swoon [swu:n] vi desmayarse

swoop [swu:p] n (by police etc) redada
♦ vi (also: ~ down) calarse

swop [swɒp] = **swap**

sword [sɔ:d] n espada; **~fish** n pez m
espada

swore [swɔ:*] pt of **swear**

sworn [swɔ:n] pp of **swear** ♦ adj
(statement) bajo juramento; (enemy)
implacable

swot [swɒt] (BRIT) vt, vi empollar

swum [swʌm] pp of **swim**

swung [swʌŋ] pt, pp of **swing**

sycamore ['sɪkəmɔ:*] n sicomoro

syllable ['sɪləbl] n sílaba

syllabus ['sɪləbəs] n programa m de
estudios

symbol ['sɪmbl] n símbolo

symmetry ['sɪmɪtrɪ] n simetría

sympathetic [sɪmpə'θetɪk] adj
(understanding) comprensivo; (likeable)
simpático; (showing support):
~ **to(wards)** bien dispuesto hacia

sympathize ['sɪmpəθaɪz] vi: **to**
~ **with** (person) compadecerse de;
(feelings) comprender; (cause) apoyar;
~r n (POL) simpatizante m/f

sympathy ['sɪmpəθɪ] n (pity)
compasión f; **sympathies** npl
(tendencies) tendencias fpl; **with our
deepest** ~ nuestro más sentido
pésame; **in** ~ en solidaridad

symphony ['sɪmfənɪ] n sinfonía

symptom ['sɪmptəm] n síntoma m,
indicio

synagogue ['sɪnəgɒg] n sinagoga

syndicate ['sɪndɪkɪt] n (gen) sindicato;
(of newspapers) agencia de noticias

syndrome ['sɪndrəʊm] n síndrome m

synopsis [sɪ'nɒpsɪs] (pl **synopses**) n

sinopsis f inv

synthesis [ˈsɪnθəsɪs] (pl **syntheses**) n síntesis f inv

synthetic [sɪnˈθetɪk] adj sintético

syphilis [ˈsɪfɪlɪs] n sífilis f

syphon [ˈsaɪfən] = **siphon**

Syria [ˈsɪrɪə] n Siria; **~n** adj, n sirio/a

syringe [sɪˈrɪndʒ] n jeringa

syrup [ˈsɪrəp] n jarabe m; (also: **golden ~**) almíbar m

system [ˈsɪstəm] n sistema m; (ANAT) organismo; **~atic** [-ˈmætɪk] adj sistemático, metódico; **~ disk** n (COMPUT) disco del sistema; **~s analyst** n analista m/f de sistemas

T, t

ta [tɑ:] (BRIT: inf) excl ¡gracias!

tab [tæb] n lengüeta; (label) etiqueta; **to keep ~s on** (fig) vigilar

tabby [ˈtæbɪ] n (also: ~ **cat**) gato atigrado

table [ˈteɪbl] n mesa; (of statistics etc) cuadro, tabla ♦ vt (BRIT: motion etc) presentar; **to lay** or **set the ~** poner la mesa; **~cloth** n mantel m; **~ of contents** n índice m de materias; **~ d'hôte** [tɑːblˈdəut] adj del menú; **~ lamp** n lámpara de mesa; **~mat** n (for plate) posaplatos m inv; (for hot dish) salvamantel m; **~spoon** n cuchara de servir; (also: ~**spoonful**: as measurement) cucharada

tablet [ˈtæblɪt] n (MED) pastilla, comprimido; (of stone) lápida

table tennis n ping-pong m, tenis m de mesa

table wine n vino de mesa

tabloid [ˈtæblɔɪd] n periódico popular sensacionalista

tabloid press

El término **tabloid press** *o* **tabloids** *se usa para referirse a la prensa popular británica, por el tamaño más*

pequeño de los periódicos. A diferencia de los de la llamada **quality press**, estas publicaciones se caracterizan por un lenguaje sencillo, una presentación llamativa y un contenido sensacionalista, centrado a veces en los escándalos financieros y sexuales de los famosos, por lo que también reciben el nombre peyorativo de "gutter press".

tack [tæk] n (nail) tachuela; (fig) rumbo ♦ vt (nail) clavar con tachuelas; (stitch) hilvanar ♦ vi virar

tackle [ˈtækl] n (fishing ~) aparejo (de pescar); (for lifting) aparejo ♦ vt (difficulty) enfrentarse con; (challenge: person) hacer frente a; (grapple with) agarrar; (FOOTBALL) cargar; (RUGBY) placar

tacky [ˈtækɪ] adj pegajoso; (pej) cutre

tact [tækt] n tacto, discreción f; **~ful** adj discreto, diplomático

tactics [ˈtæktɪks] n, npl táctica

tactless [ˈtæktlɪs] adj indiscreto

tadpole [ˈtædpəul] n renacuajo

tag [tæg] n (label) etiqueta; **~ along** vi ir (or venir) también

tail [teɪl] n cola; (of shirt, coat) faldón m ♦ vt (follow) vigilar a; **~s** npl (formal suit) levita; **~ away** vi (in size, quality etc) ir disminuyendo; **~ off** vi = **~ away**; **~back** (BRIT) n (AUT) cola; **~ end** n cola, parte f final; **~gate** n (AUT) puerta trasera

tailor [ˈteɪlə*] n sastre m; **~ing** n (cut) corte m; (craft) sastrería; **~-made** adj (also fig) hecho a la medida

tailwind [ˈteɪlwɪnd] n viento de cola

tainted [ˈteɪntɪd] adj (food) pasado; (water, air) contaminado; (fig) manchado

take [teɪk] (pt **took**, pp **taken**) vt tomar; (grab) coger (SP), agarrar (AM); (gain: prize) ganar; (require: effort, courage) exigir; (tolerate: pain etc) aguantar; (hold: passengers etc) tener

cabida para; (accompany, bring, carry)
llevar; (exam) presentarse a; **to ~ sth
from** (drawer etc) sacar algo de;
(person) quitar algo a; **I ~ it that ...**
supongo que ...; **~ after** vt fus
parecerse a; **~ apart** vt desmontar;
~ away vt (remove) quitar; (carry off)
llevar; (MATH) restar; **~ back** vt (return)
devolver; (one's words) retractarse de;
~ down vt (building) derribar; (letter
etc) apuntar; **~ in** vt (deceive) engañar;
(understand) entender; (include)
abarcar; (lodger) acoger, recibir; **~ off**
vi (AVIAT) despegar ♦ vt (remove)
quitar; **~ on** vt (work) aceptar;
(employee) contratar; (opponent)
desafiar; **~ out** vt sacar; **~ over** vt
(business) tomar posesión de; (country)
tomar el poder ♦ vi: **to ~ over from
sb** reemplazar a uno; **~ to** vt fus
(person) coger cariño a, encariñarse
con; (activity) aficionarse a; **~ up** vt (a
dress) acortar; (occupy: time, space)
ocupar; (engage in: hobby etc)
dedicarse a; (accept): **to ~ sb up on**
aceptar; **~away** (BRIT) adj (food) para
llevar ♦ n tienda (or restaurante m) de
comida para llevar; **~off** n (AVIAT)
despegue m; **~out** (US) n = **~away**;
~over n (COMM) absorción f

takings ['teikiŋz] npl (COMM) ingresos
mpl

talc [tælk] n (also: **~um powder**) (polvos
de) talco

tale [teil] n (story) cuento; (account)
relación f; **to tell ~s** (fig) chivarse

talent ['tælənt] n talento; **~ed** adj de
talento

talk [tɔ:k] n charla; (conversation)
conversación f; (gossip) habladurías fpl,
chismes mpl ♦ vi hablar; **~s** npl (POL
etc) conversaciones fpl; **to ~ about**
hablar de; **to ~ sb into doing sth**
convencer a uno para que haga algo;
to ~ sb out of doing sth disuadir a
uno de que haga algo; **~ shop**
hablar del trabajo; **~ over** vt discutir;

~ative adj hablador(a); **~ show** n
programa m de entrevistas

tall [tɔ:l] adj alto; (object) grande; **to
be 6 feet ~** (person) ≈ medir 1 metro
80

tally ['tæli] n cuenta ♦ vi: **to ~ (with)**
corresponder (con)

talon ['tælən] n garra

tambourine [tæmbə'ri:n] n pandereta

tame [teim] adj domesticado; (fig)
mediocre

tamper ['tæmpə*] vi: **to ~ with** tocar,
andar con

tampon ['tæmpən] n tampón m

tan [tæn] n (also: sun~) bronceado ♦ vi
ponerse moreno ♦ adj (colour) marrón

tang [tæŋ] n sabor m fuerte

tangent ['tændʒənt] n (MATH)
tangente f; **to go off at a ~** (fig)
salirse por la tangente

tangerine [tændʒə'ri:n] n mandarina

tangle ['tæŋgl] n enredo; **to get
in(to) a ~** enredarse

tank [tæŋk] n (water ~) depósito,
tanque m; (for fish) acuario; (MIL)
tanque m

tanker ['tæŋkə*] n (ship) buque m
cisterna; (truck) camión m cisterna

tanned [tænd] adj (skin) moreno

tantalizing ['tæntəlaizɪŋ] adj
tentador(a)

tantamount ['tæntəmaunt] adj: **~ to**
equivalente a

tantrum ['tæntrəm] n rabieta

tap [tæp] n (BRIT: on sink etc) grifo (SP),
canilla (AM); (gas ~) llave f, (gentle
blow) golpecito ♦ vt (hit gently) dar
golpecitos en; (resources) utilizar,
explotar; (telephone) intervenir; **on ~**
(fig: resources) a mano; **~ dancing** n
claqué m

tape [teip] n (also: magnetic ~) cinta
magnética; (cassette) cassette f, cinta;
(sticky ~) cinta adhesiva; (for tying)
cinta ♦ vt (record) grabar (en cinta);
(stick with ~) pegar con cinta adhesiva;
~ deck n grabadora; **~ measure** n

cinta métrica, metro

taper ['teɪpə*] *n* cirio ♦ *vi* afilarse

tape recorder *n* grabadora

tapestry ['tæpɪstrɪ] *n* (*object*) tapiz *m*; (*art*) tapicería

tar [ta:] *n* alquitrán *m*, brea

target ['ta:gɪt] *n* (*gen*) blanco

tariff ['tærɪf] *n* (*on goods*) arancel *m*; (BRIT: *in hotels etc*) tarifa

tarmac ['ta:mæk] *n* (BRIT: *on road*) asfaltado; (AVIAT) pista (de aterrizaje)

tarnish ['ta:nɪʃ] *vt* deslustrar

tarpaulin [ta:'pɔ:lɪn] *n* lona impermeabilizada

tarragon ['tærəgən] *n* estragón *m*

tart [ta:t] *n* (CULIN) tarta; (BRIT: *inf*: *prostitute*) puta ♦ *adj* agrio, ácido; ~ **up** (BRIT: *inf*) *vt* (*building*) remozar; **to ~ o.s. up** acicalarse

tartan ['ta:tn] *n* tejido escocés *m*

tartar ['ta:tə*] *n* (*on teeth*) sarro; **~(e) sauce** *n* salsa tártara

task [ta:sk] *n* tarea; **to take to ~** reprender; **~ force** *n* (MIL. POLICE) grupo de operaciones

taste [teɪst] *n* (*sense*) gusto; (*flavour*) sabor *m*; (*also*: *after~*) sabor *m*, dejo; (*sample*): **have a ~!** ¡prueba un poquito!; (*fig*) muestra, idea ♦ *vt* (*also fig*) probar ♦ *vi*: **to ~ of** or **like** (*fish, garlic etc*) saber a; **you can ~ the garlic (in it)** se nota el sabor a ajo; **in good/bad ~** de buen/mal gusto; **~ful** *adj* de buen gusto; **~less** *adj* (*food*) soso; (*remark etc*) de mal gusto; **tasty** *adj* sabroso, rico

tatters ['tætəz] *npl*: **in ~** hecho jirones

tattoo [tə'tu:] *n* tatuaje *m*, (*spectacle*) espectáculo militar ♦ *vt* tatuar

tatty ['tætɪ] *adj* (BRIT: *inf*) *adj* cochambroso

taught [tɔ:t] *pt, pp of* **teach**

taunt [tɔ:nt] *n* burla ♦ *vt* burlarse de

Taurus ['tɔ:rəs] *n* Tauro

taut [tɔ:t] *adj* tirante, tenso

tax [tæks] *n* impuesto ♦ *vt* gravar (con un impuesto); (*fig*: *memory*) poner a prueba (: *patience*) agotar; **~able** *adj*

(*income*) gravable; **~ation** [-'seɪʃən] *n* impuestos *mpl*; **~ avoidance** *n* evasión f de impuestos; **~ disc** (BRIT) *n* (AUT) pegatina del impuesto de circulación; **~ evasion** *n* evasión f fiscal; **~-free** *adj* libre de impuestos

taxi ['tæksɪ] *n* taxi *m* ♦ *vi* (AVIAT) rodar por la pista; **~ driver** *n* taxista *m/f*; **~ rank** (BRIT) *n* = **stand**; **~ stand** *n* parada de taxis

tax: **~ payer** *n* contribuyente *m/f*; **~ relief** *n* desgravación f fiscal; **~ return** *n* declaración f de ingresos

TB *n abbr* = **tuberculosis**

tea [ti:] *n* té *m*; (BRIT: *meal*) merienda *f* (SP); cena; **high ~** (BRIT) merienda-cena (SP); **~ bag** *n* bolsita de té; **~ break** (BRIT) *n* descanso para el té

teach [ti:tʃ] (*pt, pp* **taught**) *vt*: **to ~ sb sth, to ~ sth to sb** enseñar algo a uno ♦ *vi* (*be a teacher*) ser profesor(a), enseñar; **~er** *n* (*in secondary school*) profesor/a *m/f*; (*in primary school*) maestro/a, profesor/a de EGB; **~ing** *n* enseñanza

tea cosy *n* cubretetera

teacup ['ti:kʌp] *n* taza para el té

teak [ti:k] *n* (*madera de*) teca

team [ti:m] *n* equipo; (*of horses*) tiro; **~work** *n* trabajo en equipo

teapot ['ti:pɔt] *n* tetera

tear¹ [tɪə*] *n* lágrima; **in ~s** llorando

tear² [tɛə*] (*pt* **tore**, *pp* **torn**) *n* rasgón *m*, desgarrón *m* ♦ *vt* romper, rasgar ♦ *vi* rasgarse; **~ along** *vi* (*rush*) precipitarse; **~ up** *vt* (*sheet of paper etc*) romper

tearful ['tɪəful] *adj* lloroso

tear gas [tɪə-] *n* gas *m* lacrimógeno

tearoom ['ti:ru:m] *n* salón *m* de té

tease [ti:z] *vt* tomar el pelo a

tea set *n* servicio de té

teaspoon *n* cucharita; (*also*: *~ful*: *as measurement*) cucharadita

teat [ti:t] *n* (*of bottle*) tetina

teatime ['ti:taɪm] *n* hora del té

tea towel (BRIT) n paño de cocina

technical ['teknɪkl] adj técnico; **~ college** (BRIT) n ≈ escuela de artes y oficios (SP); **~ity** [-'kælɪtɪ] n (point of law) formalismo; (detail) detalle m técnico; **~ly** adv en teoría; (regarding technique) técnicamente

technician [tek'nɪʃn] n técnico/a

technique [tek'niːk] n técnica

technological [teknə'lɔdʒɪkl] adj tecnológico

technology [tek'nɔlədʒɪ] n tecnología

teddy (bear) ['tedɪ-] n osito de felpa

tedious ['tiːdɪəs] adj pesado, aburrido

teem [tiːm] vi: **to ~ with** rebosar de; **it is ~ing (with rain)** llueve a cántaros

teenage ['tiːneɪdʒ] adj (fashions etc) juvenil; (children) quinceañero; **~r** n quinceañero/a

teens [tiːnz] npl: **to be in one's ~** ser adolescente

tee-shirt ['tiːʃəːt] n = **T-shirt**

teeter ['tiːtə*] vi balancearse; (fig): **to ~ on the edge of ...** estar al borde de ...

teeth [tiːθ] npl of **tooth**

teethe [tiːð] vi echar los dientes

teething ['tiːðɪŋ]: **~ ring** n mordedor m; **~ troubles** npl (fig) dificultades fpl iniciales

teetotal ['tiː'təutl] adj abstemio

telegram ['telɪgræm] n telegrama m

telegraph ['telɪgrɑːf] n telégrafo; **~ pole** n poste m telegráfico

telepathy [tə'lepəθɪ] n telepatía

telephone ['telɪfəun] n teléfono ♦ vt llamar por teléfono, telefonear; (message) dar por teléfono; **to be on the ~** (talking) hablar por teléfono; (possessing ~) tener teléfono; **~ booth** n cabina telefónica; **~ box** (BRIT) n = **~ booth**; **~ call** n llamada (telefónica); **~ directory** n guía (telefónica); **~ number** n número de teléfono

telephonist [tə'lefənɪst] (BRIT) n telefonista m/f

telescope ['telɪskəup] n telescopio

television ['telɪvɪʒən] n televisión f; **on ~** en la televisión; **~ set** n televisor m

tell [tel] (pt, pp **told**) vt decir; (relate: story) contar; (distinguish): **to ~ sth from** distinguir algo de ♦ vi (talk): **to ~ (of)** contar; (have effect) tener efecto; **to ~ sb to do sth** mandar a uno hacer algo; **~ off** vt: **to ~ sb off** regañar a uno; **~er** n (in bank) cajero/a; **~ing** adj (remark, detail) revelador(a); **~tale** adj (sign) indicador(a)

telly ['telɪ] (BRIT: inf) n abbr (= television) tele f

temp [temp] n abbr (BRIT: = temporary) temporero/a

temper ['tempə*] n (nature) carácter m; (mood) humor m; (bad ~) (mal) genio; (fit of anger) acceso de ira ♦ vt (moderate) moderar; **to be in a ~** estar furioso; **to lose one's ~** enfadarse, enojarse

temperament ['tempərəmənt] n (nature) temperamento

temperate ['tempərət] adj (climate etc) templado

temperature ['temprətʃə*] n temperatura; **to have** or **run a ~** tener fiebre

temple ['templ] n (building) templo; (ANAT) sien f

tempo ['tempəu] (pl **tempos** or **tempi**) n (MUS) tempo, tiempo; (fig) ritmo

temporarily ['tempərərɪlɪ] adv temporalmente

temporary ['tempərərɪ] adj provisional; (passing) transitorio; (worker) temporero; (job) temporal

tempt [tempt] vt tentar; **to ~ sb into doing sth** tentar or inducir a uno a hacer algo; **~ation** [-'teɪʃən] n tentación f; **~ing** adj tentador(a); (food) apetitoso/a

ten [ten] num diez

tenacity [tə'næsɪtɪ] n tenacidad f

tenancy 573 textiles

tenancy ['tenənsı] n arrendamiento, alquiler m

tenant ['tenənt] n inquilino/a

tend [tend] vt cuidar ♦ vi: **to ~ to do sth** tener tendencia a hacer algo

tendency ['tendənsı] n tendencia

tender ['tendə*] adj (person, care) tierno, cariñoso; (meat) tierno; (sore) sensible ♦ n (COMM: offer) oferta; (money): **legal ~** moneda de curso legal ♦ vt ofrecer; **~ness** n ternura; (of meat) blandura

tenement ['tenəmənt] n casa de pisos (SP)

tennis ['tenɪs] n tenis m; **~ ball** n pelota de tenis; **~ court** n cancha de tenis; **~ player** n tenista m/f; **~ racket** n raqueta de tenis

tenor ['tenə*] n (MUS) tenor m

tenpin bowling ['tenpin-] n (juego de los) bolos

tense [tens] adj (person) nervioso; (moment, atmosphere) tenso; (muscle) tenso, en tensión ♦ n (LING) tiempo

tension ['tenʃən] n tensión f

tent [tent] n tienda (de campaña) (SP), carpa (AM)

tentative ['tentətɪv] adj (person, smile) indeciso; (conclusion, plans) provisional

tenterhooks ['tentəhuks] npl: **on ~** sobre ascuas

tenth [tenθ] num décimo

tent peg n clavija, estaca

tent pole n mástil m

tenuous ['tenjuəs] adj tenue

tenure ['tenjuə*] n (of land etc) tenencia; (of office) ejercicio

tepid ['tepɪd] adj tibio

term [tə:m] n (word) término; (period) período; (SCOL) trimestre m ♦ vt llamar; **~s** npl (conditions, COMM) condiciones fpl; **in the short/long ~** a corto/largo plazo; **to be on good ~s with sb** llevarse bien con uno; **to come to ~s with** (problem) aceptar

terminal ['tə:mɪnl] adj (disease) mortal; (patient) terminal ♦ n (ELEC)

borne m; (COMPUT) terminal m; (also: air ~) terminal f; (BRIT: also: coach ~) (estación f) terminal f

terminate ['tə:mɪneɪt] vt terminar

terminus ['tə:mɪnəs] (pl **termini**) n término, (estación f) terminal f

terrace ['terəs] n terraza; (BRIT: row of houses) hilera de casas adosadas; **the ~s** (BRIT: SPORT) las gradas fpl; **~d** adj (garden) en terrazas; (house) adosado

terrain [te'reɪn] n terreno

terrible ['terɪbl] adj terrible, horrible; (inf) atroz; **terribly** adv terriblemente, (very badly) malísimamente

terrier ['terɪə*] n terrier m

terrific [tə'rɪfɪk] adj (very great) tremendo; (wonderful) fantástico, fenomenal

terrify ['terɪfaɪ] vt aterrorizar

territory ['terɪtərɪ] n (also fig) territorio

terror ['terə*] n terror m; **~ism** n terrorismo; **~ist** n terrorista m/f

test [test] n (gen, CHEM) prueba; (MED) examen m; (SCOL) examen m, test m; (also: driving ~) examen m de conducir ♦ vt probar, poner a prueba; (MED, SCOL) examinar

testament ['testəmənt] n testamento; **the Old/New T~** el Antiguo/Nuevo Testamento

testicle ['testɪkl] n testículo

testify ['testɪfaɪ] vi (LAW) prestar declaración; **to ~ to sth** atestiguar algo

testimony ['testɪmənɪ] n (LAW) testimonio

test: ~ match n (CRICKET, RUGBY) partido internacional; **~ tube** n probeta

tetanus ['tetənəs] n tétano

tether ['teðə*] vt atar (con una cuerda) ♦ n: **to be at the end of one's ~** no aguantar más

text [tekst] n texto; **~book** n libro de texto

textiles ['tekstaɪlz] npl textiles mpl; (textile industry) industria textil

texture ['tekstʃə*] n textura
Thailand ['taɪlænd] n Tailandia
Thames [temz] n: **the ~** el (río) Támesis
than [ðæn] conj (in comparisons): **more ~ 10/once** más de 10/una vez; **I have more/less ~ you/Paul** tengo más/menos que tú/Paul; **she is older ~ you think** es mayor de lo que piensas
thank [θæŋk] vt dar las gracias a, agradecer; **~ you (very much)** muchas gracias; **~ God!** ¡gracias a Dios!; **~s** npl gracias fpl ♦ excl (also: **many ~s, ~s a lot**) ¡gracias!; **~s to** prep gracias a; **~ful** adj: **~ful (for)** agradecido (por); **~less** adj ingrato; **T~sgiving (Day)** n día m de Acción de Gracias

┌─ **Thanksgiving (Day)** ──────┐

En Estados Unidos el cuarto jueves de noviembre es **Thanksgiving Day**, fiesta oficial en la que se recuerda la celebración que hicieron los primeros colonos norteamericanos ("Pilgrims" o "Pilgrim Fathers") tras la estupenda cosecha de 1621, por la que se dan gracias a Dios. En Canadá se celebra una fiesta semejante el segundo lunes de octubre, aunque no está relacionada con dicha fecha histórica.

└──────────────────────────────┘

┌─ KEYWORD ─┐
└───────────┘

that [ðæt] (pl **those**) adj (demonstrative) ese/a, pl esos/as; (more remote) aquel/aquella, pl aquellos/as; **leave those books on the table** deja esos libros sobre la mesa; **~ one** ése/ésa; (more remote) aquél/aquélla; **~ one over there** ése/ésa de ahí; aquél/aquélla de allí
♦ pron **1** (demonstrative) ése/a, pl ésos/as; (neuter) eso; (more remote) aquél/aquélla, pl aquéllos/as; (neuter) aquello; **what's ~?** ¿qué es eso (or

aquello)?; **who's ~?** ¿quién es ése/a (or aquél/aquélla)?; **is ~ you?** ¿eres tú?; **will you eat all ~?** ¿vas a comer todo eso?; **~'s my house** ésa es mi casa; **~'s what he said** eso es lo que dijo; **~ is (to say)** es decir
2 (relative: subject, object) que; (with preposition) (el/la) que etc, el/la cual etc; **the book (~) I read** el libro que leí; **the books ~ are in the library** los libros que están en la biblioteca; **all (~) I have** todo lo que tengo; **the box (~) I put it in** la caja en la que or donde lo puse; **the people (~) I spoke to** la gente con la que hablé
3 (relative: of time) que; **the day (~) he came** el día (en) que vino
♦ conj que; **he thought ~ I was ill** creyó que yo estaba enfermo
♦ adv (demonstrative): **I can't work ~ much** no puedo trabajar tanto; **I didn't realise it was ~ bad** no creí que fuera tan malo; **~ high** así de alto

thatched [θætʃt] adj (roof) de paja; (cottage) con tejado de paja
thaw [θɔː] n deshielo ♦ vi (ice) derretirse; (food) descongelarse ♦ vt (food) descongelar

┌─ KEYWORD ─┐
└───────────┘

the [ðiː, ðə] def art **1** (gen) el, f la, pl los, fpl las (NB = el immediately before f n beginning with stressed (h)a; a+ el = al; de+ el = del); **~ boy/girl** el chico/ la chica; **~ books/flowers** los libros/ las flores; **~ postman/from ~ drawer** el cartero/del cajón; **I haven't ~ time/money** no tengo tiempo/dinero
2 (+ adj to form n) lo; lo; **~ rich and ~ poor** los ricos y los pobres; **to attempt ~ impossible** intentar lo imposible
3 (in titles): **Elizabeth ~ First** Isabel primera; **Peter ~ Great** Pedro el Grande

4 (in comparisons): **~ more he works ~ more he earns** cuanto más trabaja más gana

theatre ['θɪətə*] (US **theater**) n teatro; (also: lecture ~) aula; (MED: also: operating ~) quirófano; **~-goer** n aficionado/a al teatro

theatrical [θɪ'ætrɪkl] adj teatral

theft [θeft] n robo

their [ðɛə*] adj su; **~s** pron (el) suyo/(la) suya etc; see also **my**; **mine**[1]

them [ðɛm, ðəm] pron (direct) los/las; (indirect) les; (stressed, after prep) ellos/ellas; see also **me**

theme [θiːm] n tema m; **~ park** n parque de atracciones (en torno a un tema central); **~ song** n tema m (musical)

themselves [ðəm'sɛlvz] pl pron (subject) ellos mismos/ellas mismas; (complement) se; (after prep) sí (mismos/as); see also **oneself**

then [ðɛn] adv (at that time) entonces; (next) después; (later) luego, después; (and also) además ♦ conj (therefore) en ese caso, entonces ♦ adj: **the ~ president** el entonces presidente; **by ~** para entonces; **from ~ on** desde entonces

theology [θɪ'ɔlədʒɪ] n teología

theory ['θɪərɪ] n teoría

therapist ['θerəpɪst] n terapeuta m/f

therapy ['θerəpɪ] n terapia

KEYWORD

there ['ðɛə*] adv **1**: **~ is**, **~ are** hay; **~ is no-one here/no bread left** no hay nadie aquí/no queda pan; **~ has been an accident** ha habido un accidente
2 (referring to place) ahí; (distant) allí; **it's ~** está ahí; **put it in/on/up/down** ~ ponlo ahí dentro/encima/arriba/abajo; **I want that book** ~ quiero ese libro de ahí; **~ he is!** ¡ahí

está!
3: **~**, **~** (esp to child) ea, ea

there: **~abouts** adv por ahí; **~after** adv después; **~by** adv así, de ese modo; **~fore** adv por lo tanto; **~'s = there is**; **there has**

thermal ['θəːml] adj termal; (paper) térmico

thermometer [θə'mɔmɪtə*] n termómetro

Thermos ® ['θəːməs] n (also: ~ flask) termo

thermostat ['θəːməustæt] n termostato

thesaurus [θɪ'sɔːrəs] n tesoro

these [ðiːz] pl adj estos/as ♦ pl pron éstos/as

thesis ['θiːsɪs] (pl **theses**) n tesis f inv

they [ðeɪ] pl pron ellos/ellas; (stressed) ellos (mismos)/ellas (mismas); **~ say that ...** (it is said that) se dice que ...; **~'d = they had**; **they would**; **~'ll = they shall**; **they will**; **~'re = they are**; **~'ve = they have**

thick [θɪk] adj (in consistency) espeso; (in size) grueso; (stupid) torpe ♦ n: **in the ~ of the battle** en lo más reñido de la batalla; **it's 20 cm ~** tiene 20 cm de espesor; **~en** vi espesarse ♦ vt (sauce etc) espesar; **~ness** n espesor m; grueso; **~set** adj fornido

thief [θiːf] (pl **thieves**) n ladrón/ona m/f

thigh [θaɪ] n muslo

thimble ['θɪmbl] n dedal m

thin [θɪn] adj (person, animal) flaco; (in size) delgado; (in consistency) poco espeso; (hair, crowd) escaso ♦ vt: **to ~ (down)** diluir

thing [θɪŋ] n cosa; (object) objeto, artículo; (matter) asunto; (mania): **to have a ~ about sb/sth** estar obsesionado con uno/algo; **~s** npl (belongings) efectos mpl (personales); **the best ~ would be to ...** lo mejor sería ...; **how are ~s?** ¿qué tal?

think [θɪŋk] (*pt, pp* **thought**) *vi* pensar
♦ *vt* pensar, creer; **what did you ~ of them?** ¿qué te pareció?; **to ~ about sth/sb** pensar en algo/uno; **I'll ~ about it** lo pensaré; **to ~ of doing sth** pensar en hacer algo; **I ~ so/not** creo que sí/no; **to ~ well of sb** tener buen concepto de uno; **~ over** *vt* reflexionar sobre, meditar; **~ up** *vt* (*plan etc*) idear; **~ tank** *n* gabinete *m* de estrategia

thinly ['θɪnlɪ] *adv* (*cut*) fino; (*spread*) ligeramente

third [θɜːd] *adj* (*before n*) tercer(a); (*following n*) tercero/a ♦ *n* tercero/a; (*fraction*) tercio; (*BRIT: SCOL: degree*) título de licenciado con calificación de aprobado; **~ly** *adv* en tercer lugar; **~ party insurance** (*BRIT*) *n* seguro contra terceros; **~rate** *adj* (*de calidad*) mediocre; **T~ World** *n* Tercer Mundo

thirst [θɜːst] *n* sed *f*; **~y** *adj* (*person, animal*) sediento; (*work*) que da sed; **to be ~y** tener sed

thirteen ['θɜː'tiːn] *num* trece

thirty ['θɜːtɪ] *num* treinta

KEYWORD

this [ðɪs] (*pl* **these**) *adj* (*demonstrative*) este/a; *pl* estos/as; (*neuter*) esto; **~ man/woman** este hombre/esta mujer; **these children/flowers** estos chicos/estas flores; **~ one (here)** éste/a, esto (de aquí)
♦ *pron* (*demonstrative*) éste/a; *pl* éstos/as; (*neuter*) esto; **who is ~?** ¿quién es éste/ésta?; **what is ~?** ¿qué es esto?; **~ is where I live** aquí vivo; **~ is what he said** esto es lo que dijo; **~ is Mr Brown** (*in introductions*) le presento al Sr. Brown; (*photo*) éste es el Sr. Brown; (*on telephone*) habla el Sr. Brown
♦ *adv* (*demonstrative*): **~ high/long** *etc* así de alto/largo *etc*; **~ far** hasta aquí

thistle ['θɪsl] *n* cardo

thorn [θɔːn] *n* espina

thorough ['θʌrə] *adj* (*search*) minucioso; (*wash*) a fondo; (*knowledge, research*) profundo; (*person*) meticuloso; **~bred** *adj* (*horse*) de pura sangre; **~fare** *n* calle *f*; **"no ~fare"** "prohibido el paso"; **~ly** *adv* (*search*) minuciosamente; (*study*) profundamente; (*wash*) a fondo; (*utterly: bad, wet etc*) completamente, totalmente

those [ðəʊz] *pl adj* esos/esas; (*more remote*) aquellos/as

though [ðəʊ] *conj* aunque ♦ *adv* sin embargo

thought [θɔːt] *pt, pp* of **think** ♦ *n* pensamiento; (*opinion*) opinión *f*; **~ful** *adj* pensativo; (*serious*) serio; (*considerate*) atento; **~less** *adj* desconsiderado

thousand ['θaʊzənd] *num* mil; **two ~s** dos mil; **~s of** miles de; **~th** *num* milésimo

thrash [θræʃ] *vt* azotar; (*defeat*) derrotar; **~ about** *or* **around** *vi* debatirse; **~ out** *vt* discutir a fondo

thread [θrɛd] *n* hilo; (*of screw*) rosca ♦ *vt* (*needle*) enhebrar; **~bare** *adj* raído

threat [θrɛt] *n* amenaza; **~en** *vi* amenazar ♦ *vt*: **to ~en sb with/to do** amenazar a uno con/con hacer

three [θriː] *num* tres; **~-dimensional** *adj* tridimensional; **~-piece suit** *n* traje *m* de tres piezas; **~-piece suite** *n* tresillo; **~-ply** *adj* (*wool*) de tres cabos

threshold ['θrɛʃhəʊld] *n* umbral *m*

threw [θruː] *pt* of **throw**

thrifty ['θrɪftɪ] *adj* económico

thrill [θrɪl] *n* (*excitement*) emoción *f*; (*shudder*) estremecimiento ♦ *vt* emocionar; **to be ~ed** (*with gift etc*) estar encantado; **~er** *n* novela (*or obra or película*) de suspense; **~ing** *adj* emocionante

thrive [θraɪv] (*pt, pp* **thrived**) *vi* (*grow*) crecer; (*do well*): **to ~ on sth** sentarse muy bien a uno algo; **thriving** *adj* próspero

throat [θrəut] n garganta; **to have a sore ~** tener dolor de garganta

throb [θrɔb] vi latir; dar punzadas; vibrar

throes [θrəuz] npl: **in the ~ of** en medio de

throne [θrəun] n trono

throng [θrɔŋ] n multitud f, muchedumbre f ♦ vt agolparse en

throttle ['θrɔtl] n (AUT) acelerador m ♦ vt estrangular

through [θru:] prep por, a través de; (time) durante; (by means of) por medio de, mediante; (owing to) gracias a ♦ adj (ticket, train) directo ♦ adv completamente, de parte a parte; de principio a fin; **to put sb ~ to sb** (TEL) poner or pasar a uno con uno; **to be ~** (TEL) tener comunicación; (have finished) haber terminado; **"no ~ road"** (BRIT) "calle sin salida"; **~out** prep (place) por todas partes de, por todo; (time) durante todo ♦ adv por or en todas partes

throw [θrəu] (pt threw, pp thrown) n tiro; (SPORT) lanzamiento ♦ vt tirar, echar; (SPORT) lanzar; (rider) derribar; (fig) desconcertar; **to ~ a party** dar una fiesta; **~ away** vt tirar; (money) derrochar; **~ off** vt deshacerse de; **~ out** vt tirar; (person) echar; expulsar; **~ up** vi vomitar; **~away** adj para tirar, desechable; (remark) hecho de paso; **~-in** n (SPORT) saque m

thru [θru:] (US) = **through**

thrush [θrʌʃ] n zorzal m, tordo

thrust [θrʌst] (pt, pp thrust) n empuje m ♦ vt empujar (con fuerza)

thud [θʌd] n golpe m sordo

thug [θʌg] n gamberro/a m

thumb [θʌm] n (ANAT) pulgar m; **to ~ a lift** hacer autostop; **~ through** vt fus (book) hojear; **~tack** (US) n chincheta f

thump [θʌmp] n golpe m; (sound) ruido seco or sordo ♦ vt golpear ♦ vi

(heart etc) palpitar

thunder ['θʌndə*] n trueno ♦ vi tronar; (train etc): **to ~ past** pasar como un trueno; **~bolt** n rayo; **~clap** n trueno; **~storm** n tormenta; **~y** adj tormentoso

Thursday ['θə:zdɪ] n jueves m inv

thus [ðʌs] adv así, de este modo

thyme [taɪm] n tomillo

thyroid ['θaɪrɔɪd] n (also: ~ gland) tiroides m inv

tic [tɪk] n tic m

tick [tɪk] n (sound: of clock) tictac m; (mark) palomita; (ZOOL) garrapata; (BRIT: inf): **in a ~** en un instante ♦ vi hacer tictac ♦ vt marcar; **~ off** vt marcar; (person) reñir; **~ over** vi (engine) girar en marcha lenta; (fig) ir tirando

ticket ['tɪkɪt] n billete m (SP), tíquet m, boleto m (AM); (for cinema etc) entrada (SP), boleto (AM); (in shop: on goods) etiqueta; (for raffle) papeleta; (for library) tarjeta; (parking ~) multa por estacionamiento ilegal; **~ collector** n revisor(a) m/f; **~ office** n (THEATRE) taquilla (SP), boletería (AM); (RAIL) despacho de billetes (SP) or boletos (AM)

tickle ['tɪkl] vt hacer cosquillas a ♦ vi hacer cosquillas; **ticklish** adj (person) cosquilloso; (problem) delicado

tidal ['taɪdl] adj de marea; **~ wave** n maremoto

tidbit ['tɪdbɪt] (US) n = **titbit**

tiddlywinks ['tɪdlɪwɪŋks] n juego infantil con fichas de plástico

tide [taɪd] n marea; (fig: of events etc) curso, marcha; **~ over** vt (help out) ayudar a salir del apuro

tidy ['taɪdɪ] adj (room etc) ordenado; (dress, work) limpio; (person) (bien) arreglado ♦ vt (also: ~ up) poner en orden

tie [taɪ] n (string etc) atadura; (BRIT: also: neck~) corbata; (fig: link) vínculo, lazo; (SPORT etc: draw) empate m ♦ vt atar ♦ vi (SPORT etc) empatar; **to ~ in a bow** atar con un lazo; **to ~ a knot in sth** hacer un nudo en algo; **~ down** vt (fig: person: restrict) sujetar; (: to price, date etc) obligar a; **~ up** vt (parcel) envolver; (dog, person) atar; (arrangements) concluir; **to be ~d up** (busy) estar ocupado

tier [tɪə*] n grada; (of cake) piso

tiger ['taɪgə*] n tigre m

tight [taɪt] adj (rope) tirante; (money) escaso; (clothes) ajustado; (bend) cerrado; (shoes, schedule) apretado; (budget) ajustado; (security) estricto; (inf: drunk) borracho ♦ adv (squeeze) muy fuerte; (shut) bien; **~en** vt (rope) estirar; (screw, grip) apretar; (security) reforzar ♦ vi estirarse; apretarse; **~-fisted** adj tacaño; **~ly** adv (grasp) muy fuerte; **~rope** n cuerda floja; **~s** (BRIT) npl panti mpl

tile [taɪl] n (on roof) teja; (on floor) baldosa; (on wall) azulejo; **~d** adj de tejas; embaldosado; (wall) alicatado

till [tɪl] n caja (registradora) ♦ vt (land) cultivar ♦ prep, conj = **until**

tilt [tɪlt] vt inclinar ♦ vi inclinarse

timber ['tɪmbə*] n (material) madera

time [taɪm] n tiempo; (epoch: often pl) época; (by clock) hora; (moment) momento; (occasion) vez f; (MUS) compás m ♦ vt calcular o medir el tiempo de; (race) cronometrar; (remark, visit etc) elegir el momento para; **a long ~** mucho tiempo; **4 at a ~** de 4 en 4; **4 a la vez**; **for the ~ being** de momento, por ahora; **from ~ to ~** de vez en cuando; **at ~s** a veces; **in ~** (soon enough) a tiempo; (after some time) con el tiempo; (MUS) al compás; **in a week's ~** dentro de una semana; **in no ~** en un abrir y cerrar de ojos; **any ~** cuando sea; **on ~** a su hora; **5 ~s 5** 5 por 5; **what ~ is it?** ¿qué hora es?; **to have a good ~** pasarlo bien, divertirse; **~ bomb** n bomba de efecto retardado; **~less** adj eterno; **~ limit** n

plazo; **~ly** adj oportuno; **~ off** n tiempo libre; **~r** n (in kitchen etc) programador m horario; **~ scale** (BRIT) n escala de tiempo; **~-share** n apartamento (or casa) a tiempo compartido; **~ switch** (BRIT) n interruptor m (horario); **~table** n horario; **~ zone** n huso horario

timid ['tɪmɪd] adj tímido

timing ['taɪmɪŋ] n (SPORT) cronometraje m; **the ~ of his resignation** el momento que eligió para dimitir

tin [tɪn] n estaño; (also: ~ plate) hojalata; (BRIT: can) lata; **~foil** n papel m de estaño

tinge [tɪndʒ] n matiz m ♦ vt: **~d with** teñido de

tingle ['tɪŋgl] vi (person): **to ~ (with)** estremecerse de; (hands etc) hormiguear

tinker ['tɪŋkə*]: **~ with** vt fus jugar con, tocar

tinned [tɪnd] (BRIT) adj (food) en lata, en conserva

tin opener [-əupnə*] (BRIT) n abrelatas m inv

tinsel ['tɪnsl] n (guirnalda de) espumillón m

tint [tɪnt] n matiz m; (for hair) tinte m; **~ed** adj (hair) teñido; (glass, spectacles) ahumado

tiny ['taɪnɪ] adj minúsculo, pequeñito

tip [tɪp] n (end) punta; (gratuity) propina; (BRIT: for rubbish) vertedero; (advice) consejo ♦ vt (waiter) dar una propina a; (tilt) inclinar; (empty: also: ~ out) vaciar, echar; (overturn: also: ~ over) volcar; **~-off** n (hint) advertencia; **~ped** (BRIT) adj (cigarette) con filtro

Tipp-Ex ® ['tɪpeks] n Tipp-Ex ® m

tipsy ['tɪpsɪ] (inf) adj alegre, mareado

tiptoe ['tɪptəu]: n: **on ~** de puntillas

tire ['taɪə*] n (US) = **tyre** ♦ vt cansar ♦ vi (gen) cansarse; (become bored) aburrirse; **~d** adj cansado; **to be ~d of**

sth estar harto de algo; **~less** adj incansable; **~some** adj aburrido; **~ting** adj cansado

tissue ['tɪʃuː] n tejido; (paper handkerchief) pañuelo de papel, kleenex ® m; **~ paper** n papel m de seda

tit [tɪt] n (bird) herrerillo común; **to give ~ for tat** dar ojo por ojo

titbit ['tɪtbɪt] (US **tidbit**) n (food) golosina; (news) noticia sabrosa

title ['taɪtl] n título; **~ deed** n (LAW) título de propiedad; **~ role** n papel m principal

TM abbr = **trademark**

KEYWORD

to [tuː, tə] prep **1** (direction) a; **to go ~ France/London/school/the station** ir a Francia/Londres/al colegio/a la estación; **to go ~ Claude's/the doctor's** ir a casa de Claude/al médico; **the road ~ Edinburgh** la carretera de Edimburgo

2 (as far as) hasta, a; **from here ~ London** de aquí a or hasta Londres; **to count ~ 10** contar hasta 10; **from 40 ~ 50 people** entre 40 y 50 personas

3 (with expressions of time): **a quarter/twenty ~ 5** las 5 menos cuarto/veinte

4 (for, of): **the key ~ the front door** la llave de la puerta principal; **she is secretary ~ the director** es la secretaria del director; **a letter ~ his wife** una carta a or para su mujer

5 (expressing indirect object): **to give sth ~ sb** darle algo a alguien; **to talk ~ sb** hablar con alguien; **to be a danger ~ sb** ser un peligro para alguien; **to carry out repairs ~ sth** hacer reparaciones en algo

6 (in relation to): **3 goals ~ 2** 3 goles a 2; **30 miles ~ the gallon** ≈ 9,4 litros a los cien (kms)

7 (purpose, result): **to come ~ sb's aid** venir en auxilio or ayuda de alguien; **to sentence sb ~ death** condenar a uno a muerte; **~ my great surprise** con gran sorpresa mía

♦ with vb **1** (simple infin): **~ go/eat** ir/comer

2 (following another vb): **to want/try/start ~ do** querer/intentar/empezar a hacer; see also relevant vb

3 (with vb omitted): **I don't want ~** no quiero

4 (purpose, result) para; **I did it ~ help you** lo hice para ayudarte; **he came ~ see you** vino a verte

5 (equivalent to relative clause): **I have things ~ do** tengo cosas que hacer; **the main thing is ~ try** lo principal es intentarlo

6 (after adj etc): **ready ~ go** listo para irse; **too old ~ ...** demasiado viejo (como) para ...

♦ adv: **pull/push the door ~** tirar de/empujar la puerta

toad [təud] n sapo; **~stool** n hongo venenoso

toast [təust] n (CULIN) tostada; (drink, speech) brindis m ♦ vt (CULIN) tostar; (drink to) brindar por; **~er** n tostador m

tobacco [tə'bækəu] n tabaco; **~nist** n estanquero (a), tabaquero-a (AM); **~nist's (shop)** (BRIT) n estanco (SP), tabaquería (AM)

toboggan [tə'bɒgən] n tobogán n

today [tə'deɪ] adv, n (also fig) hoy m

toddler ['tɒdlə*] n niño/a (que empieza a andar)

toe [təu] n dedo (del pie); (of shoe) punta; **to ~ the line** (fig) conformarse; **~nail** n uña de pie

toffee ['tɒfɪ] n toffee m; **~ apple** (BRIT) n manzana acaramelada

together [tə'geðə*] adv juntos; (at same time) al mismo tiempo, a la vez; **~ with** junto con*

toil [tɔɪl] n trabajo duro, labor f ♦ vi trabajar duramente

toilet ['tɔɪlət] n retrete m; (BRIT: room) servicios mpl (SP), wáter m (SP), sanitario (AM) ♦ cpd (soap etc) de aseo; ~ **paper** n papel m higiénico; ~**ries** npl artículos mpl de tocador; ~ **roll** n rollo de papel higiénico

token ['təukən] n (sign) señal f, muestra; (souvenir) recuerdo; (disc) ficha ♦ adj (strike, payment etc) simbólico; **book/record** ~ (BRIT) vale m para comprar libros/discos; **gift** ~ (BRIT) vale-regalo

Tokyo ['təukjəu] n Tokio, Tokío

told [təuld] pt, pp de **tell**

tolerable ['tɔlərəbl] adj (bearable) soportable; (fairly good) pasable

tolerant ['tɔlərnt] adj: ~ **of** tolerante con

tolerate ['tɔləreɪt] vt tolerar

toll [təul] n (of casualties) número de víctimas; (tax, charge) peaje m ♦ vi (bell) doblar

tomato [tə'mɑːtəu] (pl ~es) n tomate m

tomb [tuːm] n tumba

tomboy ['tɔmbɔɪ] n marimacho

tombstone ['tuːmstəun] n lápida

tomcat ['tɔmkæt] n gato (macho)

tomorrow [tə'mɔrəu] adv, n (also: fig) mañana; **the day after** ~ pasado mañana; ~ **morning** mañana por la mañana

ton [tʌn] n tonelada (BRIT = 1016 kg; US = 907 kg); (metric ~) tonelada métrica; ~**s** of (inf) montones de

tone [təun] n tono ♦ vi (also: ~ **in**) armonizar; ~ **down** vt (criticism) suavizar; (colour) atenuar; ~ **up** vt (muscles) tonificar; ~-**deaf** adj con mal oído

tongs [tɔŋz] npl (for coal) tenazas fpl; (curling ~) tenacillas fpl

tongue [tʌŋ] n lengua; ~ **in cheek** irónicamente; ~-**tied** adj (fig) mudo; ~-**twister** n trabalenguas m inv

tonic ['tɔnɪk] n (MED, also fig) tónico; (also: ~ water) (agua) tónica

tonight [tə'naɪt] adv, n esta noche; esta tarde

tonsil ['tɔnsl] n amígdala; ~**litis** [-'laɪtɪs] n amigdalitis f

too [tuː] adv (excessively) demasiado; (also) también; ~ **much** demasiado; ~ **many** demasiados/as

took [tuk] pt de **take**

tool [tuːl] n herramienta; ~ **box** n caja de herramientas

toot [tuːt] n pitido ♦ vi tocar el pito

tooth [tuːθ] (pl **teeth**) n (ANAT, TECH) diente m; (of saw) muela; ~**ache** n dolor m de muelas; ~**brush** n cepillo de dientes; ~**paste** n pasta de dientes; ~**pick** n palillo

top [tɔp] n (of mountain) cumbre f, cima; (of tree) copa; (of head) coronilla; (of ladder, page) lo alto; (of table) superficie f; (of cupboard) parte f de arriba; (lid: of box) tapa; (: of bottle, jar) tapón m; (of list etc) cabeza; (toy) peonza; (garment) blusa; camiseta ♦ adj de arriba; (in rank) principal, primero; (best) mejor ♦ vt (exceed) exceder; (be first in) encabezar; **on** ~ **of** (above) sobre, encima de; (in addition to) además de; **from** ~ **to bottom** de pies a cabeza; ~ **off** (US) vt = ~ **up**; ~ **up** vt llenar; ~ **floor** n último piso; ~ **hat** n sombrero de copa; ~-**heavy** adj (object) mal equilibrado

topic ['tɔpɪk] n tema m; ~**al** adj actual

top: ~**less** adj (bather, bikini) topless inv; ~-**level** adj (talks) al más alto nivel; ~**most** adj más alto

topple ['tɔpl] vt derribar ♦ vi caerse

top-secret adj del todo secreto

topsy-turvy ['tɔpsi'təːvi] adj al revés ♦ adv patas arriba

torch [tɔːtʃ] n antorcha; (BRIT: electric) linterna

tore [tɔː*] pt de **tear²**

torment [n 'tɔːmɛnt, vt tɔː'mɛnt] n

tormento ♦ vt atormentar; (fig: annoy) fastidiar

torn [tɔːn] pp of **tear²**

torrent ['tɔrnt] n torrente m

tortoise ['tɔːtəs] n tortuga f; **~shell** ['tɔːtəʃel] adj de carey

torture ['tɔːtʃə*] n tortura ♦ vt torturar; (fig) atormentar

Tory ['tɔːri] (BRIT) adj, n (POL) conservador(a) m/f

toss [tɔs] vt tirar, echar; (one's head) sacudir; **to ~ a coin** echar a cara o cruz; **to ~ up for sth** jugar a cara o cruz algo; **to ~ and turn** (in bed) dar vueltas

tot [tɔt] n (BRIT: drink) copita; (child) nene/a m/f

total ['təutl] adj total, entero; (emphatic: failure etc) completo, total ♦ n total m, suma f ♦ vt (add up) sumar; (amount to) ascender a; **~ly** adv totalmente

touch [tʌtʃ] n tacto; (contact) contacto ♦ vt tocar; (emotionally) conmover; **a ~ of** (fig) un poquito de; **to get in ~ with sb** ponerse en contacto con uno; **to lose ~** (friends) perder contacto; **~ on** vt fus (topic) aludir (brevemente) a; **~ up** vt (paint) retocar; **~-and-go** adj arriesgado; **~down** n aterrizaje m; (on sea) amerizaje m; (US: FOOTBALL) ensayo; **~ed** adj (moved) conmovido; (fig) chiflado; **~ing** adj conmovedor(a); **~line** n (SPORT) línea de banda; **~y** adj (person) quisquilloso

tough [tʌf] adj (material) resistente; (meat) duro; (problem etc) difícil; (policy, stance) inflexible; (person) fuerte; **~en** vt endurecer

toupée [tuː'peɪ] n peluca f

tour ['tuə*] n viaje m, vuelta; (also: package ~) viaje m todo comprendido; (of town, museum) visita; (by band etc) gira ♦ vt recorrer, visitar; **~ guide** n guía m turístico, guía f turística

tourism ['tuərɪzm] n turismo m

tourist ['tuərɪst] n turista m/f ♦ cpd turístico; **~ office** n oficina de turismo

tousled ['tauzld] adj (hair) despeinado

tout [taut] vi: **to ~ for business** solicitar clientes ♦ n (also: ticket ~) revendedor(a) m/f

tow [təu] vt remolcar; **"on** or **in** (US) **~"** (AUT) "a remolque"

toward(s) [tə'wɔːd(z)] prep hacia; (attitude) respecto a, con; (purpose) para

towel ['tauəl] n toalla; **~ling** n (fabric) felpa; **~ rail** (US **~ rack**) n toallero

tower ['tauə*] n torre f; **~ block** (BRIT) n torre f (de pisos); **~ing** adj muy alto, imponente

town [taun] n ciudad f; **to go to ~** ir a la ciudad; (fig) echar la casa por la ventana; **~ centre** n centro de la ciudad; **~ council** n ayuntamiento, consejo municipal; **~ hall** n ayuntamiento; **~ plan** n plano de la ciudad; **~ planning** n urbanismo

towrope ['təurəup] n cable m de remolque

tow truck (US) n camión m grúa

toy [tɔɪ] n juguete m; **~ with** vt fus jugar con; (idea) acariciar; **~shop** n juguetería

trace [treis] n rastro ♦ vt (draw) trazar, delinear; (locate) encontrar; (follow) seguir la pista de; **tracing paper** n papel m de calco

track [træk] n (mark) huella, pista; (path: gen) camino, senda; (: of bullet etc) trayectoria; (: of suspect, animal) pista, rastro; (RAIL) vía; (SPORT) pista; (on tape, record) canción f ♦ vt seguir la pista de; **to keep ~ of** mantenerse al tanto de, seguir; **~ down** vt (prey) seguir el rastro de; (sth lost) encontrar; **~suit** n chándal m

tract [trækt] n (GEO) región f

traction ['trækʃən] n (power) tracción f; **in ~** (MED) en tracción

tractor ['træktə*] n tractor m

trade [treid] n comercio m; (skill, job)

oficio ♦ vi negociar, comerciar ♦ vt
(exchange): to ~ sth (for sth) cambiar
algo (por algo); ~ in vt (old car etc)
ofrecer como parte del pago; ~ fair n
feria comercial; ~mark n marca de
fábrica; ~ name n marca registrada;
~r n comerciante m/f; ~sman (irreg) n
(shopkeeper) tendero; ~ union n
sindicato; ~ unionist n sindicalista m/f

tradition [trə'dɪʃən] n tradición f; ~al
adj tradicional

traffic ['træfik] n (gen, AUT) tráfico,
circulación f, tránsito (AM) ♦ vi: to ~ in
(pej: liquor, drugs) traficar en; ~ circle
(US) n isleta; ~ jam n embotellamiento;
~ lights npl semáforo; ~ warden n
guardia m/f de tráfico

tragedy ['trædʒədɪ] n tragedia

tragic ['trædʒɪk] adj trágico

trail [treɪl] n (tracks) rastro, pista; (path)
camino, sendero; (dust, smoke) estela
♦ vt (drag) arrastrar; (follow) seguir la
pista de ♦ vi arrastrar; (in contest etc) ir
perdiendo; ~ behind vi quedar a la
zaga; ~er n (AUT) remolque m;
(caravana) caravana; (CINEMA) trailer m,
avance m; ~er truck (US) n trailer m

train [treɪn] n tren m; (of dress) cola;
(series) serie f ♦ vt (educate, teach skills
to) formar; (sportsman) entrenar; (dog)
adiestrar; (point: gun etc): to ~ on
apuntar a ♦ vi (SPORT) entrenarse;
(learn a skill): to ~ as a teacher etc
estudiar para profesor etc; one's ~ of
thought el razonamiento de uno; ~ed
adj (worker) cualificado, (animal)
amaestrado; ~ee [treɪ'niː] n
aprendiz m/f; ~er n (SPORT: coach)
entrenador(a) m/f; (: shoe): ~ers
zapatillas fpl (de deporte); (of animals)
domador(a) m/f; ~ing n formación f;
entrenamiento; to be in ~ing (SPORT)
estar entrenando; (fit) estar en forma;
~ing college n (gen) colegio de formación profesional;
(for teachers) escuela de formación del
profesorado; ~ing shoes npl zapatillas
fpl (de deporte)

trait [treɪt] n rasgo

traitor ['treɪtə*] n traidor(a) m/f

tram [træm] (BRIT) n (also: ~car) tranvía
m

tramp [træmp] n (person) vagabundo/
a; (inf: pej: woman) puta

trample ['træmpl] vt: to ~ (underfoot) pisotear

trampoline ['træmpəliːn] n trampolín m

tranquil ['træŋkwɪl] adj tranquilo;
~lizer n (MED) tranquilizante m

transact [træn'zækt] vt (business)
despachar; ~ion [-'zækʃən] n
transacción f, operación f

transfer [n 'trænsfə*, vb træns'fəː*] n
(of employees) traslado; (of money,
power) transferencia; (SPORT) traspaso;
(picture, design) calcomanía ♦ vt
trasladar; transferir; to ~ the charges
(BRIT: TEL) llamar a cobro revertido

transform [træns'fɔːm] vt transformar

transfusion [træns'fjuːʒən] n
transfusión f

transient ['trænzɪənt] adj transitorio

transistor [træn'zɪstə*] n (ELEC)
transistor m; ~ radio n transistor m

transit ['trænzɪt] n: in ~ en tránsito

transitive ['trænzɪtɪv] adj (LING)
transitivo

transit lounge n sala de tránsito

translate [trænz'leɪt] vt traducir;
translation [-'leɪʃən] n traducción f;
translator n traductor(a) m/f

transmit [trænz'mɪt] vt transmitir;
~ter n transmisor m

transparency [træns'pɛərnsɪ] n
transparencia; (BRIT: PHOT) diapositiva

transparent [træns'pærnt] adj
transparente

transpire [træns'paɪə*] vi (turn out)
resultar; (happen) ocurrir, suceder; it
~d that ... se supo que ...

transplant [n 'trænsplɑːnt] n (MED)
trasplante m

transport [n 'trænspɔːt, vt træns'pɔːt]
n transporte m; (car) coche m (SP),

carro (AM), **automóvil** m ♦ vt
transportar; **~ation** [-'teɪʃən] n
transporte m; **~ café** (BRIT) n bar-
restaurant m de carretera

transvestite [trænz'vestaɪt] n travestí
m/f

trap [træp] n (snare, trick) trampa;
(carriage) cabriolé m ♦ vt coger (SP) or
agarrar (AM) en una trampa; (trick)
engañar; (confine) atrapar; **~ door** n
escotilla

trapeze [trə'piːz] n trapecio

trappings ['træpɪŋz] npl adornos mpl

trash [træʃ] n (rubbish) basura; (pej):
the book/film is ~ el libro/la película
no vale nada; (nonsense) tonterías fpl;
~ can (US) n cubo (SP) or balde m (AM)
de la basura

travel ['trævl] n el viajar ♦ vi viajar ♦ vt
(distance) recorrer; **~s** npl (journeys)
viajes mpl; **~ agent** n agente m/f de
viajes; **~ler** (US **~er**) n viajero/a; **~ler's
cheque** (US **~er's check**) n cheque m
de viajero; **~ling** (US **~ing**) n los viajes,
el viajar; **~ sickness** n mareo

trawler ['trɔːlə*] n pesquero de
arrastre

tray [treɪ] n bandeja; (on desk) cajón m

treacherous ['tretʃərəs] adj traidor,
traicionero; (dangerous) peligroso

treacle ['triːkl] (BRIT) n melaza

tread [tred] (pt **trod**, pp **trodden**) n
(step) pisada; (sound) ruido de
pasos; (of stair) escalón m; (of tyre)
banda de rodadura ♦ vi pisar; **~ on** vt
fus pisar

treason ['triːzn] n traición f

treasure ['treʒə*] n (also fig) tesoro
♦ vt (value: object, friendship) apreciar;
(: memory) guardar

treasurer ['treʒərə*] n tesorero/a

treasury ['treʒərɪ] n: **the T~** el
Ministerio de Hacienda

treat [triːt] n (present) regalo ♦ vt
tratar; **to ~ sb to sth** invitar a uno a
algo

treatment ['triːtmənt] n tratamiento

treaty ['triːtɪ] n tratado

treble ['trebl] adj triple ♦ vt triplicar
♦ vi triplicarse; **~ clef** n (MUS) clave f
de sol

tree [triː] n árbol m; **~ trunk** tronco
(de árbol)

trek [trek] n (long journey) viaje m largo
y difícil; (tiring walk) caminata

trellis ['trelɪs] n enrejado

tremble ['trembl] vi temblar

tremendous [trɪ'mendəs] adj
tremendo, enorme; (excellent)
estupendo

tremor ['tremə*] n temblor m; (also:
earth ~) temblor de tierra

trench [trentʃ] n zanja

trend [trend] n (tendency) tendencia;
(of events) curso; (fashion) moda; **~y**
adj de moda

trespass ['trespəs] vi: **to ~ on** entrar
sin permiso en; **"no ~ing"** "prohibido
el paso"

trestle ['tresl] n caballete m

trial ['traɪəl] n (LAW) juicio, proceso;
(test: of machine etc) prueba; **~s** npl
(hardships) dificultades fpl; **by ~ and
error** a fuerza de probar

triangle ['traɪæŋgl] n (MATH, MUS)
triángulo

tribe [traɪb] n tribu f

tribunal [traɪ'bjuːnl] n tribunal m

tributary ['trɪbjutərɪ] n (river) afluente
m

tribute ['trɪbjuːt] n homenaje m,
tributo; **to pay ~ to** rendir homenaje
a

trick [trɪk] n (skill, knack) tino, truco;
(conjuring ~) truco; (joke) broma;
(CARDS) baza ♦ vt engañar; **to play a
~ on sb** gastar una broma a uno; **that
should do the ~** a ver si funciona así;
~ery n engaño

trickle ['trɪkl] n (of water etc) goteo
♦ vi gotear

tricky ['trɪkɪ] adj difícil; delicado

tricycle ['traɪsɪkl] n triciclo

trifle ['traɪfl] n bagatela; (CULIN) dulce

de bizcocho borracho, gelatina, fruta y natillas ♦ adv: **a ~ long** un poquito largo; **trifling** adj insignificante

trigger ['trɪgə*] n (of gun) gatillo; **~ off** vt desencadenar

trim [trɪm] adj (house, garden) en buen estado; (person, figure) esbelto ♦ n (haircut etc) recorte m; (on car) guarnición f ♦ vt (neaten) arreglar; (cut) recortar; (decorate) adornar; (NAUT: a sail) orientar; **~mings** npl (CULIN) guarnición f

trip [trɪp] n (journey) viaje m; (excursion) excursión f; (stumble) traspié m ♦ vi (stumble) tropezar; (go lightly) andar a paso ligero; **on a ~** de viaje; **~ up** vi tropezar, caerse ♦ vt hacer tropezar or caer

tripe [traɪp] n (CULIN) callos mpl

triple ['trɪpl] adj triple; **triplets** ['trɪplɪts] npl trillizos/as mpl/fpl;

triplicate ['trɪplɪkət] n: **in triplicate** por triplicado

trite [traɪt] adj trillado

triumph ['traɪəmf] n triunfo ♦ vi: **to ~ (over)** vencer; **~ant** [traɪˈʌmfənt] adj (team etc) vencedor(a); (wave, return) triunfal

trivia ['trɪvɪə] npl trivialidades fpl

trivial ['trɪvɪəl] adj insignificante; (commonplace) banal

trod [trɒd] pt of **tread**

trodden ['trɒdn] pp of **tread**

trolley ['trɒlɪ] n carrito; (also: ~ bus) (BRIT: bus) trolebús m

trombone [trɒmˈbəʊn] n trombón m

troop [truːp] n grupo, banda; **~s** npl (MIL) tropas fpl; **~ in/out** vi entrar/salir en tropel; **~ing the colour** n (ceremony) presentación f de la bandera

trophy ['trəʊfɪ] n trofeo

tropical ['trɒpɪkl] adj tropical

trot [trɒt] n trote m ♦ vi trotar; **on the ~** (fig) seguidos/as

trouble ['trʌbl] n problema m, dificultad f; (worry) preocupación f;

(bother, effort) molestia, esfuerzo; (unrest) inquietud f; (MED): **stomach** etc ~ problemas mpl gástricos etc ♦ vt (disturb) molestar; (worry) preocupar, inquietar ♦ vi: **to ~ to do sth** molestarse en hacer algo; **~s** npl (POL etc) conflictos mpl; (personal) problemas mpl; **to be in ~** estar en un apuro; **it's no ~!** ¡no es molestia (ninguna)!; **what's the ~?** (with broken TV etc) ¿cuál es el problema?; (doctor to patient) ¿qué pasa?; **~d** adj (person) preocupado; (country, epoch, life) agitado; **~maker** n agitador(a) m/f; (child) alborotador a; **~shooter** n (in conflict) conciliador(a) m/f; **~some** adj molesto

trough [trɒf] n (also: drinking ~) abrevadero; (also: feeding ~) comedero; (depression) depresión f

troupe [truːp] n grupo

trousers ['traʊzəz] npl pantalones mpl; **short ~** pantalones mpl cortos

trousseau ['truːsəʊ] (pl **~x** or **~s**) n ajuar m

trout [traʊt] n inv trucha

trowel ['traʊəl] n (of gardener) palita; (of builder) paleta

truant ['truːənt] n: **to play ~** (BRIT) hacer novillos

truce [truːs] n tregua

truck [trʌk] n (lorry) camión m; (RAIL) vagón m; **~ driver** n camionero; **~ farm** (US) n huerto

true [truː] adj verdadero; (accurate) exacto; (genuine) auténtico; (faithful) fiel; **to come ~** realizarse

truffle ['trʌfl] n trufa

truly ['truːlɪ] adv (really) realmente; (truthfully) verdaderamente; (faithfully): **yours ~** (in letter) le saluda atentamente

trump [trʌmp] n triunfo

trumpet ['trʌmpɪt] n trompeta

truncheon ['trʌntʃən] n porra

trundle ['trʌndl] vi: **to ~ along** ir sin prisas

trunk [trʌŋk] n (of tree, person) tronco; (of elephant) trompa; (case) baúl m; (US: AUT) maletero m; ~s npl (also: swimming ~s) bañador m (de hombre)

truss [trʌs] vt: ~ (up) atar

trust [trʌst] n confianza f; (responsibility) responsabilidad f; (LAW) fideicomiso ♦ vt (rely on) tener confianza en; (hope) esperar; (entrust): to ~ sth to sb confiar algo a uno; to take sth on ~ aceptar algo a ojos cerrados; ~ed adj de confianza; ~ee [trʌs'ti:] n (LAW) fideicomisario; (of school) administrador m; ~ful adj confiado; ~ing adj confiado; ~worthy adj digno de confianza

truth [tru:θ, pl tru:ðz] n verdad f; ~ful adj veraz

try [traɪ] n tentativa, intento; (RUGBY) ensayo ♦ vt (attempt) intentar; (test: also: ~ out) probar, someter a prueba; (LAW) juzgar, procesar; (strain: patience) hacer perder ♦ vi probar; to have a ~ probar suerte; to ~ to do sth intentar hacer algo; ~ again! ¡vuelve a probar!; ~ harder! ¡esfuérzate más!; well, I tried al menos lo intenté; ~ on vt (clothes) probarse; ~ing adj (experience) cansado; (person) pesado

T-shirt [ti:ʃɜ:t] n camiseta

T-square n regla en T

tub [tʌb] n cubo (SP), balde m (AM); (bath) tina, bañera

tube [tju:b] n tubo; (BRIT: underground) metro; (for tyre) cámara de aire

tuberculosis [tjubə:kju'ləusıs] n tuberculosis f inv

tube station (BRIT) n estación f de metro

tubular ['tju:bjulə*] adj tubular

TUC (BRIT) n abbr (= Trades Union Congress) federación nacional de sindicatos

tuck [tʌk] n (put) poner; ~ away vt (money) guardar; (building): to be ~ed away esconderse, ocultarse; ~ in vt

meter dentro; (child) arropar ♦ vi (eat) comer con apetito; ~ up vt (child) arropar; ~ shop n (SCOL) tienda; ≈ bar m (del colegio)

Tuesday ['tju:zdı] n martes m inv

tuft [tʌft] n mechón m; (of grass etc) manojo

tug [tʌg] n (ship) remolcador m ♦ vt tirar de; ~-of-war n lucha de tiro de cuerda; (fig) tira y afloja m

tuition [tju:'ıʃən] n (BRIT) enseñanza; (: private) clases fpl particulares; (US: school fees) matrícula

tulip ['tju:lıp] n tulipán m

tumble ['tʌmbl] n (fall) caída ♦ vi caer; to ~ to sth (inf) caer en la cuenta de algo; ~down adj destartalado; ~ dryer (BRIT) n secadora

tumbler ['tʌmblə*] n (glass) vaso

tummy ['tʌmı] (inf) n barriga, tripa

tumour ['tju:mə*] (US tumor) n tumor m

tuna ['tju:nə] n inv (also: ~ fish) atún m

tune [tju:n] n melodía ♦ vt (MUS) afinar; (RADIO, TV, AUT) sintonizar; to be in/out of ~ (instrument) estar afinado/desafinado; (singer) cantar afinadamente/desafinar; to be in/out of ~ with (fig) estar de acuerdo/en desacuerdo con; ~ in vi: to ~ in (to) (RADIO, TV) sintonizar (con); ~ up vi (musician) afinar (su instrumento); ~ful adj melodioso; ~r n: piano ~r afinador(a) m/f de pianos

tunic ['tju:nık] n túnica

Tunisia [tju:'nızıə] n Túnez m

tunnel ['tʌnl] n túnel m; (in mine) galería ♦ vi construir un túnel/una galería

turban ['tə:bən] n turbante m

turbulent ['tə:bjulənt] adj turbulento

tureen [tə'ri:n] n sopera

turf [tə:f] n césped m; (clod) tepe m ♦ vt cubrir con césped; ~ out (inf) vt echar a la calle

Turk [tə:k] n turco/a

Turkey ['tə:kı] n Turquía

turkey ['tɜːkɪ] n pavo
Turkish ['tɜːkɪʃ] adj, n turco
turmoil ['tɜːmɔɪl] n: **in ~** revuelto
turn [tɜːn] n turno; (in road) curva; (of mind, events) rumbo; (THEATRE) número; (MED) ataque m ♦ vt girar, volver; (collar, steak) dar la vuelta a; (page) pasar; (change): **to ~ sth into** convertir algo en ♦ vi volver; (person: look back) volverse; (reverse direction) dar la vuelta; (milk) cortarse; (become): **to ~ nasty/forty** ponerse feo/cumplir los cuarenta; **a good ~** un favor; **it gave me quite a ~** me dio un susto; **"no left ~"** (AUT) "prohibido girar a la izquierda"; **it's your ~** te toca a ti; **in ~** por turnos; **to take ~s (at)** turnarse (en); **~ away** vi apartar la vista ♦ vt rechazar; **~ back** vi volverse atrás ♦ vt hacer retroceder; (clock) retrasar; **~ down** vt (refuse) rechazar; (reduce) bajar; (fold) doblar; **~ in** vi (inf: go to bed) acostarse ♦ vt (fold) doblar hacia dentro; **~ off** vi (from road) desviarse ♦ vt (light, radio etc) apagar; (tap) cerrar; (engine) parar; **~ on** vt (light, radio etc) encender ♦ vt (tap) abrir; (engine) poner en marcha; **~ out** vt (light, gas) apagar; (produce) producir ♦ vi (voters) concurrir; **to ~ out to be ...** resultar ser ...; **~ over** vi (person) volverse ♦ vt (object) dar la vuelta a; (page) volver; **~ round** vi volverse; (rotate) girar; **~ up** vi (person) llegar, presentarse; (lost object) aparecer ♦ vt (gen) subir; **~ing** n (in road) vuelta; **~ing point** n (fig) momento decisivo
turnip ['tɜːnɪp] n nabo
turn: **~out** n concurrencia; **~over** n (COMM: amount of money) volumen m de ventas; (: of goods) movimiento; **~pike** (US) n autopista de peaje; **~stile** n torniquete m; **~table** n plato; **~up** (BRIT) n (on trousers) vuelta
turpentine ['tɜːpəntaɪn] n (also: turps) trementina

turquoise ['tɜːkwɔɪz] n (stone) turquesa ♦ adj color turquesa
turret ['tʌrɪt] n torreón m
turtle ['tɜːtl] n galápago; **~neck (sweater)** n jersey m de cuello vuelto
tusk [tʌsk] n colmillo
tutor ['tjuːtə*] n profesor(a) m/f; **~ial** [-'tɔːrɪəl] n (SCOL) seminario
tuxedo [tʌk'siːdəu] (US) n smóking m, esmoquin m
TV [tiː'viː] n abbr (= television) tele f
twang [twæŋ] n (of instrument) punteado; (of voice) timbre m nasal
tweezers ['twiːzəz] npl pinzas fpl (de depilar)
twelfth [twelfθ] num duodécimo
twelve [twelv] num doce; **at ~ o'clock** (midday) a mediodía; (midnight) a medianoche
twentieth ['twentɪɪθ] adj vigésimo
twenty ['twentɪ] num veinte
twice [twaɪs] adv dos veces; **~ as much** dos veces más
twiddle ['twɪdl] vi: **to ~ (with) sth** dar vueltas a algo; **to ~ one's thumbs** (fig) estar mano sobre mano
twig [twɪg] n ramita
twilight ['twaɪlaɪt] n crepúsculo
twin [twɪn] adj, n gemelo/a m/f ♦ vt hermanar; **~-bedded room** n habitación f doble
twine [twaɪn] n bramante m ♦ vi (plant) enroscarse
twinge [twɪndʒ] n (of pain) punzada; (of conscience) remordimiento
twinkle ['twɪŋkl] vi centellear; (eyes) brillar
twirl [twɜːl] vt dar vueltas a ♦ vi dar vueltas
twist [twɪst] n (action) torsión f; (in road, coil) vuelta; (in wire, flex) doblez f; (in story) giro ♦ vt torcer; (weave) trenzar; (roll around) enrollar; (fig) deformar ♦ vi serpentear
twit [twɪt] (inf) n tonto
twitch [twɪtʃ] n (pull) tirón m; (nervous) tic m ♦ vi crisparse

two [tu:] num dos; **to put ~ and ~ together** (fig) atar cabos; **~-door** adj (AUT) de dos puertas; **~-faced** adj (pej: person) falso; **~-fold** adv: **to increase ~fold** doblarse; **~-piece (suit)** n traje m de dos piezas; **~-piece (swimsuit)** n dos piezas m inv, bikini m; **~some** n (people) pareja; **~-way** adj: **~-way traffic** circulación f de dos sentidos

tycoon [tar'ku:n] n: (business) ~ magnate m

type [taip] n (category) tipo, género; (model) tipo; (TYP) tipo, letra ♦ vt (letter etc) escribir a máquina; **~-cast** adj (actor) encasillado; **~face** n letra; **~script** n texto mecanografiado; **~writer** n máquina de escribir; **~written** adj mecanografiado

typhoid ['taifɔid] n tifoidea

typical ['tipikl] adj típico

typing ['taipiŋ] n mecanografía

typist ['taipist] n mecanógrafo/a

tyrant ['taiərnt] n tirano/a

tyre ['taiə*] (US **tire**) n neumático (SP), llanta (AM); **~ pressure** n presión f de los neumáticos

U, u

U-bend ['ju:'bend] n (AUT, in pipe) recodo

udder ['ʌdə*] n ubre f

UFO ['ju:fəu] n abbr = (unidentified flying object) OVNI m

ugh [ə:h] excl ¡uf!

ugly ['ʌglɪ] adj feo; (dangerous) peligroso

UHT abbr: **~ milk** leche f UHT, leche f uperizada

UK n abbr = **United Kingdom**

ulcer ['ʌlsə*] n úlcera; (mouth ~) llaga

Ulster ['ʌlstə*] n Ulster m

ulterior [ʌl'tiəriə*] adj: **~ motive** segundas intenciones fpl

ultimate ['ʌltɪmət] adj último, final;

(greatest) máximo; **~ly** adv (in the end) por último, al final; (fundamentally) a o en fin de cuentas

umbilical cord [ʌm'bɪlɪkl-] n cordón m umbilical

umbrella [ʌm'brelə] n paraguas m inv; (for sun) sombrilla

umpire ['ʌmpaiə*] n árbitro

umpteen [ʌmp'ti:n] adj enésimos/as; **~th** adj: **for the ~th time** por enésima vez

UN n abbr (= United Nations) NN. UU.

unable [ʌn'eɪbl] adj: **to be ~ to do sth** no poder hacer algo

unaccompanied [ʌnə'kʌmpənɪd] adj no acompañado; (song) sin acompañamiento

unaccustomed [ʌnə'kʌstəmd] adj: **to be ~ to** no estar acostumbrado a

unanimous [ju:'nænɪməs] adj unánime

unarmed [ʌn'ɑ:md] adj (defenceless) inerme; (without weapon) desarmado

unattached [ʌnə'tætʃt] adj (person) soltero y sin compromiso; (part etc) suelto

unattended [ʌnə'tendid] adj desatendido

unattractive [ʌnə'træktɪv] adj poco atractivo

unauthorized [ʌn'ɔ:θəraizd] adj no autorizado

unavoidable [ʌnə'vɔidəbl] adj inevitable

unaware [ʌnə'weə*] adj: **to be ~ of** ignorar; **~s** adv de improviso

unbalanced [ʌn'bælənst] adj (report) poco objetivo; (mentally) trastornado

unbearable [ʌn'beərəbl] adj insoportable

unbeatable [ʌn'bi:təbl] adj (team) invencible; (price) inmejorable; (quality) insuperable

unbelievable [ʌnbɪ'li:vəbl] adj increíble

unbend [ʌn'bend] (irreg) vi (relax) relajarse ♦ vt (wire) enderezar

unbiased [ʌn'baɪəst] adj imparcial

unborn [ʌn'bɔːn] adj que va a nacer

unbroken [ʌn'brəukən] adj (seal) intacto; (series) continuo; (record) no batido; (spirit) indómito

unbutton [ʌn'bʌtn] vt desabrochar

uncalled-for [ʌn'kɔːldfɔː*] adj gratuito, inmerecido

uncanny [ʌn'kænɪ] adj extraño

unceremonious ['ʌnserɪ'məunɪəs] adj (abrupt, rude) brusco, hosco

uncertain [ʌn'sɜːtɪn] adj incierto; (indecisive) indeciso

unchanged [ʌn'tʃeɪndʒd] adj igual, sin cambios

uncivilized [ʌn'sɪvɪlaɪzd] adj inculto; (fig: behaviour etc) bárbaro; (hour) inoportuno

uncle ['ʌŋkl] n tío

uncomfortable [ʌn'kʌmfətəbl] adj incómodo; (uneasy) inquieto

uncommon [ʌn'kɒmən] adj poco común, raro

uncompromising [ʌn'kɒmprəmaɪzɪŋ] adj intransigente

unconcerned [ʌnkən'sɜːnd] adj indiferente, despreocupado

unconditional [ʌnkən'dɪʃnl] adj incondicional

unconscious [ʌn'kɒnʃəs] adj sin sentido; (unaware) inconsciente (de) ♦ n: the ~ el inconsciente

uncontrollable [ʌnkən'trəuləbl] adj (child etc) incontrolable; (temper) indomable; (laughter) incontenible

unconventional [ʌnkən'venʃənl] adj poco convencional

uncouth [ʌn'kuːθ] adj grosero, inculto

uncover [ʌn'kʌvə*] vt descubrir; (take lid off) destapar

undecided [ʌndɪ'saɪdɪd] adj (character) indeciso; (question) no resuelto

under ['ʌndə*] prep debajo de; (less than) menos de; (according to) según, de acuerdo con; (sb's leadership) bajo

♦ adv debajo, abajo; **~ there** allí abajo; **~ repair** en reparación

under... ['ʌndə*] prefix sub; **~age** adj menor de edad; (drinking etc) de los menores de edad; **~carriage** (BRIT) n (AVIAT) tren m de aterrizaje; **~charge** vt cobrar menos de la cuenta; **~clothes** npl ropa interior (SP) or íntima (AM); **~coat** n (paint) primera mano; **~cover** adj clandestino; **~current** n (fig) corriente f oculta; **~cut** vt irreg vender más barato que; **~developed** adj subdesarrollado; **~dog** n desvalido/a; **~done** adj (CULIN) poco hecho; **~estimate** vt subestimar; **~exposed** adj (PHOT) subexpuesto; **~fed** adj subalimentado; **~foot** adv con los pies; **~go** vt irreg sufrir; (treatment) recibir; **~graduate** n estudiante m/f; **~ground** n (BRIT: railway) metro; (POL) movimiento clandestino ♦ adj (car park) subterráneo ♦ adv (work) en la clandestinidad; **~growth** n maleza; **~hand(ed)** adj (fig) socarrón; **~lie** vt irreg (fig) ser la razón fundamental de; **~line** vt subrayar; **~mine** vt socavar, minar; **~neath** [ʌndə'niːθ] adv debajo ♦ prep debajo de, bajo; **~paid** adj mal pagado; **~pants** npl calzoncillos mpl; **~pass** (BRIT) n paso subterráneo; **~privileged** adj desposeído; **~rate** vt menospreciar, subestimar; **~shirt** (US) n camiseta; **~shorts** (US) npl calzoncillos mpl; **~side** n parte f inferior; **~skirt** (BRIT) n enaguas fpl

understand [ʌndə'stænd] (irreg) vt, vi entender, comprender; (assume) tener entendido; **~able** adj comprensible; **~ing** adj comprensivo ♦ n comprensión f, entendimiento; (agreement) acuerdo

understatement ['ʌndəsteɪtmənt] n modestia (excesiva); **that's an ~!** ¡eso es decir poco!

understood [ʌndə'stud] pt, pp of **understand** ♦ adj (agreed) acordado;

(*implied*): **it is ~ that** se sobreentiende
que

understudy [ˈʌndəstʌdɪ] n suplente
m/f

undertake [ʌndəˈteɪk] (*irreg*) vt
emprender; **to ~ to do sth**
comprometerse a hacer algo

undertaker [ˈʌndəteɪkə*] n director(a)
m/f de pompas fúnebres

undertaking [ˈʌndəteɪkɪŋ] n empresa;
(*promise*) promesa

under: **~tone** n: **in an ~tone** en voz
baja; **~water** adv bajo el agua ♦ adj
submarino; **~wear** n ropa interior (*SP*)
or íntima (*AM*); **~world** n (*of crime*)
hampa, inframundo; **~writer** n
(*INSURANCE*) asegurador(a) m/f

undesirable [ʌndɪˈzaɪrəbl] adj (*person*)
indeseable; (*thing*) poco aconsejable

undo [ʌnˈduː] (*irreg*) vt (*laces*) desatar;
(*button etc*) desabrochar; (*spoil*)
deshacer; **~ing** n ruina, perdición f

undoubted [ʌnˈdautɪd] adj indudable

undress [ʌnˈdres] vi desnudarse

undulating [ˈʌndjuleɪtɪŋ] adj
ondulante

unduly [ʌnˈdjuːlɪ] adv excesivamente,
demasiado

unearth [ʌnˈɜːθ] vt desenterrar

unearthly [ʌnˈɜːθlɪ] adj (*hour*)
inverosímil

uneasy [ʌnˈiːzɪ] adj intranquilo,
preocupado; (*feeling*) desagradable;
(*peace*) inseguro

uneducated [ʌnˈedjukeɪtɪd] adj
ignorante, inculto

unemployed [ʌnɪmˈplɔɪd] adj parado,
sin trabajo ♦ npl: **the ~s** los parados

unemployment [ʌnɪmˈplɔɪmənt] n
paro, desempleo

unending [ʌnˈendɪŋ] adj interminable

unerring [ʌnˈɜːrɪŋ] adj infalible

uneven [ʌnˈiːvn] adj desigual; (*road
etc*) lleno de baches

unexpected [ʌnɪkˈspektɪd] adj
inesperado; **~ly** adv inesperadamente

unfailing [ʌnˈfeɪlɪŋ] adj (*support*)

indefectible; (*energy*) inagotable

unfair [ʌnˈfeə*] adj: **~ (to sb)** injusto
(con uno)

unfaithful [ʌnˈfeɪθful] adj infiel

unfamiliar [ʌnfəˈmɪlɪə*] adj extraño,
desconocido; **to be ~ with** no
desconocer

unfashionable [ʌnˈfæʃnəbl] adj
pasado or fuera de moda

unfasten [ʌnˈfɑːsn] vt (*knot*) desatar;
(*dress*) desabrochar; (*open*) abrir

unfavourable [ʌnˈfeɪvərəbl] (*us
unfavorable*) adj desfavorable

unfeeling [ʌnˈfiːlɪŋ] adj insensible

unfinished [ʌnˈfɪnɪʃt] adj inacabado,
sin terminar

unfit [ʌnˈfɪt] adj bajo de forma;
(*incompetent*): **~ (for)** incapaz (de);
~ for work no apto para trabajar

unfold [ʌnˈfəuld] vt desdoblar ♦ vi
abrirse

unforeseen [ʌnfɔːˈsiːn] adj imprevisto

unforgettable [ʌnfəˈgetəbl] adj
inolvidable

unfortunate [ʌnˈfɔːtʃnət] adj
desgraciado; (*event, remark*)
inoportuno; **~ly** adv desgraciadamente

unfounded [ʌnˈfaundɪd] adj
infundado

unfriendly [ʌnˈfrendlɪ] adj antipático;
(*behaviour, remark*) hostil, poco
amigable

ungainly [ʌnˈgeɪnlɪ] adj desgarbado

ungodly [ʌnˈgɒdlɪ] adj: **at an ~ hour**
a una hora inverosímil

ungrateful [ʌnˈgreɪtful] adj ingrato

unhappiness [ʌnˈhæpɪnɪs] n tristeza,
desdicha

unhappy [ʌnˈhæpɪ] adj (*sad*) triste;
(*unfortunate*) desgraciado; (*childhood*)
infeliz; **~ about/with** (*arrangements
etc*) poco contento con, descontento
de

unharmed [ʌnˈhɑːmd] adj ileso

unhealthy [ʌnˈhelθɪ] adj (*place*)
malsano; (*person*) enfermizo; (*fig:
interest*) morboso

unheard-of [ʌn'hɜːd-] adj inaudito, sin precedente

unhurt [ʌn'hɜːt] adj ileso

unidentified [ʌnaɪ'dentɪfaɪd] adj no identificado, sin identificar; see also UFO

uniform ['juːnɪfɔːm] n uniforme m ♦ adj uniforme

unify ['juːnɪfaɪ] vt unificar, unir

uninhabited [ʌnɪn'hæbɪtɪd] adj desierto

unintentional [ʌnɪn'tenʃənəl] adj involuntario

union ['juːnjən] n unión f; (also: trade ~) sindicato ♦ cpd sindical; U~ Jack n bandera del Reino Unido

unique [juː'niːk] adj único

unison ['juːnɪsn] n: in ~ (speak, reply, sing) al unísono

unit ['juːnɪt] n unidad f; (section: of furniture etc) elemento; (team) grupo; **kitchen ~** módulo de cocina

unite [juː'naɪt] vt unir ♦ vi unirse; **~d** adj unido; (effort) conjunto; U~d Kingdom n Reino Unido; U~d Nations (Organization) n Naciones fpl Unidas; U~d States (of America) n Estados mpl Unidos

unit trust (BRIT) n bono fiduciario

unity ['juːnɪtɪ] n unidad f

universe ['juːnɪvɜːs] n universo

university [juːnɪ'vɜːsɪtɪ] n universidad f

unjust [ʌn'dʒʌst] adj injusto

unkempt [ʌn'kempt] adj (appearance) descuidado; (hair) despeinado

unkind [ʌn'kaɪnd] adj poco amable; (behaviour, comment) cruel

unknown [ʌn'nəʊn] adj desconocido

unlawful [ʌn'lɔːfʊl] adj ilegal, ilícito

unleaded [ʌn'ledɪd] adj (petrol, fuel) sin plombo

unless [ʌn'les] conj a menos que; **~ he comes** a menos que venga; **~ otherwise stated** salvo indicación contraria

unlike [ʌn'laɪk] adj (not alike) distinto de or a; (not like) poco propio de ♦ prep a diferencia de

unlikely [ʌn'laɪklɪ] adj improbable; (unexpected) inverosímil

unlimited [ʌn'lɪmɪtɪd] adj ilimitado

unlisted [ʌn'lɪstɪd] (US) (TEL) que no consta en la guía

unload [ʌn'ləʊd] vt descargar

unlock [ʌn'lɒk] vt abrir (con llave)

unlucky [ʌn'lʌkɪ] adj desgraciado; (object, number) que da mala suerte; **to be ~** tener mala suerte

unmarried [ʌn'mærɪd] adj soltero

unmistak(e)able [ʌnmɪs'teɪkəbl] adj inconfundible

unnatural [ʌn'nætʃrəl] adj (gen) antinatural; (manner) afectado; (habit) perverso

unnecessary [ʌn'nesəsərɪ] adj innecesario, inútil

unnoticed [ʌn'nəʊtɪst] adj: **to go or pass ~** pasar desapercibido

UNO ['juːnəʊ] n abbr (= United Nations Organization) ONU f

unobtainable [ʌnəb'teɪnəbl] adj inconseguible; (TEL) inexistente

unobtrusive [ʌnəb'truːsɪv] adj discreto

unofficial [ʌnə'fɪʃl] adj no oficial; (news) sin confirmar

unorthodox [ʌn'ɔːθədɒks] adj poco ortodoxo; (REL) heterodoxo

unpack [ʌn'pæk] vi deshacer las maletas ♦ vt deshacer

unpalatable [ʌn'pælətəbl] adj incomible; (truth) desagradable

unparalleled [ʌn'pærəleld] adj (unequalled) incomparable

unpleasant [ʌn'pleznt] adj (disagreeable) desagradable; (person, manner) antipático

unplug [ʌn'plʌg] vt desenchufar, desconectar

unpopular [ʌn'pɒpjʊlə*] adj impopular, poco popular

unprecedented [ʌn'presɪdəntɪd] adj sin precedentes

unpredictable [ʌnprɪ'dɪktəbl] *adj* imprevisible

unprofessional [ʌnprə'feʃənl] *adj* (*attitude, conduct*) poco ético

unqualified [ʌn'kwɔlɪfaɪd] *adj* sin título, no cualificado; (*success*) total

unquestionably [ʌn'kwestʃənəblɪ] *adv* indiscutiblemente

unreal [ʌn'rɪəl] *adj* irreal; (*extraordinary*) increíble

unrealistic [ʌnrɪə'lɪstɪk] *adj* poco realista

unreasonable [ʌn'riːznəbl] *adj* irrazonable; (*demand*) excesivo

unrelated [ʌnrɪ'leɪtɪd] *adj* sin relación; (*family*) no emparentado

unreliable [ʌnrɪ'laɪəbl] *adj* (*person*) informal; (*machine*) poco fiable

unremitting [ʌnrɪ'mɪtɪŋ] *adj* constante

unreservedly [ʌnrɪ'zɜːvɪdlɪ] *adv* sin reserva

unrest [ʌn'rest] *n* inquietud *f*, malestar *m*; (POL) disturbios *mpl*

unroll [ʌn'rəʊl] *vt* desenrollar

unruly [ʌn'ruːlɪ] *adj* indisciplinado

unsafe [ʌn'seɪf] *adj* peligroso

unsaid [ʌn'sed] *adj*: **to leave sth ~** dejar algo sin decir

unsatisfactory ['ʌnsætɪs'fæktərɪ] *adj* poco satisfactorio

unsavoury [ʌn'seɪvərɪ] (US **unsavory**) *adj* (*fig*) repugnante

unscrew [ʌn'skruː] *vt* destornillar

unscrupulous [ʌn'skruːpjʊləs] *adj* sin escrúpulos

unsettled [ʌn'setld] *adj* inquieto, intranquilo; (*weather*) variable

unshaven [ʌn'ʃeɪvn] *adj* sin afeitar

unsightly [ʌn'saɪtlɪ] *adj* feo

unskilled [ʌn'skɪld] *adj* (*work*) no especializado; (*worker*) no cualificado

unspeakable [ʌn'spiːkəbl] *adj* indecible; (*awful*) incalificable

unstable [ʌn'steɪbl] *adj* inestable

unsteady [ʌn'stedɪ] *adj* inestable

unstuck [ʌn'stʌk] *adj*: **to come ~** despegarse; (*fig*) fracasar

unsuccessful [ʌnsək'sesful] *adj* (*attempt*) infructuoso; (*writer, proposal*) sin éxito; **to be ~** (*in attempting sth*) no tener éxito, fracasar; **~ly** *adv* en vano, sin éxito

unsuitable [ʌn'suːtəbl] *adj* inapropiado; (*time*) inoportuno

unsure [ʌn'ʃʊə*] *adj* inseguro, poco seguro

unsuspecting [ʌnsəs'pektɪŋ] *adj* desprevenido

unsympathetic [ʌnsɪmpə'θetɪk] *adj* poco comprensivo; (*unlikeable*) antipático

unthinkable [ʌn'θɪŋkəbl] *adj* inconcebible, impensable

untidy [ʌn'taɪdɪ] *adj* (*room*) desordenado; (*appearance*) desaliñado

untie [ʌn'taɪ] *vt* desatar

until [ən'tɪl] *prep* hasta ♦ *conj* hasta que; **~ he comes** hasta que venga; **~ now** hasta ahora; **~ then** hasta entonces

untimely [ʌn'taɪmlɪ] *adj* inoportuno; (*death*) prematuro

untold [ʌn'təʊld] *adj* (*story*) nunca contado; (*suffering*) indecible; (*wealth*) incalculable

untoward [ʌntə'wɔːd] *adj* adverso

unused [ʌn'juːzd] *adj* sin usar

unusual [ʌn'juːʒʊəl] *adj* insólito, poco común; (*exceptional*) inusitado

unveil [ʌn'veɪl] *vt* (*statue*) descubrir

unwanted [ʌn'wɒntɪd] *adj* (*clothing*) viejo; (*pregnancy*) no deseado

unwelcome [ʌn'welkəm] *adj* inoportuno; (*news*) desagradable

unwell [ʌn'wel] *adj*: **to be/feel ~** estar indispuesto/sentirse mal

unwieldy [ʌn'wiːldɪ] *adj* difícil de manejar

unwilling [ʌn'wɪlɪŋ] *adj*: **to be ~ to do sth** estar poco dispuesto a hacer algo; **~ly** *adv* de mala gana

unwind [ʌn'waɪnd] (*irreg: like* **wind**²) *vt* desenvolver ♦ *vi* (*relax*) relajarse

unwise 592 **urn**

unwise [ʌnˈwaɪz] *adj* imprudente
unwitting [ʌnˈwɪtɪŋ] *adj* inconsciente
unworthy [ʌnˈwɜːðɪ] *adj* indigno
unwrap [ʌnˈræp] *vt* desenvolver
unwritten [ʌnˈrɪtn] *adj (agreement)* tácito; *(rules, law)* no escrito

KEYWORD

up [ʌp] *prep*: **to go/be ~ sth** subir/ estar subido en algo; **he went ~ the stairs/the hill** subió las escaleras/la colina; **we walked/climbed ~ the hill** subimos la colina; **they live further ~ the street** viven más arriba en la calle; **go ~ that road and turn left** sigue por esa calle y gira a la izquierda
♦ *adv* **1** *(upwards, higher)* más arriba; **~ in the mountains** en lo alto (de la montaña); **put it a bit higher ~** ponlo un poco más arriba or alto; **~ there** ahí or allí arriba; **~ above** en lo alto, por encima, arriba
2: **to be ~** *(out of bed)* estar levantado; *(prices, level)* haber subido
3: **~ to** *(as far as)* hasta; **~ to now** hasta ahora or la fecha
4: **to be ~ to** *(depending on)*: **it's ~ to you** depende de ti; **he's not ~ to it** *(job, task etc)* no es capaz de hacerlo; **his work is not ~ to the required standard** su trabajo no da la talla; *(inf: be doing)*: **what is he ~ to?** ¿qué estará tramando?
♦ *n*: **~s and downs** altibajos *mpl*

upbringing [ˈʌpbrɪŋɪŋ] *n* educación *f*
update [ʌpˈdeɪt] *vt* poner al día
upgrade [ʌpˈgreɪd] *vt (house)* modernizar; *(employee)* ascender
upheaval [ʌpˈhiːvl] *n* trastornos *mpl*; *(POL)* agitación *f*
uphill [ʌpˈhɪl] *adj* cuesta arriba; *(fig: task)* penoso, difícil ♦ *adv*: **to go ~** ir cuesta arriba
uphold [ʌpˈhəuld] *(irreg) vt* defender
upholstery [ʌpˈhəulstərɪ] *n* tapicería

upkeep [ˈʌpkiːp] *n* mantenimiento
upon [əˈpɒn] *prep* sobre
upper [ˈʌpə*] *adj* superior, de arriba
♦ *n (of shoe: also: ~s)* empeine *m*; **~class** *adj* de clase alta; **~ hand** *n*: **to have the ~ hand** tener la sartén por el mango; **~most** *adj* el más alto; **what was ~most in my mind** lo que me preocupaba más
upright [ˈʌpraɪt] *adj* derecho; *(vertical)* vertical; *(fig)* honrado
uprising [ˈʌpraɪzɪŋ] *n* sublevación *f*
uproar [ˈʌprɔː*] *n* escándalo
uproot [ʌpˈruːt] *vt (also fig)* desarraigar
upset [*n* ˈʌpset, *vb, adj* ʌpˈset] *n (to plan etc)* revés *m*, contratiempo; *(MED)* trastorno ♦ *(irreg) vt (glass etc)* volcar; *(plan)* alterar; *(person)* molestar, disgustar ♦ *adj* molesto, disgustado; *(stomach)* revuelto
upshot [ˈʌpʃɒt] *n* resultado
upside-down *adv* al revés; **to turn a place ~** *(fig)* revolverlo todo
upstairs [ʌpˈsteəz] *adv* arriba ♦ *adj (room)* de arriba ♦ *n* el piso superior
upstart [ˈʌpstɑːt] *n* advenedizo/a
upstream [ʌpˈstriːm] *adv* río arriba
uptake [ˈʌpteɪk] *n*: **to be quick/slow on the ~** ser muy listo/torpe
uptight [ʌpˈtaɪt] *adj* tenso, nervioso
up-to-date *adj* al día
upturn [ˈʌptɜːn] *n (in luck)* mejora; *(COMM: in market)* resurgimiento económico
upward [ˈʌpwəd] *adj* ascendente; **~(s)** *adv* hacia arriba; *(more than)*: **~(s) of** más de

urban [ˈɜːbən] *adj* urbano
urchin [ˈɜːtʃɪn] *n* pilluelo, golfillo
urge [ɜːdʒ] *n (desire)* deseo ♦ *vt*: **to ~ sb to do sth** animar a uno a hacer algo
urgent [ˈɜːdʒənt] *adj* urgente; *(voice)* perentorio
urinate [ˈjuərɪneɪt] *vi* orinar
urine [ˈjuərɪn] *n* orina, orines *mpl*
urn [ɜːn] *n* urna; *(also: tea ~)* cacharro

metálico grande para hacer té

Uruguay ['juerəgwaɪ] *n* (el) Uruguay; **~an** [-'gwaɪən] *adj, n* uruguayo/a *m/f*

US *n abbr* (= United States) EE. UU.

us [ʌs] *pron* nos; (after prep) nosotros/as; see also **me**

USA *n abbr* (= United States (of America)) EE. UU.

usage ['juːzɪdʒ] *n* (LING) uso

use [*n* juːs, *vb* juːz] *n* uso, empleo; (usefulness) utilidad *f* ♦ *vt* usar, emplear; **she ~d to do it** (ella) solía or acostumbraba hacerlo; **in ~** en uso; **out of ~** en desuso; **to be of ~** servir; **it's no ~** (pointless) es inútil; (not useful) no sirve; **to be ~d to** estar acostumbrado a, acostumbrar; **~ up** *vt* (food) consumir; (money) gastar; **~d** *adj* (car) usado; **~ful** *adj* útil; **~fulness** *n* utilidad *f*; **~less** *adj* (unusable) inservible; (pointless) inútil; (person) inepto; **~r** *n* usuario/a; **~r-friendly** *adj* (computer) amistoso

usher ['ʌʃə*] *n* (at wedding) ujier *m*; **~ette** [-'rɛt] *n* (in cinema) acomodadora

USSR *n* (HIST): **the ~** la URSS

usual ['juːʒuəl] *adj* normal, corriente; **as ~** como de costumbre; **~ly** *adv* normalmente

utensil [juːˈtɛnsl] *n* utensilio; **kitchen ~s** batería de cocina

uterus ['juːtərəs] *n* útero

utility [juːˈtɪlɪtɪ] *n* utilidad *f*; (public ~) (empresa *f* de) servicio público; **~ room** *n* ofis *m*

utilize ['juːtɪlaɪz] *vt* utilizar

utmost ['ʌtməust] *adj* mayor ♦ *n*: **to do one's ~** hacer todo lo posible

utter ['ʌtə*] *adj* total, completo ♦ *vt* pronunciar, proferir; **~ly** *adv* completamente, totalmente

U-turn ['juːˈtəːn] *n* viraje *m* en redondo

V, v

v. *abbr* = **verse**; **versus**; (= volt) v; (= vide) véase

vacancy ['veɪkənsɪ] *n* (BRIT: job) vacante *f*; (room) habitación *f* libre; **"no vacancies"** "completo"

vacant ['veɪkənt] *adj* desocupado, libre; (expression) distraído

vacate [vəˈkeɪt] *vt* (house, room) desocupar; (job) dejar (vacante)

vacation [vəˈkeɪʃən] *n* vacaciones *fpl*

vaccinate ['væksɪneɪt] *vt* vacunar

vaccine ['væksiːn] *n* vacuna

vacuum ['vækjum] *n* vacío; **~ cleaner** *n* aspiradora; **~-flask** (BRIT) *n* termo; **~-packed** *adj* empaquetado al vacío

vagina [vəˈdʒaɪnə] *n* vagina

vagrant ['veɪgrnt] *n* vagabundo/a

vague [veɪg] *adj* vago; (memory) borroso; (ambiguous) impreciso; (person: absent-minded) distraído; (: evasive): **to be ~** no declarar las cosas claramente; **~ly** *adv* vagamente; distraídamente; con evasivas

vain [veɪn] *adj* (conceited) presumido; (useless) vano, inútil; **in ~** en vano

valentine ['væləntaɪn] *n* (also: ~ card) tarjeta del Día de los Enamorados

valet ['væleɪ] *n* ayuda *m* de cámara

valid ['vælɪd] *adj* válido; (ticket) valedero; (law) vigente

valley ['vælɪ] *n* valle *m*

valuable ['væljuəbl] *adj* (jewel) de valor; (time) valioso; **~s** *npl* objetos *mpl* de valor

valuation [væljuˈeɪʃən] *n* tasación *f*, valuación *f*; (judgement of quality) valoración *f*

value ['væljuː] *n* valor *m*; (importance) importancia ♦ *vt* (fix price of) tasar, valorar; (esteem) apreciar; **~s** *npl* (principles) principios *mpl*; **~ added tax** (BRIT) *n* impuesto sobre el valor añadido; **~d** *adj* (*appreciated*) apreciado

valve [vælv] *n* válvula

van [væn] *n* (*AUT*) furgoneta (*SP*), camioneta (*AM*)

vandal ['vændl] *n* vándalo/a; **~ism** *n* vandalismo; **~ize** *vt* dañar, destruir

vanilla [və'nɪlə] *n* vainilla

vanish ['vænɪʃ] *vi* desaparecer

vanity ['vænɪtɪ] *n* vanidad *f*

vantage point ['vɑ:ntɪdʒ-] *n* (*for views*) punto panorámico

vapour ['veɪpə*] (*US* **vapor**) *n* vapor *m*; (*on breath, window*) vaho

variable ['veərɪəbl] *adj* variable

variation [veərɪ'eɪʃən] *n* variación *f*

varicose ['værɪkəus] *adj*: **~ veins** varices *fpl*

varied ['veərɪd] *adj* variado

variety [və'raɪətɪ] *n* (*diversity*) diversidad *f*; (*type*) variedad *f*; **~ show** *n* espectáculo de variedades

various ['veərɪəs] *adj* (*several: people*) varios/as; (*reasons*) diversos/as

varnish ['vɑ:nɪʃ] *n* barniz *m*; (*nail ~*) esmalte *m* ♦ *vt* barnizar; (*nails*) pintar (con esmalte)

vary ['veərɪ] *vt* variar; (*change*) cambiar ♦ *vi* variar

vase [vɑ:z] *n* florero

Vaseline ® ['væsɪli:n] *n* vaselina ®

vast [vɑ:st] *adj* enorme

VAT [væt] (*BRIT*) *n abbr* (= **value added tax**) IVA *m*

vat [væt] *n* tina, tinaja

Vatican ['vætɪkən] *n*: **the ~** el Vaticano

vault [vɔ:lt] *n* (*of roof*) bóveda; (*tomb*) panteón *m*; (*in bank*) cámara acorazada ♦ *vt* (*also*: **~ over**) saltar (por encima de)

vaunted ['vɔ:ntɪd] *adj*: **much ~** cacareado, alardeado

VCR *n abbr* = **video cassette recorder**

VD *n abbr* = **venereal disease**

VDU *n abbr* (= **visual display unit**) UPV *f*

veal [vi:l] *n* ternera

veer [vɪə*] *vi* (*vehicle*) virar; (*wind*) girar

vegan ['vi:gən] *n* vegetariano/a estricto/a, vegetaliano/a

vegeburger ['vedʒɪbə:gə*] *n* hamburguesa vegetal

vegetable ['vedʒtəbl] *n* (*BOT*) vegetal *m*; (*edible plant*) legumbre *f*, hortaliza ♦ *adj* vegetal; **~s** *npl* (*cooked*) verduras *fpl*

vegetarian [vedʒɪ'teərɪən] *adj*, *n* vegetariano/a *m/f*

vehement ['vi:mənt] *adj* vehemente, apasionado

vehicle ['vi:ɪkl] *n* vehículo; (*fig*) medio

veil [veɪl] *n* velo ♦ *vt* velar; **~ed** *adj* (*fig*) velado

vein [veɪn] *n* vena; (*of ore etc*) veta

velocity [vɪ'lɔsɪtɪ] *n* velocidad *f*

velvet ['velvɪt] *n* terciopelo

vending machine ['vendɪŋ-] *n* distribuidor *m* automático

veneer [və'nɪə*] *n* chapa, enchapado; (*fig*) barniz *m*

venereal disease [vɪ'nɪərɪəl-] *n* enfermedad *f* venérea

Venetian blind [vɪ'ni:ʃən-] *n* persiana

Venezuela [venɪ'zweɪlə] *n* Venezuela; **~n** *adj*, *n* venezolano/a *m/f*

vengeance ['vendʒəns] *n* venganza; **with a ~** (*fig*) con creces

venison ['venɪsn] *n* carne *f* de venado

venom ['venəm] *n* veneno; (*bitterness*) odio; **~ous** *adj* venenoso; lleno de odio

vent [vent] *n* (*in jacket*) respiradero; (*in wall*) rejilla (de ventilación) ♦ *vt* (*fig: feelings*) desahogar

ventilator ['ventɪleɪtə*] *n* ventilador *m*

venture ['ventʃə*] *n* empresa ♦ *vt* (*opinion*) ofrecer ♦ *vi* arriesgarse, lanzarse; **business ~** *n* empresa comercial

venue ['venju:] *n* lugar *m*

veranda(h) [və'rændə] *n* terraza

verb [və:b] *n* verbo; **~al** *adj* verbal

verbatim [və:'beɪtɪm] *adj, adv* palabra por palabra

verdict ['vɜːdɪkt] n veredicto, fallo; (fig) opinión f, juicio

verge [vɜːdʒ] (BRIT) n borde m; "**soft ~s**" (AUT) "arcén m no asfaltado"; **to be on the ~ of doing sth** estar a punto de hacer algo; **~ on** vt fus rayar en

verify ['verɪfaɪ] vt comprobar, verificar

vermin ['vɜːmɪn] npl (animals) alimañas fpl; (insects, fig) parásitos mpl

vermouth ['vɜːməθ] n vermut m

versatile ['vɜːsətaɪl] adj (person) polifacético; (machine, tool etc) versátil

verse [vɜːs] n poesía; (stanza) estrofa; (in bible) versículo

version ['vɜːʃən] n versión f

versus ['vɜːsəs] prep contra

vertebra ['vɜːtɪbrə] (pl **~e**) n vértebra

vertical ['vɜːtɪkl] adj vertical

verve [vɜːv] n brío

very ['verɪ] adv muy ♦ adj: **the ~ book which** el mismo libro que; **the ~ last** el último de todos; **at the ~ least** al menos; **~ much** muchísimo

vessel ['vesl] n (ship) barco; (container) vasija; see **blood**

vest [vest] n (BRIT) camiseta; (US: waistcoat) chaleco; **~ed interests** npl (COMM) intereses mpl creados

vet [vet] vt (candidate) investigar ♦ n abbr (BRIT) = **veterinary surgeon**

veteran ['vetərn] n veterano

veterinary surgeon ['vetrɪnərɪ] (US **veterinarian**) n veterinario/a m/f

veto ['viːtəu] (pl **~es**) n veto ♦ vt prohibir, poner el veto a

vex [veks] vt fastidiar; **~ed** adj (question) controvertido

VHF abbr (= very high frequency) muy alta frecuencia

via ['vaɪə] prep por, por medio de

vibrant ['vaɪbrənt] adj (lively) animado; (bright) vivo; (voice) vibrante

vibrate [vaɪ'breɪt] vi vibrar

vicar ['vɪkə*] n párroco (de la Iglesia Anglicana); **~age** n parroquia

vice [vaɪs] n (evil) vicio; (TECH) torno de banco

vice- [vaɪs] prefix vice-; **~-chairman** n vicepresidente m

vice squad n brigada antivicio

vice versa ['vaɪsɪ'vɜːsə] adv viceversa

vicinity [vɪ'sɪnɪtɪ] n: **in the ~ (of)** cercano (a)

vicious ['vɪʃəs] adj (attack) violento; (words) cruel; (horse, dog) resabido; **~ circle** n círculo vicioso

victim ['vɪktɪm] n víctima

victor ['vɪktə*] n vencedor(a) m/f

victory ['vɪktərɪ] n victoria

video ['vɪdɪəu] cpd video ♦ n (~ film) videofilm m; (also: ~ cassette) videocassette f; (also: ~ cassette recorder) magnetoscopio; **~ game** n videojuego; **~ tape** n cinta de vídeo

vie [vaɪ] vi: **to ~ (with sb for sth)** competir (con uno por algo)

Vienna [vɪ'enə] n Viena

Vietnam [vjet'næm] n Vietnam m; **~ese** [-nə'miːz] n inv, adj vietnamita m/f

view [vjuː] n vista; (outlook) perspectiva; (opinion) opinión f, criterio ♦ vt (look at) mirar; (fig) considerar; **on ~** (in museum etc) expuesto; **in full (of)** en plena vista (de); **in ~ of the weather/the fact that** en vista del tiempo/del hecho de que; **in my ~** en mi opinión; **~er** n espectador m/f; (TV) telespectador(a) m/f; **~finder** n visor m de imagen; **~point** n (attitude) punto de vista; (place) mirador m

vigour ['vɪgə*] (US **vigor**) n energía, vigor m

vile [vaɪl] adj vil, infame; (smell) asqueroso; (temper) endemoniado

villa ['vɪlə] n (country house) casa de campo; (suburban house) chalet m

village ['vɪlɪdʒ] n aldea; **~r** n aldeano/a

villain ['vɪlən] n (scoundrel) malvado/a; (in novel) malo; (BRIT: criminal) maleante m/f

vindicate ['vɪndɪkeɪt] vt vindicar, justificar

vindictive [vɪnˈdɪktɪv] adj vengativo

vine [vaɪn] n vid f

vinegar [ˈvɪnɪɡəʳ] n vinagre m

vineyard [ˈvɪnjɑːd] n viña, viñedo

vintage [ˈvɪntɪdʒ] n (year) vendimia, cosecha ♦ cpd de época; ~ **wine** n vino añejo

vinyl [ˈvaɪnl] n vinilo

viola [vɪˈəʊlə] n (MUS) viola

violate [ˈvaɪəleɪt] vt violar

violence [ˈvaɪələns] n violencia

violent [ˈvaɪələnt] adj violento; (intense) intenso

violet [ˈvaɪələt] adj violado, violeta ♦ n (plant) violeta

violin [vaɪəˈlɪn] n violín m; ~**ist** n violinista m/f

VIP n abbr (= very important person) VIP m

virgin [ˈvɜːdʒɪn] n virgen f

Virgo [ˈvɜːɡəʊ] n Virgo

virtually [ˈvɜːtjuəlɪ] adv prácticamente

virtual reality [ˈvɜːtjuəl-] n (COMPUT) mundo or realidad f virtual

virtue [ˈvɜːtjuː] n virtud f; (advantage) ventaja; **by ~ of** en virtud de

virtuous [ˈvɜːtjuəs] adj virtuoso

virus [ˈvaɪərəs] n (also: COMPUT) virus m

visa [ˈviːzə] n visado (SP), visa (AM)

visible [ˈvɪzəbl] adj visible

vision [ˈvɪʒən] n (sight) vista; (foresight, in dream) visión f

visit [ˈvɪzɪt] n visita ♦ vt (person: us: also: ~ **with**) visitar, hacer una visita a; (place) ir a, (ir a) conocer; ~**ing hours** npl (in hospital etc) horas fpl de visita; ~**or** n (in museum) visitante m/f; (invited to house) visita; (tourist) turista m/f

visor [ˈvaɪzəʳ] n visera

visual [ˈvɪzjuəl] adj visual; ~ **aid** n medio visual; ~ **display unit** n unidad f de presentación visual; ~**ize** vt imaginarse

vital [ˈvaɪtl] adj (essential) esencial, imprescindible; (dynamic) dinámico; (organ) vital; ~**ly** adv: ~**ly important**

de primera importancia; ~ **statistics** npl (fig) medidas fpl vitales

vitamin [ˈvɪtəmɪn] n vitamina

vivacious [vɪˈveɪʃəs] adj vivaz, alegre

vivid [ˈvɪvɪd] adj (account) gráfico; (light) intenso; (imagination, memory) vivo; ~**ly** adv gráficamente; (remember) como si fuera hoy

V-neck [ˈviːnek] n cuello de pico

vocabulary [vəʊˈkæbjulərɪ] n vocabulario

vocal [ˈvəʊkl] adj vocal; (articulate) elocuente; ~ **cords** npl cuerdas fpl vocales

vocation [vəʊˈkeɪʃən] n vocación f; ~**al** adj profesional

vodka [ˈvɒdkə] n vodka m

vogue [vəʊɡ] n: **in ~** en boga, de moda

voice [vɔɪs] n voz f ♦ vt expresar

void [vɔɪd] n vacío; (hole) hueco ♦ adj (invalid) nulo, inválido; (empty): ~ **of** carente or desprovisto de

volatile [ˈvɒlətaɪl] adj (situation) inestable; (person) voluble; (liquid) volátil

volcano [vɒlˈkeɪnəʊ] n (pl ~**es**) volcán m

volition [vəˈlɪʃən] n: **of one's own ~** de su propia voluntad

volley [ˈvɒlɪ] n (of gunfire) descarga; (of stones etc) lluvia; (fig) torrente m; (TENNIS etc) volea; ~**ball** n vol(e)ibol m

volt [vəʊlt] n voltio; ~**age** n voltaje m

volume [ˈvɒljuːm] n (gen) volumen m; (book) tomo

voluntary [ˈvɒləntərɪ] adj voluntario

volunteer [vɒlənˈtɪəʳ] n voluntario/a ♦ vt (information) ofrecer ♦ vi ofrecerse (de voluntario); **to ~ to do** ofrecerse a hacer

vomit [ˈvɒmɪt] n vómito ♦ vt, vi vomitar

vote [vəʊt] n voto; (votes cast) votación f; (right to ~) derecho de votar; (franchise) sufragio ♦ vt (chairman) elegir; (propose): **to ~ that** proponer que ♦ vi votar, ir a votar; **~ of thanks** voto de gracias; **~r** n votante m/f; **voting** n votación f

vouch [vautʃ]: **to ~ for** vt fus garantizar, responder de

voucher ['vautʃə*] n (for meal, petrol) vale m

vow [vau] n voto ♦ vt: **to ~ to do/ that** jurar hacer/que

vowel ['vauəl] n vocal f

voyage ['vɔɪdʒ] n viaje m

vulgar ['vʌlgə*] adj (rude) ordinario, grosero; (in bad taste) de mal gusto; **~ity** [-'gæriti] n grosería; mal gusto

vulnerable ['vʌlnərəbl] adj vulnerable

vulture ['vʌltʃə*] n buitre m

W, w

wad [wɔd] n bolita; (of banknotes etc) fajo

waddle ['wɔdl] vi anadear

wade [weid] vi: **to ~ through** (water) vadear; (fig: book) leer con dificultad; **wading pool** (US) n piscina para niños

wafer ['weifə*] n galleta, barquillo

waffle ['wɔfl] n (CULIN) gofre m ♦ vi dar el rollo

waft [wɔft] vt llevar por el aire ♦ vi flotar

wag [wæg] vt menear, agitar ♦ vi moverse, menearse

wage [weidʒ] n (also: ~s) sueldo, salario ♦ vt: **to ~ war** hacer la guerra; **~ earner** n asalariado/a; **~ packet** n sobre m de paga

wager ['weidʒə*] n apuesta

wag(g)on ['wægən] n (horse-drawn) carro; (BRIT: RAIL) vagón m

wail [weil] n gemido ♦ vi gemir

waist [weist] n cintura, talle m; **~coat** (BRIT) n chaleco; **~line** n talle m

wait [weit] n (interval) pausa ♦ vi esperar; **to lie in ~ for** acechar a; **I can't ~ to** (fig) estoy deseando; **to ~ for** esperar (a); **~ behind** vi

quedarse; **~ on** vt fus servir a; **~er** n camarero; **~ing** n: "no **~ing"** (BRIT: AUT) "prohibido estacionarse"; **~ing list** n lista de espera; **~ing room** n sala de espera; **~ress** n camarera

waive [weiv] vt suspender

wake [weik] (pt **woke** or **waked**, pp **woken** or **waked**) vt (also: **~ up**) despertar ♦ vi (also: **~ up**) despertarse ♦ n (for dead person) vela, velatorio; (NAUT) estela; **waken** vt, vi = **wake**

Wales [weilz] n País m de Gales; **the Prince of ~** el príncipe de Gales

walk [wɔːk] n (stroll) paseo; (hike) excursión f a pie, caminata; (gait) paso, andar m; (in park etc) paseo, alameda ♦ vi andar, caminar; (for pleasure, exercise) pasear ♦ vt (distance) recorrer a pie, andar; (dog) pasear; **10 minutes' ~ from here** a 10 minutos de aquí andando; **people from all ~s of life** gente de todas las esferas; **~ out** vi (audience) salir; (workers) declararse en huelga; **~ out on** (inf) vt fus abandonar; **~er** n (person) paseante m/f, caminante m/f; **~ie-talkie** ['wɔːkɪ'tɔːkɪ] n walkie-talkie m; **~ing** n el andar; **~ing shoes** npl zapatos mpl para andar; **~ing stick** n bastón m; **W~man** ['wɔːkmən] n Walkman ® m; **~out** n huelga; **~over** (inf) n: **it was a ~over** fue pan comido; **~way** n paseo

wall [wɔːl] n pared f; (exterior) muro; (city ~ etc) muralla; **~ed** adj amurallado/a; (garden) con tapia

wallet ['wɔlɪt] n cartera (SP), billetera (AM)

wallflower ['wɔːlflauə*] n alhelí m; **to be a ~** (fig) comer pavo

wallow ['wɔləu] vi revolcarse

wallpaper ['wɔːlpeɪpə*] n papel m pintado vt empapelar

walnut ['wɔːlnʌt] n nuez f; (tree) nogal m

walrus ['wɔːlrəs] (pl **~** or **~es**) n morsa

waltz [wɔːlts] n vals m ♦ vi bailar el

vals

wand [wɒnd] n (also: magic ~) varita (mágica)

wander ['wɒndə*] vi (person) vagar; deambular; (thoughts) divagar ♦ vt recorrer, vagar por

wane [weɪn] vi menguar

wangle ['wæŋgl] (BRIT: inf) vt agenciar

want [wɒnt] vt querer, desear; (need) necesitar ♦ n: for ~ of por falta de; ~s npl (needs) necesidades fpl; to ~ to do querer hacer; to ~ sb to do sth querer que uno haga algo; ~ed adj (criminal) buscado; "~ed" (in advertisements) "se busca"; ~ing adj: to be found ~ing no estar a la altura de las circunstancias

war [wɔː*] n guerra; to make ~ (on) (also fig) declarar la guerra (a)

ward [wɔːd] n (in hospital) sala; (POL) distrito electoral; (LAW: child: also: ~ of court) pupilo/a; ~ off (blow) desviar, parar; (attack) rechazar

warden ['wɔːdn] n (BRIT: of institution) director(a) m/f; (of park, game reserve) guardián/ana m/f; (BRIT: also: traffic ~) guardia m/f

warder ['wɔːdə*] (BRIT) n guardián/ana m/f, carcelero/a

wardrobe ['wɔːdrəub] n armario, guardarropa, ropero (esp AM)

warehouse ['wɛəhaus] n almacén m, depósito

wares [wɛəz] npl mercancías fpl

warfare ['wɔːfɛə*] n guerra

warhead ['wɔːhɛd] n cabeza armada

warily ['wɛərɪlɪ] adv con cautela, cautelosamente

warm [wɔːm] adj caliente; (thanks) efusivo; (clothes) abrigado; (welcome, day) caluroso; it's ~ hace calor; I'm ~ tengo calor; ~ up vi (room) calentarse; (person) entrar en calor; (athlete) hacer ejercicios de calentamiento ♦ vt calentar; ~-hearted adj afectuoso; ~ly adv

afectuosamente; ~th n calor m

warn [wɔːn] vt avisar, advertir; ~ing n aviso, advertencia; ~ing light n luz f de advertencia; ~ing triangle n (AUT) triángulo señalizador

warp [wɔːp] vi (wood) combarse ♦ vt combar; (mind) pervertir

warrant ['wɒrənt] n autorización f; (LAW: to arrest) orden f de detención; (: to search) mandamiento de registro

warranty ['wɒrəntɪ] n garantía

warren ['wɒrən] n (of rabbits) madriguera; (fig) laberinto

warrior ['wɒrɪə*] n guerrero/a

Warsaw ['wɔːsɔː] n Varsovia

warship ['wɔːʃɪp] n buque m o barco de guerra

wart [wɔːt] n verruga

wartime ['wɔːtaɪm] n: in ~ en tiempos de guerra, en la guerra

wary ['wɛərɪ] adj cauteloso

was [wɒz] pt of be

wash [wɒʃ] vt lavar ♦ vi lavarse; (sea etc): to ~ against/over sth llegar hasta/cubrir algo ♦ n (clothes etc) lavado; (of ship) estela; to have a ~ lavarse; ~ away vt (stain) quitar lavando; (subj: river etc) llevarse; ~ off vi quitarse (al lavar); ~ up vi (BRIT) fregar los platos; (US) lavarse; ~able adj lavable; ~basin (US ~bowl) n lavabo; ~ cloth (US) n manopla; ~er n (TECH) arandela; ~ing n (dirty) ropa sucia; (clean) colada; ~ing machine n lavadora; ~ing powder (BRIT) n detergente m (en polvo)

Washington ['wɒʃɪŋtən] n Washington m

wash: ~ing-up (BRIT) n fregado, platos mpl (para fregar); ~ing-up liquid (BRIT) n líquido lavavajillas; ~-out (inf) n fracaso; ~room (US) n servicios mpl

wasn't ['wɒznt] = **was not**

wasp [wɒsp] n avispa

wastage ['weɪstɪdʒ] n desgaste m; (loss) pérdida

waste [weɪst] n derroche m,

despilfarro; (of time) pérdida; (food)
sobras fpl; (rubbish) basura,
desperdicios mpl ♦ adj (material) de
desecho; (left over) sobrante; (coin)
baldío, descampado ♦ vt malgastar,
derrochar; (time) perder; (opportunity)
desperdiciar; ~s npl (area of land)
tierras fpl baldías; ~ **away** vi
consumirse; ~ **disposal unit** (BRIT) n
triturador m de basura; ~**ful** adj
derrochador(a); (process)
antieconómico; ~ **ground** (BRIT) n
terreno baldío; ~**paper basket** n
papelera; ~ **pipe** n tubo de desagüe

watch [wɔtʃ] n (also: wrist ~) reloj m;
(MIL: group of guards) centinela m; (act)
vigilancia; (NAUT: spell of duty) guardia
♦ vt (look at) mirar, observar; (: match,
programme) ver; (spy on, guard) vigilar;
(be careful of) cuidarse de, tener
cuidado de ♦ vi ver, mirar; (keep guard)
montar guardia; ~ **out** vi cuidarse,
tener cuidado; ~**dog** n perro guardián;
(fig) persona u organismo encargado de
asegurarse de que las empresas actúan
dentro de la legalidad; ~**ful** adj
vigilante, sobre aviso; ~**maker** n
relojero/a; ~**man** (irreg) n see **night**;
~ **strap** n pulsera (de reloj)

water ['wɔːtə*] n agua ♦ vt (plant)
regar ♦ vi (eyes) llorar; (mouth) hacerse
la boca agua; ~ **down** vt (milk etc)
aguar; (fig: story) dulcificar, diluir;
~ **closet** n wáter m; ~**colour** n
acuarela; ~**cress** n berro; ~**fall** n
cascada, salto de agua; ~ **heater** n
calentador m de agua; ~**ing can** n
regadera; ~ **lily** n nenúfar m; ~**line** n
(NAUT) línea de flotación; ~**logged** adj
(ground) inundado; ~ **main** n cañería
del agua; ~**melon** n sandía; ~**proof**
adj impermeable; ~**shed** n (GEO)
cuenca; (fig) momento crítico; ~-
skiing n esquí m acuático; ~**tight** adj
hermético; ~**way** n vía fluvial or
navegable; ~**works** n central f
depuradora; ~**y** adj (coffee etc) aguado;

(eyes) lloroso
watt [wɔt] n vatio
wave [weɪv] n (of hand) señal f con la
mano; (on water) ola; (RADIO, in hair)
onda; (fig) oleada ♦ vi agitar la mano;
(flag etc) ondear ♦ vt (handkerchief,
gun) agitar; ~**length** n longitud f de
onda
waver ['weɪvə*] vi (voice, love etc)
flaquear; (person) vacilar
wavy ['weɪvɪ] adj ondulado
wax [wæks] n cera ♦ vt encerar ♦ vi
(moon) crecer; ~ **paper** (US) n papel m
apergaminado; ~**works** n museo de
cera ♦ npl figuras fpl de cera
way [weɪ] n camino; (distance)
trayecto, recorrido; (direction) dirección
f, sentido; (manner) modo, manera;
(habit) costumbre f; **which ~? — this**
~ ¿por dónde?, ¿en qué dirección? —
por aquí; **on the** ~ (en route) en (el)
camino; **to be on one's** ~ estar en
camino; **to be in the** ~ bloquear el
camino; (fig) estorbar; **to go out of
one's** ~ **to do sth** desvivirse por
hacer algo; **under** ~ en marcha; **to
lose one's** ~ extraviarse; **in a** ~ en
cierto modo or sentido; **no ~!** (inf) ¡de
eso nada!; **by the** ~ ... a propósito ...;
'"~ **in**" (BRIT) "entrada"; '"~ **out**"
(BRIT) "salida"; **the ~ back** el camino
de vuelta; **"give ~"** (BRIT: AUT) "ceda
el paso"
waylay [weɪˈleɪ] (irreg) vt salir al paso a
wayward ['weɪwəd] adj díscolo
W.C. n (BRIT) wáter m
we [wiː] pl pron nosotros/as
weak [wiːk] adj débil, flojo; (tea etc)
claro; ~**en** vi debilitarse; (give way)
ceder ♦ vt debilitar; ~**ling** n
debilucho/a; (morally) persona de poco
carácter; ~**ness** n debilidad f; (fault)
punto débil; **to have a ~ness for**
tener debilidad por
wealth [welθ] n riqueza; (of details)
abundancia; ~**y** adj rico
wean [wiːn] vt destetar

weapon ['wɛpən] *n* arma

wear [wɛə*] (*pt* **wore**, *pp* **worn**) (*in use*) uso; (*deterioration through use*) desgaste *m*; (*clothing*): **sports/baby-** ropa de deportes/de niños ♦ *vt* (*clothes*) llevar; (*shoes*) calzar; (*damage: through use*) gastar, usar ♦ *vi* (*last*) durar; (*rub through etc*) desgastarse;

~ evening ~ ropa de etiqueta; **~ away** *vt* gastar ♦ *vi* desgastarse; **~ down** *vt* gastar; (*strength*) agotar; **~ off** *vi* (*pain etc*) pasar, desaparecer; **~ out** *vt* desgastar; (*person, strength*) agotar;

~ and tear *n* desgaste *m*

weary ['wɪərɪ] *adj* cansado; (*dispirited*) abatido ♦ *vi*: **to ~ of** cansarse de

weasel ['wiːzl] *n* (*ZOOL*) comadreja

weather ['wɛðə*] *n* tiempo ♦ *vt* (*storm, crisis*) hacer frente a; **under the ~** (*fig: ill*) indispuesto, pachucho; **~-beaten** *adj* (*skin*) curtido; (*building*) deteriorado por la intemperie; **~cock** *n* veleta;

~ forecast *n* boletín *m* meteorológico; **~man** (*irreg: inf*) *n* hombre *m* del tiempo; **~ vane** *n* = **~cock**

weave [wiːv] (*pt* **wove**, *pp* **woven**) *vt* (*cloth*) tejer; (*fig*) entretejer; **~r** *n* tejedor/a *m/f*; **weaving** *n* tejeduría

web [wɛb] *n* (*of spider*) telaraña; (*on duck's foot*) membrana; (*network*) red *f*

website ['wɛbsaɪt] *n* espacio Web

wed [wɛd] (*pt, pp* **wedded**) *vt* casar ♦ *vi* casarse

we'd [wiːd] = **we had**; **we would**

wedding ['wɛdɪŋ] *n* boda, casamiento; **silver/golden ~** (*anniversary*) bodas *fpl* de plata/de oro; **~ day** *n* día *m* de la boda; **~ dress** *n* traje *m* de novia; **~ present** *n* regalo *m* de boda; **~ ring** *n* alianza

wedge [wɛdʒ] *n* (*of wood etc*) cuña; (*of cake*) trozo ♦ *vt* acuñar; (*push*) apretar

Wednesday ['wɛdnzdɪ] *n* miércoles *m inv*

wee [wiː] *adj* (*Scottish*) pequeñito

weed [wiːd] *n* mala hierba, maleza ♦ *vt* escardar, desherbar; **~killer** *n*

herbicida *m*; **~y** *adj* (*person*) mequetréfico

week [wiːk] *n* semana; **a ~ today/on Friday** de hoy/del viernes en ocho días; **~day** *n* día *m* laborable; **~end** *n* fin *m* de semana; **~ly** *adv* semanalmente, cada semana ♦ *adj* semanal ♦ *n* semanario

weep [wiːp] (*pt, pp* **wept**) *vi, vt* llorar; **~ing willow** *n* sauce *m* llorón

weigh [weɪ] *vt, vi* pesar; **to ~ anchor** levar anclas; **~ down** *vt* sobrecargar; (*fig: with worry*) agobiar; **~ up** *vt* sopesar

weight [weɪt] *n* peso; (*metal ~*) pesa; **to lose/put on ~** adelgazar/engordar; **~ing** *n* (*allowance*): (**London**) **~ing** dietas (*por residir en Londres*); **~lifter** *n* levantador *m* de pesas; **~y** *adj* pesado; (*matters*) de relevancia or peso

weir [wɪə*] *n* presa

weird [wɪəd] *adj* raro, extraño

welcome ['wɛlkəm] *adj* bienvenido ♦ *n* bienvenida ♦ *vt* dar la bienvenida a; (*be glad of*) alegrarse de; **thank you — you're ~** gracias — de nada

weld [wɛld] *n* soldadura ♦ *vt* soldar

welfare ['wɛlfɛə*] *n* bienestar *m*; (*social aid*) asistencia social; **~ state** *n* estado del bienestar

well [wɛl] *n* fuente *f*, pozo ♦ *adv* bien ♦ *adj*: **to be ~** estar bien (*de salud*) ♦ *excl* ¡vaya!, ¡bueno!; **as ~** también; **as ~ as** además de; **to do ~** bien hecho!; **get ~ soon!** ¡que te mejores pronto!; **to do ~** (*business*) ir bien; (*person*) tener éxito; **~ up** *vi* (*tears*) saltar

we'll [wiːl] = **we will**; **we shall**

well-: ~-behaved *adj* bueno; **~-being** *n* bienestar *m*; **~-built** *adj* (*person*) fornido; **~-deserved** *adj* merecido; **~-dressed** *adj* bien vestido; **~-groomed** *adj* de buena presencia; **~-heeled** (*inf*) *adj* (*wealthy*) rico

wellingtons ['wɛlɪŋtənz] *npl* (*also: wellington boots*) botas *fpl* de goma

well: ~**-known** adj (person) conocido; ~**-mannered** adj educado; ~**-meaning** adj bienintencionado; ~**-off** adj acomodado; ~**-read** adj leído; ~**-to-do** adj acomodado; ~**-wisher** n admirador(a) m/f

Welsh [welʃ] adj galés/esa ♦ n (LING) galés m; **the** ~ npl los galeses; ~**man** (irreg) n galés m; ~**rarebit** n pan m con queso tostado; ~**woman** (irreg) n galesa

went [went] pt of **go**

wept [wept] pt, pp of **weep**

were [wə:*] pt of **be**

we're [wɪə*] = **we are**

weren't [wə:nt] = **were not**

west [west] n oeste m ♦ adj occidental, del oeste ♦ adv al norte o hacia el oeste; **the W~** el Oeste, el Occidente; **W~ Country** (BRIT): **the W~ Country** el suroeste de Inglaterra; ~**erly** adj occidental (wind) del oeste; ~**ern** adj occidental ♦ n (CINEMA) película del oeste; **W~ Germany** n Alemania Occidental; **W~ Indian** adj, n antillano/a m/f; **W~ Indies** npl Antillas fpl; ~**ward(s)** adv hacia el oeste

wet [wet] adj (damp) húmedo; (~ through) mojado; (rainy) lluvioso ♦ (BRIT) n (POL) conservador(a) m/f moderado/a; **to get** ~ mojarse; **"~ paint"** "recién pintado"; ~**suit** n traje m térmico

we've [wi:v] = **we have**

whack [wæk] vt dar un buen golpe a

whale [weɪl] n (ZOOL) ballena

wharf [wɔ:f](pl **wharves**) n muelle m

___KEYWORD___

what [wɔt] adj **1** (in direct/indirect questions) qué; ~ **size is he?** ¿qué talla usa?; ~ **colour/shape is it?** ¿de qué color/forma es?
2 (in exclamations): ~ **a mess!** ¡qué desastre!; ~ **a fool I am!** ¡qué tonto soy!
♦ pron **1** (interrogative) qué; ~ **are you doing?** ¿qué haces or estás haciendo?; ~ **is happening?** ¿qué pasa or está pasando?; ~ **is it called?** ¿cómo se llama?; ~ **about me?** ¿y yo qué?; ~ **about doing …?** ¿qué tal si hacemos …?
2 (relative) lo que; **I saw** ~ **you did/was on the table** vi lo que hiciste/había en la mesa
♦ excl (disbelieving) ¡cómo!; ~, **no coffee!** ¡que no hay café!

whatever [wɔt'evə*] adj: ~ **book you choose** cualquier libro que elijas
♦ pron: **do** ~ **is necessary** haga lo que sea necesario; ~ **happens** pase lo que pase; **no reason** ~ or **whatsoever** ninguna razón sea la que sea; **nothing** ~ nada en absoluto

whatsoever [wɔtsəʊ'evə*] adj see **whatever**

wheat [wi:t] n trigo

wheedle ['wi:dl] vt: **to** ~ **sb into doing sth** engatusar a uno para que haga algo; **to** ~ **sth out of sb** sonsacar algo a uno

wheel [wi:l] n rueda; (AUT: also: **steering** ~) volante m; (NAUT) timón m ♦ vt (pram etc) empujar ♦ vi (also: ~ **round**) dar la vuelta, girar; ~**barrow** n carretilla; ~**chair** n silla de ruedas; ~ **clamp** n (AUT) cepo

wheeze [wi:z] vi resollar

___KEYWORD___

when [wen] adv cuando; ~ **did it happen?** ¿cuándo ocurrió?; **I know ~ it happened** sé cuándo ocurrió
♦ conj **1** (at, during, after the time that) cuando; **be careful ~ you cross the road** ten cuidado al cruzar la calle; **that was ~ I needed you** fue entonces que te necesité
2 (on, at which): **on the day ~ I met him** el día en qué le conocí
3 (whereas) cuando

whenever |wɛn'ɛvə*| *conj* cuando;
(*every time that*) cada vez que ♦ *adv*
cuando sea

where |wɛə*| *adv* dónde ♦ *conj*
donde; **this is ~** aquí es donde;
~abouts *adv* dónde ♦ *n*: **nobody
knows his ~abouts** nadie conoce su
paradero; **~as** *conj* visto que, mientras;
~by *pron* por lo cual; **wherever**
|-'ɛvə*| *conj* dondequiera que;
(*interrogative*) dónde; **~withal** *n*
recursos *mpl*

whether |'wɛðə*| *conj* si; **I don't
know ~ to accept or not** no sé si
aceptar o no; **~ you go or not** vayas
o no vayas

> KEYWORD

which |wɪtʃ| *adj* **1** (*interrogative: direct,
indirect*) qué; **~ picture(s) do you
want?** ¿qué cuadro(s) quieres?;
~ one? ¿cuál?
2: in ~ case en cuyo caso; **we got
there at 8 pm, by ~ time the
cinema was full** llegamos allí a las 8,
cuando el cine estaba lleno
♦ *pron* **1** (*interrogative*) cuál; **I don't
mind ~** el/la que sea
2 (*relative: replacing noun*) que;
(: *replacing clause*) lo que; (: *after
preposition*) (el/la) que el/la, el/la cual
etc; **the apple ~ you ate/~ is on the
table** la manzana que comiste/que
está en la mesa; **the chair on ~ you
are sitting** la silla en la que estás
sentado; **he said he knew, ~ is
true/I feared** dijo que lo sabía, lo cual
or lo que es cierto/me temía

whichever |wɪtʃ'ɛvə*| *adj*: **take
~ book you prefer** coja (*SP*) el libro
que prefiera; **~ book you take**
cualquier libro que coja

while |waɪl| *n* rato, momento ♦ *conj*
mientras; (*although*) aunque; **for a ~**
durante algún tiempo; **~ away** *vt*
pasar

whim |wɪm| *n* capricho

whimper |'wɪmpə*| *n* sollozo ♦ *vi*
lloriquear

whimsical |'wɪmzɪkl| *adj* (*person*)
caprichoso/a; (*look*) juguetón/ona

whine |waɪn| *n* (*of pain*) gemido; (*of
engine*) zumbido; (*of siren*) aullido ♦ *vi*
gemir; zumbar; (*fig: complain*)
gimotear

whip |wɪp| *n* látigo; (*POL: person*)
encargado de la disciplina partidaria en
el parlamento ♦ *vt* azotar; (*CULIN*) batir;
(*move quickly*): **to ~ sth out/off**
sacar/quitar algo de un tirón; **~ped
cream** *n* nata or crema montada; **~-
round** (*BRIT*) *n* colecta

whirl |wə:l| *vt* hacer girar, dar vueltas a
♦ *vi* girar, dar vueltas; (*leaves etc*)
arremolinarse; **~pool** *n* remolino;
~wind *n* torbellino

whirr |wə:*| *vi* zumbar

whisk |wɪsk| *n* (*CULIN*) batidor *m* ♦ *vt*
(*CULIN*) batir; **to ~ sb away** or **off**
llevar volando a uno

whiskers |'wɪskəz| *npl* (*of animal*)
bigotes *mpl*; (*of man*) patillas *fpl*

whiskey |'wɪskɪ| (*US, Ireland*) *n* =
whisky

whisky |'wɪskɪ| *n* whisky *m*

whisper |'wɪspə*| *n* susurro ♦ *vi*, *vt*
susurrar

whistle |'wɪsl| *n* (*sound*) silbido;
(*object*) silbato *m* ♦ *vi* silbar

white |waɪt| *adj* blanco; (*pale*) pálido
♦ *n* blanco; (*of egg*) clara; **~ coffee**
(*BRIT*) *n* café *m* con leche; **~-collar
worker** *n* oficinista *m/f*; **~ elephant** *n*
(*fig*) maula; **~ lie** *n* mentirilla; **~ness** *n*
blancura; **~ noise** *n* sonido blanco;
~ paper *n* (*POL*) libro rojo; **~wash** *n*
(*paint*) jalbegue *m*, cal *f* ♦ *vt* (*also fig*)
blanquear

whiting |'waɪtɪŋ| *n inv* (*fish*) pescadilla

Whitsun |'wɪtsn| *n* pentecostés *m*

whizz |wɪz| *vi*: **to ~ past** or **by**
pasar a toda velocidad; **~ kid** (*inf*) *n*
prodigio

who [huː] *pron* **1** *(interrogative)* quién; ~ **is it?**, ~'s **there?** ¿quién es?; **are you looking for?** ¿a quién buscas?; **I told her** ~ **I was** le dije quién era yo **2** *(relative)* que; **the man/woman** ~ **spoke to me** el hombre/la mujer que habló conmigo; **those** ~ **can swim** los que saben *or* sepan nadar

whodun(n)it [huː'dʌnɪt] *(inf)* n novela policíaca

whoever [huː'evə*] *pron:* ~ **finds it** cualquiera *or* quienquiera que lo encuentre; **ask** ~ **you like** pregunta a quien quieras; ~ **he marries** no importa con quién se case

whole [həul] *adj (entire)* todo, entero; *(not broken)* intacto ♦ n todo; *(all):* **the** ~ **of the town** toda la ciudad, la ciudad entera ♦ n *(total)* total m; *(sum)* conjunto; **on the** ~, a **total** ~ en general; ~**food(s)** n(pl) alimento(s) m(pl) integral(es); ~**hearted** sincero, cordial; ~**meal** *adj* integral; ~**sale** n venta al por mayor ♦ *adj* al por mayor; *(fig: destruction)* sistemático; ~**saler** n mayorista m/f; ~**some** *adj* sano; ~**wheat** *adj =* ~**meal**; **wholly** *adv* totalmente, enteramente

whom [huːm] *pron* **1** *(interrogative):* ~ **did you see?** ¿a quién viste?; **to** ~ **did you give it?** ¿a quién se lo diste?; **tell me from** ~ **you received it** dígame de quién lo recibió **2** *(relative)* que; **to** ~ a quien(es); **of** ~ de quien(es), del/de la que *etc;* **the man** ~ **I saw/to** ~ **I wrote** el hombre que ví/a quien escribí; **the lady about/with** ~ **I was talking** la señora de (la) que/con quien o (la) que hablaba

whooping cough ['huːpɪŋ-] n tos f ferina

whore [hɔː*] *(inf: pej)* n puta

whose [huːz] *adj* **1** *(possessive: interrogative):* ~ **book is this?**, ~ **is this book?** ¿de quién es este libro?; ~ **pencil have you taken?** ¿de quién es el lápiz que has cogido?; ~ **daughter are you?** ¿de quién eres hija? **2** *(possessive: relative)* cuyo/a, pl cuyos/as; **the man** ~ **son you rescued** el hombre cuyo hijo rescataste; **those** ~ **passports I have** aquellas personas cuyos pasaportes tengo; **the woman** ~ **car was stolen** la mujer a quien le robaron el coche ♦ *pron* de quién; ~ **is this?** ¿de quién es esto?; **I know** ~ **it is** sé de quién es

why [waɪ] *adv* por qué; ~ **not?** ¿por qué no?; ~ **not do it now?** ¿por qué no lo haces (or hacemos *etc*) ahora? ♦ *conj:* **I wonder** ~ **he said that** me pregunto por qué dijo eso; **that's not** ~ **I'm here** no es por eso (por lo) que estoy aquí, **the reason** ~ la razón por la que ♦ *excl (expressing surprise, shock, annoyance)* ¡hombre!, ¡vaya! *(explaining):* ~, **it's you!** ¡hombre, eres tú!; ~, **that's impossible** ¡pero sí eso es imposible!

wicked ['wɪkɪd] *adj* malvado, cruel

wicket ['wɪkɪt] n *(CRICKET: stumps)* palos mpl; *(: grass area)* terreno de juego

wide [waɪd] *adj* ancho; *(area, knowledge)* vasto, grande; *(choice)* amplio ♦ *adv:* **to open** ~ abrir de par en par; **to shoot** ~ errar el tiro; ~-

angle lens n objetivo de gran angular; **~-awake** adj bien despierto; **~ly** adv (travelled) mucho; (spaced) muy; **it is ~ly believed/known that** ... mucha gente piensa/sabe que ...; **~n** vt ensanchar; (experience) ampliar ♦ vi ensancharse; **~ open** adj abierto de par en par; **~spread** adj extendido, general

widow ['wɪdəʊ] n viuda; **~ed** adj viudo; **~er** n viudo

width [wɪdθ] n anchura; (of cloth) ancho

wield [wiːld] vt (sword) blandir; (power) ejercer

wife [waɪf] (pl **wives**) n mujer f, esposa

wig [wɪg] n peluca

wiggle ['wɪgl] vt menear

wild [waɪld] adj (animal) salvaje; (plant) silvestre; (person) furioso, violento; (idea) descabellado; (rough: sea) bravo; (: land) agreste; (: weather) muy revuelto; **~s** npl regiones fpl salvajes, tierras fpl vírgenes; **~erness** ['wɪldənɪs] n desierto; **~life** n fauna; **~ly** adv (behave) locamente; (lash out) a diestro y siniestro; (guess) a lo loco; (happy) a más no poder

wilful ['wɪlful] (US **willful**) adj (action) deliberado; (obstinate) testarudo

---KEYWORD---

will [wɪl] aux vb 1 (forming future tense): **I ~ finish it tomorrow** lo terminaré o voy a terminar mañana; **I ~ have finished it by tomorrow** lo habré terminado para mañana; **you do it? — yes I ~/no I won't** ¿lo harás? — sí/no

2 (in conjectures, predictions): **he ~** or **he'll be there by now** ya habrá or debe (de) haber llegado; **that ~ be the postman** será o debe ser el cartero

3 (in commands, requests, offers): **~ you be quiet!** ¡quieres callarte?;

~ you help me? ¿quieres ayudarme?; **~ you have a cup of tea?** ¿te apetece un té?; **I won't put up with it!** ¡no lo soporto!
♦ vt (pt, pp **willed**): **to ~ sb to do sth** desear que alguien haga algo; **he ~ed himself to go on** con gran fuerza de voluntad, continuó
♦ n voluntad f; (testament) testamento

willing ['wɪlɪŋ] adj (with goodwill) de buena voluntad; (enthusiastic) entusiasta; **he's ~ to do it** está dispuesto a hacerlo; **~ly** adv con mucho gusto; **~ness** n buena voluntad

willow ['wɪləʊ] n sauce m

willpower ['wɪlpaʊə*] n fuerza de voluntad

willy-nilly [wɪlɪ'nɪlɪ] adv quiérase o no

wilt [wɪlt] vi marchitarse

win [wɪn] (pt, pp **won**) n victoria, triunfo ♦ vt ganar; (obtain) conseguir, lograr ♦ vi ganar; **~ over** vt convencer a; **~ round** (BRIT) vt = **~ over**

wince [wɪns] vi encogerse

winch [wɪntʃ] n torno

wind¹ [wɪnd] n viento; (MED) gases mpl ♦ vt (take breath away from) dejar sin aliento a

wind² [waɪnd] (pt, pp **wound**) vt enrollar; (wrap) envolver; (clock, toy) dar cuerda a ♦ vi (road, river) serpentear; **~ up** vt (clock) dar cuerda a; (debate, meeting) concluir, terminar

windfall ['wɪndfɔːl] n golpe m de suerte

winding ['waɪndɪŋ] adj (road) tortuoso; (staircase) de caracol

wind instrument [wɪnd-] n (MUS) instrumento de viento

windmill ['wɪndmɪl] n molino de viento

window ['wɪndəʊ] n ventana; (in car, train) ventanilla; (in shop etc) escaparate m (SP), vitrina (AM); **~ box** n jardinera de ventana; **~ cleaner** n

(*person*) limpiador m de cristales;
~ **ledge** n alféizar m, repisa; ~ **pane** n
cristal m; **~-shopping** n: **to go ~-
shopping** ir de escaparates; **~sill** n
alféizar m, repisa

windpipe ['wɪndpaɪp] n tráquea

wind power n energía eólica

windscreen ['wɪndskriːn] (US
windshield) n parabrisas m inv;
~ **washer** n lavaparabrisas m inv;
~ **wiper** n limpiaparabrisas m inv

windswept ['wɪndswept] adj azotado
por el viento

windy ['wɪndɪ] adj de mucho viento;
it's ~ hace viento

wine [waɪn] n vino; ~ **bar** n enoteca;
~ **cellar** n bodega; ~ **glass** n copa
(para vino); ~ **list** n lista de vinos;
~ **waiter** n escanciador m

wing [wɪŋ] n ala; (AUT) aleta;
(THEATRE) bastidores mpl; **~er** n (SPORT)
extremo

wink [wɪŋk] n guiño, pestañeo ♦ vi
guiñar, pestañear

winner ['wɪnə*] n ganador(a) m/f

winning ['wɪnɪŋ] adj (team)
ganador(a); (goal) decisivo; (smile)
encantador(a); **~s** npl ganancias fpl

winter ['wɪntə*] n invierno ♦ vi
invernar; **wintry** ['wɪntrɪ] adj invernal

wipe [waɪp] n: **to give sth a ~** vt pasar
un trapo sobre algo ♦ vt limpiar; (tape)
borrar; ~ **off** vt limpiar con un trapo;
(remove) quitar; ~ **out** vt (debt)
liquidar; (memory) borrar; (destroy)
destruir; ~ **up** vt limpiar

wire ['waɪə*] n alambre m; (ELEC) cable
m (eléctrico); (TEL) telegrama m ♦ vt
(house) poner la instalación eléctrica
en; (also: ~ **up**) conectar; (person:
telegram) telegrafiar

wireless ['waɪəlɪs] (BRIT) n radio f

wiring ['waɪərɪŋ] n instalación f
eléctrica

wiry ['waɪərɪ] adj (person) enjuto y
fuerte; (hair) crespo

wisdom ['wɪzdəm] n sabiduría, saber

m; (good sense) cordura; ~ **tooth** n
muela del juicio

wise [waɪz] adj sabio; (sensible) juicioso

...wise [waɪz] suffix: **time~** en cuanto a
or respecto al tiempo

wish [wɪʃ] n deseo ♦ vt querer; **best
~es** (on birthday etc) felicidades fpl;
with best ~es (in letter) saludos mpl,
recuerdos mpl; **to ~ sb goodbye**
despedirse de uno; **he ~ed me well**
me deseó mucha suerte; **to ~ to do
sb to do sth** querer hacer/que
alguien haga algo; **to ~ for** desear;
~ful adj: **it's ~ful thinking** eso sería
soñar

wisp [wɪsp] n mechón m; (of smoke)
voluta

wistful ['wɪstful] adj pensativo

wit [wɪt] n ingenio, gracia; (also: ~s)
inteligencia; (person) chistoso/a

witch [wɪtʃ] n bruja; **~craft** n brujería;
~-hunt n (fig) caza de brujas

KEYWORD

with [wɪð, wɪθ] prep **1** (accompanying,
in the company of) con (con+ mí, ti, sí
= conmigo, contigo, consigo); **I was
~ him** estaba con él; **we stayed
~ friends** nos quedamos en casa de
unos amigos; **I'm (not) ~ you**
(understand) no te entiendo; **to be
~ it** (inf: person: up-to-date) estar al
tanto; (: alert) ser despabilado
2 (descriptive, indicating manner etc)
con; de; **a room ~ a view** una
habitación con vistas; **the man ~ the
grey hat/blue eyes** el hombre del
sombrero gris/de los ojos azules; **red
~ anger** rojo de ira; **to shake ~ fear**
temblar de miedo; **to fill sth ~ water**
llenar algo de agua

withdraw [wɪθ'drɔː] (irreg) vt retirar,
sacar ♦ vi retirarse; ~ **to ~ money (from
the bank)** retirar fondos (del banco);
~al n retirada; (of money) reintegro;
~al symptoms npl (MED) síndrome m

de abstinencia; **~n** adj (person)
reservado, introvertido
wither ['wɪðə*] vi marchitarse
withhold [wɪð'həuld] (irreg) vt
(money) retener; (decision) aplazar;
(permission) negar; (information) ocultar
within [wɪð'ɪn] prep dentro de ♦ adv
dentro; **~ reach (of)** al alcance (de);
~ sight (of) a la vista (de); **~ the
week** antes de acabar la semana; **~ a
mile (of)** a menos de una milla (de)
without [wɪð'aut] prep sin; **to go
~ sth** pasar sin algo
withstand [wɪθ'stænd] (irreg) vt
resistir a
witness ['wɪtnɪs] n testigo m/f ♦ vt
(event) presenciar; (document)
atestiguar la veracidad de; **to bear
~ to** (fig) ser testimonio de; **~ box** n
tribuna de los testigos; **~ stand** (us) n
= **~ box**
witty ['wɪtɪ] adj ingenioso
wives [waɪvz] npl of **wife**
wk abbr = **week**
wobble ['wɒbl] vi temblar; (chair)
cojear
woe [wəu] n desgracia
woke [wəuk] pt of **wake**
woken ['wəukən] pp of **wake**
wolf [wulf] n lobo; **wolves** [wulvz]
npl of **wolf**
woman ['wumən] (pl **women**) n
mujer f; **women's lib** (inf: pej) n liberación f
de la mujer; **~ly** adj femenino
womb [wu:m] n matriz f, útero
women ['wɪmɪn] npl of **woman**
won [wʌn] pt, pp of **win**
wonder ['wʌndə*] n maravilla,
prodigio; (feeling) asombro ♦ vi: **to
~ whether/why** preguntarse si/por
qué; **to ~ at** asombrarse de; **to
~ about** pensar sobre o en; **it's no
~ (that)** no es de extrañarse (que
+ subjun); **~ful** adj maravilloso
won't [wəunt] = **will not**
wood [wud] n (timber) madera; (forest)

bosque m; **~ carving** n (act) tallado
en madera, (object) talla en madera;
~ed adj arbolado; **~en** adj de madera;
(fig) inexpresivo; **~pecker** n pájaro
carpintero; **~wind** n (MUS)
instrumentos mpl de viento de madera;
~work n carpintería; **~worm** n
carcoma
wool [wul] n lana; **to pull the ~ over
sb's eyes** (fig) engatusar a uno; **~en**
(us) adj = **~len**; **~len** adj de lana;
~lens npl géneros mpl de lana; **~ly** adj
lanudo, de lana; (fig: ideas) confuso;
~y (us) adj = **~ly**
word [wə:d] n palabra; (news) noticia;
(promise) palabra (de honor) ♦ vt
redactar; **in other ~s** en otras
palabras; **to break/keep one's ~**
faltar a la palabra/cumplir la promesa;
to have ~s with sb reñir con uno;
~ing n redacción f; **~ processing** n
proceso de textos; **~ processor** n
procesador m de textos
wore [wɔ:*] pt of **wear**
work [wə:k] n trabajo; (job) empleo,
trabajo; (ART, LITERATURE) obra ♦ vi
trabajar; (mechanism) funcionar,
marchar; (medicine) ser eficaz, surtir
efecto ♦ vt (shape) trabajar; (stone etc)
tallar; (mine etc) explotar; (machine)
manejar, hacer funcionar; **~s** n (BRIT:
factory) fábrica ♦ npl (of clock, machine)
mecanismo; **to be out of ~** estar
parado, no tener trabajo; **to ~ loose**
(part) desprenderse; (knot) aflojarse;
~ on vt fus trabajar en, dedicarse a;
(principle) basarse en; **~ out** vi (plans
etc) salir bien, funcionar ♦ vt (problem)
resolver; (plan) elaborar; **it ~s out at
£100** suma 100 libras; **~ up** vt: **to get
~ed up** excitarse; **~able** adj (solution)
práctico, factible; **~aholic**
[wə:kə'hɔlɪk] n trabajador(a) obsesivo/
a m/f; **~er** n trabajador(a) m/f, obrero/
a; **~force** n mano f de obra; **~ing
class** n clase f obrera; **~ing-class**
adj obrero; **~ing order** n: **in ~ing order**

en funcionamiento; **~man** n (irreg) n obrero; **~manship** n habilidad f, trabajo; **~sheet** n hoja de trabajo; **~shop** n taller m; **~ station** n puesto or estación f de trabajo; **~-to-rule** (BRIT) n huelga de celo

world [wə:ld] n mundo ♦ cpd (champion) del mundo; (power, war) mundial; **to think the ~ of sb** (fig) tener un concepto muy alto de uno; **~ly** adj mundano; **~-wide** adj mundial, universal; **W~-Wide Web** n: **the W~-Wide Web** el World Wide Web

worm [wə:m] n (also: earth~) lombriz f

worn [wɔːn] pp of **wear** ♦ adj usado; **~-out** adj (object) gastado; (person) rendido, agotado

worried ['wʌrɪd] adj preocupado

worry ['wʌrɪ] n preocupación f ♦ vt preocupar, inquietar ♦ vi preocuparse; **~ing** adj inquietante

worse [wə:s] adj, adv peor ♦ n lo peor; **a change for the ~** un empeoramiento; **~n** vt, vi empeorar; **~ off** adj (financially): **to be ~ off** tener menos dinero; (fig): **you'll be ~ off this way** de esta forma estarás peor que nunca

worship ['wə:ʃɪp] n adoración f ♦ vt adorar; **Your W~** (BRIT: to mayor) señor alcalde; (: to judge) señor juez

worst [wə:st] adj, adv peor ♦ n lo peor; **at ~** en lo peor de los casos

worth [wə:θ] n valor m ♦ adj: **to be ~** valer; **it's ~ it** vale or merece la pena; **to be ~ one's while (to do)** merecer la pena (hacer); **~less** adj sin valor; (useless) inútil; **~while** adj (activity) que merece la pena; (cause) digno de

worthy ['wə:ðɪ] adj respetable; (motive) honesto; **~ of** digno de

---

KEYWORD

---

would [wud] aux vb **1** (conditional tense): **if you asked him he ~ do it** si se lo pidieras, lo haría; **if you had**

asked him he ~ have done it si se lo hubieras pedido, lo habría or hubiera hecho

2 (in offers, invitations, requests): **~ you like a biscuit?** ¿quieres una galleta?; (formal) ¿querría una galleta?; **you ask him to come in?** ¿quiere hacerle pasar?; **~ you open the window please?** ¿quiere or podría abrir la ventana, por favor?

3 (in indirect speech): **I said I ~ do it** dije que lo haría

4 (emphatic): **it WOULD have to snow today!** ¡tenía que nevar precisamente hoy!

5 (insistence): **she ~n't behave** no quiso comportarse bien

6 (conjecture): **it ~ have been midnight** sería medianoche; **it ~ seem so** parece que sí

7 (indicating habit): **he ~ go there on Mondays** iba allí los lunes

would-be (pej) adj presunto

wouldn't ['wudnt] = **would not**

wound[1] [wu:nd] n herida ♦ vt herir

wound[2] [waund] pt, pp of **wind**

wove [wəuv] pt of **weave**

woven ['wəuvən] pp of **weave**

wrap [ræp] vt (also: ~ up) envolver; **~per** n (on chocolate) papel m; (BRIT: of book) sobrecubierta f; **~ping paper** n papel m de envolver; (fancy) papel m de regalo

wreak [ri:k] vt: **to ~ havoc (on)** hacer estragos (en); **to ~ vengeance (on)** vengarse (de)

wreath [ri:θ, pl ri:ðz] n (funeral ~) corona

wreck [rek] n (ship: destruction) naufragio; (: remains) restos mpl del barco; (pej: person) ruina f ♦ vt (car etc) destrozar; (chances) arruinar; **~age** n restos mpl; (of building) escombros mpl

wren [ren] n (ZOOL) reyezuelo

wrench [rentʃ] n (TECH) llave f inglesa; (tug) tirón m; (fig) dolor m ♦ vt arrancar; **to ~ sth from sb** arrebatar algo violentamente a uno

wrestle ['rɛsl] vi: **to ~ (with sb)** luchar (con or contra uno); **~r** n luchador(a) m/f (de lucha libre); **wrestling** n lucha libre

wretched ['rɛtʃɪd] adj miserable

wriggle ['rɪgl] vi (also: ~ about) menearse, retorcerse

wring [rɪŋ] (pt, pp wrung) vt retorcer; (wet clothes) escurrir; (fig): **to ~ sth out of sb** sacar algo por la fuerza a uno

wrinkle ['rɪŋkl] n arruga ♦ vt arrugar ♦ vi arrugarse

wrist [rɪst] n muñeca; **~watch** n reloj m de pulsera

writ [rɪt] n mandato judicial

write [raɪt] (pt wrote, pp written) vt escribir; (cheque) extender ♦ vi escribir; **~ down** vt escribir; (note) apuntar; **~ off** vt (debt) borrar (como incobrable); (fig) desechar por inútil; **~ out** vt escribir; **~ up** vt redactar; **~-off** n siniestro total; **~r** n escritor(a) m/f

writhe [raɪð] vi retorcerse

writing ['raɪtɪŋ] n escritura; (hand-~) letra; (of author) obras fpl; **in ~** por escrito; **~ paper** n papel m de escribir

written ['rɪtn] pp of **write**

wrong [rɒŋ] adj (wicked) malo; (unfair) injusto; (incorrect) equivocado, incorrecto; (not suitable) inoportuno, inconveniente; (reverse) del revés ♦ adv equivocadamente ♦ n injusticia ♦ vt ser injusto con; **you are ~ to do it** haces mal en hacerlo; **you are ~ about that, you've got it ~** en eso estás equivocado; **to be in the ~** tener la culpa; **what's ~?** ¿qué pasa?; **to go ~** (person) equivocarse; (plan) salir mal; (machine) estropearse; **~ful** adj injusto; **~ly** adv mal, incorrectamente; (by mistake) por error; **~ number** n (TEL): **you've got the ~ number** se ha equivocado de

número

wrote [rəʊt] pt of **write**

wrought iron [rɔːt-] n hierro forjado

wrung [rʌŋ] pt, pp of **wring**

wt. abbr = **weight**

WWW n abbr (= World Wide Web) WWW m

X, x

Xmas ['ɛksməs] n abbr = **Christmas**

X-ray ['ɛksreɪ] n radiografía ♦ vt radiografiar, sacar radiografías de

xylophone ['zaɪləfəʊn] n xilófono

Y, y

yacht [jɒt] n yate m; **~ing** n (sport) balandrismo; **~sman/woman** (irreg) n balandrista m/f

Yank [jæŋk] (pej) n yanqui m/f

Yankee ['jæŋkɪ] (pej) n = **Yank**

yap [jæp] vi (dog) aullar

yard [jɑːd] n patio; (measure) yarda; **~stick** n (fig) criterio, norma

yarn [jɑːn] n hilo; (tale) cuento, historia

yawn [jɔːn] n bostezo ♦ vi bostezar; **~ing** adj (gap) muy abierto

yd(s). abbr = **yard(s)**

yeah [jɛə] (inf) adv sí

year [jɪə*] n año; **to be 8 ~s old** tener 8 años; **an eight-~-old child** un niño de ocho años (de edad); **~ly** adj anual ♦ adv anualmente, cada año

yearn [jɜːn] vi: **to ~ for sth** añorar algo, suspirar por algo

yeast [jiːst] n levadura

yell [jɛl] n grito, alarido ♦ vi gritar

yellow ['jɛləʊ] adj amarillo

yelp [jɛlp] n aullido ♦ vi aullar

yes [jɛs] adv sí ♦ n sí m; **to say/ answer ~** decir/contestar que sí

yesterday ['jɛstədɪ] adv ayer ♦ n ayer m; **~ morning/evening** ayer por la mañana/tarde; **all day ~** todo el día de ayer

yet [jɛt] *adv* ya; *(negative)* todavía ♦ *conj* sin embargo, a pesar de todo; **it is not finished** ~ todavía no está acabado; **the best** ~ el/la mejor hasta ahora; **as** ~ hasta ahora, todavía

yew [ju:] *n* tejo

yield [ji:ld] *n* (AGR) cosecha; (COMM) rendimiento ♦ *vt* ceder; *(results)* producir, dar; *(profit)* rendir ♦ *vi* rendirse, ceder; (US: AUT) ceder el paso

YMCA *n abbr* (= Young Men's Christian Association) Asociación *f* de Jóvenes Cristianos

yog(h)ourt ['jəʊgət] *n* yogur *m*

yog(h)urt ['jəʊgət] *n* = **yog(h)ourt**

yoke [jəʊk] *n* yugo

yolk [jəʊk] *n* yema (de huevo)

KEYWORD
---

you [ju:] *pron* **1** *(subject: familiar)* tú, *pl* vosotros/as (SP), ustedes (AM); *(polite)* usted, *pl* ustedes; ~ **are very kind** eres/es *etc* muy amable; ~ **Spanish enjoy your food** a vosotros (or ustedes) los españoles os (or les) gusta la comida; ~ **and I will go** iremos tú y yo

2 *(object: direct: familiar)* te, *pl* os (SP), les (AM); *(polite)* le, *pl* les, f la, *pl* las; **I know** ~ te/le *etc* conozco

3 *(object: indirect: familiar)* te, *pl* os (SP), les (AM); *(polite)* le, *pl* les; **I gave the letter to** ~ **yesterday** te/os *etc* di la carta ayer

4 *(stressed)* **I told YOU to do it** te dije a ti que lo hicieras, es a ti a quien dije que lo hicieras; *see also* **3, 5**

5 *(after prep: NB:* con+ ti = contigo: *familiar)* ti, *pl* vosotros/as (SP), ustedes (AM); *(polite)* usted, *pl* ustedes; **it's for** ~ es para ti/vosotros *etc*

6 *(comparisons: familiar)* tú, *pl* vosotros/as (SP), ustedes (AM); *(polite)* usted, *pl* ustedes; **she's younger than** ~ es más joven que tú/vosotros *etc*

7 *(impersonal: one)*: **fresh air does**

~ **good** el aire puro (te) hace bien; ~ **never know** nunca se sabe; ~ **can't do that!** ¡eso no se hace!

---

you'd [ju:d] = **you had; you would**

you'll [ju:l] = **you will; you shall**

young [jʌŋ] *adj* joven ♦ *npl (of animal)* cría; *(people)*: **the** ~ los jóvenes, la juventud; ~**er** *adj (brother etc)* menor; ~**ster** *n* joven *m/f*

your [jɔ:*] *adj* tu; *(pl)* vuestro; *(formal)* su; *see also* **my**

you're [juə*] = **you are**

yours [jɔ:z] *pron* tuyo; *(pl)* vuestro; *(formal)* suyo; *see also* **faithfully**; **mine**[1]; **sincerely**

yourself [jɔ:'sɛlf] *pron* tú mismo; *(complement)* te; *(after prep)* tí (mismo); *(formal)* usted mismo; (: *complement)* se; (: *after prep)* sí (mismo); **yourselves** *pl pron* vosotros mismos; *(after prep)* vosotros (mismos); *(formal)* ustedes (mismos); (: *complement)* se; (: *after prep)* sí mismos; *see also* **oneself**

youth [ju:θ, *pl* ju:ðz] *n* juventud *f*; *(young man)* joven *m*; ~ **club** *n* club *m* juvenil; ~**ful** *adj* juvenil; ~ **hostel** *n* albergue *m* de juventud

you've [ju:v] = **you have**

Yugoslav ['ju:gəʊslɑ:v] *adj, n* yugo(e)slavo/a *m/f*

Yugoslavia [ju:gəʊ'slɑ:vɪə] *n* Yugoslavia

yuppie ['jʌpɪ] *(inf) adj, n* yupi *m/f*, yupy *m/f*

YWCA *n abbr* (= Young Women's Christian Association) Asociación *f* de Jóvenes Cristianas

Z, z

zany ['zeɪnɪ] *adj* estrafalario

zap [zæp] *vt (COMPUT)* borrar

zeal [zi:l] *n* celo, entusiasmo; ~**ous** ['zɛləs] *adj* celoso, entusiasta

zebra ['ziːbrə] n cebra; ~ **crossing** (BRIT) n paso de peatones

zero ['zɪərəʊ] n cero

zest [zest] n ánimo, vivacidad f; (of orange) piel f

zigzag ['zɪgzæg] n zigzag m ♦ vi zigzaguear, hacer eses

zinc [zɪŋk] n cinc m, zinc m

zip [zɪp] n (also: ~ fastener, (US) ~per) cremallera (SP), cierre m (AM) ♦ vt (also:

~ up) cerrar la cremallera de; ~ **code** (US) n código postal

zodiac ['zəʊdɪæk] n zodíaco

zone [zəʊn] n zona

zoo [zuː] n (jardín m) zoo m

zoology [zuˈɒlədʒɪ] n zoología

zoom [zuːm] vi: **to ~ past** pasar zumbando; ~ **lens** n zoom m

zucchini [zuːˈkiːnɪ] (US) n(pl) calabacín(ines) m(pl)

SPANISH VERB TABLES

1 Gerund. **2** Imperative. **3** Present. **4** Preterite. **5** Future. **6** Present subjunctive. **7** Imperfect subjunctive. **8** Past participle. **9** Imperfect. *Etc* indicates that the irregular root is used for all persons of the tense, *e.g.* **oír: 6** oiga, oigas, oigamos, oigáis, oigan.

agradecer 3 agradezco **6** agradezca *etc*

aprobar 2 aprueba **3** apruebo, apruebas, aprueba, aprueban **6** apruebe, apruebes, apruebe, aprueben

atravesar 2 atraviesa **3** atravieso, atraviesas, atraviesa, atraviesan **6** atraviese, atravieses, atraviese, atraviesen

caber 3 quepo **4** cupe, cupiste, cupo, cupimos, cupisteis, cupieron **5** cabré *etc* **6** quepa *etc* **7** cupiera *etc*

caer 1 cayendo **3** caigo **4** cayó, cayeron **6** caiga *etc* **7** cayera *etc*

cerrar 2 cierra **3** cierro, cierras, cierra, cierran **6** cierre, cierres, cierre, cierren

COMER 1 comiendo **2** come, comed **3** como, comes, come comemos, coméis, comen **4** comí, comiste, comió, comimos, comisteis, comieron **5** comeré, comerás, comerá, comeremos, comeréis, comerán **6** coma, comas, coma, comamos, comáis, coman **7** comiera, comieras, comiera, comiéramos, comierais, comieran **9** comía, comías, comía, comíamos comíais, comían

conocer 3 conozco **6** conozca *etc*

contar 2 cuenta **3** cuento, cuentas, cuenta, cuenta **6** cuente, cuentes, cuente, cuenten

dar 2 doy **4** di, diste, dio, dimos, disteis, dieron **7** diera *etc*

decir 2 di **3** digo **4** dije, dijiste, dijo, dijimos, dijisteis, dijeron **5** diré *etc* **6** diga *etc* **7** dijera *etc* **8** dicho

despertar 2 despierta **3** despierto, despiertas, despierta, despiertan **6** despierte, despiertes, despierte, despierten

divertir 1 divirtiendo **2** divierte **3** divierto, diviertes, divierte, divierten **4** divirtió, divirtieron **6** divierta, diviertas, divierta, divirtamos, divirtáis, diviertan **7** divirtiera *etc*

dormir 1 durmiendo **2** duerme **3** duermo, duermes, duerme, duermen **4** durmió, durmieron **6** duerma, duermas, duerma, durmamos, durmáis, duerman **7** durmiera *etc*

empezar 2 empieza **3** empiezo, empiezas, empieza, empiezan **4** empecé **6** empiece, empieces, empiece, empecemos, empecéis, empiecen

entender 2 entiende **3** entiendo, entiendes, entiende, entienden **6** entienda, entiendas, entienda, entiendan

ESTAR 2 está **3** estoy, estás, está, están **4** estuve, estuviste, estuvo, estuvimos, estuvisteis, estuvieron **6** esté, estés, esté, estén **7** estuviera *etc*

HABER 3 he, has, ha, hemos, han **4** hube, hubiste, hubo, hubimos, hubisteis, hubieron **5** habré *etc* **6** haya *etc* **7** hubiera *etc*

HABLAR 1 hablando **2** habla,

hablad 3 hablo, hablas, habla, hablamos, habláis, hablan **4** hablé, hablaste, habló, hablamos, hablasteis, hablaron **5** hablaré, hablarás, hablará, hablaremos, hablaréis, hablarán **6** hable, hables, hable, hablemos, habléis, hablen **7** hablara, hablaras, hablara, habláramos, hablarais, hablaran **8** hablado **9** hablaba, hablabas, hablaba, hablábamos, hablabais, hablaban

hacer 2 haz **3** hago **4** hice, hiciste, hizo, hicimos, hicisteis, hicieron **5** haré etc **6** haga etc **7** hiciera etc **8** hecho

instruir 1 instruyendo **2** instruye **3** instruyo, instruyes, instruye, instruimos **4** instruyó, instruyeron **6** instruya etc **7** instruyera etc

ir 1 yendo **2** ve **3** voy, vas, va, vamos, vais, van **4** fui, fuiste, fue, fuimos, fuisteis, fueron **6** vaya, vayas, vaya, vayamos, vayáis, vayan **7** fuera etc **9** iba, ibas, iba, íbamos, ibais, iban

jugar 2 juega **3** juego, juegas, juega, juegan **4** jugué **6** juegue etc

leer 1 leyendo **4** leyó, leyeron **7** leyera etc

morir 1 muriendo **2** muere **3** muero, mueres, muere, mueren **4** murió, murieron **6** muera, mueras, muera, muramos, muráis, mueran **7** muriera etc **8** muerto

mover 2 mueve **3** muevo, mueves, mueve, mueven **6** mueva, muevas, mueva, muevan

negar 2 niega **3** niego, niegas, niega, niegan **4** negué **6** niegue, niegues, niegue, neguemos, neguéis, nieguen

ofrecer 3 ofrezco **6** ofrezca etc

oír 1 oyendo **2** oye **3** oigo, oyes, oye, oyen **4** oyó, oyeron **6** oiga etc **7** oyera etc

oler 2 huele **3** huelo, hueles, huele, huelen **6** huela, huelas, huela, huelan

parecer 3 parezco **6** parezca etc

pedir 1 pidiendo **2** pide **3** pido, pides, pide, piden **4** pidió, pidieron **6** pida etc **7** pidiera etc

pensar 2 piensa **3** pienso, piensas, piensa, piensan **6** piense, pienses, piense, piensen

perder 2 pierde **3** pierdo, pierdes, pierde, pierden **6** pierda, pierdas, pierda, pierdan

poder 1 pudiendo **2** puede **3** puedo, puedes, puede, pueden **4** pude, pudiste, pudo, pudimos, pudisteis, pudieron **5** podré etc **6** pueda, puedas, pueda, puedan **7** pudiera etc

poner 2 pon **3** pongo **4** puse, pusiste, puso, pusimos, pusisteis, pusieron **5** pondré etc **6** ponga etc **7** pusiera etc **8** puesto

preferir 1 prefiriendo **2** prefiere **3** prefiero, prefieres, prefiere, prefieren **4** prefirió, prefirieron **6** prefiera, prefieras, prefiera, prefiramos, prefiráis, prefieran etc **7** prefiriera etc

querer 2 quiere **3** quiero, quieres, quiere, quieren **4** quise, quisiste, quiso, quisimos, quisisteis, quisieron **5** querré etc **6** quiera, quieras, quiera, quieran **7** quisiera etc

reír 2 ríe **3** río, ríes, ríe, ríen **4** rio, rieron **6** ría, rías, ría, riamos, riáis, rían **7** riera etc

repetir 1 repitiendo **2** repite **3** repito, repites, repite, repiten **4** repitió, repitieron **6** repita etc **7** repitiera etc

rogar 2 ruega **3** ruego, ruegas, ruega, ruegan **4** rogué **6** ruegue, ruegues, ruegue, roguemos, roguéis, rueguen

saber 3 sé 4 supe, supiste, supo, supimos, supisteis, supieron 5 sabré *etc* 6 sepa *etc* 7 supiera *etc*

salir 2 sal 3 salgo 5 saldré *etc* 6 salga *etc*

seguir 1 siguiendo 2 sigue 3 sigo, sigues, sigue, siguen 4 siguió, siguieron 6 siga *etc* 7 siguiera *etc*

sentar 2 sienta 3 siento, sientas, sienta, sientan 6 siente, sientes, siente, sienten

sentir 1 sintiendo 2 siente 3 siento, sientes, siente, sienten 4 sintió, sintieron 6 sienta, sientas, sienta, sintamos, sintáis, sientan 7 sintiera *etc*

SER 2 sé 3 soy, eres, es, somos, sois, son 4 fui, fuiste, fue, fuimos, fuisteis, fueron 6 sea *etc* 7 fuera *etc* 9 era, eras, era, éramos, erais, eran

servir 1 sirviendo 2 sirve 3 sirvo, sirves, sirve, sirven 4 sirvió, sirvieron 6 sirva *etc* 7 sirviera *etc*

soñar 2 sueña 3 sueño, sueñas, sueña, sueñan 6 sueñe, sueñes, sueñe, sueñen

tener 2 ten 3 tengo, tienes, tiene, tienen 4 tuve, tuviste, tuvo, tuvimos, tuvisteis, tuvieron 5 tendré *etc* 6 tenga *etc* 7 tuviera *etc*

traer 1 trayendo 3 traigo 4 traje, trajiste, trajo, trajimos, trajisteis, trajeron 6 traiga *etc* 7 trajera *etc*

valer 2 val 3 valgo 5 valdré *etc* 6 valga *etc*

venir 2 ven 3 vengo, vienes, viene, vienen 4 vine, viniste, vino, vinimos, vinisteis, vinieron 5 vendré *etc* 6 venga *etc* 7 viniera *etc*

ver 3 veo 6 vea *etc* 8 visto 9 veía *etc*

vestir 1 vistiendo 2 viste 3 visto, vistes, viste, visten 4 vistió, vistieron 6 vista *etc* 7 vistiera *etc*

VIVIR 1 viviendo 2 vive, vivid 3 vivo, vives, vive, vivimos, vivís, viven 4 viví, viviste, vivió, vivimos, vivisteis, vivieron 5 viviré, vivirás, vivirá, viviremos, viviréis, vivirán 6 viva, vivas, viva, vivamos, viváis, vivan 7 viviera, vivieras, viviera, viviéramos, vivierais, vivieran 8 vivido 9 vivía, vivías, vivía, vivíamos, vivíais, vivían

volver 2 vuelve 3 vuelvo, vuelves, vuelve, vuelven 6 vuelva, vuelvas, vuelva, vuelvan 8 vuelto

VERBOS IRREGULARES EN INGLÉS

present	pt	pp	present	pt	pp
arise	arose	arisen	dig	dug	dug
awake	awoke	awaked	do (3rd	did	done
be (am, is,	was,	been	person;		
are;	were		he/she/		
being)			it/does)		
bear	bore	born(e)	draw	drew	drawn
beat	beat	beaten	dream	dreamed,	dreamed,
become	became	become		dreamt	dreamt
begin	began	begun	drink	drank	drunk
behold	beheld	beheld	drive	drove	driven
bend	bent	bent	dwell	dwelt	dwelt
beset	beset	beset	eat	ate	eaten
bet	bet, betted	bet, betted	fall	fell	fallen
bid	bid,	bid,	feed	fed	fed
	bade	bidden	feel	felt	felt
bind	bound	bound	fight	fought	fought
bite	bit	bitten	find	found	found
bleed	bled	bled	flee	fled	fled
blow	blew	blown	fling	flung	flung
break	broke	broken	fly (flies)	flew	flown
breed	bred	bred	forbid	forbade	forbidden
bring	brought	brought	forecast	forecast	forecast
build	built	built	forget	forgot	forgotten
burn	burnt,	burnt,	forgive	forgave	forgiven
	burned	burned	forsake	forsook	forsaken
burst	burst	burst	freeze	froze	frozen
buy	bought	bought	get	got	got, (US)
can	could	(been			gotten
		able)	give	gave	given
cast	cast	cast	go (goes)	went	gone
catch	caught	caught	grind	ground	ground
choose	chose	chosen	grow	grew	grown
cling	clung	clung	hang	hung,	hung,
come	came	come		hanged	hanged
cost	cost	cost	have (has;	had	had
creep	crept	crept	having)		
cut	cut	cut	hear	heard	heard
deal	dealt	dealt	hide	hid	hidden

614

present	pt	pp	present	pt	pp
hit	hit	hit	seek	sought	sought
hold	held	held	sell	sold	sold
hurt	hurt	hurt	send	sent	sent
keep	kept	kept	set	set	set
kneel	knelt, kneeled	knelt, kneeled	shake	shook	shaken
			shall	should	—
know	knew	known	shear	sheared	shorn, sheared
lay	laid	laid			
lead	led	led	shed	shed	shed
lean	leant, leaned	leant, leaned	shine	shone	shone
			shoot	shot	shot
leap	leapt, leaped	leapt, leaped	show	showed	shown
			shrink	shrank	shrunk
learn	learnt, learned	learnt, learned	shut	shut	shut
			sing	sang	sung
leave	left	left	sink	sank	sunk
lend	lent	lent	sit	sat	sat
let	let	let	slay	slew	slain
lie (lying)	lay	lain	sleep	slept	slept
light	lit, lighted	lit, lighted	slide	slid	slid
lose	lost	lost	sling	slung	slung
make	made	made	slit	slit	slit
may	might	—	smell	smelt, smelled	smelt, smelled
mean	meant	meant			
meet	met	met	sow	sowed	sown, sowed
mistake	mistook	mistaken			
mow	mowed	mown, mowed	speak	spoke	spoken
			speed	sped, speeded	sped, speeded
must	(had to)	(had to)			
pay	paid	paid	spell	spelt, spelled	spelt, spelled
put	put	put			
quit	quit, quitted	quit, quitted	spend	spent	spent
			spill	spilt, spilled	spilt, spilled
read	read	read			
rid	rid	rid	spin	spun	spun
ride	rode	ridden	spit	spat	spat
ring	rang	rung	split	split	split
rise	rose	risen	spoil	spoiled, spoilt	spoiled, spoilt
run	ran	run			
saw	sawed	sawn	spread	spread	spread
say	said	said	spring	sprang	sprung
see	saw	seen	stand	stood	stood

615

present	pt	pp	present	pt	pp
steal	stole	stolen	**tell**	told	told
stick	stuck	stuck	**think**	thought	thought
sting	stung	stung	**throw**	threw	thrown
stink	stank	stunk	**thrust**	thrust	thrust
stride	strode	stridden	**tread**	trod	trodden
strike	struck	struck, stricken	**wake**	woke, waked	woken, waked
strive	strove	striven	**wear**	wore	worn
swear	swore	sworn	**weave**	wove, weaved	woven, weaved
sweep	swept	swept			
swell	swelled	swollen, swelled	**wed**	wedded, wed	wedded, wed
swim	swam	swum	**weep**	wept	wept
swing	swung	swung	**win**	won	won
take	took	taken	**wind**	wound	wound
teach	taught	taught	**wring**	wrung	wrung
tear	tore	torn	**write**	wrote	written

LOS NÚMEROS

NUMBERS

un, uno(a)	1	one
dos	2	two
tres	3	three
cuatro	4	four
cinco	5	five
seis	6	six
siete	7	seven
ocho	8	eight
nueve	9	nine
diez	10	ten
once	11	eleven
doce	12	twelve
trece	13	thirteen
catorce	14	fourteen
quince	15	fifteen
dieciséis	16	sixteen
diecisiete	17	seventeen
dieciocho	18	eighteen
diecinueve	19	nineteen
veinte	20	twenty
veintiuno	21	twenty-one
veintidós	22	twenty-two
treinta	30	thirty
treinta y uno(a)	31	thirty-one
treinta y dos	32	thirty-two
cuarenta	40	forty
cincuenta	50	fifty
sesenta	60	sixty
setenta	70	seventy
ochenta	80	eighty
noventa	90	ninety
cien, ciento	100	a hundred, one hundred
ciento uno(a)	101	a hundred and one
doscientos(as)	200	two hundred
doscientos(as) uno(a)	201	two hundred and one
trescientos(as)	300	three hundred
cuatrocientos(as)	400	four hundred
quinientos(as)	500	five hundred
seiscientos(as)	600	six hundred
setecientos(as)	700	seven hundred
ochocientos(as)	800	eight hundred
novecientos(as)	900	nine hundred
mil	1 000	a thousand
mil dos	1 002	a thousand and two
cinco mil	5 000	five thousand
un millón	1 000 000	a million

LOS NÚMEROS

NUMBERS

primer, primero(a), 1º, 1er (1ª, 1era)   first, 1st
segundo(a) 2º (2ª)   second, 2nd
tercer, tercero(a), 3º (3ª)   third, 3rd
cuarto(a), 4º (4ª)   fourth, 4th
quinto(a), 5º (5ª)   fifth, 5th
sexto(a), 6º (6ª)   sixth, 6th
séptimo(a)   seventh
octavo(a)   eighth
noveno(a)   ninth
décimo(a)   tenth
undécimo(a)   eleventh
duodécimo(a)   twelfth
decimotercio(a)   thirteenth
decimocuarto(a)   fourteenth
decimoquinto(a)   fifteenth
decimosexto(a)   sixteenth
vigésimo(a)   twentieth
vigésimo(a) primero(a)   twenty-first
trigésimo(a)   thirtieth
centésimo(a)   hundredth
centésimo(a) primero(a)   hundred-and-first
milésimo(a)   thousandth

Números Quebrados etc

Fractions etc

un medio   a half
un tercio   a third
un cuarto   a quarter
un quinto   a fifth
cero coma cinco, 0,5   (nought) point five, 0.5
diez por cien(to)   ten per cent

N.B. In Spanish the ordinal numbers from 1 to 10 are commonly used; from 11 to 20 rather less; above 21 they are rarely written and almost never heard in speech. The custom is to replace the forms for 21 and above by the cardinal number.

LA HORA

THE TIME

¿qué hora es?

what time is it?

es/son

it's o it is

medianoche, las doce (de la noche)	midnight, twelve p.m.
la una (de la madrugada)	one o'clock (in the morning), one (a.m.)
la una y cinco	five past one
la una y diez	ten past one
la una y cuarto or quince	a quarter past one, one fifteen
la una y veinticinco	twenty-five past one, one twenty-five
la una y media or treinta	half-past one, one thirty
las dos menos veinticinco, la una treinta y cinco	twenty-five to two, one thirty-five
las dos menos veinte, la una cuarenta	twenty to two, one forty
las dos menos cuarto, la una cuarenta y cinco	a quarter to two, one forty-five
las dos menos diez, la una cincuenta	ten to two, one fifty
mediodía, las doce (de la tarde)	twelve o'clock, midday, noon
la una (de la tarde)	one o'clock (in the afternoon), one (p.m.)
las siete (de la tarde)	seven o'clock (in the evening), seven (p.m.)

¿a qué hora?

(at) what time?

a medianoche	at midnight
a las siete	at seven o'clock
en veinte minutos	in twenty minutes
hace quince minutos	fifteen minutes ago

LA FECHA

DATES

hoy	today
todos los días	every day
ayer	yesterday
esta mañana	this morning
mañana por la noche	tomorrow night
anteanoche; antes de ayer por la noche	the night before last
antes de ayer; anteayer	the day before yesterday
anoche	last night
hace dos días/seis años	2 days/six years ago
mañana por la tarde	tomorrow afternoon
pasado mañana	the day after tomorrow
todos los jueves, el jueves	every Thursday, on Thursday
va los viernes	he goes on Fridays
"miércoles cerrado"	"closed on Wednesdays"
de lunes a viernes	from Monday to Friday
para el jueves	by Thursday
un sábado de marzo	one Saturday in March
dentro de una semana	in a week's time
dentro de dos martes	a week next/on Tuesday/Tuesday week
el domingo que viene	next Sunday
esta semana/la semana que viene/ la semana pasada	this/next/last week
dentro de dos semanas	in 2 weeks or a fortnight
dentro de tres lunes	two weeks on Monday
el primer/último viernes del mes	the first/last Friday of the month
el mes que viene	next month
el año pasado	last year
el uno de junio, el primero de junio (LAM)	the 1st of June, June first
el dos de octubre	the 2nd of October, October 2nd
nací en 1987	I was born in 1987
su cumpleaños es el 5 de junio	his birthday is on June 5th (BRIT) or 5th June (US)
el 18 de agosto	on 18th August (BRIT) or August 18th (US)
en el 96	in '96
en la primavera del 94	in the Spring of '94
del 19 al 3	from the 19th to the 3rd
¿qué fecha es hoy?, ¿a cuanto estamos?	what's the date?, what date is it today?

A FECHA

...y es 15, estamos a quince	today's date is the 15th, today is the 15th
...l novecientos ochenta y ocho	1988 - nineteen (hundred and) eighty-eight
...y hace 10 años	10 years to the day
...final de mes	at the end of the month
...final de mes	at the month end (*ACCOUNTS*)
...ariamente/semanalmente/ mensualmente	daily/weekly/monthly
...nualmente	annually
...os veces a la semana/dos veces al mes/dos veces al año	twice a week/month/year
...os veces al mes	bi-monthly
...n el año 2006 (dos mil seis)	in the year 2006
...a. de C.	4 B.C., B.C. 4
...9 d. de C.	79 A.D., A.D. 79
...en el siglo XIII	in the 13th century
...en *o* durante los (años) 80	in *or* during the 1980s
...a mediados de la década de los 70	in the mid seventies
...en mil novecientos noventa y tantos	in 1990 something

HEADINGS OF LETTERS

...9 de octubre de 1995	9th October 1995 *or* 9 October 1995

PESOS Y MEDIDAS
CONVERSION CHARTS

In the weight and length charts the middle figure can be either metre or imperial. Thus 3.3 feet = 1 metre, 1 foot = 0.3 metres, and so on.

feet		metres	inches		cm	lbs		k
3.3	1	0.3	0.39	1	2.54	2.2	1	0.4
6.6	2	0.61	0.79	2	5.08	4.4	2	0.9
9.9	3	0.91	1.18	3	7.62	6.6	3	1.
13.1	4	1.22	1.57	4	10.6	8.8	4	1.8
16.4	5	1.52	1.97	5	12.7	11.0	5	2.2
19.7	6	1.83	2.36	6	15.2	13.2	6	2.
23.0	7	2.13	2.76	7	17.8	15.4	7	3.2
26.2	8	2.44	3.15	8	20.3	17.6	8	3.
29.5	9	2.74	3.54	9	22.9	19.8	9	4.
32.9	10	3.05	3.9	10	25.4	22.0	10	4.
			4.3	11	27.9			
			4.7	12	30.1			

°C	0	5	10	15	17	20	22	24	26	28	30	35	37	38	40	50	100
°F	32	41	50	59	63	68	72	75	79	82	86	95	98.4	100	104	122	212

Km	10	20	30	40	50	60	70	80	90	100	110	120
Miles	6.2	12.4	18.6	24.9	31.0	37.3	43.5	49.7	56.0	62.0	68.3	74.6

Liquids

gallons	1.1	2.2	3.3	4.4	5.5	pints	0.44	0.88	1.7
litres	5	10	15	20	25	litres	0.25	0.5	1